U.S.IANA (1650–1950)

U.S.IANA

(1650–1950)

A SELECTIVE BIBLIOGRAPHY
IN WHICH ARE DESCRIBED
11,620 UNCOMMON AND SIGNIFICANT BOOKS
RELATING TO THE CONTINENTAL PORTION
OF THE UNITED STATES

Revised and Enlarged Edition

COMPILED BY WRIGHT HOWES

NEW YORK

R.R. BOWKER COMPANY

FOR

THE NEWBERRY LIBRARY

1962

BIBLIOGRAPHICAL NOTE

THE FIRST EDITION OF THIS WORK WAS COPYRIGHTED AND PUBLISHED

IN 1954 BY R. R. BOWKER COMPANY

SECOND EDITION 1962

REPRINTED 1963

REPRINTED 1970

REPRINTED 1978

LIBRARY OF CONGRESS CATALOG CARD NUMBER 62-10988

INTERNATIONAL STANDARD BOOK NUMBER 0-8352-0103-1

PRINTED AND BOUND IN THE UNITED STATES OF AMERICA

FOREWORD

In this country today more people, *per capita*, than ever before collect what they persist in calling—rather loosely—Americana. In the intervening years since Sabin, attention to some phases of that subject has unmistakably increased steadily and grown more widespread, deep and ardent. The subject itself, however, as a field of interest for the vast majority of our citizens has at the same time conspicuously narrowed. Towards many of its branches we have developed a marked indifference; we now give meagre attention to books relating to Canada, Mexico, our various sister republics further south, or even to those having to do with our own insular possessions in the West Indies and the Pacific.

So pronounced has become concentration on books confined to the history of the United States proper that our collectors, as a whole, can no longer be considered as collecting AMERICANA—in its broad, hemispherical and true sense—at all. They collect, instead, on only one isolated segment of that subject. They collect: U.S.IANA.

This first large-scale attempt at a bibliography exclusively devoted to books relating to human activities throughout the whole continental portion of the United States was originally issued in 1954.

There had appeared previously, over the years, countless partial studies, of like character, confined variously to books recording events occurring in separate States and regions or to those relating to single periods and phases of national affairs. From all of these, collectors and students profited greatly; through their use, the value of bibliographical reference tools became better recognized.

But fragmentary coverages—albeit of first importance for workers in those narrow, isolated fields—left something to be desired; an obvious need still remained for a more comprehensive survey, one offering historian, book-seller, and book-buyer similar information on the whole subject. To remedy this deficiency—to some extent, at least— *U.S.iana* was planned and published. Within limitations, presently to be set forth, it proposed: to explore this field of interest almost in its entirety; to satisfy curiosity concerning bibliographical essentials, relative uncommonness and commercial value of every included entry; and to present all of this—compressed into a single, compact volume.

No illusion is entertained as to any skill or excellence in the manner in which this task was performed. However laudable the motive prompting it, the actual preparation of a compilation of this unscholarly type represents almost the lowest possible form of literary endeavor, one calling for physical endurance and mechanical drudgery—but practically nothing else. The plan itself, however, must not have been unattractive. At any rate, the public—persuaded perhaps that on a neglected subject deserving attention a tolerable treatment was better than none—responded more vigorously than had been anticipated: within sixty days after publication, the entire edition—a sizable one—had completely sold out.

A survey compelled to cope with the extensive literature involved in a subject of such magnitude and scope—and forced, at the same time, to be held within the circumscribed bounds of a single volume—had to be rigidly restricted to books of a factual, serious and fundamentally historical nature, relating to human affairs only.

This calculated and deliberate limitation automatically removed from consideration almost everything of a primarily scientific, technical or imaginative nature: including text-books and juvenilia; practically all sermons and orations; bibliographies; natural histories; laws; legislative documents of a purely governmental character; most almanacs; linguistics; as well as dramatic, poetical and fictional compositions—even those dealing with historic persons and events.

Further specific exclusions—already revealed, expressly or by implication, in a carefully worded title-page—are here recapitulated for emphasis and clarification:

1. From an avowed "bibliography of books" pamphlets might technically have been omitted *in toto;* that being manifestly undesirable, those containing as many as twenty-four pages are, by compromise, arbitrarily considered "books" and entered as such. Except for a few items of transcendent importance, tracts and brochures of fewer pages— along with circulars, broad-sheets and broad-sides—are excluded. The absence of such fragile and seldom-seen ephemera should not too often prove a source of disappointment to information-seekers.

2. A blanket exclusion applies to all books printed prior to 1650. In a work aimed at contributing the greatest good to the greatest number, space devoted to the dread complexities of De Bry, Hulsius and other contemporary annalists of that shadowy era of our remote antiquity, can be alloted more profitably to material on later periods, holding today far wider popular appeal. One is forced to recognize that present-day interest is—for some unknown reason—far more centered on comparatively recent exploits and events, within our interior valleys and along the shifting rim of a far-flung Western frontier, than it is, or ever will be, in activities—equally heroic and noteworthy —confined to the Atlantic seaboard, in a long-gone and forgotten yesterday.

3. Another blanket exclusion—of books relating to our insular possessions, including, of course, Hawaii—is mildly regrettable; but the inclusion of these subjects (and the voluminous maritime literature they involve) would mean a sacrifice of space unjustifiably disproportionate to the benefits afforded a comparatively small portion of our population.

4. No reasonable man, if such exists, can regret a further blanket exclusion: that of the innumerable "common" or "insignificant" books whose original editions command current prices of less than ten dollars each. Man's brief life permits all too little time for consequential books; why, then, waste it on trivia? No mature collector buys material in that category; and books unfit for purchase are surely unfit for admittance into a selective bibliography. An unweeded garden is close kin to a jungle!

This work, then, is highly selective; aside from its rejection of common items, entirely too much so for that majestic coterie of the chosen few—the advanced collectors, specialty experts and hypercritical pedants—who, for the highly uncommon books in which alone they delight, demand a relatively unlimited inclusiveness. It should, however, prove sufficiently ample to meet, in some real measure, the needs of the less exacting group for which it is designed: that large group composed of the average collector, the average historical student, the average library-worker, the average antiquarian bookseller.

All original editions of titles selected are listed and carefully described in 11,620 numbered main entries. Their reprints and translations—with descriptions and collations less complete and less meticulously verified—are listed in about 7,000 unnumbered supplemental entries. A greater number of titles could hardly be accomodated in one portable volume.

The one obligatory requirement of a bibliographical project is fulfilled when it has met the demands of classic tradition and has supplied—as has been done here—data on the following stable, permanent, physical features of all books listed: author; title; place

6

and date of publication; size and number of volumes; pagination; and number of maps, plates and tables not counted in pagination. From such data, when correctly given, the identity and completeness of any book checked against it may be determined with absolute exactitude. All of the points involved in the requirement just noted can be adjudicated with definite precision; no danger of reversal exists. But on another question, of almost equally wide interest, that concerning the commercial value of entries, the reverse is true; on that question no bibliography desirous of permanent usefulness can attempt an exact answer. A book's current price, like that of any other commodity, is the temporary product of prevailing demand, supply, economic conditions, value of the dollar, taste and fashion, a combination of highly variable, unstable and impermanent influences; any conclusion concerning a value so generated can be safely expressed only in the inexact terms of a generalization. The appetite of a hungry man may sometimes have to be content with half a loaf; curiosity concerning the dollar value of individual books can be satisfied here only to the limited extent of a somewhat vague approximation.

Supplying that limited information has been accomplished by utilizing the following simple expedient: immediately after the collation of each entry is inserted a symbol indicating the particular group, or "value bracket", to which it belongs. There are six of these arbitrarily established brackets: the symbol "a" indicates books worth from $10.00 to $25.00; the other five "value brackets", with their symbols, are: "aa"— ($25–$100), "b"—($100–$300), "c"—($300–$600), "d"—($600–$1000), "dd"—($1000 and upwards). This formula—as shown in the more detailed tabulation given on the next leaf—not only establishes the approximate monetary values of all entries but also indicates their coincidental status, as to relative uncommonness and importance, in the hierarchy of printed books.

Disinclination to produce a volume of unwieldy dimensions has dictated all attainable frugality in the matter of space. Titles are shortened; descriptions are abbreviated and largely unpunctuated; collations are confined to essentials; and bindings—the mere protective coverings of books and not strictly integral parts of them—are gone into only in the case of occasional pamphlets where wrappers are included in the printer's pagination. It is hoped that none of these devices will defeat identification or intelligibility. In entering anonymous and obviously pseudonymous titles, the first substantive word has been used unless a proper name or place appears prominently in the title, in which case the entry is indexed under that word. This departure from usual practice, having been adopted years ago by the compiler in making the notes which form the basis of this work, is followed here. It offers the distinct advantage of presenting together various entries on the same subject. A few—generally two or three—locations of "rare" books (those graded "b" or higher) are supplied when repositories containing perfect copies are known to the compiler, but no complete census of known copies is ordinarily attempted. Absence of a location symbol does not mean that no copy of that particular title exists. It means only that this compiler has no information as to where one may be found.

Though time and labor be lavished upon it, the revision of a work of this nature can never attain anything approaching impeccability. All that can be hoped for is that it will prove to be a substantial improvement over its predecessor. In justification of this present attempt, it is submitted: that many errors have been corrected; that some unworthy titles have been deleted and replaced by others deemed more important; and that, by moving back the point of departure from 1700 to 1650, many additional and highly interesting books, printed between those dates, have now been given sanctuary. Urged against the original edition was the reasonable complaint that, in lumping the two classes of "scarce" books (the "fairly scarce" and the "quite scarce") into one "a"-bracket, little help was given the user; an additional "aa"-bracket now establishes a definite distinction between books worth from $10.00 to $25.00 and those worth from $25.00 to $100.00. Finally, entries are now numbered, not consecutively throughout, but, separately, under each letter of the alphabet. This offers the double advantage of reducing the sesquipedalian length of many numbers and of obviating all need for specifying, in a citation, whether the number cited refers to the first or to the second edition of this work.

Information and suggestions, generously supplied by interested owners of the first edition, have contributed substantially to this revision. To those contributing that aid (gentlemen and scholars all) and to Mr. Sol H. Malkin, in whose *Antiquarian Bookseller* was printed an open letter requesting such aid, the compiler is deeply grateful.

For elaborate contributions, far exceeding the call of duty, the following gentlemen should be specifically named: Mr. Jeff C. Dykes, College Park, Md.; Mr. E. B. Halbmeir, cataloger for New York's Swann Auction Galleries; Mr. Edward G. Howard, Baltimore, Md.; Mr. John J. Lipsky, Colorado Springs, Col.; Mr. John P. Love, partner in the firm of Francis Edwards, Ltd., London, Eng.; and Mr. Karl Yost, Morrison, Ill.

The compiler is also deeply obligated to Mr. Colton Storm for his herculean labor in checking Western entries against the superb copies of the Graff Collection, now being cataloged by him.

Above all, must be acknowledged the renewed, material support furnished by The Newberry Library, whose similar aid alone made possible the publication of the first edition.

The co-operation of those mentioned should be construed only as an approval of the projected plan and not of the manner in which it was carried out. All shortcomings, omissions and inaccuracies are to be attributed to the compiler's limited knowledge or to the fading memory of his advanced senescence. Even in the improved form of a revised edition, this thesaurus can be considered definitive only in one sense: it is the last that will be done by these hands.

WRIGHT HOWES

1018 N. State Street,
Chicago 10, Illinois

ABBREVIATIONS AND SYMBOLS

Places of publication, printed in italics, are not always completely written out. Boston appears as B, Cambridge, Mass. as C, London as L and Paris as P. Others are shown in shortened form [their first three or four letters only being given, such as Alb for Albany, Amst for Amsterdam]. These are generally so obvious as to present no difficulty to the reader. A few of the less obvious follow:

Des M for Des Moines	Richm for Richmond
Fredkbg for Fredericksburg	S F for San Francisco
Indp for Indianapolis	S L for Salt Lake City
Lis for Lisbon	Sav for Savannah
Liv for Liverpool	St L for St. Louis
N Hav for New Haven	St P for Saint Paul
N Lond for New London	St Ptbg for St. Petersburg
N O for New Orleans	Wmsbg for Williamsburg

Book sizes are indicated by:

F for folio	O for octavo
Q for quarto	D for duodecimo

Smaller sizes are shown in the ordinary manner.

Other abbreviations follow common practice and require no long listing, but a few may be clarified to advantage:

adds	additions	ll or lvs	leaves
anr	another	loc	located
capt t	caption title	oth	other
col	colored	p	page [or, when plurality is indicated, pages]
comp	compiler		
cont	continued	pl	plate
cor	corrected	pls	plates
facs	facsimile	rptd	reprinted
front	frontispiece	tab	table
impr	imprint [i.e. place where published]	t	title
		t-p	title page
l or lf	leaf		

Value symbols, showing relative grades of dollar value, importance and uncommonness are indicated by the following lower case letters: [When no symbol accompanies an entry, "a" value or less is to be inferred].

a – represents books that are mildly scarce, obtainable without much difficulty, at prices ranging from $10.00 to $25.00.

aa – represents books that are quite scarce, obtainable only with some difficulty, at prices ranging from $25.00 to $100.00.

b – represents books that are mildly rare, obtainable only with considerable difficulty, at prices ranging between $100.00 and $300.00.

c – represents books that are quite rare, obtainable only with much difficulty, at prices ranging between $300.00 and $600.00.

d – represents very rare books, obtainable only with great difficulty, at prices between $600.00 and $1000.00.

dd – represents superlatively rare books, almost unobtainable, worth $ 1000.00 and upwards.

For further clarification consult Foreword.

Location symbols. Many of the location symbols employed are such as should be self-explanatory. An abbreviation for a city followed by P refers to that city's Public Library; if followed by H, it means its Historical Society; if followed by U, it refers to its University. [Examples: DenvP; ChiH; ChiU]. Similarly H, S or U following an abbreviation for a State should be interpreted as meaning that particular State's Historical Society, or its State Library, or its University. [Examples: KasH, IndS, KyU]. Those listed below are the only ones requiring individual explanation:

AA	Amer. Antiquarian Soc., Worcester, Mass.
AlaA	Ala. Archives and Hist. Soc., Montgomery, Ala.
B	Bancroft Library at the Univ. of Calif., Berkeley, Calif.
BA	Boston Athenaeum Library, Boston, Mass.
BM	British Museum, London, England.
BN	Bibliothèque Nationale, Paris, France.
BP	Boston Public Library, Boston, Mass.
BurtH	Burton Hist. Collection, Detroit, Mich.
Clem	Clements Library, Ann Arbor, Michigan
G	Private Library of Everett D. Graff, Winnetka, Ill.
H	Harvard University Library, Cambridge, Mass.
Hn	Henry E. Huntington Library, San Marino, Calif.
IH	Ill. State Hist. Soc., Springfield, Ill.
JCB	John Carter Brown Library, Providence, R. I.
LC	Library of Congress, Washington, D. C.
Lincoln Life	Lincoln Life Ins. Co., Ft. Wayne, Indiana.
MH	Mass. Hist. Soc., Boston, Mass.
MoSH	Missouri State Hist. Soc., Columbia, Mo.
N	Newberry Library, Chicago, Ill.
OHP	Ohio Hist. & Phil. Soc., Cincinnati, Ohio.
Pn	Princeton Univ. Library, Princeton, N. J.
S	Private library of Thomas W. Streeter, Morristown, N. J.
StL Merc	St. Louis Mercantile Library, St. Louis, Mo.
TransU	Transylvania Univ., Lexington, Ky.
UCHO	Utah Church Hist. Office, Salt Lake City, Utah.
WRH	Western Reserve Hist. Soc., Cleveland, Ohio.
Y	Yale University Library, New Haven, Conn.

A

A., AD D'   **1**
Esquisses américaines, ou tablettes d'un voyageur aux États-Unis... *P* 1841. 18° 178 a

A., T.
Carolina; or A description... *L* 1682. *See* Ash, Thomas.

AA, PETER VAN DER, ed. & pub.   **2**
Naaukeurige versameling der gedenkwaardigste zee en land-reysen, na Oost en West-Indien... *Leyden* 1707. 0 30v pls b
—anr. ed., same impr., 1707–08. F 8v pls b
Collection of voyages from 1246 to 1696, embracing many to this continent. The plates were also issued separately, two volumes, folio.

ABBATT, WILLIAM   **3**
The crisis of the revolution... story of Arnold and André... *N Y* 1899. Q [12] 120 fold. map 70pls 2errata slips a 250copies ptd. a

ABBEVILLE, SOUTH CAROLINA.   **4**
Incidents of a journey from: to Ocola [*sic*], Florida, by an observer of small things. *Edgefield S C* 1852. O 44 a

ABBEY, JAMES   **5**
California. A trip across the plains. *New Albany Ind* 1850. D 64 c AA G NYP Y

ABBILDUNG   **6**
Abbildung nordamericanischer Länder und eingebohrner Wilden... *Erfurt* 1757. D [12] 360 pl a
—Rus. tr. *St Ptbg* 1765. O 420

[ABBOTT, JOSEPH]   **7**
The emigrant to North America.. By an emigrant farmer. *Edin* 1843. 18° 128 aa
—rptd. *Montr* 1843, 18° 116; *Edin* 1844, 18° [8] 120 a
Observations cover Canada and Illinois.

ABDY, E[DWARD] S.   **8**
Journal of a residence and tour in the United States... *L* 1835. O 3v: [12] 395; [8] 415; [8] 408 aa

ABEL, ANNIE H.   **9**
The slaveholding Indians... *Clev* 1915–19–25. O 3v: 394; 403; 419 [maps & plans incl. in paginat.] aa

ABENTHEUERLICHE
Abentheuerliche Ereignisse aus dem Leben der ersten Ansiedler an den Grenzen der mittleren und westlichen Staaten... *See* Pritts, Jos.

ABERT (LIEUTENANT [JAMES W.])   **10**
Message from the president... communicating a report of an expedition led by: on the upper Arkansas and through the country of the Camanche Indians. [Sen. Doc. 438]. *Wash* 1846. O 75 map 12pls [col. in a few copies] aa

ABERT (LIEUTENANT J[AMES] W.)   **11**
Report of the Secretary of war, communicating... a report and map of the examination of New Mexico, made by: [*Wash* 1848]. Sen. Ex. Doc. 23. O 132 map 24pls a
For another edition, accompanying Emory's *Notes of a military reconnoissance, see* that entry.

ABHANDLUNGEN   **12**
Abhandlungen über die Kolonien überhaupt, und die amerikanischen besonders. *Bern* 1779. O 152 a
Concluded that by 1879 the seat of England's government would be in America.

[ABILENE, KAS.]   **13**
A gem... Abilene... *Burlington Ia* 1887. 16° 68 [incl. wraps & pls] aa

ABINGDON [EARL OF].
A letter to the Right Honourable Willoughby Bertie, by descent:... *See* Lind, John.

ABINGDON, EARL OF   **14**
Thoughts on the Letter of Edmund Burke to the sheriffs of Bristol [John Farr and John Harris], on the affairs of America. *Oxf* [1777]. O 64 a
—5 other 1777 eds., same impr. & date, of which ed. 6 is the most complete [96p introd. added]
—anr. ed. *Dub* 1777. O 48
—Am. ed. *Lancaster Pa* 1778. O 30
The leading British supporter of colonial rights attacks Burke for temporizing.

ABNEY, A. H.   **15**
Life and adventures of L. D. Lafferty... from an adventurous boyhood in Arkansas, through a protracted life... upon the frontier of Texas... *N Y* [1875]. D 219 [incl. 4pls] aa
Purportedly a true biography; easy to read, but hard to swallow.

ABOLITION   **16**
Abolition a sedition. By a northern man. *Phil* 1838. 18° [8] 187 a
Attributed to Calvin Colton.

Abolition (The) of slavery the right of the   **17**
government under the war power. *B* 1861. D 24 a
—rptd. *B* 1862. same collat.

ABOLITIONISM   **18**
Abolitionism exposed, corrected. By a physician formerly resident in the south... *Phil* 1838. O 40 a

Abolitionism unveiled! Hypocrisy un-   **19**
masked! and knavery scourged! By a physician... resident of the south. *N Y* 1850. O 40 a

ABOTT, ABOTT A.   **20**
The life of Abraham Lincoln. *N Y* 1864. 16° [2] 11–100 aa
—anr. issue, incl. assassination details. 16° [2] 11–104 a

ABRAMS, A[LEXANDER] S.   **21**
A full... history of the siege of Vicksburg. *Atlanta* 1863. O 80 aa

ABRÉGÉ DE LA REVOLUTION...
See Dubuisson, Paul U.

ABRIDGEMENT   **22**
Abridgement (An) of the laws in force... in Her Majesty's plantations... *L* 1704. D [4] 304 aa

Abridgement (An) of the several acts... of   **23**
parliament, relating to the trade and navigation of Great Britain to, from and in the British plantations... *L* 1739. F 44 aa

ABSARAKA, HOME OF THE CROWS...
See Carrington, Mrs. Henry B.

ABSTRACTS   **24**
Abstracts of the principal regulations... in the acts of parliament relative to the trade of the British plantations. *Charlestown Mass* 1774. D 28 aa

ACADIA.   **25**
Remarks on the French Memorials concerning the limits of: *L* 1756. O [4] 110 + 2adv-p 2maps [p57–64 frequently missing] aa

ACADIE.   **26**
Considerations sur les differends des couronnes de la Grande Bretagne et de France, touchant:... fondé sur les Mémoires des commissaires de deux puissances. *Frankf* 1756. D 172 aa

ACADIE (L').   **27**
Pièces justificatives des Memoirs concernant les limites de: *P* 1754. Q [2] 646 aa

ACCOUNT
Account (An) of a late conference on the occurrences in America. *See* Steele, Joshua.

Account of a voyage up the Mississippi... from Mr. Pike's journal. *See* Pike, Zebulon M.

Account (An) of the conduct of the war in the middle colonies... *See* Galloway, Jos., *Letters to a nobleman*...

Account (An) of the earthquakes... in the   **28**
United States... 1811–1812... *Phil* 1812. D 84 a

Account (An) of the European settlements in America... *See* Burke, Wm.

Account (An) of the French settlements in   **29**
North America... By a gentleman. *B* 1746. O 26 b AA H

Account of the grand federal procession... *See* Hopkinson, Francis.

Account (An) of the interment of the remains   **30**
of 11,500 American seamen... on board... prison ships at the Wallabout, during the American revolution... *N Y* 1808. D 96 aa
—rptd. "Letters from the prisons...," *N Y* 1865. O 49 45copies ptd.; also 35copies issued in Q a

Account (An) of the late intended insurrection among... the blacks of this city... *See* Hamilton, James, Jr.

Account (An) of the rise and progress of the American war. *See* Galloway, Jos., *Letters to a nobleman*...

Account (An) of the Society for Propagating   **31**
the Gospel... *L* 1706. Q [2] 97 front. a

Account (An) of the Spanish settlements in America... *See* Campbell, John.

Accounts of shipwreck and of other disasters at sea... *See* Allen, Wm.

ACHENWALL, D. GOTTFRIED   **32**
Anmerkungen über Nord-Amerika und über dasige grosbrittanische Colonien. Aus mündlichen Nachrichten des Herrn Dr. Franklins verfasst. *Stuttgart* 1769. O 94 aa
—anr. ed. *Frankf* 1769. same collat. aa
—rptd. *Helmstedt* 1777. O 72 a
—Dutch tr. *Utrecht* 1778. Q [8] 85
Based on talks with Benj. Franklin.

ACKLEY, MARY E.   **33**
Crossing the plains and early days in California ... *S F* 1928. O 68 front. aa

ACRELIUS, ISRAEL   **34**
Beskrifning om de Swenska Församlingars Forna och Närwarande Tilstånd, uti det så kallade Nya Swerige, sedan Nya Nederland... *Stockh* 1759. Q [20] 534 aa
—Eng. tr. *Phil* 1874. O [50] 17–468 map 2pls a
Most trustworthy contemporary authority on the Swedisch settlements on the Delaware.

ACTES ET MÉMOIRES
Actes et mémoires concernant les negociations ... entre la France et les États-Unis... *See* Gebhardt, A. G.

ACTS   35
Acts passed at a Congress of the United States ... March 4th, 1789. *N Y* Childs & Swaine [1789]. F 105 d NYP
—rptd., same impr. & date. O c
First amendment to the Constitution, the so-called Bill of Rights.

ACUÑA, JUAN DE, Marqués de Casa-Fuerte   36
Reglamento para todos los presidios de las provincias internas de esta governacion... *Mex* 1729. F 36 lvs, [incl. one larger lf, double-folded] d JCB S [of 3copies located]
First of these regulations issued by Mexican viceroys or the kings themselves for the government and conduct of affairs in frontier army garrisons, all of which throw valuable light on early conditions in these remote regions. For the last of such regulations, *see Nueva España. Reglamento ... de:*

ADAIR, CORNELIA   37
My diary, August 30th to November 5th, 1874. *Bath* 1918. D 125 3pls a
Texas interest.

ADAIR, JAMES   38
The history of the American Indians... *L* 1775. Q [12] 464 map b AA N NYP Y
—rptd. *Johnson City Tenn* 1930. O [38] 508 map a
—Ger tr. *Breslau* 1782. O [8] 419 a
Best 18th century English source on the Southern tribes, written by one who traded forty years with them.

ADAIR (GENERAL JOHN).   39
Biographical sketch of: *Wash* 1830. O 24 aa
—rptd. *Harrodsburg Ky* 1831. aa
Has been attributed to Judge James Blair; also to a Mrs. White.

ADAIR (GENERAL [JOHN]), and   40
JACKSON (GENERAL [ANDREW]).
Letters of: relative to the charge of cowardice made by the latter against the Kentucky troops at New Orleans. *Lex* Thos Smith n.d. [1827?]. O 63 b ChiU Y
Anti-Jackson campaign document, based on material in McAfee's *War in the western country.*

ADAIR, W[ILLIAM] P.   41
The expediency... of organizing the Indian country into... the Territory of "Ok-la-ho-ma." [*Wash* 1876]. O 37 aa

**ADAMS, (MISS [ABIGAIL], daughter of   42
John Adams).**
Journal and correspondence of: written in France and England, in 1785. Ed. by her daughter [Mrs. Caroline Amelia (Smith) De Windt]. *N Y* 1841–2. D 2v: [12] 248; [16] 219. 3pls a
—vol. 2, rptd., with date on t-p unchanged, but pref. dated 1849 & with letters of John Q. Adams added. D [10 incl. 2adv-p] 214 219 port [of John Q. Adams] replacing the Trenton battle scene as front.

ADAMS, AMOS   43
A concise... view of the difficulties... which attended the planting [etc.] of New England... *B* 1769. O 66 aa
—*L* 1770. O [2] 68; *B* 1774; *L* 1776. a

ADAMS, AMOS   44
A dissertation... for the yeomanry of the western country. *Marietta* O 1810. D 36 aa

ADAMS, ANDY   45
The log of a cowboy... *B* 1903. D [10] 388 6pls map a

ADAMS, CHARLES F., ed.   46
Antinomianism in... Massachusetts Bay, 1636–8. *B* Prince Soc. 1894. sm Q 416 [incl. front cover] a 250 cops ptd

ADAMS, CHARLES F.   47
A chapter of Erie. *B* 1869, 16° [4] 152 a
—anr. ed., with adds., *B* 1871. D [4] 429

ADAMS, GEORGE J.   48
A lecture on the authenticity... of the Book of Mormon... *B* 1844. O 24 a

[ADAMS, H. J.]   49
Report of... commissioners for the investigation of [Kansas] election frauds... *Leavenworth* 1858. D 142 errata lf. b KasH KasStateCollege G
Report to Governor Denver concerning voting on the acceptance of the Lecompton constitution [forbidding slavery], doomed to failure by armed bands of pro-slave ruffians.

ADAMS, HANNAH   50
A summary history of New England... *Dedham* 1799. O 513 [3] a

ADAMS, HENRY, ed.   51
Documents relating to New England federalism, 1800–1815. *B* 1877. O [12] 437 a
—rptd. same impr. & collat. 1905.

ADAMS (HENRY).   52
The education of: *Wash* priv. ptd. 1907. Q [6] 453 100 cops ptd. c NYP N
—pub'd ed. *B* H.M.Co [Some cops have Mass. Hist. Soc. impr] 1918. 0 [10] 520 a

ADAMS, HENRY   **53**
History of the United States [during the Jefferson and Madison administrations, 1801–1817] *N Y* 1889–1891. D 9v: I, [8] 446 map; II, [8] 456 map; III, [8] 471; IV, [8] 500; V, [8] 428; VI, [8] 488 5 maps; VII, [8] 417 6 pls; VIII, [8] 385 16 pls; IX, [8] 369 aa
—Eng. ed. *L* 1891–2. 9v aa
—anr. ed. *N Y* 1930. 9v in 4 a
—rptd. *N Y* 1961. 9v
The most skilfully organized and most brilliantly presented interpretation of any period of our history yet attempted.

ADAMS, HENRY   **54**
The life of Albert Gallatin. *Phil* 1879. O [6] 697 [incl. map] 2ports aa
—rptd: *Phil* 1880; *N Y* 1943. a

ADAMS (ISRAEL).   **55**
A narrative of the life and travels of: *Cortland N Y* 1843. O 28 b
—anr. ed. *Utica* 1847. O 36 aa
Includes War of 1812 services.

ADAMS, J. S.   **56**
Florida; its climate, etc. *Jacksonv* 1869. O 151 a

ADAMS (JAMES CAPEN).
Adventures of: *See* Hittell, Theodore H.

ADAMS (J[AMES] C[APEN]).   **57**
Life of: *N Y* 1860. 16° 29 + 3adv-p b Hn Y
—anr. [later] issue, with adds. 53 + cover t. b
—other eds., same impr.: 1874; 1884. a

ADAMS, JAMES T.   **58**
Atlas of American history. *N Y* [1943]. O [12] 360 [incl. 147maps] a

ADAMS (MR. [JOHN]).
A brief consideration of the... services which recommend: for the presidency. *See* Gardner, John.

ADAMS (JOHN).   **59**
Correspondence of: concerning the British doctrine of impressment... *Balt* 1809. D 72 a

ADAMS, JOHN   **60**
A defense of the constitutions of government of the United States... *L* 1787. O [32] 392 a
—Am. eds.: *Phil* 1787. O [20] 3–390; *N Y* 1787. O [24] 390 [4]; *B* 1788. D [30] 317 a
—complete ed. *L* 1787–8. O 3v: [32] 392; [2] 651; [2] 528 [36] aa
—rptd. *L* 1794. O 3v: [40] 392; [4] 452; [4] 528 [36]. port aa
—anr. ed. "History of the principal republics...," *L* 1794. O 3v: [38] 392; 451; 528 [36] aa
—Am. ed. called ed. 3, *Phil* 1797. O 3v: [40] 392; [6] 451; [2] 528 [36]. port aa
—Fr. tr. *P* 1792. O 2v: [24] 547; 503 a

ADAMS (JOHN and SAMUEL).   **61**
Four letters... correspondence between...: on the important subject of government. *B* 1802. O 32 a

ADAMS, JOHN   **62**
History of the dispute with America... *L* 1784. O 90 + adv-l. a
—Dutch tr. *Amst* 1782. O [8] 156 port
Separate [and abridged] publications of his *Letters of Novanglus* which had appeared serially in a Boston paper in 1774. For later edition, *see* below *Novanglus and Massachusettensis*.

ADAMS, JOHN, [and LEONARD, DANIEL]   **63**
Novanglus and Massachusettensis; or, political essays, published in... 1774 and 1775, on the.. controversy between Great Britain and her colonies... *B* 1819. O 312 a

ADAMS (JOHN).   **64**
Political sketches inscribed to...: By a citizen of the United States. *L* 1787. O [4] 96 a

[ADAMS, JOHN]   **65**
Thoughts on government: applicable to the present state of the American colonies... *Phil* 1776. D 28 a
—rptd. *B* 1776. D 16
—abr. ed. *B* 1788.
Written in opposition to ideas advanced in Paine's *Common sense*.

ADAMS, JOHN   **66**
Twenty-six letters... respecting the revolution of America... *L* [1786]. D 87 + adv-l. at front a
—Am. eds.: *N Y* Fenno "for subscribers" 1789. D 89
—rptd. *N Y* Fenno "never before published" 1789. D 64

ADAMS (JOHN).   **67**
A vindication of the character of: in reply to the Letter of General Hamilton... *N Y* 1800. O 24 a

ADAMS (JOHN Q.) et al.   **68**
Correspondence between: concerning the charge of a design to dissolve the Union... *B* 1829. O 80 a
—ed. 2, *B* 1829. O 48
—rptd. *Wash* 1829. O 56

ADAMS, JOHN Q.   **69**
Memoirs... portions of his diary from 1795 to 1848. Ed. Charles F. Adams. *Phil* 1874–77. O 12v 3ports b AA N NYP Y 250sets ptd.

ADAMS, NATHANIEL   **70**
Annals of Portsmouth [N. H.]... *Portsmouth* 1825 O 400 a

[ADAMS, SAMUEL]   71
An appeal to the world; or, a vindication of the
town of Boston... B 1769. D 37 aa
—Eng. ed. L 1769. D [2] 58 a
—rptd. L 1770. same collat.
Attributed also to William Cooper.

ADAMS, SAMUEL   72
An oration... at the State House in Philadelphia... 1st of August, 1776. Phil ptd, L rptd
1776. O [2] 42 a
Of this oration [never delivered], there was no
Philadelphia edition [in spite of its being indicated
by title-page]; it was, in fact a London forgery
designed to show that the colonies were bent on
independence.

ADAMS, WILLIAM L.   73
Lecture on Oregon... B 1869. O 39 a

ADAMS, WILLIAM L.   74
Oregon as it is... Port Ore 1873. O 62 tabs
errata lf aa
—rptd., same impr., 1875 a
First Oregon-printed Northwestern guide.

ADAMSON, AUGUSTUS P.   75
Brief history of the Thirtieth Georgia regiment.
Griffin, Ga 1912. O 157 front aa

ADDITIONAL
Additional number (An) of letters prom [sic]
the federal farmer... See Lee, Richard H.

ADDRESS   76
Address and recommendations to the states, by
the United States in Congress assembled... Phil
1783. O 35 lvs aa
—anr. issue, with foot-note added, same impr. &
date. O 37 lvs aa
—other 1783 eds.: B O 62; Trenton D 36; Rich
O 60 aa
—anr. ed. with a Conn. report added, Hart 1783.
Q 2pts in 1: 50; 31. tab aa
—Eng. ed. L 1783. O 91 a
On the necessity of raising national revenue,
etc. Largely the work of Madison.

Address (An) of the members of... the   77
Congress of the United States, to their constituents,
on... the war with Great Britain. Alexandria 1812.
O 35 a
—other Am. eds., same date: B; Hart; Balt; N Y;
Northampton; Phil; Portsmouth.
—Eng. ed. L 1813. O

Address (The) of the people of Great Britain to
the inhabitants of America. See Dalrymple, Sir
John.

Address (An) to the Congress of the United
States... 1809. See Brown, Chas. B.

Address to the deputies of North America   78
in general congress. [Signed Freeman]. [Charleston
SC 1774]. Q 47 aa
Plea to have Congress declare boldly American
grievances.

Address (An) to the inhabitants of the British
settlements in America, upon slavekeeping. See
Rush, Benj.

Address (An) to the Parliament... of Great   79
Britain on... affairs between Spain and Great
Britain respecting their American possessions. L
Debrett 1790. O [2] 49 b LC NYP ProvL Victoria
Nootka controversy. Written under pseudonym
Zetes.

Address (An) to the people of Great Britain   80
in general... on the present crisis of American
politics. Bristol 1776. O 79 a

Address (An) to the people of the United States,
on the policy of maintaining a permanent navy.
See Bronson, Enos.

Address (An) to the public... on the present
political state of the American republicks... See
Thurston, Benj.

Address to the Rt. Hon. L-d M-sf-d...   81
respecting America... L 1775. O 35 a

ADIRONDACKS (THE).   82
Life in:... By one of the Q, C. [N Y] 1876.
O 23 a

ADMINISTRATION
Administration (The) of the colonies. See
Pownall, Thos.

ADTS, N.   83
Le Monitor et le Merrimac. P 1862. O 40 pl a

ADVENTURES   84
Adventures (The) of a captain's wife... through
the straits of Magellan to California in 1850...
N Y 1877. D 63 a

Adventures of a porcupine... See Henderson,
Archibald.

AFFAIRES DE L'ANGLETERRE   85
Affaires de l'Angleterre et de l'Amérique.
Antwerp [P ptd] 1776–9. O 24pts, divided into
15v [usually bound in 17v] b NYP Y
Edited by Franklin and others to give France a
favorable American view of revolutionary events.
A French counterpart of the English periodical,
Almon's Remembrancer.

AFFECTIONATE ADDRESS   86
Affectionate address (An) to the inhabitants of the British colonies in America. By a lover... of mankind. *N Y* 1776. O [6] 55 aa
—anr. issue [*Phil*] same yr. & collat. aa

AFRICAN RACE   87
African race (The) in the United States. An enquiry into the condition... of: By an American. *Phil* 1839. D 214 a

AFTER FORTY YEARS.
See Gorrell, Joseph R.

AFTER THE MOONSHINERS.
By one of the raiders. *See* Atkinson, Geo. W.

AGASSIZ, LOUIS   88
Lake Superior... *B* 1850. O [12] 9–428 + 4 duplicated p [239–42] and 20adv-p map 16pls [natural hist pls colored in some cops] aa

AGEE, G[EORGE] W.   89
Rube Burrow, king of outlaws... [*Cin* 1890]. D [10] 194 port a
—anr. iss has *Chi* impr

AINSWORTH, DANFORTH H.   90
Recollections of a civil engineer. *Newton Ia* 1901. O [2] 192 a

[AITKEN, JAMES]   91
From the Clyde to California... *Greenock* 1882. D [8] 152 8pls a

AITKEN, W. A.   92
A journey up the Mississippi... to Nauvoo. *Ashton Eng* ptd by Williamson [1845?]. O 56 b Y
—ed. 2, same impr. ptd. by Micklethwaite [1845?]. O 58 b Y

AKEN, DAVID   93
Pioneers of the Black hills... [*Milw* 1920?]. D 151 [incl.front]. a
Narrative by one of the twenty-eight members of Gordon's gold-seeking expedition of 1874, made in defiance of government orders.

AKERLY, SAMUEL   94
An essay on the geology of the Hudson river... *N Y* 1820. D 69 map a

AKIN (JAMES).   95
The journal of: Ed. by E. E. Dale. *Norman Okla* 1919. O 32 [cover t.] a
Seven of this 1842 ox-team party to Oregon died on the way.

ALABAMA
A Catholic history of Alabama and the Floridas. By a member of the Order of Mercy. *See* Carroll, Mother Mary Austin.

History of Co. B., 40th Alabama regiment. *See* Willett, Elbert D.

Scenes and settlers of Alabama. *See* Ravesies, Paul.

"ALABAMA (THE)"
The career of the "Alabama"... *L* 1864.   96
O 43 a

The cruise of the "Alabama"... By an officer on board. *See* Haywood, P. D.

The cruise of the "Alabama"... By one of the crew. *See* Haywood, P. D.

[ALAMAN, LUCAS]   97
Memoria presentada a los dos camaras del Congreso... por el Secretario de Estado. *Mex* [1825]. O 51 aa
Contains material on the missions in California and Texas.

[ALAMAN, LUCAS]   98
Memoria que el Secretario de Estado y del Despacho de Relaciones Esteriores e Interiores, presentado al... Congreso. *Mex* 1823. O 60 3charts b
Contains account of California and of explorations for an overland route thereto.

ALAMEDA COUNTY, CALIFORNIA.   99
History of: *Oakl* 1883. Q [4] 7-1001 pls aa

ALARM   100
Alarm; or, a plan of pacification with America ... *N Y* [*ca* 1781]. 16° 64 aa

ALASKA
Alaska, the Eldorado of the midnight sun...
See Hall, Edw. H.

Compilation of narratives of exploration   101
in Alaska. *Wash* 1900. Q 856 27maps 33pls a

Latest information about the Alaska gold fields. *See* Hiller, E. H.

New official map of Alaska and the Klondike   102
gold fields. *Chi* 1897. D 28 fold.map a
—anr. iss, same collat *Phil* 1897

ALBACH, JAMES R. [comp.]
Annals of the west. *See* Perkins, James H.

ALBANY [ORE.]... DIRECTORY...   103
Albany Ore 1878. O [19] 175 aa

ALBANY [N. Y.]
Random recollections of: *See* Worth, Gorham A.

ALBANY COUNTY [WYO.]...   **104**
Also the city of Laramie... *Laramie* 1896. O 51 map pls a

[ALCAREZ, RAMÓN, et al]   **105**
Apuntes para la historia de la guerra entre Mexico y los Estados-Unidos. *Mex* 1848. D [8] 401 [3] 27maps & pls b
—Eng. tr., ed. by A. C. Ramsey, "The other side: or notes for the history of the war between Mexico and the United States." *N Y* 1850. D [16] 458 24maps & pls aa
The original Spanish edition was suppressed by Santa Anna.

ALDEN, TIMOTHY   **106**
An account of... missions... among the Senecas... *N Y* 1827. 16° 180 port a

ALDEN, TIMOTHY   **107**
A collection of American epitaphs... *N Y* 1812–14. 16° 5v: 292; 288; 288; 288; 288 + 4 l. of subscribers. 5pls a
—vol. 1, rptd. 1814, usually found with sets, as the 1812 ed. of that vol. was issued in 4pts & is scarce.

ALDERSON, MATT W.   **108**
Bozeman; a guide... *Bozeman Mont* 1883. D 54 map aa

ALDRICH, LORENZO D.   **109**
A journal of the overland route to California! ... *Lansingburgh N Y* 1851. O 48 dd AA Y G S [all known]
—rptd. *L A* 1950. D [12] 95 map a
Reached San Diego, via Santa Fe route, Tucson and the Gila, early in December, 1849; the first printed account — aside from Pattie — of a civilian journey through Arizona.

ALDRIDGE, REGINALD   **110**
Life on a ranch... *N Y* 1884. D [8] 227 + 4adv p 4pls a
—Eng. ed. "Ranch notes [etc.]," *L* 1884, same collat. + 16adv p

ALDRIDGE, WILLIAM [ed.]   **111**
A narrative of the Lord's wonderful dealings with John Marrant... *L* 1785. O 38 aa
—eds. 2 & 3, same collat., 1785 aa
—eds. 3 & 4, with adds., 1785. O 40 aa
—rptd. *L* [1785]. O 40 aa
—ed. 5, [*L* 1785]. Q 26
—anr. ed., title altered, [*L*?] 1787. O [4] 22 aa
—ed. 6, *L* 1788. O 40 aa
—rptd. *Dub* 1790. D 32; *L* 1790 a
—ed. 7, *L* 1802. O 40
—other eds.: *Halifax* 1808; *Leeds* Davies & Co 1810; *Leeds* Preston & Co 1810; *Halifax* 1812; *York* 1812; *Brighton* 1813; *Halifax* 1813; *Newry* 1813; and 12 others before 1840.

The wide and sustained popularity of this historically unimportant captivity can only be explained by its appeal to a fanatically religious age. Marrant's book was, however, one of the earliest written by an American Negro.

ALEGRE, FRANCISCO X.   **112**
Historia de la Compañia de Jesús en Nueva España. *Mex* 1841–2. Q 3v: [8] 460; [6] 476; 310. 2ports aa
For continuation, see Dávila y Arrillaga, José M.

ALER, F. VERNON   **113**
History of Martinsburg and Berkeley County, W. Va... *Hagerstown* 1888. O 438 [incl.front] a

ALEXANDER, EDWARD P.   **114**
Military memoirs of a Confederate... *N Y* 1907. O [18] 634 map 3pls a
—rptd. 1908. same impr. & collat.
—Eng. ed. "The American civil war," same collat., *L* 1908.

ALEXANDER, HARTLEY B.   **115**
L'art et la philosophie des Indiens... *P* 1926. O [8] 118 26 pls a

ALEXANDER, HARTLEY B.   **116**
Sioux Indian painting... *Nice France* [ca 1938]. F 2v: 10; 6. 50col.pls b N NYP Y 400copies ptd.

ALEXANDER, JAMES E.   **117**
Transatlantic sketches... *L* 1833. O 2v: [24] 384; [16] 320. map 10pls a
—rptd. *Phil* 1833. O 378 + adv pp

ALEXANDER, JESSE H.   **118**
Indian horrors of the fifties... *Synarep Wash* [ptd *Yakima*] n.d. [1916]. O 170 front. a

ALEXANDER, J[OHN] B.   **119**
Biographical sketches of the early settlers of the Hopewell section [N.C.]. *Charlotte* 1897. O 104 port a

ALEXANDER, JOHN H.   **120**
Mosby's men. *N Y* 1907. O 180 a

ALEXANDER, T[ONY]   **121**
Experiences of a trapper... *Linnton Ore* 1924. O 118 + adv-p a

ALEXANDER, TONY   **122**
Practical hunter's and trapper's guide... *N Y* [1887]. D 121 pls a

[ALEXANDER, WILLIAM, LORD STIRLING]   **123**
The conduct of Major Gen. Shirley... *L* 1758. O [8] 131 aa

Relates to the attack on Niagara, etc. Ascribed also to Gen. Shirley, but probably by Alexander, his secretary.

[ALEXANDER, WILLIAM, LORD STIRLING]   **124**

Memoirs of the principal transactions of the last war between the English and French in North America... *L* 1757. O [8] 102 aa
—ed. 2, *L* 1758 aa
—Am. ed. *B* 1758. O [4] 9–80 aa

Ascribed also to the British commander, William Shirley, whose conduct of the campaign [against Louisbourg and the island of Cape Breton] is defended.

ALEXANDRE, PHILIP L.   **125**

Alexandre's compendium... Oklahoma City in detail, Oklahoma Territory in general, Kiowa and Comanche country in particular. *Okla City* 1901. 16° [4] 208; [6] 209; aa

ALEXIS   **126**

Alexis (The grand duke)... in the United States... *C* 1872. O [4] 224 port aa

Hunting expedition on the plains and large-scale destruction of the vanishing buffalo.

ALLGEMEINE GESCHICHTE

Allgemeine Geschichte der Länder und Völker von America. *See* Schröter, Johann F.

ALGIERS.   **127**

A short account of: with... view of the origin of the rupture between Algiers and the United States... *Phil* 1794. O [2] 46 map a
—ed. 2, *Phil* 1794. O 50 map
—enl. ed. "A short history of Algiers...," *N Y* 1805. 24° 106 [2]

ALIANO, JACOPI

Chronicles of Ohio... *See* Allen, James.

ALL THE MEMORIALS

All the Memorials of the courts of Great Britain and France... *See Memoires des commissaires du roi*...

ALLAN (COLONEL JOHN)...   **128**

Memoir of: *Alb* 1867. O 32 a

ALLAN, WILLIAM   **129**

The Army of Northern Virginia in 1862. *B* 1892. O [10] 537 4maps port aa

ALLAN, WILLIAM   **130**

History of the campaign in the Shenandoah valley... *Phil* 1880. O 175 9maps on 6pls a
—rptd. "Stonewall Jackson's campaign...," *L* 1912. O [16] 284 8maps [on 7 sheets]

[ALLARDICE, ROBERT B.]

Agricultural tour in the United States... *See* Barclay, Robt.

ALLEN, MISS A. J. [comp.]   **131**

Ten years in Oregon. Travels and adventures of Doctor E. White and lady... *Ithaca* 1848. D 399 [incl. port] a
—anr. issue, port. omitted, paginat. extended to 430 [with extracts from Fremont]
—rptd., same collat., 1850, with altered title, *N Y* 1859.

White, fervent Presbyterian missionary and political propagandist, describes his trip out, in 1842, and back, in 1845, as well as his part in the civic organization of Oregon.

ALLEN (ELIZA)   **132**

Allen (Eliza), the female volunteer. [*Cin* 1851]. O 68 a

ALLEN, ETHAN   **133**

An animadversory address to the inhabitants of... Vermont... *Hart* 1778. O 24 c AA BA JCB

ALLEN, ETHAN   **134**

A brief narrative of the proceedings of the government of New-York, relative to their obtaining the jurisdiction of that large district of land to the westward from Connecticut river, which... had been patented by... New Hampshire ... *Hart* [1774]. O 211 c AA BA MH Y

ALLEN, ETHAN, and FAY, JONES   **135**

A concise refutation of the claims of New-Hampshire and Massachusetts Bay to the territory of Vermont... *Hart* [1780]. O 29 c AA Hn Y

ALLEN, ETHAN   **136**

A narrative of [his] captivity... *Phil* Bell 1779. O [2] 46 c
—rptd: *B* 1779. O 40 b AA NYP; *N Y* 1779 b
—anr. ed. *Phil* Mentz 1779. O 64 b NYH
—other eds.: *Newbury* 1780. O 80 b; *Norwich* 1780. same collat. b; *Walpole* 1807. D 158 [2] a; *Alb* 1814. D 144; *Burl Vt* 1838; *B* 1845; *Burl* 1846; *Burl* 1849; *Dayton* 1849.

ALLEN, ETHAN   **137**

A vindication of the opposition of the inhabitants of Vermont to the government of New York, and of their right to form into an independent state... [*Dresden*] 1779, sm Q 172 b AA LC Hn NYP Y

One of the earliest non-legal Vermont imprints, Dresden (now Hanover, New Hampshire) being then in Vermont.

ALLEN, REV. ETHAN   **138**

Historical notices of St. Ann's parish in Ann-Arundel county, Md... *Balt* 1857. D 131 + errata slip a

ALLEN, REV. ETHAN   **139**
Maryland toleration... early history of Maryland... *Balt* 1855. O 64 a

[ALLEN, LIEUT. G. N.]   **140**
Mexican treacheries and cruelties... *B* 1847. O 32 aa
—rptd., same impr., 1848. a
Reasonably uncommon; utterly worthless.

ALLEN, GOV. HENRY W.   **141**
Official report relative to the conduct of Federal troops in western Louisiana... 1863 and 1864... *Shrevept* 1865. O 89 aa

ALLEN, IRA   **142**
The natural and political history of... Vermont ... *L* 1798. O [8] 300 map[not issued in all copies]b

ALLEN, IRA   **143**
Particulars of the capture of the ship Olive Branch... with a cargo of arms... destined for supplying the militia of Vermont... with the proceedings... before the High Court of Admiralty... Vol. I. *L* 1798. O [6] 406 b
—vol. II, issued later, without t-p & unfinished [ending with p368], was also ptd, possibly at *Phil*, in 1804, & is sometimes found with v. I. aa
—anr. ed. calling itself v. II, but really complete in itself as it includes a resumé of v. I. *Phil* 1805. O [30] 551 aa
—"Concise summary of the Second volume...," *Phil* 1806. O 24 aa
—rptd. *Phil* 1807. O aa
An Admiralty "cause célèbre"; Allen's ship was seized on suspicion that its cargo was going to Ireland. For an earlier edition, see below, *Twenty thousand muskets...*

ALLEN, IRA   **144**
Some miscellaneous remarks... on a small pamphlet, dated in the convention... of New York, October 2, 1776... And some reasons... why the District of the New-Hampshire Grants had best be a state. *Hart* 1777. Q 26 b H NYH

[ALLEN, IRA]   **145**
Twenty thousand muskets!!! Particulars of the capture of the ship Olive Branch... *L* 1797. O [4] 106 aa
For amplification, see above, *Particulars of the capture...*

ALLEN, IRA   **146**
A vindication of the conduct of the general assembly of... Vermont... *Dresden* [now Hanover *N H*] 1779. D 48 b Hn

ALLEN, JAMES   **147**
Chronicles of Ohio... snatched from oblivion

and rendered into English, from... Chaldaic, by ... Jacopi Aliano... *Columbus* 1841. O 30? [no perfect copy known] aa
Harrison campaign political pamphlet.

ALLEN, LIEUT. [JAMES] and   **148**
SCHOOLCRAFT, HENRY R.
Expedition to the northwest Indians... in 1832. [Wash 1834]. O 68 map a
A one-page correction list issued at Chicago in 1835 was the first Chicago imprint.

ALLEN, JOEL A.   **149**
The American bisons... *C* 1876. Q [10] 246 map & 12pls [each with lf of letter press] b G LC NYP Y
—anr. ed. *Sans* map and pls, issued as vol. I, pt. 2, Memoirs, Ky. Geol. Survey. aa
—abr. ed. "History of the American bison," without pls, from 9th annual report, U.S. Geol. Survey, *Wash* 1877. O [2] 443–587 a

ALLEN, JOHN   **150**
Uncle John Allen's rambles in the Rockies... *Hermitage Tenn* 1917. D 94 a
Crossed the plains in 1866, prospected a bit, then for thirty years hunted throughout the West.

[ALLEN, REV. JOHN]   **151**
An essay on the policy of appropriations... by the government... for purchasing, liberating and colonizing, the slaves... *Balt* 1826. O 40 a

ALLEN, LEWIS L.   **152**
Pencillings of scenes upon the Rio Grande... *N Y* 1848. D 48 a

ALLEN, L[EWIS] L.   **153**
A thrilling sketch of... the distinguished chief Okah Tubbee... of the Choctaw nation... *N Y* 1848. D 43 a
First part [all published] of a contemplated series. *See* also Tubbee, Laah C. M. E.

ALLEN, O[BRIDGE]   **154**
Guide book and map to the gold fields of Kansas and Nebraska and Great Salt Lake City. *Wash* 1859. D 68 map[ptd. later & probably not issued with the book, but found in one copy] c WisH Y [of 3copies known]
For what is probably the proper book for this map, *see* Gunnison, John W., and Gilpin, William.

ALLEN, PAUL   **155**
A history of the American revolution. *Balt* 1819. O 2v: [12] 592; [14] 510 a
—rptd., same collat. *Balt* 1822.
Allen's name on title-page, but actually written by John Neal.

19

ALLEN, PAUL [ed.]
History of the expedition under... Lewis and Clark. *See* Lewis, Meriwether, and Clark, William.

ALLEN, T. S., comp.   156
Directory of... Mineral Point [Wis.] for 1859. Containing also a sketch of the history... *Mineral Point* 1859. O 64 aa

ALLEN, THADDEUS   157
An inquiry into the views... of the leading men in the origination of our Union... Vol. I & v. II, pt. 1 [all.]. *B* 1847–8. O v. 1 553; v. 2, pt. 1 555–662 aa

[ALLEN, THOMAS]   158
The commerce and navigation of the valley of the Mississippi... *St L* [1847]. O 32 aa

ALLEN, THOMAS   159
Pacific railroad commenced. *St L* 1850. O 46 b NYP StLP Y

ALLEN, WALTER   160
Governor Chamberlain's administration in South Carolina... *N Y* 1888. O [16] 544 port a

ALLEN, WILKES   161
History of Chelmsford [Mass.]... *Haverhill* 1820. O 192 a. 400 cops ptd

ALLEN, WILLIAM, of Eng.   162
The American crisis: a letter... on the present alarming disturbances... a complete plan of restoring the dependence of America upon Great Britain... *L* 1774. O [4] 72 a

[ALLEN, WILLIAM] 1784—1868   163
Accounts of shipwreck and of other disasters at sea... *Brunswick Me* 1823. D [24] 335 a

ALLEN, WILLIAM, 1784—1868   164
The history of Norridgewock [Maine]... *Norridgewock* 1849. D 252 6pls eng.t. a

ALLEN, WILLIAM A.   165
Adventures with Indians and game. *Chi* 1903. O 302 27pls[22 incl. in paginat.] front. a

ALLEN, WILLIAM A.   166
The Sheep Eaters. *N Y* 1913. D 78 6pls a

ALLEN, WILLIAM B.   167
History of Kentucky... *Louisv* 1872. O 449 port a

ALLEY, B. F., pub.   168
Linn county, Oregon, descriptive... *Albany Ore* [1889]. O 111 a

ALLEY, B. F., and   169
MUNRO-FRASER, J. P.
Washington Territory... *Olympia* 1886. O 142 tab a

ALLEYNE, C. H.   170
A description of Polk county, Florida... *Sanford Fla* 1885. D 44 a

ALLGEMEINE...   171
Allgemeine amerikanischer Kriegsgeschichte, an den Flüssen Ohio, St. Laurenz... *Frankf* 1756. D [18] 121 + 3adv-p a map 2pls aa

ALLHANDS, J. L.   172
Gringo builders... [*Ia C*] 1931. O 284 [13] a

ALLISON (CLAY) OF THE WASHITA...
See Clark, O. S.

ALLISON, [EDWIN H.]   173
The surrender of Sitting Bull... *Dayton* 1891. D 85 aa

ALLISON, J.   174
Trans-continental letters... across the plains to Colorado, Salt Lake and California. *Milw* 1871. D 67 b Y

ALLSOP, ROBERT [ed.]   175
California and its gold mines... *L* 1853. 16° 149 aa

[ALLSTON, JOSEPH]   176
A short review of the late proceedings at New Orleans. [Charleston?] 1807. O 42 [1] aa
—rptd. *Rich* 1807. O 35 aa
Defense of Burr by his son-in-law, excoriating both Wilkinson and Jefferson.

ALMBERT, ALFRED d'   177
Flânerie parisienne aux États-Unis. *P* 1856. D [4] 279 a
Urges criminal prosecution against writers praising the U.S.

[ALMON, JOHN?]   178
An appendix to the Review of Mr. Pitt's administration. *L* 1763. O 36 a
—other eds.: *L* 1763. O 40; *L* 1763. O 116

[ALMON, JOHN] ed.   179
A collection of interesting, authentic papers, relative to the dispute between Great Britain and America... causes and progress of that misunderstanding... 1764–1775. *L* 1777. O 280 [3] aa
Usually cited as *Prior documents*, from its running title, these papers were intended to accompany the 17 volumes of *The remembrancer*, described below.

[ALMON, JOHN]?   180
An impartial history of the late war... 1749–
1763. *L* 1763. D [4] 9–421 6pls aa
—ed. 2, same impr., date & collat. aa

ALMON ([JOHN])...   181
Memoirs of: *L* 1790. O 262 a

[ALMON, JOHN] ed.   182
The remembrancer; or, impartial repository of
public events, from 1775 to 1784. *L* 1775–84.
O 17v each separately paged, with separate t-p;
some with separate index; 2maps in v. I, 2maps
in v. IV, & port of Franklin in v. V. b AA JCB
NYP TorP
Volume one only was reprinted—three times in
1775—in larger format, and an undated octavo
edition without maps was issued later.
A complete set should include volume noted
above, *A collection of interesting... papers*; some
sets include also Almon's 1776 or 1778 edition of
the *Journal... of Congress, held at Philadelphia,
May 10, 1775*.

[ALMON, JOHN?]   183
A review of Lord Bute's administration... *L*
1763. O 116 port a

[ALMON, JOHN?]   184
A review of Mr. Pitt's administration. *L* 1762.
O 141 a
—ed. 2, with adds., same impr. 1763. O [8] 7–150
6ports.
—ed. 3, same impr. & date. O 152
—ed. 4, *L* 1764.
—ed. 5, *L* 1766.

ALMONTE, GENERAL JUAN N.   185
Memoria del Ministerio de Estado... del
gobierno supremo de Mexico. *Mex* 1846. O 44
tables aa
Largely concerned with the Texas war and the
attitude of the United States.

ALMONTE, [GEN.] JUAN N.   186
Noticia estadistica sobre Tejas... *Mex* 1835.
O 96 [4] + 3 tabs b N Y
Official report based on extensive travel.

ALRIC, HENRY J. A.   187
Dix ans... dans les deux Californies. *Mex* 1866.
Q 53 errata slip aa

ALSOP, GEORGE   188
A character of the province of Mary-land...
L 1666. 16° [20] 118 map port dd H LC N
—rptd. *N Y* 1869. O 125 map port a
—anr. ed. *Clev* 1902. O 113 map port

[ALSOP, RICHARD] ed.   189
A narrative of the adventures and sufferings of
John R. Jewitt... during a captivity... among the
savages of Nootka sound... *Middletown* Loomis
& Richards 1815. D 203 2pls aa
—anr. issue, impr. Seth Richards a
—later Am. eds.: *N Y* [*ca* 1815]; *Middletown* 1816;
N Y 1816; *Middletown* 1820; *Ithaca* 1849; *N Y*
1849; *Ithaca* 1857.
—Eng. eds.: *Wakefield & L* 1816; same 1820;
Edin 1824.
For the author's original *Journal*, amplified by
Alsop into above *Narrative, see* Jewitt, John R.

ALTAMIRANO, PEDRO I.   190
Informe historico... por las missiones de la
Compania de Jesus de la Nueva-España: en el
expediente... sobre... missiones de Sinaloa,
Sonora y otras... [*Madrid ca* 1755]. O 44 dd Y

ALTER, J. CECIL   191
James Bridger... *S L C* [1925]. O [18] 546
18pls aa
—enl. ed. *Columbus* O 1951. O 601 18pls a

ALTON [ILL.]
General city directory... of: 1858. *See* McEvoy
& Bowron, pubs.

ALVAREZ, FRANCISCO, ed.   192
Noticia del establecimiento y poblacion de las
colonias inglesas en la America Septentrional...
Madrid 1778. sm Q 196 aa
Compiled from various sources.

ALVORD, LIEUT. BENJAMIN   193
Address before the Dialectic Society of the
Corps of Cadets in commemoration of the...
officers... who fell in the battles... in Florida...
N Y 1839. O 62 a

ALVORD, CLARENCE W., and   194
BIDGOOD, LEE
The first explorations of the trans-Allegheny
region by the Virginians. *Clev* 1912. O 275 [incl.
2maps & 4facs] aa

ALVORD, CLARENCE W.   195
The Mississippi valley in British politics... *Clev*
1917. O 2v: 358; 396. 4maps [incl. in paginat.] aa

AMADOR COUNTY, CALIFORNIA.   196
History of: *Oakl* 1881. Q 344 pls b B Hn N
CalS

AMBLER, CHARLES H.   197
The life and diary of John Floyd, governor of
Virginia... and the father of the Oregon country.
[*Rich* 1918]. D 248 port a

AMBLER, CHARLES H.   **198**
Sectionalism in Virginia... *Chi* 1910. D [10] 366
12maps a

AMERICA
America and France... message of the   **199**
President [i.e., John Adams]... covering the full
powers to, and dispatches from, the Envoys... to
the French republic. *B* 1798. O 71 a
—Eng. ed. "American state papers... documents...," *L* 1798. sm Q 30

America and the americans. By a citizen of the
world. *See* Boardman, James.

America compared with England.... *See* Russell,
Robt. W.

America dissected... *See* MacSparran, James

America (L') geografico-storico politica...   **200**
descrizione, e nome d'ogni provincia... *Venice* 1785.
Q 3v: [16] 322; [8] 288; [12] 236 aa

America pois'd in the balance of justice   **201**
... the mother country and her colonies... considered in a new light... By P—oplicola H—istor-
icus. [*L*] 1776. Q 40 2pls a

America vindicated from... charge of in-   **202**
gratitude and rebellion... By a friend... *Devizes
Eng* 1774. O [4] 48 a

AMERICAN
American alarm (The)... for the rights, and
liberties, of the people... *See* Skillman, Isaac.

American and British chronicle (The) of   **203**
war and politics... 1773–1783... *L* [1783]. O 64
lvs aa

American anecdotes [on the revolution,   **204**
etc.]. By an American. *B* 1830. D 2v: 300; 300 a
Attributed to Freeman Hunt.

American annual register (The), or, historical
memoirs of the United States, for... 1796. *See*
Callender, James T.

American atlas. *Phil* 1795. *See* Carey, Mathew.

American atlas (The). *N Y* 1796. *See* Reid, John.

American atlas (The); or, a geographical
description... *See* Jefferys, Thos., *A general
topography*...

American (The) bloody register... *B* 1784.   **205**
No. 1 [all] 16° 30 aa
—rptd. t changed. *Worc* 1784. a

American coast pilot (The)... *See* Furlong,
Laurence.

American crisis (The). By a citizen of the   **206**
world... *L* 1777. O [4] 31 a

American crisis (The). By the author of Common
sense. *See* Paine, Thos.

American field of Mars (An)... *See* Eggleston,
Benjamin.

American gazetteer (The)... account of   **207**
all the parts of the new world... *L* 1762. D 3v: [24]
324; 348; 348 6maps aa
—Ital. ed. "Il gazzettiere americano...," *Leghorn*
1763. Q 3v: [24] 217; 256; 253; 78maps and pls b

American husbandry. *L* 1775. *See* Young,
Arthur.

American independence the interest and glory of
Great Britain... *See* Cartwright, John.

American mariners (The), or the Atlantic
voyage... *See* Davis, John.

American memoranda... during a short tour in
... 1843. *See* Lumsden, James.

American military pocket atlas (The)...   **208**
L Sayer & Bennet [1776]. O 8 6fold.maps a

American naval battles: being a complete
history... *See* Kimball, Horace, *The naval
temple*...

American Nepos (The):... lives of... men, who
have contributed to the discovery,... of America.
See Wilmer, James J.

American pilot (The). [*B*] J[ohn] Norman   **209**
1793. F [6] 11maps b LC
—rptd. *B* 1794, F [4] 11maps aa
—anr. ed. *B* W[illiam] Norman 1798. F [6]
9maps aa
—rptd. *B* 1803. F [8] 11maps aa

American pioneer (The)... 1842–3. *See* Williams,
John S.

American political and military biography   **210**
... n.p. 1825. D 424 a

American querist (The)... By a North-American.
See Cooper, Myles.

American register (The); or, summary review...
See Walsh, Robt.

American remembrancer (The)... relative... to the treaty with Great Britain. *See* Carey, Mathew.

American review (The) of history and politics... *See* Walsh, Robt.

American (The) shooter's manual... *See* Kester, Jesse Y.

American sketches. By a native of the   211
United States. *L* 1827. D [18] 412 a

American slavery, in reference to the present agitation... By an adopted citizen. *See* Scholte, Henry P.

American spy (The); or, freedom's early sacrifice ... *See* Simms, Jephtra R.

American spy (An). Letters written in London by: *See Letters written in London...*

American state papers. Documents, legis-   212
lative and executive, of the Congress of the United States... Ser. I & II. *Wash* 1832–61. F 38v b N NYP Y
Classified as: Foreign Relations, 6v; Indian Affairs, 2v; Finance, 5v; Commerce and Navigation, 2v; Military Affairs, 7v; Naval Affairs, 4v; Post-Office, 1v; Public Lands, 8v; Claims, 1v; Miscellaneous, 2v.

American state papers. Important documents and dispatches... *See America and France...*

American traveller (The) and emigrant's   213
guide... *Shrewsbury* 1817. O [2] 22 front. a

American traveller (The); or, observations on the present state... of the British colonies... By an old and experienced trader. *See* Cluny, Alex.

AMERICANS
Americans against liberty... *See* Serle, Ambrose.

Americans (The) as they are; described in a tour through the valley of the Mississippi. *See* Postl, Karl.

Americans defended by an American. *See* Cary, Thos. G.

Americans (The) roused, in a cure for the spleen... *See* Sewall, Jonathan.

AMERICANUS EXAMINED...
By a Pennsylvanian. *See* Fisher, Jabez.

AMERICA'S APPEAL   214
America's appeal to the impartial world... their resorting to arms... vindicated. *Hart* 1775. O 72 aa

AMERIKA!   215
Treuer Rathgeber und Führer des deutschen Auswanderers nach den Vereinigten Staaten... *Kreuznach* 1849. O [4] 96 map a

AMERIKA   216
Amerika und die Auswanderung dahin sum Bedenten... *Leip* 1834. O 93 aa
—rptd. same impr., 1835. O a

AMERIKANISCHE JAGD
Amerikanische Jagd- und Reiseabenteuer... Von Armand. *See* Strubberg, Friedrich Armand.

AMÉRIQUAIN (L')
Amériquain (L') aux Anglois, ou observations... a divers ministres d'Angleterre... *See* Vincent, N.

AMÉRIQUE
Amérique (De l') et des Americains... *See* Bonneville, Zacharie de Pazzi de.

Amérique (L') du nord... *See* Bibliothèque Américaine...

Amérique (L'), ou guide utile aux person-   217
nes qui veulent connoître ce pays... *Belfort* 1824. Q 28 aa

AMES, AZEL   218
The Mayflower and her log... *B* 1901. Q [22] 375 11pls a
—ed. 2, enl., *B* 1907. Q 385 pls

AMES, JOHN HENRY   219
Lincoln, the capital of Nebraska. A complete history [etc.]. *Lincoln* 1870. O 30 + 6adv-p a

AMES, NATHANIEL   220
Nautical reminiscences. *Prov* 1832. D 216 a

AMIS, MOSES N.   221
Historical Raleigh... *Raleigh* 1902. D 230 [incl. port & advs] a
—rptd. 1913.

AMORETTI, CARLO
Viaggio dal Mare Atlantico al Pacifico... *See* Ferrer Maldonado, Lorenzo F.

AMPÈRE, J[EAN] J.   222
Promenade en Amerique: États Unis... *P* 1855. O 2v: [12] 421 + 4adv-p; [4] 425 a
—rptd. *P*: 1856; 1860; 1867; 1874; 1887.
This distinguished scientist covered the east and the south, and as far west as Cincinnati and Chicago.

AMPHLETT, WILLIAM   223
The emigrant's directory to the western states ... *L* 1819. D [8] 208 b ChiH LC N Y

AMPUDIA, GENERAL PEDRO DE   224
Ante el tribunal de la opinion, por los primeros sucedos ocurridos en la guerra á que nos provoca ... el gobierno de los Etados Unidos... *San Luis Potosi* 1846. O 27 b
Narrative of the beginning of the Mexican War, including movements on the Rio Grande.

AMSDEN, CHARLES A.   225
Navaho weaving. *Santa Ana Calif* 1934. O [18] 261 123 pls [incl. 7 in color] aa
—rptd. *Albuquerque* 1948. O [20] 263 a

[ANBUREY, THOMAS]   226
Travels through the interior parts of America ... By an officer... *L* 1789. O 2v: [36] 467; [4] 558. map 7pls facs aa
—rptd. *L* 1791. O 2v: [12] 414; 492. map 7pls; *L* 1792. same collat., but au. named. a
—Am. ed. *B* 1923. O 2v map 575 copies ptd.
—Fr. trs.: *P* 1790. O 2v map; 1792 O 2v map; *P* 1793. O 2v [4] 336; [4] 455 4maps and pls
—Ger. eds.: "Reisen im Inneren von Nordamerika...," *Berlin* 1792. O [8] 372 3maps & pls; same impr and date. O [10] 444 3maps and pls
Capt. Anburey served with Burgoyne, but this account of his travels was largely plagiarized from Burnaby, Smyth and others.

ANDERSON (MR.)
The history of the life and adventures of....
See Kimber, Edw.

ANDERSON, EPHRAIM McD.   227
Memoirs... including the campaigns of the First Missouri Confederate brigade. *St L* 1868. O [4] 436 [2] 9 pls aa

ANDERSON, FULTON, et al   228
Addresses... before the Virginia state convention, February, 1861. *Rich* 1861. O 64 a
Plea for Virginia to join her seceding sister states.

[ANDERSON, JAMES]   229
Free thoughts on the American contest... *Edin* 1776. O 59 a
Severe condemnation of the colonies and of Paine's *Common sense.*

ANDERSON, JAMES   230
The interest of Great-Britain with regard to her American colonies... *L* 1782. O [8] 136 [36] a
Asserts that settling the colonies was unwise and all subsequent aid impolitic; they were a detriment to British trade and power. However, he submits a plan for pacification.

ANDERSON, JOHN E., and   231
HOBBY, WILLIAM J.
The contract for the purchase of western territory... considered... *Augusta Ga* 1799. O 93 2 lvs. [of errata, &c.] inserted after t-p aa
—anr. issue. O 91 aa

ANDERSON, MRS. MABEL W.   232
The life of General Stand Watie, the only Indian brigadier general of the Confederate army ... [*Pryor Okla* 1915]. O 58 [incl. pls] a
—ed. 2, 1931. O 85

ANDERSON, MELISSA G.   233
The story of a Kansas pioneer... [*Mt Vernon O*] 1924. O 61 a

ANDERSON, OSBORNE P.   234
A voice from Harper's Ferry... with incidents prior and subsequent to its capture by Captain Brown... *B* 1861. D 72 aa
—rptd. *Wash* 1873. O 24 a

ANDERSON, RUFUS   235
Memoir of Catherina Brown, a Christian Indian of the Cherokee nation... *B* 1825. 16° 180 front. a
—ed. 2, same impr. & date. 16° 144 front.
—other eds.: *Cin* 1827; *B* 1828.
—rptd. *Phil* 1832.
—Eng. ed.: *Glas* 1825 front.

ANDERSON, W. F.   236
Map of southern Idaho and the adjacent regions. With an accompaniment... by Chas. Drayton Gibbes. *S F* [1880]. O 55 fold. map a

ANDERSON ([WILLIAM J.])   237
Life and narrative of: twenty-four years a slave ... *Chi* 1857. D 81 a

ANDRADE, JUAN J.   238
Documentos... sobre la evacuacion de... San Antonio de Bejar... *Monterrey* 1836. O 24 b B G Hn Y
Official papers on withdrawal of this garrison force from Texas.

ANDRÉ [MAJOR JOHN].
Case of:... candidly represented, with remarks ... *See* Inglis, Chas.

ANDRÉ, MAJOR [JOHN]   239
Journal [1777–1778]. Ed. by H. C. Lodge. *B* Bibliophile Soc. 1903. Q 2v: [20] 136; [10] 80. 3eng.t. 2ports 7facs 38maps [some fold., some double p.] a 467copies ptd.
First printing of this military journal which lay undiscovered in England until 1902.

ANDRÉ (MAJOR [JOHN]).   **240**
Papers concerning the capture... of: Ed. H. B.
Dawson. *Yonkers* 1866. O [8] 246 a

ANDRÉ (MAJOR JOHN).   **241**
Proceedings of a board of general officers...
respecting: *Phil* 1780. O [2] 21 b AA Hn NYP Y
iss. 1 : p 1 misnumbered
—other 1780 eds.: *Exeter* O 15 NYP; *Hart* D 32;
N Y O 13 NYP; *Prov* n.d. O 16 AA; *Norwich*
D 16 all b value.
—anr. ed. "The trial of:" *Palmer* 1810. O 24 a
—anr. ed. "Minutes of a court of inquiry upon the
case of:" *Alb* 1865. Q [4] 66 port 100 copies [of
which 10 on L. P.] a
—anr. ed. "Andreana. Containing the trial... of:"
Phil 1865. O [4] 67 [4] 12pls 175 copies [25 on
L. P.]
—Eng. ed. *Dub* 1781. aa

ANDRÉ (MAJOR [JOHN]).
Vindication of the captors of: *See* Benson,
Egbert.

ANDREAS, A[LFRED] T.   **242**
Historical atlas of Dakota. *Chi* 1884. F [4]
13–212 map of Dakota. aa
Contains historical sketches and plat maps of
every county.

ANDREAS, A[LFRED] T.   **243**
History of Chicago... *Chi* 1884–6. Q 3v: 648;
[40] 49–780; [14] 876. 3maps 36pls[one double-p.,
one fold.] aa

ANDREAS, A[LFRED] T.   **244**
History of... Kansas. *Chi* 1883. F 1616 map
pls aa

ANDREAS, A[LFRED] T.   **245**
History of... Nebraska. *Chi* 1882. Q [8] 1506
fold map pls aa

ANDREE, KARL T.   **246**
Geographische Wanderungen. *Dresden* 1859.
O 2v in 1 : [8] 336; [2] 358 a

ANDREE, KARL T.   **247**
Kartenwerk zu Nord-Amerika... *Braunschweig*
1854. Q [4] 28 18 maps a
Intended to accompany author's *Nord-Amerika*.
See below. For original edition *see* under actual
author, Lange, Henry.

ANDREE, KARL T.   **248**
Nord-Amerika in geographischen und ge-
schichtlichen Umrissen. *Braunschweig* 1851. O [14]
810 4 pls + atlas Q [4] 28 18maps aa
—ed. 2, same impr. 1854. same collat. aa
German settlements in Texas, the Central
West, etc. For separate edition of atlas *see*
preceding entry.

ANDREIS (FELIX de...).   **249**
Sketches of the life of: *Balt* 1861. D 276 port a
Biography of the Vicar-General of the Diocese
of New Orleans, with account of Catholicism in
the United States.

ANDREW, JAMES O.   **250**
Miscellanies... *Louisv* 1854. D 395 a
—ed. 2, *Nashv* 1855. D
Describes trips to Ark., Tex. and the Central
West.

[ANDREWS, CHARLES]   **251**
The prisoner's memoirs; or Dartmoor prison...
N Y 1815. D 283 pl a
—issue 1, prisoner's name not given on t-p
—issue 2, prisoner's name on t-p
—rptd. *N Y* 1852. D 152
Edited by Philip R. Hopkins.

ANDREWS, CHARLES M.   **252**
The colonial period of American history. *N Hav*
1934–6–7–8. O 4v: [14] 551; [10] 407; [14] 354;
[14] 477 aa
Profound, exhaustive and dependable survey
of the various American settlements in the 17th
century and of England's commercial and political
policy towards them.

ANDREWS, C[HRISTOPHER] C.   **253**
Minnesota and Dacotah... tour through the
north west... *Wash* 1857. D 215 map a
—eds 2, 3 & 4, same impr. & date.

ANDREWS, ELIZA F.   **254**
The war-time journal of a Georgia girl, 1864–5.
N Y 1908. O [8] 387 16pls a

ANDREWS, ETHAN A.   **255**
Slavery and the domestic slave-trade in the
United States. *B* 1836. D [12] 9–201 a

ANDREWS, GARNETT   **256**
Reminiscences of an old Georgia lawyer.
Atlanta 1870. O 104 a

ANDREWS, ISRAEL W.   **257**
Washington county and the early settlement of
Ohio. *Cin* 1877. O 83 a

ANDREWS, JOHN   **258**
The conduct of Holland... examined. *L* 1782.
O 162 a
Remonstrance against Holland's siding with
the colonists and an exposition of French cunning
and duplicity.

ANDREWS, JOHN   **259**
History of the war with America... 1775–1783.
L 1785–6. O 4v: [4] 448; [2] 445; [2] 445; [2] 416
[60] + subscriber's list, 14p. 31pls&maps aa

25

ANDREWS, JOHN D.   260
Eight years in the toils: sketches from a gambler's life. *Butte* 1890. D 225 port a

[ANDREWS, P. AND JOHN] engs.   261
A set of plans and forts in North America...
[*L*] 1763. obl Q eng.t. index 30plans c LC
—2d ed., same impr. & collat. 1765. c N NYP
Best collection of its kind at the period. Sometimes cited under publisher's name, Rocque, Jean and Mary Ann.

ANDREWS, SIDNEY   262
The south since the war... *B* 1866. D [8] 400 a

ANDREWS, WILLIAM L.   263
The Bradford map... *N Y* 1893. O 115 fold.
map 10 pls b 10copies on Jap. P. LC NYP
—anr. issue of 142copies on plate paper aa
See below, *James Lyne's survey...*

ANDREWS, WILLIAM L.   264
Fragments of American history... *N Y* 1898.
D [22] 5–69 14pls a 30copies on Jap., & 80 on hand made paper aa

ANDREWS, WILLIAM L.   267
James Lyne's survey... of the city of New York... in 1731... *N Y* 1900. O [12] 3–38 3maps a 170 cops on hand made paper a 32 cops on Japan paper aa

ANDREWS, WILLIAM L.   268
New Amsterdam... *N Y* 1897. O [32] 13–142 [2] maps pls b 30copies on Jap. paper with extra pls LC N NYP; 170 cops on hand made paper. a

ANDREWS, WILLIAM L.   269
New York as Washington knew it... *N Y* 1905.
O [16] 92 [2] [incl. pls] a 32copies on Jap. paper aa 135 cops on hand made pap. a

ANDROS, THOMAS   270
The old Jersey captive... *B* 1833. 16° 80 a
—rptd. "The museum of remarkable... events," *Clev* 1844. D: *N Y* 1857. D

ANDROS TRACTS (THE).   271
Ed. W. H. Whitmore... *B* Prince Society 1868, 1869, 1874. sm Q 3v: 215; 346; 257 a some copies on L.P. aa

ANDROSSE (SIR EDMUND) et al.   272
A narrative of the proceedings of: during his government in New England. By several gentlemen ... of his Council. [*B*] 1691. D 48 b BA MassH
—anr iss sm Q 12 d
Attributed to Increase Mather and to William Stoughton. Probably the work of the latter.

ANECDOTES
Anecdotes américaines, ou histoire abrégée...
See Hornot, Ant.

Anecdotes anglaises et américaines... *See* Espinasse de Langeac.

[ANGEL, MYRON] ed.   273
History of Nevada... *Oakland* 1881. Q 680 116pls tab b
—rptd. *S F* 1958. same collat. a
Exhaustive work on this state and its fifteen counties.

ANGEL, MYRON, ed.   274
History of Placer county, California. *Oakl* 1882.
Q 416 pls b N

[ANGEL, MYRON]   275
History of San Luis Obispo county [Calif.].
Oakland 1883. Q 391 pls b B Hn

ANGEL, MYRON   276
La Nevada orientale... *P* 1867. D [8] 164 [in Eng. & Fr.] aa
—anr. ed. [in Eng. only], *L* 1868. 16° [4] 80 a

ANGELO, C. AUBREY   277
Idaho: a descriptive tour... *S F* 1865. D 52 + 12adv-l. errata slip d CalS NYP Pn
—rev. ed. "Sketches of travel in Oregon and Idaho." *N Y* 1866. O 181 + 7adv-l. map d Pn OreH Y

ANGLICANO (JACOBO).
Fortune's favourite... memoirs of: *See* Annesley, James, *Memoirs of an unfortunate young nobleman...*

ANMERKUNGEN   278
Anmerkungen aus der neuen und alten Welt bei Belegenheit der Beschreibung des Siebenjährigen Seekrieges zwischen England und den amerikanischen Staaten... *Berlin* 1788. D 482 [2] aa

ANNALES   279
Annales de l'Association de la Propagation de la Foi... collection faisant suite à toutes les éditions des Lettres edifiantes *P* & *Lyons* [some later vols. *Lyons* impr. only] 1823–90. O 62v + Index [1822–53, pub. 1854] b N NYP Y
—Eng. tr.[in part], *L* 1841–5. O 6v aa
—Ital. tr., pub. at Lyons, simultaneously with the Fr. ed. b
For series to which these annual volumes were supplementary, see *Lettres edifiantes.* For similar American series see note to *Quebec. Notices sur les missions...*

ANNESLEY (JAMES).   280
The case of:... a sequel to the Memoirs of an
unfortunate young nobleman. *L* 1745. D [4] 215 a
—rptd. *L* 1756.
—abr. ed. n.p. 1756. O 38
See also, below, A plain historical account of the
tryal between... James Annesley...

[ANNESLEY, JAMES]   281
Memoirs of an unfortunate young nobleman,
returned from a thirteen years slavery in America,
where he had been sent by... his cruel uncle...
L 1743. D 2v: [4] 277 + 7adv-p; [4] 235 aa
—anr. ed. "Fortune's favourite...," n.p. 1744.
O a
—ed. 2, rev., "The history of an unfortunate
young nobleman...," *L* 1769. O
For a third volume, or sequel, *see* above *The*
case of... James Annesley. Scott's *Guy Mannering*
was based on this fight for an inheritance and an
earldom.

ANNESLEY (JAMES).   283
A plain historical account of the tryal between:
... and... the Earl of Anglesea... *L* 1744.
O 227 a
—oth. eds: "The trial..." *L* 1744. D 336; *L* 1744
F 260

ANNEWALT, E. H., comp.   284
Mount Pleasant city directory... historical
sketch... *Burlington* 1870. O 67 + 7adv-l. pl aa

ANNO REGNI GEORGII III   285
Anno Regni Georgii III Regis Magnae Britan-
niae... At the Parliament begun... the nineteenth
day of May... 1761... to the tenth day of January
1765, being the fourth session of the twelfth
Parliament... *L* Baskett 1765. O 66 aa. Some copies
in F b
—Am. eds.: *B* 1765. F 24; *Phil* [1765]. O 40;
Annap [1765]. F [2] 16; *N Lond* 1765. F 32;
[*Woodbridge N J* 1765]. O 40 ea b
Contains the momentous "Act for granting and
applying certain Stamp duties..."

ANNUAL REGISTER
Annual register (The) of Indian affairs... 1835.
See McCoy, Isaac.

ANSTED, DAVID T.   286
The gold-seeker's manual... guide to all persons
emigrating to the... gold regions of California.
L 1849. D 96 a
—rptd. *N Y* 1849. same collat.
—ed. 2, *L* 1849. D 172 + 4adv-p

ANSWER   287
Answer (The) to a Colonel's letter. By a wooden-
legged soldier. Wherein some American matters
are slightly touched upon. *L* 1766. O 36 a

Answer to a dialogue between a Federalist and a
Republican... *See* Desaussure, Henry W.

Answer (An) to a pamphlet, call'd The conduct
of the ministry impartially examined... *See*
Shebbeare, John.

Answer (An) to a pamphlet, entitled   288
Taxation no tyranny... *L* 1775. O 63 a
Probably by John Wilkes.

Answer (An) to the declaration of the American
Congress. *See* Lind, John.

Answer (An) to the pamphlet... The   289
conduct of the Paxton men... *Phil* 1764. O 28 b
For defense of the conduct of these murderers,
to which this replies, *see* Barton, Thomas.

Answer (An) to War in disguise... *See* Morris,
Gouverneur.

ANTICIPATION
Anticipation: ... the substance of His M——y's
most gracious speech... *See* Tickell, Rich.

ANTIGALLICAN
Antigallican (The); or, the lover of his own
country... By a citizen of New England. *See*
Lowell, John.

ANTILLES.
Souvenirs des: Voyage... aux États-Unis, etc.
See Montlezun, Baron de.

ANTRIM, JOSHUA   290
The history of Champaign and Logan counties
[O.]... *Bellefontaine* 1872. D 460 front. a

APERCU
Apercu de la situation intérieure des États-
Unis... Par un Russe. *See* Poletica, Pierre.

APOSTÓLICOS AFANES
Apostólicos afanes de la Compañia de Jesus...
por un Padre de la misma sagrada religion...
Barcelona 1754. *See* Ortega, José.

APPEAL   291
Appeal (An) to reason and justice, in behalf of
the British Constitution... In which the... contest with the revolted colonies is impartially considered... *L* 1778. O [4] 176 a
Bewails colonial ingratitude to an indulgent
mother-country.

Appeal (An) to the American people...   292
account of the persecutions of the Church of Latter
Day Saints... by the inhabitants of... Missouri.
Cin Glezen & Shepard 1840. 16° 84 b Y
—ed. 2, rev., same date & impr. Shepard & Stearns.
D 60 b Y

Appeal (An) to the government and congress of the United States... By an American citizen. *See* Bronson, Enos.

Appeal (An) to the justice... of the people of Great Britain... *See* Lee, Arthur.

Appeal (An) to the people of the United States. By a Georgian. *Sav* 1825. O 85 aa   293

APPENDIX
Appendix (An) to The present state of the nation... *See* Knox, Wm.

APPLEGATE, JESSE   294
Recollections... *Roseburg Ore* 1914. O 99 aa
—rptd., with adds., "A day with the cow column ...," *Chi* Caxton Club 1934. D [18] 208 300copies ptd. a
Embraces account of the great Oregon migration of 1843. Applegate established the southern route to Oregon.

APPLER, AUGUSTUS C.   295
The guerrillas of the west... exploits of the Younger brothers... *St L* 1875. D [4] 208 pls b
—rptd. *St L* 1876. D 244; *Osceola, Mo* 1877.; *St L* 1878. D 215 aa
—anr. ed. "The true life of the Younger brothers". *Chi* 1880. D 287 a
—rptd. "Train and bank robbers" [James brothers added] *Chi* 1882. D 2 pts in 1: [4] 358; 287 12 pls [in add. to 2 fronts. incl. in pagination]; same, 1884.

APPLETON, NATHANIEL   296
A sermon... occasioned by the surrender of Montreal... *B* 1760. O 36 aa

APPLETON'S RAILROAD
Appleton's railroad and steamboat companion ... *See* Williams, Wellington.

APPLICATION   297
Application (An) of some general political rules to the present state of Great Britain, Ireland and America... *L* Almon 1766. O 86 a
Has been attributed to a Mr. Gretrix, of Dublin.

APUNTES
Apuntes para la historia de la guerra entre Mexico y los Estados-Unidos. *See* Alcarez, Ramón.

ARBUTHNOT [A.] & AMBRISTER [R. C.]
An official account of the trial and execution of:... *See* Davis, Paris M.

ARBUTHNOT (A.) & AMBRISTER (R. C.)   298
The trials of: charged with exciting the Seminole Indians... *L* 1819. O [4] 80 a

ARCHBOLD, MISS ANN   299
A book for the married and the single... especially designed for steamboat passengers. *E Plainfield O* 1850. 16° 192 aa
Narrative of midwestern travel.

ARCHDALE, JOHN   300
A new description of... Carolina: with a brief account of its discovery, settling [etc.]. *L* 1707. Q [8] 32 b N NYP
—Am. ed. *Charleston* 1822. O 33 [14] aa
Archdale, one of the proprietors of this colony, served as Governor, 1695–7.

ARCIS, M. H.   301
La Californie telle qu'elle est, etc. [incl. tr. of Vizetelly's "Four months among the gold-finders"] *Ingouville* [1849]. O 40 45 aa

ARENDS, FRIEDRICH   302
Schilderung des Mississippithales; oder, des Westens der Vereinigten Staaten... *Emden* 1838. O [16] 631 aa
—Dutch ed. "Het Mississippi-Dal...," *Groningen* 1839. O [8] 354 [1] a

ARFWEDSON, CARL D.   303
De colonia Nova Svecia... *Upsala* 1825. Q [4] 34 map a

ARFWEDSON, CARL D.   304
The United States and Canada. *L* 1834. O 2v: [8] 433; [8] 418. 2pls aa
—Swed. ed. "Förenta Staterna och Canada," *Stockh* 1835. D 2v in 1. D 674 a

ARGUMENT   305
Argument (An) in defence of the... right claimed by the colonies to tax themselves... *L* 1774. O [8] 163 + 4adv-p a
Said to have been written by a Mr. Parker.

ARGYLE, ARCHIE.   306
Cupid's album. *N Y* 1866. D [4] 332 aa
Narrative of a journey overland from St. Joseph.   Author's real name: Annie Argyle.

ARICKAREE INDIANS (THE).   307
Correspondence relative to hostilities of: General Gaines to the Secretary of War. [In Sen. Doc. 1 & H. Doc. 2, 18th Cong., 1st Sess.] *Wash* 1823. O 55–108 aa
Complete pagination of these documents is 206 + 23 folding tables.

ARISTOCRACY IN AMERICA...
See Grund, Francis J.

ARIZONA
   Arizona: its agricultural, mineral and   308
other resources... n.p. [1867?]. 16° 40 a

   Gold, silver, lead and copper mines of   309
Arizona: [*Phil* 1867] 16° 40 b

   History of Arizona Territory:... *S F*   310
Elliott & Co. 1884. F [8] 25–322 [2] map 62pls b

   Memorial and affidavits showing outrages... by
the Apache Indians, in the Territory of Arizona:...
See Dobbin, M. D.

   Resources of Arizona territory:... with a
description of the Indian tribes; ancient ruins...
S F 1871. *See* Safford, A[nson] P. K.

   The resources of Arizona:... [1881]. *See*
Hamilton, Pat'k.

   The Territory of Arizona:... 1874. *See* Safford,
A[*nson*] P. K.

ARIZPE, JOSÉ I., and PADILLA,   311
J[UAN] A.
   [Nota estadistica... dcl... Coahuila y Tejas...]
No t.p. [Saltillo? or Mex? 1827.] D 10, + 14fold
tabs b S TxU Y

ARIZPE (RAMOS DE).
   Idea... sobre la conducta... de: *See* Ramos
de Arizpe, Miguel.

ARKANSAS
   Journal of a tour to Arkansas and the Indian   312
territory. *N Y* 1844. O 74 map aa
   Tour of observation made by an agent of the
Episcopal Church.

   Mysteries and miseries of Arkansas: or, a defence
of the loyalty of the state. By a refugee. *See* Demby,
James W.

ARKANSAS VALLEY, COLORADO.   314
   History of: *Chi* 1881. Q [8] 11–889 178 pls aa

ARMAND [pseud.]
   See Strubberg, Friedrich Armand.

ARMES, ETHEL   315
   The story of coal and iron in Alabama. *Birm*
(ptd *N Y*) 1910. O [34] 581 33pls aa
   Many copies burned.

ARMES, GEORGE A.   316
   Ups and downs of an army officer... *Wash*
1900. O [20] 784 port a

[ARMROYD, GEORGE]   317
   A connected view of the whole internal navigation of the United States... *Phil* 1826. O 192
10maps aa
—best. ed., enl., *Phil* 1830. O 617 fold. map
2profiles aa
   Leading early authority on the subject.

ARMSTRONG, A. N.   318
   Oregon... *Chi* 1857. D 147 aa

ARMSTRONG, BENJAMIN G.   319
   Early life among the Indians... *Ashland Wis*
1892. D 266 [incl. front] 15 pls a

[ARMSTRONG, GEN. JOHN]   320
   An enquiry respecting the capture of Washington
[D. C.]... *Wash* 1816. 16° 32 a

ARMSTRONG, GEN. JOHN   321
   Notices of the war of 1812. *N Y* 1836–40.
D 2v: 260; [4] 244 + slip containing pub's. notice
inserted in front of v.I a some copies of v.I are
dated 1840

ARMSTRONG, MOSES K.   322
   History and resources of Dakota, Montana and
Idaho. *Yankton* 1866. D 72 map dd H N Y
—rptd. [Pierre 1928]. D 62 a
   First history of Dakota.

ARMSTRONG, PERRY A.   323
   The piasa ... *Morris, Ill.* 1887. O 48 a

ARMSTRONG, PERRY A.   324
   The Sauks and the Black Hawk war...
Splingfield [*sic*] 1887. O [20] 7–726 [incl. pls] a

ARNOLD ET SIR HENRY CLINTON.
   Complot d': *See* Barbé-Marbois, Francois.

ARNOLD (MAJOR GENERAL   325
[BENEDICT]).
   Proceedings of a general court martial... for
the trial of:... *Phil* 1780. F 55 c 50 copies ptd H
MH NYP Y
—rptd. *N Y* 1865. O [30] 182 port a 100 copies
+ 35 on L. P. aa

ARNOLD, CHARLES H.   326
   The new and impartial history of North and
South America, and of the present... war. *L*
Hogg [1782]. D [12] 25–276 front. a
—rptd: *L* [1783] D [12] 25–282 front; *L* 1790;
L 1796

ARNOLD, HENRY V.   327
   The early history of Ransom county ... [N.D.].
Larimore 1918. D 74 plan aa

ATHERTON, WILLIAM   366
Narrative of the suffering and defeat of the northwestern army under General Winchester . . . *Frankf Ky* 1842. 16° 152 a

ATKINS, SAMUEL   367
Kalendarium Pennsilvaniense . . . *Phil* 1685. D 40 dd PaH [of 2 cops loc]
This almanac, for 1686, was the first product of the Pennsylvania press.

ATKINSON, GEORGE H.   368
The northwest coast . . . *Port Ore* 1878. O 56 map a
By a missionary who came to Oregon in 1848. Called "second edition" as it first appeared serially in a newspaper.

[ATKINSON, GEORGE W.]   369
After the moonshiners . . . *Wheeling W Va* 1881. D 239 [incl. front.] 16pls a
Account of government attempts to suppress illicit stills in the southern mountain regions.

ATKINSON, GEORGE W.   370
History of Kanawha county, [W. Va.] . . . *Charleston* 1876. O [6] 5–338 7pls a 300 copies ptd.

ATLANTA DIRECTORY   371
Atlanta directory . . . [with historical sketch by G. B. Haygood] for 1859–60. *Atlanta* 1859. O 230 aa
First directory and first history of Atlanta. *See* also, Barnwell, V. T.

ATLANTE DELL' AMERICA . . .   372
Leghorn 1777. F [15] 38maps 6pls[one, of Quebec, not listed] b N NYP
—anr. issue, with *Pescia* impr. b Y
Maps taken from Italian edition of *The American gazetteer, q.v.*

ATLANTE NOVISSIMO.
See Des Barres, Jos. F. W.

ATLANTIC CITY   373
Atlantic City: its early and modern history. By Carnesworthe [*pseud.*]. *Phil* 1868. 16° 96 a
—rptd., same impr. 1888.
First history of this city.

ATLANTIC
Atlantic Neptune (The).
See Des Barres, Joseph F. W.

Atlantic pilot (The)
See De Brahm, John G. W.

ATLAS
Atlas Ameriquain Septentrional.
See Jefferys, Thos., *A general topography of North America . . .*

Atlas to accompany the offcial records of the Union and Confederate armies. *See* Cowles, Calvin D.

ATSON, WILLIAM   374
Heart whispers . . . with sketches of a tour through nine southern states . . . *Memphis* 1859. 16° [18] 27–368 aa

[ATTELLIS SANTANGELO,   375
GIDEON DE]
The Texas question reviewed by an adopted citizen . . . *N Y* 1844. O 28 a

ATTEMPT   376
Attempt (An) to demonstrate the practicability of emancipating the slaves of the United States . . . By a New-England man. *N Y* 1825. O 75 a

Attempt (An) to shew, that America must be known to the ancients . . . *See* Mather, Samuel.

ATTUCKS (CRISPUS) et al.
The trial of the British soldiers for the murder of: *See* Hodgson, John.

ATWATER, CALEB   377
A history of . . . Ohio . . . *Cin* 1838. O 403 a
—ed. 2, *Cin* [1838.] O 407
—ed. 3, *Cin* 1858. O

[ATWATER, CALEB]?   378
Mysteries of Washington City, during the session of the 28th Congress. *Wash* 1844. 16° 218 [1] a

ATWATER, CALEB   379
Remarks made on a tour to Prairie de Chien . . . *Columbus* 1831. 16° [8] 296 a
—anr. issue, unsold sheets of above, with new title: "The Indians of the north-west . . . or remarks, [etc.]," *Columbus,* n. d. [1831].
—rptd. 1850. same collat.

ATWATER (CALEB).   380
The writings of: *Columbus* 1833. O 408 10pls a
Reprints, with slight additions, his *Remarks . . . on a tour to Prairie du Chien* [see above] and his *Description of the antiquities discovered in the western country* [from Am. Antiq. Soc. Colls., V.I, 1820].

ATWATER, H. COWLES   381
Incidents of a southern tour . . . *B* 1857. O 120 aa

AUBIN, MRS. PENELOPE   382
The life of Charlotta Du Pont . . from her own memoirs . . . , how she was trepan'd by her stepmother to Virginia . . . *L* 1723. D [6] 282 aa
—rptd. 1736, same collat a
Of dubious authenticity.

AUCHINLECK, G. 383
A history of the war between Great Britain and the United States . . . 1812–1814. *Tor* 1855. O [7] 408 [3] a

AUDOUARD, MME. OLYMPE 384
A travers l'Amérique. Le far-west. *P* 1869. 18° 370 port a

AUDOUARD, MME. OLYMPE 385
A travers l'Amérique. North America. États-Unis . . . *P* 1871. D 372 a

AUDUBON (JOHN J.) 386
Journal of: . . . 1820–1821. *B* 1929. O [10] 234 [2] port facs a 225 cops ptd.

AUDUBON (JOHN J.) 387
Journal of: . . . 1840–1843. *B* 1929. O [6 5–7] 179 [2] front. a 225 cops ptd.

AUDUBON (JOHN J.) 388
Letters of: 1826–1840. *B* 1930. O 2v: [8] 277; 278 [1] a 225copies ptd.

AUDUBON (JOHN J.)
The life of: ed. by his widow. *See* Buchanan, Rob't.

AUDUBON, JOHN J. 389
Ornithological biography . . . with delineations of American scenery and manners. *Edin* 1831–39. O 5v aa
—Am. ed. *Phil*, same date & collat.
—rptd. *N Y* 1926. O 349 port map a
—Fr. ed. "Scènes de la nature dans les États-Unis . . .," *P* 1857. O 2v: [6] 460; 512
Issued, without plates, to serve as text for the folio edition of his *Birds*.

AUDUBON, JOHN W. 390
Illustrated notes of an expedition through Mexico and California. *N Y* 1852. F [4] 48 4col pls dd G Hn NYP Y
—anr. issue, pls not col. b
—rptd. with adds. and re-titled "Western journal." *Clev* 1906. O 249 [incl. 6pls] map + 10 adv.p aa
The 1852 edition was part one of a contemplated larger work abandoned from lack of encouragement; the four plates, in colored state, are of outstanding beauty.

AUDUBON, MARIE R., ed. 391
Audubon and his journals. *N Y* 1897. O 2v: [14] 532; [8] 554 [1]. 46pls aa
—rptd. same impr. & collat. 1900 a
—Eng. ed., same collat., *L* 1898. a

AUFFORDERUNG 392
Aufforderung und Erklärung in Betreff einer Auswanderung . . . in die Nordamerikanischen Freistaaten. *Giessen* 1833. O 28 a
—ed. 2, with adds., same impr. & date. O 56

AUGER, EDOUARD 393
Voyage en Californie [1852–3]. *P* 1854. D [4] 238 a

AUGUSTA [GA.] DIRECTORY . . . 394
Augusta 1841. D 82 + 36adv-p a
First Augusta directory, with historical sketch.

AUGUSTA [GA.] 395
Journal of the congress of the four southern governors . . . with the Five Nations of Indians, at: *Charlestown S C* 1764. Q [2] 45 dd GaU NYP [of 3copies known] 50copies ptd.

AUSFÜHRLICHE NACHRICHTEN
Ausführliche Nachrichten (Der) von der Saltzburgischen Emigrantem . . . *See* Urlsperger, Saml.

[AUSTIN, BENJAMIN] 396
Constitutional Republicanism, in opposition to fallacious Federalism . . . *B* 1803. O 327 a

[AUSTIN, BENJAMIN] 397
Thoughts on the situation of the . . . settlers . . . in the northwestern counties of Pennsylvania. *Phil* 1810. O 30 a

AUSTIN, J. 398
Summer trip to California. [*Prov* 1896]. O 32 a 100copies ptd.

AUSTIN, JAMES T. 399
The life of Elbridge Gerry . . . *B* 1828–9. O 2v: [16] 520; [8] 408. port a

AUSTIN, MRS. MARY 400
The land of little rain . . . *B* 1903. O [16] 280 [2] front. a

[AUSTIN, MOSES] 401
A summary description of the lead mines in Upper Louisiana . . . *Wash* 1804. O 22 b AA LC
First United States' book on Missouri.

AUSTIN, STEPHEN F. 402
An address delivered . . . in . . . Louisville . . . *Lexington* 1836. D 30 b

AUSTIN, STEPHEN F. 403
Esposición al público sobre los asuntos de Tejas. *Mex* 1835. D 32 dd LC Y G TxU
Vindication of himself and Texas from charges of disloyalty to Mexico written by him while a virtual prisoner in Mexico.

AUSTIN, STEPHEN F. 404
Map of Texas . . . with descriptive notes. *Phil* 1830 F 30sections b G
—rptd., same impr., 1835; 1836. aa

AUSTIN, [NEVADA].   **405**
Harrington's directory of the city of: . . . With a
historical . . . review . . . by Myron Angel. *Austin*
1866. O 119 b NYP Y

AUSTRALIA   **406**
Australia, Vancouver's Island and California.
Perils, pastimes and pleasures of an emigrant in:
L 1849. D [2] 606 a

AUSWANDERER   **407**
Auswanderer (Der) am Niederrhein. *Meurs*
1849–50. O 8nos in 1: 170 aa

AUSZÜGE AUS BRIEFEN AUS   **408**
NORD-AMERIKA . . .
Ulm 1833. D 214 [incl. front wrap] pl aa
Letters written home by members of a German
family who travelled through the North in 1824
and settled in Louisiana.

AUTHENTIC   **409**
Authentic copies of the provisional and prelimi-
nary articles of peace . . . between Great Britain,
France, Spain and the United States . . . *L* 1783.
O [4] 28 a

Authentic exposition (An) of the "K. G. C."   **410**
"Knights of the Golden Circle"; or, a history of
secession from 1834 to 1861 . . . *Indp* 1861.
O 80 aa
—anr. ed. [*Louisv* 1862]. O *See* also under Ku-
Klux-Klan.

Authentic history (An) of remarkable per-   **411**
sons . . . including . . . the iniquities of the pretended
prophet Joe Smith . . . *N Y* 1849. O 64 aa

Authentic narrative (An) of facts relating to   **412**
the exchange of prisoners taken at the Cedars . . .
L 1777. O [4] 50 b LC N
—Fr. tr. *Montr* 1873. O 44 a
Congress had refused to ratify the exchange
cartel made by Arnold and the British on the
grounds that the American prisoners had been
maltreated by their captors.

Authentic papers from America: submitted   **413**
to the dispassionate consideration of the public.
L 1775. O [2]. 33 errata slip aa

AUTHENTISCHE RELATION   **414**
Authentische Relation von dem Anlass, Fort-
gang und Schlusse . . . in Germantoun gehalten.
(16.) Continuations: Authentische Nachricht . . .,
(16); Zuverlässige Beschreibung der dritten Con-
ferenz der Evangelischen Religionen . . . in Pennsylvania, ([2] 43–56; Vierte general Versammlung

der Kirche . . ., ([2] 59–76); Grundliche An-und
Aufforderung . . ., ([2] 79–90). *Phil* B. Franklin
1742. Q 5pts b NYP
For further accounts of Moravian conferences,
see Muller, Johann J.

AUTOBIOGRAPHY
Autobiography of an English soldier . . . *See*
Ballentine, Geo.

AUZIAS-TURENNE, RAYMOND   **415**
Voyage au pays des mines d'or. Le Klondike.
P 1898. D [6] 318 [2] port a
—eds. 2 & 3, *P* 1899. D 2 maps

AVERETTE, MRS. ANNIE, tr.   **416**
The unwritten history of old St. Augustine . . .
copied from the Spanish Archives. [*St Augustine*
1907?]. 16° 16 [incl. initial blank lf] 233 front. a

AVERILL, CHARLES E.   **417**
Kit Carson, the prince of the gold hunters . . .
B [1849]. O [4] 8–124 b Y
—rptd. *N Y* [1849]. O 100 aa
Fictionalized biography.

AVERILL, CHARLES E.   **418**
Life in California . . . *B* 1849. O 108 aa
—ed. 2, *B* 1850. O 100 a
—rptd. *B* n.d. [1865]. D [4] 9–100
Sequel to his *Kit Carson* . . .

AVERILL, CHARLES E.   **419**
The Rob Roy of the Rocky mountains. *N Y*
1849. O 96 aa
—rptd. "The hunters of the west . . .," *N Y* [1857].
same collat. aa
Another sequel to author's *Kit Carson* . . .

AVERY, A.   **420**
Handbook . . . of New Mexico [and Durango,
Colorado] . . . *Denver* 1881. D 106 [14] fold. map
2 pls b G

AVERY, ELROY McK.   **421**
A history of the United States . . . *Clev* 1904–10.
O 7v[all] + index vol. *Tarrytown* 1915. In all, 8v
maps pls facs aa

AVERY, ISAAC W.   **422**
The history of . . . Georgia . . . 1850–1881 . . .
N Y [1881]. O [12] 754 errata slip map [not in all
copies] 41pls a
—anr. issue, no index, thus ending with p715.

AVERY, RUFUS, and   **423**
HEMPSTEAD, STEPHEN
Narrative of Jonathan Rathbun, with . . .
accounts of the capture of Groton fort . . . and the

sacking and burning of New London . . . [*N Lond?* 1840?]. D [4] 80 aa
—rptd. *N Y* 1911. a

AVERY, SAMUEL 424
The Susquehannah controversy examined . . . *Wilkesbarre* 1803. D 142 b LC

AVIRETT, JAMES B. 425
The memoirs of General Turner Ashby and his compeers. *Balt* 1867. D 408 port a

AYER, I. WINSLOW 426
The great north-western conspiracy . . . to plunder and burn Chicago . . . *Chi* 1865 O 112 a
—eds. 2 & 3. *Chi* 1865. same collat.
—anr. ed. "The great treason plot . . .," *Chi* [1895]. O 453

AYER, I. WINSLOW 427
Life in the wilds of America . . . *Grand Rapids* 1880. O 528 [incl front] a

AYERS, ELISHA 428
Journal of travel in different parts of the United States . . . [*Preston Conn*] 1847. O 52 aa
Travels, beginning in 1788, extended to Pittsburgh, Ohio, Kentucky and Tennessee.

AYERS, NATHANIEL M. 429
Building a new empire . . . [early Nebraska, etc.] *N Y* [1910] D 221 pls a

[AYSCOUGH, SAMUEL] 430
Remarks on the Letters from an American farmer . . . pointing out the pernicious tendency of these letters to Great Britain. *L* 1783. O [2] 26 a

B

B. (A.) 1
Six letters of: on the difference between Great Britain and the United States . . . *L* 1807. O 48 aa

B., J.
The English party's excursion to Paris . . . *See* Bill, John.

B., J.C. 2
Voyage au Canada . . . 1751 à 1761. *Queb* 1887. O 255 a
Printed for the first time from the contemporary Ms of a French soldier stationed at Ft. Duquesne.

B., J. M. DE . . .
Lettres sur les États-Unis . . . *See* Bins de St. Victor, Jacques M.

B., R.
The English empire in America . . . See Burton, Rob't.

B., R.
The English heroe: or, Sir Francis Drake revived. *See* Burton, Robert.

B., W. D.
Rosecrans' campaign . . . *See* Bickham, Wm. D.

BABB, T[HEODORE] A. 3
In the bosom of the Comanches . . . told by a surviving captive. *Amarillo* [1912]. D 145 a
—ed 2 *Dallas* 1923

BABBITT, CHARLES H. 4
Early days at Council Bluffs. *Wash* 1916. O 96 a

BABBITT, E. L. 5
The Allegheny pilot . . . historical matter . . . *Freeport Pa* 1855. O 64 + 14adv-p 16 maps aa

BABCOCK, RUFUS [ed.] 6
Forty years of pioneer life; memoir of John Mason Peck . . . *Phil* [1864]. D 360 port a
Backwoods life in Tennessee, Louisiana, Missouri and Illinois.

BABER, D. F. ed. 7
The longest rope; the truth about the Johnson County cattle war . . . as told by Bill Walker. *Caldwell Idaho* 1940. O 320   port a
—ed 2 same impr and collat 1947.

BABSON, JOHN J. 8
History of . . . Gloucester [Mass.] . . . *Gloucester* 1860. O [12] 610 fold. map pls a
Portion of the edition burned.

BABSON, JOHN J. 9
Notes and additions to the History of Gloucester. Ser. I & II [all]. *Gloucester* 1876–91. O [4] 94; [2] 187 a

BACA, MANUEL C. DE 10
Historia de Vicente Silva; sus cuarenta bandidos, etc. *Las Vegas* 1896. D [10] 128 30pls aa
—rptd. same impr, n.d. D [8] 97 aa
—Eng. tr. *Wash* 1947. Q [6] 78 500cops ptd a

[BACHE, BENJAMIN F.], pub. 11
Remarks occasioned by the late conduct of Mr. Washington . . . *Phil* 1797. O [4] 84 a
Vicious effort to depreciate the abilities of a great man.

BACHE, WILLIAM   **12**
Historical sketches of Bristol Borough [Pa.].
Bristol 1853. 16° 60 a

BACHELER, ORIGEN   **13**
Mormonism exposed . . . *N Y* 1838. D 48 front.
aa

BACKUS, ISAAC   **14**
An abridgment of the church history of New-
England . . . *B* 1804. O 272 a
Because of additions contained, may be conside-
red a fourth volume of his earlier 3-volume work,
see below.

BACKUS, ISAAC   **15**
A history of New-England, with particular
reference to the . . . Baptists . . . *B* 1777, *Prov* 1784,
B 1796. O 3v: [8] 544 [16]; [16] 432; 335 + adv-1.
b AA NYP Y
—rptd. *Newton Mass* 1871. O 2v a

BACON, ALVIN Q.   **16**
Thrilling adventures of a pioneer boy while a
prisoner of war. n.p. [*ca* 1875] O 32 a
Thrice captured and re-captured by Confederates,
was finally successful and rejoined his Illinois
regiment just in time to get killed at Vicksburg.

[BACON, ANTHONY]   **17**
Considerations on the . . . state of the New
England colonies . . . *L* 1769. O 39 a

[BACON, ANTHONY]   **18**
A short address to the government, the merchants . . . and the colonists in America . . . on the
present state of affairs. *L* 1775. O [2] 40 a

[BACON, ANTHONY?]   **19**
The true interest of Great Britain, with respect
to her American colonies . . . *L* 1766. O [4] 51 a

BACON, EDWARD   **20**
Among the cotton thieves. *Det* 1867. O 300 aa

BACON, GEORGE W.   **21**
The life . . . of Abraham Lincoln . . . *L* 1865.
D [8] 183 port map [at rear] a
—anr. issue, identical but different map [at front] a
—anr. ed. wraps. D 120 port [on cover] no map
—Dutch tr. *Amst* 1865. D

BACON, OLIVER N.   **22**
A history of Natick [Mass.]. *B* 1856. O [2] 261
pl a

BACQUEVILLE DE LA POTHERIE,   **23**
CLAUDE C. L.
Histoire de l'Amérique-Septentrionale . . . *P*
1722. D 4v: [14, incl. eng. t] 15–216 [erroneously
numb 126] 227–370; [2] 168, 173–356 [7]; [12] 158,

157–310 [6]; [2] 271 [5]. 3maps 25pls b AA NYP
Y N
—rptd., with new t-p, au's name omitted, "Voyage
de l'Amérique . . .," *Amst* 1723. D 4v same collat.
except "Epitre," "Avertissement" and "Privilege"
omitted. b N
—anr. ed., au.'s name and original reading of t-p
restored, *P* 1752. D 4v same collat, as in 1722 ed.
Some copies carry date 1753. b
Material on Indians of the Lake regions said to
be based on lost manuscripts of Nicholas Perrot.
Claims advanced as to an earlier [1616] edition
entitled *Nouveau voyage du Canada* . . . may be
dismissed as a bibliographical myth, at least until
a copy has been produced. For English translation
see Blair, Emma H.

BADEAUX, J[EAN] B.   **24**
Journal des operations de l'armée américaine
lors de l'invasion du Canada en 1775–6. *Montr*
1871. O 43 a

BADGER (REV. JOSEPH).   **25**
A memoir of: . . . *Hudson O* 1851. D 185 + 3
adv p a
Came to Ohio in 1801.

BADGER, JOSEPH E.   **26**
Joaquin, the saddle king: a romance of Murietta's
first fight. *N Y* Beadle 1881. Q 29 aa

BADIA, MARC A.   **27**
Compendio della guerra nata per confini in
America tra la Francia e l'Inghilterra . . .
Amst 1763. D [16] 168 port aa

[BADIN, STEPHEN T.]   **28**
Origine et progrès de la mission du Kentucke . . .
par un témoin oculaire. *P* 1821. O [2] 32 a
Badin was the first priest ordained in the United
States.

[BÄGERT, JACOB]   **29**
Nachrichten von der amerikanischen Halbinsel
Californien . . . *Mannheim* 1772. D [16] 358 errata
1. fold.map 2 pls [not issued in all copies] b
—rptd. 1773. aa; Sp tr *Mex* 1942 D [44] 262 [4] a
—Eng tr *Berkeley* 1952. D 218

BAGLEY, CLARENCE B.   **30**
In the beginning . . . *Seattle* 1905. O 90 a

BAILEY, ISAAC   **31**
American naval biography. *Prov* 1815. D 257 a

BAILEY, J. T.   **32**
An historical sketch of . . . Brooklyn. *Bklyn*
1840. D 72 map a

BAILEY, JAMES N.   **33**
Sketches of Indian character . . . Leeds 1841.
O 64 a

BAILEY (ROBERT). 34
The life and adventures of: *Rich* 1822. O [4]
9–348 [2] port 3pls a
—rptd. 1828.
Autobiography of an engaging scoundrel. A
Southern prototype of Stephen Burroughs.

BAILEY, WASHINGTON 35
A trip to California in 1853. [*Leroy Ill*] 1915
O 50 port aa

BAILEY, WILLIAM 36
Records of patriotism, etc. *Wash* [ptd at *Stamford, Eng.*] 1825. D [16] 216 a
—rptd. same impr & collat 1826.
Based largely on Alex. Garden's *Anecdotes of the Revolutionary War*, this bitterly anti-British compilation from an English pen had to be issued with a counterfeit American imprint.

BAILEY, WILLIAM F. 37
The story of the first trans-continental railroad . . . [*Fair Oaks, Pa* 1906]. D 164 a

[BAILLIE, HUGH] 38
An appendix to a letter to Dr. Shebbeare. To which are added, Some observations on . . . Taxation no tyranny . . . *L* 1775. O 80 a

BAILLIE, HUGH 39
A letter to Dr. Shebear . . . refutation of his arguments concerning the Boston and Quebec Acts . . . *L* 1775. O [2] 54 a

BAILY, FRANCIS 40
Journal of a tour in unsettled parts of North America in 1796–7. *L* 1856. O [12] 439 aa
Mississippi valley in the days of Boone.

BAINES, EDWARD 41
History of the late war, between the United States and Great Britain; with . . . appendix . . . by Ebenezer H. Cummins. *Balt* 1820. D 167 [47] a

BAIRD, CHARLES W. 42
Chronicle of a border town. History of Rye [N. Y.] . . . *N Y* 1871. O [18] 570 map a

BAIRD, CHARLES W. 43
History of the Huguenot emigration to America. *N Y* [1885]. O 2v: [2] 354; [2] 448. 15maps & pls a

BAIRD, GEORGE M. P. 44
The story of Barney May, pioneer [in the Fraser river gold regions]. O 61 pls 100 copies ptd. aa

[BAIRD, ROBERT] 45
View of the valley of the Mississippi . . . *Phil* 1832. D [12] 341 15 maps & plans a
—ed. 2, *Phil* 1834. D [12] 372 15 maps & plans
Attributed also to Richard Bache and Robert Bache.

BAKANOWSKI, ADOLF 46
Moje Wspomnienia . . . [My memoirs]. *Lwow* [*Lemberg*] 1913. O [6] 226 a
Missionary activities in the first Polish settlement in the United States, near San Antonio, Texas.

BAKER, D. W. C. comp. 47
A Texas scrap-book . . . *N Y* [1875]. O 657 [incl. illus.] front. a
—rptd. *N Y* 1887.
—anr. ed. *Austin* 1936.

[BAKER, DELPHINE P.] 48
Solon; or the rebellion of '61 . . . *Chi* 1862. O 74 a

BAKER, HOZIAL H. 49
Overland journey to Carson valley, Utah. *Seneca Falls N Y* 1861. O 38 port dd AA G Y [of 4copies known]

BAKER (LOUISA).
The adventures of: *See* West, Mrs.LucyBrewer.

BAKER (LOUISA).
An affecting narrative of: *See* West, Mrs. Lucy Brewerl.

[BAKER, S.] 50
Outline history of an expedition to California . . . *N Y* 1849. obl. 16° 32 lvs+cover t. b LC NYH S Y

BAKER, WILLIAM 51
A concise description of middle Tennessee. ed. 2. *McMinnville* 1868. O 127 a

BAKER, WILLIAM S. 52
Itinerary of General Washington [1775–1783]. *Phil* 1892. O [4] 334 port a

BAKER, WILLIAM S. 53
Washington after the revolution [1784–1789]. *Phil* 1898. O [2] 416 a

BALBONTIN, MANUEL 54
La invasion americana. 1846 à 1848. *Mex* 1883. O 137 4maps a

BALCH, THOMAS 55
Les Francais en Amérique . . . 1777–1783. *P* 1872. O [8] 238 [2] map 3pls a
—Eng. tr., with added vol. on French regiments and officers, *Phil* 1891-5. O 2v: maps port

BALCH, THOMAS, ed. 56
Letters and papers relating chiefly to the provincial history of Pennsylvania . . . *Phil* 1855. D [138] 312 a
Usually cited as the "Shippen Papers."

BALCH, THOMAS, ed.   57
Papers relating chiefly to the Maryland line during the Revolution. *Phil* 1857. O [4] 219 150 cops ptd a

BALDWIN, MRS. ALICE B.   58
Memoirs of . . . Frank D. Baldwin . . . *L A* 1929. O [16] 204 12pls a
General Baldwin campaigned against Indians all over the West and was the only officer to receive twice the Medal of Honor.

BALDWIN, BENJAMIN F.   59
Notices of the campaign of the Tennessee volunteers . . . 1836-7. *Nashv* 1843. O 30 b TennH[only copy located]

BALDWIN, EBENEZER   60
Annals of Yale college . . . to 1831. *N Hav* 1831. O [8] 324 a
—ed. 2, to 1838. same impr. 1838. O [8] 343 port.

BALDWIN, HENRY   61
A general view of the origin and nature of the constitution and government of the United States. *Phil* 1837. O [6] 197 a

BALDWIN, JOSEPH G.   62
The flush times of Alabama and Mississippi . . . *N Y* 1853. D [12] 330 + 6 adv p 4 pls aa

BALDWIN (THOMAS).   63
Narrative of the massacre, by the savages, of the wife and children of: . . . *N Y* 1835. O 24 fold col front. aa
—rptd. *N Y* 1836, same collat.; *N Y* 1837. a
Perhaps based on some actual incident of border horror in early Kentucky, but unconvincingly and rhapsodically presented.

BALESTIER, J[OSEPH] N.   64
The annals of Chicago. *Chi* 1840. D 24 c AA ChiH G NYP
—rptd. *Chi* 1876. O 48; *Chi* 1879. same collat. a
First history of this metropolis, and one of its earliest imprints.

BALL, CHARLES   65
Slavery in the United States . . . *Lewistown Pa* 1836. D 400 a
—rptd: *N Y* 1837. D [2] 517; *Pitt* 1853; 1854.
—anr. ed. "Fifty years in chains . . .," *Indp* 1859. D 430
—Eng. ed. "The life of a Negro slave . . .," *L* 1846. O 245
—Ger. tr. *Berlin* 1854. O 2v: [4] 236; [4] 196
One of the few personal narratives of southern slaves that sounds veracious.

BALL, J. P.   66
Ball's mammoth pictorial tour of the United States. Comprising views of the . . . slave trade . . . *Cin* 1855. O 56 fold.pl aa

BALL, NICHOLAS   67
The pioneers of '49 . . . *B* 1891. O [16 incl front] 288 + adv-p 7 pls a

BALL (NICHOLAS).   68
The voyages and travels of: 1838–53. *B* 1895. O 38 port a

BALL, T[IMOTHY] H.   69
A glance into the great south-east; or, Clarke county, Alabama . . . 1540–1877. *Grove Hill Ala* [ptd. *Chi*] 1882. D 782 map aa

BALL, T[IMOTHY] H.   70
Lake county, Indiana . . . *Chi* 1873. D 364 map a
—rptd. *Crown Point* 1884.

BALL, T[IMOTHY] H.   71
Northwestern, Indiana . . . *La Porte* 1900. D 570 2maps port a
Amplification of his *Lake county*.

BALLANCE, C[HARLES]   72
The history of Peoria. *Peoria* 1870. D [8] 271 a

BALLARD, COLIN R.   73
The military genius of Abraham Lincoln . . . *L* 1926. O [8] 246 front. 19 maps [on 17 sheets] a
—Am ed *N Y* [1952]

[BALLARD, D. P.]   74
Washington Territory and the far northwest . . . *Chi* [1889]. O 60 a

[BALLARD, WILLIAM]   75
Sketch of the history of Framingham, Mass . . . *B* 1827. O 71 a

BALLENSTEDT, C. W. T.   76
Beschreibung meiner Reise nach dem Goldminen Californiens. *Schöningen* 1851. D 103 aa

[BALLENTINE, GEORGE]   77
Autobiography of an English soldier in the United States army. *L* 1853. D 2v: [2] 306 + 24adv-p; [2] 313 + 16adv-p a
—Am. ed.: *N Y* 1853. D [12] 9–288 2pls; 1854.
—anr. ed. "The Mexican war . . .," *N Y* 1860. same collat.
Served at Ft. Pickens, Florida, and with Scott from Vera Cruz to Mexico City.

BALLINGER, R. H.   78
Does it pay? A book on the stock industry of southwestern Kansas. *Larned Kas* 1883. O 48 + adv pp. aa

BALLOU, ROBERT   79
Early Klickitat valley days . . . [*Goldendale, Wash.* 1938] O 496 a

BALTHASAR (JUAN ANTONIO).   80
Carta del: en que dà noticia de la exemplar vida . . . del ferveroso missionero . . . Francisco Maria Picolo. [*Mex* 1752]. Q 88 d Hn JCB N
Sabin 2986 lists, without collation or location, a 1730 edition of this life of one of the earliest California missionaries; he also lists, by same author, lives of two other California Jesuits—Nicolas de Tamaral [1752], and Lorenzo Carranco [1751].

BALTIMORE.   81
An exact . . . narrative of the events which took place in: on the 27th and 28th of July last . . . n.p. [1812?]. 18° 71 aa

BALTIMORE.   82
Interesting papers relative to the recent riots at: *Phil* 1812. O 89 aa
This shameful affair began with the destruction of a Federal newspaper opposed to the war of 1812 and ended with the killing of one of the proprietors and fatal injuries to General Henry Lee.

BALTIMORE.   83
Picture of: . . . *Balt* Lucas [1832]. 18° 249 map plan pls a

BALTIMORE.   84
Proceedings of sundry citizens of: . . . for the purpose of devising . . . means of improving . . . intercourse between that city and the western states. *Balt* 1827. O 39 aa
Resulted in the construction of the first western railway, the Baltimore and Ohio.

BALTIMORE.   85
Remarks on the intercourse of: with the western country . . . *See* Howard, J.T.E.

BALTIMORE AND OHIO RAILROAD (THE).
A history and description of: By a citizen of Baltimore. *See* Smith, Wm. Prescott.

BANCROFT, AARON   86
An essay on the life of George Washington . . . *Worc* 1807. D [12] 552 port a
—Am. ed. 2, "Life of George Washington . . .," *B* 1826. D 2v: 223; 218. 2pls
—rptd. several times
—Eng. ed. "Life of George Washington . . .," *L* 1808. O [12] 560 port

[BANCROFT, EDWARD]   87
Remarks on the Review of the controversy between Great Britain and her colonies . . . *L* 1769. O [4] 126 a
—Am. ed., au. named, *N Lond* 1771. O 130
Defends colonial rights.

BANCROFT, GEORGE   88
History of the United States [to 1782]. *B* 1834–74. O 10v maps & ports aa
—rptd. several times, both in Eng. & Am. a
—rev. ed. [to 1789], with omissions, *N Y* 1883–5. O 6v a
—tr. into Dutch, Fr., Ger., and other languages.

BANCROFT, GEORGE   89
Reply of the United States to the case of . . . Her Britannic Majesty . . . [*Berlin* 1872]. Q 120 a
This case, in which the German Kaiser as arbitrator decided in favor of the United States, involved the Northwestern boundary, the San Juan Island trouble, etc.

BANCROFT, HUBERT H.   90
History of Alaska. *S F* 1886. O [38] 775 map aa
—rptd. same impr & collat 1890. a
—anr. ed. *N Y* 1959, same collat.
Includes the most comprehensive English account of Russian America.

BANCROFT, HUBERT H., ed.   91
Works. *S F* 1882–1891. O 39vols: 1–5, Native races; 6–8, Cent. Amer.; 9–14, Mexico; 15–16, North Mexico and Texas; 17, Ariz. and New Mex.; 18–24, Calif.; 25, Nev., Col. and Wyo.; 26, Utah; 27–28, Northwest coast; 29–30, Ore.; 31, Wash., Idaho and Mont.; 32, Brit. Columbia; 33, Alaska; 34, Calif. pastoral; 35, Calif. inter pocula; 36–37, Popular tribunals; 38, Essays, etc.; 39, Literary industries. b
Colossal co-operative undertaking; nothing approaching it has ever been attempted in this country. Several of the volumes went through various reprints.

BANCROFT, JOSEPH, comp.   92
Census of . . . Savannah . . . with historical notices . . . *Sav* 1848. O 56 pl a
—ed. 2, with commercial directory added, same date & impr. D 96 [incl advs] map a

BANDELIER, ADOLPH F. A.   93
Contributions to the history of the southwestern portion of the United States. *C* 1890. O [10] 206 map a
Early northward expansion from Mexico: Cabeca de Vaca, Nizza and Villazur; volume V, Papers of the Archaeological Institute of America, American series.

BANDELIER, ADOLPH F. A.   94
The delight makers . . . *N Y* [1890]. D 490 a
—eds 2 & 3: *N Y* 1916; 1918.

BANDELIER, ADOLPH F. A.   95
Final report of investigations among the Indians of the southwestern United States. Pts. 1 & 2[all]. *C* 1890–92. O 2v: [8] 323; [8] 591. map 13pls a

Volumes III and IV, Papers of the Archaeological Institute of America, American series. Most important work of its nature on Arizona and New Mexico; based on original sources, historical and archaeological.

BANDELIER, ADOLPH F. A.   96
The gilded man . . . *N Y* 1893. D [6] 302 a

BANDELIER, ADOLPH F. A.   97
Historical introduction to studies among the sedentary Indians of New Mexico. *B* 1881. O [4] 135 11pls a
—ed. 2, same impr. & collat., 1883.
Volume I, Papers of the Archaeological Institute of America, American series.

BANDITTI (THE) OF THE ROCKY MOUNTAINS . . .
See Idaho.

BANKS, CHARLES E.   98
The history of Martha's Vineyard . . . *B* 1911–25. O 3v: 535; [2] 209 147 74 82 68 35 27 18; [16] 565. 47maps & pls aa
Volume three [devoted to genealogy] has imprint of Edgarton.

BANKS, CHARLES E.   99
The planters of the commonwealth . . . *B* 1930. O [20] 3–231 9pls a 750copies ptd.
Supplements and corrects previously published lists.

BANKS, CHARLES E.   100
The Winthrop fleet of 1630 . . . *B* 1930. O [26] 119 12maps & pls a 550copies ptd.

BANKS, HENRY   101
A memorial to the Congress of the United States, relating to revolutionary events. *Frankf Ky* 1827. D 71 b NYP

BANKS, HENRY   102
Observations shewing the benefits of . . . a turnpike road from Lexington in Kentucky to James river in Virginia . . . *Frankfort* 1819. O 56 aa

BANKS, HENRY   103
A review of political opinions . . . for the benefit of the people of Kentucky. *Frankf Ky* 1822. O [8] 83 aa

BANKS, HENRY   104
The vindication of John Banks, of Virginia . . . and . . . of General Henry Lee . . . *Frankf Ky* 1826. O 88 b AA NYP TransU
In defending his brother and Lee, General Nathaniel Greene and his biographers—Caldwell and Johnson—are pilloried as scoundrels and liars.

[BANNISTER, SAXE]   105
Remarks on the Indians of North America . . . *L* 1822. O [2] 64 a

BANNON, ARTHUR H.   106
A hunter's summer in the Yukon Territory. *Columbus* 1911. D 48 8pls a

BANTA, D[AVID] D.   107
A historical sketch of Johnson County, Indiana. *Chi* 1881. O 170 a

BANTA, S. E., ed.   108
Buckelew, the Indian captive . . . *Mason Tex* [1911]. D [2] 112 pl a
—rptd. *Bandera Tex* [1925]. O [2] 7–188 [5] pl

BANTA, WILLIAM   109
Twenty-seven years on the frontier. *Austin* 1893. D [16] 270 aa
—rptd. *Council Hill Okla* [1933]. D [8] 224 [2] front. a

BANVARD, JOHN   110
Description of [his] Panorama of the Mississippi . . . *B* 1847. O 48[incl. wraps] aa
—anr. ed., with adds., *N Y* 1862. O 38 a
—Eng. eds.: *L* 1848; *L* 1849; both: O 48 [incl.wraps] a
—rptd. *L* 1850. O 32; *L.* 1852. same collat.
Painted on three miles of canvas, covering 1200-miles of river, from the Missouri's mouth to New Orleans.

BARAGA, F[REDERIC]   111
Abrégé de l'histoire des Indiens de l'Amérique Septentrionale. Traduit de l'Allemand. *P* 1837. D 296 b
—rptd. *P* 1843. same collat. aa

BARBARITIES   112
Barbarities of the enemy exposed . . . *Troy* 1813. D 178 errata l. a
—other eds.: *Worcester* 1814. D 192; *Lex* 1814. D 124

[BARBAROUX, CHARLES O., and   113
LARDIER, J. A.]
Voyage du Général Lafayette aux États-Unis . . . *P* 1824–5. O 3pts in 1: 364 port aa
—anr. ed. *Brus* 1825. 16 3v a
—anr. ed. *P* 1826. O [6] 3–30, 364 [2] map port a

[BARBÉ-MARBOIS, FRANCOIS,   114
Marquis de]
Complot d'Arnold et de Sir Henry Clinton . . . *P* 1816. D [4] 44 184 map 2ports a
—rptd. *P* 1831. D [4] 48 164 map 2 ports. [not iss in all cops]
—Eng. tr. in *American Register*, v.2

BARBÉ-MARBOIS, FRANCOIS, 115
Marquis de
Histoire de la Louisiane . . . *P* 1829. O [6] 485
map aa
—Eng. tr. *Phil* 1830. O [18] 15–456 aa

BARBER (MISS, wife of "Squatting Bear.") 116
The true narrative of the five years' suffering
and . . . adventures of: . . . *Phil* Barclay [1873?].
O [4 incl. cover t.] 19–94 97–108[9pls incl. in
paginat.] a
—rptd. *Phil* [1880].
Probably as spurious as are the medical remedies contained.

BARBER, REV. DANIEL 117
The history of my own times. *Wash* 1827–8. O
2pts in 1 : 48; 32 a
—same, pt. 3, *Frederick Md* 1832. O

BARBER (DARIUS). 118
Narrative of the tragical death of: and his seven
children . . . butchered by the Indians in Camden
County, Georgia . . . the captivity and sufferings
of Mɪs. Barber [etc.]. *B* Hazen [ca 1818]. D 24
front. b 4 perfect copies known

BARBER, JOHN W., and 119
HOWE, HENRY
All the western states and territories . . . *Cin*
1867. O 704 map port a
—rptd. same impr. 1868. O 733 map port

BARBER, JOHN W. 120
Connecticut historical collections . . . *N Hav*
[1838]. O 560 map 6pls a
—ed. 2, same impr. [1846]. O 576 map pls.
—best. ed. *N. Hav.* [1849] O [6] 5–584 map 12pls
[3 in color]

BARBER, JOHN W., and 121
HOWE, HENRY
Historical collections of . . . New Jersey . . . *N Y*
1844. O 512 2 col.fronts. map 8 pls a
—other eds. [with *N Y* or *N Hav* impr.]: 1845;
1846; [1852]; 1857; 1868.

BARBER, JOHN W., and 122
HOWE, HENRY
Historical collections of . . . New York . . . *N Y*
1841. O 608 map 10pls a
—rptd.: *N Y* 1842; 1844; 1845; 1851; *Cooperstown*
1846.

BARBER, JOHN W. 123
Historical collections . . . relating to the history
. . . of evry town in Massachusetts . . . *Worc* 1839.
O 624 map front. 16 pls a
—other eds.: *Worc* 1841. O 632 map pls: *Worc*
1844. O 624 map pls; *Worc* 1848.

BARBER, JOHN W. 124
The history and antiquities of New England,
New York, New Jersey and Pennsylvania . . . *Hart*
1840. O 576 pls a
—other eds. [with *Hart*, *Port*, or *Worc* impr.]:
1841; 1843; 1846; 1847; 1848; 1856.

BARBER, JOHN W. 125
History and antiquities of New Haven . . .
N Hav 1831. D 120 map 6col pls a
—rptd. 1846.
—ed. 2, same impr. 1856. D 180 5 pls
—ed. 3, enl., *N Hav* 1870.

BARBER, J[OHN] W., ed. 126
Interesting events in the history of the United
States . . . *N Hav* 1828. D [6] 216 a
—rptd. *B* n.d. same collat.
—ed. 3, "Incidents in American history . . .." *N Y*
1847. D 404
—Ger. tr. *Darmstadt* 1849. O [8] 288

BARBER AND BAKER [pub.] 127
Sacramento illustrated. *Sacr* 1855. O 36 32views
[incl. in text] b 6 cops loc
—rptd. *Sacr* 1950. F [14] 135 a 300copies ptd. a

BARBEY, THÉODORE 128
Le Texas. [*P*] 1841. O [2] 22 map aa

BARBOUR COUNTY, KANSAS. 129
Osage troubles in: *Topeka* 1875. O 68 a

[BARCIA CARBALLIDO Y ZÚÑIGA, 130
ANDRÉS GONZALEZ DE]
Ensayo cronologico, para la historia general de
la Florida . . . *Madrid* [1723]. F [40] 368 [54] tab
b N NYP
Covers early explorations in the whole continent
north of Mexico and east of the Pacific coast. It
was issued to accompany —as Part II—Barcia's
edition of Garcilaso de la Vega's *La Florida del
Inca*, published the same year, and is the principal authority on Florida itself during its two
centuries of undisputed Spanish supremacy, 1567–
1763.

BARCIA CARBALLIDO Y ZÚÑIGA, 131
ANDRÉS GONZALEZ DE, ed.
Historiadores primitivos de las Indias Occiden-
tales . . . *Madrid* 1749. F 3v: [4] 128 173 57 [18] 50
43 [18] 70 [4]; 226 [60] 214 [46]; [8] 176 [28] 179–
237 [14] 31 [18] 107 [34] 48 c 1500copies ptd, but
all but about 200 were junked as waste-paper.
N NYP Y
Though devoted chiefly to narratives relating to
Mexico and South America, contains Cabeza de
Vaca's *Relacion*, along with Ardoino's defense of
its authenticity.

BARCLAY, ROBERT   132
Agricultural tour in the United States . . . *Edin*
1842. D [24] 181 a
Dedication signed R. Barclay-Allardice.

BARD, JOHN   133
A letter to the proprietors of the great Nine-
Partner's tract . . . Duchess County [N. Y.] N Y
1751. *O* 28 b Hn[only copy located]

BARDE, ALEXANDRE   134
Histoire des comités de vigilance aux Attakapas.
St Jean Baptiste La 1861. O [6] 3–428 b AA LaU
LC NYP
Prose masterpiece of the ante-bellum South,
concerning the extra-judicial proceeding of the
outraged citizenry of Lafayette and Vermillion
parishes, La., against organized ruffians.

BARDE, FREDERICK S.   135
Life and adventures of "Billy" Dixon of Adobe
Walls, Texas panhandle . . . *Guthrie* [1914]. D 320
[incl. pls] a
—rev. ed. *Dallas* [1927]. O [18] 251 pls

BARHAM, WILLIAM, comp.   136
Descriptions of Niagara . . . *Gravesend* [1847].
O 180 2pls a

BARKER, EUGENE C.   137
The life of Stephen F. Austin . . . *Nashv* 1925.
O [15] 551 2maps plan 6ports a some copies on L. P.
—rptd Austin 1949

BARKER (JACOB).   138
Incidents in the life of: . . . with historical
facts . . . *Wash* 1855. O [6] 285 2pls a

[BARKER, JACOB]   139
The rebellion: its consequences . . . *N O* 1866.
O 231 port a
—anr. ed., same impr. & date. O 248 port

BARKER, JAMES N.   140
Sketches of the primitive settlements on the river
Delaware. *Phil* 1827. O 62 a

BARLER, MILES   141
Early days in Llano [Tex.]. [*Llano ca* 1898]. 16°
68 cover t. only b Tx U [only copy known]
—rptd. [*ca* 1905]. 16° 49 a
—anr ed n.p. n.d. 16° 76

[BARLOW, JOEL]?   142
Observations generales et impartiales sur
l'affaire du Scioto. *P* 1790. O 27 b JCB

BARLOW (JOEL).   143
The political writings of: *N Y* 1796. D 258 a

BARLOW (JOEL)   144
Barlow (Joel) to his fellow citizens in the United
States. Letters I and II. [*P* 1799?], O 2v: 55; 102 aa
[Some cops of letter I have only 32 p]
—Eng. ed. "Letters from Paris . . .," *L* 1799. O 2v:
32; 36 aa
—anr. Eng. ed. *L* 1800. O 116 aa
—Am. eds. of Letter I only: [*Phil* 1799–1800]. D;
[1800–01]. D Ea have 32 p. a
—anr. Am. ed., with a letter to Washington added,
"Two letters . . .," *N Hav* 1806. D 118 aa

BARLOW, J[OHN] W., and HEAP, D. P.   145
Report of reconnaissance . . . of the upper Yel-
lowstone in 1871. [Sen. Exec. Doc. 66]. *Wash* 1872.
O [2] 43 fold.map a

BARNARD (CAPT. CHARLES H.)   146
A narrative of the sufferings . . . of: in a voyage
round the world . . . 1812–1816 . . . seizure of his
vessel by an English crew at the Falkland islands,
etc. *N Y* 1829. O 296 map 6pls aa
Appendix contains account of Colter's adventures in the Yellowstone valley.

BARNARD, EVAN G.   147
A rider of the Cherokee strip. *B* 1936. O [20]
233 8 pls a

BARNARD, F[REDERICK] A. P.   148
No just cause for a dissolution of the Union . . .
Tuscaloosa 1851. O 36 a

BARNARD, GEORGE N.   149
Photographic views, illustrative of the civil
war . . . *N Y* n.d. Q 285photos b

BARNARD, GEORGE N.   150
Photographic views of Sherman's campaign . . .
N Y [1866]. F [2] 61views b

BARNARD, DR. J. H.   151
Journal . . . giving an account of Fannin massacre. *Goliad* [1912?]. O [2] 36 a

BARNES, CHARLES M.   152
Combats and conquests of immortal heroes.
San Antonio 1910. O 268 front a

BARNES, DEMAS   153
From the Atlantic to the Pacific, overland . . .
N Y 1866. D 136 front. a

BARNES, JOHN S., ed.   154
The logs of the Serapis-Alliance-Ariel, *N Y*
1911. Q [44] 138[incl.pls] a 300copies ptd.

BARNES, JOSEPH   155
Remarks on Mr. Fitch's reply to Mr. James
Rumsey's pamphlet. *Phil* 1788. O [16] 16 aa

BARNES, WILL[IAM] C.   156
Tales from the X-Bar horse camp. *Chi* 1920. D
[12] 218 18pls a

BARNES, WILLIAM C.   157
Western grazing grounds ... *Chi* 1913. D 390
pls a

BARNEY, JOSHUA   158
Report of the survey of a route from St. Louis to
the big bend of the Red river. [*Wash* 1853]. O 59
map a

BARNEY, LIBEUS   159
Early day letters from Auraria. *Denver* [1907]
O 88 port b
—rptd *San José* 1959. O [6] 11–99 map pl a

BARNEY, MARY, ed.   160
A biographical memoir of ... Commodore
Joshua Barney ... *B* 1832. O [16] 328 port a

BARNUM, H. L.   161
The spy unmasked; or, memoirs of Enoch
Crosby, alias Harvey Birch, the hero of Mr.
Cooper's tale ... *N Y* 1828. O [6] 9–206 + 2adv-p
map 5pls aa
—ed. 2, *Cin* 1831. D 216 port a
—rptd., abr., *N Y* 1864. 16° 312
—Eng. ed. *L* 1828. D 2v: 234; 222 a
—rptd. *L* 1829. same collat.
—anr. ed. *N Y* [ptd *L*] 1829. D 2v in 1 3pls

BARNUM (JAMES H.)   162
The traveller's guide, or life of: ... by himself.
Gt Barrington 1847. O 52 b Hn Y
Mississippi Valley travels and adventures, trips
to the Missouri, etc.

BARNWELL, V. T., comp.   163
Atlanta city directory ... for 1867. *Atlanta*
1867. O 288 aa
First "post-bellum" Atlanta directory, with the
historical sketch by Colonel Haygood, contained
in the first directory of 1859, considerably amplified. For that first directory see Atlanta.

BAROUX (ABBÉ L.)   164
Lettre de: à M. J. Denève ... supérieur du Col-
lège américain de Louvain. *Orleans* 1863. D 68 a
Baroux worked 16 years as missionary among
the Michigan Indians.

BAROUX, ABBÉ L.   165
Notice sur la mission des Pottowatomies dans
l'état du Michigan. *Caen* 1859. O 48 aa

BARR, JAMES [F.]   166
A correct ... narrative of the Indian war in
Florida ... *N Y* 1836. D 32 b LC N NYP

[BARRATT, JOSEPH] ed.   168
The Indian of New England ... *Middletown
Conn* 1851. D 24 a
—eds. 2 & 3, same impr., date & collat.

BARREIRO, ANTONIO   169
Ojeada sobre Nuevo-México ... *Puebla* 1832.
O 42 [14] 3tabs c B G NYP
For enlarged edition, *see* Pino, Pedro B.

[BARREIRO, MIGUEL]   170
Resumen instructivo, que publica el comisario
de division del exército de operaciones sobre
Tejas ... *Matamoras* 1837. O 36 2tabs b B m S Y
Face-saving explanation for Mexico's failure
against the despised Texans in 1836-7.

BARRELL, GEORGE   171
Notes of voyages ... in a career of thirty years
at sea. *Springfield Ill.* 1890. O 223 b N Y
Only record of his voyage to the North-west
coast and California, 1824–5.

BARRETT, JOSEPH O.   172
History of Traverse county [Minn.] ... *Brown's
Valley* 1881. O 32 a

BARRETT (SELA H.)   173
Journal of: ... *Pomeroy*, O. 1847. 16° 32 aa

BARRETT, THOMAS   174
Great hanging at Gainesville ... *Gainesville Tex*
1885. D [4] 31 a

BARRETT, WALTER [pseud.]
The old merchants of New York. *See* Scoville,
Jos. A.

BARRETT-LENNARD, CHARLES E.   175
Travels in British Columbia ... [and a trip to
California] *L* 1862. O [12] 307 pl a

BARRIE, ROBERT and GEORGE   176
Cruises, mainly in the ... Chesapeake. *Phil*
1909. O [10] 276 map 58pls a

BARRINGTON, DAINES   177
Miscellanies. *L* 1781. Q [12] 557 2ports 7maps
& charts aa
Contains the journal of Maurelle, pilot with the
fleet commanded by Don Juan de la Bodega, while
exploring the coast northward of California in
1775; this portion was also issued in separate form.
See Maurelle, Francisco A.

[BARRINGTON, DAINES]   178
Proofs that Great Britain was successful against
each of her numerous enemies before the late
victory of ... Rodney. *L* 1782. [1] 39 a

43

BARRON (CAPTAIN JAMES) . . .   179
Proceedings of a court of enquiry upon: . . .
Wash 1822. O 111 a

BARRON (COMMODORE JAMES) et al.
Proceedings of the general court martial . . . for
the trial of: *Wash* 1822. O 496 a

BARRON (MRS. JANE).   180
Life of: *Dayton, O.* 1857. O 93 b

BARRON, SAMUEL B.   181
The Lone Star defenders: a chronicle of the
Third Texas cavalry . . . *N Y* 1908. D [6] 3–276
11pls a

[BARRON, WILLIAM]   182
History of the colonization of the free states of
antiquity, applied to the present contest between
Great Britain and her American colonies . . . *L*
1777. Q [8] 151 a
—Fr. tr., with adds., *Utrecht* 1778. O [8] 248
Justifies colonial taxation as an ancient practice.

BARROW, SIR JOHN, 1764-1848   183
The life of Richard, Earl Howe . . . *L* 1838. O
[16] 432 port 2facs a

BARROW, JOHN, 1808-98   184
Facts relating to north eastern Texas . . . from
notes made during a tour . . . *L* 1849. O 68 map
b N

BARROWS, JOHN R.   185
Ubet. *Caldwell Ida* 1934. D 278 a
One of the best cowboy narratives.

BARROWS, WILLARD   186
Notes on Iowa Territory. *Cin* 1845. 16° 46 map
b G IaH [of 3 cops loc]

BARROWS, WILLIAM   187
Eight weeks on the frontier. [*B* 1876]. 16°
24 + cov. t. aa

[BARROWS, WILLIAM]   188
The general; or, twelve nights in the hunter's
camp. . . . *B* 1869, 16° [4] 268 front. a
—rptd. *B* 1870.
Adventures of General Willard Barrows, who
crossed the plains to California in 1850 and to
Idaho and Montana in the '60s.

[BARRY, HENRY]   189
The Strictures on the Friendly address examined . . . [*B* ?] 1775. O 14 aa
+anr. ed. *B* 1775. O 20 aa
—rptd. as "The general attacked by a subaltern...,"
with Lee's "Strictures" included, *N Y* Rivington
[1775]. O 25 aa
For pamphlet attacked, *see* Lee, Charles.

BARRY, JOHN S.   190
A historical sketch of . . . Hanover, Mass. *B*
1853. O 448 pl a

[BARRY, JOSEPH]   191
The annals of Harper's Ferry . . . *Hagerstown*
1869. O 64 a
—ed. 2, *Martinsburg W Va* 1872. O 126

BARRY, T. A., and PATTEN, B. A.   192
Men and memories of San Francisco in the
"spring of '50." *S F* 1873. D 296 2 pls a
—rptd. "San Francisco . . . 1850," *S F* 1947. Q

BARRY (THOMAS).   193
Narrative of the singular adventures and captivity of: among the Monsipi Indians, in the unexplored regions of North America. *Sommers Town*
Neil 1800. D 60 front. aa
—rptd. *Manch* n.d. (1801?) 16 48° aa
—ed. 2, "The singular adventures . . .," [*L*] 1802.
D 62 [incl. col. front.] aa
Unquestionably questionable.

BARRY, WILLIAM E.   194
The blockhouse and stockade fort. *Kennebunk*
Me 1915. Q [8] 50 [20] 5pls a 34copies ptd.

BARRY, WILLIAM J.   195
Up and down; or, fifty years . . . in Australia,
California, etc. *L* 1879. D [14] 308 + 32adv-p
11pls a
Four chapters on two lengthy California trips,
1849 and 1852.

BARSUKOV, IVAN I.   196
Innokenti, Metropolit Moskovskii i Kolo-
menskii po ego Sochineneim Pisjmam i Rozskazam
Sovremennikov. [Biography of Innocent, Metropolitan of Moscow, etc.]. *Moscow* 1883. O 769 3pls
aa
See also Veniaminov, Ivan Y.

BARTHOLF, J. F., and   197
BOGGESS, F. C. M.
South Florida . . . With a narration of incidents
of the Seminole . . . war. *Jacksonville* 1881. D 76 a

BARTLETT, DAVID V. G.   198
The life . . . of Abraham Lincoln. *N Y* Dayton
1860. D 150 pref. dated June 1, words "Authorized
Edition" not on front cover a
First biography exclusively on Lincoln.

BARTLETT, JOHN R.   199
A history of the destruction of His Britannic
Majesty's schooner Gaspee . . . *Prov* 1861. O 140
a 125copies ptd.

[BARTLETT, JOHN R.]   200
Official despatches . . . connected with the Commission to . . . mark the boundary between the United States and Mexico. Sen. Ex. Doc. 119 [*Wash* 1852]. O 515 7maps a

BARTLETT, JOHN R.   201
Personal narrative of explorations . . . in Texas, New Mexico, California, &c . . . with the United States and Mexican Boundary Commission . . . 1850–1–2–3. *N Y* 1854. O 2v: [24] 506; [20] 624, map 16pls [front. belonging to v.2 was placed in v. 1 and only one geyser pl, not two as listed, is found in v.2, that deficiency being made up by an unlisted view of Tucson] aa
—Eng. ed., same collat. *L* 1854. aa
—anr. issue, 2v. in 1, same collat. except for omission of Tucson view, resulting in only 15 pls, *N Y & L* 1856. a

BARTLETT, JOHN R., ed.   202
Records of the colony of Rhode Island and Providence Plantations . . . *Prov* 1856–65. O 10v: 549; [4] 609; [8] 595; [4] 622; [4] 594; [4] 629; [4] 643; [4] 661; [4] 763; [4] 527. 4ports a 50copies issued on L. P. aa

BARTLETT, JOHN R.   203
Report on the . . . boundary line between the United States and Mexico. Sen. Ex. Doc. 41. [*Wash* 1853]. O 31 5maps a

BARTLETT, JOSIAH   204
An historical sketch of Charlestown [Mass.] *B* 1814. O 24 a
—rptd. 1880

BARTLETT, M. R.   205
A statistical . . . view of the United States . . . *Roch* 1837. 16° 48 a

[BARTLETT, NAPIER]   206
A soldier's story of the war; including the marches and battles of . . . Louisiana troops . . . *N O* 1874. O [2] 259 251–252 [2] 13 [36] + 6adv-p 9pls aa
—rptd. "Military record of Louisiana," *N O* 1875. O 64 30 40 [12] 259 9pls aa
Both editions issued also without plates. Pagination often varies.

BARTLETT [LIEUT.]   207
W[ASHINGTON] A.
A portion of the evidence . . . in the case of: n.p. [1856]. O 32 a

BARTLETT (LIEUT. WASHINGTON A.)   208
Reply of: to the testimony taken before the Naval Committee [on charges of misconduct in the conquest of California] . . . *Wash* 1856. O 71 aa

BARTLETT, WILLIAM H.   209
American scenery . . . *L* 1840. Q 2v: [10 incl. eng.t.] 140; [6 incl. eng.t.] 106 map port 117pls aa
—rptd. several times
—Ger tr "America in Bildern" *L* n.d. O 2v in 1, same pls a
Originally issued in 30 parts. A few copies of the plates, without text, were issued in folio.

BARTLETT, WILLIAM P., ed.   210
Livermore valley, California. *Livermore* 1878. O 26 + 12adv-p a

BARTON, BENJAMIN S.   211
New vieuws of the origin of the tribes . . . of America. *Phil* 1797. O [12] 109 83 a
—ed. 2, enl., *Phil* 1798. O [30] 109 133 [32]
+Eng. ed. *L* 1798.
Pioneer investigation into American philology by an American.

BARTON, BENJAMIN S.   212
Observations on some parts of natural history, to which is prefixed, an account of . . . vestiges of an ancient date . . . in different parts of North America. Pt. I[all]. *L* [1787]. O [4] 76 map a

BARTON, BENJAMIN S.   213
Papers relative to certain American antiquities. *Phil* 1796. Q [4] 39 2pls a

BARTON, BENJAMIN S.   214
Remarks on the speech attributed, by Mr. Jefferson, to Logan. [*Phil* 1806]. O [8] 24 a
Separate printing from *Phil. Med. Trans.*

BARTON, CHARLES C.   215
Manifest of the charge . . . against Jesse Duncan Elliott . . . for unlawful conduct . . . n.p. 1839. O 2pts in 1: 46; 24 a

BARTON, JAMES L.   216
Address on the early reminiscences of western New York and the lake region . . . *Buf* 1848. O 69 errata slip a
—ed. 2, same impr. & date.

BARTON, JAMES L.   217
Commerce of the lakes . . . *Buf* 1847. O 80 fold.tab a
—ed. 2, same impr. & date.
—rptd., t. shortened, *Buf* 1851. O 51

BARTON, JAMES L.   218
Lake commerce . . . *Buf* 1846. O 34 tab a
—ed. 2, with adds., same impr. & date. O 32 fold.tab
—eds. 3 & 4, same impr. & date.

[BARTON, THOMAS]   219
The conduct of the Paxton-Men . . . with some remarks upon the narrative . . . lately published . . . *Phil* 1764. D [2] 34 b NYH NYP PhilL

Attempt to exculpate the back-country Pennsylvanians from accusations in Franklin's *Narrative of the late massacres.*

BARTON, WILLIAM   220
Observations on the progress of population . . . in the United States. *Phil* 1791. Q [2] 38 a

BARTON, WILLIAM   221
The true interest of the United States . . . considered. *Phil* Carey 1786. O 43 aa
—anr. issue, ptd. by Cist, same date. O [4] 31 aa

BARTRAM, JOHN   222
Observations on the inhabitants, [etc.] in . . . travels from Pensilvania to Onondaga, Oswego . . . *L* 1751. O [2] 94 map b AA N NYP Y
—rptd. *Roch* 1895. O 94 map 2pls a 300 copies ptd.

Bartram, an eminent botanist, accompanied Conrad Weiser on this friendly mission to the Iroquois. Included is a latter from Peter Kalm giving the first scientific description of Niagara Falls. For his Florida journal see Stork, William.

BARTRAM, WILLIAM   223
Travels through . . . Carolina, Georgia . . . Florida . . . *Phil* 1791. O [36] 522 map 8pls b
—Eng. ed. *L* 1792. O [24] 520 [12] map 8pls b
—rptd. 1794. same collat., except 8 instead of 12 final p. aa
—anr. ed. *Dub* 1793. O [24] 520 [12] map 8pls aa
—Dutch tr. *Haarlem* 1794–7. O [30] 695 map 3pls a
—rptd. *Amst* 1797. map pl
—Fr. tr. *P* [1799–1801]. O 2v: [6] 457 [1]; [4] 436 [1]. map 4pls tab
—Ger. tr. *Berlin* 1793. O [28] 501 map 8pls

Extensive travels, in the early years of the Republic, through the southern frontiers and among the Creeks and Cherokees. A work of high character well meriting its wide esteem.

BASCOM, MAJ. DICK   224
The carpet-bagger in Tennessee. [*Clarksville Tenn* 1869]. O [2] 208[incl. advs] aa

BASCOM, FLAVEL   225
A historical discourse . . . settlement of Galesburg, Illinois. *Galesbg* 1866. 0 39 aa

BASKIN, R. N.   226
Reminiscences of early Utah. [*S L C*] 1914. O 252 6ports a

Written to correct false statements in Whitney's history of this state.

BASS (SAM) the . . . train robber . . .   227
Life and adventures of: *Dallas* 1878. O 110 [2] b

—rptd. *Dallas* 1878. [actually ptd at Austin much later than 1878] O 89 blue wraps a
—anr ed [*Austin*] Gammel n.d. tan wraps
—rptd. *Bandera* 1926.
—anr. ed. *Houst* 1952. D 89 4pls

Attributed to a Dallas journalist named Morrison.

BASS (SAM) the bandit.   228
A sketch of: *Dallas* 1880. *See* Martin. Chas. L.

BASS, WILLIAM W., ed.   229
Adventures in the canyons of the Colorado by . . . James White and W. W. Hawkins. *Grand Canyon* 1920. D 38[incl.front.] a

BASTEROT, FLORIMOND JACQUES,   230
vicomte de
De Québec à Lima . . . en 1858–9. *P* 1860. D [8] 338 a

Travelled West to Minnesota, attended a Lincoln-Douglas debate in Illinois and visited Missouri and Kansas.

BATCHELDER, GEORGE A.   231
A sketch of the history and resources of Dakota Territory. *Yankton* 1870. O 56 map b H N Y
—rptd. *Pierre* 1928. O 71 a

One of the earliest works on the Dakota-Wyoming frontier.

BATCHELDER (JAMES).   232
Notes from the life and travels of: [including a trip across the continent]. *S F* 1892. D 335 port a

BATCHELOR, CHARLES W.   233
Incidents in my life . . . *Pitt* 1887. Q 262 12 pls aa
—rptd. same impr. 1895. a

Activities of an old-time steamboat man on the Ohio, Mississippi and Missouri rivers, from the '40's to the '70's.

BATES, ED[MOND] F.   234
History . . . of Denton county [Texas]. *Denton* [1918]. O [4, 9–16] 412 5pls aa

BATES, W. R.   235
The history . . . of the Saginaws. *E Saginaw* 1874. O 133 + 26 adv p [8 at front, 18 at end] panorama a

BATTEN, JOHN M.   236
Reminiscences of two years in the United States navy [1864–6]. *Lancaster Pa* 1881. D 125 a
—enl. ed. "Random thoughts . . .," *Pitt* 1896. D 320 port.

BATTLE, KEMP P.   237
Sketches of the early history of . . . Raleigh . . . *Raleigh* 1877. O [2] 71 a
—enl. ed., same impr., 1893. O 144

BATTLEFIELDS 238
Battlefields of the south . . . By an English combattant . . . *L* 1863. D 2v: [44] 340; 400 2maps aa
—Am. ed. *N Y* 1864. O [28] 517 2maps a

BATTLES AND LEADERS OF THE CIVIL WAR
See Johnson, Rob't U. and Buel, Clarence C.

BATTY, JOSEPH 240
Over the wilds to California; or, eight years from home. *Leeds Eng* 1867. 16° [4] 64 aa

BAUDISSIN, ADELBERT 241
Der Ansiedler im Missouri-Staate. Den deutschen Auswanderer gewidmet. *Iserlohn* 1854. O [4] 181 map aa

BAUDRY DES LOZIERES, LOUIS N. 242
Second voyage à la Louisiane . . . *P* [1803]. O 2v: [18] 415; [4] 411 aa
Sequel to next entry.

B[AUDRY DES] L[OZIERES], 243
[LOUIS N.]
Voyage à la Louisiane . . . 1794–1798 . . . *P* [1802]. O [8] 382 map aa

BAUGHMAN, THEODORE 244
Baughman, the Oklahoma scout. Personal reminiscences . . . *Chi* 1886. D 215[incl. front.] 11pls aa
—rptd. *Chi* n.d. same collat. a

BAUGY, LOUIS HENRY DE 245
Journal d'une expédition contre les Iroquois en 1687. *P* 1883. O 211 a
Describes Denonville's campaign against the Iroquois and expeditions to Michilmackinac and the Illinois country.

BAUMBACH, LUDWIG C. W. VON 246
Briefe aus den Vereinigten Staaten . . . mit besonderer Rücksicht aus deutsche Auswanderer. *Cassel* 1851. D [4] 192 pl a
—enl ed "Neue Briefe aus den Vereinigten Staaten" . . . *Cassell* 1856. O [14] 336 a

[BAUSMAN, WILLIAM] 247
The idle and industrious miner. *Sacr* 1854. O 24 b
Ascribed also to Alonzo Delano.

BAXTER, JAMES P. ed. 248
The British invasion from the north . . . 1776–7, with the journal of Lieut. William Digby . . . *Alb* 1887. Q [6, 5–8] 412 5pls a

BAXTER, JAMES P. 249
The pioneers of New France in New England. *Alb* 1894. sm Q [2] 450 a

BAXTER, JAMES P. 250
Sir Ferdinando Gorges and his province of Maine. *B* Prince Soc 1890. Q 3v: [10] 353; [8] 271; [10] 353. 2maps 6pls aa 250 cops ptd.

BAXTER, WILLIAM 251
Pea Ridge and Prairie Grove . . . incidents of the war in Arkansas. *Cin* 1864. 16° 262 a
—rptd same impr 1867.

BAXTER, WILLIAM E. 252
America and the Americans. *L* 1855. 16° [4] 244 a

BAXTER, WILLIAM E. 253
The social condition of the southern states . . . *L* 1862. D 28 a

BAY CITY, MICHIGAN. 254
History . . . of: *Bay City* H. S. Dow 1875. O 96 [24] a

BAYARD, FERDINAND M. 255
Voyage dans l'intérieur des Etats-Unis . . . *P* Cocheris 1797. O [18] blank l. 336 a
—ed. 2, enl., *P* Batilliot [1798]. O [26] 349[error for 347, p345–346 being omitted]

BAYARD (COLL. NICHOLAS). 256
An account of the . . . tryal of: *N Y* 1702. F [4] 44 c Hn NYP
—ed. 2, with adds., *L* 1703. F 32 b JCB NYP
Bayard, New York mayor in 1685, was accused of treason by political enemies, sentenced to death and saved only by the Crown's decree that the proceedings were illegal.

BAYARD, NICHOLAS, and 257
LODOWICK, CHARLES
A narrative of an attempt made by the French . . upon the Mohaques country . . . *N Y*, Bradford, 1693. smF 14 dd Lond. Pub. Record O [only cop known]
—rptd. *N Y* 1903. smF [8] 14 500 cops ptd a
—Eng. ed. "A journal of the late actions of the French at Canada . . ." *L* 1693. O [4] 22 dd Hn JCB
—rptd. *N Y* 1868. O [10] 7–56 175 cops ptd [25 on L.P.] a
This was Frontenac's expedition against the Iroquois, during which Schenectady was threatened. The first book printed in New York.

BAYARD, SAMUEL J. 258
Life of George Dashiell Bayard . . . *N Y* 1874. D 337[incl.front.] map pl a
Includes army services in Kansas, Utah and Wyoming, 1857–60.

[BAYARD, SAMUEL J.] 259
A sketch of the life of Com. Robert F. Stockton . . . *N Y* 1856. O 210 [131] port a

BAYLEY, JAMES R.   **260**
Memoirs of the Right Reverend Simon Wm. Gabriel Bruté, first bishop of Vincennes . . . *N Y* 1860. O [12] 9–223 [2] 9pls aa 50 copies ptd.
—rptd. *N Y* 1861. D a

BAYLIES, FRANCIS   **261**
An historical memoir of the colony of New Plymouth. *B* 1830. O 4pts in 2v: [12] 322; [10] 286 [2]; [4] 193; [4] 170 a
—rptd., with adds., ed. S. G. Drake, *B* 1866. O 5pts in 2v: [12] 322; [3–10] 286; [8] 193; [4] 170; 145. 2maps 2 ports fold. lf.

BAYLIES, FRANCIS   **262**
A narrative of Major General Wool's campaign in Mexico . . . *Alb* 1851. O 78 port a

BAYLIES (FRANCIS)   **263**
Report on the north west coast . . . *Wash* 1826. O 26 aa

BAYLIES (FRANCIS)   **264**
Second report on the north west coast . . . *Wash* 1826. O 22 aa

[BAYLY, WILLIAM]   **265**
The original astronomical observations . . . in the course of a voyage [by Capt. James Cook] . . . wherein the north west coast of America and the north east coast of Asia . . . were explored. *L* 1782. Q [12] 352 b
Attributed also to John Rickman.

[BAYNTON OR BAYNTUN,   **266**
MAJ. BENJAMIN]
Authentic memoirs of William Augustus Bowles, ambassador from . . . Creeks and Cherokees to the court of London. *L* 1791. 16° [10] 79 b H N NYP Y
Restless and enterprising Maryland-born adventurer who abandoned civilization, became chief of the Lower Creeks and almost succeeded in establishing an independent empire.

[BAYSWATER, J. W.]   **267**
Perils, pastimes, and pleasures of an emigrant in New Zealand, Vancouver's island and California. *L* 1849. O [2] 404 a

[BEADLE, CHARLES]   **268**
A trip to the United States in 1887. [*Oxf*] 1887. O [6] 210 map a
Visited Oregon, California, etc.

BEADLE, J[OHN] H.   **269**
The undeveloped west; or, five years in the territories. *Phil* National Pub. Co. [1873]. O [2] 15–824 + 8 adv p 7 pls a

BEADLE (WILLIAM [A.])   **270**
A narrative of the life of: . . . the "horrid massacre" of himself and family . . . *Hart* 1783. O 24 [incl. eng.t.] aa
—rptd. *Windsor Vt* 1795. D 24 a

[BEALE, EDWARD F.]   **271**
Wagon road from Fort Defiance to the Colorado river [1857–8] . . . [*Wash* 1858]. O 87 map a

BEALE, EDWARD F.   **272**
Wagon road—Fort Smith to Colorado river, 1858–9 . . . [*Wash* 1860]. O 91 map a

BEALE, G[EORGE] W.   **273**
A lieutenant of cavalry in Lee's army. *B* 1918. D 231 a
Served with Stuart, Hampton and Fitz Hugh Lee.

BEALE, R[ICHARD] L. T.   **274**
History of the Ninth Virginia cavalry . . . *Rich* 1899. O 192 port aa

BEALE and PHELAN, comps.   **275**
City directory and history of Montgomery, Ala. *Montg* 1878. O 207 aa
First directory of this city. The history, by M. P. Blue, is important.

BEALL (JOHN YATES).
Memoir of: *See* Lucas, Daniel B.

BEALL (JOHN Y[ATES]).   **276**
Trial of: as a spy . . . *N Y* 1865. O 94 a

BEAMISH, NORTH L.   **277**
The discovery of America by the Northmen . . . *L* 1841. O [16] 239 [11] fold. 1. 2maps pl a
Chiefly translated from Rafn's *Antiquitates Americanae.*

BEAN, EDWIN F.   **278**
History and directory of Nevada county, California. *Nevada Calif* 1867. O [12] 424 b

BEARDSLEY, LEVI   **279**
Reminiscences . . . early settlement of Otsego County [N. Y.] . . . *N Y* 1852. O [10] 575 port a

BEATSON, R. S.   **280**
The plains of Abraham . . . *Gibralter* 1859. O 48 map 2ports aa

BEATTY, CHARLES   **281**
The journal of a two-month's tour . . . among the frontier inhabitants of Pennsylvania and . . . among the Indians to the westward . . . *L* 1768. O 110 b AA H N NYP Y
—rptd. as app. to Brainerd's *Journal, Edin* 1798, some copies separately ptd [with either *Edin* or *L* impr] 1798. O 56 aa

—Ger. tr. "Tagebuch einer zween Reise . . .," *Leip* 1771. O 157 aa
—Swed tr Stockh. 1772. O a
First account of Indian towns in southeast Ohio.

BEATTY, JOHN   282
The citizen-soldier; or, memoirs of a volunteer. *Cinci* 1879. D 401 a
—rptd, "Memoirs of a volunteer". *N Y* 1948 D

BEAUBIEN'S CLAIM   283
Beaubien's claim in the case of Jackson. Opinions of the Supreme Court of . . . Illinois in: *Chi* 1837. O 26 b ChiH
First Chicago literary production.

BEAUCHAMP (JEREBOAM O.)   284
The confession of: . . . *Bloomfield Ky* 1826. D 108 113–134 b KyH LC N Y
—rptd., with title variants, various times.

BEAUCHAMP (JEREBOAM O.)   285
The life of: . . . hung at Frankfort, Kentucky, for the murder of Col. Solomon P. Sharp . . . *Frankf* 1850. O [4] 24 aa
—rptd. *Louisv* 1851. a

BEAUCHAMP (JEREBOAM O.)   286
The trial of: for the murder of Colonel Solomon P. Sharp . . . *N Y* 1826. O 38 b
For another account, *see* Dana, J. G., and Thomas, R. S.

[BEAUFOY, MARK]   287
Tour through parts of the United States and Canada. *L* 1828. O [8] 141 aa

BEAUJOUR, [LOUIS A.] FÉLIX DE   288
Aperçu des États-Unis . . . 1800–1810. *P* 1814. O 274 map 17tabs a
—Eng. tr. *L* 1814. O [20] 363 map 17tabs

BEAUMARCHAIS, PIERRE A. C. DE   289
Observations sur Le mémoire justificatif de la cour de Londres. *L & Phil* 1779. O 56 aa
—rptd., same impr., 1780. a
For title to which this is a reply *see* Gibbon, Edward.

[BEAUMARCHAIS, PIERRE A. C. DE]   290
La voeu de toutes les nations . . . dans l'abaissement et l'humiliation de la Grand-Bretagne. [*P*?] 1778. O [4] 3–74 a
—ed. 2, cor. [*P*? 1778]. O [2] 74

BEAUMONT, WILLIAM   291
Experiments . . . on the gastric juice . . . *Plattsburgh* 1833. O 280 b LC N NYP
—rptd. *B* 1834. same collat. b
—ed. 2, cor. *Burlington Vt* 1847. D 304 aa
—anr. ed., ed. by Osler, *C* 1929. O [40] 280 port facs a

—Eng. ed. *Edin* 1838. D [20] 319 aa
Most important American contribution to medical science.

BEAUREGARD, GEN. G[EORGE] T.   292
Official report of the "Battle of Manassas." *Rich* 1861. D 29 aa

BEAUREGARD, GEN. G[EORGE] T.   293
Report of the defence of Charleston. *Rich* 1864. O 93 aa

[BECHERVAISE, JOHN?]   294
Thirty-six years of a seafaring life. *Portsea* 1839. O 336 aa
Visited California in 1826 and 1827, with Captain Beechey.

BECK, MRS. HENRY H.   295
On the Texas frontier. *St L* [1937]. D 295 a

BECK, JOHN B.   296
An historical sketch of the state of medicine in the American colonies . . . *Alb* 1842. O 35 a
—ed. 2, same impr. 1850. O 63

BECK, LEWIS C.   297
A gazetteer of . . . Illinois and Missouri . . . *Alb* 1823. O 352 map 5pls b LC N NYP Y
One the earliest American books describing in detail the Illinois settlement and the adjacent country west of the Mississippi.

[BECKLEY, JOHN J.]   298
Address to the people of the United States: with an epitome of the public life . . . of Thomas Jefferson. *Phil* 1800. O 32 a
—other eds.: *Newport* 1800 [2 eds.] O 32; *Rich* 1800. O 38; *Wilm Del* 1800. "Epitome of the life. . . of Thomas Jefferson,"; *Worc* 1802. O 32

BECKWITH, E[DWARD] G.   299
Report of exploration of a route for the Pacific railroad, near the 38th and 39th parallels, from the mouth of the Kansas to . . . the great basin. [*Wash* 1855]. O [4] 149 a
For series [House Executive Document 129] of which this formed a part, and which contained a map and a profile relating to this report, *see Pacific railroad explorations.*

BECKWITH, E[DWARD] G.   300
Report of explorations for the Pacific railroad, on the line of the forty-first parallel . . . [*Wash* 1855]. O 136 a
For series [House Executive Document 129] of which this formed a part, *see Pacific railroad explorations.*

BECKWITH, PAUL   301
Creoles of St. Louis. *St L* 1893. O 169 5fold. charts aa

BECKWOURTH (JAMES P.)
Life and adventures of: See Bonner, T. D.

BEDFORD, HILORY G. 303
Texas Indian troubles. *Dallas* 1905. O 249 aa
The author lived for fifty years on the Texas frontier.

BEDFORD, N. H. 304
History of: ... *B* 1851. O 364 map a

BEEBE, GILBERT J. 305
A review and refutation of Helper's "Impending crisis." *Middletown N Y* 1860. D 64 aa

BEEBE, HENRY S. 306
History of Peru, Illinois. *Peru* 1858. 16° [4] 162 errata 1f aa

BEECHER, EDWARD 307
Narrative of riots at Alton ... *Alton* 1838. D 159 a

BEECHER (LIEUT. FREDERICK H.) 308
Memorial of: *Portl, Me* 1870. Q 47 port b
Beecher was killed by Cheyennes on the Arickaree fork of the Republican in Kansas in 1868 at what is now called the battle of Beecher's Island.

BEECHEY, FREDERICK W. 309
Narrative of a voyage to the Pacific and Beering's strait ... 1825–6–7–8. *L* 1831. Q 2v: [22] 392; [8] 393–742 3maps 23pls b issue on L. P. b N NYP Y
—rptd. *L* 1831. O 2v: [28] 472; [6] 452. 3maps 23pls aa
—new ed. 1831. O 2v: [22] 472; [4] 452. 3maps 23pls a
—Am. ed. *Phil* 1832. O 493
Interesting accounts of Monterey and San Francisco before the American conquest. For the zoölogical data gathered on this voyage *see* Richardson, Sir John. For botanical data *see* Hooker, Sir William J. The California portion was issued by Grabhorn in folio, San Francisco, 1941.

BEER, GEORGE L. 310
British colonial policy, 1754–1765. *N Y* 1907. O [12] 328 [2] a
—rptd. *N Y* 1933. same collat.

BEER, GEORGE L. 311
The old colonial system, 1660–1754. Vols. I & II [all], ending at 1688. *N Y* 1912. O 2v: [18] 381; [8] 382 a
—rptd. *N Y* 1933. O 2v
Sequel to next entry.

BEER, GEORGE L. 312
The origins of the British colonial system, 1578–1660. *N Y* 1908. O [10] 438 a

BEERS, GEORGE A. 313
Vásquez ... with ... account of the capture, trial and execution of the noted bandit. *N Y* De Witt [1875]. O 141 aa
Lurid, but reasonably authentic.

BEESON, JOHN 314
A plea for the Indians; with facts and features of the late [Rogue river] war in Oregon. *N Y* 1857. D 144 aa
—ed. 2, same impr., date & collat. a
—ed. 3, same impr. & collat. 1858.
For similar title, *see* Plea (*A*) *for the Indians.*

BEGINNING 315
Beginning (The). progress and conclusion of the late war ... *L* 1770. Q [2] 32 map aa

BEGLEY, REV. JOHN 316
The western missionary priest. [*Wichita* 1894]. O 205 port a

BEHR, OTTOMAR VON 317
Guter Rath für Auswanderer nach den Vereinigten Staaten ... mit besonderer Berücksichtigung von Texas ... *Leip* 1847. O [4] 107 aa
—Dutch tr. *Arnheim* 1849. O a

BELANI, H. E. R. [pseud.]
Die Auswanderer nach Texas ... *See* Haeberlin, Carl L.

BELCHER, EDWARD 318
Narrative of a voyage round the world ... 1836–1842. *L* 1843. O 2v: [40] 387; [8] 474. 3maps 19pls aa
Visited California, the Columbia river and the northwest coast.

BELCHER (JONATHAN). 319
A conference held at Deerfield ... August 1735, by and between: ... and ... chiefs of the Cagnawaga ... and other Indian tribes. *B* 1735. sm Q [20] c AA

BELCHER (JONATHAN). 320
A conference of: ... with Edewakenk, chief sachem of the Penobscot tribe, [*et al*] at Falmouth in Casco bay, July 1732. [*B* 1732]. Q 23 [no t-p] errata slip c AA H [of 6copies known]
—Eng. ed., t. slightly changed from preceding capt. t., *L* [1732]. O 28 b N

[BELISLE, ORVILLA S.] 321
The prophets; or, Mormonism unveiled ... *Phil* 1855. D [6] 11–412 aa

BELKNAP, JEREMY 322
American biography ... *B* 1794–8. O 2v: 416; [4] 476 aa
—rptd. *N Y* 1843. 18° 3v: 370; 333; 315

BELKNAP, JEREMY   323
The history of New Hampshire. *Phil* 1784, *B*
1791–2. O 3v: [8] 361 [84]; 494; 480 [8]. map aa
—rptd. *B* 1792–3. map aa
—anr. ed. [*Dover*] 1812. O 3v: 351; 377; 354. map a
—ed. 2, enl., *B* 1813. same collat. but different map
—anr. ed. with notes by Farmer, v.I[all]. *Dover*
1831. O [16] 512 port [contains complete text of
the historical portion only – geographical portion
forming v. 3 of oth. eds. omitted]

BELL, A, W.   323a
The state register . . . account of Louisiana, from
its earliest settlement as a territory . . . *Baton Rouge*
1855. O 164 a

[BELL, ANDREW]   324
Men and things in America . . . the experience of
a year's residence . . . *L* 1838. D [8] 296 a

BELL, HORACE   325
Reminiscences of a ranger, or early times in
southern California. *L A* 1881. O [6] 9–457 aa
—rptd. *Santa Barbara* 1927. D pls a
The most readable historical narrative of early
southern California.

BELL, JAMES G.   326
A log of the Texas-California cattle trail . . .
[*Austin*] 1932. O 78 [2] a

BELL, JOHN T.   327
History of Washington county, Neb.; its early
settlement [etc.]. *Omaha* 1876. O 64 + 6adv-p a

BELL, LANDON C.   328
The old free state . . . Lunenburg county and
southside Virginia. *Rich* [1927]. O 2v: 623; 644.
3maps 4pls facs a

BELL, MANUEL A.   329
South side view of Cotton is king; and the philosophy of American slavery. *Atlanta* 1860. O 47 a

BELL, SOLOMON [pseud.]
Tales of travels west of the Mississippi. *See*
Snelling, Wm. J.

BELL, THOMAS W.   329a
A narrative of the capture . . . of the Mier pris-
oners . . . *De Soto County Miss* 1845. 16° 108 d
TxU [only cop kn]
One of the few accounts written by an actual
prisoner at this Mexican fortress.

BELL, WILLIAM A.   330
New tracks in North America. A journal of
travel and adventure . . . in the survey for a
southern railroad to the Pacific . . . *L* 1869. O 2v:
[68] 236; [10] 322. 2maps 24pls aa
—ed. 2, same impr., 1870. O 2v in 1: [70] 564
2maps 24pls a

BELL, WILLIAM S.   331
Old Fort Benton . . . *Helena* 1909. O 31 a

[BELLEGARDE, L'ABBÉ   332
JEAN B. M. DE]
Histoire universelle des voyages . . . Par M. Du
Perier. *P* 1707. D [12] 50 [6] 458 aa
—rptd., au. cor. named, *Amst* 1708. 16° map 6pls a
—anr. ed., au. cor. named, *P* 1711.
—Eng. ed. "A general history of all voyages . . .
By Mons. Du Perier," *L* 1708. O [10] 364 [8]
6pls aa
—anr. Eng. ed., au. cor. named, "A complete col-
lection of voyages . . . into North and South
America . . .," *L* 1711. O [8] 364 [8] 6pls aa
Contradictory to its title, all voyages given were
to America.

BELLEGARRIQUE, A.   333
Les femmes d'Amérique. *P* 1853. 16° 96 a

BELLEGRAVE (HENRIETTA DE).   334
The true and affecting history of: . . . her shipwreck . . . rescue by a party of Indians . . . *N Y*
1821. D 40 aa
—rptd., same impr. & collat.: 1823; 1828. a
Fictitious.

[BELLEMARE, EUGENE L. G. DE]   335
Impressions de voyages et aventures dans le
Mexique, la Haute Californie . . . *Brus* 1851. O
410 aa

BELLEVILLE, ILL.   336
Revised ordinances of: with a brief history . . .
by John Reynolds . . . *Belleville* 1862. O 191 [12]
aa

BELLIN, [JACQUES N.]   337
Remarques sur la Carte de l'Amérique Septentrionale . . . *P* 1755. Q 131 aa
Map referred to was in Bellin's *Hydrographie
française* . . .

BELTRAMI, J. [i.e., Giacomo] C.
Constantino Beltrami da Bergamo, *See* Rosa,
Gabriele.

BELTRAMI, J. [i.e., Giacomo] C.   338
La découverte des sources du Mississippi et de
la rivière Sanglante . . . *N O* 1824. O [8] 328 errata
slip aa
—Eng. ed., enl., "A pilgrimage in Europe and
America, leading to the discovery of the sources of
the Mississippi . . .," *L* 1828. O 2v: [76] 472 [4];
[2] 546 [4]. port map 2plans 3pls errata slip aa

BELUZE, JEAN P.   339
La colonie icarienne à Saint-Louis. *P* 1857.
D 24 b

BELUZE, JEAN P.   340
Départ de Nauvoo du fondateur d'Icarie avec les vrais Icariens. *P* 1856. D 23 b

BELUZE, JEAN P.   341
Lettre sur la colonie icarienne . . . *P* 1856. D 46 b

BELUZE, JEAN P.   342
Notre situation à Saint-Louis. *P* 1857. D 23 b

BENDER, TEX
Ten years a cowboy. *See* Post, Chas. C.

BENDER (THE) HOTEL HORROR . . .   343
The five fiends; or: *Phil* 1874. O 61 aa
Sensational account of a series of sickening murders perpetrated by a cold-blooded Kansas family.

BENEDICT, DAVID   344
History of the Baptist denomination in America. *B* 1813. O 2v: 606; 556 [24] a
—rev. ed., with some omissions, *N Y* 1848. O [8] 970 port
—rptd., same impr. & collat., 1849.

BENEZET, ANTHONY   345
A caution . . . to Great Britain and her colonies in a short representation of the state of the enslaved Negroes . . . *Phil* 1766. O 35 a
—rptd., with adds., *Phil* 1767. O [4] 52 4
—Eng. eds., all *L* O 46: 1767; 1784; 1785.

[BENEZET, ANTHONY?]   346
A mite cast into the treasury: or, observations on slave-keeping . . . *Phil* 1772. D [4] 24 a
—rptd., same impr. [1785]. D

BENEZET, ANTHONY   347
The potent enemies of America laid open: . . . spirituous liquors and the slavery of the negroes. *Phil* [1774]. D [2] 48 83 16 a

[BENEZET, ANTHONY]   348
Serious considerations on several important subjects: viz. on war . . . on slavery . . . *Phil* 1778. D 48 a

[BENEZET, ANTHONY]   349
Some observations on the . . . Indian natives of this continent. *Phil* 1784. D 59 a

BENHAM, GEN. H. W.   350
Recollections of Mexico and the battle of Buena Vista. *B* 1871. O 27 a

[BENJAMIN, J. J. [i.e., Israel J.] 351
Drei Jahre in Amerika . . . *Hannover* 1862. O 3pts in 1[pt. 3 in 2sections]: [16] 384; [8] 168; [8] 69; [2] 132. port aa
—Eng tr *N Y* 1956 O 2v a
Of considerable interest on California, the Mormons and the Northwest.

BENJAMIN, L. N. ed.   352
The St. Albans raid; or, investigations into the charges against Lieut. Bennett H. Young and command . . . *Montr* 1865. O [4] 480 a
—anr. issue, same date & collat., carries *B* impr.

BENJAMIN, MARCUS   353
John Bidwell, pioneer . . . *Wash* 1907. Q [4] 52 5pls a

BENNETT, EMERSON   354
Leni-Leoti; or, adventures in the far west. *Cin* 1849. O [2] 11–118 + 2 adv p aa
—rev. ed. same impr. 1850. O 110 a
Sequel to the author's *The prairie flower*, in which the hero's adventures are continued to 1844. Written by Bennett himself, hence undiluted fiction.

BENNETT, EMERSON   355
The prairie flower; or, adventures in the far west . . . *Cin* 1849. O [4] 9–128 b H N Y
—rev. ed. same impr. 1850; 1851. a
It seems probable that this romance was really written by Sidney W. Moss, who accompanied Hastings to California in 1842, so some of the incidents may be factual.

BENNETT, ESTELLINE   356
Old Deadwood days. *N Y*, Sears [1928]. D [12] 300 pls a
—rptd. same impr & pub. 1929
—anr ed. *N Y*, Scribner, 1935

BENNETT, FREDERICK D.   357
Narrative of a whaling voyage round the globe . . . *L* 1840. O 2v: [16] 402; [8] 395. map 2pls aa
During this three year's voyage (1833–6), California was visited.

BENNETT, JAMES   357a
Overland journey to California . . . in 1850. [*N Y* 1932]. D 45 + cov.t. a 200copies ptd.

BENNETT, JOHN C.   358
The history of the saints; or, an exposé of Joe Smith and Mormonism. *B* 1842. D [2] 344 5pls [3 of which were counted in pagination] aa
—eds. 2 & 3, same impr., date & collat. a

BENNETT, NATHANIEL   358a
Report of cases . . . in the Supreme Court of California. With a history of the alcalde system . . . account of San Francisco and its provisional government. *S F* 1851. O [12] 657 errata 1f a
Later editions omitted the historical portion.

[BENNETT, THOMAS H.]   359
A voyage from the United States to South America . . . Embracing . . . an eighteen months cruise in a Nantucket whaleship . . . *Newburyport* 1823. O 80 500copies ptd. aa
—ed. 2, same impr., date & collat. a

—ed. 5, "Chili and Peru in 1824," *B* 1824. O [2] 5–80

Ascribed also to Washington Chase who took out the copyright.

BENSCHOTER, GEO[RGE] E.   359a
Book of facts concerning the early settlement of Sherman county [Neb.] . . . *Loup City Neb* [ca 1897]. D [4] 76 a

[BENSON, EGBERT]   360
Vindication of the captors of Major André. *N Y* 1817. D 99 a
—rptd. *N Y* 1865. O [10] 134 115cops [35 on L.P.]
—anr. ed. *N Y* [Sabin] 1865. O 84 250cops [50 on L.P.]

BENSON, HENRY C.   360a
Life among the Choctaw and sketches of the southwest. *Cin* 1860. D 314 aa

BENT, JOSEPH A.   361
Hand-book of Kansas . . . *Chi* 1869. D 77 fold. map a

[BENTALOU, PAUL]   362
Pulaski vindicated from an unsupported charge . . . in Judge Johnson's sketches of . . . Maj. Gen. Nathanael Greene. *Balt* 1824. O 34 [3] a
—rptd., au. named, t. altered. *Balt* 1826. O 41

[BENTHAM, EDWARD]   363
De tumultibus Americanis . . . *Oxf* 1776. O [4] 36 a
—Eng. ed. "The honor of the University of Oxford defended, against the . . . aspersions of E[dmun]d B[urk]e; with . . . observations on the present rebellion . . .," *L* [1776?]. O [4] 36

BENTON, JESSE   364
An address to the people of the United States, on the presidential election. *Nashv* 1824. D 34 aa
Venomous attempt to discredit Jackson; by the same hand that twelve years earlier fired the bullet his body still carried.

BENTON, NATHANIEL S.   365
A history of Herkimer county [N. Y.] . . . *Alb* 1856. O [6] 5–497 + 3adv-p 3maps[large one not in all copies] 2pls a

BENTON, MR. [THOMAS H.]   366
Discourse of: . . . on the physical geography of the country between Missouri and California . . . [*Balt* 1854]. O 16 aa
—anr. issue, with slight adds., *Wash* 1854. O 24 aa
—rptd. *Wash* 1855. O 21 a

[BENTON, THOMAS H.]   367
Historical and legal examination of that part of the decision . . . in the Dred Scott case, which declares the unconstitutionality of the Missouri compromise act . . . *N Y* 1857. O [4] 3–193 a
—rptd. 1858; 1860.

BENTON (COL. [THOMAS H.])   368
Letter from: to the people of Missouri. Central . . . highway from the Mississippi river to the Pacific. [*Wash* 1853]. O 24 running t. only a
—anr. ed [St L 1853[O 15
A portion of this speech had been previously printed [Washington, 1849] in an eight-page tract.

BENTON, THOMAS H.   369
Selections of editorial articles . . . on the subject of Oregon and Texas . . . 1818–19. *St L* 1844. O 45 b G LC WisH Y [only cops loc]

BENTON, THOMAS H.   370
The torch light. An examination of the origin . . . of the opposition to the administration, and an exposition of the official conduct of: . . . [*St L*] 1826. O [8] 88 b LC MoH WRH [of 4 cops loc]

BENWELL, J.   371
An Englisman's travels in America . . . *L* [1853?]. D [8] 231 front. a
—rptd. *L* 1857. D
Spent four years in the slave states and loathed their "peculiar institution."

BERGHAUS, HEINRICH K. W.   372
Die Vereinigten Staaten . . . geographisch-statistisch vorzugweise nach Van der Straten-Ponthoz geschildert, mit besonderer Rücksicht aus die deutsche Auswanderung . . . *Gotha* 1848. O [8] 98 2maps aa

BERGHOLD, ALEXANDER   373
Indianer-rache, oder, die schreckenstage von Neu-Ulm, im jahre 1862. *New Ulm Minn* 1876. O 112 a
—ed 2 *Graz* 1892. D 186 map
—Eng. tr "The Indian's revenge [etc.]," *S F* 1891. D 240 7pls

BERKELEY, GRANTLEY F.   374
The English sportsman in the western prairies. *L* 1861. O [14] 431 + 16 adv p 9pls a
Buffalo hunting around Fort Riley and western Kansas.

BERKH, VASILII N.   375
Kronologicheskaia istoriia otkrytiia Aleutskikh ostrovov . . . [Chronological history of the Aleutians and account of the Russian fur trade]. *St Ptbg* 1823. O [4] 169 map aa

BERKH, VASILII N.   376
Kronologicheskaia istoriia vsiekh . . . poliarnyia strany s prisovokupl . . . [Chronological history of voyages to polar lands]. *St Ptbg* 1821–3. O 2v in 1: 356 2maps 10pls aa

[BERKH, VASILII N.] 377

Pervoe morskoe pouteschestvie Rossiian pred-priniatoe dlia reshenia geografisheskoi zadachi: Soediniaetsa li Aziia s Amerikoiu . . . 1727–8–9 . . . *St Ptbg* 1823. O [4] 126 map fold. tab b

Account of the Bering and Chirikov voyage in which Asia and America were proven uncon-nected.

BERKH, VASILII N. 378

Puteshestvie po sievermoi Amerikie . . . *St Ptbg* 1808. sm Q [14] 196 map aa

Translations from both Hearne and Mackenzie.

BERKSHIRE, MASSACHUSETTS.

A history of the county of: By gentlemen in the county . . . *See* Field, David D., and Dewey, Chester.

BERLANDIER, LUIS, and CHOVEL, R. 379

Diario de viage de la comision de limites . . . baja la direccion del . . . D. Manuel de Mier y Teran . . . *Mex* 1850. O 298 [2] port aa

Journal of the Mexican Boundary Commission, 1827–1831.

BERNARD, DAVID 380

Light on Masonry . . . embracing the reports . . . in relation to the abduction of William Morgan. *Utica* 1829. D 552 [36] 2pls a

[BERNARD, GOV. FRANCIS] 381

Copies and extracts of . . . newspapers printed in New England . . . referred to in the Letters transmitted from Francis Bernard . . . n.p. [1765?]. F [6] 108 aa

BERNARD, GOV. [FRANCIS] et al. 382

Letters to . . . the Earl of Hillsborough from: . . . *B* 1769. F 83 aa

—rptd. *Salem* 1769. Q a

—Eng. ed. *L* [1769]. O 165 + 8adv-p

The letters contained in this and the following collection cover one and a half years and repre-sent New England political dissensions for that period.

BERNARD, GOV. [FRANCIS] et al. 383

Letters to the ministry from: . . . *B* 1769. O 108 a

—Eng. ed. *L* [1769]. O 146

On the turbulent state of affairs in Boston result-ing from the Stamp Act.

BERNARD, GOVERNOR [FRANCIS] 384

Select letters on the trade and government of America . . . *L* Payne 1774. O [10] 130 a

—ed. 2, *L* Payne 1774. O [12] 130

—anr. ed. *L* Bowyer &c. 1774. O [10] 85

Discusses the taxation issue, and calumniates the colonists.

[BERNHARD, KARL, Duke of 385
Saxe-Weimar-Eisenach]

Reise . . . durch Nord Amerika. *Weimar* 1828. O 2v[usually bound in 1]: [34] 317; [6] 324 + 4adv p 9maps & plans 4pls aa

—Dutch tr. *Dordrecht* 1829. O 2v: [16] 468; [4] 514 7maps & pls a

—Eng. tr. *Phil* 1828. O 2v in 1: [4] 9–212; 238 + 2 adv p a

BERNHARDI, MME. CHARLOTTE, tr. 386

Memoir of . . . Admiral Adam John de Krusen-stern, the first Russian circumnavigator. Ed. Sir John Ross. *L* 1856. O [8] 75 port a

BERNHEIM, GOTTHARDT D. 387

History of the German settlements . . . in North and South Carolina . . . *Phil* 1872. D [16] 25–557 a

[BERQUIN, H. K.] 388

Considerations relative to a southern confeder-acy . . . *Raleigh* 1860. O 40 a

[BERQUIN-DUVALLON] 389

Vue de la colonie espagnole du Mississippi, ou des provinces de Louisiane et Floride occidentale . . . *P* 1803. O [20] 318 5 [4] 2maps aa

—ed. 2, *P* 1804. Same collat., au. named. a

—anr. ed., au. named, *P* 1805. a

—Eng. ed. "Travels in Louisiana . . .," *N Y* 1806. D [8] 181 aa

—Ger. ed. "Schilderung von Louisiana . . .," *Weimar* 1804. O [28] 344 map a

BERRY, HARRISON 390

Slavery and abolitionism, as viewed by a Georgia slave . . . *Atlanta* Lynch 1861. O [8] 46 port a

—anr. issue, Franklin Ptg. House, same date. O 41 [2] port

BERRY, THOMAS F. 391

Four years with Morgan and Forrest . . . *Okla C* 1914. D [3–15, incl. front.] 476 13pls a

BERTHOUD, EDWARD L. 392

Jefferson county Colo; a statistical review . . . *Golden* 1868. O 8 aa

—enl. ed. "Statistical review of Jefferson county," *Golden City* 1882. O [2] 32 2pls

BERTIN, GEORGES 393

Joseph Bonaparte en Amérique . . . *P* 1893. 16° [16] 423 port a

BERTON, FRANCIS 394

Un voyage sur le Colorado. *S F* 1878. O 64 19maps & pls 50copies ptd. aa

—Eng tr *LA* 1953. 300 cops ptd a

BESANCON, L. A. 395

Annual register of . . . Mississippi, for the year 1838 . . . *Natchez* 1838. D 232 + 11 adv p fold. map a

BESCHKE, WILLIAM   **396**
   The dreadful sufferings . . . of an overland party
of emigrants to California. *St L* 1850. O [2, 6–10]
13–72 4pls[2 on 1 lf.] b
—other issues [no 2 copies agree in collat.] have 60
and 70 p.; no priority established. b
—rptd. [*N O* 1946].
   Romantic improbabilities purporting to be
based on the diary of George Adam, one of the
adventurers. Professor Beschke's inventive genius,
here first demonstrated, later fructified in his 1865
patents for ironclad ships and turrets.

BESCHRYVINGE   **397**
   Beschryvinge van eenige voorname Kusten in
Oost- en West-Indien: als Zueriname, Nieuw-
Nederland, Florida . . . *Leeuwarden* 1716. sm Q [2]
150 eng.t. aa

BESKRIFNING   **398**
   Beskrifning öfver de Engelska colonierne
i Nord-America . . . *Stockh* 1777. O 32 map aa

BESOM, A.   **399**
   Pawnee county, Nebraska . . . *Atchison* 1878.
16° 80 + 3adv-p map a

BESSON, J. A. B.   **400**
   History of Eufaula, Alabama . . . *Atlanta* 1875.
O 32 [5] a

BESTE, J[OHN] RICHARD   **401**
   The Wabash: or, adventures of an English gentleman's family in the interior of Amrica . . . *L*
1855. D 2v: [12] 329; [8] 352. 2pls aa

BETAGH, WILLIAM   **402**
   A voyage round the world . . . chiefly to cruize
on the Spaniards in the great South ocean . . . *L*
1728. O [16] 342 [4] map b
—ed. 2, same collat., 1737.
   Narrative of Shelvocke's buccaneering expedition of 1719 by one of his officers, differing greatly
from Shelvocke's own account, and exhibiting
bitter animosity against that commander. Betagh
himself never got to California.

BETHEL, JOHN D., & CO., comps.   **403**
   A general business and mining directory of
Storey, Lyon, Ormsby and Washoe counties,
Nevada . . . *S F* 1875. O 355 aa

BETHEL.   **404**
   Official reports of the battle of: *Rich* 1862. O 31 a

BETTINGER, J. B., tr.   **405**
   Guide des emigrants aux États-Unis. Traduit de
l'Allemand [of Traugott Bromme's Reisen . . .].
Havre 1834. D [12] 127 a
   For another French edition, *see Guide de
l'emigrant . . .*

BEUKMA (K. JZ.)   **406**
   Brieven van: bevorens landbouwer op de boer-
derij Castor, in het kerspel Zuurdijk, gemeente
Leens, doch verhuisd naar de Vereenigde Staaten
. . . *Groningen* 1835–8. O 3v in 1 : [4] 33; [4] 88; [2]
48. map pl aa
—rptd., same sheets, but cover t. gives *Amst* impr.
& 1849 date a

BEVENS, W. E.   **407**
   Reminiscences of a private . . . n.p. [*ca* 1912]
O 58 front a
   Served with the First Arkansas infantry.

BEVERIDGE, ALBERT J.   **408**
   Abraham Lincoln, 1809–1858. *B* 1928. O 2v:
[28] 607; [7] 741. 62pls ltd.ed.[of 500 sets] on hand
made paper b
—anr. ed. "Manuscript ed." [of 1000sets]. O 4v
62pls & l. of MS aa
—trade ed. O 2v 29pls a
—standard library ed. O 4v 62pls a
   Most thorough investigation for the period
covered.

BEVERIDGE, ALBERT J.   **409**
   The life of John Marshall. *B* 1916–19. O 4v: [28]
506 [2]; [20] 594 [2]; [24] 644 [2]; [20] 608 [2].
38pls a
—anr. issue, "Autographed ed." same impr., date
& paginat., but ptd. on H.M.paper & with 60pls aa
—same, "Standard Library ed." on ordinary
paper, but containing 60pls a

[BEVERLEY, ROBERT]   **410**
   The history and present state of Virginia . . .
By a native [etc.]. *L* 1705. O 4pts in 1 : [32] 104; 40;
64; 84 + 4adv-p. eng.t. 14pls fold. tab b MH N
NYP
—ed. 2, rev., with adds. and omissions, *L* 1722.
O [8] 284 [24] + 4adv-p front. 14pls aa
—Am. eds: *Rich* 1855. O [20] 264 front. 14pls a;
Chapel Hill 1947. O [26] 366 pls
—Fr. tr. *P* [ptd. *Orleans*] 1707. D [10 incl. eng.t.]
416 [18] 14pls fold. tab a
—rptd. *Amst* 1707. D [8 incl. eng.t.] 432 [16] fold.
tab 14pls; *Amst* 1712; *Amst* 1718.
   After John Smith, the first account of this
colony, the first one penned by a native and the
best contemporary record of its aboriginal tribes
and of the life of its early settlers.

[BEVIER, ABRAHAM G.]   **411**
   The Indians. Or narratives of massacres and
depredations . . . during the American revolution.
By a descendant of the Huguenots. *Rondout N Y*
1846. D 79 aa

BEVIER, ROBERT S.   **412**
   History of the First and Second Confederate
brigades . . . *St L* 1879. O 480 [27] port aa

BEY, ALI [pseud.]
Extracts from a journal of travels in North America . . . See Knapp, Saml. L.

BEYER, ED[WARD]   **413**
Album of Virginia. *Rich* 1856. obl F [40pls & decorated t.] + octavo vol. describing pls[issued separately] b
—rptd., same impr. & collat., 1857; 1858 b AA NYP

BEYER, EDWARD   **414**
Cyclorama. Reisebilder . . . durch die Vereinigten Staaten . . . *Meiszen* [ca 1860] D 62 [2] a

BEYER, MORITZ, and KOCH, LOUIS   **415**
Amerikanische Reisen. *Leip* 1839–41. D 4pts 38sheets aa
—enl. ed. "Lebensbilder und Reisen in Amerika . . .," *Leip* 1850. D 2v: [10] 447; [4] 437 a

BEYER, MORITZ   **416**
Das Auswanderungsbuch oder Führer und Rathgeber bei der Auswanderung nach Nordamerika . . . *Leip* 1846. O [12] 236 pl aa
—rptd. 1846. a
—ed. 3, enl. *Leip* 1850. O [12] 297 2maps
—Dutch ed. "Het boek der landverhuizers . . .," *Amst* 1846. O [8] 120

BIARNÈS, ADOLPHE   **417**
Le droit des gens: la France et les Yankees. *Nantes* 1866. O 98 a

BIBAUD, F. M. M.   **418**
Biographie des sagamos illustrés de l'Amérique Septentrionale . . . *Mont* 1848. O 309 aa

BIBLE BOY   **419**
Bible boy (The) taken captive by the Indians . . . *Phil* [1845]. 16° 35 front. a

BIBLIOTHÈQUE AMÉRICAINE . . .   **420**
9nos.[all]. *P* 1807. O nos 1 & 2, 195; no. 3, 123; no. 4, 127; nos 5 & 6, 234; nos. 7, 8 & 9, 384. 6fold.tabs aa
Includes bitterly critical letters, written from 1795 to 1803 by a French resident, predicting early dissolution of the nation. The first four numbers were issued under title *A'amérique du nord*. A table of contents was added in 1808.

BICKHAM, GEORGE   **421**
The British monarchy . . . *L* 1743. sm F [8] 280. [incl. 68 describing American colonies], aa
—rptd: 1747; 1748. aa

[BICKHAM, WILLIAM D.]   **422**
Rosecrans' campaign with the . . . Army of the Cumberland . . . *Cin* 1863. D 476 map a

BICKLEY, GEORGE W. L.   **423**
History of the settlement and Indian wars of Tazewell county, Virginia. *Cin* 1852. O 267 [incl. pls & map] aa

BIDDLE (CHARLES).   **424**
Autobiography of: 1745–1821. *Phil* 1883. O [4 7–14 incl blank lf] 423 a

BIDDLE, CLEMENT   **425**
The Philadelphia directory . . . *Phil* 1791. O [20] 188 aa

BIDDLE, MRS. ELLEN McG.   **426**
Reminiscences of a soldier's wife . . . *Phil* 1907. D 259 14pls a

BIDDLE, HENRY D., ed.   **427**
Extracts from the journal of Elizabeth Drinker, 1759–1807. *Phil* 1889. O 423 a

BIDDLE, JOHN   **428**
A discourse . . . on the anniversary of the Historical Society of Michigan. *Det* 1832. O 31 a

[BIDDLE, RICHARD]   **429**
Captain Hall in America. *Phil* 1830. O 120 a
—Eng. ed. "A review of Capt. Basil Hall's Travels . . .," *L* 1830. O 149
—ed. 2, same impr. & date.

[BIDDLE, RICHARD]   **430**
A memoir of Sebastian Cabot . . . *Phil* 1831. O [8] 327 a
—Eng. ed. *L* 1831. O [8] 5–333 errata slip
—Eng. ed. 2, *L* 1832. same collat., but no errata slip, error being cor. by replacing lf. 77–78 with new lf.
—rptd. *Phil* 1915. O [14] 5–327 2ports
Author is said to have ordered both American and English editions destroyed; the infrequent appearance of the American edition would indicate that its publishers obeyed.

[BIDWELL, BARNABAS]   **431**
The Susquehannah title stated . . . *Catskill* 1796. O 115 aa
Defends Connecticut's claim in her controversy with Pennsylvania over the Wyoming Valley.

BIDWELL, JOHN   **432**
Echoes of the past . . . *Chico Calif* [1914] D [4] 91 pl a
The three articles contained herein were reprintde in his *Addresses, reminiscennes . . .*, see under the editor, Charles C. Royce.

BIDWELL, JOHN   **433**
A journey to California. [*St L?* or *Liberty Mo?* 1843?]. D 36 [?] dd B [only cop kn]
—anr. ed. *S F* 1937. Q [10] 48 a

First published narrative of an overland trip to California made with the purpose of settling. Only known copy of the original edition has no title-page and may have been so issued. Though Bidwell dates his journal 1842, it may not have been printed until 1843 or 1844.

BIERCE, L. V.   **434**
Historical reminiscences of Summit county [O.]. *Akron* 1854. D 158 aa

BIGELOW, FRANCIS H.   **435**
Historic silver of the colonies . . . *N Y* 1917. O [26] 476 front. a

BIGELOW, JOHN   **436**
Retrospections of an active life. *N Y* 1909–13. O 5v a

BIGELOW, TIMOTHY   **437**
Journal of a tour to Niagara falls in . . . 1805. *B* 1876. O [20] 121 a

BIGGAR, HENRY P.   **438**
The early trading companies of New France . . . *Tor* 1901. O [12] 308 map 600copies ptd. aa

[BIGGERS, DON H.]   **439**
From cattle range to cotton patch . . . *Abilene, Tex* [ca 1908] D [4] 156 errata slip at p83 front aa
—rptd. *Bandera* 1944. O 80 a

[BIGGERS, DON H.]   **440**
History that will never be repeated. [*Ennis Tex* 1902]. O 83, pls a
—anr. ed., with adds., "Pictures of the past . . .," *Colorado Tex* [1903]. O 2pts in 1: 75; 83, pls

BIGGERS, DON H.   **441**
Shackleford county [Texas] sketches. *Albany Tex* 1908. Q 37 lvs [incl. front] aa

[BIGGS, JAMES]   **442**
The history of . . . Miranda's attempt to effect a revolution in South America . . . *B* 1808. D [12] 300 a
—rptd. *B* 1809. D
—ed. 2, *B* 1810. D [12] 312
—ed. 3, *B* 1811. same collat.
—Eng. ed., au. named, *L* 1809. O [16] 312

BIGGS (WILLIAM).   **443**
Narrative of: while . . . a prisoner with the Kickapoo Indians, then living . . . on the west bank of the Wabash river . . . n.p. 1825. O 22 d N WisH [only cops kn]   *LL. State His. L.*
—rptd. [*N Y*] 1922. O 36 a 86 copies ptd. [5 on Jap. P.]
A captivity relation of special interest for its account of southern Illinois in the first two years of American occupation.

BIGHAM, R. W.   **444**
California goldfield scenes . . . *Nashv* 1886. D 283 a

BIGLER, GOV. JOHN   **445**
Message to the Legislature of . . . California on the overland route from the Mississippi river to the Pacific . . . *Sacr* 1855. O 40 aa

BILBO, W. N.   **446**
The past, present and future of the Southern Confederacy. *Nashv* 1861. O 47 aa
Utters the prophesy that as absolutism cost Charles the First his head, it may also cost Abe the First his.

BILDER . . . DER NORD-   **447**
AMERIKANER . . .
Bilder aus dem gesellschaftlichen Leben der Nord-Amerikaner. *Reutlingen* 1835. O 254 pl aa
—anr. ed. "Erzählungen aus dem . . . Leben der Nord-Amerikaner". same impr 1842. a
—rptd. "Erzählungen und Bilder aus Amerika". *Erfurt* 1852. O 98 8pls

BILL, EDWARD L.   **448**
The last of the Danvers . . . *N Y* [1894]. D [6] 173 front. a
Contains an overland narrative.

B[ILL], J[OHN]   **449**
The English party's excursion to Paris . . . to which is added, a trip to America . . . *L* 1850. D [6] 557 a
The American trip extended through southern and mid-western states.

BILL OF RIGHTS (THE)
See Acts passed at a Congress of the United States . . . March 4th, 1789.

BILLINGS, JOHN S.   **450**
A report on barracks and hospitals, with descriptions of military posts. [Circ. 4, Surg. Gen. Office]. *Wash* 1870. Q [34] 494 13maps & plans aa
—anr. ed. "Report on the hygiene of the . . . army, with descriptions of military posts," *Wash* 1875. Q [60] 567 map 12plans [To this Circ. 8 were added 95 new posts] aa

BILLON, FREDERIC L.   **451**
Annals of St. Louis . . . *St L* 1886–8. O 2v: [8] 500; [4] 465. 18pls a some copies on L. P. aa
By a settler of 1825; based on personal knowledge, French and Spanish official documents and Chouteau and Gratiot family papers.

[BILSON, B.]   **452**
The hunters of Kentucky; or the trials and toils of traders and trappers during an expedition to the Rocky Mountains, New Mexico and California. *N Y* 1847. O 100 + 4adv-p b G NYP Y

Shameless piracy of James O. Pattie's overland narrative, Bilson's sole contribution being a differently worded title-page, and a changing of the names of Pattie and son to those of Ben Bilson and son.

BILTON, THOMAS   453
Journal of a voyage ... to Virginia ... *L* 1715. O [4] 28 b H
—rptd. 1722. b

BINET, G.   454
Neuf mois aux États-Unis ... *Geneva* 1862. D 184 aa
Scarce-but sketchy.

BINGHAM, HELEN M.   455
History of Green county, Wisconsin. *Milw* 1877. D 310 front. a
In preparing this history of the lead region, over fifty settlers of the 1820's and 1830's were interviewed.

BINGHAM, WILLIAM   456
A letter from an American, now resident in London, to a member of Parliament ... containing strictures on Lord Sheffield's pamphlet on the commerce of the American states ... *Phil* 1784. O 2pts in 1: 48; [2] 29–48 a
—Eng. ed. *L* 1784. O

BINS DE ST. VICTOR, JACQUES M.   457
Lettres sur les États-Unis ... *P* 1835. O 2v: [14] 355; [4] 359 aa
—Ger. tr. *Berl* 1835. O 2v: [16] 293; [24] 272 a
Observations by a French royalist, unsympathetic to American life under Jacksonian democracy.

BIOGRAPHY
Biography of the signers to the declaration of independence. *See* Sanderson, John, *ed.*

BIORCK, TOBIAS E.   458
Dissertatio gradualis, de plantatione ecclesiae Svecanae in America ... *Upsala* [1731]. Q [8] 34 map b Hn NYP
This first book by a native-born American to be published in Sweden gives interesting data on the Swedish settlements on the Delaware.

BIRCH, W[ILLIAM]   459
The city of Philadelphia ... in 1800. *Springland Cot Pa* 1800. obl Q [6] plan eng.t. 27col.pls [some cops have 28 or 29 pls] dd LC NYH NYP
—rptd. same impr. 1802. d
—oth. eds: *Phil* 1841. aa; *Phil* 1908. a
Cf. Childs, C. G., *Views in Philadelphia* ...

BIRCH, W[ILLIAM]   460
The country seats of the United States ... *Springland Pa* 1808. Pt. I[all]. obl Q [8] 20col.pls [incl.eng.t.] c LC Y

[BIRD, H. M.?]   461
A view of the relative situation of Great Britain and the United States ... *L* 1794. O [4] 43 a

[BIRD, ISABELLA]   462
The Englishwoman in America. *L* 1856. D 464 a

BIRGE, JULIUS C.   463
The awakening of the desert ... *B* [1912]. D 492 25pls a
—ed. 2 [4 add. p. inserted before text]

BIRKBECK, MORRIS   464
An address to the farmers of Great Britain, with an essay on the prairies of the western country ... *L* 1822. O 52 aa

BIRKBECK, MORRIS   465
An appeal to the people of Illinois on the question of a convention. *Shawneetown* 1823. O 25 b BA G

BIRKBECK, MORRIS   466
Extracts from a supplementary letter from the Illinois ... [and a] reply to the remarks of William Cobbett. *N Y* 1819. O 29 aa
—Eng. ed. *L* 1819. O [4] 36 aa

BIRKBECK, MORRIS   467
Letters from Illinois. *Phil* 1818. D 154 [incl initial adv p] 2maps aa
—ed. 2, *Phil* 1818. O [18] 126 2maps a
—anr. issue, *B* 1818. same collat.
—Eng. ed. *L* 1818. O [16] 114
—other 1818 Eng. eds.: 2 at *L*; 2 at *Dub* O [16] 112; anr. at *Belf*
—Fr. ed. *P* 1819. O [18] 156 map

BIRKBECK, MORRIS   468
Notes on a journey in America ... to the Territory of Illinois ... *Phil* 1817. D [2] 189 [incl 2 initial blank pp] aa
—rptd. *Phil* 1819. D a
—Eng. ed. 1, *L* 1818. O [4] 144 map[apparently not in all copies]
—other 1818 Eng. eds. O: 3 at *L*; others at *Cork* & [*Belf*]; 4 at *Dub*[by Courtney, by Haydock, 2 by Larkin]
—Ger. tr. *Jena* 1818. D
—Dutch tr. *Amst* [1820].

BIRMINGHAM CITY DIRECTORY ...   469
Atlanta 1883. O 294 a
First directory of this city, with historical sketch.

BISHARD, M. M., comp.   470
Business directory of the towns on the Des Moines Valley railroad ... *Des M* 1869. D 144 a

[BISHOP, ABRAHAM]   471
Georgia speculation unveiled; in two numbers. *Hart* 1797. O 39 a

—complete ed., 4 nos., *Hart* 1797–8. O 2pts; [paged continuously to 144] aa
Cf.. under Georgia, *State of facts* . . .

BISHOP, ABRAHAM 472
Oration, in honor of the election of . . . Jefferson, and the . . . acquisition of Louisiana . . . [*Hart*] 1804. O 24 aa

[BISHOP, ABRAHAM?] 473
Strictures on an pamphlet, entitled, "An examination of the president's reply to the New-Haven remonstrance . . ." *Alb* 1801. O 38 a

BISHOP, A[LBERT] W. 474
Loyalty on the frontier . . . *St L* 1863. D 228 a

[BISHOP, FRANCIS A.] 475
Report of the chief engineer on the survey of the Placerville and Sacramento railroad. *S F* 1863. O 47 aa

BISHOP, J[AMES] LEANDER 476
A history of American manufactures . . . *Phil* 1861, 1864, 1866. O 3v: [4, 7–12] 642 [1]; [2] 11–826; [6] 14–574 ports aa
—ed. 2, *Phil* 1866. O 3v: [2] 7–642; 13–654; [6] 14–574. ports a
—ed. 3, rev., *Phil* 1868. O 3v ports aa

BISHOP, JUDSON W. 477
History of Fillmore county, Minnesota . . . *Chatfield* 1858. D 40 map aa

BISHOP, ROBERT H. 478
An outline of the history of the church in . . . Kentucky . . . [1783–1823]. *Lex* 1824. D 420 aa
Most important ecclesiastical history of the early West.

BISHOP, W. W. 479
A journal of twelve months campaign of Gen. Shields' brigade, in Mexico . . . *St L* 1847. O 48 b G H

BISHOPE, GEORGE 481
New England judged . . . the sufferings of the . . . Quakers, 1650–1660. *L* 1661. smQ 176 + [Appendix]: [2] 177–198. b JCB N Y
—same, the second part [continuing the narrative to March 1661]. *L* 1667. smQ 148 errata slip b JCB Y
—anr. ed. [containing both parts, slightly abbreviated, with a new appendix and Whiting's answer to Cotton Mather's 1702 *Church History of New England*]. *L* 1703–02. O [10] 498, 212 [12] + adv pp. aa
Most exhaustive contemporary indictment of God-fearing Puritans driven by insensate religious fervor to sickening brutalities against other religious fanatics who dared to differ from themselves. Witch-hunting was bad; this was worse.

BISMARCK. 482
Directory of: . . . also history of Burleigh county. *Bismarck* 1879. O 40[incl. preliminary adv-1.] [2] 41–144 aa

BIXBY, L. A. 483
A statistical and chronological view of the United States . . . *Roch* 1843. D 68 [3] a

BLACK, AMOS, and WHITE, V. 484
Directory of Osage City [Kas.] . . . with a historical and business review. *Osage City* 1887. O 96 a

[BLACK, CHAUNCEY F.] ed. 485
Some account of the work of Stephen J. Field. [*N Y*?] 1881[copyright date 1882]. O 63 464 a
—enl. ed. 1895. O 63 522 198 [4]

[BLACK, ROBERT] 486
A memoir of Abraham Lincoln . . . *L* 1861. D 126 port + 18 adv p
First biography of Lincoln published outside of the United States.

BLACK, WILLIAM L. 487
A new industry [*i.e.* Angora goats.] *Ft. Worth* [1900] D 523 front a

BLACK, WILLIAM P., et al 488
War sketches . . . *Muldrow Okla* 1895. 16° 232 [incl.initial blank lf & 3ports] aa

BLACK HAWK. 489
An account of the Indian chief Black Hawk . . . with the . . . narrative of a lady who was taken prisoner . . . *Phil* 1834. O 26[incl.front cov. & pl] a
Copyrighted by Zephaniah Keach.

Life of Black Hawk dictated by himself. *See* Patterson, J. B.

BLACK HILLS (THE).
Gold in the Black Hills see Smith, D.N.

The golden land . . . history . . . of the 490
Black Hills gold region. *Chi* [1875]. O 104 map aa

New map and guide to the Black Hills 491
Chi Rand McN. 1875. 16° 32 fold.map a

BLACKBIRD, ANDREW J. 492
History of the Ottawa and Chippewa Indians of Michigan . . . *Ypsilanti* 1887. 16° 128 a
—rptd. *Harbor Springs* 1897. D 94

BLACKFORD, DOMINIQUE DE 493
Précis de l'état . . . des colonies angloises dans l'Amérique . . . Milan 1771. D 99 a

[BLACKLOCK, THOMAS?] 494
Remarks on the nature and extent of liberty . . . and on the justice and policy of the American war . . . *Edin* 1776. O 70 a
Ascribed also to Dr. Adam Ferguson.

BLACKMAN'S [LOUISA] ESCAPE   495
Blackman's (Louisa) escape from the Mormons. *Indp* 1867. O 23 a

BLACKMAR, FRANK W.   496
Spanish institutions of the southwest. *Balt* 1891. O [26] 353 map 31pls a

BLACKMORE, WILLIAM
Colorado: its resources... *L* 1869. *See* that title.

BLACKWATER CHRONICLE (THE)
See Kennedy, Philip Pendleton.

BLADA, V. [pseud.]
See Volck, Adalbert J.

BLAIR, ED   497
History of Johnson county, Kansas. *Lawrence* 1915. O 489[incl.pls] a

BLAIR, EMMA H., ed.   498
The Indian tribes of the upper Mississippi valley ... *Clev* 1911–12. O 2v: 372; 412. 15pls[incl. in paginat.] aa
Translation of accounts by Nicholas Perrot, Bacqueville de la Potherie, etc.

[BLAIR, JAMES, ed.]   499
Notices of the harbor at the mouth of the Columbia river. n.p. n.d. [*Lancaster Pa*? or *Wash*? 1846]. O 22 map aa
Disputes Captain Wilkes' opinion as to the danger in approaching this harbor.

BLAIR, SAMUEL   500
A short... narrative, of the... revival of religion in... New-Londonderry, and other parts of Pennsylvania. *Phil* [1744]. D 46 aa

BLAKE, WILLIAM J.   501
The history of Putnam County, N. Y.... *N Y* 1849. D [4] 13–368 a

**BLAKE, WILLIAM P., and JACKSON,   502
CHARLES T.**
The gold placers of the vicinity of Dahlonega, Georgia... and an historical notice of gold mining in Georgia. *B* 1859. O 45 aa

BLANCHARD (CLAUDE).   503
The journal of: commissary of the French auxiliary army sent to the United States. Tr. Wm. Duane. *Alb* 1876. O [16] 207 a
—original Fr. ed. "Journal de campagne...," *P* 1869. O 32
—enl. Fr. ed. "Guerre d'Amérique...," *P* 1881. O [12] 217
—anr issue, same impr & date. O 134

BLANCHARD, J.   504
Memoir of Rev. Levi Spencer... pastor... at Canton, Bloomington, and Peoria. *Cin* 1856. 16° 192[incl. port] a

BLANCHARD, JEAN P[IERRE]   505
Journal of my forty-fifth ascension... the first performed in America... *Phil* 1793. O 27 pl b AA NYP
—Fr. tr., same impr., date & collat. aa
First successful aerial flight made in this country.

[BLANCHARD, JEAN P[IERRE]]   506
The principles, history, and use, of air-balloons ... *N Y* 1796. O 46·pl b AA BP NYP

BLANCHARD, P., and DAUZATS, A.   507
San Juan d'Ulua... et d'un apercu général sur l'état actuel du Texas, par M. E. Maissin. *P* 1839. sm Q [12] 591 18pls aa

BLANCHARD, RUFUS   508
The discovery and conquest of the north-west, including the early history of Chicago... *Wheaton Ill* 1879. O 484 [2] 30 [4] 7maps & pls a Also issued in 6 parts aa
—rptd. same impr. & collat. 1880. [some copies bear *Chi* impr.] a
—anr. ed. *Chi* 1881. O 768 11maps & pls [some copies bear *Wheaton* impr.]
—enl. ed. *Chi* 1898–1900. O 2v: 685[incl. front., 2 pls & fold. map]; 689. The 2 vols. contain 2 maps & 41 pls. not incl. in paginat. [vol.2, though dated 1900, did not appear until 1903].

BLANCHARD, RUFUS   509
Handbook of Iowa. *Chi* 1867. 16° 92 map a
—ed. 2, same impr., 1869.

BLANCHARD, RUFUS   510
History of Illinois, to accompany an historical map... *Chi* 1883. O 128 huge fold.map a

[BLANCHET, FRANCIS N.]   511
Historical sketches of the Catholic church in Oregon... 1838–1878. *Port Ore* 1878. D [5]–186 cover t. b OreH WashU
—anr. ed. [*Port Ore* 1884?]. O 72 aa
—ed. 2, *Ferndale Wash* 1910. O 72 cap.t. only a
Blanchet went to Oregon in 1838 and became the first Bishop of that diocese.

[BLANCHET, FRANCOIS X.]   512
Dix ans sur la côte du Pacifique... *Quebec* 1873. D 100 aa
Ascribed also to Jean B. A. Brouillet. Blanchet, nephew of Bishop Blanchet, went to Oregon in 1863.

BLAND, [*pseud*]   513
A southern document. To the people of Virginia ... *Wytheville* 1861. O 32 [cov-t only] aa

[BLAND, EDWARD]   514
The discovery of New Brittaine . . . from Fort
Henry, at the head of Appamattuck river in Vir-
ginia . . . *L* 1651. smQ [8] 16 map front d LC Hn
JCB
—rptd. *N Y* 1873. O [8] 16 a
Early promotional tract.

BLAND, COL. [HUMPHREY]   515
An abstract of military discipline . . . *B* 1755.
16° [4] 67 aa
Condensed from the larger *Treatise* by this
author, published earlier in England.

BLAND, RICHARD   516
The colonel dismounted; or, the rector vindicated. [*Wmsbg* 1764] [2] 30 [17] b AA LC [only
cops kn–both imperfect]

BLAND, RICHARD   517
An inquiry into the rights of the British colonies
. . . *Wmsbg* [1766]. O [31] aa
—rptd. *L* 1769. O 19[error for 23] aa
—rptd. *Rich* 1922. O [10] 37 100copies ptd. a

BLAND, RICHARD   518
A letter to the clergy of Virginia . . . *Wmsbg*
1760. O [6] 20 aa
Upholds the Assembly's attack on church
property.

BLAND (COLONEL THEODORICK, JR)   519
The Bland papers . . . a selection from the
manuscripts of: *Petersburg* 1840–3. O 2v: [40]
160; [4] 9–130 aa
Important collection of material on the Revolution.

BLAND, WILLIAM   520
The awful doom of the traitor . . . full disclosure
of the character . . . of General Lopez, who decoyed . . . our best and bravest citizens to an . . .
untimely grave in Cuba. *Cin* 1852. O 32 b N

[BLANE, WILLIAM N.]   521
An excursion through the United States and
Canada . . . By an English gentleman. *L* 1824. O
[4] 511 2maps tab errata lf aa
—rptd. "Travels through the United States . . .,"
L 1828. O [4] 511 2maps tab a
Visited Ohio, Kentucky, Indiana and Illinois.

BLANKENSHIP, GEORGIANA M., comp.   522
Early history of Thurston county, Washington . . . *Olympia* 1914. O 392 24pls a
—rptd. 1916. same impr. & collat.

BLASPHEMY
Blasphemy (The) of abolitionism exposed . . .
By Amor Patriae. *See Comparison of slavery with
abolitionism* . . .

BLASCHKE, EDUARDO   523
Topographia medica portus Novi-Archangel-
scensis, sedis principalis coloniar um Rossicarum
in Septentrionali America. *St Ptsbg* 1842. O [4]
82 [4] pl 6tabs fold-plat fold-map c
Describes what is now the city of Sitka.

BLATCHFORD (JOHN).   524
Narrative of remarkable occurrences in the life
of: . . . as a prisoner in the late war . . . *N Lond*
1788. O 22 b
—ed. 2, same impr. 1794. D 23 aa
—rptd., with adds., *N Y* 1865. O 127 2pls a

BLATCHLY, A.   526
Mining . . . in the Reese river region [of] . . .
Nevada. *N Y* 1867. D 48 aa

BLATCHLY A., et al]   527
The silver districts of Nevada. *N Y* 1865. O 37
map cov.t.only aa

BLEDSOE, A[NTHONY] J.   528
History of Del Norte county, California . . .
Eureka Cal 1881. O 176 [3] + 29adv-p dd
With the possible exception of Cox, *Annals of
Trinity County*, the rarest California local history.

BLEDSOE, A[NTHONY] J.   529
Indian wars of the northwest . . . *S F* 1885. O
5–505 errata slip at p9 aa
—rptd *Oakl* 1956 O 292 map a
Best record of the California Indian troubles to
1865.

BLEECKER, ANN ELIZA   530
The history of Maria Kittle. *Hart* 1797. D 70 b
AA N Y
—rptd. 1802. aa

BLEECKER [ANN ELIZA].   531
The posthumous works of: . . . *N Y* 1793. D
[12] 375 port aa
Includes, in fictionized form, captivity of Maria
Kittlehuyne [Maria Kittle], 1744–8.

BLEEKER (CAPT. LEONARD).   532
The order book of: . . . in the campaign of 1779.
N Y 1865. Q 138 a 250 copies [50 on L. P.]

[BLESSINGTON, JOSEPH P.]   533
The campaigns of Walker's Texas division, by a
private soldier . . . *N Y* 1875. O 314 aa

BLISS, EDWARD   534
A brief history of the new gold regions of Colo-
rado . . . with hints . . . to intending emigrants.
N Y 1864. O 30 map c ColH G NYP Y

BLISS, LEONARD   535
The history of Rehoboth . . . Massachusetts . . .
B 1836. O [6] 294 [1] a

BLOCK, BISKOP   **536**
Rimelig formodning at de oprindelige Amerika-nere nedstamme fra en mongolisk Aet, som i en meget tidlig Verdenalder er kommen over fra det nordösllige Asia til det nordvestlige Amerika. *Copenh* 1804. D 37 aa

[BLODGET, SAMUEL]   **537**
Economica: a statistical manual for the United States . . . *Wash* 1806. O [8] 202 [14] a
—ed. 2, *Wash* 1810. O [8] 202 [14] 8

[BLODGET, SAMUEL]   **538**
Thoughts on the increasing wealth . . . of the United States . . . *Wash* 1801. O 40 fold. tab. a
Predicts that this nation will become the most powerful in the world.

[BLODGET, WILLIAM]   **539**
Facts and arguments respecting the great utility of an extensive plan of inland navigation in Ame-rica . . . *Phil* 1805. O 62 map a
Ascribed also to Turner Camac.

BLODGETT (HENRY W[ILLIAMS]).   **540**
Autobiography of: *Waukegan Ill* 1906. O [2] 102 aa
Came to Chicago in 1830; was an intimate friend of John Kinzie and one of the pioneer settlers of Waukegan.

BLODGETTE, GEORGE B.   **541**
Early settlers of Rowley, Massachusetts . . . *Salem* 1887. O 239 aa
—rev. ed. *Rowley* 1933. O [14] 472 map 30pls 250copies ptd. a

BLOIS, JOHN T.   **542**
Gazetteer of . . . Michigan . . . with a succinct history . . . *Det* 1838. D 418 errata slip aa
—rptd: 1839; [1840] a

BLOKOM [or BLOK], G. K.   **543**
[In Russian] A short geographical . . . descrip-tion of California . . . its inhabitants . . . with the geological survey of the . . . gold region. *St Ptbg* 1850. O [4] 132 map b Y

BLOOD, KATIE E.   **544**
Memoirs of a forty-niner. *N Hav* 1907. O 27 a
Narrative of an 1849 trip to California by the author's father, John E. Brown.

[BLOODGOOD, SIMEON DE WITT], ed.   **545**
The sexagenary; or, reminiscences of the . . . revolution. *Alb* 1833. D 203 a
—rptd. *Alb* 1866. O 234 3ports Also 50 copies on L.P.

BLOOMINGTON . . . MINNESOTA.
A sketch of the town of: 1857. *See* Brewster, Wm.

[BLOME, RICHARD]   **546**
The present state of his majesties . . . territories in America . . . *L* 1687. O [8] 262 + 18 lvs of astronomical tables port 8maps b H LC N
—Fr. tr., "L'Amérique angloise . . ." *Amst* 1688. D [4] 332 [2] 7maps aa
—anr. Fr. tr., "Description etc." *Amst* 1715. D 68 [2] a
—Ger tr "Englischem America . . ." *Leip* 1697. D
A popular but unreliable guide which did much to attract emigration to these shores.

BLOUDY TENENT [THE] . . .
See Williams, Roger.

[BLOUIN, DANIEL]   **547**
A memorial . . . against Lieutenant Colonel John Wilkins . . . commandant of the English settlements in the Illinois country . . . n.p. [1771?], O 527 b NYH
Blouin's memorial is followed by four other pieces, all concerning events in this region from 1768 to 1771, each with separate titles and text in English and French.

BLOUNT [WILLIAM].   **548**
Proceedings on the impeachment of . . . *Phil* 1799. O 102 aa
Reveals the conspiracy to secure Louisiana and Florida for England.

BLOUNT [WILLIAM].   **549**
Report of the committee . . . appointed to pre-pare . . . articles of impeachment against: . . . [*Phil* 1797]. O [8] 3–16 [160] aa
Some copies contain an additional *Further report*, issued same year. This treasonable United States senator from Tennessee conspired with In-dians and British to seize the Spanish Floridas and erect there a British colony.

[BLOWE, DANIEL]   **550**
A geographical, historical [etc.] view of the United States . . . *L* 1820. O [8] 3–746 [16] 3maps tab port aa
—rptd., au. named, word "historical" dropped from title, *Liv* [1820?]. O 758 [36] port 2maps 4plans tab a

BLOWFIELD, T. M. [comp.]   **551**
Echoes from the Sioux. [*Sioux Falls* 1886]. D [4] 48 cover t.only aa

[BLUE, DANIEL]   **552**
Thrilling narrative of the adventures . . . of Pike's Peak gold seekers. *Chi* 1860. D 23 d LC N Y [only cops kn]
—ed. 2, *Morrison Ill* n.d. [ca 1890]. D 21 + wraps b

BLUETT, THOMAS   **553**
Some memoirs of the life of Job . . . a slave about two years in Maryland . . . *L* 1734. O 63 fold port [not in all cops] aa

BLUMHARDT, CHRISTIAN G.   556
Vie de David Zeisberger ... *Neuchatel* 1844.
D 184 a

BLUNT, EDMUND M.   557
Stranger's guide to the city of New York ...
historical sketch ... *N Y* 1817. D [17] 14–306 plan
3pls a
—rptd., same impr. 1818; 1822.

BLUNT, EDMUND M.   558
Traveller's guide to and through ... Ohio, with
sailing directions for lake Erie. *N Y* 1832. 16°
16 map b
—ed 2 *N Y* 1833. 32° 28 + 4 adv p map aa

BLUNT, EDMUND M.
See under Furlong, Laurence, *The American
coast pilot* ...

BLUNT, JOSEPH   559
A historical sketch of the formation of the confederacy ... provincial limits and the jurisdiction
... over Indian tribes ... *N Y* 1825. O [6] 116 a

[BLYTH, STEPHEN C.]   560
History of the war between the United States
and Tripoli ... *Salem* 1806. D 144 a

[BOARDMAN, JAMES]   561
America and the Americans. *L* 1833. O 430 a

BOARDMAN (TIMOTHY).   562
Log-book of: during a cruise from New London,
Connecticut, to Charleston, South Carolina and
return in 1778. *Alb* 1885. Q 88 a

[BOBO, WILLIAM M.]   563
Glimpses of New York city. *Charleston S C*
1852. D 215 a

BODINE, L. T.   564
Kansas illustrated ... *KC* 1879. O 40 [8] pls aa

[BODMAN, ALBERT H.]   565
The hand-book of Chicago, or stranger's guide
... *Chi* [1859?]. 16° 129 map a

BÖRNSTEIN, HEINRICH   566
Die Geheimnisse von St. Louis. *Cassell* 1851. O
10pts[usually bound in 2vols]. aa
—Eng. tr. "The mysteries of St. Louis ...," *St L*
1852. sq D 4pts in 1[paged consecutively]: [2] 357
[i.e. 359] eng.t. front .aa
—rptd., same impr. & collat., 1853. aa
In fictional form, presenting the startling thesis
of a Jesuit conspiracy, with the aid of Southern
malcontents, to dismember the Union and replace
it with an American Catholic monarchy; also portrays an overland trip to California.

BÖSCHE, EDUARD T.   567
Allgemeine Beschreibung der Erde und ihrer
Bewohner ... *Phil* 1840. O [4] 793 map aa

BOGARDUS, J. P.   568
The Stockton city directory ... with a historical
sketch ... *S F* 1856. O 96 b

BOGGESS, F. C. M.   569
A veteran of four wars ... and ... unwritten
history of the Florida Seminole Indian wars.
Arcadia Fla 1900. D 90 port aa

BOGGS, MAE H., comp.   570
My play house was a Concord coach. *Oakl Cal*
[1942] Q 763 maps pls aa
Contains a mass of historical information on
Northern California, from 1822 to 1888.

BOIES, HENRY L.   571
History of De Kalb county, Illinois. *Chi* 1868.
O [2] 23–530 map 20pls a
First comprehensive Illinois county history.

BOILLOT, LEON   572
Aux mines d'or du Klondike ... *P* 1899. O [2]
256 map front 36pls aa
—rptd. *P* 1909. a

BOLDUC, JEAN-BAPTISTE Z.   573
...Lettre et journal. [Written while on a mission
to the Columbia river in 1842]. *Quebec* [ca 1843].
D 95 b Most of ed. destroyed by fire. N WashU Y
—Deuxième lettre et journal. *Quebec* 1845. D 28 b
MontU Y

BOLIN, JOHANN   574
Beskrifning öfwer Nord-Amerika Förenta Stata
... [Swedish emigrant's guide]. *Wexjo* 1853. D 364 a

[BOLLAN, WILLIAM]   575
Coloniae Anglicanae illustratae; or, the acquest
of dominion, and the plantation of colonies ... in
America, examined ... Pt. I [all]. *L* 1762. Q [10
incl. adv-l.] 142 b AA H N NYP Y

[BOLLAN, WILLIAM]   576
Continued corruption, standing armies, and
popular discontents considered; and the establishment of the colonies in America ... examined ...
L 1768. Q 82 pl aa

[BOLLAN, WILLIAM]   577
The freedom of speech and writing upon public
affairs, considered ... *L* 1766. Q [2] 160 aa
—rptd., in part. as "A succinct view of the origin
of our colonies ... whereby the nature of the
empire established in America ... may be clearly
understood ...," *L* 1766. O [2] 46 a
Bollan was the able English agent of Massachusetts.

[BOLLAN, WILLIAM]? 578
The importance and advantage of Cape Breton truly stated . . . *L* 1746. O [8] 156 2maps b
—Ger. tr. *Leip* 1747. O 174 2 maps aa
—Dutch tr *Delft* 1746. O [16] 192 2maps aa

BOLLER, HENRY A. 579
Among the Indians. Eight years in the far west: 1858–1866. *Phil* 1868. D 428 map [probably not issued in all copies] b MontH N NYP Y
Most authoritative narrative of fur-trading among the plains Indians of the upper Missouri, for the period.

BOLLES, ALBERT S. 580
The financial history of the United States, 1774–1885. *N Y* 1879–83–86. O 3v: [8] 371; [10] 621; [12] 585 a; ed 2 1884–6. 3v
—enl. & revised ed. *N Y* 1891–4. O 3v: [12] 371; [10] 621; [12] 585

BOLLES, ALBERT S. 581
Industrial history of the United States. *Norwich Conn* 1878. O [12] 936 a
—rptd. same impr: 1879; 1881

BOLLES, ALBERT S. 582
Pennsylvania, province and state . . . 1609–1790. *Phil* 1899. O 2v: [10] 582; [6] 532. 2ports a

BOLTON, HERBERT E. [ed.] 583
Anza's California expeditions. *Berkeley* 1930. O 5v: [24] 529; [16] 473; [22] 436; [14] 552; [20]426 14maps 106pls 47facs aa
Monumental work containing translations of the original MS. diaries of Anza, Díaz, Garcés, Font and Palóu relating to the 1773 and 1774 expeditions and the founding of both Monterey and San Francisco.

BOLTON, HERBERT E. 584
Athanase de Mézières amd the Louisiana-Texas frontier, 1768–80. *Clev* 1914. O 2v: 351; 392. map 2facs[one incl. in paginat.] aa
First publication of these manuscripts.

BOLTON, HERBERT E., ed. 585
Font's complete diary: a chronicle of the founding of San Francisco. *Berkeley* 1931. O [20] 552 20maps, pls & facs a
—rptd. same impr. & collat. 1933 .
Font left both a short official account and this elaboration of it. Both were incorporated in Bolton's *Anza's California expeditions*, 1930; the shorter diary was also published, with Spanish and English texts, Berkeley 1913.

BOLTON, HERBERT E. [ed.] 586
Fray Juan Crespi . . . *Berkeley* 1927. O [64] 402 6maps 4pls facs aa

BOLTON, HERBERT E. 587
The rim of Christendom; a biography of Eusebio Francisco Kino . . . *N Y* 1936. O [16] 644 8maps 12pls 3facs aa
—rptd *N Y* 1960 O maps & pls a

BOLTON, HERBERT E., ed. 588
Spanish exploration in the southwest, 1542–1706. *N Y* 1916. O [14] 487 3maps a
Two thirds of these contemporary narratives and reports were either never before printed in any language or are their first appearance in English.

BOLTON, HERBERT E. 589
Texas in the middle eighteenth century . . . *Berkeley* 1915. O [10] 501 12maps & pls a

BOLTON, NATHANIEL 590
A lecture on the early history of Indianapolis and central Indiana . . . *Indpl.* 1853. O 29 a
—rptd same impr 1897

BOLTON, ROBERT 591
A history of the county of Westchester [New York] . . . *N Y* 1848. O 2v: [32] 559; [2] 582. 4maps & pls 21pedigree charts a
—enl. ed., rev. by C. W. Bolton, t. slightly altered, *N Y* 1881. O 2v

BOMAR, TOM 592
Glimpses of Grayson county [Tex.]. *Sherman* 1894. O 28 aa

BONANZA KINGS 593
Bonanza kings (The)! . . . a plain history of swindles. *S F* 1878. O 38 pl a

BONDAGE 594
Bondage a moral institution, sanctioned by the Scriptures . . . By a southern farmer. *Macon Ga* 1837. O 78 front. a

BONDI (AUGUST). 595
Autobiography of: 1833–1907. *Galesburg* 1910. O 178 13pls a
Narrative of an Austrian Jew who operated with John Brown in the Kansas border war from 1856 to 1858.

BONDUEL, FL[ORIMOND] J. 596
Souvenir d'une mission indienne . . . *Tournai* 1855. O 44 map 4pls a

BONDUEL, FL[ORIMOND] J. 597
Tableau comparatif entre la condition morale des tribus indiennes de l'état du Wisconsin: ou mémoire partiel de l'état des missions . . . du diocése de Milwaukie . . . *Tournai* 1855. O 27 2pls aa
Bonduel was missionary among the Menominees, in Wisconsin.

BONE, J. H. A.   598
Petroleum and petroleum wells . . . oil regions of
Pennsylvania, West Virginia, Kentucky and Ohio.
N Y 1865. 16° 95 a
—ed. 2, enl., *Phil* 1865. 16° 153

BONIFACE, JOHN J.   599
The cavalry horse and his pack. *KC* 1903. D [22]
538 front a

BONNELL, GEORGE W.   600
Topographical description of Texas. To which
is added an account of the Indian tribes. *Austin*
1840. 16° [8] 7–150 b BA N Y

BONNER, T. D. [ed.]   601
Life and adventures of James P. Beckwourth.
N Y 1856. D 537 [incl. pls] front. aa
—Eng. ed., Am. sheets with new t-p, *L* 1856. front.
omitted. a
—Fr. tr "Le chasseur." *P* 1860. 18° [10] 504
Highly colored, but basically authentic, narra-
tive of a noted mountain character.

[BONNET, ABBÉ J. E.]   602
Réponse aux . . . questions . . . sur les États-
Unis . . . par un habitant de la Pennsylvanie. *Lau-*
sanne 1788. O 2v: 23 [72] 312; 469 aa
—anr. ed., au. described as "un citoyen des États-
Unis", *Lausanne* 1795. O 2v: 312; [2] 469 aa
—rptd., au. named, "États-Unis . . . à la fin du
18th siècle," *P* Maradan [1802]. O 2v: [12] 7–24
[62] 313; [4] 470 a

BONNET, M.-E.   603
Tableau des États-Unis . . . au commencement
du 19th siècle. *P* 1816. O [8] 175 map a

BONNET, MAJOR STEDE   604
Bonnet, Major Stede, and other pirates . . . The
trials of: . . . at Charles-Town, in . . . South Carolina . . . *L* 1719. F [6] 50 b H NYP

BONNEVILLE, ZACHARIE DE   605
PAZZI DE]?
De l'Amérique et des Américains . . . *Berlin*
1771. D 80 aa
—rptd. same impr. 1772. 16° 116 a
Attributed also to Pierre Poivre and Dom
Pernety.

BONNEY, EDWARD   606
The banditti of the prairies . . . *Chi* 1850. O [4]
9–195[incl. illus.t. & pls] c G MH WisH
—anr. ed. *Chi* 1853. b Y
—rptd., "25th thousand" [probably pub's. hyper-
bole], *Chi* 1856, same collat. b LC Y
—other eds.: 1857; 1858. b
—rptd. *Phil* Peterson n.d. [1855?] O 224; *Chi* 1881;
Chi Homewood Pub. Co. [1890]. D 248; *Rockfd*
[1890] O 89 a

Sensational account of the tracking down of
these confederated criminals—mostly Mormons—
who murdered Colonel Davenport at Rock Island
and terrorized the upper Mississippi valley, from
1843 to 1848.

BONREPOS, [RIQUET] DE   607
Description du Mississippi . . . *Rouen & P*
[1720]. O 46 b LC NYP
—rptd. *Rouen* 1772. aa
Also found included in *Relations de la Louisiane*,
under Tonty, *q.v.*

BONSAL, STEPHEN   608
Edward Fitzgerald Beale . . . *N Y* 1912. O [14]
312 19pls a

[BONY, MONSIEUR]   609
Vie de Mgr. Jean-Marie Odin, archeveque de la
Nouvelle Orleans. *P* 1896. O 227 a
Before his transference to the See of New
Orleans in 1861, Odin had been, since 1847, bishop
of Texas.

BOOCOCK, JOHN   610
The town of Huron . . . Michigan . . . *N Y* 1837.
O 34 map a

BOOGHER, WILLIAM F.   611
Gleanings of Virginia history . . . *Wash* 1903.
O 443 a

BOOK
Book for all Travellers. See Cuming, Samuel.

Book (A) of commandments, for the government
of the Church of Christ. *See* Smith, Jos.

Book (The) of nullification. By a spectator of the
past. *See* Memminger, C. G.

Book of the prophet Stephen. *See* White,
Richard G.

BOON (COLONEL DANIEL).
The adventures of: . . . 1786. *See* Trumbull,
Henry.

BOONE (DANIEL, the Kentucky rifleman).
The adventures of: *See* Hawks, Francis L.

BOOTH, EDWIN G.   612
In war time. Two years in the Confederacy, etc.
Phil 1885. O [6] 3–141; [12] 142–221 pls aa

[BOOTH, GEORGE W.]   613
Personal reminiscences of a Maryland soldier
. . . *Balt* 1898. O 177 a

BOOTH (JOHN WILKES).
The life, crime, and capture of: . . . See Townsend, George A.

BOOTH, JOHN WILKES.   **614**
Private confession of the murder of President Lincoln, and his terrible oath of vengeance; furnished by an escaped confederate. [cover t.] [*L* 1865]. O 16 aa
—Fr. tr., with adds., *P* 1865. D 266 [6] aa

BOOTH, MARY L.   **615**
History of the city of New York. *N Y* 1859. O 846 a
—rptd. *N Y* 1860. O 850; *N Y* 1866.
—anr. ed., with adds., *N Y* 1867. O 2v: 892 front. also 100copies on L.P.

BOOTY, JAMES H.   **616**
Three months in Canada and the United States. *L* 1862. O [4] 94 only a few copies ptd. aa

BORCKE, HEROS VON   **617**
Die grosse Reiterschlacht bei Brandy Station . . . *Berlin* 1893. O 179 [incl 13 pls] 5maps aa

BORCKE, HEROS VON   **618**
Memoirs of the Confederate war . . . *Edin* 1866. O 2v: [10] 323; [8] 318. map aa
—rptd. *Phil* 1867. D [10] 438 map aa
—anr. ed. *N Y* 1938. O 2v map a
—Ger. tr "Zwei Jahr im Sattel . . .," *Berlin* 1886. O map 2ports O 2v in 1: [8] 282; [6] 304 map 2ports aa

BORDEN, W. W.   **619**
The past and present of Leadville . . . *New Alb* [1879]. D 50 aa

BORDER STATES [THE] . . .
See Kennedy, John P.

BORDMAN, PAUL   **620**
Facts for Klondikers . . . *L A* 1897. D 36 a

BORRETT, GEORGE T.   **621**
Letters from Canada and the United States . . . *L* 1865. D [4] 294 a
—rptd. "Out west; . . . letters from Canada and the United States," *L* 1866. same collat.

BORTHWICK, J. D.   **622**
Three years in California. *Edin* 1857. O [8] 384 + 6adv p 8col. pls aa
—rptd. *Oakland* 1948. O 8pls a
Faithful picture of mining experiences made graphic by fine plates.

BOSQUI, EDWARD   **623**
Memoirs. [*S F* 1904]. O 281 c B G 50 cops ptd
—rptd. *Oakland* Grabhorn 1952. O 181 a 350 copies ptd.
Reminiscences of a pioneer printer, who came to California in 1850.

[BOSS, HENRY R.]   **624**
Sketches of the history of Ogle County, Ill., and the early settlements of the north-west. *Polo Ill* 1859. 16° [4] 80 [incl 5adv p] aa

BOSSHARD, HEINRICH   **625**
Auschauungen und Erfahringen in Nord-amerika. *Zurich* 1853–5, D 3v in 1[paged continuously] 1151 2maps pl a
Letters from Fla, Pa and Wis.

BOSSU, M[ONS. JEAN BERNARD]   **626**
Nouveaux voyages aux Indes Occidentales . . . *P* 1768. D 2v: [20] 244; [4] 264 [incl.9adv-p]. 4pls b
—ed. 2, same place, date & collat. aa
—anr. ed. *Amst.* 1769. D 2v: [20] 187; 193 [6]. 4pls aa
—anr. ed. *Amst* [but ptd in *P*] 1777.D 2 pts in 1 [16] 392 4 pls aa
—ed. 3, enl., *P* 1789. D 2v 4pls aa
—Dutch tr. *Amst* 1769. O 2v: 224; 227 4pls a
—Eng. tr "Travels through . . . Louisiana . . .," *L* 1771. O 2v: [8] 407; [4] 432 b
—Am. ed., abr., "The Arkansas," *Ft Smith* 1850. [first printing there] D 18 aa
—Ger. trs.: *Frankf* 1771–4. O 2v; *Helmstadt* 1776. O 2v in 1: [14] 207: 192 a
—Rus. tr. *Moscow* 1783. D 2v a
This officer's first and second tours of service among the Indians from Alabama to Illinois. For comments, too critical of the ministry, Bossu was imprisoned and his book banned for awhile in France; this probably accounts for the scarcity of the first edition, of which Sabin found no record.

BOSSU, M[ONS. JEAN BERNARD]   **627**
Nouveaux voyages dans l'Amérique Septentrionale . . . *Amst* [but ptd in *P*] 1777. O [16] 392 4pls aa
—rptd. 1778, same sheets with new t.
Of this account [of Bossu's third tour through Louisiana] there is no English translation.

BOSTON
An appeal to the world: or, a vindication of the town of Boston. *See* Adams, Sam'l.

A fair account of the late unhappy distrurbance at Boston . . . *See* Maseres, Francis.

A letter to a friend, giving a concise . . . representation of the hardships . . . the town of Boston. is exposed to . . . *See* Chauncy, Charles

Life in town, or: the Boston Spy . . . By an   **628**
Athenian. *B* 1844. O 56 a

Remarks on the practicability . . . of establishing a railroad . . . from Boston to the Connecticut river. *See* Hale, Nathan.

Report of a committee of the inhabitants   629
of Boston on the rights of the colonists . . . *B* 1772.
O 36 a

Report of a French Protestant refugee, in   630
Boston. *Bklyn* 1868. sm Q 42 a

A reprospect of the Boston tea party. *See*
Thatcher, Benj.

Selections from the chronicle of Boston.   631
. . . [*B* 1822]. O 132 a
Written in Biblical style.

A short narrative of the horrid massacre   632
in Boston. . . . the fifth day of March, 1770. *B*
1770. O 38 [80, 79–81] b N
—anr. issue, incl. "Additional observations . . .,"
B 1770. O 48 [83] b AA Y
—anr. issue, with adds. same impr. & date. O 48
[88] b AA
—rptd: *Phil* 1770. O; *N Y* 1849. O 122 pl plan;
Alb 1870. a
—Eng. eds.: *L* Dilly 1770. O 166 pl; *L* Bingley
1770. O 38 [83] pl aa
Probably written by James Bowdoin, chairman
of the committee preparing the account.

Sketches of Boston. *See* Homans, Isaac Smith.

A trip to Boston in a series of letters . . . *See*
Wines, Enoch C.

The votes and proceedings of the . . . inha-   633
bitants of Boston. [Oct. 28, Nov. 2 & 20, 1772]. *B*
[1772]. O [4] 43 aa
—Eng. ed. with pref. by Franklin, *L* 1773. O
[12] 43

BOTH SIDES   634
Both sides of the question: or, a candid and
impartial enquiry into a certain doubtful charac-
ter . . . remarkably acquited [*sic*] by a C . . . t
M . . . l. *L* Mechell [1749]. O 28 aa
—ed. 2, with t-p slightly altered, same collat., *L*
Mumfort [1749]. aa
Severe critique of Oglethorpe's conduct of
Georgia affairs and of his St. Augustine expedition.

BOTSCHAFT   635
Botschaft über den Vertrag zwischen den Vereinigten Staaten. [*Bern*? 1851?]. O 43 a

BOTTA, CARLO   636
Storia della guerra dell' independenza degli
Stati Uniti . . . *Parigi* 1809. O 4v: [22] 363; [4]
543; [4] 553; [4] 477 a
—rptd. 20 times before 1860
—Fr. tr., & best ed., *P* 1812–13. O 4v: [6 96] 409;
[4] 593; [4] 603; [4] 550, port 12maps

—Eng. tr. *Phil* 1820. O 3v: 448; [6] 567; [12] 503
—many reprints
—Eng. ed. *Glas* 1844. O 584
Most valuable history of the Revolution up to
its date.

BOTTEN-HANSEN, PAUL   637
Mormonismens Historie . . . *Christiania* 1853.
O [6] 52 a

BOUCHACOURT, CH[ARLES]   638
Notice industrielle sur la Californie . . . *P* 1849.
O 72 a
Largely translation of official documents on the
gold discovery.

[BOUCHER, JONATHAN]   639
A letter from a Virginian to the members of
Congress to be held at Philadelphia . . . [*N Y?
Phil?*] 1774. D [2] 29 aa
—rptd: *B* 1774. O 24; *B* 1774. O 50; *B* 1774. O 31
—Eng. ed. *L* 1774. O [6] 60
Appeasement plea.

BOUCHER, JONATHAN   640
Reminiscences of an American loyalist, 1738–
1789. *B* 1925. O [12] 201 port a 575 copies ptd.
First publication from the manuscript.

BOUCHER, JONATHAN   641
A view of the causes and consequences of the
American revolution. *L* 1797. O [8] 94 [2] 596 aa

BOUDINOT, ELIAS, 1740-1821   642
Journal; or historical recollections. *Phil* 1894.
Q [8] 97, facs a 350copies ptd. [25 on L.P. with
adds] aa

BOUDINOT, ELIAS, 1740-1821   643
A star in the west . . . attempt to discover the
long lost ten tribes of Israel . . . *Trenton N J* 1816.
O [4] 312 a

BOUDINOT, ELIAS, d. 1839   644
Letters relating to Cherokee affairs. *Athens Ga*
1837. D 66 aa

[BOUDINOT, ELIAS C.]   645
The manners, customs . . . of the civilized Indians of the Indian Territory. n.p. [1872?]. O 431.
capt.t.only aa

BOUDINOT, ELIAS C.   646
Speech in behalf of a territorial government for
the Indian territory [replying to William P. Ross's
speech against such action]. *Wash* 1872. O 30 aa

BOUDINOT, ELIAS C.   647
A territorial government for the civilized Indians
of the Indian territory. n.p. [1873]. O 26 aa
This lecture includes much Cherokee history and
folk-lore.

BOUGHTON, JOSEPH S.   **648**
The Kansas hand-book. *Lawrence* 1878. 16°
112 a

BOUGHTON, JOSEPH S.   **649**
The Quantrell raid . . . *Lawrence* 1884. D 36
[incl cover-t] aa
—anr. iss. "The Lawrence massacre . . ." same
impr & collat n.d. [1884?] aa
—rptd. same impr & collat 1885. aa
First appearance was in *"Lawrence directory
for 1865"*.

BOUIS, AMEDÉE T.   **650**
Le whip-poor-will, ou les pionniers de l'Oregon.
P 1847. D 427 aa
Fiction.

BOURGEOIS, [AUGUSTE A.] tr.
Voyage aux États-Unis . . . *See* Davidson, G.
M., *The fashionable tour*.

[BOURGEOIS, NICOLAS L.]   **651**
Voyages intéressans dans différentes colonies
francaises, espagnoles, anglaises . . . *L* 1788. O [9]
507 aa
—Ger. tr. *Leip* 1789. O a
Contains information on Massachuetts, New
York, Louisiana, New Mexico, Porto Rico, etc.;
the author lived 30 years in America.

BOURKE, JOHN G.   **652**
An Apache campaign in the Sierra Madre . . .
N Y 1886. D [6] 112 + 4adv p 12pls aa
—rptd *N Y* [1958] D 128

BOURKE, JOHN G.   **653**
Mackenzie's last fight with the Cheyennes . . .
Governor's Island N Y 1890. O 44 aa

BOURKE, JOHN G.   **654**
On the border with Crook. *N Y* 1891. O [16]
491 7pls aa
—ed. 2, 1892, same collat; anr ed 2 *N Y* 1902 a
—rptd. *Columbus O* 1951. O

BOURKE, JOHN G.   **655**
The snake-dance of the Moquis . . . a journey
from Santa Fe . . . *L* 1884. O [18 incl. front.] 371
31 pls aa
Printed in Edinburgh; some copies have N.Y.
imprint.

BOURNICHON, JOSEPH   **656**
Sitting-Bull, le héros du désert: scènes de la
guerre indienne . . . *Tours* 1879. O 308 aa
—ed. 2, same impr. 1885. O 324 a
Account not only of the Sioux war, but also of
the Black Hills.

BOUYER, A. C. [pseud.]
Les tribulations d'un chercheur d'or. *See* Cour-
cier, Adrien.

BOWDITCH, NATHANIEL   **657**
The new American practical navigator . . .
Newburyport E. M. Blunt 1802. O 590 [6] [incl.tabs
& diagrams] 7pls map b N
—ed. 2, same impr. 1807. O 312 276 613–679[incl.
tabs & diagrams] 12pls & charts aa
—rptd. ten times by 1838.
First accurate navigator's guide. The publisher,
Blunt, had issued, in 1799, a *New American navigator*, modelled on an English treatise of 1772, J.
H. Moore's *The new practical navigator*. Bowditch
planned revision only, but finding so many errors
was compelled to produce an entirely new work.
Earliest issue of the first edition has page ninety-six
incorrectly numbered ninety-five.

[BOWEN, ABEL]   **658**
The naval monument . . . battles fought between
the navies of the United States and Great Britain
during the late war . . . *B* 1816. O [18] 316 [error
for 320] [2] errata slip 26pls a
—rptd. *B* 1830. O [14] 328 26pls
—rev. ed., with adds., *B* 1836.
—other eds.: *N Y* [1837]; *N Y* 1838; *B* 1838;
B 1840

BOWEN, DANIEL   **659**
A history of Philadelphia . . . *Phil* 1839. O [4]
200 + 15adv-p a

BOWEN, ELE [i.e., Eli] ed.   **660**
The coal regions of Pennsylvania . . . *Pottsville*
1848. O [4] 72 32, maps front. a

BOWEN, ELE [i.e., Eli]   **661**
Rambles in the path of the steam horse . . .
historical and descriptive view . . . of the travelled
route from Baltimore to Harper's Ferry . . . Cincinnati and Louisville, *Phil* 1855. O [8 incl. eng t]
432[incl.pls] a

BOWEN, ELIZA A.   **662**
Story of Wilkes County [Ga.]. [*Washington Ga*
ca 1897]. O 108 108–127 [ending abruptly there,
though some extend through p134, also
ending abruptly] b Emory GaU
—rptd. *Marietta* 1950. O 192 front a
First edition of this unfinished history appeared
originally in a local paper and a few copies only
were issued in separate form, sewed and with no
title-page.

BOWEN, J. B. comp.   **663**
The Wheeling directory . . . *Wheeling* 1839. O
[36] 19–90 [2] aa

BOWIE COUNTY [TEXAS] 664
Bowie county [Texas]: a discriptive [*sic*] . . .
history by an emigrant. n.p. n.d. [*ca* 1850]. O *ca*
64 b no copy known of this first Texas county
history.

BOWLAND, JAMES M. 665
Pioneer recollections . . . in Sandusky county.
Fremont O 1903. D [2] 31 pls a

BOWLBY, RICHARD 666
Kansas, the seat of war in America. *L* 1856.
O 36 aa

BOWLES (WILLIAM AUGUSTUS).
Authentic memoirs of: *L* 1791. *See* Baynton,
Maj.

BOWLES (GEN. W[ILLIAM] 667
A[UGUSTUS]).
The life of: . . . *N Y* 1803. O 31 b AA GaU NYP
Reprinted from the London annual, *Public
characters for 1802*; entirely different biography
from that of Maj. Baynton [*q.v.*].

[BOWNAS, SAMUEL]
An account of the captivity of Elizabeth Hanson. *See* Hanson, Elizabeth.

BOWNAS (SAMUEL). 668
An account of the life, travels . . . of: *L* 1756.
O [8] 3–198 + 2adv-p aa
—ed. 2, *L* 1761. O [8] 198 a
—anr. ed. *L* 1795. O [8] 196
—Am eds: *Phil* 1759. O [10] 242; same [with Jno.
Richardson's travels added] *Phil.* 1759. O [10] 242;
[6] 220; *Stanford, N. Y.* 1805. O 306 [2]
Includes some particulars of the captivity of
Elizabeth Hanson, later elaborated into the narra-
tive listed under her name.

BOWRON, WATSON [comp.] 669
The first annual directory of . . . Burlington
[Ia.], for 1859 . . . also a succinct history of the
city [etc.]. *Burlington* 1859. D 108 b
The first business directory of this city appeared
in 1856; of each only one copy is located.

BOWRON, WATSON, comp. 670
Henry county [Iowa] directory for 1859–60.
Containing a history . . . *Burlington* [1859]. D 132
aa

BOX, CAPT. MICHAEL J. 671
Adventures and explorations in new and old
Mexico . . . *N Y* 1861. D 344 b
—rptd., same sheets with new t-p, same collat &
impr. 1869. a

[BOYCE, JAMES R.] 672
Facts about Montana Territory and the way to
get there. [*Helena* 1872]. O 24 aa

BOYD (BELLE) IN CAMP AND PRISON.
See Hardinge, Belle B.

[BOYD, JOHN P.] 673
Documents and facts relating to military events,
during the late war [of 1812]. n.p. n.d. [1815]. O 24
capt.t.only a
Defence of the author's conduct in commanding
his brigade under Wilkinson at the disastrous
battle of Chrysler's Farm, 1813.

BOYD, MRS. ORSEMUS 674
Cavalry life in tent and field . . . *N Y* 1894. D 376
port a

BOYER, LIEUT. JOHN 675
A journal of Wayne's campaign . . . *Cin* 1866.
Q 23 a
Published as appendix to Jacob's *Life of Cresap*,
but also issued separately.

[BOYKIN, EDWARD M.] 676
The falling flag. Evacuation of Richmond, etc.
By an officer of the rear guard. *N Y* 1874. D 67 aa

BOYLE (CAPTAIN ROBERT).
The voyages and adventures of: . . . *See* Chetwood, Wm. R.

BOYNTON, C[HARLES] B., and 677
MASON, T. B.
A journey through Kansas; with sketches of
Nebraska. *Cin.* 1855. D [10] 216 map aa
—eds. 2 & 3 same impr., date & collat. a

BOYNTON, EDWARD C. 678
History of West Point . . . *N Y* 1863. O [20]
9–408 + 12 adv p 10maps & pls a Also 100copies
on L.P. dated 1864
—ed. 2, *N Y* 1871.
—Eng. ed. *L* 1864; *L* 1866.

BOYNTON, W[ASHINGTON] W. 679
The early history of Lorain county [Ohio].
Elyria 1876. O 35 aa
—rptd. *clev* 1892 a

BOZMAN, JOHN L. 680
A sketch of the history of Maryland, during the
first three years after its settlemant . . . *Balt* 1811.
O 388 port a
—best ed. "The history of Maryland . . . 1633–
1660," *Balt* 1837. O 2v: [12] 9–314; 728 a

BRABANT, A. J. 681
Vancouver island and its missions, 1874–1900.
n.p. [*ca* 1900]. O 89 a 70 cops ptd

BRACHT, VIKTOR 682
Texas im Jahre 1848 . . . *Elberfeld* 1849. O [14]
322 aa
—Eng. tr. *San Antonio* [1931] O [26] 223 2pls a

BRACKENRIDGE, H[ENRY] M.   683
Early discoveries by Spaniards in New Mexico
... *Pitt* 1857. O 48 b N NYP Y

BRACKENRIDGE, H[ENRY] M.   684
History of the late war between the United
States and Great-Britain ... *Balt* 1816. D 359
6pls a
—ed. 2, *Balt* 1817. D 363 6pls
—ed. 3, rev., *Balt* 1817. D 360 6pls
—rptd. many times
—Fr. tr. *P* 1820. O 2v: [4] 310; [4] 317. map
—rptd. *P* 1822.
—Ital. tr. *Milan* 1821. O 448 map

BRACKENRIDGE, HENRY M.   685
History of the western insurrection in western
Pennsylvania ... 1794. *Pitt* 1859. O 336 a
Defends his father for defending the frontier
"Whiskey Rebellion."

BRACKENRIDGE, HENRY M.   686
Mexican letters written during the progress of
the late war ... No. I[all]. *Wash* 1850. O 85 aa

BRACKENRIDGE, HENRY M.   687
Recollections of persons and places in the west.
Phil [1834]. D 244 a
—ed. 2, enl. *Phil* 1868. D 331 + 4adv p

BRACKENRIDGE, H[ENRY] M.   688
Views of Louisiana ... [including journal of his
voyage up the Missouri with Manuel Lisa, 1811].
Pitt 1814. O 304 b
—anr. ed. containing only the Missouri river
journal, *Balt* 1815. D [8] 247 aa
—ed. 2, rev. & enl. 1816. D [8] 247
—anr. ed. containing only "Views of Louisiana,"
Balt 1817. D 323 aa
—Ger. ed. [complete], *Weimar* 1818. O a

BRACKENRIDGE, H[UGH] H.   689
Gazette publications. *Carlisle Pa* 1806. D 348 a

BRACKENBRIDGE, HUGH H.   690
Incidents of the insurrection in the western parts
of Pennsylvania ... 1794. *Phil* 1795. O 3pts in 1:
[2] 5–124; 5–84; 5–154 aa
Erratic pagination resulted from printers having
planned for 3 volumes.

BRACKETT, ALBERT G.   691
General Lane's brigade in central Mexico. *Cin*
1854. D 336 pl port a
Operations of this command—including Hay's
Texas Rangers—in the Puebla region.

BRACKETT, ALBERT G.   692
History of the United States Cavalry ... *N Y*
1865. D 337 [incl. front. & 6maps & pls] + 2adv-p a

[BRACKETT, GEORGE A.]   693
A winter evening's tale. *N Y* 1880. O 31 9pls b N
Experiences in the 1862 Sioux war.

BRADBURY, CHARLES   694
History of Kennebunk Port [Me.] ... *Kennebunk* 1837. D 301 pl a 500copies ptd.

BRADBURY, JOHN   695
Travels in the interior of America ... [including
a trip up the Missouri with Hunt's Astorian party
and return with Brackenridge]. *Liv* 1817. O [12]
9–364 errata slip aa
—ed. 2, *L* 1819. O [14] 17–346 map b
—Am. ed., ed. Thwaites, *Clev* 1904. O 326 map a

BRADDOCK (MAJOR-GENERAL)   696
The expedition of: to Virginia ... *L* 1755. O [2]
29 b Hn JCB
By some Grub Street hack who never saw
America.

BRADFORD, ALDEN   697
History of Massachusetts, for two hundred
years, 1620–1820. *B* 1835. O 480 map a

BRADFORD, ALDEN   698
History of Massachusetts, 1764–1820 ... *B*
1822–5–9. O 3v: 414; 376; 327 a

[BRADFORD, ALDEN]   699
A particular account of the battle of Bunker or
Breed's hill. *B* 1825. O 26 a
—ed. 2, same impr. 1825. O 27

BRADFORD, JOHN
Notes on Kentucky. *See* Stipp, G. W., *The
western miscellany.*

[BRADFORD, SAMUEL F.]   700
The imposter detected, or a review of some of the
writings of Peter Porcupine, by Timothy Tickletoby ... *Phil* 1796. O 2pts in 1: 51; 23 a
—ed 2 same impr. date & collat.

BRADFORD, T[HOMAS] G.   701
An illustrated atlas ... of the United States ...
B [1835]. Q [6] 170 40maps aa
—rptd: same impr. & collat., 1839; 1842.

BRADFORD (MAJOR WARD).   702
Biographical sketches of the life of: ...
[Fresno? 1893]. 16° 95 port a
Life in Nevada gold fields, Indian troubles, etc.

BRADFORD, WILLIAM   703
History of Plymouth Plantation. Ed. Charles
Deane. *B* 1856. O [20] 476 a
—rptd. *B* 1898. Q [78] 555 pls facs; rptd. same
collat. 1899.

—best ed. *B* 1912. O 2v: [16] 452; [14] 462. 62maps & pls[some fold.]
—anr. ed., ed. S. E. Morison, *N Y* 1952. O [44] 448 [16] 4maps
—Eng. ed. in facs. of MS, *L* 1896. F [22] 535 facs aa
One of the best narratives of colonization ever penned.

BRADFORD, WILLIAM J. A.   704
Notes on the northwest, of valley of the upper Mississippi ... *N Y* 1846. D [8] 302 a

BRADLEY, GLENN D.   705
The story of the Santa Fe. *B* [1920]. O 288 [16] pls a
A sixteen-page supplement of notes, issued separately by the author, is inserted in some copies.

BRADLEY, JAMES   706
The Confederate mail carrier ... *Mexico Mo* 1894. D 275 15pls a

BRADLEY, JOSHUA   707
Accounts of religious revivals in many parts of the United States, 1815–1818. *Alb* 1819. 24° 300 a

BRADLEY, R. T.   708
The outlaws of the border ... [including reprint of Edwards, *Noted guerillas*]. *St L* 1880. D 302 aa

BRADLEY, STEPHEN R.   709
Vermont's appeal to the candid and impartial world ... *Hart* [1780]. O 51 b AA Hn Y

BRADLEY, THOMAS H.   710
O'Toole's mallet; or, the resurrection of the second national city of the United States ... n.p. n.d. O 65 aa
—ed. 2, same collat., *Seattle* 1894. a
Account of the founding of Port Angeles on Puget Sound, called by residents "the second national city," being located on a federal reserve; lots were sold in 1894 under the hammer by O'Toole, Register of the United States Land Office.

[BRADSTREET, LIEUT. COL. JOHN]   711
An impartial account of ... Bradstreet's expedition to Fort Frontenac ... By a volunteer ... *L* 1759. O [4] 60 b H LC N NYP
—rptd. *Tor* 1940. O 32 map front. a
One of the best contemporary accounts of the war, possibly written by Bradstreet himself.

BRADY, CYRUS T.   712
Indian fights and fighters ... *N Y* 1904. D [24] 423 27pls a

BRADY, CYRUS T.   713
Northwestern fights and fighters. *N Y* 1907. O [26] 373 23pls a

BRADY, WILLIAM   714
Glimpses of Texas. *Houston* 1871. D 104 [2] map a
Worth-while immigration booklet.

BRADY, WILLIAM [N.]   715
The naval apprentice's kedge anchor ... *N Y* 1841. O 328 front. 8folds. pls aa
—rptd. "The kedge-anchor, or young sailor's assistant," same impr. 1847. O 9pls; 1848; and later. a

BRAHM, WILLIAM G. DE
See De Brahm, John G. W.

BRAIN, J. C.   716
The new descriptive route book and traveller's guide to the great west ... towns, stations, country ... on the Pittsburgh, Fort Wayne and Chicago R. R. ... *Chi* 1859. D 104 aa

BRAINERD, DAVID   717
Mirabilia Dei inter Indicos, or the ... work of grace amongst ... Indians in the provinces of New-Jersey and Pennsylvania ... *Phil* [1746]. O [10] 253 a some copies on better paper b AA NYP
—Eng. ed. "An abridgement of ... Brainerd's journal among the Indians," *L* 1748. D [6, 3–110 [4] a
—rptd. *Phil* 1748; *Worc* 1793.
—many later eds., Eng. & Am., generally accompanying Jonathan Edwards' biog. of Brainerd.
—Dutch tr. *Utrecht* 1756. O

BRAKE, HEZEKIAH   718
On two continents ... *Topeka* 1896. O 240 2ports a
Experiences in Minnesota, New Mexico and Kansas in the '50's and '60s.

BRAMAN, D. E. E.   719
Information about Texas. *Phil* 1857 D 192 a
—rptd., same impr. & collat. 1858

BRANAGAN, THOMAS   720
Serious remonstrances ... to the citizens of the northern states ... on the recent revival of the slave trade ... *Phil* 1805. D 133 a

BRANCH, [EDWARD] DOUGLAS   721
The cowboy and his interpreters. *N Y* 1926. O [12] 278 front. a

BRANNAN, JOHN, comp.   722
Official letters of ... officers of the United States during the war with Great Britain ... 1812–15. *Wash* 1823. O 510 a

BRANSTETTER, PETER L.   723
Life and travels ... *St Joseph Mo* [1913]. D 203 port a
Crossed the plains to California in 1850.

BRANTLEY, WILLIAM H.   724
Three capitals [St. Stephens, Huntsville and
Catawba, Ala.] . . . n p 1947. O 265 map 500cops
ptd a

BRATT, JOHN   725
Trails of yesterday, *Lincoln Neb*[ptd. *Chi*] 1921.
O [12] 302 22pls a
A cow-puncher's experiences in the Platte valley.

BRAUN, JOHANNES   726
Circular Schreiben an die Einwohner von
Rockingham und Augusta, und den benachbarten
Counties. *Harrisonburg Va* 1818. D [10] 4–409 [2] aa
Largely concerned with slavery in Virginia.

BRAUNS, ERNST [L.]   727
Ideen über die Auswanderung nach Amerika . . .
Gottingen 1827. O [32] 880 pl aa

BRAUNS, ERNST [L.]   728
Neudeutschland in Westamerika . . . *Lemgo*
1847. O [14] 90 a

BRAUNS, E[RNST L.]   729
Praktische Belehrungen und Rathscläge für
Reisende und Auswanderer nach Amerika.
Braunschweig 1829. O [4[492 [3] aa

BRAUNS, E[RNST L.]   730
Skizzen von Amerika . . . *Halberstadt* 1830. D
[8] 408 a

[BRAUW, J. DE]?   731
Herinneringen eener Reize naar Nieuw York . . .
in den Jaren 1831 en 1832. *Leyden* 1833. O [2]
220 [2] a
Also attributed to C. R. T. Krayenhoff.

BRAWLEY, BENJAMIN G.   732
A social history of the American Negro . . . *N Y*
1912. O [16] 420 a
—rptd. *N Y* 1921. O

[BRAXTON, CARTER]   733
Address to the convention of . . . Virginia, on
the subject of government . . . *Phil* 1776. D 25 a

[BRAXTON, CARTER M.]   734
Map of the battlefield of Fredericksburg, explained by extracts from official reports . . . *Lynchburg* 1866. O 44 fold.map aa

BRAY, MRS. ELIZABETH, ed.   735
Judge G. C. R. Mitchell. Memoirs and memo-
rials . . . *Davenport* 1915. O [2] 96 10pls a
Early Iowa, etc.

BRAYTON (MATTHEW).   736
The Indian captive. A narrative of the adventures . . . of: *Clev* 1860. 16° 68 c AA N Y
—rptd. *Fostoria O* 1896. 16° 70 a

After being stolen as a lad in northwestern Ohio,
successively traded to various western tribes, and
finally adopted by the Snakes, he wandered with
them as far as California and Oregon. Basically
authentic, though confused in its details and geography, it is one of the most remarkable and—in
spite of its relatively late publication date—one of
the rarest items belonging to captivity literature.
Mr. E. J. Wessen concludes, from evidence uncov-
ered, that this narrative was actually written by
John H. A. Bone.

BRAYTON (PATIENCE).   737
A short account of the life . . . of: . . . *N Y* 1801.
16° 135 aa
—rptd., same date, *New Bedford*; *N Y* 1802.
Contains her trip from New Jersey to Savannah,
in 1771.

BRAZELTON, B. G.   738
History of Hardin county, Tennessee. *Nashv*
1885. D 135[incl.front] a

BREAKENRIDGE, WILLIAM   739
Helldorado: bringing the law to the mesquite.
B 1928. O [20] 256 21pls a

BREARLY, W. H.   740
Recollections of the east Tennessee campaign . . .
Det 1871. O 43 a

BREAZEALE, J. W. M.   741
Life as it is . . . sketches of the exploration and
first settlement of . . . Tennessee [etc.] *Knoxv* 1842.
D 256 aa

BRECK, SAMUEL   742
Sketch of the internal improvements . . . made
by Pennsylvania; with observations upon . . . their
extension. *Phil* 1818. O 48 [1] a
—ed. 2, rev., same impr. & date. O 82 map
Emphasizes Philadelphia's strategic position for
trade with the rising West.

BREESE, SIDNEY   743
The early history of Illinois . . . *Chi* 1884. O [14]
422 port 3 maps a

BREESE, SIDNEY   744
Report, relative . . . a national railroad from the
Mississippi to the Columbia river. [*Wash* 1846].
O 51 2fold.maps a

BREMER, FREDERIKA   745
Die Heimath in der Neuen Welt . . . *Stuttgart*
1853. D 3v: [10] 462; [14] 520; [14] 534 a
—Dutch tr. *Haarlem* 1854. O 2pls
—Eng. tr. *L* 1853. D 3v: 1346 fronts
—Am. ed. *N Y* 1853. D 2v: [12] 654; rptd 1854.
—Swed. tr. *Stockh* 1853–4. D 3v:
Detailed and amiable record of an extensive tour.

BRENT, JOSEPH L.   **746**
Memoirs of the war between the states. [*N O*] 1940. O 238 port a

[BRENTON, E. B.]   **747**
Some account of the public life of the late Lieutenant-General Sir George Prevost . . . *L* 1823. O [4] 197 100 [2] a
Defends his campaigns on the Great Lakes.

BRENTS, J. A.   **748**
The patriots and guerillas of Tennessee and Kentucky . . . *N Y* 1863. D 171 2pls a

BREVARD, CAROLINE M.   **749**
A history of Florida . . . *Deland Fla* 1924. O 2v: [22] 293; [8 incl. initial blank l.] 309. 2maps 2ports a

BREVARD COUNTY [FLA.]   **750**
Brevard county [Fla.]; a brief description. [*Titusville*] 1888. D 40 a
—ed. 2, same impr., 1889. D 71 2maps

BREVOORT, ELIAS   **751**
New Mexico. Her natural resources [etc.] *Santa Fe* 1874. O 176 + errata slip + 2adv p a

BREVOORT, JAMES C.   **752**
Verrazano the navigator . . . *N Y* 1874. O 161 2maps a 250copies ptd.

BREWER, CHARLES   **753**
Reminiscences [of Alaska, etc.]. n.p. [*B*] [1884]. O 67 a

BREWER (LUCY).
The adventures of: *See* West, Mrs. Lucy Brewer.

BREWER (MISS LUCY).
The female marine, or adventures of: *See* West, Mrs. Lucy Brewer.

BREWER, WILLIAM H.   **754**
Up and down California . . . 1860–1864. *N Hav* 1930. O [30] 601 map 32pls aa
—rptd. same impr [1931]. a
—ed. 2, *Berkeley* 1939.

BREWER, WILLIS   **755**
Alabama: her history . . . 1540–1872. *Montg* 1872. O 712 a
Best general history of this state; admirable supplement to Pickett.

BREWSTER, JARVIS   **756**
An exposition of the treatment of slaves in the southern states . . . *New Brunswick* 1815. O 34 a

[BREWSTER, WILLIAM]   **757**
A sketch of the town of Bloomington . . . Minnesota. *St P* 1857. D 24 map b

BREWSTER & WRAY [pubs.]   **758**
Directory of Guthrie . . . *Guthrie* 1889. D 70 [incl. adv-pp] b NYP
When issued the town was only three months old.

BRICE, JAMES   **759**
Reminiscences of ten years experience on the western plains . . . *K C* [1905]. O 24 cover t.only aa

BRICE, JAMES R.   **760**
History of the revolutionary war . . . account of the captivity . . . of Captain Diets, and John and Robert Brice . . . taken prisoners . . . by the British, Indians and Tories . . . Vol. I [all.] *Alb* 1851. O 48 aa
Curious, but inconsequential.

BRICE, WALLACE A.   **761**
History of Fort Wayne . . . *Ft Wayne* 1868. O [16] 324 33 7pls a

BRICKELL, JOHN   **762**
The natural history of North Carolina . . . *Dub* 1737. O [6, 3–16] 408 map 4pls h Hn LC
—ed. 2, *Dub* 1743, same collat. aa
—rptd. [*Raleigh* 1910]. O [4] 418 map 4pls a
Shameless piracy from John Lawson's *History of Carolina, q.v.*, with travel portion omitted and slight additions.

BRIDEL, LOUIS   **763**
Le pour et le contre, ou avis à ceux qui se proposent de passer dans les Etats-Unis . . . *P* 1803. D [4] 162 [2] map aa
—Eng. tr. *Buff* 1914. D 56 map 25 copies ptd separately from Buffalo Hist. Soc. Pub. 18 a
—Ger. tr. *Basel* 1804. O 88 map a
This Swiss pastor who lived in America 20 years describes particularly western New York and Kentucky.

[BRIDGE, ISAAC]   **764**
Providential aspect and salutary tendencies of the existing crisis. *N O* 1681[*i.e.* 1861]. O 36 aa

BRIDWELL, J. W., comp.   **765**
The life and adventures of Robert McKimie, alias "Little Reddy", from Texas . . . desperado of the Black Hills region . . . *Hillsboro O* 1878. O 56 [incl front wrap] b Y

BRIEF
Brief enquiry (A) into the true nature . . . of our federal government . . . By a Virginian. *See* Upshur, Abel P.

Brief examination (A) of the plan and   **766**
conduct of the northern expedition in America . . . and of the surrender of . . . Burgoyne. *L* 1779. O 52 b
Severe attack. For others *see* under Burgoyne.

Brief extract (A) . . . of important argu-   767
ments . . . in support of the supremacy of the
British legislature and their right to tax the Americans. By a livery-man. *L* 1775. O [2] 48 a

Brief popular account (A) of all the finan-   768
cial panics . . . in the United States. By members
of the New York press. *N Y* 1857. D 59 a

Brief remarks on the defence of the Halifax libel
. . . *See* Otis, James.

Brief review (A) of the rise, progress, serv-   769
ices and sufferings, of New England . . . *L* 1774.
O 32 a
—rptd., same collat. *Norwich* 1774.

BRIEFE
Briefe aus Amerika fur deutsche Auswanderer . . .
See Köhler, Carl.

Briefe aus Amerika von einem Basler   770
Landmann . . . *Aarau* 1806. D 127 aa

Briefe aus den Vereinigten Staaten . . . *See* Jörg,
Eduard.

Briefe des gegenwärtigen Zustander von Nord
America. *See* Sprengel, Matthias C.

BRIEVEN
Brieven uit en over de Vereenigde Staten . . .
See Swalue, E. B.

[BRIGGS, CHARLES W.]   771
The reign of terror in Kansas : as encouraged by
President Pierce, and carried out by the southern
slave power . . . *B* 1856. O 34 b BA G Y [only
copies located]

[BRIGGS, JASON W. et al]   772
A word of consolation to the scattered saints.
[*Janesville Wis* 1853]. O 24 capt.t. only aa

BRIGGS, L[LOYD] VERNON   773
California and the west . . . [*B*] 1931. O [14]
214 44pls aa

BRIGGS, L[LOYD] VERNON   774
History of shipbuilding on North river, Plymouth county, Massachusetts . . . *B* 1889. O [16]
421 51pls aa

BRIGHAM, ALASCO D. [comp.]   775
Aurora [Ill.] city directory, for 1858–1859.
Aurora 1858. O 120 + 6adv-p[4 front, 2 rear] aa
Includes historical sketch.

BRIGHAM, ALASCO D. [comp.]   776
Janesville city directory, history . . . for 1859–
60. *Janesville* 1859. D 128 aa
First Janesville directory.

BRINCKERHOFF (DICK).   777
Life and adventures of: [in California and
Nevada in the 'fifties]. *Custar, O.* 1915. O 31 a

BRINTON, DANIEL G.   778
A guide-book of Florida and the south . . .
Jacksonville 1869. D [6] 9–136 fold.map a

BRINTON, DANIEL G.   779
Notes on the Floridian peninsula . . . *Phil* 1859.
D [8] 13–202 a
Contains the first attempt at a Florida biblio-
graphy; only 100 copies said to have been printed.

BRISBIN, GENERAL JAMES S.   780
The beef bonanza . . . *Phil* 1881. D 222 8pls a

BRISBIN, GEN. JAMES S., ed.   781
Belden the white chief; or twelve years among
the wild Indians . . . *Cin* 1870. O bound in blue
clo., gilt Indian on front cover. 513[incl.pls]
front. a
—anr. ed., same impr., date & collat., bound in
brown clo., Indian on front cover blind-stamped
—rptd., "million ed.," same date, impr. & collat. D
—best ed., with adds., "Stories of the plains," *St*
L 1881. D 541
—rptd. same impr 1882. D

BRISSOT DE WARVILLE, JACQUES-PIERRE
The commerce of America with Europe. *See*
Clavière, Etienne.

BRISSOT DE WARVILLE, JACQUES-   782
PIERRE
Examen critique des voyages dans l'Amérique
de . . . Chastellux . . . *L* 1786. O 143 aa
—Eng. tr., with adds. by au., *Phil* 1788. O [2] 89 b
—Eng. ed. *L* 1788. O aa

BRISSOT, DE WARVILLE, JACQUES-   783
PIERRE
Mémoire sur les noirs de l'Amérique Septentrio-
nale. *P* 1789. O 56 a

BRISSOT DE WARVILLE, JACQUES-   784
PIERRE
Nouveau voyage dans les États-Unis . . . *P* 1791.
O 3v: [4] 52 395; [4] 460; [28] 448. tab a some
copies ptd in large type aa
—Eng. tr. *L* 1792. O [4] 483 [4] a there were 2
issues of t-p [one short text, the other longer
text]
—other Eng. eds.: *Dub* 1792. O [8] 483; with adds.,
L 1794. O [64] 348 port
—Eng. ed. 2, cor., *L* 1794. O 2v: [12] 416; [2] 64,
348. port tab
—Am. eds: *N Y* 1792. D 264 [8] tab a; *B* 1797. O
276 [4] tab
—Dutch tr. *Amst* [1794]. O 3v

—Ger. trs.: *Berlin* 1792. O; *Dürkheim* 1792; *Heidelberg* 1792; *Reutlingen* 1797.
—anr. Ger. tr. *Bayreuth* 1793–6. 3v
—Swed. tr. *Stockh* 1799. D [4] 328
A favorable view of America, attracting to its shores many Europeans. Most of the Paris and London eds. include Claviére's book *q.v.*

BRISTED, JOHN   **785**
The resources of the United States... *N Y* 1818. O [16] 506 a
—Eng. ed. "America and her resources," *L* 1818. same collat.
—Fr. ed. "Les États-Unis...," *P* 1826. O 2v: 380; 320
—Ger. ed. "Der Hilfsquellen der Vereinigten Staaten...," *Weimar* 1819. O

BRISTOL, C. C.   **786**
Traveller's guide through the United States... To which is added the routes to California. *Buf* 1850 16° 48 b Y

BRISTOL, RHODE ISLAND.
Tales of an old sea port;... sketch of the history of: *See* Munro, Wilfred H.

BRISTOW, G. O.   **788**
Lost on Grand river. *Nowata* [*Okla*] 1900. D [2] 131 aa
Outlaw operations in old Indian Territory.

BRITISH
British Empire [The] in America...
See Oldmixon, John

British influence on the affairs of the United States... *See* Wolcott, Oliver.

British mechanic's and labourer's hand   **789**
book (The) and true guide to the United States... *L* 1840. D [6] 288 map 9pls a
—rptd. "The British emigrant's guide to the United States...," *L* 1847. 16° [4] 288 pls map

BRITTISCHE REICH   **790**
Brittische Reich in America (Das)... oder Kurzgefasste Beschreibung der Engländischen Pflanzstädte sammt ihrer Macht, Geschichte und Handlung in Nord-America... *Sorau* 1761. Q 48 front 3 maps aa
—rptd same impr & collat 1771. a

BROCK, ROBERT A.   **791**
Vestry book of Henrico parish... *Rich* 1874. Q [18] 3–222 a 100copies ptd.

BROCK, R[OBERT] A.   **792**
Virginia and Virginians... *Richm* 1888. D 2v: 408[incl.pls]; 409–813[incl.pls] 3 ports a

[BROCK, SALLIE A.]   **793**
Richmond during the war... *N Y* 1867. D [4] 9–389 a
Author's married name was Putnam.

BROCKWAY, REV. THOMAS   **794**
America saved; or divine glory displayed in the late war... *Hart* [1784]. O 24 a

[BROCKWAY, REV. THOMAS]?   **795**
The European traveller in America... *Hart* 1785. O 40 a
Attributed also to Jo Young. Of minor significance but uncommon.

BRODHEAD, JOHN R.   **796**
History of the State of New York... *N Y* 1853–71. O 2v: [16] 801; [16] 680. map a
—vol. 1 was rptd., same collat & impr. 1859.

BRODIE, WALTER   **797**
Pitcairn's Island, and the islanders, in 1850... and a few hints upon California... *L* 1851. D 260 4pls a
—ed. 2, same impr., date & collat.

BROMME, TRAUGOTT   **798**
Gemälde von Nord-Amerika... *Stuttgart* 1838–42. O 16parts 44pls aa
—re-iss. same impr 1839–42. a
—ed 2, "Des Universums Neue Welt... same impr & date O 796 48pls
—anr. iss. "Nordamerikas Bewohner" same impr & collat 1839.

BROMME, TRAUGOTT   **799**
Plan einer in Nord-Amerika zu gründen deutschen Kolonie. *Balt* 1834. D 26 a
The proposed colony was for western Michigan.

BROMME, TR[AUGOTT]   **800**
Reisen durch die Vereinigten Staaten... *Leip* [some cops carry *Balt* impr] 1834–5. D 3v: [12] 334; [10] 381; [6] 466 map pl 2tabs aa
—anr. ed. "Wohlfeile Hand-Bibliothek für Auswanderer". *Leip* 1838. D 6v 3maps a
—rptd. "Neustes vollständigstes Hand-und Reise-Buch für Auswanderer". *Bayreuth* 1840. O
—anr. ed. *Bayreuth* 1848. O [12] 555 tab
—6 oth. later eds., with various titles, and abridged as "Rathgeber", "Wegweiser", "Leitfaden", etc.
Based on actual travels this constituted the most extensive source of information for emigration-minded Europeans. There were, in addition to French translations, extracted portions devoted to individual states or regions: Alabama and Mississippi, Illinois and Missouri, Florida, Louisiana, Michigan, etc.

BROMWELL, WILLIAM J.   **801**
History of immigration to the United States... 1819–1855. *N Y* 1856. O [3] 12–225 a

BRONCHO, JOHN [pseud.]
See Sullivan, John H.

BRONSON, EDGAR B.   802
Reminiscences of a ranchman. *N Y* 1908. D [6]
314 a 2nd ptg same impr & collat. 1909.
—rev. ed., *Chi* 1910. O 369 pls.
—anr. ed. "Cowboy life on the western plains,"
N Y n.d. D 369 pls

[BRONSON, ENOS]   803
An address to the people of the United States,
on the policy of maintaining a permanent navy.
Phil 1802. O 51 a
Ascribed also to Albert Gallatin.

[BRONSON, ENOS]   804
An appeal to the government and congress . . .
against the depredations . . . by American privateers on the commerce of nations at peace with us.
N Y 1819. O 100 a

BRONSON, FRANCIS S.   805
. . . Traveler's directory, from New-York to
New-Orleans . . . *La Grange Ga* 1845. 16° 32 aa
—anr. ed. *N Y* 1845. 16° 64 a

BROOKE, FRANCIS T.   806
A narrative of my life. *Rich* 1849. 16° 90 aa

BROOKE, H. K.   809
Annals of the revolution: or, a history of the
Doans. *Phil* [1848]. 16° 84 a

[BROOKE, ROBERT?]   810
Remarks and conjectures on the voyage of the
ships Resolution and Discovery, in search of a
northerly passage from Kampschatka to England,
after the death of Capt. James Cook . . . *L* 1780.
O 48 aa

[BROOKES, IVESON L.]   811
A defence of southern slavery against the attacks
of Henry Clay and Alex'r. Campbell. *Hamburg
S C* 1851. O 46 [2] a

BROOKES, IVESON L.   812
Defence of the south, against the reproaches . . .
of the north . . . *Hamburg S C* 1850. O [4] 32 a

BROOKLYN DIRECTORY . . . 1822.
See Spooner, Alden.

BROOKS, B. F. C.   813
Memphis; her great men . . . as secession
leaders, editors and tools . . . *Memphis* 1864. O
86 aa

BROOKS [BRYANT B.]   814
Memoirs of: cowboy, trapper . . . *Glendale
Calif* 1939. O 370[incl. pls] aa 150 copies ptd.

BROOKS, ELISHA   815
A pioneer mother in California . . . how the
emigrants crossed the plains . . . *S F* 1922. D 61
2ports a

BROOKS, J. TYRWHITT
Four months among the gold-finders in California. *See* Vizetelly, Henry.

BROOKS, SARAH M.   816
Across the isthmus to California in '52. *S F*
1884. D 79 a
—rev. ed. *B* 1886.

BROSS, WILLIAM   817
Address on the resources of the far west . . .
N Y 1866. O 30 a

[BROSS, WILLIAM]   818
Rock Island and its surroundings . . . *Davenport*
[but ptd at Chicago] 1854. O 36 aa Some copies
carry *Chi* impr., some *Rock Islsnd.*

BROTHERHEAD, WILLIAM, ed.   819
The book of the signers . . . *Phil* 1861. Q [8]
114[incl.pls & facs] a
—anr issue, on L.P., with proof plates [only
99copies] aa
—ed. 2, with adds., *Phil* 1865. Q [26] 53–834 60pls
a 160copies ptd. a
—rptd. "The centennial book of the signers," *Phil*
[1875?]. F [8] 295[incl.pls] port aa
For an earlier work, on which this was based,
see Sanderson, John.

BROTHERS, THOMAS   820
The United States . . . as they are. *L* 1840. O [8]
517 a
Bitter disparagement of democracy by an Englishman who lived here fifteen years.

BROUGHTON, WILLIAM R.   821
A voyage of discovery to the north Pacific ocean
. . . *L* 1804. Q [20] 394 + adv lf 3charts 6pls c N
NYP OreH SeattleP Y
—Fr. tr. *P* 1807. O 2v: [38] 244 [2]; [4] 342 +
errata lf 4pls 3maps aa
—Ger. tr. *Weimar* 1805. Q [20] 352 2maps pl tab
Visited Nootka and sailed down the coast to
California; in further explorations he solved what
La Perouse had first attempted, the puzzle of the
Aleutians, Japan and Korea. Great Britain's claim
to the Oregon country was based largely on
Broughton's exploration of the mouth of the
Columbia. For another account of this expedition,
see Vancouver, George.

BROUILLET, JEAN B. A.   822
Protestantism in Oregon; account of the murder
of Dr. Whitman and the . . . calumnies of H. H.
Spaulding. *N Y* 1853. D [4] 107 c G OreH WashU Y

—ed. 2, with J. Ross Browne's "The late Indian war in Oregon . . .," *Wash* 1858. O 66 a see Browne, John Ross.

—anr. ed. 2, "Authentic account of the murder of Dr. Whitman . . .," *Port Ore* [1869]. D 108 b N OreH WashU Y

—ed. 3, *Ferndale* 1912. O 40 a

Convincing refutation of the accusation that Catholics instigated this massacre.

BROWER, J. V.   823

Memoirs of explorations in the basin of the Mississippi. *St Paul* 1898–1904. Q 8v aa 300 cops ptd.

Volume I, Quivira; II, Harahey; III, Mille Lac; IV, Kathio; V, Kakabikansing; VI, Minnesota; VII, Kansas; VIII, Mandan.

BROWN, A. J.   824

History of Newton county, Mississippi . . . *Jackson* 1894. O [16] 472 + errata lf aa

BROWN, AARON V.   825

A report on the Oregon territory . . . and the advisability of extending government and laws to that territory. *Wash* 1844. O 27 Ho. Doc. 308 a

BROWN, ALEXANDER   826

The first republic in America . . . *B* 1898. O [25] 688 port a

BROWN, ALEXANDER   827

The genesis of the United States . . . *B* 1890. O 2v: [2, 5–38] 524; [2] 525–1157. 111pls aa

—Eng. ed., same sheets, *L* 1890. a

BROWN (BENJAMIN).   828

Testimonies for the truth . . . witnessed in the travels and experiences of: *Liv* 1853. O 32 b N

Experiences with the Mormons in Missouri and as a member of the first Utah exodus.

BROWN, C. EXERA   829

Gazetteer of the Chicago and Northwestern railway . . . and of the Union Pacific . . . a guide and business directory. *Chi* 1869. O 360 map aa

Describes towns along these two systems from Chicago to Ogden.

[BROWN, CHARLES BROCKDEN]   830

An address to the Congress . . . on the utility and justice of restrictions upon foreign commerce . . . *Phil* 1809. O [8] 97 [i.e. 95] a

[BROWN, CHARLES BROCKDEN]   831

An address to the government of the United States, on the cession of Louisiana to the French. *Phil* 1803. O [2] 92 aa

—new ed. 1803. O 56 a

Urges the seizure of this French territory for the protection of our Western people.

[BROWN, CHARLES BROCKDEN]   832

Monroe's embassy . . . in relation to our claims to the navigation of the Mississippi . . . *Phil* 1803. O 57 aa

BROWN, CHARLES R.   833

The old Northwest Territory: its forts, missions, and trading posts. *Kalamazoo* 1875. O 32 map a

[BROWN, DAVID]   834

The planter: or, thirteen years in the south. *Phil* 1853. D 276 a

Defends the institution of slavery.

[BROWN, EDWARD?]   835

Notes on the origin and necessity of slavery. *Charleston S C* 1826. O 48 a

BROWN, EDWARD M.   836

An ocean voyage and around Cape Horn, 1849–50. n.p. 1900. D 67 a

BROWN, GEORGE L.   837

The centennial history of Butler county, Neb. *Lincoln* 1876. O 34 map a

BROWN, GEORGE W.   838

The truth at last. History corrected. Reminiscences of old John Brown . . . *Rockford Ill* 1880. O 80 [2] a

John Brown stripped of his halo by a leading abolitionist.

BROWN, HENRY   839

The history of Illinois . . . *N Y* 1844. O [10] 492 map + 10 adv p a

Chronologically the first, intrinsically the worst, history of this state.

BROWN, HENRY   840

A narrative of the anti-Masonic excitement, in . . . New York . . . *Batavia* 1829. D [8] 244 a

BROWN, IGNATIUS   841

. . . History of Indianapolis, 1818–1868. *Indp* [1868]. O 100 a

BROWN, J. ROBERT   842

Journal of a trip across the plains . . . to California, 1856. *Columbus* 1860. O 119 c Pn Y [only copies known]

BROWN, JACOB   843

Miscellaneous writings [on western Pennsylvania in pioneer times]. *Cumberland* 1896. O 325 port a

BROWN, JAMES, of Kentucky   844

An address to the public . . . exposing the . . . falsehoods contained in the pamphlet of Elisha I. Hall. *Lex* Bradford [ca 1803]. D 62 [3] a

Hall, former Secretary of State of Tennessee, is charged by Brown, Secretary of State of Kentucky, with being a cowardly poltroon and thief.

BROWN, J[AMES] C.   845
Calabazas, or amusing recollections of an Arizona city. *S F* 1892. D 251 aa

BROWN, J[AMES] HENRY   846
Political history of Oregon . . . Vol. I [all]. *Port Ore* 1892. O [8] 462 map 2ports 2facs tab b
Practically entire edition burned or lost at sea?

BROWN, J[AMES] H[ENRY]   847
The Salem [Ore.] directory . . . with a history . . . *Salem* 1871. O 128 86 diagram b G Y
This first directory of Salem, by an 1847 pioneer, sketches overland expeditions, from 1829.

BROWN, JAMES S.   848
California gold . . . history of the first find . . . *Oakl* 1894. D 20 [incl port] + wraps 55cops ptd aa
By a co-worker with Marshall at the time of the discovery.

BROWN, JAMES S.   849
Life of a pioneer . . . *S L C* 1900. O [20] 9–520 port 2pls aa

BROWN, JESSE, and WILLARD, A. M.   850
The Black hills trails . . . *Rapid City S D* 1924. O [12] 17–572 2pls aa

BROWN (THE JOHN) INVASION . . .
See Drew, Thos.

BROWN (JOHN) agitator.   851
The life, trial and conviction of: . . . *N Y* [1859]. O [2] 7–100 8pls a
—new ed., with adds., "The life, trial and execution . . .," same impr. [1859]. O [2] 7–108 8pls

BROWN, JOHN E.   852
Memoirs of a forty-niner . . . *N Hav* 1907. O 28 aa
Day-by-day journal of his overland trip.

BROWN, JOHN HENRY [of Calif.]   853
Reminiscences and incidents. "The early days" of San Francisco . . . 1845–1850. *S F* [1886]. O 53 lvs. map b B CalS G Y
—rptd. *S F* [Grabhorn 1933]. O a 25cops signed aa
—rptd. *Oakland* 1949. O 150 map pl 500 cops a

BROWN, JOHN HENRY and   854
SPEER, WILLIAM S.
Encyclopedia of the new west . . . *Marshall Tex* 1881. Q 611 269 77 38 13 [6] 90ports aa
Biographies of leading men of Arkansas, Colorado, Indian Territory, New Mexico and Texas.

BROWN, JOHN HENRY [of Texas]   855
History of Dallas county [Tex.] *Dallas* 1887. D 114 + 2adv-p a
John H. Cochran issued what he called a supplement to this, Dallas 1928, in an octavo volume of 296 pages.

BROWN, JOHN HENRY [of Texas]   856
History of Texas. *St L* [1892–3]. O 2v: 631 + 2 index p after t-p; 591. 25pls aa

BROWN, JOHN HENRY [of Texas]   857
Indian wars and pioneers of Texas . . . *Austin & St L* [1896]. O 762 124pls aa

BROWN, JOHN HENRY [of Texas]   858
Life . . . of Henry Smith, the first American governor of Texas. *Dalles* 1887 O 395 port. a
—rptd Austin 1935

BROWN, JOHN M[ATHIAS]   859
Brief sketch of the first settlement of the county of Schoharie, by the Germans. *Schoharie N Y* 1823. O 23 b
—anr. ed. *Cobleskill N Y* 1891. O 52 a
Rarest New York county history.

BROWN, LONDON   860
An old time cowboy. n.p. n.d. 16° 82 [1] cover t.only a

BROWN, NAT. P., and DALLISON,   861
JOHN K., pubs
Nevada, Grass valley and Rough and Ready directory . . . with an historical sketch of Nevada County [California]. Vol. I[all]. *S F* 1856. O [6] 133 [18] b
—rptd. *S F* 1862. aa

[BROWN, PAUL]   862
The radical; and advocate of equality . . . *Alb* 1834. O 170 a

BROWN, PAUL   863
Twelve months in New-Harmony . . . *Cin* 1827. O 128 b IndS WisH

BROWN, PHILIP F.   864
Reminiscences of the war of 1861–1865. [*Roanoke* 1912]. O 53 a
—rptd. *Rich* 1917. O 62 port

BROWN (SAMUEL).   865
A thrilling narrative of the . . . sufferings . . . of: Ed. by J. F. McGaw, *Urichsville O* 1852. D 63 c G

BROWN, SAMUEL R.   866
Views on Lake Erie . . . *Troy* 1814. O 96 aa
—anr. ed., enl., "Views of the campaigns of the northwestern army . . .," *Troy* 1814. D 156 aa

—rptd., same collat., *Burl N J* 1814; *Phil* 1815. front.added a
—best ed. "Authentic history of the second war for independence," *Auburn* 1815. D 2v: 228 [96]; 264 [132] aa

BROWN, SAMUEL R. 867
The western gazetteer; or emigrant's directory. *Auburn N Y* 1817. O 352 errata slip[of 3 lines] a
—issue 2, with 4-line errata
—anr. issue, with adds. 360p
—ed. 2, *Auburn* 1820. O 360
—foreign eds.: *Belfast* 1819 O 399 map; *L* 1820.
One of the earliest American-printed emigrant's guides.

BROWN (TARLETON, a Captain in 868
the revolutionary army).
Memoirs of: *N Y* 1862. O 64 3 pls a 100 cops ptd

BROWN (THOMAS) of Mass. 869
A plain narrative of the uncommon sufferings... of: ... *B* 1760. O 27 d MH N [of 4 known copies]
—ed. 2, same impr., date & collat. c LC
—ed. 3, *B* 1760. D 24 c N [only perfect copy known]
Narrative of a glutton for punishment who enjoyed three separate captivities by both Indians and French. Sickeningly rare, terrifically thrilling.

BROWN, WILLIAM, of Leeds 870
America: a four years' residence in the United States and Canada ... *Leeds* 1849. O [4] 108 a
Two of his four years spent in Ohio.

BROWN, WILLIAM H[ENRY]. 1808-83 871
Portrait gallery of distinguished American citizens. *Hart* 1845. F 111 27pls b LC PhilL
—rptd. same impr. & collat. 1846. b AA NYP Y
—anr. ed. *N Y* 1931. same collat. aa 600 copies ptd.[200 with add. set of pls]

BROWN, WILLIAM H[ENRY], 1836-1910 872
The history of the first locomotives in America ... *N Y* 1871. O [10] 9–242 10pls a
—rev. ed. same impr. 1874.
—abr. ed. *Phil* [1877]. O 48, pls

BROWN, WILLIAM H[UBBARD] 873
An historical sketch of the early movement in Illinois for the legalization of slavery ... *Chi* 1865. O 44 a
—rptd. *Chi* 1876. D 30 [2]

BROWN, W[ILLIAM] W[ELLS]. 874
Narrative of: a fugitive slave. *B* 1847. D 110 port a
—rptd. several times
—Dutch tr. *Zwolle* 1850. O port

BROWN COUNTY, WISCONSIN.
History of: *See* Swisher, Mrs. Bella French.

BROWNE, J[OHN] ROSS 875
Adventures in the Apache country; a tour through Arizona [etc.]. *N Y* 1869. D [3] 6–535 a
—rptd. 1871; 1878.
—Ger. tr. *Jena* 1877. D 474

BROWNE, J[OHN] ROSS 876
Crusoe's island ... with sketches of adventure in California and Washoe. *N Y* 1864. D 436 a
—rptd:, same impr., 1871; 1872; 1875.

BROWNE, J[OHN] ROSS 877
Etchings of a whaling cruise ... *N Y* 1846. O [16] 580 + 8adv-p 13pls aa
—Eng. ed., Am. sheets with new t-p, *L* 1846. aa

BROWNE, J[OHN] ROSS 878
Report on the late Indian war in Oregon and Washington. [Sen. Exec. Doc. 40]. *Wash* 1858. O 66 aa
—anr. ed. [Ho. Exec. Doc. 38]. same impr, date & collat aa
—anr. ed. [Ho. Exec. Doc. 39] .*Wash* 1858 O 48 a
Brouillet's *Protestantism in Oregon* was included in the two 66-page editions.

BROWNE, PETER A. 879
Lecture on the Oregon Territory. *Phil* 1843. O 20 + wraps b

BROWNING, MESHACH 880
Forty-four years of the life of a hunter ... *Phil* 1859. D [18] 13–400 12 pls a called rev. ed. but the first ed. in book form
—rptd: *Phil* 1860; 1865; 1870.

BROWNLOW, WILLIAM G. 881
Americanism contrasted with foreignism, Romanism and bogus democracy ... in which certain demagogues in Tennessee ... are shown up in their true colors. *Nash* 1856. O 208 a

BROWNLOW, WILLIAM G. 882
Helps to the study of Presbyterianism ... To which is added a brief account of the life and travels of the author. *Knoxv* 1834. D 299 aa

BROWNLOW, WILLIAM G. 883
A political register ... the princples [*sic*] of the Whig and Locofoco parties ... *Jonesborough Tenn* 1844. O 349 aa

BROWNLOW (PARSON [WILLIAM G.]) 884
Portrait and biography of: ... *Indp*. 1862. D 72 a some cops carry *Cin* impr.

BROWNSON, ORESTES A. 885
The American republic; its constitution, tendencies and destiny. *N Y* 1866. O [16] 439 a

BRUCE (PETER H.)   886
Memoirs of: *L* 1782. O [12] 446 aa
—rptd. *Dub* 1783. O [16] 527 a
—Ger. tr. *Leip* 1784. O a
Military adventures in Europe and America;
including two stays in South Carolina in 1741 and
1745.

BRUCE, PHILIP A.   888
Economic history of Virginia in the seventeenth
century. *N Y* 1896. O 2v: [20] 634; [6] 647. map a
—rptd: *N Y* 1907. O 2v; *N Y* 1935 O 2v

BRUCE, PHILIP A.   889
Institutional history of Virginia in the seventeenth century... *N Y* 1910. O 2v: [14] 707; [6]
698 + 4adv-p a

BRÜCKNER, G.   890
Amerikas Geographie und Naturgeschichte. *St
L* [1858]. O [4] 201 3pls 2 charts a
—anr. ed. "Amerikas wichtigste Charakteristik
...," same impr. & collat. [1858].
—anr. ed. *Ghent* 1858.

BRUFF, J[OSEPH] G.
Gold rush... *See* Read, Georgia W., and
Gaines, Ruth.

BRUFFEY, GEORGE A.   891
Eighty-one years in the west. *Butte* 1925. D 152
port a

BRUMMELKAMPF, A[NTHONY] and   892
VAN RAALTE, A. C.
Landverhuizing... *Amst* 1846. O [4] 56 a
—rptd. several times, same impr., date & collat.

BRUMMITT, STELLA W.   893
Brother Van. *N Y* [1919]. D [10] 172 [3] 2pls by
C. M. Russell a

[BRUN, JEAN B.]   894
Le triomphe du nouveau monde... *P* 1785. O
2v: [10] 242; [4] 298 [8] a

BRUNCKOW (FREDERIC).   895
Report of: [concerning the Sonora Exploring
and Mining Co. of Arizona]. *Cin* 1859. O 48 map
front. aa

BRUNNER, DAVID B.   896
The Indians of Berks county, Pennsylvania...
Reading 1881. O 177 34pls a

BRUNSON (REV. ALFRED).   897
A western pioneer; or, incidents of the life and
times of: *Cin* 1872–9. O 2v: 418; 413 aa

BRUNSWICK [MAINE].
A description of:... by a gentleman of South
Carolina. *See* Putnam, Henry.

BRYAN, EDWARD B.   898
Letters to the southern people... in relation to
the African slave trade. *Charleston* 1859. O 89 a

BRYAN, CAPT. ROGER B.   899
An average American army officer... *San
Diego* 1914. 16° 167[incl. front wrap, front. &
preliminary blank lf] aa

[BRYAN, SAMUEL]?   900
The genuine principles of the ancient... English constitution... With some observations,
on their peculiar fitness, for the united colonies. By
Demophilus. *Phil* 1776. O 46 [1] aa
Contains earliest appearance, in book form, of
the Declaration of Independence; advertisement
at end is dated July 8th, 1776.

BRYAN, WILLIAM S., and   901
ROSE, ROBERT
A history of the pioneer families of Missouri;
with... sketches... relating to early days... *St
L* 1876. O [4] 528 2ports aa
—rptd., with index, [*Columbia Mo* 1935]. O [18]
569 [incl.pls] a

BRYANT, CHARLES S.   902
A history of the... massacre by the Sioux...
in Minnesota... *Cin* 1864. D 504 a
—later printings, with A. B. Murch as co-au. added
to t-p, same impr., date & collat.
—rptd. *Cin* 1868.

BRYANT, EDWIN   903
What I saw in California... journal of a tour
... across the continent... and through California... 1846–7. *N Y* 1848. D 455 aa
—ed. 2, same collat., *N Y* 1848. a
—ed. 3, *N Y* 1849.
—eds. 4, 5, appendix added same impr. 1849.
D 480
—ed. 6, same, with fold.map added.
—Eng. ed: abr. *L* 1849: D 144map [not same as
in Am. ed.]; D [8] 208 map
—best ed. [incl. Wierzbicki's *California as it is*]
Launcestown Tasmania 1850. c
—anr. ed., with adds., *Santa Ana Calif* 1936. O
—Fr. tr. *Brus* 1849. D 4pls; *P* [1849]. D; *Brus*
1850. 16°
—for Swed. tr. *see* "Californien: en Skildring...."
—Dutch tr. see "Californien en Skildring".

BRYCE (MRS, CAMPBELL).   904
The personal experiences of: during the burning
of Columbia, S. C.... *Phil* 1899. D 53 a

BRYCE, GEORGE   905
The remarkable history of the Hudson'ᵉ Bay
Company... *L* 1900. O [22] 502 31maps & pıs a
—rptd. *L* 1902. same collat.
—ed. 2, *L* 1904. O [22] 502 31maps & pls

—ed. 3, *L* 1910. O [24] 504 31maps & pls
All three editions are also found bearing imprints both of New York and of Toronto.

BRYCE, JAMES   **906**
The American commonwealth. *L* 1888. O 3v:
[32 incl. initial blank l.] 592; [12] 683; [10] 699,
map aa
—rptd., same impr. & date. O 2v. a
—many later reprints [all omitting the chap. on the
Tweed ring]
Remains the most authoritative study of American political and social institutions.

BUACHE, J[EAN] N[ICOLAS]   **907**
Mémoire sur les pays de l'Asie et de l'Amérique,
situés au nord de la Mer du Sud *P* 1775. Q 22 map
b LC Y
Objects to some conclusions voiced by Robert
de Vaugondy in his similarly entitled pamphlet of
1754.

BUACHE, PHILIP   **908**
Considerations géographiques et physiques sur
les nouvelles-découvertes au nord de la grande
mer, appelleé . . . la Mer du Sud. *P* 1753–54. Q
3pts in 1: 7, 6–158 16maps on 12pls dd N NYP Y
—some copies are accompanied by a 4-p. list of
maps, dated 1755, and a 3-p. "Exposé des découvertes au nord . . ."
In addition to its Northwest interest [Russian
and Spanish discoveries and Del Fonte's apocryphal one] deals also with California, New Mexico
and Louisiana.

[BUACHE, PHILIP]   **909**
Explication de la carte des nouvelles découvertes
au nord de la Mer du Sud. *P* 1752. Q [2] 18, fold.
map by de L'Isle[in some copies, but probably
sold separately] b LC NYP Y
—Ger. ed. "Erklärung der charte . . .," *Berlin*
1753. 16° 48 aa
See also Müller, Gerhard F., *Lettre d'un officier
de la marine Russienne* . . ., which is a reply to this
pamphlet, and severely critical of the de L'Isle map
of 1752.

[BUCHANAN, FRANKLIN]   **910**
In relation to the claims of the officers of the late
Texas navy. *N Y* n.d. O 44 a

BUCHANAN, JAMES, British consul   **911**
Sketches of the history . . . of the North American Indians . . . *N Y* 1824. 16° 2v. 182; 156 a
—rptd. *N Y* 1825. same collat.
—Eng. ed., omitting au.'s "plan for melioration,"
L 1824. O [12] 371 map

BUCHANAN, ROBERT, ed.   **912**
The life and adventures of John James Audubon
. . . *L* 1868. O [8] 366 port a

—Am. ed., with some alterations & no "adventures' in t., ed. by Mrs. Audubon, *N Y* 1869. D
443 port
—anr. ed. *N Y* 1871. D

BUCHANAN, W. JEFFERSON   **913**
Maryland's hope: her trials and interests in connexion with the war. *Rich* 1864. O 62 a
Sequel to the author's fifteen-page pamphlet of
1863, *Maryland's crisis*, both advocating Confederate affiliation.

BUCHON, J. A. C.
Atlas géographique . . . des deux Amériques . . .
traduit de l'atlas exécuté en Amérique . . . *See*
under Carey, Henry C., and Lea, J.

BUCK, DANIEL   **914**
Indian outbreaks. *Mankato* 1904. O 284 9pls a

BUCK, IRVING A.   **915**
Cleburne and his command. *N Y* 1908. D 382 a

BUCK, SOLON J.   **916**
The Granger movement . . . *C* 1913. O [12] 384
4maps tab a
—rptd., same impr. & collat., 1933.

BUCK, WILLIAM J.   **917**
History of Bucks county [Pa.] . . . *Willow Grove
Pa* 1855. O 118 [24] pls a

BUCK, WILLIAM J.   **918**
History of Montgomery county [Pa.] . . . *Norristown* 1859. O 124 [4] a

BUCK, WILLIAM J.   **919**
History of the Indian walk, performed for the
proprietaries of Pennsylvania in 1737 . . . *Phil*
1886. D 269 a 210copies ptd.

BUCK, WILLIAM J.   **920**
Local sketches . . . pertaining to Bucks and
Montgomery counties, Pennsylvania. [*Phil*] 1887.
D [6] 9–340 a 200copies ptd.

BUCKINGHAM, J[AMES] S.   **921**
America, historical, statistic and descriptive. *L*
Fisher [1841]. O 3v: [16] 504; [14] 563; [12] 569
[20]. port map
—Am. ed. *N Y* 1841. O 2v: 515; [14] 9–516. port
Devoted to New England, New York, Pennsylvania and Maryland.

BUCKINGHAM, J[AMES] S.   **922**
The eastern and western states . . . *L* Fisher
[1842]. O 3v: [16] 573; [8] 536; [10] 495. 15pls a
Covers the Ohio and upper Mississippi valleys.

BUCKINGHAM, JAMES S.   **923**
The slave states of America. *L* Fisher &c. [1842].

O 2v: [24] 487 [error for 587]; [12] 588. 8pls 8adv-p[front of v. 1] a
—anr. issue, with index added to v.2, carrying paginat. to 600

BUCKINGHAM, JOSEPH T., ed.   924
Miscellanies . . . from the public journals. *B* 1822–4. D 2v: 268; 255. port a

BUCKINGHAM, JOSEPH T.   925
Personal memoirs . . . of editorial life. *B* 1852. D 2v: [2] 256; 255. port a

BUCKINGHAM, JOSEPH T.   926
Specimens of newspaper literature: with personal memoirs . . . *B* 1850. D 2v: [16] 348; [2] 356. 2ports a
—rptd., same impr. & collat., 1852.

BUCKNER, SAMUEL   927
The American sailor: a treatise on . . . seamanship . . . *Newport* [1790]. O [4] 96 aa
First American work of its kind.

BUCKSKIN MOSE
Buckskin Mose; or, life from the lakes to the Pacific . . . *See* Perrie, Geo. W.

BUCYRUS . . . DIRECTORY . . .   928
Bucyrus, Galion, and Crestline [Ohio] directory for 1875–6. Containing . . . history of Crawford county. *Bucyrus* 1875. O 180 a

BUDD, THOMAS   929
Good order established in Pennsylvania and New-Jersey . . . [*Phil*] 1685. smQ 40 d JCB NYP N [of 10 cops loc[
—rptd: *N Y* 1865; *Clev* 1902. a
Second product of the Pennsylvania press.

BUDD, WILLIAM H.   930
History of Martin county, Minnesota. *Fairmont* 1897. O 124 port a

BÜCHELE, C.   931
Land und Volk der Vereinigten Staaten . . . *Stuttgart* 1855. O [8] 622 a

[BUECHLER, JOHANN U.]   932
Land-und Seereisen eines St. Gallischen Kantonbürgers nach Nordamerika . . . *St. Gallen* 1819. D 228 aa
—ed. 2, *Chur* [183–?]. O a
—Dutch tr. *Haarlem* 1819. D [10] 221
Describes trip down the Ohio and Mississippi.

BUEL, J[AMES] W.   933
The border bandits . . . *St L* Linahan 1881. D 252 [2] 148[incl. front. & pls] a
—anr. issue, "The border outlaws . . .," same collat. & date, *St L* Hist. Pub. Co.

—rptd., same impr. & date. D 412[incl. front. & pls] + 4p notice, dated March 10, that "Heroes of the plains," will be pub. "June or July." In front. of this issue the ports of the Youngers, supplied by Cole Younger in Feb., are larger than in the previous printings.
—anr. issue, pub. date of "Heroes" given as "July 1st."
—anr. issue, contains add. train robbery of July 15, 1881.
—anr. ed., same impr., 1882. D 476[incl. front. & pls]
—*Hart* 1882; *Cin* 1882.

BUEL, J[AMES] W.   934
Heroes of the plains . . . *St L* 1881. O [4] 9–548 [incl. front. & pls] a
—rptd., same collat and impr.: 1882; 1883; 1884.
—other eds.: *Phil* 1886; *Phil* [1891].

BUEL, J[AMES] W.   935
Life and . . . adventures of Wild Bill . . . *Chi* 1880. D 93 front. b LC N
—rptd: 1888; 1891. aa

BÜLOW, [ADAM HEINRICH] D. VON   936
Der Freistaat von Nordamerika . . . *Berlin* 1797. D 2v: [6] 309; 286 a
Violent denunciation of the republic by one of the earliest European visitors.

BUENA VISTA [COLO.]   937
Buena Vista [Colo.] . . . mining camps . . . *Buena Vista* 1882. O 37 a

BÜTTNER, J[OHANN] G.   938
Das jedem nach den Vereinigten Staaten . . . *Bayreuth* 1849. D [10] 69 a

BÜTTNER, JOHANN C.   939
Nordamerikanischer Krieger, eine selbstbiographie. *Camenz* 1828. O [20] 137 aa
—ed. 2 enl. "Büttner der Amerikaner . . ." same impr & date. O [20] 137 [6] 126 port aa
—Eng. tr., abr. "Narrative, etc." *N Y* [*ca* 1912] O [6] 69 port a
After many hardships in Pennsylvania as an indentured servant, served awhile in the American army, then deserted to the Hessians.

BÜTTNER, J[OHANN] G.   940
Der Staat Ohio . . . Beschreibung für Auswanderer . . . *Bayreuth* 1849. D [8] 206 aa

BÜTTNER, J[OHANN G.]   941
Die Vereinigten Staaten . . . *Hamburg* 1844. O 2v: [14] 440; [2] 450. tab a
—anr. ed. "Briefe aus und über Nordamerika . . .," *Dresden* 1845. O 2v in 1: [14] 440; [2] 450. tab
—rptd. 1847. O 2v: [6] 440; 450. tab

BUFFALO [N.Y.]
A directory for the village of: . . . 1828. *See* Crary, L. P., pub.

BUFFALO BILL   941a
Buffalo Bill and his wild west companions . . . *Chi* [1893]. D [6 incl.front.] 234 a

BUFFALO CREEK RESERVATION.   942
Indian council held at: *Balt* 1842. O 83 a
Negotiations by which the Ogden Land Company acquired vast tracts in Western New York

BUFFUM, E. GOULD   943
Six months in the gold mines . . . *Phil* 1850. D 5–172 + 44adv p aa
—Eng. ed. *L* 1850. D [12] 244 a
Authoritative source on the early period of the gold discoveries by a resident of California at the time.

[BUGG, FRANCIS]   944
News from Pennsilvania . . . passages in the government of the Quakers in that province . . . *L* 1703. O 36 b BM NYP

BUHOUP, JONATHAN W.   945
Narrative of the . . . army of Chihuahua, commanded by Brigadier General Wool. *Pitt* 1847. 16° 168 aa

BULGER (CAPTAIN ANDREW [H.])   946
An autobiographical sketch of the services of: . . . *Bangalore* 1865. Q [2] 29 + app in 4sections: 11; 4; 4–6; 4 aa
Bulger, as British commandant at Prairie du Chien, had control over the upper Mississippi valley, 1814-15.

BULL (JOHN) IN AMERICA.
See Paulding, James K.

BULL RUN AND MANASSAS . . .   947
A narrative of the battles of: . . . *Charleston S C* 1861. O 32 + cov.t. b Duke LC [only cops loc]

BULLITT, THOMAS W.   948
My life at Exmoor. *Louisv* 1911. O [8] 132 pls a
Kentucky plantation life before the war.

BULLOCH, JAMES D.   949
The secret service of the Confederate States in Europe. *L* 1883. O 2v: [10] 460; [6] 438 errata slip in v. 1 aa
—Am. ed., from sheets of Eng. ed., *N Y* 1884. aa
—rptd *N Y* 1959. O 2v a

BULLOCK, W[ILLIAM]   950
Sketch of a journey through the western states . . . *L* 1827. D [42] 135 map plan aa
—rptd. *Phil* 1857. D a

BUNDY (S. G.)   951
Autobiography of: n.p. [*ca* 1912] D 148 1 a
Prior to service in the Civil War lived in Wisconsin and Nebraska; later a missionary to the Ponca branch of the Omaha tribe.

BUNKER . . . HILL.
A particular account of the battle of: By a citizen of Boston. *See* Bradford, Alden.

BUNN (MATTHEW).   952
A journal of the adventures of: . . . *Prov* for the au. [1796]. O 24 dd N [only copy known]
—rptd. *Litchfield* 1796. O 24 d BurtH Y
—other eds., with varying titles: *Walpole N H* 1796. d no perfect copy known; n.p. [*Prov?*] 1797. D 36 d AA Hn; *Peacham* 1806. O 55 c no perfect copy known; *B* 1806. Burt H c; *Batavia* 1827 D 71 b WRH NYS; *Batavia* 1828. D 59 b AA LC
Gives account of St. Clair's Ohio disaster and Bunn's Indian captivity thereafter.

BUNNELL (DAVID C.)   953
The travels and adventures of: . . . containing an accurate account of the battle of lake Erie [etc.]. *Palmyra N Y* 1831. D 199 map 2pls aa

BUNNELL, LAFAYETTE H.   954
Discovery of the Yosemite, and the Indian war of 1851 . . . *Chi* Revell [1880]. D 331 map port 6pla a
—anr. ed., with changes & adds., same impr. [1880]. D 349 + 4adv-p map port 6pls
—several reprints

"BUNNY" [*pseud*]   954a
Two years a cowboy . . . *L* 1887. D 128 a

BURCH, L[AWRENCE] D.   955
Kansas as it is . . . *Chi* 1878. D 142 fold.map a

BURCH, L[AWRENCE] D.   956
Nebraska as it is . . . *Chi* 1878. D 164 [20] map a

BURD PAPERS (THE)   957
Ed. by Lewis B. Walter [*Pottsville*] 1897–9. O 3v: 136; 80; 253. 3ports small ed. aa
Letters of Edward Burd and William Allen on colonial Pennsylvania and material on Braddock's expedition. The three volumes were issued separately, but are usually cited as a single work.

BURDER, GEORGE   958
The Welch Indians . . . a people . . . said . . . to inhabit a . . . country on the west side of the Mississippi . . . *L* [1797]. O 35 a

BURGE (MISS SADAI C.)   959
Journal of: [*Atlanta* 1950]. D 3–79[incl. 5pls] a

[BURGES, SIR JAMES B.]   960
Narrative of the negotiations occasioned by the dispute between England and Spain . . . in 1790. priv. ptd [*L* 1791]. O [8] 307 capt.t.only BM Prov Arch Victoria b
Exhaustive treatment of the Nootka Sound controversy, title to the northwest coast, etc., prepared by the Under Secretary of State while negotiations were in progress. The most valuable secondary source on this affair.

BURGOYNE (LIEUTENANT GENERAL).   961
An inquiry into . . . the conduct of: . . . *L* 1780. O 50 + adv-1. aa
—ed. 2, same impr. & date. a

BURGOYNE (LIEUT. GEN.)   962
A letter from: to his constituents, upon his late resignation . . . *L* 1779. O [2] 37 a
—rptd., in 5 other eds.—same impr., date & collat.

BURGOYNE (LIEUT. GEN.)   963
A letter to: occasioned by a second edition of his State of the expedition from Canada. *L* 1780. O 32 aa

BURGOYNE (LIEUT. GEN.)   964
A letter to: on his Letter to his constituents. *L* 1779. O [2] 35 a

BURGOYNE (JOHN).   965
Orderly book of: . . . *Alb* 1860. Q [34] 221 map 5pls a 110 copies (10 on L. P.]

BURGOYNE'S STATE . . .   966
Burgoyne's [General] State of the expedition from Canada. Remarks on: *L* 1780. O [2] 60 a
Defends the Ministry. The military disaster was all the fault of the General.

BURGOYNE'S [LIEUT. GEN.]
Letter to his constituents. A reply to: . . . *See* Germaine, Geo.

BURGOYNE (GEN.)   967
Reponse à un des articles des Annales politiques de M. Linguet concernant la defaite du: *L* 1778. O 23 a

BURGOYNE, JOHN   968
A state of the expedition from Canada . . . *L* 1780. Q [8] 140 62 [2] 5 maps tab aa
—ed. 2, *L* 1780. O [12] 192 109 6maps tab aa
His chief defense against all charges.

BURGOYNE'S (GEN.) SPEECHES.   969
The substance of: . . . with an appendix, containing General Washington's letter [to him] . . . *L* 1778. O [4] 42 [6] aa
—5 other *L*, & one *Dub*, eds., same date. a

BURGOYNE, JOHN   970
A supplement to the State of the expedition from Canada . . . *L* 1780. Q [2] 26[incl. plan] b
—rptd. *N Y* 1865. Q 26 75copies ptd. a
Original edition was published without Burgoyne's authorization.

BURK, JOHN [DALY]   971
The history of Virginia . . . *Ptbg Va* 1804–5–16. O 4v: [8] 348; 335 [62]; 469; [8] 538 [17] b AA H N NYP Y
Vol. 4 was the joint work of Skelton Jones and Louis H. Girardin, aided by Thomas Jefferson; most copies of that volume were burned.

[BURKE, AEDANUS]   972
An address to the freemen of . . . South Carolina . . . *Phil* 1783. O 32 a

[BURKE, AEDANUS]   973
Considerations on the . . . order of Cincinnati . . . *Charles-Town SC* 1783. O 32 aa
—anr. ed. au.'s name surmised on t-p, *Phil* 1783. O 16 aa
—other 1783 eds.: *Hart* n.d. O 23; *N Y* O 16; *Hart* O 23: *Newport* n.d. O 16 a

[BURKE, EDMUND]?   974
An account of the European settlements in America . . . *L* 1757. O 2v: [10] 3–312; [4] 3–300 [20]. 2maps aa
—rptd., in 9eds., *L* or *Dub*, before 1800. a
—best ed. *L* Stockdale 1808. Q 482 2maps
—same impr. and date O 2v: 378; 352 2maps
—Fr. tr. *P* 1767. D 2v: [20] 384; [4] 352. 2maps
—Ger. tr. *Leip* 1775. 16° 2v: [14] 452; [8] 424 [8]. map
—Dutch tr. *Amst* n.d. O 2v
—Ital tr. *Venice* 1763. O 2v 3maps
Best contemporary account. Actually written by William Burke, but usually ascribed to his more famous kinsman who gave substantial help.

[BURKE, EDMUND]?   975
An impartial history of the war in America between Great Britain and her colonies . . . *L* 1780. O [12] 608 [44] map 13ports aa
—anr. issue, *Carlisle* 1780. same collat. aa some copies of this issue had the ports. col. b
—anr. issue, *L* 1780, had only 31p in app. a

BURKE (EDMUND).   976
A letter from: . . . to John Farr and John Harris . . . on the affairs of America. *Bristol* 1777. O 79 a
—rptd. *L* 1777 O [2] 75
—4 other eds. same year.

[BURKE, EDMUND]   977
Observations on a late State of the nation . . . *L* 1769. Q [2] 97 aa

—eds. 2, 3 & 4, same impr. & date. O [4] 155 a
—anr. ed. *Dub* 1769. O [2] 114
For pamphlet attacked and a rejoinder to this attack, *see* Knox, William.

BURKE (EDMUND).   **978**
Second thoughts; or, observations upon Lord Abingdon's Thoughts on the Letter of: to the sheriffs of Bristol. By the author of the Answer to Mr. Burke's Letter. *L* 1777. O 74 a
—ed. 2, same impr., date & collat.

BURKE (EDMUND).   **979**
The speech of: on . . . conciliation with the colonies . . . *L* 1775. Q [4] 65 b NYP Y
—eds. 2 & 3, same impr. & date. O [4] 107 a
—*Dub* 1775. O
—Am. eds.: *N Y* 1775. O [6] 71; *Phil* 1775. aa

BURKE, EDMUND   **980**
Speech on American taxation, April 19, 1774. *L* 1774. Q [4] 58 b
— rptd. *Bristol* 1774. D; *L* 1774. O 96 a
—eds. 2 & 3, *L* 1775. same collat.
—ed. 4, same collat. & impr. 1776.
—rptd. *Bristol* [1777].
—Am. eds.: *N Y* 1775. O 63; *Phil* 1778. O [4[76 aa

BURKE, EMILY P.   **981**
Reminiscences of Georgia. [*Oberlin O*] 1850. D [8] 252 port aa

BURKE, JOHN M.   **982**
"Buffalo Bill" from prairie to palace. *Chi* 1893. D 275 a

BURKE (WILLIAM,   **983**
a soldier of the revolution).
Memoir of: *Hart* 1837. D 126 a

BURKE, W[ILLIAM] S., comp.   **984**
Directory of . . . Council Bluffs, and emigrants' guide to the gold regions . . . *Council Bluffs* 1866. O [24] 32 + 16adv-p[8 front, 8rear] map c G NYP WisH Y

BURKE, W[ILLIAM S.] and ROCK, J.   **985**
The history of Leavenworth . . . *Leavenworth* 1880. O 88 + 14adv-p[interspersed] aa

[BURKE, WILLIAM S.] comp.   **986**
Military history of Kansas regiments during the war . . . With accounts of the campaigns in Wyoming, along the Platte . . . *Leavenworth* 1870. O 466 aa

BURKE W[ILLIAM] S.   **987**
An outline history of Council Bluffs. *Chi* 1867. O 31 b

BURKITT, LEMUEL, and READ, JESSE   **988**
Concise history of the Kehukee Baptist Association [N.C.] . . . *Halifax* 1803. 16° 319 a
—rev. ed. *Phil* 1850. 16° 351

BURKLEY, FRANK J.   **989**
The faded frontier. *Omaha* 1935. O 436 [6] a

BURLAGE, JOHN and HOLLINGS-   **990**
WORTH, J.P.
Abstract of valid land claims . . . from the records of the general land office [etc.] of Texas. *Austin* 1859. O [8] 670 aa

BURLEIGH, WILLIAM H.   **991**
The Republican pocket pistol . . . arguments for freedom. *N Y* 1860. D 36 43 2ports a

[BURLEND, REBECCA]   **992**
A true picture of emigration; or, fourteen years in the interior of North America . . . *L* [1848]. 16° 64 [incl. covers] a
—rptd., ed. Quaife, *Chi* 1936. 16° [32] 167 map port
Account of an English family pioneering in Pike County, Illinois.

BURLINGTON, [IOWA].   **993**
Business directory . . . of: *Burlington* 1856. D [10] 48 [14] b IaH MinnH

BURLINGTON AND MISSOURI . . .   **994**
Burlington and Missouri river railroad lands (the). Views and descriptions of: . . . *Burl* [1872]. O 40 map 20pls aa

BURNABY, ANDREW   **995**
Travels through the middle settlements in North America in 1759 and 1760. *L* 1775. Q [8] 106 [2] aa
—rptd. *Dub* 1775. D [22] 206 + errata lf a
—ed. 2, *L* 1775. O [16] 198 [2] a
—ed. 3 [and best] *L* 1778. Q [20] 209 map 2pls b
—rptd. *L* 1798, same collat. aa
—Fr. tr. *Lausanne* 1778; *Hague* 1778. D [2] 181 [2] a
—Ger. tr. *Hamburg* 1776. D [16] 192
—Am ed *N Y* 1904. D 265 map pl a

BURNET, JACOB   **996**
Letters relating to the early settlements of the Northwestern Territory. *Cin* 1839. O 334 port plan a
—anr. issue, without port, pub. as Pt. 2, Vol. 1, Trans., Hist. & Philos. Soc. of Ohio.

BURNET, JACOB   **997**
Notes on the early settlement of the Northwestern Territory. *Cin* 1847. O 501, incl port[not issued in all copies] a
—anr. issue, same collat., *N Y* 1847. a
Amplification of his *Letters* listed above.

[BURNET, WILLIAM]   **998**
A letter from a Romish priest in Canada to one who was taken captive in her infancy, but . . . returned to this her native land . . . *B* 1729. D [4] 26 b Clem LC
Captured by Indians in 1689 and sold to the French, this New England girl escaped and returned home in 1714.

[BURNETT, PETER H.]?   **999**
Address to the inhabitants of New Mexico and California on the omission of Congress to provide them with territorial governments. *N Y* 1849. D 56 b B N NYP Y

BURNETT, PETER H.   **1000**
Recollections . . . of an old pioneer. *N Y* 1880. O [14] 448 + 6adv-p aa
—rptd. "An old California pioneer," *Oakland* 1946. O [4] 287 3maps facs a
Covers early days in both Oregon and California.

BURNEY, JAMES   **1001**
A chronological history of north-eastern voyages of discovery . . . [including explorations along the northwest coast of America made by Bering, Cook, Tschirikov, *et al*]. *L* 1819. O [8] 310 2maps aa

BURNEY, JAMES   **1002**
A chronological history of the discoveries in the South sea . . . including a history of the buccaneers . . . *L* 1803–17. O 5v: [22] 391; [16] 482; [10] 437 [18] 580; [8] 237. 47maps & pls c N NYP Y
Monumental and valuable synthesis, from original sources, of Pacific maritime activities, 1520–1764, including those—of Alarcon, Cabrillo, Drake, Viscaino, *et al*—along the California coast. The preceding item supplements this work.

BURNS, JABEZ   **1003**
Notes of a tour in the United States and Canada . . . *L* 1848. 18° 180 a

BURNS, JAMES R.   **1004**
Battle of Williamsburg . . . *N Y* 1865. 24° 119 a

BURNS, JOHN H.   **1005**
Memoirs of a cow pony . . . *B* [1906]. D 178 [incl.pls] aa

BURPEE, LAWRENCE J.   **1006**
The search for the western sea; . . . the exploration of north-western America. *L* 1908. O [60] 651 6maps 51pls aa
—Am. ed., same collat., *N Y* 1908. aa
—Canad. ed., same collat. *Tor* [1908]. aa
—rev. ed. *Tor* 1935. O 2v a
—rptd. *N Y* 1936. O 2v

BURR (AARON).   **1007**
The amorous intrigues of: *N Y* n.d. D 100 a

BURR (COLONEL AARON).   **1008**
The examination of: before the chief justice . . . *Rich* 1807. O 46 a

BURR (AARON).
An examination of the various charges . . . against: . . . *See* Van Ness, Wm. P.

BURR (AARON).
A letter to: . . . on the . . . baneful effects of duels. By Philanthropos. *See* Ladd, Wm.

BURR (AARON) et al.   **1009**
Message from the President . . . transmitting a copy of the proceedings, and of the evidence exhibited, on the arraignment of: . . . *Wash* 1807. O [4] 332 [222] aa

BURR (COL. [AARON]).
A narrative of the suppression by: of the History of the administration of John Adams. *See* Cheetham, James.

BURR (AARON) and   **1010**
HAMILTON (ALEXANDER).
Particulars of the late duel . . . between: . . . *N Y* 1804. O 32 a

BURR (AARON).   **1011**
The private journal of: during his residence . . . in Europe. Ed. M. L. Davis. *N Y* 1838. O 2v: 451; [2] 9–453. pl a
—rptd. [on thinner paper], *N Y* 1856.
—oth eds: *N Y* 1859 2v; *N Y* 1860. 2v
—best ed., unexpurgated, *Roch* 1903. O 2v: [20] 501; [4] 503. ports b AA N NYP 250copies ptd. aa

BURR (COL. [AARON]).   **1012**
Strictures upon the Narrative of the suppression, by: of Wood's History of the administration of John Adams. By a Yeoman. n.p. n.d. O 26 a
For the *Narrative* evoking this pamphlet, *see* Cheetham, James.

BURR (AARON).   **1013**
The trial of: [reported by T. Carpenter]. *Wash* 1807–8. O 3v: [2] 148 [incl 2 prelim. blankp] 137; 465; 416 [48] b N KyS NYP Y
—[reported by D. Robertson] *Phil* 1808. O 2v: [10] 596; [4] 539 a

BURR (AARON).   **1014**
The trial of: To which is added an account of the subsequent proceedings . . . with notes by J. J. Coombs. *Wash* 1864. O [52] 392 a

BURR (AARON).
A view of the political conduct of: *See* Cheetham, James.

BURR, REV. AARON　　　　　**1015**
A discourse . . . at New-Ark . . . on . . . late encroachments of the French and their designs against the British colonies . . . *N Y* 1755. Q 41 aa

BURR, DAVID H.　　　　　　**1016**
The American atlas. n.p. [*ca* 1840?]. F [2] 13fold.maps[col.] pl aa

BURR, DAVID H.　　　　　　**1017**
An atlas of . . . New York. *Ithaca* 1829. F [4] 7–29 120 [incl 52 maps] aa
—anr iss. with *N Y* impr aa
—rptd. *N Y* 1838. O 98 58maps aa
—anr. ed. *Ithaca* 1839. F [40] 122 [incl 52maps] aa
—rptd. same impr 1841. F [4] 7–29 120 [incl 52maps] aa
Text by Simeon de Witt.

BURR, WILLIAM　　　　　　**1018**
Descriptive and historical view of Burr's moving mirror of the lakes . . . from Lake Erie to the Atlantic. *N Y* 1850. O 48 a

BURRALL, W. T.　　　　　　**1019**
A trip to the far west of British Columbia. *Wisbech* [1891]. O 26 a

BURRIS (MARTIN).　　　　　**1020**
True sketches of the life and travels of: on the western plains, the Rocky mountains, [etc.]. [*Salina Kas*] 1910. O 67 port 250copies ptd. aa

[BURROUGH, EDWARD]　　　**1021**
A declaration of the . . . persecution of the . . . Quakers, in New-England . . . *L* [1660]. SmQ 32 b JCB LC NYP

BURROUGHS (STEPHEN).　　　**1022**
Memoirs of: *Hanover N H* 1798. O [4] 8–296 aa
—V.2. *B* 1804 aa
—other eds. *Otsego* 1810. 16° 100; *Alb* 1811, with adds. D 396; *N Y* 1811. 16°; Greenfield 1812; *Brookfield* 1814. 16° 107; *B* 1832. 16°; *B* 1835. D 2v
Picaresque adventures, perhaps somewhat exaggerated, of a New England rogue.

BURROWS, J[OHN] M. D.　　　**1023**
Fifty years in Iowa . . . 1838–1888. [*Davenport*] 1888. D [12] 182 2ports aa
—rptd., with adds., "The early days of Rock Island and Davenport," *Chi* Lakeside 1942. 16° [20] 315, incl ports a

BURROWS (RUBE) and his gang . . .　　**1024**
Complete official history of: *Birmingham, Ala* [*ca* 1890] D 141 + 3adv-p aa

BURSON, CAROLINE M.　　　**1025**
The stewardship of Don Esteban Miró. *N O* 1940. O [12] 327[incl. front.] aa

BURT, S[ILAS] W., and BERTHOUD,　　**1026**
E[DWARD] L.
The Rocky mountain gold regions . . . *Denver* 1861. D 131 2maps No perfect copy known. dd
—ed. 2, identical with ed. 1 except that maps were omitted, 8 adv-p and final unnumb. p. were added and cover t. reads "second edition" and gives Charles Collins as author. c ColH S G

BURT (WILLIAM A.) and　　　**1027**
HUBBARD (BELA).
Reports of: on the geography . . . of . . . the mineral region of the south shore of lake Superior . . . *Det* 1846. D [6] 109 map chart aa
First investigation into Michigan's mineral wealth. *See* also Houghton, Jacob, for a second edition of this book.

BURTHE, M.　　　　　　　**1028**
Contre Laussat. *N O* 1804. O 34 b only 1 cop kn.

BURTON, AMOS　　　　　　**1029**
A journal of the cruise of the United States ship Susquehanna, 1860 3. *N Y* 1863. O 177 a

BURTON, HARLEY T.　　　　**1030**
A history of the J A Ranch. *Austin* 1928. O [10] 147 map port aa

BURTON (SERGEANT JONATHAN).　**1031**
Diary and orderly book of: 1775–1776. *Concord N H* 1885. O 38 a

BURTON, LEWIS W.　　　　　**1032**
Annals of Henrico parish . . . Virginia . . . *Rich* [1904]. O [6] 542 [4] 221 36pls a

BURTON, RICHARD F.　　　　**1033**
The city of the saints . . . *L* 1861. O [12] 708 3maps[on one sheet] plan 8 pls a
—ed. 2, same impr. & collat. 1862.
—Am. ed. *N Y* 1862. O [12] 574 map plan front. [other pls incl. in paginat.]

B[URTON], R[OBERT]　　　　**1034**
The English empire in America . . . *L* 1685. D [4] 209 2maps 2pls b N
—by 1739 there were 7 oth London and 2 Dublin eds. ea. a
Robert Burton seems to have been a pseudonym for the publisher, Nathaniel Crouch.

[B]URTON, [R]OBERT　　　　**1035**
The English heroe: or, Sir Francis Drake revived . . . *L* 1687. D [2] 206 port b
—rptd. many times, 23 eds by 1762
—Ger tr "Der Englische Held, etc." *Leip* [1690] O
Based largely on Fletcher's *World encompassed* [pub'd 1628] and on Nichol's *Sir Francis Drake revived* [pub'd 1626], this account of Drake's cicumnavigation and visit to California seems to

have struck English popular fancy more forcibly than did earlier and worthier narratives.

[BURTON, WARREN]   1036
The district school as it was . . . *B* 1833. D 156 aa
—rev ed. *N Y* 1838. same collat a
—anr ed. *B* 1850. D 206
—rptd. *N Y* 1928. D 190

BUSBY, ALLIE B.   1037
Two summers among the Musquawkies, relating to the early history of the Sac and Fox tribe. *Vinton Ia* 1886. D 238 errata slip aa

BUSCH, MORITZ   1038
Wanderungen zwischen Hudson und Mississippi . . . *Stuttgart* 1854. O 2v in 1: [8] 390; [8] 381 a
Trenchant observations on the Middle West, etc.

[BUSHE, GERVAISE P.]   1039
The case of Great-Britain and America . . . *L* 1769. O [4] 35 aa
—ed. 2, cor., same impr. & date. O [4] 43 a
—rptd., same date & collat. *Dub*
—Am. eds.: *Phil* 1769. O [2] 16; *B* n.d. O 15 aa
Attributed also to George B. Butler. Urges that England abandon colonial taxation, and that the colonies be permitted to act voluntarily.

BUSHNELL, CHARLES I., ed.   1040
Crumbs for antiquarians . . . *N Y* 1862–66. O 10pts in 2v: 17; 41; 65; 65; 80; 57; [4] 71; 98; 127; 86. 12pls a
All of the ten *Crumbs* were also issued separately.

BUSHNELL, CHARLES I.. ed.   1041
The destructive operation of foul air, tainted provisions . . . upon human constitutions; exemplified in the . . . cruelty of the British to the American captives at New York . . . *N Y* 1865. O 28 a
30copies ptd.

BUSHNELL, CHARLES I.   1042
Narrative of the life and adventures of Levi Hanford, a soldier of the revolution. *N Y* 1863. O 80 2pls a

[BUSHNELL, HORACE]   1043
California, its characteristics and prospects . . . n.p. n.d. [*B* 1858]. O 43 aa
—anr. ed. [*Hart* 1858]. same collat. a
—rptd., t. slightly altered, *S F* 1858. O 32 aa

BUSHNELL, JOSEPH P.   1044
Business & resident directory of Council Bluffs . . . history . . . *Council Bluffs* 1898 [error for 1868] O 120 aa
Map mentioned on title-page was apparently not included.

BUSTAMANTE, CARLOS M. DE   1045
Campañas del general D. Felix Maria Calleja . . . *Mex* 1828. O [8] 200 [24] 4maps with lf. explaining them port b B N Y
Includes account of Colonel Gutierrez's Texas campaign of 1812–13. Intended to supplement his *Quadro historico* . . .

BUSTAMANTE [CARLOS M. DE].   1046
El gabinete mexicano durante el segundo període de la administratión de: . . . *Mex* 1842. sm Q 2v: [6] 216 [8]; 249 [10] 46 aa
Gives the Mexican side of the Santa Fe expedition and surrender of the Texans to General Armijo.

BUSTAMANTE, CARLOS M. DE   1047
El nuevo Bernal Diaz del Castillo, ó sea historia de la invasion de los Anglo-Americanos en Mexico. *Mex* 1847. O 2v in 1: [2] 162 [2]; 236 [4]. port aa

BUTCHER, S[OLOMON] D.   1048
Pioneer history of Custer county, Nebraska . . . *Broken Bow* [ptd.Denver] [1901]. O 403 + errata lf and 5adv-p aa

BUTE'S (LORD) ADMINISTRATION.
A review of: . . . *See* Almon, John.

[BUTEL-DUMONT, GEORGE M.]   1049
Histoire et commerce des colonies angloises dans l'Amérique septentrionale . . . *L* 1755. D [24] 336 a
—anr. ed. *Hague* 1755. D [16] 246
—Eng. tr. *See* Huske, John.
—Ger. tr. *Frankf* 1755. D [16] 238
—Span. tr. *Madrid* 1768. D
Attributed also to De Forbonnais.

BUTLER, CALEB   1050
History of the town of Groton . . . *B* 1848. O [20] 9–499 2maps 4pls a

BUTLER, FRANCES A.   1051
Journal. *L* 1835. D 2v: 252; 218 a
—Am. ed., omitting pref., *Phil* 1835. D 2v: [6] 13–252; 218
—Fr. ed. "Journal of a residence in America," *P* 1835. O [6] 326
For another book by this author, *see* Kemble, Frances A.

BUTLER, FRANCIS G.   1052
A history of Farmington . . . Maine . . . *Farmington* 1885. O [2] 683 + errata l. & 12 ruled p.for memos 27pls a
Most of the edition burned.

BUTLER, JAMES   1053
American bravery displayed in the capture of fourteen hundred vessels . . . *Carlisle Pa* 1816. D 322 [8] a

BUTLER, JAMES D.   1054
Nebraska. Its characteristics . . . [*Neb City* 1871]. D 24 a
—anr. ed. n.p. [1873]. D 40

BUTLER, JAMES D., ed.   1055
The new found journal of Charles Floyd, a sergeant under Captains Lewis and Clark. *Worc* 1894. O 30 a
Separate printing from American Antiquarian Society *Proceedings*.

BUTLER, JOHN C.   1056
Historical record of Macon and central Georgia . . . *Macon* 1879. D 351 inserted slip at p348 errata lf 2pls aa

BUTLER, MANN   1058
An appeal from the misrepresentations of James Hall, respecting the history of Kentucky and the west . . . *Frankfort* 1837. O 32 a

BUTLER, MANN   1059
A history of . . . Kentucky. *Louisv* 1834. D [1?] 396 port aa
—ed. 2, enl., *Cin* [or *Louisv*] 1836. D [16 13–72] 551 aa
Disputes many of Marshall's findings; contains the *Journal* of Col. George Croghan, one of the earliest accounts in English of the Ohio country, previously appearing only in magazine form.

BUTLER, MANN   1060
An oration . . . at Fort Gibson, Mississippi, consisting principally of a sketch of the rise of the State of Mississippi, from . . . 1539, to the present time. *Frankfort Ky* 1837. O 24 a

BUTLER, LIEUT. WILLIAM F.   1061
Report . . . of his journey from Fort Garry to Rocky Mountain House. [*Ottawa*? 1871?]. F 23 [no t-p] c Y
—anr. issue, no priority established, *Ottawa* 1871. O [2] 29 c G
Semi-official report on the Indian trade in Manitoba and the Saskatchewan, bitterly indicting the evil influence of Montana traders among the Blackfeet, Crees and Assiniboines.

BUTTERFIELD, CONSUL W.   1062
An historical account of the expedition against Sandusky . . . *Cin* 1873. O [10] 403 port a

BUTTERFIELD, CONSUL W.   1063
History of Brulé's discoveries . . . *Clev* 1898. O [12] 184 map a
Sequel to his *John Nicolet*, below.

BUTTERFIELD, CONSUL W.   1064
History of Seneca county [O.] . . . *Sandusky* 1848. D 252 a 2000 copies ptd, 1300 burned

BUTTERFIELD, CONSUL W.   1065
History of the discovery of the northwest by John Nicolet in 1634 . . . *Cin* 1881. D 113 + 8 adv-p a

BUTTERFIELD, CONSUL W.   1066
History of the Girtys . . . Thomas, Simon, James and George . . . *Cin* 1890. O [14] 426 aa
—rptd. *Columbus O* 1950. O same collat a

BUTTERFIELD, CONSUL W., ed.
A short biography of John Leith . . . *See* Jeffries, Ewel.

BUTTERFIELD, CONSUL W.   1067
The Washington-Crawford letters . . . concerning western lands . . . *Cin* 1877. O 107 a

BUTTERFIELD, CONSUL W.   1068
The Washington-Irvine correspondence . . . *Madison Wis* 1882. O [8] 430 map 2ports a

BUTTERFIELD, F. E., and   1069
RUNDLETT, C. M., comps.
Directory of the city of Dallas . . . [with history] . . . [*St L* 1875]. O 140 port + adv-l. before t. aa

BUTTERWORTH, WILLIAM   1070
Three years adventures . . . in England, Africa, the West Indies, South Carolina and Georgia. *Leeds* 1823. D [12] 492 port errata-l. aa
—rptd., same collat., *Leeds* 1831. aa
—anr. issue, same collat., *Leeds* n.d. [1831?]. aa
Butterworth's real name was Henry Schroeder.

BUTTLES (JOEL).   1071
Extracts from the diary of: [*Newport* 1889]. sm Q 47 a
Describes conditions in early Ohio, to which he moved in 1804.

BUTTRICK, DANIEL S.   1072
Antiquities of the Cherokee Indians . . . *Vinita* 1884. O [6] 20 a

BUTTRICK (TILLY).   1073
Voyages, travels and discoveries of: *B* 1831. D 58 c H LC N Y
Includes a trip to the Ohio valley in 1814 and another to New Orleans, returning overland to Cincinnati.

BYERS, WILLIAM N., and   1074
KELLOM, JOHN H.
A hand book of the gold fields of Nebraska and Kansas . . . *Chi* 1859. D [2] 113 [15] map c Hn Y
—rptd *Denv* 1949

[BYFIELD, SHADRACH]   1075
A narrative of a light company soldier's service . . . during the late American war; together with

some adventures amongst the Indian tribes . . . 1812–14. *Bradford* 1840. O 57 aa
—rptd *N Y* 1910 a

BYRD, A. J.   **1076**
History . . . of Johnson county [Tex.] . . . *Marshall* 1879. O 232 aa

BYRD, WILLIAM   **1077**
The Westover manuscripts . . . *Petersburg Va* 1841. O [4] 144 aa
—rptd., ed. Wynne, "History of the dividing line and other tracts," *Rich* 1866. O 2v in 1: [19] 233; [6] 276. map & pl 200 copies[20 on L. P.] aa
—best ed., ed. Bassett, "Writings," *N Y* 1901. Q [10 9-88] 461 4pls ltd. ed.[of 500cops, 15 on L. P.] aa

BYRNE, BERNARD J.   **1078**
A frontier army surgeon . . . Colorado in the eighties. [*Cranford N J* 1935]. O 160 3pls 130copies ptd. aa

BYRNE, BERNARD M.   **1079**
Letters on the climate . . . of Florida. *Ralston Pa* n.d. O 15 aa
—rptd. *Jacksonville* 1851. O 28 aa
—enl ed "Florida and Texas . . .," *Ocala Fla* 1866. O 40 aa

BYRNE, WILLIAM S.   **1080**
Directory of Grass Valley township for 1865, containing . . . historical sketch . . . [*S F?*] 1865. O [30] 144 b

C

C., B. R.
A trip to the rockies. *See* Corwin, B. R.

C., J.
The siege of Penobscot . . . *See* Calef, John.

C., J.-B.
Notice sur la colonization aux États-Unis . . . *See* Claes, Jean-Baptiste.

C., T.
Entertaining passage relating to King Philip's war . . . *See* Church, Thos.

C., T. E.
A guide to Pomarede's . . . panorama of the Mississippi . . . *See* Courtney, T. E.

CABALLERIA Y COLLEL, JUAN   **1**
History of San Bernardino valley . . . 1810–51. *San Bernardino* 1902. O 130 a

CABALLERIA Y COLLEL, JUAN   **2**
History of . . . Santa Barbara. Tr. Edmund Burke. *Santa Barbara* 1892. D [4] 111 aa
—rptd., same impr., 1928. a

[CABELL, MARGARET C.]   **3**
Sketches and recollections of Lynchburg [Va.]. *Rich* 1858. D 363 a

CABET (ÉTIENNE).   **4**
Colonie icarienne. Guerre à mort de l'opposition contre le citoyen: . . . et mémorable séance de la nuit du 12 au 13 Mai 1856 . . . *Nauvoo* 1856. O 72 aa

CABET, ÉTIENNE   **5**
Colonie icarienne . . . sa constitution, ses lois, sa situation matérielle . . . *P* 1856. D 240 aa

CABET, ÉTIENNE   **6**
Colonie ou république icarienne . . . son histoire . . . *P* 1852. 16° 59 b
—ed. 2, *P* 1854. aa
—rptd. *P* 1855. a
—Eng. tr. *Nauvoo* 1852. O 20 b G Y
—Ger. tr. *Nauvoo* 1853. aa

CABET, ÉTIENNE   **7**
Compte-rendu . . . sur l'état de la colonie icarienne . . . *P* 1854. 16° 32 aa

CABET, ÉTIENNE   **8**
Départ de Nauvoo du fondateur d'Icarie avec les vrais Icariens. *P* 1856. D 23 aa

CABET, ÉTIENNE   **9**
Icarie. *p* 1849. O 16 aa
—continued as "Réalization d'Icarie. Nouvelles de Nauvoo," *P* 1849–50. O 17–144 aa

CABET, ÉTIENNE   **10**
Progrès de la colonie icarienne établie à Nauvoo . . . *P* 1854. 16° 31 aa

CABET, ÉTIENNE   **11**
Réalization de la commonauté d'Icarie. *P* 1847. D 412 aa

CABET, ÉTIENNE   **12**
Supplément à l'almanach icarien pour 1848. Specialement consacré à la description du Texas . . . *P* [1847]. D 214 3maps aa

CABOT (SEBASTIAN).
Memoir of: . . . *See* Biddle, Richard.

CACKLER, CHRISTIAN   **13**
Recollections of an old settler. [*Kent O* 1874]. O 38 b few copies known N

—ed. 2, [*Kent*] 1904. O 56 port a

Narrative of a pioneer who settled in Ohio's Western Reserve in 1804.

CADOGAN, GEORGE   14

The Spanish hireling detected . . . a refutation of the . . . falsehoods in a late pamphlet . . . "An impartial account of the late expedition against St. Augustine under General Oglethorpe." *L* 1743. O [2] 68 aa

This defense of Oglethorpe was answered by the author of *An impartial account in A full reply to Lieut. Cadogan's Spanish hireling detected, q.v.*

CADWALADER, JOHN   15

A reply to General Joseph Reed's "Remarks on a late publication in the Independent Gazetteer," . . . *Phil* 1783. O 54 aa

—rptd. *Trenton* 1846. D 36 a

For pamphlet here answered, *see* Reed, Joseph.

CADY, JOHN H.   16

Arizona's yesterdays. [Patagonia, Ariz] 1915. D 127 pl a

—rptd. [*LA* 1923.]

[CAHOONE, SARAH S.]   17

Sketches of Newport and its vicinity . . . *N Y* 1842. D 213 a

CAIN, JOSEPH, and BROWER, ARIEH C.   18

Mormon way-bill, to the gold mines . . . Fort Hall, Salt Lake, and Los Angelos [*sic*] . . . including . . . various cut-offs . . . *G S L C* 1851. 16° 40 dd G Y [of 4 cops kn]

First overland guide printed west of Missouri.

CAIRD, SIR JAMES   19

Prairie farming in America . . . *L* 1859. D [8] 128 map a

—Am. ed. *N Y* 1859. D 130

CAIRO [ILL.]   20

Prospectus and engineers report, relative to the city of: *St L* 1839. O [8] 36 aa

CALDWELL, CHARLES   21

Memoirs of the life . . . of the Hon. Nathanael Greene . . . *Phil* 1819. O [24] 452 [1] port 2facs a

CALDWELL, J. F. J.   22

The history of a brigade of South Carolinians known first as "Gregg's" and subsequently as "Mc Gowan's brigade." *Phil* 1866. D 247 addenda 1f inserted at p38 aa

One of the best chronicles of a Confederate military organization.

CALDWELL, JOHN E.   23

A tour through . . . Virginia . . . *N Y* 1809. O 31 aa

—Eng. ed. *Belf* 1810. O 63 a

[CALEF, JOH]   24

The siege of Penobscot by the rebels . . . *L* 1781. O [4] 44 2charts on 1 sheet b BA H NYP

CALEF, ROBERT   25

More wonders of the invisible world . . . *L* 1700. sm Q [12] 156 errata list [not in all copies] b AA BP MH NYP Y

—Am. ed. *Salem* 1796 [but not pub. till 1797]. D 318 [2] a

—rptd. *Salem* 1823. D 312; *B* 1828. 16° 333

Antidote to the hysterical credulity of contemporary religious passion. The first copy to reach Boston was publicly burned.

CALEF (ROBERT).

Some few remarks, upon a scandalous book . . . by one: . . . *See* Mather, Cotton and Increase.

[CALHOUN, A. P., et al]   26

An appeal to the state rights party of South Carolina . . . on the present conditions of public affairs. *Columbia* 1858. O [12] 36 a

CALHOUN, ARTHUR W.   27

A social history of the American family. *Clev* 1917. O 3v: 348; [6] 9–390 + errata slip; 411 aa

—rptd. *N Y* 1945. O 3v in 1 a

CALHOUN (JAMES S.)   28

Official correspondence of: while Indian agent at Santa Fe . . . *Wash* 1915. O 554 4maps a

CALHLUN, JOHN C.   29

Correspondence with General Andrew Jackson on . . . the Seminole war. *Wash* 1831. O 52 a

CALHOUN (JOHN C.)   30

Life of: . . . *N Y* 1843. O 74 port a

CALHOUN (JOHN C.) and   31
BUCHANAN (JAMES).

Oregon: the claim of the United States . . . as stated in the letters of: . . . *L* 1846. O [6] 3–55 16 map aa

CALHOUN (JOHN C.)   32

The works of: [Ed. by R. K. Cralle]. *N Y* [1851]–5. O 6v: [8] 406; [8] 652; [8] 648; [8] 578; [8] 461; [8] 445 aa

—all vols. rptd. several times, 1853–60; also 1883.

CALHOUN, WILLIAM L.   33

History of the 42nd Regiment, Georgia Volunteers. [*Atlanta* 1900]. O 46 port a

CALHOUN COUNTY [MICH.]   34

Calhoun county [Mich.] business directory for 1869–70 . . . historical sketch . . . *Battle Creek* Rust 1869. O 425 fold.map aa

CALIFORNIA 35
An account of California and the wonderful gold regions. *B* [1849]. O 32 c Hn S Y
Not seriously informative. Possibly compiled by the publisher, J. B. Hall; whoever wrote it had never been to California.

Adventures in California . . . *See* Huntley, Sir Henry V.

All about California . . . *S F* 1870. O 96 + 36 advs a
—ed. 2, same impr. & date. O 64 [16] + 30 adv-p map
—other eds., same impr.: 1871; 1875.
Written in part by John S. Hittell.

Alta California embracing notices of the 37 climate . . . of northern Mexico and the Pacific seaboard; also, a history of . . . operations of the United States . . . 1846–7. By a Captain of Volunteers. *Phil* 1847. O 64 aa

The bonanza mines . . . of California . . . *See* Dewey, Squire P.

California and her gold regions, compiled from the best sources. *See* Duganne, Augustine J. H.

California characters, and mining scenes . . . By Whittlestick. *See* Williston, H. C.

California Crusoe [The]; or, the lost treasure found. *See* Richards, R.

California, dess Klimat, och Guldminor, 38 jemte räd for utvandrare . . . [Wrapper title: Californien en skildring . . .]. *Stockh* 1850. D 205map pl a
A Swedish version of Edwin Bryant's *What I saw in California.*

California, from its Discovery. By a traveller. 1848. *See* Kells, C. E.

California gold regions . . . how to get there 39 and what to take . . . *B* [1849]. O 48 b
—other issues, *N Y* and other cities. b
Probably compiled by the publisher, F. M. Pratt.

California guide book (The); comprising 40 Col. Fremont's Geographical account . . . Major Emory's Overland journey . . . *N Y* 1849. O 30 3–83 186 2maps aa
—for anr. issue of a part of this, *see* below, "Notes of travel in California . . ."

California illustrated . . . By a returned Californian. *See* Letts, J. M.

California, its characteristics and prospects . . . *See* Bushnell, Horace.

California: its gold and its inhabitants. 2v. 1856. *See* Huntley, Sir Henry V.

California: its past history; its present position; [etc.]. *See* Fleming, G. A.

California: its present condition and future 41 prospects, with . . . account of the gold regions. By a scientific gentleman . . . resident in California. *Adelaide Australia* 1850. O 52 [4] aa

California: its situation and resources . . . 42 *L* 1849. O 32 a

California sketches, with recollections of the gold mines. *See* Kip, Leonard.

California und seine Goldminen . . . *Kreuz-* 43 *nach* 1849. O 32 aa

Coleccion de articulos con respecto a Cali- 44 **fornia:** *Santiago Chile* 1849. O 28 b Hn one copy known

Coleccion de los principales trabajos en 45 **que se ha ocupado la junta nombrado para meditar y proponer** . . . **los medios** . . . **para promover el progreso de la cultura y civilizacion de los territorios de la Alta y de la Baja California.** [*Mex*] 1827. D 7pts in 1: "Dictamen," 16p; "Arreglo de las missiones," 11p; "Colonizacion estrangera," 8p chart; "Colonizacion de nacionales," 18p 3tabs; "Plan politico mercantil," 14p; "Proyecto para el establecimiento de una compania de comercia . . . cuyo punto centrico debe ser Monterey," 14p; "Iniciativa del ley . . . para el major arreglo del gobierno de los territorios de Californias," 44p. d B Hn Y
Covers the ambitious grand strategy of the Junta de Fomento de Californias looking to California colonization and the establishing at Monterey of a commercial capital to dominate the whole Pacific trade.

Diario historico de los viages . . . **hechos al norte de la California:** *Mex* 1770. *See* Constansó, Miguel

Disputatio geographica de vero Californiae . . . *See* Gmelin, Johan G.

The emigrant's guide to California: . . . 46 Also some useful information for . . . overland travellers through Texas . . . By a traveller recently returned from California. *L* Pelham Richardson [*ca* 1850]. O 65 [13] map b G Y
Miscellaneous information compiled, probably by the publisher, from various sources, but basically a piratical translation of Schmolder's *Wegweiser für Auswanderer, q.v.* For a re-translation into German, *see* below *Californien. Der Führer für Auswanderer nach:*

Exploits of the Attorney-General in Cali- 47
fornia: *N Y* 1860. O 30 aa
Criticizes United States Attorney-General
Black's conduct in handling California land claims.

From England to California: Life among 48
the Mormons and Indians ... *Sacr* 1868. D 146
c B only copy located.

From ocean to ocean ... diary of a three month's
expedition from Liverpool to California: ... *See*
Flowers, R. W.

From the Clyde to California: *See* Aitken, James.

Gids naar California: Bevattende een ver- 49
slag van de luchtstreek ... *Amst* 1849. D 38 map aa

The gold regions of California: ... *L* 50
Baily [1849]. O 79 map aa

Guide to the gold regions of California: ... 51
L 1850. 18° 36 aa

An historical journal of the expedition ... to
the north of California: *L* 1790. *See* Costansó,
Miguel.

Historia Cristiana de la California: *See* under
Californie.

Laws for the better government of California: 52
S F 1848. O 68 dd CalS Hn [only copies known].
Regulations imposed on this Territory under
American military occupation and first English
book printed there; nearly all copies destroyed.

Life in California: By an American. 1846. *See*
Robinson, Alfred.

Message from the President ... on the sub- 53
ject of California and New Mexico: [H. Exec. Doc.
17]. *Wash* 1850. O 977 maps a

Misrepresentations of early California 54
history, corrected ... *S F* 1894. O 37a
Issued by the Society of California Pioneers in
remonstrance to unpalatable truths contained in
H. H. Bancroft's histories.

Mysteries of California: Being an accurate 55
journal of one who has seen the elephant. *Syracuse*
1850. O 52 b

Northern California, Scott and Klamath rivers
... By a practical miner. *See* Metlar, George W.

Notes of travel in California: ... *N Y* 1849. 56
O [30, incl map] 3–83 a
—Eng. eds.: *L* 1849. O 312; *Dub* 1849. D; *L* 1856.
D 2v

Made from Fremont's and Emory's reports. For
another, enlarged issue, *see* above, *California guide
book* ...

Notes on California and the Placers: ... By one
who has been there. *See* Delavan, James.

Outline history of an expedition to California: ...
See Baker, S.

Pictorial view of California: *See* Letts, J. M.

Reglamento para la Compañia Cosmopolitan 56a
Protectora de la Industria en la Alta California:
Mex 1834. D 59 b

Reglamento provisional para el gobierno 57
interior de la ecma. diputacion territorial de la Alta
California: *Monterey* Zamorano 1834. 16° 18 aa
First book printed in California; the only
earlier printing was a broadside—from the same
press and with the same date—*Aviso al publico.*

The shortest route to California: illustrated 58
by a history of explorations of the great basin of
Utah ... *Phil* 1869. O 58 aa

A sketch of the route to California, China 59
and Japan via the Isthmus of Panama ... *S F*
1867. D 105 aa

The Volcano diggings; a tale of California law:
By a member of the bar. *See* Kip, Leonard.

CALIFORNIAE SITU ET CONDITIONE.
Disputatio geographica de vero: *See* Gmelin,
Johan G.

CALIFORNIAS
Noticias de la provincia de Californias: ... *See*
Sales, Luis.

Reglamento para el gobierno de la provincia 60
de Californias: *Mex* 1784. F [2] 38 d N NYP
—ed 2 *Mex* 1838. O [4] 297 [38] b
—rptd. *Santa Clara* 1874. O 68 all but 6 copies
burned c
—Eng. tr. & original Sp. text, *S F* Grabhorn 1929.
O 2v: [2] 57; [2] 62 aa 300 cops ptd.
This *Reglamento* remained in force until Mexico
became independent. It embodied for the first time
laws governing Upper California.

CALIFORNIE 61
Histoire Chrétienne de la Californie: Par ...
la Comtesse de ... *Plancy* 1851. D [2] 289 [2] 2pls
aa
—Sp. tr. *Mex* 1864. D 238 5pls a

Voyage en Californie: 1850-1 ... *See* Saint-
Amant, Pierre Ch. de.

CALIFORNIEN   62
Almanach Californien: guide . . . pour tout le monde sur la Californie . . . *P* Martimon [1850]. 16° 160 aa

Authentische Nachrichten über Californien   63
und dessen gold reichthum . . . *Bremen* 1849. D 24 map aa
—Swed tr—see next entry.

Beretning om Californien og dets Guldrig-   64
dom. *Christiania* 1849. 16° 125 map a

Californien, dessen Minen, Ackerbau,   65
Handel und Gewerbe . . . *N Y* 1851. 16° 32 a

Californien en skildring . . .
See California, dess Klimat, och Guldminor . . .

Der Führer für Auswanderer nach Califor-   66
nien: *Leip* 1849. D [16] 88 map pl a
For prior English edition, *see* above, *California. The emigrant's guide to:*

Nachrichten von der amerikanischen Halbinsel Californien. *See* Bägert, Jacob.

Rathgeber für auswanderer nach Californien: *See* Uhlenhuth, E.

CALL, RICHARD E.   67
The life and writings of Rafinesque. *Louisv* 1895. Q [12] 227 2pls 3facs a

CALLAHAN, JAMES M.   68
The diplomatic history of the southern Confederacy. *Balt* 1901. O 304 a

CALLAO TO SAN FRANCISCO.
Journal of a voyage from: By Long Tom. *See* Downes, S. T.

[CALLENDER, JAMES T.]   69
The American annual register, or historical memoirs of the United States, for . . . 1796. *Phil* 1797 O [8] 288 a
—rptd., "The history of the United States for 1796 . . .," same impr. and date O [8] 312 [Also issued in 8 weekly nos.]
Chapters 5 and 6, charging him with financial dishonesty, forced Hamilton to issue his "Reynolds pamphlet."

CALLENDER, [JAMES] T.?   70
Letters to Alexander Hamilton, king of the Feds . . . *N Y* 1802. O 64 a
—rptd. *N Y* 1866. O [4] 89 60copies ptd[20 on L.P.]

CALLENDER, JAMES T.   71
The political register. Vol. I in 2 pts [all]. *Phil* 1795. O [8] 549 a

[CALLENDER, JAMES T.]   72
The prospect before us . . . *Rich* 1800–01. O 3pts in 2v: 184; 152; 96 a

CALLENDER (JAMES T.)   73
Trial of: for sedition . . . [capt. t. only] n.p. [*Rich*?] n.d. [1800?]. O 76 a

CALLENDER, JOHN   74
An historical discourse on . . . affairs of the colony of Rhode Island . . . *B* 1739. O [16] 121 aa
—ed. 2, enl. [in R. I. Hist. Colls., V. 4] *Prov* 1838. O 270 [2] a
—ed. 3, "The early history of Rhode Island". *B* 1843. O 270 facs

CALLISON, JOHN J.   74a
Bill Jones of Paradise Valley, Oklahoma; his life and adventures for over forty years in the great southwest . . . [*Chi* 1914]. D 328 front a

CALM ADDRESS (A)
Calm address (A) to the people of the eastern states. By the author of the Olive Branch . . . *See* Carey, Mathew.

CALVIN, MARTIN V.   75
Augusta [Ga.] directory, for 1865–6. Containing a . . . history . . . *Augusta* 1865. O 98 aa

CAMAC, TURNER   76
Facts and arguments respecting the great utility of an extensive plan of inland navigation in America. *Phil* 1805. O 61 map a

CAMACHO, SEBASTIEN   77
Memoria de los ramos del Ministerio de Relaciones Interiores y Esteriores de la Republica . . . *Mex* 1826. Q 33 + errata p b
Organization of California missions, Indian troubles, etc. Wrapper title only.

CAMBRAY, LOUIS-MARIE-JOSEPH   78
Réminiscences . . . d'un ancien chirurgien de corsaires . . . pendant les années 1800–1803. *Cambrai* 1856. O 200 a
Describes a visit to New Orleans.

CAMBRIDGEPORT AND EAST CAMBRIDGE.
Two hundred years ago; or, a brief history of: By S. S. S. *See* Simpson, S. S.

CAMDEN (CHARLES).   79
Autobiography of: . . . *S F* 1916. O 173 port pls 50copies ptd. aa
Includes California experiences, 1849–50.

[CAMM, JOHN]   80
A review of The rector detected, or, the colonel reconnoitred. Pt I [all] *Wmsbg* 1764. O 29 aa
For book reviewed see Carter, Langdon.

CAMP, CHARLES L. [ed.]   **81**
James Clyman, American frontiersman. *S F* 1928. O [6, incl. port on verso of 1/2 t.] 9–251 3maps port b MontH N OreH NYP Y
—rptd. with considerable adds. *Port Ore* 1960. O 400 17maps & pls 1000 cops ptd aa
One of the most trustworthy narratives of the far west, for the period 1842–6; the only Oregon overland journal of 1844.

CAMP, MORTIMER M.   **82**
Life and adventures of a New England boy. *N Hav* [1893]. D 129 pls aa

CAMPAÑA   **83**
Campaña contra los Americanos del Norte . . . por un official de infanteria. Pt I [all]. *Mex* 1846. O 48[incl. 5tabs on 8p] 2plans aa
Criticizes Arista and other commanders for military ineptitude along the Rio Grande and at Palo Alto and Resaca de la Palma.

CAMPANIUS HOLM, TOMAS   **84**
Kort beskrifning om Provincien Nya Swerige [etc.]. *Stockh* 1702. Q [14 incl. eng. t-p] 190 [2] 7maps & pls b AA N NYP Y
—Eng. tr. "Description of New Sweden . . .," *Phil* 1834. O [6] 5–166 5maps & pls a
Best early account of settlements on the Delaware. The author, never in America, got information from settlers.

CAMPBELL, A.   **85**
A glance at Illinois . . . *La Salle Ill* 1856. O 32 a

[CAMPBELL, ALBERT H., et al]   **86**
. . . Reports upon the Pacific wagon roads . . . [*Wash* 1859]. O 125 6maps aa
Issued both as House Executive Document 108 and as Senate Executive Document 36; former has priority.

CAMPBELL, ALEXANDER   **87**
Delusions! An analysis of the book of Mormon. *B* 1832. O 24 aa
—Eng. ed. "Mormonism weighed in the balances . . ." *L* [1850]. same collat a

CAMPBELL, ARCHIBALD   **88**
A voyage round the world . . . *Edin* 1816. O 288 map aa
—Am. eds.: *N Y* 1817. D map; *N Y* 1819. D 219 map; *Charleston S C* 1822. D; *Roxbury* 1825. D map a
—Dutch tr. *Amst* 1818. O
—Ger. tr. *Jena* 1817. O 162
Includes adventures on the Northwest coast.

CAMPBELL, CHARLES   **89**
History of . . . Virginia. *Phil* 1860. O [2] 11–765 a

CAMPBELL, CHARLES   **90**
Introduction to the history of . . . Virginia. *Rich* 1847. O 200 [8] a

CAMPBELL, G. L.
A relation . . . of a late expedition to the gates of St. Augustine . . . *See* Kimber, Edw.

CAMPBELL, SIR GEORGE   **91**
White and black. The outcome of a visit to the United States. *L* 1879. O [18] 442 [40] a
—Am. ed. *N Y* 1879. O [18] 420

CAMPBELL, JAMES Y.   **92**
History of Anderson county [Kas.]. [*Garnett Kas* 1876?]. O 40 a

[CAMPBELL, JOHN] LL.D.   **93**
A concise history of the Spanish America . . . *L* 1741. O [12] 330 a some copies on L.P. aa
—rptd. "A complete history of Spanish America . . .," *L* 1742. same collat. aa
—anr. ed. "The Spanish Empire in America . . .," *L* 1747. O [12] 330 aa
—best ed., with adds., "An account of the Spanish settlements in America . . .," *Edin* 1762. O [16] 512 map aa
—Dutch trs.: *Amst* 1745–6; *Amst* 1750. a

CAMPBELL, JOHN, LL.D.   **94**
Lives of the admirals and other eminent British seamen . . . *L* 1742–4. O 4v aa
—ed. 2, rev. & enl., *L* 1750. O 4v: [4] 543; [2] 476 [24]; 488; [2] 453 [16] aa
—several later eds.

CAMPBELL, JOHN A.   **95**
Recollections of the evacuation of Richmond. *Balt* 1880. O 27 a

CAMPBELL, JOHN A.   **96**
Reminiscences . . . relating to the civil war during 1865. *Balt* 1887. O 68 a

CAMPBELL, J[OHN] L.   **97**
Idaho: six months in the new gold diggings . . . *Chi* 1864. O 62[incl.advs] + [2 add. adv-p] map d Hn Pn
—anr. issue, with *N Y* impr., O 52 + 14adv-p map c N Y
—anr. ed. "Idaho and Montana gold regions . . .," *Chi* 1865. D [6] 6–52 [16] + 15 adv-p interspersed, map ptd on verso of t-p, no copyr. notice at foot of t-p c Hn Y
—same, anr. issue, with copyr. notice on t-p b
—anr. ed. "Great agricultural and mineral west . . .," *Chi* 1866. O 22adv-p [4] 15–78 + 22 adv-p map b Y
—anr. ed. *Chi* Western News Co [1867]. 16° 98 b
Campbell's industry also produced a twelve-page traveller's guide to the Idaho and Colorado

mines, with two maps, Chicago 1864. Some copies of the first edition have Chicago imprint on wrappers, others give New York imprint. Editons listed above do not exhaust the bewildering variants.

[CAMPBELL, JOHN P.]　　　　　　　　　98
The passenger; or a religious ramble through Kentucky and Ohio. *Lex* 1804. D 2pts in 1: 20; 22 b N PresbyH[only cops loc]

[CAMPBELL, JOHN P.] ed.　　　　　　　99
The southern business directory . . . Vol. I [all]. *Charleston S C* 1854. O 404 173 a

CAMPBELL, J[OHN] W.　　　　　　　　100
A history of Virginia . . . *Phil* [1813]. D 310 a
—anr. ed. *Petersburg Va* 1813, same collat.

CAMPBELL, P[ATRICK]　　　　　　　　101
Travels in the interior inhabited parts of North America . . . 1791–2 . . . *Edin* 1793. O [10] 388 3pls tab c AA N NYP Y
—rptd. *Tor* Champlain Soc. 1937. O [22] 326 [12] pls 550copies ptd. aa

CAMPBELL, WILLIAM PARKER　　　　102
The escape and wanderings of John Wilkes Booth, until ending of the trail by suicide in Oklahoma . . . *Okla C* [1922]. D [6] 142 aa
—some copies have a leaf, p. 143–4, added. aa

CAMPBELL, WILLIAM W.　　　　　　103
Annals of Tryon county . . . border warfare of New York during the revolution . . . *N Y* 1831. O 191 [78] map facs a
—ed. 2, "The border warfare of New York . . .," *N Y* 1849. D 396 map a
—rptd. *Cherry Valley* 1880.

CAMPER, CHARLES, and　　　　　　　104
KIRKLEY, J. W.
Historical record of the First Regiment Maryland Infantry . . . *Wash* 1871. D [10] 312 a

CAMPION, J. S.　　　　　　　　　　105
On the frontier . . . *L* 1878. O [16] 372 [incl. 8pls] a
—ed. 2, same impr., date & collat.

CANADA　　　　　　　　　　　　　106
The four kings of Canada: . . . lately arriv'd from North America . . . description of their country . . . *L* 1710. O 47 b N
—abr. ed. *Wakefield* [ca 1800]. O 8 a
These were Iroquois chiefs taken to London by Col. Schuyler of Albany. Portraits of these sachems engraved contemporaneously at London in folio, did not form a part of this account.

A letter from a Romish priest in Canada to one who was taken captive . . . *See* Burnet, Wm.

Mission du Canada: relations inédites . . . *See* Martin, Felix, and Montezon, F. de.

Notes upon the south western boundary line of Lower Canada and New Brunswick. . . . and the United States . . . *See* Stuart, Andrew.

On the origin and progress of the North West Company of Canada: . . . *See* Atcheson, Nathaniel.

Relation des affaires du Canada: en 1696,　107
et des missions des Peres de la Compagnie de Jesus jusqu'en 1702. *N Y* 1865. O 42 aa
—enl. ed. *N Y* 1865. O 73 100copies ptd.
Forms Number 19 of Shea's "Cramoisy series." Includes letters by Jesuit missionaries written from Detroit and Illinois.

Succinct account of the treaties . . . relating to the boundary line between . . . Lower Canada and New Brunswick and the United States . . . *See* Stuart, Andrew.

A tour through Upper and Lower Canada. By a citizen of the United States. *See* Ogden, John C.

Voyage au Canada: Par J.C.B. See B., J.C.

CANAJOHARY
Canajohary und Palatine, an der Mohawk-Rivier. Handbuch für meine Freunde in den Districten von: *See* Runckler, Seb.

CANDID . . .　　　　　　　　　　　108
Candid and impartial considerations on the preliminary articles of peace with France and Spain, and the provisional treaty with the United States. By a country gentleman. *L* 1783. O [2] 53 a

Candid examination (A) of the mutual claims of Great Britain, and the colonies . . . *See* Galloway, Jos.

Candid examination (A) of the objections to the treaty . . . between the United States and Great Britain . . . *See* Smith, Wm. L.

Candid retrospect (The): or, the American war examined . . . *See* Smith, Wm., Jr.

Candid thoughts; or, an enquiry into the　109
causes of national discontents . . . since the commencement of the present reign. *L* 1781. O 73 aa
Accuses the colonies of filial ingratitude, asserts that their taxation was just and expedient, that the war, unavoidable and necessary, was bungled by Lord North's timidity and General Howe's incapacity, dissipation and treachery.

[CANDLER, ISAAC]　　　　　　　　　110
A summary view of America . . . the result of

observations . . . during a journey in the United States. *L* 1824. O [8] 503 a
Travelled down the coast to No. Carolina.

CANFIELD, CHAUNCEY L., ed.   111
The diary of a forty-niner. *N Y* and *S F* 1906. O [22 incl. map] 231 a
—rptd. *B* 1920. D [18 incl. map] 253

CANFIELD, T. H. [comp.]   112
Business directory of . . . Oswego, Labette county, Kansas, containing a history of the town [etc.]. *Oswego* 1870. O 32 map aa

CANFIELD (THOMAS H.)   113
Life of: . . . *Burl Vt* [ptd in Chi] 1889. Q 48 port aa

CANFIELD, THOMAS H.   114
Northern Pacific railroad; partial report . . . of the reconnoissance . . . between lake Superior and the Pacific . . . [*N Y?*] 1870 O 96, 44 2maps b G NYP WashU Y
Printed for distribution to directors only, presenting facts and operations which at the time it was inadvisable to make public.

CANNON, GEORGE Q.   115
Writings from the "Western Standard" . . . *Liv* 1864. O [16] 512 aa
Selections recording important Mormon events of 1856 and 1857.

CANNON, J. P.   116
Inside of rebeldom. *Wash* 1899. O 288 [incl. front.] a
—rptd. same impr. 1900.

CANO, GABRIEL DE CARDENAS Z.
Ensayo cronologico . . . See Barcia Carballido y Zuñiga, author's real name.

CANOVA, ANDREW P.   117
Life and adventures in south Florida. *Palatka* 1885. O 186 aa
—rptd. *Tampa* 1906. D 160 port a

CANTON, FRANK M.   118
Frontier trails . . . *B* 1930. D [18] 237 12pls a

CANTONWINE, ALEXANDER   119
Star forty-five, Oklahoma . . . [*Okla City*] 1911. O 334 front. a

CANTRELL, OSCAR A.   120
Sketches of the First Regiment Georgia Volunteers . . . *Atlanta* 1864. O 73 b Duke Emory [only cops loc]

CAPE BRETON
An accurate journal . . . during the late expedition against Cape Breton. See Pepperell, Sir William.

The great importance of Cape Breton dem-   121
onstrated . . . With the reasons that induced the people of New England to subdue this . . . rival . . *L* 1746. O [8] 72 2maps [on 1 sheet] b

The importance and advantage of Cape Breton truly stated . . . *See* Bollan, Wm.

The importance of Cape Breton consider'd;   122
in a letter . . . from an inhabitant of New England. *L* 1747. O [2] 73 aa

CAPELLINI (G[IOVANNI]).   123
Relazione di un viaggio scientifico fatto . . . nell' America settentrionale dal: *Bologna* 1864. O 44 map a
—enl. ed., "Ricordo di un viaggio . . ." same impr 1867. D [12] 279 + 3adv-p

[CAPEN, NAHUM?]   124
The republic of the United States; its duties . . . Embracing also a review of the late war between the United States and Mexico . . . *N Y* 1848. O [12] 322 a
Ascribed also to David Henshaw.

CAPERS, HENRY D.   125
The life and times of C. G. Memminger. *Rich* 1893. O 604 pls a
Best account of the Confederacy's finances; also brings out the growth of secession thought from 1832 to the formation of the Confederacy.

CAPERS, HENRY D.   126
Recollections of the civil service of the Confederate government. Pt. 1[all]. *Atlanta* 1887. O 48 a
Account of frenzied finance in the Confederacy, by the Chief Clerk of its Treasury Department.

CAPITULATION (THE)
Capitulation (The); or, a history of the expedition conducted by William Hull . . . By an Ohio volunteer. *See* Foster, James.

CAPRON, E[LISHA] S.   127
History of California . . . *B* 1854. D [12] 356 map a

CARAMAN, GEORGES J. V. R., comte de   128
Les États-Unis il y a quarante ans. *P* 1852–4. O 54 31 30 20 a
Reprinted from the *Revue contemporaine*. The author accompanied the French minister to this country in 1811.

CARAYON, AUGUSTE   129
Bannissement des Jésuites de la Louisiane . . . *P* 1865. O [12] 136 a

CARDELLE, CARA [comp.]
Letters from an early settler of Texas. *See* Dewees, Wm. B.

CARDENAS Z CANO, GABRIEL DE
Ensayo cronologico, para la historia general de la Florida. *See* Barcia Carballido y Zuniga, Andrés González [from which Cardenas z Cano was anagrammatically formed].

CARDOZO, JACOB N.   130
A plan of financial relief . . . *Atlanta* 1863. O 37 a

CARDOZO, J[ACOB] N.   131
Reminiscences of Charleston. *Charleston S C* 1866. D 144 a

CAREW (MR. BAMFYLDE MOORE).   132
The life and adventures of: . . . with his travels twice through . . . America. *L* 1745. D 240 b
—anr. ed. *Exeter, Eng.* 1745. D [6, incl port] 152 aa
—rptd. "An apology for the life of Mr. Bamfylde Moore Carew". *L* [1749] D 149 a
—later Eng. eds. too numerous to list.
—Am. eds. *Phil* 1773; 1827. a
For misdemeanors in his native England this inveterate rogue was transported to Maryland, escaped and operated confidence games among colonial suckers from Virginia to Connecticut, — the memorable first of a long line of such artists who have continued to flourish in this climate. His purported autobiography appears to have been written by either Robert Goadby or his wife.

CAREY, HENRY C. AND LEA, J. [pubs]   133
A complete historical . . . American atlas . . . *Phil* 1822. F [6] 118 lvs [incl 46 maps + 2pls] aa
—rptd, same no of maps and pls, *Phil* 1823; 1825; 1827 aa
—Eng ed., abr. "The geography, etc. of America." *L* 1823. O 447 18maps and pls
—Fr tr, "Atlas géographique . . ." *P* 1825. [18] 125lvs [incl 63 maps and pls] aa
—Ger tr, "Atlas von America . . ." *Weimar* 1824–9. F [2] 45 maps [pub'd separately] aa

[CAREY, JOHN L.]   134
Some thoughts concerning domestic slavery . . . *Balt* 1838. 18° [2] 5–115 a
—ed. 2, au. named, *Balt* 1839. same collat.

CAREY, MATHEW [pub.]   135
American atlas. *Phil* 1795. F [2] 21maps b AA LC
—rptd., same impr. & collat, 1800. same impr. 1805. F [2] 21maps aa
—anr. ed. *Phil* 1809. F [2] 26maps aa
First American atlas printed in the United States; maps were first engraved for the American edition of Guthrie's *Geography*, Phil 1794. *Cf.* Reid, John, *The American atlas.*

CAREY, MATHEW   136
American minor atlas. *Phil* 1806. O [2] 20maps a

CAREY, MATHEW   137
American pocket atlas . . . *Phil* 1796. D 118 + starred dupl. p13–16 19maps aa
—ed. 2, enl., *Phil* 1801. D [8] 114 19maps fold.tab a
—ed. 3, *Phil* 1805. D [4] 114 20maps tab
—ed. 4, *Phil* 1814. D [4] 168 23maps 2fold. tabs [some copies dated 1813]

[CAREY, MATHEW] ed.   138
The American remembrancer . . . essays, [etc.] relative . . . to the treaty with Great Britain. *Phil* 1795–6. O 12nos. in 3v: 288; 288; 312 a

CAREY, MATHEW   139
Autobiographical sketches: containing a view of the rise and progress of the American system. Vol. I[all]. *Phil* [1829]. D [16] 156 a

[CAREY, MATHEW]   140
Essay on railroads. [*Phil* 1830]? O 26 [incl.diags] caption t. only a

CAREY, MATHEW   141
Essays on political economy . . . applied particularly to the United States. *Phil* 1822. O [14] 10–546 [10] a

[CAREY, MATHEW]   142
Thirteen essays on the policy of manufacturing in this country . . . *Phil* 1830. O [2] 30 a

[CAREY, T. J.]   143
Klondike and all about it. *N Y* 1896. D 144 map diag. a
—rptd. [*ca* 1897].

[CAREY, THOMAS] comp.   144
History of the pirates . . . *Haverhill* 1825. D 276 front aa
—rptd. *N Y* 1827; *Hart* 1827 a
—oth *Hart* eds.: 1829; 1834; 1835
—enl ed., events to 1835. *Hart* [1836] D 298 [incl front] 7pls
—later eds.: *Hart* 1850; *Hart* 1855; *N Y* 1860
An earlier edition may have appeared at Norwich 1814. For similar compilations — based as is this on Johnson's classic on the subject — see Ellms, *The history of the pirates* and *History and lives of the . . . pirates.*

[CARLET, JOSEPH A.]   145
Quelques considérations sur l'Amérique. *P* 1823. O 28 a

CARLETON (GENERAL SIR GUY).
A list of the officers serving . . . under the command of: *See* Rivington, James.

CARLETON, JAMES H.   146
The prairie log books. [Dragoon campaigns in 1844–5 to the Pawnee country and Rocky mountains]. *Chi* 1943. O [18] 295 map 350cops ptd a

CARLETON, JAMES H.   147
Report on . . . the massacre at Mountain Meadows, in Utah . . . *Little Rock* True Democrat 1860. O 32 c G Pn S Y [only copies known]
—anr. issue, with "Senate document" on t-p & impr. of ohnson [*sic*] and Yerkes. c ArkU KasU [only cops loc]
—rptd. H. R. 605, *Wash* 1902. O 17 a
—anr ed *Little Rock* 1889 O 24 a
Full account of this inhuman holocaust, in which perished at Mormon hands over 125 California-bound emigrants from Arkansas and Missouri. *See* also entry under Mountain Meadows.

CARLETON, LATHAM C.   148
Texas Joe: or, army life on the frontiers. *N Y* [1868]. D 100 pl a

CARLETON, ROBERT [pseud.]
The new purchase . . . *See* Hall, Baynard R.

[CARLI, COMTE GIOVANNI R.]   149
Delle lettere Americane. *Cosmopoli* 1780. 16° 2v: 275 [8]; 318 [10] a
—enl. ed. *Cremona* 1781–3. O 3v: [32] 232; [8] 269; [10] 214 [3]
—Fr. ed. "Lettres américaines . . .," *B & P* 1788. [actually ptd at *P*]. O 2v: [24] 520; [6] 536. map
—rptd. *P* 1792. O 2v map
—Ger. ed. "Briefe über Amerika," *Gera* 1785. D 3v: 468; 502; 368. map
—Sp. ed. "Les cartas Americanas," *Mex* 1821–2. Q 3v
Confutes de Pauw's *Recherches* . . . *sur les Américains*, and ascribes the origin of the American natives to the Atlantides.

CARLIER, AUGUSTE   150
De l'esclavage dans ses rapports avec l'union américaine. *P* 1862. O [16] 495 a

CARLIER, AUGUSTE   151
Histoire du peuple américain . . . et de ses rapports avec les Indiens . . . jusqu'a la révolution . . . *P* 1864. O 2v: [32] 456 [1]; [4] 512 [1] a

CARLISLE, EARL OF, CLINTON, SIR HENRY, et al   152
Letters and other papers relating to the proceedings of His Majesty's Commissioners . . . to treat . . . upon the means of quieting the disorders . . . in certain of the colonies . . . [*N Y*] Rivington [1778]. O 58 b NYP Y

CARMICHAEL, JOHN   153
A self-defensive war lawful, proved in a sermon . . . before Captain Ross's company of militia . . . *Phil* 1775. O 34 a
—anr. ed. *Lancaster* [1775].

CARMICHAEL, MARY H., comp.   154
Pioneer days. *N Y* 1917. D [12] 196 7pls a

CARO, RAMÓN M.   155
Verdadera idea de la primera campaña de Tejas . . . despues de la acción de San Jacinto. *Mex* 1837. O [8] 162 b H N Y
By Santa Anna's secretary; contains that officer's official report of this campaign. In reliability as a contemporary Mexican source on the Texas revolution ranks with Filisola's *Memorias*; it is highly critical of Santa Anna.

CAROLINA
An account of the province of Carolina: . . . *See* Wilson, Samuel.

Allerneuste Beschreibung der Carolina . . .: *Hamburg* 1712. *See* Lawson, John.

Ausführlich- und umständlicher Bericht von Carolina . . . *See* Kocherthal, Joshua.

Carolina described more fully than heretofore . . . **from the several relations of that place** . . .   156
Dub 1684. O 56 Hn NYP [of 4 cops loc] c

Carolina in the olden time. By the octogenarian lady . . . *See* Poyas, Mrs. Eliz. A.

The case of protestant dissenters in Carolina: . . . *See* Defoe, Dan'l.

Neue Nachricht alter und neuer Merckwurdig-keiten . . . **von der Landschafft Carolina** . . .   157
Zurich 1734. O 80 aa

Nouvelle relation de la Caroline: par un gentilhomme françois . . . *Hague* [1686]. D 36 c JCB MassH   158

Nummehro (Der) in den Neuen Welt . . . **Beschreibung des gegenwärtigen Zustande der** . . . **Provinz Carolina.** *Bern* 1734. O 46 aa   159

Party-tyranny . . . **as now practised in Carolina:** *See* Defoe, Danl.

The present state of Carolina: with advice to the setlers. By R. F. *L* 1682. Q 36 c Hn[only copy located]   160

CARPENTER, HERMAN   161
Three years in Alaska. *Phil* [1901]. D 105 a

CARPENTER, L[EWIS] C.   162
Tourist's guide to Colorado . . . *Denver* 1879. D 80 a

CARPENTER, RUSSELL L.   163
Observations on American slavery, after a year's tour in the United States. *L* 1852. O [6] 69 a

[CARPENTER, STEPHEN C.] 164
Memoirs of the Hon. Thomas Jefferson . . .
[*N Y*] 1809. O 2v: [4] 404; [2] 434 a
Venomously critical; said to have been suppressed.

CARPENTER, S[TEPHEN] D. 165
Logic of history . . . Results of slavery agitation
and emancipation . . . with chapters on despotism,
usurpations and frauds. Ed. 2. *Madison Wis* 1864.
O [4] 351 aa
Voices the unregenerate Copperhead belief that
abolition Republicans strove to effect sectional
rupture and did not want the Union restored.

CARR, JOHN [of Tenn.] 166
Early times in middle Tennessee. *Nashv*, for
author, 1857. 16° 248 aa
—iss 2, *Nashv*, for E. Carr, 1857 aa
—rptd, *Nashv* 1958. O [6] 112 a

CARR, JOHN, 1827-96 167
Pioneer days in California. *Eureka Calif* 1891.
O [4] 11–452 port aa
—rptd. *Louisiana Mo* n.d. a

CARR, SPENCER 168
A brief sketch of La Crosse, Wisconsin. *La
Crosse* 1854. O 28 aa
—rptd. same impr. 1917. a
First La Crosse imprint.

CARRASCO Y GUISASOLA, 169
FRANCISCO, ed.
Documentos referentes al reconocimiento de la
costas de las Californias . . . *Madrid* 1882. O 2pts
[continuously paged] 214 aa
First publication of material on Viscaino's
explorations, 1584–1602.

CARREY, EDMOND, and 170
FRIGNET, ERNEST
États-Unis d'Amérique. Les états du north-west
et Chicago. *P* 1871. O 88 10pls aa
The plates—actual photos taken just before the
fire—are of great local importance.

CARRIGAN, MRS. WILHELMINA 171
Captured by the Indians . . . pioneer life in Minnesota. *Forest City S D* 1907. O [4] 3–42 pl aa
—rptd. [*Buffalo Lake Minn*] 1912. D 48 [20] a

CARRINGTON, FRANCES C. 172
My army life and the Fort Phil. Kearney massacre. *Phil* 1910. O 318 3maps 39pls a
—rptd., same impr. & collat., 1911.
By the second wife of General Carrington; her
first husband fell with Fetterman in the massacre.

CARRINGTON, HENRY B. 173
History of Indian operations on the plains . . .
[*Wash* 1881]. O 56 a
—rptd. same impr. & collat. 1887.

CARRINGTON, HENRY B. 174
The Indian question . . . *B* 1884. O 32 2maps a
—rptd. *B* 1909. O 32 2maps 2pls
Includes General Carrington's report on the
Fort Phil Kearney massacre.

[CARRINGTON, MRS. HENRY B.] 175
Absaraka, home of the Crows . . . experience of
an officer's wife on the plains . . . *Phil* 1868. D 284
map aa
—ed. 2, same impr. & collat., 1869. a
—ed. 3, enl., *Phil* 1878. D [20] 13–378 2maps 15pls
—four other eds. by 1896.
Editions after 1869 had variant sub-titles: i.e.,
"land of massacre" and "or, Wyoming opened."

[CARRINGTON, MRS. HENRY B.] 176
Ocean to ocean. The Pacific railroad and adjoining territories, with distances and fares . . . *Phil*
1869. 18° 32 map a
Usually attributed to Mrs. Carrington, but
probably by her husband.

CARROLL'S CLAIM 177
Carroll's (Miss Anna E.) claim before Congress,
in connection with the Tennessee campaign of
1862. [*Wash* 1873]. O 55 a
Asks remuneration for suggesting this decisive
plan.

CARROLL, B[ARTHOLOMEW] R., ed. 178
Historical collections of South Carolina. *N Y*
1836. O 2v: [82] 9–533; 576. map a

CARROLL (CHARLES, of Carrollton). 179
Journal of: during his visit to Canada in 1776 . . .
Balt 1845. O 84 a some copies on L.P. Q
—rptd. *Balt* 1876. O 110[incl.front.] port

CARROLL, GEORGE R. 180
Pioneer life in and around Cedar Rapids . . .
1839–1849. *Cedar Rapids* 1895. D [12] 251[incl.
pls] a

[CARROLL, MOTHER MARY A.] 181
A Catholic history of Alabama and the Floridas.
Vol. I[all]. *N Y* 1908. O 373 a

[CARSON, CHRISTOPHER] 182
Kit Carson's own story . . . Ed. Blanche C.
Grant. *Taos N M* 1926. O 138[incl.pls] + adv-p a
—rptd. "Kit Carson's autobiography," ed. M. M.
Quaife, *Chi* 1935. 16° [38] 192 port facs

CARSON (CHRISTOPHER).
The life and times of: . . . *See* Ellis, Edward S.

CARSON, J[AMES] H. 183
Early recollections of the mines . . . *Stockton*
1852. O 64 map[by Gibbes] c Hn N NYH
—rptd. *Oakland* 1950. O 113 2maps a 750 copies
ptd.

First book printed in Stockton, and only a few copies known. Called "second edition" on cover title because it had been issued previously as a newspaper supplement.

CARSON, THOMAS   **184**
Ranching, sport and travel . . . *L* 1911. O 320 [incl.front.] 15pls a
—Am. ed. [same sheets] *N Y* [1912?].

CARTA   **185**
Carta de un ciudadano Mexicano a un oficial del ejercito Norte-Americano . . . *Atlixco* 1847. D 28 aa

Cartas edificantes . . . *See Lettres edificantes* . . .

CARTER (E. S.)   **186**
The life and adventures of: . . . *St Joseph Mo* 1896. D 145 b N Y

CARTER, H. L.   **187**
A descriptive hand-book to the two lands of gold . . . Australia and California . . . *L* [1853]. D 38 aa

CARTER, HOWELL   **188**
A cavalryman's reminiscences of the civil war. *N O* [*ca* 1900]. D 212 [incl ports] a

CARTER, LANGDON   **189**
The rector detected . . . defense of the two-penny act . . . *Wmsbg* 1764. O 40 aa

CARTER, RICHARD   **190**
A short sketch of the author's life . . . *Versailles Ky* 1825. O 2pts in 1: 499 aa
Early Kentucky physician.

CARTER, ROBERT G.   **191**
Four brothers in blue. *Wash* 1913. O [14] 509 front and pl 100cops ptd aa

CARTER, ROBERT G.   **192**
The Mackenzie raid from Texas into Mexico. *Wash* 1919. O 63 a
Punitive chase of hostile Texas Indians by the Fourth Cavalry, in 1873, which didn't bother to halt at the international border.

CARTER, ROBERT G.   **193**
Massacre of Salt Creek prairie . . . *Wash* 1919. O 48 [incl wraps] aa

CARTER, ROBERT G.   **194**
The old sergeant's story; winning the west from the Indians and bad men . . . *N Y* 1926. O 220 8 pls a

CARTER, ROBERT G.   **195**
On the border with Mackenzie; or, winning west

Texas from the Comanches . . . *Wash* [1935]. O [18] 418 [2] 419–542 3ports a
—rptd. *N Y* 1961.

CARTER, ROBERT G.   **196**
On the trail of deserters . . . *Wash* 1920. O 60 a 250copies ptd.

CARTER, ROBERT G.   **197**
Pursuit of Kicking Bird . . . in the Texas "bad lands" . . . *Wash* 1920. O 44 100 copies ptd. aa

CARTER, ROBERT G.   **198**
Tragedies of Cañon Blanco; a story of the Texas panhandle . . . *Wash* 1919. O 97 port a

CARTER, W. A.   **199**
History of Fannin county, Texas. *Bonham* 1885. D 128 + 16adv-p a

CARTER, W. C., and GLOSS-   **200**
BRENNER, A. J.
History of York county [Pa.]. *York* 1834. D 183 [30] front. a

CARTER, WILLIAM   **201**
A genuine detail of the several engagements . . . during the years 1775 and 1776 . . . the blockade of Boston . . . *L* 1784. Q [2] 50 errata slip plan c BA N NYP Y
—ed. 2, same impr. & collat., with errata cor., 1785. b

CARTER, W[ILLIAM] H.   **202**
Old army sketches. *Balt* 1906. D 203 5pls a

CARTMELL, T[HOMAS] K.   **203**
Shenandoah valley pioneers . . . [*Winchester* 1909]. O [8] 587 20pls aa

CARTUYVELS, JEAN-LOIIS-U.   **204**
Aux émigrants belges. Colonie de St Marie . . . Pennsylvania. *St Trond* 1850. O 32 map aa

CARTWRIGHT, DAVID W.   **205**
Natural history of western wild animals . . . also, narratives of personal adventure . . . *Toledo* 1875. D [12] 280 19pls aa
—ed. 2, same collat., 1875. a

[CARTWRIGHT, JOHN]   **206**
American independence the interest and glory of Great Britain . . . *L* 1774. O [20] 72 a
—new ed., with adds., *L* 1775. O [22] 72 15 30 52 map aa
—Am. ed. *Phil* 1776. O 125 aa
Urges British recognition of American independence; the two countries then to form a union, beneficial to both. The 1775 edition, with map, suggested that when population warranted the region west of the Ohio should be subdivided into separate colonies.

[CARTWRIGHT, JOHN]   207
A letter to Edmund Burke . . . controverting the
principles of American government, laid down in
his . . . speech on American taxation . . . L 1775.
O 30 a
Separate printing of a portion of the additions
contained in the 1775 edition of his *American
independence* . . .

[CARTWRIGHT, JOHN]   208
The memorial of common sense, upon the pres-
ent crisis between Great Britain and America . . .
L 1778. O 29 a

CARTWRIGHT (PETER).   208a
Autobiography of: . . . *N Y* 1856. D 526 +
2adv-p port a
—rptd. 1857; and many times later.

CARTWRIGHT, W[ILLIAM] C.   209
Gustave Bergenroth . . . *Edin* 1870. D [16] 315 a
Contains his California experiences in 1850, including his formation of a motley crew of unsavory adventurers, one of whom was executed by
Vigilantes. Leaving California in 1851, he ultimately earned international fame as a scholar.

CARUTHERS, E[LI] W.   210
Revolutionary incidents . . . in the "Old North
State" [North Carolina]. Ser. 1 & 2. *Phil* 1854–6.
D 2v: 431; 448. 2maps pl a

CARUTHERS, E[LI] W.   211
A sketch of the life of the Rev. David Caldwell
. . . including . . . revolutionary transactions and
incidents . . . *Greensboro N C* 1842. O 302 [2] a

[CARUTHERS, WILLIAM A.]?   212
The lives of Sir Walter Raleigh and Capt. John
Smith with an account of the Governors of Virginia . . . *Shepherds'-Town*[now W. Va.] 1817. 16°
122 a

CARVALHO, S[OLOMON] N.   213
Incidents of travel and adventure in the far west:
with Col. Fremont's last expedition . . . *N Y & L*
1856. D [4] 7–380 earlier date than *N Y* ed., but
really formed from its sheets, with new t-p, and
with front. omitted. aa
—anr. ed. *N Y* 1857. same collat., with front. a
—anr. issue, same impr. & date. D [4] 250 130
front.[different one]
—rptd. 1858; 1859; 1860.
Carvalho accompanied Fremont's fourth expedition as artist. Preliminary pages five and six, containing dedication to Mrs. Fremont, were suppressed in all early editions.

CARVER, HARTWELL   214
Proposal for a charter to build a railroad from
lake Michigan to the Pacific ocean. *Wash* 1847.
O 38 aa

One of the earliest transcontinental projects,
with critical comments on the plans of Whitney
and Wilkes.

CARVER, JOHN [pseud.]
Sketches of New England . . . *See* Dodge, N. S.

CARVER, JONATHAN   215
Travels through the interior parts of North America . . . 1766–8. *L* 1778. O [20] 544 2maps4 pls aa
—rptd. *Dub* 1779. O [20] 508 map 2pls aa
—ed. 2, *L* 1779. O [24] 544 2maps 4pls [a 5th pl —
"tobacco plant" — found inserted in some cops
was not issued with this ed] aa
—ed. 3, *L* 1780. O [26] 543 port 2maps 5pls aa
—same, issue 2, [best ed.], with biog. & index
added, *L* 1781. O [10] 22 [24incl.blank lf] 544 [20]
port 2maps 5pls[4col.] b
—Am. & other Eng eds.: *Phil* 1784. O 217; 1789;
1792; 1794; *Portsmouth N H* 1794; *Phil* 1795;
1796; *B* 1797; *Edin* 1798. map; *Charlestown Mass*
1802; *Glas* 1805; *Edin* 1807; 1808; *Phil* 1812;
Walpole N H 1813; *N Y* 1838 [best Am. ed., being
rptd. from issue 2 of the *L* ed. of 1781, with new t.,
"Travels in Wisconsin"]. O 376 port 2maps 5pls;
Minneap 1956 O
—Dutch tr. *Leyden* 1796. O 2v: [28] 248; [4] 280
[16]. 6pls [4col.] map a
—Fr. tr. *P* 1784. O [24 28] 451 map; *Yverdon* 1784.
D [26] 436 a
—Ger. tr. *Hamburg* 1780. D [24] 456 map a
Carver penetrated farther into the West than any
other English explorer before the Revolution. Like
his French predecessor—Verendrye—he was seeking a transcontinental waterway, but, aside from
exploring some tributaries of the Mississippi, he
made no substantial contributions to geographical
knowledge; his book, however, stimulated curiosity concerning routes to the Pacific, later satisfied
by Mackenzie and Lewis and Clark. The tobacco
plant plate, added first to the third edition, is sometimes found inserted in copies of the first and
second editions. It belongs properly to neither.

CARVER (DR. WILLIAM F.)   215a
Life of: *B* 1878. D 177 b G LC
Captive for sixteen years with the Indians;
became the world's champion rifle shot.

[CARY, THOMAS G.]   216
Americans defended by an American . . . *L*
1844. O 38 a

CASE, C[HRISTOPHER] F.   216a
History and description of Lyon county [Minn.].
Marshall Minn 1884. O 98 map a

CASE   217
Case (The) and claim of the American loyalists
impartially stated and considered. [*L*] ptd. by order
of their agents 1783. O [2] 38 a
—anr. issue, *L* Wilkie 1783. same collat.

A 16-page pamphlet, *The particular case of the Georgia loyalists*, was issued at London in 1783 to accompany the above.

Case (A) decided in the Supreme Court of   217a the United States, February, 1793, in which was discussed the question "Whether a state be liable to be sued by a private citizen of another state?" *Phil* 1793. O [2] 120 [1] aa
—anr. ed. *B* 1793. O 80 a
In this suit, brought by Chisholm against the State of Georgia, was involved for the first time the problem of state sovereignty. The specific finding— that a State could be so sued—was of minor significance; it was ignored by the defendant, and, by a 1798 amendment, such suits were precluded. However, the "*obiter dicta*" assertion that State sovereignty was limited under the Constitution, had far-reaching implications of the greatest magnitude. It reversed the theory, hitherto unquestioned, that States were independent sovereign republics confederated for some purposes only, but not to the extent of affecting their sovereignty. Years of bitter argument had to pass until the arbitrament of arms handed down a final decision.

Case (The) of Great-Britain and America... *See* Bushe, Gervaise P.

Case [of William Trent and other traders   218 who were despoiled by the Indians near Fort Pitt in 1763]. [*L* 1770?]. Q 8 [24] capt.t. only b NYP
Cf. Wharton, Samuel, *View of the title to Indiana* ...

Case (The) stated on philosophical ground,   218a between Great Britain and her colonies ... *L* 1777. O [38] 130 a
—rptd. *L* 1778. O 166
Spirited argument favoring the plea of the colonies for independence.

CASEY, CHARLES   219
Two years on the farm of Uncle Sam ... *L* 1852. D [10] 311 a

CASLER, JOHN O.   219a
Four years in the Stonewall brigade. *Guthrie* 1893. D 495 fold.facs aa
—rptd: *Girard Kas* 1906. D 365 3ports[on 2sheets]; *Marietta Ga* 1951 a

CASLER, MELL[YER]   220
A journal ... of a journey to California in 1859, by the overland route ... *Toledo* 1863. D [4] 48 c Y [only copy known]

CASLO (ANTHONY).   220a
Life of: a Bonaparte soldier ... in the armies of France, Spain, England and the United States. *Det* 1856. O 76 a

CASS, LEWIS   221
A discourse ... at the first meeting of the Historical Society of Michigan. *Det* 1830. O 52 aa

[CASS, LEWIS]   221a
Inquiries respecting the history [etc.] of the Indians ... *Det* 1823. 16° 64 b AA Clem
Issued previously—about 1820—at Detroit in two separate pamphlets: *Inquiries ...*, and *Additional inquiries ...*

CASS (GENERAL LEWIS).   222
Life of: comprising ... services in the northwest ... *See* Nicholson, C.A.P.

CASS (GEN. LEWIS).
Outlines of the life ... of: *See* Schoolcraft, Henry R.

CASS.   222a
The county of: and the city of Fargo [N. D.]. A sketch, historical ... *Fargo* 1888. D 48 map a

CASSEDAY, BEN   223
The history of Louisville ... *Louisv* 1852. D 255 [38] map a

CASSLER, LAFAYETTE   223a
Thrilling experiences of frontier life in the early days of western Oklahoma. *Cin* [*ca* 1910?]. D 197 a

CASTAÑARES, MANUEL   224
Coleccion de documentos relativos al Departamento de Californias. *Mex* 1845. O 70 + wraps aa
Cover title dated 1846. Information on missions and the pious fund, Russian establishments, a gold discovery in 1843, &c.

CASTAÑEDA DE NÁGERA, PEDRO DE   224a
Relation du voyage de Cibola, entrepris en 1540 ... *P* 1838. O [20] 392 aa
Issued as volume IX, Termaux-Campan's first series of *Voyages, relations* ... First appearance in any language of the chief source on Coronado's expedition, previously known of only from meager accounts found in Ramusio, Herrera, Gomara and Venegas. Coronado and his men were, aside from De Vaca, the first Europeans to visit Texas, and preceded all others into New Mexico, Arizona and Colorado. For English translation of Castañeda [with other material on Coronado] see Winship, George P.

CASTELLANOS, HENRY C.   225
New Orleans as it was ... *N O* 1895. D [8] 350 pls a

CASTELNAU, FRANCIS, comte de   225a
Vues et souvenirs de l'Amérique du Nord. *P* 1842. Q [8] 166 [2] 35pls [one of which is duplicated as a col front] aa

—rptd: same collat., *P* 1844; *P* 1852. aa
First book to contain a view of Chicago; other views range from Florida to the great lakes.

[CASTERA, F.]   226
The trials of the Honb. James Workman, and Col. Lewis Kerr ... on a charge of ... setting on foot, within the Unites States, an expedition for the conquest ... of Mexico. *N O* 1807. D 180 aa

CASTETS, ÉMILE   227
Mexique et Californie ... *P* 1886. D [4] 219 a

CASTIGLIONI, LUIGI   228
Viaggio negli Stati Uniti ... 1785–6–7 ... *Milan* 1790. O 2v: [12] 403; [6] 402. 3tabs 5maps 9pls aa
—Ger. tr., vol.I[all], *Memmingen* 1793. O [16] 495 8pls(& plans a
First Italian traveller through the South. Merits an English translation.

CASTLE (EDWARD H.)   229
Life of: *Chi* 1893. D 29 port pls aa
Recollections of a California '49er.

CASTLEMAN, ALFRED L.   230
The Army of the Potomac ... *Milw* 1863. D [6] 288 a

CASTLEMAN, JOHN B.   231
Active service. *Louisv* 1917. O [2] 269 60pls & facs a

[CASTRO, HENRY]   232
Le Texas en 1845. Castroville ... sur la rivière Medina ... *Antw* 1845. O 24 pl plan aa
—anr. issue, same impr. & date. O 43 aa
—anr. ed., text in both Fr. & Ger., n.p.,n.d. O 39 aa
Some editions of this promotion tract give author's name. Castro, Napoleonic veteran, founded Castroville.

CASWALL, HENRY   233
America and the American church. *L* 1839. D [20] 368 4pls map a
—rptd. *L* 1849.
—ed. 2, *L* 1851. D [12] 400 [2] maps & pls

CASWALL, HENRY   234
The city of the Mormons; or, three days at Nauvoo ... *L* 1842. 16° [4] 82 aa
—ed. 2, enl., *L* 1843. 16° [4] 88 front. a

CASWALL, HENRY   235
The prophet of the nineteenth century; or, the rise ... of the Mormons ... *L* 1843. O 278 pl + 2 adv-p a

CASSWELL, HENRY   236
The western world revisited. *Oxf* 1854. 16° [16] 351 a

CATAWBA AND CHEROKEE INDIANS [THE].   237
A treaty with: ... *Wmsbgh* 1756. Q [14] 25 b NYH NYP VaH

CATES, CLIFF D.   238
Pioneer history of Wise county [Tex.] ... *Decatur* 1907. O 471[incl.advs.] aa

CATLIN, GEORGE   239
An account of an annual religious ceremony practised by the Mandan tribe ... *L* 1865. O 67 b NYP Pn Y
Only 50 copies were circulated in separate form of this unauthorized edition of what the author later issued as *O-Kee-pa* [etc.], but the publishers—Philobiblon Society—bound identical copies in volume VIII of their *Miscellanies.*

CATLIN, GEORGE   240
Last rambles amongst the Indians of the Rocky mountains and the Andes. *L* 1867. 16° [12] 361 8 pls a
—Am eds, Eng sheets with *N Y* impr: 1867; 1868.

CATLIN, GEORGE   241
Letters and notes on ... American Indians. *L* 1841. O 2v: [8] 264; [8] 266. 3maps 309pls[not 312 as t-p states: there were no pls 23, 113, 114, 137, 142, 149, 159, 246 or 247, but nos 101 1/2, 210 1/2 and 3 unnumb pls were added]. Some copies carry Wiley and Putnam's imprint, others state "Pub. by the author," all have errata slips in v.I. aa
—Am. ed., Eng. sheets—even to errata slip—with new t-p, *N Y* 1841. aa
—many later eds., some with titles altered; a few copies of the *L* eds. of 1844, 1846, 1857 and 1866 had pls hand-col. b
—anr. ed., first with pls printed in color, *L* 1876. O 2v aa
—for Ger. tr. of text *see* below, "North American Indian portfolio."

CATLIN, GEORGE   242
Life amongst the Indians ... *L* 1861. 16° [10] 339 14pls a
—rptd. *L* 1867. 16° [12] 339 14pls
—Am ed, Eng sheets, *N Y* 1867. 16° [12] 339 14pls
—Fr tr, *P* 1863. 16°; ed 2, *P* 1866. 16°
Though this and No. 240 [its sequel] were written for boys, both give episodes in the author's life not found elsewhere.

CATLIN, GEORGE   243
North American Indian portfolio. *L* 1844. F [2] 18 25col pls c *N Y* some copies have plates mounted on card-board, loose in portfolio NYP
—anr. ed. *L* Catlin [1845]. F 12 25cols.pls b N
—Am. ed. *N Y* 1845. F 16 25col pls c N NYP Y
—ed. 2, *L* [1845?]. F no text, only t-p & lf. of contents 31pls[25 numb., 6 umnnub.] with pls col b with pls uncol[as probably issued] a

—Ger. ed. "Die Indianer Nord Amerikas und die während . . .," *Brus* [1846]–1848. O [10] 382 errata lf 24col pls b
—rptd. same impr. [1850]–1851. O 24pls [one only col.] aa

As graphic delineations of Indian hunting and dancing scenes, these plates rank next to those of Bodmer. Text of German edition is translation of *Letters and notes* . . .

CATLIN, GEORGE   **244**
O-Kee-pa: a religious ceremony; and other customs of the Mandans. *L* 1867. O [8] 52 13col pls b
—Am. ed. [Eng. sheets with *Phil* t-p], same collat., 1867. aa

Authorized version of an earlier garbled and surreptitious issue—*see* above *An account* [etc.]— but, being for public consumption, with the lascivious details of the bull dance omitted. Some copies, however, carry [inserted] a separate printing of that rite entitled *Folium reservatum*, three pages.

CATTERMOLE, E. G.   **245**
Famous frontiersmen, pioneers and scouts . . . *Chi* 1883. D 540 + 4adv-p front a
—rptd., same impr. & collat., 1884; and later.

CATTLE RANCHES AND CATTLE   **246**
RAISING ON THE PLAINS.
B, Brooks [1881] 16° 43 aa

[CAUSTEN, JAMES H.]   **247**
View of the claim of American citizens . . . assumed by the United States, in the Louisiana convention of the 30th April, 1803, *Wash* 1829. O 141 aa

CAVE, WILL   **248**
Nez Perce Indian war of 1877 . . . *Missoula* n.d. O 24 port a

CAVEAT (A)   **249**
Caveat (A); or considerations against the admission of Missouri, with slavery, into the Union. *N Hav* n.d. O 40 a

CAVELIER, JEAN
Relation du voyage . . . par feu M. Robert Cavelier, sieur de la Salle . . . See La Salle, Jean Cavelier de.

[CAWTHORNE, J.]   **250**
A plan of reconciliation with America . . . *L* 1782. D [2] 48 a

[CAZNEAU, MRS. WILLIAM L.]   **251**
Eagle Pass; or, life on the border. *N Y* 1852. D 188 a

[CAZNEAU, MRS. WILLIAM L.]   **252**
Texas and her presidents. *N Y* 1845. 16° 122 a

CEDARHOLME (MRS. CAROLINE).   **253**
A narrative of the dangerous journey of: across the deserts to Arizona. *St P* 1872. O 32 aa
—anr. ed. *Indp*, same date. O 45 aa

CÉLIZ, FRAY FRANCISCO   **254**
Diary of the Alarcon expedition into Texas, 1718–19. Tr. F. L. Hoffman. *L A* Quivira Soc 1935. O [12] 124 8pls 2maps a

First publication in book form, in any language. Céliz accompanied this expedition which established Spanish government and missions in the region.

CENSUS OF THE UNITED STATES   **255**
[3rd census]. [*Wash* 1812?]. F 90 lvs a

For earlier issues *see Return of the whole number of persons* . . .; later enumerations followed every decade, under varying titles; the tenth, of 1881.

CENTRAL PACIFIC
Central Pacific railroad of California. For early reports, *see* Judah, Theo. D.

Railroad communication across the conti-   **256**
nent, with an account of the Central Pacific railroad of California: . . . *N Y* 1868. O 32[incl. map & tabs] a

CENTZ, P. C. [pseud.]
Davis and Lee . . . *See* Sage, Bernard J.

[CERISIER, ANTOINE M.]   **257**
Le destin de L'Amérique, ou dialogues . . . dans lesquels on developpe la cause des événéments . . . relativement a cette guerre . . . *L* [probably ptd in Europe] n.d. [1780?]. D 124 a
—Dutch ed. "Het Oor in het Kabinet . . .," *L* [1780?]. O

Purports to be translation from the English, but actually an original work consisting of imaginary conversations between North, Bute, Franklin and others. The Dutch edition was probably printed in Holland.

[CERISIER, ANTOINE M.]   **258**
Observations impartiales d'un vrai Hollandois . . . réponse au Discours d'un soidisant bon Hollandois à ses compatriotes. [Together with "Suite" to same]. *Arnhem* [1778–9]. O 2v: [4] 60; [4] 74 a

[CHALESME, M. DE]   **259**
Récit fidele . . . de toutes les particularitez qui sont dans l'Amérique . . . *Poitiers* 1676. D 60 c N Phil. Lib. Co.

CHALFANT, W[ILLIE] A.   **260**
Outposts of civilization [in early California and Nevada]. *B* [1928]. D 193 a

CHALFANT, W[ILLIE] A. 261
The story of Inyo [Calif.]. *Chi* 1922. D [18] 358
errata slip map a
—rptd. *LA* 1933 D 430
Best history of the California region east of the
Sierras, the Owens Valley and Death Valley.

CHALKLEY (THOMAS). 262
A collection of the works of: ... *Phil* 1749. O
[16] 590 + blank 1. opp. p.326 aa
—rptd. often in America and England, some giving
only his "Journal." a
His *Journal* describes preaching trips to Quaker
settlements from New England to Carolina and
voyages, as a sea-captain, to the West Indies.

CHALMERS, GEORGE 263
An estimate of the comparative strength of
Great Britain ... *L* 1782. Q 190 a
—rptd., with 2nd app. added, same impr. & date.
Q 197
—enl. ed., same impr. 1786. O 250
—rptd. 1794.
—other eds.: *L* 1802; *L* 1810; *Edin* 1812. O 443
The later editions show how British trade was
benefitted by American independence.

CHALMERS, GEORGE 264
An introduction to the history of the revolt of
the colonies. Vol. I [all]. *L* 1782. O [2] 496 b H
NYP [of 5copies known, complete with title-lf]
—Am. ed.—and first to contain v.II—*B* 1845. O
2v[usually bound in 1]: [36] 414; [18] 376 a
Of the first edition—suppressed by the author—
only a few copies are extant, most of them being
without the title-leaf.

[CHALMERS, GEORGE?] 265
The life of Thomas Pain [sic] ... Ed. 2. *L* 1791.
O 35 port a
—ed. 3, same impr. & date. O [2] 129
—several rpts. by 1793: also several abridged versions
—anr. ed. *Dub* 1791. D 69; also *Dub* [1792?]. O 135
—Am. ed., Paine's name on t-p spelled cor., *B*
1796. O 40
Chalmers never acknowledged authorship.

CHALMERS, GEORGE 266
Political annals of the present united colonies.
Book I [all]. *L* 1780. Q [10] 695 aa

CHALMERS, LIONEL 267
An account of the weather and diseases of South
Carolina. *L* 1776. O 2v: [8] 222; [4] 224. 2tabs b
—Ger. tr. *Stendal* 1796. O 2v aa

CHAMBERLAIN, HOPE S. 268
History of Wake county. N. C. *Raleigh* 1922.
O 302[incl. port] a

[CHAMBERLAIN, WILLIAM H., et al] 269
History of Yuba county, California ... *Oakland*
1879. Q [6] 21–150 maps pls b

CHAMBERS, ANDREW J. 270
Recollections ... n.p. [1947]. D 40 aa small ed.
ptd.
Crossed the plains in 1845 and fought in the
Oregon Indian wars of 1855–1856.

CHAMBERS, JOHN, [second Gov., 271
Iowa Territory]
Autobiography. Ed. by J. C. Parish. *Iowa City*
1908. Q [14] 49 3ports a 400 cops ptd

CHAMBERS, MARGARET W. 272
Reminisences [sic]. n.p. [1903]. O 48 b G OreH
WashU Y
Written in 1894; includes account of her 1851
overland journey. The authoress was the wife of
Andrew J. Chambers, *see* above.

CHAMBERS (T. J.) 273
Exposition of the part taken by: in the difficulties
of Texas ... and his views ... upon separating
Texas from Coahuila ... *Brazoria* 1833. D 27 b
S [only cop kn]

CHAMBERS, THEODORE F. 274
The early Germans of New Jersey ... [*Dover*
1895]. O [16] 667 3maps 61pls a

CHAMBERS, WILLIAM [of Eng.] 275
Things as they are in America. *L* 1854. O [6]
364 a
—Am. ed., same date & collat. *Phil*

CHAMBERS, WILLIAM, [of Texas] 276
Sketch of the life of Gen. T. J. Chambers of
Texas. *Galv* 1853. O 63 aa
—ed. 2, rev. & enl., *Galv* 1853. O 63 [36] a

CHAMISSO, LOUIS C. A. von 277
Bemerkungen und Ansichten auf einer Ent-
deckungs-Reise ... auf dem Schiffe Rurick ...
Weimar 1821. Q [2] 240 fold.tab 2maps 13pls b
—rptd. "Reise um die Welt ...," *Leip* 1836. O 2v
aa
—Eng. ed. [Calif. portion only], "A sojourn at San
Francisco bay ...," *S F* 1936. aa 250 cops ptd.
For other accounts of this voyage to the North-
west coast and California, *see* Choris, and also
Kotzebue's voyage of 1815–18.

CHAMPIGNY, [JEAN], chevalier de 278
État-présent de la Louisiane ... *Hague* 1776.
O 147 [2] b
—ed. 2, *Amst* 1781. same collat. b
From material furnished by an English officer
with troops which took possession after the cession
of this colony to England.

[CHAMPIGNY, JEAN, chevalier de]   279
La Louisiane ensanglantée . . . *L* 1773. O [20]
124 [32 32] aa
—anr ed Amst 1781. a
Particulars of the revolt against Spanish authority, 1768–9.

[CHAMPION, J.]   280
Reflections on the state of parties . . . and the
necessity . . . of the present war with America. *L*
1747[error for 1776]. O [4] 64 aa
—ed. 2, "Reflections on the state of parties . . . and
the necessity . . . of suppressing the American
rebellion," *L* 1746 [error for 1776]. same collat. a

[CHAMPION, RICHARD]   281
Considerations on the present situation of
Great Britain and the United States . . . to expose
the dangerous tendency of the arguments . . . in a
late pamphlet . . . by Lord Sheffield. *L* 1784. O [8]
3–157 errata slip a
—ed. 2, au. named, with adds., *L* 1784. O [34]
274 36

CHAMPLIN, REV. JAMES   282
Early biography, travels . . . *Columbus O* 1842.
D 192 a
—ed. 2, same impr. [1842]. D 206

CHANDLER, JOSEPH E.   283
The colonial architecture of Maryland, Penna,
and Virginia. *B* 1892. F [6] 50pls a

CHANDLER, PELEG W.   284
American criminal trials. *B* 1841–4. D 2v: [12]
436; [8] 387 a

[CHANDLER, THOMAS B.]   285
What think ye of the Congress now? . . . how far
the Americans are bound to abide by . . . decisions
of the late Continental Congress . . . *N Y* 1775.
O 48 [4] aa
—rptd. *L* 1775. O [2] 90 a
Tory pamphlet severely critical of the rebel Congress. Attributed also to Myles Cooper.

CHANDLESS, WILLIAM   286
A visit to Salt Lake; being a journey across the
plains and a residence in the Mormon settlements.
L 1857. D [12] 346 map a
Some copies have no advertisement pages; some
have sixteen dated April 1857; others twenty-four
dated 1858.

CHANNING, GEORGE G.   287
Early recollections of Newport, R. I . . . 1793–
1831. *Newport* 1868. 16° 284 a

CHAPELLE, HOWARD I.   288
The Baltimore clipper . . . *Salem* 1930. Q [12]
192 + adv-p 36 pls aa

CHAPELLE, HOWARD I.   289
The history of American sailing ships. *N Y* 1935.
O [20] 400 23pls[16double-p] a also 121copies on
L.P., Q aa

CHAPELLE, HOWARD I.   290
The history of the American navy . . . *N Y*
[1949]. Q [24] 558 17pls 32fold.plans a

CHAPMAN, ARTHUR   291
The pony express . . . *N Y* 1932. O 319 8pls a

CHAPMAN, ISAAC A.   292
A sketch of the history of Wyoming . . . *Wilkes-
barre* 1830. D 210 a
First history of this valley.

CHAPMAN, J. BUTLER   293
History of Kansas and emigrant's guide. *Akron*
1855. D 116 c G KasH MiamiU MoH [only cops
loc]
Only volume I published. Map called for was
separately pubd with a 3-page Explanation.

CHAPMAN, JOHN A.   294
History of Edgefield County [S. C.] . . . *Newbury S C* 1897. O 521 [6] map a

CHAPMAN, S., pub.
Handbook of Wisconsin. See Wisconsin. Hand-
book of:

CHAPMAN, SAMUEL D.   296
History of Tama county, Iowa . . . *Toledo* 1879.
O [8] 13–296 a

CHAPMAN, THOMAS J.   297
Old Pittsburgh days. *Pitt* 1900. D 237 a

CHAPMAN, THOMAS J.   298
The valley of the Conemaugh [Pa.] *Altoona*
1865. 16° 202 a

CHAPPE D'AUTEROCHE, [JEAN]   299
Voyage en Californie pour l'observation du
passage de Vénus sur le disque du soleil . . . *P*
1772. Q [4] 170 [2] plan 3pls fold.tab aa
—Eng. tr., with adds. on Newfoundland, *L* 1778.
O [8] 215 plan aa
Aside from astronomical data of little impor-
tance.

CHAPPELL, ABSALOM H.   300
Miscellanies of Georgia . . . *Columbus Ga* 1874.
O 3pts in 1: [4] 73 [2]: 137; 24 a
—re-issued, same sheets with new t-pp., *Atlanta*
1900. a

CHAPPELL, PHILLIP E.   301
History of the Missouri river. n.p. 1904. O [2] 98 aa
—anr ed, [*K C* 1905]. O [2] 98 4pls a

CHAPTER (A) OF AMERICAN HISTORY. 302
Sketches of the revolutionary war . . . Written
by an old sailor . . . *Columbus O* 1853. O 54 a

CHARDON, [FRANCIS A.] 303
Journal at Ft. Clark, 1834–9 . . . Ed. by Annie
H. Abel. *Pierre S D* 1932. O [46] 458 2pls a

CHARLESTON [S. C.] 304
Directory and . . . guide for . . .: *Charleston*
1819. D 98 56 aa

CHARLES-TOWN, SOUTH-CAROLINA.
Extracts from the proceedings of the court of
Vice-Admiralty in: . . . *See* Laurens, Henry.

CHARLESTON, S.,C. 305
Proceedings of the State Rights Association,
at: . . . *Charleston* 1830. D 56 a

CHARLESTON, [S. C.]
Reflections, occasioned by the late disturbances
in: By Achates. *See* Pinckney, Thos.

CHARLESTON [S. C.] 306
Charleston [S. C.] and the towns of Hamburg
and Augusta. Report of a . . . committee to enquire
into the cost . . . of a railroad communication between: *Charleston* 1828. O 32 aa
First railroad to operate in America.

CHARLESTON [S. C.]
The siege of: by the British . . . *See* Hough,
Franklin B.

CHARLEVOIX, P. FRANCOIS-XAVIER 307
Histoire et description . . . de la Nouvelle
France, avec le journal historique d'un voyage . . .
dans l'Amérique . . . *P* 1744. Q 3v: [34] 64, 664;
[20] 582; [24, 14] 543. 28 maps 96pls[on 22 sheets]
b AA H N NYP Y some copies on fine paper
[collat. given varies in sequence in different copies,
depending on vagaries of printer or binder]
—anr. ed. *P* 1744. D 6v: [14] 454; [2] 501; [2] 465;
[2] 388; [30] 456; [2] 434 [4]. 28 maps 96pls[on 44
sheets] aa
—Eng. tr. [of historical portion] with notes, by
Shea, *N Y* 1866–72. Q 6v: 18maps 15pls 4facs
25copies on L. P. aa
—rptd. *N Y* 1900. same collat. aa
—Ger. tr. *Leip* 1756. Q [8] 648 [40] 18maps a
The principal work of this great Jesuit traveller
and historian and the pre-eminent authority on
the French period in the west. For English translations of his Journal of travels see below.

CHARLEVOIX, P. FRANCOIS-XAVIER 308
Journal of a voyage to North America . . . *L*
1761. O 2v: [8] 128 145–382; [8] 380 [22]. map b
—rptd. *Chi* 1923. O 2v: [26] 362; [10] 383 map aa
—anr. ed., different tr., "Letters to the Dutchess

[*sic*] of Lesdigueres . . . account of a voyage to
Canada . . . and Louisiana . . .," *L* 1763. O [16]
384 map[generally missing and probably not inserted in all copies] aa
—rptd., same collat., 1764. aa
—best Eng ed. *Dub* 1766. O 2v: [8] 48, 228; [4] 336
[20]. 8maps 2pls b N NYH NYP

CHARLTON, THOMAS U. P. 309
Life of Major General [James] Jackson. Part I
[all]. *Augusta Ga* 1809. O [10] 70 b BA CharlestonL
[of 3copies known]
—rptd. [*Atlanta* 1898]. O [10] 215 a

CHARTERS (THE) 310
Charters (The) of . . . Virginia, Maryland, Connecticut, Rhode-Island, Pennsylvania, Massachusetts Bay and Georgia. To which is prefixed . . .
proceedings of the . . . colonies in consequence of
the late stamp act. *L* 1766. Q [2] 18 16 6 4 6 6 9 7
map[dated 1763] aa
—rptd. "The charters of the British colonies . . .,"
L Almon [1774]. O [2] 142 a
—anr. ed. *Dub* 1776, same collat.
First collected edition of these colonial charters.

CHAS, JEAN, and LEBRUN, M. 313
Histoire . . . de la révolution de l'Amérique . . .
P [1801]. O [16] 458 a
—rptd., same impr. & collat. [1802].

CHASE, BENJAMIN 314
History of Old Chester [N. H.]. *Auburn N H*
1869. O [16] 702 map 15ports a

CHASE, C[HARLES] M. 315
The editor's run in New Mexico and Colorado
. . . [observations on territorial history] . . . *Lyn-
don* [1882]. O 233 + 3adv-p a

**CHASE, FREDERICK, and
LORD, JOHN K.** 316
A history of Dartmouth college and . . . Hanover, New Hampshire. *C* 1891–1913. O 2v: [14]
682; [8] 725. 31pls a

CHASE, LUCIEN B. 317
History of the Polk administration. *N Y* 1850.
O 512 a

CHASE, OWEN 318
Narrative of the shipwreck of the whale-ship
"Essex" . . . *N Y* 1821. D 128 c
—rptd. *L* 1935. 275cops ptd a

CHASE, PHILANDER 319
Reminiscences. [capt. t. only]. *Peoria* Davis
1841–2, *N Y* Craighead 1843–4. O 5 pts in 7nos:
480; 400 b G
—anr.ed., unsold sheets of the above priv. ptd. ed.,
with 2 t-p added, *N Y* Blake 1844. O 2v aa

—ed.2, enl., brings events to 1847, *B* 1848. O 2v:
[12] 548; [6] 564. port 4pls a
Autobiography of high interest concerning Ohio,
Michigan and Illinois affairs.

CHASE, SALMON P.   320
A sketch of the history of Ohio. *Cin* 1833. O [2]
40 aa
First separate publication of the first general
history of this state; it appeared earlier prefixed to
the author's *Statutes of Ohio* [with title leaf and
paged 9 to 48] under title *A preliminary sketch of
the history of Ohio.* b

CHASE, THOMAS   321
Sketches of the life ... of Paul Jones. *Rich*
1859. D 58 a
Some of the author's information came from his
grandfather who served under Jones.

CHASLES, PHILARÈTE   322
Études sur la litterature et les moeurs des Anglo-
Américains ... *P* [1851]. 16° [12] 515 a
—Eng. tr. *N Y* 1852. D [12] 312

[CHASTELLUX, FRANCOIS J.,   323
marquis de]
Discours sur les avantages ... qui résultent ...
de la découverte de l'Amérique. *L* 1787. O [8] 68 a
—rptd. "Quelle à été l'influence de l'Amérique
...," *P* 1792. O 86

CHASTELLUX (the Marquis de).
Remarks on the travels of: *See* Simcoe, John G.

[CHASTELLUX, FRANCOIS J.,   324
marquis de]
Voyage de Newport à Philadephie [*sic*] ... *Newport* [1781]. Q [4] 188 c less than 30 copies ptd H
NYP [of 6 cops loc]
—unauthorized ed. "Voyage en Amerique ...,"
[*Cassell*] 1785. D 191 aa
—rptd. n.p. [*P*?] 1785. O 228 aa
—rptd. *P & Brus* 1786. O 136 aa
—complete & authorized ed. "Voyages dans
l'Amérique ...," *P* 1786. O 2v: [8] 390; [4] 362
[2]. 2maps 3pls aa
—ed. 2, *P* 1788–91. O 2v: [8] 408; [4] 251, i.e., 351.
2maps 3pls aa
—Eng. ed. "Travels in North America ...," *L*
1787. O 2v: [16] 462; [12] 432. 2maps 3pls aa
—ed. 2, same date, impr. & collat. aa
—rptd. *Dub* 1787. O 2v: [16] 462; [16] 430. 2maps
3pls aa
—Am. ed., with adds., *N Y* 1827. O 416 some
copies on L. P. a
—rptd., same collat. & impr. 1828. a
—Ger tr: *Hambg* 1785. D [8] 152; 3 others in
1786 a
In its completed form constitutes the first trustworthy record of life in the United States.

CHATEAUBRIAND, FRANCOIS A. R.,   325
vicomte de
Oeuvres inédites [vols 6 & 7] ... Voyages en
Amérique, en France, et en Italie. *P* 1827. O 2v:
[4, 92] 306; [4] 396 a
—1st separate ed "Voyages en Amérique et en
Italie," *P* 1828. O 2v: [10] 400; [6] 423
—rptd., "Voyage en Amérique," *Brus* 1828. 16° 2v
—many later Fr. eds. under various titles
—Eng. ed. "Travels in America and Italy," *L* 1828.
O 2v: [6] 356 + 4 adv p; [4] 429 + 2adv-p
—Ger. tr. *Freiburg* 1828. 16° 2v
—Ital. tr. *P* 1836. 16° 3v
—Sp tr *Madr* 1846. O
The distinguished author, fascinated by Indian
character, roamed in 1791 throughout our in-
terior frontiers, from western New York to the
Floridas.

CHATEAUBRIAND, FRANCOIS A. R.,   326
vicomte de
Souvenirs d'Italie, d'Angleterre et de l'Amérique
... *L* 1815. O 2v: [14] 262; [4] 298 [4] aa
—Eng. ed. "Recollections ...," *L* 1815. O 2v: [12]
258; [4] 314 a
—anr. ed. *L* 1816. O 2v
—Am. ed. *Phil* 1816. O [4] 9–364
—Ger. tr. *Dresden* 1816. O
A luminous preface sketches maritime discovery
from the earliest time to Bering, Vancouver,
Mackenzie, Lewis and Clark, Pike and School-
craft.

CHATHAM (THE EARL OF).   327
Letter to: concerning his speech ... To which
are subjoined reflections on His Majesty's ...
speech from the throne, and an index to peace with
America. *L* 1777. O 54 a
Views British victory as impossible.

CHATHAM (LORD).
A letter to: concerning the present war ... By
a gentleman of the Inner Temple. *See* Dawes,
Matthew.

CHAULMER, CHARLES   328
Le nouveau-monde ou l'Amérique chrestienne
... *P* 1659. D 2pts in 1: [12, 56] 432; [2] 360 c
Bost. Athenaeum N

CHAUMONOT (PIERRE J.).   329
La vie du: *N Y* 1858. sm Q 108 a 100 copies ptd.
First printing of the autobiography of a Jesuit
missionary, written in 1688, with his labors among
Hurons and Iroquois.

CHAUNCY, CHARLES   330
A letter to a friend, containing remarks on ...
a sermon ... by John, Bishop of Landaff [*sic*] ...
B 1767. O 56 a
—Eng. ed., with suppl., *L* 1768. O 80

[CHAUNCY, CHARLES]   331
A letter to a friend, giving a concise . . . account
. . . of the Ohio defeat . . . *B* 1755. Q [15] c JCB
NYP
—Eng. ed. *Bristol* 1755. O [4] 30 b N NYP
—anr. ed. *L* 1755. O 28 b AA
Earliest account in book form of Braddock's
defeat. Has been erroneously ascribed to Timothy
Walker.

[CHAUNCY, CHARLES]   332
A letter to a friend, giving a concise . . . repre-
sentation of the hardships . . . the town of Boston
is exposed to . . . *B* 1774. O 35 a
Ascribed also to Timothy Walker, as it is signed
T. W.

[CHAUNCY, CHARLES]   333
Two letters to a friend, on the present critical
conjuncture of affairs . . . *L* 1755. O [2] 54 b AA
N Y
Reprints his *First letter* [on Braddock's defeat]
and his *Second letter* [on Sir William Johnson's
victory at Lake George], both of which had been
printed at Boston earlier in the year; the *Second
letter* contained only 16 pages and hence is not
entered separately in this work.

[CHEETHAM, JAMES]   334
Answer to Alexander Hamilton's Letter concer-
ning . . . John Adams. *N Y* 1800. O 32 a
Attributed also to Uzall Ogden.

CHEETHAM, JAMES   335
A letter to a friend on the conduct of the adher-
ents to Mr. Burr. *N Y* 1803. O 72 a

CHEETHAM, JAMES   336
The life of Thomas Paine . . . *N Y* 1809. O 347 a
—Eng. ed. *L* 1817. O 187

[CHEETHAM, JAMES]   337
A narrative of the suppression by Col. Burr of
the History of the administration of John Adams
. . . *N Y* 1802. O 72 a
—ed. 2, rev., *N Y* same date & collat.
—ed. 3, *Balt* [1802?]. same collat.
For reply see Wood, John, *A correct statement.*

CHEETHAM, JAMES   338
Nine letters on . . . Aaron Burr's political defec-
tion . . . *N Y* 1803. O 139 a
For earlier edition *see* below, *A view of the
political conduct . . .*

CHEETHAM, JAMES   339
A reply to Aristides. *N Y* 1804. O 134 a
For book replied to, *see* Van Ness, William P.,
An examination of charges against Burr.

[CHEETHAM, JAMES]   340
A view of the political conduct of Aaron Burr.
N Y 1802. O 120 a
For later edition *see* above, *Nine letters . . .*

CHENEY, T[HESEUS] APOLEON   341
Historical sketch of the Chemung Valley [N. Y.].
Watkins N Y 1868. O [12] 59 a

CHEROKEE STRIP BRAND BOOK . . .   342
KC 1881. 16° 66 [incl advs] b
—anr ed., *Caldwell* 1886. 16° 48 [incl init blank lf]
aa

CHEROKEE
The case of the Cherokee nation against the state
of Georgia. *See* Peters, Richard.

A faithful history of the Cherokee tribe of Indians:
. . . *See* Stambaugh, Saml. C.

Memorial of the Cherokee representatives   343
submitting the protest . . . of the treaty . . . at New
Echota . . . [H. Doc. 286]. *Wash* [1836?]. O 167 a

Some observations on the two campaigns   344
against the Cherokee Indians. In a second letter from
Philopatrios. *Charles-Town S C* 1762. O 88 fold.
tab b PhilL

Treaties between the United States . . . and   345
the Cherokee nation from 1785. *Tahlequah* 1870. O
144 [1] a
—other eds.: *Tahlequah* 1884. O 140 [1]
—same [in Cherokee]. O 118

CHEROKEES   346
An enquiry into the origin of the Cherokees: *Oxf*
1762. O [2] 27 aa
The learned author satisfied himself that this
tribe stemmed from Japhet.

Treaty with the Cherokees October 7th, 1861.
See Pike, Albert.

CHERRY, CUMMINGS   347
Cincinnati and Sonora Mining Association:
maps and reports of the San Juan del Rio Ranche
. . . *Cin* 1866. O 138 2fold.maps aa
Includes personal narrative of his trip along the
southern border of Arizona.

CHESAPEAKE (THE).   348
American evidences upon the capture of: *L* 1808.
O [4] 75 a

CHESAPEAKE AND OHIO   349
History of the Chesapeake and Ohio R.R. *Rich*
1868. O 49 a

**Proceedings of the Chesapeake and Ohio   350
canal convention** . . . *Wash* 1827. O 112 2fold.tabs a

CHESNEY, C. C.   351
A military view of . . . campaigns in Virginia and
Maryland [through the battle of Chancellorsville].
L 1863. D [12] 231 2maps errata slip a
—ed. 2 [continuing through 1863], t. slightly altered, *L* 1864-5. D 2v: [12] 231; [8] 234 + 2adv-p.
7maps errata slip aa

CHESNUT, MARY BOYKIN   352
A diary from Dixie. *N Y* 1905. D [22] 424 +
2adv-p 16pls a
—rptd *N Y* 1929.

CHESTER, GREVILLE J.   353
Transatlantic sketches. *L* 1869. D [16] 405 a
Describes Chicago, Cincinnati, Pittsburgh and
early reconstruction conditions in the South, from
St. Louis to New Orleans and Mobile.

CHESTERTON, GEORGE L.   354
Peace, war and adventure . . . *L* 1853. D 2v: [12]
282; [8] 326 a
Served with the British at Washington, Baltimore and New Orleans, in 1814.

[CHETWOOD, WILLIAM R.]   355
The voyages and adventures of Captain Robert
Boyle . . . To which is added, the voyage . . . of
Richard Castleman . . . with a description of the
city of Philadelphia . . . *L* 1726. O [10] 374 pl aa
—ed. 2, same impr. & collat. 1727. a
—rptd., same impr. & collat. 1728.
—other eds.: *L* 1735; *Wolverhampton* 1744; *L* 1762;
L 1769; *L* 1772; *L* 1777; *Edin* 1778 & 1780; *L* 1787.
—Am. ed. *Greenfield Mass* 1794. D 244
—Fr. tr. *Amst* 1730. D 2v: [8] 341; 276 +table
[of 6 lvs] 8 pls
—Ger. tr. *Leip* 1793. O
—Ital. tr. *Venice* 1734. D 447
Though Boyle's narrative is purely imaginary,
that of Castleman seems to be factual.

[CHETWOOD, WILLIAM R.]   356
The voyages, dangerous adventures . . . of Captain Richard Falconer . . . *L* 1720. O [8] 72 136 179
front. aa
—rptd. many times—in England: 1724; 1726;
1727; 1728; 1734; 1735; 1744; 1762; 1764; 1777;
1780; 1785. a
—Am. ed. *Greenfield Mass* 1794. D 244
Tremendous—but undoubtedly imaginary—
adventures. Attributed also to Benjamin Victor
and Daniel Defoe.

CHEVALIER, [LOUIS] EDOUARD   357
Histoire de la marine francaise pendant la
guerre de l'indépendance américaine . . . *P* 1877.
O [4] 517 [2] a

CHEVALIER, MICHEL   358
Histoire et description des voies de communication aux États-Unis . . . *P* 1840–41. O 2v: [14]
544; [4] 582 [15] + atlas vol[of 19 maps] Q aa
—to above was added, 1857, "Table analytique
des matières." Q 53
Most elaborate early foreign work on American
railroads and canals. The text volumes issued originally in parts; cover-title of last part carries 1843
date.

CHEVALIER, MICHEL   359
Lettres sur l'Amérique du Nord. *P* 1836. O 2v:
[20] 472; [4] 528. map a
—rptd. often at *P & Brus*, of which ed. 3 is best: *P*
1838. O 2v: [16] 439; 535. map
—ed. 3, rptd. *Brus* 1838. 16° 3v
—Eng. tr., with omissions, "Society, manners and
politics in the United States," *B* 1839. O [4] 467
—Ger tr *Leip* 1837 D 4v

CHEVES, LANGDON   360
Speech in the southern convention, at Nashville
. . . [*Nashv*] 1850. O 36 a
One of the earliest of radical secession utter-
ances, practically an appeal to arms.

CHICAGO   361
An act to incorporate the city of Chicago. *Chi*
1837. O 23 dd G[only copy known]
—anr. issue, adding on p.23, a suppl.act of March
4th d ChiH
First separate printing of the first Chicago charter and first important book printed there.

**Amendments to the city charter [of Chi-   362
cago]** capt. t. n.p. n.d. [*Chi* 1842]. O 30 b ChiH S

**Biographical sketches of the leading men   363
of Chicago:** *Chi* 1868. sm Q [2] 693 97photos a

Charter of Chicago: with the various   364
amendments . . . *Chi* 1847. O 32 b ChiH MH [of
3copies known]
—anr. ed. *Chi* 1849. O 116

Chicago as it is. A strangers' and tourists'   365
guide . . . *Chi* 1866. 16° 129 14adv-lvs [3 at front,
11 at rear] map 24 pls a

Chicago avant, pendant et après l'incendie.   366
Par Fortunio, témoin . . . dans ce grand drame . . .
P 1871. 18° 35 a

Chicago; her commerce and railroads.   367
Chi 1853. O 29 [wrapper t.only] aa
—anr. issue, "Illustrated annual review . . ."
Continued annually, under various titles,
through 1865.

Chicago illustrated, 1866-7. *See* Jevne and Almini.

A guide to the city of Chicago: *Chi* [Zell]   368
1868. 16° 196 map 24pls a
—anr. iss. 108p & 11maps

The hand-book of Chicago: or stranger's guide...
See Bodman, Albert H.

The laws and ordinances of... Chicago   369
Chi 1839. O 46 [6] b ChiH [of 3 cops loc]
Contains a sketchy business directory added as
an afterthought, pages 41–46; the city ordinances
alone were first printed—in 21 pages—Chicago,
1837. For another business directory see Griswold,
David D.

Official proceedings of the Democratic   370
national convention, held in 1864, at Chicago. *Chi*
1864. O 64 a

Out of town... the suburban towns... of
Chicago. *See* Runnion, J. B.

Proceedings of the harbor and river con-   371
vention, held at Chicago. *Chi* 1847. D 79 aa
Held to protest President Polk's veto of a bill
asking appropriation for Chicago harbor development. For the Committee's report *see Memorial.
To the Senate*...

Proceedings of the national ship-canal   372
convention, held at... Chicago. *Chi* 1863. O 248 a

Proceedings of the... Republican conven-   373
tion held at Chicago. 1860. [*Chi* 1860]. O 44 [capt.t.
only] a
—anr. ed.[*Alb* 1860]. O [2] 153

The railroads, history and commerce of   374
Chicago. *Chi* 1854. O 72 a
—ed. 2, same impr. & date. O 80
—Ger. tr. same impr. & date. O 79
Fore-runner of the *Annual review of commerce
...*, which was continued for years. See above
Chicago; her commerce...

Transactions of the Chicago Academy of   375
Sciences. Vol. I, pts. I & II[all]. *Chi* 1867–69.
Q [12] 129 map 19pls[12 in col.]; 131–337 port
34pls[some col.] b ChiU G LC

Uebersicht der Geschichte und des Han-   376
dels von Chicago. *Chi* 1856. O 62 aa

CHICKAMAUGA.   377
Official report of the battle of: *Rich* 1864. O 234 a

CHILD, ANDREW   378
Overland route to California... *Milw* 1852. 24°
61 d Hn N S Y [of 5 cops loc]
—rptd. *L A* 1946. O [10] 60 [4] map 5pls a 775
copies[25signed] a
One of the earliest dependable "plains guides,"
based on its author's experience.

CHILD, DAVID L[EE]   379
The taking of Naboth's vineyard, or history of
the Texas conspiracy... for the dismemberment
and robbery of... Mexico. *N Y* 1845. O 32 aa
Abolitionist argument against annexation.

[CHILD, DAVID LEE]   380
The Texan revolution... [*Wash* ca 1843]. O 84
[capt. t.] aa
Includes attack on Commodore Jones' conduct
in California.

CHILD, FRANK S.   381
South Dakota... gleanings of a journey...
N Y 1888. D 67 aa

CHILD, SIR JOSIAH, et al   382
Select dissertations on colonies and plantations
By...: *L* 1775. O [6] 113 a

CHILDS, C. G., engraver   383
Views in Philadelphia and its vicinity. *Phil* 1827–
[1830]. Q 39 lvs [incl. eng.t.] + 2 lvs plan 24pls
Some copies on L.P. aa
Originally issued in parts. *Cf.* Birch, William,
The city of Philadelphia...; also Wild, J. C.

CHILDS, JAMES E.   384
History of Waseca county, Minnesota...
Owatonna 1905. O 847 a
Contains eye-witness accounts of Sioux massa-
cres, etc.

CHILLICOTHE [O.]   385
Business directory of: for 1855–6... and [its]
history. *Chillicothe* 1855. D 78 [12] 2pls aa

CHILTON, FRANK B., comp.   386
Unveiling... of monument to Hood's Texas
brigade... history... *Houston* 1911. O 373 pls a

CHIPMAN, DANIEL   387
The life of Col. Seth Warner, with an acccount
of the controversy between New York and Vermont, 1763–1775. *Burl Vt* 1858. 16° 84 a

CHIPMAN, DANIEL   388
Memoir of Colonel Seth Warner [with life of
Ethan Allen, by Jared Sparks]. *Middlebury* 1848.
16° 226 a

CHIPMAN, NATHANIEL   389
Sketches of the principles of government...
Rutland 1793. D [4] 292 a
—rptd. "Principles of government...," *Burl Vt*
1833. O [8] 330

CHITTENDEN, HIRAM M.   390
The American fur trade of the far west... *N Y*
1902. O 3v: [26] 482; [10] 483–892; [4] 893–1029.
map plan 3facs 6pls aa

—rptd., with omissions, ed. S. Vinton, *N Y* 1935. O 2v: [30] 482; [4] 483–1014. fold.map 16pls; anr ed Stanford Univ 1954. O 2v a

CHITTENDEN, HIRAM M., ed.　　　391
History of early steamboat navigation on the Missouri river; life and adventures of Joseph La Barge. *N Y* 1903. O 2v: [14] 248; [8] 249–461. 16maps & pls aa

CHITTENDEN, HIRAM M., ed.　　　392
Life, letters and travels of Father Pierre-Jean De Smet . . . *N Y* 1905. O 4v: [16] 402; [8] 403–794; [6] 795–1212; [6] 1213–1624. map 13pls 3facs aa

CHITTENDEN, NEWTON H.　　　393
Travels in British Columbia and Alaska . . . *Victoria Can* 1882. O 84 a

CHOCTAW NATION (THE).　　　394
Papers respecting the rights and interests of: . . . *Wash* 1855. O 88 a

CHOIR, MELODY　　　396
Pioneer directory of . . . Seattle and King county; history . . . *Pottsville Pa* 1878. O 125[incl. map] b WashS WashU Y
Second directory of Seattle.

CHORIS, LOUIS　　　397
Voyage pittoresque autour du monde . . . *P* 1821–23. F 22pts divided into 7sections, each paged separately 3maps on 2sheets port 104pls[in some copies, all col.; in some, many col.; in some, none col.] all pls col. c G Y
Elaborately handsome work by the artist with Kotzebue's 1816 expedition in which a long visit was made to the Pacific coast from California to Bering's sea.

CHORPENNING, GEORGE　　　398
Chorpenning (George) *vs.* the United States. The case of: *Wash* 1874. O 56 aa
—enl. ed. "Statement . . . of claim . . .," *Wash* 1889. O 103

CHORPENNING (GEORGE).　　　399
The case of: . . . [*Wash* 1880]. O 67 aa
Argument, by F. W. Hughes, before the Judiciary Committee of the House, presenting the whole story of the earliest overland mail and pony express operations.

CHOVEL, RAFAEL　　　400
Diario du viage de la comision de limites que puso el gobierno de la republica, bayo la direccion de . . . Manuel de Mier y Teran. *Mex* 1850. O 298 aa

CHRISTIAN ADVOCATE (THE)
By a Tennessean. *See* Haywood, John.

CHRISTIE, ROBERT　　　401
Memoirs of the administration of the colonial government of Lower-Canada, by Sir James Henry Craig, and Sir George Prevost . . . comprehending . . . operations . . . during the late war with the United States. *Quebec* 1818. O 150 [9] aa
—rptd. "The military and naval operations in the Canadas . . .," *N Y* 1818. D 235 aa

[CHRISTY, DAVID]　　　402
Cotton is king; or, the culture of cotton, and its relation to agriculture . . . and to the free colored people . . . *Cin* 1855. D 210 a
—ed. 2, enl., au.named, *N Y* 1856. D 298
Attempts to show the impossibility of abolition success.

CHRISTY (WILLIAM).　　　403
Proceedings in case of the United States versus: on a charge of having set on foot a military expedition in New Orleans, against . . . Mexico . . . *N O* 1836. O 55 b G

CHRONICON EPHRATENSE . . .
See Gass, Jacob, and Miller, Johann P.

CHRONOLOGICAL ANNALS OF THE WAR.
See Dobson, John.

CHURCH, BENJAMIN
History of King Philip's war . . . *See* Church, Thos.

CHURCH, JERRY　　　404
Journal of travels . . . *Harrisburg* 1845. O 72 + adv-p b Y
—ed. 2, *Burl N J* 1857. D 83 aa
—rptd. *Harrisburg* 1933. O 89 + 4adv-p a
Rambled through Ohio, Indiana and Michigan.

[CHURCH, THOMAS]　　　405
Entertaining passages relating to King Philip's war . . . By T. C. *B* 1716. Q [4] 120 dd AA LC N NYP Y
—ed. 2, "Entertaining history of King Philip's war," with biog. of Benj. Church added and au. named, *Newport* 1772. O [4] 199 2ports[by Paul Revere] b AA BA Hn Y Some copies bound with Morton's *New England's memorial*, same date.
—ed. 3, with adds., *B* 1825. 304 a
—rptd. 1827; 1828; 1829. many other eds.
—best modern ed., by H. M. Dexter, *B* 1865. Q 2v: [16] 205; [34] 203. map 285copies ptd [35 on L.P.]
Most popular early account of this war, based on information obtained from the author's father, a participant.

CHURCHES QUARREL ESPOUSED (THE).
See Wise, Rev. John.

CHURCHILL, MRS C[AROLINE] M.   406
"Little sheaves" . . . [travel in the California and
Nevada towns and mining camps]. *S F* 1874. D
99 a

CHURCHILL, FRANKLIN H.   407
Sketch of Bvt. Brig. Gen. Sylvester Churchill,
Inspector General U. S. army. *N Y* 1888. O [6] 201
correction slip a
Active in Florida and Mexican wars.

CINCINNATI   408
Celebration of the forty-fifth anniversary of the
first settlement of Cincinnati and the Miami country.
. . . . *Cin* 1834. O 52 aa
Includes notable reminiscences by William
Henry Harrison.

Cincinnati directory (The) . . . By a citizen.   **409**
Cin 1819. D [10] 156 plan aa
First directory of any Ohio city; contains histor-
ical data.

Cincinnati past and present. See Joblin. M.

Memorial of the citizens of Cincinnati to   **410**
the Congress of the United States, relative to the
navigation of the Ohio and Mississippi. *Cin* 1843.
O 36 a
James Hall had a part in drafting this plea for
removing river obstacles.

Narrative of the late riotous proceedings   **411**
against the liberty of the press in Cincinnati . . .
Cin 1836. O 48 [2] a

Recollections of Cincinnati: . . . *See* Worth,
Gorham A.

CIST, CHARLES   412
Cincinnati in 1841: its early annals . . . *Cin*
1841. D 300 + 88adv-p 8pls a

CIST, CHARLES [comp.]   413
The Cincinnati miscellany, or antiquities of the
west . . . *Cin* 1845–6. O 2v: 272; 364 [4] b
Above two volumes were all published of this
annual.

CIVIL PRUDENCE   414
Civil prudence recommended to the thirteen
united colonies . . . *Norwich* 1776. O 55 a

CLACK, MRS. LOUISE   415
Our refugee household. *N Y* 1866. D 226 a

[CLAES, JEAN-BAPTISTE]   416
Notice sur la colonization aux États-Unis . . .
Brus 1856. O 67 a

CLAIBORNE, JOHN F. H. [ed.]   417
Life and times of Gen. Sam Dale . . . *N Y* 1860.
D 233 + 6adv-p 13pls[incl. in paginat.] a
Personal adventures of Alabama's most notable
Indian fighter.

CLAIBORNE, JOHN F. H.   418
Life . . . of John A. Quitman . . . *N Y* 1860. O
2v: 400; 392. port map a

CLAIBORNE, JOHN F. H.   419
Mississippi as a province, territory and state . . .
Vol. I [all]. *Jackson* 1880. O [24] 545 [1] 7ports aa

CLAIBORNE, JOHN F. H.   420
A sketch of Harvey's scouts . . . Jackson's division. *Starkville Miss* 1885. O [2] 24 a

CLAIBORNE, NATHANIEL H.   421
Notes on the war in the South; with . . . lives of
Montgomery, Jackson, Sevier, *et al. Rich* 1819.
16° 112 aa
Inconsequential, but scarce.

CLAIM (THE)
Claim (The) of the American loyalists reviewed
. . . *See* Galloway, Jos.

CLAIM (THE)
Claim (The) of the colonies to an exemption
from internal taxes . . . *See* Knox, Wm.

CLAP (CAPT. ROGER).   422
Memoirs of: . . . *B* 1731. O [6] 34 [10] b AA
H NYP NYS
Of this important early New England autobiog-
raphy there have been six reprints, two in the
18th century.

CLAP, THOMAS   423
The annals . . . of Yale-College . . . *N Hav*
1766. O [4] 124 aa

CLAPP, JOHN T.   424
A journal of travels to and from California.
Kalamazoo 1851. O 67 d G Y 3copies known
Day-by-day account of an 1850 crossing, from
Council Bluffs to Sacramento.

CLAPP, THEODORE   425
Autobiographical sketches and recollections,
during a thirty-five years' residence in New-
Orleans. *B* 1857. O [8] 419 port a
—ed. 2, *B* 1858. Same collat.

CLAPP, W. WARLAND   426
A record of the Boston stage. *B* 1853. 16° [14]
479 a

**[CLAPPE, LOUISE AMELIA   427
KNAPP SMITH]**
The Shirley letters from the California mines.
S F Russell 1922. O [52] 350 [2] 8pls 450copies ptd.
also special issues, one of 50, the other of 200,
copies aa
—anr. ed. *S F* Grabhorn 1933. O 2v: [20] 142 [6];
[20] 144 [6] 500copies ptd. aa
First appearing serially in the *Pioneer Magazine*
under the pseudonym of "Dame Shirley," in 1854–
5, these letters present a vivid and unexcelled picture of every-day life in the mines.

CLARENCE, C. W.   428
A biographical sketch of . . . Ralph Farnham . . .
sole survivor of . . . Bunker hill. *B* 1860. D 48
[incl.port] a

[CLARK, AUSTIN S.]   429
Reminiscences of travel, 1852–65. *Middletown*
[*ca* 1865]. O 54 port aa
Experiences in California and Idaho mining
regions. Ascribed erroneously to Isbell, F. A.

CLARK, C[HARLES] M.   430
A trip to Pike's Peak . . . *Chi* 1861. O [10] 134
[2] 18pls b N Pn Y
—rptd. *San Jose* 1958. O [10] 129 50cops ptd a
About the best contemporary account of this
gold rush.

CLARK, DANIEL   431
Proofs of the corruption of Gen. James Wilkinson, and of his connexion with Aaron Burr. *Phil*
1809. O [2] 150 199 aa

CLARK, FRANCIS D.   432
The First Regiment of New York Volunteers
commanded by Col. Jonathan D. Stevenson in the
Mexican war, 1846–1848. *N Y* 1882. O 94 2ports aa
—app. to above, *N Y* 1883. O 16

CLARK, GEORGE R.   433
Sketch of his campaign in the Illinois . . . *Cin*
1869. O 119 port Some cops on L.P. a
—rptd. *Cin* 1907.
This first account by Clark also appeared, along
with his later *Memoir* and other germane documents, in Vol. VIII, Ill. Hist. Colls. Springfield
1912, — easily the best edition. The *Memoir* itself,
edited by Quaife, was pub'd in the Lakeside Clas-
sics, *Chi* 1920.

CLARK, HIRAM C.   434
History of Chenango county [N.Y.] *Norwich
N Y* 1850. O 120 a 100copies ptd.

CLARK, ISAAC   435
Miscellany, in prose and verse. *Nashv* 1812. 16°
[16] 9–120 c G Hn WisH[of 5copies known]
Describes trips to various parts of the country,
from Alabama to Illinois.

CLARK, JAMES A.   436
The Wyoming valley . . . *Scranton* 1875. O [8]
236 25pls a

CLARK, JOEL W.   437
Miniature of Dansville village [N. Y.]. *Dansville*
1844. D 72 a

CLARK, JOHN [1609-1676]   438
Ill newes from New-England: or a narative [*sic*]
of [her] persecution . . . *L* 1652. smQ [20] 76 c Hn
JCB LC
—iss. 2, word "narative" in title spelled correctly b

CLARK, JOHN   439
Considerations on the purity of the principles of
William H. Crawford . . . To which is added some
remarks upon the introduction of Africans into
this state . . . *Augusta Ga* 1819. O 208 errata slip aa
—rptd., with pref., *N Y* 1823. O 78 a

CLARK (REV. JOHN).
"Father Clark"; . . . sketches and incidents of:
See Peck, John M.

CLARK, JOHN A.   440
Gleanings by the way . . . *Phil* 1842. D 352 a
Observations made on trips through the Ohio
and Mississippi valleys.

CLARK, JONAS   441
The fate of blood-thirsty oppressors . . . A sermon . . . to commemorate the murder, bloodshed,
and commencement of hostilities between Great-
Britain and America . . . *B* 1776. O 31 [8] aa

CLARK, JOSEPH G.   442
Lights and shadows of sailer life . . . including
. . . events of the U. S. exploring expedition. *B*
1847. D 324 a
—rptd. *B* 1848. same collat. with 6pls added
Chapters on the Sandwich islands and on the
Pacific coast.

CLARK, JOSHUA V. H.   443
Onondaga . . . with notes on the several towns
in the county, and Oswego. *Syracuse* 1849. O 2v:
[16] 402; [4] 392 [2] 10pls map a

CLARK, DR. MARTIN V. B.   444
The centennial sketch of Clay county, Nebraska
. . . *Sutton Neb* [1876]. O [2] 22 aa

[CLARK, O. S.]   445
Clay Allison of the Washita . . . Recollections of
Colorado, New Mexico and the Texas panhandle
. . . [*Attica Ind*] 1920. O [2] 38 some cops have
3 inserted lvs aa
—rptd. 1922. O 135 a
—anr ed *Houston* 1954

CLARK, THOMAS   **446**
Sketches of the naval history of the United States . . . *Phil* 1813. D [16] 13–178 [139] front. a
—anr. issue, t. slightly altered, same impr. & collat., 1814.
—ed. 2, enl., "The naval history of the United States . . .," *Phil* 1814. D 2v: 239; [4, 7–12] 17–255 2pls

CLARK, WILLIAM   **447**
The mania of emigrating to the United States and its disadvantages developed . . . Pt. I [all]. *L* 1820. O a

CLARK, GEN. WILLIAM   **448**
Memorial and documents in relation to Indian depredations upon the citizens of Missouri. *Wash* 1826. O 90 fold.tabs aa

CLARK, WILLIAM P.   **449**
Indian sign language . . . *Phil* 1885. O 443 map + 4adv-p a
—rptd. [San José 1959] O 440

CLARKE, ADÈLE   **450**
. . . John Clarke: his adventures . . . *Montreal* 1906. O 47 5pls a
Clarke, a partner of Astor, was at Astoria from 1811 to 1813.

CLARKE, ASA B.   **451**
Travels in Mexico and California . . . *B* 1852. D 138 b AA N Y
Went via central Mexico, Arizona and the Gila to Los Angeles, thence north to the mines.

CLARKE (GEORGE).   **452**
Voyage of: to America. Ed. E. B. O'Callaghan. *Alb* 1867. Q [81] 126 pl a 100 copies ptd.

CLARKE, H. C.   **453**
The Confederate States almanac . . . for 1862. *Vicksburg* [1861]. D 176 a

CLARKE, H. C.   **454**
Diary of the war for separation . . . to the battle of Shiloh . . . *Vicksburg* 1862. D 56 aa
—enl. ed. "including Walker's narrative of the battle of Shiloh," same impr. & date. D 191 a
—anr. issue, *Augusta Ga* 1862. same collat.

CLARKE, HENRY   **455**
A history of the Sabbatarians or Seventh Day Adventists in America . . . *Utica* 1811. D 196 [4] a
—rptd., same impr., 1813. D

CLARKE, JOHN, Lieut. of Marines   **456**
An impartial and authentic narrative of the battle . . . on Bunker's hill . . . *L* 1775. O [2] 32 c
—ed. 2, with adds., *L* 1775. O [2] 36 b NYS
—Am. ed. [*N Y* 1868]. O a 99copies ptd. a

CLARKE (LEWIS).   **457**
Narrative of the sufferings of: during a captivity . . . among the Algerines of Kentucky . . . *B* 1845. D 108 port a
—anr. ed. "Narratives of the sufferings of Lewis and Milton Clarke . . . during a captivity . . . among slaveholders of Kentucky," *B* 1846. D 144 2ports
—rptd. same impr. & collat. 1854.

CLARKE, PETER D.   **458**
Origin and traditional history of the Wyandotts . . . *Tor* 1870. 16° [6] 158 a

CLARKE, PEYTON N.   **459**
Old King William homes and families . . . *Louisv* 1897. O [8] 211 11 pls a

[CLARKE, WILLIAM]   **461**
Observations on the . . . conduct of the French . . . encroachments upon the British colonies in North America . . . To which is added, wrote by another hand; observations [etc.]. *B* 1755. Q [12] 47 [15] b AA BA Hn NYP Y
—Eng. ed., au. named, *L* 1755. O [10] 54 aa
The added observations were by Franklin.

CLARKSON, THOMAS S.   **462**
A biographical history of Clermont or Livingston Manor . . . *Clermont N Y* 1869. O 319 5pls a 150copies ptd.

CLAUSSON, NIELS C.   **463**
Undersogelse om Americas opdagelse har mere skadet end gavnet det menneskelige Kien. *Copenh* 1785. D [4] 160 a

CLAVERS, MRS MARY [pseud.]
See Kirkland, Mrs. Caroline M.

CLAVIÈRE, ETIENNE, and BRISSOT   **464**
DE WARVILLE, JACQUES P.
De la France et des États-Unis . . . *L* 1787. O [48] 344 a
—rptd. n.p. [*ca* 1787]. D [24] 448
—Eng. ed. "Considerations on the relative situations of France and the United States . . .," *L* 1788. O [18, 34] 326 port
—anr. Eng. ed. "The commerce of America with Europe . . .," *L* 1794. O [54] 348 port
—Am. ed. *N Y* 1795. D [36] 228 port
This title was also issued as a volume of both French and English editions of *Nouveau voyage dans les États-Unis, q.v.*, under Brissot de Warville, Jacques P.

CLAVIGERO, FRANCISCO J.   **465**
Storia della California. *Venice* 1789. O 2v: 276 [2]; 212 [2], map b B N NYP Y
—Sp. ed., with Palou's life of Serra added, "Historia de la Antigua ó Baja California," *Mex* 1852. O [14] 252 [6] [map mentioned not issued] aa

—Eng. ed. abr. "Historical outline of Lower California," *S F* 1862. O 79 a

Essentially confined to Lower California affairs, but contains official license for Salvatierra and Kino's expedition and account of the founding of the Mission at San Francisco.

[CLAXTON, CHRISTOPHER]   466
Naval monitor . . . observations on the naval actions with America . . . *L* 1815. D [12] 235 a
—rptd. *L* 1833. D [2] 263

CLAY (CASSIUS M.)   467
The life . . . of: Vol. I[all]. *Cin* 1886. O 600 7pls a

CLAY, CASSIUS M.   468
Writings . . . Ed. by Horace Greeley. *N Y* 1848. O 536 port a

CLAY, JEHU C.   469
Annals of the Swedes on the Delaware. *Phil* 1835. 16° 180 port a
—rptd. *Phil* 1854.
—ed. 2, enl., *Phil* 1858. D 179 2pls

CLAY, JOHN   470
My life on the range . . . *Chi* [1924]. O [8] 366 [2] 17pls aa

CLAY, JOHN   471
New world notes . . . *Kelso, Scotl* 1875. 16° [8] 200 + 4adv-p aa
Chapters on Va., Ill., Ia., Neb., Col., etc.

CLAYSON, EDWARD   472
Historical narratives of Puget sound . . . [*Seattle* 1911]. D 106 port a

[CLAYTON, AUGUSTIN S.]   473
A vindication of the . . . policy of . . . Georgia. *Athens* 1827. O [10] 9–90 b NYP

CLAYTON, WILLIAM   474
Journal . . . journey of the . . . Mormon pioneers, from Nauvoo to . . . Great Salt Lake. *S L C* 1921. D [10] 376 port a
From this day-by-day account, the official historian of the Mormon exodus prepared his famous *Guide*. A 28-page index was issued in 1942 at Salt Lake City.

CLAYTON, WILLIAM   475
The Latter-Day Saints' emigrants' guide. *St L* 1848. D 24 dd G Hn N Y
—rptd., in facs., *S L C* n.d. [1921] D 24 a
Best guide for the itinerary covered, Council Bluffs to Salt Lake.

CLEAR CREEK AND BOULDER   476
VALLEYS, COLORADO.
History of: . . . *Chi* 1880. Q [12] 17–713 pls aa

CLELAND, ROBERT G.   477
The cattle on a thousand hills. Southern California, 1850–1870. *San Marino Calif* 1941. O [14] 327[incl.pls] a
—rptd same impr 1951. O [18] 13–365

CLEMENS, ORION   478
City of Keokuk in 1856 . . . also, a sketch of the Black Hawk war [etc.] *Keokuk* 1856. D 44 aa
This is same as following entry, with directory portion omitted.

CLEMENS, ORION   479
Keokuk city cirectory, for 1856–7 . . . Also, a sketch of the Black Hawk war [etc.] *Keokuk* 1856. D 112 + 41adv-p aa
By the brother of "Mark Twain." First Keokuk directory.

[CLEMENS, SAMUEL L.]   480
Life on the Mississippi. *B* 1883. O 624 [incl. pls] "Osgood" at bottom of spine; p441, cut of au. being cremated; p443, caption for building pictured given as "St. Louis Hotel" few copies had gilt edges. aa
—Eng. ed., pub. 5days prior to Am. ed., *L* same date, D [28] 563 advs dated March, 1883. a
—Canadian pirated ed. [portion only], *Tor* 1876. D date in Arabic; verso of 1/2 t. blank; t. on front cover stamped diagonally

[CLEMENS, SAMUEL L.]   481
Roughing it. By Mark Twain [*pseud.*] *Hart* 1872. O 591 + 1adv-p 8pls [incl 2 fronts] Some copies had gilt edges aa
—later issues show a battered "M" in line 1 of Contents, a damaged "y" in "My," first word of Chap. I, and missing words from lines 20/21, p. 242 a
—Eng. ed. and actual ed. 1, issued a week prior to Am. ed., *L* 1872. D 2v: [v.I "Roughing it," v.II "Innocents at home."] a
Valuable as an autobiographical chapter in the author's life and as a vidid portrayal of Nevada mining life in the '60s.

CLEMENT, JOHN   482
Sketches of the first emigrant settlers in Newton township, Old Gloucester County, West New Jersey. *Camden* 1877. O 442 errata 1. 3maps port a

[CLEMENT, SAMUEL]   483
Truth is no slander . . . *Natchez* 1827. D 72 a
Rabid condemnation of Andrew Jackson's conduct at the battle of New Orleans, urging his unfitness for the Presidency.

CLEMENTS, J. I.   484
The Klondyke . . . A complete guide to the gold fields. *L A* 1897. D 98 map + 2adv-p a

117

CLEVELAND, RICHARD J.   **485**
A narrative of voyages and commercial enterprises. *C* 1842. D 2v: [16] 249; [8] 240 aa
—ed. 2, enl. *C* 1843. D 2v in 1: [40] 249; [8] 244 a
—ed. 3, *B* 1850. D 407 4pls
—ed. 4, "Voyages . . . of the sons of New England," *N Y* 1855.
—Eng. eds.: *L* 1842; *L* 1843.
Includes voyages to California and the Northwest coast, 1799–1802.

CLEVELAND, STAFFORD C.   **487**
History and directory of Yates county, N.Y. Vol I [all] *Penn Yan* 1873. O [28] 766 [13] maps & pls aa

CLEVELAND, PAST AND PRESENT.
See Joblin, M.

CLEVELAND.
A directory of: . . . 1837. *See* McCabe, Julius F. B.

CLEVER, CHARLES P.   **488**
New Mexico: her resources . . . *Wash* 1868. O 48 [incl wraps] a

CLIFT, G. GLENN   **489**
History of Maysville and Mason county [Ky.] Vol.I[all]. *Lex* 1936. O [10] 461 map a

CLINCH, BRYAN J.   **490**
California and its missions . . . *S F* 1904. O 2v: 228; 538. 2 fronts.incl. in paginat. aa
Almost the entire edition destroyed in the San Francisco fire.

CLINTON, DE WITT   **491**
Correspondence on the importance . . . of a railroad from New York to New Orleans . . . *N Y* 1830. O [4] 23 aa

CLINTON (GEORGE)   **492**
A treaty between: and the Six . . . Nations . . . held at Albany . . . August and September, 1746. *N Y* 1746. F 23 b BA NYP

CLINTON (SIR HENRY) and   **493**
CORNWALLIS (EARL).
Correspondence between: [*N Y* 1781]. O 76 [4] a
—Eng. ed. [*L* 1783].

CLINTON (LIEUT. GEN. SIR HENRY).   **494**
A letter from: to the commissioners of public accounts, relative to some observations . . . which may be judged to imply censure on the late commanders . . . in America. *L* 1784. O 31 + explanatory slip [in some copies] a

[CLINTON, SIR HENRY]   **495**
Memorandums . . . respecting plunder taken after a siege . . . [*L*] 1794. O [4] 106 aa

Concerning capture of Charleston and sale of American property.

CLINTON (LIEUTENANT-GENERAL   **496**
SIR HENRY)
Narrative of: relative to his conduct . . . in North-America . . . *L* 1783. O [4] 115 errata slip a
—5 other Eng. eds., same yr.
—ed. 7, *L* 1785. O [4] 87
—Am. ed. *N Y* 1783. Q [2] 39
—rptd. *Phil* 1866. O 250 cops ptd.

CLINTON'S (SIR HENRY)   **497**
CO-OPERATIONS
Clinton's (Sir Henry) co-operations with Sir Peter Parker, on the attack of Sullivan's Island . . . A narrative of: *N Y* [1780? 1781?]. O 39 b N NYH NYP

CLINTON, SIR HENRY   **498**
Observations on Mr. Stedman's History of the American war. *L* 1794. Q [4] 34 aa
—rptd. *N Y* 1864. same collat. a

CLINTON, LIEUT. GEN. SIR HENRY   **499**
Observations on some parts of the Answer of Earl Cornwallis to Sir Henry Clinton's Narrative. *L* 1783. O [4] 35 114 fold.tab a
—rptd. same impr. & collat., 1783
—Am. ed. *Phil* 1866. O [8] 35 116 tab 200 copies ptd.

CLINTON'S (SIR HENRY) NARRATIVE.
A reply to: . . . *See* Cornwallis, Earl.

CLINTON [IA.] DIRECTORY   **500**
Clinton [Ia.] directory . . . and a historical sketch . . . *Clinton* 1869. O 166 aa
Its first history as well as its first directory.

[CLUNY, ALEXANDER]   **501**
The American traveller; or, observations on the present state . . . of the British colonies . . . *L* 1769. Q [8] 122 map pl b AA JCB N NYP Y
—anr. issue, differs only in not having au.'s printed signature to dedication b
—rptd. [*L*] 1770. D 89 aa
—Am. ed. [*Phil*] 1770. D 90 aa
—Fr. tr., *see* under Mandrillon, Jos., "Le voyageur américain . . ."
—Ger. ed., from Fr. ed., "Reisen durch Amerika . . .," *Leip* 1783. O 238 a
A survey of Anglo-American trade just prior to the Revolution, showing that the colonies were no drain on British economy.

CLYMAN (JAMES) . . . frontiersman.
See Camp, Chas. L.

COAHUILA AND TEXAS   **502**
Constitution of the United Mexican States: the

general colonization law, and the colonization law of the state of Coahuila and Texas. *Natchez* 1826. O 51 c S [only copy known]

Laws and decrees of the state of Coahuila 503 and Texas. To which is added the constitution of said state ... *Houston* 1839. O 354 [8] 7 aa
—Sp tr same impr, date & collat aa

COAHUILA Y TEJAS   504
Constitucion política del estado libre de Coahuila y Tejas *Mex* 1827. 16° 108 [2] c Hn TxU
—rptd. *Leona Vicario* [i.e. Saltillo] n.d. [1829] b G S [only cops kn]
—Eng. tr. *Natchitoches* 1827. D 48 dd NYP S TxU Y
—anr. Eng. ed. *Chillicothe* 1829. O 34 [some copies have a 35-p. "Constitution of the Mexican States," bound in] c G S
—anr. Eng. ed., with adds., *N Y* 1832. O 113 aa
First Texas constitution, as a Mexican state.

Memoria en que el gobernador del ... 505 Coahulla y Tejas: da cuenta de los ramos de su administracion ... *Leona-Vicario* 1833. O 7 + 15 statistical tables b Y

Nota estadistica remitida por el gobierno 506 supremo del estado de Coahuila y Tejas: con arreglo de la Constitucion Federal. *Mex* 1826. sm Q 99 aa

COALE, CHARLES B.   507
The life and adventures of Wilburn Waters ... embracing early history of southwestern Virginia ... *Rich* 1878. O [14] 17–265 aa

[COALE, EDWARD J.]?   508
An original memoir on the Floridas ... *Balt* 1821. O 43 aa
Example of early Fla. promotional literature.

COBB, GOVERNOR [HOWELL]   509
Governor Cobb, to Governor Means, on the boundary between Georgia and South Carolina. *Columbia S C* 1852. O 23 a

COBB, JOSEPH B.   510
Mississippi scenes ... *Phil* 1851. D [8] 13–250 + 6adv-p aa
—ed. 2, same impr., date & collat. a

[COBB, JOSIAH]   511
A green hand's first cruise ... with a residence of five months in Dartmoor. *Balt* 1841. D 2v: [8] 13–278; 329 a
—anr. issue, same date & collat. *B*

COBB, SANFORD H.   512
Story of the Palatines ... *N Y* 1897. O 319 a

COBB, THOMAS R. R.   513
An historical sketch of slavery ... *Phil* 1858. O [4] 23–302 a
Separate printing of a portion of his larger work of same date, *An enquiry into the law of Negro slavery in the United States*, of which volume one only appeared.

COBBET, THOMAS   514
Civil magistrates power in matters of religion ... with a brief answer to a ... pamphlet called Ill news from New-England ... by John Clark ... *L* 1653. Q 2pts in 1: [12] 108; 52 c N

COBBET (sic) (MR. WILLIAM).   515
British honour and humanity ... exemplified in the modest publication ... of: ... by a friend to regular government. *Phil* 1796. O 58 a
Attributed to both John Swanwick and Mathew Carey.

COBBETT, WILLIAM   516
The emigrant's guide ... including ... letters from English emigrants now in America ... *L* 1829. D [20] 153 a
—rptd., same impr. & collat. 1830; 1838.

[COBBETT, WILLIAM]   517
A letter to the infamous Tom Paine ... By Peter Porcupine. Ed. 2, *Phil* [1796]. O 64 + 5adv-p a
—Eng. ed. *L* 1797. O 23

COBBETT, WILLIAM   518
Letters on the late war ... *N Y* 1815. O 407 port a
—anr. ed. "Letters on the American war ...," *Phil* 1815. D [8] 400

[COBBETT, WILLIAM]   519
The life and adventures of Peter Porcupine ... *Phil* 1796. O 58 + adv-p a
—ed. 2, same impr. & date. O 56
—rptd. *Phil* 1797. D 58
—Eng. ed. "The life of William Cobbett, by himself," *L* 1809. O

[COBBETT, WILLIAM]   520
The life of Thomas Paine ... *L* 1797. O [2] 60 a
—Am. ed. *Phil* 1797. D 60

[COBBETT, WILLIAM]   521
A little plain English ... on the treaty, negotiated with his Britannic Majesty, and on the conduct of the President ... *Phil* 1795. O [8] 111 a rptd. B 1795
—ed. 2, *Phil* 1796. O [8] 77
—Eng. ed. *L* 1795. O 110

[COBBETT, WILLIAM]   522
A New-Year's gift to the Democrats; or obser-

vations on . . . "A vindication of Mr. Randolph's resignation." *Phil* 1796. O 71 a
—ed. 2, same impr., date & collat.
—ed. 3, *Phil* 1798. same collat.

COBBETT, WILLIAM   **523**
The pride of Britannia humbled; or, the queen of the ocean unqueen'd, "by the American cock boats," . . . *N Y* 1815. D 216 front a
—new ed. *Phil* 1815. same collat.
—rptd. *Cin* 1817. same collat.

[COBBETT, WILLIAM]   **524**
The trial of republicanism . . . injurious and debasing consequences of republican government and writen constitutions . . . *L* 1801. O 63 a

COBBETT, WILLIAM   **525**
A year's residence in the United States . . . *N Y* Clayton & Kingsland 1818–19. 16° 3 separate pts, consecutively paged, 432 aa
—anr. issue, *N Y* for the au. 1818–19. 16° 3pts in 1 same collat. a
—rptd., same collat. *N Y* 1819.
—Eng. eds.: *L* 1818–19. D 3pts port; *L* 1819. O 3pts in 1 map; *Belf* 1818. D; *L* 1822. 16° map; *L* 1828. D 370 map
Hulme's *Journal*, embracing account of Birkbeck's Illinois settlement, is contained in the third part; for earlier printing of extracts from that journal *see* Smith, Thomas, of Liverpool.

COBLER, FRANK, and SWANWICK,   **526**
T. F., comps.
Tucson and Tombstone . . . directory . . . with other . . . information concerning both cities. *Tucson* 1883. O 224 [2] aa

COCHRAN, MRS. M. A.   **527**
Posie; or, from reveille to retreat. *Cin* 1896. D 194 front. a

COCHRANE, CAPT. JOHN D.   **528**
Narrative of a pedestrian journey through Russia and Siberian Tartary . . . to the frozen sea and Kamtchatka, 1820–23. *L* 1824. O [8] 564 2fold. maps a
—ed. 2, enl., same impr. & date. O 2v: [16] 428; [4] 344 + lf. of binder's directions 3maps 6pls [2col.]
Journal of a year's residence on the shores of Bering's Sea, offering much on the explorations of Wrangel, Vassilieff and Kotzebue, and on the trade carried on by the Russian-American Fur Company. An Appendix in Ed 2 ridicules Captain Burney's theory of a probable junction of the American and Asiatic continents.

COCHRANE, JOSEPH   **529**
Centennial history of Mason county, Illinois . . . *Springfield* 1876. O 352 a

CODE NOIR (LE)   **530**
Code noir (Le), ou recueil des réglemens . . . concernant le gouvernement . . . la discipline et le commerce des negrés dans les colonies francoises. *P* 1740. 16° 504 b
—other eds., same impr.: 1742; 1743; 1752; 1767. b
—most complete ed. *P* 1788. 16° 648 aa
—Am. ed. *N O* 1778. b
Includes edicts applicable to Louisiana slaves; in force until 1803, when the colony was ceded to the United States.

CODY (WILLIAM F.)   **531**
The life of: . . . an autobiography. *Hart* [1879]. O 365 port aa
—anr. ed., amplified to include his later exploits and those of Boone, Crockett and Carson, "Story of the wild west . . .," *Phil* [1888]. O 766 col.front a
Probably ghost-written by Prentiss Ingraham.

CODY, WILLIAM F.   **532**
True tales of the plains. *N Y* Empire Book Co. 1908. D [4] 259 16pls a
—anr. issue, same date & collat., with 6adv-p added, *N Y* Cupples & Leon.

COE, CHARLES H.   **533**
Juggling a rope . . . also the truth about Tom Horn, "king of the cowboys" . . . *Pendleton Ore* 1927. D 114 front. a

COE, GEORGE W.   **534**
Frontier fighter . . . who fought and rode with Billy the Kid. *B* 1934. O [16] 220 7pls a
—rptd. Albuquerque [1951]

COEUR D'ALENE COUNTRY (THE).   **535**
A report on the labor unions of: with reference to the crimes . . . *Wardner Ida* 1899. O 47 a

COFFEEN, H[ENRY] A.   **536**
Vermilion county [Ill.], historical . . . *Danville Ill* [1871?] D 116 map aa

COFFIN, CHARLES   **537**
History of the battle of Breed's hill . . . *Saco* 1831. O 38 a
—rptd. *Port* 1835. O 36

COFFIN, CHARLES C.   **538**
The history of Boscawen and Webster . . . *Concord N H* 1878. O [32] 666 map a

COFFIN (ELIJAH).   **539**
The life of: with a reminiscence, by his son, Charles F. Coffin . . . [*Cin*?]. 1863. O 307[incl. blank lf before text] port a
Contains the day-by-day journal kept by this pioneer Indiana Quaker on travels in Kansas, Iowa, Carolina, etc., 1848–61.

COFFIN (LEVI).   **540**
Reminiscences of: the reputed president of the underground railroad . . . *Cin* Western Tract Soc. [1876]. O [8] 712 2ports a
—ed. 2, *Cin* 1880. O [8] 732 2ports
—Eng. ed. *L* 1876. O

COFFIN, LEWIS A., and   **541**
HOLDEN, ARTHUR C.
Brick architecture of the colonial period in Maryland and Virginia. *N Y* 1919. Q 29 118pls a

COGGESHALL, GEORGE   **542**
A history of American privateers . . . *N Y* 1856. O [56] 438 8pls a
—ed. 2, same impr., date & collat.
—ed. 3, enl. *N Y* 1861. O [56] 482 pls

COGHLAN (MRS. [MARGARET]).   **543**
Memoirs of: . . . *L* 1794. D 2v: [26] 152; [2] 172 aa
—rptd. *Dub* 1794. D [20] 171; *Cork* 1794. 16° [16] 138 a
—Am. ed. *N Y* 1795. D 184 p3–6 of Preface suppressed in many copies
—rptd. *N Y* 1864. O [8] 158 120copies[20 on L.P.]
Narrative of a lady famous for her affair with Colonel Burr in the Revolution.

COGSWELL, LEANDER W.   **544**
History . . . of Henniker . . . New Hampshire . . . *Concord* 1880. O 808 fold.map 21pls a

COHEN, MYER M.   **545**
Notices of Florida and the campaigns. *Charleston SC* 1836. D 240 map port a

COKE, E[DWARD] T.   **546**
A subaltern's furlough . . . in various parts of the United States . . . *L* 1833. O [12] 486 map 13pls a
—Am. ed. *N Y* 1833. D 2v: [4] 9–222; [4] 188. [pls called for were issued separately; *see* next entry].

COKE, EDWARD T.   **547**
Views in North America. n.p. [N Y]? ptd., *L* Hullmandel [1833]. Q 12pls aa
Intended to accompany the American edition of *A subaltern's furlough.*

COKE, HENRY J.   **548**
A ride over the Rocky mountains to Oregon and California . . . *L* 1852. O [10] 388 [2] port aa
On this perilous 1850 trip undertaken for sheer adventure by two young English sportsmen, two of their seven companions perished; the survival of any was a miracle.

COKE, HENRY J.   **549**
Tracks of a rolling stone. *L* 1905. O [6] 349 port + 2adv-p a

—ed. 2, same impr. & date. O [8] 360 port
Incorporates some details of his 1850 overland trip not given in his earlier book.

COKE, THOMAS   **550**
Extracts from the journals of [his] three visits to America. *L* 1790. D 120 [12] a
—anr. ed., embracing 5 visits to America, *L* 1793. D 195
—rptd., *Dub* 1816 D [4] 272; *L* 1817
Only his first, third, fourth and fifth trips were to the continent; the others were to the West Indies.

COKE, REV. DR. [THOMAS]   **551**
Journal of [his] fourth tour on the continent of America. *L* 1792. D 23 a
Visited Virginia, Carolinas and Georgia.

COKE, THE REV. THOMAS, THE   **552**
REV. FRANCIS ASBURY, et al.
Minutes of several conversations between: at a conference, begun at Baltimore . . . Composing a form of discipline for the . . . Methodist Episcopal Church in America. *Phil* 1775. D 35 aa
The first Methodist *Discipline*, the foundation of this church in the United States.

COKER (DANIEL).   **553**
Journal of: . . . *Balt* 1820. O 52 aa
Describes the trip under the leadership of this Maryland Negro, of 90 colonists to West Africa, the first fruition of the American Colonization Society's efforts to solve the problem of American freedmen.

COKER, JAMES L.   **554**
History of company "E", Sixth S. C. infantry. *Charleston* 1899. D 210 150cops ptd aa

COLBERT, E.   **555**
Chicago. Historical . . . sketch of the Garden City . . . *Chi* 1868. O 120 a
Sometimes bound with Bross, William, *History of Chicago* . . .

COLBURN, J. G. W., ed.   **556**
The life of Sile Doty . . . noted thief and daring burglar . . . *Toledo* 1880. O 269 3pls b
—rptd. *Det.* 1948 D [16] 288 port. a
A predatory profession, practised chiefly in Michigan, Indiana and Ohio, and told of with gusto by the old rogue at seventy-five; his horrified family succeeded in destroying many copies.

COLBY, CHARLES   **557**
Hand-book of Illinois . . . *N Y* 1854. 18° 36map a
—rptd. same impr. & collat. 1855.

COLBY, GEN. L. W.   **558**
Report . . . on the Indian campaign . . . at the Pine Ridge agency. *Lincoln* 1891. O 23 map aa

COLDEN (CADWALLADER). **558a**
The conduct of: ... [*L*] 1767. O [4] 2–66 b H Y
—Am. ed. [*N Y*] 1767. O [4] 2–56 b AA N NYP
Vindication of his conduct concerning the Stamp Act, etc., with special reference to the New York riots.

COLDEN, CADWALLADER **559**
An explication of the first causes of action in matter, and of the cause of gravitation. *N Y* 1745. D [6] 44 c ColumbiaU Hn NYP
—Eng. ed. *L* 1746. D 75 b NYP
—Eng. ed. 2, enl., *L* 1751. aa
—rptd., t. altered, *L* 1752. aa
—Fr tr *Bordeaux* 1751. D a
First New York scientific publication.

COLDEN, CADWALLADER **560**
The history of the Five Indian Nations ... *N Y* 1727. D [20] 119 dd JCB N NYP [of 10 known copies]
rptd., ed. Shea, *N Y* 1866. O [42] 18 141 map port a 125 copies[25 on L.P.] a
—Eng. ed., considerably altered, but with adds., *L* 1747. O [20] 90 [4] 91–204 283 map aa
—Eng. ed. 2, same sheets with new t-p, *L* 1750. some copies undated aa
—Eng. ed. 3, *L* 1755. D 2v: [16] 260; [4] 251 [8]. map a
First history of the Iroquois Confederation and first historical work printed in New York.

[COLDEN, CADWALLADER] ed. **561**
Papers relating to an act of assembly of ... New-York; for encouragement of the Indian trade ... *N Y* 1724. F [2] 24map [first one made in N.Y.]. dd NYP 2copies known
Incporporated in the second [London] and later editions of Colden's *History of the Five Indian nations*.

COLDEN, CADWALLADER D. **562**
Memoir ... at the celebration of the completion of the New York canals. *N Y* 1825–6. Q [8] 408 [2] 47maps & pls 8facs aa

COLDEN, CADWALLADER D. **563**
A vindication of the steam boat right, granted by the state of New York ... *Alb* 1818. D 178 a
—rptd. *N Y* 1819. O 96

COLE, ARTHUR C. **564**
The Whig party in the south. *Wash* 1913. D [12] 392 6 pls a

COLE (CORNELIUS). **565**
Memoirs of: ... *N Y* 1908. O [10] 354 port a

COLE, CYRENUS **566**
A history of the people of Iowa. *Cedar Rapids* 1921. O [16] 572 2maps 8pls a

COLE, DAVID **567**
History of Rockland county, N. Y. *N Y* 1884. O 344 [75] maps & pls aa

COLE, J. R. **568**
History of Greenbrier county [W. Va.]. *Leesburg* [1917]. O 347 a

COLE, MAJOR WILLIAM L. **569**
California ... *N Y* 1871. O 103 aa
Cover title is dated 1872.

COLEMAN (ELDER R. J.) **570**
Life and ministrial labors of: *Little Rock* 1894. 16° [6] 80 port errata lf a

[COLEMAN, ROBERT M.] **571**
Houston displayed, or, who won the battle of San Jacinto? *Velasco* 1837. D 38 b S TxU [of 3copies known]
—rptd [Houston 1841] same collat b

[COLEMAN, WILLIAM] ed. **572**
A collection of the facts and documents, relative to the death of ... Alexander Hamilton ... *N Y* 1804. O [4] 238 a
—abr. ed. same impr. & date. O 46
—anr. ed. complete, *B* 1904. O 276 430 copies ptd.

[COLEMAN, WILLIAM]? **573**
An examination of the president's reply to the New-Haven remonstrance ... *N Y* 1801. O 69 a
—anr. ed. *N Hav* 1801.
Ascribed also to Wm Cranch.

COLEMAN, WILLIAM H., comp. **574**
Historical sketch book and guide to New Orleans ... *N Y* 1885. D [4] 324 map[14 × 10 3/4] front. a
—issue 1: Hearn's name omitted at foot of p299; if in wraps, front cover has an alligator holding a sign in its mouth, and at bottom words "Exposition edition."
—issue 2: Hearn's name at foot of p299; map larger [37 1/2 × 27]
Map not issued in all copies.

COLESON, ANN **575**
Narrative of her captivity among the Sioux ... *Phil* 1864. O [2] 19–28 33–46 53–58 63–70 front. 3pls [actually 40 pp of text] a
—anr. issue, same impr., date & collat., but carries wrap. & copyright date of 1866
—rptd. 1866; 1875; 1877; [1882]
—Norw. tr. "Fangenskap bland Sioux-Indianeren ...," *Minneap* n.d. D 61

COLLECTION **576**
Collection d'estampes representant les differents evenemens de la guerre qui a procuré l'indépendance aux États Unis ... *P* Godefroy & Ponce [1784?

1786?]. Q eng.t. 16pls [nos. 6, 9, 11, 13, 15, 16 not numb. at top] b NYP
anr.issue, no separate t-p [pl one, "Précis . . .," serving as such, with its reading: "Recueil d'estampes . . .,"] *P* Ponce & Godefroy [1784? 1786?]. Q 16 numb.pls aa
—rptd. *P* 1918. Q 16pls a
Some copies of orig. ed. were printed on Large Paper in folio. First French book with a title-page mentioning the United States.

Collection (A) of authentic discoveries . . . *L* 1763. *See* under *Voyages (The), adventures and discoveries of the following circum-navigators . . .*

Collection (A) of Indian anecdotes. *Con-*   **577** *cord N H* 1837. 64° 192 a

Collection (A) of interesting . . . papers, relative to the dispute between Great Britain and America . . . *See* Almon, John.

Collection (A) of modern and contemporary voyages and travels. *See* Phillips, Sir Richard.

Collection of papers containing Declaration   **578** **of independence**; Treaty of alliance between France and the United States . . . *N Y* [1784]. O 96 b

Collection of papers . . . relating to the   **579** **proceedings of His Majesty's commissioners . . .** *N Y* 1778. O [2] 55 [19] + [in some copies] 8p "Proposed Appendix" a

Collection (A) of papers, relative to half-   **580** **pay . . . to officers of the army . . .** *Fish-Kill* 1783. Q 36 b BA N NYP Y
—rptd. *B* 1783. Q 24 aa
—anr. ed., *see* Washington, Geo., "The last official address . . ."
Contains Washington's famous Newburgh address which quelled a threatened revolt by discontented officers.

Collection (A) of state papers relative to   **581** **the first acknowledgement of the sovereignty of the United States . . . and the reception of their Minister by . . . the States General of the United Netherlands.** *Hague* 1782. O 96 aa
—Eng. ed., with adds., *L* 1782. O [4] 100 a

Collections (A) of sundry publications . . .   **582** **in relation to the attack . . . upon the private armed brig General Armstrong . . .** 1814. *N Y* 1833. D [4] 55[mispaged 46] a

COLLES, CHRISTOPHER   **583**
Proposal of a design for the promotion of the interests of the United States . . . by means of inland navigable communication . . . *N Y* 1808. O 22 pl map in some copies aa

COLLES, CHRISTOPHER   **584**
A survey of the roads of the United States . . . [*N Y*] 1789. sm Q 84eng. pls[incl. t-p] Of the 83 road-maps nos 34-39 are found in no copies and were evidently not issued. Some copies have, inserted, a fold. sheet of "Proposals" for this work. c AA LC NYP
Colles was the originator of the Erie canal plan; the maps represent the best engraving done in this country up to this time. In 1785 Colles issued a fourteen-page *Proposals for the speedy settlement of . . . lands on the western frontiers of New York . . .*, his first agitation for this scheme of inland navigation.

COLLINS, CHARLES [comp.]   **585**
City directory of Leavenworth: embracing . . . historical data . . . *Leavenworth* [1866]. D 260 aa
—anr. ed. [1868]. D 188[incl. advs] map a

COLLINS, CHARLES   **586**
History and directory of the Black Hills . . . *Central City Dak* 1878. O 91 + 4adv-p b SDH Y [only 3copies known]
First book printed in the Black Hills.

COLLINS, CHARLES [comp.]   **587**
Mercantile guide and directory for Virginia City, Gold Hill, Silver City and American City . . . with sketches . . . historical and statistical matter [etc.]. *Virginia Nev* [*S F* ptd] 1864–5. O 386 + 15adv-p at front b LC

COLLINS, CHARLES [comp.]   **588**
. . .Omaha directory . . . and an appendix containing . . . historical data . . . [*Omaha* 1866]. O lf of title [80] 97–204 [incl. advs] b G NYP Y
—[2nd directory] *Omaha* 1868. O 224 [incl. advs] map pl aa

COLLINS, CHARLES
The Rocky mountain gold regions . . . *See* Burt, Silas W., and Berthoud, Edward L.

COLLINS, DANIEL   **589**
Narrative of the shipwreck of the brig Betsy . . . and murder of five of her crew, by pirates, on the coast of Cuba. *Wicasset Me* 1825. O 52 a

COLLINS, DENNIS   **590**
The Indians' last fight; or, the Dull Knife raid . . . [*Girard Kan*, 1915]. O 326[incl. front.] 7pls aa

[COLLINS, ELIZABETH]   **591**
Memories of the southern states. *Taunton Eng* 1865. D [6] 116 aa

COLLINS, HUBERT E.   **592**
Warpath and cattle trail [in Oklahoma, etc.]. *N Y* 1928. O [22] 296 a
—rptd. *N Y* [1933]

[COLLINS, JAMES] 593
Autobiography of a revolutionary soldier. Ed. by John M. Roberts. *Clinton La* 1859. D [4] 176 aa
—rptd 1945 O 32 a
Scouting services at King's Mountain and the Cowpens, with later adventures on the Georgia and Tennessee frontiers.

COLLINS, J[OHN] S. 594
Across the plains in '64. *Omaha* 1904. D 151 aa
—ed. 2, & best, containing later frontier experiences, *Omaha* 1904–11. D 2pts in 1: 151; 152 9pls aa
For ten years Collins was Post Trader at Ft. Laramie; he incorporates much unwritten history on the early trans-Missouri region.

COLLINS, LEWIS 595
Historical sketches of Kentucky. *Maysville* 1847. O [16] 560 map pl aa
—rptd, *Maysville & Cin* 1847; *Cin* 1849. O 514 map; same impr 1850. a
—enl ed, by Richard H. Collins *Covington* 1874. O 2v: aa; rptd in one vol, with omissions *Louisv* 1877. a
—oth 2v eds: *Covingt* 1878: 1882: *Louisv* 1924. aa

COLLINS (MRS. NAT) the cattle queen 596
of Montana
Comp. by Charles Wallace. *St. James Minn* [ptd. *Chi*] 1894. O 249 32pls[3 by Russell] b G LC 1000 cops ptd [most of them burned]
—rev. ed. *Spokane* [1902?]. O 260 pls aa

COLLINS, LIEUT. R. M. 597
Chapters from the unwritten history of the war between the states. *St L* 1893. D 335 aa

COLLINS, S. H. 598
The emigrant's guide to . . . the United States . . . *Hull Eng* 1829. D [4] 134 map a
—ed. 2, same impr., collat. & date
—ed. 3, same impr. 1830.
—ed. 4, same impr. n.d. D [4] 180 map
Editions one and two can only be distinguished when in original boards.

COLLISON, JOHN, and BELL, W. A. 599
The Maxwell land grant . . . in Colorado and New Mexico . . . *L* 1870. O 32 [incl front wrap] map aa

COLLISON, WILLIAM H. 600
In the wake of the war canoe . . . adventure amongst the savage . . . tribes of the Pacific coast. *L* 1915. O 351 map 16pls a
—Am. eds.: same collat. *Tor* n.d.; *N Y* n.d.

COLLOT, GEORGES H. V. 601
A journey in North America, containing a survey of the countries watered by the Mississippi, Ohio [etc.]. *P* 1824–6. Q 2v: [12] 310; 372 + atlas [36maps & pls] dd LC N
—rptd. *Florence* 1924–6. O 2v + atlas Q 36maps & pls aa
—[in Fr.] with app. to v. 2 not in the Eng. tr. *P* 1824–6. O 2v: [14] 416 [2] 427 [72] + atlas [36maps & pls] d LC N NYP
Gen. Collot's survey—the most detailed of the western interior up to his time—was made in 1796, probably in concert with Genet's abortive scheme for involving that section in attacking the Spanish possessions in Florida and Louisiana. Both English and French editions were printed simultaneously, in 1805, but not published till 1826, at which time all but 100 copies of the English and 300 of the French were deliberately destroyed.

COLLYER, ROBERT H. 602
Lights and shadows of American life. *B* [1844?]. O 40 cov.t.only a

COLNETT (CAPTAIN JAMES). 603
The journal of: aboard the Argonaut . . . 1789–1791. *Tor* Champlain Soc. 1940. O [32] 328 21maps & pls aa 550 cops ptd

COLNETT, JAMES 604
A voyage to the south Atlantic and . . . into the Pacific . . . *L* 1798. Q [26] 179 port [not in all copies] 9maps & pls b B N NYP Y
Attempting to establish an English furtrading post on Nootka, Colnett's crew was seized and imprisoned by Spaniards, precipitating a controversy which came close to resulting in war. First complete edition, said to have been written by William Combe. It was preceded by a sixteen-page abridged version printed at Trenton, 1787, and reprinted [27 pages] Philadelphia, 1797.

COLONEL DISMOUNTED (THE) . . .
See Bland, Richard.

COLONIAE ANGLICANAE ILLUSTRATAE.
See Bollan, Wm.

COLONIE ICARIENNE . . .
See Cabet, Étienne.

COLORADO 605
Colorado brand book. No. 1. *Denver*, ptd. *Chi*, [*ca* 1884]. 16° [8] 61 b G
—supplementary brands, for 1885, *Denver* [1885] 16° 92 [2] b G

Colorado brand book . . . *Denv* [1887]   605a
D [6] 314 [6] + 3adv-p b

Colorado condensed . . . *Denv* 1881. O 40 a   606

Colorado; its resources, parks and pros-   607
pects as a new field for emigration . . . *L*, priv ptd 1869. Q 2v: [2] 55; [6] 133 [16]. 3maps a
—pub'd ed *L*, Sampson, Low. 1869 Q [2] 217 3 maps 5 pls a

First annual report of the Union Colony   608
of Colorado: including a history of . . . Greeley.
N Y 1871. O 40 map[in some copies] a

The geopgraphy, description [etc.] of cen-   609
tral and southern Colorado. *Pueblo* 1869. D 32 b
ColH H

Gypsy days in Colorado, California, Florida. *See*
Ledyard, L. Wolters.

Historical and descriptive treatise of Fre-   610
mont and Custer counties . . . *Cañon City* [ptd in
Chi?] 1879. O 136 [incl advs] aa

The Rocky mountain directory and Colo-   611
rado gazetteer: for 1871 . . . *Denver* [ptd *Chi* 1870].
O 442 + 202 adv-pp [not incl. in paginat] a

Routes of travel in Colorado: . . . *Denver*   612
1874. 16° 66 a

Western Colorado and her resources . . .   613
[*Aspen* 1891]. O 73 + adv-pp map a

The westward march of emigration . . . in   614
its bearing upon the near future of Colorado and
New Mexico. *Lancaster Pa* 1874. O 53 a

COLORADO SPRINGS . . .   615
Among the mountains; a guide book to: *Colo
Springs* 1873. D 137 [3] fold.map a

COLT, MRS. MIRIAM [DAVIS]   616
Went to Kansas . . . *Watertown N Y* 1862. D 294 a

COLT, NELSON   617
The Devil's Hole, with an account of the visits
made to it in 1679 by De La Salle . . . *Lockport*
1844. D 24 a
—anr. ed. *Niagara City N Y* 1859. D 15

COLT (SAMUEL).   618
Armsmear: the home, the arms and the armory
of: . . . *N Y* 1866. Q 399 map pls b

COLTON, C[ALVIN]   619
Tour of the American lakes, and among the
Indians . . . in 1830 . . . *L* 1833. D 2v: [32] 316;
[8] 387 a

[COLTON, CALVIN]   620
A voice from America to England. *L* 1839. O
[12[321 a
Four chapters deal with slavery and the uncon-
stijutional tactics of abolition societies.

COLTON, J[OSEPH] H. [pub.]   621
The emigrant's handbook . . . directions . . .
especially to those designing to settle in the great
western valley . . . *N Y* 1848. 16° 136 map a

—Eng. ed. *L* 1848. 16° map
See also similar publications entered under the
name of Smith, John Calvin.

COLTON, J[OSEPH] H. [pub.]   622
The State of Indiana delineated . . . *N Y* 1838.
18° 92 + adv-p map[pub separately & found inserted in only a few copies] b ChiU N NYP Y

COLTON, J[OSEPH] H. [pub.]   623
Traveler and tourist's guide book through the
United States . . . *N Y* 1850. 16° [14] 250 2maps[1
fold.] a
—rptd.: 1851; 1852; 1854; 1855; 1856
—anr. ed., comp. R. S. Fisher, *N Y* 1857. 16° 354
map; same impr 1860.
Essentially same as the various handbooks listed
under Smith, John Calvin. Includes material on
California, Oregon and Texas, with overland
routes, etc.

COLTON, J[OSEPH] H. [pub.]
The western tourist, [etc.]. *See* Smith, John
Calvin.

COLTON, WALTER   624
Deck and port . . . *N Y* 1850. D 408 front. 4col.
pls[lith. by Sarony] a
—issue 2, identical except that map was added, the
4 pls are lith. by Sarony & Major and end papers
are blank, while those of issue 1 were ptd.
—other eds.: *N Y* 1854. same collat.; *N Y* 1860.
D 408 front.

COLTON WALTER   625
Three years in California. *N Y* 1850. D 456
12pls fold. facs. a
—rptd. 1851; 1852; 1854; 1856; 1859.
—anr. ed., title changed to "The land of gold."
1860.
Colton was alcalde of Monterey; his narrative is
interesting and valuable.

COLUMBIA, S. C.   626
Proceedings of the state rights meeting, in Columbia, S. C. *Columbia* 1830. O 46 a

Sack and destruction of the city of Columbia, S. C.
See Simms, Wm. G.

Who burnt Columbia? Pt.1[all]. *Charle-*   627
ston 1873. D 121 a
Depositions of claimants against the government and of Generals Sherman and Howard for
the defense.

COLUMBIA RIVER   628
Message from the President . . . communicating
. . . documents relating to an establishment made
at the mouth of the Columbia river. H. Doc. 45.
Wash 1823. O 65 aa

Message from the President . . . **relative**   629
**to the British establishments on the Columbia and
the state of the fur trade** . . . Sen. Doc. 39. *Wash*
1831. O 36 aa
Contains Pilcher's trip—probably at government instigation—to the far North-west, as well as others made by Jackson, Sublette and Jedidiah Smith to the Wind River headwaters, Ft. Vancouver, etc.

Notices of the harbor at the mouth of the Columbia river. *See* Blair, James.

COLUMBUS [OHIO] . . . DIRECTORY
Columbus [Ohio] business directory for 1843–4.
See Siebert, John.

COLUSA COUNTY [CALIF.]   630
Colusa county annual and directory . . . **with
historical** . . . **sketches** . . . *Colusa* 1876. O102 aa

COLUSA COUNTY   631
**Illustrations descriptive of its scenery, etc. With
historical sketch** . . . *SF* 1880. F [4] 7–196 pls b
B CalS
—ed. 2, *Oakl* 1887. F 104 aa

COLVILLE, SAMUEL, comp.   632
Marysville [Calif.] directory for . . . 1853.
Marysville 1853. O 133 b Hn NYP 2copies known
—same, for 1855, *S F* 1855. O [30] 96 [8] aa
Both editions contain historical sketches; the original issue was the first book printed in this town.

COLVILLE, SAMUEL, comp.   633
Sacramento directory for 1853–4 . . . with a history . . . *Sacr* 1853. O [4] 40 [2] 110 [14] aa
—same, for 1854–5. *S F* 1854. O 116 + 64 adv-p aa

COLVILLE, SAMUEL, comp.   634
San Francisco directory. Vol. I[all]. *S F* 1856.
O [82] 307 [2] map aa
In most copies, the list of Vigilantes, pages 226–227, was covered over by advertising.

COLVOCORESSES, GEORGE M.   635
Four years in a government exploring expedition . . . [commanded by Captain Charles Wilkes.]
N Y 1852. D 372 + 3adv-p 20pls[15 incl. in paginat.] a
—rptd. 4 times by 1855.

COLYER (VINCENT).   636
Report of: on peace with the Apaches of New
Mexico . . . *Wash* 1872. O 58 a
Includes a sickening account of the massacre, perpetrated by Tucson citizens and their Indian allies, of eighty-five friendly Apaches.

COMAN, KATHARINE   637
Economic beginnings of the far west . . . *N Y*
1912. O 2v: [20] 418; [10] 450. 4maps 47 pls a
—rptd., same impr., 1925. O 2v in 1

COMBATTANTS FRANCAIS   638
Les combattants francais de la guerre américaine, 1778–83. *P* 1903. Q [22] 327 pls a
—Am. ed., Sen.Doc. 77, *Wash* 1905. Q [2] 453 10pls

COMBE, GEORGE   639
Notes on the United States . . . during a phrenological visit, 1838–40. *Edin* 1841. D 3v: [38] 372
[3]; [2] 400 [1]; [2] 488 [1] + 6 adv-p. map a
—Am. ed. *Phil* 1841. D 2v: [26] 13–374; [2] 9–405

COMBS (GENERAL LESLIE).   640
Narrative of the life of: embracing incidents in the early history of the north-western territory.
N Y 1852. O 23 port cover t.only aa
—anr. ed. [*Wash*] 1852. O 20 aa
—rptd. *Wash* 1855. O 24 a

COMETTANT, [JEAN P.] OSCAR   641
L'Amérique telle qu'elle est; voyage anecdotique de Marcel Bonneau dans le nord et le sud des États-Unis . . . *P* 1864. 16° [4] 392 a
—best ed. "Voyage pittoresque . . .," *P* 1866. O
[8] 469 + 2 adv-p 22 pls[4 col.] aa
—rptd. with only 4pls

COMETTANT, [JEAN P.] OSCAR   642
Trois ans aux États-Unis. Étude de moeurs et coutumes . . . *P* 1857. 16° [4] 364 a
—anr. ed. *Brus* 1856-7. 16° 2v
—ed. 2, cor., *P* 1858. 16° [4] 392
—rptd. "Le nouveau-monde, scenes de la vie américaine," *P* 1861. 16° [16] 375
—later eds.: 1863; 1864; 1868; 1870.
—Sp. tr. *Madrid* 1858. Q 288 4pls; *Vera Cruz* 1859,
O 279

COMMENTS   643
Comments on the convention with Spain [relating to Nootka sound, etc.]. *L* 1790. Q 28 b
BritColProvL PortOreL

COMMERCE
Commerce (The) and navigation of the valley of
the Mississippi . . . *See* Allen, Thos.

COMMERCIAL DIRECTORY   644
Commercial directory . . . of the Union . . . *Phil*
1823. Q [8] 242 [2] 41 map 7 pls aa

Commercial directory of the western states   645
and rivers . . . *St L & Chi* 1867. Q [20] 1197 85 73 a

COMMON SENSE
Common sense: addressed to the inhabitants of
America . . . *See* Paine, Thos.

Common sense: in nine conferences be-   646
tween a British merchant and a candid merchant
of America . . . tracing the several causes of the
present contests . . . *L* 1775. Q [10] 117 aa
Arguments supposed to have converted the
"candid" Yankee seem quite unconvincing.

COMMONS, JOHN R., ed.   647
A documentary history of American industrial
society. *Clev* 1910–11. O 11v ports b N NYP

COMMUNICATIONS   648
Communications from several states on the
Resolutions of the legislature of Virginia, respec-
ting the Alien and Sedition laws . . . *Rich* [1800].
D 104 a
Amplified from an earlier undated tract of
twenty pages with same title, printed at Richmond
about 1799.

COMPARISON (A)   649
Comparison (A) of slavery with abolitionism . . .
By Amor Patriae. *N Y* 1848. O 16 a
—enl. ed. "The blasphemy of abolitionism exposed
. . .," *N Y* 1850. O 24

COMPENDIOUS   650
**Compendious account (A) of the most important
battles of the late war,** to which is added, the
curious adventures of Corporal Samuel Stubbs . . .
B 1815. D 24 port b AA LC
—rptd., same place & collat., 1817. aa
Cf. Lathrop, John. *A compendious history* . . . of
which this is, in part, an abridgment.

Compendious history (A) of the late war. *See*
Lathrop, John.

COMPLEAT HISTORY (A)
Compleat history (A) of Spanish America . . .
See Campbell, John.

Compleat history (A) of the late war . . . *See*
Wright, John.

COMPLETE . . .   651
**Complete and accurate account (A) of the very
important debate in the House of Commons** . . . in
which the cause of Mr. Fox's resignation, and the
great question of American independence came
under consideration . . . *L* 1782. O [4] 61 a
—eds. 2 &3, same impr., date & collat.
—Am. ed. *Phil* 1845. O

Complete collection (A) of all the protests   652
of the Peers of Parliament . . . on the great questions of the cause and issue of the war . . . *L* 1782.
O 126 a

Complete (A) historical . . . American atlas . . .
See Carey, Henry C., and Lea, J.

Complete history (A) of the origin and   653
progress of the late war . . . *L* 1763. O 2v: [4] 358;
[2] 359–771 aa
—rptd. *L* 1764. O 2v in 1 same paginat. aa
For similar title—ascribed, as is this, to Edmund
Burke—*see* Wright, John.

Complete history (A) of the present war   654
. . . 1756–1760. *L* 1761. D [4] 548 aa

COMPRESSED VIEW (A)
Compressed view (A) of the points to be discus-
sed, in treating with the United States . . . *See*
Atcheson, Nathaniel.

COMPTON, RICHARD J., ed.   655
Pictorial St. Louis . . . *St L* 1876. obl. Q 215
110pls b LC

COMSTOCK, JOSEPH   656
The tongue of time and star of the states . . .
American antiquities . . . *N Y* 1838. O 487 a

COMSTOCK, WILLIAM   657
The life of Samuel Comstock, the terrible whaleman . . . mutiny and massacre of the officers of the
ship "Globe" . . . *B* 1850. D [4] 115 front. aa

COMSTOCK, WILLIAM   658
A voyage to the Pacific, descriptive of customs
. . . on board Nantucket whale ships. *B* 1838. 16°
72 aa

CONARD, HOWARD L.   659
"Uncle Dick" Wootton . . . *Chi* 1890. O 474
[incl.front. & adv-p at end] 2 pls not incl. in paginat. aa
—rptd. *Columbus* 1950. O 500 copies ptd. a

CONCERNING STEAM BOATS:
Documents without comments. *See* Ogden,
Aaron.

CONCESSIONS
Concessions to America, the bane of Britain . . .
See Marryat, Jos.

CONCILIATION (A)   660
Conciliation (A) with America: adapted to the
constitutional rights of the colonies and the supremacy of Great Britain. *L* 1778. O 55 a

Conciliation with America, the true policy   661
of Great Britain. By a friend to British manufactures. *L* 1811. O 31 a

CONCILIATORY . . .   662
**Conciliatory address to the people of Great
Britain and of the colonies on the present . . . crisis.**
L 1775. O [4] 56 a

Conciliatory bills (The) considered. *L*   663
1778. O 39 a
The Ministry white-washed.

Conciliatory hints, attempting . . . **to remove
party-prejudices** . . . By Philodemus. *See* Tucker,
Thos. T.

CONCISE . . .
**Concise account (A) of voyages for the discovery
of a north-west passage** . . . By a sea officer. *See*
Pickersgill, Lieur. Richard.

**Concise historical account (A) of all the British
colonies in North-America** . . . *See* Wein, Paul.

Concise history (A) of the Spanish America . . .
See Campbell, John.

CONCLIN, GEORGE, pub.
A book for all travelers . . . *See* Cumings, Sam'l.,
The western navigator.

CONCLIN GEORGE [comp.]
New river guide . . . *See* Cumings, Sam'l.

[CONDIE, THOMAS]   664
Biographical memoirs of the illustrious Gen.
George Washington . . . *Phil* Charless & Ralston
1800. 16° 243 aa
—ed. 2, *Phil* Folwell 1800. 16° 217 a
—ed. 3, *Phil* Folwell 1801. 16° 217
—ed. 4, *Phil* Johnson & Warner 1809. 16° 143;
anr.ed. *N Hav* 1809, same collat.
—anr. ed. 4, *Brattleborough* 1811. 16° 211; and
many other eds.
For similar title *see* under Corry, John. *See* also
Trumbull, James; for a plagiarized version, *see*
Kingston, John.

CONDITION OF THE INDIAN TRIBES   665
Report of the . . . special committee appointed
under joint resolution of March 3rd, 1865 . . .
Wash 1867. O 532 a
Lurid details of Chivington's sickening massacre
of unoffending Indians at Sand Creek, Colorado.
cf. The Sand Creek massacre.

CONDUCT   666
**Conduct (The) of a noble commander in America,
impartially reviewed** . . . *L* 1758. O [2] 45 aa
—ed. 2, same impr., date & collat. a
Vindication of Lord Loudoun's conduct of the
war, in 1756–7, probably written by himself, but
also ascribed to J. E. Campbell.

Conduct (The) of Great Britain respecting   667
neutrals. *Phil* 1807. O 72 a

**Conduct (The) of the late administration exam-
ined** . . . *See* Lloyd, Chas.

Conduct (The) of the late ministry . . . *See*
Moreau, Jacob N., *Mémoire contenant les précis
des faits* . . .

Conduct of the ministry impartially exa-   668
mined . . . *L* 1756. O 68 aa
—ed. 2, same impr., date & collat. a
Remonstrance, addressed to London merchants, against imprisoning of British traders on
the Ohio.

[CONDY, JONATHAN W.]?   669
A description of the river Susquehannah . . .
Phil 1796. O [4] 60 map aa

CONE, ANDREW, and JOHNS,   670
WALTER R.
Petrolia: history of the Pennsylvania petroleum
region . . . *N Y* 1870. O 652 12pls aa

CONFEDERATE   671
The Confederate. By a South Carolinian . . .
Mobile [1863]. D 102 aa
Issued in 12 numbers.

Confederate war etchings. By V. Blada. *See*
Volck, Adalbert J.

Constitution of the provisional govern-   672
ment of the Confederate States . . . *Montg* 1861.
O 15 aa

Experience of a Confederate States prisoner . . .
Rich 1862. *See* West, Beckwith.

Journal of the general council of the Prot-   673
estant Episcopal church in the Confederate States.
Augusta Ga 1862–3. O 3pts in 1: 305 aa

Provisional and permanent Constitutions   674
. . . **with the Acts** . . . **of the first session of the provisional Congress of the Confederate States.** *Montg*
1861. O 160 aa
—other eds.: *Milledgeville Ga* 1861. O; *Rich* 1861.
O a
—rptd., with Acts of the 1st and 2nd sessions of
the provisional Congress [enacted at Montgomery]
and the 3rd session [enacted at Richmond], *R*
1861. O a

Uniform and dress of the army of the   675
Confederate States. *Rich* 1861. F [10] 15pl[9 col]
errata slip c Duke Emory
Some copies have an added tipped-in strip
illustrating field caps. Contained in General Order
No. 9, Adjutant and Inspector General's Office.
Reprinted, with naval uniforms added. *N Y* 1960
[O 72 23 pls]

CONFESSIONS   676
Confessions, trials . . . of the most cold blooded

murderers... executed in this country... *B*
1840. D 408 a
—anr. issue, same impr. & collat., 1841.
—rptd. *Hart* 1844. D 420[incl.front.]

CONGER, O. T., ed.   677
Autobiography of a pioneer: or, the travels, *etc.*
of Rev. Samuel Pickard... *Chi.* 1866. D 403 a
Iowa and Illinois in the 'forties.

CONGRESS (THE) CANVASSED...
See Seabury, Sam'l.

CONN, WILLIAM
Cowboys and colonels. See Mandat-Grancy.

CONNECTED VIEW (A)
Connected view (A) of the... internal navigation
of the United States... *See* Armroyd, George.

CONNECTICUT   678
Connecticut Gore title (The), stated and consid-
ered... *Hart* 1799. O 80 aa
—anr. ed. "The rise, progress and effect...,"
Hart 1802. a
Advocates Connecticut's right, based on royal
grants, to this strip of land on the southwest border
of New York, known as "the Connecticut gore".

**An examination of the Connecticut claim to lands
in Pennsylvania.** *See* Smith, *Provost* Wm.

A general history of Connecticut... By a
gentleman of the province. *See* Peters, Sam'l.

An historical narrative... showing the   679
**cause and rise of the Strict Congregational churches
in Connecticut:...** *Prov* 1781. D 44 a

The politics of Connecticut:...   680
By a Federal Republican. *Hart* 1817. O 36 a
Attributed to a Mr. Richards.

The public records of the colony of Con-   681
necticut:... 1636–1767. Ed. J. H. Trumbull and
Charles J. Hoadly. *Hart* 1850–81. O 12v aa

Record of service of Connecticut men in   682
the... revolution... *Hart* 1889. Q 3pts in 1: [18]
780; [2] 170; [2] 171–180 a

Report of the committee to whom was   683
**referred the consideration of accepting from...
Connecticut a cession of the territory west of Pennsylvania...** *Wash* 1800. O 31 a

The right of the Governor... of Con-   684
**necticut to claim and hold the lands within the limits
of their charter, lying west of...** New-York...
Hart 1773. O 47 b AA BP N NYP
Attributed to Samuel Mather.

The security of the rights of citizens of   685
Connecticut considered. *Hart* 1792. O 102 a

Sketch of Connecticut forty years since. *See*
Sigourney, Mrs. Lydia H.

Some seasonable considerations for the   686
good people of Connecticut. *N Y* [Bradford] 1694.
SmQ 50 dd [only 1 cop loc]
One of the earliest N.Y. imprints. Attributed to
Gershom Bulkeley. For reply see below, *Their
Majesties colony of Connecticut vindicated...*

Their Majesties colony of Connecticut   687
**... vindicated from the abuses of a pamphlet...
intituled [*sic*] Some seasonable considerations for
the good people of Connecticut...** *B* 1694. D 43
b LC NYP
For the pamphlet complained of, see above,
*Some seasonable considerations for... people of
Connecticut.*

CONNELLEY, WILLIAM E.   688
...Doniphan's expedition and the conquest of
New Mexico and California... *Topeka* 1907. O
[16] 670 2fold.maps front. a some cops carry *KC*
impr.

CONNELLEY, WILLIAM E.   689
Quantrill and the border wars... *Cedar Rapids*
1910. O 542 port. 2maps a
—rptd *N Y* 1956

CONNELLEY, WILLIAM E.   690
Wild Bill and his era... *N Y* 1933. O [14] 229
12pls a

CONNOLLY (JOHN).   691
A narrative of the transactions, imprisonment,
and sufferings of:... *L* 1783. O [2] 62 b
—rptd. *N Y* 1889. a
Compensation sought by a royalist for imprisonment in America resulting from attempts to
form a Virginia regiment for the King.

CONOVER, MRS. CHARLOTTE R.   692
Concerning the forefathers: a memoir, with per-
sonal narrative and letters of... Col. Robert
Patterson and Col. William Johnston, *N Y* 1902.
O [18] 432 [20] 18pls a
Both of these pioneers were prominent figures
in the early Ohio Valley.

CONRAD, AUGUST   693
Schatten und Lichtblicke aus amerikanischen
Leben während des Secessiones-Krieges. *Hannover*
1879. O [2] 205 aa
—Eng. ed., in part, "The destruction of Columbia,
S. C.," *Roanoke* 1902. O 31 a

[CONRAD, ROBERT T.]   694
General Scott and his staff . . . *Phil* 1848. D [6]
11–224 ports a
—rptd. same impr. & collat. 1849.

CONRAD, T. N.   695
The rebel scout . . . *Wash* 1904. D 220 a

CONSAG, FERNANDO
See under Konsag.

CONSIDÉRANT, VICTOR [P.]   697
Au Texas. *P* 1854. O [2] 194 2maps aa
—ed. 2, enl., *Brus* 1855. D [4] 344 map 4tabs aa
—anr. ed., abr. *P* [1856?]. 16° 35 a
—Ger. tr. "Auswanderung nach Hoch-Texas,"
with adds. Zurich. 1855. O 3v: 50; 32; 52
Optimistic report of his visit to Texas and colonization plans. As a result of these extravagant
promises, Considerant was able to acquire 57,000
acres near Dallas and to establish there — at Reunion — his Fourier communal experiment.

CONSIDERANT, VICTOR [P.]   698
Du Texas. *P* 1857. O 80 aa
—rptd. *P* 1859. a
Relates the failure of the Fourier colony near
Dallas.

CONSIDÉRANT, VICTOR [P.]   699
European colonization in Texas . . . *N Y* 1855.
O 38 a

CONSIDÉRANT, VICTOR [P.]   700
The great west. A new social and industrial life
in its fertile region. *N Y* 1854. O [4] 60 a

CONSIDERATIONS
Considerations on behalf of the colonists. *See*
Otis, James.

Considerations on the American stamp   701
act, and on the conduct of the Minister who planned
it. *L* 1766. O [2] 38 a
Recommends repeal of the obnoxious act.

Considerations on the American war . . .   702
L 1776. O 60 aa
For different pamphlet with this title, *see* Wil-
liams, Joseph.

Considerations on the Attorney-General's   703
propositions for a bill for the establishment of
peace with America. By an old member of parliament . . . *L* 1782. O 58 a

Considerations on the Bank of North America.
See Wilson, James.

Considerations on the commencement of   704
the civil war in America . . . By an American. *L*
1775. O [4] 46 aa

Considerations on the dependencies of Great
Britain . . . *See* Langrishe, Sir Hercules.

Considerations on the expediency of admitting
representatives from the American colonies into the
. . . House of Commons. *See* Maseres, Francis.

Considerations on the great western canal . . .
See Haines, Chas. G.

Considerations on the impropriety . . . of   705
renewing the Missouri question . . . By a Pennsylvanian. *Phil* 1820. O 88 a

Considerations on the Indian trade. *See* Ogden,
Peter S.

Considerations on the measures . . . with respect
to the British colonies . . . *See* Robinson, Matthew,
Baron Rokeby.

Considerations on the mode and terms of a   706
treaty of peace with America. *L* 1778. O 30 aa
—ed. 2, same impr., date & collat. aa
—Am. eds.: *Phil* 1779. O 16; *Hart* 1779. O 23 aa

Considerations on the nature and extent of the . . .
authority of the British parliament. *See* Wilson,
James.

Considerations on the . . . order of Cincinnati . . .
By Cassius. *See* Burke, Aedanus.

Considerations on the points lately brought into
question as to the . . . right of taxing the colonies . . .
See Pownall, Thos.

Considerations on the present situation of Great
Britain and the United States . . . *See* Champion,
Richard.

Considerations on the present state of affairs between England and America. *See* Dalrymple, Alex.

Considerations on the propriety of imposing taxes
in the British colonies . . . *See* Dulany, Daniel.

Considerations on the provisional treaty with
America . . . *See* Kippis, Andrew.

Considerations on the . . . removal of the seat of
government. By Aristides. *See* Hanson, Alex. C.

Considerations on the . . . state of the New England colonies . . . *See* Bacon, Anthony.

Considerations on the trade and finances of this
kingdom . . . *See* Whately, Thos.

Considerations relative to a southern confederacy
. . . By a citizen of North Carolina. *See* Berquin,
H. K.

Considerations relative to the North American colonies. *See* Fothergill, John.

Considerations upon the American enquiry . . . *See* Dallas, Robt.

Considerations upon the French and **707** American war . . . *L* 1779. O 44 aa

Considerations upon the rights of the **708** colonists to the privilege of British subjects . . . *N Y* 1766. O [4] 1–4, 9–27 aa
Declares that the colonists will oppose any infringement upon their rights as freeborn Englishmen.

CONSOLATORY THOUGHTS
Consolatory thoughts on American independence . . . *See* Tod, Thos.

CONSOLIDATION:
An account of parties in the United States. *See* Cooper, Thos.

CONSTANT, L.   709
Texas. Das verderben deutscher Auswanderer . . . *Berlin* 1847 O 32 aa

CONSTANT, MLLE. R. DE, tr.   710
Journal de la femme d'un missionaire dans les prairies . . . *Geneva* 1857. D 154 a
Purports to be translated from the English.

CONSTANT, RILLIET   711
Auszuge aus Briefen eines amerikanischen Colonisten über die Schweizercolonie Highland bei St. Louis. *Berne* 1849. D 58 fold.map tab aa

CONSTITUTION   712
Constitution (The) defended, and Pensioner exposed; in remarks on The false alarm [by Samuel Johnson]. *L* 1770. O [2] 31 a

Constitution for the United States of **713** America. We the people of the United States, in order to form a more perfect union . . . do ordain and establish this: [*Phil* 1787]. F 4 dd [Issued 2 days after adoption by convention]
—anr. ed. with adds. [*Phil*] printed by Dunlap & Claypoole [1787]. F 6 d Hn Y
—anr. ed. [*Phil*] printed by Dunlap & Claypoole [1787]. F 4 [Issued as an extra by the Pennsylvania Packet, etc. c
—other 1787 eds.: *Alexandria* Richards & Co. n.d. F 3 b; *Hart* 16° 16 b; *Prov* John Carter n.d. F 2 b; *B* D 32 b NYP Y; *Trenton* a; *N Y* F c; *Portsmouth* n.d. a; *Rich* sm Q 12 b; *New Brunswick* b NYP Y; *Phil* O a
—for anr. ed. *see* "Result of the deliberations of the federal convention . . ."
—Eng. eds., *see* "Plan of the new constitution . . ."
History's most remarkable political document.

CONSTITUTIONAL   714
Constitutional means (The) for putting an end to the disputes between Great-Britain and the American colonies. *L* 1769. O 33 a

Constitutional right (The) of the legisla- **715** ture of Great Britain to tax the . . . colonies in America . . . *L* 1768. O [16] 60 a

CONSTITUTIONALIST [THE] . . .
See Ford, Timothy.

CONSTITUTIONS [THE]   716
Constitutions (The) of the several independent states . . .; the declaration of independence; the articles of confederation . . . *Phil* Bailey 1781. D [2] 226 200 copies ptd. aa
—later Am. eds.: *B* 1785; *N Y* 1786; *Phil* 1791; *Phil* 1800; *Lex* 1813. a
—Eng. ed. *L* 1782. O [8] 168; rptd., with adds., *L* 1783. a
—Eng. ed. 2, with adds., incl. "Declaration of rights," *L* 1783. O [36] 472 [2] port
—other Eng. eds.: *Dub* 1783; *Glas* 1783.
—Fr. ed. "Constitutions des treize États-Unis de l'Amérique," *Phil* [ptd at *P*] 1783. O [4] 540 600 copies ptd.[100 on L. P.] aa
—rptd., with longer t., same impr. & date a
—anr. Fr. ed., with 1787 Federal constitution added, *P* 1792. O 2v: [4] 324; 317
The French translation was made by the Duc de la Rochefoucault, at Franklin's suggestion, with over fifty footnotes by the latter, and shows on title the United States seal [eagle and stars and stripes], its first appearance in a book. For an earlier French collection, *see Recueil des loix constitutives* . . .

CONTEST
Contest (The) in America between Great Britain and France. By an impartial hand. *See* Mitchell, John.

CONTESTACIONES   717
Contestaciones habidas entre el supremo gobierno Mexicano, el general en gefe del ejercito Americano . . . *Mex* 1847. D 36 aa
—iss 2, Herrera letter added, same impr & date aa

CONTINUED CORRUPTION
Continued corruption, standing armies, and popular discontents . . . *See* Bollan, Wm.

CONTRA COSTA COUNTY,   718
CALIFORNIA
History of Contra Costa county, California . . . *SF* 1882. Q 710 pls b

Illustrations of Contra Costa county, **719** California with historical sketches. *Oakl* [1878]. Obl F 54 2maps 64pls b

CONTROVERSY
Controversy (The) between Great Britain and her colonies reviewed . . . *See* Knox, Wm.

CONVERSE, LORING   720
Notes of what I saw . . . [including a trip to California and Mexico, with sketches of Arizona and New Mexico]. *Bucyrus* 1882. O 454 pls a

[CONWAY, CORNELIUS]   721
The Utah expedition . . . with incidents of travel on the plains, [etc.]. By a wagonmaster . . . *Cin* 1858. O 48 c LC Y [only copies located]

CONWAY (GENERAL [HENRY S.])   722
The speech of: . . . on moving in the House of Commons . . . a bill for quieting the troubles . . . in America . . . *L* 1781. O [4] 51 a

CONWAY, MONCURE D.   723
Barons of the Potomack and the Rappahannock, *N Y* Grolier Club 1892. O [18] 290 [2] 7pls 3facs a 363copies[3 on vell.] a

CONWAY, MONCURE D.   724
The life of Thomas Paine . . . *N Y* 1892. O 2v: [20] 380; [4] 489. 2pls a
—Eng. ed., with adds., *L* 1909. O 352

CONYERS, JOSIAH B.   725
A brief history of the leading causes of the Hancock mob, in the year 1846. *St. L* 1846. D 84 b AA G BP [only cops kn]

COOK (ANN, late Mrs. [Jereboam   726
A. Beauchamp]).
Letters of: to her friend in Maryland, containing [a] short history of the life of that remarkable woman. *Wash* 1826. D 91 a

COOK, DARIUS B.   727
Six months among Indians . . . in the forests of Allegan county, Michigan . . . 1839–40 . . . *Niles Mich* 1889. D [4] 101 pl aa

COOK, DAVID J.   728
Hands up; or, twenty years of detective life in the mountains and on the plains . . . *Denver* 1882. O 285 32pls b G LC
—enl. to cover 35 years, *Denver* 1897. O 442 port a
The rarity of the original edition has been explained as resulting from most copies having been used for gun wadding in an Indian scare. Probably ghost-written by Thos. F. Dawson.

COOK, J. H.   729
Guide book . . . giving the early history of St. Louis . . . *St L* 1867. 16° 44 map a

[COOK, JAMES]
An authentic narrative of a voyage to the Pacific . . . By an officer on board the Discovery . . . *Phil* 1783. *See* under Rickman, John.

[COOK, JAMES]
Journal of Captain Cook's last voyage to the Pacific . . . 1776–1780. *L* 1781. *See* Rickman, John.

COOK, CAPTAIN JAMES, et al
The original astronomical observations . . . *See* Bayly, Wm.

COOK (CAPT. JAMES).
Remarks and conjectures on the voyage of the ships Resolution and Discovery . . . after the death of: . . . *See* Brooke, Robt.

COOK, JAMES, and KING, JAMES   729a
A voyage to the Pacific . . . for making discoveries . . . to determine the position and extent of the west side of North America . . . 1776–1780. *L* 1784. O 3v: [10, 96] 421; [14] 549; [14] 556 [2] + Atlas F 87maps & pls [24 in text vol., 63 in atlas] b
—eds. 2 & 3, same collat. 1785. aa
—anr. ed. *L* 1784. O 4v: [16] 370; [12] 359; [12] 400; [12] 310 [36 28] + 2 adv-p. 2maps 49pls aa
—anr. ed. Dub 1784. O 3v: [8] 98 421; [14] 549; [12] 559, port 26maps & pls fold.tab a
—Fr. tr. *P* 1785. Q 4v: [8] 132 440; [4] 422; [4] 488; [4] 554. 88maps & pls [in separate vol] a
—Ger. tr. *Nürnberg* 1786. O 2v map 2pls
Official account of the first voyage attempting an adequate examination and charting of our northwest coast; on Cook's discovery of Nootka, England based her claim to that region. Following the publication in above forms, various abridged editions, issued in one, two, three and four octavo volumes, were issued in New York, Worcester, Philadelphia, London, Dublin, and several French and German editions on the continent. For unofficial versions *see* under William Ellis, John Ledyard, John Rickman and Henry Zimmerman. Cook's two earlier voyages were confined to discoveries in the South Pacific. The official publication of the first, edited by Hawkesworth, appeared in 1773, three volumes quarto, 52 maps and plates; that of the second, by Cook himself, in 1777, two volumes quarto, 87 maps and plates.

COOK, JOHN R.   730
The border and the buffalo . . . *Topeka* 1907. O [12] 352[incl. pls] a
—rptd., ed. Quaife, *Chi* 1938. 16° [44] 480 port

COOK (JOSEPH W.)   730a
Diary and letters of: *Laramie* 1919. D 137 a

[COOK, MRS. MARY L. (REDD)]   731
Ante bellum; southern life as it was. *Phil* 1868. D 322 a

COOK & SARGENT, pubs.   732
Prairie versus bush. Iowa as an emigrant field. *Davenport* 1859. O 24 fold.map a

COOKE, EDWARD   **733**
A voyage to the South sea, and round the world
... 1708–11. *L* 1712. O [24] 456 [12 incl. 2 adv-p]
20maps & pls aa
—ed. 2, *L* 1712. O 2v: [22] 432 [10]; [32] 328 [8].
27 maps & pls 3fold. tabs. b N
—rptd. 1718 [with new t-p]; 1726 [with only 2pls] aa
Originally issued hurriedly in one volume, with
the voyage home compressed into the final chapter, in order to be on the market before the appearance of a rival publisher's account of the same
voyage by Woodes Rogers. More leisure permitted
for the second edition an amplification of that final
chapter into a second volume; that chapter was
at the same time deleted from the 2nd edition of
volume one.

[COOKE, JOHN E.]   **734**
The life of Stonewall Jackson ... By a Virginian.
Rich 1863. D 305 port + 6adv-p aa
—anr. ed., same collat., different port, *N Y* 1863. a
—Eng. ed. *L* 1863.
Cover of New York edition erroneously attrib-
utes authorship to John M. Daniels.

[COOKE, JOHN E.]   **735**
Wearing of the gray ... personal portraits,
scenes and adventures of the war. *N Y* 1867. O 601
10pls a rptd *Augusta Ga* 1870
—anr. ed. *Bloomington* Ind 1959

COOKE, JOHN H.   **736**
A narrative of events in the south of France, and
of the attack on New-Orleans. *L* 1835. D [4] 319 a

COOKE, MRS. LUCY [R.]   **737**
Crossing the plains in 1852 ... *Modesto Calif*
1923. O 94 2pls aa

COOKE, PHILIP ST. GEORGE   **738**
The conquest of New Mexico and California.
N Y 1878. D [6] 307 map aa
—rptd. *Oakl* 1952. O map a
Essentially a sequel to his *Scenes and adven-
tures.*

COOKE (PHILIP ST. GEORGE).   **739**
Report from the Secretary of War, communi-
cating ... the official journal of: from Santa Fe to
San Diego ... [*Wash* 1849]. O 85 a
First publication of the complete journal of this
famous march of the Mormon Battalion; only
extracts from it had been included in the 1847
edition of Emory's *Reconnaissance.*

COOKE, LIEUT. COL. PHILIP   **740**
ST. GEORGE
Scenes and adventures in the army. *Phil* 1857.
D 432 aa
—rptd. 1859. same collat., but t-p gives au. rank
of Col. aa

Personal narrative of service in the West with
the 2nd Dragoons, escorting Santa Fe traders and
Oregon emigrants, etc., 1829–45.

COOL THOUGHTS
Cool thoughts on the consequences ... of American independence ... *See* Galloway, Jos.

COOL THOUGHTS
Cool thoughts on the present situation of our
public affairs ... *See* Franklin, Benj.

COOLIDGE, A[USTIN] J., and   **741**
MANSFIELD, J. B.
A history ... of New England ... Vol. I [all].
Maine, New Hampshire and Vermont. *B* 1859. O
[28] 1024 3maps 22pls a
—rptd., same impr. & collat., 1864.
—Separate histories—Maine, New Hampshire and
Vermont—were published in 1860.

COOLIDGE, DANE   **742**
Fighting men of the west. *N Y* [1932] O 343 pls a

COOLIDGE, LOUIS A.   **743**
Klondike and the Yukon country ... *Phil* 1897.
D 213 + 15 adv-p 2maps 18pls a

COOMBS, FREDERICK   **744**
The dawn of the millenium ... *N Y* [1869]. O
[6] 26 lvs p. 29–143 lvs aa
Meaningless vaporings of a half-mad San
Francisco photographer; of value only because of
illustrations depicting early California scenes and
events.

COOPER, JAMES FENIMORE   **745**
The American democrat; or hints on the social
and civic relations of the United States ... *Cooperstown N Y* 1838. D 192 a

COOPER, JAMES FENIMORE   **746**
The battle of lake Erie ... *Cooperstown* 1843.
D 118 a

[COOPER, JAMES FENIMORE]   **747**
The chronicles of Cooperstown [N. Y.] *Coo-
perstown* 1838. D 100 a
See also Livermore, Samuel T., with whose
History of Cooperstown these *Chronicles* are incor-
porated.

COOPER, JAMES FENIMORE   **748**
The history of the navy of the United States ...
Phil 1839. O 2v: 394; 482. map plan a
—ed. 2, cor., *Phil* 1840. O 2v: 438; 417. pl
—anr ed contd to 1853. *N Y* 1853. O 3v in 1: 276;
248; [4] 7–100 errata 1f 2maps 5ports
—Eng. ed. *L* 1839. O 2v: [48] 456; [12] 558 [2]
3ports 2 maps

—other eds.: *P* Baudry 1839. O 2pls; *P* Galignani 1839. O 2v 2pls
—Fr. tr. *P* 1845–6. O 3v
—Ger. tr. *Frankf* 1840. 16° 4v

COOPER, J[AMES] F[ENIMORE]   749
Lives of distinguished American naval officers . . . *Phil* 1846. D 2v: 252; 264 4ports [not iss in all cops] a
—anr iss. 2v in 1
—anr ed., *Auburn, N.Y.* 1846. D 2v: 252; 264 4ports [in some cops]
—rptd *N Y* 1849. D 2v

[COOPER, JAMES FENIMORE]   750
Notions of the Americans . . . *L* 1828. O 2v: [24] 459; [12] 477 a
—Am. ed. *Phil* 1828. D 2v: [12] 340; 359
—rptd.: *Phil* 1838. D 2v; *N Y* 1850. D 2v
—Fr. tr. *P* 1828. D 4v
—Ger. tr. *Stuttgart* 1828. O 4v

COOPER, JOHN   751
An historical . . . sketch of Croydon, N. H. . . . *Concord N H* 1852. O 52 a

COOPER (JOSEPH W.)   752
Life and adventures of: among the . . . Indians . . . *Albany Ga* [1879]. D 39 aa

[COOPER, MYLES]   753
The American querist: . . . questions proposed relative to the present dispute between Great Britain, and her . . . colonies. [*N Y*] 1774. O [4] 31 aa
—ed. 2? [called ed. 10] *N Y* 1774. same collat. a
—rptd: *B* 1774. O 31; *L* 1775 a
A copy of the first printing was burned at New York by the Sons of Liberty. Attributed also to Thomas B. Chandler.

[COOPER, MYLES]?   754
A friendly address to all reasonable Americans . . . *N Y* 1774. O [56] + errata p aa
—anr. issue, without errata p. *America* [N Y] 1774. O 55 aa
—anr. ed., abr., *N Y* 1774. O 24 a
—Eng. eds: [ascribed to "A. W. Farmer"] *L* 1774. O 56; *Dub* 1774. a
Discussion of colonial actions regarding tea duties. Also attributed to Thomas B. Chandler, probably the likeliest candidate.

COOPER, MYLES   755
National humiliation and repentance recommended, and the cause of the present rebellion in America assigned . . . *Oxf* 1777. Q [2] 24 a
+ed. 2, *Edin* 1778. O 20
Violent Tory sermon preached at Oxford University.

[COOPER, REV. SAMUEL]   756
The crisis . . . [*B*] 1754. O 15 aa
—Eng. ed. *L* 1756. O a
—anr. Eng. ed. "The crisis, or a full defence of the colonies . . . the mother country cannot lay any arbitrary tax upon the Americans . . .," *L* 1766. O 30 a

[COOPER, THOMAS]   757
Consolidation. An account of parties in the United States . . . 1787 to the present period. *Columbia S C* 1824. O [2] 17+4+4 a
—ed. 2, au. named, same impr. 1830. O 37 errata slip
A second part—containing five essays—was published at Columbia, 1834.

COOPER, THOMAS   758
Political arithmetic. [*Phil* 1801?]. D 40 a

COOPER, THOMAS   759
Political essays . . . *Northumberland Pa* 1799. O 64 a
—ed. 2, enl., *Phil* 1800. O [4] 88

COOPER, THOMAS   760
Some information respecting America. *L* 1794. O [4] 240 map errata l. a
—rptd. *Dub* 1794; *L* 1795. map in both of these reprints
—Fr. ed. "Renseignemens . . .," *P* 1795. O 292; *Hamburg* 1795. O [20] 218 74 map

COOPER, REV. [WILLIAM]   761
The history of North America . . . *L* 1780. 16° [8] 13–184 6pls aa
—rptd., same impr. & collat., 1789. a
—Am. eds: *Benningt Vt* 1793 D 184 6 pls; *Lansingbg N Y* 1795. 16° [8] 159 6pls; *Benningt* 1800. D 184 6pls

COOPER, WILLIAM   762
A guide in the wilderness; or, the history of the first settlements in the western counties of New York . . . *Dub* 1810. O [2] 71 c Hn NYP [of 5 cops kn]
—rptd. *Roch* 1897. O [8] 41 a 300 copies

COOPERSTOWN [N. Y.]
The chronicles of: See Cooper, James F.

COOS BAY [ORE.]   763
Settlement and early settlers of: . . . by a pioneer resident . . . *Marshfield Ore* 1879. O 38 aa

COPIES   764
Copies and extracts of documents on . . . British impressments of American seamen. *L* 1812. O 61 a
—Am. ed. *N Y* 1813. O 64

Copies and extracts of . . . newspapers printed in New England . . . referred to in the Letters transmitted from Francis Bernard . . . *See* Bernard, Francis.

COPLEY, JOHN M.   765
A sketch of the battle of Franklin . . . *Austin* 1893. 16° 206 4pls a

COPLEY, JOSIAH   766
Colorado, and its relations to Kansas. *Lawrence* 1873. D 30 b 2 cops loc
—ed. 2, same impr., date & collat. aa 1 cop loc.

COPLEY, JOSIAH   767
Kansas and the country beyond . . . *Phil* 1867. O 86 [10] map a

COPPEY, HYPOLITE   768
Monsieur de Raousset en Sonore. *Mex* 1855. O 48 b

COPPINGER, JOSÉ   769
Manifesto . . . demonstrado el injusto y violento proceder . . . en San Augustin de Florida, despojandole de orden de la autoridad gobernante . . . despues de la entrega de la provincia à los Estados Unidos . . . *Phil* 1821. O 36 aa

COPWAY (GEORGE).   770
The life, history and travels of: *Alb* 1847. O [8] 5–224 front. a
—ed. 2, *Phil* 1847. D 158 front.
—Eng. ed. "Recollections of a forest life . . .," *L* 1850. D 256
—Eng. ed. 2, *L* 1854. D [12] 248
—rptd., same collat., *L* [1855].

COPWAY, GEORGE   771
Organization of a new Indian territory east of the Missouri . . . *N Y* 1850. O 32 a

COPWAY, GEORGE   772
The traditional history . . . of the Ojibway nation. *L* 1850. D [12] 298 a
—Am. ed. *B* 1851. D 266 2pls
—rptd. *B* 1851.

CORAM, ROBERT   773
Political inquiries: to which is added, a plan for the establishment of schools throughout the United States. *Wilm Del* 1791. O 108 aa

CORDIER, A. H.   774
A Wyoming big game hunt. *K C* 1907. D 56 aa

CORDOVA, JACOB
See De Cordova.

COREY, ALLEN   775
Gazetteer of the county of Washington, N. Y. . . . *Schuylerville* 1849–50. O [4] 200 227–264 17 maps a

[CORNELIUS, ELIAS]   776
The little Osage captive: an authentic narrative. *B* 1822. 16° [4] 4–108 2pls a
—Eng. ed. *York* 1824. 16° 182 + 2adv-p 2pls
—later Am edr: *B* 1832; 1837
In some copies of the York edition the final "4" in the date had become so broken as to resemble "1," hence the myth of an 1821 printing.

CORNELL, MRS. CHARLOTTE   777
[HAWLEY]
Reminiscences of a private life. *N Y* 1893. O 38 a
California resident from 1852.

CORNER, WILLIAM   778
San Antonio de Bexar. *San Antiono* 1890. O [8] 166 + 27 adv-p map 16pls a

CORNEY, PETER   779
Voyages in the northern Pacific . . . 1813–1818, between the northwest coast of America . . . and China. *Honolulu* 1896. D [12] 84 75–138 [5] a
First separate printing; of California, Oregon and Russian-American interest.

CORNWALL, BRUCE   780
Life sketch of Pierre Barlow Cornwall. *S F* 1906. O [10] 87 6ports a
Describes his 1848 overland journey to California.

CORNWALLIS, EARL   781
An answer to that part of the narrative of Lieutenant-General Sir Henry Clinton, which relates to the conduct of Lieutenant-General Earl Cornwallis. *L* 1783. O [24] 260 errata slip fold.tab at p236 + 4adv-p aa
—ed 2 *L* 1783. O a
—Am ed *Phil* 1866. O [12] 260

CORNWALLIS (EARL).   782
Examination of: before a committee of the House of Commons, upon Sir William Howe's papers. *L* 1779. O 60 aa

[CORNWALLIS, EARL]   783
A reply to Sir Henry Clinton's Narrative, wherein . . . errors are pointed out and the conduct of Lord Cornwallis fully vindicated. *L* 1783. O 109 a
—eds 2&3, *L* 1783. same collat.
—Am. ed. *N Y* 1783. sm Q [2] 40 a

CORNWALLIS, KINAHAN   784
A panorama of the new world: travels. *L* 1859. D 2v: [8] 430; 390 a
Of negligible North American interest.

CORONADO'S EXPEDITION . . .
See Castañeda de Nagera.

CORRECT COPIES 785
Correct copies of the two protests against the bill to repeal the American Stamp act . . . *P* [i. e. *L*] 1766. O 24 aa
—anr. issue, the two protests ptd. separately, same impr. & date. O 2pts: 16; 15 aa

CORRESPONDENCE 786
Correspondence and offcial proceedings relating to the expeditions against the [Oregon] Indians. [Ore. H. Doc. 19]. *Salem* 1855. O 68 b OreH WisH

Correspondence between this government 787 and that of Great Britain on . . . the territory west of the Rocky mountains. [H. Doc. 199]. *Wash* 1828. O 77 aa

Correspondence in relation to the capture of the British brigs Detroit and Caledonia . . . *See* Elliott, Jesse D.

Correspondence relating to the massacre 788 of immigrants by the Snake Indians. In August 1854. *Salem Ore* 1854. O 25 b OreH OreS

CORRESPONDENCIA
Correspondencia entre la legacion de Mexico y los Estados Unidos sobre el paso del Sabina . . . *See* Gaines, el General.

CORRILL, JOHN 789
A brief history of the Church of Christ of Latter Day Saints . . . *St L* 1839. O [4] 7–50 b AA NYP WisH Y

CORRY, JOHN 790
The life of George Washington . . . *L* Kearsley 1800. D 228 [3] aa
—rptd. *L* Myers 1800. D [8] 228; *Dub* 1800. D 228 [2] port; *Dub* 1801. a
—new ed. [i.e., ed. 2], *L* Crosby [1802]. D 57 [2] port; rptd. 1802
—Am eds: *Phil* 1801. D 204 [4]; *N Y* Hyer 1807. D 216; *N Y* Low 1807. D 349 [7] port; *N Y* 1809 D 239 [12] port
—many later Am. eds., some abr. giving no au., under t.: "Biographical memoirs of the illustrious General George Washington," same t. as the biography of Washington by Thos. Condie [*q.v.*].
The first full-length English biography of Washington.

[CORSAN, W. C.] 791
Two months in the Confederate States . . . *L* 1863. O [4] 299 aa
An Englishman's judicious observations.

CORTAMBERT, LOUIS [R.] 792
Voyage au pays des Osages . . . *P* 1837. O 94 aa

C[ORWIN], B. R. 793
A trip to the rockies. *N Y* 1889. D 63 3pls a
—rptd same impr 1890.

COSAS DE LOS ESTADOS UNIDOS. 794
Par Nazareno. *N Y* 1864 O 364 port a

[COSTANSÓ, MIGUEL] 795
Diario histórico de los viages . . . hechos al norte de la California . . . [*Mex* 1770]. F [2] 56 dd JCB N NYP Y
—rptd. *Mex* 1950. O 71 a 110copies
—Eng. ed. with important adds., *L* 1790. Q [4] 76 8maps[on 4 sheets] dd Hn NYP
—anr. issue, probably the earlier, with only 4maps [on 2 sheets] d BM JCB
—anr. ed. *S F* Grabhorn 1934. O aa 500cops pld
—Ger. tr. *Tubingen* 1792. F 32 map b Y
Account of the Portola expedition and the establishment of the first settlements in upper California, at San Diego and Monterey. The original Spanish edition was immediately suppressed by Spain to keep its information from the rest of the world. Intrinsic importance and superlative rarity, combined with its status as the first book devoted entirely to California, place this item, either in Spanish or English, in the top rank of memorable and desirable California books. A preliminary account of this expedition—*Extracto de noticias del puerto de Monterrey*—had appeared at Mexico earlier in the year, in two issues [Folio, six pages; Quarto, eight pages].

COTHERN, WILLIAM 796
History of ancient Woodbury, Connecticut . . . *Waterbury* 1854–79. O 3v: [12] 833; [2 10] 841–1610; 706 [2]. map 5pls[one an adv-card] a
The compiler devoted thirty-two years to this task, an all-time endurance record among local historians.

COTTON, A[LFRED] J. 797
"Cotton's Keepsake": " with autobiographical sketch . . . and a condensed history of the early settlement of Ohio and Indiana . . . *Cin* 1858. D 526 port a
Earliest history of Dearborn County, Indiana.

COTTON, MRS. SARAH E., and 798
HANLEY, ELVIRA J.
Gen. David Thomson . . . a memorial volume . . . n.p. [1922]. O 56 a
Based on the General's papers; he was, it is claimed, the actual slayer of Tecumseh at the battle of the Thames, in 1813.

COTTON IS KING . . .
By an American. *See* Christy, David.

COUCH, NEVADA 799
Pages from Cherokee Indian history as identi-

fied with Samuel A. Worcester ... *St L* [1884].
O 25 a
—eds. 2 & 3, same impr. [1885?]. O 27

COUES, ELLIOTT, ed.   **800**
Forty years a fur trader on the upper Missouri
... 1833–72. By Charles Larpenteur. *N Y* 1898.
O 2v: [28] 236; [10] 237–473. 18maps & pls aa
—anr. ed., ed. Quaife, *Chi* 1933. 16°

COUES, ELLIOTT, ed.
New light on the early history of the ... northwest. *See* Henry, Alex., and Thompson, David.

COUES, ELLIOTT, ed.   **801**
On the trail of a Spanish pioneer; the diary ...
of Francisco Garcés ... *N Y* 1900. O 2v: [30] 312;
[8] 313–608. 3maps 5facs 12pls aa

COULTER, JOHN   **802**
Adventures in the Pacific ... *Dub* 1845. D [12]
290 a
—continued in: "Adventures on the western coast
of South America, and the interior of California
...," *L* 1847. D 2v: [14] 288 + 32adv-p; [12] 278
+ 2adv-p a

COUNCIL, WILLIS D.   **803**
Dottings of adventure in the wild far West.
Mobile 1881. D 37 aa
—rptd. *Brownsville, Tex.* 1955. same collat. a

COUNSEL   **804**
Counsel for emigrants ... with ... letters from
Canada and the United States. *Aberdeen* 1834. D
[4] 140 map a
—ed. 2, enl., same impr. 1835. D 156 map
—ed. 3, same impr., 1838. D map
—rptd. *L* 1839.
Ascribed to John Mathison, the book's publisher.
For additions to this guide *see Sequel to the Counsel for emigrants.*

[COURCIER, ADRIEN]   **805**
Les tribulations d'un chercheur d'or. *P* n.d. O
247 pls a

COURTAULD, GEORGE   **806**
Address to those ... disposed to remove to the
United States ... Including remarks on Mr. Birk-
beck's opinions ... *Sudbury* [ptd.*L*] 1820. O 40 a

[COURTNEY, T. E.]   **807**
A guide to Pomarede's ... panorama of the
Mississippi ... *N Y* 1849. O 84 8pls b
—anr. ed. *St L* 1850. O 84 8pls a

COURTNEY, WILLIAM A., ed.   **808**
The genesis of South Carolina: 1562–1670.
Columbia 1907. Q 239 6maps [3fold.] 6pls a

COURTRIGHT, GEORGE S.   **809**
An expedition against the Indians in 1864.
Lithopolis O [1911]. 16° 31 a
Address before a G. A. R. group, largely taken
from the earlier pamphlet by George H. Pettis,
Kit Carson's fight ...

COUTANT, CHARLES G.   **810**
History of Wyoming. Vol I [all] *Laramie* 1899.
O [24] 17–712 map 76pls aa
A useful index — of 4 leaves — was issued at
Cheyenne in 1941.

COUTS, CAVE J.   **811**
From San Diego to the Colorado in 1849. *L A*
1932. 16° [8] 270 3maps on 2sheets a

COWAN, WILLIAM B.   **812**
A description of Grand Tower, on the Missis-
sippi ... *N Y* 1839. O 43 map b

[COWDERY, DR. JONATHAN]   **813**
American captives in Tripoli; or, Dr. Cowdery's
journal   during his late captivity. *B* 1806. D
34 aa
—ed. 2, *B* 1806. D a

COWDERY, OLIVER   **814**
Letters ... on the origin of the Book of Mormon
and the rise of the Church ... *Liv* 1844. O 48 aa

[COWELL, EBENEZER]   **815**
A concise view of the controversy between the
proprietors of East and West-Jersey ... *Phil* 1785.
D [6] 18 b Hn NYP

COWLES, CALVIN D., comp.   **816**
Atlas to a accompany the Official records of the
Union and Confederate armies. *Wash* 1891–5. F
2v: 29 154maps 21pls aa

COWLES, E. B.   **817**
History ... of Berrian County, Michigan ...
Buchanan Mich 1871. O 384 a

COX, G. W.   **818**
Pioneer sketches ... of Montague county,
Texas. [*Montague* 1911]. D 44 aa
—rptd [*St Jo Tex* 1958]

COX, ISAAC   **819**
The annals of Trinity county [Cal.]. *S F* 1858.
O 206 d CalU H Y [of 7 cops loc]
—rptd. 1926; 1940. a
Earliest California county history.

COX, JAMES, ed.   **820**
Historical and biographical record of the cattle
industry ... *St L* 1895. Q 743 col. front. 16pls b
N NYP Pn
—rptd *N Y* 1959 Q 2v 500 cops aa

COX, JOHN E.   821

Five years in the . . . army. *Owensville Ind* 1892. O [4 incl. port] 171 aa

Campaigns in Dakota and Wyoming, 1875–77.

COX, ROSS   822

Adventures on the Columbia river . . . *L* 1831. O 2v: [24] 368; [8] 400. aa

—eds. 2 & 3 followed in 1832, t. slightly altered. O 2v: [20] 233; [6] 350 aa

—Am. ed. *N Y* 1832. O [15] 25–335 adv-l. before t-p a

The narratives of Cox, Alexander Ross and Franchere are chief sources for fur trading history in the early Oregon country.

COX, SANDFORD C.   823

Recollections of the early settlement of the Wabash valley. *Lafayette Ind* 1860. O 160 a

[COX, ZACHARIAH]   824

An estimate of commercial advantages by way of th' Mississippi and Mobile rivers, to the western cou. . y . . . and the commencement . . . of a settlement on the Ohio river to facilitate the same . . . *Nashv* 1799. D 70 b LC OHP [of 4 known copies]

Earliest known Nashville imprint.

COXE, DANIEL, [ed.]   825

A collection of voyages and travels . . . *[L]* 1741. O 3pts in 1: [6] 142; [8] 86; [54] 122. 3maps a

Part 3, the editor's own work on "Carolana," was issued separately, as shown below.

COXE, DANIEL   826

A description of the English province of Carolana . . . *L* 1722. O [54] 122 map c LC N NYP

—ed. 2, same sheets with new t-p, *L* 1726. map b Y

—rptd., same collat., *L* 1727. b AA; *L* 1741, with adds. map b

—Am. ed. *St L* 1840. O [6] 90 map aa

Bold assertion of the rights of England to the entire gulf region [Ga., Fla., Ala., Miss. and La.] which had been granted to the author's father, with a description based on a residence there. Coxe was the first American Masonic Grand Master. His book first agitated a confederation of the colonies against French aggressions, later adopted as Franklin's "Albany Plan." and was the first English account of Louisiana.

[COXE, RICHARD S.]   827

The extent and value of the . . . rights of the Hudson's Bay Company in Oregon . . . *[Montr* 1849]. O [2] 51 aa

COXE, TENCH   828

A brief examination of Lord Sheffield's Observations on the commerce of the United States. *Phil* Carey, Stewart & Co. 1791. O 48 a

—enl. ed. *Phil* Carey 1791. O [8] 136

—Eng. ed. *L* 1792. O [8] 127 + 4 tabs

[COXE, TENCH]   829

An enquiry into the principles on which a commercial system for the United States . . . should be founded . . . *[Phil]* 1787. O 52 a

[COXE, TENCH]   830

An examination of the conduct of Great Britain respecting neutrals . . . *Phil* 1807. O 72 a

—ed. 2, *B* 1808. same collat.

COXE, TENCH   831

An important statement of facts relative to the invalidity of the pretensions of Connecticut claimants to Pennsylvania lands. *Lancaster* 1801. O 40 aa

[COXE, TENCH]   832

Thoughts on the subject of naval power in the United States . . . *Phil* 1806. O 35 a

COXE, TENCH   833

A view of the United States . . . *Phil* 1794. O 513 a

—Eng. eds.: *L* 1795. O [16] 512 3tabs; *Dub* 1795. O [16] 439

COXE, WILLIAM   834

Account of the Russian discoveries between Asia and America. *L* 1780. Q [22] 344 [14] 4maps pl aa

—ed. 2, same impr, date, format & collat. a

—ed. 3, with "A comparative view of the Russian discoveries . . ." added. *L* 1787. O [8] [5–28] 388 [28] 417–454 [2] 4maps pl aa

—ed. 4, enl. *L* 1803. O [24] 18–500 + 4adv-p 5maps pl. Of this ed some cops were iss on L.P. in Q with 1804 date.

—Fr. tr. *Neuchatel* 1781. O [24] 320 4maps pl

—anr. Fr. ed. *P* 1781. O [24] 314 4maps pl

—Ger. tr. *Frankf* 1783. O [16] 409 [8] 3maps pl

Largely a translation, but with considerable additions, of Johann L. Schulze's *Neue Nachrichten* [q.v.], this account, devoted to explorations after Behring and Tschirikoff, in 1741, forms a valuable supplement to Gerhardt Müllers *Nachrichten* [q.v.] who concluded his work with those earlier navigators.

COXE, WILLIAM   835

A comparative view of the Russian discoveries with those made by Captains Cook and Clerke . . . *L* 1787. Q 31 b

This supplement to the author's *Account of the Russian discoveries* was incorporated in the 1787 octavo edition of that title; some quarto copies were issued separately for owners of the earlier editions.

COYNER, DAVID H.   836

The lost trappers . . . scenes and events in the Rocky mountains . . . *Cin* 1847. D 255 + 6adv-p aa

—rptd. 1850; 1853; 1856; 1858; 1859.

Thrilling narrative, but not of unquestioned veracity.

COZZENS, SAMUEL W.   838
The marvellous country; or, three years in Arizona and New Mexico. *B* 1873. O 532 map 27pls[incl. eng.t.] aa
—rptd. *B* n.d. same collat. a
—anr. ed. *B* 1876. O 548 map 27pls[incl. eng.t.]
—Eng ed *L* 1875 O a
—Fr tr *P* 1876 D 359

CRABB (COLONEL) AND HIS   839
ASSOCIATES.
Official information . . . in relation to the execution of: [Ex. Doc. 64]. *Wash* 1858. O 84 a

CRADLEBAUGH, JOHN   840
Utah and the Mormons. [*Wash*] 1863. O 67 capt.t.only aa
Official inquiry into the Mountain Meadows massacre and other outrages.

CRAIG, R. F.   841
The rough diamond: pen pictures of eventful scenes . . . *K C* 1880. D 214 port a

CRAIG, JOHN R.   842
Ranching with lords and commons; or, twenty years on the range . . . *Tor* [1903]. D 293 front. 16pls aa
Financial skulduggery connected with the operation of a great cattle company in the Northwest. For a different picture, *see* Alexander S. Hill's *From home to home.*

CRAIG, NEVILLE B.   843
Exposure of . . . the many misstatements in H. M. Brackenridge's History of the whiskey insurrection. *Pitt* 1859. 18° [6] 80 a

CRAIG, NEVILLE B.   844
The history of Pittsburgh . . . *Pitt* 1851. D 312 2maps a
—rptd same impr 1917. D 3maps

CRAIG, NEVILLE B.   845
Lecture upon the controversy between Pennsylvania and Virginia, about the boundary line. *Pitt* 1843. O 30 a

CRAIG, NEVILLE B. [ed.]   846
The olden time; a monthly publication devoted to . . . information in relation to the early exploration . . . of the country around the head of the Ohio. Vols. I and II [all]. *Pitt* 1846-8. O 2v: [8] 576; [4] 572. map pl in 24 original monthly nos. b; bound aa
—ed. 2, with index, *Cin* 1876. O 2v: [4] 582; [2]; 580, map pl errata lf [in v I] aa
The first edition is seldom found complete with

the final number, many copies having been confiscated at the printer's on a creditor writ. Unrivalled collection of Ohio Valley sources.

CRAIG, NEVILLE B.   847
Sketch of the life . . . of Isaac Craig . . . during the revolutionary war. *Pitt* 1854. 18° 70 a

CRAIG, NEVILLE B. [ed.]   848
Washington's first campaign . . . Braddock's defeat, [etc.]. *Pitt* 1848. O 32 map aa

CRAIGHEAD, ERWIN   849
From Mobile's past . . . *Mobile* 1925. 16° 258 port a

CRAKES, SYLVESTER   850
Five years a captive among the Black-feet . . . *Columbus* 1858. O 224 6pls b N Y
Utterly devoid of plausibility, though a few incidents may have been based on some actual captivity.

CRAM, JACOB   851
Journal of a missionary tour in 1808 through New Hampshire and Vermont. *Roch* 1909. O 37 a
200 copies ptd.

CRAM, T[HOMAS] J.   852
Memoir upon the northern inter-oceanic route . . . between . . . Puget sound . . . and . . . the St. Lawrence gulf . . . *Det* [1869]. O 35 map plan aa

CRAM, THOMAS J.   853
Topographical memoir . . . relative to the Territories of Oregon and Washington. *Wash* 1859. [H. Doc. 114]. O 126 aa

CRAMER, CHARLES   854
Etwas über die Natur-Wunder in Nord-America. *St Ptbg* 1837–40. O 2v: 40; [4 14] 5–86 [4]. 10maps & pls aa

[CRAMER, ZADOK]   855
The Ohio and Mississippi navigator . . .
—eds. 1 & 2. No copies known to have been pub'd by Cramer, but there was a similar work, *The Ohio navigator*, of which two eds. were issued in 1798. *See* that title.
—ed. 3, *Pitt* 1802. D 40 c AA PittU Y [only copies known]
—ed. 4, [first to include the Mississippi] "The navigator," *Pitt* 1804. D 62 c BP [of 2 copies known]
—other eds., all pub'd at *Pitt*: ed. 5, 1806. D 94 b; ed. 6, enl., with Lewis and Clark material, 1808. D 156 aa; ed. 7, 1811. D 295; ed. 8, 1814. D 360; ed. 9, 1817. D 307; ed. 10, 1818. D 305; ed. 11, 1821. D 283; ed. 12, 1824. D 275
Most widely used guide to western waters in the early period, both before and after the application

of steam in 1807. *See* also *Mississippi (the)*. *Notes on the navigation of*: and *Mississippi navigator (The)*; *revised and corrected*.

CRAMP, W. E. H.   856
The journal of a grandfather. [*St L* 1912]. O 239 15pls aa
Colonel Cramp served in the Confederate army and was later active in the Texas cattle industry.

[CRANDALL, WARREN D.]   857
History of the ram fleet and the Mississippi marine brigade . . . *St L* 1907. O 464 [28] port aa

CRANE, CHARLES J.   858
The experiences of a colonel of infantry. *N Y* 1923. O [12] 578 3ports a

CRANE, EDWARD A.   859
Examples of colonial architecture in Charleston . . . and Savannah . . . *B* 1895. F [2] 52pls aa

CRANE, GEORGE B.   860
A life history . . . *San Jose* 1886. D [2 blank lvs. 3–14] 3–243 port[pasted on front end paper] aa
Recollections of old-time life in New York, the South, Central West and California.

CRANE, JAMES M.   861
The past, the present and the future of the Pacific. *S F* 1856. O 79 aa

CRANE, VERNER W.   862
The southern frontier. *Durham N C* 1928. O [16] 391 front. map a

CRANE, WILLIAM C.   863
Centennial address embracing the history of Washington county, [Texas]. *Galv* 1876. O 40 a

CRANE, WILLIAM C.   864
Life . . . of General Samuel Houston. *Phil* 1884. O 2v in 1: 672 6pls a

CRANFILL, J[AMES] B.   864a
Chronicle . . . *N Y* [1916] O [12] 496 37pls a

CRANTZ [or CRANZ], DAVID   865
Alte und neue Brüder-historie, oder, kurz gefasste Geschichte der evangelischen Brüder-unität. *Barby* 1771. D [16] 868 [55] a
—ed. 2, same impr. & collat., 1772.
—Eng. tr. by Benj. La Trobe, *L* 1780. O [16] 622 [85] + 2 lvs. [one of errata, one of adv]
Covers Moravian activities in Georgia, Carolina, Pennsylvania, etc., from 1734.

[CRARY, C. G.]   866
Pioneer and personal reminiscences. *Marshalltown Ia* 1893. O 105 aa

CRARY, L. P., pub.   867
A directory for the village of Buffalo . . . To which is added a sketch of [its] history. *Buf* 1828. 18° 55 map aa
First directory. Later editions appeared in 1837, 1841, 1842, 1844, 1847, etc.

CRAVEN COUNTY [S. C.]   868
Historical and social sketch of: n.p. [1852]. O 52 aa

CRAWFORD, CHARLES   869
Observations upon Negro slavery. *Phil* 1784. D 24 a
—ed. 2, same impr. 1790. D
—Eng. ed. *Tunbridge Wells* n.d. O 42

CRAWFORD, CHARLES H.   870
Scenes of earlier days in crossing the plains to Oregon . . . *Petaluma Cal* 1898. D 186 port aa

CRAWFORD, J. MARSHALL   871
Mosby and his men . . . *N Y* 1867. D 375 7ports a

CRAWFORD, LEWIS F., ed.   872
Rekindling camp fires; the exploits of Ben Arnold [Connor] . . . as Indian fighter . . . *Bismarck N D* [1926]. O [2] 324 map 10pls a also 100special copies, signed.

CRAWFORD, LUCY   873
History of the White mountains . . . [*Port Me*] 1846. 18° 204 [1] a
—rptd. *Port* 1883. 16° 230; *Port* 1886. 16° 228

CRAWFORD, MEDOREM   874
. . . Journal; an account of his trip across the plains with the Oregon pioneers of 1862. *Eugene Ore* 1897. O 26 a
The only diary of the first large emigrant train to Oregon; it was issued previously at Washington, 1863, in fourteen pages [Senate Executive Document 17].

CRAWFORD, THERON C.   875
An American vendetta; a story of barbarism in the United States. *N Y & Chi* [1888]. D 185[incl. front.] a
Account of the Hatfield-McCoy feud on the Kentucky and West Virginia border.

CRAWFORD (WILLIAM H.)   876
Sketches of the life . . . of: By Americanus. *Alb* 1824. O 38 a

CREEK-INDIAN (A).
The speech of: . . . *See* Smith, Provost Wm.

CREEK INDIANS.   877
Letter from the Secretary of War, transmitting documents in relation to hostilities of: [H. Doc. 276]. *Wash* [1836]. O 413 caption t.only aa

CREIGH, ALFRED 878
History of Washington county, Pennsylvania.
[*Wash Pa* 1870]. O 386 [121] a
—ed. 2, rev., *Harrisburg* 1871. O 375 132 a

CREMONY, JOHN C. 879
Life among the Apaches. *S F* 1868. D 322 aa
—rptd: *Tucson* 1951. D 372 a; same impr 1954.
—ed. 2, with illus. added, *S F* [1885]. D a
A cavalry officer's adventures on the frontiers of
Texas, Arizona and New Mexico.

CRESPEL, EMANUEL 880
Voiages . . . dans le Canada . . . *Frankf* 1742.
D [10] 3–158 b LC NYP
—ed. 2, same impr. 1752. D [8] 135 aa
—anr. ed., notes added, "Voyage au Nouveau
monde . . ." *Amst* 1757. D [10] 240 [erroneously
paged 140] aa
—rptd., *Quebec* 1884. D [22] 136 [40] port
—Eng. tr., "Travels in North America . . ." *L*
1797. D [28] 187 aa
—Ger. tr., *Frankf* 1751 D [8] 112
This priest accompanied, in 1728, a punitive
expedition against the Fox Indians [in present
Wisconsin]. His observations form an important
sequel to the earlier relations of Sagard and Le
Clercq. In the first edition all copies are initialed on
page eleven by the editor, Louis Crespel.

CREUZBAR, ROBERT [comp.] 881
Route from the Gulf of Mexico and the lower
Mississippi Valley to California and the Pacific
ocean. *N Y* 1849. 16° 40 + 1 adv-p 5maps c N
NYH Pn Y [of 6 cops loc]
Some few copies seem to have been issued with
a sixth map. The best authority on the route
described.

CREVECOEUR, FERDINAND F. [comp.] 882
Old settler's tales . . . sketches of the early settle-
ment and settlers of . . . Pottawatomie and . . .
Nemaha counties, Kansas . . . *Onaga Kas* 1902.
O 162 a

[CREVECOEUR, MICHEL- 883
GUILLAUME SAINT JEAN DE]
Letters from an American farmer . . . *L* 1782.
O [16] 318 [2] + 8adv-p 2maps b
—rptd. *Dub* 1782. D [8] 256 2maps; *L* 1783. O [16]
326 [2] 2maps; *Belf* 1783. D [8] 208 2maps a
—Am. eds.: *Phil* 1793. D 240; *Phil* 1798. D 260;
N Y 1904. O 392
—Fr. tr., with adds., *P* 1784. O 2v: [32] 422 [2];
[8] 400 [2] a
—anr. issue paged [24] 422 [2]; [4] 392 a
—rptd. *Maestricht* 1785. D 2v: [14] 458; [8] 432;
n.p. 1785. D 2v a
—best Fr. ed.—and most complete of all eds.—*P*
1787. O 3v: [34] 478 [4]; [2] 438 [6]; [2] 593. 5maps
4pls aa

—Dutch tr. "Brieven van eenen Amerikaenschen
Landman," *Leyden* 1784. O [16] 328 a
—Ger. trs: "Sittliche Schilderungen von Amerika
. . . .," *Leip & Leignitz* 1784. D [10] 462 2maps;
Leip 1788–[1789]. D 3v pl a
Description of American life of great influence
in attracting European immigration in the post-
revolutionary period. As literature unexcelled by
any American work of the eighteenth century.

[CREVECOEUR, MICHEL- 884
GUILLAUME SAINT JEAN DE]
Voyage dans la Haute Pennsylvanie . . . *P* 1801.
O 3v: [32] 427; [14] 434; [12] 409. 11 maps & pls
4tabs a some copies on L.P., with pls in separate
atlas aa
—Ger. tr. *Berlin* 1802. O 472 2pls a
Original work of this author, presented under
the guise of a translation.

CREWE, E. O. 885
Gold fields of the Yukon . . . *Chi* [1897]. O 61
2maps a

CRICHTON, KYLE S. 886
Law and order, ltd . . . life of Elfego Baca . . .
Santa Fé 1928. O [8] 219 pls 2000 cops ptd of which
375 were signed.
Only account of this outlaw pal of Billy the Kid.

CRICHTON, VISCOUNT 887
A tour in British North America and the United
States . . . *Dub* 1864. O 63 a

CRIPPLE CREEK MINING 888
Cripple Creek mining district (the). History and
description of: . . . *Cripple Creek* 1894. O 161
view aa

CRISIS
Crisis (The). *L* 1775–6. *See* Moore, Wm.

Crisis (The): on the origin and conse- 889
quences of our political dissensions . . . By a citizen
of Vermont. *Alb* 1815. O 96 a

Crisis (The); or, essays on the usurpations of the
federal government. By Brutus. *See* Turnbull,
Robt. J.

Crisis (The): or nullification unmasked. *See*
Pendleton, Edmund.

Crisis (The); or thoughts on slavery; 890
occasioned by the Missouri question. Nos. 1 and 2
[all]. *N Hav* 1820. O 2pts: 14; 19 a

Crisis (The). *Scire volunt, secreta domus atque
inde timeri. See* Cooper, Saml.

CRITICAL MOMENT   891
Critical moment (The) on which the salvation or destruction of the British empire depends. Containing the rise . . . of our American disputes. By Janus. *L* 1776. O 121 aa
Places the blame on administration policies.

[CROCCHIOLA, FATHER STANLEY]   892
The grant that Maxwell bought. [*Denv* 1952] Q [8] 236 map 15pages of plates 250 cops ptd aa

[CROCCHIOLA, FATHER STANLEY]   893
Raton chronicle. *Denv* 1948. O 146 pls 500cops ptd a

[CROCCHIOLA, FATHER STANLEY]   894
Socorro the oasis. *Denv* 1950. O 418 pls 500cops ptd a

CROCKET, GEORGE L.   895
Two centuries in east Texas . . . *Dallas* [1932]. O [12] 372 aa

CROCKETT, DAVID   896
An account of [his] tour to the north and down east . . . *Phil* 1835 D 234 + 34adv-p port. a
—rptd., *N Y* 1845, same collat.
Has been ascribed to his friend, Augustin S. Clayton, of Georgia.

CROCKETT, DAVID   897
Almanack, of wild sports in the west . . . *Nashv* [1834]. O 48 [incl. covers] 6pls aa
—later *Nashv* eds.: annually, under various titles, from [1835] to [1855]. Some eds. carry *N Y* impr.; some, *Phil*; some *B* aa

CROCKETT, DAVID
Exploits and adventures in Texas . . . *See* Smith, Richard Penn.

CROCKETT (COLONEL DAVID).   898
The life and adventures of: *Cin* 1833. D 113 aa
—new ed. "Sketches and eccentricities of Col. David Crockett," *N Y* 1833. D [4] 24–209 a
—anr. issue, same impr. & date. 16° 209
Spurious biography, not authorized by Crockett; attributed to James S. French. *See* also below Crockett's *Narrative* . . . the authorized biography

CROCKETT, DAVID   899
The life of Martin Van Buren . . . *Phil* 1835. D 209 + 24adv-p a
—rptd. [as eds. 10 & 16, prob. eds. 2 & 3] same collat. *Phil* 1836; *Phil* 1837.
—anr. ed. *Cin* 1839. same collat.
Possibly written by Augustin S. Clayton.

CROCKETT (COL. DAVID).   900
A narrative of the life of: written by himself. *Phil* 1834. D 211 + 22 adv-p aa
—rptd. repeatedly, about 15 eds. before 1850 [incl 2 Eng eds of 1834 and 1836]

The authorized biography, probably ghost-written by Thos. Chilton, of Ky., at Crockett's dictation; issued to check-mate the spurious publication of 1833.

CROFUTT, GEORGE A., AND CO.   901
Great trans-continental railroad guide . . . from the Atlantic to the Pacific . . . *Chi* 1869. 16° 244 16pls aa
—rptd. *Chi* 1870. same collat. a
—anr. ed. "Great trans-continental tourists' guide . . .," *N Y* 1870. 16° 208 map 16pls
—anr. ed. *N Y* 1871. D 215 map pls
The compiler was H. Wallace Atwell.

CROGHAN (COL. GEORGE).   902
Journal of: . . . sent . . . to explore the country adjacent to the Ohio river . . . *Burlington N J* 1831. O 38 a 100copies ptd. as a separate from the "Journal of Geology."
—rptd. 1875, same impr & collat.

CROGHAN, GEORGE   903
Journal of his trip to Detroit in 1767 . . . *Ann Arbor* 1939. O [8] 61 a

CROGHAN (GEORGE).   904
Minutes of conferences held at Fort Pitt under the direction of: . . . with . . . the Ohio and other western Indians. *Phil* 1769. F 22 b PaH

[CROGHAN, JOHN]   905
Rambles in the Mammoth Cave . . . *Louisv* 1845. D [12] 9–101 6pls errata slip fold.map a

CROIX ([CARLOS F.]) marquis de.   906
Correspondence du: . . . 1737–1786. *Nantes* 1891. Q [12] 336 [4] 2ports 550 copies ptd [50 on Holland paper, numb.] aa
Previously unpublished material on the Portola expedition to California, etc., during the period when the Marquis was Viceroy of Mexico.

[CROKER, JOHN WILSON]   907
The letters on the . . . naval war with America . . . *L* 1813. O [4] 104 a

CROLL, PHILIP C.   908
Ancient . . . landmarks in the Lebanon valley [Pa.]. *Phil* 1895. O 334 port a

[CROLY, DAVID G.] et al   909
Miscegenation: the theory of the blending of the races, applied to the . . . white man and Negro. *N Y* 1864. D [2] 72 a
First work advocating this solution to the race problem.

CROME, A[UGUST] F. W.   910
Etwas über die Grösse, Volksmenge, Clima und Fruchtbarkeit des . . . nordamerikanischen Freystaats. *Dessau* 1784. O [8] 64 aa

CROMWELL, O.   911
Directory, guide . . . of the city of Charleston
[S. C.]. *Charleston* 1829. 16° 107 aa

CRONKRIGHT, W. G., pub.   912
Souvenir Board of Trade, Ponca City [Okla.]
Ponca City [1895]. O unpaged text 21pls aa

CROOK (GEN. GEORGE).   913
Annual report of: *Prescott Ariz* 1883. D 43 aa
Covers the Apache campaign and capture of
Geronimo.

CROOK (GEN. GEORGE).   914
Annual report of: . . . 1885. n.p. n.d. [*L A?* 1885].
16° 41 + cov.t. aa

[CROOKS, RAMSAY]?   915
Indian trade . . . [*Detroit?* 1820?]. O 14 10 b Y

CROOM, WENDELL D.   916
The war history of Company "C" . . . 6th Georgia regiment. *Fort Valley Ga* 1879. O [4] 37 aa

CROSBY, JAAZANIAH   917
History of Charlestown in New Hampshire . . .
Concord 1833. O 41 a

CROSS, FRED J.   918
The free lands of Dakota . . . *Yankton* 1876. O 32
[incl wraps] aa

CROSS, FRED J.   919
Information for persons seeking a home in the
west. Dakota Territory as it is. *Sioux Falls* 1875.
O 45 [3] b

[CROSS, HENRY]   920
An answer to an invidious pamphlet, intituled A
brief state of the province of Pennsylvania . . . *L*
1755. D [2] 80 aa
For pamphlet attacked, *see* Smith, *Provost
William.*

CROSS, MRS. JANE T. H.   921
Duncan Adair: or, captured in escaping. A story
of one of Morgan's men. *Macon Ga* 1864. O 51 a

CROSS, JOSEPH   922
Camp and field. Papers from the portfolio of an
army chaplain. 4books in 3v *Macon & Columbia*
1864. Books 1 & 2 *Macon.* 16° [10 incl. front cover]
13–141; 160[incl. front cover]. Books 3 & 4 in 1v
Columbia. D 380 + covers b BA Emory

CROSS, O[SBORN]   923
A report, in the form of a journal, of the march
of the regiment of Mounted Riflemen to Oregon
. . . *Phil* Sherman 1850. O 228 map 36pls c G
—anr. ed., in "Report of the Quartermaster General for 1850," [Sen. Exec. Doc 1], in which it occu-

pies pp. 126–244, with 37pls[in some copies only
34, 35, or 36] & no map *Wash* 1850 aa
—anr. issue [H. R.], pls omitted. a
—anr. ed., with separate t., *Wash* 1850. O [4] 218 a
The Philadelphia issue was of a few copies only,
made up for the author, and can hardly be considered an edition. A twelve-page abstract, with
caption title only, preceded this *Report.*

CROSWELL (JOSEPH).   924
Sketches of the life . . . of: for more than forty
years . . . an itinerant preacher . . . *B* 1809. D 96 a

CROTHERS, SAMUEL   925
Strictures on African slavery. *Rossville* O 1833.
O 46 a

CROUCH, CARRIE J.   926
Young county [Texas] . . . history . . . *Dallas*
1937. O [14] 339 a

CROUSE, RUSSEL   927
Mr. Currier and Mr. Ives. *N Y* 1931. O [14] 138
46pls[32col.] a

CROWE [PAT]:   928
His story, etc. *N Y* 1907. D 252 5pls a

CROWELL (SETH).   929
The journal of: . . . his travels as a Methodist
preacher, for twelve years. *N Y* 1813. D 108 a

[CROWLEY, THOMAS]   930
Letters and dissertations on various subjects . . .
L 1782. O 130 aa
—anr. ed. *L* n.d. [1782?]. O 258 a
Largely on the Stamp Act and other American
disputes. Four of the pieces had been published in
1774, in a ten-page pamphlet, *Dissertations on the
grand dispute* . . .

CROWQUILL, ALFRED [pseud.]
A good natured hint about California . . . *See*
Forrester, Alfred H.

CROY, DUC DE   931
Mémoire sur le passage par le nord . . . *P* 1782.
Q 23 a
Concludes that for practical purposes the tried
routes to the Pacific—around Cape Horn or Cape
of Good Hope—are best, regardless of whether a
Northwest passage exists.

CROY, C. G.   932
Pioneer and personal reminiscences. *Marshall-
town Ia* 1893. O 105 a
Early days in Ohio, Kentucky, etc.

CROZAT (MR.)   933
A letter to a member of the P—t of G—t B—n,
occasioned by the priviledge granted . . . to: *L*
1713. sm Q 44 b JCB N

143

Summarizes the commercial and political importance of Louisiana and the Mississippi valley. One of the earliest, if not the earliest, English book on the subject.

CROZIER, R[OBERT] H.   **934**
The bloody junto; or, the escape of John Wilkes Booth . . . *Little Rock* 1869. O 146 aa

CROZIER, R[OBERT] H.   **935**
The Confederate spy: a story . . . *Gallatin Tenn* 1866. D 406 aa
—rptd., same collat., *Louisv* 1871; 1885. a

CRUIKSHANK, ERNEST A.   **936**
Documents relating to the invasion of Canada and the surrender of Detroit, 1812 . . . *Ottawa Can* 1912. O [8] 258 2maps a

CRUMPTON (H. J., and W. B.)   **937**
The adventures of: . . . *Montg* 1912. D 238 2ports a
Overland trip, in 1849, over the Southern route from Fort Smith to California.

CRUMRINE, BOYD   **938**
History of Washington county, Pennsylvania . . . *Phil* 1882. Q [6] 13–1002 8maps 71pls aa

CUBA   **939**
Apuntes historicos acerca de la expedicion piratica que invadio la isla de Cuba: *N O* 1850. O 32 [8] 52 [4] aa

The history of the late expedition to Cuba. By one of the participants. *See* Davis, Capt. J. C.

CUFFEE (PAUL).   **940**
Memoir of: . . . *Liv* 1811. O 12 aa
—rptd. same impr. & date. D 24; *York* 1812. D 36
—anr. ed. *L* 1840. 16° 64 port a
—Am. eds.: *Phil* 1816. O 12; *Vernon* 1839. D 21
Includes Revolutionary and War of 1812 services of this Massachusetts Negro, whaling, etc.

CULBERTSON, THAD.**EUS A.**   **941**
Journal of an expedition to the Mauvaises Terres . . . [occupies 61p. in the 5th Annual Report, Smithsonian Inst.]. *Wash* 1851. O a
—rptd *Wash* 1952. D [8] 164
Explored the Bad Lands and ascended the Missouri to a point several hundred miles north of Ft. Pierre. First account of those regions since Prince Maximilian of Wied.

CULLEY, JOHN H.   **942**
Cattle, horses and men of the western range. *L A* [1940]. O [16] 337 pls aa
By the manager of the Bell ranch in New Mexico.

CULLUM, GEORGE W.   **943**
Campaigns of the war of 1812–15 . . . *N Y* 1879. O 412 port a

CULVER, HENRY B.   **944**
The book of old ships . . . *N Y* 1924. Q [26] 306 2pls[one col.] a

CULVER, J. HORACE [comp.]   **945**
The Sacramento city directory. *Sacramento* 1851. D 96 b
First directory of this city.

CULVER, J. Z., and CO. [pub.]   **946**
Fort Scot [Kas.] city directory for 1869–70, containing . . . reminiscences of its early days . . . *Ft Scott* [ptd *Chi*] 1869–70. D 88 aa
—for 1871–2, *Ft Scott*, n.d. a

CUMING, F[ORTESCUE]   **947**
Sketches of a tour to the western country . . . *Pitt* 1810. D 504 b AA N NYP Y
—rptd., ed. Thwaites, *Clev* 1904. O 377 a
Excellent and extensive observations on pioneer conditions throughout the Ohio and lower Mississippi valleys.

CUMINGS, SAMUEL   **948**
The western navigator . . . *Phil* 1822. 2v: v.I F [2] 33charts[on 27pls] v.II O [4] 232 [6] b AA N WRH [all cops loc]
—rptd. frequently in 1v., under various titles: "Western pilot," "New River guide," "River guide," "Traveller's companion," "Book for all travellers," etc. From 1825 to 1866 there were over 20 of these; in later issues Cumings' name was replaced by those of the publishers—Conclin or James. Poetic justice to one whose book was based, without credit, on Cramer's "Navigator". aa

CUMMING, KATE   **949**
A journal of hospital life in the Confederate army . . . *Louisv* [1866] 0 200 a

CUMMINGS, HENRY   **950**
A sermon . . . at Lexington on the 19th of April, 1781 . . . the anniversary of the commencement of hostilities . . . *B* 1781. O 39 a

CUMMINS, EBENEZER H.
See Baines, Edw.

CUMMINS, [JAMES R.]   **951**
Jim Cummins' book . . . story of the James and Younger gang . . . *Denver* 1903. D 192 13pls aa

CUMMINS, MRS. SARAH J. W.   **952**
Autobiography and reminiscences. [*La Grande Ore* 1914]. O 63 port a

—rptd. several times, but with different impr. [*Walla Walla*]
Crossed the plains to Oregon in 1845.

CUNNINGHAM, EDITH P.   953
Owl's nest . . . *C* 1907. O [12] 323 13pls 2tabs a
Account of the Cincinnati home of James H. Perkins, incorporating material on intellectual life in early southern Ohio.

CUNNINGHAM, EUGENE   954
Triggernometry; a gallery of gunfighters . . . *N Y* 1934. O [20] 441 21pls a
—rptd.: *Caldwell Ida* 1941; 1947; 1952.

CUNNINGHAM, G. A.   955
History of Neenah [Wis.]. [*Neenah*] 1878. O 254 [53] 5pls[incl. in paginat.] a

CUNNINGHAM, J. O.   956
A history of the early settlement of Champaign County, Ill . . . *Urbana* 1876. O 24 a

CUNNINGHAM, SUMNER A.   957
Reminiscences of the 41st Tenn. regiment. *Shelbyville, Tenn.* [ca 1867] O 57 aa

CUNYNGHAME, ARTHUR [A. T.]   958
A glimpse at the great western republic . . . *L* 1851. D [4] 337 a
—rptd. *L* 1852. 16° 152; *L* 1863. D [4] 337

CURE (A) FOR THE SPLEEN . . .
See Sewall, Jonathan.

CURLEY, EDWIN A.   959
Glittering gold; the true story of the Black hills. *Chi* 1876. O 128 map + 16adv-p b G LC Y
—ed 2 Guide to the gold hills *Chi* 1877. O 136 + 20adv-p b

CURRIE, WILLIAM, M. D.   960
An historical account of the climates and diseases of the United States . . . *Phil* 1792. O [6] 409 [5] aa

CURRIE, REV. WILLIAM   961
A treatise on the lawfulness of defensive war . . . *Phil* 1748. O [18] 119 aa

CURRY, GEORGE L., comp.   962
Correspondence, resolutions and memorials of the [Oregon] Legislative Assembly . . . *Salem* 1857. O 65 b Hn Y

CURRY, JOHN P.   963
Observations and experiences among the mineral regions of Nevada . . . *N Y* 1865. O 24 front. b Y

CURSORY REFLECTIONS   964
Cursory reflections on the consequences . . .

should Mr. Jefferson and Mr. Burr have equal votes . . . *N Y* 1801. D 25 a

CURTIS, EDWARD S.   965
The North American Indian. *N Y* [ptd. in Mass.] 1907–30. Q 20v [text] + 20portfolios of pls dd N NYP Y 500sets [pub'd. at $ 3850⁰⁰]

CURTIS, STEPHEN   966
Brief extracts from the journal of a voyage performed by the whale ship M[ercury], of New Bedford . . . *B* 1844. O 46 aa

CURTISS, DANIEL S.   967
Western portraiture, and emigrant's guide . . . *N Y* 1852. D 351 + 18 adv-p map a
—Ger tr same impr & date

CURTIUS.
Letters of: 1851. *See* Grayson, Wm. J.

CURWEN, MASKELL C.   968
A sketch of the history of . . . Dayton. *Dayton* 1850. D 64 map aa
Calls itself "second edition", having previously appeared as part of Odell's *Dayton directory*, same year.

CURWOOD, JAMES O.   969
The great lakes . . . *N Y* 1909. O [16] 227 72pls map a

CUSHING, CALEB   970
Oregon Territory: report [and supplemental report]. *Wash* 1839. O 2v: 51; 61. map aa
Includes reports from Wyeth, Slacum and Kelley.

CUSHING, FRANK   971
Almost a life, or saved by the Indians [in New Mexico]. [*N Y ca* 1879]. O 32 a

CUSHING, FRANK H., comp.   972
Zuni folk tales . . . *N Y* 1901. O [18] 474 12pls a
—rptd. *N Y* 1931. O [36] 474 [2] 12pls

CUSHING, JACOB   973
Divine judgments upon tyrants . . . Sermon preached at Lexington . . . in commemoration of the . . . war and rapine . . . perpetrated . . . by British troops in that town on the nineteenth of April, 1775. *B* 1778. O 28 a

CUSHING, S. W.   974
Wild oats sowings . . . *N Y* 1857. D 483 [incl. 4pls] aa
Fascinating autobiography of an adventurer; embracing experiences as a soldier at San Jacinto and as a sailor in the Texas navy.

CUSHMAN, DAVID Q.   975
The history of ancient Sheepscot and Newcastle [Maine] . . . *Bath Me* 1882. O [18] 458 map 2pls a

145

CUSHMAN, H[ORATIO] B.   976
A history of the Choctaw, Chickasaw and
Natchez Indians. *Greenville Tex* 1899. O 607
port aa
The author lived among these tribes from 1820
to 1890.

CUSHMAN, SAMUEL   977
The gold mines of Clear Creek county, Colorado. *Denver* 1876. D 116 aa

CUSHMAN, SAMUEL, et al   978
The gold mines of Gilpin county, Colorado.
Central City 1876. D 136 cover-t.only aa

CUSICK, DAVID   979
Sketches of ancient history of the Six Nations...
Lewiston N Y 1827. D 28 b N NYP Y
—ed. 2, *Tuscarora Village* [i.e. *Lewiston*] but ptd.
Lockport 1828. D 36 4pls[on one sheet] aa
—ed. 3, *Lockport* 1848. O 35[incl.4pls] a

CUSTER, ELIZABETH B.   980
"Boots and saddles" ... *N Y* 1885. D 312 a
—anr. issue, same impr., date & paginat., with
map & port added.

CUSTER, GEORGE A.   981
My life on the plains ... *N Y* 1874. O 256
8pls a
—rptd., same collat., *N Y* 1876.
—later eds., enl., issued at *St L* from 1883 to 1891,
with t., "Wild life on the plains ..."
—anr ed *Chi* 1952. 16°

[CUSTER, GENERAL GEORGE A.]   982
The Northern Pacific railroad: character and
climate of the country it traverses ... n.p. [1871–
4?]. O 32 [capt.t.only] aa
Reply to General Hazen's denunciation of this
region. Hazen countered with *Our barren lands, q.v.*

CUTLER, CARL C.   983
Greyhounds of the sea: the story of the American clipper ship. *N Y* 1930. Q [4 28] 3–592 30pls
[8col.] a
—rptd *N Y* n.d.

[CUTLER, JERVIS]   984
Topographical description ... of Ohio, Indiana
Territory, and Louisiana ... [including journal of
Charles Le Raye who, in 1801, while a captive with
Sioux on the upper Missouri, made trips to the
Yellowstone and Big Horn rivers]. *B* 1812. D 219
errata sheet 5pls[among them the earliest view of
Cincinnati] b AA N NYP Y
The highly interesting Le Raye journal is of
questionable authenticity.

CUTLER, JULIA P., ed.   985
Life and times of Ephraim Cutler ... *Cin* 1890.
O [6] 353 3pls a

[CUTLER, MANASSEH]   986
An explanation of the map which delineates that
part of the Federal lands, comprehended between
Pennsylvania west line, the rivers Ohio and Sioto
[*sic*], and lake Erie ... and now ready for settlement. *Salem* 1787. O 24 b NYP WisH Y
—rptd. *Newport* 1788. O 24 b
—anr. ed. "Ohio in 1788 ...," *Columbus O* 1888.
D 104 a
—Fr. tr. *P* 1789. O 30 aa
First comprehensive description of the present
state of Ohio. The map which it explained was not
issued with either French or English copies; it
was published in both languages, but sold separately.

CUTLER (MANASSEH).   987
Life, journals and correspondence of: *Cin* 1888.
O 2v: [12] 524; [4] 496 + 12adv-p. 3pls a

CUTRIGHT, W. B.   988
The history of Upshur county, West Virginia ...
[*Buchannon, W. Va.*] 1907. O 607 300 cops ptd
aa

CUTTS, JAMES M.   989
Conquest of California and New Mexico...
1846–7. *Phil* 1847. D 264 port eng.t. [and 4maps &
plans incl. in paginat.] aa
—anr. ed., in wraps, with date 1848 on front cover
aa
—rptd. 1855. a

D

D., C.   1
Le Champ-d'Asile, au Texas, ou notice ... sur
la formation de cette colonie ... *P* Tiger [1820].
16° 107 fold pl aa

D., O.
Die unbekante Neu Welt ... *See* Dapper,
Olfert.

DABNEY, R[OBERT] L.   2
Life of ... Stonewall Jackson. *L* 1864–6. D 2v:
[6] 333; [16] 527. port aa
—Am. ed., t. slightly altered, *N Y* 1866. O [12]
732 port a
Written by a member of Jackson's staff, with the
help of Jackson's family. Next to Henderson, his
most authoritative biography.

DABNEY, R[OBERT] L.   **3**
True courage: a discourse commemorative of
Lieut. General Thomas J. Jackson. *Rich* 1863. D
26 aa
—ed. 2, with biog. added, same impr. & date.
D 32 aa

DABRY DE THIERSANT, CLAUDE   **4**
De l'origine des Indiens du nouveau monde et de
leur civilization. *P* 1883. Q [4] 358 [2] a

DACUS, J[OSEPH] A.   **5**
Annals of the great strikes . . . *St L* 1877. D 480
11pls a
—anr. issue, same date & collat., *Chi*

DACUS, J[OSEPH] A.   **6**
Life and adventures of Frank and Jesse James.
St L 1880. D 383[incl. pls] a
—oth. issues same date & collat., *Indp*; *Chi*
—enl. ed. with biogs. of the Youngers added, *St
L* 1881. D [4] 442[incl. pls]
—new ed. *Cin* 1882. D [20 incl.front. & lf of ports]
13–498
rptd. *N Y* 1882. D [20 incl.front. & lf of ports]
13–520 most complete ed.
—rptd. *St L* 1882. D [4] 458[incl.pls]
—anr. issue. D [4] 496[incl.pls]

DACUS, ROBERT H.   **7**
Reminiscences of Company H, First Arkansas
mounted rifles. *Dardanelle Ark* 1897. O 48 aa

[DAGGETT, THOMAS F.]   **8**
Billy Le Roy, the Colorado bandit. *N Y* Fox
1881. O 66 aa
—rev. ed. "The life and deeds of Billy Le Roy,
alias the Kid . . .," same impr. & date. aa
—rptd., with original t. restored, same impr. 1883.
O 66 + 10adv-p aa
Sensational and unauthentic, but the first of the
fictionalized biographies of this hoodlum.

[DAGGETT, THOMAS F.]   **9**
The outlaw brothers, Frank and Jesse James . . .
N Y Fox [1881?]. O 67 28pls aa

DAHLBERG, C. V.   **10**
Settlement of the Blue valley, in the vicinity of
Randolph [Kas.]. n.p. [1923]. D 31 a

DAKOTA
The Black hills of Dakota. *Deadwood* [1881]. *See*
Van Cise, Edwin.

Dakota: how to go and what to do when   **11**
you get there. *Milw* 1882. O 32 map pl a
—Ger. tr *Milw* n.d. map pl

The early history and rapid progress of that   **12**
wonderland, central Dakota. n.p. n.d. [*Chi* 1882?]
O 32 capt.t.only aa

Gold fields of Dakota and Wyoming. *Chi*   **13**
1877. O 86 + advs aa

History of southeastern Dakota . . . *Sioux*   **14**
City 1881. O 392 + 8adv-p a

New map and guide to Dakota and the Black
Hills. *See* Maguire, Henry N.

Northern Dakota: its soil, climate . . .   **15**
Fargo 1877. O 24 map aa

Southern Dakota, the Black Hills . . .   **16**
By an early pioneer . . . *Chi* 1875. D 32 [incl. wrap-
pers] map b Y

DAKOTAS (THE).   **17**
Table of distances in: *Wash* 1875. O 28 3fold.
maps 3tabs a

DALCHO, FREDERICK   **18**
An historical account of the . . . Episcopal
church in South-Carolina. *Charleston S C* 1820.
O [8] 613 [3] aa

[DALCHO, FREDERICK]   **19**
Practical considerations . . . relative to the slave
population of South Carolina . . . *Charleston* 1823.
O 38 a

DALE, EDWARD E.   **20**
The range cattle industry . . . *Norman Okla*
1930. O 216[incl. pls] aa
—rptd. same impr 1960. O [16] 207 a

DALE, HARRISON C.   **21**
The Ashley-Smith explorations and the discovery of a central route to the Pacific, 1822–1829.
Clev 1918. O 352[incl. maps & pls] aa
—rptd. *Glendale* 1941. a

DALE, HENRY   **22**
Adventures . . . of the Younger brothers . . .
N Y 1890. D 191[incl. front.] a

DALL, WILLIAM H.   **23**
Alaska and its resources . . . *B* 1870. O 628 map
15pls a
—Eng. ed., *L* 1870. same collat.

DALL, W[ILLIAM] H., et al   **24**
The Yukon Territory . . . *L* 1898. O [14 incl.
front.] 438 map 21pls a

[DALLAS, ALEXANDER J.]   **25**
An exposition of the causes and character of the
late war with Great Britain. *Phil* 1815. O 82 a
—other 1815 eds., all O: *Concord N H* 108; *B* 47;
Middlebury Vt 55[and anr. issue 59]; Wash 47;
Wash 72; *L* 101
—Fr tr "Manifeste etc *P* 1816. O 136

Attributed also to President Madison. Official vindication of the Government.

[DALLAS, ALEXANDER J.]   **26**
Features of Mr. Jay's treaty . . . *Phil* 1795. O [2] 51 a

DALLAS, SIR GEORGE   **27**
A biographical memoir of . . . Sir Peter Parker . . . killed . . . near Baltimore . . . 1814. *L* 1815. Q [2] 111 port a
—ed. 2, same impr. & collat. 1816.

[DALLAS, ROBERT, JR.]   **28**
Considerations upon the American enquiry. *L* 1779. O [2] 55 a
—rptd. same impr. & date
Severely critical of the conduct of British commanders. Attributed also to Thos. Dallas.

DALLIBA, JAMES   **29**
A narrative of the battle of Brownstown . . . during the campaign under . . . Hull. *N Y* 1816. O 37 aa Issued also in parts.

DALLY, JOSEPH W.   **30**
Woodbridge [N.J.] and vicinity . . . *New Brunswick*, 1873 O 391 a Issued also in 12 pts.

DALLY, NATHAN   **31**
Tracks and trails . . . of a Minnesota territorial pioneer. *Walker Minn* [1931]. O [6] 138 map front. a

[DALRYMPLE, ALEXANDER]   **32**
Considerations on the present state of affairs between England and America. *L* 1778. O [4] 39 a
Advocates a middle ground; no war, no colonial independence.

DALRYMPLE, ALEXANDER   **33**
Plan for promoting the fur-trade and securing . . . by uniting the operations of the East-India and Hudson's-Bay Companys. *L* 1789. Q [4] 32 b ProvArchVictoria Y [only copies located]

DALRYMPLE, ALEXANDER   **34**
The Spanish Memorial of the 14th June considered. *L* 1790. O 41 aa
Concerning the Nootka sound controversy.

DALRYMPLE, A[LEXANDER]   **35**
The Spanish pretensions fairly discussed. *L* 1790. O 19 b LegisL Victoria N NYP
Violently British presentation of the Nootka controversy.

[DALRYMPLE, SIR JOHN]   **36**
The address of the people of Great Britain to the inhabitants of America. *L* 1775. O [4] 60 a
Conciliatory plea, written for colonial consumption.

[DALRYMPLE, SIR JOHN]   **37**
The rights of Great Britain asserted against the claims of America: being an answer to the declaration of the General Congress. *L* 1776. O 92 a
—rptd., in 9 other eds., same yr., pub. at *L, Edin & Dub*
—Am. ed. *Phil* 1776. O 92 [4] fold tab
—Fr. tr. 1776.
Attributed variously to Lord George Germaine, Sir James Mackintosh, James McPherson and Henry Mackenzie. For another *Answer*, *see* Lind, Jonathan.

DALTON, EMMETT   **38**
Beyond the law . . . *N Y* 1918. D [12] 190 front aa

DALTON, EMMETT   **39**
When the Daltons rode. *N Y* 1911. O [8] 313 8pls a
—rptd. *N Y* [1937].

DALTON BROTHERS (THE) . . .   **39a**
By an eye-witness. *Chi* 1892. D 220 [incl front] + 4adv p a

DALTON, WILLIAM   **40**
Travels in the United States, and part of upper Canada. *Appleby* 1821. D [8] 256 a

DALY, JAMES   **41**
For love and bears. A description of a hunting trip [to northern Idaho]. *Chi* [1886]. obl O 144 port a
Author was Frank S. Gray.

DALZELL, J. M.   **42**
John Gray . . . the last soldier of the revolution . . . *Wash* 1868. O 64 a

DAMES, WILHELM   **43**
Der Staat Wisconsin . . . *Neures* 1849. O 29 a

DAMON, SAMUEL C.   **44**
A trip from the Sandwich islands to lower Oregon and upper California. *Honolulu* 1849. Q 56 b G Y
—rptd. *S F* Grabhorn 1927. O [12] 86 port aa
This description of conditions in the Columbia river region, San Francisco, etc., appeared in vol. VII of a Honolulu periodical, *The Friend*, and the book was made from its sheets, with title-page added.

DANA, CHARLES A., ed.   **45**
The United States illustrated . . . *N Y* [ca 1855]. Q 2v: letter press & 77pls aa

DANA, EDMUND   **46**
A description of the bounty lands in . . . Illinois: also a description of the principal roads and routes . . . *Cin* 1819. D 108 aa Some copies have, inserted, fold-map, not issued with the book b

DANA, EDMUND   **47**
Geographical sketches on the western country:
designed for emigrants and settlers . . . *Cin* 1819.
D 312 aa

DANA, J. G., and THOMAS, R. S.   **48**
A report of the trial of Jereboam O. Beauchamp
. . . for the murder of Col. Solomon P. Sharp . . .
Frankf Ky Hodges [1826]. O 153 b BP KyH
Most famous of American criminal trials, the
inspiration of a novel by Simms and poems by Poe
and Chivers.

[DANA, RICHARD H.]   **49**
Two years before the mast . . . *N Y* 1840. 16°
483. Issue 1: white or tan clo.; only 105 titles in ser.
listed on rear cover; in copyr. notice, letter "i" [in
"in"] dotted; p. 9 has heading in perfect type. c
NYP Y
—issue 2: same except more titles listed in enumer-
ation of series b N NYP
—issue 3: gray or black clo.; more titles listed;
type damage to copyr. notice and on p. 9. aa
—new ed., incl. author's later California visit in
1859, *B* 1869. D [8] 470 a
—Eng. eds: *L* 1841 O [4] 124; *Glas* 1842. 16° aa
This account of California in 1835 and 1836 sur-
passed in popularity all other books relating to
that state.

DANE COUNTY, WISCONSIN.   **50**
Statistics of: with a business directory . . . of
Madison. *Madison* 1851. O 24 front. a
—rptd., same impr. 1852. O 16 [incl. front. & illus]
—anr. ed. "Statistics of Madison and Dane County," same impr. & collat. 1853.

DANFORTH, SAMUEL   **51**
A brief recognition of New-Englands' errand
into the wilderness . . . *C* 1671. O [4] 23 c AA BP

[DANIEL, FREDERICK S.]   **52**
Richmond howitzers in the war . . . *Rich* 1891.
D 155 aa

DANIEL (JOHN M.)   **53**
The Richmond Examiner during the war; or, the
writings of: . . . *N Y* 1868. O 232 a
—rptd., same impr. & collat. 1869.

DANIEL, JOHN M.   **54**
Character of Stonewall Jackson. *Lynchburg*
1868. O 63 a

DANIEL, R. JACKSON   **55**
The trials and hair-breadth escapes of R. J. and
Bud Daniel in Arkansas. [*Atlanta* 1885]. O 84 a

DANIELS, ARTHUR M.   **56**
A journal of Sibley's Indian expedition . . . 1863
. . . *Winona* 1864. D 52 b G only 2 copies located

DANIELS, WILLIAM M.   **57**
A correct account of the murder of . . . Joseph
and Hyrum Smith . . . *Nauvoo* 1845. O 24[incl.
wrappers] c NYP Y
—anr. issue, same impr., date & collat., but 2pls
added c G LC
Author was an eye-witness of this tragedy.

DANKERS, JASPER, and SLUYTER, PETER
Journal of a voyage to New York . . . see Murphy, Henry C.

D'ANVILLE, JEAN B. B.   **58**
Mémoires sur la carte intitulée Canada, Louisiane, et les terres anglaises. *P* 1755. Q 26 map aa
—anr. ed. same impr & collat 1756. aa

(D[APPER], O[LFERT]), tr.   **59**
Die unbekante Neu Welt, oder Beschreibung des
welt-teils America . . . *Amst* 1673. F [8, incl eng-t]
658 [22] 54maps & pls c BA N
German translation from the Dutch of Montanus [*q.v.*] and issued by the translator as one of
the twelve parts of his collection of voyages
[pub'd 1670–88]. He names himself as author and
offers no shadow of credit to Montanus; the same
shabby plagiarism was practised by the English
translator, John Ogilby [*q.v.*]

DARBY, JOHN F.   **60**
Personal recollections . . . *St L* 1880. O [4] 480
port a 500 cops ptd

DARBY, WILLIAM   **61**
The emigrant's guide to the western and southwestern states and territories . . . *N Y* 1818. O [6]
311 [13] 3maps 2tabs aa

DARBY, WILLIAM   **62**
A geographical description of . . . Louisiana,
etc. *Phil* 1816. O 270 [17] map aa
—ed. 2, enl. to incl. Miss. & Ala. *N Y* 1817. O 356
[4] 2 maps and [with some cops] large fold. map in
separate folder [which was sold separately] aa
Some copies of the 1816 edition contain a list of
subscribers.

DARBY, WILLIAM   **63**
Geographical, historical and statistical repository. Vol. I, nos. 1 & 2 [all]. *Phil* 1824. O 136 6fold.
maps & profiles a

DARBY, WILLIAM   **64**
Memoir on the . . . history of Florida . . . *Phil*
1821 O [12] 5–92 map aa

DARBY, WILLIAM, and   **65**
DWIGHT, THEODORE
A new gazetteer of the United States . . . *N Y*
1832. O [4] 9–630 a
—rptd. *Hart* 1833. O 608 map
—ed. 2, rev., same impr. 1834. O; 1836. O

DARBY, WILLIAM   66
A tour from . . . New York, to Detroit . . . *N Y*
1819. O 228 64 [7] 3maps[only 1 in some copies]
errata slip aa

DARBY, WILLIAM   67
View of the United States . . . *Phil* 1828. 16° [4]
622 14maps a
—anr.—best—issue, with index [carrying paginat.
to 654] 12adv-p same impr., date & maps

DARLEY, ALEXANDER M.   68
The Passionists of the southwest . . . *Pueblo*
1893. O 59 port a
—rptd. *B* 1894.
First full account of the unusual sect of Peni-
tentes.

DARLEY, FELIX O. C.   69
Scenes in Indian life . . . *Phil* 1843. obl Q 5pts:
[usually bound in 1 vol.] 14pls aa

DARLINGTON, MARY C., ed.   70
Fort Pitt and letters from the frontier. *Pitt* 1892.
O 312 3maps 3pls 300 copies [100 on L. P.] aa

DARLINGTON, MARY C.   71
History of Colonel Henry Bouquet and the western frontiers of Pennsylvania, 1747–64. [*Pitt*
1920]. O 224 7pls 600copies ptd. a

DARLINGTON, WILLIAM M. [ed.]   72
Christopher Gist's journals, with notes . . .
Pitt 1893. O [2] 7–296 7maps some copies on
L.P. aa
First printing of the second journal—of 1751–2
—and first publication containing the complete
series of three. Gist's explorations were among the
earliest made by Americans into Ohio and Kentucky. For his first journal—of 1750—*see* Pownall,
Thomas, *A topographical description*. His third
journal—of 1753—had previously appeared only
in the 1836 volume of the *Massachusetts Historical
Society Collections*.

DARNALL [or Darnell], ELIAS   73
A journal, containing . . . account of the hardships . . . of those heroic Kentucky volunteers,
commanded by General Winchester . . . 1812—13
. . . *Paris Ky* 1813. O [2] 57 [8] b LC NYP PiHU
WisH [only copies known]
—anr. ed. *Frankfort Ky* 1814. D 64 b NYP [only
copy known]
—anr. ed. *Shelbyville Ky* 1814. O 39 b WisH
—other eds.: *Phil* 1834. 16° 87 aa; *Phil* 1854. 16°
100 a

DARTMOOR PRISON.
The prisoner's memoirs, or: *See* Andrews,
Chas.

[D'ARUSMONT, MME. FANNY   74
(WRIGHT)]
Views of society and manners in America . . .
By an English-woman. *L* 1821. O [10] 523 a
—ed. 2, *L* 1822. O [10] 483 map
—Am. ed. *N Y* 1821. O [12] 388
—Am. ed. 2, *N Y* 1821. same collat.
—Dutch tr. *Amst* 1822. O 2v
—Fr. tr. *P* 1822. O 2v: [14] 351; [6] 359
—Ger. tr. *Berlin* 1824. 16° 2v
—Swed tr *Stockh* 1826. O

DASHKEVICH, ANTHONY   75
Archangelo-Mickhailovskii pravoslavnyi sobor
v Sitkhie (The Russian cathedral . . . at Sitka).
N Y 1899. D 71 aa
History of this church from 1848 to the Ameri-
can purchase of Alaska; in both Russian and
English text.

DASSIÉ, LE SIEUR   76
Description generale des costes de l'Amérique
. . . Rouen 1676. D [18] 421 c BA
—anr ed., same impr 1677. Same collat except no
errata lf in prel. portion. c N
—rptd at Havre 1680; 1691. b
This compilation describes both the Atlantic and
the Pacific maritime regions, with account of inhabitants, etc. Section on California and New Mexico
is exhaustive for the period.

DAUBENY, CHARLES [G. B.]   77
Journal of a tour through the United States . . .
1837–8. *Oxf* 1843. D [6] 231 map aa 100 copies ptd

[DAVEIS, C. STEWART]   78
The north-eastern boundary of the United
States. *B* 1832. 16° 100 a
Ascribed also to Nathan Hale.

[DAVEISS, JOSEPH H.]   79
An essay on Federalism. [*Frankf?* 1810?] D 64
caption t. only a
Usually bound with the author's *Sketch of a bill
for an uniform militia* . . ., which bears imprint and
date shown.

DAVEISS, JOSEPH H.   80
A view of the President's conduct, concerning
the conspiracy of 1806. *Frankfort Ky* 1807. O 64 aa
—rptd. *Cin* 1917.
Severely critical of Jefferson's actions in the
mysterious Burr affair.

[DAVENANT, CHARLES]   81
An essay upon the government of the English
plantations on the continent of America . . . *L*
1701. O [32] 86 [2] c AA N NYP Y
Ascribed also to Rob't Beverley, aided by Wm
Byrd.

DAVENPORT, B. M.   **82**
Resources of Nebraska . . . *Nebraska City* 1869.
O 24 a

DAVENPORT [IOWA] . . .   **83**
Davenport [Iowa] city business directory.
Davenport Patton 1853. D 48 b DavenportPL
IaMasonic [only cops loc]

DAVENPORT . . . DIRECTORY . . .   **84**
Davenport [1855]. D 40 [8] 26 + 36adv-p b only
4copies located.
First directory of this town.

DAVID, ROBERT B., ed.   **85**
Malcolm Campbell, sheriff, reminiscences . . .
Casper Wyo [1932]. D [8] 7–361 [5] 20pls a

DAVID, URBAIN   **86**
Les Anglais à la Louisiane en 1814 et 1816 . . .
N O 1845. O 60 aa

DAVIDSON, ALEXANDER, and   **87**
STUVÉ, BERNARD
A complete history of Illinois . . . *Springfield Ill*
1874. O [10] 944 a
—rptd., same impr.; 1876; 1877.
—ed. 2, same impr. 1884. O [14] 1040 [10] 33pls

DAVIDSON, GEORGE   **88**
The Alaska boundary. *S F* 1903. Q 235 map port
small ed. a

DAVIDSON, GEORGE   **89**
The tracks and landfalls of Bering and Chirikof
on the northwest coast . . . [*S F*] 1901. O 44 map a

DAVIDSON, GORDON C.   **90**
The North West Company. *Berkeley* 1918. O
[12] 349 6maps & pls aa

[DAVIDSON, I. G,]   **91**
Oregon and the Pacific Northwest . . . scenery
along the line of the Northern Pacific railroad . . .
Port Ore [*ca* 1879]. F 41 col.t-p 53photos b Spo-
kaneP Y

DAVIDSON, RICHARD O.   **92**
A disclosure of the discovery of . . . the aerostat;
or, a new mode of aerostation. *St L* 1840. D 32 a

DAVIDSON, R[OBERT]   **93**
An excusion to the Mammoth Cave and the
barrens of Kentucky . . . *Lex* 1840. 24° 148 a
—ed. 2, same collat. *Phil* 1840.

DAVIDSON, ROBERT   **94**
History of the Presbyterian Church in . . . Kentucky. *N Y* 1847. O [12] 372 [8] a

DAVIES, BENJAMIN   **95**
Some account of . . . Philadelphia . . . *Phil* 1794.
D [4] 93 fold.tab. eng.plan[issued separately, in-
serted in some copies] aa

DAVIES, EBENEZER   **96**
American scenes and Christian slavery: a
recent tour of four thousand miles in the United
States. *L* 1849. O [12] 324 a
—rptd. *L* 1853.
Though revolted by slavery, the pious observer
revelled in attending slave auctions, of which he
gives the most circumstantial account in all literature.

[DAVIES, GEN. HENRY E.]   **97**
Ten days on the plains. *N Y* [1872]. O 68 [incl
init blank lf] map aa A few cops were issued with
18 photos inserted. b
Best account of General Sheridan's great buffalo
hunt of 1871.

DAVIES, J. J., comp.   **98**
History and business directory of Madison
county, Iowa. *Des M* 1869. O 254 pl map a

DAVIESS, MRS. MARIA T.   **99**
History of Mercer and Boyle counties, Ken-
tucky. *Harrodsburg* 1924. O 176 port a
First appearing serially in a local paper in the
early eighties, this is its first edition in book form.

DÁVILA, F. T.   **100**
Sonora histórico y descriptivo . . . desde la
llegada de los españoles hasta nuestros dias. *Noga-
les* 1894. O [4] 328 a

DÁVILA Y ARRILLAGA, JOSÉ M.   **101**
Continuación de la Historia de la Compañia de
Jesús en Nueva España del P. Francisco Javier
Alegre. *Puebla Mex* 1888–9. Q 2v: 334; 370 a

DAVIS, A. C.   **102**
Frauds of the Indian office. *Wash* 1867. O 36 a

DAVIS, ANDREW McF.   **103**
The journey of Moncacht-Ape . . . across the
continent . . . *Worc* 1883. O 30 a
Study into the credibility of this legend of a 1700
overland trip to Oregon. Separate printing from
American Antiquarian Society *Proceedings*.

DAVIS, CARLYLE C.   **105**
Olden times in Colorado. *L A* 1916. O [16] 448
47pls map a

DAVIS, CHARLES G.   **106**
Ships of the past. *Salem* 1929. O [12] 170 +
adv-p 31pls 12fold.plans at end a also 97 copies on
L.P.

[DAVIS, DANIEL] 107
An address to the inhabitants of the District of Maine, upon the subject of their separation from ... Massachusetts. By one of their fellow citizens. *Port Me* 1791. O 54 aa

DAVIS, DUKE 108
Flashlights from mountains and plain. *Bound Brook N J* 1911. D [6] 13–266 2pls [not incl. in paginat.] + 3adv-p a

DAVIS, EUGENE, reporter 109
Can a Negro hold office in Georgia? ... Arguments ... and the decision ... in the case of Richard W. White ... *vs* ... Wm. J. Clemens. *Atlanta* 1869. O 179 a

DAVIS, F[RANKLIN] C., pub. 110
Great western business guide; or, the Pittsburgh, Fort Wayne and Chicago railway, and its connections. *Phil* 1861. 16° 284 2 maps pl b 4cops loc.
Contains route to Pike's Peak.

DAVIS, GEORGE, b. 1821 111
Recollections of a sea wanderer's life ... his trip to California in 1849 ... *N Y* 1887. D [8] 408[incl. pls] aa

DAVIS [COL.] GEORGE T. M. 112
An authentic account of the massacre of Joseph Smith, the Mormon prophet ... *St L* 1844. O 47 b NYP Y [only cops kn]

DAVIS (COL. G[EORGE] T. M.) 113
Autobiography of: ... *N Y* 1891. D 395 [incl initial blank lf] a

DAVIS, HENRY T. 114
Solitary places made glad ... experiences for thirty-two years in Nebraska. *Cin* 1890. D 422 port a
Davis also crossed the plains in 1850 and spent two years in California.

DAVIS, HORACE 115
Record of Japanese vessels driven upon the northwest coast ... *Worc* 1872. O 22 pls a

[DAVIS, CAPT. J. C.] 116
The history of the late expedition to Cuba ... *N O* [1850]. O 64 b
—anr. issue, with adds., *N O* 1850. O [2] 89 aa

DAVIS, JAMES D. 118
The history of ... Memphis ... *Memphis* 1873. D 320 front. a

DAVIS (JEFFERSON). 119
Life of: from authentic sources. By a South Carolinian. *L* 1865. D [4] 96 a

DAVIS, JEFFERSON 120
The rise and fall of the Confederate government. *N Y* 1881. O 2v: [24] 707 + 2 adv-lvs; [20] 808 + 2adv-lvs 14 maps 19pls a
—rptd *N Y* 1958. O 2v

DAVIS, JEFFERSON 121
Speeches delivered during the summer of 1858. *Balt* 1859. O 56 a
Davis issued these ten speeches because of misrepresentations concerning them; he is willing "to stand or fall by their contents."

[DAVIS, JOHN] b. 1774 122
The American mariners ... To which are added naval annals ... *Salisbury Eng* [1822]. D [12] 384 a

DAVIS, JOHN, b. 1774 123
Travels ... in the United States ... 1798–1802. *L* [ptd *Bristol*] 1803. O [8] 454 aa
—rptd., with changes, "Personal adventures ...," *L* 1816. roy O 96 a
—anr. ed., same collat. & impr., 1817.
—Am. ed. *N Y* 1909. O [12] 429
—anr. ed., ed. J. V. Cheney, *B* Bibliophile Soc. 1910. O 2v 487copies ptd.

DAVIS, J[OHN E.] 124
Mormonism unveiled ... by a deluded brother of the sect. *Bristol Eng* 1855. D 48 aa
—rptd. *Bristol* 1856; *Cardiff* 1858. aa
Describes trip from Louisiana to Utah and sojourn there.

DAVIS [JOSHUA] 125
Narrative of: an American citizen who was pressed and served on ... six ships of the British navy ... *B* 1811. D 72 a

DAVIS, MATTHEW L. 126
Memoirs of Aaron Burr ... *N Y* 1836. O 2v: 436; 453. 2ports facs a
—rptd. *N Y* 1837; *N Y* 1858.

DAVIS, NICHOLAS A. 127
The campaign from Texas to Maryland. *Rich* 1863. D 168 2pls b Emory LC
—rev. ed. *Houston* 1863. D 87 aa

DAVIS, PARIS M. 128
An authentick history of the late war between the United States and Great Britain ... *Ithaca* 1829. D 360 a
—rptd., with t. reading "authentic," *N Y* 1836. D 360 5pls

DAVIS, P[ARIS] M. 129
The four principal battles of the late war ... *Harrisburg* 1832. O 32 pl a
Extracted from his *Authentick history*, above.

[DAVIS, PARIS M.?]   **130**
An official account of the trial and execution of Arbuthnot & Ambrister . . . n.p. 1825. D 45 aa

DAVIS, PARIS M.   **131**
An official and full detail of the great battle of New Orleans . . . *N Y* 1836. D 60 pl a

DAVIS, REUBEN   **132**
Recollections of Mississippi . . . *B* 1889. O [6] 446 port a
—rptd., same impr.: 1890; 1891.

DAVIS, ROBERT   **133**
The Canadian farmer's travels in the United States . . . *Buf* 1837. D 108 aa
Visited Ohio, Indiana and Michigan.

[DAVIS, SAMUEL B.]   **134**
Escape of a Confederate officer from prison . . . *Norfolk Va* 1892. D 72 a
Includes later service under Wirz at Andersonville prison.

DAVIS, STEPHEN   **135**
Notes of a tour in America . . . *Edin* 1833. 18° 150 a

DAVIS, WILLIAM HEATH   **136**
Sixty years in California . . . *S F* 1889. O [22] 639 aa
—anr. ed. with adds., "Seventy-five years in California." *S F* 1929. Q [32] 422 44 maps & pls several issues, all ltd.; the Argonaut ed., of 100copies, has add. pls & p. of au's original MS. aa
Most valuable Californian reminiscences.

DAVIS, WILLIAM J., ed.
The partisan rangers of the Confederate States army . . . *See* Johnson, Adam R.

DAVIS, WILLIAM M.   **137**
Nimrod of the sea, or, the American whaleman. *N Y* 1874. O 403 a

DAVIS, WILLIAM W.   **138**
The civil war and reconstruction in Florida. *N Y* 1913. O [24] 769 aa

DAVIS, WILLIAM W. H.   **139**
El Gringo; or, New Mexico and her people. *N Y* 1857. D 432 front. a
—rptd S Fé 1938

DAVIS, W[ILLIAM] W. H.   **140**
The history of Bucks county, Pennsylvania . . . *Doylestown* 1876. O 875 [54] 39pls & maps aa
—ed. 2, *N Y* 1905. O 3v aa

DAVIS, WILLIAM W. H.   **141**
The Spanish conquest of New Mexico. *Doylestown Pa* 1869. O 438 map port aa

DAVIS, WINFIELD J.   **142**
History of political conventions in California . . . *Sacr* 1893. O [6] 711 errata slip a

[DAVISON, GIDEON M.]   **143**
The fashionable tour: or, a trip to the Springs, Niagara . . . *Saratoga* 1822. 24° 165 a
—rptd., same impr.: 1825; 1828; 1830; 1833; 1834.
—later eds., au. named, "The traveller's guide through the middle and northern states," same impr. 1837; 1840; 1848.
—Fr. ed. "Tournée à la mode dans les États-Unis," *P* 1839. O [8] 199 map
—anr. Fr. ed. "Voyage aux États-Unis . . .," *P* 1834. map
Later editions contained map and plates.

[DAVISON, GIDEON M.]   **144**
Routes and tables of distances . . . in the Traveller's guide through the northern and middle states . . . *Saratoga Springs* 1833. 16° 24 fold.map a

DAVISON [ETC] COUNTIES, DAK.   **145**
Carefully compiled facts concerning: . . . [*Mitchell* 1883]. O [6incl. wrapper t. & 2 adv-p] 6 24 + 3adv-p a

[DAVYDOV, GAVRILLA I.]   **146**
Dvukratnoe puteshestvie v. Ameriku . . . *St Ptbg* 1810–12. D 2v: 287; 234 c NYP WashU Y
—Ger. tr. "Reise der . . . flottenofficiers . . . von durch Sibirien nach Amerika . . .," *Berlin* 1816. D [58] 253 b NYP Y
Account of two voyages to Alaska, the Aleutian islands, etc.

[DAWES, MATTHEW]   **147**
A letter to Lord Chatham, concerning the present war . . . *L*[1776?]. O 60 a

DAWES, RUFUS R.   **148**
Service with the Sixth Wisconsin . . . *Marietta, O.* 1890. O 330 19ports a

DAWES, THOMAS, JR.   **149**
An oration . . . to commemorate the bloody tragedy of the 5th of March, 1770. *B* 1781. Q 23 aa

DAWSON, CHARLES   **150**
Pioneer tales of the Oregon trail and Jefferson county, Nebraska. *Topeka* 1912. O [16] 488 map pl aa

DAWSON, FRANCIS W.   **151**
Reminiscences of Confederate service. *Charleston S C* 1882. O 180 100copies ptd aa

DAWSON, HENRY B.   **152**
The assault on Stony Point . . . *Morrisania N Y* 1863. O [8] 156 250copies a

DAWSON, HENRY B., et al   153
Major-General Israel Putnam ... *Morrisania*
N Y 1860. O 169 a 250copies ptd[some burned]

DAWSON, HENRY, B., ed.   154
Record of the trial of Joshua Hett Smith, Esq.,
for ... complicity in the treason of Benedict Arnold. *Morrisania* 1866. O [6] 116 a 50copies ptd

DAWSON, HENRY B., and   155
DAVIS, WILLIAM J.
Reminiscences of New York City ... *N Y* 1859.
D 350 a 50copies ptd

DAWSON, HENRY B.   156
The Sons of Liberty in New York. [*N Y*] 1859.
O 118 a For private circulation.

DAWSON, HENRY B.   157
Westchester county, N. Y., during the ... revolution. *Morrisania* 1886. Q [6] 281 map port a

DAWSON, MOSES   158
A historical narrative of the civil and military
services of Major General Harrison ... *Cin* 1824.
O [8] 464 [8] errata slip of 15 lines b anr iss with
24 line errata slip aa
Not only the principal contemporary authority
on Harrison, but also one of the most exhaustive
and dependable sources on events of the War of
1812 in the western country, Tecumseh's uprising,
etc. A few copies on Large—and thinner—Paper.

DAWSON, NICHOLAS ["CHEYENNE"]   159
California in '41. Texas in '51. [*Austin ca* 1901].
D 119 [5] port b G NYP Y 50cops ptd
—rptd. "Narrative of ... "Cheyenne" Dawson,"
S F Grabhorn 1933. O [12] 100 [7] aa 500 cops ptd
Crossed the Rockies, 1841, with first Calif.
settlers.

DAWSON, SARAH M.   160
A Confederate girl's diary. *B* 1913 D [20] 440
[2] 8pls a

DAWSON, THOMAS F., and   161
SKIFF, F. J. V.
The Ute war: a history of the White River mas-
sacre [etc.] *Denver* 1879. O 184 + 8adv-p c N
NYP Y
After Hollister's *History of the First Col. Regi-
ment*, the rarest Colorado imprint.

DAY, SAMUEL P.   162
Down south; or, an Englishman's experience at
the seat of the American war. *L* 1862. D 2v: 827
[paged continuously] 2 ports a

DAY, SHERMAN   163
Historical collections of ... Pennsylvania ...
N Hav 1843. O 708 a

DAY, THOMAS   164
Reflections upon the present state of England,
and the independence of America. *L* 1782. O [4]
102 2adv-p a
—ed. 2, same impr., date & collat.
—ed. 3, with adds., *L* 1783. O [2] 129
—several other eds.
Acknowledgment of American independence
England's best policy.

DAYS FOREVER FLOWN
See Haselhurst, Mrs. May A.

DAYS
Days of yore; or shadows of the past. By the
ancient lady. *See* Poyas, Mrs. Eliz. A.

DAYTON, EDSON C.   165
Dakota days ... 1886–1898. *Clifton Spgs, N Y*
[Htfd ptd] 1937. O [10] 128 map pl 300 cops ptd aa

DEAN, HENRY C.   166
Crimes of the civil war ... *Balt* 1868. O [8] 512 a
—anr. ed. same impr. 1869. O [8] 539

DEAN, JAMES   167
An alphabetical atlas, or gazetteer of Vermont
... *Montpelier* 1808. O 44 a

DEAN (CAPT. JOHN) and company.   168
Narrative of the sufferings ... of: in the Nottingham-Galley ... cast away on Boon Island,
near New England ... *L* [1711]. D [6] 23 b H NYP
—Am. ed. *B* 1711. O b
—later Eng. eds., with adds., all *L*. O: 1726; 1727;
1730; 1738. a
—Am. ed. *Morrisania N Y* 1863. O [8] 156
For another account, blaming Captain Dean,
see Langman, Christopher.

DEAN, JOHN W., ed.   169
Captain John Mason, founder of New Hampshire ... *B* Prince Society 1887. sm Q [14] 492 map
2pls tab a 250copies ptd.

DE ANDREIS (REV. FELIX).
Sketches of the life of: *See* Semeria, J. B.

[DEANE, CHARLES] ed.   170
Records of the council for New England. *C*
1867. O 10 [16] 11–83 a

DEANE, SAMUEL   171
History of Scituate, Massachusetts ... *B* 1831.
O [4] 406 [2] a Many copies burned
—rptd. 1899.

DEANE, SILAS   172
An address to the ... citizens of the United
States ... *Hart* 1784. D 30 aa
—Eng. ed., with adds., t. altered, *L* 1784. O [4] 95 aa
—rptd. *N Lond* 1784. O 54; anr. issue, Q 38 a

DEANE (SILAS). 173
   Papers in relation to the case of: now first published from the original manuscripts. *Phil* Seventy-Six Soc. 1855. O [4] 17–201 [4] a 250 cops ptd

DEANE, SILAS 174
   Paris papers . . . intercepted letters to his brothers . . . *N Y* [1782]. D [12 32] 141 [2 24, i.e. 34] b AA JCB NYP
   The publication of these private letters [advocating reconciliation with England] ruined Deane with his countrymen. They were written in the heat of bitterness engendered by the suspicions of Congress as to his conduct in buying war supplies in France and had appeared first in a Tory journal of 1781. For separate printing of the appendix, *see Declaration (A) of independence . . .*

DEARBORN, H[ENRY] A. S. 175
   Defense of Gen. Henry Dearborn, against the attack of Gen. William Hull. *B* 1824. O 28 a
   Hull's alibi for surrendering Detroit was that Dearborn failed to keep the British occupied at Niagara.

DEARBORN, H[ENRY] A. S. 176
   Letters on the internal improvements and commerce of the west. *B* Lewis 1839. O 75 a
   —anr. issue, *B* Dutton, etc. 1839. O 120

DEARBORN, NATHANIEL 177
   Boston notions . . . account of "that village" from 1630 to 1847 . . . *B* 1848. 18° [20] 7–426 [2] 30pls a

DEATHERAGE, CHARLES P. 178
   Early history of greater Kansas City . . . Vol. I [all]. *K C* 1927. roy O 700 map a

DEATON, E. L. 179
   Indian fights on the Texas frontier . . . *Hamilton Tex* 1894. O 199 port[on cover] a
   —rptd. *Ft Worth* 1927. O [14] 161

DEATON, L. B. 180
   Eleven months of exile life in southern Illinois. *Chi* priv. ptd. 1862. O 128 aa

DE BAETS, MAURICE 181
   Mgr. [Monseigneur] Seghers, l'apotre de l'Alaska. *Ghent* 1896. O 237 port facsm maps a
   —anr. ed. same impr 1897. O 283 port
   Biography based on letters written from Vancouver, Oregon and Alaska.

DEBAR, J. H. 182
   The West Virginia handbook and immigrant's guide . . . *Parkersburg* 1870. O 200 fold.map a

DE BARTHE, JOE 183
   The life and adventures of Frank Grouard . . . *St Joseph, Mo.* [1894] O 545 68pls aa

—rptd. *Buffalo, Wyo.* n.d. D [2] 326 no pls a
—anr ed., *Norman, Okla.* 1958.

DEBOUCHEL, V. 184
   Histoire de la Louisiane . . . *N O* 1841. D 197 aa

DE BOW, J[AMES] D. B. 185
   The industrial resources of the southern and western states . . . *N O* 1852–53. O 3v: [8] 464; [4] 560; [4] 584 [10] aa
   —Eng. ed. *L* 1854. O 3v aa
   —ed. 2, "Encyclopaedia of the trade . . . of the United States, more particularly of the southern and western states . . .," *N Y* 1854. O 2v a
   —ed. 3, "The industrial resources . . . of the United States . . .," *N Y* 1854. O 3v in 1 aa
   —anr. issue [in part], "Cotton commerce and the southern states," *Wash & N O* 1856. O 560 a
   —issued also under t.: "The southern states . . .," *Wash* same date & collat.

[DE BOW, JAMES D. B.] 186
   The interest in slavery of the southern non-slaveholder . . . *Charleston S C* 1860 O 30 aa

[DE BOW, JAMES D. B.] 187
   The political annals of South Carolina. *Charleston S C* 1854. O 50 aa

[DE BRAHM, JOHN G. W.] 188
   The Atlantic pilot. *L* 1772. O [8] 25 3maps fold tab b GaU LC

DE BRAHM, JOHN G. W. 189
   History of the province of Georgia . . . *Wormsloe Ga* [Phil ptd] 1849. Q 57 6maps aa 49 copies ptd.
   Written in 1772, but here first printed.

DECALVES [or De Calves] 190
DON ALONSO, pseud.
   New travels to the westward, or, unknown parts of America. Being a tour of almost fourteen months. Containing an account of the country, upwards of two thousand miles west of the Christian parts of North-America . . . *B* Folsom [1788] D [10] 7–44 c AA Hn
   —anr. ed. *Norwich* 1788. D 34 [Evans erroneously lists a 1789 Norwich ed.] b Y
   —rptd. *Norwich* 1790. b
   —anr. ed. n.p. 1795. 16° [2] 58 b
   —other eds.: [*Dover N H*] 1796. O 34; *N Lond* 1796. D 36; *Norwich* [1796]; *B* [1796] b
   —anr. ed. with added "History of Charles Mortimer," n.p. 1797. D 81 b
   —other eds.: *Hudson* 1797; *Rutland* 1797; *Schenectady* 1797; *Hudson* 1799; *Hudson* 1801; *Hart* 1801; *Danbury* 1802; *Lex* 1802; *Cooperstown* 1803; *Greenwich Mass* 1805. aa
   —Ger. ed. "Eine ganz neue und sehr merkwürdige Reisebeschreibung . . .," *Phil* 1796. O 82 [2] a

**DECALVES [or De Calves],   191
DON ALONSO, pseud.**
Travels to the westward, or the unknown parts of America . . . 1786–7. Containing an account of the country to the westward of the . . . Mississippi . . . *Keene N H* 1794. D 35 b JCB
—ed. 2, *Keene*, for the purchaser, 1795. O 35 b AA JCB
—anr. issue, *Keene* Blake & Co. 1795. D 35 b JCB
—anr. ed. *Port Me* 1796. D 28 aa
—anr. ed. "2nd Dover ed." [for 1st Dover ed. of 1796 *see*, above, under "New travels . . ."] [*Dover* 1797]. O 39 aa
—anr. ed. "3rd Dover ed." [*Dover* 1797?]. D 41 aa
—anr. ed. *Rutland* 1797. D 48 aa
—anr. ed. *Windsor* 1797. D 36 aa
Decalves gives the fantastic narrative of an overland trip from New Orleans to the northwest coast in 1786–7. The journey described was undoubtedly imaginary and consequently he did not obtain, as claimed, from John Vandeleur's lips the story of his 7-year captivity among the Indians of the northwest coast; but the Vandeleur story, incorporated in all editions of the Decalves' narrative, undoubtedly has factual basis. For other accounts of it *see* Van Leason, James, *A narrative of a voyage*, and Vandeleur, John, *A history of the voyages* [etc.].

DECATUR . . . AND BARRON   192
Decatur, Commodore Stephen, and Barron, Commodore James. Correspondence between: . . . *B* 1820. O 22 a
—anr. ed. *Wash* 1820. O 26
—other eds. *Rich* n.d. O; *Charleston S C* 1820. O
Led to the famous duel in which Decatur was killed.

DECATUR, ILLINOIS.   193
History of: . . . *Decatur* 1871. O 51 aa

DECENNIUM LUCTUOSUM . . .
See Mather, Cotton.

**[DECKER, WILLIAM R.   194
(MUSTANG BILL)]**
Our great Indian war. The miraculous lives of Mustang Bill, and Miss Marion Fannin . . . among the hostile Sioux . . . *Phil* Barclay n.d. [1876?]. O [2] 19–78 [2] [incl. pls] aa
—rptd. same impr.[1881]; 1885. aa

DECLARATION   195
Declaration (The) and address of His Majesty's suffering loyalists to the people of America. *L* 1782. Q [6] 32 a

Declaration (A) by the representatives of   196
the United States . . . in general congress assembled. *Phil* Dunlap [1776]. Broadside. d NYP 4copies known

First printing of the Declaration of Independence [of July 4th, 1776]. For its first printing in book form, *see* Bryan, Samuel.

**Declaration (A) of independence . . . at   197
Philadelphia in 1776.** With a counter-declaration... [*N Y* 1782?]. D [2] 24[i.e. 34] b LC
Tory propaganda; issued both separately and as an appendix to another Tory pamphlet of the same year, Silas Deane's *Paris papers*.

A declaration of the . . . persecution of the Quakers . . . *See* Burrough, Edw.

**Declaration (A) of the representatives of   198
the United Colonies . . . setting forth the causes . . . of their taking up arms** . . . *Phil* Bradford 1775. O 13 b
—other 1775 Am. eds.: *Bristol*; *Newport*; *Prov*: *Watertown*. aa
—1776 Am. eds.: *Newport*; *Salem*. a
—Eng. ed., with adds., *L* 1775. O [6] 3–32 a
The London edition was secretly issued, with no printer shown, as propaganda for American sympathizers.

DE CORDOVA, J[ACOB]   199
Lecture on Texas . . . *Phil* 1858. D 32 a

DE CORDOVA, JACOB   200
Lectures on Texas and cotton cultivation . . . *L* 1858. O 58 a
—anr. ed. "Texas; her capabilities . . .," *Manch* 1858. D 114
—Am ed *Phil* 1858. D 32

DE CORDOVA, J[ACOB]   201
The State of Texas; her capabilities . . . *Galv* [1858?]. D 68 a
—enl. ed. "Texas: her resources . . .," *Phil* 1858. D 371
—anr. issue, same impr. & date, with index added. D 375
Intended as a companion to the author's separately printed map published by Colton, New York, 1857. An earlier form of this map, by Creuzbar, prepared in 1847, copyrighted in 1848 and engraved by J. M. Atwood in New York, was published by De Cordova, Houston, 1849.

DE CORDOVA, J[ACOB]   202
The Texas immigrant and traveller's guide book. *Austin* 1856. D 103 aa

DE COSTA, BENJAMIN F.   203
A narrative of events at Lake George . . . to the close of the revolution. *N Y* 1868. O 75 a 75copies ptd

DE COSTA, B[ENJAMIN] F.   204
Sketches of the coast of Maine . . . *N Y* 1869. Q 231 pl a 24copies ptd

DE COSTA, BENJAMIN F.   **205**
Verrazano the explorer: a vindication . . . *N Y*
1880. [cover t.1881]. Q 82 3maps 2ports a

DEEDES, HENRY   **206**
Sketches of the south and west . . . *L* 1869. O
[6] 170 a
Travelled through the South, to Chicago, etc.;
shows decided Southern sympathy.

DEERFIELD, MASSACHUSETTS.
A brief sketch of the first settlement of: . . . By
one of the descendants of the first settlers . . . *See*
Hoyt, Elihu.

DEERING, RICHARD   **207**
Louisville, her commercial . . . advantages. Including . . . history . . . *Louisv* 1859. O 99 a

DEFEBAUGH, JAMES E.   **208**
History of the lumber industry in America. *Chi*
1906–09. O 4v pls aa

DEFENCE (A)   **209**
Defence (A) of southern slavery . . . in which
much of the false philanthropy and mawkish senti-
mentalism of the abolitionists is . . . refuted. By a
southern clergyman. *Hamburg S C* 1851. O 46 [2] a

DEFENCE
Defence of the alien and sedition laws . . . By
Virginiensis. *See* Lee, Chas.

**Defence (A) of the people . . . confutation   210
of . . . a late huge, angry pamphlet called Faction
detected** . . . *L* 1744. O [2] 150 a
For pamphlet attacked, *see* Perceval, John.

**Defence (A) of the Resolutions and address   211
of the American congress, in reply to Taxation no
tyrrany** . . . *L* [1775]. O [2] 96 a

**Defence (A) of the treaty . . . between the United
States and Great Britain** . . . By Camillus. *See*
Hamilton, Alex.

DEFENSE
Defense des Recherches philosophiques sur les
Américains. Par M. de P . . . *See* Pauw, M. Cor-
neille de.

DEFINITIVE TREATY   **212**
**Definitive treaty (The) between Great Britain and
the United States . . . signed at Paris, the 3rd day
of September 1783.** n.p. 1783. O 22 b Clem JCB Y
—Eng. ed. *L* 1783. O 12 aa
Though not formally ratified until January 14,
1784, the terms embodied in this preliminary printing first acknowledged to the world the existence
of the United States as a nation. On the title-page
was shown its seal—the eagle device and "E pluri-

bus unum"—its first appearance, unless preceded
by the French edition of the *Constitutions of the
several states*, printed at Paris the same year.

Definitive treaty (The) . . . **between His   213
Britannick Majesty, the most Christian king, and
the King of Spain . . . at Paris, the 10th day of
February, 1763** . . . *L* 1763. Q 48 aa
—Am. ed. *Charlestown* 1763. Q [4] 3–13 aa
—Fr. tr. *P* 1763. Q a
—Sp. & Fr. tr. *Madrid* 1763. Q
—Portuguese tr. *Lis* 1763. Q
These final terms, by which France relinquished
her North American claims and Spain ceded Flo-
rida, gave England undisputed possession of the
territory of the present United States from the
Mississippi to the Atlantic. For preliminary ar-
rangement, signed the year previous, *see Prelimi-
nary articles of peace* . . .

[DEFOE, DANIEL]   **214**
The case of Protestant dissenters in Carolina . . .
L 1706. Q 42, blank lf 67 b N NYP NYS
Contains fourteen tracts at end including John
Ash's *The present state of affairs in Carolina*, first
published in 1682.

[DEFOE, DANIEL]   **215**
Party-tyranny . . . as now practised in Carolina
. . . *L* 1705. Q [2] 30 b Y

DE FOREST, JOHN W.   **216**
History of the Indians of Connecticut . . . *Hart*
1851. O [26] 509 map a
—rptd., same collat., *Hart* 1852; *Hart* 1853; *Alb*
1871.
Best account of these tribes.

DE FOREST, T. R.   **217**
Olden time in New York . . . *N Y* 1833. D 54 a

DEFOURI, JAMES H.   **218**
Historical sketch of the Catholic church in New
Mexico [and Arizona]. *S F* 1887. O 164 aa

DEFOURI, JAMES H.   **219**
The martyrs of New Mexico . . . lives and deaths
of the earliest missionaries in the territory . . . *Las
Vegas* 1893. O [4] 78 aa

DE GROOT, HENRY   **220**
Sketches of the Washoe silver mines . . . *S F*
1860. O 24 + 4adv-p b N Y
Earliest tract on Nevada; issued before that
Territory was officially established. De Groot also
published, in 1884, his sixteen page *Recollections of
California mining life.*

DE HAM, VICTOR   **221**
Conseils à l'émigrant belge aux États-Unis . . .
Brus 1849. D 96 map aa
—Dutch tr. au's name not given. Same impr, date
& collat. a

DE HASS, CARL   222
Wisconsin . . . *Elberfeld Ger* 1848. D 92 map
pl aa
—rptd. same impr. 1849. D 140 map pl aa

DE HASS, WILLS   223
History of the early settlement and Indian wars
of western Virginia . . . *Wheeling* 1851. O 416 5pls
aa
Valuable compilation based on reliable sources.

DE KRAFFT, JOHANN C. P. VON   224
Journal . . . 1776–1784. *N Y* 1883. O [8] 217 [10]
6pls a
War diary of a Hessian officer.

DELAFIELD, JOHN   225
A brief topographical description of the county
of Washington, in . . . Ohio. *N Y* 1834. O 39 pl b
First Ohio county history.

DELAFIELD, JOHN   226
An inquiry into the origin of the antiquities of
America . . . *N Y* 1839. Q 102 105–142 11pls
[1fold.] a
—anr. issue, same collat., *Cin* 1839.
The folding plate is often lacking.

DELAFIELD, MAJOR JOSEPH   227
The unfortified boundary. A diary of the first
survey of the Canadian boundary line from St.
Regis to the Lake of the Woods . . . *N Y* 1943. O
[12] 491 13maps & pls[some fold.] a 1000copies
ptd

DELANEY, CALDWELL   228
Deep south. *Mobile* 1942. O 72 lvs [incl. front. &
pls] a 200copies ptd.

DELANEY, MRS. MATILDA J.   229
A survivor's recollections of the Whitman massacre. [*Spokane* 1920]. D 46 port a

DELANO, ALONZO   230
Life on the plains and among the diggings.
Auburn 1854. D 384 4pls no mention on t-p of no.
of thousands ptd aa
—rptd. *NY* 1854; 1857; 1859; 1861; 1936
One of the best "forty niner" narratives.

[DELANO, ALONZO]   231
Old Block's sketch book . . . *Sacr* 1856. O [6]
78 [incl. pls] c G NYP Y
—rptd *Santa Anna* 1947. O 91 a

[DELANO, ALONZO]   232
Pen knife sketches; or chips of the Old Block . . .
Sacr 1853. O 112 [incl. pls] b N Y
—ed. 2, same impr., date & collat. aa
—rptd. *S F* [Grabhorn] 1934. Q 550cops ptd a

DELANO, AMASA   233
A narrative of voyages in the northern and
southern hemispheres . . . *B* 1817. O 598 map
2ports aa
—ed. 2, *B* 1818. a

DELANO, JUDAH   234
The Washington [D. C.] directory . . . *Wash*
1822. 16° [20] 13–148 aa
First directory of this city.

DELANO (REUBEN).   235
Wanderings and adventures of: . . . twelve years
on a whaleship. *Worc* 1846. O [4] 13–102 3pls a
—rptd. *N Y* 1846. O

DELAPLAINE, J[OSEPH] pub.   236
Delaplaine's repository of the lives and portraits
of distinguished American characters. *Phil* 1815–
[16]. Q 2v in 1[all]: [16] 223; 148. front. 18ports a

[DELAVAN, JAMES]   237
Notes on California and the placers . . . *N Y*
1850. O 128 2pls b LC Y
—rptd *Oakl* 1956 a 700 cops ptd

DELAWARE
The biographical history of Dionysius, tyrant of
Delaware: . . . By Timoleon. *See* Tilton, James.

Brief sketch of the military operations on   238
the Delaware during the late war . . . *Phil* 1820.
D 96 map aa

Ways and means for the inhabitants of Delaware:
to become rich. *See* Rawle Francis.

DE LEON, EDWIN   239
La verité sur les États Confédérés . . . *P* 1862.
O 32 port a
Propaganda pamphlet by a Confederate agent to
induce French recognition.

DE LEON, THOMAS C.   240
Belles, beaux and brains of the 60's. *N Y* [1909].
O [20] 9–464 port a Binding of first issue gold-
stamped.

DE LEON, THOMAS C.   241
Four years in rebel capitals . . . *Mobile* 1890. O
[14] 11–376 a
—rptd., same impr., 1892. O 12 376 port

DELESSERT, EUGENE   242
Les mines d'or de la Californie. *P* 1849. O 20 +
wraps b NYH

DELESSERT, EUGENE   243
Voyages dans les deux océans . . . 1844 à 1847.
Brésil, États-Unis . . . *P* 1848. O [8] 326 [2] 2maps
15pls aa

DE L'ISLE, [JOSEPH N.] 244
Nouvelles cartes des découvertes de l'Amiral de Fonte [*et al*] dans les meres septentrionales . . . *P* 1753. Q [4] 60 4maps b NYP Y
—rptd. *P* 1754. b
In some copies of the 1753 edition a supplement [on the passage of Mercury, May 6, 1753] extends pagination to seventy-six. Includes one of the earliest accounts of Bering's second voyage.

[DELIUS, EDOUARD] 245
Wanderungen eines jungen Norddeutschen durch Portugal, Spanien und Nord-Amerika . . . 1827–1831. *Hamburg* 1834. D 4v: [6] 192; 192; 192; 195 aa

DELLE LETTERE AMERICANE.
See Carli, Giovanni R.

DELONY, LEWIS S. 246
Forty years a peace officer . . . [ranger and Waco detective chief]. [*Abilene, Tex* 1907] O [2] 61 port wrap-t only aa

[DEMBY, JAMES W.] 247
Mysteries and miseries of Arkansas . . . *St L* 1863. D 88 aa
Tribulations of a loyal Arkansas journalist compelled to fly to St. Louis for safety.

DEMBY, J[AMES] W. 248
The war in Arkansas . . . *Little Rock* 1864. 4pts [all pub] D 64 b H Hn [only cops loc]

DÉMEUNIER, JEAN N. 249
L'Amérique indépendante . . . avec un précis de l'histoire de chaque province . . . *Ghent* 1790. O 3v: [2] 231; [2] 196; [2] 226 [4]. map a
—suppl. [to above], *Ghent* 1791. O [2] 120

DÉMEUNIER, JEAN N. 250
Essai sur les États-Unis. *P* 1786. Q [2] 89 a

[DEMING, EBENEZER]? 250a
Western emigration; a narrative of a tour to . . . "Edensburgh" [Illinois] by Major Walter Wilkey . . . *N Y* Sackett, etc. 1839. O 24[incl. front.] a
—anr. issue, same collat. & date, *N Y* Claiborne.
Imaginary tour to, and residence in, an imaginary town, written as a burlesque exposé of emigration projects.

DEMOCRATIC . . . CONVENTION 251
Democratic national convention of 1860 . . . at Charleston and Baltimore . . . *Clev* 1860. O 188 a

DEMOPHILUS, pseud.
The genuine principles of the ancient . . . English constitution . . . *See* Bryan, Saml.

DENISON, E. S. 252
Yosemite views . . . [*S F* 1881] O 104 lvs [incl 2 maps & 50 pls] no text a

DENKSCHRIFTEN 252a
Denkschriften der russischen geographischen Gessellschaft zu St. Petersburg. Vol. I [all]. *Weimar* 1849. O [6] 652 4maps aa
Contains account of Sagoskin's voyage to the islands of the northwestern coast.

[DENNIS, JOHN] 253
An address to the people of Maryland, on the origin . . . of French agression . . . *Phil* 1798. O 78 [4] a

DENNY, ARTHUR A. 253a
Pioneer days on Puget sound. *Seattle* 1888. D 83 errata slip [many cops were burned] aa
—rptd. same impr 1903. D 103 [13] map 36pls 850 cops a

DENNY (MAJOR EBENEZER). 254
Military journal of: . . . in the revolutionary and Indian wars. *Phil* 1859. O 288 2 ports 4 plans a

DENNY (GEORGE) 255
Denny (George); or sketches of life in the far west. By Chinquopin. *S F* 1856. D 80 a

DENSON, A. C[LARK] 256
Westmoreland: or secession ferocity . . . *St L* 1865. D 48 a
Account of the firing by Federals into the civilian steamboat "Westmoreland," near Memphis, in 1862.

DENSON, JESSE 257
The chronicles of Andrew . . . account of General Jackson's victories . . . *Lex* 1815. D 35 a
—anr. ed., priority not established, *Milledgeville Ga* 1815. D 38
—for rpt. *see* Hillard, Isaac, "A wonderful and horrible thing . . ." [1822 ed.].

DENTAN, REV. 258
Voyage du missionaire . . . *Lausanne* 1838. O 29 fold.map b
Worked among the Indians at Mackinac, Prairie du Chien, etc.

DENTON, DANIEL 259
A brief description of New York . . . *L* 1670. smQ [6] 21 [Date on title page was so close to bottom margin that rebound copies usually have had it cut off by the binder] dd LC N NYS
—rptd. *N Y* 1845 O [22] 58 + 20 adv-p; *Clev* 1902. 250 cops ptd a
First publication on this city to be printed in English.

DENVER   **260**
   Denver City and Auraria, the commercial empo-
rium of the Pike's Peak gold region in 1859. [*St L*
1860]. D 44 [incl. advs.] map pl b ColH Hn
—anr. issue, with more advs., carries paginat. to
75 b S
—reprint in facs of the 44-p issue, [*Glendale* 1942]. a

   Directory of . . . Denver for 1873. *Denver*   **261**
1873. O [12] 18–264 b 1 cop loc

   Guide to Denver, Utah [etc.] . . . *See* Woolworth, S. B.

   History of Denver, Arapahoe County, and   **262**
Colorado . . . *Chi* 1880. Q 652 pls aa

DE PAUW (M.)
   Dissertation sur l'Amérique . . . de: *See* Pernety,
Antoine J. D.

[DE PEYSTER, ARENT S.]   **263**
   Miscellanies; by an officer. Vol. I [all]. *Dumfries*
1813. Q 277 b OHP N NYP
—rptd., with large adds., *N Y* 1888. O 2pts in 1:
80; 202 [6], map plan 4pls a
By the British commander of forts Detroit and
Niagara in the revolution. Pages 232–277 relate
chiefly to affairs in the Old Northwest.

De PEYSTER, JOHN W.   **264**
   La royale. *N Y* 1872–4. O 7pts in 2v: 70; 150.
3maps 4ports a 100copies ptd.
   Military analyses of the final operations of the
Army of the Potomac, severely critical of Grant.

DE PUY, HENRY W.   **265**
   Ethan Allen and the Green-mountain heroes of
'76 . . . *Buf* 1853. D 428 map 2 ports a
—anr. issue, same date & collat., *B*
—rptd. *N Y* 1860. same collat.

DE QUILLE, DAN [pseud.]
   History of the big bonanza. *See* Wright, Wm.

DE QUILLE, DAN [pseud.]
   A history of the Comstock silver lode . . . *See*,
Wright, Wm.

DERBY, E[LIAS] H[ASKET]   **266**
   The overland route to the Pacific . . . *B* 1869.
O 97 a
Day-by-day journal of observations on a trip
over the Union Pacific and Central Pacific lines.

[DERENNE, GEORGE W. -J.]   **267**
   Observations on Doctor Stevens's History of
Georgia. *Sav* [*Phil* ptd] 1849. O 28 a 105 copies
ptd[5 on L. P.]

DERIENNI (THE)
   Derienni [The]; or, land pirates of the isthmus
. . . *See* Orton, A. R.

DE ROOS, FRED[ERICK] F.   **268**
   Personal narrative of travels in the United States
and Canada . . . *L* 1827. O [12] 207 14pls & plans a
—ed. 2, same impr., date & collat.
—ed. 3, same impr. & date. O [12] 235 14 pls &
plans

DE RYEE, WILLIAM, and   **269**
MOORE, R. E.
   The Texas album, of the eighth legislature . . .
Austin 1860. O 198 unnumb. lvs 99 photos b

[DESAUSSURE, HENRY W.]   **270**
   Answer to a dialogue between a Federalist and a
Republican . . . *Charleston* 1800. O 36 a
   Ascribed also to Charles Pinckney.

DES BARRES, JOSEPH F. W.   **271**
   The Atlantic neptune. *L* 1774–82. F 4v in 2 [6
t-pp, 2 contents lvs, 2 reference lrs, 6 ptd sheets]
93maps[on 184sheets] 140views[on 46sheets] dd
LC
—Ital. ed. "Atlante novissimo," *Venice* 1775–85.
F 4v 218maps c
Executed at the expense of the British government. Probably the most magnificent collection of
views and hydrographic charts ever published. Certainly the best American maps of the revolutionary
period. The number of maps varies in different
copies, as do the even rarer views, many of which
are finely colored. Any copy collating approxi-
mately as above is desirable.

DES BARRES, JOSEPH F. W.   **272**
   A statement . . . Respecting his services. The
utility of his . . . Atlantic neptune . . . n.p. [1795].
F [10] 99 b JCB NYP

DE SCHWEINITZ, EDMUND A.   **273**
   The life and times of David Zeisberger . . . *Phil*
1870. O 747 a
—rptd. same impr. & collat. 1871.

DESCRIPTION
   **Description exacte de la guerre entre l'Anglois
et la France,** etc. See Kort en bondigh Verhael.

   Description . . . of the air-ship City of   **274**
New York . . . to be employed in aerial voyages to
Europe . . . *N Y* 1859. 16° 24 aa

   Description (A) of the English and   **275**
French territories, in North America . . . an explanation of a new map . . . *Dub* 1755. O 28 plan aa
—anr. ed., same impr. 1756. D 32 fold.map plan aa

Description (A) of the golden islands ... *See* Montgomery, Sir Robt.

DESERET.
Constitution of the State of: *See* under Mormon.

[DESGEORGES, ABBÉ]   276
Monseigneur Flaget, Évêque de Bardstown et Louisville ... *P* 1851. O 328 port a
—anr. ed., au. named, *P* 1855. O 388
See also Grelische, Henry.

DE SHIELDS, JAMES T.   277
Border wars of Texas. *Tioga Tex* 1912. O 400 a

DE SHIELDS, JAMES T.   278
Cynthia Ann Parker. The story of her capture at the massacre of the inmates of Parker's Fort ... her recapture [etc.]. *St L* 1886. D 80 front. 3ports a
—rptd. *San Antonio* 1934. D 66

DE SHIELDS, JAMES T.   279
Frontier sketches. *St L* 1883. D 80 a

DESLANDES, LE CHEVALIER   280
Discours sur la grandeur et l'importance de la révolution ... dans l'Amérique Septentrionale. *Frankf* 1785. D [8] 6–183 a

DE SMET, [PIERRE-JEAN]   281
Cinquante nouvelles lettres, *P* 1858. D [10] 502 errata-l aa
—rptd. *Brus* 1860. 18° a
—Eng. tr., *see*, below "Western missions ..."

[DE SMET, PIERRE-JEAN] et al   282
Indian missions ... under the care of the Missouri Province of the Society of Jesus. *Phil* 1841. D 34 aa
His first and rarest book; consists of translations from the Lyons edition of *Annales de la propagation de la foi.*

DE SMET, PIERRE-JEAN   283
Letters and sketches; with a narrative of a year's residence among Indian tribes of the Rocky mountains. *Phil* 1843. D [12 incl. front.] 13–252 11other pls & fold. allegorical lf b
—anr. issue with paginat.: 244 [12] aa
—Fr. ed. *see* below, "Voyages aux Montagnes Rocheuses."

DE SMET, [PIERRE-JEAN]   284
De Smet et Vercruyse, P. P., missionaires belges aux montagneuses rocheuses. Lettres des: *Ghent* n.d. [ca 1846] 16° 48 map a

DE SMET, PIERRE-JEAN   285
New Indian sketches. *N Y* 1863. 16° 175 [incl. front.] pl. aa
—rptd. 1865, 1870, 1881, 1885.

DE SMET, PIERRE-JEAN   286
Oregon missions and travels over the Rocky mountains, 1845–6. *N Y* 1847. D 408 [incl.front. & eng.t.] [4] map 12pls aa
—same, later issue, pls omitted a
—Fr. tr., with adds., by De Smet, *Ghent* [1848]. D [6 incl.eng.t. 14] 9–389 3maps 15pls a
—rptd. 1849. same impr. & collat.
—anr. Fr. tr. by Bourlez, *P.* 1848. D [8 incl. eng.t.] 7–408 13pls
—Dutch tr. *Ghent* 1849. D 423[incl. front. & eng.t.] 3maps 14pls

DE SMET, PIERRE-JEAN   287
Voyage au Grand-Désert, en 1851. *Brus* 1853. 18° 2pts in 1v: 36; 71. b Bibliot. Royal, Brussels S G
—rptd. in his "Cinquante nouvelles lettres," above

DE SMET, PIERRE-JEAN   288
Voyages aux Montagnes Rocheuses ... *Malines* 1844. D [4] [3–6] 304 port map 18 pls a
—several other Fr. eds. and one Ital. ed. appeared before 1860.
—Eng. ed. *see* above, "Letters and sketches."
—Ger tr. *St L* 1865. D [4] 220
—Dutch tr. *Deventer* [1844?] D 69

DE SMET, PIERRE-JEAN   289
Western missions and missionaries. *N Y* Kirker 1863. D [4] 7–532 + 8 adv-p a
—rptd., same collat. with port. added, *N Y* Strong [*ca* 1870]
—anr. ed., same collat., port., *N Y* Kenedy n.d.
Translation of his "Cinquante nouvelles lettres," above. Publication intended earlier, as shown by 1859 copyright date, but delayed till 1863 because of the business failure of the original publisher. A portrait is only found in some few copies of the 1863 edition.

DESPERADOES OF THE SOUTHWEST
See Arrington, Alfred W.

DESPOTISM
Despotism; or, the last days of the American republic. By invisible Sam. *See* Vose, Reuben.

DESTIN [LE] DE L'AMÉRIQUE.
See Cerisier, Antoine M.

DETAIL
Detail (The) and conduct of the American war ... *See View (A) of the evidence relative to the conduct of the American war.*

Detail (A) of some particular services ... in America ... *See* Town, Ithiel.

DETALLE
Detalle de las operaciones ocurrida en la defensa de la capital ... *See* Santa-Anna, Antonio López de.

DETROIT
Diary of the siege of Detroit. *See* Hough, Franklin B.

Directory of Detroit: *Det* 1857. See McCabe, Julius P.B.

Sketches of the city of Detroit . . . *See* Roberts, Robt. E.

A thrilling narrative . . . of the late 290
Detroit riot . . . *Det* 1863 O 24 a
Race riot, with great destruction of property.

DEUBRAY, COL. X. B.   290a
A sketch of the history of [his 26th] regiment of Texas cavalry. *Austin* 1884. O 26 aa

DE TUMULTIBUS AMERICANIS.
See Bentham, Edw.

DEUTHER, CHARLES G.   291
The life and times of . . . John Timon, first Roman Catholic Bishop of . . . Buffalo. *Buf* 1870. O 338 2pls a
Includes his missionary activities in Missouri and Texas, 1819–1842.

DEUTSCHEN [DIE] IN AMERIKA.
Berlin 1859. *See* Hollenberg, W. N.

DEUX-PONTS, WILLIAM DE   291a
My campaigns in America . . . 1780–1. *B* 1868. O [18] 176 150 copies a 25 copies on L. P. a
Served with Rochambeau.

DE VEAUX, S[AMUEL]   292
The falls of Niagara, or tourist's guide . . . *Buf* 1839. 18° [8] 17–169 map 4pls a
—rptd. many times as "The travellers' own book . . ."

[DEVENS, SAMUEL A.]   293
Sketches of Martha's Vineyard . . . *B* 1838. 16° [8] 208 a
Includes travels into Maine, New York, Virginia, etc.

DEVINNY, V.   294
The story of a pioneer . . . incidents pertaining to the early settlements of Colorado. *Denver* 1904. D 164 pls a

DEVOL, GEORGE H.   295
Forty years a gambler on the Mississippi. *Cin* 1887. O 300 aa some cops have *N Y* impr
—rptd: *N Y* 1892. same collat; *N Y* [1926]

DE VOTO, BERNARD   296
Across the wide Missouri . . . *B* 1947. O [28] 483 81pls[some col.] on 48sheets a
—also 265 signed copies. aa

DEW, THOMAS R.   297
Review of the debate [on slavery abolition] in the Virginia legislature of 1831–2. *Rich* 1832. O 133 a
—rptd., same collat., *Wash* 1833.
—ed. 2, "An essay on slavery," *Rich* 1849. O 115

DEWEES, F[RANCIS] P.   298
The Molly Maguires . . . *Phil* 1877. O [6 9–11] 9–380[incl. map] a

DEWEES, WILLIAM B.   299
Letters from an early settler of Texas . . . *Louisv* 1852. D 312 + 8adv-p 250 copies aa
—anr. ed. *Louisv* 1854. D 312 4maps & pls aa
—anr. ed. [called 2nd ed.] *Louisv* [ptd. *New Albany Ind*] 1858, same paginat. but no map or pls a

DEWEY, D.   300
Early Waupaca county [Wis.]. *Waupaca* 1855. O 96 aa

DEWEY, J. J.   301
Knox county [Illinois] directory. [With historical sketches of the townships]. *Galesburg* 1868. O 257 map 4pls aa
First history of this county.

[DEWEY, SQUIRE P.]   302
The bonanza mines of Nevada . . . [*S F*] 1878. O 78 a
—ed. 2, "The bonanza mines . . . of California . . .," [*S F* 1880]. O [6] 3–87

[DE WITT, CHARLES G.]   303
Periodical sketches . . . *N Y* 1820. O 36 a
Narrative of atrocities perpetrated by New York Indians.

DE WITT, DAVID M.   304
The assassination of . . . Lincoln . . . *N Y* 1909. O [12] 302 + 4adv-p a

DE WITT, DAVID M.   305
The impeachment . . . of Andrew Johnson . . . *N Y* 1903. O [8] 646 + 2adv-p a

DE WITT, DAVID M.   306
The judicial murder of Mary E. Surratt. *Balt* 1895. D [6] 259 a

DE WITT, EDNA N.   307
Lest we forget . . . *Gonzales* n.d. O 88 a
History of the De Witt colony in Texas, by its founder's grand-daughter.

[DE WITT, ROBERT M.], pub.   308
The life of Joaquin Murietta, the marauder of the mines . . . *N Y* 1865. O 160 aa
—anr. ed. *N Y* 1888. D 206 + adv-lf a
—rptd. same impr. 1889.
Attributed to Henry L. Williams.

DEWITZ, PAUL W. H.   **309**
Notable men of Indian Territory . . . *Muskogee*
[1905]. O [26] 186 a

D' WOLF, JOHN   **310**
A voyage to the north Pacific . . . more than half
a century ago. *C* 1861. O [4] 147 c 100copies ptd
Brit.Col.Leg.L N NYP Y
Captain D'Wolf, Herman Melville's uncle, took
the Bristol brig "Juno" to Sitka in 1805; sold her
to the Russian governor and returned with Langsdorff by way of Siberia and St. Petersburg. *See* also
Munro, Wilfred H., *Tales of an old sea port* . . .

DE WOLFF, J. H.   **311**
Pawnee Bill . . . his experience . . . on the western plains . . . n.p. 1902. O 108 [incl. pls] a

DEXTER, A. HERSEY   **312**
Early days in California. [*Denver*] 1886. D 214 aa

DIALOGUE
**Dialogue (A) concerning the slavery of the Afri-
cans** . . . *See* Hopkins, Saml.

Dialogue on the principles of the [Eng-   313
lish] constitution and legal liberty, compared with
despotism:** applied to the American question . . .
L 1776. O 92 a

DIARY OF A SOUTHERN REFUGEE
By a lady of Virginia. *See* McGuire, Mrs.
John P.

DICEY, EDWARD   **314**
Six months in the Federal States . . . *L* 1863. O
2v in 1: [10] 310; [6] 326 + 4adv-p a

DICK, EVERETT N.   **315**
The sod-house frontier, 1854–90 . . . *N Y* 1937.
O [20] 550 32pls a
—rptd *N Y* 1943

DICKENS, CHARLES   **316**
American notes . . . *L* 1842. D 2v: [4, 12–16]
308; [8] 306 + 6adv-p at end of each v. aa
—Am. eds. *N Y* 1842: by Wilson, n.d. O 46; by
Winchester, O 46; by Harper, O 92 a
—many later Eng. & Am. eds.; as well as trs. into
Danish, Dutch, Ger. and other languages.

DICKENSON [Dickinson], JONATHAN   317
God's protecting providence . . . in the remark-
able deliverance of divers persons . . . *Phil* 1699.
O [12] 96 c N NYP [of 5 perfect copies known]
—Am. ed. 2, *Phil* Franklin 1735. no copy known,
if pub.
—other Am. eds., some with variant titles ("Re-
markable deliverance of Robert Barrow . . .,"
"Narrative of a shipwreck in the Gulph of Florida
. . .,"): *Phil* 1751. O [8] 80 b NYP; *Phil* 1791. D

123 b; *Dover N H* 1792. O [12] 112 b; *Stanford
N Y* 1803. D 96; *Burl* 1811; *Salem O* 1826. D 120 aa
—Eng. ed. *L* 1700. O [10] 90 + 8adv-p b Hn N Y
—anr. issue collates [10] 86 + 8adv-p b N
—rptd. *L* 1701. same collat. aa
—other Eng. eds.: *L* 1720. O [10] 94 [12]; *L* 1734;
L 1741; *L* 1759; *L* Hinde [1772]; *L* 1787; *L* 1790.
D 136 aa
—Ger. trs.: *Germantown* 1756; *Frankfurt* 1774.
—Dutch tr. *Leyden* [1707]. O map 3pls aa
The original edition of this popular narrative of
a captivity among Florida Indians was the first
book of general interest printed in Philadelphia.

DICKENSON, LUELLA   **318**
Reminiscences of a trip across the plains in 1846
. . . *S F* 1904. D 118[incl. pls] b N Y
The Dickensons got through to the Truckee
valley just ahead of the snows which trapped the
Donner party.

DICKERSON, OLIVER M.   **319**
American colonial government, 1696–1765 . . .
Clev 1912. O 390 a

DICKERSON, PHILIP J.   **320**
History of Andarko [Okla.] . . . [*Andarko* 1901].
D 60 [incl.advs] a

DICKERSON, PHILIP J.   **321**
History of the Osage Nation . . . *Pawhuska* 1906.
D 144 + cover t. aa

DICKERSON, PHILIP J.   **322**
History of Tulsa . . . *Tulsa* 1903. D 36 + cover
t. a

DICKERT, D. A.   **323**
History of Kershaw's brigade. *Newberry S C*
1899. O 584 [8] pls aa

DICKEY, JOHN M.   **324**
A brief history of the Presbyterian church in . . .
Indiana. *Madison Ind* [1828?]. D 24 b Ind S Presb.
Hist. Soc. [only cops known]

DICKINSON, CAPT. HENRY C.   **325**
[2nd Va. Cavalry]
Diary of: *Denv* n.d. O 189 225cops ptd aa

[DICKINSON, JOHN]   **326**
An essay on the constitutional power of Great
Britain over the colonies . . . *Phil* 1774. O [8] 128 a
—Eng. ed. "A new essay . . . on the constitutional
power of Great Britain . . .," *L* 1774. O [8]
126 [1]

DICKINSON, JOHN, and LEE, ARTHUR   327
The Farmer's and Monitor's letters to the inhabitants of the British colonies. *Wmsbg* 1769. sm Q
98 aa

[DICKINSON, JOHN]   328
The late regulations respecting the British colonies . . . *Phil* 1765. O 38 a
—Eng. eds.: *L* 1765. O 62; *L* 1766. O [4] 39

[DICKINSON, JOHN]   329
Letters from a farmer in Pennsylvania, to the inhabitants of the British colonies. *Phil* 1768. O 146 [2] aa
—rptd. *B* 1768. O 146 [2] a
—*N Y* 1768. D 118
—ed. 2, *Phil* 1768. O 71
—ed. 3, *Phil* 1769. O [2] 104
—other eds.: *Wmsbg* 1769; *Phil* 1774.
—Eng. ed. *L* 1768. O [8] 118; rptd., with 29-p app., [*Dub*] 1768. a
—anr. Eng. ed. *L* 1774. O 136
—Fr. tr. *Amst* 1769. O [28] 258
Earliest serious study into colonial legal rights.

[DICKINSON, JOHN]   330
The letters of Fabius, in 1788, on the federal constitution; and, in 1797, on the present situation . . . *Wilm Del* 1797. O [4] 203 aa

DICKINSON, (JOHN).   331
The political writings of: . . . *Wilm Del* 1801. O 2v: [16] 416; 384 + 7 lvs [of errata & subscriber's names] a
—rptd., same impr. & collat. 1814.

[DICKINSON, JOHN]   332
Remarks on a late pamphlet entitled Plain truth. *Phil* 1776. O 31 aa
For pamphlet referred to, *see* Galloway, Joseph.

DICKINSON, JOHN   333
A reply to a piece called the Speech of Joseph Galloway . . . *Phil* 1764. O [4] 45 [13] aa
—Eng. ed. *Y* 1765. O [4] 62 [1] a

DICKINSON, JOHN   334
A speech in the . . . Assembly of . . . Pennsylvania . . . on occasion of a petition . . . praying His Majesty for a change of the government of this province [from a proprietary to a royal one]. *Phil* 1764. O [12] 45 a
—ed. 2, same impr. & date. O [12] 30
—Eng. ed. *L* 1764. O [16] 31

DICKISON, MARY E.   335
Dickison and his men. Reminiscences of the war in Florida. *Louisv* 1890. O 266 13 pls aa

DICKSON, W. JONATHAN   336
La guerre d'Amérique . . . avec . . . la biographie de J. Wilkes Booth. *P* 1865. 16° 240 aa
—ed. 2, same impr., date & collat. a

DIDIMUS, HENRY [pseud.]
New Orleans as I found it. *See* Durrell, Edw. H.

DIEHL, LOUIS   337
Meine Schicksale und Erlebnisse in Nordamerika . . . *Darmstadt* 1851. O [6] 96 a

DIELITZ, THEODOR   338
Amerikanische Reisebilder . . . *Berlin* [1853]. D [8 incl. eng.t.] 336 7pls aa
—ed. 2, *Berlin* 1856. D 8pls[incl.eng.t.] aa
Includes his trip to Santa Fe and experiences in the California mines.

DIENST, ALEXANDER   339
The navy of the republic of Texas. *Temple Tex* 1909. O 150 [7] aa

DIETRICHSON, J[OHANNES]   340
VILHELM C.
Reise blandt de norske Emigranter i "de forenede nordarmerikanske fristater." *Stavanger* 1846. O 128 aa
Describes Norwegian settlements in Wisconsin and Illinois.

DIETZ, AUGUST   341
The postal service of the Confederate States . . . *Rich* 1929. O [12] 439 2col.pls diagram aa

DILLIN, JOHN G. W.   342
The Kentucky rifle . . . *Wash* 1924. Q [8] 124 [6] aa
—rptd. same impr. 1946 a

DILLON, JOHN B.   343
The history of Indiana . . . Vol. I [all]. *Indp* 1843. O [12] 456 a
—rptd. "History of the early settlement of the North-west Territory," *Indp* 1854, same collat. a
—anr. ed. "A history of Indiana . . .," *Indp* 1859. O [12] 637 2maps 4pls a

DILLON, JOHN B.   344
Oddities of colonial legislation in America . . . *Indianap* 1879. O 784 port a

DIMSDALE, THOMAS J.   345
The vigilantes of Montana . . . *Va City* 1866. D 228 + 4adv-p b G NYP WisH Y
—ed. 2, *Va Cty* 1882. D 241 aa
—many later reprints a
—best ed., with a history of southern Montana, ed. A. J. Noyes, *Helena* [1915]. O 290 26pls 4facs a
Not only the first, but textually the most important, book ever printed in Montana. For its first reprinting see Warner Frank W. in whose *Montana Territory* it was incorporated.

DINKINS, JAMES   346
. . . Personal recollections and experiences of the Confederate army. *Cin* 1897. D 280 a

DIOMEDI, ALEXANDER   347
Sketches of modern Indian life. [Woodstock Md? 1894?] O 79 aa
Experiences of a Catholic missionary among Montana, Idaho, Oregon and Washington Indians. Written in 1879 but here first printed

DIPLOMACY
Diplomacy (The) of the United States . . . *See* Lyman, Theo.

DISCOVERY   348
Discovery (A) of a large, rich and plentiful country, in the North America . . . *L* Boreham [*ca* 1720]. O [4] 22 + 2adv-p b NYP
Propaganda, based on Hennepin, to excite interest in the South Sea Company.

Discovery of a nation of Welshmen in the interior of America . . . *See interestina narratives* . . .

DISPASSIONATE THOUGHTS
Dispassionate thoughts on the American war . . . *See* Tucker, Josiah.

DISPUTE (THE)   349
Dispute (The) with America, considered in a series of letters from a cosmopolite to a clergyman . . . *L* [1812]. O [8] 220 a

[DISRAELI, BENJAMIN]   350
The life of Paul Jones, from . . . documents in the possession of John Henry Sherburne . . . *L* 1825. D [12] 320 a
Disraeli's first literary work.

DISSERTATION (A)
Dissertation (A) on the political union and constitution of the thirteen United States . . . by a citizen of Philadelphia. *See* Webster, Pelatiah.

DISSERTATIONS
Dissertations on government, the affairs of the bank . . . *See* Paine, Thos.

Dissertations on the first principles of government . . . *See* Paine, Thos.

DISTRICT SCHOOL [THE] AS IT WAS.
See Burton, Warren

DISTURNELL, J[OHN], pub.   351
The emigrant's guide to New Mexico, California, and Oregon . . . *N Y* 1849. 16° 45 + adv-l. map[pub. by Colton] b
—issue 2—and best—with map pub. by Disturnell b N Y
—ed. 2, *N Y* 1850. 16° [8] 3–80 map b

DISTURNELL, J[OHN], pub.   352
Guide through the middle, northern and eastern states . . . *N Y* June 1847. 16° 80 map a

—rptd., same collat.: *N Y* July 1847; *N Y* Jan. 1848.

DISTURNELL, JOHN, pub.   353
The northern traveller . . . Hudson river . . . *N Y* 1844. 16° 84 2maps front. a

DISTURNELL, JOHN pub.   354
Tourists guide to the upper Mississippi river . . . *N Y* 1866. 16° 84 + 16 adv-p fold.map a
—rptd. *N Y* 1868. 16° 93 fold.map

DISTURNELL, J[OHN], pub.   355
A trip through the lakes . . . *N Y* 1857. D 406 [incl. front. 2 pls & adv-pp] 2maps 3pls a

DISTURNELL, JOHN, pub.   356
The Troy directory, for the year 1829 . . . *Troy* 1829. 16° [18] 15–70 aa
First directory of this city.

DISTURNELL, JOHN, pub.   357
Upper lakes of North America . . . *N Y* 1857. 16° 200 + 4adv-p a
—rptd., with changes, "The great lakes or inland seas . . .," *N Y* 1863. 16° 162 map
—several later eds.

DISTURNELL, JOHN [pub.]   358
The western traveller . . . *N Y* 1844. D 90 2 maps 3pls a

DISTURNELL, W. C., comp.   359
Arizona business directory and gazetteer . . . *S F* 1881. O 327 aa

[DIX, JOHN A.]   360
Report of the organization . . . of the Union Pacific Railroad Co. *N Y* 1864. O [6] 58 [8 8 14 20 4] 2fold.maps a

DIX ANS SUR LA CÔTE DU PACIFIQUE.
See Blanchet, Francois X.

[DIXON, —]   361
Transatlantic rambles . . . twelve months' travel in the United States . . . *L* 1851. D [8] 168 a
Gives considerable attention to the South, from Charleston to New Orleans.

DIXON ("BILLY").
Life and adventures of: *See* Barde, Frederick S.

[DIXON, EDWARD H.]   362
The terrible mysteries of the Ku-Klux-Klan. A full exposé . . . *N Y* 1868. O 56 aa

DIXON, GEORGE   363
Further remarks on the voyages of John Meares . . . *L* 1791. Q 80 b Y
Substantiates charges made in his *Remarks*, to

which Meares had replied in his *Answer* . . . For reprint of the three pamphlets *see* Howay, Frederick W.

DIXON, GEORGE   364
Remarks on the voyages of John Meares . . . *L* 1790. Q 37 b Y
Strictures on his geographical and other statements. For Meares' refutation *see* his *Answer* . . .

DIXON, GEORGE   365
A voyage round the world . . . particularly to the north-west coast of America . . . 1785–1788. *L* 1789. Q [32] 360 48 22pls & charts aa
—issue 2 on large and thick paper, with some pls col. and much of the errata cor. aa
—ed. 2, *L* 1789, same collat. aa
—Fr. tr. by Lebas, *P* 1789. Q [2] 499 47 22pls & charts a
—rptd. *P* 1789. D 2v 22pls & charts
—Dutch tr. *Amst* 1795. O map 9pls[incl. lf. of music] a
Ghost-written by William Beresford, but usually cited as by Capt. Dixon. For abridged editions *see* Portlock, Nathaniel, and Dixon, George.

DIXON, SAM H., and KEMP, LOUIS W.   366
The heroes of San Jacinto. *Houston* 1932. O 462 8pls a

DIXON [ILL.]   367
City directory, for 1869–70. *Chi* Western Pub. Co. [1869]. O 120 a

DIXON AND LEE COUNTY.   368
History of . . . *Dixon* 1870. O 33 a

DIXON AND LEE COUNTY.   369
History of: *Dixon* 1880. O 66 + 22adv.-p a

DIXON AND PALMYRA [ILL.]   370
History of: 1827–1880. *Dixon* 1880. O 66 map 4pls a

DOANE, GUSTAVUS C.   371
Report upon the so-called Yellowstone expedition of 1870. Sen. Exec. Doc 51. [*Wash* 1873]. O 40 a

DOBBIN, M. D., comp.   372
Memorial and affidavits showing outrages . . . by the Apache Indians, in the Territory of Arizona . . . *S F* 1871. O 32 aa

DOBBS, ARTHUR   373
An account of the countries adjoining to Hudson's Bay . . . *L* 1744. Q [4] 211 map b AA BA N NYP Y some copies issued on L. P. (9" × 11^1/$_2$") NYP
Contains information on the lake region obtained from the Indian trader, Joseph La France; an

abstract of all voyages and discoveries between the northwest coast and Asia, etc.

DOBIE, JAMES F.   374
Coronado's children . . . *Dallas* [1930]. O [16] 367 pls a Dedication to his father as "A cowman . . ."
—later issues, dedication: "A clean cowman . . ."

DOBIE, J[AMES] F.   375
The longhorns. *B* 1941. O [24] 388 17 lvs containing pls & explanatory text inserted between p346–347 a also ltd.issue, signed, of 265copies aa

DOBIE, JAMES F.   376
A vaquero of the brush country . . . *Dallas* 1929. O [16] 314 6pls a iss. 1 has redundant word ["River"] aft "Rio Grande" on endpaper map
—rptd twice, same date & impr, with redundancy corrected

[DOBSON, JOHN]   377
Chronological annals of the war [1755–1763]. *Oxf* 1763. O [16] 327 [8] fold.tab aa

DOCK, CHRISTOPHER   378
Eine einfältige und grundlich abgefasste Schul-Ordnung . . . *Germantown* 1770. O [8] 54 b
—ed. 2, same impr. & date. O [6] 34 aa
First American work on educational management and methods.

DOCUMENTARY HISTORY   379
Documentary history of slavery in the United States. By a native of Maryland. *Wash* 1851. O 64 a

DOCUMENTS
Documents and facts relating to military events, during the late war [of 1812]. *See* Boyd, James P.

Documents . . . and . . . views of the In-   380
dian trade. *Wash* 1816. F 128 8tabs aa

Documents in relation to the boundary of   381
the United States west of the Rocky mountains . . . *Wash* 1828. O 83 a

Documents relative to Indian affairs . . .   382
N Y Clayton & Kingsland [1817?]. O 28 b AA BA
Treaty between this infant Republic and the Six Nations, with speeches of the chiefs, etc.

Documents relative to the Indian trade . . .   383
Wash 1822. O 62 10fold. tabs aa

Documents relative to the negotiations   384
for peace between the United States and Great Britain. *Phil* 1814. D 63 map a

Documents tending to prove the . . . advantage of rail-ways . . . over canal navigation. *See* Stevens, John.

Documents to accompany the Message of 385
the President. [Sen. Exec. Doc. 1]. *Wash* 1823. O
108 aa
Document L. (pages 55–108) gives General
Gaines' report, to Secretary of War Calhoun.
*Correspondence relative to hostilities of the Aricka-
ree Indians* [attack on Ashley's fur traders and
other outrages].

DODD, A. CHARLES 386
The contrast; or, strictures on . . . parts of
Doctor Price's "Additional observations on civil
liberty . . ." *L* 1777. O [6] 56 a

DODD, STEPHEN 387
The East-Haven [Conn.] register . . . *N Hav*
1824. D 200 a

DODD, WILLIAM E. 389
Life of Nathaniel Macon. *Raleigh* 1903. D [8
13–16] 443 a

DODDRIDGE, JOSEPH 390
Notes, on the settlement and Indian wars, of the
western parts of Virginia and Pennsylvania . . .
Wellsburgh Va 1824. D [10] 5–316 aa
—rptd., with adds: *Alb* 1876. D [4] 331 a; *Pitt*
1912. O 320 front.
Best of the many secondary sources on these
border wars.

DODGE, GEORGE A. 391
A narrative of a whaling voyage . . . *Salem* 1882.
D 30 a
Voyage made in 1831, with a brief stay at Mon-
terey.

DODGE, GRENVILLE M. 392
Biographical sketch of James Bridger . . . *K C*
[1905]. O 18 [2] [incl.2pls] aa
—anr. issue, *N Y* 1905. O 27 3pls[one fold.] a

DODGE, GRENVILLE M. 393
How we built the Union Pacific railway . . .
Council Bluffs [1908?]. O 171 30pls a
—anr. issue, identical, except printer's name on
p. before t-p
—rptd. [*N Y*? 1910?]. O [2] 5–171 30pls

[DODGE, GRENVILLE M. 394
Letter from the Secretary of the Interior, transmitting . . . Gen. Dodge's Report to the President
of the Union Pacific for 1867. [H. Exec. Doc. 331].
Wash 1868. O 71 a
—anr. ed., slightly different t., same impr. & date.
O 85
—same, for 1868–9. *Wash* 1870. Ho Doc 132 O 61

DODGE, GRENVILLE M. 395
Report of the chief engineer of the Union Pacific
Railway . . . on lines crossing the Rocky moun-
tains. *N Y* 1867. O 33 4pls fold. profile a

DODGE, GRENVILLE M. 396
Report of the chief engineer of the Union Pacific
. . . with . . . reports of division engineers, for
1866. *Wash* 1868. O 123 fold.map 6pls[incl.in
paginat.] aa

DODGE, GRENVILLE M. 397
Romantic realities . . . *N Y* 1888. O 49 a
—anr. ed. *Omaha* 1889. O 24
—rptd., same impr. & collat., 1891.
—anr. ed., with adds., *N Y* 1899. O 50

DODGE (COLONEL [HENRY]).
Journal of the march of a detachment of dra-
goons, under the command of: *See* Kingsbury,
Gaines P.

DODGE, J. R. 398
Red men of the Ohio valley . . . *Springfield O*
1859. D [10] 435 aa
—rptd., same collat., 1860. a

DODGE (JOHN). 399
A narrative of the capture and treatment of: by
the English at Detroit . . . *Phil* 1779. D 22 dd
PhilL [only cop kn]
—ed. 2, "An entertaining . . . narrative [etc.]."
Danvers 1780. O 32 d AA N NYP
—rptd. *Cedar Rapids* 1909. Q 64 a

DODGE, ORVIL 400
Pioneer history of Coos and Curry counties,
Oregon. *Salem* 1898. O 468 [103] pls a

DODGE, RICHARD I 401
The Black hills . . . *N Y* 1876. D 151 + 4adv-p
map 14pls a

DODGE, RICHARD I 402
A living issue . . . *Wash* 1882. O 37 aa
Portions of *Our wild Indians* deemed by its
publishers too impolitic to feed to the public.

DODGE, RICHARD I 403
Our wild Indians . . . *Hart* 1882. O [40] 29–653
[incl. 17pls in black & white] 2ports 6col pls a
—rptd., same impr. & collat., 1883.
—Ger tr *Vienna* 1884. O [8] 330 16pls

DODGE, RICHARD I 404
The plains of the great west . . . *N Y* 1877. O
[56] 448 map 19pls a
—Eng. eds "Hunting grounds of the great west
. . .," *L* 1877. O [58] 448 map 19pls; *L* 1878, same
collat

DODSON, CHARLES W. 405
Life and adventures of Smith Maythe [or Mays]:
the notorious robber of the west . . . *Cin* 1841. O
48 a

DOLLARD, ROBERT   **406**
Recollections of the civil war and going west . . . *Scotland S D* 1906. O [10 incl errata lf] 5–296 6pls a

DOMENECH, EM[M]ANUEL H. D.   **407**
Erinnerungen aus Amerika, insbesondere aus Texas. Aus dem tagebuche von Emanuel Domenech. *Marburg* 1856. D [4] 95 aa

DOMENECH, EMMANUEL H. D.   **408**
Journal d'un missionaire au Texas et au Mexique. *P* 1857. O [12] 477 errata lf map a
—ed. 2, *P* 1872. D [12] 417 no map
—Eng. ed., with omissions, "Missionary adventures in Texas and Mecixo," *L* 1858. O [16] 366 map + 26adv-p aa

DOMENECH, EMMANUEL H. D.   **409**
Manuscrit pictographique américain . . . *P* 1860. O [8] 119 + 228facs pages of what the Abbé thought was an ancient Indian MS aa
Classic example of a would-be savant being deluded. For its exposé *see* Petzholdt, Julius.

DOMENECH, EMMANUEL H. D.   **410**
Seven years' residence in the great deserts of North America. *L* 1860. O 2v: [24] 446 + 2adv-p; [12] 466 + 24adv-p, map 58pls aa
—ed. 2, *L* 1869. O 2v map pls a
—Fr. ed. "Voyage pittoresque, &c." *P* 1862. Q [6] 608 40 pls
—rptd. *P* n.d., same collat

DOMENECH, EMMANUEL H. D.   **411**
La vérité sur le livre des sauvages. *P* 1861. O 54 10pls a
Defends the authenticity of his *Manuscrit pictographique americain* . . .

DOMENECH, EMMANUEL H. D.   **412**
Voyage dans les solitudes américaines. Voyage au Minnesota. *P* 1858. 16° 224 a

DOMESTIC MANNERS   **413**
Domestic manners (The) of the Americans; or, characteristic sketches . . . By recent travelers. *Glas* 1836. D 60 a
—rptd., with new t., "Five hundred curious . . . narratives . . .," *Glas* 1838. same collat.

DONAGHEY (GEORGE W.)   **414**
Autobiographical sketch of: [*Little Rock* 1924]. O 31 port a
Youthful range and trail driving days of an Arkansas governor.

DONALD, JAY   **415**
Outlaws of the border . . . *Cin* 1882. D 520 6pls a
—ath issues same date & collat: *Phil*; *Chi*; *Cin*

DONALDSON, THOMAS C., ed.   **416**
The George Catlin Indian gallery . . . *Wash* 1886. O 939 3ports 139pls 2 maps a
—rptd. *Wash* 1887.
In Part V of the Smithsonian Report for 1885.

DONALDSON, THOMAS C.   **417**
The public domain. Its history . . . *Wash* 1880. O [10] 544 5maps a
—ed. 3—and best—*Wash* 1884. O [12] 516 [2] 517–1343 17maps & plans
—anr. issue, Author's ed., same impr. & date. O [12] 1343 maps plans diags

DONALDSON, THOMAS C, ed.   **418**
Report on Indians taxed and not taxed . . . *Wash* 1894. Q [6] 683 19cold pls + 5 oth maps & pls aa

DONCK, ADRIAEN VAN DER   **419**
Beschryvinge van Nieuw-Nederlandt . . . *Amst* 1655. smQ [8] 100 [4] d JCB LC N
—ed. 2, same impr 1656. smQ [8] 100 [12] map c LC NYP
The engraved view of fort New Amsterdam found in the text of the first edition was omitted in the second.

[DONCK, ADRIAEN VAN DER]   **420**
Vertoogh van Nieu-Neder-Land. *Hague* 1650. smQ 49 d Hn JCB N
—Eng trs: *N Y* 1854. Q [8] 190 125 cops a; *Alb* 1856. Q [6] 66
By New York's first lawyer and the most highly important contemporary description and history of that Dutch province.

DONIOL, HENRI   **421**
Histoire de la participation de la France à l'établissement des États-Unis . . . *P* 1886–99. Q 5v: [4 10] 707; [4 2] 864; [4 10] 868; [4 12] 722; [4 6] 722 [3]. 16pls + suppl.to vol.V: [4 2] 259–398 [2] aa

DONKIN, MAJOR [ROBERT] pub.   **422**
Military collections and remarks. *N Y* 1777. O [32] 264 front. b N NYP Y
For the benefit of the families of "the valiant soldiers . . . butchered when peacably marching to and from Concord the 19th April 1775, by the rebels." Leaf 189/190 usually deleted or the portion excised which suggests that small-pox be smeared on arrows for shooting rebels.

DONNAVAN, C[ORYDON]   **423**
Adventures in Mexico . . . during a captivity of seven months . . . *Cin* 1487 [error for 1847]. O 112 aa
—rptd. *B* 1848. D 132 port a
—Ger. tr. *Kutztaun Pa* 1848. O 144
Three chapters on Texas.

DONNE, W[ILLIAM] BODHAM, ed. 424
The correspondence of King George the Third with Lord North, from 1768 to 1783. *L* 1867. O 2v: [92] 370 [2]; 752 a

DONNELL, WILLIAM M. 425
Pioneers of Marion county [Ia.]. *Des M* 1872. O 346 + adv-p a

DONNELLY, IGNATIUS 426
A pamphlet in reference to Nininger City, Dakota County, [Minn.]. *Phil* 1856. O 32 2maps a
—Ger tr. same impr & date O 36 2maps

DONOHO, MILFORD H. 427
Circle-Dot; a true story of cowboy life . . . *Topeka* 1907. D 256 front. a

DOOLITTLE, [BENJAMIN] 428
A short narrative of mischief done by the French and Indian enemy on the western frontiers of the Massachusetts-Bay . . . *B* 1750. O [2] 22 b AA NYP PhiL

DOOM [THE]
Doom [The] of slavery in the Union: its safety out of it. *See* Townsend, John.

DORNIN, GEORGE D. 429
Thirty years ago. 1849–1879. n.p. [1879]. O 62 2ports b
Reminiscences of gold-rush days, etc.

DOUBLEDAY, C[HARLES] W. 430
Reminiscences of the "filibuster" war in Nicaragua. *N Y* 1886. D [10] 226 + 2adv-p map a
The author, personal friend of Walker, commanded a company in two of his expeditions.

DOUGHERTY, EDWARD 431
The Rio Grande valley. *Brownsville* 1867. O 30 aa

DOUGHTY, ARTHUR G. 432
The siege of Quebec . . . *Quebec* 1901–02. O 6v maps & pls aa
—anr iss. on hand-made paper aa

DOUGHTY, J. and T., pubs 433
The cabinet of natural history and American rural sports. *Phil* 1830–34. O 29monthly pts[usually bound in 3v] 57pls[54col.] c
First American colored sporting prints. Volume three had only four numbers.

DOUGLAS, C[LAUDE] L. 434
Cattle kings of Texas. *Dallas* [1939]. O 376[incl. front.] pl a

DOUGLAS, DAVID 435
Journal . . . during his travels in North America, 1823–1827. *L* 1914. O [8] 364 port aa 500copies ptd. Rptd *N Y* 1959. O a
Douglas explored the Oregon country, named

the Cascade range, and first described the fir tree now known under his name. *See also* Hooker, Sir William J., *A brief memoir of . . . David Douglas . . .*

DOUGLAS, (JUDGE [STEPHEN A.]), and BLACK, (ATTORNEY-GENERAL [JEREMIAH S.])
Remarks on popular sovereignty, as maintained and denied respectively by: By a southern citizen. *See* Johnson, Reverdy.

[DOUGLASS, WILLIAM] 436
A summary . . . of the first planting . . . of the British settlements in North America . . . *B* 1749–51[i.e. 1752]. O 2v: [10] 568; [4] 416 b AA N NYP Y Vol. II was reissued, 1753 [1758?], with app.: O [4] 440
—Eng. ed. *L* 1755. O 2v: [10] 568; [6] 416 + 8adv-p. map[by D'Anville, pub. Jefferys] not in all copies aa
—rptd. *L* 1760. same collat. map[by Huske] aa
First American history of the whole country. The Boston edition was also issued in parts [36 for vol. I, 26 for vol. II]. A vast reservoir of untrustworthy information.

DOW, GEORGE F., and EDMONDS, JOHN H. 437
The pirates of the New England coast . . . *Salem* 1923. O [22] 394 29pls a also L.P. issue of 85copies, Q aa

DOW, GEORGE F. 438
Slave ships and slaving. *Salem* 1927. O [38] 350 + adv-p 50pls a also 97copies on L.P., Q aa

DOW, GEORGE F. 439
Whale ships and whaling . . . *Salem* 1925. O [12] 446[incl.pls] + adv-p front. a also L.P. issue of 97copies, Q aa

DOW, LORENZO 440
History of Cosmopolite; or, the four volumes of Lorenzo's journal concentrated in one . . . also the "Journey of life," by Peggy Dow. *N Y* 1814. D 360 port aa
—ed. 2, enl., *Phil* 1815. O 554 port a
—ed. 3, further enl., *Phil* 1816. D 700 [incl. 2ports at front]
—ed. 4, "The dealings of God, man and the devil . . .," *Norwich* 1833. O 704, 2ports a
—many reprints under variant titles
For first edition, *see* next entry.

DOW (LORENZO). 441
The life and travels of: . . . *Hart* 1804. D 308 aa
—Eng. ed. "The travels and providential experiences . . .," ed. 2, *Liv* 1806. D 240 a
—many later eds., under various titles [*see* preceding entry].
Most widely travelled and most eccentric of early American gospel ranters.

DOW, PEGGY   **442**
Vicissitudes exemplified; or, the journey of life. *N Y* 1814. 16° 124 port aa
—anr. ed. *Phil* 1815. 16° 264[incl.port] a
—rptd. "Vicissitudes in the wilderness . . .," *Norwich Conn* 1833. D 214 port
Describes one of the most amazing trips ever made by a woman; down the Ohio from Wheeling to Natchez on the Mississippi, thence overland through the hostile Creek country to the Georgia settlements, Carolina and Virginia. Some editions were incorporated with Dow, Lorenzo, *History of Cosmopolite, q.v.*

DOWD, JEROME   **443**
Life of Zebulon Vance. *Charlotte* 1897. O [6] 493 13pls a

DOWD, JEROME   **444**
The Negro in American life. *N Y* 1926. O [20] 647 a

DOWN, ROBERT H.   **445**
A history of the Silverton country [Ore.]. *Port* 1926. O [8] 258 front. a
First Oregon local history to be based on modern research methods.

[DOWNES, S. T.]   **446**
Journal of a voyage from Callao to San Francisco. *Liv* 1852. D [5] 3–54 front. a

DOWNES, SAMUEL   **447**
The testament of the twelve patriarchs . . . *Manchester* 1843. 16° 102 aa

DOWNIE, WILLIAM   **448**
Hunting for gold . . . *S F* 1893. O 407 front. aa
Unassuming but valuable reminiscences of an inveterate miner and pioneer.

DOWNING, MAJOR JACK   **449**
The life of Andrew Jackson . . . *Phil* 1834. D [4, 7–12] 263 a
Written by some unknown imitator of Seba Smith, under his pseudonym.

DOWNS, E[DWARD] C.   **450**
Four years a scout and spy . . . *Zanesville* 1866. O [8, 6–12] 404[incl. 10pls] + adv lf a
—rptd., t.altered: *N Y* 1868; 1870; 1873

DOWNS, S[OLOMON] W.   **451**
Speech . . . on the annexation of Texas. *N O* [1844]. O 64 a

DOWSE, THOMAS   **452**
The new northwest. Montana . . . *Chi* 1879. Q 22 + wrps aa
—rptd., same impr. & collat., 1880. aa

DOY (JOHN, of Lawrence, Kansas).   **453**
The narrative of: . . . *N Y* 1860. D 132 aa
—anr. issue, *B* 1860. same collat. aa

DOYLE, J[OHN] A.   **454**
The English in America. *L* 1882–1907. O 5v: [16] 556; [16] 442; [16] 532; [16] 563; [16] 630. 4fold.maps aa
—Am. ed. "English colonies in America," *N Y* same date. O 5v aa
Volume I, Virginia, Maryland and Carolinas; II and III, Puritan colonies; IV, Middle colonies; V, The colonies under the House of Hanover.

DOYLE, JOHN T.   **455**
Some account of the Pious fund of California . . . *S F* 1880. O 11pts in 1: [6] 14 20; 68; 8; 40; 12; 32; 8; 32; 38; 20; 7 b LC NYP

DOYLE, JOSEPH B.   **456**
Frederick William von Steuben and the . . . revolution . . . *Steubenville O* 1913. O [18] 399 21pls a 600 copies ptd.

DOYLÉ, WILLIAM   **457**
Some account of the British dominions beyond the Atlantic . . . Pt. I [all]. *L* [1770]. O [20] 87 [2] map c JCB LC N NYP Y
Early British claim to the Northwest coast, with suggestion that Alaska be named Hyperborea, that Canada be called Sebastia, etc.

DRAGOON CAMPAIGNS
Dragoon campaigns to the Rocky mountains . . . By a Dragoon. *See* Hildreth, James.

DRAKE, BENJAMIN, and   **458**
MANSFIELD, EDWARD D.
Cincinnati in 1826. *Cin* 1827. D 100 2pls a

DRAKE, BENJAMIN   **459**
The life . . . of Black Hawk . . . *Cin* 1838. D 252 [incl 2 ports] aa
—rptd. same impr. 1839. a
—9 other *Cin* eds. prior to 1860.

DRAKE, BENJAMIN   **460**
Life of Tecumseh . . . *Cin* 1841. D 235 aa
—5 other *Cin* eds. prior to 1860. a

DRAKE, BENJAMIN   **461**
Tales and sketches of the Queen City. *Cin* 1838. D 180 aa
—rptd., same collat., *Cin* 1839. a

DRAKE, DANIEL   **462**
An anniversary discourse on the . . . Western Museum Society . . . *Cin* 1820. 16° 36 aa

DRAKE, DANIEL   **463**
Discourse on the history [etc.] of the west . . . *Cin* 1834. O 56 aa

DRAKE, DANIEL   464
Discourses . . . before the Cincinnati Medical Library Association. *Cin* 1852. D 93 aa
One discourse is on early Cincinnati physicians and society.

DRAKE, DANIEL   465
Natural and statistical view . . . of Cincinnati and the Miami country . . . *Cin* 1815. D 251 [4] 2maps aa

DRAKE, DANIEL   466
Notices concerning Cincinnati. *Cin* 1810. O 28 [4] + p29–60[issued a few months later and not in all copies] c OHP Y
Most desirable—and elusive—of Ohio local chronicles.

DRAKE, DANIEL   467
Pioneer life in Kentucky. *Cin* 1870. O [46] 263 port some copies on L.P. aa
—rptd., same impr. & collat. 1873 a
—anr. ed. *N Y* [1948]. D [24] 257 9pls

DRAKE, DANIEL   468
Remarks on the importance of promoting literary and social concert, in the valley of the Mississippi . . . *Louisv* 1833. O 26 aa
Fearing a possible dissolution of the Union, Drake proposes to circumvent disaster to the West by a solidarity of that section so that it might act in decisive concert when necessary.

DRAKE, DANIEL   469
A systematic treatise, historical [etc.], on the principal diseases of the interior valley of North America . . . *Cin* 1850. O [16] 878 19maps & pls b Y
—ser. 2, *Phil* 1854. O [20] 17–985 aa

DRAKE, EDWIN L.   470
The annals of the Army of the Tennessee . . . Vol. I[all]. *Nashv* 1878. O [6] 434 [100] fold.map aa
Issued originally as a periodical; later the numbers were bound, with a summary of battles added, shown here as supplemental pages 100.

DRAKE, EUGENE B., comp.   471
Jimeno's and Hartnell's indexes of land concessions . . . *S F* 1861. O 18 69 b N NYP

DRAKE, FRANCIS S., ed.   472
The Indian tribes of the United States [condensed from Schoolcraft]. *Phil* 1884. Q 2v: 458; 455. 100pls aa

DRAKE, JAMES V.   473
The life of General Robert Hatton . . . *Nash* 1867. O [12] 458 port a

DRAKE, RICHARD   474
Revelations of a slave smuggler . . . 1807–57. *N Y* 1860. O 98 a

DRAKE, SAMUEL G.   475
The history and antiquities of . . . Boston . . . 1630–1670. *B* 1856. roy O [10] 840 20pls a
—ed. 2, same impr. 1857. O [12] 816 20pls
Originally issued in sixteen parts.

DRAKE, SAMUEL G.   476
Indian biography . . . *B* 1832. D [2] 348 [2] pl a
—ed. 2, *B* 1833. O 5bks in 1: [4] 22; 110; 124; 47; 135. front.
—ed. 3, enl., "Biography and history of the Indians . . .," *B* 1834. O 518 [30] 8pls
—7 other eds. by 1851.
—ed. 15, "The aboriginal races . . .," *Phil* 1860. O 736

DRAKE, SAMUEL G. [ed.]   477
Indian captivities . . . a collection of the most remarkable narratives . . . *B* 1839. D 360[incl. front.] a
—rptd. "Tragedies of the wilderness . . .," *B* 1841. D 360
—anr. ed., same collat., *B* 1846.
—later eds.—"Indian captivities or life in the wigwam,": *Auburn* 1850; *Auburn* 1851; *Buf* 1853; *N Y* & *Auburn* 1855; *B* 1856; *N Y* & *Auburn* 1856.

DRAKE, SAMUEL G.   478
The old Indian chronicle . . . *B* 1836. D [4] 208 front. 500 copies ptd. aa
—rptd. *B* 1867. sm Q [12] 333 map a

DRAKE, SAMUEL G.   479
A particular history of the five years French and Indian war . . . 1744–1749, sometimes called Governor Shirley's war. *Alb* 1870. Q 312 port a
—anr. issue, identical, but with *B* impr.

DRAKE, SAMUEL G.   480
Result of some researches . . . for information relative to the founders of New England . . . *B* 1860. Q 143 map 2pls a
—ed. 2, *B* 1862. Q [12] 148
—ed. 3, *B* 1865. Q [22] 148 pls Also 75 L.P. copies

DRAKE, SAMUEL G., ed.   481
The witchcraft delusion in New England . . . *Roxbury* 1866. Q 3v: [102] 247; [30] 212; 244 a
Some copies on L.P.

DRANNAN, WILLIAM F.   482
Thirty-one years on the plains and in the mountains . . . *Chi* Rhodes & McClure 1899. D [2] 7–586 + 8adv-p 73pls aa
—rptd., same impr. & collat.: 1900; 1901 a

—later eds., pub. by Thos. W. Jackson, *Chi* n.d. D 654[incl. pls]

Reminiscences—chiefly of adventures that never happened—by a senile braggart.

DRANNAN, WILLIAM F.   **483**
Drannan, William F., chief of scouts . . . *Chi* 1910. D [6] 17–407[incl.pls] a
—rptd. *ad nauseam*
Additional fabrications by this hoary-headed father of liars.

DRAPER, ELIAS J.   **484**
An autobiography of . . . a pioneer of California. *Fresno* 1904. O 76 port aa
Includes account of his overland journey.

DRAPER, LYMAN C.   **485**
King's mountain and its heroes. *Cin* 1881. O 612 map 10pls aa
—rptd.: *N Y* 1929. 500copies ptd.; 1954. a
This author's most notable work and one of our great historical monographs.

DRAPER, LYMAN C.   **486**
Madison, the capital of Wisconsin, its growth, progress . . . *Madison* 1857. O 48 a
For similar title, *see* under Madison.

DRAPER, ROBERT E.   **487**
Sacramento directory . . . *Sacr* 1866. O 201 aa

DRAPER, SETH   **488**
Voyage . . . from Boston around Cape Horn to San Francisco, 1849, *Prov* 1870. D 80 aa

[DRAPER, SIR WILLIAM]   **489**
The thoughts of a traveller upon our American disputes. *L* 1774. O 27 a
Plea for forbearance; to exercise a legal right not always wise.

DRAYTON, JOHN   **490**
Letters . . . during a tour through the northern and eastern states. *Charleston S C* 1794. O [16] 3–138 3pls b AA N NYP Y
—rptd. 1810. b

DRAYTON, JOHN   **491**
Memoirs of the American revolution . . . *Charleston S C* 1821. O 2v: [28] 430; [2] 400. port 2maps aa

DRAYTON, JOHN   **492**
A view of South Carolina . . . *Charleston* 1802. O [4] 252 + 1. of postscript[added later and not in all copies] map 2plans 3pls tabs aa 500 cops ptd
—Ger tr *Weimar* 1808. O [10] 406 map tab a

[DRAYTON, WILLIAM]   **493**
The south vindicated from the treason and fanaticism of the northern abolitionists. *Phil* 1836. D [10] 13–314 a

[DRAYTON, WILLIAM H.]   **494**
A letter from Freeman of South Carolina, to the deputies . . . in the high court of Congress at Philadelphia. *Charleston S C* 1774. sm Q 47 b BA JCB NYP Y

DREDGE, JAMES   **495**
The Pennsylvania railroad: its organization . . . *L* 1879. F [16] 274 map port 82pls a
—anr. issue has impr. *N Y & L*

DREW, ADMIRAL [ANDREW]   **496**
A narrative of the capture and destruction of the steamer "Caroline" . . . *L* for priv. circulation 1864. O 31 a

DREW, C[HARLES] S.   **497**
An account of the origin . . . of the Indian war in Oregon. [Doc. 59]. *Wash* 1860. O 48 a

DREW, C[HARLES] S.   **498**
Official report of the Owyhee reconnoissance . . . 1864 . . . *Jacksonville Ore* 1865. O [2] 29 [4] c B N Y
First exploration of this part of Idaho.

[DREW, THOMAS]   **499**
The John Brown invasion . . . *B* 1860. O 112 port a

DREWE (MAJ. EDWARD).   **500**
The case of: *Exeter Eng* 1782. O [6] 102 a
Drewe served with the British at Bunker's Hill; his court-martial was for neglect of duty.

DREWE, MAJ. EDWARD   **501**
A letter to a young officer . . . *N Y* 1778. Q 24 aa
—enl. ed., au. named, "Military sketches . . .," *Exeter Eng* 1784. O [2] 156 aa

[DRIGGS, GEORGE W.]   **502**
Opening of the Mississippi; or two years' campaigning in the south-west. A record of the . . . 8th Wisconsin Volunteers. *Madison* 1864. O 141 a

DRING, THOMAS   **503**
Recollections of the Jersey prison-ship. *Prov* 1829. D 168 pl a L.P. cop aa
—rptd. *N Y* 1831; *Morrisania N Y* 1865. O [22] 201 3pls map 2diagrams also 50copies on L. P. a

DRINKER (ELIZABETH).
Extracts from the journal of: *See* Biddle, Henry D., *ed.*

[DRINKER, JOHN]   **504**
Observations on the late popular measures. *Phil* 1774. O 24 aa
Urges opposition to a tyrannical Parliament, but deplores such mob action as the tea riots.

DRIPS, SERGEANT J[OSEPH] H.   505
Three years among the Indians in Dakota. *Kimball S D* 1894. O [6 incl blank lf] 139 b N NYP Y
Campaigned under Sully in the Upper Missouri country.

DRISCOLL, FREDERICK   506
The twelve days' campaign . . . the final campaign of the late war. *Montr* 1866. O 103 map aa

DROITS
Droits (Les) de la Grande-Bretagne établis contre les prétentions des Américains . . . *See* Dalrymple, Sir John.

DROUIN DE BERCY   507
L'Europe et l'Amérique comparées. *P* 1818. O 2v: [6] 432; [4] 452 6pls a

DROWN, S[IMEON] DE WITT, comp.   508
The Peoria directory for 1844, . . . with a history. *Peoria* 1844. D 124 fold.map aa
First directory and first history of Peoria.

DROWN, S[IMEON] DE WITT   509
. . . record and historical view of Peoria . . . to which is added a business directory . . . *Peoria* 1850. D 164 + 44adv-p aa

DROWNE, SOLOMON   510
Journal of a cruise in . . . 1780 in the privatesloop of war, Hope. *N Y* Moreau 1872. O [4] 27 lvs. [4] 27pls a
—anr. issue, *N Y* [Moreau & Drowne] same date. Q 27 lvs. port

DRUMHELLER, DANIEL M.   511
"Uncle Dan" . . . tells thrills of western trails in 1854. *Spokane* 1925. D [12] 131 2ports a

DRURY, REV. P. SHELDON, ed.   512
The startling . . . narrative of . . . Henry Madison, and his . . . accomplice, Miss Ellen Stevens . . . executed by the vigilance committee of San Francisco . . . *Phil* [1857]. O 36[incl.2pls & cover t.] aa
—other issues, same sheets with new t-p, giving *Charleston S C* and *Cin* imprints aa
—rptd. *Phil* 1865. a
A few facts and lots of ambroidery.

DRYSDALE, ISABEL   513
Scenes in Georgia. *Phil*[1827]. 16° 83 [incl. front.] a
—rptd., same impr. & collat., n.d.[*ca* 1850?] .

[DUANE, JAMES]?   514
A state of the right of the colony of New-York with respect to its eastern boundary on Connecticut river . . . *N Y* 1773. F 28 b AA H Hn NYP
Also printed in the *Journal of the General Assembly of New York for* 1773, p.93–118. *See* also *A narrative of the proceedings . . . concerning the lands to the westward of Connecticut river*, with which this title is frequently bound and to which it is essentially an appendix.

[DUANE, WILLIAM]   515
A letter to Washington by Jasper Dwight, of Vermont [*pseud.*] *Phil* 1796. O 48 a
—anr. issue, with longer t., same impr., date & collat.
Transcends in bitterness even Paine's invective. Duane's book-keeper, a Pole named Treziulney, has been cited as author.

DUANE, WILLIAM J.   516
Letters . . . to the people of Pennsylvania, respecting the internal improvements. *Phil* 1811. O [2] 125 a

DUANE, WILLIAM J.   517
Mississippi question. Report of a debate in the Senate of the United States . . . concerning the violation of the right of deposit in the island of New Orleans. *Phil* 1803. O [2] 198 a
Influential showing of the necessity for acquiring Louisiana.

[DUANE, WILLIAM J.]   518
The Mississippi question fairly stated . . . *Phil* 1803. O [4] 48a
Attributed also to Wm. Duane.

DUANE, WILLIAM J.   519
Politics for American farmers . . . *Wash* 1807. D [2] 200 a
—anr iss. same impr & date. O [2] 96

DUBOC, GUSTAVE   520
Les nuées Magellaniques. I. Voyage au Chili, au Pérou, et en Californie à la pêche de la baleine. II. Le requin, ou la mer du sud. *P* 1853. O 2v: 200; 93 aa
Includes account of a short stay at Monterey in 1835.

DU BOIS, JOHN VAN D.   521
Campaigns in the west, 1856–1861. *Tucson* 1949. Q [14] 124 16pls fold.map 300 copies ptd. by Grabhorn aa

DU BOIS, WILLIAM E. B.   522
The suppression of the African slave trade to the United States, 1638–1870. *N Y* 1896. O [12] 335 a

DuBOSE, JOHN W.   523
General Joseph Wheeler and the Army of Tennessee. *N Y* 1912. O 476 7pls a

DUBOSE, JOHN W.   524
Life and times of William Lowndes Yancey . . . *Birm Ala* 1892. O [16] 752 9pls aa

—rptd. *N Y* 1942. O 2v: [14] 406; [6] 346. port a
Authoritative historical contribution; analyzing the development of the extreme States Rights theory in the deep South, from 1834 to 1864.

DU BOSQUE, MONS.   **525**
The history of America . . . Tr. from the French. *L* 1770–71. O 2v: [12] 387; [6] 384 aa
—ed. 2, *L* 1771. O 2v a

DUBROCA, LOUIS   **526**
L'itinéaire des Francais dans la Louisiane; contenant l'histoire . . . *P* 1802. 16° [4] 104 map b AA LC Y

DUBUISSON, [CHARLES R.]   **527**
Official report . . . of the war which took place at Detroit, in 1712 . . . *Det* 1845. O 24 aa

[DUBUISSON, PAUL U.]   **528**
Abrégé de la révolution de l'Amérique angloise . . . 1774–8, par M. xxx, américain. *P* 1778. D [4] 452 a
—rptd. *Yverdon* 1779. D [12] 345
—Ger. tr. *Bern* 1779. O [12] 352
—ed. 2, same impr. 1784. O [8] 374
—Ital. tr., with adds., *Venice* 1782–4. O 3v in 1; [8] 263; 183; [4] 199 4maps pl
Day-by-day account of events from Gage's arrival at Boston until French recognition.

DUBUQUE (JULIEN).   **529**
Memorial . . . praying for the confirmation of the title to a tract of land granted to: . . . *St L* 1845. O 28 aa

DUBUQUE   **530**
Dubuque city directory . . . Also general and historical information. *Dubuque* [1856]. D 201 [16] b IaH WisH
—anr. issue, identical except for change of advertiser's name on p. 186 from "Gilbert and Buchanan" to "Gilbert and Bauman." b
—anr. issue, identical with preceding except that front. is added and a calendar for 1857 placed on verso of t-p. aa

Dubuque and Pacific Railroad Company   **531**
(the). Documents of: . . . *Dubuque* 1858. O 72 aa

Dubuque and Pacific Railroad Company   **532**
(the). Report of: . . . *Dubuque* 1858. O 45 fold.map aa

DUCLOS [CAPT. FRANCIS].   **533**
A brief sketch of: . . . particularly during the American revolution . . . *St Albans* 1824. O 26 aa

DUDEN, GOTTFRIED   **534**
Bericht über eine Reise nach den westlichen Staaten . . . und einen mehrjährigen Aufenthalt am Missouri . . . *Elberfeld* 1829. O [16] 348 aa
—rptd. *St. Gallen* 1833.
—ed. 2, enl., *Bonn* 1834. O [58] 404 map
Exerted great influence in attracting European emigration to the Middle West.

[DUDLEY, PAUL]   **535**
An essay on the merchandize of slaves, . . . *B* 1731. O [8] 63 aa
—Eng. ed., *L* 1732. O [6] 35 [35] a

DUDLEY, W[ILLIAM] H.   **536**
The National Park from the deck of a cayuse . . . *Butte* 1886. D [10] 132 a

DUDLEY, W[ILLIAM] L., pub.   **537**
Grand Forks and North Dakota manual . . . Historical . . . sketches . . . *Grand Forks* 1885. D 146 a

DUER, WILLIAM A.   **538**
Reminiscences of an old New Yorker . . . *N Y* 1867. O 102 a 35copies ptd.

DUER, WILLIAM A.   **539**
Reply to Mr. Colden's Vindication of the steamboat monopoly . . . *Alb* 1819. O 184 [28] a

DUFEY, P. J. S.   **540**
Résumé de l'histoire des révolutions de l'Amérique septentrionale . . . *P* 1826. 16° 2v: [4] 371; [4] 452 aa
—rptd., title slightly altered. *P* 1827 D 2v. same collat a

DUFFIELD, GEORGE, ed.
Travels in the two hemispheres. *See* that title.

DUFFIELD, GEORGE C.   **541**
Memories of frontier Iowa. *Des M* 1906. O [4] 54 port a 250 cops ptd
The author's family settled west of the Des Moines river, in 1837.

DUFLOT DE MOFRAS, EUGENE   **542**
Exploration du territoire de l'Orégon, des Californies [etc.], 1840–1–2. *P* 1844. O 2v: [16] 524; [4] 514 8pls + atlas F [6] 26maps & pls [on 19 lvs] c LC N NYP Y
—Eng. tr. by Wilbur [of Pacific coast portion] *Santa Ana Cal* 1937. O 2v: [3–44] 273; [3–12] 353. 2maps 8pls a
Issued under French government auspices, it forms an admirable supplement to Humboldt's account of the same region and is the only early illustrated work on the Pacific coast comparable in beauty to the *Voyage pittoresque* of Choris or to Litké's account of the Russian survey of the northwest coast.

DUFLOT DE MOFRAS, EUGÈNE   543
L'Oregon. *P* 1846. O 44 aa

DUFUR, A. J.   544
Statistics of ... Oregon ... *Salem Ore* 1869.
O 128 tab aa

[DUGANNE, AUGUSTINE J. H.]   545
California and her gold regions ... *Phil* 1849.
16° 70 b

DU HAILLY, L., [pseud.]
Campagnes et stations sur les côtes de l'Amérique ... *See* Vanéechout, Édouard P.

DU HALDE, JEAN-BAPTISTE   546
Description géographique ... de la Chine et de
la Tartarie chinoise. *P* 1735. F 4v: [68] 592; [8]
726; [8] 567; [6] 520. 50maps 14pls aa sets with
Atlas [*see* below] b N Y
—rptd. *Hague* 1736. Q 4v: [80] 488 [31]; [6] 834;
[6] 652; [4] 606 [129]. 52maps & pls aa
—Eng. tr. *L* 1736. Q 4v aa
—2 other Eng. eds. followed
—Ger. tr. *Rostock* 1747–56. Q 5v
First book describing any part of Alaska, containing a synopsis of Bering's unpublished report
of his first voyage of 1728. D'Anville's *Nouvel
atlas de la Chine*, folio, published at The Hague,
1737, to accompany the work, reproduced Bering's
original map, along with forty-one others.

DUHAUT-CILLY, A[UGUSTE B.]   547
Voyage autour du monde ... à la Californie et
aux Iles Sandwich ... 1826–9. *P* 1834–5. O 2v:
[14] 410; [4] 438. 2errata l. 3pls, fold. tab b
—Ital. tr. [with Botta's observations on Cal. Indians added] *Turin* 1841. O 2v: [16] 296; 393 [2].
4pls aa
—rptd. *Naples* 1842 O 566 no pls. a
Most extensive contemporary account of California's missions and settlements in this period,
over 300 pages being devoted to the author's seven
month's stay.

DUKE, BASIL W.   548
History of Morgan's cavalry. *Cin* 1867. O 578
port a
—rev. ed. "Morgan's cavalry ...," *N Y* 1906. O
441 9maps 4ports a
—rptd *Bloomingt Ind* 1960

DUKE, BASIL W.   549
Reminiscences. *N Y* 1911. O 512 port a

[DULANY, DANIEL]   550
Considerations on the propriety of imposing
taxes in the British colonies ... [*Annap*]? 1765.
Q [55] aa
—ed. 2, *Annap* 1765. same collat. aa

—other eds.: *N Y* 1765. O 55; *B* [1765]. O 48;
[Phil 1765] a
—2 oth Am eds, both cautiously imprinted "*North
America*", one undated, with 48 p, the oth. dated
1765, with 90 p. a
—Eng ed *L* 1766. O [6] 69 [error for 81] a
—Eng. ed. 2, same impr. & date, but paginat.
error cor.
Forceful argument against taxation without
representation.

[DULIEU, MARIE-HENRI J.]   551
Souvenirs d'Amérique. Par Théodore Vance
[*pseud.*]. *Brus* 1860. D 247 aa
—enl. ed., "Mississippi et Indiana etc.", au's real
name given. same impr 1862. D 310 a
—anr iss, same sheets. *P* n.d.
Author resided here, chiefly in New Orleans and
the South, 1838–1847.

DULUTH, MINN.   552
Duluth: its location, etc. *Duluth* 1871. O 54 +
3adv p maps a

DUMAS, ALEXANDRE, ed.   553
Californie. Un an sur les bords du San-Joaquin
et du Sacramento ... redigées sur les récits d'un
émigrant. *Brus* 1852. 16° 2v: 122; 133 a

DUMMER, JEREMIAH   554
A defence of the New England charters. *L* 1721.
O [5] 80 b
—rptd. *L* 1728. aa
—Am. ed. *B* 1721. D 44 aa
—rptd.: *B* 1745; *B* 1765; *L* [1765]. a
Notable contribution to colonial political
thought, voicing the theory that, by reason of their
contractual nature, these charters could not now,
after the colonists had fulfilled their obligation by
redeeming the wilderness, be abrogated and
government restored to the Crown.

[DUMMER, JEREMIAH]   555
A letter to a friend in the country, on the late
expedition to Canada ... *L* 1712. O 22 b
—anr ed., same impr and date, with title "A letter
to a noble lord, concerning the late expedition to
Canada ..." O 26 b NYP Y
—Am ed., *B* 1712. D 24 b
—rptd *B* 1746. D 23 aa
Massachusetts defended against Hovenden
Walker's accusations.

DUMONT [DE MONTIGNY], M.
Mémoires historiques sur la Louisiane ... *See*
Le Mascrier, J. B.

[DUNBAR, JOHN B.]   556
The Pawnee Indians. A sketch. [*N Y* 1883]. O
92 a

DUNBAR, SEYMOUR   **557**
A history of travel in America . . . *Indp* ptd. by
Braunworth [1915]. O 4v: [54] 340; [6] 341–740;
[6] 741–1124; [6] 1125–1530, 2maps 12 col. pls a
—L.P. issue, Q same collat. 250copies aa
—rptd., identical except without printer's name
—anr. ed. *N Y* 1937. O 4v in 1

DUNBAR, WILLIAM
Discoveries made in exploring the Missouri,
Red river and Washita . . . *Natchez* 1806. *See*
Lewis and Clark, *Message of the President.*

DUNCAN, JAMES   **558**
Animadversions on the principles of the New-
Harmony Society. *Indp* 1826. D 40 aa

DUNCAN, JAMES   **559**
A treatise on slavery. *Vevay Ind* 1824. O 88 aa
Rptd, same date: *Cin*; *N Y* a
First Indiana anti-slavery publication.

[DUNCAN, JOHN M.]   **560**
A Sabbath among the Tuscarora Indians . . .
Glas 1819. 24° 69 pl a
—ed. 2, same impr. 1821. 24° 69 pl

DUNCAN, JOHN M.   **561**
Travels through part of the United States and
Canada . . . *Glasgow* 1823. D 2v: [16] 334; [12]
384. aa
—Am. ed. *N Y* 1823. D 2v a

DUNCAN, R. S.   **562**
A history of the Baptists in Missouri. *St L* 1882.
O 937[incl.front.] a

DUNCAN, WILLIAM, comp.   **563**
The New York directory . . . *N Y* 1791. D [8]
146 [2] 71 plan b NYP
Fourth directory of this city.

DUNCUMB, [JOHN]   **564**
Account of Mr. Mathew's trip to America. *L*
[*ca* 1825] D 28 pl a
For another account see Smith, James.

DUNCUMB, JOHN   **565**
The British emigrant's advocate . . . for the use
of emigrants and travellers in British America and
the United States . . . *L* 1837. D [6] 362 map 2pls
aa

DUNDASS (SAMUEL R.)   **566**
Journal of: . . . including . . . route to California
. . . 1849. *Steubenville O* 1857. D 60 c G IndU Y

DUNHAM, JACOB   **567**
Journal of voyages . . . *N Y* 1850. D 243 [incl.
12pls] a
—rptd. *N Y* 1851. same collat.

DUNIWAY, MRS. ABIGAIL J.   **568**
Captain Gray's Company; or, crossing the
plains and living in Oregon. *Port Ore* 1859. D 342
b AA G LC NYP Y
Romance, in the form of journal entries, embodying an 1850 overland trip based on the author's
own experience in 1852. The first literary production written and printed in Oregon.

[DUNKLE, JOHN J.]   **569**
Prison life during the rebellion . . . By Fritz
Fuzzlebug [pseud.]. *Singer's Glen Va* 1869. O 48 a

DUNLAP, WILLIAM   **570**
A history of the American theatre. *N Y* 1832. O
[8] 420 + 4adv-p & errata slip a
—Eng. ed. *L* 1833. Q 2v: [12] 412; [6] 387
—rptd., with front. added & bound in 1v., otherwise same collat., impr. & date.

DUNLAP, WILLIAM   **571**
History of the . . . arts of design in the United
States. *N Y* 1834. O 2v: 435; [8] 480 a
—rptd. *B* 1918. O 3v
An American Vasari.

DUNLAP, WILLIAM   **572**
History of the New Netherlands . . . *N Y* 1839–
40. O 2v: 487; 282 [248]. 3maps pl errata lf a

DUNLOP, W. S.   **573**
Lee's sharpshooters . . . *Little Rock* 1899. O 488
port a

DUNLOP, DR. [WILLIAM]   **574**
Recollections of the American war, 1812–14 . . .
Tor 1905. D [8] 112 port a 250copies ptd.
—ed. 2, same impr. 1908. D [12] 112[incl. port]

DUNN, JACOB PIATT   **575**
Massacres of the mountains. A history of the
Indian wars of the far west. *N Y* 1886. O [9] 784
map aa rptd *N Y* 1958 a
Best single volume covering the subject.

DUNN, JAMES E.   **576**
Indian Territory, a pre-commonwealth. *Indp*
1904. D [2] 9–250 front. a

DUNN, JOHN   **577**
History of the Oregon Territory and British
North American fur trade. *L* 1844. O [8] 359 map b
—rptd. *L* 1846. same collat. aa
—Am. ed. *Phil* 1845. 16° [8] 13–236 a
Practically a history of Hudson's Bay Co.
operations in the North-west; by one of their
men.

DUNN, J[OHN] B.   **578**
Perilous trails of Texas. *Dallas* [1932] O [10] 163
errata slip 4pls a

DUNNINGTON, GEORGE A.   579
History . . . of the county of Marion, W. Va. . . .
Fairmont W Va 1880. D 162 a

DUNT, DETLEF   580
Reise nach Texas . . . *Bremen* 1834. D [8] 158
[2] b S
First German book exclusively on Texas.

DUNTON, JOHN   581
Letters written from New-England, A. D. 1686
. . . Now first published . . . *B* Prince Soc. 1867. Q
[24] 340 a 140copies [20 on L. P.]
Interesting picture of New England life in the
seventeenth century, but chiefly plagiarized from
Josselyn, Mather and others.

DUNTON (JOHN).   582
The life and errors of : . . . *L* 1705. O [18] 463
200–251 aa
—rptd. *L* 1818. O 2v paged continuously : [32] 776
port a
Curious experiences of a London bookseller in
Boston.

DU PONCEAU, PETER S.   583
A discourse on the early history of Pennsylvania
. . . *Phil* 1821. O 38 a

DU PONCEAU, PETER S., and   584
FISHER, J. FRANCIS
A memoir of the history of the . . . treaty made
by William Penn with the Indians . . . 1662. *Phil*
1836. O 63 a

DU PONCEAU, M. [PETER S.]   585
Mémoire au . . . prétensions du gouvernment sur
l'alluvion du la fleuve Mississippi. *N O* 1808. O 52 a

DUPONCEAU (MR. [PETER S.])   586
Reply to : [on the New Orleans batture]. [*N O*
1809]. O 67 [capt.t] aa
—Fr. tr., same impr., date & collat. a

DU PONCEAU, PETER S.   587
A review of the cause of the New Orleans batture . . . *Phil* 1809. O [2] 52 aa
Answer to Thierry's *Examination of the claim
of the United States.*

DU PONT (CAPT. S[AMUEL] F.)   588
Extracts from private journal-letters of : . . .
during the war with Mexico. *Wilm Del* 1885. O
[6] 444 b small ed. ptd. G Y
Privately printed account of California naval
operations, where Du Pont commanded Stockton's
flagship, the "Congress."

DU PONT (REAR ADMIRAL   589
[SAMUEL F.])
Official dispatches and letters of : . . . 1846–8 ;
1861–3. *Wilm Del* 1883. O [4] 531 b LC N NYP Y

DUPORTAIL (M.)
Love and patriotism! Or, the . . . adventures of :
See Louvet de Couvray, Jean B.

DUPRÉ, E   590
Atlas of the city and county of St. Louis . . . *St
L* 1838. O [4] 30maps aa

DURAND (JAMES R.)   591
The life and adventures of : . . . 1810–1816, in
which time he was impressed on board the British
fleet . . . *Bridgeport* 1817. D 83 aa
—rptd. *Roch* 1820. D 129 a
—anr ed *N Hav* 1926. O [16] 140

DURANT (THOMAS C.)   592
Report of : . . . in relation to the operations . . .
[of the Union Pacific railroad] to the close of . . .
1865. *N Y* 1866. O [2] 64 a

DURANT, THOMAS C.   593
Report of : . . . in relation to the surveys and
exploration [for a route through Wyoming Terri-
tory] . . . to the close of 1864. *N Y* 1866. O 8 24 12
15 4fold.maps 14pls aa

DUREAU, JEAN B.   594
Les États-Unis en 1850. Notes et souvenirs. *P*
1891. D [4] 540 a
First printing of this survey of American life
written in 1851, the fruit of a three-year's residence. Twelve chapters are given to slavery and
the Mississippi Valley.

DURO, CAESARIO F.   595
Don Diego de Penalosa y su descubrimiento del
. . . Quivira. *Madrid* 1882. O 160 a
Proves this pretended expedition to have been a
hoax. *See* Freytas, Nicolas de.

DU ROI (LIEUT. [AUGUST W.])   596
Journal of : . . . *N Y* 1911. O [6] 189 2facs a
Translation of an unpublished manuscript by a
Hessian officer on the Saratoga campaign and
subsequent prison life.

DU RU (PAUL).   597
Journal of : . . . *Chi*, Caxton Club 1934. O [10]
74 [2] a
Translation by Ruth L. Butler of an unpublish-
ed Ms by a missionary accompanying Iberville to
Louisiana in 1700.

[DURRELL, EDWARD H.]   598
New Orleans as I found it . . . *N Y* 1845. O 125 a

DU SIMITIÈRE. [PIERRE EUGÈNE]   599
Portraits des généraux . . . célèbres dans la révo-
lution. *P* 1781. Q [2] 13ports[of Washington,
Steuben, Gates, Arnold, *et al*] b
—Eng. ed. "Thirteen portraits of American legisla-

tors, patriots and soldiers . . .," *L* [1783]. Q 13ports aa

—to this Eng. ed. were added 2 other series, same impr. & date; complete set: F 3v 60pls b

DUSTIN, FRED   600
The Custer tragedy . . . *Ann Arbor* 1939. Q [22] 251 3maps 200copies ptd. aa

—anr iss [16cops ptd] leath. bound, signed b

DUTTENHOFER, A.   601
Bereisung der Vereinigten Staaten . . . *Stuttgart* 1835. O [8] 134 [2] 15maps & pls aa

DUVAL, JOHN C.   602
The adventures of Big-foot Wallace, the Texas ranger . . . *Phil* 1871. D 291 6pls aa

—eds. 2 & 3, same impr. & collat., 1872; 1873.

—anr. ed. 3, *Macon Ga* 1885, same collat. a

—rptd., with fanciful impr. & date of *Macon Ga* 1870. [*Austin* n.d. ,but after 1900].

—anr. ed. *Austin* 1935. O [16] 309 pls

DUVAL, JOHN C.   603
Early times in Texas [2 pts. in 1, pt. 1, "Adventures of Jack Dobell"; pt 2, "The young explorers"] *Austin* 1892. D 135; 253 [incl. blank lf before app.] a

—rptd. same impr. 1935. same collat.

—anr ed *Austin* 1947

DUVALLON
Vue de la colonie espagnole du Mississippi . . . *See* Berquin-Duvallon.

DUVERGIER DE HAURANNE, ERNEST   604
Huit mois en Amérique . . . *P* 1866. D 2v: [12] 439; 503 a
Travelled extensively as far West as the Mississippi.

DU VERNOY, GUSTAVE   605
Freude nach Leid, oder die Ansiedler in Texas . . . *Regensburg* 1866. O 340 a

—rptd. same impr. 1868. O 346

DUYCKINCK, EVERT A.   606
National portrait gallery of eminent Americans. *N Y* [1864–7]. Q 2v: [4] 470; [4] 470. ports a

DWIGHT, JASPER, of Vt. [*pseud*]
A letter to Washington. *See* Duane, Wm.

[DWIGHT, THEODORE, JR.]   607
The northern traveller; . . . routes to Niagara . . . *N Y* 1825. D [2] 222 16maps 4pls a

—ed. 2, *N Y* 1826. 16° [6] 382 19maps & 8pls

—ed. 3, *N Y* 1828. 16° [6] 403 19maps 11 pls

—ed. 4, with information added [on Pa. & N. Eng.], *N Y* 1830. D [8] 19maps 9pls 444

—rptd. *N Y* 1831. same collat.

—ed. 5, with app.[on the west], *N Y* [1834]. 16° 432 19maps 12pls[incl.eng.t.]

—ed. 6, au. named, *N Y* 1841. D [8] 250 17maps
For similar title *see* Disturnell, John.

[DWIGHT, THEODORE, JR.]   608
Sketches of scenery and manners in the United States . . . *N Y* 1829. D 188 9pls a

—rptd. "Life and manners in the United States," *N Hav* 1836. D

[DWIGHT, THEODORE, JR.]   609
Things as they are . . . notes of a traveller through . . . the middle and northern states. *N Y* 1834. D 252 [incl. front.] 4pls a

—ed. 2, au. named, "Summer tours, or notes of a traveller . . .," *N Y* 1847.

—Eng. ed. "Travels in America," *Glas* 1848.

DWIGHT, TIMOTHY   610
A sermon . . . occasioned by the capture of the British army . . . under Cornwallis . . . *Hart* Patten [1781]. O 34 a

DWIGHT, TIMOTHY   611
A statistical account of the towns . . . in the state of Connecticut. No. 1[all], covering New Haven only. *N Hav* 1811. O [12] 84 a

DWIGHT, TIMOTHY   612
Travels in New England and New York . . . *N Hav* 1821–2. O 4v: 524; 527; 534; 527 + errata slip 3maps aa

—Eng. ed. *L* 1823. O 4v: [32] 483; [12] 504; [12] 574; [12] 514. port 3maps a

DWINELLE, JOHN W.   613
Address on the acquisition of California. *S F* 1866. O 34 errata lf aa

DWINELLE, JOHN W.   614
The colonial history of . . . San Francisco . . . [author's legal brief used in the U. S. District Court in support of San Francisco's suit against the U. S. for land on which the city was built]. *S F* 1863. O 3 lvs [incl. map] 102 115 b Y

—ed. 2, propably never issued

—ed. 3, [containing add. material used after the suit was transferred to the U. S. Circuit Court] *S F* 1866. O 45 slip of arrata [on p. 44] 34 errata lf 106 391 [2] 3pls 2maps fold. map inserted in some copies does not properly belong to them c G NYP Y

—ed. 4, sheets of ed. 3, with new t-p. *S F* 1867. b Y In some copies 4 extra lvs after p. 365

—anr. ed. *San Diego* 1924.
Basic book for the beginnings of this city, with documents not available elsewhere.

DWYER, CHARLES P.   615
History of Buffalo. Pt.1[all]. [*Buf*] 1852. O [12] 16 aa

DWYER, CHARLES P.   616
Memoir of Commodore O. H. Perry . . . including a faithful sketch of the great battle of lake Erie . . . *Clev* 1860. O 32 a

DYE, JOHN S.   617
The adder's den; or, secrets of the great conspiracy to overthrow liberty in America . . . *N Y* 1864. O 128 a
—enl. ed. "History of the plots and crimes . . .," *N Y* 1866. O [6] 364 [4]
—rptd. *Phil* 1868.

DYER, CHARLES E.   618
Historical address before the old settlers society of Racine County. *Racine* 1871. O 84 aa

DYER, MRS. D. B.   619
"Fort Reno," or picturesque "Cheyenne and Arrapahoe army life," before the opening of Oklahoma. *N Y* 1896. D 216 10pls aa
The author's husband, Oklahoma City's first mayor, resented certain allusions to his conduct and succeeded in destroying many copies.

[**DYER, ELIPHALET**   620
Remarks on Dr. Gale's Letter to J. W., Esq. n.p. 1769. O 27 aa

Relative to the dispute between New York and Connecticut, concerning Susquehannah lands. For reply *see* Gale, Benjamin, *Observations* . . .

DYER, J. E.   621
Dakota: the observations of a tenderfoot. [*Fargo*] 1884. O 129 + 15adv-p pl diag map [wrapper t. only] b

DYER, REV. JOHN L.   622
The snow-shoe itinerant . . . *Cin* 1890. D 362 5pls a
—ed. 2, enl., *Cin* 1891. D 374 15 pls
Dyer was the Peter Cartwright of the Rocky mountain region.

DYER, JOHN W.   623
Reminiscences; or, four years in the Confederate army . . . *Evansville Ind* 1898. O 323 pls a

DYER, T. J.   624
Old Kiowa in history and romance . . . n.p. 1934. D 25 port a

DYK, WALTER   625
Son of old man Hat. *N Y* [1938[. D]14] 378 aa

E

EAGER, SAMUEL W.   1
An outline history of Orange county [N. Y.] . . . *Newburgh* 1846–7. O [2] 652 [4] errata slip a

EAMES, CHARLES B.   2
Down the Mississippi . . . a steamboat trip from Evansville, Indiana, to the gulf . . . and return. [*Evansville*] priv ptd 1878. 16° [6] 63 5pls aa

EAMES, WILBERFORCE, ed.   3
John Eliot and the Indians, 1652–1657. *N Y* 1915. Q 31 lf. port 20pls [each with separate lf. of description] a 150copies ptd.
Sumptuous printing of two unpublished letters written by Eliot from Roxbury, and an account of his various books.

EARDLEY-WILMOT, JOHN   4
Historical view of the Commission for enquiring into the losses . . . of the American loyalists . . . *L* 1815. O [8] 204 pl a

EARLE, ALICE M.   5
Two centuries of costume in America, 1620–1820. *N Y* 1903. O 2v: [20] 338; [24] 389–824 + 3adv-p. 98pls a
—rptd. 2v in 1, same impr. & collat. 1910.

EARLE, E. W.   6
Reminiscenes of the Sioux Indian massacre in 1862. [*Fairfax Minn* 1907?]. D [47] 4pls a

EARLE, J. P.   7
History of Clay county [Texas]. [*Henrietta* 1900] O [4] 64 aa

EARLE, SWEPSON   8
The Chesapeake bay country. *Balt* 1923. O 510 [2] [pls incl. in paginat.] fold. map aa
—ed. 2, rev., same impr. 1924. O [10] 13–519 [incl.pls] fold. map a
—ed. 3, *Balt* 1929. Q 520 [incl.pls] fold.map
—ed. 4, same impr. 1934. Q 522

EARLE, SWEPSON, and   9
SKIRVEN, PERCY G.
Maryland's colonial eastern shore. *Balt* 1916. Q [20] 204 map aa

[**EARLE, THOMAS**]   10
comp., 1796–1849
The life, travels and opinions of Benjamin Lundy, including his journeys to Texas . . . *Phil* 1847. D 316 [incl. port] map aa

EARLE, THOMAS, 1796–1849   **11**
Treatise on railroads and internal communications . . . *Phil* 1830. O 120 2maps 4pls aa
First book on the subject written in this country.

EARLY, JUBAL A.   **12**
Autobiographical sketch and narrative of the war between the states. *Phil* 1912. O [26] 496 13pls aa
—rptd "War memoirs" *Bloomingt* 1960 a

EARLY, JUBAL A.   **13**
The campaigns of General Robert E. Lee. *Balt* 1872. O 47 a

EARLY, JUBAL A.   **14**
A memoir of the last year of the war for independence in the Confederate States. *Tor* 1866. O 144 aa
—rptd: *Lynchburg* 1867. O 136; *N O* 1867. O 112; *Augusta Ga* 1867. O a

EASTBURN (ROBERT).   **15**
A faithful narrative of the many dangers . . . of: during his captivity among the Indians . . . *Phil* 1758. D 46 c AA N NYP
—anr. ed. *B* 1758. O [4] 35 b PaH Y
—for 1828 reprint, *see* Green Ashbel.
—anr. ed. *Clev* 1904. O 76 a

EASTLICK, MRS. LAVINA   **16**
Thrilling incidents of the Indian war of 1862 . . . *Lancaster* [ptd. *Minneap*] 1864. O 37 b LC MinnH 3copies located

EASTMAN, MRS. MARY [HENDERSON]   **17**
The American aboriginal portfolio . . . *Phil* [1853]. Q 84 [incl. eng. t-p] 26pls aa

EASTMAN, MRS. MARY [HENDERSON]   **18**
Chicôra and other regions . . . *Phil* 1854. Q [4] 21 9–126 21pls a
—anr. ed. "The American annual . . .," *Phil* n.d. same collat.

EASTMAN, MRS. MARY [HENDERSON]   **19**
Romance of Indian life . . . *Phil* 1852. O 310 12col.pls a
—rptd., same impr. & collat. 1853.

EASTON, REV. H.   **20**
A treatise on the intellectual character . . . of the colored people of the United States . . . *B* 1837. O 54 [1] a
Omission of the sermon mentioned in title is explained on final leaf.

EASTON, JOHN   **21**
A narrative of the causes which led to Philip's

Indian war . . . Ed. F. B. Hough. *Alb* 1858. Q [26] 207 map 125 copies [25 on L.P.] aa

EASTON.   **22**
Minutes of conferences . . . with the Indians at Easton . . . July and November, 1756 . . . *Phil* 1757. F 32 dd Y

Minutes of conferences . . . with the Indians   **23**
at Easton . . . July, and August, 1757. *Phil* 1757. F 24 dd N NYP Y

Minutes of conferences, held at Easton, in   **24**
October 1758, with . . . the Mohawks . . . *Phil* 1758. F 31 dd N NYP PaH Y
—ed. 2, *Phil* 1759. same collat. d Y
—anr. ed. "Minutes of a treaty . . .", *Woodbridge N J* 1758. F 35 dd

EATON, CYRUS   **25**
Annals of . . . Warren [Me.] . . . *Hallowell* 1851. D [12] 437 2maps port[incl.in paginat.] a
—ed. 2, same impr. 1877. D [16] 680 maps pls

EATON, CYRUS   **26**
History of Thomaston . . . Maine. *Hallowell* 1865. D 2v: [12] 468; [4] 472 a

EATON, JOHN H.   **27**
Candid appeal to the American public, in reply to Messrs. Ingham, Branch and Berrien, on the dissolution of the late Cabinet. *Wash* 1831. O 55 a

EATON, JOHN H.
The life of Andrew Jackson . . . See Reid, John, and Eaton, John H.

EATON, M[OSES]   **28**
Five years on the Erie canal . . . *Utica* 1845. 16° [2] 156 a

EATON, MRS. RACHEL C.   **29**
John Ross and the Cherokee Indians . . . *Menasha Wis* 1914, O [12, incl final blank lf] 212 aa
—anr. ed. *Muskogee Okla* 1921. O [6] 153 a

EATON, S[AMUEL] J. M.   **30**
Petroleum: a history of the oil regions of Venango county, Pa . . . *Phil* 1866. D 299 fold.map pls a

[EATON, WILLIAM]   **31**
Interesting detail of the operations of the American fleet in the Mediterranean . . . *Springfield*. [1805]. O 31 aa

EATON (THE LATE GEN. WILLIAM).
The life of: . . . *See* Prentiss, Chas.

EBENEZER IN . . . GEORGIEN. 32
Kurzgefasste Nachricht von dem Etablissement derer [der?] Salzburgischen Emigranten zu: . . . *Hamburg* 1777. O 44 aa

EBERLEIN, HAROLD D. 33
The colonial homes of Philadelphia . . . *Phil* 1912. O [4] 366 [4] pls a

ECCLESTON, ROBERT 34
Overland to California on the southwestern trail, 1849 . . . *Berkeley* 1950. O [24] 260 2 maps port a 750 cops ptd

ECKENRODE, HAMILTON J., and 35
CONRAD, B.
James Longstreet, Lee's war horse. *Chapel Hill* 1936. O [8] 3–399 front. a

ECKENRODE, HAMILTON J., ed. 36
List of the colonial soldiers of Virginia. *Rich* 1917. O 91 a

ECKENRODE, HAMILTON J., ed. 37
List of the revolutionary soldiers of Virginia. *Rich* 1912–13. O 2v: a

ECKENRODE, HAMILTON J. 38
The political history of Virginia during the reconstruction. *Balt* 1904. O 128 a

ECKENRODE, HAMILTON J. 39
The revolution in Virginia. *B* 1916. D 311 a

ECKENRODE, HAMILTON J. 40
Separation of church and state in Virginia. *Rich* 1910. O 164 a

ECONOMICA
Economica: a statistical manual for the United States . . . *See* Blodget, Saml.

ECONOMICAL CAUSES
Economical causes of slavery in the United States . . . By a South Carolinian. *See* Middleton, H.

EDDIS, WILLIAM 41
Letters from America . . . comprising occurrences from 1769 to 1777 . . . *L* 1792. O [50] 455 aa

EDDY, MARY BAKER 42
Science and health. *B* 1875. D. 456 errata lf 1000 cops ptd [lf 367–8 pasted on stub] c
—ed. 2, labelled "vol.2," *Lynn* 1878. D [6] 144 141–167 errata slip front. c [many cops suppressed]
—ed. 3, rev. *Lynn* 1881. D 2v b rptd 1883 with front added aa
—ed. 6, rev., with "Key to the Scriptures" added, *B* 1883. D 2v front aa
—ed. 21, rev. *B* 1886. D 590 port aa
—ed. 50, with index added, *B* 1891. 16° [12] 651 aa

EDEN, WILLIAM, BARON AUCKLAND 43
Four letters to the Earl of Carlisle . . . *Edin* 1779, O 86 a
—ed. 2, *L* same date. O [4] 163
England urged to continue the war until colonial resistance is crushed.

EDES (PETER). 44
A diary of: . . . written during his confinement in Boston by the British . . . after the battle of Bunker hill. *Bangor* 1837. D 24 aa
—rptd. 1901. a

EDGE, FREDERICK M. 45
The Alabama and the Kearsarge . . . account . . . from information furnished . . . by the . . . prisoners of the Confederate privateer. *L* 1864, 16° 48 aa
—Am. ed. "An Englishman's view of the battle between the Alabama and the Kearsarge," *N Y* 1864. O 48 a
—anr. ed. *B* 1870. O 24 a

EDMONDS, GEORGE [pseud.]
Facts and falsehoods concerning the war on the south. *See* Meriwether, Mrs. Elizabeth A.

EDMUNDS, A. C. 46
Pen sketches of Nebraskans . . . *Lincoln* [*Omaha* ptd] 1871. D 511 20pls [all mounted photos] a
There were two states of the frontispiece, one having two miniature portraits in left hand border.

EDSALL (JOHN). 47
Incidents in the life of: *Catskill* 1831. 16° 156 a
Served with Miranda's expedition and, later, in the United States navy, under Perry and McDonough in the War of 1812.

EDWARD, DAVID B. 48
The history of Texas . . . *Cin* 1836. D 336 map a
Conditions just prior to the Revolution described by an actual observer.

EDWARDS, A. 49
The city of Fargo; with an account of Cass county . . . *Fargo* 1883. O 40 map aa

EDWARDS, CHARLES 50
Texas and Coahuila . . . *N Y* 1834. O [6] 50 [2] map b LC NYP Y
By a prominent advocate of Texas colonization.

EDWARDS, EDWARD 51
The life of Sir Walter Raleigh . . . [*L*] 1868. O 2v: [56] 723; [98] 530. port facs 3 pedigree tabs a

EDWARDS, FRANK S. 52
A campaign in New Mexico with Colonel

Doniphan. *Phil* 1847 [copies in wraps have cov.t. dated 1848]. D 184 map + 22adv-p aa
—rptd: 1848; 1849. a
—Eng. ed. *L* 1848. D [8] 134 + 2adv-p map a

EDWARDS, JOHN N.   **53**
Noted guerillas; or the warfare of the border ... *St L* 1877. O [4] 9–488 + 2adv-p front. 12pls aa

EDWARDS, JOHN N.   **54**
Shelby and his men ... *Cin* 1867. O 551 map pl a
—rptd, *K C* 1897. D 461 port

EDWARDS, JOHN N.   **55**
Shelby's expedition to Mexico ... *K C* 1872. O 139 aa
—rptd., with adds., "John N. Edwards. Biography ...," *K C* 1889. D a

EDWARDS, JONATHAN, 1703–58   **56**
An account of the life of ... David Brainerd ... from his own diary ... *B* 1749. O [20] 316 + adv-l. a
—Eng. ed., with his journal while with Indians, etc., *Edin* 1765. O [12] 504
—rptd., under various titles, numerous times. *See* also under Brainerd.

EDWARDS, JONATHAN, 1703–58   **57**
A faithful narrative of the surprising work of God in the conversion of many hundred souls in Northampton ... in New England. *L* 1737. D [16] 132 a
—ed. 2, *L* 1738. D [16] 126
—rptd. *Edin* 1738. O [24] 93
—Am. ed., styled ed. 3, new pref. by J. Sewall, *et al, B* 1738. 16° [16] 79
—many later eds., Eng. & Am., with slightly variant titles.

EDWARDS, JONATHAN, JR., 1745–1801   **58**
The injustice and impolicy of the slave trade ... [*N Hav*?] 1791. O [2] 37 a
—rptd., with adds., *Prov* 1792. O 60

EDWARDS, JONATHAN, 1847–1929   **59**
Marcus Whitman, M. D., the founder of the Pacific northwest ... *Spokane* 1892. O 48 ports a

EDWARDS, JOSEPH L.   **60**
Centennial history of Pawnee county, Nebraska. *Pawnee City* [1876]. O 50 [incl initial blank lf] aa

EDWARDS, LOUISA M.   **61**
A pioneer home maker ... Louisa Maria Montgomery. n.p. 1903. O 67 a
Includes her journey to Ohio in 1807 and her life there to 1866.

EDWARDS (MONROE [D.])   **62**
Life and adventures of: *N Y* 1848. O 152 + 8 adv-p port aa
—anr. issue, same date & collat. *Phil* aa
—rptd. *N Y* 1849. O a
Accomplished swindler, forger and Texas adventurer.

EDWARDS (MUNROE [sic?] [D.])   **63**
The life of the celebrated: ... By a Texian. *B* 1842. D 33 aa

EDWARDS, MORGAN   **64**
Materials towards a history of the Baptists in Pennsylvania [and Jersey] ... *Phil* 1770–92. D 2v [all]: 132; 155. pl aa

EDWARDS, GOV. [NINIAN W.]   **65**
Communication to both Houses of Illinois Legislature ... [*Kaskaskia* 1814]. O 24 caption t. only c S [only copy located]
This message, largely concerned with the War of 1812 on the western frontier, was the first pamphlet printed in Illinois.

EDWARDS, PHILIP L.   **66**
California in 1837 ... *Sacr* 1890. D 47 aa
—rptd. "The diary of Philip Leget Edwards ...," *S F* Grabhorn 1932. O [6] 47 front. 500copies ptd a
Originally issued serially in an 1860 California magazine.

EDWARDS, PHILIP L.   **67**
Sketch of the Oregon Territory; or emigrant's guide. *Liberty Mo* 1842. D 20 dd Y [only copy known]
—rptd. [*K C*] 1951. a
First guide to the Pacific coast.

EDWARDS, RICHARD, comp.   **68**
Commercial directory of the western states and rivers ... *St L* 1867-8. O 1371 a

EDWARDS, RICHARD, and   **69**
HOPEWELL, M.
Great west and her commercial metropolis ... *St L* 1860. O 604 116pls a

EDWARDS, SAMUEL E.   **70**
The Ohio hunter ... *Battle Creek* 1866. 16° 240 [incl. front] b
—ed. 2, same collat. & impr., 1880. aa
—ed. 3, same impr., 1893 a

EDWARDS, T. A.   **71**
The last was trail of the Modocs ... *Erie* 1884. O 110 aa
—rptd. under t. "Daring Donald McKay; or, the last war trail of the Modocs." *Erie* 1885 a

EDWARDS, WELDON N.   72
Memoir of Nathaniel Macon . . . *Raleigh* 1862.
O 22 + wraps a

EDWARDS, W. F., pub.   73
Tourists' guide and directory of the Truckee
basin . . . *Truckee Calif* 1883. D 138 + 36adv-p
aa
First book on this region.

EELKING, MAX VON   74
Die deutshen Hülfstruppen im nord-amerika-
nischen Befreiungskriege, 1776–83. *Hanover Ger*
1863. O 2v: [12] 397; 271 a
—Eng. tr., somewhat abr., ed. Rosengarten,
"German allied troops . . .," *Alb* 1893. O 360 port

EELKING, MAX VON [ed.]   75
Leben und Wirken des . . . Friedrich Adolph
Riedesel . . . *Leip* 1856. O 3v: [16] 288; [10]
450; [4] 400. map port a
—Eng. tr. by Wm. L. Stone, "Memoirs and
letters, and journals of Major-General Riedesel,
during his residence in America," *Alb* 1868. O 2v:
[8] 307; 284. 2pls a Also 50 copies on L. P.

EFFECT [THE] OF SECESSION.
See Lord, Daniel.

EGAN, WILLIAM M., ed.   76
Pioneering the west, 1846 to 1878 . . . *Richmond
Utah* 1917. D 302 pl a
A 12-page index was pub'd in 1942.

EGERSTRÖM, C. AX.   77
Berättelse om en färd till Kalifornien . . . *Stockh*
1859. D 326 a

EGGERLING, H. W. E.   78
Kurze Beschreibung der Vereinigten Staaten . . .
Wiesbaden 1832. D [14] 279 a
—ed. 2, enl., "Beschreibung der Vereinigten Staaten . . .," *Mannheim* 1833. D 344

[EGGLESTON, BENJAMIN]   79
An American field of Mars . . . Vol.I[all]. *Clev*
1839. D 464 a
—anr. ed., possibly the 1st, "The wars of America . . .," same collat. *Balt* 1839.

EGLE, WILLIAM H.   80
An illustrated history of . . . Pennsylvania . . .
Harrisburg 1876. O 1186 a
—ed. 2, same impr. 1877. O 2v
—ed. 2, rev,, *Phil* 1880 .O
—ed. 3, *Phil.* 1883, O 1204

EGLE, WILLIAM H., ed.   81
Notes and queries relating to Pennsylvania.
Phil 1883–98. 5ser. in 8v b AA
—ser. 1 & 2 [originally ptd. 1883–4], rptd. 1894–5. a

EGMONT, JOHN PERCEVAL, EARL OF   82
A journal of the transactions of the Trustees
for Establishing the Colony of Georgia. *Wormsloe
Ga* 1886. Q [10] 494 b 49copies ptd.
For other titles of this author see Perceval,
John.

EHRENBERG, HERMAN   83
Texas und seine Revolution . . . *Leip* 1843. O [4]
258 aa
—rptd. "Der Freiheitskampf in Texas im Jahre
1836", *Leip* 1844. 16° [6] 294 aa
—anr. ed. "Fahrten u. Shicksale eines Deutschen
in Texas," *Leip* 1845. O [4] 258 + 2adv-p aa
By the leading surveyor, map maker and explorer
of the early Southwest. He was with Fannin in
the Texas revolution, narrowly escaping the
massacre of that command; went to Oregon in
1844 and to California in the gold rush; in the
'50's explored Arizona for the Sonora Mining
Co. and met death there at the hand of the
Indians in 1866.

EICKMEYER, RUDOLF   84
Letters from the southwest . . . [*N Y*] 1894.
O 111 a

EIGHT WEEKS ON THE FRONTIER
See Barrows, William

EINIGE WORTE   85
Einige Worte für Auswanderungs-lustige . . .
Bielefeld 1849. O 72 a

ELDERKIN, JAMES D.   86
Biographical sketches . . . of a soldier of three
wars. *Det* 1899. D [4] 202 3pls a

ELDORADO COUNTY, CALIFORNIA.   87
Historical souvenir of: *Oakl* 1883. Q 272 pls b
B Hn

ELGIN   88
History of . . .Elgin: *Chi* 1867. D 41 a

History of Elgin: . . . *Elgin* 1875. O 114 a   89

ELIOT (JOHN, the apostle of the Indians).
The life of: . . . *See* Wilson, John.

ELKINS, JOHN M.   90
Life on the Texas frontier. *Beaumont, Tex.* 1908.
O 108 front aa

ELLENBECKER, JOHN G.   91
The Jayhawkers of Death valley. *Marysville
Kas* 1938. O 130 pl a
Contains information on the tragic first emi-
gration over the southern route not found in the
previous accounts by Manly and Stephens.

ELLET, MRS. [ELIZABETH F. L.]   92
Domestic history of the ... revolution. *N Y*
1850. D 308 a
—rptd., same impr. & collat. 1851.

ELLET, MRS. [ELIZABETH F. L.]   93
The women of the ... revolution ... *N Y*
1848–50. D 3v: 348; 312; 396. 7pls a
—vols. 1 & 2 were rptd. several times

ELLICOTT (ANDREW).   94
The journal of: ... *Phil* 1803. Q [8] 300 [mis-
paged 299] 151 + errata lf 14maps & pls aa
—rptd. same impr & collat 1814 aa
First thorough American survey of the lower
Mississippi and Gulf regions.

ELLICOTT, ANDREW   95
The unfortunate controversy between the war-
rantees and the actual settlers on the lands ...
lying north and west of the Ohio and Allegheny
rivers ... *Lancaster Pa* 1810. D 28 aa

[ELLIOT, GEORGE H.]   96
The Presidio of San Francisco ... [*Wash* 1874].
D 39 b
Privately printed and based on Mexican docu-
ments destroyed in the 1906 disaster.

ELLIOT (JAMES).   97
The poetical and miscellaneous works of: ...
Greenfield Mass 1798. D 271 [5] b AA BA N
NYP Y 300 copies ptd.
Contains a journal of his 3-years' army service,
1793–6, on the Ohio frontier.

ELLIOT, JONATHAN   98
The debates ... on the adoption of the Federal
constitution as recommended by the general
convention at Philadelphia ... *Wash* 1827–30.
O 4v: [8] 358 [8]; 33–487; [8] 17–322; [8] 272
404 [4] a
—ed. 2, with Madison's notes, etc., added, *Wash*
1836–45. O 5v: [16] 508; [12] 556; [12] 663;
[12] 639; [22] 641 a
—rptd.; *Phil* 1854; 1859; 1861; 1866; 1896; 1901.

ELLIOT, JONATHAN   99
Historical sketches of the ten miles square
forming the District of Columbia ... *Wash* 1830.
D 554 pl a

ELLIOT, W. J.   100
The Spurs. [*Spur, Tex.*] 1939. D [12] 274 map
3 pls a
For another history of the ranch of that name
see Holden, Wm. C.

[ELLIOT, WILLIAM]   101
The Washington guide ... *Wash* 1822. 18° [12]
138 map a

—rptd. *Wash* 1823.
—ed. 2, with adds., *Wash* 1826. 18° [8] 150
—other eds., same impr.: 1830; 1837. 18° [12]
310 map & pls

ELLIOTT, A. B.   102
Traveller's handbook across the continent ...
Troy 1870. D 88 aa

ELLIOTT, REV. [CHARLES]   103
History of the great secession from the Methodist ... Church ... in the organization of ... the
"Methodist ... Church South." *Cin* 1855. O
1144 a

ELLIOTT, REV. CHARLES   104
Indian missionary reminiscences, principally of
the Wyandot nation ... *N Y* 1837. 18° 216 [incl.
prelim. blank lf]
—ed. 2. *N Y* 1850. 16° 216[incl. prelim. blank lf]

ELLIOTT, REV. CHARLES   105
The life of the Rev. Robert B. Roberts ... of the
Methodist ... Church. *Cin* 1844. D 407 port a
—rptd. *N Y* 1853. D
Includes his trip to Arkansas and Kansas.

ELLIOTT, REV. CHARLES   106
South-western Methodism ... *Cin* 1868. D 469
port a

ELLIOTT, DAVID S.   107
Last raid of the Daltons ... at Coffeyville,
Kansas. *Coffeyville* 1892. D 72[incl. port] aa

ELLIOTT, E. N. ed.   108
Cotton is king, and pro-slavery arguments ...
Augusta Ga 1860. O [16] 908 5ports a

ELLIOTT (COM. JESSE D.)
A biographical notice of: ... By a citizen of
New York. *See* Jarvis, Russell.

[ELLIOTT, COM. JESSE D.]   109
Correspondence in relation to the capture of
the British brigs Detroit and Caledonia ... 1812.
Phil 1843. O 29 front. a
For similar title on the same affair, *see* Towson,
Nathan.

ELLIOTT, R[ICHARD] S.   110
Industrial resources of western Kansas and
eastern Colorado. *St L* 1871. O 32[including front
wrap] a

ELLIOTT, RICHARD S.   111
Notes taken in sixty years. *St L* 1883. O [4] 336
port[not in later issues] a
Council Bluffs Indian agent, 1834; with Doniphan's expedition, 1846.

ELLIOTT, WILLIAM   112
Carolina sports, by land and water . . . *Charleston* 1846. D 172 aa
—rptd.: *N Y* 1850. same collat.; *N Y* 1859. D [8] 11–292 + 5 adv-p 6pls; *Columbia* 1918
—Eng. ed. *L* 1867. D [4] 3–292 + 2adv.-p. no pls. a

ELLIS, ALBERT G.   113
Hand-book of Stevens Point and the upper Wisconsin . . . early settlement [etc.]. *Stevens Point* 1857. D 45 + 17adv-p aa

ELLIS, ALBERT G.   114
Some account of the advent into Wisconsin. *Madison* 1856. O 449 aa

ELLIS (DANIEL), the great Union   115
guide of east Tennessee.
Thrilling adventures of: . . . *N Y* 1867. O 430 a

[ELLIS, EDWARD S.]   116
The life and times of Chirstopher Carson . . . *N Y* Beadle n.d. D 94 aa
—rptd same impr + collat 1861. a

[ELLIS, FRANKWILL]   117
History and future of Minnehaha County, Dakota, and city of Sioux Falls. [Wrapper title only]. *Sioux Falls* [1887]. O 26 map aa

ELLIS, G. A.   118
New Britain. A narrative of a journey . . . to a country . . . in the vast plain of the Missouri . . . *L* 1820. O [8] 336 aa
Allegorical fantasy in which is elaborated the author's theory for a Utopian society.

ELLIS, JOHN B.   119
Free love and its votaries; or, American socialism unmasked . . . *N Y* [1870]. O 502 [incl. front] 12pls a

ELLIS, LEONARD B.   120
History of New Bedford [Mass.]. *Syracuse* 1892. O 732 [4] 175 2maps 65pls a

ELLIS, SAMUEL W.   121
The emigrant's guide to Texas . . . with a table of distances, *N O* 1839. D 50 b l copy known.

ELLIS, WILLIAM   122
An authentic narrative of a voyage . . . by Captain Cook and Captain Clerke . . . 1776–1780 . . . *L* 1782. O 2v: [12] 360; [8] 348. map 21pls aa
—ed. 2, same collat. 1783. a
—ed. 3, same collat. 1784.
—Dutch tr. *Frankt* 1783. O [4] 324 map
In defiance of the Admiralty's insistence that no private journal of this voyage be retained, those kept by several members were published

anonymously; Ellis was the only Englishman who had the temerity to admit authorship. First edition, though dated 1782, was printed in December, 1781. Rickman's *Journal, q.v.*, was dated 1781 and probably precedes this Ellis account.

ELLISON (JAMES).   123
The afflicted family and awful effects of intemperance deleniated [*sic*] in a brief relation of . . . the unfortunate family of: in their attempted remove, in . . . 1841, from Pennsylvania to . . . Missouri, when, through the beastly inebriation of their father, three of the children perished by reason of hunger and cruel neglect. *N Y* 1842. O 23 a
Apparently—and happily—only one copy is known to exist.

ELLISTON, ROBERT H.   124
The history of Grant County . . . Kentucky. *Williamstown Ky* 1876. O 37 a

ELLISTON, THOMAS   125
Slavery and secession in America, historical and economical. *L* 1861. D [18] 371 map a
—ed. 2, enl., *L* 1862. D [36] 371

[ELLMS, CHARLES] comp.   126
The pirate's own book . . . *B* 1837. D 432 front. engt.t. b
—ed. 2, same date & collat., *Portland* aa
—rptd. *Phil* 1839; 1840; 1841; 1842; *Portland* 1855; 1856; 1859. a
—anr. ed. *Salem Mass* 1924. D [14] 470 front. also 100copies on L.P.
Most popular American compilation on this subject; includes transactions to 1835. For an earlier compilation, with some identical chapters, *see* Carey, Thomas.

ELLS, B. F., ed.   127
The western miscellany. Vol. I [all]. *Dayton* 1848–9. O 384[incl.front] aa
Contains, among other material, a *History of Oregon*, in three installments, embodying information gathered by Slacum for the government in 1836.

ELLSWORTH, HENRY W.   128
Valley of the upper Wabash. Indiana . . . *N Y* 1838. D [12] 175 map 2pls plan a

ELLSWORTH, SPENCER   129
Records of the olden time [in Putnam and Marshall counties, Ill.]. *Lacon* 1880. O [2] 9–772 [incl.pls] fold.,map a
Four chapters are included on the blood-chilling sufferings of the Donner party in 1846.

ELLSWORTH COUNTY, KANSAS.   130
Compendious history of: . . . *Ellsworth* 1879. D 59 + 3adv p aa

185

ELLSWORTH AND PACIFIC   131
Ellsworth and Pacific railroad (The): . . . information as to the routes . . . west of Kansas. *Leavenworth* [1868]. O 30 b G NYP

ELMWOOD, ELNATHAN [pseud]
A Yankee among the nullifiers . . . *See* Greene, Asa.

EL PASO, TEXAS.   132
The city and county of: . . . *El Paso* 1886. O 84 map aa

ELSNER, [CHRYSOSTOM] HEINRICH   133
Die Befreiungs-kampf der nord-amerikanischen Staaten . . . *Stuttgart* 1835. O 768 eng.t. 8ports a
—ed. 2, *Stuttgart* 1838. O, same collat

ELY, ELISHA, pub.   134
A directory for the village of Rochester . . . to which is added, a sketch of the history of the village [by Jesse Hawley]. *Roch* 1827. D 142 + 14adv-p map aa
First directory and first history of this city. For separate issue of the history, *see* Hawley, Jesse.

ELY, WILLIAM   135
The Big Sandy valley [Ky.] . . . *Catlettsburg Ky* 1887. D 500 front. a

ELZAS, BARNETT A.   136
The Jews of South Carolina . . . [*Charleston* 1903]. O 4pts facs [caption t.to pts. 1–3, cover t.to pt. 4] a
—best ed., *Phil* 1905. O 352 11pls 175 copies ptd. aa

EMBURY, AYMAR   137
The Dutch colonial house . . . *N Y* 1913. O [16] 108 pls a
—rptd. same collat. *N Y* 1919.
—anr. ed. "Building the Dutch colonial house," *N Y* 1929. same collat.

EMERSON, CHARLES L.   138
Rise and progress of Minnesota Territory. *St P* 1855. O 64 b G [of 4 cops kn]

EMERY, SAMUEL H.   139
History of Taunton, Massachusetts . . . *Syracuse* 1893. O 768 110 + suppl. dated 1894, of 13p 2maps 50pls aa

EMIGRANT [THE] TO NORTH AMERICA.
See Abbott, Joseph.

EMIGRANT'S GUIDE
Emigrant's guide (The), or a picture of   140
America . . . divested of democratic colouring . . . By an old scene painter. *L* 1816. O 77 aa

Emigrant's guide (The), or pocket geogra-   141
phy of the western states . . . *Cin* 1818. 16° 266 aa

Emigrant's guide (The): or, sketches of Canada, with some of the northern and western states . . . *See* Fraser, Wm.

EMIGRANT'S HANDBOOK [THE]. 1848.
See Colton, Jos. H.

EMIGRATION
Emigration to America candidly considered . . . *See* Rickman, Thos C.

EMIGRATOR'S GUIDE   142
Emigrator's guide (The) to the British settlements and United States . . . *L* [*ca* 1819]. D 108 a

EMMERT, D. B.   143
Wichita city directory . . . historical sketches . . . *K C* 1878. O 144[incl.front board cover & advs] 3mounted photo views aa

EMMONS, GEORGE F.   144
The navy of the United States . . . 1775-1853 . . . *Wash* 1853. Q [6] 208 [1] a

EMORY, W[ILLIAM] H., LIEUT-COL.   145
Notes of a military reconnoissance, from Fort Leavenworth . . . to San Diego [including reports by Abert, Cooke and Johnston]. [House Exec. Doc. 41]. *Wash* 1848. O 614 64 pls 6maps & plans [incl. large fold. map, not in all copies] a
—anr. ed., au.'s rank given also as Lieut. Col., omitting Johnston's Journal, and abridging Cooke's report. [Sen. Exec. Doc. 7]. Same impr. & date. O 416 40pls 4maps & plans [incl. large map in pocket] aa
—same, issue 2, au.'s rank given as Brevet Maj. a
—rptd. Emory only, *N Y* 1848. O 230 maps pls; *Albuqurque* 1951.
That the House edition has priority is indicated by the fact that many copies were seemingly issued before the large map was available. The plates of scenery in the Senate edition were lithographed by Weber & Co.; in the House edition these are usually all done by C. B. Graham, though in some copies the 24 plates in Abert's report were executed, in a superior manner, anonymously.

EMORY, WILLIAM H.   146
United States and Mexican boundary survey . . . [Sen. issue]. *Wash* Nicholson 1857-8. Q 4 pts in 2v: [16] 258; [8] 174; [6] 270 78; 62 33 35 86 [2]. 2maps[one fold.] fold. chart fold.profile 346pls [of which 33 contain 66 sketches] aa
—anr. issue [H. R.], *Wash* Wendell 1857-9. Q same collat. aa

ENCARNACION PRISONERS . . . 1848.
See Scott, John.

ENCYCLOPEDIA OF THE NEW WEST
See Brown, John Henry, and Speer, Wm. S.

[ENGEL, E. BAILLI D']   147
Essai sur cette question . . . comment l'Amérique
a-t-elle été peuplée . . .? *Amst* 1767. Q [18] 610 aa
—anr ed same impr. & date D 5v [generally
bd in 4v]: [30] 454; [4] 388; [8] 360; [2] 228
[4] a
American natives indigenous, coevally created
with the rest of humanity, but somehow escaping
the calamity of the deluge.

ENGEL, SAMUEL   148
Anmerkungen über den Theil von Cap. Cook's
Reise-Relation, so die meerenge zwischen Asia
und Amerika ansiehet . . . n. p. 1780. D [2] 30 aa
—Fr. ed. "Remarques sur la partie de la relation
. . .," *Geneva* 1781. Q 26 map
—anr. Fr. ed. *Berne*. same date & collat.

[ENGEL, SAMUEL]   149
Mémoires et observations . . . sur la situation
de pays septentrionaux de l'Asie et de l'Amérique
. . . *Lausanne* 1765. Q [22] 268 [8] 2 maps b
—rptd. "Extraits raisonnés des voyages . . ."
Lausanne 1779. Q [24] 268 2maps aa
—Ger. ed. tr. by au. with adds. "Geographische
und kritische Nachrichten . . ." *Mietau* [&c.]
1772. Q [18] 368 2maps aa
—anr. issue, giving author's name
—most complete ed *Basel* 1777. Q 2v 5maps aa
   Contains accounts of the Cabrillo, De Fonte
and De Fuca exploring voyages up the Pacific
coast and definitively refuted the conception of
Californian insularity.

ENGELANDS DWAASHEID   150
Engelands Dwaasheid in den tegenwoordigen
oorlog van het begin der onlusten met America
tot op de oorlogsverklaring aan Holland. n.p.
[1781]. O 23 a

ENGELHARDT, G., comp.   151
   Reise des Kaiserlich-Russischen Flotten-
Lieutenants Ferdinand von Wrangel längs der
Nordküste von Sibirien und auf dem Eismeere . . .
1820–24. *Berlin* 1839. O 2v: map tabs b
—rptd. *Leip* 1885. O [12] 212 map port a
—Eng. tr., abr., *L* 1840. O [138] 413 map tab a
—rptd., with adds., *L* 1844. O [20] 525 map port
—Am. eds., abr., *N Y* 1841 D 302 map; 1845;
1855.
—Fr. ed. "Le nord de la Siberie," *P* 1843. O 2v
map 2pls
—Russ. ed., complete "Puteshestvie po Siever-
nym . . .," *St Ptbg* 1841. O 2v 4maps

ENGELHARDT, ZEPHYRIN   152
The Franciscans in Arizona. *Harbor Springs
Mich* 1899. O 236 [10] map a

ENGELHARDT, ZEPHYRIN   153
The Franciscans in California. *Harbor Springs
Mich* 1897. O [20] 517 front a

ENGELHARDT, ZEPHYRIN   154
The missions and missionaries of California . . .
S F 1908–16. O 5v[incl. index] maps & pls a
—vol. 1 only, rptd. 1912.

ENGELS, L.   155
Nordamerika-Ohio. Reise nach Nordamerika.
Beobachtungen und Erfahrungen in Ohio 1848
and 1849 . . . *Elberfeld* 1850. O [4] 108 aa

ENGLAND AND AMERICA.
A comparison . . . *See* Wakefield, Ed. G.

ENGLANDISCHEN PFLANZETÄDTE   156
Englandischen Pflanzetädte in Nord-America
. . . *Stuttgart* 1755. D [14] 216 a

ENGLISH, WILLIAM H.   157
Conquest of the country northwest of the
Ohio . . . *Indp* 1896. Q 2v: 586; 587–1186 [incl.
pls] a
—rptd., same impr. & collat. 1898.

ENGLISHMAN (THE)   158
Englishman (The); or, letters found in the
state of Tennessee. Supposed to be the production
of an Englishman, travelling through the United
States as a spy. *Rogersville Tenn* 1815. 16° 80 b
LC NYP [only copies known]

ENGLISHMAN'S ANSWER (AN)
Englishman's answer (An) to the address from
the delegates, to the people of Great-Britain . . .
See Lind, John.

ENGLISHWOMAN (THE) IN AMERICA.
See Bird, Isabella.

ENNEMOSER, FRANZ J.   159
Eine Reise vom Mittelrhein . . . nach den nordamerikanischen Freistaaten. *Kaiserslautern* 1857.
D [4] 127 a
—oth eds: same impr 1865. D 160; [*Mainz*] 1865,
same collat; *Kaiserslautern* 1866.
Travelled largely in the south.

ENOS, A. A.   160
Across the plains in 1850. [*Stanton Neb ca*
1905]. large O [4] 56 wrapper t. only aa

ENQUIRY (AN)
An enquiry into the causes of our ill   161
success in the present war. *L* 1757. O 48 aa

Enquiry (An) into the causes of the alienation
of the Delaware and Shawanese Indians from the
British interest . . . *See* Thomson, Charles.

Enquiry (An) into the constitutional authority of the supreme federal court . . . By a citizen of South Carolina. *See* Ford, Timothy.

Enquiry (An) into the principles . . . of certain public measures. *See* Taylor, John, of Va.

Enquiry (An) into the principles on which a commercial system for the United States . . . should be founded . . . *See* Coxe, Tench.

Enquiry (An) whether the absolute inde-   162 pendence of America is not to be preferred to her partial dependence . . . *L* Bew (1770?). O 38 [1] a

Enquiry (An), whether the guilt of the present civil war, ought to be imputed to Great Britain or America. *See* Roebuck, John.

ENSIGN, M.   163 Colorado Springs, Manitou and vicinity. *Colo Springs* 1878. D 56 aa

ENSIGN('S) . . . GUIDE   164 Ensign, Bridgman and Fanning's lake and river guide . . . with thrilling scenes in border warfare . . . *N Y* 1856. 16° 144 map a —rptd., same impr. & collat., 1858.

ENSIGN AND THAYER   165 Traveller's guide through . . . Ohio, Michigan . . . *N Y* 1849. 16° 33 map aa —oth eds, *N Y* 1854. 16°; *N Y* 1857. 16° 36 map a

ENTICK, JOHN   165a The general history of the late war . . . in Europe, Asia, Africa and America. *L* 1763–4. O 5v: [4] 495; 464; 480; 480: 469 [27]. 8 maps 41ports aa —rptd., same format & impr; 1765; 1766; 1775; 1779. a

EPHRATA.   166 Pencillings about: By a visitor. *Phil* 1856. O 24 a —rptd. *Phil* 1860.

ERES, RUSO D' *See* Ruso d'Eres, Charles Dennis.

ERIE CANAL Documents relating to the western termi-   167 nation of the Erie canal . . . *Black Rock* 1822. D 60 fold. map aa.

Facts and observations in relation to the   168 origin and completion of the Erie canal: *N Y* 1825. O 36 a —ed. 2, *Prov* 1827. O 32

ERLAUTERUNGEN   169 Erlauterungen über die Unternehmung eines Land-Ankaufs in den Vereinigten Staaten . . .

[*Aarau Switzerland* 1804]. 16° 24 [capt.t.only] b Explanation of a colonization project in the Central West.

ERNST, FERDINAND   170 Bemerkungen auf einer Reise durch das Innere de Vereinigten Staaten . . . Hildesheim 1820. O [8] 183 pl aa —Dutch tr "Waarnemingen op eene Reize . . ." *Amst* 1821. D 2v: 54; [2] 49–96 a

ERSKINE, MRS. GLADYS S.   171 Broncho Charlie; the story of Charlie Miller, the last of the pony express riders . . . *N Y* [1934] O [16] 316 24maps & pls a —Eng ed *L* n.d.

[ERSKINE, JOHN]   172 Reflections on the rise, progress . . . of the present contentions with the colonies. *Edin* 1776. D [4] 54 a

ERWIN, MILO   173 The history of Williamson county, Illinois . . . also, a complete history of its "bloody vendetta" . . . *Marion Ill* 1876. D [8] 286 aa —rptd. [1914]. O 238 a

ERZÄHLUNGEN   174 Erzählungen und Bilder aus Amerika. *Erfurt* 1852. O 98 8col.pls a

ESCAPE Escape of a Confederate officer from prison . . . *See* Davis, Saml. B.

ESCOTT, G. S.   175 History and directory of Springfield . . . [Mo.]. *Springfield* 1878. O 273 map aa

ESCUDERO, JOSÉ A., ed. Noticias . . . de Nueva-Mexico. *See* under Pino, Pedro B.

ESCUDERO, JOSÉ A.   176 Noticias estadisticas . . . de Chihuahua. *Mex* 1834. Q 253 160 [mispaged 260] aa

ESCUDERO, JOSÉ A.   177 Noticias estadisticas de . . . Durango. *Mex* 1849. smQ 72 aa

ESCUDERO, JOSÉ A.   178 Noticias estadisticas de Sonora y Sinaloa. *Mex* 1849. Q 148 map 6 tabs aa Includes present Arizona, just prior to the Gadsden purchase.

ESHLEMAN, HENRY F.   179 Historic backgrounds and annals of the Swiss and German pioneer settlers of south-eastern Pennsylvania. *Lancaster* 1917. O [4] 386 a

ESPINASSE DE LANGEAC,   180
CHEVALIER DE L'
Anecdotes anglaises et américaines . . . 1776 à
1783. *P* 1813. D 2v: 298; 324 a

ESPINOSA DE LOS MONTEROS,   181
CARLOS
Esposicion. sobre las provincias de Sonora y
Sinaloa . . . *Mex* 1823. O [4] 44 2tabs [one fold] b
—rptd. same impr 1825 aa

ESPINOSA, ISIDRO F. DE   182
Chrónica apostólica y seraphica de todas los
colegios, *etc.*, de esta Nueva-España, de missio-
neros Franciscanos . . . Parte primera [all]. *Mex*
1746. F [100] 590 [24] b JCB N NYP Y
Covers establishment of Texas missions and
expeditions of Alonso de Leon and of the Marquis
de Aguayo. For what passes as a 2nd part, *see*
Arricivita, Juan D.

ESPINOSA, ISIDRO F. DE   183
Nuevas empressas del peregrino americano
septentrional Atlante . . . *Mex* 1747. O [22] 46 a
Issued to supplement following entry.

ESPINOSA, ISIDRO F. DE   184
El peregrino septentrional Atlante . . . *Mex*
1737. Q [38] 456 [4] pl c JCB N NYP Y
—rptd., *Valencia* 1742. Q [10] 412 [4] pl b
Life of Padre Antonio Margil, with account of
the founding by him of Texas missions in 1716.
In some copies of the original edition, title-page
is printed in red and black.

ESPINOSA Y TELLO, JOSÉ   185
Memorias sobre las observaciones astronómicas,
hechas por los navegantes Españoles . . . *Madrid*
1809. Q 2v in 5pts: [8] 170; [8] 184; [32] 224;
[20] 199; [6] 320. 5 fold.pls b NYP
Includes, among other Spanish exploring
voyages up the Pacific coast, Malaspina's 1791
expedition to Alaska, etc., which the author
accompanied. For another book ascribed to
Espinosa *see* Galiano.

ESPY (JOSIAH).   186
Memorandum of a tour made by: in . . . Ohio
and Kentucky . . . in 1805. [Together with] Two
western campaigns in the war of 1812, by Samuel
Williams. [And] The leatherwood god, by R. H.
Taneyhill. *Cin* 1870. O 3 pts in 1: [8] 29; 58;
53 a some L.P.copies
Forms Number 7 of Clarke's Ohio Valley
Historical Series, and carries the general title
Miscellanies.

ESQUISSE INTÉRESSANTE   187
Esquisse intéressante du tableau fidele des
causes qui ont occasioné les révolutions . . . de
'Amérique septentrionale . . . *Phil* 1783. O 124 aa

ESQUISSES AMÉRICAINES
Esquisses américaines, ou tablettes d'un voyageur aux États-Unis . . . Par Ad. d'A *See* A., Ad. d'

ESSAI
Essai sur cette question: . . . comment l'Amérique a-t-elle été peuplée . . .? *See* Engel, E. Bailli d'

Essai sur le commerce de Russie, avec l'histoire
de ses découvertes . . . *See* Marbault, Mons. de.

ESSAY   188
Essay (An) in defence of slave holding . . .
in the southern states . . . By a citizen of New
York. *N Y* 1837. D 32 a

Essay (An) in vindication of the continental
colonies . . . By an American. *See* Lee, Arthur.

Essay (An) on currency. *Charleston*   189
S C 1734. O 24 b Charleston L [only cop kn]
—rptd. [*Charleston S C* 1934]. O 24 100 copies
ptd. aa
First Carolina book.

Essay (An) on federalism. *See* Daveiss, Jos. H.

Essay on rail roads. *See* Carey, Mathew.

Essay (An) on the constitutional power of Great
Britain over de colonies . . . *See* Dickinson, John.

Essay on the effects of slaverny on the moral   190
character . . . of a nation . . . *Hart* 1793. O 66 a

Essay (An) on the interests of Britain in   191
regard to America: or, an outline of the terms on
which peace may be restored . . . *L* 1780. O 23 a

Essay [An] on the merchandize of slaves . . .
By a gentleman. *See* Dudley, Paul.

Essay (An) on the policy of . . . purchasing,
liberating and colonizing . . . slaves. By a citizen of
Maryland. *See* Allen, Rev. John.

Essay (An) on the seat of federal government . . .
See Webster, Pelatiah.

Essay (An) on the trade of the northern   192
colonies of Great Britain in North America. *Phil*
1764. O [4] 38 aa
—rptd., same date & collat., *L* a

Essay (An) upon government, adopted by   193
the Americans. Wherein, the lawfulness of revo-
lutions, are demonstrated . . . *Phil* 1775. O 125 aa

Essay (An) upon the government of the English
plantations on the continent of America . . . By an
American. *See* Davenant, Chas.

ESSAYS 194

Essays on the origin of the federal government
... it emanates not from the people collectively, but from the people of the respective states ... *Charleston S C* 1830. O 28 a

**Essays ... on the real and relative in-   195
terests of imperial and dependent states, particularly those of Great Britain and her dependencies:** displaying the probable causes of and a mode of compromising the present disputes ... *Newcastle* 1777. O [10] 148 fold.tab aa

ESSEX JUNTO (THE) 196

Essex junto (The) and the British spy; or, treason detected. *Salem* 1812. O 36 a

ESTADOS-UNIDOS MEXICANOS

Coleccion de constituciones de Estados-Unidos Mexicanos. *Mex* 1828. *See* Galván Rivera, Mariano.

**Constitucion federal de los Estados-Unidos   197
Mexicanos.** ... [*Mex* 1824]. Q [4] 28 [2] b BA
—anr. ed. [*Mex* 1824]. D [22] 62 [8] pl copies usually have a 12-p "Acta constitutiva," with separate t-p, added a
The first constitution of the Mexican Republic under which operated our present southwestern states, from Texas to California. The *Acta constitutiva*—establishing the Provisional government and outlining the federal system on which it was based—operated from January 31 to October 4, when superseded by the *Constitucion*.

ESTAING (M. [CHARLES HECTOR] 198
le comte d').

Extrait du journal d'un officier ... de l'escadre de: [*P*?] 1782. O [2] 158 port a
—anr. issue. O 126 port[not same as in issue 1] a
—anr. issue. O [2] 94
—rptd. *Amst* 1783. O [2] 72
—Eng. tr., *see* Jones, Chas. C., "The siege of Savannah, in 1779"
The unidentified author [possibly Captain Walsh, the Chevalier O'Connor] is highly critical of the conduct of his superior. A defense against his charges appeared at Brussels in 1782: *Le campagne en Amárique de ... Estaing*.

ESTES, GEORGE 199

The rawhide railroad ... *Canby, Ore.* [1916] O 54 aa
—ed. 2, *Troutdale, Ore.* [1924] O a
Utilizing leather-covered wooden rails, this pioneer line in the Walla Walla valley came to an inglorious end when winter came and hungry wolves devoured the tracks.

ESTES, MATTHEW 200

A defence of negro slavery ... in the United States. *Montg* 1846. 24° 260 a

ESTEVA, JOSÉ I. 201

Memoria sobre el estado de la hacienda publica ... *Mex* [1825] Q 52 [2] b
Covers the history of California missions from 1726, the pious fund, etc.

ESTLIN, J[OHN] B. 202

A brief notice of American slavery, and the abolition movement. *Bristol Eng.* 1846. 24° 40 a
—ed. 2, *L* [1853]. 24° 54

ESTVÀN, B[ELA] 203

War pictures from the south. *L* 1863. D 2v: [16] 310; [10] 320. map 10pls a
—Am. ed. *N Y* 1863. D [8] 352
—Ger. tr. *Leip* 1864. O 2v in 1: [28] 435
This Hungarian imposter claiming to having been a Confederate cavalry colonel was a noncombatant hospital orderly.

ESTWICK, SAMUEL 204

A letter to the Reverend Josiah Tucker, in answer to his Humble address and earnest appeal ... *L* 1776. O 125 a

ÉTAT

État (De l') et du sort des colonies ... *See* Sainte-Croix, Guillaume E. J. G. de Clermont-Lodève.

État politique actuel de l'Angleterre ...   205
Vol. I[all[. n.p. [P] 1757. 16° 3 pts in 1: [8] 176; [4] 177–394; [4] 395–462 fold.map aa
Gives information gathered from every available source on the current war both in Europe and America. Attributed to Edmé J. Genet.

ÉTATS CONFÉDÉRÉS

États Confédérés d'Amérique (Les), visités en 1863 ... *See* Girard, Chas. F.

ÉTATS-UNIS (LES)

États-Unis (Les) et l'Angleterre, ou souvenirs ... *See* Lee, Wm.

[ETCHES, JOHN C.] 206

An authentic statement of all the facts relative to Nootka sound. *L* 1790. O [2] 26 b N OreU WashU Y

[ETCHES, JOHN C.] 207

A continuation of An authentic statement of all the facts relative to Nootka sound ... *L* 1790. O 34 b NYP
Etches was surpercargo with Meares, and one of the owners of the ships captured by the Spanish.

ETHELL, HENRY C. 208

The rise and progress of civilization in the hairy nation [and] history of Davis County Iowa. *Bloomfield Ia* 1883. O 144 aa

ÉTOURNEAU, M[ONS]. 209
De Paris au nouveau monde ... narration d'un voyage de dix ans. *P* 1857–9. 16° 3v: [2] 312; 315; 408 a

ETZENHOUSER, R. 210
From Palmyra ... to Independence ... *Independence Mo* 1894. D [4] 444 a

EUROPEAN TRAVELLER (THE)
European traveller (The) in America ... *See* Brockway, *Rev.* Thos.

EUSTACE (MAJOR-GENERAL 211
[JOHN S.])
Exile of: ... from the kingdom of Great-Britain ... *L* 1797. O [18] 48 a

[EUSTACE, MAJOR-GENERAL 212
JOHN S.]
Lettres ... sur les crimes du roi George III. *P* l'imprimerie des Sans-Culottes [1794]. O 2pts in 1v: [12] 80; 135 a
—Eng. tr. *P* Jansen [1794]. O

EUSTACE (MAJOR-GENERAL 213
J[OHN] S.)
Official and private correspondence of: ... Pt. I [all]. *P* 1796. O [6] 152 aa
Exiled from England, Eustace came to America with the French army, serving as aide-de-camp to Generals Lee and Sullivan and as Adjutant General with Georgia troops.

[EVANS, CALEB] 214
A letter to ... John Wesley occasioned by his Calm address to the American colonies. *L* 1775. D 24 a
—rptd. *Bristol* 1775. same collat.
—new ed., with adds., *L* 1775. D [8] 24
Colonial rights warmly defended.

EVANS, CALEB 215
Political sophistry detected ... remarks on the Rev. Mr. Fletcher's ... "American patriotism." *Bristol Eng* 1776. D 36 a

EVANS, CALEB 216
A reply to the Rev. Mr. Fletcher's vindication of Mr. Wesley's Calm address to our American colonies. *Bristol, Eng* [1775?]. D 103 a

EVANS, ELWOOD 217
The re-annexation of British Columbia to the United States, right, proper, [etc.]. *Olympia* [1870]. O 24 aa

EVANS, ELWOOD 218
Washington Territory; her past, her present, [etc.]. *Olympia* 1877. O 51 aa

EVANS, ESTWICK 219
Essay on state rights ... Ser. 1 [all]. *Wash* 1844. O 40 aa
Calls itself second edition; possibly had appeared previously in some periodical.

EVANS, ESTWICK 220
A pedestrious tour, of four thousand miles, through the western states and territories ... *Concord N H* 1819. D 256 port b AA KyU N NYP Y
Visited Pittsburgh, Detroit, New Orleans, etc. In some copies is inserted a leaf giving copyright dated January 18, 1819, apparently to correct the regular one on verso of title which bears date December 10, 1818.

EVANS, ISRAEL 221
A discourse ... at Easton to the ... soldiers of the western army, after their return from an expedition [under Sullivan] against the Five Nations ... *Phil* 1779. O 40 aa
—rptd. [*Easton* 1914]. O a

EVANS, ISRAEL 222
A discourse delivered near York in Virginia, on ... the surrender of the British army ... before the ... New York troops and the division, under ... Lafayette. *Phil* 1782. O [46] aa

EVANS, JA[ME]S A. 223
Report of: of exploration [for Union Pacific R. R.] from Camp Walsach to Green river. [*Montrose Pa* 1865]. O 24 b Pn Y
First white man to thread Laramie canyon.

EVANS (GOV. [JOHN]), of Colorado. 224
Reply of: To ... Report ... Massacre of Cheyenne Indians ... *Denv* 1865. O 16 [6] capt-t only b Hn LC [of 4 cops kn]
This exculpation of the author — and Chivington — includes Mrs. Ewbank's account of her captivity.

EVANS, JONATHAN, comp. 225
A journal of the life, travels ... of William Savery. [Includes account of a tour with Heckewelder to Sandusky in 1793]. *Phil*, Evans [1837] D 485 aa
—rptd *Phil*, Friends Book Store [1837] same collat a
—Eng. ed. *L* 1844. D [8] 316 a

EVANS, LEWIS 226
Geographical ... essays ... containing an analysis of a map of the middle ... colonies. *Phil* 1755. Q [4] 32 map[issued prior to book, but should accompany it] b AA NYP Y
—ed. 2, *Phil* 1755, same collat. b AA N NYP Y
—Eng. ed. *Phil* ptd, sold in *L* 1755. Q same collat. b NYP Y

For republication of both map and analysis, *see* Pownall, Thomas, *A topographical description*... The first state of this map [which was improved from one printed at Philadelphia in 1749, and reprinted in 1752] measures 20 $^1/_4$ × 26 $^3/_4$ inches, bears Philadelphia imprint and 1755 date; the second state, London 1758, measures 23 × 32 $^1/_2$ inches. It was based on actual surveys or reliable information, gave valuable data on the Western country [then claimed by France] and was the best cartographical delineation of the colonies available at its time. Both American and English editions of *Essays* and *Map* should be accompanied by the second series of *Essays*, *see* below.

EVANS, LEWIS   **227**
Geographical... essays. No. II. *Phil* 1756. Q 43 b NYP N
—Eng. ed. *L* 1756. Q 35 b Y
Answered objections made to his map and original volume of Essays and gave new material on the French claims, with proposals for resisting them.

[EVANS, THOMAS]   **228**
An address to the people of Virginia, respecting the alien and sedition laws. *Rich* 1798. 16° 64 [4] a

EVANS, THOMAS   **229**
A series of letters addressed to Thomas Jefferson... *Phil* 1802. O 170 a

[EVARTS, JEREMIAH]   **230**
Essays on the present crisis in the present condition of the... Indians. *B* 1829. O 112 a
—rptd. *Phil* 1830. O 116

EVENTS IN INDIAN HISTORY
See Wimer, James.

EVEREST, ROBERT   **231**
A journey through the United States and part of Canada. *L* 1855. O [12] 178 a

EVERETT (EDWARD).   **232**
Address of: at the consecration of the National Cemetery at Gettysburg... with the dedicatory speech of President Lincoln... *B* 1864. O 88 map a
First authorized edition of Lincoln's address.

EVERETT, EDWARD   **233**
An oration delivered on the battlefield of Gettysburg... *N Y* 1863. O 48 b IllH NYP Y
First appearance of Lincoln's Gettysburg address in book form, antedated only by a 16-page Washington pamphlet, *The Gettysburg solemnities*,

which included a somewhat garbled version and of which only two copies are known.

EVERETT, FRANKLIN   **234**
Memorials of the Grand River valley [Mich.]. *Chi* 1878. O [10 incl. front.] 546 [74] a

EVERETT, H[ORACE]   **235**
Regulating the Indian department... [report from the committee on Indian affairs]. *Wash* [1834]. O 131 map aa

EVERHART, J. F., comp.   **236**
Quincy [Ill.] city directory for 1855–6. *Quincy* 1855. D. 143 + 12 adv-p aa
Includes historical sketch.

EVERSHAW, MARY   **237**
Five years in Pennsylvania. *L* 1840. D [2] 227 a
Sad story of an English girl who came to this country in 1830 and met with nothing but tribulation.

EWELL, JAMES   **238**
The medical companion... also a concise... history of the capture of Washington. ed. 3. *Phil* 1816. O [16] 694[i.e., 698] a
Earlier and later editions did not contain the historical portion.

EWELL, THOMAS T.   **239**
A history of Hood county, Texas... *Granbury Tex* 1895. O [4] 160 [8] + 6 interspersed adv-p aa
—rptd, 1956.

EXAMEN
Examen des Recherches philosophiques sur l'Amérique ... *See* Pernety, Antoine J. D.

Examen du gouvernement d'Angleterre, comparé aux constitutions des États-Unis ... *See* Stevens, John.

EXAMINATION   **240**
Examination (An) into the conduct of the present administration ... And a plan of accommodation with America. By a member of parliament. *L* 1778. O [2] 69 aa
—ed. 2, *L* 1779, same collat. a

Examination (An) of the British doctrine which subjects to capture a neutral trade not open in time of peace ... *See* Madison, James.

Examination (An) of the conduct of Great Britain respecting neutrals ... *See* Coxe, Tench.

Examination [An] of the conduct of the Executive ... towards the French republic ... By a citizen of Pennsylvania. *See* Gallatin, Albert.

Examination (An) of the Constitution   241
for the United States. By an American citizen . . .
Phil 1788. O 33 a

Examination (An) of the late proceedings in
Congress respecting the official conduct of the
Secretary of the Treasury . . . *See* Taylor, John
[of Va.].

Examination (The) of the President's message . . .
December 7, 1801. *See* Hamilton, Alex.

Examination (An) of the President's reply to the
New-Haven remonstrance . . . *See* Coleman, Wm.

Examination (An) of the riphts of the   242
colonies, upon principles of law. By a gentleman
at the bar. *L* 1766. O 42 a
Ascribed to John Wilson.

Examination of the Russian claims to the
northwest coast of America. *See* Sturgis, Wm.

Examination of the treaty . . . between the
United States and Great Britain . . . By Cato. *See*
Livingston, Robt. R.

EXAMINER (THE) EXAMINED.   243
A letter from a gentleman in Connecticut, to
his friend in London. In answer to a letter from a
gentleman in London to his friend in America:
intitled, The claim of the colonies to an exemption
from internal taxes . . . examined. *N Lond* 1766.
O 24 aa
Attributed to Ebenezer Devotion.

EXCURSION (AN)
Excursion (An) through the United States and
Canada . . . By an English gentleman. *See* Blane,
Wm. N.

EXPEDIENCY (THE)   244
Expediency (The) of securing our American
colonies by settling the country adjoining the . . .
Mississippi [etc.]. *Edin* 1763. D 68 b H

EXPERIENCE
Experience preferable to theory . . . *See* Hutchinson, Thos.

EXPLICATION
Explication de la carte des nouvelles décou-
vertes au nord de la mer du Sud. *See* Buache,
Philip.

EXPOSÉ   245
Exposé de l'évantualités d'un guerre entre les
États Unis et l'Angleterre. *P* 1845. O 60 b NYP Y
3copies known

This war—over Texas and Oregon—considered
almost certain.

Exposé des droits des colonies britan-   246
iques pour justifier le projet de leur independance.
Amst 1776. O [4] 43 74 a

EXPOSITION
Exposition (An) of the causes and character of
the late war with Great Britain. *See* Dallas,
Alex J.

Exposition of the motives of the conduct of the
King of France towards England . . . *See* Gibbon,
Edw.

Exposition (An) of the weakness . . . of the government of the United States. *See* Mercer, Chas. F.

EXTRACT
Extract of a letter from a gentleman in America
. . . on the subject of emigration. *See* Cooper,
Th., *Thoughts on emigration.*

EXTRACTS   247
Extracts from the votes and proceedings of . . .
Continental Congress . . . Philadelphia . . . 5th of
September 1774. *Phil* Oct. 24, 1774. O [36] aa
—oth. issues, *Phil* Oct. 27, 1774: D [32] [36];D 23;
D [28] 36; O [4] 11 50 a
—other Am. eds. of 1774; *Annap; B; Hart;
N Lond; N Y; Newport; Norwich; Prov; Wmsbg*
—Am. eds. of 1775; *N Y* [2issues, of which one
contains Journal complete]; *Prov*
—Eng. eds. *L* 1774: O [4] 82 + 2adv-p; O [2] 59
—other Eng. eds. "Journal of the proceedings . . .,"
[i.e., the portions not included in the previously
ptd. "Extracts . . .,"] *L* Dilly 1775. O [2] 66; rptd.
same impr., date & collat., Almon.
The forerunner of the Declaration of Independence. For complete proceedings see *Journal* . . .

Extracts from the votes and proceedings   248
of . . . Continental Congress . . . Philadelphia, 10th
of May, 1775. *N Y* 1775. O [4] 192 a
For complete form *see Journal.*

EYES (THE)
Eyes (The) opened, or Carolinians convinced . . .
See Smith, Wm. L., *A candid examination . . .*

EYMA, LOUIS X.   249
Scènes de moeurs et de voyages dans le nouveau
monde. *P* 1862. 16° 392 a

EYMA, LOUIS X.   250
La vie dans le nouveau monde. *P* 1862. 16°
355 a

EYRE, JOHN　　　　　　　　　　　251
The beauties of America. *Buf* 1836. D 72 aa
—for reprint, *See* next entry.

EYRE, JOHN　　　　　　　　　　　252
The Christian spectator . . . a journey from
England to Ohio . . . *Alb* 1838. 16° 84 a

EYRE, JOHN　　　　　　　　　　　253
The European stranger in America. *N Y* 1839.
D 84 a

A continuation of the author's *The Christian
spectator.*

EYRE, JOHN　　　　　　　　　　　254
Travels . . . *N Y* 1851. D 372 a
—rptd. *N Y* 1852. Same collat.
Contains the author's previous books—*The
Christian spectator* and *The European stranger in
America*—with the addition of his travels through
the eastern states.

F

F., R.　　　　　　　　　　　　　　1
The present state of Carolina . . . *L* 1682. O 36
b Hn NYP

FABIUS.
The letters of: *see* Dickinson, John.

FABLE, EDMUND　　　　　　　　　2
Billy the Kid . . . *Denv* [1881] O 83 b.
The rarest and one of the earliest of several
worthless fictionalized biographies of this lethal
juvenile delinquent. Happily, only one copy survives and no reprint has been perpetrated. For a
similar atrocity see Daggett, Thos. F.

FABRICIUS
Fabricius: or, letters to the people of Great
Britain . . . *See* Galloway, Jos.

FACTION
Faction detected, by the evidence of facts . . .
See Perceval, John, Earl of Egmont.

FACTS
Facts and arguments respecting . . . inland
navigation in America . . . By a friend to national
industry. *See* Blodget, Wm.

Facts and documents, relating to the . . .　3
controversy, between America and Great Britain . . .
By a friend of truth . . . *B* 1813. O 31 a

FADEN, WILLIAM, pub.　　　　　　4
Atlas of battles of the American revolution . . .
[*L* 1793]. F 23maps b ChiH H [of 4 cops loc]

[FADEN, WILLIAM] pub.　　　　　5
The North American atlas . . . *L* 1776. F t-p
38maps on 44sheets dd
—anr. ed. *L* 1777. F [4] 27maps on 63
sheets[in some copies 23maps on 54sheets; in
others 30maps on 34sheets] d NYP
—anr iss, same impr. & date. F [4] maps on 39
sheets d

[FAIRBANKS, CHARLES]　　　　　6
The old soldier's story . . . 1813–1814. *Haverhill*
1861. O 20 + wraps a

FAIRBANKS, GEORGE R.　　　　　7
The early history of Florida. An introductory
lecture . . . before the Florida Historical Society
. . . *St Augustine* 1857. O 32 a

FAIRBANKS, GEORGE R.　　　　　8
History of Florida . . . 1512–1842. *Phil* 1871.
D 350 + 10 adv-p a

FAIRBANKS, GEORGE R.　　　　　9
The history . . . of St. Augustine . . . *N Y* 1858.
O [12] 9–200 7pls a
—ed. 2, 1868.
—ed. 3, *Jacksonville* 1881. O [8] 117 map 4pls
—rptd. same impr. 1898.

FAIRBANKS, GEORGE R.　　　　　10
The Spaniards in Florida. *Jacksonville* 1868
O 120 + 15 adv-p a

FAIRFIELD, ASA M.　　　　　　11
Pioneer history of Lassen county, California . . .
S F [1916] O [12] 507 map a

FALCKNER [or FALKNERN], DANIEL　　12
Curieuse Nachricht von Pensylvania . . . *Frankft*
1702. D [14] 58 b N PaH PhilP
Most influential promotion tract for German
emigration to this country at the period. It was
also issued as the second part of the German,
translation of Gabriel Thomas' *Historical account
of Pensilvania, q.v.*

FALCONBRIDGE, ALEXANDER　　13
An account of the slave trade on the coast of
Africa. *L* 1788. O 55 a
—ed. 2, *L* 1788. D 72

FALCONER (CAPTAIN RICHARD).
The voyages, dangerous adventures . . . of: *See*
Chetwood, Wm. R.

FALCONER, THOMAS   **14**
Expedition to Santa Fe ... its journey from
Texas ... with particulars of its capture. *N O*
1842. D 12 c N TxU
—rptd., with adds., ed. F. W. Hodge. "Letters
and notes on the Texas-Santa Fe expedition ...,"
N Y 1930. O 159 port a
This narrative was appended to the seventh
edition of Kendall's *Santa Fe expedition.*

FALCONER, THOMAS   **15**
Notes of a journey through Texas and New
Mexico ... 1841–2. [*L* 1844]. D 28 capt.t.only aa
Separate printing from *Journal of the Royal
Geographical Society*, volume thirteen, part two.
It was included in the 1930 reprint of Falconer's
similar *Expedition to Santa Fe*, above.

FALCONER, THOMAS   **16**
On the discovery of the Mississippi, and on the
south-western. Oregon, and north-western boundary ... *L* 1844. O [6] 98[incl errata lf] 100 map aa
—anr. issue, without map. D a
Weightiest exposition of British claims to
Oregon and contains the first English translation
of La Salle's report and of Tonty's 1693 *Memoire.*
See under Tonty for other relations by him.

FALCONER, THOMAS   **17**
The Oregon question ... British claims ... in
opposition to the pretensions of ... the United
States ... *L* 1845. O 46 map errata slip a
—ed. 2, with 4p. postscript but no map, *L* 1845. O 50
—anr. issue, with a second postscript. O 50 4
—rptd. *L* 1852.
—Am. ed. *N Y* 1845. O 40 map
Both *Postscripts*—one of four and one of
twelve pages—were separately issued in 1845.

FALDING, F. J.   **18**
Notes of a journey round the world ... *Shef-
field* 1876. D 208 a
Considerable attention given to Californis and
the West.

FALKENSTEIN, [CONSTANTINE] KARL   **19**
Thaddaus Kosciuszko: nach seinem offentlichen
und hauslichen Leben. *Leip* 1827 a
—ed. 2, *Leip* 1834. O [18] 376 port facs
—Fr. tr. *P* 1839. O [8] 303

FALLING FLAG (THE).
Evacuation of Richmond. Retreat and surrender at Appomattox. By an officer of the rear
guard. See Boykin, Edw. M.

FALMOUTH IN CASCO-BAY   **20**
The conference with the Eastern Indians, at
the ratification of the peace, held at Falmouth,
in Casco-Bay. July and August, 1726. [*B* 1726?].
Q 23 c LC MH NYP

Conference with the Eastern Indians, at   **21**
the further ratification of the peace, held at: Falmouth, in Casco-Bay. July 1727. [*B* 1727?]. Q
31 c MH NYP
—rptd. *B* 1754. Q b

A journal of the proceedings at two confer-   **22**
ences ... held at: Falmouth in Casco-Bay ... between ... William Shirley ... and the chiefs of the
Norridgwalk Indians ... *B* 1754. F 27 c AA MH N

THE FALSE ALARM
False alarm (the). *L* Cadell 1770. *See* Johnson,
Saml.

False alarm (The), adressed to ... Richard   **23**
Rigby ... By Cincinnatus. *L* Coghlan 1782. O [4]
106 [2] aa
—anr. issue, same collat. & date. *L* Wilkie. a
Attempts to belittle British military reverses in
America.

False alarm (The): or, the Americans mis-   **24**
taken. *L* 1775. O 22 a

FANATICISM, AND ITS RESULTS.
By a southerner. *See* Mc Cabe, James D.

FANEUIL HALL.   **25**
Address of the committee appointed by a
public meeting held at: for ... considering the
recent case of kidnapping ... *B* 1846. O 42 a

FANNING [COLONEL DAVID].
A fan for: and a touch-stone to Tryon ... *See*
Husband, Harmon.

FANNING (COLONEL DAVID).   **26**
The narrative of: ... his adventures in North
Carolina, 1775–1783. *Rich* 1861. Q [26] 92 b
60copies ptd. [10 on thick paper]
—rptd. *N Y* 1865. O [26] 86 a 250 copies ptd.[50
on L. P.] a
—*Tor* 1908. O [6] 55; *N Y* 1912 300cops.
The original edition was the first book printed
in the Confederacy.

FANNING, EDMUND   **27**
Voyages round the world ... *N Y* 1833. O 499
5pls aa
—Eng. ed. *L* 1834. O same collat. aa
Different work from next entry; but both give
account of the first naval exploring expedition
sponsored by the United States government,
commanded by the author.

FANNING, EDMUND   **28**
Voyages to the south seas ... north-west
coast ... *N Y* 1838. D 324 front. aa
—4 other eds., same impr., date & collat. a
—anr. ed. *Salem* 1924. O 32pls also 97 copies on
L.P., Q a

In this narrative, Captain Fanning gives an account of the destruction of Astor's ship, the "Tonquin," at Nootka Sound. Really a second edition—and so named on title—of preceding entry.

[FANNING, NATHANIEL]   29
Narrative of the adventures of an American navy officer who served . . . under the command of Com. John Paul Jones . . . *N Y* 1806. D 270 b H NYP
—rptd. "Memoir of the life of Captain Nathaniel Fanning," *N Y* 1808. D 270 aa
—rptd., ed. J. S. Barnes, *N Y* 1912. O [32] 258 300copies ptd. a
Earliest authoritative account of Jones' Revolutionary actions.

FAR WEST (THE)
Far west (The): a sketch of Illinois . . . *See* under Mitchell, Saml. A. *Illinois in* 1837.

Far west (The): its present, past and future. *See* Tefft, B. F.

Far west (The); or, a tour beyond the mountains. *See* Flagg, Edmund T.

FARDON, G. R.   30
San Francisco album . . . *S F* [1856]. Q 30 photos, with t-p & index aa
First San Francisco book containing photographic views.

[FARGO, FRANK F.]   31
A true . . . history of the assassination of James King . . . *S F* Sullivan [1856]. O 26 [cover t.only] aa
For similar title, *see* Rivors, C.

FARGO CITY DIRECTORY.   32
Fargo 1881. O 103 + 10adv-p aa only one cop loc.

FARÍA, FRANCISCO XAVIER DE   33
Vida. Y heroycas virtudes del . . . Pedro de Velasco . . . *Mex* 1753. O [14] 170[i.e. 178] b G JCB NYP TxU

FARIBAULT COUNTY, MINNESOTA: 34
Its history . . . *Faribault* 1868. D 24 aa

FARISH, THOMAS E.   35
Central and southwestern Arizona . . . [*Phoenix*] 1889. O [2] 48 pl a
Contains historical data.

FARISH, THOMAS E.   36
The gold hunters of California. *Chi* 1904. D 246 pls a

FARISH, THOMAS E.   37
History of Arizona. *Phoenix* 1915–20. O 8v [incl. Index vol. of 64p] pls b

FARISH, THOMAS E.   38
Southeastern Arizona . . . *Phoenix* 1889. O 47 a
Contains historical data.

FARMER, JOHN, and MOORE,   39
JACOB B., eds.
Collections, topographical, historical . . . relating principally to New Hampshire . . . *Concord* 1822,3,4. O 3v: 296 [7]; [2] 387 103 [6]; [4] 388 88 [9] aa
Volume I was reprinted in 1831. Titles of volumes II and III differ slightly from that of volume I as entered above.

FARMER, JOHN   40
Emigrants guide [etc.] of the surveyed part of Michigan. *Alb* 1830. 24° 32 map [separately sold but inserted in some copies] b N
—ed. 2, *Alb* 1831. aa
—anr. ed. *Det* 1835. a
—enl. ed. 1836.
First gazetteer of this Territory.

FARMER, JOHN, and MOORE, JACOB B.   41
A gazetteer of . . . New Hampshire. *Concord N H* 1823. D 276 map a

FARMER, JOHN   42
A genealogical register of the first settlers of New England . . . *Lancaster Mass* 1829. O 352 port a

FARMER, SILAS   43
The history of Detroit and Michigan . . . *Det* 1884. O [46] 1024 front. aa
—ed. 2, biog. vol. added, *Det* 1889. O 2v pls aa
—ed. 3, "History of Detroit and Wayne county and early Michigan," *Det* 1890. O 2v fold.map pls a

FARMER (THE)
Farmer (The) refuted . . . in answer to a letter from A. W. Farmer . . . *See* Hamilton, Alex.

FARMER'S . . .
Farmer's letter (A) to the people. *See* Lincoln, Levi.

Farmer's and Monitor's letters (The) to the inhabitants of the British colonies. *See* Dickinson, John, and Lee, Arthur.

Farmer's handbook and emigrant's guide to   44 northern Shawnee . . . counties [Kas.]. *North Topeka* 1879. D 32[incl.advs] aa

FARNAM, HENRY W.   **45**
Henry Farnam. [*N Hav* 1889]. D 136 [2] front.
a 100copies ptd.

[FARNESWORTH, FREDERICK?]   **46**
An adventure on the banks of the Ohio...
story of Mrs. Eliza Williamson... *B* 1818. 16°
24 front aa

FARNESWORTH, FREDERICK, ed.   **47**
The man of the mountain... narrative of
Mr. William Warland... *B* 1818. O 24 front. a

FARNHAM, THOMAS J.   **48**
History of Oregon territory... *N Y*,Winchester,
1844. O 80 map aa
—ed. 2, *N Y*, Taylor, n. d. [ca 1844] a
—rptd. same impr, 1845. O 83
Vehement presentation of the superiority of
America's claims to Oregon over those of England.

FARNHAM, THOMAS J.   **49**
Travels in the Californias... *N Y* 1844. O
4pts paged continuously 416 map pl h
—anr. issue, bd. in 1v. aa
—rptd. with titles altered, "Life... in California
...," etc., same collat., 1846; 1847. a
—other eds., with adds., 1849; and later.
—anr. ed. "Early days in California...," *Phil* 1859.
—rptd. *Oakland* 1947. O [16] 166 map facs
Essentially a sequel to his *Travels in the great
western prairies.*

FARNHAM, THOMAS J.   **50**
Travels in the great western prairies... *Poughkeepsie* 1841. D 197 b
—rptd. *Poughkeepsie* [in some copies "Plough-
keepsie"] 1843; *N Y* [Wiley] 1843; *N Y* [Greeley]
1843. O 112 + wrap.t. a
—Eng-& best-ed. *L* 1843. D 2v: [24] 297; [8]
315 + adv.1. in v.1 aa
—Ger.tr. "Wanderungen über die Felsengebirge
in das Oregon-Gebiet," *Leip* 1846. D [8] 310 a

FARNSWORTH, OLIVER [pub.]   **51**
The Cincinnati directory... By a citizen. [*Cin*]
1819. D 156 plan b AA LC N NYP WisH Y
First Cincinnati directory.

FARNSWORTH, R. W. C., ed.   **52**
A southern California paradise... *Pasadena*
1883. D 132 a
—ed. 2, same impr. & date. D 142
First history of this place.

FARRELL, NED E.   **53**
Colorado, the Rocky mountain gem... *Chi*
1868. 16° 72 map front. b G LC NYP Y

FARROW, EDWARD S.   **54**
American small arms... *N Y* 1904. O [2] 408 a

FARROW, EDWARD S.   **56**
Mountain scouting... *Phil* 1881. D 248 36 aa
—anr. issue, same collat. & date, *N Y* aa
—rptd. "Camping on the trail...," *Phil* [1902[.
D [4] 7-284 pls a

FASHIONABLE TOUR
Fashionable tour (The): or, a trip to the
Springs... *See* Davison, Gideon M.

FAUCHET, JOSEPH   **57**
Coup d'oeil sur l'état actuel de nos rapports
politiques avec les Etats-Unis. *P* 1797. O 42 a
—Eng. tr. *Phil* 1797. O 31 a
Fauchet replaced Genet as Minister to the
United States.

FAUQUIER [VA.]   **58**
Six weeks in:... by a visiter. *N Y* 1839. 18°
67 pl a

FAUVEL-GOURAUD, J. B. G.   **59**
L'Hercule et la Favorite, ou la capture de
l'Alexandre, et des pirates bordelais... à New-
Port... suivi d'un apercu sur les moeurs...
americaines... *P* 1840. O 2v: [12]; 524 [4]; 580.
2 pls aa

FAUX, W[ILLIAM]   **60**
Memorable days in America... journal of a
tour to the United States... *L* 1823. O [16]
488 pl aa
Bitterly unfavorable.

FAVEZ, L.   **61**
Fragments sur les Mormons... *Lausanne*
1854-6. D 2v: 84; 82 a

FAY, [HEMAN] A., comp.   **62**
Collection of the official accounts... of all the
battles... 1812-1815. *N Y* 1817. O 295 a

FAY, T. C., comp.   **63**
Mobile directory, or strangers' guide for 1839
Mobile [1839]. D 104 96 aa
For first directory, *see* Mobile.

FAY, THEODORE S., ed.   **64**
Views in New York, and its environs, taken
on the spot... by Dakin. *N Y* 1831-[1834]
8parts [all] Q 46 eng t. map 15 pls a

FEARON, HENRY B.   **65**
Sketches of America... *L* 1818. O [8] 462 a
—ed. 2, *L* 1818. O [2, 5-12] 454
—ed. 3, *L* 1819. O [16] 454
—Ger. ed. "Skizzen von Amerika," *Jena* 1819.
Unflattering picture of the western frontier.

FEARS, JESSE, ed.   **66**
Confession of Richard H. Shuck, a member

of the Owen and Henry county marauders, of ...
Kentucky. *Frankf* 1877. O 35 a

FEATHERSTONHAUGH, G[EORGE] W.   67
A canoe voyage up the Minnay Sotor ... *L*
1847. O 2v: [14] 416; [8] 351. 2 maps 2pls aa
—re-issued, 2v in 1, without the maps a

FEATHERSTONHAUGH, G[EORGE] W.   68
Excursion through the slave states ... *L* 1844.
O 2v: [30] 358; [10] 394 + 16adv-p. map 2eng
t. aa
—Am. ed. *N Y* 1844. O 168 a

FEDERALIST (THE)   69
Federalist (The): containing some strictures
upon ... "The pretensions of Thomas Jefferson
to the Presidency ..." *Phil* 1796. O 2pts: 48; 27 a
Vigorous defence of Jefferson in reply to
William L. Smith's pamphlet; probably by Tench
Coxe.

Federalist (The) ... essays in favour of the new
Constitution ... *See* Hamilton, Alex.

FÉDIX, P. A.   70
L'Orégon et les côtes de l'océan pacifique du
nord ... *P* 1846. O 258 map b N NYP OreH
WashU Y
Proposes that world powers maintain Oregon
as an independency to serve as an international
trade center for the Pacific.

FEDRIC, FRANCIS   71
Slave life in Virginia and Kentucky; or, fifty
years of slavery in the southern states. *L* 1863.
D [8] 115 a

FELSENHART, J.,   72
Les colonies anglaises de 1574 à 1660 ... et epi-
sode de l'emigration belge en Virginie. *Ghent* 1868.
O [8] 94 a

FELT, JOSEPH B.   73
The annals of Salem. *Salem* 1827. O 611 a
Issued first in 6 nos. a
—ed. 2, enl. *Salem* 1845–9. D 2v: [6] 5–535; 662
2 maps 3 pls.

FELT, JOSEPH B.   74
The customs of New England ... *B* 1853.
O [2] 208 a

FELTMAN (LIEUT. WILLIAM).   75
The journal of: ... 1781–82. Including the
march into Virginia, and the siege of Yorktown.
Phil 1853. O 48 a

FEMALE REVIEW (THE)
Female review (The): or, memoirs of an
American young lady ... *See* Mann, Herman.

FENDERICH, CHARLES   76
Portfolio of living American statesmen. *Wash*
[1837]. F [2] 70pls a

FENTON (COL. JAMES).   77
Journal of the military tour by the Pennsylvania volunteers and militia under command of:
to the frontiers of Pennsylvania and New York,
Lake Erie ... and from thence to Greenbush
garrison. By a volunteer in the regiment. *Carlisle
Pa* [1814? 1815?]. O 52 b IndU [only copy located
—may lack one or two final pages.]

FERGUS, ROBERT, pub.   78
Fergus' historical series. *Chi* 1876–1903. D
35pts b AA N Y
Important collection of feminiscences, historical
sketches, etc., relating to Chicago and the region
around.

FERGUS FALLS [MINN.]   79
Coarse fodder (bran, chips and sawdust ...)
raked up by an old settler ... relating to: *Minneap*
1881. O 24 map a

[FERGUSON, DR. ADAM] 1724–1816   80
Remarks on a pamphlet ... by Dr. Price,
intitled [*sic*[, Observations on the nature of civil
liberty ... *L* Cadell 1776. O [2] 61 a
—anr. ed. "Remarks on Dr. Price's Observations ...," *L* Kearsley 1776. O [4] 76

FERGUSON, ADAM, LL.D.   81
Biographical sketch or memoir of Lieutenant-
Colonel Patrick Ferguson ... *Edin* 1817. O 36
port a

FERGUSON, ROBERT   82
America during and after the war. *L* 1866. D [22]
280 a

FERGUSON, DR. T.   83
A complete history of the present civil war
between Great Britain and the united colonies ...
L 1779. O 358 aa

FERGUSON, THOMPSON B.   84
The jayhawkers. A tale of the border war.
Guthrie 1892. O [4] 415 a

FERGUSON, WILLIAM   85
America by river and rail ... *L* 1856. O [8]
511 2pls a
South to Carolina, west to Iowa.

FERGUSSON, ADAM   86
Practical notes ... during a tour in Canada,
and a portion of the United States ... *Edin* 1833.
D [16] 379 map a
—ed. 2, with adds., *Edin* 1834. D [16] 426 map
Includes visits to Baltimore, Washington,
western New York and Michigan.

FERGUSSON (MAJOR D[AVID]).   87
. . . Report of: on the country . . . and the
route between Tucson and Lobos bay, Arizona.
Sen. Exec. Doc.1.[*Wash* 1863]. O 22 3maps a

[FERGUSSON, JAMES]   88
Notes of a tour in North America in 1861.
[*Edin* 1861]. D [4] 100 a

F[ERNAGUS] D[E] G[ELONE]   89
Manual-guide des voyageurs aux États-Unis
. . . *P* 1818. D 196 aa

FERNÁNDEZ DE SAN SALVADOR,   90
AUGUSTIN P.
Los Jesuitas quitados y restituidos al mundo.
Historia de la antigua California. *Mex* 1816. 16°
[10] 213 a

FERNANDEZ DE TAOS   91
A review of the boundary question . . . *Santa
Fe* 1853. O 32 b one copy known.

FERNOW, BERTHOLD   92
The Ohio valley in colonial days. *Alb* 1890.
O 299 a

FERRALL, S[IMON] A.   93
A ramble of six thousand miles through the
United States . . . *L* 1832. O [12] 360 + 14adv-p
facs a
Author's name was actually O'Ferrall. Valuable
source for the Ill, and Ind. frontier.

FERRAN [AUGUSTO] and   94
BATURONE [JOSÉ]
Album Californiano . . . *Havanna* [ca 1849–50].
Q 12pls b *NYH*
Issued in three parts, of four plates each,
with wrappers; in two states, with plates colored
or uncolored.

FERRER MALDONADO (LORENZO).   95
Viaggio dal Mare Atlantico al Pacifico per la
via del Nord-Ouest fatto dal: Tradotto da una
manoscritto spagnuolo inedito da Carlo Amoretti.
Milan 1810. Q [4] 72 3maps aa
—rptd. n.p. 1810. same collat. aa
—anr. ed. *Milan* 1811. Q [4] 98 3maps errata lf.
describing 3rd map a
—rptd. *Bologna* 1812. Q [4] 96 3maps
—Fr. tr. *Plaisance* 1812. Q [8] 84 [4] 12maps[on
5sheets] a
This spurious voyage through Polar seas from
the Atlantic to the west coast of America, claimed
to have been made in 1588 by a famous Spanish
navigator, excited much controversy when first
published in 1810, but is no longer defended. A
nineteen-page Appendix was issued at Milan,
1813. *See* also L., B.V., *Die Glaubwürdigkeit* . . .

FERRI-PISANI, [MARCEL VICTOR   96
PAUL CAMILLE]
Lettres sur les États-Unis . . . *P* 1862. 16° [4]
455 a

FERRIS, BENJAMIN   97
A history of the original settlements on the
Delaware . . . *Wilm Del* 1846. O [12] 312 7maps
&pls a

FERRIS, BENJAMIN G.   98
Utah and the Mormons . . . from personal
observation . . . *N Y* 1854. D 347[incl.front.]
3pls a

FERRIS, MRS. BENJAMIN G.   99
The Mormons at home; with . . . incidents of
travel from Missouri to California . . . *N Y* 1856.
D [8] 299 + 4adv-p a

FERRIS, WARREN A.   100
Life in the Rocky mountains [1830–1835]. Ed.
Paul C. Phillips. *Denver* 1940. O [98] 365 map
5 pls aa
—anr. ed., ed. J. C. Alter, *S L C* [1940]. O 284
map 4pls a
First full-length description of the Yellowstone
region.

FERRY, GABRIEL [pseud.]
Impressions de voyages . . . see Bellemare,
Eugene L. G. de

FERRY, HYPOLITE [i.e., Hippolyte]   101
Description de la Nouvelle-Californië . . . *P*
1850. D [4] 386 8maps & pls aa
—anr. ed., same yr., same collat a
—Ital. tr. *Venice* 1851. O 340 pls

FERSLEW, WILLIAM C. L. E., comp.   102
. . . Kane county gazetteer . . . *Geneva Ill* 1857.
D [4] 48 [2] 49–198 + adv-l. aa

FERSLEW, WILLIAM C. L. E., comp.   103
. . . Rockford city register. No. 1. *Rockford*
1857. D [16] 25–136 + adv-l. at front aa

FESSENDEN, G[UY] M.   104
The history of Warren, Rhode Island. *Prov*
1845. 16° 125 a

FESSENDEN, THOMAS G.   105
Some thoughts on the present dispute between
Great Britain and America. *Phil* 1807. O 91 aa
Defends England's attitude on our neutrality
and hints that France was behind Burr's con-
spiracy.

FETHERSON, F. M.   106
Yarns round a prairie camp fire: or tales of
wild adventure in the far west. *L* [1860?]. D 61 a

FEVRET DE ST.-MÉMIN,   **107**
CHARLES B. J.
The St.-Mémin collection of portraits . . . principally of distinguished Americans . . . *N Y* 1862. F [8] 104 760ports[on 63pls] b NYP 100 cops ptd.

FEW
Few notes [A] respecting the United States . . .
See Stokes, C.

Few political reflections [A] submitted to the consideration of the British colonies. *See* Wells, Richard.

FIBBLETON, GEORGE [pseud.]
Travels in America. *See* Greene, Asa.

FICKER, CHRISTIAN T.   **108**
Freundlicher Rathgeber für alle, welche nach Amerika und vorzugsweise nach Wisconsin auswandern wollen. *Leip* 1853. D [4] 124 b N
By a German immigrant farmer in Wisconsin advocating that state as the most desirable for his countrymen.

FIDFADDY, FREDERICK A. [pseud.]   **109**
The adventures of Uncle Sam, in search after his lost honor . . . *Middletown Conn* 1816. D 142 a
Political allegory against the Democrats, chiefly concerned with War of 1812 affairs. The first book to symbolize the United States by the phrase "Uncle Sam."

FIDLER, ISAAC   **110**
Observations on professions, literature, manners . . . in the United States and Canada . . . *L* 1833. D [8] 434 + 10adv-p a
—Am. ed. *N Y* 1833. D [8] 13–247[mispaged 248]
Sweeping disparagement of a republic whose citizens were neither gentlemen nor scholars.

FIELD, DAVID D.   **111**
A history of . . . Haddam and East Haddam [Conn.]. *Middletown* 1814. O 48 a
—rptd. *N Y* 1892. O 200copies ptd.
—best ed *N Y* 1914

[FIELD, DAVID D., and DEWEY,   **112**
CHESTER]
A history of the county of Berkshire, Massachusetts . . . *Pittsfield* 1829. D 468 2maps 5pls a

FIELD, DAVID D.   **113**
A statistical account of the county of Middlesex, in Connecticut. *Middletown* 1819 O 154 a

FIELD, JOSEPH E.   **114**
Three years in Texas. Including a view of the . . . revolution . . . the principal battles [etc.]. *Greenfield Mass* 1836. D 36 b N S

—anr. ed., same impr. & date. D 47 b G LC
—anr. issue, same collat., *B* 1836. b Y
—rptd. *Austin* 1936. O 59 a
Field was one of two survivors of the Goliad massacre.

FIELD (STEPHEN J.)   **115**
Biographical notice of: . . . [By H. J. Field]. [*S F* 1892]. O 112 a

FIELD (STEPHEN J.)   **116**
Character and career of: as it is known in California. Field's infamy is Judge S. Terry's vindication. n.p. [1889?]. O 76 cover t.only a
Answer to Judge Field's *Personal reminiscences.*

FIELD, STEPHEN J.   **117**
Personal reminiscences of early days in California . . . n.p. [*S F* ?1880]. O [6] 248 aa
—anr. ed., with Gorham's account of Terry's attempted assassination of Field, [*Wash* 1893]. O [6] 472; also incl. in 1895 ed. of Chauncey F. Black's "Some account of the work of . . . Field," *q.v.* a
—anr. iss. smaller type. O [6] 406.

FIELD (STEPHEN J.)   **118**
A sketch of the life of: . . . *N Y* 1880. O 36 a

FIELD (STEPHEN J.)
Some account of the work of: *See* Black, Chauncey F.

FIELD, THOMAS W.   **119**
Historic and antiquarian scenes in Brooklyn . . . *Bklyn* priv. ptd. 1868. O [8] 96 map 11pls a only 100copies issued; of which there were 2 issues of p.23–26.

FIELD NOTES . . .
See Stevens, W. H.

FIELDER, HERBERT   **120**
The disunionist . . . the propriety of separation and the formation of a southern United States. n.p. 1858. O 72 a

FIELDER, HERBERT   **121**
A sketch of the life and times . . . of Joseph E. Brown. *Springfield Mass* 1883. O [4] 785 port a

FIGUEROA, JOSÉ   **122**
Manifiesto a la republica Mejicana . . . *Monterey* Zamorano 1835. D [2] 184 errata 1f dd B G Hn Y
—Eng. tr. [*S F*] 1855. O [2] 105 c B H NYP Y
—rptd' *Oakl* 1952 .O a
Second California printed book, first one of importance; in it Figueroa records and defends his administration of California affairs, 1833–1835.

FILISOLA, VICENTE   123
Analysis del Diario militar del General D.
José Urrea . . . *Matamoras* 1838. O 180 b S T x U
[only perfect cops loc].

FILISOLA, VICENTE   124
Manifiesto á la nacion. *Leona Vicaria Mex* 1836.
O 3–42 b S TxU Y [of 4 cops kin].
Relates largely to the Texas war.

FILISOLA, VICENTE   125
Memorias para la historia de la guerra de Tejas
[to June 1836] *Mex* Rafael 1848–9. D 2v: 587;
625 b N Y
—anr. issue, same impr. & date. D 2v in 1: 602
+ errata lf.; 625. Vol. I contains paginat. errors
and errata lf not found in 2v issue, hence this
issue may be the first. b Y

FILISOLA, VICENTE   126
Memorias para la historia de la guerra de
Tejas [to Oct. 1837]. *Mex* Cumplido 1849. O
2v: 512, *i.e.* 502 [2]; 267 b B NYP S Y
May be considered, though not so stated, as an
enlarged second edition of the preceding entry,
continuing the annals to the latter part of 1837,
but also containing the earlier events [to San
Jacinto] as given in the other. Both reprint valuable papers, the earlier volume including Almonte's
Statistical report on Texas, [*q.v.*]. The two together offer the most comprehensive history,
from the Mexican point of view, of the war for
Texas independence. General Filisola was active
on this frontier from 1833, was Santa Anna's
second-in-command, and led the Mexican army
on its retreat from San Jacinto.

FILISOLA, VICENTE   127
Representacion dirigida al Supremo Gobierno,
en defensa de su honor y aclaracion de sus opera-
ciones como General en Gefe del ejército sobre
Tejas. *Mex* 1836. O 82 b N NYP Y
—Eng. ed., "Evacuation of Texas . . .," *Columbia
Tex* 1837. D. [8 incl. blank lf] 3–68 c BA G Hn S Y
The English edition was, aside from legal
publications, the first book printed in Texas.
Account of the battle of San Jacinto and retreat to
Mexico by Santa Anna's second in command.

FILLEY (WILLIAM).   128
Life and adventures of: . . . stolen from his
home in Jackson, Mich., by the Indians . . . *Chi*
Fergus 1867. O 96 7 pls b
—ed. 2, *Chi* Filley & Ballard 1867. O 112 [incl.
8pls] aa
Remained in captivity 29 years.

FILSON, JOHN   129
The discovery, settlement [etc.] of Kentucke . . .
Wilm Del 1784. O 118 with map [which was ptd
at Phil., sold separately & not issued with the

book]dd AA N LC PhilL without map d N Y
—rptd *Lousv* 1934 O [12] 118 map a
—Eng. ed. *L* 1793. O 67 5adv.-p map[by Hutchins]
b N NYP Y
—Fr. tr. with adds. *P* 1785. O [20] 234 map aa
—Ger. trs: *Frankf* 1785. O 254; *Nuremb* 1789. O
124; *Leip* 1790. O 124 a
First book on Kentucky and most notable
product from the pen of a Western pioneer.
Cf. Imlay, Gilbert, and Trumbull, Henry.

FINAN, P.   130
Journal of a voyage to Quebec . . . with recol
lections of Canada, during the late American
war . . . 1812–14. *Newry* 1828. D [6] 400 errata slip a

FINCH, J[OHN]   131
Travels in the United States and Canada . . .
L 1833. O [16] 455 errata slip a

FINCH, MARIANNE   132
An Englishwoman's experience in America.
L 1853. O [8] 386 a
—rptd. *L* 1857.

FINDLEY, WILLIAM   133
History of the insurrection, in the four western
counties of Pennsylvania . . . 1794 . . . *Phil* 1796.
O 328 a

FINDLEY, WILLIAM   134
Observations on "The two sons of oil" . . .
Pitt 1812. D 366 errata slip a

[FINDLEY, WILLIAM]   135
A review of the revenue system . . . under the
federal constitution . . . *Phil* 1794. O [4] 130 a

FINERTY, JOHN F.   136
War-path and bivouac, or the conquest of the
Sioux . . . *Chi* [1890]. O [22] 25–460 map 18pls a
—rptd. without maps or pls, *Chi* n. d.
—anr ed *Chi* 1955. D [56] 379 12pls

FINEST PART [THE] OF AMERICA.
See Varlo, Charles.

FINLAY, HUGH   137
Journal . . . kept during his survey of the post
offices between Falmouth . . . Massachusetts, and
Savannah . . . *Bklyn* 1867. Q [28] 94 2maps
175copies[25 on L.P.] aa

FINLAYSON, ARCHIBALD W.   138
A trip to America . . . *Glas* 1879. O 54 a

[FINLAYSON, DUNCAN]   139
Traits of American-Indian life and character.
By a fur trader. *L* 1853. D [16] 220 + 16 adv-p b
—rptd. *S F* Grabhorn 1933. O 107 6pls a 500
copies ptd.

Attributed also to another Hudson's Bay Co. trader, Peter Skene Ogden, as many of his adventures in the Oregon country are related.

FINLEY, A[NTHONY], pub.   **140**
A new American atlas. *Phil* 1826. F [4] 15maps aa

FINLEY, ALEXANDER C.   **141**
The history of Russellville and Logan county, Kentucky... Vol. I [all]. *Russellville* 1878–90. O 5pts in 3: 60; 100; 63 aa
One wonders how the author could have remained in this community after perpetrating such unvarnished personal commentaries.

FINLEY, ISAAC J., and   **142**
PUTNAM, RUFUS
Pioneer record of the early settlers... of Ross county, Ohio. *Cin* 1871. O 148 a

FINLEY (JAMES B.).   **143**
Autobiography of: or, pioneer life in the west. *Cin* 1853. D 455[incl. front. & 7pls] a
—rptd., same impr.: 1854; 1857

FINLEY, JAMES B.   **144**
History of the Wyandotte mission at Upper Sandusky... *Cin* 1840. D 432 a

FINLEY, JAMES B.   **145**
Life among the Indians... *Cin* 1857. D 548 2ports a
—rptd., same collat., 1860; 1868.

FINLEY, JAMES B.   **146**
Sketches of western Methodism... *Cin* 1854. D 551 port a

FIRST   **147**
First book [The] of the American chronicles of the times. Chaps. 1–6 [all]. *Phil* [1774–5]. D 70 aa
—rptd. [5 chaps. only], same date, *B* D 58; Norwich. same collat. aa
—anr. ed. [4 chaps. only], same date. *Prov* D 32 aa
Covers, in scriptural style, events of 1774; each chapter was also issued separately.

First impressions of America. *See* Walter, John.

First impressions of the new world... *See* Trotter, Isabella.

First steamship pioneers. [*S F* 1874]. Q   **147a**
[14] 393 11 pls[in some copies only] a

FISCH, GEORGES   **148**
Les États-Unis en 1861. *P* 1862. D 238 a
—Eng. ed. "Nine months in the United States...," *L* 1863. D [16] 166 a

FISCHER, JOSEPH   **148a**
Die Entdeckungen der Normannen... *Freiburg* 1902. O [12] 126 front. 10maps a
—Eng. ed. "The discoveries of the Norsemen in America...," *L* 1902. large O [24] 130 [2] front. 10maps.
—rptd. same impr. & collat. 1903.
—Am. ed. *St L* 1903.

[FISH, REEDER McCANDLESS]   **149**
The grim chieftain of Kansas [Jim Lane]... By one who knows. *Cherryvale Kas* 1885. 16° [4] 145 b

FISHER, ELIJAH   **149a**
Journal while in the war for independence. *Augusta Me* 1880. O 29 a

FISHER, ELWOOD   **150**
Lecture on the north and the south... *Charleston S C* 1849. O 24 a
—ed. 2, same impr., date & collat.
—other eds., same date: *Rich* O 31; *Cin* O 64

FISHER (EZRA).   **150a**
Correspondence of: n.p. [1919]. O 492 a
Largely on early Oregon missions.

FISHER, GEORGE   **151**
Memorials... [to the Congress] of Texas... *Houston* 1840. O 87 + 21fold-p b B G NYP Y
Concerning General Mexia's 1835 expedition against Tampico, the first armed demonstration by Texans against Mexico.

[FISHER, JABEZ]   **151a**
Americanus examined, and his principles compared with those of the approved advocates for America. *Phil* 1774. O 24 a
"Americanus" was the pseudonym used by Caleb Evans in his *Letter to John Wesley. q.v.*

FISHER, ORCENETH   **152**
Sketches of Texas in 1840... *Springfield Ill* 1841. 16° 64 b G IH LC [of 4 copies known]

FISHER, RICHARD S.   **152a**
Indiana:... its geography, etc. *N Y* 1852. D 126 map a
—rptd. same impr & collat 1854.

[FISHER, VARDIS, ed.]   **153**
Idaho; a guide... *Caldwell Ida* 1937. D 431 15maps 128 pls [on 64 sheets] aa

FISHER, WILLIAM [comp.]   **153a**
New travels among the Indians... taken partly from the communications... of Captains Lewis and Clark and partly from other authors... *Phil* 1812. D 300 2ports a some copies have 2t-p aa

—anr. issue, "An interesting account of the voyages and travels of Captains Lewis and Clark ...," *Balt* 1812. D 326 2ports [incl. in paginat.] a
—rptd. *Balt* 1813. 16° 266 2ports 4pls[in some copies only 3]
For an earlier edition of this spurious or unauthorized account of Lewis and Clark, *see* Lewis and Clark, *Travels.*

FISK (JAMES) JR.
A life of: *N Y* 1868. *See* Stafford, Marshall P.

FISK, CAPT. JAMES L.   154
Expedition from Fort Abercrombie to Fort Benton ... H. Exec. Doc. 80. [*Wash* 1863]. O 36 a
In some copies is inserted a map, which was printed later. aa

FISK (CAPTAIN [JAMES L.])   154a
Expedition of: to the Rocky mountains ... [Sen. Doc.]. *Wash* 1864. O 38 a
—anr. issue, [House Doc.], *Wash* 1864. O 39
Captain Fisk commanded an escort for an Idaho emigrant party.

FISK, CAPT. JAMES L.   155
Idaho; her gold fields and the routes to them. *N Y* 1863. 16° 99 map b G MinnH WisH

FISKE, FRANK B.   155a
The taming of the Sioux ... *Bismarck* [1917]. O 186 [incl. blank lf & front] a

FITCH, FRANKLYN Y., ed.   156
Life, travels and adventures of Alonzo De Milt ... among the Indians ... in the gold mines ... *N Y* [1883]. D [2] 228 + 48 adv-p 12pls a

FITCH, JOHN, 1743–98   156a
The original steam-boat supported; or, a reply to Mr. James Rumsey's pamphlet ... *Phil* 1788. O [34] [20]
—issue 1, with cor. by hand & Rumsey's plan incl. aa
—issue 2, cor. by type & omitting Rumsey's plan, same impr. & date. O 34

FITCH, MICHAEL H.   157
Ranch life and other sketches. Vol. I [all]. *Pueblo* 1914. D 309 [2] a 150 cops ptd

[FITCH, THOMAS]   158
Reasons why the British colonies ... should not be charged with internal taxes by authority of Parliament ... *N Hav* 1764. O [39] b AA NYP Y

FITCH [THOMAS] & CO., pub.   159
Directory of ... Placerville, Upper Placerville, El Dorado, Georgetown and Coloma, containing a history ... *Placerville* 1862. D 128 correction slip aa

FITE, EMERSON D., and FREEMAN, ARCHIBALD   160
A book of old maps ... *C* 1926. F [16] 299 [incl. 74maps] col. map as front. aa

FITE, EMERSON D.   161
Social and industrial conditions in the north during the civil war. *N Y* 1910. O [8] 318 a

FITHIAN, PHILIP V.   162
Journals and letters ... 1767–1774. *Princeton* 1900. O [24] 320 8pls aa
—Journals, 1775–76, *Princeton* 1934. O [18] 279 2 maps a
—Journals, 1773–74, *Wmsbg* 1943. O [14 incl. front] 323 7 pls a

FITZGERALD, ROSS   163
A visit to the cities and camps of the Confederate States. *L* 1865. D [6] 300 map aa

FITZHUGH, GEORGE   164
Cannibals all! or, slaves without masters. *Rich* 1857. D 379 + 4adv-p aa
Influenced profoundly southern belief in Negro inferiority.

FITZHUGH, GEORGE   165
Sociology for the south; or, the failure of free society. *Rich* 1854. D 310 aa
First work on sociology produced in this country.

FITZ-JAMES (ZILLAH)   166
Fitz-James (Zillah) the female bandit of the southwest ... *Little Rock* [ptd. Buffalo?] 1852. O 32 [incl. front] aa
—anr. ed., same collat., *N Y* n.d. aa
For her male consort, *See* Long, Green H.

FITZMAURICE, JOHN W.   167
"The shanty boy," or, life in a lumber camp ... discriptions [*sic*] ... in the lumbering shanties of Michigan and Wisconsin. *Cheboygan* 1889. O 246 + 12adv-p [4 front, 8 rear] b Burton LC N Y
As a narrative of the lumbering industry unequalled; as a picture of Michigan pioneer life comparable to Nowlin's *The bark covered house.*

FIVE YEARS IN THE WEST ...
By a Texas preacher. *See* Allen, Wm. M.

FLACK, CAPT.   168
A hunter's experience in the southern states ... *L* Longmans 1866. *See* St. John, Percy B.

FLAGET, MONSEIGNEUR [BENEDICT J.]
Évêque de Bardstown et Louisville. Sa vie ... par le prêtre qui accompagnait le prélat ... *See* Desgeorges, Abbé.

[FLAGG, EDMUND T.]   169
The far west; or, a tour beyond the mountains . . . *N Y* 1838. D 2v: [16] 13–263; [12] 9–241 aa
Extensive travels, by an Ohio journalist, through Missouri and Illinois.

FLANDRAU, CHARLES E.   170
Narrative of the Indian war of 1862–1864 . . . in Minnesota, n.p. n.d. O 90 a

FLANIGAN, J. H.   171
Mormonism triumphant! . . . a reply to Palmer's Internal evidence against the Book of Mormon. *Liv* 1849. O 32 a

FLEISCHMANN, C[ARL] L.   172
Erwerbszweige, fabrikwesen und handel der Vereinigten Staaten . . . *Stuttgart* 1850. O [10] 616 a
—ed. 2, same impr., 1852. O [4] 612 [5–10] 613–616

FLEISCHMANN, C[ARL] L.   173
Neuste officielle Berichte an die Regierung der Verein. Staaten über die . . . Californiens. *Stuttgart* 1850. D [8] 64 b NYP Y
A translation of Thomas Butler King's *Report* . . ., *q.v.*

FLEISCHMANN, C[ARL] L.   174
Der nordamerikanische Landwirth . . . *Frankf* 1848. O [14] 399 a
—ed. 2, same impr. 1852. O [14] 400 fold. map

FLEISCHMANN, C[ARL] L.   175
Wegweiser und Rathgeber nach und in den Vereinigten Staaten . . . *Stuttgart* 1852 O [4] 500 map aa
—rptd. same impr & date a

FLEMING, E. B.,   176
Early history of Hopkins county, Texas . . . n.p. 1902. D 183 aa

FLEMING, FRANCIS   177
Memoir of Capt. C. Seton Fleming, of the 2nd Fla. Inf., C. S. A. . . . *Jacksonv* 1884. O 125 aa

[FLEMING, G. A.]   178
California: its past history; its present position; [etc.]. *L.* 1850. O [8] 270 eng.t. 9pls map all col. by hand c Y
One of the fullest and most interesting of contemporary accounts. The complete complement of nine plates is not found in all copies: the ordinary issue had only three. b

FLEMING, ROBERT   179
Sketch of the life of Elder Humphrey, first Baptist missionary to the Cherokee Indians . . . [*Phil*?] 1852. 16° 103 port a

FLEMING, W. S.   180
A historical sketch of Maury county [Tenn.]. *Columbia Tenn* 1876. O [2] 65 a

FLEMING, WALTER L.   181
Civil war and reconstruction in Alabama. *N Y* 1905. O [24] 816 + adv-p 12 pls aa

FLEMING, WALTER L.   182
Documentary history of reconstruction. *Clev* 1906–7. O 2v: [20] 493; [18] 3–480. 9facs aa
—rptd. *N Y* 1950. O 2v in 1 a

FLEMING (WILLIAM, and ELIZABETH).   183
A narrative of the sufferings . . . of: . . . taken captive by . . . Indians . . . in Pennsylvania [etc.]. *Phil* no printer named, for the benefit of the unhappy sufferers [1756]. D 28 d 1 copy known [Brinley]
—other 1756 eds. [priority not determined]: *Phil* Jas. Chattin, for the unhappy sufferers, D 28 d no perfect copy known; *B* O 20 c AA MH; *Lancaster* c Evans [no collat. given]; *N Y* c Evans[no collat. given]
—ed. 2, *Phil* Jas. Chattin 1756. c Evans [no collat. given]
—Ger. tr. *Lancaster* 1756. 16° 29 b AA N PaH

FLEMING, [WILLIAM H.], &   184
TORREY, comps.
The Twin Cities directory; including Davenport . . . Rock Island . . . Moline . . . *Davenport* 1856. D 144 aa

[FLETCHER, MISS A.]   185
Within Fort Sumter; or, a view of Major Anderson's garrison family for one hundred and ten days. By one of the company. *N Y* 1861. D 72 a

FLETCHER (BENJAMIN) . . .   186
An account of the treaty between: and the Indians of the Five Nations . . . *N Y* 1694. Q 39 c BM
First Indian treaty printed in N.Y.

FLETCHER, CHARLES H.   187
Jefferson county, Iowa. *Fairfield Ia* 1876. O 36 aa

FLETCHER, DANIEL C.   188
Reminiscences of California and the civil war. *Ayer Mass* 1894. O 196 port a

FLETCHER (EBENEZER).   189
A narrative of the captivity [etc.] of: *Amherst* 1798. O 26 c NHH NYP [of 3 known copies]
—rptd. *Windsor Vt* 1813. D 22 b AA LC N
—anr. ed., styled "ed. 4," rev. & enl., *New Ipswich N H* 1827. D 24 b AA N
—rptd., same place, same collat., n.d. [1828?]. aa
—anr. ed., ed. Bushnell, with notes, *N Y* 1866. O 86 port a

Fletcher was captured by Indians while serving in the 1777 campaign against Burgoyne.

**FLETCHER, LIEUT.-COLONEL   190
[HENRY C.]**
History of the American war . . . *L* 1865–6. O 3v: [16] 454 + adv-l; [12] 446 + adv.l-; [14] 550. 20pls 7 maps a

FLETCHER, REV. J[OHN]   191
American patriotism farther confronted . . . *Shrewsbury Eng* 1776. D [8] 130 aa
—rptd. *L* 1777. a

FLETCHER'S . . . ARGUMENTS   192
Fletcher's (The Rev. John) arguments . . . in his "Vindication of the Calm address" in defence of the assumed right . . . to tax America, considered. By a member of the Rev. Mr. Wesley's Society. *L* 1776. O 70 a

FLETCHER, REV. JOHN   193
A vindication of the Rev. Mr. Wesley's "Calm address to our American colonies" . . . *L* [1776]. D [4] 70 a
—rptd. *Dub* 1776. O

FLETCHER, WILLIAM A.   194
A rebel private, front and rear . . . *Beaumont Tex* 1908. O 193[incl.port] aa
—rptd. *Austin* 1954 a
Best personal narrative by a Confederate private. Most of the edition was destroyed by fire.

FLEURIEU, C[HARLES] P. C.   195
Voyage autour du monde . . . 1790–2. *P* [1798–1800]. Q 4v: [12 144] 628 [3]; [16 incl. initial blank l.] 676 [2]; [12] 432 [2]; [10] 159. 15maps pl tab b JCB N
—anr. ed. *P* [1798–1800]. O 5v [300] 294 [1]; [6] 530; [8] 475; [8] 494 [2]; [12] 560 [4] + Atlas Q [15maps pl] b
—Eng. tr. *L* 1801. Q 2v: [140] 361; [12] 503 105 + Atlas [8maps] b
—anr. issue, same impr. & date. O 2v: [16] [192] 536; [14] 663 105 + Atlas Q [8maps] aa
—Ger. ed. "Die neuste Reise um die Welt . . .," *Leip* n.d. O 2v map pl aa
This French circumnavigation, under Marchand, was preceded only by Bougainville's. It added considerably to the scanty knowledge of Northwest America and included a scholarly survey of earlier maritime explorers.

FLICKINGER, ROBERT E.   196
Pioneer history of Pocahontas county [Ia.]. *Fonda Ia* 1904. O [24] 9–990 a

FLINT, HENRY M.   197
The railroads of the United States; their history . . . *Phil* 1868. D 452 a

FLINT, JAMES   198
Letters from America, containing observations on the . . . western states. *Edin* 1822. O [8] 330 + 2 adv-p aa
—Am. ed., ed. Thwaites, *Clev* 1904. O a

FLINT, TIMOTHY   199
Biographical memoir of Daniel Boone, the first settler of Kentucky . . . *Cin* 1833. D 267 port aa
—other *C*in eds.: 1834; 1840; 1841; 1842; 1846; 1849; 1850; 1851; 1854; 1856; 1857; 1858. a
—rev. ed. "Life and adventures of Daniel Boone . . .," *Cin* 1868. D 256 map 3pls

FLINT, TIMOTHY   200
A condensed geography and history of the western states . . . *Cin* 1828. O 2v: 592; 520 errata slip aa
—ed. 2, enl., "The history and geography of the Mississippi valley . . .," *Cin* 1832. O 2v in 1: 464; 276 a
—ed. 3, *Cin* 1833. O 2v in 1: 469; 310
—rptd. *Cin* 1839.

FLINT, TIMOTHY   201
Indian wars of the west . . . *Cin* 1833. D 240 a
—rptd., same impr. 1838.

FLINT (TIMOTHY).   202
Journal of: from the Red river, to the Ouachitta . . . in Louisiana, in 1835. [*Alexandria La* 1835]? D 31 b LC [only cop loc]
—rptd. in "Waldie's Library," *Cin* 1836; some copies carry *Phil* impr. a

FLINT, TIMOTHY   203
The lost child. *B* 1830. 16° 121 a
—rptd. "Little Henry, etc." *B* 1847 16° 143 a
Adventures of Henry Howe, stolen from his Arkansas home and found five years later in New Orleans.

FLINT, TIMOTHY   204
Recollections of the last ten years . . . in the valley of the Mississippi. *B* 1826. O [2] 395 aa
—rptd. N Y 1932. D 380 facsm a

FLORIDA
Account of East Florida: . . . its future importance . . . *See* Stork, Wm.

An account of the surveys of Florida: . . . *See* Lorimer, John.

**The case of the inhabitants of East Flo-   205
rida:** . . . *St Augustine* 1784. O [4] 58 d JCB S [only copies located]
First book printed in Florida, with possible exception of Samuel Gale's *Essay . . . on public credit*, of the same date. Protest by Florida loyalists against this province being ceded to Spain.

Coleccion de varios documentos para la historia de la Florida y tierras adjacentes: *See* Smith, Buckingham.

A concise narrative of General Jackson's first invasion of Florida: By Aristides. *See* Van Ness, Wm. P.

Crisis del Ensayo a la historia de la Florida: *See* Salazar, Joseph de.

A description of East Florida: ... *L* 1769. *See* Stork, Wm.

Documentos historicos de la Florida y la   206
Louisiana: siglos XVI al XVIII. *Madrid* 1913. Q [8] 466 errata l. a

Documents in proof of the climate and   207
soil of Florida: ... *N Y* 1832. O 28 aa
—enl. ed. *N Y* 1835, O 68 [4] aa

Ensayo cronologico, para la historia general de la Florida. *See* Barcia Carballido y Zuniga, Andrés González de.

Florida and Taxas ... comparing the soil, climate ... *See* Byrne, Bernard M.

Florida colonist [The], or settler's guide.   208
Jacksonville [1870]. O 68 a
—ed. 2, enl., same impr. 1871. O [2] 86 map

Florida: its climate, etc. *Jacksonv* 1868.   209
O 68 aa
—enl ed, same impr 1869. O [4] 151 a
—anr ed *N Y* 1869. O 128 map pl
—rptd *Jacksonv* 1870. O 69 map pl

Florida pirate [The], or, an account of a   210
cruise in the schooner Esparanza ... *N Y* Borradaile 1823. D 24 col.port a
—anr. ed., ship's name given correctly as "Esperanza," Johnstone & Van Norden, same date. D 24 2pls
This pirate, a colored man named Manuel, was hanged at Charleston.

Notices of East Florida: with an account   211
of the Seminole nation ... By a recent traveller [etc.[. *Charleston* 1822. D 106 aa
Authorship has been ascribed to a Colonel Simmons.

Ordinances adopted by the convention of   212
West Florida: *Natchez* 1810. O 32 b BP NYH

Sketches of the Indian war in Florida: 213
N Y 1837. O 24 3pls[incl. in paginat] b NYP

A true and authentic account of the Indian war in Florida: *See Seminole war [the]. An authentic narrative of:* ...

Verscheyde Scheeps-togten na Florida: 214
door Pontius, Ribald, Laudonniere, Gourgues en andere ... *Leyden* Vander Aa 1706. O [2] 171 [18] map 33pls a

The war in Florida: ... its causes [etc.]. By a late staff officer. *See* Potter, Woodburn.

FLORIDAS   215
Message from the President ... communicating the correspondence ... in relation to the treaty for the session of the Floridas: *Wash* 1820. O 32 [8] a

An original memoir on the Floridas: ... By a gentleman of the south. *See* Coale, Edw. J.

FLORIDE (LA).
Recueil de pièces sur: ... *See* Ternaux-Compans, Henri.

FLORY, J[ACOB] S.   216
Thrilling echoes from the frontier ... *Chi* 1893. D [6] 17-248 + 2 adv-p 8pls a

FLOWER, GEORGE   217
The errors of emigrants ... and a description of the ... English settlement in Illinois ... *L* [1841]. D 64 aa

FLOWER, GEORGE   218
... History of the English settlement in Edwards county, Illinois ... *Chi* 1882. O [4] 10, 9–402 2ports a

FLOWER, RICHARD   219
Letters from Lexington [Ky.] and the Illinois ... *L* 1819. O 32 b AA LC N Y

FLOWER, RICHARD   220
Letters from the Illinois; containing an account of the English settlement at Albion ... *L* 1822. O 76 b
Supplements his earlier *Letters from Lexington and the Illinois.*

[FLOWERS, R. W.]   221
From ocean to ocean ... diary of a three month's expedition from Liverpool to California ... [*L*] 1871. O 108 a

FLOYD (CHARLES).
The new found journal of: *See* Butler, James D.

FOGG (MAJOR JEREMIAH).   222
Journal of: during the expedition of Gen. Sullivan ... *Exeter N H* 1879. O [2] 24 a 150copies ptd.

FOLLETT, FREDERIK 223
History of the press of western New York ...
Roch 1847. O [2] 76 a

FOLSOM, BENJAMIN 224
A compilation of biographical sketches of ...
officers in the American navy. *Newburyport* 1814.
O 187 a

FOLSOM, GEORGE 225
History of Saco and Biddeford ... Maine.
Saco 1830. D 331 map pl aa

[FOLSOM, GEORGE F.] 226
Mexico in 1842. *N Y* 1842. 16° 256 map aa
Includes account of Texas and a narrative, by
Franklin Coombs, of the Texas expedition against
Santa Fe. Ascribed also to Charles J. Folsom,
publisher of the book.

FOLSOM, JAMES M. 227
Heroes and martyrs of Georgia ... in the
revolution of 1861. Vol. I [all[. *Macon* 1864. O
164 aa

FOLSOM, W. H. C. 228
Fifty years in the northwest [*i.e.* the Minnesota-
Wisconsin region]. [*St P*] 1888. O [44] 763 16pls a

FOND DU LAC COUNTY [WIS.] 229
Centennial directory of: ... *Fond du Lac* 1876.
O 412 a

FONT'S ... DIARY
Font's [Pedro] complete diary. *See* Bolton,
Herbert E.

FONTAINE, FELIX G. DE 230
History of American abolitionism ... with a
history of the Southern Confederacy ... *N Y* 1861.
O 66 a
—anr. issue, same date, impr. & collat., but with
shortened title.

[FONTAINE, FELIX G. DE] 231
Marginalia; or gleanings from an army note-
book. By "Personne." *Columbia S C* 1864. O
[8] 248 + 8adv-p[incl. covers] a

FONTAINE, JAMES 232
A tale of the Huguenots; or, memoirs of a
French Huguenot family. *N Y* 1838. D [12] 266 a
—anr. ed. enl. "Memoirs of a Huguenot family
...," *N Y* 1853. D 512 2 ports aa
—rptd. *N Y* 1872; [1900] .a
Includes original journal of travels in Virginia,
New York, etc., 1715-16. The 1853 ed. gives an
account, written in 1756, of a plan to explore the
far west by way of the Missouri, fore-shadowing
by 50 years that of Lewis and Clark.

FONTANE, MARIUS É. 233
La guerre d'Amérique. Récit d'un soldat du
sud. *P* [1866–70]. D 2v: [4] 304; [2] 265. map a
—Ital. tr. *Milan* 1870. D 400

FONTE [OR FUENTE] (ADMIRAL DE).
The great probability of a north west passage
... from observations on the letter of: *See*
Jefferys, Thos.

FONTE [FUENTE] (L'AMIRAL DE).
Nouvelles cartes des decouvertes de: ... *See*
De L'Isle, Jos. N.

FONTENAY, MARIE
L'autre monde. *See* Grandfort, Marie F. de.

FONTICELLI, ANTONIO 234
Americologia; ossia osservazioni storiche ...
Con un breve ragguaglio delle ultime scoperte
fatte dai Russi nel mar Pacifico. *Genoa* 1790.
D 123 a

FOOS, JOSEPH 235
The highway of all nations. *Columbus O* 1820.
O 24 b BA Y
First book advocating American settlement of
the Pacific coast.

FOOTE, HENRY S. 236
Bench and bar of the south and the south-west
St L 1876. O [8] 264 a

FOOTE, HENRY S. 237
Casket of reminiscences. *Wash* 1874. O [4] 498
aa

FOOTE, HENRY S. 238
Texas and the Texans: or advance of the
Anglo-Americans to the southwest ... *Phil* 1841.
D 2v: [8] 13–314; 403 aa
—rptd. *Austin* 1935. D 2v a
Though no map was issued with the first
edition, Young's map [published by Mitchell] is
so frequently found inserted as to breed the con-
jecture that the publisher had acquired copies
made to accompany a never-published but contemplated third volume, and that he disposed of
them to later buyers of the two volumes, for
insertion therein.

FOOTE, HENRY S. 239
War of the rebellion ... observations upon the
causes, course and consequences of the late civil
war ... *N Y* 1866. D [2] 440 port a

FOOTE, WILLIAM H. 240
Sketches of North Carolina ... *N Y* 1846. O
557 a
—rptd. 1912.

FOOTE, WILLIAM H.   **241**
Sketches of Virginia. [Series I]. *Phil* 1850. O
[8] 568 port a
—[Series II] *Phil* 1855. O 596 port a
—rev. ed. 1856.

FORBES, ALEXANDER   **242**
California: a history ... *L* 1839. O [16] 352
port map 9pls errata slip b
—rptd. *S F* 1919. O [26] 372 map 10pls 250
copies ptd. aa
—anr. ed. *S F* 1937. O [32] 230 map front. 2facs
First book in the English language devoted
exclusively to California and of permanent value
on its Indians and early missions.

FORBES, JAMES G.   **243**
Sketches, historical [etc]. of the Floridas ...
N Y 1821. O 226 + adv-l. map[not issued in all
copies] a

FORBES, ROBERT B.   **244**
Personal reminiscences. *B* 1876. D [8] 382 [5] a
—rptd., with pls added, *B* 1878; *B* 1892. D 412
4pls
Maritime experiences; including a voyage to
California in 1825 and later visits there.

FORCE, PETER, ed.   **245**
American archives. [Ser. IV, v. 1–6; ser. V,
v. 1–3] all published. *Wash* 1837–53. Q 9v maps
facs b
More volumes, covering other periods of the
seventeenth and eighteenth centuries, were planned, but only the above nine [six of the Fourth and
three of the Fifth series] appeared.

FORCE, PETER   **246**
The Declaration of Independence, or notes on
Lord Mahon's History ... *L* 1855. O 66 a

FORCE, PETER, ed.   **247**
Tracts ... relating principally to the origin,
settlement, and progress of the colonies in North
America ... to 1776. *Wash* 1836–46. O 4v b
AA B N NYP Y
—rptd. *N Y* 1947. O 4 vois aa
—rptd. [in part] "American colonial tracts ...,"
18nos in 2v [all], *Syracuse* Humphrey 1897–8. a
Some of these 52 tracts appeared here in print
for the first time; all are separately paged, the
reprinted ones with title-pages.

FORD, GUY S., ed.   **248**
Essays in American history dedicated to Frederick Jackson Turner. *N Y* 1910. O 293 a

FORD, HENRY A.   **249**
The history of Putnam and Marshall counties
... *Lacon Ill* 1860. 16° [8] 160 aa

FORD, HENRY C.   **250**
Etchings of the Franciscan missions of California ... *N Y* 1883, F 28 24pls b only 50copies
ptd. Pub'd at $150 [00]

FORD, PAUL L., ed.   **251**
Essays on the Constitution ... 1787–1788.
Bklyn 1892. O [8] 424 a 500copies ptd.

FORD, PAUL L., ed.   **252**
Pamphlets on the Constitution. *Bklyn* 1888. O
[12] 451 a 500copies ptd.

FORD, SALLY [R.]   **253**
Raids and romance of Morgan and his men.
Mobile 1863. O 318 b [no cop kn]
—ed. 2, same impr. 1864. O 332 + 2adv.-p aa
—rptd. *N Y* 1864. D 417[incl.port] a
Chiefly historical, but considerably fictionalized.
Federal soldiers devoured this incendiary appeal
for Southern independence; Rosecrans, fearing
its effect, banned its being read by a general order
of June, 1864.

FORD, THOMAS   **254**
A history of Illinois ... *Chi* 1854. D [2] 447 +
6adv-p a
—rptd., ed. Quaife, *Chi* 1945–6. 16° 2v

[FORD, TIMOTHY]   **255**
The constitutionalist ... *Charleston S C* 1794.
O 55 aa

[FORD, TIMOTHY?]   **256**
An enquiry into the constitutional authority of
the supreme federal court, over the several states
... *Charleston S C* 1792. O 49 aa

FORDHAM, ELLIAS P.   **257**
Personal narrative of travels in Virginia, etc;
and of a residence in the Illinois Territory: 1817–
1818. *Clev* 1906. O 248 + 10adv p 4pls [incl. in
paginat[. a
First printing of this account of life in Birkbeck's
Illinois colony.

FORE AND AFT
Fore and aft; or, leaves from the life of an
old sailor. By "Webfoot." *See* Phelps, Wm. D.

FOREMAN, GRANT   **258**
Indian removal; the emigration of the Five
Civilized Tribes ... *Norman Okla* 1932. O 415
20 maps & pls aa
—ed 2, same impr. & collat [1953] a

FOREMAN, GRANT   **259**
Indians and pioneers ... the American southwest before 1830. *N Hav* 1930. O [18] 348 map
8pls a
—rev. ed. *Norman Okla* 1936. O [18] 302 map 8pls

FOREMAN, GRANT 260
Pioneer days in the early southwest ... *Clev* 1926. O 349[incl. pls] fold.map aa

FORENSIC DISPUTE [A]
Forensic dispute (A) on the legality of enslaving the Africans ... *See* Parsons, Theo., and Pearson, Eliphalet.

FOREST, P[RUDENT] 261
Voyage aux États-Unis d'Amérique en 1831. *Lyon* 1834. O 95 a

FORMAN, HENRY C. 262
Early manor and plantation houses of Maryland ... *Easton* 1934. Q 271 front, a

FORMAN, SAMUEL S. 263
Narrative of a journey down the Ohio and Mississippi in 1789-90. *Cin* 1888. O 67 a
Written at the age of 94. What a man!

FORNEY, JOHN W. 264
What I saw in Texas. *Phil* [1872]. O 92 a

FORREST, EARLE R. 265
Arizona's dark and bloody ground. *Caldwell*, 1936. D 370 pls a
—rptd. with adds same impr 1948.

[FORREST, MICHAEL] 266
The political reformer ... *Phil* 1797. O 73 a

FORREST, WILLIAM S. 267
Historical ... sketches of Norfolk ... [Va.]. *Phil* 1853. O [32] 496 pl a

[FORRESTER, ALFRED H.] 268
A good natured hint about California ... *L* Bogue [1849]. obl O [8] 35pls a

FORSTER, JOHANN REINHOLD 269
Geschichte der Entdeckungen und Schiffahrten im Norden ... *Frankf* 1784. O [24] 446 449–596 [2] 2maps front aa
—rptd., au's. initials "J. H.," *Berlin* n.d. same collat.
—Eng. ed. "History of the voyages and discoveries made in the north ...," *L* 1786. Q [24] 490 [16] + adv-l. 3 maps aa
—rptd. *Dub* 1786. O [24] 489 [30] map a
—Fr. tr. *P* 1788. O 2v: [16] 399; [12] 410. 3maps a

FORSTER, JOHANN REINHOLD, tr.
Tagebuch eine Entdekkungs-Reise nach der sud-see ... [1776–1780] ... unter ... Cook, Clark, Gore und King. See under Rickman, John, of whose account this is a trans.

FORSYTH, GEORGE A. 270
The story of the soldier. *N Y* 1900. D [6] 390 + 10adv-p 6pls a

FORSYTH, GEORGE A. 271
Thrilling days in army life ... *N Y* 1900. D [8] 3–197 + 2adv-p 16 pls a

FORSYTH, JAMES W., and GRANT, F. D. 272
Report of an expedition up the Yellowstone ... *Wash* 1875. O 17 fold.map 5pls a

FORT DEFIANCE
Fort Defiance to the Colorado river. Wagon road from: See Beale, Edw. F.

FORT DUQUESNE
Fort Duquesne (Old); a tale ... of the first settlers at the forks of the Ohio. *See* McKnight, Chas.

FORT SCOTT ... DIRECTORY 273
Fort Scott [Kansas] city directory ... for 1865–6. Containing ... a sketch of the city, a chapter on Price's raid [etc.]. [*Ft. Scott* 1865]. O 78 aa

FORT SILL COUNTRY (THE) ... 274
Duncan Okla 1894. O 31 map a

FORT SMITH 275
Fort Smith and Sebastian county. Hand book of: *Chi* 1887. Q 36 aa

FORT SMITH, ARKANSAS 276
Fort Smith, Arkansas: its history ... n.p. [*Ft Smith*?] [*ca* 1893]. O 28 a
—anr. issue, n.p. n.d. O 23

FORT SUMTER. 277
The battle of Fort Sumter and first victory of southern troops ... *Charleston S C* 1861. O 32 aa
—anr. issue, same date & impr. O 35 map aa
For similar title, *See* Smyth, Thomas.

Within Fort Sumter; or, a view of Major Anderson's garrison family ... *See* Fletcher, Miss A.

FORT SUTTER PAPERS (THE).
A transcript of: *See* Kern, Edw. M.

FORTIER, ALCÉE 278
A history of Louisiana. *P & N Y* 1904. Q 4v: [20] 268; [14] 342; [14] 272; [14] 299. 52pls 1200sets ptd[200 on H.M. paper, with some pls in two states] aa

FORTS HENRY AND DONELSON. 279
Report of the special committee on the ... military disaster at: ... *Rich* 1862. O 194 a

FOSS (JOHN). 280
Journal of the captivity ... of: several years a prisoner in Algiers ... *Newburyport* 1798. D 189 aa
—ed. 2, same impr. & collat., n.d. [*ca* 1798]. a

FOSSETT, FRANK   281
Colorado: a historical, descriptive and statistical work. *Denver* 1876. D [2] 470 [10] + 7adv-p 16pls a
—rptd, same impr 1878, 8p1el-p
—anr. ed., re-written, "Colorado, its ... mines ...," *N Y* 1879. D [8] 540 maps & pls
—rptd. same impr. *N Y* 1880.

FOSTER, CHARLES   282
The gold placers of California ... *Akron* 1849. 16° 52, 55–56, 59–60, 63–94, 97–98, 101–106 map c S few copies known
A California guide compiled from various sources, with overland routes briefly treated. The five pagination breaks represent pages planned to have been occupied by sections of the map, each of the five sections constituting two pages.

FOSTER, REV. G. L.   283
The past of Ypsilanti ... *Det* 1857. O 48 aa

FORSTER, GEORGE E.   284
Literature of the Cherokees ... *Ithaca* 1889. D [4] 70 28 12 + 7adv-p a

FOSTER, GEORGE E.   285
Remisniscences of travel in Cherokee lands. An address ... Ithaca, N.Y. ... 1898. *Ithaca* 1899. D [8] 76 a
—ed. 2, enl., "Story of the Cherokee bible ... address ... Ithaca, 1897," [also contains his 1898 adress] *Ithaca* 1899. D [6 3–10] 89 port

FOSTER, GEORGE E.   286
Sequoyah ... biography of the greatest of redmen ... *Phil* 1885. D [20] 244 6pls a
—rptd. *Ithaca* 1899. same collat.

FOSTER, GEORGE G. [ed.]   287
The gold mines of California ... *N Y* 1848. O map aa
—rptd., "Gold regions of California," same collat., *N Y* 1848. aa
—best ed., with fold.map in place of the single p. map of the earlier eds., *N Y* 1849. aa

[FORSTER, JAMES]   288
The capitulation; or, a history of the expedition conducted by William Hull ... By an Ohio volunteer. *Chillicothe* 1812. D 78 [6] c IndH N NYP WisH
Earliest Ohio book of national historical importance; First account of this inglorious surrender.

FOSTER, JAMES S.   289
Outlines of history of the Territory of Dakota ... *Yankton* 1870. O 127 map c G MinnH Y
—rptd. *Pierre* 1928. O 110 [2] a

FOSTER, LILLIAN   290
Wayside glimpses, north and south. *N Y* 1860. D 250 a

FOSTER (MATTHEW WATSON).   291
Biographical sketch of: 1800–1863. By J[ohn] W. F[oster]. *Wash* 1896. O 86 port a
Life in the Ohio and Mississippi valleys from 1817 to 1860.

FOSTER, MRS. R[OXANA] C., ed.   292
The Foster family, California pioneers. [*San José* [1889]. D 46 [type-script text] front aa
—enl. ed. with add journal [via Panama] [*Santa Barbara* 1925]. D 285[incl. pls] b
Contains three overland journals—1489, 1852, 1853.

[FOTHERGILL, JOHN]   293
Considerations relative to the North American colonies. *L* 1765. O 48 a
Condemns the Stamp Act as a precursor of revolution.

FOTHERINGHAM, H.   294
Elwood [Kans.] directory, for ... 1860–61. *St Joseph Mo* 1860. O 28 b
Situated across the Missouri from St. Joseph, Mo., this upstart town presents its rival claim as an outfitting point for Pike's Peak adventurers.

FOUR
Four dissertations, on the reciprocal advantages of a perpetual union between Great-Britain and her American colonies ... *See* Smith, *Provost* William.

Four essays on the right and propriety of secession ... By a member of the bar of Richmond. *Rich* 1861. *See* Lyons, James

Four letters on interesting subjects. *Phil*   295 1776. O 24 aa
Possibly by Thomas Paine.

FOURNEL, HENRI   296
Coup-d'oeil historique et statistique sur le Texas. *P* 1841. O 57 map aa

FOURTH   297
Fourth letter to the people of England ... *L* M. Cooper 1756. O 43 a
Not to be confused with Shebbeare's own pamphlet of the same year, with similar title; this pamphlet was an answer to the first three Shebbeare *Letters*.

Fourth letter (A) to the people of England ... *See* Shebbeare, John.

FOWLER (JACOB). 298
The journal of: . . . from Arkansas through the Indian territory . . . to the sources of the Rio Grande del Norte, 1821–2. Ed. by Elliott Coues. *N Y* 1898. O [24] 183 front. a
First American traveller over much of the route. 950 copies printed.

FOWLER, JOHN 299
Journal of a tour in . . . New York . . . *L* 1831. D [12] 333 a

FOWLER, REGINALD 300
Hither and thither; or, sketches of travel on both sides of the Atlantic. *L* 1854. O [8] 272 errata slip a

FOWLER (CAPT. S[MITH] W.) 301
Autobiographical sketch of: . . . *Manistee Mich* 1877. D [4] 37 a
—anr. ed., with cancel t-p adding unsold copies of his Speeches which had appeared a yr. earlier. D [4] 37 61
Came to Michigan in 1843; describes visits to Kansas and Nebraska.

FOWLER, WILLIAM C. 302
History of Durham, Connecticut . . . *Hart* 1866. O 144 a

FOX, EDGAR B., and DUDLEY, W. T. 303
History and directory of Green Lake and Waukesha counties and the city of Ripon. *Berlin Wis* 1869. O 144 front. a

FOX, JAMES D. 304
A true history of the reign of terror in southern Illinois [in the civil war] . . . *Aurora* 1884. O [8] 60 a

FOX, RICHARD K. 305
The outlaw brothers, Frank and Jesse James . . . *N Y* [1881]. O 67 28pls a

FOX, TRUMAN B. 306
History of Saginaw county [Mich] . . . *E. Saginaw* 1858. 0 [2] 80 aa
First history of this county.

FOX, WILLIAM F. 307
Regimental losses in the civil war . . . *Alb* 1889. Q [6] 595 a

FOX-BOURNE, HENRY R. 308
English seamen under the Tudors. *L* 1868. O 2v: [16] 304; [12] 314. 4maps a

FOXCROFT, THOMAS 309
Observations, historical and practical, on the rise and primitive state of New-England . . . *B* 1730. O [6] 46 aa

FRAMINGHAM, MASS.
Sketch of the history of: . . . *See* Ballard, Wm.

FRANCHÈRE, GABRIEL 310
Relation d'un voyage à la côte du Nord-ouest . . . [and employment there with Astor's Fur Co.], 1810–14. *Montr* 1820. O 284 c AA N NYP Y
—ed. 2 [in Eng. tr.] with added chap. & app., *N Y* 1854. D 376 + 8 adv-p 3pls aa
Most important source on the Astor adventure.

FRANCIS, CHARLES and J. M. 311
Sport among the Rockies. Troy 1889. O 134 48mounted photos 15cops ptd b

FRANCIS, CONVERS 312
An historical sketch of Watertown in Massachusetts. C 1830. O 151 a

FRANCIS, FRANCIS, JR. 313
Saddle and moccasin . . . *L* 1887. O [11] 322 + 42 adv-p a
An Englishman's experiences in 1882, in New Mexico, Arizona, etc.

FRANCIS, JOHN W. 314
New York during the last half century. *N Y* 1857. O 232 27 a
Later enlarged into the entry following.

FRANCIS, JOHN W. 315
Old New York; or, reminiscences of the past sixty years. *N Y* 1858. D 384 a 100 copies on L.P.
—anr. ed., with memoir of au., *N Y* 1865. O [136] 400 3pls.
—rptd., same impr. & collat. 1866.

FRANK, B. F., and CHAPPELL, H. W. 316
The history and business directory of Shasta, California. *Redding* 1881. D 180 aa

"FRANKLIN".
Letters of: on the conduct of the executive, and the treaty . . . with the court of Great Britain. *See* Oswald, Eleazer.

FRANKLIN (BENJAMIN).
Autobiography of: *See* below, *Mémoires de la vie privée* . . .

FRANKLIN [BENJAMIN] 317
Franklin [Benjamin[before the privy council . . . on behalf of . . . Massachusetts, to advocate the removal of Hutchinson and Oliver. *Phil* priv.ptd. 1859. O [6] 134 pl a

[FRANKLIN, BENJAMIN] 318
Cool thoughts on the present situation of our public affairs . . . *Phil* 1764. O 22 aa

FRANKLIN (DOCTOR [BENJAMIN]).   319
The examination of: . . . relating to the repeal
of the . . . stamp act . . . [*Phil*? 1766]. O 16 aa
—other eds.: *B* [1766]. O 23; *N Y* 1766. O 16;
Wmsbg 1766. a
—Eng. ed. [*L* 1766]. O 50 no t-p aa
—anr. Eng. ed. [*L*] 1767. O [2] 50 a
—Fr. tr. *Strasburg* n.d. O 35 a
—Ger. tr. *Phil* 1766. O 43 a

FRANKLIN, BENJAMIN   320
Experiments and observations on electricity . . .
[with Pt.2] Supplemental experiments . . . [and Pt.
3] New experiments and observations. *L* 1751-3-4.
Q 3pts in 1: [4] 86 [2]; [2] 89-108; [4] 111-154,
pl b NYP
—ed. 2, "New experiments . . .," [this t. for all
3pts], *L* 1754. Q 3pts in 1: [2] 86; [2] 89-110;
[4] 111-154. pl aa
—ed. 3, *L* 1760-65. Q 3pts in 1[3rd pt. called
ed.4]: [6] 86; [2] 89-110; [2] 111-154. pl aa
—ed. 4 [1st complete ed.], "Experiments and
observations . . .," *L* 1769. Q [6] 496 [really 508]
[14] errata l. 7pls b AA N NYP
—anr. ed. *C* 1941. O [28] 453 2pls facs a
—Fr. ed. "Expériences et observations . . .," *P*
1752. 16° [24] 70 [10] 222 [29] pl aa
—anr. Fr. ed. *P* 1756. D 2v 2pls a
—Ger. ed. "Briefe von der Elektricität . . .," *Leip*
1758. D [26] 354 pl
America's first great scientific contribution.

[FRANKLIN, BENJAMIN]?   321
An inquiry into the nature and causes of the
present disputes between the British colonies . . .
and their mother-country . . . *L* 1769. O [4] 76
b NYP Y
—ed. 2, same impr., date & collat. aa

FRANKLIN (BENJAMIN).   322
Letters to: from his family and friends . . . Ed.
by W. Duane. *N Y* 1858 [some copies dated 1859].
O 195 2pls a 260copies[10 on L.P.]

FRANKLIN (BENJAMIN).   323
Mémoires de la vie privée de: écrité par lui-
même . . . *P* 1791. O 2pts in 1: [8] 156; 207 [of
which the last 3p are incorrectly numb 360-363
b AA N NYP Y
—Ger. tr. "Jugendjahre . . .," *Berlin* 1792. O 214;
Weimar 1794; *Tübingen* 1795 aa; *Groningen* 1798-
1800. O 2v in 1 a
—Swed. tr "Enskildta Lefwerne . . .," *Stockh*
1792. D 218 front. a
—Eng. tr "The private life of . . . Franklin . . .,"
L 1793. O [16] 324 aa
—Eng. ed. 2, "Works . . .," different tr.
with 35 of his essays, *L* 1793. D 2v a
—Am. ed. "Works of . . . Franklin, consisting of
his life . . .," *NY* Tiebout & Obrian for H. Gaine
[1794]. 16° 2v in 1 [no 1-2 t. for v2] port eng.t.

—issue 1: binder's instructions placed just a
trifle above the middle of final page b AA NYP
—issue 2: binder's instructions moved up to
make room for adv aa
—other Am. eds.: *Phil* 1794; *N Y* T. & J. Swords
1794; *Danbury* 1795; *Salem* 1796; *Charlestown*
1796; *N Y* 1797; *Alb* 1797; *N Y* 1798. a
—enl. ed. "Memoirs of the life . . . of Franklin . . .
continued to the time of his death by W. T.
Franklin," *L* 1818-19. Q 3v: [10] 450 [89]; [24]
449; [14] 570. map 8pls facs a
—anr. issue. O 6v
—Fr. tr. *P* 1818-19. Q 3v
—1st complete ed., "Autobiography of . . .
Franklin," ed. by J. Bigelow, *Phil* 1868. D 410
port a 100copies on L.P. aa
—best ed., giving 4texts, ed. M. Farrand, *Berkeley
Calif* 1949. O [40] 422 a

FRANKLIN (the late DR. BENJAMIN).   324
Memoirs of: with a review of his . . . "Infor-
mation to those who would wish to remove to
America." *L* 1790. O 94 port aa
For the pamphlet here censured, *See* below,
Two tracts . . .

[FRANKLIN, BENJAMIN]   325
A memorial of the case of the German emigrants settled in . . . Pennsilvania and the back
parts of Maryland, Virginia . . . *L* 1754. Q 20 [8]
b NYP Y

[FRANKLIN, BENJAMIN]   326
A modest enquiry into the nature and necessity
of a paper currency. *Phil* 1729. O 36 c
His first American publication, preceded only
by a 1725 London-printed *Dissertation on liberty*.

[FRANKLIN, BENJAMIN]   327
A narrative of the late massacres in Lancaster
county . . . of a number of Indians . . . [*Phil*]
1764. O 31 b N NYP Y
Unprovoked wholesale murder of friendly
Indians, perpetrated by a frenzied mob of Pennsylvania frontiersmen—the so-callled PaxtonBoys.

FRANKLIN, BENJAMIN   328
Philosophical and miscellaneous papers . . . *L*
1787. O [6] 186 3pls map aa

[FRANKLIN, BENJAMIN]   329
Plain truth: or, serious considerations on the
present state of . . . Philadelphia and . . . Pennsylvania. [*Phil*] 1747. O 22 b AA H PhilL Y
—ed. 2, same impr. & date. O 22 [2] aa
—Ger. ed. "Die lautere Wahrheit . . .," [*Phil*]
n.d. O 20 a

FRANKLIN, BENJAMIN   330
Political, miscellaneous and philosophical pieces
. . . *L* 1779. O [12] 567 [7] port 3pls tab some
copies on L.P. aa

[FRANKLIN, BENJAMIN]   331
Some account of the Pennsylvania hospital . . .
[and] Continuation of the account . . . *Phil*
1754–61. Q 2v: 40; 41–77 b AA NYP Y
—rptd. *Phil* 1817. O 144 144–145 [p50 misnumb.
53] a

FRANKLIN (DR. [BENJAMIN]).   332
Two letters from: to the Earl of Shelburne . . .
L [1782]. O [2] 31 a
Probably not written by Franklin.

[FRANKLIN, BENJAMIN]   333
Two tracts: information for those who would
remove to America. And, remarks concerning
the savages . . . *L* 1784. O 39 a
—eds. 2 & 3, same yr. & collat.
—anr. ed. *Dub* 1784. O 30
The second tract, *Remarks . . .*, had been
previously published at Birmingham, same year
[16 pages]; both tracts were originally issued in
French and English at Paris, 1794.

FRANKLIN (DR. BENJAMIN).
Vida del: 1798. *See* Garces de Marcilla, Pedro.

FRANKLIN, BENJAMIN
Works . . . *L* 1793. *See* above, *Mémoires de la
vie privée* . . .

FRANKLIN, JAMES   334
The philosophical and political history of the
thirteen United States . . . *L* 1784. O [12] 156 a
—rptd. t. altered, *L* 1784 O [2] 101 a
First history of the United States.

FRANKLIN, J[OHN] BENJAMIN   335
A cheap trip to the great Salt Lake City.
Ipswich Eng [1860?]. D 32 a
Most—possibly all—copies are called either
"third" or "fourth" edition.

[FRANKLIN, WILLIAM]   336
A humble attempt at scurrility . . . *Quilsilvania*
[i.e., Pennsylvania] 1765. O 48 b NYP PhilL
Defence of Benjamin Franklin by his son.

FRANKLIN COUNTY [OHIO].   337
A brief history . . . of: to accompany Wheeler's
map. *Columbus* [1840?]. 16° 229 a

FRANKS, DAVID, comp.   338
The New York directory . . . *N Y* 1786. D 82
dd Hn NYP
—rptd; *N Y* 1851. D 82 map; *N Y* 1876 map a
First directory of this city. The second followed,
New York 1787, D 58. c. For the third, *see* Hodge,
Allen and Campbell, publishers.

FRANKS, J. M.   339
Seventy years in Texas . . . *Gatesville Tex* 1924.
O 134 port a

FRANKS, LAN [pseud.]
See Biggers, Don R.

FRASER, CHARLES   340
Reminiscences of Charleston [S. C.]. *Charleston*
1854. O 119 a

[FRASER, WILLIAM]   341
The emigrant's guide; or, sketches of Canada,
with some of the northern and western states . . .
Glas 1867. D 72 a

FREDERICKSBURG.
Map of the battle field of: etc. *See* Braxton,
Carter M.

FREE
Free and calm consideration (A) of the . . . misunderstanding . . . between the Parliament . . .
and these colonies . . . *See* Prescott, Benj.

Free and candid review (A), of . . .   343
"Observations on the commerce of the American
states" . . . *L* 1784. O 108 a
For work reviewed, *see* Holroyd, John B.

Free enquiry (A) into the causes . . . for   344
laying on the embargo. By a citizen of Vermont.
Windsor Vt 1808. O 28 a

Free remarks on the spirit of the federal   345
constitution . . . By a Philadelphian. *Phil* 1819. *See*
Walsh, Robert.

Free thoughts on the American contest . . . *See*
Anderson, James.

Free thoughts on the proceedings of the Continental Congress . . . *See* Seabury, Sam'l.

Free trade and sailor's rights . . . victories   346
of Hull, Jones. Decatur, Bainbridge . . . *Phil* 1813.
O 58 a

FREEDOM
Freedom (The) of speech and writing, upon
public affairs . . . *See* Bollan, Wm.

FREEMAN OF SOUTH CAROLINA [pseud].
A letter from: to the deputies . . . in the high
court of Congress . . . *See* Drayton, Wm. H.

FREEMAN [pseud].   347
Some fugitive thoughts on a letter signed:
addressed to the deputies . . . in the high court
of Congress . . . By a back settler. *South Carolina*
1774. Q 36 a

FREEMAN, DOUGLAS S. [ed.]   348
Lee's dispatches . . . 1862–5. *N Y* 1915. O [64]
400 port map a

—anr. issue, identical except for words "second impression" on verso of t-p

FREEMAN, DOUGLAS S.   **349**
Lee's lieutenants... *N Y* 1942-3-4. O 3v: [58] 773; [46] 760; [48] 862. 2maps 24 pls[incl. in paginat.] a

FREEMAN, DOUGLAS S.   **350**
R. E. Lee: a biography. *N Y* 1934-5. O 4v: [18] 647; [14] 621; [14] 559; [10] 594. 64pls & facs aa

FREEMAN, DOUGLAS S.   **351**
The south to posterity... *N Y* 1939. O [12] 235 a
—rptd *N Y* 1951

FREEMAN, FREDERICK   **352**
The history of Cape Cod... *B* 1856-8. O 2v: 803; 803. ports aa
—rptd.: same impr. & collat., 1858-62; 1860-62; 1869. aa
First issued in ten parts.

FREEMAN, GEORGE D.   **353**
Midnight and noonday... incidents happening in and around Caldwell, Kansas... 1871-1890. Caldwell 1890. O 405 16pls aa
—rptd. with authenticating certificate added, same impr 1892. O 406 16pls

FREEMAN, JAMES W., ed.
Prose and poetry of the live stock industry. *See* that title.

FREEMAN, SAMUEL   **354**
The emigrant's handbook and guide to Wisconsin... *Milw* 1851. O 148 [incl.advs] aa
—Ger. tr. *Milw* 1852. O 134 a

FREEMAN [THOMAS[and   **355**
CUSTIS [PETER].
An account of the Red river in Louisiana... from the returns of:... who explored the same in... 1806. [*Wash* 1807?] O 63 2tabs dd B BA
This expedition into Spanish territory was a part of Jefferson's plan to explore the Louisiana Purchase. Due to the strained relations with Spain over the vexed boundary issue, the pamphlet was probably secretly printed in a mere handful of copies for the guarded use of high government officials.

FREEPORT, Ill.   **356**
Freeport, [Ill.] directory [*Chi* 1867]. D 126 [10] aa

The present advantages and future pros-   **357**
pects of the city of Freeport, Ill.:... *Freeport* 1857. D 48 map aa

[FREER, R. L.]   **358**
Memoirs, extracts of speeches, diary of a journey to America... *Hereford Eng* 1866. O 294 3pls a

FREJES, FRANCISCO   **359**
Historia breve de la conquista de los estados independientes del imperio Mejicano. [*Zacatecas*] 1838. Q [6] 166 [2] b LC NYP
—ed. 2, *Mex* 1839. D [8] 302 [2] aa
—rptd. *Guadalajara* 1878. O 277 [2] a
Includes data on Texas and present Arizona. The 1878 edition is usually bound with this author's *Conquista de Jalisco* of same date, a reprint of the original edition of 1833.

FRELIGH, J. H.   **360**
The true position, interests and policy of the south. Union or secession: which is best? *Memphis* January 1861. O 35 aa

FREMANTLE, LIEUT. COL.   **361**
[ARTHUR J. L.]
Three months in the southern states... *Edin* 1863. D [10] 316 6ports aa
—Am. eds.: *N Y* 1864. D 309 port a; *Mobile* 1864. O 158 aa

FRÉMAUX, LEON J.   **362**
New Orleans characters. *N O* 1876. F 17col.pls [incl eng t.] b

FREMONT, JESSIE B.   **363**
A year of American travel. *N Y* 1878. 18° 190 [incl. preliminary advs] + 2adv-p a
—rptd *S F* 1960. O 135 450 cops ptd.
Account of California in 1849, including three letters from her husband describing the horrors of his ill-fated last expedition.

FREMONT (JOHN C.)   **364**
California claims: report of the Committee to which was referred the Memorial of: praying an investigation... *Wash* 1848. O 83 aa
Fremont states that the Bear Flag Revolution was launched on his discovery that Mexico was on the eve of transferring California to England.

FREMONT (LIEUT. COL. J[OHN] C.)   **365**
Defence of: before the military court martial ... [*Wash* 1848]. O 78 Jincl. cover t.] aa

FREMONT, JOHN C.   **366**
Geographical memoir upon Upper California, in illustration of his map of Oregon and Washington. [Sen. Misc. Doc. 148] *Wash* 1848. O 67 map by Preuss[not issued in all copies, if in any, but intended to accompany the pamphlet] a
—anr. issue [H.R. Misc. Doc 5], same impr. 1849. O 40 map[different from that described above]

His third expedition. For another edition, *see* McCarty, William.

FREMONT, JOHN C.   367
Memoirs of my life. Vol. I [all.] *Chi* 1887. Q [10, 13–20] 655 7maps 82pls aa
Embraces his first three exploring expeditions and the part played by him in the conquest of California. Issued also in 10parts, wrappers.

FREMONT (JOHN C.)   368
The memorial of: praying an investigation of the claims of citizens of California, for money and supplies furnished for the use of the United States . . . *Wash* 1848. O 83 aa
Adduces proof that the Bear Flag revolution was precipitated to thwart Great Britain, Mexico being on the verge of transferring California to that power.

FREMONT (LIEUT. COL. [JOHN C.])   369
Message from the President, communicating the proceedings of the court-martial . . . of: . . . [Exec. Doc. 33]. *Wash* 1848. O 447 aa

FREMONT, JOHN C.   370
Report of the exploring expedition to the Rocky mountains . . . 1842, and to Oregon and north California . . . 1843–4. [Ptd. for Senate]. *Wash* 1845. O 693 22pls 5maps[incl. large fold. one in pocket] aa
—anr. issue [H. R.], scientific data omitted, same impr. & date. O 583 22pls 5maps a
—other 1845 eds.: *Wash* Taylor. O 278 2 maps; *Wash* Polkinghorn. O 278
—other eds.: *Syracuse* 1846. O 305; *N Y* 1846, O 186 map port
—best ed. *Syracuse* 1847. O 427 large map by Rufus Sage 2pls b
—Eng. ed., with omissions and different pls from those in the *Wash* ed., *L* 1846. O 324 [2] map pls a
Contains his first and second expeditions.

FREMONT, JOHN C.   371
A report on an exploration . . . between the Missouri river and the Rocky mountains . . . [Sen. Doc. 243] *Wash* 1843. O 207 map 6pls aa
His first expedition.

FRENCH, BELLA
See Swisher, Mrs. Bella French.

FRENCH, BENJAMIN F., ed.   372
Historical collections of Louisiana. *N Y & Phil* 1846, 1850-1—2–3. O 5v: [10] 222 + 6adv-p facs; [8] 301 map; [2] 252 facs; [80] 268 + 8adv-p map facs; [8] 291 port b
—for separate issue of vol. 4, *see* Shea, John G., "Discovery and exploration of the Mississippi valley."

FRENCH, BENJAMIN F.   373
Historical collections of Louisiana and Florida. *N Y* 1869–75. O 2v: [6] 362 facs; [18] 300 aa
This series supplemented the original series shown above. Both series were reprinted at N. Y. in 1961.

FRENCH, CAPT. W. J.   374
Wild Jim, the Texas cowboy . . . *Antioch* [*Ill.*] 1890. O 76 port aa

FRENCH, WILLIAM   375
Some recollections of a western ranchman . . . *L* [1927]. O [8] 284 + 8adv-p aa
—rptd., same impr. & collat., 1928 a
—Am. ed., same collat., *N Y* [1928]? a
—rptd *N Y* 1961
By the brother of Field Marshal Sir John French. Only about half of his manuscript said to have been included. Too bad!

FRENCH . . .
French encroachments exposed; or, Britain's original right . . . *See* Payne, J.

French policy defeated . . . account of all   376
the hostile proceedings of the French, against the . . . British colonies in America . . . *L* 1755. O [2] 114 2maps aa
—rptd., same collat. & impr., 1760.

[FRENEAU, PHILIP]   377
Letters on various . . . subjects . . . *Phil* 1799. O 142 + adv-p a

FRERE, REV. JOHN   378
The history of the Mormonites, or Latter Day Saints . . . *L* 1850. D 24 a

FRESNO COUNTY, CALIFORNIA.   379
History of: *S F* 1881. Q 246 pls b

FREWEN, MORETON   380
Melton Mowbray and other memories. *L* 1924. O [12] 311 16pls aa
Ten chapters on the author's disastrous cattle enterprise on Powder river, Wyoming.

FREYTAS, NICOLAS DE   381
The expedition of Don Diego Dionisio de Penalosa . . . from Santa Fé to the river Mischipi and Quivira in 1662. *N Y* 1882. O 102 a
After his removal as Spanish Governor of New Mexico in 1668, Penalosa interested France in undertaking the conquest of that province. The narrative, here translated from a 17th century MS., of a fictitious journey, ascribed to a non-existent author, was presumably written by Penalosa himself, to impress French authorities with the wealth of the region described and his experience and knowledge thereof. There seems

little doubt that if La Salle's last voyage had been successful, it would have been followed by another French expedition under this imposter.

FRIBERT, LAURITZ J.   382
Haandbog for Emigranter til Amerikas Vest . . . [*Christiania* 1847]. O 100 aa

FRICKMANN, A.   383
Côte occidentale de l'Amérique du Nord . . . de l'Oregon et du territore de Washington . . . *P* 1872. O 112 a

FRIDGE, IKE   384
History of the Chisum war . . . cowboy life on the frontier. Ed. Jodie D. Smith *Electra Tex* [1927]. O 71 port aa

FRIEDRICHSBURG
Friedrichsburg, die colonie . . . in Texas. Von Armand. *See* Strubberg, Friedrich Armand.

FRIENDLY ADDRESS (A)
Friendly address (A) to all reasonable Americans . . . *See* Cooper, Myles.

FRIGNET, ERNEST   385
La Californie . . . *P* 1866. O [16] 479 a
—ed. 2, *P* 1867. O [30] 479 map

FRIGNET, ERNEST, and   386
CARREY, EDMOND
Les états du nord-ouest et Chicago. *P* 1871. O 88 10photographic views aa
Issued just prior to the fire, the views are important.

FRINK, F. W.,   387
A record of Rice county, Minnesota, in 1868 . . . *Faribault* 1868. D 24 aa
—rptd. same impr. 1871. D 32 a

FRINK, MARGARET A.   388
Journal of the adventures of a party of California gold-seekers . . . [*Oakland* 1897]. D 131 b
A few cops. priv ptd.

FRISTOE, WILLIAM   389
History of the Ketochton Baptist Association. *Staunton* 1808. D 162 a

FROEBEL, JULIUS   390
Aus Amerika. Erfahrungen, Reisen und Studien. *Leip* 1857–[1858]. D 2v: [16] 550; [16] 616 aa
—Eng. ed. "Seven years' travel . . ." *L* 1859. O [16] 587 8pls aa
—Fr. ed. "A travers l'Amérique." *Brus* 1861. D 3v: 344; 380; 358 a
Describes several trips over the Santa Fe Trail and a journey from Tucson and the Gila to Los Angeles.

FROEBEL, JULIUS   391
Die deutsche Auswanderung und ihre cultur-historische Bedeutung. *Leip* 1858. O [6] 103 a

FROST, DONALD McK., ed.   392
Notes on General Ashley, the overland trail and South pass. *Worc* 1945. O 159 fold. map a
—L. P. issue, of 50copies. Q aa
—anr ed *Barre Mass.* 1960. O 149 map a
Contains the letters of Daniel T. Potts who was in the Rocky Mountains with Ashley's men from 1822 to 1827.

FROST, GRIFFIN   393
Camp and prison journal . . . *Quincy Ill* 1867. D [8 incl. front.] 304 + 2adv.-p aa
Day-by-day narrative of a Missouri Confederate, published to show that Federal prisons were not guiltless of atrocities. All but 100 copies burned.

FROST, JOHN   394
Heroic women of the west. *Phil* 1854. D 348 6pls a
—rptd. *Phil* 1869. D
Among many others, includes the Tennessee captivity of Jane Brown and family in 1788.

FROST, JOHN   395
History . . . of California . . . *Auburn* 1850. O 508 16pls + 4adv-p aa
—rptd., same impr. 1851; 1853; 1855; *N Y* n.d. a
Hasty and unreliable compilation.

FROST, M. O.   396
Regimental history of the Tenth Missouri volunteer infantry. *Topeka* n.d. D 317 aa

FROTHINGHAM, OCTAVIUS B.   397
Transcendentalism in New England. *N Y* 1876. O [10] 305 front. a

FRY, F[REDERICK]   398
Traveler's guide . . . of the great north-western territories . . . *Cin* 1865. D 264 + 12adv-l. b
Earliest accounts of the Idaho and Montana mines, visited in 1862 to 1864.

FRY, JAMES B.   399
Army sacrifices . . . Sketches . . . illustrating the services and experiences of the regular army . . . on the Indian frontier . . . *N Y* 1879. D [4] 254 + 2adv-p aa
—rptd., illus. added, *N Y* 1887 a

FRY, JAMES B.   400
Descriptions of posts and stations in the military division of the south. *Louisv.* 1870. O 56 a

FÜRSTENWÄRTHER, M. VON 401
Der Deutsche in Nord America. *Stuttgart* 1818.
D 124 aa
One of the earliest German emigration aids.

FULKERSON, H. S. 402
A civilian's recollections of the war between
the states. *Baton Rouge* 1939. O [10] 253 300cops
ptd a

FULKERSON, H. S. 403
Random recollections of early days in Mississippi. *Vicksb* 1885. O 158 aa
—rptd. *Baton Rouge* 1937. O [12] 158 235 cops
ptd a

FULL 404
Full and particular answer (A) to all the calumnies . . . in a pamphlet called a Fourth letter to the
people of England. *L* 1756. O [2] 61 a
For pamphlet attacked, *see* Shebbeare, John.

Full reply (A) to Lieut. Cadogan's Spanish 405
hireling . . . wherein "The impartial account of the
late expedition to St. Augustine" is clearly vindicated . . . *L* 1743. D [8] 63 aa
By the author of *The impartial account . . .*,
q.v. under Oglethorpe, Gen. James.

Full vindication (A) of the measures of Congress
. . . in answer to a letter under the signature of
A. W. Farmer. *See* Hamilton, Alex.

FULLER, C. L. [comp.] 406
Pocket map and compendium of statistics
accompanied by a . . . history of the Black Hills
of Dakota . . . *Rapid City* 1887. D 56 map b SD
Hist.

FULLER, MRS. EMELINE L. 407
Left by the Indians . . . [*Mt. Vernon Ia* 1892].
16° [4] 41 [incl. ports] cover t. only aa
—rptd. *N Y* 1936. 16° port 200 copies ptd.
Only account by a survivor of the sufferings
of the 1860 Utter-Myers emigrating party of
fifty-four members, all but fifteen of whom perished from hunger or were killed by Indians on the
Snake river in Idaho. Among overland disasters,
equalled in horror only by that of the Donner
party; cannibalism was resorted to in both cases.

FULLER, HUBERT B. 408
The purchase of Florida . . . *Clev* 1906. O 399
19adv-p 2maps a

FULLER, S[ARAH] M[ARGARET]
Summer on the lakes. *See* Ossoli, Sarah M.

FULLMER, JOHN S. 409
Assassination of Joseph and Hiram Smith.
Liv 1855. O 40 aa

FULTON, A[LEXANDER] R. 410
The free lands of Iowa . . . description of the
Sioux City land district. *Des M* 1869. D 44 [3]
map a

FULTON, ALEXANDER R. 411
The red men of Iowa . . . *Des M* 1882. O 559
26pls aa

FULTON, ALEXANDER R. 412
Sketches of the northwest, including . . . historical account of Iowa. *Des M* 1878. O 256 pls a

FULTON, AMBROSE C. 413
A life's voyage; a diary of a sailor on sea and
land . . . *N Y* 1898. D [8] 555 15pls aa

FULTON, FRANCES I. S. 414
To and through Nebraska . . . *Lincoln* 1884.
16° 273 a

FULTON, R. L., comp. 415
Truckee basin and lake Tahoe directory, for
1884-5. *Reno* [1884]. D 163 + advs aa
First book printed in the divorce capital of
the world.

FULTON, ROBERT 416
Letters . . . on sub-marine navigation and
attack . . . *L* 1806. O [8] 37 aa

FULTON, ROBERT 417
Torpedo war and submarine explosions . . .
N Y 1810. obl. Q 58 [3] 5pls b
—anr. ed. "Letter to the Secretary of the Navy . . .
on the practical use of the torpedo . . .," *Wash*
1811. O 55 aa
—Fr. ed. "De la machine infernale maritime . . .,"
P 1812. O 5pls aa

FULTON, ROBERT 418
A treatise on the improvement of canal navi-
gation . . . *L* 1796. Q [16] 144 17pls + 2adv-lvs
aa
—Fr. tr. *P* 1799. O [12] 247 7pls & maps a
—Portug. tr *Lisb* 1800. 17pls aa

FULTON CITY, ILLINOIS. 419
Sketches of the early history . . . of: . . . *Fulton
City* 1856. O 32 aa

FURBER, GEORGE C. 420
The twelve months volunteer . . . in the campaign in Mexico . . . *Cin* 1848. O 640 [incl.pls]
map aa
—rptd., same impr: 1849; 1850; 1851; 1857. a

FURLONG, LAURENCE 421
The American coast pilot . . . *Newburyport*,
Blunt & March, 1796. O [8] 125 b AA NYP
—rptd, same impr, Blunt, 1797. O aa

—ed. 2, same impr. 1798. O 172 [8] 177–240 aa
—ed. 3, same impr. 1800. O 252 a
—ed. 4, same impr. 1804. O 386 [6] 11charts
—rptd. often—in both Fr. and Eng. eds.—under
name of pub, Edmund M. Blunt.

FURMAN, GABRIEL   **422**
Antiquities of Long Island . . . *N Y* 1874. O 478 a
—rptd. same impr. & collat. 1875.

FURMAN, GABRIEL   **423**
Notes . . . relating to . . . Brooklyn. *Bklyn* 1824.
D 119 aa
—rptd. *Bklyn* 1865. Q [34] 120 [39] 120 copies,
20 on L. P. a

[FURMAN, GARRETT]   **424**
Long Island miscellanies. *N Y* 1847. D 185
6pls a

FURNAS, ROBERT W., pub.   **425**
Brownville and Nehama county, [Neb.] . . .
Brownville 1859. D 99 a

FURTHER EXAMINATION
Further examination (A) of our present American measures . . . *See* Robinson, Matthew.

FUZZLEBUG, FRITZ [pseud.]
Prison life during the rebellion . . . *See* Dunkle,
John J.

G

G., G.
A letter to: *L* 1767. *See* Grenville, George.

G., CAPT. J. C.
Lee's last campaign. *See* Gorman, John C.

G., S.
A glass for the people of New England . . .
See Groome, S.

"GAFF" [pseud.]   **1**
Rambles through the great Kansas valley and
in eastern Colorado. *K C* 1878. O [2] 84 + 22adv-p
map aa

GAFFARAL, PAUL   **2**
Histoire de la Floride francaise. *P* 1875. O [12]
522 2 maps a

GAGE'S INSTRUCTIONS   **3**
Gage's (General [Thomas]) instructions, of
22nd February 1775, to Captain Brown and Ensign d'Berniere . . . with a curious narrative . . . of
their doings . . . also, an account of the transactions of the British troops, from the time they
marched out of Boston . . . till their confused
retreat back . . . *B* 1779, O 20 b AA BA MH
Contains de Berniere's narrative of his operations as a spy, later plagiarized and issued as *A
journal kept by Mr. John Howe . . . , q.v.*

GAGE (GENERAL [THOMAS]).   **4**
A narrative, of the excursion and ravages of
the King's troops under the command of: . . .
Worc [1775]. O 23 c AA Hn NYP Y
One of the earliest sources on the Concord and
Lexington affair, and the first book printed at
Worcester. Author may have been Rev. William
Gordon.

GAGNON, [FREDERICK] ERNEST [A]   **5**
Louis Jolliet, découvreur du Mississippi . . .
Quebec 1902. O [16] 284 a
—ed. 2, *Montr* 1912. O [6] 11–364 port
—ed. 3, same impr. 1926. O [6] 11–301 port

GAINES (EL GENERAL).   **6**
Correspondencia . . . sobre el paso del Sabina
por las tropas que mandabo: *Phil* 1836 O [22]
59 map [earliest of the Republic of Texas] b Y
—anr. ed., *Mex* 1837 O [30] 122 aa
—Fr. tr., *P* 1837 O [32] 91 map aa
Probably by Manuel E. Gorostiza, Mexican
minister at Washington. For reply *see* Weaver,
William A.

GAINES, EDMUND P.   **7**
Plan for the defence of the western frontier.
[H. R. 311]. [*Wash* 1838]. O 58 map a

GAINES, FRANCIS P.   **8**
The southern plantation . . . *N Y* 1925. O [10]
243 a

GAINES (MYRA) vs. CHEW   **9**
(ROLF) et al.
A full report of the . . . suit of: to recover the
property of Daniel Clark . . . *N O* 1850. O 80 a

GALATIAN, ANDREW B.   **10**
History of Elmira . . . *Elmira* 1868. O [8]
280 33 a

GALATIAN, ANDREW B.   **11**
History of Scranton . . . *Scranton* 1867. O
416 a

GALAUP, JEAN F., Comte de la Perouse
See La Perouse.

GALE, BENJAMIN   **12**
Doctor Gale's Letter to J. W., Esq . . . *Hart*
1769. D 34 aa
Relates to Connecticut's Susquehanna claims.
For reply *See* Dyer, Eliphalet, *Remarks* . . .

GALE, BENJAMIN   **13**
Observations on a pamphlet, entitled Remarks
on Dr. Gale's Letter to J. W., Esq. . . . *Hart* [*ca*
1769]. D 40 aa
A reply to Dyer, Eliphalet, *Remarks* . . .

GALE'S . . . LETTER
Gale's (Dr. [Benjamin]) Letter to J. W., Esq.
Remarks on: *See* Dyer, Eliphalet.

GALE, GEORGE   **14**
Upper Mississippi; or, historical sketches of
the mound-builders, the Indian tribes [etc.]. *Chi*
1867. D 460[incl. 13pls] port aa

GALENA, Ill.   **15**
Directory of Galena, Illinois: 1847. *See* Seymour,
Wm. N.

Galena [Ill.] city directory . . . and sketch   **16**
of Galena and the lead trade. *Galena* 1858. D 139 aa

Galena (The) and Chicago Union Railroad   **17**
Company.
First annual report of: . . . *Chi* 1848. O [2] 23 aa
Second annual report. *Chi* 1849. O [2] 20 [2] aa
Third annual report. *Chi* 1850. O [8] 16 16 a
For first *Survey* of this pioneer road *see* Morgan,
Richard P.

[GALIANO, DIONISIO ALCALÁ]   **18**
Relación del viage hecho por las goletas Sutil
y Mexicana en el año de 1792 para reconocer el
estrecho de Fuca . . . *Madrid* 1802. Q [16] 168
185 fold.sheet of missions + atlas F 4p 9maps
8pls dd N NYP Y
—rptd. *Madrid* 1958 Q 2V 17maps and pls
—Eng. ed. "A Spanish voyage to . . . the northwest coast . . .," *L* 1930. O [14] 142 map 6pls aa
—Apendice [to above], by José de Espinosa y
Tello. *Madrid* 1806. Q 20 c Y.
Important voyage up the Pacific coast—and the
last to be undertaken by Spain—; written probably by the commander, Galiano, but attributed
also to José de Espinosa y Tello. and to Cayetano
Valdés. The "Introduccion," giving a splendid
historical sketch of earlier Spanish explorations
in the same region, was the work of the maritime
authority, Navarrette. These two Spanish ships
cooperated with Vancouver.

GALINÉE, RENÉ DE BREHANT DE   **19**
Exploration of the great lakes, 1669–1770. Part I
[all]. *Tor* 1903. O [38] 89 5maps 10 pls plan facs a
First English translation of this narrative of a

trip along the shores of Lake Erie to Detroit
river and Sault Ste. Marie. La Salle accompanied
this party for some time.

GALL, LUDWIG   **20**
Meine Auswanderung nach den Vereinigten
Staaten . . . *Trier* 1822. O 2v: [10] 408; [4] 428 [2].
9maps & pls tab a
After a year's residence in the Ohio valley the
author found little basis for recommending it to
emigrants.

GALLAGHER, WILLIAM D.   **21**
Facts and conditions of progress in the northwest . . . *Cin* 1850. O 85 a

GALLAND, I[SAAC]   **22**
. . . Iowa emigrant . . . *Chillicothe O* 1840. O
32map b LC N WisH
—rptd. [*Iowa City* 1950]. O [14] 28 map a

[CALLAND, ISAAC]   **23**
Villainy exposed. [Keokuk?] 1836. 0 75 c G.
For reply *see* Kilbourne, *Strictures.*

[GALLATIN, ALBERT]   **24**
An examination of the conduct of the executive
. . . towards the French republic . . . *Phil* 1797
O [6] 72 a

GALLATIN, ALBERT   **25**
Letters . . . on the Oregon question . . . *Wash*
1846. O 30 a
—best ed. "The Oregon question," *N Y* 1846.
O 75
—rptd. n.p. n.d., same collat.

GALLATIN, ALBERT   **26**
Letter . . . transmitting a report . . . to establish
the Treasury Department. *Wash* 1805. Q [4] 6 +
16tabs [some fold] a

GALLATIN, ALBERT   **27**
Report on . . . public roads and canals. *Wash*
1808. O 123 a
—ed. 2 *Phil* same date & collat.

GALLATIN, ALBERT   **28**
The right of the United States . . . to the north-
eastern boundary . . . *N Y* 1840. O [10] 180
8maps [on 6 sheets] a

GALLATIN, ALBERT   **29**
A sketch of the finances of the United States.
N Y 1796. O [4] 9–205 3tabs a

GALLATIN, ALBERT   **30**
A synopsis of the Indian tribes . . . east of
the Rockies. [In Am. Antiq. Soc. Colls., v. 2] *C*
1836. O [32] 574 errata 1. map[best of western
country up to this time] aa

GALLATIN, ALBERT   31
Writings. Ed. Henry Adams. *Phil* 1978–80. O
3v: [14] 707; [10] 666; [4] 646. 2fold.tabs aa
—rptd. *N Y* 1960. O 3v a
Important source on the political and financial
history of the early republic.

GALLATIN, E. L.   32
What life has taught me. *Denver* [1900]. O [2]
215 port aa
Reminiscences of the maker of the famous
Western saddle carrying his name; includes ac-
count of his trip from Denver to Virginia City,
Montana, in 1864.

GALLOWAY, DAVID H., comp.   33
Directory of . . . Savannah, for 1849. *Sav* 1848.
D 72 b GaU [only copy known]
First regular directory of this city.

[GALLOWAY, JOSEPH]   34
A candid examination of the mutual claims of
Great Britain, and the colonies . . . *N Y* 1775. O
[2] 62 a There were 2 issues; one with, the other
without, errata on verso of t-p aa
—anr. ed., with "A reply to an address to the
author . . .," *N Y* 1780. D a
—Eng. ed., also with "A reply . . .," *L* 1780. O 116 a
One of the most famous Tory tracts, upholding
unlimited parliamentary supremacy. In several
colonies copies were officially burned. It was
answered in *An address to the author of A candid
examination*, which in turn evoked Galloway's *A
reply to An address . . .*, see below.

[GALLOWAY, JOSEPH]   35
The claim of the American loyalists reviewed
and maintained . . . *L* Almon [1783]. O [8] 5–126 aa
—rptd. *L Wilkie* 1783. O [8] 138 a
—ed. 2, *L* 1788.

[GALLOWAY, JOSEPH]   36
Cool thoughts on the consequences . . . of
American independence . . . *L* 1780. O [4] 70 +
adv-p a
—Fr. ed. "Réflexions impartiales . . .," *L* 1780.
D; *Amst* 1781. O [2] 70

GALLOWAY (JOSEPH).   37
The examination of: . . . before the House of
Commons . . . *L* 1779. O [2] 85 a
—ed. 2, same impr. & collat., 1780.
—Dutch tr. *Amst* 1781. O 107
—Am. ed., ed. Balch. *Phil* Seventy-Six Soc. 1855.
O [4] 86 250 copies ptd

[GALLOWAY, JOSEPH]   38
Fabricius: or, letters to the people of Great
Britain: on the absurdity . . . of defensive operations only in the American war . . . *L* 1782. O
[4] 111 aa

[GALLOWAY, JOSEPH]   39
Historical and political reflections on the rise
. . . of the American rebellion . . . *L* 1780. O
[8] 135 + adv-p a
In many copies passages on pages 38–39 and
107 are crossed out. *Cf.* Wesley, John, *Reflections . . .*

[GALLOWAY, JOSEPH]   40
A letter from Cicero to the Right Hon. Lord
Viscount H[ow]e . . . *L* 1781. O [4] 43 aa
Scathing attack on both Admiral Lord Richard
Howe and his brother Gen. Sir William Howe for
the failure of their operations in America.

[GALLOWAY, JOSEPH]?   41
A letter to the people of America, lately printed
at New York . . . *L* 1778. O [4] 74 aa
Reconcilliation and submission urged as
America's only salvation. The author condemns
General Howe's generalship at the battles of
Long Island and White Plains, and his failure to
move against Valley Forge.

[GALLOWAY, JOSEPH]   42
A letter to the . . . Viscount [Richard] H . . . e, on
his naval conduct in the American war, *L* 1779.
O [4] 50 a
—ed. 2, cor. *L* 1781. O [4] 50
—anr. ed. [abr. by John Wesley], "An extract
from A letter . . .," *L* 1781. D 27
—ed. 2, same impr., date & collat.

[GALLOWAY, JOSEPH]   43
Letters to a nobleman on the conduct of the
war in the middle colonies. *L* 1779. O [8] 101
plan a
—rptd *Dub* 1779
—ed. 2, *L* 1779. same collat.
—eds. 3 & 4, *L* 1780. same collat.
—anr.ed. [abr. by John Wesley] "An account of
the conduct of the war, etc." *L* 1780. D 56
—ed.2, same impr. and date D 28 [error for 56]
—ed.5, slightly rev., "An account of the rise and
progress of the American war," *L* 1780. D 56
—Am. ed. *See* below "A short history, *etc.*"

[GALLOWAY, JOSEPH]   44
Observations upon the conduct of S[ir]
W[illia]m H[ow]e at the White Plains . . . *L* 1779.
O 44 a
—Am. ed., au. named, *Phil* 1780. D Ascribed also
to Israel Mauduit.

[GALLOWAY, JOSEPH]   45
Plain truth: or, a letter to the author of Dispas-
sionate thoughts on the American war . . . *L* 1780.
O [8] 76 + adv-p a
Ascribed also to George Chalmers, Alexander
Hamilton, Charles Inglis, and *Provost* William
Smith.

[GALLOWAY, JOSEPH]   46
Political reflections on the royal, proprietary, and charter governments of the American colonies . . . *L* 1782. O [4] 259 aa
—rptd. "Political reflections on the late colonial governments . . .," *L* 1783. O [6] 259

GALLOWAY, JOSEPH   47
A reply to An address to the author of . . . "A candid examination of the mutual claims of Great Britain, and the colonies" . . . *N Y* 1775 [not pub until 1777]. O 42 b BA LC NYP
—rptd. with his. "A candid examination . . .," *N Y* 1780 aa
—Eng. ed., also with "A candid examination . . .," *L* 1780. O 116 aa
Practically all copies of original edition destroyed by a New York mob.

[GALLOWAY, JOSEPH]   48
A reply to observations of Lieut. Gen. Sir William Howe, on . . . Letters to a nobleman . . . *L* 1780. O [4] 149 + 3adv-p a
—abr. ed. "An extract . . .," *L* 1781. D 104
—ed. ?, with adds., *L* 1781. O [4] 157
The *Observations* here answered were contained in Howe's *Narrative* . . .

GALLOWAY, JOSEPH   49
A short history of the war in America, during the command of Sir William Howe . . . *Phil* 1787. D [2] 106 aa
This American edition of the author's *Letters to a nobleman* incorporates several of Galloway's pamphlets.

GALLOWAY (JOSEPH).   50
The speech of: in answer to the speech of John Dickinson . . . *Phil* 1764. O 35 [4] 45 aa
—Eng. ed. *L* 1765. O [2] 92

[GALT, JOHN M.]   51
Political essays [on Texas annexation, etc.]. [*Wmsbg* 1852] O 3pts in 1: 38 a

GALVÁN RIVERA, MARINO, comp.   52
Coleccion de constitutiones de Estados-Unidos Mexicanos. *Mex* 1828. 16° 3v: b LC NYP Y
Includes constitution of the state of Coahuila and Texas.

GALVESTON
Galveston Bay and Texas land company [The]. Address to the reader of the documents relating to: . . . *See* Sumner, Wm. H.

Galveston directory . . . 1859–60. *See* Richardson, W. and D.

GALVEZ, BERNARDO DE
Diario de las operaciones . . . contra la Plaza de Panzacola. *See* Panzacola.

GAMBIER (VICE-ADMIRAL).   53
A narrative of facts relative to the conduct of: during his late command in North America . . . *L* 1782. [O] 4 73 a

GAMMAGE, W. L.   54
The camp, the bivouac, and the battlefield . . . a history of the Fourth Arkansas regiment . . . *Selma Ala* 1864. O 164 aa
—rptd. *Van Buren Ark* 1958. O 150 a

[GANILH, ANTHONY]   55
Mexico versus Texas, a descriptive novel . . . *Phil* 1838. D 348 aa
—ed. 2, au. named as A. T. Myrthe, "Ambrosio de Letinez; or the first Texian novel," *N Y* 1842. D 2v: 202; 192 aa
First Texan novel in English; a French novel, *L'heroine du Texas*, was published at Paris in 1819; *See* that title under Texas.

GANO (the late REV. JOHN,   56
of Frankfort [Ky.])
Biographical memoirs of. . . . *N Y* Tiebout 1806. 16° 151 a
—anr. issue, ptd. by Southwick &c.
Gano served as chaplain in the Revolution and came to Kentucky in 1787

GANTT, EDWARD W.   57
Address [attacking Albert Pike] to the people of Arkansas. *Little Rock* 1860. O 24 aa
—rptd. [*Phil* 1863]. O 29 a

GARCÉS, FRANCISCO
On the trail of a Spanish pioneer . . . *See* Cones, Elliott.

[GARCES DE MARCILLA, PEDRO]   59
Vida del Dr. Benjamin Franklin . . . *Madrid* 1798. O [22] 216 eng. t. a

GARCIA, GENARO, ed.   60
Dos antiguas relaciones de la Florida. *Mex* 1902. Q [6 3–102] 266 [2] a 500copies ptd.
A 1568 account of the Menendez expedition against French Huguenots and another relation on the Florida Indians.

GARDEN, ALEXANDER   61
Anecdotes of the revolutionary war, with sketches of . . . persons the most distinguished, in the southern states . . . *Charleston S C* 1822. O [6, 9–12] 459 [incl. errata l. & 9p subscribers' list] aa
—ser. 2. t. slightly altered, *Charleston* 1828. D [12] 240 [12 incl. errata lf] 240 aa
—both series, with adds. by Thos. W. Field, *Bklyn* 1865. Q 3v: [8] 438; 32 [5]; [10] 223 [6] 150 copies ptd. + 25 on L. P. aa

GARDINER, MISS ABIGAIL
History of the Spirit Lake massacre! . . . *See* Lee, L. P.

GARDINER, LION   62
A history of the Pequot war . . . *Cin* 1860. Q [2] 36 a
—best ed. "Relation of the Pequott warres . . .," *Hart* 1901. O [30] 33 facs 102 copies ptd.
The Cincinnati edition was issued as a separately paged appendix to Pennhallow's *Indian wars*, but some copies were bound separately.

GARDINER, RICHARD, ed.   63
Memoirs of the siege of Quebec . . . *L* 1761. Q [2] 39 b H JCB

[GARDNER, ALEXANDER]   64
Photographic sketch book of the war. *Wash* [1865–6]. obl. F 2v: 53; 53. 100 pls [incl. 2 fronts]
—rptd., ed. E. B. Eaton, "Original photographs . . .," *Hart* 1907. obl F 126 [2] pls aa
—anr ed *N Y* [1959] F 224 pls

GARDYNER, GEORGE   65
A description of the new world. *L* 1651. D [8] 189 d Hn NYP [of 6 cops in U.S.]
Based on the author's actual visit to Virginia, etc.

GARLAND, HAMLIN   66
The book of the American Indian. *N Y* 1923. F [10] 274 35pls by Remington aa

GARNER, JAMES W.   67
Reconstruction in Mississippi. *N Y* 1901 O [14] 422 aa

GARNIER, PIERRE   68
Voyage médicale en Californie. *P* 1854. O 43 aa

GARRARD, LEWIS H.   69
Memoir of Charlotte Chambers. *Phil* 1856. O [60] 135 aa
Consists largely of letters, relating to the early settlement of southern Ohio, written by Mrs. Chambers from her Cincinnati home, 1797–1821.

GARRARD, LEWIS H.   70
Wah-To-Yah, and the Taos Trail. *Cin* 1850. D [8] 349 b
—anr. ed. *S F* Grabhorn 1936. O [18] 290 [1] 550 copies ptd. aa
—rptd., ed. R. P. Bieber, *Glendale Calif* 1938. O 380 [incl. map & pls] a

GARRETSON (MR. FREEBORN).   71
The experience and travels of: . . . *Phil* Cruikshank 1791. 16° 252 a
—anr. ed. *Phil* Hall same date. D 276

GARRETT, LEWIS   72
Recollections of the west . . . *Nashv* 1834. 16° 240 b G LC WisH.
Frontier life in Ky. and Tenn.

GARRETT, PAT F.   73
The authentic life of Billy, the kid . . . *Santa Fe* 1882. O 137 front, errata slip b G Y
—rptd., ed. M. G. Fulton, *N Y* 1927. O [32] 233 port a
First genuine biography of America's most spectacular example of juvenile delinquency, purportedly by the sheriff who shot him, but actually ghost-written by a journalist friend, Marshall A. Upson.

GARRETT, WILLIAM   74
Reminiscences of public men in Alabama . . . *Atlanta* 1872. O 809 a

GARSIDE, ALSTON H.   75
Cotton goes to market . . . description of a great industry. *N Y* 1935. O [20] 411 pls diags a

[GASS, JACOB, and MILLER, JOHAN P.]   76
Chronicon Ephratense . . . *Ephrata* 1786. Q [6] 250 [2] issue 1, no community seal on t-p; issue 2, seal pasted on t-p; issue 3, seal ptd. on t-p b LC Pa H
—Eng. tr. *Lancaster* 1889. O [16] 288 a
Chief source for the history of this Pennsylvania cloister founded by Conrad Beissel.

GASS, PATRICK   77
Journal of voyages and travels. *Pitt* 1807. D 262 b
—rptd., same place & collat., 1808. aa
—eds. 2 & 3, same collat., but with 6pls, *Phil* 1810 [&] 1811. a
—ed. 4, same collat., with map added, *Phil* 1812. aa
—Eng. ed.—and best—*L* 1808. O [4] 381 b
—anr. ed. *Chi* 1904. O [56] 298 port 6pls [map mentioned on t-p not issued] some copies on L.P. a
—Fr. tr., ed. Tardieu, with notes and adds, *P* 1810. O [18] 443 map [best of Lewis and Clark route done up to this date]
Earliest full first-hand narrative of the Lewis and Clark expedition, preceding the official account seven years.

GATCHELL, H[ORATIO] P.   78
Western North Carolina; its agricultural resources . . . *Milw* 1870. D 24 errata slip a
—rptd., t. slightly altered, *N Y* 1885. D 32 [incl. front].

GATES, CHARLES M., ed.   79
Five fur traders of the northwest . . . narrative of Peter Pond, *et al* . . . *Minneap* 1933. O [8] 298 a

[GATFORD, LIONEL]   **80**
Public good without private interests . . . the present sad state of . . . Virginia . . . *L* 1657. Q [20] 26 d JCB N NYP [only cops loc]
—rptd. *P* 1866. a

GATSCHET, ALBERT S.   **81**
A migration legend of the Creek Indians . . . *Phil* 1884; *St L* 1888. O 2v: [2] 251; [2] 207. 2maps pl a
Of Vol II, a separate from Transactions, Academy of Science of St. Louis, only a few copies were issued. Highly important contribution to the history of the southern Indian. Title chosen was misleading and totally inadequate.

GAULD, GEORGE, cartographer   **82**
An account of the surveys of Florida . . . *L* 1790. Q [4] 27 map [on 2sheets] aa
—anr. ed. "Observations on the Florida kays [*sic*], reef and gulf . . .," *L* 1796. Q 28 aa
Text ascribed to Dr. John Lorimer.

GAUSE, HARRY T.   **83**
A detailed description of the scenes and incidents connected with a trip through . . . Colorado. [*Wilm Del* 1871]. D 205 a

GAYARRÉ, CHARLES E. A.   **84**
Essai historique sur la Louisiane. *N O* 1830–31. 16° 2v: [4] 210; [6] 231 [6] a

GAYARRÉ, CHARLES E. A.   **85**
Histoire de la Louisiane. *N O* 1846–47. O 2v: [14] 377; [8] 427 aa
Different work from his later history in English. Covers French period only.

GAYARRÉ, CHARLES E. A.   **86**
History of Louisiana. [French domination, 2v. 1854; Spanish domination, 1854; American domination, 1866]. *N Y* 1854–66. O 4v: 540; [12] 380; [12] 649; [8] 693, map aa
—rptd. *N Y* 1866. O 4v in 3 aa
—ed. 2, *N O* 1879. O 4v aa
—ed. 3 *N O* 1885. O 4v: 540; 383, 649; 693. maps aa
—anr. ed., with bibliog. & index added, *N O* 1903, O 4v port & maps aa
First two volumes—*French domination*—had previously appeared, New York, 1851–2, respectively entitled *Louisiana its colonial history* . . ., and *Louisiana . . . as a French colony, See* below.

GAYARRÉ, CHARLES E.A.   **87**
Lousiana; its history as a French colony . . . *N Y* 1852. O [12] 17–380 map a

GAYARRÉ, CHARLES E. A.   **88**
Romance of the history of Louisiana . . . *N Y* 1848. D 265 a

—enl. ed. "Louisiana; its colonial history and romance," *N Y* 1851. O 546

GAZETTEER   **89**
Gazetteer and business directory of the new southwest . . . *St L* 1881. O 224 [4] map a

GAZZETTIERE AMERICANO [IL] . . .
See American gazetteer . . .

GEARY (MAJOR GEN. JOHN W.)   **90**
Sketch of the early life of: . . . his trip to California in 1849 . . . *Phil* 1866. O 32 a

[GEBHARDT, A. G.] ed.   **91**
Actes et mémoires concernant les negociations . . . entre la France et les États-Unis . . . 1793–1800. *L* 1807. D 3v: [6] 368; 451; 481 [3] a
—Eng. ed. "State papers relating to the diplomatic transactions between the American and French governments . . .," *L* 1816. D 3v same paginat.

[GEE, JOSHUA]   **92**
The trade and navigation of Great-Britain considered . . . *L* 1729. O [18] 147 b
—ed. 2, au. named *L* 1730. O [18] 147 aa
—ed.3, enl. *L* 1731. O [24] 164 aa
—5 oth. eds. between 1738 and 1768 a
—Fr. tr. *P* 1749. D a
Largely concerning England's American colonies.

[GEFFS, IRVIN]   **93**
The first eight months of Oklahoma City. By Bunky. *Okla City* 1890. O 110 b G OklaH
—rptd. *Okla City* 1939. a

GELLINE, P. L.   **94**
Journal de mer d'un voyage à la Nouvelle-Orleans . . . *P* 1842. O 40 b No cop loc in U.S.

GEMELING, JOHAN G.
See Gmelin.

GENERAL
General [The] attacked . . . *See* Barry, Henry.

General [The]: or, twelve nights in the hunters' camp . . . *See* Barrows, Wm.

General opposition [The] of the colonies   **95** to . . . the stamp duty . . . *L* 1766. sm Q 40 aa some copies on L.P.

General outline [A] of the United States   **96** . . . her resources and prospects . . . *Phil* 1824. O 238 engs called for not issued a
—rptd. same impr. 1825.

General topography of North America . . . *See* Jefferys, Thos.

General view of the late war between the   97
United States . . . and Great Britain. n.p. [1815?].
16° 118[incl. preliminary blank l.] aa

General view [A] of the rise . . . of the   98
American navy . . . *Bklyn* 1828. D [8] 13–484
[incl. tabs] a
Chiefly exploits in war of 1812.

GENESEE   99
An account of the soil . . . in North America.
And particularly the lands . . . known by the name
of the Genesee tract. n.p. 1791. sm Q [1] 37 map b
AA NYP

Bericht über den Genesee-Distrikt *See New York
and Pennsylvania. An account of the soil . . . of:*

Description of the Genesee country . . . *See*
Williamson, Chas.

A view of the present situation of . . . the Genesee
country: *See* Williamson, Chas.

GENET, EDMOND C.   100
Memorial on the upward forces of fluids . . .
Alb 1825. O 112 5pls tab b
First American work on aviation.

GENTY, L'ABBE L[OUIS]   101
L'influence de la découverte de l'Amérique
sur le bonheur du genre-humain. *P* [ptd at *Orléans*]
1787, O [10] 352 [2] errata l. a
—ed. 2, same impr. 1788. same collat., with
front.&map added
—ed. 3, *Orleans* 1789. D 2v: [8 36] 292; 296
A philosopher's warning that unless some of
the evils be diminished and some advantages
fostered, no benefits would accrue to either the
old world or the new.

GENTZ, FRIEDRICH VON   102
The origin and principles of the American
revolution . . . *Phil* 1800. O 73 a

GENUINE PRINCIPLES
Genuine principles [The] of the ancient English
constitution . . . By Demophilus. *See* Bryan,
Samuel

GEOGRAPHICAL   103
Geographical and historical description [A] of
the principal objects of the present war in the
West Indies . . . *L* 1741. O [8] 192 map a
Contains three chapters on English attacks on
Florida, from Drake to Oglethorpe.

Geographical, commercial, and political   104
essays . . . *L* 1812. O [12] 323 aa
Includes remarks on Gass's *Journal* and other
papers of American interest.

Geographical, historical [etc.] view [A] of the
United States . . . *See* Blowe, Dan'l.

GEOGRAPHISCHE . . . NACHRICHTEN
Geographische und kritische Nachrichten . . .
über die Lage der nördlichen Gegenden von
Asien und Amerika . . . 1772. *See* Engel, Samuel.

GEORGE III (ROI).
Lettres . . . sur les crimes du: . . . par un officier
americain. *See* Eustace, Major-General John S.

GEORGE, HENRY   105
Our land and land policy, national and state.
S F 1871. O 48 fold.map aa
His first book; vigorous remonstrance against
indiscriminate land concessions to corporate
bodies.

GEORGE, HENRY   106
Progress and poverty: an enquiry into the cause
of industrial depression . . . and the remedy.
S F 1879. D 512 + slip asking that no reviews be
ptd. issue 1: "Author's edition." b 200copies ptd.
—issue 2, trade ed., same impr. & date. aa
The single tax theory is only incidental in this
significant American contribution to economic
and sociological thought.

GEORGE, HENRY, of Ky.   107
History of the 3rd, 7th, 8th and 12th Kentucky,
C.S.A. *Louisv* 1911. O 193 aa

GEORGE, ISAAC   108
Heroes and incidents of the Mexican war;
containing Doniphan's expedition . . . *Greensburg
Pa* 1903. D 296 6pls aa

GEORGE, N[OAH] J. T.   109
A concise . . . journal of the late war with
Great-Britain, to which is added a short account
of the war with Algiers. n.p. n.d. [*ca* 1815]. 24°
plans aa
—anr. ed. *Haverhill* 1821. aa

GEORGE, NOAH J. T.   110
A memorandum of the Creek Indian war.
Meredith N H 1815. D 24 b AA [only copy loc]

GEORGE, N[OAH] J. T.   111
A pocket . . . gazetteer of . . . Vermont. *Haverhill N H* 1823. 16° 264 a

GEORGIA
An account showing the progress of the colony
of Georgia: *See* Martyn, Benj.

A brief account of the causes that have retarded
the progress of . . . Georgia. *See* Stephens, Thos.

The case of the Georgia sales on the Mississippi.
See Harper, Robert G.

Cursory remarks on men and measures in   112
Georgia. n.p. 1784. O [2] 30 a

Documents accompanying the Report of   113
the commissioners . . . for the amicable settlement of
limits with the state of Georgia. *Wash* 1803. O 27 a
Contains Documents "G" and "K" and intended to accompany *Report of the commissioners*,
entered below.

Documents . . . relating to the boundary   114
line between . . . Georgia and Florida. [Misc. Doc.
25]. *Wash* 1855. O [12] 396 a

Examination of the controversy between   115
Georgia and the Creeks . . . *N Y* 1825. O 30 a

The general account of all the monies . . .   116
expended by the Trustees for Establishing the
Colony of Georgia. . . . *L* 1736. F 29 a

Georgia speculation unveiled. *See* Bishop,
Abraham.

Grant to the Georgia Mississippi Com-   117
pany . . . the constitution thereof, [etc.]. *Augusta*
1795. O 28 aa
—anr. ed. "by desire of the purchasers in Connecticut," *Augusta* 1795. O 39 aa
—anr. ed. "by order of the directo [*sic*]," *Augusta*
1795. O 40 aa

An impartial enquiry into the state and utility
of the province of Georgia. *See* Martyn, Benj.

The letters of a farmer to the people of   118
Georgia: or, the constitutionality . . . of the late
sales of western lands . . . *Charleston S C* 1796.
O 41 aa

The letters of Sicilius on . . . the late sale of
western lands in Georgia: *See* Jackson, James.

Message from the President accompanying   119
certain articles of agreement and cession . . . [and]
Report of the commissioners . . . for the amicable
settlement of limits with the state of Georgia:
[*Wash* 1804]. O 140 a
—anr. issue, with Act of Georgia Legislature
added. O 156
Complete *Report* here first published.

Neuste und richtigste Nachricht von der . . .
Georgia: *See* Martyn, Benj., *a new . . . account
of South Carolina and Georgia.*

A new voyage to Georgia: By a young gentleman.
See Tailfer, Pat'k.

Observations on Doctor Steven's History of
Georgia: *See* De Renne, Geo. W.-J.

Proceedings of the convention of the   120
Equal Rights and Educational Association of
Georgia: Macon, Oct. 29th, 1866. *Augusta* 1866.
O 25 a
For later convention, *See Proceedings of the
American Equal Rights Association.*

Proceedings of the Freedmen's convention   121
of Georgia: Jan. 10th, 1866 . . . *Augusta* 1866. O 40 a
First ex-slave convention—inspired doubtless
by politically minded "carpet-baggers"—in which
was established the Equal Rights Association.

Progress of the colony of Georgia: . . .   122
contrast to "State of the colony of Georgia."
[*L*] 1743. O 24 10 aa

Reasons for establishing the colony of Georgia:
See Martyn, Benj.

Report of the attorney general to to [*sic*]   123
Congress: communicating . . . documents relative
to . . . title to the land situate in the south western
parts . . . and claimed by certain companies under a
law of the state of Georgia: *Phil* 1796. O 171 aa

Report of the commissioners . . . for the   124
amicable settlement of limits with the state of
Georgia: . . . *Wash* 1803. O 22 [2] 5–92 a
See also above, *Documents accompanying the
Report . . .*, and *Message from the President . . .*

Report of the committee [of the S. C.   125
Assembly] appointed to examine into the proceed-
ings of the people of Georgia: . . . *Charlestown* 1736.
SmQ 120 + errata lf. c GaU JCB MassH NYH
Dispute over Georgia's inroads into Carolina's
Indian trade. The earliest American-printed
book relating to Oglethorpe's colony.

State of facts shewing the right of certain   126
companies to the lands lately purchased by them
from the state of Georgia [*Phil?*] 1795. O 64 aa

A state of the province of Georgia. *See* Stephens,
Wm.

A true account of the colonies of Nova   127
Scotia, and Georgia. [*L* ? 1774?]. O 24 aa

A vindication of the recent . . . policy of the
state of Georgia . . . *See* Clayton, Augustin S.

GÉRARD, A. G.   128
Itinéraire de Québec à Chicago. *Montr* 1868.
O [4] 170 pl a

GERKE, HEINRICH C.   129
Der nordamerikanische Rathgeber, nebst den,
in den Jahren 1831 und 1832 . . . *Hamburg* 1833.
D 598 a

GERMAIN [*sic*] (LORD G[EORGE]). 130
Correspondance du: avec les généraux Clinton, Cornwallis, *et al. Berne* 1782. O [16] 304 port 2tabs aa
—rptd. *L* 1784. same collat. a
Apparently there was no English edition.

GERMAINE (LORD GEORGE). 131
A letter to: *L* 1776. O 38 + adv-l. a
Urges discontinuance of the American war as hopeless. This is entirely different from the pamphlet of similar title next described.

GERMAINE (LORD GEORGE). 132
A letter to: giving an account of the origin of the dispute between Great Britain and the colonies . . . *L* 1778. O 84 a
Advocates peace, but not on the terms of American independence. "The Americans are in a state of insanity . . . everything done by them in that condition should be held void . . ."

[GERMAINE, LORD GEORGE] 133
A reply to Lieut. Gen. Burgoyne's Letter to his constituents . . . *L* 1779. O [4] 46 a
—eds. 2 & 3, same impr., date & collat.
Ascribed also to Sir John Dalrymple.

GERSTÄCKER, FRIEDRICH 134
Amerikanische-Wald-und Strombilder. *Leip* 1849. O 2v: 205; 224 a
—anr. ed. *Ghent* 1856. O [4] 444
—anr. ed. *Leip* 1862. D 2v: [4] 218; [4] 219

GERSTÄCKER, FRIEDRICH 135
Californische Skizzen. *Leip* 1856. O [4] 379 a
—Fr. ed. "Scenes de la vie Californienne," *Geneva* 1859. D 262 + adv-p 6 pls a
—rptd. same impr. 1860.
—Eng. ed. "Scenes of life in California," *S F* Grabhorn 1942. O [14] 188 pls 500copies ptd. a
—anr. Eng. ed. "California gold mines," *Oakland* 1946. O []14] 150 map pls 500copies ptd.

GERSTÄCKER, FRIEDRICH 136
Der deutschen Auswanderer Fahrten und Schicksale. *Leip* 1847. O [4] 334 map aa
—rptd., same impr. & collat., 1849; 1854 .a
—Dutch ed. "Lotgevallen en Ontmoetingen . . .," *Amst* 1847. O [4] 352 map pl a
—Eng. eds.: "The wanderings and fortunes of some German emigrants," *N Y* 1848. D 3–270; *L* 1848. D [8] 310; *L* 1850. same collat .a
Attempt to establish a German colony on the Mississippi.

GERSTÄCKER, FRIEDRICH 137
Gold! Ein Californisches Lebenbild aus dem Jahre 1849. *Leip* 1858. D 3v: [6] 327; [6] 322; [6] 341 aa

GERSTÄCKER, FRIEDRICH 138
Kalifornien's Gold u. Quecksilber-District . . . *Leip* 1849. O 32 map a
—3 other eds., same year

GERSTÄCKER, FRIEDRICH 139
Das kleine Goldgraber in Californien. *Ghent* 1857. 16° [6] 346 6pls a

GERSTÄCKER, FRIEDRICH 140
Mississippi-Bilder, Licht-und Schattenseiten transatlantischen Lebens. *Dresden* 1847–8. D 3v: [4] 343; [4] 386; [4] 371 aa
—rptd. *Leip* 1853–6. 16° 3v: [4] 352; [6] 414; [6] 363 a
—Eng. ed. "Western land and western waters," *L* 1864. O [12] 388 a

GERSTÄCKER, FRIEDRICH 141
Nach Amerika! . . . *Jena* 1855. O 6v: [12] 260; 258; 296; 263; 274; 252. 32pls a
—anr. ed. *Leip* 1855. same collat.

GERSTÄCKER, FRIEDRICH 142
Streif-und Jagdzüge durch die Vereinigten Staaten . . . *Dresden* 1844. D 2v: [8] 311; [4] 323 a
—anr. ed. *Leip* 1856. D 2v in 1 same collat.
—Eng. tr. "Wild sports in the far west," *L* 1854. D [12] 396 8pls
—rptd. *L* 1856; 1862. 16°
—Am. eds.: *B* 1859; 1866. D
Experiences in Arkansas, etc.

GERSTÄCKER, FRIEDRICH 143
Wie ist es denn nun Eigentlich in Amerika? . . . *Leip* 1849. 16° [8] 127 a
—rptd., same impr. & collat., 1853.

GERSTNER, CLARA VON 144
Beschreibung einer Reise durch die Vereinigten Staaten . . . *Leip* 1842. D [12] 456 aa
Travelled throughout the South from Virginia to Louisiana and to Illinois, Kentucky and Ohio.

GERSTNER, FRANZ ANTON VON 145
Berichte aus den Vereinigten Staaten . . . über Eisenbahnen, Dampfschiffahrten, Banken . . . *Leip* 1839. Q [4] 67 aa

GERSTNER, FRANZ ANTON VON 146
Die innern Communicationen der Vereinigten Staaten . . . *Vienna* 1842–3. Q 2v: [8] 376; [4] 339. map 34pls aa

GESCHICHTE
Geschichte der englischen Kolonien in Nordamerika . . . *See* Klausing, Anton E.

Geschichte der Kriege in und ausser Europa 147
vom Aufange des Austandes der brittischen Kolonien

in Nordamerika an . . . **1776.** [*Nurnberg*] Gabriel N. Raspe 1777–84. sm Q 30pts[usually bound in 7vols.] 10 maps & pls [only 8 in some cops]

Compiled—probably by the publisher—from German newspapers and other contemporary sources. Ascribed also to Christopher Korn.

Geschichte des amerikanischen Kriegs von   148 1812 . . . *Reading* 1817. O [8] 273 port a

To some copies a folding plate of the battle of New Orleans was added.

Geschichte und Handlung der englischen Colonien . . . *See* Butel-Dumont.

GETZENDANER, W. H. and   149 DICHMAN, A. M.

A brief . . . history of Parson's Texas cavalry brigade . . . *Waxahachie Tex.* 1892. O 96 aa

GEVERS DEYNOOT, W. T.   150

Aanteekeningen op eene Reis door de Vereenigde Staten . . . c Canada. *Hague* 1860. O [12 incl eng t.] 264 6pls aa

Travels extended to Minnesota and Missouri.

GIBBES, R[OBERT] W.   151

Documentary history of the American revolution . . . chiefly in South Carolina, in 1781–1782. *Columbia S C* 1853. O [16] 288 a

—enl. ed., covering years 1764–1782. *N Y* 1855–57. O 2v: [12] 292; [12] 293 aa

[GIBBON, EDWARD]   152

Mémoire justificatif pour servir de réponse à l'Exposé . . . de la cour de France. *L* 1779. Q [2] 32 aa

—rptd., same impr., 1780. a

—Eng.tr. "Exposition of the motives . . ." L. 1780 Q aa

Reply to the exposition, justifying French assistance to America, which had appeared at Madrid [in French] earlier in 1779. For reply see Beaumarchais, Pierre A. C. de.

GIBBS, MIFFLIN W.   153

Shadow and light. An autobiography . . . *Wash* 1902. D 372 aa

Describes an overland trip to California, in 1850, made by this educated negro, with later experiences in California and British Columbia.

GIBSON, J. WATT   154

Recollections of a pioneer . . . [*St Joseph Mo* 1912]. O 216 port aa

GIBSON, JAMES   155

A journal of the late siege by the troops from North America, against the French at Cape Breton . . . *L* 1745. O [2] 50 fold.plan b AA JCB N NYP Y

—rptd. "Narrative . . .," *L* 1785. aa

—Am. ed. "A Boston merchant of 1745 . . .,." *B* 1847. D 102 a

GIBSON, JOHN, pub.

Guide and directory for . . . Louisiana . . . *See* Louisiana.

[GIDDINGS, MAJOR LUTHER]   156

Sketches of the campaign in northern Mexico . . . *N Y* 1853. D 336 map plan a

Ascribed also to M. E. Curwen.

GIDDINS, EDWARD   157

An inquiry into the causes of the rise and fall of the lakes . . . *Lockport N Y* 1838. O 31 a

GIDEON, D. C.   158

Indian Territory . . . *N Y & Chi* 1901. Q [16] 956 2pls aa

GIFT, GEORGE W.   159

Facts about Napa county . . . *Napa City Calif* 1876. O 64 map aa

GIFT, GEORGE W.   160

Settler's guide . . . *Benicia Calif* 1854. O 32 b

—rptd. *Stockton* 1857. O 24 b Y

GILBERT, AMOS   161

Memoir of Fanny Wright, the pioneer woman in the cause of human rights. *Cin* 1855. D 86 a

GILBERT (BENJAMIN).

A narrative of the captivity . . . of: *See* Walton, Wm.

GILBERT, FRANK T.   162

History of San Joaquin county [Calif.] . . . *Oakland* 1879. Q 142 6maps 171pls aa

[GILBERT, OLIVE]   163

Narrative of Sojourner Truth. *B* 1850. D 144 port a

—several reprints

GILBERT, R. R.   164

Confederate letters. *Austin* 1894. O 75 a

[GILES, FRYE W.]   165

Historical sketch of Shawnee county, Kansas. *Topeka* 1876. D 68 errata slip a

GILES, FRYE W.   166

Thirty years in Topeka . . . *Topeka* 1886. O 412 front. [100 copies ptd] aa

GILES (JOHN).   167

Memoirs of odd adventures [etc.] in the captivity of: . . . *B* 1736. O [2] 40 [4] c H N [of 4 known copies]

—rptd., with adds., *Cin* 1869. O 64 a 250 copies ptd

GILES, L[EONIDAS] B.   **168**
Terry's Texas rangers. [*Austin*] 1911. D 105 aa

GILL, JOHN   **169**
Reminiscences of . . . a private soldier in the Confederate army. *Balt* 1904. O 136 [2] port a

GILL, OBADIAH, et al   **170**
Some few remarks upon a scandalous book . . . by one Robert Calef . . . *B* 1701. D 72 b AA H N NYP

GILL (WILLIAM).   **171**
California letters of: written in 1850 to his wife . . . *N Y* [1922]. Q 43 map port b G LC NYP 100copies ptd.

GILLELAND, J. C.   **172**
The history of the late war between the United States and Great Britain . . . *Balt* 1817. D 151 a
—ed. 2, same impr. & date. D 191 a
—ed. 3, same impr. 1818. 16° 175

GILLELAND, J. C.   **173**
The Ohio and Mississippi pilot . . . *Pitt* 1820. D 2pts in 1: 46[incl. 16maps]; 47–274 aa
—anr. ed., without the geography, "The Ohio pilot," *Pitt* 1826. 16° 34 aa
Borrowed largely from the earlier Cramer's *Navigator*, and furthermore doesn't live up to its title, only the Ohio being charted.

GILLELEN, F. M. L.   **174**
The oil regions of Pennsylvania . . . *Pitt* 1865. O 67 map 16 charts aa

GILLEM, COL. ALVAN C.   **175**
Report on the Modoc war . . . *Benicia Barracks Cal* 1874. D 24 aa
—rptd. [*Wash*] 1877. [Sen. Exec. Doc. 1]. O 18 a
Earliest account of this disastrous campaign.

GILLESPY, JOHN C., ed.   **176**
History of Green Lake county [Wis.] . . . as related by old pioneers . . . *Berlin Wis* 1860. D 120 [incl. advs] aa

GILLETT, JAMES B.   **177**
Six years with the Texas Rangers . . . *Austin* [1921]. D 332 8pls aa
—rptd: *N Hav* 1925. O; ed. Quaife, *Chi* 1943. 16° a

GILLETTE, CHARLES   **178**
A few historic records of the church in the diocese of Texas, during the rebellion . . . *N Y* 1865. O 131 a

GILLIAM, ALBERT M.   **179**
Travels over the table lands . . . of Mexico . . . including a description of California . . . *Phil* 1846. O 455 3maps 10pls aa
—rptd. *Aberdeen Scot* 1847. D 312 a

GILLILAND, WILLIAM   **180**
Pioneer history of the Champlain valley . . . *Alb* 1863. O 231 a 26copies on L.P.

GILLMORE, PARKER   **181**
Adventures afloat and ashore. [Largely devoted to life and sport on Chesapeake bay] *L* 1873. D 2v: [10] 297; [10] 267 + 16adv-p 2 fronts a

GILMAN, MRS. CAROLINE, ed.   **182**
Letters of Eliza Wilkinson, during the . . . possession of Charleston, S. C., by the British . . . *N Y* 1839. D 108 a

GILMAN, MRS. CAROLINE   **183**
The poetry of travelling in the United States . . . *N Y* 1838. D [10] 430 a

[GILMAN, CHANDLER R.]   **184**
Legends of a log-cabin. *N Y* 1835. D [4] 277 a

[GILMAN, CHANDLER R.]   **185**
Life on the lakes . . . *N Y* 1836. D 2v: [4] 270; [4] 275. 2pls aa
Ascribed sometimes to Charles Lanman and sometimes to Margaret Fuller Ossoli; to the latter through confusion with her *Summer on the lakes.*

GILMER, GEORGE R.   **186**
Sketches of some of the first settlers of upper Georgia . . . *N Y* 1855. O 587 port aa
—rptd. *Americus Ga* 1926. O 458 a

GILMOR, HARRY   **187**
Four years in the saddle. *L* 1866. D [8] 310 a
—Am. ed. *N Y* 1866. D 291 [incl front]

GILMOR, ROBERT   **188**
Memoir . . . of Robert Gilmor of Baltimore . . . [*Balt* 1840]. O 46 port a

[GILPIN, HENRY D.]   **189**
A northern tour: . . . to Saratoga . . . *Phil* 1825. 16° [8] 279 fold.map a

GILPIN, JOSHUA   **190**
A memoir on the . . . Chesapeake and Delaware canal . . . *Wilm Del* 1821. O [4] 50 72 5maps a

GILPIN, WILLIAM, 1724-1804   **191**
Memoirs of Josias Rogers . . . *L* 1808. O [8] 184 front. a
British naval officer in the revolution.

GILPIN, WILLIAM, 1822-94   **192**
The central gold region . . . *Phil* 1860. O 194 6maps a
—rptd., with adds., "Mission of the American people . . .," *Phil* 1873. O 217 6maps
—rev. ed., same impr., 1874. O 223 6maps

GILPIN (WILLIAM) 1822-94 193
History of the life of: *S F* 1889. O 62 map
port a
Overland to Oregon, 1843; with Doniphan in
New Mexico; Governor of Colorado; etc.

GILPIN, WILLIAM, 1822-94 194
Notes on Colorado ... [*L* 1870]. D 52 a
—ed. 2, same collat. & impr., [1871].

GILSON, WILLIAM R. 195
Up-hill in Canada and south California. *Montr*
1923. O 86 a

[GIRARD, CHARLES F.] 196
Les États Confédérés d'Amérique visités en
1863 ... *P* 1864. O 160 map a

GIRARD, JUST [pseud.]
Les aventures d'un capitaine francais ... *See*
Roy, Just J. E.

GIRDLESTONE, THOMAS 197
Facts tending to prove that General [Charles]
Lee was ... the author of Junius. *Yarmouth & L*
1813. O [8] 138 errata slip port 2facs a
Some of the letters contained relate to his Amer-
ican experiences.

[GIROD-CHANTRANS, JUSTIN] 198
Voyage d'un Suisse dans différentes colonies
d'Amérique pendant la dernière guerre ... *Neu-*
chatel 1785. O [8] 416 tab aa
—rptd., same sheets with new t-p, *L* 1786. aa
—Ger. ed. "Reisen eines Schweizers ...," *Leip*
1786. O 304 a
Travels chiefly restricted to Santo Domingo.

GIST, CHRISTOPHER
Journals. *See* Darlington, William M.

GIVEN, ABRAHAM 199
Overland trip to California in 1850. *Frankfort*
Ind [*ca* 1900]. O 24 a

GLADSTONE, THOMAS H. 200
Kansas; or, squatter life and border warfare ...
L 1857. D [8] 295 map 2pls a
—ed 2 *L* 1858, same collat
—Am. ed. "The Englishman in Kansas ...," *N Y*
1857. D 328
—Ger. ed. "Bilder und Skizzen aus Kansas ...,"
Leip 1857. O; rptd. 1860.

GLANCE (A) AT THE TIMES ... 201
By a Yankee. *Phil* 1827. D 52 a

GLASSCOCK (LEMUEL). 202
The life and travels of: [*Maysville Ky* 1841]?
O 27 aa

GLEED, CHARLES S. 203
The Kansas memorial ... *K C* 1880. O 261
fold.map front. a

GLEESON, WILLIAM 204
History of the Catholic church in California. *S F*
1872-1. O 2v: [15] 446; 351. 4 maps & plans 9pls
b LC
—anr. ed. 2v in 1. 1872. Made from sheets of ed. 1
salvaged from the fire which had destroyed many
copies. b

[GLEIG, GEORGE R.] 205
A narrative of the campaigns of the British army
at Washington and New Orleans ... *L* 1821. O [4]
377 + errata lf a
—later Eng. eds.: *L* 1826; 1827; 1836; 1837; 1847;
1861
—Am. ed. *Phil* 1821. O 431
—Ger tr *Celle* 1832. D [12] 371

[GLEN, DR. JAMES] 206
A description of South Carolina ... *L* 1761. O
[8] 110 + 2adv-p c N NYP Y
As a general history preceded only by Hewatt's
Account of South Carolina and Georgia ... Has
been ascribed to Governor James Glenn of South
Carolina.

GLENN, THOMAS A. 207
Merion in the Welsh tract ... *Norristown* 1896.
O [12 incl blank lf] 394 [2] 21 pls a

GLENN, THOMAS A. 208
Some colonial mansions and those who lived in
them ... Ser. I & II. *Phil* 1898–1900. O 2v: [22]
17–482; [14] 19–504. 20pls + 20explanatory lvs. a

GLISAN, RODNEY 209
Journal of army life ... *S F* 1874. O [12] 511
21pls tab a
Served in Oklahoma, Washington and Oregon.

GLOVER, THOMAS 210
An account of Virginia ... *Oxf* 1904. O 31 a
250copies ptd.
First separate printing; appeared previously
only in *Transactions of the Royal Society*, 1677.

[GMELIN (or GEMELING), 211
JOHAN G.]
Disputatio geographica de vero Californiae situ
et conditione. *Marburg* [1739]. D 30 c B [of a few
copies known]

GMELIN [or GEMELING], JOHAN G. 212
Reise durch Siberien, 1733–1743. *Göttingen*
1751–2. O 4v: [14] 467; [35] 652; [24] 584; [4] 692
[8]. 23maps & pls b NYP Y
—Dutch tr. *Haarlem* 1752-7. O 4v map pls aa

—Fr. tr. abr., *P* 1767. D 2v: [22] 430; [8 erratically numb.] 324 [4]. 2pls aa

One of the earliest accounts of Bering's voyage to the Northwest mainland, written by the botanist of the expedition. For other accounts, *see* Müller, Gerhard F.

GOBLE, BENJAMIN 213

Narrative of incidents in the life of an Illinois pioneer . . . *Moline* 1881. O 35[incl. in some cops only an inserted front. (photo of au.)] b MolineP RockIslandP

GODDARD, G. H. 214

Report . . . on a reconnaissance of the . . . immigrant roads over the Sierra Nevada, and a survey of the eastern boundary of California. *Sacr* 1856. O 334 tab aa

GODFREY, CARLOS E. 215

The commander-in-chief's guard . . . *Wash* 1904. O 302[incl.front.] 6pls 9facs[2fold.] a

GODLEY, JOHN R. 216

Letters from America. *L* 1844. D 2v: [24] 272; [8] 243 + 5 adv-p a

GÖBEL, GERT 217

Länger als ein Menschenleben in Missouri. *St L* [1877]. O [8] 234 aa

Autobiography of a pioneer who settled in Missouri in 1834.

GÖCKING, G. G. GÜNTHER 218

Vollkommene Emigrations-Geschichte von denen aus dem Ertz-Biszthum Sallzburg . . . *Frankf* 1734–7. Q 2v: [20] 822; [12] 888 [72]. 2maps 2pls aa

Includes emigration to Georgia by this sect.

[GOENS, R. M. VAN] 219

Politiek Vertoog . . . [*Utrecht*] 1781. F 151 a
—unauthorized ed., same date. O [2] 346 [1]

Disapproves of the assistance indirectly given to the American colonists by Holland during the Revolution.

GÖRLING, ADOLPH 220

Die Neue Welt. Skizzen von Land und Leuten der . . . Freistaaten. *Leip* 1848. D 614 [10] 69pls aa

Includes a comprehensive historical account of the Ohio Zoarites, along with extensive descriptions of many towns, etc., in the Ohio and Mississippi valleys.

GOFF, LYMAN B. 221

An 1862 trip to the west. [*Pawtucket* 1926]. D 158 10pls aa

Overland adventures from St. Paul to Fort Garry and among the Sioux.

GOLD IN THE BLACK HILLS . . .

See Smith, D. N.

GOLDEN LAND (THE)

Golden land (The) . . . history . . . of the Black hills gold region. *See Black hills gold region.*

GOLDER, FRANK A. 223

Russian expansion on the Pacific . . . *Clev* 1914. O 368[incl. maps & pls] aa

GOLDMANN, FREIDMUND 224

Briefe aus Wisconsin . . . *Leip* 1849. D [8] 96 aa

GOLDSBOROUGH, CHARLES W. 225

The United States' naval chronicle. Vol. I [all]. *Wash* 1824. O 396 + errata slip pasted on last p. a

GOLDSBOROUGH, W. W. 226

The Maryland line in the Confederate States army. *Balt* 1869. D 357 9ports a
—enl. ed. [*Balt* 1900]. O 371 21pls

[GOLDSMITH, J.] 227

The present state of the British empire in Europe, Asia, Africa and America . . . *L* 1768. O [8] 486 5maps pl aa

GOLDSMITH, REV. J. [pseud.]

A view of the character . . . of the North-Americans . . . *See* Phillips, Sir Richard.

GOLDSMITH, OLIVER 228

Overland in forty-nine . . . *Detroit* 1896. D 148 9pls b LC N

GOLDSON, WILLIAM 229

Observations on the passage between the Atlantic and Pacific . . . *Portsmouth Eng* 1793. Q [12] 162 map b N Y

GOLOVIN, IVAN 230

Stars and stripes; or, American impressions. *L* 1856. D 312 a
—Am. ed. *N Y* same date & collat.

American democracy examined by a Russian political exile and found by no means perfect.

GOLOVNIN, VASILII M. 231

Memoirs of a captivity in Japan, 1812–1813 . . . Eng ed 2, *L* 1824. O 3v: [4] 302; 348; 302 aa

Earlier Russian, German, French and English editions contained only the captivity narrative: to the edition listed was added Admiral Shishkov's account of the fur-trading voyages of Kyvostov and Davydov to the Northwest coast of America, 1804–7.

GOLOVNIN, VASILII M. 232

Putéshestvie vokroug svieta po poveleniiu Gosudaria . . . 1817–19. *St Ptbg* 1822. Q 2v: [12] 512 44; [10] 206 127 2 fold tabs 15maps & pls b LC NYP Y

On this Russian voyage around the world the northwest coast and California were visited. Golovnin was severely critical of the Russian-American Company for conditions among both settlers and natives. This is his most important work.

GOLOVNIN, VASILII M.   233
Sokrashcennyia zapiski flota . . . o plavanni ego na shlieupie Dianie . . . *St Ptbg* 1819. Q 146 3maps aa
Account of a Russian voyage in 1811 to the Kurile Islands, etc., completing Aleutian discoveries by La Perouse, Broughton and Krusenstern. Information on this voyage was also included in the admiral's *Putéshestvie* . . . entered above.

[GOMEZ DEL PALACIO] FRANCISCO]   234
Claims of Mexican citizens against the United States for Indian depredations . . . *Wash* 1871. O 162 + cov.t. aa
—Sp. tr. *Mex* 1872. D 259 a
—anr. issue, same impr. & date. O 172 + cov.t.

GOOD
Good fetched out of evil: a collection of memorables relating to our captives. *See* Williams, John.

GOOD HUMOR
Good humor; or, a way with the colonies . . . *See* Tod, Nicholas.

GOODE, G[EORGE] B.   235
Virginia cousins . . . *Rich* 1887. O [36] 526 + 10[4 after p32, 6 after p50] 5 lvs. [one each at 32, 36, 50, 110 & 164] slip at p302. map pl 51ports 2pedigree charts aa

GOODE, WILLIAM H.   236
Outposts of Zion . . . *Cin* 1863. D 464 front. a
—rptd. 1864, same collat
Experiences of a frontier missionary, in Kansas, Nebraska, etc.

[GOODENOW, STIRLING]   237
A brief topographical and statistical manual of the state of New York. *Alb* 1811. O 34 a
—ed. 2, enl. *N Y* 1822. O 88

GOODHART, BRISCOE   238
History of the Independent Loudon Virginia rangers, U. S. Vol. cavalry, 1862–65. *Wash* 1896. D [6] 234 19pls a

GOODHUE, JOSIAH F.   239
History of . . . Shoreham, Vermont . . . *Middlebury* 1861. O [6] 198 [2] a

GOODLANDER, C. W.   240
Memoirs and recollections . . . of the early days of Fort Scott . . . *Ft Scott Kan* 1899. 16° 79 port pls aa
—rptd., same impr., 1900. 16° 147 30pls a

GOODMAN, THOMAS M.   241
A thrilling record . . . *Des M* 1868. D 66 aa
Account of the Centralia massacre by Bill Anderson's guerillas, told by one of the few Federal soldiers who escaped.

GOODMANE, W. F.   242
Seven years in America. *L* 1845. O 32 a
Compares Canada with the states [and Texas].

GOODNIGHT, CHARLES, et al
Pioneer days in the southwest . . . *See* under Hart, John A., *History of pioneer days in Texas and Oklahoma* . . .

GOODPASTURE, ALBERT V.   243
Overton county [Tenn.]. *Nash* 1877. O 27 a

GOODRICH, S[AMUEL] G.   244
Recollections of a lifetime . . . *N Y* 1851. O 2v: 542; 563 a
—rptd., same collat. & impr. 1857.

[GOODRICKE, HENRY]   245
Observations on Dr. Price's theory . . . of civil liberty . . . *York Eng* 1776. O [8] 147 a
—Dutch tr. *Leyden* 1777. O

[GOODRICKE, HENRY]   246
A speech on some political topics . . . intended to have been delivered in the House of Commons . . . *L* 1779. D [8] 71 a
Discusses at length complaints of the colonies.

GOODWIN, CARDINAL L.   247
The trans-Mississippi west. *N Y* 1922. O [14] 528 6maps a

GOODWIN, H. C.   248
Pioneer history; or Cortland county and the border wars of New York . . . *N Y* 1859. D 456 3pls a

GOODWIN, W. A. R.   249
Historical sketch of Bruton church, Williamsburg, Virginia. [*Petersburg*] 1903. O 183 16pls a

GOOKIN, DANIEL   250
Historical collections of the Indians in New England . . . *B* 1792. O pp. 141–227 of Mass. Hist. Soc. Colls., V. I. aa
—rptd. *B* 1806. same collat. a
—anr ed *B* 1859, same collat a

GOOKIN, FREDERICK W.   251
Daniel Gookin, 1612–1687 . . . his life and letters . . . *Chi* 1912. O [16 incl.front.] 208 [1] 10pls a 202copies ptd.

GORDON, JAMES B.   252
An historical . . . memoir of the North Ameri-

can continent; its nations and tribes . . . *Dub* 1820.
Q [126incl.port] 305 errata slip & pub.'s note
inserted a some copies on L.P. aa
  Two chapters on New Mexico, California and
Northwest coast.

GORDON (MR. JOHN).
  The case of: with respect to . . . certain lands in
East Florida . . . *See* Walker, Fowler.

GORDON, MARQUIS L.   253
  Experiences in the civil war . . . *B* 1922. Q [14]
3–72 pls a Small ed.

[GORDON, PATRICK?]   254
  The history of the war in America, between
Great Britain and her colonies . . . *Dub* 1779–85.
O 3v: [8] 5–41 [2] 2–352 349–399; 427 [4]; [16] 432.
map tab b N NYP

GORDON, SAMUEL   255
  Recollections of old Milestown, Montana. *Miles
City* 1918. O [2] 46 18pls aa

GORDON, WILLIAM   256
  The history of rise, progress and establishment
of the independence of the United States . . . *L*
1788. O 4v: [26] 504; [8] 584; [8] 499; [8] 446 [34].
9maps & plans a some copies on thick paper aa
—Am. eds.: *N Y* 1789. O 3v: [12] 25–443; [10]
25–474; [36] 17–446. 2maps; *N Y* 1794. O 3v: 431;
460; 448 a
—rptd. *N Y* 1801. O 3v
  First full-scale history of this war by an American; to its preparation Jefferson contributed some
aid.

[GORDON-MILLER, WILLIAM L.]   257
  Recollections of the United States army . . . By
an American soldier . . . *B* 1845. 18° [12] 167[incl.
8pls] a
—ed. 2, same impr., date & collat.
  See also Hildreth, James, *Dragoon campaigns* . . .

GORGES, FERDINANDO   258
  America painted to the life . . . *L* 1658–59. smQ
4 parts in 1: [6] 52; [2] 58; [4] 236, numb. in error
239; [4] 52 [20, incl 3 adv-p] double-page map,
and, in some few cops, a fldg front but whether
this was issued regularly in the book is questionable. dd AA N NYP
  Most important early account of the present
Maine. The publisher [N. Brooke] issued also Edw.
Johnson's *History of New England*, in 1654; he
utilized unsold sheets of that work to form the third
part of Gorges' work without proper explanation.

GORHAM, GEORGE C.   259
  The story of the attempted assassination of
Justice Field . . . n.p. n.d. O 198 a

—rptd. in the 1893 ed. of Field's "Personal reminiscences . . ."
  Some copies of orig. ed. have correction slips
pasted over certain passages.

GORIN, FRANKLIN   260
  The times of long ago. Barren county [Ky.]
Louisv 1929. O 131 a
  Written in 1876, by the first white child born in
this county and owner of the Mammoth Cave, but
here first published in book form.

G[ORMAN], CAPT. J[OHN] C.   261
  Lee's last campaign. *Raleigh* 1866. 16° 59 a
—ed. 2, same impr. & date. 16° 71

GORMAN, SAMUEL   262
  The Pueblo Indians . . . *N Y* 1860. O 25 a

[GOROSTIZA, MANUEL E.]   263
  Dictámen leido . . . en el Consejo de Gobierno
sobre la cuestion de Tejas. *Mex* 1844. D [4] 21 aa
  Urges an attempt to recover Texas before increased population makes the task too formidable.

GOROSTIZA (M[ANUEL] E.),
late envoy . . . from Mexico.
  Examination of a pamphlet . . . circulated by:
See Weaver, Wm. A.

[GORRELL, JOSEPH R.]   264
  After forty years [including 1865 trip from St
Paul to Montana]. np nd. O 39 aa

GORRELL, J[OSEPH] R.   265
  A trip to Alaska. *Newton Ia* 1905. D 40 aa

[GOSCH, JOSIAS L.]   266
  Washington und die amerikanische Revolution.
Giesen 1807. 16° [2] 280 a
—rptd. "Washington und die nordamerikanische
Revolution," *Giesen* 1810. D
—rptd. *Giesen* 1817; *Giesen* 1818.

GOSS, C. CHAUCER   267
  Bellevue, Larimer and Saint Mary [Neb.], their
history [etc.]. *Bellevue* 1859. D 48 maps [cover t.
only] bNeb H [of 3 cops loc]
  First imprint of Bellevue, one of the American
Fur Co's earliest trading posts.

GOSSE, PHILIP H.   268
  Letters from Alabama, chiefly relating to natural history. *L* 1859. 16° [12] 306 a

GOSSELMAN, CARL A.   269
  Resa i norra Amerika. *Nyköping* 1835. O 2v:
[8] 326; [14] 332 aa

[GOTTLIEB, G. A.]   269a
  Nachrichten und Erfahrungen über die Ver-

einigten Staaten . . . gesammelt auf einer Reise in den Jahren 1806 bis 1808 von einem Rheinländer. *Frankf* 1812. D [4, 3–4] 260 fold.tab pl aa
—rptd. same impr. & collat. 1814.

GOTTSCHALK, LOUIS M.   270
Notes of a pianist; during . . . tours in the United States, Canada . . . *Phil* 1881. O 480 port a
Tours through the East, Middle West and Far West by a musical prodigy from Louisiana, who Chopin predicted would become the king of pianists.

GOUGHNOUR, E.   271
Across the plains in '49. n.p. [*Libertyville Ia ca* 1910]. D [2] 54 port b G [only 6cops ptd]

GOULD, DANIEL   272
A brief narration of the sufferings of the . . . Quakers . . . [*N Y* 1700]. Q 38 aa

GOULD, EMERSON W.   273
Fifty years on the Mississippi . . . *St L* 1889. O [16] 750 front. errata p aa
—rptd. *Columbus O* 1951. same collat. a

GOULD, JAY   274
History of Delaware county and border wars of New York . . . *Roxbury* [ptd *Phil*] 1856. O [16] 426 port a
Many copies destroyed by fire and some of those escaping that fate were bought up and destroyed by the author.

GOULD (JAY).   275
Life and death of: and how he made his millions. *N Y* [*ca* 1892]. D 208 a

GOULD, JAY   276
The Missouri Pacific Railroad Company . . . history of the title to its property . . . *N Y* 1884. O 48 a

GOULDER, WILLIAM A.   277
Reminiscences . . . of a pioneer in Oregon and Idaho. *Boise* 1909. D 376 port a
Goulder ascended the Missouri with Benton and Robidoux in 1844.

[GOULDING, JOHN?]   278
Statistics of the woolen manufactories in the United States . . . *N Y* 1845. D 190 a

GOVE, CAPT. JESSE A.   279
The Utah expedition, 1857–8. *Concord N H* 1928. O 442 5pls a
—L.P. issue, same impr., date & collat. Q 50copies ptd. aa

GRABER, H. W.   280
The life record. A Terry Texas ranger, 1861–5 . . . [*Dallas* 1916]? D 442 [incl.port] aa small ed. ptd.

GRABOWSKI, STANISLAUS   281
Die Regulatoren von San Francisco. *Berlin* [*ca* 1850]. 16° 348 aa

GRACE (HENRY).   282
The history of the life and sufferings of: . . . during . . . captivity among the savages of North America . . . *Basingstoke* 1764. O 56 dd N NYP [of 6 cops loc]
—ed. 2, same collat., 1765. c N [of 2 cops loc]
Patterned after Peter Williamson's similar narrative, but far less credible.

GRACE, JOHN N., and JONES, R. B.   283
A new history of Parker county [Texas] . . . *Weatherford Tex* 1906. O 206 + 20adv-p pls a

GRADY (MR.)   284
A description of the famous new colony of Georgia, in South Carolina . . . in a letter from: . . . *Dub* 1734. D [6] 3–138 aa
Fanciful hoax relating in no sense to Georgia except for a 1733 letter from Oglethorpe.

GRAHAM, JAMES   285
The life of General Daniel Morgan . . . *N Y* 1856. D 475 port a
—rptd., same impr. & collat.: 1858; 1859.
By General Morgan's grand-son.

GRAHAM (LIEUTENANT COLONEL   286
[JAMES D.])
Report of the Secretary of War, communicating . . . the report of: on the subject of the boundary line between the United States and Mexico. [Sen. Exec. Doc. 121]. [*Wash* 1852]. O 250 2maps profile a

GRAHAM, JAMES J., ed.   287
Memoir of General [Samuel] Graham, with notices of the campaigns in which he was engaged from 1779 to 1801. *Edin* 1862. D [20] 318 2maps 5pls a 100copies ptd.
Graham served, as Captain, with Cornwallis in Carolina and Virginia.

GRAHAM, JOHN A.   288
A descriptive sketch of the present state of Vermont . . . *L* 1797. O [8] 187 2-line errata port aa
—iss 2, same except has 6-line errata

GRAHAM, MRS. M[ARTHA] M.   289
The polygamist's victim . . . experiences of the author . . . *S F* 1872. D 72 b B G H
—rptd. "Life of Martha Morgan," *S F* 1875. b UCLA
For another book by this authoress, *see* Morgan, Mrs. Martha M.

GRAHAM, MARY   290
Historical reminiscences of one hundred years ago . . . *S F* 1876. D 40 aa

Account of San Francisco's first mission—Mission Dolores—and of Maria de la Concepcion Arguello, the betrothed of Rezanov.

GRAHAM, WILLIAM A.   **291**
Gen. James Graham . . . *Raleigh* 1904. O 385 map 12pls a
Includes Revolutionary correspondence.

GRAHAM, W[ILLIAM] A.   **292**
The story of the Little Big Horn: Custer's last fight. *N Y* Century [1926]. O [34] 174 26maps & pls a
—ed. 2, *Harrisburg* [1941]. O [42] 178 [44] maps pls

GRAHAME, JAMES   **293**
History of the rise . . . of the United States, till . . . 1688. *L* 1827. O 2v: [18] 531; [8] 529 a
—Am. ed. *N Y* 1830. O 2v
—anr. Am. ed. *B* 1833. O 2v

GRAHAME, JAMES   **294**
The history of the United States, from the plantation of the British colonies till their revolt . . . *L* 1836. O 4v: [24] 451; [8] 448; [8] 436; [8] 462 a
—Am. eds.: *Phil* 1845; *B* 1845; and several later

GRAND FORKS . . . MANUAL   **295**
Grand Forks and North Dakota manual for 1885 . . . *Grand Forks* 1885. D 146 map a

GRANDFORT, MARIE F. DE   **296**
L'autre monde. *P* 1855. 16° [8] 259 [2] + 18 adv-p a
—ed. 2, *P* 1857. D [4] 272 [2]
—Eng. tr. *N O* 1855. O 144 [2]
Conclusions concerning America even more malicious than those of Mrs. Trollope. For reply, *see Inconnue* (*L'*) . . . and also Ligeret de Chazy, *Les Creoles.*

GRANDGUILLOT, A.   **297**
La reconnaissance du sud. *P* 1861. O [2] 310 [1] a
Defends southern secession.

GRANDPIERRE, JEAN H.   **298**
Quelques mois de séjour aux États-Unis . . . *P* 1854. D 207 [4] a
—Dutch tr. "Eenige maanden in de Vereenigde Staten," *Amst* 1854. O [12] 174 [2]
—Eng. tr. "A Parisian pastor's glance at America," *B* 1854. 16° 132

GRANGER, ERASTUS, and   **299**
RED JACKET
Public speeches . . . at the village of Buffalo . . . respecting the part the Six Nations would take in the present war against Great Britain. *Buf* 1812. D 32 a
First book printed in Buffalo.

[GRANGER, GIDEON]   **300**
An address to the people of New-England [defending Jefferson's administration]. *Wash* 1808. O 38 a
—rptd., 1809: *Alb*; *Trenton*; *Phil*; *Portsmouth*
—anr. ed. n.p. n.d.[1809?] D 36 capt.t.only

[GRANGER, GIDEON]   **301**
A vindication of the measures of the present administration . . . *Wash* 1803. O 20 a
—rptd. same year: *Trenton*. Q 16; *Wilm Del.* D 36; *Hart.* O 32; *Portsmouth.* O 23; *Utica*

GRANGER, J. T.   **302**
A brief biographical sketch of . . . Major-General Grenville M. Dodge. *N Y* 1893. O 128 port a

[GRANT, MRS. ANNE McV.]   **303**
Memoirs of an American lady [i.e., Mrs. Philip Schuyler] . . . *L* 1808. D 2v: [12] 322; [8] 344 aa
—ed. 2, 1809. same collat. a
—ed. 3, 1817.
—Am. ed.: *B* 1809. D 2v: [4] 158; [2] 161
—other *Am. eds*: *N Y* 1809. D 344; *N Y* 1836; *N Y* 1846; *Alb* 1876; *N Y* 1901. D 2 v 300 cops ptd

GRANT, BLANCHE C., ed.
Kit Carson's own story . . . *See* Carson, Kit.

GRANT, FREDERICK J.   **304**
History of Seattle . . . *N Y* 1891. O 526 53ports a

GRANT, JEDEDIAH M.   **310**
A collection of facts relative to the course taken by Elder Sidney Rigdon, in . . . Ohio, Missouri, Illinois . . . *Phil* 1844. D 48 b Y

GRANT (ULYSSES S.)   **311**
Report of . . . : 1864–5. *Wash* 1865. O 44 a
—rptd. *N Y* [1865]. O 77 port
—other eds.: *Wash* 1866. O 44; *N Y* Beadle [1866]. 16° 87

GRANT, WILLIAM H.   **312**
Observations on the western trade and its influence . . . *Poughkeepsie* 1846. O 40 aa

GRANTHAM, SIR THOMAS   **313**
An historical account of some memorable actions . . . *L* 1714. O 71 c Hn [only copy known]
—rptd., with t. somewhat extended, *L* 1716. same collat. b JCB LC VaH [only cops kn]
—anr. ed. *Rich* 1882. O [8] 71 a
Bacon's rebellion, etc.

GRASSE, ALEXANDRE-F.-A., comte de   **314**
Notice biographique sur l'amiral comte de Grasse . . . *P* 1840. O 48 a

[GRASSE, FRANCOIS J. P., comte de]   **315**
Journal d'un officier de l'armée navale en Amérique en 1781 & 1782. *Amst.* 1783. O 72 b MH

Anonymous account, written in the interest of de Grasse—and possibly by him. An English translation is included in the second entry below.

GRASSE ([FRANCOIS J. P.] comte de).   316
Mémoire du: sur le combat du 12 Avril, 1782... [*P?* or *Amst* 1782]. Q 26 [2] 8fold. plans b LC NYP
Attempt at exoneration by the French admiral for his defeat in the West Indies.

GRASSE ([FRANCOIS J. P.] comte de).   317
The operations of the French fleet under:... *N Y* Bradford Club 1864. O 216 2pls a 150copies ptd.
Includes translations of two anonymous French accounts: the favorable *Journal* described above [No. 315], along with an unfavorable one previously unpublished.

GRASSI, GIOVANNI A.   318
Notizie varie sullo stato presente della republica degli Stati Uniti... *Rome* 1818. D [8] 120 fold.tab a
—ed. 2, *Milan* 1819. O 146
—ed. 3, enl., *Turin* 1822. O 140 fold tab

GRATTAN, THOMAS C.   319
Civilized America. *L* 1859 O 2v: [20] 444; [8] 518 2 maps a
—ed. 2, same impr. & date. O 2v: [40] 444; [8] 518 errata slip 2maps a

GRATWICK, CAPT. G. F.   320
A trip west and back. *Exeter Eng* 1891. O 80 25copies ptd. aa
Letters describing a tour of the Eastern states.

GRAVES, H. A.   321
Andrew Jackson Potter, the fighting parson of the Texas frontier... *Nash* 1881. D 471 port aa
—anr. ed., same impr. & collat. 1882. a
—rptd. 1883; 1890.

GRAVES, RICHARD S.   322
Oklahoma outlaws... [*Okla C* 1915?]. D [4] 132 a

[GRAVES, S. H.]   323
On the "White Pass" pay-roll, by the president of the White Pass and Yukon route. *Chi* 1908. D 258 15pls aa
History of the first Alaska railroad.

GRAVES, W[ILLIAM]   324
Two letters... respecting the conduct of Rear-Admiral[Thomas] Graves in North America... in 1781. [*L* 1782?]. Q 32 map b N NYP Y
—anr. ed. n.d. Q 40 map b N NYP
—anr. ed., with app., n.d. Q 48 [14 9–19] map b N Y
—rptd. *Morrisania N Y* 1865. Q [4] 40 a 100 copies ptd

GRAVIER, GABRIEL   325
Découvertes... de Cavelier de la Salle... *P* 1870. O [12] 412 4maps & pls a
—anr. issue, *Rouen*, same date & collat.

GRAVIER, HENRI   326
La colonization de la Louisiane à l'epoque de Law. *P* 1904. O [8] 78 [2] 2 maps a

GRAVIER, JAQUES   327
Relation de ce qui s'est passé dans la mission... au pays des Ilinois... 1693–1694. *N Y* 1857. D 66 a 100copies ptd.
First printing of one of the earliest accounts of affairs at Kaskaskia.

GRAVIER (JAQUES).   328
Relation... du voyage du: en 1700 depuis le pays des Illinois jusqu'à l'embouchure du Mississippi. *N Y* 1859. D 68 a 100 copies ptd

[GRAY, ANDREW B.]   329
Charter of the Texas Western Railroad Company and extracts from reports of Col. A. B. Gray... on the survey of the route... to California. *Cin* 1855. O 40 map aa
Incorporated as the Texas Western, in 1852; reincorporated, soon, as the Vicksburg and El Paso, then known for a while as the Texas Western; later, in 1856, the Southern Pacific R. R. of Texas; in 1872 merged into the Texas and Pacific R. R.

GRAY (A[NDREW] B.)   330
Report of the Secretary of the Interior... communicating a report... of: relative to the Mexican boundary. [Ex. Doc. 55]. *Wash* 1855. O 50 2maps errata lf a

GRAY, A[NDREW] B.   331
Survey of a route for the Southern Pacific R.R. *Cin* 1856. O 110 3maps 32pls errata slip b AA G NYP Y
Best edition of Gray's *Survey*, enlarged and with a series of unrivalled Southwestern views.

[GRAY, ANDREW B.]   332
Texas Western Railroad. Survey of route... in connection with the Pacific Railway... *Cin* 1855. O 108 errata slip aa

GRAY, EDWARD H.   333
Narrative of a Confederate prisoner... [*Dub*] n.d. O 24[incl.wraps] cov.t.only aa

[GRAY, HENRY M.]?   334
Judges and criminals... History of the Vigilance Committee of San Francisco... *S F* 1858. 16° 100 b G Hn [only cops loc]

GRAY, J.   335
A brief, historical... review of East Tennessee... *Leith* 1842. O 71 map 2pls aa

[GRAY, JOHN]   336
Doctor Price's notions of the nature of civil liberty . . . contradictory to reason . . . *L* 1777. O [4] 123 a

[GRAY, JOHN]   337
Remarks on the New essay of the Pennsylvania farmer . . . *L* 1775. O [2] 62 a

GRAY, JOHN W.   338
Life of John Bishop . . . pioneer in the first settlements of middle Tennessee . . . *Nash* 1858. D 236 + 2adv lvs aa

GRAY, THOMAS G.   339
America defended . . . with answers to inquiries concerning the books of Dickens and Marryat. *B* 1844. O 60 a

GRAY, THOMAS R. [ed.]   340
The confessions of Nat Turner, the leader of the late insurrection in Southampton, Va. . . . *Balt* 1831. D 23 a
—rptd. *Rich* 1832; *N Y* 1861; *Ptbg Va* [ca 1881].

GRAY, WILLIAM F.   341
From Virginia to Texas, 1835. *Houston* 1909. O [8] 230 aa

GRAY, WILLIAM H.   342
A history of Oregon, 1792–1849 . . . *Port Ore* 1870. O 624 front. iss 1: red clo has 1 errata slip; iss 2: black clo has 2 errata slips a
—enl. ed., with his Ore. journal, *Port* [*N Y* ptd. ca 1923]. Q [2] 706 pls aa
Undependable and biased, but, as the product of a pioneer of 1838, cannot be ignored.

GRAY, WILLIAM H.   343
The moral and religious aspect of the Indian question . . . *Astoria Wash* 1879. O 2v: [2] 36; 32 aa
Bitter arraignment of the Catholics for inciting Indians against Protestant settlers in Oregon.

[GRAYDON, ALEXANDER]   344
Memoirs of a life, chiefly passed in Pennsylvania . . . *Harrisburg* 1811. D 378 errata lf a
—anr. ed. *Phil* 1845. O [24] 13–504
—rptd., same impr. & collat. 1846.
—Eng. ed. *Edin* 1822. O [8] 431

GRAYJACKETS (THE)
Grayjackets (The) and how they lived . . . *See* McCabe, James D.

[GRAYSON, WILLIAM J.]   345
Letters of Curtius . . . *Charleston S C* 1851. O 53 a

GREAT-BRITAIN   346
Great-Britain undeceived in the conduct of government and views of America . . . and a plan for the speedy termination of the . . . contest . . . *L* 1778. D 128 aa
Advocates a brutal prosecution of the war, terrifying the colonists into submission.

GREAT
Great Britain's right to tax her colonies . . . By a Swiss. *See* Zubly, John J.

Great conspiracy (The). Full account of the assassination plot . . . *See* under Lincoln, Abraham, *The terrible tragedy* . . .

Great Falls, Montana, historic and scenic.   347
By the Tribune. *Great Falls* [1899]. Q 78 pl [by Russell] cover t. only aa

Great national object. Proposed connection of the eastern and western waters . . . *See* Lacock, Abner.

Great panic (The) . . . incidents connected   348
with two weeks of the war in Tennessee. By an eye-witness. *Nash* 1862. O 36 aa
Effect on the public of the fall of Fort Donelson.

Great steam-duck (The) . . . an invention   349
for aerial navigation. *Louisv* 1841. 16° 32 b
—rptd. *Tarrytown N Y* 1919; *N Y* 1928. a
The pioneer American attempt in this field.

Great Union Pacific railroad excursion   350
. . . *Chi* 1867. O 64 a
—rptd. *N Y* same date. O 84

GREAVES, JOHN   351
Tour through parts of the United States and Canada. *L* 1828. O 141 a
Includes travels through northwestern New York.

GRECE, CHARLES F.   352
Facts and observations respecting Canada, and the United States . . . comparative view of the inducements . . . in those countries. *L* 1819. O [16] 172 aa

GREELEY, HORACE   353
A history of the struggle for slavery extension or restriction . . . *N Y* 1856. O [4] 164 a

GREELEY, HORACE   354
Letters from Texas . . . *N Y* 1871. O 56 a

GREELEY, HORACE   355
An overland journey from New York to San Francisco . . . *N Y* 1860. D 386 + 10 adv-p a

GREELEY, COLORADO.   356
First annual report of the Union colony of: including a history . . . *N Y* 1871. O 40 a

GREEN, ADAM T.   357
Seventy years in California. *S F* 1923. O [8] 42
port a

GREEN, MRS. ANNIE MARIA   358
Sixteen years on the great American desert . . .
Titusville Pa 1887. O 84 aa

GREEN, ASHBEL   359
Memoirs of Rev. Joseph Eastburn . . . *Phil* 1828.
D [6] 208 port a
Contains reprint of the 1758 narrative of East-
burn's captivity among the Indians.

GREEN (EZRA . . . surgeon . . . under   360
John Paul Jones).
Diary of: *B* 1875. O 28 port a

GREEN, FRANK W.   361
Notes on New York, San Francisco . . . *Wakefield Eng* 1886. O [6] 173 a

[GREEN, H. T., and TENNISON, O. M.]   362
Report and map of the superintendent and engineer of the Smoky Hill Expedition . . . *Leavenworth* 1861. 18° 20 + cover t. map dd S Y [3copies
known]

[GREEN, JACOB?]   363
Observations: on the reconciliation of Great-
Britain, and the colonies . . . *Phil* 1776. O 40 aa
—anr. issue, with comma after "Observations" aa
—anr. ed. *N Y* 1776. O 16 a

GREEN, JOHN [pseud.]
Remarks in support of the New chart of North
and South America . . . *See* Mead, Bradock.

GREEN, JOHN PATTERSON   364
Recollections of the inhabitants, localities,
superstitions and Ku Klux outrages of the Carolinas . . . *Clev* 1880. D 205 a

GREEN, J[ONATHAN] H.   365
Gambling unmasked . . . . *Phil* [some cops have
N Y impr] 1844. D 193 [incl pls] aa
—rptd, *Phil* 1847. D [2] 312 a
—oth eds, with variant titles, "The gambler's life",
etc.
A reformed gambler's adventures among
brother card-sharps, counterfeiters, etc., along the
lower Mississippi, from Kentucky to Louisiana.

GREEN, J[ONATHAN] H., ed.   366
The life, trial, death, etc, of Samuel H. Calhoun,
the soldier murderer [including his earlier Arizona
career]. *Cin* 1862. 16° 92 2ports aa

GREEN, J[ONATHAN] H.   367
The secret band of brothers; or, the American
outlaws . . . *Phil* 1847. D 192 4pls a

—rptd, with adds: *Phil* 1848, D 312 4pls; *N Y*
1850, D 240; *Phil* [*ca* 1858].
Sequel to his *Gambling unmasked.*

GREEN, JONATHAN S.   368
Journal of a tour on the northwest coast in . . .
1829. *N Y* 1915. O [4] 7–104 160 copies ptd[10 on
Jap. vell.] aa

GREEN, RALEIGH T.   369
Genealogical and historical notes on Culpepper
county, Virginia . . . *Culpepper Va* 1900. O [14
6–8] 120 [2] 160 [28] port a
Includes an enlarged edition of Slaughter's
History of St. Mark's parish.

GREEN, SAMUEL B.   370
A pamphlet on equal rights . . . *St Joseph Mo*
1856. O 24 a
Upholds slave-owner's rights to his property.

GREEN, THOMAS J.   371
Journal of the Texian expedition against Mier
. . . *N Y* 1845. O 487 [incl init. blank lf] 13pls aa
—rptd. *Austin* 1935. O 481 map a

GREEN, THOMAS J.   372
Reply to the speech of Gen. Sam Houston in the
Senate . . . [*Wash* 1854]. O 67 aa

GREEN, THOMAS M.   373
Historic families of Kentucky. *Cin* 1889. O 304
port a
—rptd *Balt* 1959

GREEN, THOMAS M.   374
The Spanish conspiracy . . . Containing proofs
of the intrigues of James Wilkinson . . . *Cin* 1891.
O 406 [2] a

GREEN HAND'S FIRST CRUISE [A] . . .
By a Younker. *See* Cobb, Josiah.

GREENBURG, DAN W.   375
Sixty years; a brief review. The cattle industry in
Wyoming . . . *Cheyenne* 1932. O 73 aa

[GREENE, ASA]   376
Travels in America. By George Fibbleton . . .
N Y 1833. D 216 a
Travesty on Isaac Fidler's book of the same
title.

[GREENE, ASA]   377
A Yankee among the nullifiers . . . *N Y* Stodart
1833. 16° 152 a
—ed. 2, *N Y* Pearson 1833. 16° 143

GREENE, CHARLES W.   378
A complete business directory of New Mexico
. . . *Santa Fe* 1882. O 256 aa

GREENE, CHARLES W.   379
A sketch of Kingston [N.M.] . . . *Kingston* 1883.
O 48 aa

GREENE, GEORGE W.   380
The life of Nathanael Greene . . . *N Y* 1867–
71. O 3v: [24] 583; [10] 514; [14] 571. 4maps port a
—vol. I, rptd. 1871. same collat.

GREENE (REV. JESSE).   381
Life . . . and . . . writings of: . . . Ed. by Mary
Greene. *Lexington Mo* 1852. D 280 port a
This itinerant Methodist preacher served in the
War of 1812 and travelled widely through the old
southwest.

GREENE, JOHN P.   382
Facts relative to the expulsion of the Mormons
. . . from the state of Missouri. *Cin* 1839. O 43 aa
By a cousin of Brigham Young and eye-witness
of the events described.

GREENE, MAX   383
The Kanzas region. *N Y* 1856. D 168 173–192 +
adv-pp[6, 8 or 12] 2maps aa

GREENE, TALBOT   384
American nights' entertainments . . . from pen-
cilings of a United States senator: entitled: A
winter in the federal city . . . *Jonesborough Tenn*
1860. 16° 266 a

GREENE, TALBOT   385
The bivouac; or, life in the central army of Kentucky . . . No.I[all]. *Bowling-Green Ky* 1861. O
40 aa

GREENE, VIRGIL E.   386
Central and western Idaho . . . *Boise* 1886. O
122 a

GREENE, W. P.   387
The Green river [Ky.] country. *Evansville Ind*
1898. D 164 a

GREENHOW, ROBERT [T.]   388
The history of Florida, Louisiana, Texas, and
California . . . Vol. I[all]. *N Y* 1856. O [4] 556 b LC
Only seven copies privately printed from the
stereotype plates left uncompleted at the author's
death. Covers events to 1769.

GREENHOW, ROBERT [T.]   389
Memoir . . . on the northwest coast of North
America . . . *Wash* 1840. Sen. Doc. 174. O [12]
228 map a
—rptd. *Phil* 1840; *N Y* 1840.
—anr. ed. "The geography of Oregon and California . . .," *B* 1845. O 140 map;
—enl. ed., "The history of Oregon and California
. . .," *B* 1844. O [18] 482 map
—rptd. *L* 1844. same collat.

—ed. 2, adding an answer to Falconer's *Strictures*,
B 1845. O [20] 492 map
—ed. 3, *N Y* 1845, same collat.
—ed. 4, *B Little* 1847. same collat. but no map; anr.
issue, *B Freeman* 1847. same collat.
Leading contemporary authority, well documented. Greenhow's *Answer to the Strictures of* . . .
Falconer was also issued separately [Washington
1845, seven pages].

GREENHOW, MRS. ROSE O'N.   390
My imprisonment and the first year of abolition
rule at Washington. *L* 1863. D [10] 352 port +
2adv-p aa
Famous Confederate spy whose information
helped win the first battle of Bull Run and who
was said by McClellan to have known his plans
better than Lincoln or his cabinet.

GREENLEAF, A. B.   391
Ten years in Texas. *Selma* 1881. O 131 2pls cov.
t.only aa

GREENLEAF (MISS MARY C.).   392
Life and letters of: *B* [1858]. D 446 port aa
Description of missionary labors among the
Chickasaws in Arkansas and Oklahoma.

GREENLEAF, MOSES   393
A statistical view of . . . Maine . . . *B* 1816. O
154 map a
—enl. ed. "A survey of . . . Maine . . .," *Port Me*
1829. O 468 + atlas[of 7pls] aa

GREENWOOD, ISAAC J.   394
Captain John Manley, second in rank in the
United States navy, 1776–1783. *B* 1915. O [30] 174
col. front. 9pls a 100copies ptd.

GREENWOOD COUNTY, KANSAS.   395
Handbook . . . of: *Chi* 1886. O 30 a

GREER, GEORGE C.   396
Early Virginia immigrants, 1623–1666. *Rich*
1912. D 376 a

GREER, JAMES K.   397
Bois d'Arc to barbed wire . . . *Dallas* 1936. O
[14] 428 aa

GREER, JAMES K.   397a
Grand prairie. *Dallas* [1935]. O [8] 284 pls a

GREER, JAMES K.   398
A Texas ranger and frontiersman. The days of
Buck Barry, etc. *Dallas* 1932. O [14] 254 2maps
7pls a

GREGG, ALEXANDER   398a
A few historic records of the church in the dio-
cese of Texas, during the rebellion . . . *N Y* 1865.
O 131 a

GREGG, ALEXANDER   399
History of the old Cheraws . . . the aboriginees
of the Pedee . . . first white settlements [etc.], 1730–
1810 . . . *N Y* 1867. O [8] 546 4maps aa
—rptd. *Columbia* 1925. O [8] 629 front. 28 maps
& pls a

GREGG, ASA   400
Personal recollection of the early settlement of
Wapsinonoc township and the murder of Atwood
by the Indians. With . . . directory of . . . West
Liberty, Iowa. *West Liberty* [*ca* 1875]. O 28 +
14adv-p b G N

GREGG, JOSIAH   401
Commerce of the prairies . . . *N Y* 1844. D 2v:
320; 318. 6pls 2maps b N NYP Y
—anr. issue, carries impr. *N Y & L* b
—ed 2 *N Y* 1845 same collat aa
—anr. ed. 2, index and glossary added, *N Y* 1845.
2v: 323; 327 [no pp 319–321] 2maps 6pls + 24
adv-p b
—same, 2nd issue, omitting fold. map [of Indian
terr. &c.] aa
—rptd. at *Phil*; 1849; 1850; 1851; 1855; 1856; all
without fold. map
—rptd. in 1v, with altered title and omitting pref.,
glossary and index: *Phil* 1856 map 4pls; 1857,
same collat aa
—anr. ed., ed. Quaife, *Chi* 1926. 16° a
—Ger. eds: *Leip* 1845; *Stuttgart* 1847 [and] 1851.
D 2v 2maps 2pls; *Dresd* 1848. O map pl a
Chief contemporary authority on the Santa Fé
trade-route and traffic.

GREGG, ROBERT D.   402
The influence of border troubles on relations be-
tween the United States and Mexico, 1876–1910.
Balt 1937. O 200 a

GREGG, THOMAS   403
History of Hancock county, Illinois . . . *Chi*
1880. Q [6] 17–1036 map front. aa
Best history of the Mormons in Illinois, written
by an eye-witness of many of the events described.

GREGG, THOMAS   404
The prophet of Palmyra. Mormonism . . . *N Y*
1890. D [16 incl. front.] 552 9pls facs [with explanatory lf] a

[GREGG, WILLIAM J.]   405
The early pioneers of the west. *Terre Haute* 1891.
O 60 aa
The author settled at Paris, Illinois, in 1827.

GREGORY, JOHN   406
Industrial resources of Wisconsin. *Milw* 1855.
16° 329 + 2[errata & adv] aa
—rptd. [*Milw*] See-Bote 1870. O 320 a
—anr. ed. *Milw* News Co. 1872. O 272

Planned originally for issuance in parts, by Gregory and Rounds in Chicago, but publication
abandoned there in 1853, after only 3 parts had
appeared; unsold sheets of those parts, with the
balance added resulted in the first complete edition
as above, with title page carrying imprint of the
Star Printing Office.

GREGORY, JOSEPH W.   407
Guide for California travellers; via the isthmus
of Panama. *N Y* 1850. O 46 aa
—rptd. *S F* 1949. O 22 map 375copies ptd. a

GREGORY, SAMUEL   408
History of Mexico; with an account of the Texan
revolution . . . *B* 1847. O 100 a

GRELISCHE, HENRY   409
Essai sur la vie et les travaux de Mgr . . . Flaget,
Évêque de Bardstown et de Louisville. *P* 1851. O
192 port aa
Work of the first Western bishop, whose diocese,
in 1811, comprised Kentucky, Ohio. Michigan,
Indiana, Illinois and Missouri. *See* also Desgeor-
ges, Abbé.

GRENVILLE, GEORGE
The regulations . . . concerning the colonies . . .
See Whately, Thos.

GRENVILLE, RICHARD and GEORGE   410
The Grenville papers . . . Ed. W. J. Smith. *L*
1852–3. O 4v: [48] 494; [20] 535; [228] 397; [18]
592 aa

G[RENVILLE] G[EORGE].   411
A letter to: *L* 1765. O [2] 96 a
A reply to Lloyd, Charles, *The conduct of the late
administration . . . q.v.*

GREWINGK, CONSTANTINE C. A.   412
Beitrag zur Kenntniss der orographischen . . .
Beschaffenheit der Nord-West-Küste Amerikas . . .
St Ptbg 1850. O 351 5maps 4pls aa

GREY, F[REDERICK] W.   413
Seeking fortune in America. *L* 1912. O [14]
308 + 4adv-p front a

[GREY, ISAAC]   414
A serious address to such . . . Quakers . . . as
profess scruples relative to the present government
. . . *Phil* Bell 1778. O [6] 42 [2] aa
—ed. 2, *Phil* Styner & Cist, same date. O 48 a
—Eng. ed, *L* 1788. a
Written to strengthen this sect's faint support of
the patriot cause, the original edition was suppressed by Quakers and loyalists, but a second edition
was immediately issued.

GREY, WILLIAM
A picture of pioneer times in California. 1881.
See White, Wm. F.

**GRIERSON (COL. B. H., commanding   415
District of New Mexico).**
Annual report of: [1886–7]. [*Santa Fe?*] 1887.
D 18 lvs. [variously paged] cov.t.only aa

GRIERSON, COL. B. H.   416
Annual report . . . District of Arizona [1887–8].
[*Santa Fe?*] 1888. D 14lvs variously paged] blue-
print map a

GRIERSON (COLONEL B. H.)   417
Annual report of: comprising a summary of
events in the Department of Arizona . . . 1888–
1889. [*L A?*] 1889. D [2] 34 + roster, etc.[of 38lvs
variously paged] 8 blue-print maps aa
Some copies issued without roster.

GRIERSON (GENERAL B. H.)   418
Report of: . . . a summary of events in the De-
partment of Arizona . . . Sept. 1889–July 1890. [*L
A?*] 1890. D 34lvs [incl. roster, etc.] 3maps aa
This Department embraced also New Mexico
and Southern California.

GRIESINGER, [KARL] THEODORE   419
Lebende Bilder aus Amerika. *Stuttgart* 1858.
O [6] 346 a
—enl. ed. "Land und Leute . . .," same impr. 1863.
O [4] 882 map
—rptd. "Freiheit und Sclaverei . . ." *Stuttg* 1862.
D 2 pts in 1: [4] 480; [4] 481–882
Stresses the seamy side of American life.

GRIEVANCES (THE)
Grievances (The) of the American colonies candidly examined . . . *See* Hopkins, Stephen.

GRIEVE, JAMES, tr.
History of Kamchatka and the countries adjacent . . . *See* Krashcninnikov, Stefan P.

GRIFFIN, AUGUSTUS   420
Griffin's journal. The first settlers of Southold
[L. I.]. *Orient L. I.* 1857. D 312 port aa

[GRIFFIN, GEORGE B.]   421
Pocket guide of Los Angeles . . . history . . .
L A [1886]. 16° 94 a

GRIFFIN, JOHN S.   422
A historic sketch descriptive of Jesuit warfare
. . .*Hillsboro Ore* [ptd *Keene N H*] 1881. O 49 aa
Almost outdoes Rev. Spalding's sweeping indict-
ment of the Catholic church for complicity in the
Whitman massacre.

GRIFFIN, MARTIN I. J.   423
The history of Commodore John Barry. *Phil*
1897. O [6] 262 [14] 7pls 3facs a 200 copies ptd.
—anr. ed. "Commodore John Barry . . .," *Phil*
1903. O [12] 424 pls 600copies ptd.

[GRIFFITH, MAURICE]
. . . Discovery of a nation of Welshmen in the
interior of America . . . *See Interesting narratives
and discoveries, including Maurice Griffith's* . . .

GRIFFITH, THOMAS W.   424
Annals of Baltimore. *Balt* 1824. O 240 errata-lf
pl a
—ed. 2, with "Sketches of . . . Maryland," *Balt*
1821–33. O 2v in 1 2pls

GRIFFITH, THOMAS W.   425
Sketches of the early history of Maryland. *Balt*
1821. O 77 pl a
—ed. 2, with "Annals of Baltimore," *Balt* 1821–33.
O 2v in 1 2pls

GRIFFITH, WILLIAM   426
Historical notes of the American colonies and
revolution . . . *Burl N J* 1843. O 300 [6] a

GRIFFITHS, D., JR.   427
Two years residence in the new settlements of
Ohio . . . *L* 1835. D 197[incl. list of subscribers]
front. b N NYP Y

GRIMES, GEN. BRYAN, C. S. A.   428
Extracts from letters to his wife . . . *Raleigh*
1883. O 138 aa
—rptd. same impr. 1884. O 134 a

GRIMES (WILLIAM, the runaway slave).   429
Life of: . . . *N Y* 1825. D [4] 68 a

GRIMSHAW, WILLIAM A.   430
History of Pike county [Ill.] . . . *Pittsfield Ill*
[1877]. O 46 aa

GRINNELL, GEORGE B.   431
Bent's Fort and its builders. n.p. n.d. O 64 map
pls a

GRINNELL, GEORGE B.   432
The Cheyenne Indians: their history . . . *N Hav*
1923. O 2v: [10] 358; [8] 430. map 48 pls aa

GRINNELL, GEORGE B.   433
The fighting Cheyennes. *N Y* 1915. O [10] 431
11maps & plans a
—rptd *Norman Okla* 1956. O [18] 454 5pls

[GRINNELL, JOSIAH B.]   434
The home of the Badgers; or a sketch of the
early history of Wisconsin . . . By Oculus. *Milw*
1845. D 36 c G NYP WisH

—ed. 2, "Sketches of the west, or the home of the Badgers: comprising an early history of Wisconsin ...," *Milw* [ptd *N Y*] 1847. O 48 map b

The first edition, though bearing a Milwaukee imprint, was actually printed at Prairieville [now Waukesha] and was the earliest commercial printing done there.

GRISSON, WILHELM   **435**
Beiträge zur Charakteristik der Vereinigten Staaten ... *Hamburg* 1844. O [14] 480 aa

GRISWOLD, DAVID D.   **436**
Statistics of Chicago ... with a business ... directory ... [*Chi* 1843]. O 24 b CrerarL IH
First Chicago business directory.

[GRISWOLD, J.] comp.   **437**
James' rail road and route book for the western and southern states. *Cin* 1853. 16° [12] 11–68 + 6adv-l. a
—pub. also with James' "Traveller's companion," *q.v.*, under Cumings, Saml.

[GRISWOLD, RUFUS W.]   **438**
Washington and the generals of the ... revolution. *Phil* 1847. D 2v: 324; 336. 16 ports a
—rptd. *Phil* 1848. D 2v
Griswold was assisted by Simms, Ingraham and others.

GRISWOLD, WAYNE   **439**
Kansas: her resources ...; or the Kansas pilot ... *Cin* 1871. O [2] 95 a

GRONE, A. C[ARL] E. VON   **440**
Briefe über Nord-Amerika und Mexico ... *Braunschweig* 1850. O [10] 110 a

G[ROOME], S.   **441**
A glass for the people of New-England ... their abominable ways and cursed contrivances ... ever since they usurped authority to banish, hang, whip and cut off ears ... of the dissenters from them in religious matters ... [*L*] 1676. SmQ 43 c JCB

GROOTE TAFEREEL (HET)   **442**
Groote Tafereel (Het) der Dwaasheid, vertoonende de Opkomst ... [*Amst*] 1720. F [2] 26 [10] 52 26 29–32 77pls[many fold.] aa
—anr. issue, F [2] 26 52 26 29–32 8 77pls aa
Evidently issued in separate sections before being assembled into one volume; hence copies vary both in pagination and in plates.

GROSS, S[AMUEL] D.   **443**
A discourse on the life ... of Daniel Drake, M. D. *Louisv* 1853. O 92 a

GROSS, SAMUEL D.   **444**
Lives of eminent American physicians and surgeons of the nineteenth century. *Phil* 1861. O 836 [incl.port] aa

GROVE, JAMES P.   **445**
Life ... of John S. Moseby [*sic*] ... Colonel in the rebel army. [*Urbana O* 1865]? 16° 32 aa

GROVE, MR. [JOSEPH]   **446**
A letter to a right honourable patriot; upon the glorious success at Quebec ... *L* 1759. O [2] 58 b JCB

GROVER, LA FAYETTE [ed.]   **447**
The Oregon archives: including the journals, governors' messages and public papers ... from the earliest attempt ... to form a government ... *Salem Ore* 1853 [ptd 1854] O 333 [2] b N NYP OreH Y
Historically the most important issue of the early Oregon press; preceded only by publications of a strictly legal nature.

GROVER (LAFAYETTE).   **448**
Report of: ... on the Modoc war ... *Salem Ore* 1874. O 68 a

GRUND, FRANCIS J.   **449**
The Americans in their moral, social, and political relations. *L* 1837. O 2v: [8] 365; [4] 418 a
—Am. ed. *B* 1837. D [2] 9–423
—Ger. tr. *Stuttgart* 1837. O [8] 444

GRUND, FRANCIS J., ed.   **450**
Aristocracy in America ... *L* 1839. D 2v: [12] 319; [8] 331. 4 ports a
—Ger. tr. *Stuttgart* 1839. O 2v: [4] 223; 240. 2ports

GRUND, FRANCIS J.   **451**
Handbuch und Wegweiser für Auswanderer nach den Vereinigten Staaten ... *Stuttgart* 1843. O 251 map a
—ed. 2, *Stuttgart* 1846. O [4] 278 map

GÜNTHER, F. B.   **452**
Berichte über Ost-Tennessee und die deutsche Ansiedelung. *Stuttgart* 1849. O 48 aa

GUERIN, (MRS. E. J.)   **453**
An autobiography. Mountain Charley, or the adventures of: ... *Dubuque* 1861. O 45 b one copy located
Sensational, but basically veracious narrative of a Colorado counterpart of "Calamity Jane."

GUERNSEY, ORRIN, and   **454**
WILLARD, JOSIAH F.
History of Rock county [Wis.] ... *Janesville* 1856. O [12] 350 5pls aa

GUERRA, P. JOSEPH   **455**
... Relacion breve de la vida exemplar del V.P.F. Antonio Margil de Jesus. *Mex* [1726]. O [20] 56 b
Funeral sermon on the great pioneer missionary to Texas Indians, throwing considerable light on his labors in that field.

GUEST, MOSES   456

Poems . . . to which are annexed extracts from a journal kept by the author while he followed the sea [etc.]. *Cin* 1823. D [4] 160 [pl, called for by both Sabin and Thomson, is not in all copies, if in any] aa

—ed. 2, same collat. except for addition of port and leaf before t-p containing acrostic poem on Lafayette dated "Sept. 13, 1824," *Cin* 1824. a

Guest, a revolutionary soldier, came to Cincinnati in 1817 and gives some account of his residence there. His voyages were to the Georgia and Carolina coasts.

GUIDE DE L'EMIGRANT   457

Guide de l'emigrant aux États-Unis. *Lausanne* 1849. D 191 aa

Based on Traugott Bromme's German emigrant's guide (*Taschenbuch*), but adds numerous letters from Swiss settlers in Tennessee and Illinois. *See* also Bettinger, J. B.

GUILD, JOSEPHUS C.   458

Old times in Tennessee . . . *Nash* 1878. O 503 aa

GUILD, REUBEN A.   459

History of Brown University . . . *Prov* 1867. sm Q [4] 443 5pls 310copies[10 on L.P.] a

GUNN, LEWIS C. and LE BRETON, ELIZABETH

Records of a California family . . . see Marston, Anna L.

GUNN, O[TIS] B.   461

New map and hand-book of Kansas and the gold mines. *Pitt* 1859. 71 [incl. advs.] map dd G Hn NYP Y

—rptd. *Denver* 1952. a

—later issues of the map only: *Lecompton* 1861 b; 1864; *Lawrence* 1866. aa

GUNNISON, JOHN W., and   462
GILPIN, WILLIAM

Guide to the Kansas gold mines at Pike's Peak. *Cin* 1859. D 40 5adv-p map c ColH KCPL

GUNNISON, JOHN W.   463

The Mormons . . . in the valley of the Great Salt lake: a history . . . *Phil* 1852. D 168 [incl. front.] + 27adv-p aa

—rptd.: same impr., date & collat. 1853; 1856 a

—Ger. tr. *Dresden* 1857.

GURNEY, JOSEPH J.   464

A journey in North America . . . *Norwich Eng* 1841. O [2] 416 a

GUROWSKI, ADAM G.   465

Diary [1861–5]. *B, N Y, Wash* 1862–4–6. D 3v: [2] 315; 348; 413 aa

GUTHRIE . . . COUNTY [OKLA.]   466

Business and resident directory of: *Guthrie* [1892]. D 152 aa

GUTIÉRREZ DE LARA, JOSÉ   467
BERNARDO M.

Breve apologia . . . de las imposturas calumniosas . . . en un folleto . . . *Monterrey* 1827. D [2] 44 b S

—rptd. *Mex* 1915. a

Important account, by one of its leaders, of the Gutiérrez-Magee expedition into Texas, in 1812–1813.

GUYER, ISAAC D.   468

History of Chicago . . . *Chi* 1862. O 200 5pls a

GUYER, JAMES S.   469

Pioneer life in west Texas. *Brownwood Tex* 1938. D [12] 185 a

GYOT, PAULINE   470

Amitié et devouement ou trois mois à la Louisiane. *Tours* 1845. 16° [12] 276 aa

—anr. ed. "Trois mois à la Louisiane," *Tours* 1857. D 191 a

—rptd. same impr. 1859; 1861.

GWATHMEY, JOHN H.   471

Historical register of the Virginians in the revolution . . . *Rich* 1938. O 872 a

GYLES, JOHN

Memoirs of odd adventures . . . *See* Giles John.

H

H., E. M.

Ranch life in California. *L* 1886. *See* Hertslet, Evelyn M.

H., E. P.

A tale of home and war. *See* Howland, Mrs. E. P.

H., L. F. L.

Le Champ-d'Asile: tableau . . . du Texas. *See* L'Heritier, Louis F.

HABERMEHL, JOHN   1

Life on the western rivers, 1811–1900. *Pitt* [1901] D 222 [2] small ed a

[HACHARD, MARIE MADELEINE]   **2**
Relation du voyage des dames religeuses de Rouen à la Nouvelle Orléans . . . *Rouen* 1728. D 100 c
—anr. iss, same impr & date has add chap carrying paginat to 128 c
—rptd. *Rouen* 1865. D [12] 70 [20] a
—anr. ed. Ed by Gravier. *P* 1872. O [64, incl blank lf preceding 2nd t-p] 123 100cops ptd.
For another account of the establishment of New Orleans' first convent school see Tranchepain, Marie de St. Augustin.

HACKLEY (RICHARD S.)   **3**
Titles and legal opinions thereon, of lands in East Florida, belonging to: *Bklyn* 1822. O 122 b
—ed 2, *Fayetteville, N C* 1826. O 71 aa

HACO, DION   **4**
J. Wilkes Booth, the assassinator of . . . Lincoln. *N Y* 1865. D [4 incl.front cov.] 15–102 aa

HADDEN, JAMES   **5**
A history of Uniontown . . . Pennsylvania. [*Uniontown*] 1913. O 824 a

HADDEN (LIEUT. JAMES M.)   **6**
A journal kept in Canada and upon Burgoyne's campaign . . . by: . . . *Alb* 1884. Q [100] 581 4maps & plans 2facs errata slip a
First printing of an unpublished manuscript. Fullest British account of this campaign.

HADDOCK, WILLIAM J.   **7**
A reminiscence. The prairies of Iowa. *Iowa City* 1851. sm Q [4] 71 50 cops ptd aa

HADLEY, LEWIS F.   **8**
A list of the primary gestures in Indian sign-talk . . . *Anadarko Indian Ter* 1887. O 32 lvs. only 19 copies ptd, being proofs given out for the purpose of obtaining corrections b LC
—complete ed. "Indian sign-talk . . .," [*Chi* 1893]. O [22] 206 lvs [57 lvs] port aa

HAEBERLIN, CARL L.   **9**
Die Auswanderer in Texas . . . *Leip* 1841. O 3v: [2] 332; [2] 302; [2] 316 aa
—Dutch tr., "De landverhuizers naar Texas . . . *Groningen* 1842. O 2v. a
Historical romance.

HAFEN [LE ROY R., and GHENT, W. J.   **10**
Broken Hand, the life story of Thomas Fitzpatrick, chief of the mountain men. *Denver* 1931. O 316 map 8pls aa
—same, L.P. issue of 100copies b

HAFEN, LEROY R.   **11**
The overland mail . . . *Clev* 1926. O 361 [incl. map & 7pls] aa

HAGERMAN, HERBERT J.   **12**
A statement in regard to certain matters concerning . . . political affairs in New Mexico . . . [*Roswell*] 1908. O 113 a
Defense of his gubernatorial conduct, with a discussion of mining and timber-land frauds.

HAGERTY, FRANK H.   **13**
A dictionary of Dakota . . . soon to become two states. *Aberdeen* [1888?] .O 32 aa

HAGERTY, FRANK, H.   **14**
The Territory of Dakota . . . *Aberdeen* 1889. O 3pts in 1: 119; 90; 102 aa

HAHNEL, CARL F.   **15**
Wahreit . . . über Amerika . . . *Leip* 1851. 16° 162 a

HAILEY, JOHN   **16**
The history of Idaho. *Boise* 1910. O [10] 395 + 5adv-p port a

[HAINES, CHARLES G.]   **17**
Considerations on the great western canal, from the Hudson to lake Erie. *Bklyn* 1818. O 58 a
—ed. 2, same impr. & date. O 81

[HAINES, CHARLES G.] ed.   **18**
Public documents relating to the New York canals . . . to connect the . . . lakes with the Atlantic . . . *N Y* 1821. O [52] 485 map a

HAINES, ELIJAH M.   **19**
The American Indian . . . *Chi* 1888. O [2]7–821 fold map a

HAINES, ELIJAH M.   **20**
Historical and statistical sketches of Lake county . . . Illinois . . . *Waukegan* 1852 [ptd Feb.-1853] *N Y* 16° 112 front. errata lf b
Earliest Illinois county history.

HAINES, HELEN   **21**
History of New Mexico . . . *N Y* 1891. O [20] 631[incl.pls] aa

HAINES, HIRAM   **22**
The state of Alabama . . . resources . . . *P* 1867. O 120 a
—Fr. tr., same impr. & date. O 128

HAIR, JAMES T., comp.   **23**
Gazetteer of Madison county [Ill.] . . . historical sketches of Alton City . . . *Alton* 1866. O [4] 9–292 + adv-lf & 2inserted notices[at p91 & at end] pl aa

HAIR, JAMES T., comp.   **24**
Iowa state gazetteer, embracing . . . historical sketches of counties, cities . . . *Chi* 1865. O 722 + 76 adv-p aa

—ed. 2, same impr. 1866. same collat
First—and best—gazetter of this state; an encyclopedia of historical data.

HAIRDRESSER'S EXPERIENCE (A) . . .
See Potter, Eliza.

HAKLUYT, RICHARD   25
A discourse concerning western planting. Ed. by Charles Deane. *C* ptd for Maine Hist. Soc. 1877. O [64] 253 5facs a
First printing from a manuscript copy of the earliest elaborate argument for American colonization.

HAKLUYT, RICHARD   26
Early voyages, travels and discoveries of the English nation. A new edition, with additions. *L* for R. H. Evans, 1809–1812. Q 5v: [34] 670 [2]; [22] 684; [16] 623; [6] 612; [4] 595 aa
The complete text of the original edition of 1599–1600 is supplemented by 14 similar voyages not included in either Hakluyt or Purchas. Only 325 copies printed [75 being on large paper].

HAKLUYT, RICHARD   27
A selection of curious, rare, and early voyages . . . chiefly published by: or, at his suggestion, but not included in his . . . compilation . . . *L* R. H. Evans, 1812. Q 807 aa
Separate printing of the additions found in vol. IV and V of this publisher's edition of Hakluyt's voyages, listed above.

HALBERT, HENRY S., and   28
BALL, TIMOTHY H.
The Creek war of 1813 and 1814. *Chi* 1895. D 331 [3] fold map [not issued in all copies] 4ports aa
Careful and detailed monograph on Alabama's last border war.

HALE, CHARLES R.   29
Innocent of Moscow, the apostle of Kamchatka and Alaska . . . [*Davenport*] 1888. O 23 a

HALE, JOHN, 1636-1700   30
A modest enquiry into the nature of witchcraft . . . *B* 1702. D 176 c AA BP Hn NYP
—rptd. *B* 1771. O 158 b
Hale had witnessed and approved the Salem persecutions of 1692, but seems now doubtful of their legality and justice.

HALE, JOHN, of N.Y.   31
California as it is . . . a tour by the overland route [to California in 1849]. *Roch* 1851. D 40 dd G F.Rosenstock Y [all known]
—rptd. [*S F*] Grabhorn, 1954. Q [28] 51 map 6pls 150cops ptd aa

HALE, JOHN P.   32
Trans-Allegheny pioneers . . . *Cin* 1886. D [4] 7–330 11pls facs aa
—ed. 2, *Charleston W Va* 1931. D 340 a

[HALE, NATHAN]   33
Notes . . . during an excursion to the highlands of New Hampspire . . . *Andover* 1833. D 184 a

[HALE, NATHAN]   34
Remarks on the practicability . . . of establishing a railroad . . . from Boston to the Connecticut river. *B* 1827. O 71 aa
One of the earliest of such projects; carriages horse-drawn.

HALE, SALMA   35
Annals of . . . Keene [N. H.] . . . to 1790. *Concord* 1826. O 69 a
—enl. ed., con. to 1815, *Keene* 1851. O 120 map

HALE, WILL [pseud]
Twenty-four years a cowboy. *See* Stone, William H.

HALE and EMORY, pubs
Marysville [Calif.] city directory . . . 1853. *See* Colville, Sam'l.

HALEY, J. EVETTS   36
Charles Goodnight, cowman . . . *B* 1936. O [16] 485[incl.front.] a
—rptd. *Norman Okla* 1949, same collat.

HALEY, J. EVETTS   37
Charles Schreiner . . . story of a country store. *Austin* 1944. O [14] 73 front. a

HALEY, J. EVETTS   38
Jeff Milton, a good man with a gun. *Norman, Okla* 1948. O [14] 430 map pls Iss 1: port of Jno. Greenaway, p 421, inverted a

HALEY, J. EVETTS   39
The X I T ranch of Texas . . . *Chi* 1929. O [16] 261 [2] 2maps 30pls[containing 62 illus] aa
—rptd. with deletions, *Norman Okla* 1953

HALFERN, ALBERT VON   40
Scenen aus den Kämpfen der Indianer Floridas gegen die Weissen; oder, der Letzte der Seminolen . . . *Dresden* 1846. 16° 311 aa
—ed. 2, same impr. & collat. 1848. a

HALIFAX
Brief remarks on the defence of the Halifax libel . . . *See* Otis, James.

A defence of the Letter from a gentleman   41
at Halifax to his friend in Rhode Island. *Newport* 1765. O 31 aa
—in issue 1, last p. erroneously numb. as 30
Probably by author of item next below.

A letter from a gentleman at Halifax to his   **42**
friend in Rhode Island, containing remarks upon a
pamphlet, entitled The rights of colonies examined.
Newport 1765. O 22 aa
For pamphlet mentioned *see* Hopkins, Stephen.
The "gentleman at Halifax" has been identified as
Martin Howard, Jr. For reply to this *Letter* see
Otis, James, *A vindication* . . .

HALKETT, JOHN   **43**
Historical notes respecting the Indians of North
America . . . *L* 1825. O [8] 408 a
—rptd. *L* 1826.

HALL, A. J., pub.   **44**
Early and authentic history of Omaha. *Omaha*
1870. O 64 + 8interspersed adv-pp. aa

HALL, REV. B. M.   **45**
The life of Rev. John Clark . . . *N Y* 1856. D 276
+ 6adv-lvs port a
Clark was Methodist missionary at Green Bay,
1832–6; and presiding elder at Chicago, 1836–54;
with an interim transfer to Texas.

HALL, CAPT. BASIL   **46**
Forty etchings, from sketches . . . in North
America. *Edin* 1829. Q [6] 40pls on 20 l. 20 l. map a
—3 other eds. issued by 1830.

HALL'S [CAPT. BASIL] TRAVELS
Hall's (Capt. Basil) Travels in North America.
A review of: By an American. *See* Biddle, Rich.

HALL, CAPT. BASIL   **47**
Travels in North America . . . *Edin* 1829. D 3v:
[8] 421; [6] 432; [8] 436. map tab a
—ed. 2 same impr, date & collat
—rptd., with slight changes and 9-p app., *Edin*
1830. D 3v map tab
—Am. ed. *Phil* 1829. D 2v: 322; [4] 9–329
—Fr. trs.: *P* 1834. O 2v map; *Berlin* 1834. O 2v:
Brus 1835. D 2v

[HALL, BAYNARD R.]   **48**
The new purchase; or seven and a half years in
the far west [i.e. Indiana]. *N Y* 1843. D 2v: [12]
300; [8] 316 + 12adv-p aa
—rptd. *New Albany Ind* [1855]. D 471 4pls a
—anr. ed. *Princeton* 1916. O [32] 522 map pls
—Eng. ed., t. slightly altered, *L* 1855. D 471

HALL, BENJAMIN F.   **49**
The land owner's manual . . . *Auburn* 1847. O
477 a
—rptd. "The early history of the northwestern
states . . .," *Buf* 1849. O 477

HALL, BENJAMIN H.   **50**
History of eastern Vermont . . . *N Y* 1858. O
[14] 799 a

—rptd., same collat., *Alb* 1865. Also L.P. ed., 50
copies. Q 2v: [14] 366; [4] 367–799. facs

HALL, CARROL D., ed.   **51**
Journal of a voyage from Boston to San Francisco, in 1849. *Redwood City* 1933. O 40 a 75copies
ptd.

HALL, CHARLES B., eng.   **52**
Military records of general officers of the Confederate States . . . *N Y* 1898. F [10] 108 108ports
b N NYP WisH

HALL, CHARLES S.   **53**
Life and letters of Samuel Holden Parsons,
Major-General in the revolution . . . *Binghamton*
1905. O [14] 601 plan a 500 copies ptd.

[HALL, EDWARD H.] 1858-1936   **54**
Alaska, the Eldorado of the midnight sun . . .
N Y 1897. D 62 front. map a

HALL, EDWARD H[EPPLE]   **55**
The great west: emigrants' . . . hand-book to . . .
California and Oregon . . . *N Y* 1864. D 89 map aa

HALL, EDWARD H[EPPLE]   **56**
The great west: travelers' . . . hand-book to the
western . . . states and territories . . . *N Y* 1865. D
198 map [2 adv-lvs at front and 5 at end] aa
—rptd., with t. somewhat altered, *N Y* n.d. [1866?].
D 181 map a
—Eng. ed. *L* 1870. D [8] 124 + 7adv-p a
Hall also issued at London—in 1856, 1857 and
1858—an annual entitled *Ho! for the west!* containing information on Canada and the middle
west, [octavo, 32 p.].

HALL, E[DWARD] H[EPPLE]   **57**
The northern counties gazetteer . . . a guide to
northern Illinois . . . *Chi* 1855. O [2 4 3–8 8] 17–
208 + 128adv-p aa

HALL, EDWIN   **58**
The ancient . . . records of Norwalk, Connecticut . . . *Norwalk* 1847. D 320 3maps 4pls a
—ed 2 same impr 1865. O 320 map 2pls

HALL, FAYETTE   **59**
The secret . . . history of the war . . . showing
how Abraham Lincoln came to be President . . .
N Hav 1890. O 56 port 2pls a
—anr. ed. "The Copperhead, or the secret . . .
history of our Civil war . . .," *N Hav* 1902. O 63 a
Continuation of this bitter disparagement of
Lincoln was planned, but never issued.

[HALL, FAYRER]   **60**
The importance of the British plantations in
America . . . *L* 1731. D [6] 114 b
Fine survey of trade in southern colonies.

HALL (MISSES FRANCES and ALMIRA).   61
Narrative of the capture and . . . escape of: . . .
St L?] 1832. O 24 [incl.pl] Narrative begins "The
present year (1832)" aa
—rptd. same collat. 1833. a
—anr. ed. [1833]. O [4 incl. front.] 7–26 Narrative
begins "The preceding year" a
—anr. ed. n.p. 1834. O 24[incl.front].
—anr. ed. *N Y* 1835. O 21
—anr. ed. with adds. n.p. [1836]. O 26 aa
Probably by William P. Edwards in whose name
it was copyrighted. Internal evidences point to him
as also the perpetrator of similar questionable
captivities ascribed to Mrs. Hannah Lewis and
Mrs. Jane Lewis, *q. v.* The correct names of the
Hall sisters were Rachel and Sylvia.

HALL, LIEUT. FRANCIS   62
Travels in Canada, and the United States, in
1816–17. *L* 1818. O [4] 543 map a
—ed. 2, *L* 1819. O [12] 421 map
—Am. ed. *B* 1818. O 332
Unflattering description of American life and
character.

HALL, FREDERIC   63
The history of San José . . . *S F* 1871. O [16] 537
fold.map 4pls aa

HALL, FREDERICK   64
Letters from the east and from the west. *Wash*
[1840]. O [12] 168 a

HALL, FREDERICK   65
Statistical account of . . . Middlebury [Vt.]. Pt.
1 [all]. *B* 1821. O 38 a

HALL, HARVEY, comp.   66
The Cincinnati directory for 1825 . . . *Cin* 1825.
D 137 plan aa
Second directory of this city, more uncommon
than the first, of 1819; gives nativity of each
citizen.

HALL, HENRY   67
The history of Auburn [N.Y.]. *Auburn* 1869. D
[16] 580 a

HALL, HILAND   68
The history of Vermont . . . *Alb* 1868. O [12] 522
map a Also L. P. issue of 50copies.

HALL, J.   69
Travels and adventures in Sonora . . . *Chi* 1881.
O 302 aa
Includes travels, etc., in California and Arizona.

HALL, JAMES, 1744-1826   71
A brief history of the Mississippi territory . . .
Salisbury N C 1801. 24° [2] 70 b LC NCU NYP Y
First history of Mississippi, with some particu-

lars of the author's travels from Nashville through
the Chickasaw country.

HALL, JAMES, 1793-1868   72
The Harpe's head: a legend of Kentucky. *Phil*
1833. D [6] 256 + 36adv-p aa
—Eng. ed. "Kentucky: a tale," *L* 1834. D 2v:
rptd. *L* 1845. a

HALL, JAMES, 1793-1868   73
Legends of the west. *Phil* 1832. D [8] 266 +
adv-p aa
—ed. 2, *Phil* 1833. D 257 a
—rev. ed. *N Y* 1853. D 435
—rptd., with 2pls added, *N Y* 1854.
—other eds.: *Cin* 1857; *Cin* 1869; 1871; 1874.

HALL, JAMES, 1793-1868   74
Letters from the west . . . *L* 1828. O [6] 385 +
adv-p aa
—rptd., same collat., *L* 1830.
His first book; pirated from *The portfolio.*

HALL, JAMES, 1793-1868   75
A memoir of the public services of William
Henry Harrison . . . *Phil* 1836. 18° 323 port a

HALL, JAMES, 1793-1868   76
Reply to strictures on Sketches of the west . . .
Phil 1838. D 24 aa
This reply to Mann Butler's attack is a separate
printing of the preface to Hall's 1838 edition of
Statistics of the west, see below.

HALL, JAMES, 1793-1868   77
The romance of western history . . . *Cin* 1857.
D 420 [12] port + 12adv-p port a
—rptd.: 1869; 1871; 1885.
Assembled from his other books.

HALL, JAMES, 1793-1868   78
Sketches of history, life and manners in the west
. . . Vol. I [all]. *Cin* 1834. D 263 aa
—reissued, with vol. II added, *Phil* 1835. D 2v:
282 [2]; 276. pl; in some cops V II has St. L impr
For a castigation of this *see* Mann Butler's
Appeal . . .

HALL, JAMES, 1793-1868   79
Statistics of the west, at the close of . . . 1836.
Cin 1836. D [18] 13–284 + 2adv-p a
—rptd. 1837, same impr & collat
—anr. ed. "Notes on the western states," *Phil*
1838. D [24] 13–304[incl.tabs]
—other eds.: "The west; its commerce . . .," *Cin*
1848. D [8] 328; "The west; its soil . . .," *Cin* 1848.
D 260

HALL, JAMES, 1793-1868   80
Tales of the border. *Phil* 1834. D [2] 276 aa
—ed. 2, "Border tales," *Phil* 1835. same collat. a

HALL, JAMES [ed.], 1793-1868   **81**
The western souvenir ... for 1829. *Cin* [1828]
16° [2] 324 6pls b AA N NYP Y
First literary annual published in the west.

HALL, JAMES, 1793-1868   **82**
The wilderness and the war-path. *N Y* 1846. D
[8] 174 + 10 adv-p.
—Eng. ed., same date & collat. *L.*

HALL, JAMES N., and NORDHOFF,   **83**
CHARLES B., eds.
The Lafayette Flying Corps. *B* 1920. O 2v: [20]
514; [12] 362. 2col. fronts. 32pls [26col.] aa

[HALL, CAPT. JOHN]   **84**
The history of the civil war in America. Vol.I
[all]. *L* Payne 1780. O [12] 413 map aa
—anr. issue, same date & collat., *L* Sewall 1780. aa
—ed. 2, *L* Payne 1780. O [12] 467 map aa
  Ascribed also to Major William C. Hall. Covers
campaigns of 1775–6–7.

HALL, J[OHN] L.
Journal of the Hartford Union Mining and
Trading Company. *See* Webster, George G.

HALL, J[OHN] W.   **85**
Marine disasters on the western lakes ... *Det*
1870. D 120 a
—rptd. "Record of the western lakes ...," *Toledo*
1878. O

HALL, P. C.   **86**
A Negro's opinion in a little book on big things.
Vicksburg 1884. O 38 a
Upholds rule of the tax-payer and state's rights.

HALL, THOMAS W.   **87**
Recollections of a grandfather. [*Oak Park Ill
ca* 1895]. D 48 small ed. aa
Describes his 1849 trip to California and life in
the mines.

HALL, T[IMOTHY] D.   **88**
Hudson [Wis.] and its tributary region. *Hudson*
1857. D 24 plan aa
First separate issue; originally in Wisconsin
Historical Collections, volume III.

HALL, WILLIAM   **89**
The abominations of Mormonism exposed ...
Cin 1852. 16° 155 aa

HALL, WILLIAM A.   **90**
The historic significance of the southern revolution ... *Petersburg Va* 1864. O 45 a

HALL, WILLIAM M.   **91**
Speech ... railroad to Pacific ... *Chi* 1847. O 22
aa 3cops loc

—enl. ed. *N Y* [1853]. O 68 a
Advocates the route proposed by George Wilkes. This speech—one of the earliest on the subject—appeared first in the *Proceedings of the Harbor and River Convention, see* under *Chicago.*

HALL, WINCHESTER   **92**
The story of the 26th Louisiana infantry ... n.p.
[*ca* 1890?] O [8] 228 [2] map aa

HALL-WOOD, MARY C. F.   **93**
Santa Barbara as it is. *Santa Barbara* [1884]. O
101 fold.chart a

HALLAGER, MORTEN   **94**
Udforlige og troevaerdige efterretninger om de
fra Rusland ... *Copenh* 1784. 16° [16] 350 aa
Account of the Russian discoveries of Bering
and Chirikov, etc.

HALLER (MAJOR GRANVILLE O.)   **95**
The dismissal of: ... also, a brief memoir of his
military services ... *Paterson, N J* 1863. O 84 +
errata lf aa
Served on the plains and in Oregon, from 1848
to 1859.

[HALLOCK, CHARLES]   **96**
A complete biographical sketch of "Stonewall"
Jackson. *Augusta Ga* 1863. O 38 [4] aa
—rptd. "Sketches of Stonewall Jackson," *Halifax
Can* 1863. a
First life of Jackson.

HALLOCK, CHARLES   **97**
Vacation rambles in northern Michigan. [*Grand
Rapids* 1878?]. O 5–58 [2] [incl. adv-pp] a

HALLUM, JOHN   **98**
Biographical ... history of Arkansas ... Vol.
I[all]. *Alb* 1887. O [14] 581 port aa
Of the 147 biographical sketches, Albert Pike
contributed fourteen, including one of himself.

HALSELL, H. H.   **99**
Cowboys and cattleland. *Nashv* [1937]. D 276
6pls a

HALSEY, FRANCIS W.   **100**
The old New York frontier ... *N Y* 1901. O [14]
432 2maps 14pls a
—rptd., same collat. & impr., 1902.

HALSEY, JOHN J.   **101**
History of Lake county, Illinois. [*Phil*] 1912. Q
[16] 872 2maps aa
Best Illinois county history.

HALSTEAD, MURAT   **102**
The caucuses of 1860 ... *Columbus* 1860. O [4]
232 4-line errata slip a

HALTON, RICHARD W.   **103**
History . . . of Angelina county, Texas. *Lufkin* [1888?]. 16° 66 + 32adv-p. b

HALTON, RICHARD W.   **104**
History . . . of Nacogdoches county, Texas. *Nacogdoches* 1880. D 73 + advs. b

HAMBLETON, CHALKLEY J.   **105**
A gold hunter's experience. *Chi* 1898. D [2] 116 [2] aa

HAMBLETON, JAMES P.   **106**
A biographical sketch of Henry A. Wise, with a history of the political campaign in Virginia in 1855 . . . *Rich* 1856. O [36] 509 port a
—anr. issue, "A history of the political campaign . . .," same impr., date & paginat., but no port

HAMBLIN, GEORGE W.   **107**
The Kansas guide . . . *Ottawa Kas* 1871. O 62 [1] a
A map was separately issued.

HAMBLIN, P. R.
United States criminal history . . . See St. Clair, Henry.

HAMBURG, SOUTH CAROLINA . . .   **108**
Origin of the town of: *Augusta Ga* 1837. O 18 18 [2] aa

HAMBURG NACH PHILADELPHIA.   **109**
Reise von: *Hannover* 1800. 16° 208 a
Down the sea-board, Mass. to Carolina.

HAMILTON [pseud.]   **110**
Review of a late pamphlet, under the signature of "Brutus." *Charleston S C* 1828. O 105 a
For work reviewed *see The crisis: or, essays on the usurpations of the federal government.*

HAMILTON (MAJOR-GENERAL ALEXANDER).
A collection of the facts and documents, relative to the death of: *See* Coleman, Wm.

HAMILTON (GENERAL [ALEXANDER]) and BURR (COL. [AARON])
A correct statement of the late . . . affair of honor, between: . . . *See* Wills, Thos.

[HAMILTON, ALEXANDER]   **111**
A defence of the treaty . . . between the United States . . . and Great Britain . . . *N Y* 1795. O 139 a
Also ascribed to Stephen Higginson and to Robert R. Livingston.

[HAMILTON, ALEXANDER]   **112**
The examination of the President's [Jefferson's] message . . . December 7, 1801. *N Y* 1802. O 127 a

First separate edition; title-page statement "revised and corrected" refers only to its previous newspaper appearance.

[HAMILTON, ALEXANDER]   **113**
The Farmer refuted . . . in answer to a letter from A. W. Farmer intitled A view of the controversy between Great-Britain and her colonies. *N Y* 1775. O [4] 78 b AA BA LC N NYP Y
Hamilton's second work; a rejoinder to Samuel Seabury's answer to his first work—*A full vindication* . . .—which had replied to that author's *Free thoughts on the proceedings of . . . Congress.*

[HAMILTON, ALEXANDER, et al]   **114**
The Federalist . . . essays in favour of the new Constitution . . . *N Y* 1788. D 2v: [6] 227; [6] 384 c AA BA N Y some copies uncut; some on large and thick paper d NYP
—re-issued, same sheets, new t-p, 1799. b AA NYP
—anr. ed., rev. & cor., with adds., *N Y* 1802. O 2v: [8] 318; [5] 351 aa
—Fr. tr. *P* 1792. O 2v: [52] 366; [4] 511 aa
—rptd., same yr., omitting the long introd. by the tr. aa
Most famous and influential American political work. Written in collaboration with Jay and Madison.

[HAMILTON, ALEXANDER]   **115**
A full vindication of the measures of Congress . . . in answer to a letter under the signature of A. W. Farmer. *N Y* 1774. D [35] b AA N NYP Y
Hamilton's first publication, written, at the age of seventeen, in answer to Samuel Seabury's *Free thoughts on the proceedings of . . . Congress.*

HAMILTON'S LETTER
Hamilton's Letter concerning . . . John Adams. An answer to: *see* Cheetham James.

HAMILTON (ALEXANDER).   **116**
Letter from: concerning the public conduct . . . of John Adams . . . *N Y* ptd. by Hopkins 1800. O 54 aa
—rptd. 3 times, *N Y* same date. a
—other eds.: *Phil* [1800]. O 54 [8]; *B* 1809. O 56

[HAMILTON, ALEXANDER]   **117**
A letter from Phocion . . . on the politics of the day. *N Y* 1784. O 23 aa
—other eds., same impr. & date: 12 or 19p aa
—rptd.: *Newport* 1784. D 12; *Phil* 1784. O 15; *B* 1784. O 23; *B* 1784. O 19 a
Advocates justice and toleration for Tories.

HAMILTON (MAJOR-GENERAL   **118**
[ALEXANDER]).
A letter to: containing observations on his Letter, concerning the public conduct . . . of John Adams . . . By a citizen. *N Y* 1800. O 32 a

—anr. ed., probably the 1st, *Salem Mass* 1800. D
28 [2]
Ascribed to Uzal Ogden.

[HAMILTON, ALEXANDER]   **119**
Letters of Pacificus . . . in justification of the
President's proclamation of neutrality. *Phil* 1796.
O 60 a
—rptd. *Wash* 1845. O 102
For reply, *see* Madison, James, *Letters of Hel-
vidius.*

HAMILTON, ALEXANDER   **120**
Observations on certain documents contained in
. . . "The history of the United States, for the year
1796." *Phil* Fenno 1797. O 38 [58] a
—rptd., same impr. & collat. 1800; *N Y* 1800. same
collat.; *Phil* Pro Bono Publico [1800]. same collat.
Known as the "Reynold's pamphlet"; in it Hamilton confessed a personal irregularity in order to
defend his public probity. The reprints of 1800
were published by his enemies.

HAMILTON (MAJOR-GENERAL   **121**
ALEXANDER).
The official . . . papers of: Vol. I[all]. *N Y* 1842.
O [4] 496 a

HAMILTON, ALEXANDER   **122**
Report . . . containing a plan for the further sup-
port of public credit . . . *Phil* 1795. O 90 10 tabs aa
—Eng. ed. *L* 1795. O 96 5tabs a

[HAMILTON, ALEXANDER]   **123**
Report . . . on the subject of manufactures . . .
[*Phil*] Childs & Swaine [1791]. F [4] 58 b AA N
—several Am. reprints a
—Eng. eds.: *Dub* 1792. O 88 a; *Dub* 1793. same
collat.; *L* 1793. O [4] 129 a
One of the great American state papers, "the
Magna Carta of industrial America."

[HAMILTON, ALEXANDER]   **124**
A second letter from Phocion: to the . . . citizens
of New York . . . *N Y* 1784. O 43 aa
—anr ed *Phil* 1784 a

HAMILTON, DR. ALEXANDER   **125**
Itinerarium . . . from Annapolis through Delaware, Pennsylvania . . . 1744. *St L* 1907. O [28] 264
fold.map 6pls 22facs a 487copies ptd.
—rptd. with adds Chapel Hill 1948 O [32 incl
front] 267 8pls

HAMILTON, B. B.   **126**
Historical sketch of Jersey county, Illinois . . .
Jacksonville Ill 1876. O 36 aa

HAMILTON, EDWARD [pseud.]
The life of Paul Jones. *See* Mackenzie, Alexander S.

[HAMILTON, H. W.]   **127**
Rural sketches of Minnesota . . . *Milan O* 1850.
O 40 aa

HAMILTON, HENRY S.   **128**
Reminiscences of a veteran. *Concord* 1897. D
[10] 180 4pls a
Narrative of western army life in the 'fifties.

HAMILTON, J. G. DE R.   **129**
Reconstruction in North Carolina. *N Y* 1914.
O [10] 683 map a

[HAMILTON, GOV. JAMES]   **130**
An account of the late intended insurrection
among . . . the blacks of this city . . . *Charleston
S C* 1822. O 48 a
—ed. 2, same impr., date & collat.
—ed. 3, same impr. & date. Q 49
—anr. ed. "Negro plot . . .," *B* 1822. O 50
—rptd.[as ed. 2], same impr., date & collat.
Contemporary account of the Vezey uprising.

HAMILTON (GOV. [JAMES]) and   **131**
CALHOUN [HON. JOHN C.]
Important correspondence, on the subject of
state interposition, between: *Charleston S C* 1832.
D 27 a
—rptd. "Correspondence . . .," n.p. [1832]. O
capt.t.only

HAMILTON (JAMES A.)   **132**
Reminiscences of: or, men and events . . . *N Y*
1869. O [10] 647 a

[HAMILTON, PATRICK]   **133**
The resources of Arizona . . . Indian tribes,
early history . . . [*Florence Ariz* 1881]. D 71 aa
—anr. ed., au. named, *Prescott* 1881. O 120 a
—ed. 2, enl. *S F* [1883]. O 275 18pls a
—anr. ed., further enl., *S F* 1884. D 415 + 14adv-p
fold.map 19pls a

HAMILTON, PETER J.   **134**
Colonial Mobile . . . *B* 1897. O [14] 446 [1]
14maps & pls aa
—rev. ed. 1910. O [30] 594 60maps & pls a
—rev. & enl. ed. *Mobile* 1952. O same collat
Most valuable secondary work on the early
history of the Gulf coast.

HAMILTON, MRS. S. WATSON   **135**
A pioneer of "fifty three". [Rhyming account of
a trip from Iowa, via Ft Boise to Oregon].
Albany, Ore 1905. D 139 aa
Only 3 copies survived the burning of author's
home.

[HAMILTON, SAMUEL S.] comp.   **136**
Indian treaties, and laws . . . relating to Indian
affairs. Compiled and published under orders of

the Department of War ... *Wash* 1826. O [20] 529 a
—rptd., with suppl. giving add. treaties to 1831, same impr. & date [but obviously ptd in 1831]. O [20] 661
Includes abstracts of all treaties made by the United States, along with much historical data. *See* also *Treaties between the United States* ... *and* ... *Indian tribes.*

HAMILTON, SCHUYLER   137
History of the national flag ... *Phil* 1852. D [8] 13–115 15col.pls a

[HAMILTON, THOMAS]   138
Men and manners in America. *Edin* 1833. D 2v: [12] 393; [6] 402 a
—eds. 2 & 3, same impr. 1834.
—new ed., with adds., *Edin* 1843. D [36] 454 port
—Am. ed. 1, *Phil* 1833. O 410; Am. ed. 2, same impr. & date. D [6] 208
—Fr. tr. *P* 1834. D 2v 2pls [16] 311; [4] 380 2pls
—Ger. tr. *Mannheim* 1834. O 2v

HAMILTON, WILLIAM T.   139
My sixty years on the plains. *N Y* 1905. O 244 8pls[6 by Russell] aa
—ed. 2, 1905.
—ed. 3, 1909.
—oth eds: *Columbus O* 1951; Norman Okla 1960 D

[HAMMETT, SAMUEL A.]   140
A stray Yankee in Texas. *N Y* 1853. D [2] 416 eng.t. front. a

HAMMOND, HENRY   141
History of Harrison county, W. Va ... *Morgantown* [1910]. O 451 pls a

HAMMOND, ISAAC B.   142
Reminiscences of frontier life. *Port Ore* 1904. D 134 port aa
Most of the edition "scrapped" to a paper mill.

[HAMMOND, JABEZ D.]   143
Letter to ... Calhoun, on the annexation of Texas. *Cooperstown* 1844. O 34 a

HAMMOND, JOHN   146
Leah and Rachel [i.e. Virginia and Mary-land]: ... present condition, etc. *L* 1656. O [6] 32 dd Hn H JCB LC

HAMMOND, JOHN   147
["In memoriam."] *Chi* 1890. O 90 3ports a
Includes his 1849 trip to California over the southern route.

HAMMOND, JOHN M.   148
Colonial mansions of Maryland and Delaware. *Phil* 1914. O [14] 304 65pls a

[HAMPSON, J.]   149
Reflections on the present state of the American war ... *L* 1776. O [2] 30 aa
British might inevitably victorious; advises the misguided rebels to sue for peace at once.

HANCE, C. H.   150
Reminiscences of one who suffered in the lost cause. [*L A* 1915?] O 37 aa

HANCOCK (JEAN, Président du Congress).   151
Discourse de: ... *Phil* 1776. O 32 aa
A scurrilous satire, probably by Fréville, actually printed at the Hague as British propaganda.

HANCOCK (JOHN).
Ten chapters in the life of: *See* Higginson, Stephen.

[HANCOCK, RICHARD R.]   152
Hancock's diary; or, a history of the Second Tennessee Confederate cavalry. *Nashv* 1887. O [16] 644 2pls a

HANCOCK, WILLIAM   153
An emigrant's five years in the free states of America. *L* 1860. D [6] 321 map front. a

HANCOCK COUNTY [N. H.]   154
The unmasked nabob of: ... *Portsmouth* 1796. D 24 aa
Protest against General Henry Knox's land claim. Attributed to Charles Peirce.

HANDLY, JAMES   155
The resources of Madison county, Montana. [*S F* 1872]. O 61 aa
Incorporates routes to the mines, business directory, etc.

HANDSAKER, SAMUEL   156
Pioneer life. *Eugene Ore* 1908. D 104 2 pls 2facs aa
Contains his 1853 overland journal and experiences in the Rogue River war.

HANGER, GEORGE   157
An address to the army; in reply to Strictures, by Roderick MacKenzie ... on Tarleton's History of the campaigns of 1780 and 1781. *L* 1789. O [16] 138 [8] aa

HANGER (GEORGE).   158
The life, adventures ... of: ... *L* 1801. O 2v: [4] 339; [4] 475 + 4adv-p a
—Am. ed. *N Y* 1801. O 2v in 1
Includes his services as Tarleton's second in command in the Revolution. Ghost-written by William Combe.

HANNA, CHARLES A.   159
Historical collections of Harrison county ... Ohio ... *N Y* 1900. O [8] 636 map 2pls a

HANNA, CHARLES A.   160
Ohio valley genealogies . . . *N Y* 1900. O [44] 128]incl.front.] a

HANNA, CHARLES A.   161
The Scotch-Irish; or, the Scot in North Britain, North Ireland and North America. *N Y* 1902. O 2v: [12] 623; [6] 602. 3maps aa

HANNA, CHARLES A.   162
The wilderness trail; or, the ventures and adventures of the Pennsylvania traders on the Allegheny path . . . *N Y* 1911. O 2v: [28] 383; [10] 447. 81maps & pls aa

HANNA, JOHN S. [ed.]   163
A history of the life and services of Capt. Samuel Dewees . . . *Balt* 1844. D 360 port a

HANNA, REV. WILLIAM   164
History of Greene county, Pa. [1682–1781]. n.p. 1882. O 350 a

HANNIBAL, PETER M.   165
Thrice a pioneer . . . *Blair Neb* [1901]. D [6] 202 a

HANS, FREDERIC M.   166
The great Sioux nation . . . *Chi* [1907]. O 575 [incl.front.] a

HANSEN, P.   167
Situation de la Belgique en 1849, et moyens de l'amélior . . . *Mons* [1849] D 167 aa
Contains remarks on benefits of emigration to the United States by Count Julien Visart de Bocarme, formerly Governor of Java, who resided in Arkansas from 1835 till his death in the early 1840's.

[HANSON, ALEXANDER C.]   168
Considerations on the . . . removal of the seat of government. *Annap* [1786]. D 62 aa

[HANSON, ALEXANDER C.]   169
Political schemes and calculations . . . *Annap* 1784. O [6] 38 aa

[HANSON, ALEXANDER C.]   170
Remarks on the proposed plan of a federal government . . . *Annap* [1788]. D 42 aa

HANSON (ELIZABETH).   171
God's mercy . . . exemplified in the captivity and redemption of: . . . *Phil* 1728. D 40 No perfect copy known
—ed. 2, *Phil* 1754. D 24 b PaH
—ed. 3, *Danvers Mass* [1780]. O 32 aa
—anr. ed. 3, *Stanford N Y.* 1803. 16° 23 a
—anr. ed. "The remarkable captivity . . . of Elizabeth Hanson," *Dover N H* 1824. D

—Eng. ed.: "An account of the captivity of Elizabeth Hanson . . .," *L* 1760. O [2] 28 + adv-l. b N NYP Y
—Eng. ed. 2, same collat. & impr. aa
—new ed. *L* 1782. D 26 [2]; rptd. *L* 1787. D 28; *Cork* 1791. D 22; and several later eds. aa
Text of American editions—differing from English versions based on conversations with Mrs. Hanson by Samuel Bownas and Samuel Hopwood —may have been written by herself.

HANSON, G. W.   172
Early days in Nebraska. *Cedar Rapids* 1916. O 47 a

HANSON, GEORGE A.   173
Old Kent, eastern shore of Maryland . . . *Balt* 1876. Q 383 [36] 5pls some copies on L.P. aa

HANSON, J. W.   174
History of . . . Danvers [Mass.] . . . *Danvers* 1848. O 304 a

HANSON, J. W.   175
History of Gardiner, Pittston and West Gardiner [Me.] . . . *Gardiner* 1852. D 343 pls a

HANSON, J. W.   176
History of the old towns Norridgewock and Canaan . . . [Me.]. *B* 1849. D 372 4pls a

HANSON, JOSEPH M.   177
The conquest of the Missouri . . . life . . . of Captain Grant Marsh. *Chi* 1909. O [14] 458 map 29pls a
—other eds., same impr. & collat.: 1910; 1912.

HARBAUGH, H.   178
The life of Rev. Michael Schlatter . . . his travels . . . in Pennsylvania . . . services as chaplain in the French and Indian war and . . . the revolution. *Phil* 1857. D [32] 26–375 front. a

HARBISON (MASSY).   179
Narrative of the sufferings of: . . . her captivity . . . cruelties of the Indians [etc.]. *Pitt* 1825. 16° 66 b N NYP
—rptd. *Pitt* 1828. 16° 98 aa
—ed. 4, enl. *Beaver Pa* 1836. D 192 aa
—anr. ed. *Meadville* 1847. D a
Important narrative on the Ohio-Pennsylvania frontier, with account of St. Clair's defeat.

HARDEN, EDWARD J.   180
The life of George M. Troup. *Savannah* 1859. O [8] 536 [22] port a

HARDEN, SAMUEL, comp.   181
Early life . . . in Boone county, Indiana . . . [*Indp* 1887]. O 498 35pls a

HARDEN, SAMUEL 182
History of Madison county, Indiana . . . *Markleville Ind* 1874. O [12] 17–411 a

HARDIE, JAMES 183
The American remembrancer . . . *Phil* 1795. D [8] 259 fold chart aa
—enl. ed. "The new universal biographical dictionary, and American remembrancer of departed merit . . .," *N Y* 1801–05. O 4v 26 ports b AA NYP

HARDIE, JAMES 184
The description of the city of New York . . . *N Y* 1827. D [6] 360 map aa

HARDIE, JAMES, comp. 185
The Philadelphia directory and register. *Phil* 1793. O [12] 234 b
—ed. 2, *Phil* 1794. O [6] 232 map b

HARDIE, JAMES 186
A short account of . . . Philadelphia . . . *Phil* 1794. O 40 map aa

HARDIE (JAMES A.) 187
Memoirs of: *Wash* 1877. D 79 port aa
Experiences in California in 1847 as second in command of Stevenson's regiment, and later operations against the Spokane Indians.

HARDIN (JOHN WESLEY). 188
The life of: . . . as written by himself. *Seguin Tex* 1896. D 144 a
Opposite page three of first issue is a cut of Hardin's brother Joe, mistitled John W. Hardin. Iss 2 [and best] has full page portrait of John W. Hardin inserted.

HARDING, BENJAMIN 189
A tour through the western country . . . *N Lond* 1819. O [4] 17 c AA ChiH G

[HARDINGE, BELLE B.] 190
Belle Boyd in camp and prison. *L* 1865. D 2v: [12] 291; [16] 280. port aa
—Am. ed. *N Y* 1865. D 464 a
Autobiography of an adventuress and bogus Confederate heroine.

HARDMAN, FREDERICK, ed. 191
Scenes and adventures in Central America [*i.e.* Louisiana, Texas and northern Mexico]. *Edin* 1852. O [10] 298 a
—rptd. "Frontier life; or, scenes . . . in the southwest," *Auburn* 1853. D 376
Apparently translated from some book by the German Karl Postl. In later editions Hardman's first name is given as Francis.

HARDY, JOHN 192
Selma: her institutions . . . *Selma* 1879. O 200 a
—rptd Selma 1957

HARDY, LIEUT. [RICHARDSON] 193
The history and adventures of the Cuban expedition . . . *Cin* 1850. 16° 94 a

HARE, GEORGE H. 194
Guide to San Jose and vicinity . . . its early history . . . *San Jose* 1872. 16° 85 [27] 2maps a

HARE (JOSEPH [T.]) 195
The dying confession of: . . . *Balt* 1818. O 23 a
—rptd., t.slightly altered, *Phil* 1818. O 24
—anr. ed., slightly abr., *Auburn N Y* 1818. O 16

HARE (JOSEPH T.)
The life and adventures of: *See* Howard, H. R.

HAREMS (LES) DU NOUVEAU-MONDE.
See Ward, Maria.

HARFORD, JOHN S. 196
Some account of the life . . . of Thomas Paine . . . *Bristol Eng* 1819. O [8] 92 a
—rptd., same impr., 1920. O 110

HARGRAVES, E. H. 197
Australia and its gold fields . . . *L* 1855. D [16] 240 map port a
Includes his California experiences in 1849.

HARLAN, JACOB W. 198
California, '46 to '48. *S F* 1888. O 242 port aa
—rptd. *Oakland* 1896. port a
Harlan arrived overland to California in 1846 just in time to join Fremont's battalion.

HARLOW, ALVIN F. 199
Old post bags: the story of the sending of a letter . . . *N Y* 1928. O [18] 500 44pls a

HARLOW, ALVIN F. 200
Old towpaths: the story of the American canal era. *N Y* 1926. O [16] 403 48pls a

HARLOWE, ALVIN F. 201
Old waybills: the romance of the express companies. *N Y* 1934. O [14] 504 49pls a
—rptd. *N Y* 1937

HARLOW, NEAL 202
The maps of San Francisco bay . . . *S F* Grabhorn 1950. Q [12] 141 21pls 375copies ptd. aa

HARMAN, S. W. 203
Hell on the border . . . history of the . . . criminal court at Fort Smith . . . and of crime and criminals in the Indian Territory. *Ft Smith* Phoenix Pub Co [1898]. O [14] 720 port b
—rptd., greatly abr., same impr. [*ca* 1920]. O 320 a

HARMAR (BRIG. GEN. JOSIAH). 204
The proceedings of a court of inquiry, held at the . . . request of: to investigate his conduct, as

commanding officer of the expedition against the Miami Indians . . . *Phil* 1791. F [4] 31 b

HARMON, DANIEL W.   **205**
Journal of voyages and travels . . . from Montreal nearly to the Pacific . . . [including 19 years as a fur-trader with the Northwest Co.]. *Andover* 1820. O 432 port map errata slip b
—rptd.: N Y 1903. 16° map port; *Toronto* 1957 D port a
Editor Daniel Haskel took some liberties with the narrative and the moral and religious undertones woven into it are hardly consistent with life on the Indian frontier. An important book in spite of Mr. Haskel.

HARMONIE.   **206**
Gedanken ueber die Bestimmung der: [*New Harmony Ind* 1824]. D 96 b
First publication of this Community.

HARNEY, GEN. WILLIAM S.   **207**
Proceedings of a council held at Fort Pierre with nine tribes of Sioux Indians. [Ex Doc 130] *Wash* 1856. O 40 a

[HARPER, ROBERT G.]   **208**
Case of the Georgia sales on the Mississippi, considered . . . *Phil* 1797. O [4] 109 aa
—rptd. *Phil* 1799. Q 91 aa
—anr. issue, *Phil* 1799. O [4] 109 aa

HARPER, ROBERT G.   **209**
Observations on the dispute between the United States and France . . . *Phil* 1797. O [2] 102 a
—ed. 2, same impr. & date. O 79
—Eng. ed. *L* 1797. O 162
—rptd. 19 times by 1799, in Eng. & Am.
—Fr. tr., *L* 1798. O [18] 127

HARPER, ROBERT G.   **210**
Observations on the North American Land Company . . . in Philadelphia . . . to which are added, Remarks on American lands . . . particularly the pine lands of the southern and western states. *L Galabin* 1796. O 149 aa
—anr. issue. O [8] 145
—anr. ed. *L Bannell & Savante*, same date. O 149

HARPER, ROBERT G.   **211**
A short account of the principal proceedings of Congress . . . and a sketch of the state of affairs between the United States and France . . . *Phil* 1798. O 22 a
—Eng. ed. *L* 1798. O 25
—same impr. & collat. 1799.

HARPER, ROBERT G.   **212**
. . . Speech to the citizens of Baltimore, on the expediency of . . . a connexion between the Ohio . . . and the waters of the Chesapeake . . . *Balt* 1824. O 78 fold.map a

HARPER, CHANCELLOR WILLIAM C.   **213**
Memoir on slavery . . . *Charleston S C* 1838. O 61 errata slip a

HARPER, CHANCELLOR   **214**
[WILLIAM C.] et al
The pro-slavery argument . . . *Charleston S C* 1852. D [4] 490 a
—rptd. *B* 1852. D; *Phil* 1853. D

HARPER'S FERRY.
The annals of: . . . By Josephus. *See* Barry, Joe.

HARPER'S FERRY.   **215**
Correspondence relative to the insurrection at: *Annap* 1860. O 79 a

HARRELL, JOHN M.   **216**
The Brooks and Baxter war: . . . the reconstruction period in Arkansas. *St L* 1893. O [8] 3–276 a

HARRINGTON, ELISHA [pub.]   **217**
The Utica directory: to which is added . . . account of the village . . . *Utica* 1828. D 99 + 16 adv-p & errata p map aa
Second directory of this city and first containing historical sketch.

HARRINGTON, GRANT W.   **218**
Annals of Brown county Kansas . . . *Hiawatha Kas* 1923. O 564 [54] pls a

HARRINGTON, W. P., and   **219**
ANGEL, MYRON
. . . Directory of the city of Austin [Nevada]. With a historical . . . review of Austin and the Reese river mining region. *Austin* 1866. O [6] 23–118 [3–16] b G LC NYP Y [only copies known]

HARRIOTT, JOHN   **220**
Struggles through life . . . *L* 1807. D 2v: [24] 375; [12] 347. port a
—ed. 2, *L* 1808. D 2v 2pls
—ed. 3, *L* 1815. D 3v: [26] 443; [12] 428; [10] 479. 3pls
—Am. eds.: *Phil* 1809. D 2v: [4] 304; [2] 267
—*N Y* 1809. D 2v same collat.
The author operated farms in New York and Rhode Island and seems to have acted as agent in a gigantic British scheme to purchase from Georgia seventeen million acres bordering on the Mississippi. This, tied in with intrigues to acquire Florida from Spain and to take over the disaffected Western country from the United States, undoubtedly had for object the confinement of the United States to the Eastern seaboard.

HARRIS, ALBERT W.   **221**
The cruise of a schooner. [*Chi* 1911]. D [14] 266 36pls map[incl. in paginat.] aa
Overland journey from California to Wisconsin in 1910.

HARRIS, ALEXANDER   **222**
A review of the political conflict in America . . . a survey of the struggle of parties which destroyed the republic, and virtually monarchised its government. *N Y* 1876. O 517 a

HARRIS, BRANSON L.   **223**
Some recollections of my boyhood. *Indp* [1908]. O [2] 70 port a
Lived in Indiana from 1817.

HARRIS (MRS. CAROLINE).   **224**
History of the captivity of: [by Texas Comanches]. *N Y* 1838. O 24 [incl. front.] b G LC NYP Y
—rptd. *Rochester* 1848. O 39 b
Cf., Narrative of Mrs. Clarissa Plummer.

HARRIS, CHARLES H.   **225**
History of the Venango oil regions . . . *Titusville Pa* 1866. D [6] 108 2pls a

HARRIS, D. W., and HULSE, B. M.   **226**
History of Claiborne parish [La.] . . . *N O* 1886. D [8] 7–264 a

HARRIS, J. MORRISON   **227**
A paper upon California . . . *Balt* 1849. O 32 a

HARRIS, JAMES S.   **228**
Historical sketches. Seventh regiment North Carolina troops. n.p. [*ca* 1893] O 70 aa

[HARRIS, JOSEPH]   **229**
The naval atalantis . . . flag officers [and] post-captains . . . during the last war. *L* 1788–1789. O 2pts in 1 : [8] 196; [8] 126 [1] aa
Of the 91 officers covered — most of whom served in America — several are unmercifully criticised or lampooned, notably Viscount William Howe, Lord of the Admiralty. The two parts were probably also issued separately.

[HARRIS, N. SAYRE]   **230**
Journal of a tour in the "Indian Territory" . . . *N Y* 1844. O [4] 74 3maps aa
Observation tour in behalf of the Episcopal Church, from Arkansas to Ft. Leavenworth.
The report had previously appeared, in June 1844, with one map, as an Extra to *Spirit of Missions*.

HARRIS, MRS. SARAH H.   **231**
An unwritten chapter of Salt Lake, 1851–1901. *N Y* 1901. D 89 aa

HARRIS, THADDEUS M.   **232**
Biographical memorials of James Oglethorpe. *B* 1841. O [22] 424 map 3pls a

HARRIS, THADDEUS M.   **233**
The journal of a tour into the territory north-

west of the Alleghany mountains . . . *B* 1805. O 271 5maps & pls [incl first separate map of Ohio] aa

HARRIS, W. A.   **234**
The record of Fort Sumter . . . *Columbia* 1862. O 50 addendum slip after p-12 aa

HARRIS, W. B.   **235**
Pioneer life in California. *Stockton* 1884. O 98 b

[HARRIS, WILLIAM] 1720-70   **236**
An historical . . . account of Hugh Peters . . . *L* 1751. O 72 port a
—rptd. *L* 1818. Q 41 port

HARRIS, WILLIAM   **237**
Mormonism portrayed: its errors . . . exposed . . . *Warsaw Ill* 1841. O 64 c G Hn NYP
Said to have been ghost-written by Thomas C. Sharp.

HARRIS, REV. W[ILLIAM] R.   **238**
The Catholic church in Utah . . . *S L C* [1909]. O [18] 350[incl. front.] map 25pls a
Contains first English translation of Escalante's account of his Utah discoveries.

HARRIS, WILLIAM T.   **239**
Remarks made during a tour through the United States . . . *Liv* [1819]. O 74 aa
—rptd. *L* 1821. D 196 aa
—Ger. tr. *Weimar* 1822. O [8 i.e. 6] 236 a
Highly favorable commentary, based on extensive investigations through Ohio, Kentucky, Indiana and Illinois.

HARRIS, WILLIAM W.   **240**
The battle of Groton Heights . . . 1781. *N Lond* 1870. O [12] 123 a 100copies ptd
—enl. ed., same impr. 1882. O

HARRISON and WINCHESTER [GENERALS].
Historical details, having relation to the campaign of the northwestern army under: *See* Winchester, James.

HARRISON (LIEUTENANT [E. J.])   **241**
The thrilling . . . narrative of: . . . prisoner at Goliad . . . *Cin* 1848. O 30 d G [of 2 cops kn]

HARRISON, FAIRFAX   **242**
Virginia land grants . . . *Rich* 1925. O 184 aa

[HARRISON, JESSE B.]   **243**
Review of the slave question . . . showing that slavery is the essential hindrance to the prosperity of slave-holding states . . . *Rich* 1833. O 48 a

HARRISON, WALTER   **244**
Pickett's men . . . *N Y* 1870. D 202 2pls a

HARRISON, WILLIAM HENRY   245
A discourse on the aborigines of the valley of
the Ohio . . . *Cin* 1838. O 51 map aa
—rptd. *B* 1840. D 47 a

HARRISON (MAJOR GENERAL   246
WILLIAM HENRY).
Life of: . . . civil and military services . . . *Phil*
1840. O 96 4pls a

HARRISON (GOV. [WILLIAM HENRY]). 247
Message of the President . . . transmitting two
letters from: reporting the particulars . . . of the
expedition . . . against the hostile Indians on the
Wabash. *Wash* 1811. O 24 fold chart aa
Account of his victory at Tippecanoe.

HARRISON (WILLIAM HENRY).
A sketch of the life and public services of: . . .
See Jackson, Isaac R.

HARRISON (MAJOR GENERAL   248
WILLIAM HENRY).
Sketch of the life of: n.p. [1836?]. D 39 a

HARRISSE, HENRY   249
Les Corte-Real et leurs voyages au nouveau-
monde. *P* 1883. O [12] 272[incl. facs] front. fold.
map[in portfolio] a

HARRISSE, HENRY   250
Découverte et évolution cartographique de
Terre-Neuve et des pays circonvoisine . . . *P* 1900.
Q [4 72] 420 26maps a 380 cops ptd

HARRISSE, HENRY   251
The discovery of North America . . . *L* 1892. Q
[12] 804 + 2adv-p 23maps b N 380 copies[40
copies, in 2v, on Hand Made Paper; 10 on Jap.
Paper; 10 on Whatman Paper]

HARRISSE, HENRY   252
Jean et Sébastien Cabot . . . *P* 1882. O [4] 400
map a
Some conclusions here advanced were altered in
his later English version—*see* below—and the
claims of Sebastian utterly discredited.

HARRISSE, HENRY   253
John Cabot, the discoverer of North America
. . . *L* 1896. O [12] 503 9maps & facs 14adv-p a
Also 25cops on L.P.
The author's definitive conclusions on this
subject.

HART, ADOLPHUS M.   254
History of the discovery of the valley of the
Mississippi. *St L* 1852. D 155 a
—ed. 2, identical, but with *Cin* impr.
—anr. ed. enl. "History of the valley of the Mississippi," *Cin* 1853. D 286

HART, ALBERT B., ed.   255
The Varick court of inquiry to investigate the
implication of Col. Varick in the Arnold treason.
B 1907. Q 217 port eng.t. 6facs a 470copies ptd.

HART, ALFRED A.   256
The traveller's own book . . . via the . . . Chicago, Burlington & Quincy R. R. . . . [*Chi* 1870].
obl. 16° 34 [10] 14pls 3maps b
First transcontinental railroad guide.

HART, CHARLES H.   257
Catalogue of the engraved portraits of Washington. *N Y* Grolier Club 1904. Q [26] 406 [1] 20pls
425copies ptd. aa

HART, JOHN A., et al   258
History of pioneer days in Texas and Oklahoma
. . . [*Guthrie* 1906]. D [2] 249 12 pls aa
—anr. ed., with 2chaps.[on Ark.] added, [*Guthrie*
1909?]. D [4] 271 12pls aa
—enl. ed. "Pioneer days in the southwest . . .,"
same impr. 1909. D 320 12pls a
—anr. issue, same impr., date & paginat., but
with 16pls[incl.col.front.] a
—ed. 2 [really ed. 3], same impr., date & collat., but
with 20pls a

HART, STEPHEN H., and   259
HULBERT, ARCHER B., eds.
Zebulon Pike's Arkansaw journal . . . *Col
Springs* [1932]. O [96] 200 4maps 3pls a

[HART, WILLIAM]   260
An appeal to the people: or, an exposition of the
official conduct of Return J. Meigs, Governor of
. . . Ohio. n.p. [*Cin*?] 1812. D 94 aa

HARTFORD . . .   261
Hartford convention)The) in an uproar! . . . By
Hector Benevolus. *Windsor Vt* 1815. O 46 [2]
front. b AA NYP Y

**Letters developing the character and views of the
Hartford convention** By "One of the convention."
See Otis, Harrison G.

The proceedings of a convention of dele-   262
gates . . . convened at Hartford. Dec. 15th 1814.
Hart Hosmer 1815. O 39 a
—anr. issue, *Hart* for Andrus & Starr 1815. same
collat.
—anr. issue, *Hart* 1815. O 36
—other eds., same yr.: *Alb*; *B*; *Newburyport*; *N
Hav*

[HARTHILL, ALEXANDER]   263
The river Mississippi, from St. Paul to New
Orleans . . . *N Y* [1859]. D 120 a

HARTLEY, CECIL B.   **264**
Hunting sports in the west . . . *Phil* 1859. D 320
eng.t. a
—rptd. often

HARTLEY, CECIL B.   **265**
Life and adventures of Lewis Wetzel . . . *Phil*
1859. D 320 a
—anr. ed., same impr. & collat., 1860.
—rptd., t. slightly changed, *Phil* 1869.

HARTLEY, DAVID   **266**
Letters on the American war . . . *L* 1777. O 92 a
—rptd. 7 times by 1779.
Favors reconciliation.

HARTLEY, DAVID   **267**
Substance of a speech in Parliament upon the
state of the nation and the present civil war with
America. *L* 1776. Q [2] 24 a
—ed. 2, same impr., date & collat.

HARTMAN, GEORGE W.   **268**
A private's own journal . . . of the battles in
Mexico . . . *Greencastle Pa* 1849. D 35 aa

HARTMANN, DR. CARL F. A.   **269**
Geographisch-statistische Beschreibung von Californien . . . *Weimar* 1849. O 2v: [16] 174; [4] 266.
maps & pls aa

HARTMANN et MILLARD   **270**
Le Texas, ou notice historique sur le Champ
d'Asile . . . *P* 1819. O [10] 135 plan b
—Eng tr *Dallas* [1937] O 180 3pls aa

HARTSUFF, GEORGE L.   **271**
Outline description of the posts . . . in the mili-
tary division of the Missouri . . . *Chi* 1870. D 93 aa
For later issues, *see* under Sheridan, Philip H.

HARTWELL, HENRY, et al   **272**
The present state of Virginia . . . *L* 1727. O [4]
95 b H N NYP
—rptd. *Wmsbg* 1940. O [74] 105 pls a

HARVEY, AUGUSTUS F.   **273**
Nebraska as it is . . . *Lincoln* 1869. D 37 [2] aa
First book printed in Lincoln.

HARVEY, AUGUSTUS F., ed.   **274**
Sketches of the early days of Nebraska City . . .
St L 1871. D 30 aa
Author's initial on title-page erroneously given
as "E".

HARVEY, HENRY   **275**
History of the Shawnee Indians . . . *Cin* 1855. D
316 pref. dated "Sept. 21," t. on spine "History of
the Shawnee Indians" aa
—issue 2, port added, pref. dated "ninth month,"

t. on spine "Harvey's History of the Shawnee Indians" a

HARWOOD, THOMAS   **276**
History of New Mexico Spanish and English
missions of the Methodist . . . church. *Albuquerque*
1908–10. D 2v: [8] 376; [16 incl.initial blank] 451
+ adv-p aa
Printed by Indian students at the Mission press.
For another book on the work of this mission, *see*
Kellogg, Harriet S., *Life of Mrs. Harwood.*

[HASELHURST, MRS. MAY A.]   **277**
Days forever flown. *N Y* 1892. O 401 25 pls a
Travels through Alaska and the Northwest.

HASENCLEVER (PETER merchant).   **278**
The remarkable case of: . . . *L* 1773. D [2] 97 c
LC [of 2copies known]
Complaint addressed to Parliament by a New
Jersey potash and iron manufacturer.

HASKEL, DANIEL, and   **279**
SMITH, J. CALVIN
A complete . . . gazetteer of the United States
. . . *N Y* 1843. O 752 a
—rptd., same impr.: 1844; 1845; 1847; 1850.

HASKELL, BURNETTE G.   **280**
Kaweah, a co-operative commonwealth . . .
Tulare county, [Calif.]. *S F* 1887. 16° 16 a
—enl. ed. "Pen picture of Kaweah . . .," *S F* 1889.
D 32 aa

HASKETT, WILLIAM J.   **281**
Shakerism unmasked, or, the history of the
Shakers . . . *Pittsfield* 1828. O 300 a

HASKIN, MAJOR WILLIAM L.   **282**
History of the First Regiment of Artillery, from
. . . 1821 . . . *Ft Preble Me* [ptd. *Portland*]. 1879.
O [16] 668 a
Over half of the volume devoted to personal
reminiscences by officers.

HASKINS, C. W.   **283**
The argonauts of California. By a pioneer. *N Y*
1890. O [2] 501 aa
Contains an index of 35,000 pioneers arriving
prior to 1850.

HASKINS, R. W.   **284**
New England and the west . . . *Buf* 1843. D 36 a

HASSAM, LOREN   **285**
A historical sketch of Lafayette, Indiana . . .
Lafayette 1872. O 88 a

HASSLER, EDGAR W.   **286**
Old Westmoreland: a history of western Penn-
sylvania during the revolution. *Pitt* 1900. O [4 6]
5–200 a

HASTINGS, FRANK S.   **287**
A ranchman's recollections . . . *Chi* 1921. D [14]
235 14pls a

HASTINGS, LANSFORD W.   **288**
Emigrants' guide to Oregon and California. *Cin*
1845. O 152 dd B G NYP Y
—ed. 2, *Cin* 1845. c
—rptd., variously entitled "New description . . ."
and "New history . . .," with 8 p. & front. added,
1847; 1848. b
—other eds. with 168 p. & front: 1849; 1852; 1857. b
Includes his 1842 overland trip to Oregon and
his 1843 trip from Oregon to California. Historically, the first California guide book.

HASTINGS, SALLY   **289**
Poems . . . To which is added a . . . tour to the
west. *Lancaster* 1808. D 220 aa

HASWELL, ANTHONY [ed.]   **300**
Memoirs and adventures of Captain Matthew
Phelps . . . Particularly in two voyages from Connecticut to the river Mississippi . . . *Bennington Vt*
1802. D [4] 210 64 [14] b

HATFIELD, EDWIN F.   **301**
History of Elizabeth, New Jersey . . . *N Y* 1868.
O 701 8pls a

HATFIELD and DEERFIELD.   **302**
Papers concerning the attack on: by . . . Indians
from Canada, 1677. *N Y* Bradford Club 1859. O
[8] 82 map a 100 copies ptd.
First printing from original manuscripts.

HATHEWAY, O. P., and TAYLOR,   **303**
J. H. [comps.]
Chicago city directory . . . for 1849–50. *Chi*
1849. D 264 b ChiH G LC
Sixth Chicago directory.

HAUPT, HERMAN   **304**
Reminiscences . . . *Milw* 1901. O [40] 331 a
On railroad transportation of Federal troops
and supplies.

HAUSER, M[iska] [i.e. MICHAEL]   **305**
Aus dem Wanderbuch . . . Briefe aus Californien
und Australien. *Leip* 1859. D 2v in 1: 475 aa
—ed. 2, same impr. 1860. a
The California letters are dated San Francisco,
March to December, 1853.

HAVEN, C[HARLES] C.   **306**
Annals of the city of Trenton . . . *Trenton* 1866.
O 31 a

HAVEN, C[HARLES] C.   **307**
Washington and his army during their march
through . . . New Jersey. *Trenton* 1856. O 56 a

HAVEN, CHARLES T., and   **308**
BELDEN, FRANK A.
A history of the Colt revolver . . . *N Y* 1940. Q
[24] 711[incl.front. & pls] aa

HAVEN, SAMUEL F.   **309**
Archaeology of the United States . . . *Wash*
1856. Q [4] 168 errata slip a

HAVERLY, CHARLES E.   **310**
Klondyke and fortune . . . *L* [1898]. D [8] 736 a

HAWES, A. G.   **311**
A historical sketch . . . of . . . Leavenworth . . .
Leavenworth 1857. D 32 aa

HAWES, MRS. A[NGELICA] H.   **312**
The grafted bud: a memoir of Angelica Irene
Hawes. *N Y* 1853. 16° 102 pl aa
—rptd. *B* n.d. a
Of Michigan interest; Sault Ste. Marie, Ft Wil-
kins, etc.

HAWES, GEORGE W., comp.   **313**
Illinois state gazetteer and business directory for
1858–9. *Chi* [1858]. O [36 incl. preliminary blank
l.] 444[incl.pl.] a

HAWES, GEORGE W. AND CO.   **314**
Missouri state gazetteer . . . for 1865. *St L* [ptd
Indp 1865]. O [36] 418 3–112 fold.map b G
Final 112 pages consisted of unsold sheets of the
rare 1860 edition of Villard's guide to the Pike's
Peak gold mines, *q.v.*

HAWES, H. W.   **315**
A comparison of the bars and harbors of the
Gulf of Mexico, from the . . . Mississippi to Vera
Cruz; and of the mines . . . in California, Nevada
. . . *Lavaca Tex* 1869. O 22 [2] + cover t. a

HAWES, HORACE   **316**
The missions in California and the rights of the
Catholic church to the property . . . *S F* 1856. O 46
errata slip c

HAWKE, SIR EDWARD   **317**
Authentic register of the British successes . . .
from the taking of Louisbourgh . . . *L* 1760. D [6]
126 aa

HAWKINS, BENJAMIN   **318**
Sketch of the Creek country . . . 1798–9. [In Ga.
Hist. Colls., v.3, pt. 1]. *Savannah* [ptd. *N Y*] 1848.
O 88 aa
This self-styled volume 3, part 1, Georgia Histo-
rical Collections, was issued at the expense of W.
B. Hodgson and is really an "extra" in the series
of this Society; its regular volume 3 was published
in 1873.

HAWKINS (CHRISTOPHER). 319
The adventures of: ... and escape from the Jersey prison ship. *N Y* 1864. O 316 8pls a 75cops ptd.

HAWKINS, JOHN P. 320
Memoranda concerning ... the Hawkins family ... [*Indp* 1913]. O 137 17pls aa
Includes account of General Hawkins' army experiences in Minnesota and Nebraska, with much on General Canby and the Modoc war.

HAWKINS, THOMAS S. 321
Some recollections of a busy life. *S F* 1913. O 161 pls aa 300cops ptd.

[HAWKS, FRANCIS L.] 322
The adventures of Daniel Boone, the Kentucky rifleman. *N Y* 1843. 16° 174 [22] a
—rptd. same impr.: 1844; 1846.

HAWKS, FRANCIS L. 323
Contributions to the ecclesiastical history of the United States ... [Virginia and Maryland]. *N Y* 1836–9. O 2v: [2] 332; 523 a

HAWKS, FRANCIS L., and 324
PERRY, WILLIAM S., eds.
Documentary history of the Protestant Episcopal Church, in the United States ... *N Y* 1863–4. O 2v: [2] 328; 359 a

HAWKS, FRANCIS L. 325
History of North Carolina. *Fayetteville* 1857–8. O 2v: 254; 591. 8maps port pl aa
—ed. 2, same impr., date & collat. aa
—ed. 3, same impr. & collat. 1859. a

HAWKS, FRANCIS L., et al 326
Revolutionary history of North Carolina ... *Raleigh* 1853. D 237 a

HAWLEY, A. T. 327
The climate, resources ... of Humboldt county, California ... *Eureka* 1879. O 42 + 12adv-p aa

HAWLEY, A. T. 328
Condition, progress and advantages of Los Angeles city and county ... *L A* 1876. O [2] 144 a

HAWLEY, MRS. CHARLOTTE 329
CORNELL
Reminiscences of a private life ... *N Y* 1893. O 38 a
Authoress crossed the Isthmus to California in 1852.

HAWLEY, D. E., comp. 330
Sedalia [Mo.] city directory, for 1879–80 ... historical sketch ... *Sedalia* 1879. O 220 fold.map aa

[HAWLEY, JESSE] 331
Rochester in 1827. *Roch* 1828. D [4] 71-156 map 14adv-p aa
For earlier issue, *see* Ely, Elisha. Pagination begins at page seventy-one because original plan was to prefix a directory.

HAWLEY, WALTER A. 332
The early days of Santa Barbara. *N Y* 1910. O 105 5pls a
—rptd., in altered form, *Santa Barbara* 1920.

HAWLEY, ZERAH 333
A journal of a tour through Connecticut [etc.], including a year's residence in that part of ... Ohio, styled New Connecticut or Western Reserve. *N Hav* 1822. D 158 aa
Attempt to stem the tide of emigration to Ohio by accentuating its every unlovely feature.

HAWTHORNTHWAITE, SAMUEL 334
Adventures among the Mormons ... *Manch* 1857. O 132 a

HAY (JOHN). 335
Letters of: and extracts from[his] diary. *Wash* ptd but not pub 1908. O 3v: [24] 393; [2] 368; [2] 350 b N Y
—rptd., in part, "Lincoln and the civil war ...," *N Y* 1939. O [14] 348 front. a

HAY, THOMAS R. 336
Hood's Tennessee campaign. *N Y* 1929. O 272 2maps a

HAYDEN, F[ERDINAND] V. 337
Sun pictures of Rocky mountain scenery ... *N Y* 1870. Q [8] 150 + atlas vol[30 mounted photos] aa

HAYDEN, FERDINAND V. 338
The Yellowstone national park [etc.]. *B* 1876. F [6] 48[incl. 2maps] 15col pls[by Moran] b G Y

HAYDEN, HORACE E. 339
Virginia genealogies ... *Wilkes-Barre* 1891. Q [18] 759 12ports aa
—rptd. *Wash* 1931. Q 758 a; *Balt* 1859. a

HAYDEN, HORACE H. 340
Geological essays; or, an enquiry into some of the geological phenomena ... in various parts of America ... *Balt* 1820. O [8] 412 a

HAYDEN, MARY J. 341
Pioneer days. *San José* 1915. D 49 front. b
Tells of her 1850 overland trip to Oregon, Indian wars, etc.

HAYDEN (WILLIAM). 342
Narrative of: ... his travels ... whilst a slave, in the south. *Cin* 1846. D 156 a

HAYES, CHARLES W., ed.   343
George Edward Hayes, a memorial. *Buf* 1882.
O 174 port b G N Y
Describes an eventful trip across the plains in
1850.

HAYES, CHARLES W.   344
A long journey; the story of Daniel Hayes. *Portland Me* 1876. 16° 76 a 100copies ptd.
Indian captivity of this Connecticut man, 1705–
1712.

HAYES, E. L.   345
Illustrated atlas of the upper Ohio river and
valley . . . *Phil* 1877. obl F 231 maps pls a

HAYMOND, CREED   346
The Central Pacific Railroad . . . *Wash* [1888].
O 181 a
—anr. ed. [*S F* 1888]. O 286
Argument, delivered before a Senate committee,
defending this carrier from attacks by Crocker,
Huntington and Stanford. Practically a history of
the overland railroad project.

HAYMOND, HENRY   347
History of Harrison county, W. Va . . . *Morgantown* [1910] O [8] 451 pls a

HAYNES, FREDERICK E.   348
Third party movements since the civil war . . .
Iowa City [1916]. O [12] 564 a

HAYNES, LEMUEL   349
The nature . . . of true republicanism . . . [*Rutland Vt*] 1801. D 24 a

HAYNES, MARTIN A.   350
Gen. Scott's guide in Mexico . . . Col. Noah E.
Smith. *Lake Village N H* 1887. O 58 aa

HAYS, GILBERT A., comp.   351
Life and letters of Alexander Hays . . . *Pitt* 1919.
O 732 9pls aa
After serving in the Mexican War, this West
Pointer resigned, crossed the plains in 1850 and
spent some time in the mines.

HAYWARD, ARTHUR H.   352
Colonial lighting. *B* [1923]. O [26] 159 100pls aa
206 cops ptd.
—rev. ed. *B* 1927. O [24] 168 83pls

HAYWARD, JOHN   353
The Columbian traveller . . . principally relating
to the United States. *B* [1833]. Q 40 4maps a

HAYWARD, JOHN   354
The New England gazetteer . . . *B* 1839. O 510
3pls a
—rptd. 13 times by 1841.

HAYWARD, JOHN   355
A view of the United States . . . *N Y* Day [1832].
O 21 lvs. [incl.cov.t.] a
—ed. 2, *N Y* Collins [1832]. same collat.
For later edition *see* above, *The Columbian
traveller* . . .

HAYWARD, SILVANUS   356
History of . . . Gilsum, New Hampshire. *Manchester N H* 1881. O 468 2maps 71pls a 250copies
ptd.

[HAYWOOD, JOHN]   357
The Christian advocate. By a Tennessean. *Nashv*
1819. D [6] 5–357 tab aa
Largely devoted to Indian antiquities; supports
a Caucasian origin of our aborigines.

HAYWOOD, JOHN   358
The civil and political history of Tennessee, from
its settlement up to 1796. *Knoxv* 1823. O [6] 504 +
copyright slip between t-p & pref b
—rptd., with sketch of au., *Nashv* 1891. O 518;
same impr. & collat. 1915. a

HAYWOOD, JOHN   359
The natural and aboriginal history of Tennessee,
up to . . . 1768. *Nashv* 1823. O [8] 390 [54] b AA
BA N NYP Y
Of great value on the pre-Caucasian period, its
people and antiquities.

HAYWOOD, MARSHALL D.   360
Governor William Tryon . . . in the province of
North Carolina . . . *Raleigh* 1903. O 223 5pls a

[HAYWOOD, P. D.]?   361
The cruise of the "Alabama" . . . *Liv* 1863. O 48
port aa
—rptd. "Our cruise on the . . . 'Alabama' . . .,"
[*L* 1863?]. O 64 a
—anr. ed. n.p. 1864. O 56
—enl. ed. *B* 1886. D 150 2maps pl
Ascribed also to George T. Fullam.

HAZARD, EBENEZER   362
Historical collections . . . materials for an history of the United States . . . *Phil* 1792–4. Q 2v:
[4] 639 [10]; [4] 654 aa

HAZARD, LUCY L.   363
The frontier in American literature. *N Y* Crowell
[1927]. D 308 a
—rptd. *N Y* 1941.

HAZARD, SAMUEL   364
Annals of Pennsylvania . . . 1609–1682. *Phil*
1850. O [8] 664 a

HAZARD, SAMUEL, ed.   365
The register of Pennsylvania . . . *Phil* 1828–36.

O 16v: v.I, [4] 448; v.II, [8] 386; v.VI, [8] 432; other vols. each [8] 416 b AA N NYP Y
Issued originally in 390 numbers.

[HAZARD, THOMAS R.]   366
The Jonny-Cake letters . . . by "Shepherd Tom." *Prov* 1882. D 449 a

HAZARD, THOMAS R.   367
The Jonny-Cake papers of "Shepherd Tom." *B* 1915. O [22] 430 map pls 600cops ptd a

HAZARD, THOMAS R.   368
Nailer Tom's diary . . . *B* 1930. Q [24] 808 400 cops ptd a

HAZELDINE, WILLIAM C.   369
Report on Bernalillo county, New Mex. *Albuq* 1881. O 31 aa

HAZELTON, JOHN H.   370
The Declaration of Independence: its history. *N Y* 1906. O [12] 3–629 12pls a

HAZEN, R[EUBEN] W.   371
History of the Pawnee Indians . . . [*Fremont Neb*] 1893. D 80 pl a

HAZEN, (MAJOR GENERAL [WILLIAM B.])
Hazen (Major General [William B.]), on his post of duty . . . reviewed. *See* Sargent, John O.

HAZEN, GEN. W[ILLIAM] B.   372
Our barren lands . . . *Cin* 1875. O 53 aa
In this and another pamphlet of eighteen pages published at St. Paul the same year, *Some corrections of "life on the plains,"* Hazen could see no economic possibilities in Dakota and the northern interior. For a scathing reply, *see* Sargent, John O.

HEAD, JAMES W.   373
History . . . of Loudon county, Virginia. [*Wash* 1908]. O 186 port a

HEAD, THOMAS A.   374
Campaigns . . . of the 16th Tenn. Infantry Regiment. *Nashv* 1885. O 488 front. a

HEADLEY, JOHN W.   375
Confederate operations in Canada and New York. *N Y* 1906. O 480 17ports a

HEADLEY, RUSSELL, ed.   376
History of Orange county, New York. *Middletown N Y* 1908. O [10] 17–997 [20] [incl.front.] pls a

[HEALD, HENRY]   377
A western tour, in a series of letters . . . during a journey through Pennsylvania, Ohio, Indiana, and into . . . Illinois and Kentucky . . . [*Wilm Del* 1819?]. O 91 capt. t. c. G NYP PittU

HEAP, GWINN H.   378
Central route to the Pacific, from the valley of the Mississippi to California. *Phil* 1854. O 136 13pls map[not inserted in all copies] advs at back [paged 1–46 in some copies, 17–32 in others] b
—rptd *Glendale Cal* 1957. O

HEARD, ISAAC V. D.   378a
History of the Sioux war and massacres . . . *N Y* 1863. D 354 [incl. pls] + 2 adv-p a
—rptd. 1864; 1865.

HEART (CAPT. JONATHAN).   379
Journal of: on the march . . . to Fort Pitt, 1785. Ed. by C. W. Butterfield. *Alb* 1885. sm Q [16] 94 a 150copies ptd.
First U.S. military expedition into the west.

HEARTSILL, W[ILLIAM] W.   380
Fourteen hundred and 91 days in the Confederate army . . . Or camp life; day-by-day, of the W. P. Lane Rangers. [*Marshall Tex* 1874–6]. O [8] 265 19pls[containing 61 pasted-in photos of members of this outfit] b N NYP TxS
Printed by the author, page-by-page, on a handpress; one of the rarest journals by a Confederate combatant.

HEATH (MAJOR-GENERAL [WILLIAM]). 381
Memoirs of: *B* 1798. O 388 a
—rptd. *N Y* 1901. O [10] 401 [3] 2ports some copies on L.P.
—anr. ed. *N Y* 1904. D 435

HEBARD, GRACE R., and   382
BRININSTOOL, E. A.
The Bozeman trail . . . *Clev* 1922. O 2v: 346; 306. 2fold.maps[other maps & pls incl. in paginat.] aa

HEBARD, GRACE R.   383
Sacajawea, a guide and interpreter of the Lewis and Clark expedition. *Glendale* 1933. O 340[incl.pls & maps] aa
—rptd same impr 1957. a

HEBARD, GRACE R.   384
Washakie . . . Indian resistance of the covered wagon and . . . railroad invasions . . . *Clev* 1930. O 338[incl. 7maps & 16pls] + adv-p aa

HEBERT, FRANK   385
Forty years prospecting . . . in the Black hills . . . [*Rapid City* 1921]. O [10] 199 7pls a

HEBERT, WILLIAM   386
A visit to the colony of Harmony, in Indiana . . . *L* 1825. O 35 b LC Y

HEBISON, W[ILLIAM] C.   387
Early days in Texas and Rains county. *Emory Tex* 1917. O [2] 50 aa

HECKE, J. VALENTIN 388
Reise durch die Vereinigten Staaten . . . *Berlin*
1820–21. O 2v: [10] 228; [16] 326+2adv-p front. aa

HECKENDORN and WILSON, pubs. 389
Miners and business men's directory . . . of Tuolumne . . . counties . . . *Columbia Calif* 1856. O
[6] 104 front. d G NYP

HECKEWELDER, JOHN 390
An account of the . . . Indian nations, who once
inhabited Pennsylvania . . . *Phil*1818. O [6] 3-348 aa
—anr. ed. same impr. 1819. O [6] 465 errata lf [In
Am. Phil. Soc. Procdgs] a
—rptd., t. altered, *Phil* 1876. O 465 port a
—anr ed *Phil* 1881
—Fr. tr., with adds., by Du Ponceau, *P* 1822. O
[4] 571 a
—Ger. tr. by Schulze, *Göttingen* 1821. O [48] 582
[2] a

HECKEWELDER, JOHN 391
Names given by . . . Delaware Indians to . . .
places . . , in . . . Pennsylvania, New Jersey, Maryland and Virginia . . . *Phil* 1833. Q 48 a
—rptd. in Am. Phil Soc. Trans., vol 4 [1834].
—anr. ed. *Bethlehem Pa* 1872. O 58

HECKEWELDER, JOHN 392
A narrative of the mission . . . among the Dela-
ware and Mohegan Indians . . . 1740–1808 . . .
Phil 1820. O [12] 17–430 port errata slip aa
—best ed., ed. Connelley. *Clev* 1907. Q [18] 3–616
3maps 5pls a some copies on L. P. aa
Standard authority on the Moravian missions in
Pennsylvania, Ohio, etc.

HECKEWELDER, JOHN 393
Reise von Bethlehem in Pensilvanien bis zum
Wabashflusz . . . *Halle* 1797. D 94 aa
—Eng. tr. *Phil* 1883. a

HEDENDAAGSCHE HISTORIE 394
Hedendaagsche Historie, of tegen woordige
staat van America . . . *Amst* 1765–69. O 3v: [4] 676
[22]; 685 [18]; 620 [16] 16maps and plans 12pls
[incl 3eng-titles] aa
Vol III on Canada and the United States.

HEILPRIN, ANGELO 395
Alaska and the Klondike . . . *L* 1899. O [10]
315 3maps 35pls a
—anr. issue, same collat. & date, *N Y*

HEINRICH, PIERRE 396
La Louisiane sous la Compagnie des Indes,
1717–31. *P* [1908]. O [80] 298 map a
Based on French archival studies.

HEINZELMANN, FRIEDRICH 397
Reisebilder und Skizzen . . . auf die Länder des

mejicanischen Golfes und Californien. *Leip* 1851.
O [8] 476 map pl aa
Travels in Texas, New Mexico and California.

HEISTAND, HENRY O. S. 398
The Territory of Alaska . . . *K C* 1898. D 195
3maps 16pls aa

HELM, MRS. MARY S. 399
Scraps of early Texas history. . . . *Austin* 1884.
O [12] 198 [2] a

HELPER, HINTON R. 400
The impending crisis of the south . . . *N Y* 1857.
D 420 a
—rptd., same date; also 1859 & 1860.
—abr. eds., "Compendium of the impensing crisis
. . .," *N Y* 1859. O 214; same impr. 1860.
Voicing the conclusion that slavery was econom-
ically unsound, this work of a southern "poor
white", officially banned in the South, vied in
popularity and influence with the sentimental
Uncle Tom's cabin.

HELPER, HINTON R. 401
The land of gold. Reality versus fiction. *Balt*
1855. D 300 a
—best ed., with 13pls added, *Phil* 1855. a

HELPER, HINTON R. 402
The Negroes in Negroland . . . in America . . .
N Y 1868. D 254 a

HELVIDIUS.
Letters of: . . . in reply to Pacificus . . . *See*
Madison, James.

HEMENWAY, ABBY M., ed. 403
The Vermont historical gazetteer . . . *Burlington
Vt* 1867–91. O 5v 125pls[more in some copies] b
[V.5 is the scarce one]
Originolly issued in parts. An index volume,
containing 1118 pages of text, was added, Rutland,
1923. a

HEMPSTEAD, FAY 404
A pictorial history of Arkansas . . . *St L* 1890.
O [12 5–10] 17–1240 front. 2 maps a

HEMPSTEAD (JOSHUA). 405
Diary of: . . . 1711–1758. With an account of a
journey made from New London to Maryland.
N Lond 1901. O [14] 750 front. facs a 500copies ptd
Some copies include a separately printed supple-
mentary sheet giving a list of criminals.

[HENDERSON, ARCHIBALD] 406
The adventures of a Porcupine . . . genuine memoirs of a notorious rogue . . . *Phil* 1796. O 47
front. a
Scurrilous lampoon on William Cobbett and
his *Life and adventures of Peter Porcupine, q.v.*

HENDERSON, GEORGE F. R.   407
The campaign of Fredericksburg. *L* 1886. D
[20] 143 4maps 2pls aa
—rptd: *L* 1919; *L* 1900. a

HENDERSON, G[EORGE] F. R.   408
Stonewall Jackson and the . . . civil war . . . *L*
1898. O 2v: [18] 550 + 32adv-p; [8] 641 + adv-p.
33maps 2ports aa
—ed. 2, with 14p. introd. by Wolsely added, *L*
1899. O 2v

HENDERSON, JOHN G.   409
Early history of the "Sangamon country" . . .
notes on the first settlements in . . . Morgan, Scott
and Cass counties [Ill.]. *Davenport Ia* 1873. O 33
errata lf aa

HENDERSON, THOMAS   410
An easy system of geography . . . designed for
schools. *Lex Ky* 1813. D 213 aa
—ed 2 same impr, date & collat
Appendix devoted chiefly to the Mississippi
Valley and the Old Northwest.

HENDRY & FELL, comps.   411
Residence and business directory of Billings,
Montana . . . history . . . *Minneap* 1883. O 96[incl.
front.] aa

HENLEY (COLONEL DAVID).   412
Proceedings of a general court-martial . . . upon
the trial of: [accused by General Burgoyne of ill
treatment of the British soldiers]. *B* 1778. sm Q 88
b AA N NYP
—Eng. ed. *L* 1778. O [4] 147 aa
—ed. 2, same impr., date O [4] 156 aa

HENLEY, G. F.   413
Guide to the Yukon-Klondike mines . . . [*Victoria Can* 1897]. D 63 a
—rptd. *N Y* 1898. D 60

HENLEY (PETER).   414
The life of: . . . his travels and adventures in
America . . . *Calne Eng* 1799. O 64 aa
After service in the French and Indian war,
distinguished by two desertions, Henley lived in
Massachusetts under the name of Robertson,
joined the Revolutionary army and lost his right
hand at Bunker's Hill.

HENNEPIN, LOUIS   415
Description de la Louisiane . . . *P* [veuve Huré]
1683. D [12] 312; 107 map c AA Hn N
—In 1684 sheets of this 1683 ed. were slightly altered
in 2 issues: the first merely adding a numeral I to
the date; the second substituting a new t-p with
1684 date and Auroy's imprint.
—ed. 2, *P* [Auroy] 1688. Same collat but typographically different. b H

—Dutch tr. "Ontdekking van Louisiania" [eng-t],
"Beschryving van Louisiania" [ptd-t] to which was
added Deny's "Beschryving der Kusten van Noord
America" *Amst* 1688. Q [4] 158 [6]; [4] 200 [4]
map 7pls [incl eng-t] b
—Eng. tr. by Shea *N Y* 1880. O [54] 41–407 map
pl facsm 250 cops ptd aa
—Eng. tr. by Cross. *Minneap* 1938. O [22] 190
front a
—Ger. tr. *Nurembg* 1689. O 425 map aa
—rptd. same impr 1692. 16° 427 map a
—anr Ger ed Bremen 1690. D a
—Ital. tr. *Bologna* 1686. D [12] 396 map b
First and most important of the writings of this
rascally friar, giving a fairly reliable account of his
genuine voyage up the Mississippi from the Illinois
to the falls he named St. Anthony's [including his
captivity there among the Sioux Indians]. It was
the first book to use the name Louisiane, albeit
that name had been given to this region previously
by La Salle and was not Hennepin's invention as
claimed by him.

HENNEPIN, LOUIS   416
Nouvelle découverte d'un très grand pays . . .
dans l'Amérique . . . *Utrecht* 1697. D [70] 506 +
10 starred p, all numb 313 2maps eng-t 2pls [incl
first view ever made of Niagara Falls] b Hn LC N
—ed. 2, same collat *Amst* 1698. b
—oth. Fr. eds., some with title "Voyage curieux",
all with added voyage, by La Borde, to West
Indies: *Amst* 1701; *Hague* 1704; *Leyden* 1704. ea a
—Dutch tr. "Nieuwe Ontdekkinge van een groot
Land . . ." *Amst* 1699. Q [26] 220 [14] 2maps pl a
—oth. Dutch eds: *Amst* 1702; *Leyden* 1704; *Rotterd* 1704; *Amst* 1711; same impr 1712. ea a
—Eng. tr. 2pts in 1 [second pt giving tr of au's
third book, "Nouveau Voyage"] *L* 1698. Of this,
2 issues, priority not definately adjudicated, of
equal value & desirability but textually so pronouncedly variant as to require the following
separate collats:
—"Bon" issue [line 1 of the 5 printers, shown on
t-p, ending with "Bon" — first 3 letters of Bonwick] Probably first iss. O [22] 300; [32] 178 [2]
303–355 2maps 7pls [incl eng front] b Hn LC
MinnU
—"Tonson" issue [that printer's name ending first
line of impr] probably second issue, but pls &
typography somewhat improved. O [22] 244; [32]
228 2maps 7pls [incl front] b Hn LC MinnU
—Eng. ed. 2, *L* 1699. O [22] 240; [24] 216 2maps
7pls [incl front] b
—rptd. *Chi* 1903. O 2v: paged continuously, [64]
353 2maps 7pls a
—Ger. tr. "Neue Entdeckung . . ." *Bremen* 1699.
D [46] 382 map 3pls a
—rptd. "Neue Reise . . ." *Nurnbg* 1739. D 425
2maps
—anr. ed. "Reisen . . ." *Bremen* 1742. D [22] 382
2maps 3pls

In this second book Hennepin adds, to his actual voyage up the Mississippi, a pretended one down that stream prior to La Salle, an imposture which has consigned him to eternal obloquy.

HENNEPIN, LOUIS   417
Nouveau voyage d'un pays plus grand que l'Europe . . . *Utrecht* [Schouten] 1698. D [70, incl final blank lf] 389 map 4pls b LC MinnU
—anr. iss. ptd by Voskuyl, same date & collat b Hn
—Dutch tr. "Aenmerckelycke historische Reys-Beschryvinge door verscheyde Landen . . ." *Utrecht* 1698. Q [32, incl eng-t] 142 [misnumb 242] [18] map 4pls b
—Eng. tr. incorporated in the 1698 Eng ed of his "Nouvelle découverte" [*q.v.*]
—Ger. tr. "Neue Reise . . ." *Bremen* 1698. O [46] 288 map 4pls a
—oth. Ger. eds: *Bremen* 1699; *Leip* 1720; *Nurembg* 1739. ea a
—Sp. tr. [abr] "Relacion de un pais . . ." *Brus* 1699. D [12] 86 map 2pls a
This third book of the recreant Franciscan priest was hastily prepared to capitalize on the enormous success of his iniquitous *Découverte*, of which it was presumably a continuation. Based on various contemporary sources, it is made up of information concerning the manners and customs of the Indians and of La Salle's extraordinary labors in the far reaches of Canada's new frontier.

HENNI, J. M.   418
Ein Blick in's Thal des Ohio oder Briefe über den Kampf und das Wiederaufleben der katholischen Kirche im fernen Westen der Vereinigten Staaten . . . *Munich* 1836. O 128 aa

HENRY, THE BRITISH SPY!
Documents from: *See* Seaver, Eben.

HENRY (ALEXANDER, [d. 1814] the   419
younger) and THOMPSON (DAVID).
New light on the early history of the greater northwest. The journals of: . . . Ed. by E. Coues. *N Y* 1897. O 3v: [28] 446; [6] 447–916; [6] 917–1027. port 4maps, &c[in pocket at end] 1100 copies ptd.[100 on L.P.] aa

HENRY, ALEXANDER, 1739-1824   420
Travels and adventures . . . 1760–6. *N Y* 1809. O [8] 330 port[not issued in the earliest copies, but collectors insist on its presence] b
—rptd., with notes, ed. Jas. Bain, *B* 1901. O [44] 347 6maps & pls some copies carry *Tor* impr. aa
Authentic narrative of fur-trading among Indians of the upper lakes. A miraculous escape from massacre during Pontiac's war, captivity, &c.

HENRY, J. T.   421
The early and later history of petroleum . . . its

development in western Pennsylvania . . . *Phil* 1873. O 607 5pls 27 ports aa
First comprehensive history of the infancy of this industry.

HENRY, JAMES P.   422
The Arkansas gazetteer . . . and emigrant's guide. *Little Rock* 1873. D 123 a

HENRY, JOHN J.   423
An accurate . . . account of the hardships . . . of that band of heroes who traversed the wilderness in the campaign against Quebec in 1775. *Lancaster* 1812. D 225 aa
—rev. ed. "Campaign against Quebec . . .," *Watertown* 1844. D 212 a
—rptd., with memoir of au., "Account of Arnold's campaign against Quebec . . .," *Alb* 1877. D [14] 198 map a

HENRY, JOSEPH   424
A statement . . . respecting the condition and treatment of slaves, in . . . Vicksburg and its vicinity . . . *Medina* O 1839. D 24 a

HENRY, M[ATTHEW] S.   425
History of the Lehigh valley . . . *Easton* 1860. O [12] 436 map 31pls[one incl. in paginat.] a
Originally issued in five parts; most copies of part five were burned, so complete sets in that form are rare.

HENRY, ROBERT S.   426
The story of the Confederacy. *Indp* [1931]. O [8] 11–314 12pls[one double p.] a

HENRY, STUART O.   427
Conquering our great American plains . . . *N Y* [1930]. D [16] 395 a

HENRY (WILLIAM).   428
Account of the captivity of: in 1755, and of his residence among the Senneka [*sic*] Indians six years and seven months . . . *B* 1766. Q 160 no copy known d

HENRY, WILLIAM S.   429
Campaign sketches of the war with Mexico. *N Y* 1847. D 331 a
—rptd., same impr. & collat., 1848.

HENRY, WILLIAM W.   430
Patrick Henry: life, correspondence and speeches. *N Y* 1891. O 3v: [24] 622; [16] 652; [4] 672. port aa

HENSHAW (COL. WILLIAM).   431
The orderly book of: . . . 1775. *B* 1877. O [14] 86 port a
—enl. ed. "The orderly books of: . . .," *B* 1881. O [14] 167 port facs

HENTZ, J. P.   **432**
Twin Valley [Ohio]; its settlement . . . *Dayton* 1883. 16° 288 a

HERBERT, ARTHUR   **433**
Sketches . . . of movements of the Seventeenth Virginia infantry. *Balt* [*ca* 1870]. O [2] 41 + cov. t. a
—rptd., same collat., n.p. [1909?].

HERBERT, CHARLES   **434**
A relic of the revolution . . . sufferings . . . of all the American prisoners captured on the high seas . . . *B* 1847. 18° [4] 258 pl a
—rptd "The prisoners of 1776". *B* 1854. 16° 264

HERFF, DR. [FERDINAND] VON   **435**
Die geregelte Auswanderung des deutschen Proletariats mit besonderer Beziehung auf Texas. *Frankf* 1850. O 68 b BM

HERMANN, ISAAC   **436**
Memoirs of a veteran . . . in the war between the states. *Atlanta* 1911. O 285 port a

HERMANN, RICHARD   **437**
Julien Dubuque; his life and adventures. *Dubuque* 1922. O 91 a

HERMES, K. H.   **438**
Die Entdeckung von America durch die Isländer im zehnten und elften Jahrhunderte. *Braunschweig* 1844. O [8] 134 pl a

HERNDON, MRS. SARAH [RAYMOND]   **439**
Days on the road; crossing the plains in 1865. *N Y* 1902. D [16] 270 port a

HERNDON, WILLIAM H., and   **440**
WEIK, JESSE W.
. . . Lincoln: the true story of a great life . . . *Chi* [1889]. D 3v: [20] 199 + 5adv-p; [4] 205–418 + 6adv-p; [4] 423–638 + 4adv-p. 63pls aa
—ed. 2, *Chi* 1890. same collat. a
—ed. 3, ed. by H. White, with adds., *N Y* 1892. D 2v: [28] 331; [10] 348 + 2adv-p. 30pls
Based on Herndon's intimate, first-hand knowledge, this will always be the most authoritatave single source for Lincoln's early period.

HERRICK, FRANCIS H.   **441**
Audubon the naturalist . . . *N Y* 1917. O 2v: [42] 451; [16] 494. 53pls a
—rptd. *N Y* 1938. O

[HERRING, ELBERT?]   **442**
Touchstone to the people . . . on the choice of a president. *N Y* 1812. O 56 a
—issue 2, errata list added on p56.

HERRING, JAMES, and   **443**
LONG-ACRE, JAMES B., eds.
The national portrait gallery of distinguished Americans. *N Y* 1834–9. roy O 4v 144ports, accompanied by biogs. a some L. P. copies Q
—anr. issue, *Phil* H. Perkins, same dates & collat.
—anr. ed. *Phil* Longacre 1837. same collat.
—later eds., with inferior impressions of pls, issued at *Phil*, both by Rice and by Rutter; anr. ed. by Rich & Hart, 4v in 3.
For similar title—*National portrait gallery of eminent Americans . . .*, *see* Duycinck, Evert A.

HERRMANN, FRIEDRICH   **444**
Die Deutschen in Nord-amerika. *Lübben* 1806. O [8] 192 a

[HERTSLET, EVELYN M.]   **445**
Ranch life in California. *L* 1886. 16° [4] 172 2pls a

HERZ, HENRI   **445a**
Mes voyages en Amérique. *P* 1866. 16° 328 port a

HESSE, N.   **446**
Das westliche Nordamerika in besonderer Beziehung auf die deutschen Einwanderer . . . *Paderborn* 1838. O [22] 244 map[of pt. of Mo.] aa
Chiefly on Missouri; some information on Arkansas and Texas.

HESSE-WARTEG, ERNST VON   **447**
Prairie-fahrten. Reise-skizzen aus den nordamerikanischen Prairen . . . *Leip* 1878. [D [8] 167 [8] incl. pls a

HESSELIUS, ANDREAS   **448**
Kort Berettelse om then Swenska Kyrkios närwarande tilständ i America . . . *Norkiöping* 1725. Q 24 b JCB N NYP
By the pastor of the Swedish church in Pennsylvania.

HEUSTIS (CAPTAIN DANIEL D.)   **449**
A narrative of the adventures and sufferings of: . . . in Canada and Van Diemen's Land . . . with travels in California . . . *B* 1847. O 168 front aa
—ed. 2, *B* 1848. aa

HEUSTIS, JABEZ W.   **450**
Physical observations . . . on the topography and diseases of Louisiana. *N Y* 1817. O 165 a

HEVERLY, C. F.   **451**
History of the Towandas . . . *Towanda Pa* 1886. D [6] 362 port a

HEWATT [or Hewat], ALEXANDER   **452**
An historical account of the rise and progress of

the colonies of South Carolina and Georgia. *L* 1779. O 2v: [16, incl. final blank 1.] 347; [10] 329 [last p. mis-numb. 309] b
Earliest history of this region.

HEWES (GEORGE R. T.)
Traits of the tea party . . . memoir of: . . . By a Bostonian. *See* Thatcher, Benj. B.

HEWETT, D[ANIEL]   **453**
The American traveller . . . an account of all the great post roads . . . *Wash* 1825. 16° 440 + starred p373-396 a

HEWETT, D[ANIEL]   **454**
A gazetteer of the New-England states . . . *N Y* 1829. D 84 a

HEWITT, GIRART   **455**
Minnesota: its advantages . . . *St P* 1867. O 36 aa
—rptd., same impr. & collat., 1868. aa

HEWITT, JOHN H.   **456**
Shadows on the wall; or, glimpses of the past . . . *Balt* 1877. D 249 a

HEWITT, JUDGE RANDALL H.   **457**
Notes by the way. Memoranda of a journey across the plains [from Illinois to Washington Territory]. *Olympia* 1863. D 58 dd B N Pn [of 6 copies known]
—ed. 2, *Olympia* 1872. b rptd Seattle 1955 a
—ed. 3, greatly enl. by Judge Hewitt's nephew and namesake, with t. "Across the plains and over the divide . . ." *N Y* [1906] D [10] 521 + 12adv-p map 58pls [in some copies a 59th pl-captioned "Variegated"-faces p. 230] port aa

HEWSON, JOHN   **458**
A brief history of the revolution . . . *Phil* 1843. O 110 [1] a

HEY, RICHARD   **459**
Observations on the nature of civil liberty, and the principles of government. *L* 1776. O [4] 70 a

HIATT, ISAAC   **460**
Thirty-one years in Baker county [Ore.]: a history of the county, 1861–1892. *Baker City* 1893. O 208 a

HIATT, JAMES M.   **461**
The war for the Democratic succession . . . battle of Rogue's Run . . . *Indp* 1866. O 80 aa
Satirical account of "Copperhead" activities in Indiana and Illinois, with a vicious attack on Andrew Johnson.

HIBERNICUS   **462**
Hibernicus; or, memoirs of an Irishman . . . before and since his emigration . . . *Pitt* 1828. D 251 a

HICKCOX, JOHN H.   **463**
An historical account of American coinage. *Alb* 1858. O [8] 151 5pls a 205copies [5 on L.P.]

HICKMAN, GEORGE   **464**
History of Marshall county [Dak.] . . . *Britton Dak* 1886. O 5-lvs[incl. 6 illus] + 20 adv-p a

HICKMAN (WILLIAM A.)   **465**
Brigham's destroying angel; . . . life, confession . . . of: Ed. J. H. Beadle. *N Y* 1872. D 219 + 5adv-p port a
—rptd. often

HICKS, ELIAS   **466**
Observations on the slavery of the Africans . . . *N Y* 1811. D 24 a
—rptd. *N Y* 1814. D [4] 23

HIGGINS, GEORGE   **467**
The king of counties. Miami county [Kas.]; her towns, etc. *Paola* 1877. O 32 aa

[HIGGINSON, STEPHEN]   **468**
The writings of Laco . . . *B* 1789. O 39 aa
—rptd. "Ten chapters in the life of John Hancock," *N Y* 1857. O 68
Annihilating attack on Hancock.

HIGGINSON, THOMAS W.   **469**
A ride through Kansas . . . [*N Y* 1856]. D 24 caption t.only a

"HIGH PRIVATE"
"High private" (The) . . . By "Corporal of the guard." *See* Lombard, A.

HILDEBRAND (SAMUEL S.)   **470**
Autobiography of: the renowned Missouri "bushwacker" . . . Comp. by James W. Evans and A. Wendell Keith. *Jeff C* 1870. D 312[incl.8pls] a

[HILDRETH, JAMES]   **471**
Dragoon campaigns to the Rocky mountains . . . By a dragoon. *N Y* 1836. O 288 aa
First active service of this newly organized regiment, commanded by Col. Dodge; from St. Louis to Ft. Gibson and the Pawnee villages. According to the third edition of Wagner-Camp, the real author was an Englishman, William L. Gordon-Miller, Hildreth being merely the man who arranged publication.

HILDRETH, RICHARD   **472**
The history of the United States . . . *N Y* 1849–51–52. O 6v: [26] 33–570; 579; [2] 592 [1]; 704; 686; 740 a
—rev. ed. *N Y* 1854-5. O 6v
—Dutch tr. *Hague* 1854-7. O 6v

HILDRETH, SAMUEL P.   **473**
Biographical and historical memoirs of the early
. . . settlers of Ohio . . . *Cin* 1852. O 539 6pls a
—rptd. t. altered *Cin* 1854. O [4] 6–539 no pls
Col. Meig's *Journal*, announced on title as being
annexed, is found in no copies.

HILDRETH, SAMUEL P.   **474**
Contributions to the early history of the northwest . . . *Cin* Poe & Hitchcock 1864. 16° 240 a
—rptd. *Cin* Hitchcock & Walden, n.d. same collat.

HILDRETH, SAMUEL P.   **475**
Original contributions to The American pioneer.
Cin 1844. O [4] 144 2pls a
Only a small number issued in this separate form.

HILDRETH, SAMUEL P.   **476**
Pioneer history . . . first examinations of the
Ohio valley . . . early settlement of the Northwest
Territory . . . *Cin* 1848. O [13] 525 map 8pls a
—ed. 2, 1850.
Of the original edition many copies were des-
troyed in a fire, of ed 2 apparently no copies
escaped.

HILGARD, THEODORE E.   **477**
Meine Erinnerungen. [*Heidelberg* 1860?]. D [2]
380 pls a
Spent twenty-five years in southern Illinois.

HILL, A. J.   **478**
History of Company E of the Sixth Minnesota
. . . [in the Sioux campaign]. *St P* 1899. O 45[incl.
port] a

HILL, ALEXANDER S.   **479**
From home to home . . . wanderings in the
northwest . . . *L* 1885. O [10] 432 + 32adv-p 2maps
25pls a
—ed. 2, same impr., date & collat., but no advs.
—Am. ed., same collat. & date, *N Y* O [12] 432
2maps 25pls
For attack on the questionable practices of Hill's
Canadian ranch, *see* Craig, John R. The operations
of this cattle combine extended into the United
States.

HILL, MRS. ALICE P.   **480**
Tales of the Colorado pioneers. [Illus. by Eugene
Field]. *Denver* 1884. D 319 aa
—rev. ed. "Colorado pioneers . . .," [*Denver*
1915]. D [16] 544 front.

HILL, EMMA S.   **481**
A dangerous crossing. *Denv* 1924. D [8] 206
2pls a

HILL, IRA   **482**
Antiquities of America explained. *Hagerstown*
1831. 16° 131 a

[HILL, ISAAC]   **483**
Brief sketch of the life, character and services of
Major General Andrew Jackson . . . *Concord*
1828. D 51 port a

HILL (JAMES; otherwise, James Hind;   **484**
otherwise, James Actzen).
The trial (at large) of: for . . . setting fire to the
rope-house, in His Majesty's dockyard at Portsmouth. Taken in short hand by Joseph Gurney. *L*
Kearsley [*ca* 1777]. F 40 aa
—anr. ed. "The trial of James Hill, alias John the
painter . . . Taken in short hand by a gentleman at
the trial," *L* Corrall [*ca* 1777]. O 55 port aa
—anr. ed., called ed. 2, with adds., n.p. 1777. D 94
port pl aa
—anr. ed., called ed. 3, "The life of James Aitken
. . .," *Winton* Wilkes n.d. O 62 port a
—rptd. *Portsmouth* n.d.
—anr. ed. "The whole of the proceedings . . .
Taken in short hand by William Blanchard," *L*
n.d.
Famous attempt at sabotaging British stores intended for use against the Colonists, undertaken,
by this Scotch-American, either for patriotic motives of reprisal for destruction of American property; for monetary reward offered him by Silas
Deane; or for both.

HILL, JIM D.   **485**
The Texas navy . . . *Chi* 1937. O [16] 224 4pls a

HILL, JOSEPH J.   **486**
The history of Warner's ranch . . . *L A* 1927.
O [14] 221 [incl.9pls] 2ports a 1300copies ptd.[300
for presentation]

HILL, LUTHER B., ed.   **488**
A history of . . . Oklahoma. *Chi* 1908. roy O 2v:
[18] 555; [8] 533. 4maps 48pls a
—anr ed, same impr *Chi* 1909 2v: [20] 603; [12]
505 pls a; rptd, different paginat 1910

[HILL, MARK L.]   **489**
A narrative shewing the promises made to the
officers of the . . . continental army . . . *Elizabeth-
Town* 1826. O 48 a

HILLARD, E[LIAS] B.   **490**
The last men of the revolution . . . *Hart* 1864.
D 64 12pls[6 col.] facs [not in all cops] a

HILLARD, ISAAC   **491**
A wonderful and horrible thing is committed in
the land . . . *Poughkeepsie* 1814. O 96 aa
—rptd. with add. of "The chronicles of Andrew,
containing . . . account of Gen. Jackson's victories
in the south, by Jesse Denson," *Hamilton* O 1822.
O 118 a
For earlier edition of *The chronicles of Andrew*,
see Denson, Jesse.

[HILLER, E. H.]   492
Latest information about the Alaska gold fields
. . . *Juneau* [1897]. D 56 a

HILLIARD D'AUBERTEUIL,   493
M[ICHEL R.]
Essais historiques et politiques sur les Anglo-
Américains. *Brus* 1781–2. O 2v in 4pts: [16] 198;
[12] 199–441; [12] 208; [14] 209–436 18maps & pls
aa
—best ed. *Brus* 1782. Q 2v: [12] 303; [6] 307.
18maps & pls aa
—anr. ed. *Brus* 1784. O 2v: [12] 303; [4] 315.
18maps & pls a
—Ger. tr. *Hamburg* 1783. O 2v: 148 188; 178 176 a

HILLIARD D'AUBERTEUIL, M[ICHEL R.]
Histoire de l'administration de Lord North . . .
See North, *Lord.*

HILLSBORO . . . DIRECTORY
Hillsboro and Hill county [Tex.] directory [The]
. . . *See* Reavis, S. A.

HILLSBOROUGH (the Right   494
Honourable the Earl of).
A letter to: on the connection between Great
Britain and her American colonies . . . *L* 1768.
O 47 aa
—rptd. *Dub* 1768. O 40 a
Ascribed to George Canning, Sr.

HILLSBOROUGH (the Right   495
Honourable the Earl of).
A letter to: on the present situation . . . in Amer-
ica . . . *L* 1769. O [1] 117 b NYP
—Am. ed. *B* 1769. D 55 aa
Exposition of American rights; probably by
Samuel Adams. Ascribed also to James Bowdoin.

HILLYARD, ISAAC
A wonderful and horrible thing is committed in
the land . . . *See* Hillard, Isaac.

HILLYARD, M. B.   496
Letters descriptive of the climate . . . of central
Mississippi . . . *McComb City* 1876. O 203 a

HILTON [or HYLTON], WILLIAM   497
A relation of a discovery . . . on the coast of
Florida . . . *L* 1664. smQ [4] 34 dd H JCB LC NYP
[of 6 cops in America]
First English description of South Carolina.

HIMES, JOSHUA V.   498
Mormon delusions and monstrosities . . . *B*
1842. D 90 aa

HINCHCLIFFE, JOHN   499
Historical review of Belleville, Illinois . . . *Belleville* 1870. O 80 a

HINCHMAN, WALTER   500
Sketches and poems: 1845–1920. n.p. 1920. O
253 map pls aa
Account of Indian adventures, etc., by a member
of Palmer's 1867 exploring expedition to select a
southern railroad route to California.

HINDMAN, DAVID   501
The way to my golden wedding. *St Joseph Mo*
1908. D [6] 200 2pls a
Trip to Illinois in 1846 and another in 1849 to
California.

HINDMAN (MAJOR GENERAL   502
[THOMAS CARMICHAEL]).
Report of: of his operations in the Trans-Missis-
sippi district . . . *Rich* 1864. O 26 aa

HINDS, WILLIAM A.   503
American communities . . . Economy, Zoar. . .
Oneida N Y 1878. D 176 2 pls a
—enl. ed., *Chi* 1902. D 433
—rptd *Chi* 1908

HINES (DAVID T.)   504
The life, adventures . . . of: . . . *N Y* 1840. D 195 a

HINES, GUSTAVUS   505
A voyage round the world; with a history of the
Oregon mission, and notes of . . . residence on
the plains, bordering on the Pacific::: *Buf* 1850.
D [6] 9 437 a
—rptd. with port, added and new t. "Life on the
plains of the Pacific . . .," *Buf* 1851. D [8] 437
—other eds. with variant t. "Oregon: its history,
etc."; "Wild life in Oregon."
Hines arrived in Oregon in 1840 and his narrative is useful on the early period.

HINES, CAPT. THOMAS H.   506
Thrilling narrative of the escape of Gen. John
H. Morgan . . . [*Columbus O*] 1887. D 38 port aa

HINKLE, JAMES F.   507
Early days of a cowboy on the Pecos. *Roswell
N M* 1937. O 35 [incl front wrap] 35copies ptd. aa

HINMAN, R[OYAL] R.   508
A catalogue of the names of the first Puritan
settlers of . . . Connecticut . . . *Hart* 1846. O 367
port a 1846–8. O 336 port a
—ed. 2, enl., t.slightly altered, *Hart* 1852–6. O 884
ports aa
Never completed beyond the name Danielson;
the supplement to the second edition, however,
included, the Hinman family.

HINMAN, ROYAL R.   509
A historical collection . . . of the part sustained
by Connecticut during the . . . revolution . . . *Hart*
1842. O 644 2 ports a

HINMAN (THE REV. S[AMUEL] D.)   510
Journal of: [while on a mission to the Santee Sioux]. *Phil* 1869. D [18] 87 a

HINMAN, WILBUR F.   511
Corporal Si Klegg and his "pard." ... *Clev* 1887. O [20] 704 a
—rptd. often

HINTON, JOHN H., ed.   512
The history and topography of the United States. *L* 1830–2. Q 2v: [22] 476; [10] 580. 99maps & pls aa
—ed. 2, *L* 1834. Q 2v: [18] 520; [10] 580. 99maps & pls a
—ed. 3, *L* 1842. Q 2v: [20] 501; [10] 580. maps & pls
—ed. 4, most complete ed., with 17chaps. on Calif. & 3 on Texas, *L* [1850]. Q 2v 67 maps & pls
—Am. ed. *B* 1834. Q 2v: [14] 427; [12] 508 map 40pls
—several later Am. eds.
Originally issued in monthly parts. Some copies of the first English edition were issued in folio; some had plates on India paper.

HINTON, RICHARD J.   513
The hand-book to Arizona ... *S F* 1878. D [4] 432 adv-lf 102 + 43adv-p 4maps 16pls a

[HINTON, RICHARD J.]   514
Rebel invasion of Missouri and Kansas ... *Chi* 1865. O [4] 351]incl.pls] a
—ed. 2, same impr., date & collat.

HINTS
Hints to emigrants ... with copious extracts from the journal of Thomas Hulme ... *See* Smith, Thos., of Liverpool.

HISTOIRE   515
Histoire de la dernière guerre ... 1756–1763. Nouvelle edition. *Berlin* 1768. 16° [8] 182 aa
—new ed. *Cologne* 1769. 16° 192 2maps eng.t. a
—anr. ed., same impr. & collat. 1770.

Histoire de la dernière guerre, entre le Grande-Bretagne, et les États-Unis ... *See* Leboucher, Odet-Julien.

Histoire de la fondation des colonies des anciennes républiques ... *See* Barron, Wm.

Histoire de la guerre contre les Anglois ... *See* Poullin de Lumina.

Histoire de la guerre d'Amérique. Divi-   516
sées par années ... *L* 1783. O [32] 151 a

Histoire et commerce des colonies angloises dans l'Amérique septentrionale ... *See* Butel-Dumont, George M.

HISTORIA
Historia del establecimiento y commercio de las colonias Inglesas ... *See* Butel-Dumont, George M.

HISTORICAL
Historical and political reflections on the rise ... of the American rebellion. 1780. *See* Galloway, Jos.

Historical anecdotes ... in a series of   517
letters from America, in the years 1777-8 ... *L* 1779. O [6] 85 aa
Loyalist affairs in New York City.

Historical essay (An) on the English constitution ... Wherein the right of parliament, to tax our distant provinces, is explained ... *See* Ramsay, Allan.

Historical register (The) of the United States ... *See* Palmer, Thos. H.

Historical remarks on the taxation of free states ... *See* Meredith, Sir Wm.

Historical review (An) and directory of   518
North America ... By a gentleman ... returned from a tour of that continent. *Dub* 1789. 18° 2v: [28] 268; [10] 377. 2fold.tabs a
—rptd. *Cork* 1801. same collat.

HISTORISCH-STATISTISCHE NOTIZ
Historisch-statistische Notiz der gross-brittanischen Colonien in America ... *See* Schirach, G. B. von.

HISTORISCHE   519
Historische und geographische Beschreibung der zwölf vereinigten Kolonien ... *Bunzlau* [1777]. 16° [8] 140 [4] aa

Historische und geographische Beschrei-   520
bung des an dem grossen Flusse Mississippi ... gelegenen herrlichen Landes Louisiana ... *Leip* 1720. O [6] 84 map port b
—ed. 2, "Ausführliche ... Beschreibung ...," same impr. & date. 16° [6] 102 map aa
—ed. 3, same impr. & date. O [6] 102 map port aa
Some copies of the third edition contain an eleven-page appendix, *Remarques* ..., with Frankfurt imprint. For similar work, in English and French, *see Mississippi. A full and impartial account of the company of*:

Historische und politische Betrachtungen   521
über die Colonien besonders in Rücksicht auf die Englisch-Amerikanischen. *Bern* 1779. O [4] 152 a

Historischer Abrisz der in Nord Amerika vorgefallenen Staats Veränderung ... 1774–1778. Dubuisson, Paul U., *Abrégé de la révolution* ...

HISTORY   **522**
History and explanation of the Russian lands . . .
along the Pacific coast . . . n.p. [ca 1860]. O 32 a

History and lives of the most notorious   **523**
pirates and their crews . . . L 1725. 16° [12] 156
[incl.front.] aa
—ed. 3, L 1729. D [8] 132 aa
—other L eds.: 1740; 1765; n.d. [ca 1825]. a
—Am. ed. N Y 1824.
Many of these pirates operated along our Eastern seaboard. Evidently a condensation of Charles
Johnson's General history of the pirates, q.v. For
later Americab editions see Carey, Thomas, History
of the pirates. Sabin mentions a similar title as
having possibly been published by Bradford, N.Y.
1724

History (A) of all the engagements by sea   **524**
and land . . . during the American revolution . . .
Manch 1787. O [4] 436 aa

History (The) of America . . . extracted from the
. . . Encyclopedia. See Morse, Jedidiah.

History of North America; comprising, a . . . view
of the United States, [etc.]. See Talbot, John.

History (The) of North America. Contain-   **525**
ing an exact account . . . L Millar, etc. 1776. D
[4] 284 map a

History of North America, from the first discovery . . . By Sylvanus Americanus. See Nevill,
Sam'l.

History (The) of North and South America, containing, an account . . . See Young, W. A.

History (The) of the American revolution,   **526**
including an impartial examination of the causes . . .
Charleston S C 1806. O v.I[all completed]: [10]
384 [7] + 1no.[of v.II] 24 aa

History of the American war of 1812. See
McCarty, Wm.

History (The) of the British dominions in   **527**
North America . . . L 1773. Q 2v in 1: [12] 297;
275. map aa
—Ger. tr. "Geschichte der englischen Colonien in
Nordamerika . . .," see Klausing, Anton E.

History (The) of the Britisch empire . . .   **528**
1765, to the end of 1783, containing an impartial
history of the . . . American revolution. Phil 1798.
O 2v: 475; 452 59. 2ports aa
—ed. 2, same impr. & collat., 1803. a

History (The) of the civil war in America. By an
officer of the army. 1780. See Hall, Capt. John.

History of the colonization of the free states of
antiquity . . .See Barron, Wm.

A history of the Federal and Democratic   **529**
parties in the United States . . . by a citizen of
Wayne county, Ind. Richmond, Ind. 1837. O 56 a

History of the great lakes. See Mansfield, John B.

History (A) of the Indian wars . . .particularly in
New England. See Sanders, Daniel G.

History of the late war, between the United States
and Great-Britain . . . See Brackenridge, Henry M.

History (The) of the Moravian missions among
the Indians . . . By a member . . . L 1838. See
Loskiel, Geo. H.

History (The) of the new world . . . Dub   **530**
[1776]. 24° 180 a
—rptd. Dub 1787.

History of the organization of the Method-   **531**
ist Episcopal Church South . . . Nashv 1845. O 275 a
Statement explaining the reasons leading to the
separation effected at the Louisville convention of
the same year.

History (The) of the origin, rise and pro-   **532**
gress of the war in America . . . B 1780. O 90 [con-
tinued as] The history of the rise and progress of
the war in North-America . . .B 1780. O 381 [34]
[concluded as] The history of the war in America
. . . Vol. II. B 1780. O 84 [4] In all, 3v[usually
bound in 2v, the first 2v together being probably
intended as v.I] b AA Hn WisH Y
All three title-pages indicate that this Boston
edition was reprinted from a London edition; in
reality it seems to have been constructed from
several English sources, notably William Russell's
History of America and Burke's An impartial
history of the war in America, both of which were
based on volumes of The annual register.

History of the pirates . . . Haverhill 1825. See
Carey, Thos.

History of the ram fleet . . . See Crandall,
Warren D.

History (The) of the United States for 1796. See
Callender, James T., American annual register
(The).

History of the United States, from their   **533**
first settlement, to . . .1815. N Y 1825. D [4] 337 a
—Eng. ed. L 1826. O [4] 467

History of the war between the United States and
Tripoli . . . See Blyth, Stephen C.

History (The) of the war in America, between Great Britain and her colonies, from its commencement . . . *See* Gordon, Patrick.

HITCHCOCK, ENOS   **534**
A discourse on the causes of national prosperity . . . *Prov* 1786. Q 28 a

HITCHCOCK, ETHAN A.   **535**
Fifty years in camp and field . . . *N Y* 1909. O [16] 514 port a

HITCHCOCK, ETHAN A.   **536**
Fraud in relation to the settlement of the claims of the half breed relatives of the Winnebago Indians . . . n.p. [1839?]. O 48 a
Exposure of the Pennsylvania political giant Simon Cameron and his co-plunderers by a subaltern disbursing officer at St. Louis. Cameron when in Lindoln's Cabinet saw to it that Hitchcock, whose rank then entitled him to the highest command, was side-tracked.

HITCHCOCK, ETHAN A.   **537**
A traveler in Indian territory . . . *Cedar Rapids* 1930. O 270 fold.map 5pls a

[HITTELL, JOHN S.]   **538**
The future of Vallejo, California. *Vallejo* 1868. O 32 a

HITTELL, JOHN S.   **539**
A history of . . . San Francisco . . . *S F* 1878. O 498 aa

[HITTELL, JOHN S.]   **540**
The prospects of Vallejo [Calif.] . . . *Vallejo* 1871. O 56 [incl advs] map a

[HITTELL, JOHN S.]   **541**
The resources of Vallejo [California] . . . [*Vallejo*] 1869. O [2] 72 + 3adv-p 2maps a

HITTELL, JOHN S.   **542**
Yosemite: its wonders . . . *S F* 1868. D 59 map 20photo.pls aa

HITTELL, THEODORE H. [ed.]   **543**
Adventures of James Capen Adams, mountaineer and grizzly bear hunter, of California. *S F* 1860. D 378 12pls aa
—rptd. *B* 1860, same collat.; *B* 1861. a
Enjoyed—and merited—wide popularity. For another brief biography, *see* under Adams, James C.

HITTELL, THEODORE H.   **544**
History of California. *S F* 1885–97. O 4v: [4] 9–799; [4] 7–823; 981; [4] 17–858 aa
—other eds. 1897; 1898. aa
By a capable historian who used, for the Spanish period, documents since destroyed.

HOAGLAND, EDWARD, et al   **545**
Report to the convention to frame a constitution . . . of Kansas. *Wyandotte* 1859. O 27 aa
—rptd. 1861. a
Recites over 400 outrages in the border troubles between pro-slavers and free-staters.

HOAGLON, W. S., comp.   **546**
History and statistics of Jackson county, Kansas . . . *Holton* 1876. D 31 aa

HOBART, CHAUNCEY   **547**
History of Methodism in Minnesota. *Red Wing Minn* 1887. D [6] 5–397 20ports a
First history of Methodism in this state, written largely from personal knowledge.

HOBART, CHAUNCEY   **548**
Recollections of my life . . . in the northwest. *Red Wing Minn* 1885. D 409 port errata slip a
Missionary labors in Illinois, Winconsin, Iowa and Minnesota. Of two later editions, all copies of the second edition were burned.

[HOBART-HAMPDEN, AUGUSTUS C.] **549**
Never caught. Personal adventures . . . in blockade-running during the American civil war. By Captain Roberts [*pseud.*]. *L* 1867. 16° [4] 123 aa
—rptd., with adds., "Sketches from my life," *L* 1887. D [6] 282 port a
Author later known to fame under his Turkish title, Hobart Pasha.

HOBBS, JAMES   **550**
Wild life in the far west . . . *Hart* 1872. O 488 col.front 20pls aa
—rptd. same impr. & collat.: 1873; 1874; 1875. aa
Hobbs was a companion of Kit Carson, Kirker and other mountain men of the Southwest.

[HOBBY, WILLIAM J.]?   **551**
Remarks upon slavery; occasioned by attempts made to circulate improper publications in the southern states. By a citizen of Georgia. *Augusta Ga* 1835. O 32 a
—ed. 2, same impr. & date.
—rptd. *Phil* 1835.

HOBSON, MRS. E[LIZABETH] C. **552**
Recollections of a happy life. *N Y* 1914. D 258 a
Narrative of California life in Vigilante days.

HOCKERSMITH, L. D.   **553**
Morgan's escape . . . *Madisonville Ky* 1903. O 75 a

HODDER, JAMES   **554**
Arithmetic . . . *B* 1719. 16° 12, 216, port b
This 25th edition of a work issued originally at London in 1661, was the first on its subject printed in the United States.

HODGE, ALLEN and CAMPBELL, 555
publishers
The New-York directory and register . . . for
1789. *N Y* 1789. D 144 map c AA NYP
The third New York directory; another by same
publisher followed in 1790. For earlier issues, *see*
under Franks, David.

HODGE, FREDERICK W. 556
Handbook of American Indians north of
Mexico. *Wash* 1907–10. O 2v: [10] 972; [4] 1221.
map aa
—rptd: same impr. & collat. 1912; *N Y* 1959 aa

HODGES, M. 557
The life and times . . . of the adventurous . . .
Captain Kirby. *Cin* 1865. O 32 front aa

HODGES, WILLIAM R. 558
Carl Wimar . . . *Galv* 1908. O 37[incl.port]
12pls a
Painter of Indians and scenes on the upper Missouri in the 1840's.

[HODGKINSON, JOHN]? 559
Letters on emigration. By a gentleman, lately
returned from America. *L* 1794. O [4] 76 aa
America, weighed on unfriendly scales, found
wanting.

HODGSON, ADAM 560
Remarks during a journey through North America . . . *N Y* 1823. O 335 a
—best ed. "Letters from North America during a
tour . . .," *L* 1824. O 2v: [18] 405; [8] 460 map pl
2errata slips some copies of v.2 have app. [461–
473] aa
Unbiased observations.

HODGSON, JOHN, reporter 561
The trial of William Wemms, James Hartegan,
et al [other British soldiers implicated in the "Boston massacre"] *B* 1770. O 217 aa
—Eng. ed. *L* [1771]. O 216 aa
—anr. Am. ed. "The trial of the British soldiers . . .
for the murder of Crispus Attucks, Samuel Gray,
et al . . .," *B* 1807. O 120 a
—rptd. *B* 1824. D 146; *Alb* 1870. a
One of the notable American trials.

HODGSON, JOSEPH 562
The cradle of the Confederacy; or, the times of
Troup, Quitman and Yancey . . . *Mobile* 1876. O
[8, 13–16] 528 a
Political history of the deep South from the
Southern view point.

HODING, SARA 563
A land log book . . . from the journal kept by
the author . . . in the United States. *L* 1836. D [2]
278 [2] aa

[HÖEN, M. W.] 564
Das Verlangte, nicht erlangte Canaan bey den
Lust-Gräbern; oder ausführliche Beschreibung von
der unglucklichen Reise derer jüngsthin aus
Teutschland nach dem Engelländischen in America gelegenen Carolina und Pennsylvanien wallen-
den Pilgrim . . . *Frankf* 1711. O [16] 127 c Hn NYP
—rptd. *Hamburg* 1712. O 384 [2] b

HÖHNE, FRIEDRICH 565
Wahn und Ueberzeugung. Reise . . . in Weimar
über Bremen nach Nordamerika und Texas,
1839–41. *Weimar* 1844. 16° [10] 436 [2] map 3pls
aa

HOFFMAN, C., comp. 566
Zeitschrift für Auswanderer nach Amerika . . .
Stolberg 1847. D 48 a

HOFFMAN, CHARLES F. 567
Wild scenes in the forest and prairie. *L* 1839. D
2v: [8] 292; [4] 284. pl aa
—rptd. *L* [1842?]. D 2v in 1: [2] 292; 284. pl a
—Am. ed. *N Y* 1843. D 2v in 1: [8] 13–207; [4]
13–210 a
—Ger. tr.: *Dresden* 1845. D 2v: [4] 194 [2]; [2]
202 [2]; *Leip* 1860. D 2v a

[HOFFMAN, CHARLES F.] 568
A winter in the west. By a New-Yorker . . . *N Y*
1835. D 2v: [4] 337; [4] 346 aa
—ed. 2, *N Y* 1835. D 2v: [12] 282; [8] 286 a
—Eng. ed. "A winter in the far west," *L* 1835. D
2v: [12] 336; [8] 340 a

HOFFMAN, OGDEN 569
Reports of land cases . . . for the northern district of California . . . 1853–1858. Vol. I [all]. *S F*
Hubert 1862. O 458 + 146 b G NYP
—iss 2 pub by Whitney. b

HOFFMANN, H. 570
Californien, Nevada und Mexico . . . *Basel* 1871.
O [4] 426 [2] a
—rptd., same impr. 1874. same collat.

HOGAN, EDMUND 571
The prospect of Philadelphia and check on the
next directory. Pt. I [all]. *Phil* 1795. O 180 aa
—ed. 2, same impr. & collat. 1796. a

[HOGAN, JOHN] 572
Thoughts about the city of St. Louis . . . *St L*
1854. O 80 17pls a
—anr. issue, cov.t. dated 1855, with fold. panorama added. aa

HOGAN, JOHN J. 573
On the mission in Missouri, 1857–68. *K C* 1892.
D [4] 231 [error for 211] a

[HOGG, THOMAS E.]   574
Authentic history of Sam Bass and his gang . . .
Denton, Tex. 1876. O 146 [incl wrps] 3cops loc. b
—rptd. *Bandera, Tex.* 1926. O 56; 1932 D 192 a

HOLABIRD, LT. COL. SAMUEL B.   575
Report of a reconnaisance made in the Department of Dakota . . . *Wash* 1870. O 32 a

HOLBROOK, SAMUEL F.   576
Threescore years: an autobiography . . . *B* 1857.
O 504[incl.front.] a

[HOLBROOK, SILAS P.]   577
Sketches by a traveller. *B* 1830. D [4] 315 aa
Includes experiences in Oregon and Alaska.

HOLCOMBE, HENRY   578
The first fruits, in a series of letters [many narrat-
ing events during a residence in Savannah, Ga,
1799–1810] *Phil* 1812. D 228 [12] front aa

HOLCOMBE, HOSEA   579
A history of . . . the Baptists in Alabama . . . *Phil*
1840. D 375 aa

HOLDEN, A[USTIN] W.   580
A history of the town of Queensbury [Glens
Falls] New York. *Alb* 1874. O [10] 519 20pls a

HOLDEN, WILLIAM C.   581
Alkali trails; or social and economic movements
of the Texas frontier. *Dallas* [1930] O [10] 253 a

HOLDEN, WILLIAM C.   582
Rollie Burns . . . account of the ranching industry on the south plains. *Dallas* [1932] D [8] 253
front bound in tan clo. a
—iss. 2, contains no front & is bound in green clo.

HOLDEN, WILLIAM C.   583
The Spur ranch [in Texas]. *B* [1934]. O 229
diags a
For another book on this ranch see Elliot W. J.

HOLDITCH, ROBERT   584
The emigrant's guide to the United States . . .
L 1818. O [4] 124 + 4adv-p a

HOLGATE, JEROME B.   585
Atlas of American history . . . *C* 1842. F [10]
6maps a
—anr. issue, same date, *N Y.* F [19] 6maps

HOLINSKI, ALEXANDER J. J.   586
La Californie . . . *Brus* 1853. D [16] 414 aa
—ed. 2, same impr., date & collat. a
—rptd. 1855, same collat. a

HOLLAND, EDWARD   587
To the Yukon and the Klondike gold fields. *S F*
1897. D 56 map a

[HOLLAND, EDWIN C.]   588
A refutation of the calumnies . . . against the
southern and western states, respecting . . . slavery
among them. *Charleston S C* 1822. O 86 [1] aa

HOLLAND, HENRY W.   589
William Dawes, and his ride with Paul Revere
. . . *B* 1878. O [8] 128 12pls fold.tab 100copies
ptd. aa

HOLLAND, JOSIAH G.   590
History of western Massachusetts . . . *Springfield* 1855. D 2v: 520; 619. map a

[HOLLENBERG, W. N.]   591
Die Deutschen in Amerika. Mittheilungen des
Berliner Vereins für die ausgewanderten Deutschen der evangelischen Kirche in Westen Nord-
amerikas. *Berlin* 1859. O 40 a

HOLLEY, FRANCES C.   592
Once their home, or our legacy from the Dahko-
tahs . . . *Chi* 1890. O 406 29pls a
—eds. 2 & 3, *Chi* 1891 & 1892. O 420 [5] 32pls

HOLLEY, MRS. MARY AUSTIN   593
Texas. Observations, historical, geographical
and descriptive . . . *Balt* 1833. D 167 map b
—enl. ed. *Lex* 1836. D [10] 410 map aa
—anr. ed. *Balt* 1838. aa
—anr. ed. *Austin* 1935 map a
By Stephen F. Austin's cousin. The 1833 edition
— earliest book on Texas in the English language
— was written to promote emigration; that of
1836, re-written, was essentially a different work
seeking to encourage United States recognition.

HOLLEY, ORVILLE L.   594
A gazetteer of . . . New York . . . *Alb* 1842. D
479 map pl a
—rptd. 1848.

HOLLIDAY, F. C.   595
Life and times of Rev. Allen Wiley; containing
sketches of early Methodist preachers in Indiana
. . . *Cin* 1853. D 291 a

HOLLIDAY, GEORGE H.   596
On the plains in '65 . . . cavalry service among
the Indians of Nebraska, Colorado, Dakota . . .
n.p. 1883. D 97[incl.port] b G NYP Y

HOLLINGSWORTH (JOHN).   597
The journal of: of the First New York Volunteers . . . 1846–1849. *S F* 1923. O [10] 61 port a
300cops ptd

[HOLLIS, THOMAS] ed.   598
The true sentiments of America: . . . *L* 1768. O
82 [2] 83–158 aa
—rptd. *Dub* 1769. O 120 a

Consists of documents relating to taxation disputes between Massachusetts and Governor Bernard.

HOLLISTER, G. H.   **599**
The history of Connecticut ... *N Hav* 1855. O
2v: 508; 663. 17ports a
—ed. 2, enl., *Hart* 1857. O 2v: 613; 758. 17ports
—rptd.: 1858; 1859.

HOLLISTER, H. [M. D.]   **600**
Contributions to the history of the Lackawanna
valley. *N Y* 1857. D 328 map port a
—ed. 2, re-written, "History of the Lackawanna
valley . . .," *N Y* 1869. O 442 front.
—ed. 3, same collat., *Scranton* 1875.
—two other eds.

HOLLISTER, OVANDO J.   **601**
History of the First Regiment of Colorado Volunteers. *Denver* 1863. D 178 d AA N Y
—rptd. "Boldly they rode . . .," *Lakewood Colo*
1949. a
Leading authority on early Colorado Indian
wars and rarest book printed in that state.

HOLLISTER, OVANDO J.   **602**
The silver mines of Colorado. *Central City* 1867.
D [8] 87 b G U S Geol Surv Y
—enl. ed. "The mines of Colorado . . .," *Springfield Mass* 1867. D [7] 450 map a

HOLLISTER, URIAH S.   **603**
The Navajo and his blanket. *Denver* 1903. smQ
144 col.pls aa

HOLLOWAY, J. N.   **604**
History of Kansas . . . *Lafayette Ind* 1868. O 584
front a

HOLLY, ISRAEL   **605**
God brings about his holy and wise purpose . . .
illustrated in a sermon, preached at Suffield . . .
after the report arrived that the people of Boston
had destroyed a large quantity of tea . . . *Hart*
1774. Q 24 b NYP Y [of 3copies known].

HOLM, CAMPANIUS T.
Kort Beskrifning om Provincien Nya Swerige . . .
See Campanius Holm, Tomas.

HOLMAN, WOODFORD C.   **606**
Twenty-four years' residence in California and
Oregon. *St L* 1870. O 25 a

HOLMES, ABIEL   **607**
American annals . . . 1492–1806. *C* 1805. O 2v:
[4] 484; 541. a
—Eng. ed. *L* 1808. O 2v map
—anr. Eng. ed., with adds., *L* 1813. O 2v: [6] 412;
[2] 457. 2maps
—ed. 2—and best—"The annals of America . . .
1492–1826," *C* 1829. O 2v: [16] 584; [4] 599 a

[HOLMES, ALEXANDER]   **608**
The deplorable state of New-England ... [*L*]
1708. O [8] 39 b H Hn NYP
—Am. eds.: [*B*] 1720. 16° 36; *B* 1721. same
collat. aa
Vigorous arraignment of Gov. Dudley. Ascribed
also to Cotton Mather, who probably shared in its
preparation, John Wise and John Higginson. For
similar pamphlet, *see* New-England. *A memorial of
the present deplorable state of*:

HOLMES, GENERAL [D. H.], et al   **609**
Report of the battle of Helena . . . *Rich* 1864.
O 64 aa

HOLMES, EZEKIEL   **610**
Report of an exploration . . . of the territory on
the Aroostook river . . . *Augusta Me* 1839. O 79 a

HOLMES, ISAAC   **611**
An account of the United States . . . from actual
observation, during a residence of four years . . .
L [1823]. O [8] 476 map tab a

HOLMES, JOSEPH T.   **612**
Quincy [Ill.] in 1857 . . . *Quincy* 1857. 16° 69 a

HOLMES CHIEF JUSTICE OLIVER W.   **613**
Speeches. *B* 1891. O [6] 55 aa
—other eds.: *B* 1896. O [6] 69; *B* 1900. O [6] 86 a
—rptd., same impr.: 1913; 1918; 1934. each O
[6] 103

HOLMES, ROBERTA E.   **614**
The southern mines of California . . . *S F* Grabhorn 1930. F [10] 60 maps pls 250cops ptd a

[HOLROYD, JOHN B., Earl of Sheffield]   **616**
Observations on the commerce of the American
states . . . *L* 1783. O 75 a
—ed. 2, with adds., *L* 1783. O [4] 122 5tabs
—enl. ed. *L* 1784. O [16] 288 11tabs
—rptd. *Dub* 1784.
—ed. 6, *L* 1784. O [52] 345 [24] 29tabs
—Am. eds.: *Phil* Bradford 1783. O 77; *Phil* Bell
1783. with adds. O [2] 78 62
—Fr. trs.: *L* 1788. O [16] 336; *Rouen* 1789. Q; *P*
1796 O
Pointed out superciliously the helpless position
of American commerce, and thus influenced the
shaping of England's trade policy from 1783 to
1789, so detrimental to American commerce and
shipping interests as to contribute greatly to the
formation of a Federal union, better able, than
were the separate federated states, to retaliate
against British maritime might.

HOLT, MISS [C. E.]   **617**
An autobiographical sketch of a teacher's life
. . . in the northern and southern states, California . . . *Quebec* 1875. O 104 errata lf aa

HOLTON, E. D.   **618**
Travels with jottings. From midland to the Pacific. *Milw* 1880. O 94 port a 50copies ptd.

HOMER, JONATHAN   **619**
Description and history of Newton [Mass.]. [*B* 1798]. O 28 a

HONE (PHILIP).   **620**
The diary of: 1828–51. *N Y* 1889. O 2v: [10] 400; [2] 426. port a
—enl ed *N Y* 1927. O 2v. rptd 2v in 1, 1936.

HONOR (THE)
Honor (The) of the University of Oxford defended . . . *See* Bentham, Edw.

HOOD, GEORGE   **621**
A history of music in New England . . . *B* 1846. 16° 252 + 3p of testimonials a

HOOD, JOHN B.   **622**
Advance and retreat . . . *N O* 1880. O 358 map 2ports a
—rptd *Bloomingt Ind* 1959

HOOKER, SIR WILLIAM J.   **623**
The botany of Captain Beechey's voyage . . . 1825–1828. *L* 1841. Q [4] 485 99pls aa

HOOKER, SIR WILLIAM J.   **624**
A brief memoir of the life of Mr. David Douglas, with extracts from his letters [and journal]. *L* [ca 1837]. O 104 b Y
First printed in *The Companion to Hooker's Botanical Magazine*, Vols I & II, London, 1835–1836. O 2v 34pls 28 cold, of which above is a separate printing. Also appeared in *Hawaiian Spectator*, 1839. *Cf.* Douglas, David, *Journal.*

HOOKER, SIR WILLIAM J.
Companion to Hooker's Botanical Magazine. *See* Douglas, David, note.

[HOOPER, JOHNSON J.]   **625**
Some adventures of Captain Simon Suggs . . . and other Alabama sketches. *Phil* 1845. D 201 front aa
—rptd., same impr. & collat., 1846. a
—many later eds., with t. slightly altered.

HOOTON, CHARLES   **626**
St. Louis' Isle, or Texiana . . . *L* 1847. O [16] 204 6pls aa

HOOVER (DAVID).   **627**
Memoir of: a pioneer of Indiana . . . *Richmond Ind* 1857. O 44 aa

HOPEWELL, M[ENRA]   **628**
Legends of the Missouri and Mississippi. Parts 1 to 3 [all] *L* Beadle, 1862–3. 16° aa

—rptd. *L*, Ward Lock, [1874] 16° 506 [incl front] aa
At least some of the interesting river legends collected by this St. Louis physician appeared first in the columns of the *Missouri Republican* during 1858, but, in book form, there was no American edition.

HOPKINS, C. T.   **629**
Ship building on the Pacific coast . . . *S F* 1874. O 48 a

HOPKINS, GERARD T.
A mission to the Indians . . . to Fort Wayne, in 1804 . . . *See* Tyson, Martha E.

HOPKINS, JEREMIAH [pseud.]
Sketch of the life of Thomas Singularity . . . *See* Singularity, Thos.

HOPKINS, SAMUEL   **630**
An address to the people of New-England . . . importance of attaching the Indians to their interest . . . *Phil* 1757. O 27 b NYS PaH Y
A reprint of the concluding part of his *Historical memoirs*, below, thus a continuation of its abridged version there entered.

[HOPKINS, SAMUEL]   **631**
A dialogue concerning the slavery of the Africans . . . *Norwich Conn* 1776. O 63 a
—rptd. *N Y* 1785. D 72

HOPKINS, SAMUEL   **632**
Historical memoirs, relating to the Housatunnuk Indians . . . *B* 1753, sm Q [6] 182 b AA H N NYP Y
—abr. ed. *Phil* 1757. O 40 b BP MH

[HOPKINS, STEPHEN]   **633**
The rights of colonies examined. Published by authority. *Prov* 1765 [ptd 1764]. O 24 b AA Hn N NYP Y
—anr. issue, without "Published by authority" on t-p b AA
—Eng. ed., omitting a few paragraphs on p38. "The grievances of the American colonies candidly examined," *L* 1766. O 48 aa
Ascribed also to Silas Downer and to Samuel Ward. Replied to in Martin Howard's famous twenty-two-page *Letter from a gentleman at Halifax*, Newport 1765, *q.v.* under Halifax.

[HOPKINSON, FRANCIS]   **634**
Account of the grand federal procession . . . July 4, 1788 . . . [*Phil* 1788] O [2] 22 a

HOPKINSON, FRANCIS   **635**
The pathetic . . . narrative of Miss Perine, of the massacre and destruction of Indian Key village . . . *Phil* 1841. O 28 b

[HOPKINSON, JOSEPH]   636
What is our situation? and what our prospects?
A few pages for Americans. [*Phil* 1798?]. O 40 a
—Eng. ed., t. slightly altered, *L* 1799. same collat.

[HOPLEY, CATHERINE C.]   637
Life in the south . . . By a blockaded British
subject . . . *L* 1863. D 2v: [16] 428; [8] 404 map aa
Attributed also to Sarah L. Jones a pseudonym
used by this authoress. Best picture of plantation
life in early years of the war.

[HOPLEY, CATHARINE C.]   638
"Stonewall" Jackson . . . A biographical sketch.
By the author of "Life in the south." *L* 1863.
D [14] 178 map a
—ed. 2, same impr., date & collat.

HOPPE, JANUS, and ERMAN, A. F.   639
Californiens Gegenwart und Zukunft . . . *Berlin*
1849. O [8] 152 2maps aa
—Danish tr. "Californien, dets Nutig og Frem-
tid," *Copenh* 1850. O map a

HORE, MAURICE P.   640
Sketches . . . of the seat of the federal government . . . Virginia . . . during a residence of fifteen
years. *Cork* 1832. O 95 aa

HORN, HOSEA B.   641
Overland guide, from . . . Council Bluffs . . . to
the City of Sacramento. *N Y* 1852. 16° 78[incl.
advs] map + 18adv-p at end b G
—issue 2, *N Y* 1852. 16° 83[incl.adv-p] map +
18adv-p at end b G Y
—rptd., with different map & add.advs, *N Y*
[1853]. 16° 84 + 24adv-p map aa
Best hand-book for the central route available
at the time. The first issue has no newspaper comments on page eight.

HORN (MRS SARAH ANN).   642
A narrative of the captivity of: [by Comanche
Indians in Texas]. *St L* 1839. D 60 c N NYP Y
—rptd., omitting prelim. note by E. House [stating
he had written the narrative from Mrs. Horn's
dictation] and a few final observations on the
habits of the Comanches, *Cin* 1851. O 32 aa
—anr. ed. *Cin* [1853], same collat. aa
Cf. Narrative of Mrs. Clarissa Plummer.

HORN, STANLEY F.   643
The Army of Tennessee. *Indp* [1941]. O 503
11pls a

HORNBECK, ROBERT   644
Roubidoux's ranch in the 70's . . . *Riverside, Cal*
1913. O 230 ports a

HORNECKER, MARTIN   645
Buffalo hunting on the Texas plains in 1877.
n.p. 1929. O 36 a

HORNER, WILLIAM B.   646
The gold regions of Kansas and Nebraska. *Chi*
1859. O 67 + 7adv-p 2maps d G NYH LC Y [only
cops kn]
—rptd *Denv* 1949 a

HORNER, W[ILLIAM] B., and   647
CORNWALL, I. S., pubs.
Horner's American railroad and steamboat trav-
elling guide . . . *Chi* [1854]. D 48 map aa

[HORNOT, ANT.]   648
Anecdotes américaines, ou histoire abrégée des
principaux événements . . . depuis sa découverte
. . . *P* 1776. D [16] 782 a

[HORRY, CHARLES L. P.]   649
A five minutes answer to Paine's Letter to
Gen'l. Washington . . . *L* 1797. O [4] 3–44 a

HORRY, PETER   650
The life of General Francis Marion. [Ed. M. L.
Weems]. *Phil* 1809. D 242 b no copy known
—ed. 2, *Balt* 1814. D 270 a
—ed. 3, *Balt* 1815.
—ed. 4, *Phil* 1816.
—Eng. ed., abr., *Devon* 1835. 18° 324
General Horry furnished the facts, Parson
Weems the rhetoric; so much of it that Horry became indignant and disclaimed all connection with
the book. Unabashed, Weems continued its publication through many editions.

HORSFORD, EBEN N.   651
John Cabot's landfall in 1497, and the site of
Norumbega. *C* 1886. Q 42 8maps 2 pls a

[HORSMANDEN, DANIEL]   652
A journal of the proceedings in the detection of
the conspiracy . . . for burning the city of New
York . . . *N Y* 1744. Q [10] 206 blank lf [16] c AA
Hn NYP Y
—Eng. ed., t.altered, *L* 1747. O [8] 425 [7] b
NYP Y
—rptd.: *N Y* 1810. O 385 [7] a; *N Y* 1851. O 96
Chief source on the "Negro Plot" of 1741; of
the 174 indicted two thirds were found guilty, on
what seems frail evidence, 20 being hanged and 13
being burned at the stake.

HORTON, THOMAS F.   653
History of Jack county [Tex.] *Jacksboro* [1932].
O [4] 166 a most of edition burned.

HOSACK, DAVID   654
Memoir of De Witt Clinton . . . *N Y* 1829. Q
[24] 21–530 port plan some cops on L.P. a

HOSKINS, JAMES   655
Narrative of a voyage . . . to the United States
. . . *Penzance* 1813. O 49 a

HOSKINS, NATHAN   656
Notes upon the western country ... Ohio, Indiana, Illinois ... Michigan ... *Greenfield* 1833.
D 108 c G LC NYP WRH
Interesting and valuable description; all too brief.

HOSKYNS-ABRAHALL, JOHN   657
Western woods and waters ... *L* 1864. D [32]
420 map pl table inserted slip a
Hiawatha-inspired verses on Indian legends; accompanied by over 200 pages of informative historical notes on the great lakes region.

HOSMER, H. P.   658
Kate Clayton, the Indian captive of Cherry valley ... *Roch* 1855. D 90 c

HOSMER, H[EZEKIAH] L.   659
Early history of the Maumee valley. *Toledo* 1858. D 9–70 aa
Separate printing from the Toledo directory, *see* below.

HOSMER, HEZEKIAH L.   660
Montana; an address ... *N Y* 1866. O 23 cover t.only aa

HOSMER, H[EZEKIAH] L., and   661
HARRIS, W. H. [comps.]
Toledo directory. Containing: Early history of the Maumee valley... *Toledo* 1858. D 294 2maps aa

HOSMER, JOHN ALLEN   662
A trip to the states by the way of the Yellowstone and Missouri. *Va C Mont* 1867. D [2] 82 [12] d G MontU Y [of 9copies known]
First narrative of travel printed in Montana. Reprinted, in part, in vol 12, *Missoula Frontier.*

HOSMER, MRS. MARGARET   663
The child captives. A true tale of life among the Indians of the west. *Phil* [1870]. 18° 230 3pls aa

HOTCHKIN, A.   664
Concise history of the town of Maryland [N.Y.] ... *Schenevus* 1876. O 66 a

HOTCHKIN, JAMES H.   665
A history of the purchase and settlement of western New York ... *N Y* 1848. O [16] 600 pl a

HOTCHKISS, CHARLES F.   666
On the ebb: a few log-lines from an old salt. *N Hav* 1878. D 127 a
Reminiscences of a California '49er.

HOTCHKISS, GEORGE W.   667
History of the lumber and forest industry of the northwest. *Chi* 1898. Q 754[incl.port] a

HOTCHKISS, JED[EDIAH] and   668
ALLAN, WILLIAM
The battlefields of Virginia ... *N Y* 1867. O 152 5maps port a

HOTTEN, JOHN C.   670
Original lists of persons of quality ... who went from Great Britain to the American plantations. *L* 1874. O 580 + adv-p aa
—Am. eds: [*N Y* 1880]. O 580; *N Y* 1932 a

HOUCK, LOUIS   671
A history of Missouri from the earliest explorations ... *Chi* 1908. O 3v: [18] 404; [10 7–8] 418; [10] 380. 6pls[all in v.I] aa

HOUCK, LOUIS, ed.   672
The Spanish regime in Missouri; a collection of papers and documents ... *Chi* 1909. O 2v: [26] 414; [10] 460. 8ports aa

HOUGH, EMERSON   673
The story of the cowboy. *N Y* 1897. D [12] 349 + 6adv-p 10pls[6 by Russell] a

HOUGH, EMERSON   674
The story of the outlaw ... *N Y* 1907. D [14] 401 17pls a
—issue 2, identical except no printer's rules top of prelim. p. 5.

HOUGH, FRANKLIN B. [ed.]   675
Diary of the siege of Detroit in the war with Pontiac ... *Alb* 1860. Q [28] 304 136 copies ptd [10 on L. P.] aa
The diarist was Lieutenant Jehu Hay. Here first printed from his MS.

HOUGH, FRANKLIN B.   676
A history of Jefferson county ... New York. *Alb* 1854. O 601 pls a

HOUGH, FRANKLIN B.   677
A history of Lewis county ... New York ... *Alb* 1860. O [4] 319 21ports a
—rptd. *Syracuse* 1883. O [8] 11–606 [37] pls

HOUGH, FRANKLIN B.   678
A history of St. Lawrence and Franklin counties, New York ... *Alb* 1853. O 720 [incl.pls] 3maps front. a

HOUGH, FRANKLIN B.   679
The northern invasion of October 1780 ... *N Y* Bradford Club 1866. O 224 [3] map pl a 75 copies ptd.

HOUGH, FRANKLIN B.   680
Notices of Peter Penet and of his operations among the Oneida Indians ... *Lowville N Y* 1866. O 36 map a 50copies ptd.

HOUGH, FRANKLIN B., ed.   **681**
Papers relating to Pemaquid . . . Maine . . . *Alb*
1856. O [8] 136 a
—anr. issue, in vol.5, *Maine Hist. Colls.*

HOUGH, FRANKLIN B., ed.   **682**
Papers relating to the island of Nantucket . . .
Alb 1856. sm Q [18] 163 map a 150copies ptd

HOUGH, FRANKLIN B., ed.   **683**
Proceedings of a convention of delegates from
several of the New England states . . . 1780 . . .
Alb 1867. sm Q 80 pl a

HOUGH, FRANKLIN B., ed.   **684**
The siege of Charleston, by the British fleet and
army . . . *Alb* 1867. O 224 2ports a 100copies ptd.

HOUGH, FRANKLIN B., ed.   **685**
The siege of Savannah, by . . . forces, under the
command of Gen. Lincoln and the Count d'Estaing . . . 1779. *Alb* 1866. O 187 port a 100copies ptd.
For similar title see Jones, Chas. C.

HOUGHTON, H. H.   **686**
A historical account of the lead mines of the
north-west. *N Y* 1866. O 49 fold.map a

HOUGHTON, JACOB   **687**
The mineral region of lake Superior . . . early
history . . . *Buf* 1846. D [4] 9–191 2maps[on one
fold.sheet] errata slip aa
See also Burt, Wm. A., and Hubbard, Bela, for
first edition of this book.

**HOUGHTON, JACOB, and
BRISTOL, T. W., eds.**
Reports . . . on the . . . mineral regions of lake
Superior. *See* Burt, Wm. A., and Hubbard, Bela.

HOUSE, E.
A narrative of the captivity of Mrs. Horn . . .
See Horn, Mrs. Sarah Ann.

HOUST, REV. ANTHONY P.   **688**
Kratke dejiny a seznam Cesko-Katolickych osad
spoj. Stateck Americkych . . . Josefa Hessouna.
St L 1890. O 542 a
Czech settlements in the United States.

HOUSTON, ANDREW J.   **689**
Texas independence. *Houst* 1938. O [10] 17–300
7pls 11maps [in pocket] 500 signed cops. a
By the son of Sam Houston.

HOUSTON [SAM] DISPLAYED . . .
By a farmer *See* Coleman, Robt. M.

HOUSTON (SAM).
The life of: . . . *N Y* 1855. *See* Lester, Chas.
Edwards.

HOUSTON, SAM   **690**
The malfeasance . . . of J. C. Watrous, Judge of
the Federal Court in Texas . . . *N Y* 1860. O 100 a
Exposé of Texas land frauds.

HOUSTON COUNTY, MINNESOTA   **691**
Houston county, Minnesota: its advantages . . .
Hokah 1858. 16° 34 + 6adv-p aa

HOUSTOUN, MRS. [MATILDA C.]   **692**
Hesperos, or travels in the west. *L* 1850. D 2v:
[8] 294; [8] 280 [8] + adv-p 2pls a
—anr. ed. *L* [*ca* 1855]. D 2v in 1 4pls
Her second American trip.

HOUSTON, MRS. [MATILDA C.]   **693**
Texas and the gulf of Mexico . . . *L* 1844. O 2v:
[8] 314; [8] 360 10pls aa
—Am. ed. *Phil* 1845. 16° 288 [incl front] a
Her first trip; largely devoted to Texas, with
Louisiana and Florida data.

HOUZEAU, JEAN C.   **694**
La terreur blanche au Texas . . . *Brus* 1862. D
96 a

HOVEY, ALVIN P.   **695**
Centennial historical sketch of Posey County,
Indiana. [*Mt Vernon Ind* 1876]. O 24 [12] a

HOW (DAVID).   **697**
How, David, a private in . . . Sargent's regi-
ment . . . in the American revolution. Diary of:
Morrisania N Y 1865. O [16] 51 a 250copies ptd.

HOW (NEHEMIAH).   **698**
A narrative of the captivity of: . . . *B* 1748. D 23
b AA BP
—issue 2, How's obituary moved to p.22 and 2-p.
list of subscribers added, *B* 1748. D 22 [2] b N
NYP
—rptd. *Clev* 1904. O 72 facs a 267 copies ptd.
Captures by Indians in the French war, this
Vermonter was imprisoned in Quebec where he
died after writing his valuable narrative.

HOW TO GO WEST . . .   **699**
Chi 1872. O 73[incl. adv-pp] 3fold,maps a
—rptd. same impr. 1873. O 78 maps

HOWARD, H. R. [ed.]   **700**
The history of Virgil A. Stewart, and his adventures in capturing . . . the great western land
pirate and his gang. *N Y* 1836. D 273 [incl. initial blank
lf] aa
—rptd. 1837; 1847, with illus; 1839 a
—anr. ed. "Pictorial life and adventures of John
A. Murrell," *N Y* 1848. O 126 a
Compiled with Stewart's assistance. For another account of this desperado, *see* Walton,
Augustus Q.

[HOWARD, H. R.]   701
  The life and adventures of Joseph T. Hare, the bold robber . . . *N Y* 1847. O 107 a
  —rptd. 1849.
  One of the most notorious of early outlaws, who operated for eighteen years throughout the southern states. *See* also Hare, Jos. T.

[HOWARD, J. E.]   702
  Remarks on the intercourse of Baltimore with the western country. *Balt* 1818. O 30 map aa

HOWARD, SERGEANT J. W.   703
  Howard, Sergeant J. W., member of Company B, 5th U. S. Cavalry. The life story of: n.p. [1903?]. O 24 aa

HOWARD, JAMES   704
  A trip to America [Chicago and the west]. *Bedford, Eng* [1867] O 60 a

HOWARD, JAMES Q.   705
  The life of Abraham Lincoln . . . *Columbus*, Follett, 1860. D 102 b Clem IH
  —iss 2: Columbus, Anderson, 1860 aa
  —Ger tr same impr & date, D 57 [cov t only] first Lincoln biography in a foreign language aa

HOWARD, McHENRY   706
  Recollections of a Maryland Confederate soldier. *Balt* 1914. O [2] 423 fold.map 11pls a

HOWARD, MARTIN, JR.
  See Halifax. *A letter from a gentleman at*:

HOWARD, OLIVER O.   707
  Annual report [Nez Perce campaign]. *Ft Vancouver Wash* 1879. D 61 aa

HOWARD, OLIVER O.   708
  Annual report of the Division of the Pacific. *S F* 1887. D 23 aa

HOWARD, OLIVER O.   709
  Famous Indian chiefs I have known. *N Y* 1908. D [10] 344[incl.pls] front. a
  —rptd. same impr. & collat. 1912.

HOWARD, OLIVER O.   710
  My life and experiences among our hostile Indians . . . *Hart* [1907]. O 570 2pls[others incl. in paginat.] a

HOWARD, OLIVER O.   711
  Nez Perce Joseph. *B* 1881. O [14] 274 2maps 2ports a

HOWARD (GENERAL O[LIVER] O.)   712
  Report of: . . . *Vancouver Barracks Wash* 1879. D 26 aa

HOWARD (O[LIVER] O.   713
  Report of: Oct. 15, 1878. *Ft Vancouver* 1879. D 53 aa

HOWAY, F[REDERICK] W., ed.   714
  The Dixon-Meares controversy . . . *Tor* [1929]. O [16] 156 [2] [incl.front. & maps] 500copies ptd. a

HOWBERT, IRVING   715
  The Indians of the Pike's Peak region . . . *N Y* 1914. D [10] 230 4pls a
  —enl. ed. "Memories of a lifetime in the Pike's Peak region . . .," *N Y* 1925. D [6] 298 front.

HOWE, EBER D.   716
  Autobiography . . . of a pioneer printer. *Painesville O* 1878. O 59 + cov.t. a
  Worked in Cleveland's first printing house, 1818; witnessed the launching of the first lake steamer, "Walk-on-the-Water," etc.

HOWE, E[BER] D.   717
  Mormonism unvailed . . . *Painesville O* 1834. D 290 pl b
  —rptd., sheets of ed. 1 with new t-p, "History of Mormonism . . .," *Painesville* 1840. aa
  First elaborate critique of this sect, the first to exploit the Spaulding manuscript and the best contemporary account of Mormon activities in Ohio.

HOWE, FRANCES R.   718
  The story of a French homestead in the old northwest. *Columbus* 1907. D 165 2fold. maps aa
  Most of the edition deliberately burned by the eccentric authoress.

HOWE, GEORGE   719
  The Scotch-Irish and their first settlements on the Tyger river . . . in South Carolina. *Columbia* 1861. O 31 a

HOWE, HENRY   720
  Historical collections of Ohio. *Cin* 1847. O 582 map a
  —ed. 2, *Cin* 1848. O 599 map
  —rptd. 1849; 1850; 1851.
  —other eds.: *Cin* 1857. O 620 map; *Cin* 1869. O [2] 599 map
  —enl. ed.: *Columbus* 1890. O 3v in 2: 750 [26]; 634; 612; Columbus 1896

HOWE, HENRY   721
  Historical collections of the great west . . . *Cin* 1851. O 2v in 1: [10] 33–440 a
  —rptd., same impr. & collat.: 1852; 1853.
  —other eds. with adds., *Cin* 1854. O 440; *Cin* 1855. O 448
  —anr. ed., enl., *N Y* 1857. O 576; rptd., same impr. & collat. 1859.

HOWE, HENRY   **722**
Historical collections of Virginia . . . *Charleston S C* 1845. O [2] 544 eng.t. col. front. map 18pls aa
—rptd. with adds: 1846; 1847; 1849; 1852; 1856. a

HOWE (MRS. JEMIMA).   **723**
A genuine and correct account of the captivity . . . of: *B* 1792. O 20 aa
—rptd. *Watertown* 1830. 16° 16 a
—Eng. ed., re-written, "The affecting history of Mrs. Howe . . .," *L* [1815]. D 28 front. a

HOWE, JOHN   **724**
The emigrants' new guide . . . description of the United States . . . *Leeds* 1822. O 52 a

HOWE (JOHN) British spy.   **725**
A journal kept by: during the revolutionary war . . . *Concord N H* 1827. D 44 aa
Thinly disguised plagiarism of the genuine spy narrative of Ensign de Bernière found in *Gen. Gage's instructions, q.v.*

HOWE, OCTAVIUS T., and   **726**
MATTHEWS, FREDERICK C.
American clipper ships, 1833–58. *Salem* 1926–7. Q 2v: [16] 372 + adv-p; [12] 373–780. 58pls aa

HOWE ([RICHARD], LORD).
A candid and impartial narrative of the transactions of the fleet under: *See* O'Beirne, Thos. L.

H[OW]E ([RICHARD], the Right Hon. Lord Viscount).
A letter from Cicero to: . . . *See* Galloway, Jos.

H[OW]E ([RICHARD], the Right Honourable Viscount).
A letter to: . . . *See* Galloway, Jos.

HOWE (LORD VISCOUNT [RICHARD]).
Three letters to: *See* Mauduit, Israel.

HOWE (MAJOR GENERAL [ROBERT]).   **727**
Proceedings of a general court martial . . . for the trial of: . . . *Phil* 1782. F 31 b AA BP NYP
Absolved Howe from all blame in the fall of Savannah in 1778, and affords the best account of that disaster.

HOWE (SIR WILLIAM).   **728**
Campaignes militaires du: en Amérique . . . *Hague* 1781. O [8] 70 116 aa
—anr. ed. same date & collat. *Rotterdam*

HOWE (LIEUT. GENERAL [WILLIAM]).
An extract from a Reply to the Observations of: . . . *See* Wesley, John.

HOWE (LIEUT. GEN. SIR WILLIAM).   **729**
The narrative of: . . . relative to his conduct . . .

in North America; to which are added, some observations upon a pamphlet, entitled, Letters to a nobleman. *L* 1780. Q [2] 110 aa
—ed. 2, same impr. & date. Q [4] 110 aa
—ed. 3, same impr. & collat., 1781. a

H[OWE] (S[IR] W[ILLIAM]).
Observations upon the conduct of: at the White Plains . . . *L* 1779. *See* Galloway, Jos.

HOWE'S ACCOUNT
Howe's (Gen. [William]) account of his procedings on Long Island. Remarks upon: *See* Mauduit, Israel.

HOWE (LIEUT. GEN. SIR WILLIAM).
A reply to the observations of: on . . . Letters to a nobleman . . . *See* Galloway, Jos.

HOWE (LIEUTENANT-GENERAL SIR WILLIAM).
Three letters to: *See* Mauduit, Israel.

HOWE (SIR WILLIAM).   **730**
Two letters from Agricola to: . . . *L* 1779. O 63 a

HOWELL, GEORGE R.   **731**
The early history of Southampton, L. I., New York. *N Y* 1866. D 318 a
—ed. 2,+and best, *Alb* 1887. D [8] 473

HOWELL (PETER).   **732**
The life and travels of: . . . *Newbern N C* [1849]. 16° [4] 320 port aa

HOWELL (READING) et al.   **733**
Copy of a report from: [on exploration of the headwaters of the Delaware, Lehigh, Schuylkill . . . rivers]. *Phil* 1791. O 33 a

HOWELLS, WILLIAM C.   **734**
Recollections of life in Ohio . . . *Cin* 1895. O 207 a

HOWELLS, WILLIAM D.   **735**
Lives and speeches of Abraham Lincoln and Hannibal Hamlin. *Columbus* 1860. D 94 blank l. 97–154 157–170 bound in wraps, with cut of Lincoln on front cover, view of Wigwam on rear cover and pub's announcement on inside of rear cover, stating that "materials . . . have been furnished from the intimate friends of Mr. Lincoln." b AA G [only copies known]
—anr. issue, no priority established, same impr., date & collat., except that rear cover is blank, with no text or view, that view being found on p95. b IllH[of 5copies known]
—enl. ed., clo., same impr. 1860. D 406 errata slip, p74; no period after O in impr.; letter "i" missing, last line, p46. 2ports a

HOWGILL, FRANCIS   736
The Popish inquisition . . . in New-England . . .
L 1659. SmQ [2] 72 b BP NYP Hn
Vehement excoriation of the New England
church hierarchy for its inhumanity to Quakers.

HOWISON, JOHN   737
Sketches of Upper Canada . . . and some recollections of the United States . . . *Edin* 1821. O [18]
339 a
—ed. 2, *Edin* 1822. O 9–353
—ed. 3, *Edin* 1825. same collat.

HOWISON, NEIL M.   738
Oregon: report of an examination . . . [*Wash*
1848]. House Misc. Doc. 29. O 36 a
The flag, taken ashore when, in 1846, Howison's
vessel was wrecked in the Columbia, was the first
to wave over Oregon.

HOWISON, ROBERT R.   739
A history of Virginia . . . *Phil* 1846–*Rich* 1848.
O 2v: 496; 528 aa

HOWITT, EMANUEL   740
Selections from letters written during a tour
through the United States . . . *Nottingham* [1820].
D [22] 230 aa
Takes a dim view of the Republic, especially the
backwoods regions.

H[OWLAND], MRS. E. P.   741
A tale of home and war. *Port Me* 1888. D 200
[incl.port] a
Experiences of the family of missionary Wor-
cester Willey among the Cherokees of the Indian
Territory during the civil war.

HOWLAND, S. A.   742
Steamboat disasters and railroad accidents in
the United States . . . *Worc* 1840. D [8] 13–408
[incl.pls] a
—ed. 2, same impr., date & collat.
—anr. ed., rev., no au. named, same impr. 1843.
D 408 [incl. 9 illus]
—rptd., same impr. & collat. 1846.

HOWLETT, W[ILLIAM] J.   743
Life of . . . Rev. Joseph P. Machebeuf, pioneer
priest . . . *Pueblo Colo* 1908. O 419 10pls a
Describes his trip in 1851 from New Orleans to
Santa Fe and his work there and at Albuquerque
until transferred to Colorado in 1860.

HOXSE, JOHN   744
The Yankee tar . . . and the cruises of the U. S.
frigate Constellation . . . *Northampton* 1840. 16°
200[incl.front.] a

HOYT, COMFORT   745
Memoirs of Dolly E. Hoyt, who died on the
Arkansas river . . . on her passage to the Osage
nation. *Danbury Conn* 1828. 16° 107 aa
Contains this young lady's journal of the trip
made by her small party, through Pennsylvania by
wagon and down the Ohio and Mississippi, to the
Arkansas.

HOYT, E[PAPHRAS]   746
Antiquarian researches: . . . the Indian wars in
the country bordering Connecticut river . . . *Greenfield Mass* 1824. O [14] 312 pl aa

HOYT, HENRY F.   747
A frontier doctor . . . *B* 1929. O [16] 260 16pls a

HUBBARD, CAROLINE   748
The history of . . . Manitowoc, Wis., 1850–60.
Manitowoc n.d. D 50 aa

HUBBARD (GURDON S.)   749
Incidents and events in the life of: Ed. by H. E.
Hamilton. *Chi* 1888. O [2] 189 port aa
—rptd. *Chi* Lakeside 1911. 16° [28] 182 port a
Lived through the panorama of Chicago's
history from an 1818 trading post to a world
metropolis.

HUBBARD, JEREMIAH   750
Forty years among the Indians . . . *Miami Okla*
1913. D 200 aa
Life of a Quaker missionary among various
tribes in Kansas, Missouri and Oklahoma.

HUBBARD, JOHN M.   751
Notes of a private [in Forrest's cavalry].
Memphis 1909. D [6] 189 2pls a
—rptd. *St L* 1911. D

HUBBARD, JOHN N.   752
Sketches of border adventures, in the life . . .
of Moses Van Campen . . . *Dansville N Y* 1841.
D 310 aa
—anr. issue, *Bath N Y*, same date & collat. a
—rptd., same collat., *Bath* 1842. [2 issues, with
minor differences] a
—rev. & enl. ed. *Fillmore N Y* 1893. D [22] 337
9pls facs
For separate account of his 1780 Indian captivity, *see* Van Campen, Moses.

HUBBARD, ROBERT   753
Historical sketches of Roswell Franklin and
family . . . *Dansville N Y* 1839. 16° 103 b AA N
NYP

HUBBARD, REV. WILLIAM   754
A general history of New England . . . to 1680.
C 1815. O [14] 676 a
—ed. 2, *B* 1848. O [20] 7–676
First printing of the original manuscript.

HUBBARD, REV. WILLIAM   755
The happiness of a people . . . recommended in a sermon . . . *B* 1676. Q [8] 63 b BPL H

A sermon so dull could not be marketed even in that pious age; to dispose of the unsalable sheets the publisher [John Foster] bound some copies, as *lagniappe*, at the end of his *Narrative of the troubles with the Indians* [see next item], in which they are frequently found. The only redeeming virtue of this exhortation is that it was the first production of a Boston press.

HUBBARD, REV. WILLIAM   756
A narrative of the troubles with the Indians in New-England . . . *B* 1677. smQ [14] 132, [8, 7–12], 88 fold map [with hilly parts at the right described correctly as "White Hills"]. Errata of 10 lines on last p. dd Hn
—iss. 2, some slight textual changes and 12-line errata at end. dd H Hn JCB N
—Eng. ed. "The present state of New-England. Being a narrative of the troubles with the Indians . . ." *L* 1677. smQ [14] 132 [12] 88 map shows hilly section at the right as "Wine Hills". d
—Am. ed. 2, *Newpt* 1772. b
—abr. ed. *B* 1775. D [8] 288 a
—oth. eds: *Worc* 1801. D 410; *Norw* [1802]. D 228; *Stockbridge* 1803. O 375 [6]; *Danbury* 1803. D 275; *Brattleborough* 1814. D 359
—best ed. *Roxbury* 1865. Q 2v: [34] 292; 303 map. 350 cops [50 on L.P.] a

A corner-stone authority on the subject. Map in original edition was the first American map made in this country.

HUBBARDTON, VERMONT.   757
Sketches of the history of: By an old man . . . *Rutland* 1855. D [4] 64 a

HUBBELL (SETH) AND FAMILY.   758
A narrative of the sufferings of: in his beginning a settlement in the town of Wolcott . . . Vermont. *Danville* 1824. D 24 aa
—rptd., same impr. & collat.: 1826; 1827; 1829 aa

HUBLEY, BERNARD   759
The history of the American revolution. Vol. I [all]. *Northumberland Pa* 1805. O [4] 606 [1] + 8p all numb 192 b

First documentary presentation of events covered.

HUDSON, CHARLES   760
History of . . . Lexington . . . Massachusetts . . . *B* 1868. O 2pts in 1: 449; 296. 22pls a Also 20copies issued on tinted paper
—best ed. *B* 1913. O 2v: [24] 583 + 8p. of corrigenda; [8] 898. 33pls

HUDSON, DAVID   761
History of Jemima Wilkinson . . . *Geneva N Y* 1821. D 208 [20] a
—rptd., *Bath N Y* 1844. 16° 288 port

This remarkable preacheress, born in R.I., 1760, was the first religious charlatan of her sex in America. No author named in the 1844 edition.

HUDSON, EDUARD M.   762
Der zweite Unabhängigkeits-Krieg in Amerika. *Berlin* 1862. O 78 [2] a
—ed. 2, same impr. & date. O [8] 100
—Eng. ed. "The second war of independence in America," *L* 1863. O [2] 177
—Eng. ed. 2, same impr. & date. O [8] 132

HUDSON, FREDERIC   763
Journalism in the United States, 1696–1872. *N Y* 1873. O [4] 789 a

HUDSON, COL. JOSHUA H.,   764
26th S. C. Inf.
Sketches and reminiscences . . . *Columbia, S C* 1903. O 190 a

HUDSON RIVER PORTFOLIO.
See Wall, Wm. G.

[HÜBNER, MARTIN]?   765
Politique Danois (Le), ou l'ambition des Anglais démasquée par leurs pirateries . . . où l'on prouve . . . de quelle importance il est pour . . . d'abattre l'orgueil de ce peuple . . . *Copenh* 1756. D [4] 364 [1] b N NYP Y
—ed. 2, same impr. 1759. D aa

Includes, among England's piratical encroachments upon the rights of other nations, Washington's operations on the Monongahela in 1754.

HÜLSEMANN, JOHANN G.   766
Geschichte der Democratie in den Vereinigten Staaten . . . *Göttingen* 1823. O [24] 388 a

HUGHES, F. W.
The case of George Chorpenning . . . *See* under Chorpenning.

HUGHES, GEORGE W.   767
Memoir . . . of the march of a division . . . under the command of Brigadier General John E. Wool, from San Antonio . . . to Saltillo . . . [*Wash* 1846]. O 67 map 4pls aa
—rptd. "Operations in Texas and Mexico," *Wash* 1850. O 67 2maps 8pls 250copies ptd.

HUGHES, JOHN T.   768
California; its history . . . *Cin* [1848]. D 105 + adv-lf b G
—rptd., with adds., same impr. 1849. D 144 aa

The 1848 edition is sometimes found bound with Joel Palmer's *Journal of travels*.

HUGHES, JOHN T. 769
Doniphan's expedition . . . *Cin* 1847. O [8 incl. front wrapper] 9–144 c G Y [of 5cops kn]
—ed. 2, *Cin* 1848. O same collat. aa
—best ed., bound in clo., *Cin* 1848. D 407 map port] of Doniphan] aa
—same, issue 2, adding port of Price and list of illus. aa
—rptd. O-in wrappers—same impr.: 1849; 1850; n.d. [*ca* 1851]. a
Doniphan's and Kearney's conquests gave the United States its claim to New Mexico and Arizona, finally acquired by the Gadsden Purchase. The 1847 edition has on front wrap no date and no words "Cheap edition".

HUGHES (LIEUT. MATTHEW). 770
A sketch of the life of: . . . serving on the Niagara frontier during the late war . . . *Alexandria* 1815. O 56 aa

HUGUENOTS (THE)
Huguenots (The) in France and America . . . *See* Lee, Hannah F.

HUISH, ROBERT, comp. 771
A narrative of the voyages and travels of Captain Beechey to the Pacific, and Behring's straits . . . 1825–1828 . . . *L* Wright [1836]. O [8] 704 map 9pls a

HULBERT, ARCHER B., ed. 772
The crown collection of photographs of American maps. Ser. 1 : *Clev* 1904–09. F 5v [of 239maps] + index [0 43]; ser. 2 : [*Harrow Eng* 1909–12]. F 5v [of 250maps]; ser. 3 : [*L* 1914–16]. Q [of 250maps] c LC N NYP

HULBERT, ARCHER B. 773
Historic highways of America. *Clev* 1902–5. O 16v maps pls Some sets on L. P. aa

HULBERT, ARCHER B. 774
The old national road . . . *Columbus* 1901. O 151 a

HULBERT, ARCHER B. 775
Red-men's roads . . . of the central west. *Columbus O* 1900. O 37 7maps 4pls a

HULING, EDMUND J. 776
Reminiscences of gun boat life in the Mississippi squadron. *Saratoga Springs* 1881. 16° [4] 86 a

HULL, AUGUSTUS L. 777
Annals of Athens, Georgia. *Athens* 1906. O [14 + errata 1.] 495 2ports 7pls a

HULL, AUGUSTUS L. 778
The campaigns of the Confederate army. *Atlanta* 1901. D 107 2maps pl a

HULL, JOHN S. 779
Remarks on the United States . . . *Dub* [1801?]. O 72 aa
Severely condemnatory.

HULL, WILLIAM 780
Memoirs of the campaign of the northwestern army . . . 1812 . . . *B* 1824. O 229 [10] a

HULL (BRIG. GEN. WILLIAM). 781
Report of the trial of: . . . *N Y* 1814. O [7] 4-156 [119, 29] a

HULL (BRIG. GEN. WILLIAM). 782
Trial of: . . . *B* 1814. O 28 a

HULLAH, JOHN 783
The train robber's career. A life of Sam Bass . . . *Chi* 1881. D 178 4pls aa

HULSWITT, IGNATZ VON 784
Tagebuch einer Reisen nach den Vereinigten Staaten . . . *Munster* 1828. O [4] 379 aa
Describes a trading voyage to the Northwest coast and experiences suspiciously similar to those of John Jewitt.

HUMASON, W. L. 785
From the Atlantic surf, to the Golden Gate . . . *Hart* 1869. O 56 a

HUMBLE ENQUIRY
Humble enquiry into the nature of the dependency of the American colonies . . . *See* Zubly, John J.

HUMBOLDT, FRIEDRICH H. A., 786
Baron von
Essai politique sur . . . la Nouvelle Espagne. [Complete in itself but formed Pt III of Humboldt and Bonpland's "Voyage aux régions équinoxiales du nouveau continent"] *P* 1811–1812. Q 2v: [14] 350 [6]; [8] 351–904 [2] + Atlas F [8] 21maps & pls [on 28sheets] b N NYP Some cops on L.P.
—anr iss, same impr & date O 5v: [8] 456 map; [4] 522 pl; [4] 420; [4] 564 [2]; [4] 350 + 2adv-p aa
—Some sets accompanied by the Atlas described above. b
—ed 2, *P* 1825–1827. O 4v: [18] 471 [4]; [4] 500; [4] 479; [4] 503 map plan a
—Eng tr, *L* 1811. O 4v: [20] 290; [4] 532; [6] 494; [2] 374 [99] 2maps, 2tabs + Atlas O 9maps and pls aa
—rptd. same impr & collat 1814; 1822. ea a
—Am ed, *N Y* 1811. O 2v [all]: [12 92] 221; 377
—Ger ed, "Versuch über de politische Zustand des . . . Neu-Spanien." *Tubingen* 1809–1814. O 5v: text only; no atlas a
—Sp tr, abr. "Minerva Ensayo politico . . ." *Madr* 1818. O 2v: 448; 462 [2] a
—oth Sp eds, *P* 1822. O 4v: *P* 1827. O 5v: *P* 1836. Q 5v

—best Sp ed, *Mex* 1941. Q 4v: 381; 460; 409; 383 4pls 20plans + Atlas 36 pp. 14 pls & maps
Of superlative California importance.

HUMBOLDT, FRIEDRICH H. A. VON   787
Examen critique . . . de la géographie du nouveau continent. *P* 1814–19. F [12] 562 39maps b
—anr. ed. *P* 1836–9. O 5v: [28] 362; 373; 407; 336; 263. 4maps aa
—rptd., with slight changes, *P* [1839]. O 2v 2maps a
—Ger. ed. "Kritische Untersuchengen . . .," *Berlin* 1836–52. O 3v: same impr. 1852. O 3v a
Classic of historical scholarship on early American geographical discovery.

HUMBOLDT COUNTY,   788
CALIFORNIA.
History of: *SF* 1881. F 218 pls b SFP
—anr. ed. same impr and collat 1882. b B CalS

HUME, JAMES B. and THACKER,   789
JOHN N.
Report [of these Wells, Fargo operatives], covering a period of fourteen years . . . *S F* 1885 O 91 aa
Gives description, record and prison sentences of over 200 train and stage robbers.

HUMFREVILLE, J[AMES] L.   790
Twenty years among our savage Indians . . . *Hart* 1897. O 674[incl.pls] port aa
—ed. 2, *Hart* 1899. O [64] 49–674 port [other pls incl.in paginat.] a
—rptd. *N Y* [1899]. same collat.
—rptd., t.altered, *N Y* [1903]. O [2, 11–36] 45–479 port[other pls incl.in paginat.]
The 1903 edition was re-written and reset throughout, with different illustrations.

HUMILIATIONS . . .
B 1697. *See* Mather, Cotton

HUMPHREYS, A[NDREW] A., and   791
WARREN, G[OUVERNEUR] K.
An examination . . . of the reports of exploration for railroad routes . . . to the Pacific . . . *Wash* 1855. O 116 [1] a
For series [House Executive Document 129] of which this formed a part, and which contained a map relating to this report, *see Pacific railroad explorations.*

HUMPHREYS, A[NDREW] A.   792
Preliminary report concerning explorations . . . in Nevada and Arizona . . . *Wash* 1872.
See Wheeler, Geo. M.

HUMPHREYS, DAVID   793
The conduct of General Washington, respecting the confinement of Capt. Asgill . . . *N Y* Holland Club 1859. O 35 small edition a

HUMPHREYS, DAVID   794
An essay on the life of . . .Israel Pntnam . . . *Hart* 1788. D 187 a
—rptd. *Middletown* 1794. D 168; *Phil* 1798. 16° 125
—many later eds., with variant titles.

HUMPHREYS, DAVID   795
An historical account of the . . . Society for the Propagation of the Gospel in Foreign Parts . . . *L* 1730. O [32] 356 2maps [of Carolina & of New England] aa

HUNDLEY, DANIEL R.   796
Social relations in our southern states. *N Y* 1860. D 367 a
This—the ablest answer to abolition propaganda—came too late to be effective and furthermore most copies were burned prior to distribution.

HUNNICUTT, JAMES W.   797
The conspiracy unveiled. The south sacrificed; or, the horrors of secession. *Phil* 1863. D [14] 13–454 port a

HUNT, CHARLES H.   798
Life of Edward Livingston. *N Y* 1864. O [24] 448 2ports a also 75copies on L.P.

HUNT, CORNELIUS E.   799
The Shenandoah; or the last Confederate cruiser. *N Y* 1867. D 273 [incl. front.] a

HUNT, ELVID   800
History of Fort Leavenworth. *Ft L* 1926. O 298 10pls 11maps a

HUNT, FREEMAN   801
Lives of American merchants . . . *N Y* 1856-8. O 2v: [48] 33–576; 13–605. 19ports a

HUNT, GEORGE W.   802
A history of the Hunt family . . . *B* 1890. D 79 aa
Contains much on early California and Oregon, Indian adventures, etc.

HUNT, GILBERT J.   803
The late war between the United States and Great Britain. *N Y* 1816. D [12] 15–334 10pls a
—rptd. "The historical reader . . .," *N Y* 1819. D 233 5pls

HUNT, ISAAC   804
The political family . . . reciprocal advantages . . . from an uninterrupted union between Great Britain and her . . . colonies. No. I [all]. *Phil* 1775. O 32 aa
—anr. issue, "The family compact . . .," same impr. & date. a
Isaac Hunt, father of Leigh Hunt and Philadelphia clergyman, for his appeasement utterances, was drummed out of town to the tune of "Yankee Doodle."

HUNT, JAMES H.   **805**
A history of the Mormon war . . . *St L* 1844. D
304 b CalU LC
—anr. ed. "Mormonism . . .," [with app. by G. W.
Westbrook, on Mormon disturbances in Ill. and
the death of Joseph Smith] *St L* 1844. D [6]
5–304 36 errata lf b G NYP Y

HUNT, JOHN W.   **806**
The Wisconsin almanac and annual register.
No 1. *Milw* 1856. D 96 aa
First Wisconsin almanac.

HUNT, JOHN W.   **807**
Wisconsin gazetteer . . . *Madison* 1853. O 256
map a

HUNT, MEMUCAN   **808**
Address to the people of Texas, soliciting the
payment of his claims . . . With a few of his . . .
papers in behalf of what he deemed the best interests of Texas in 1836 . . . *Galv* 1851. O 84 aa

HUNT, RICHARD S., and   **809**
RANDEL, JESSE F.
Guide to the republic of Texas . . . N Y 1939 16°
64 + 2adv-p map aa
—anr. ed., "A new guide to Texas . . ." *N Y* 1844
16° 64 map aa
—rptd., same impr. & collat., 1845; 1846.

HUNTER, C. L.   **810**
Sketches of western North Carolina . . . *Raleigh*
1877. O [16] 357 errata lf a

HUNTER, GEORGE   **811**
Reminiscences of an old timer . . . *S F* 1887. O
[26] 454 16pls aa
—rptd., with adds.: *Battle Creek* 1888; 1889; O
[26] 508 pls a

HUNTER, HIRAM A. [ed.]   **812**
A narrative of the captivity and sufferings of
Isaac Knight from Indian barbarity . . . *Evansville
Ind* 1839. D 34 c Hn N OHP [of 4cops loc]
Captured in Kentucky, 1793, Knight endured
two years of captivity in the Great Lakes region.
This was the first book printed in Evansville.

HUNTER, JOHN DUNN   **813**
Manners and customs of several Indian tribes
. . . west of the Mississippi . . . to which is prefixed
. . . a residence of several years among them. *Phil*
1823. O 402 aa
—Eng. ed. "Memoirs of a captivity among the Indians. To which is added, some account . . . of the
territory westward of the Mississippi," *L* 1823. O
[10] 448 a

—new ed., with port. added, *L* 1823. O [12] 440 +
14adv-p at front port, dated 1823, faces right
—ed. 2, with different port. facing left, *L* 1823.
—ed. 3, with adds., *L* 1824. O [12] 468 port dated
1824
—Ger. tr. *Dresden* 1824. D 3v in 1: [8] 182; 174;
192. 2maps a
—Dutch tr.: *Dordrecht* 1824. O [4] 315; [*Amst*
1824?].
—Swed. tr. *Mariefred* 1826. O 320 [2]

HUNTER, J[OHN] MARVIN, and   **814**
ROSE, NOAH H.
The album of gun-fighters. *Bandera, Tex.* 1951.
Q [14] 236 pls a

HUNTER, J[OHN] MARVIN   **815**
Pioneer history of Bandera county . . . *Bandera,
Tex* [1922] O 288 [4] a

HUNTER, J[OHN] MARVIN, ed.   **816**
The trail drivers of Texas . . . [*San Antonio* 1920–
23]. O 2v: 498; [2] 496 + adv-p 2ports b
—set with v. 1 in 2" ed [494 p], ptd 1924 aa
—ed 2, with adds *Nashv* 1925. O 2v in 1: [16]
1044 [incl pls] aa

HUNTER, JOHN W.   **817**
Rise and fall of the mission San Saba [Texas] . . .
[*Mason Tex* 1906]? O 84 fold. plan a

HUNTER, JOSEPH   **818**
Collections concerning the early history of the
founders of New Plymouth . . . *L* 1849. O [2] 70 a
—enl. ed. "Collections concerning the church . . .
at Scrooby . . .," *L* 1854. O [16] 205

HUNTER, LOUIS C.   **819**
Steamboats on the western rivers. *C* 1949. O
[14] 684 maps a

HUNTER, SAMUEL J.   **820**
The hunter's and trapper's . . . historical guide
. . . *St L* 1869. O 208 aa
Predominantly featured is game of the plains and
Rockies, including the wild Indian, of whom "it is
better to take a dozen of their scalps rather than
lose one Christian one."

HUNTINGTON, D. B.   **821**
Vocabulary of the Utah and Sho-sho-nee . . .
dialects . . . Including a brief account of . . .
Wahker, the Indian land pirate. *S L C* 1872. D
32 aa

HUNTINGTON, REV. E[LIJAH] B.   **822**
History of Stamford, Connecticut . . . *Stamford*
1868. O [8] 492 19pls a

HUNTINGTON, GEORGE 823
Robber and hero. The story of the raid on the First National bank . . . by the James-Younger band . . . *Northfield Minn* 1895. D [8] 119 13pls a

HUNTINGTON COUNTY [IND.] 824
Historical sketch of: *Huntington* 1877. O 41 a

[HUNTLEY, SIR HENRY V.] 825
California: its gold and its inhabitants. *L* 1856. D 2v: [4] 303; [2] 286 small ed. ptd. aa
—rptd. "Adventures in California . . .," *L* n.d. D 2v in 1 same collat., except vol.2 has no t-p a

HUNTON (EPPA). 826
Autobiography of: *Rich* 1933. O [20] 268 port a 100 copies ptd.
Hunton commanded a brigade in Pickett's Confederate division.

HURD, JOHN C. 827
The law of freedom and bondage in the United States. *B* 1858 62. O 2v: [48] 617; [44] 800 a
Most profound legalistic treatise on slavery.

HURLBURT, HENRY H. 828
Chicago antiquities . . . *Chi* 1881. O 673 eng.t. 10maps[one fold.] a

HURLBURT, J. S. 829
History of the rebellion in Bradley county, east Tennessee. *Indianap* 1866. O 280 [24] fold.map a

[HURLBURT, S. S.] 830
Early days at Racine, Wisconsin . . . *Racine* 1872. O 23 a

HURON, MICHIGAN. 831
The town of: . . . *N Y* 1837. O 32 map a

HURST, M. B. 832
History of the Fourteenth Regiment Alabama Volunteers . . . *Rich* 1863. D 48 aa

HURT-BINET, MARC-GABRIEL 833
Neuf mois aux États-Unis . . . *Geneva* 1862. 16° 184 a

[HUSBAND or HUSBANDS?, 834
HARMON or HERMAN?]
A continuation of the . . . differences . . . in the province of North-Carolina. [*Newbern?*] 1770. 16° 39 b Hn

HUSBAND, HARMON 835
A fan for Fanning, and a touch-stone to Tryon. Containing an impartial account of the rise . . . of Regulation in North-Carolina. *B* 1771. O 80 b NYP
Issued originally in 10 weekly parts. Ascribed also to Shubal Stearns.

HUSBAND, HARMON 836
An impartial relation of the . . . cause of the recent differences . . . in the province of North Carolina . . . [*Newbern?*] 1770. 16° 104 b JCB
Of the first importance concerning pre-revolutionary political tumults and the formation of "Regulators."

HUSE, CALEB 837
The supplies for the Confederate army. *B* 1904. D 36 port a

[HUSE, CHARLES E.] 838
Sketch of the history of Santa Barbara . . . *Santa Barbara* 1876. O 49 + 2adv-p a

HUSE, WILLIAM 839
History of Dixon county, Nebraska . . . *Norfolk Neb* 1896. O [12] 9–372 map 6pls [other pls incl. in paginat.] a

[HUSKE, JOHN] 840
The present state of North America . . . Pt. I [all]. *L* 1735 [i.e. 1755]. Q [2] 64 map [in some copies, but probably not issued with book] b
—ed. 2, *L* 1755. O [4] 88 aa
—rptd. *Dub* 1755. aa
—Am. ed. *B* 1755. D [2] 64 + adv-p aa
—Am. ed. 2, same impr., date & collat. aa
Chiefly translated from Butel-Dumont's *Histoire et commerce* . . .

HUSTON, CHARLES 841
An essay on the history . . . of original titles to land in . . . Pennsylvania. *Phil* 1849. O 484 a

HUSTON, GEORGE 842
Memories of eighty years [in Kentucky]. [*Morganfield Ky* 1904]. D [8] 153 port a

HUTCHINS, JAMES 843
An earnest appeal for justice. [cover t. differs]. *Black River Falls Wis* 1876. O 62 aa
Includes a condensed history of Mormonism.

HUTCHINS (JAMES). 844
Outline sketch of the travels of: *Black River Falls Wis* 1871. O 123 + cover t. b Y

HUTCHINS, THOMAS 845
An historical . . . description of Louisiana and West Florida . . . *Phil* 1784. O 95 b AA N NYP Y

HUTCHINS, THOMAS 846
A topographical description of Virginia, Pennsylvania . . . the rivers Ohio . . . Mississippi [etc.]. *L* 1778. O [4] 68 tab 2plans fold map[sold separately & not issued with the book, but found, inserted, in some copies] d H N NYP WRH without fold. map b Y

—issue 1, with Hutchins described on t-p as "Captain in the 60th Regiment."
—issue 2, cor., *L* 1778. O [4] 68 tab 2plans c AA LC N NYP
—Am. ed. *B* 1787. O [4] 30 [2] tab 2plans c AA ChiP H NYP
—anr. ed., ed. by Hicks, with biog. & bibliog., *Clev* 1904. O 143 tab 2plans fold. map 2facs 260 copies ptd]20 on hand-made paper] aa
—Fr. tr. *P* 1781. O 68 [4] 3maps&plans [on 2sheets] 2tabs a

Valuable source for the western country during the late British period, written by the first—and only—official geographer of the United States, the originator of our range system of land surveys.

[HUTCHINSON, E.]   847
Startling facts for native Americans called "know nothings" . . . dangers to American liberty . . . from foreign influence. *N Y* 1855. D 112 [incl. front.] a
—anr. ed. "'Young Sam' or native American's own book . . .," *N Y* 1855. O [2] 119

HUTCHINSON, FRANCIS   848
An historical essay concerning witchcraft . . . *L* 1718. O [20] 270 aa
—ed. 2, with adds., *L* 1720. O [34] 336 a

Includes the New England cases and attacks Cotton Mather's arguments.

HUTCHINSON, K. M.   849
A memoir of Abijah Hutchinson, a soldier of the revolution. *Roch* 1843. O 22 b N NYH [only copies located]

Includes his captivity among Canadian Indians.

[HUTCHINSON, THOMAS]?   850
The case of the provinces of Massachusetts-Bay and New-York respecting the boundary line . . . *B* 1764. F 30 tab b AA NYP [of 5perfect cops loc]

HUTCHINSON (THOMAS), OLIVER (ANDREW), et al.   851
Copy of letters sent to Great Britain by: . . . *B* 1773. O 40 [8 incl. 2blank p] a
—anr. ed. "The representations . . . contained in certain letters . . .," *B* 1773. O [2] 94 a
—anr. ed. *Phil* 1773. O 51
—*Salem* 1773. O 30
—Eng. ed., with changed t. & adds., *L* 1774. O [2] 134 a
—ed. 2, *L* 1774. O [4] 142
—rptd. *Dub* 1774. O 77

Publication of these letters—copies of which Franklin had secured in London—fanned revolutionary sentiment in America more than any other book of the period.

[HUTCHINSON, THOMAS]?   852
Experience preferable to theory. An answer to Dr. Price's Observations on the nature of civil liberty . . . *L* 1776. O [2] 102 a

HUTCHINSON, THOMAS   853
The history of . . . Massachusetts-Bay. *B* 1764. O [8] 566
—cont. as v.2, *B* 1767. O [8] 539
—cont. as "A collection of original papers . . .," *B* 1769. O [4] 576
—concluded as v.3[though actually v.4], *L* 1828. O [4] 551 16p of pref. and dedication were issued in some copies, making 20 prelim. p. complete set [4v.] b AA NYP Y

Above 4 volumes constitute the complete work. There were early reprints of vols. I and II issued both in England and America. The *Collection of original papers* [really vol. 3, being an elucidating appendix to vols. I & 2] was reprinted, in 1865, by the Prince Society, as *The Hutchinson papers*, 2vols., quarto, 160 copies. For a further continuation, *see* Minot, George R.

HUTCHINSON (THOMAS), *et al.*
The representations of: See, above, *Copy of letters* . . .

HUTCHINSON, THOMAS   854
Speeches to the General Assembly of the Massachusetts-Bay . . . *B* 1773. O [2] 126 a

[HUTCHINSON, THOMAS]   855
Strictures upon the Declaration of the Congress at Philadelphia . . . *L* 1776. O 32 a

Justifies parliamentary imposition of duties and taxes, but questions the wisdom of exercising the right and thus accelerating rebellion. Believes, however, that the colonies would, in time, have found other grounds for attaining their purpose.

HUTCHISON, J. R.   856
Reminiscences . . . during . . . forty-five years in Mississippi, Louisiana and Texas. *Houston* 1874. D 218 a
—iss 2, with 5 add articles, D 262

HYDE, EZRA   857
History of . . . Winchenden [Mass.] . . . *Worc* [1849]. D 136 a
Most of the edition burned.

HYDE, GEORGE E.   858
The early Blackfeet . . . *Denv* 1933. O 45 75cops ptd aa

HYDE, GEORGE E.   859
Notes on the Arikara Indians . . . *Denv* 1934. O 48 75cops ptd aa

HYDE, GEORGE E.   860
The Pawnee Indians . . . *Denv* 1934. O 2v: 54;
50 100cops ptd aa

HYDE, GEORGE E.   861
Rangers and regulars. *Denv* 1933. O 47 50cops
ptd a
—rptd. *Columbus*, O 1952. D 143 post

HYDE, GEORGE E.   862
Red Cloud's folk . . . *Norman Okla* 1937. O [12]
332[incl.maps] port aa
—rptd *Norman Okla* 1957.

HYDE, S. C.   863
Historical sketch of Lyon County, Ia. *Lemars Ia*
1872. 16° 40 plan aa
—rptd., same collat., *Sioux City* 1873. a

HYPOCRISY UNMASKED . . .
See Johnson, Saml.

HYPOCRITE (THE)   864
Hypocrite (The); or sketches of American
society from a residence of forty years. By Aesop.
N Y 1844. O 120 port aa

I

IDAHO   1
The banditti of the Rocky mountains, and vigilance
committee in Idaho. *Chi* 1865. O 143[incl. 10pls] +
6adv-p b WashU Y
—anr. issue [priority undetermined] *N Y* 1865.
same collat b LC
Both issues are paged erratically and styled
"twentieth thousand," obviously a publisher's
hyperbole. Presents the same events as later given
more fully and more authentically in Dimsdale's
Vigilantes of Montana. Possibly written by John
L. Campbell.

History of Idaho territory . . . *S F* Elliott   2
1884. Q 304 2maps 69pls 2facs tab aa
First full-scale history of Idaho.

Idaho; A guide . . . *Caldwell, Ida* 1937. *See*
Fisher, Vardis.

Idaho directory . . . [1864]. *See* Owens, George.

Marks and brands of the Central Idaho   3
Stock Grower's Association . . . *Boise* 1885. 16°
28 b G

[IDE, SIMEON]   4
A biographical sketch of . . . William B. Ide:
with . . . account of one of the largest emigrating
companies . . . to the Pacific coast . . . account of
"the virtual conquest of California . . . by the Bear
Flag party," as given by its leader . . . [*Claremont
N H* 1880]. 16° [4] 3–240 b N NYP Y
—rptd., "The conquest of California," *S F* Grabhorn 1944. a 500copies ptd.
The original edition printed on a handpress by
the author at 86 years of age was probably small.
It is sometimes cited [following the half-title]as
Scraps of California history never before published.
Some copies are bound with *Who conquered Cali-
fornia, see* below under Ide, William B.

IDE (WILLIAM B.)
A biographical sketch of: . . . *See* Ide, Simeon.

IDE, WILLIAM B.   5
Who conquered California? . . . *Claremont N H*
Simeon Ide [1880?]. 16° 137 8 [2] b
Sometimes bound with Simeon Ide's *Biographi-
cal sketch of William B. Ide, q.v.*

IDLE . . . MINER
Idle and industrious miner (The). *See* Bausman,
Wm.

IKIN, ARTHUR   6
Texas: its history [etc.] . . . for the use of the
British merchant, and as a guide to emigrants . . .
L 1841. 16° [8] 100 map b N NYP TxH Y
—rptd. with Calif, material added, [34] 100 map aa
Written by the first Texan consul in London to
attract purchasers of Texas land, then being sold
at seven shillings an acre.

ILES, ELIJAH   7
Sketches of early life and times in Kentucky,
Missouri and Illinois. *Springfield Ill* 1883. O 64
port aa
Major Iles went to western Missouri in 1818; in
1821 established the first store in Springfield, Illinois; commanded the company in the Black Hawk
war in which Lincoln served.

ILLINOIS
An account of the proceedings of the Illinois and
Ouabache Land Companies. *See* Smith, *Provost
Wm.*

Documents relating to the organization of the   8
Illinois Central Railway Company. *N Y* 1851. Q
141 map aa
—ed. 2, *N Y* 1852. O 148 facs aa
Practically a history of the first year of this road.

Illinois annual register . . . and western busi- **9**
ness directory. *Chi* 1847. D 120 + 36 adv-p +
12p.calendar b ChiH WisH

Illinois Central railway, a historical sketch **10**
. . . with statistical notes on . . . Illinois . . . Chicago, [etc.]. *L* 1855. O 44 aa

Illinois in 1837 . . . *See* Mitchell, Saml. A.

Invitation sérieuse aux habitants des Illinois **11**
par un habitant des Kaskaskias. *Phil* 1772. O 15
c 1 copy known
—rptd., with adds., *Prov* 1908. O [30] 53 a 100
cops ptd

Les matinées de Beaucaire ou recits d'une prome-
nade sur l'Illinois . . . *See* Lumen, Dr.

Memorial of the Illinois and Wabash Land
Companies . . . *See* Smith, *Provost* Wm.

Opinion of the Supreme court of Illinois on
Beaubien's claim, in the case of Jackson, on the
demise of Murray M'Connell vs. De Lafayette. By
Justice Smith. *See* Smith, Theophilus W.

Reminiscences of early life in Illinois. *See* Till-
son, Christina H.

Sketches of Illinois. *Phil* 1838. *See* Mitchell,
Saml. A.

IMLAY, GILBERT   **12**
A topographical description of the western territory . . . *L* 1792. O [20] 247 aa
—rptd. *Dub* 1793. D [24] 249 a
—ed. 2, enl. *L* 1793. O [22] 433 [20] 3maps &
plans tab aa
—Am. ed *N Y* 1793 D 2v: 260; 204 3maps & plans aa
—ed. 3—and best—further enl. *L* 1797. O [12]
598 [30] 4maps & plans b
—Ger. tr. [*Berlin*] 1793. O [16] 168 a
    In its final 1797 form, embodying many original
narratives and the entire works of Filson and Hutchins, this work gave the most complete information on the trans-Alleghany region available at the
end of the 18th century. Some editions give Imlay's
Christian name as George.

IMPARTIAL
Impartial account (An) of . . . **Bradstreet's expe-**
dition to Fort Frontenac . . . By a volunteer. *See*
Bradstreet, John.

Impartial and correct history (An) of the war
between the United States and Great Britain. *N Y*
1815. *See* O'Connor, Thos.

Impartial enquiry [An] . . . See Mississippi (The
great river).

Impartial history (An) of the late glorious **13**
war . . . *Manch* 1764. O [2] 358 aa
—rptd: *L* 1764. same collat.; *Manch* 1767. same
collat.; *L* 1767. same collat. a

Impartial history (An) of the late war . . . *See*
Almon, John.

Impartial history (An) of the war in America . . .
L 1780. *See* Burke, Edmund.

Impartial history (An) of the war in America . . .
B 1781–4. *See* Murray, Rev. James.

Impartial inquirer (The) . . . By a citizen of Mass.
B 1811. *See* Lowell, John.

Impartial reflections on the conduct of the **14**
late administration and opposition, and of the American colonies . . . *L* [1782]. O 84 a

Impartial review (An) of the . . . **controversy** **15**
between . . . **the Federalists, and Republicans** . . .
Phil 1800. O 50 a
    Ascribed to Charles Pettit.

Impartial view (An) of the conduct of the **16**
ministry in regard to the war in America . . . *L*
1756. O 52 a

Impartial view (An) of the real state of the **17**
black population of the United States . . . *Phil*
1824. O 26 a

IMPORTANCE (THE)
Importance (The) of gaining . . . **the friendship of**
the Indians . . . *See* Kennedy, Archibald.

Importance (The) of the British plantations in
America . . . *See* Hall, Fayrer.

IMPOSTER (THE) DETECTED . . .
By Timothy Tickletoby. See Bradford, Samuel F.

IMPRESSIONS OF THE WEST AND SOUTH.
See Kingsford, Wm.

IN PERILS BY MINE OWN COUNTRYMEN
By a clergyman . . . *See* McNamara. John.

IN VINCULIS
In vinculis; or, the prisoner of war . . . By a
Virginia Confederate. *See* Keiley, A. M.

INCH-BY-INCH   **18**
Inch-by-inch, or guide of guides. *Topeka* 1878.
O 39 a
    Ascribed to H, Hall.

INCIDENTS   **19**
Incidents and sketches connected with the early
history of the west. *Cin* [1847]. O 72 10pls a
    Fragmentary and historically useless.

INCIDENTS OF BORDER LIFE . . .
See Pritts, Joseph.

INCONNUE (L')   20
Inconnue (L') à Madame de Grandfort et à
Madame L . . . [*N O* 1860?]. 16° 29 a

INDEPENDANCE [L'] DES ANGLO-   20a
AMERICAINS
Independance (L') des Anglo-Americains . . .
utile a la Grand-Bretagne. [*P*] 1782. 16° [2] 82 a

INDEPENDENCY   21
Independency the object of the Congress in
America . . . *L* 1776. O [2] 70 a

INDEPENDENT CITIZEN [THE].
See Martin, Francois-Xavier

INDIAN   22
Indian anecdotes and barbarities . . . *Barre Mass*
1837. O 40 [incl. front.] b AA N
—rptd. *Palmer* 1841. aa
—other eds. "Indian atrocities . . .," *B A I*
Wright [1845?]. O 32 [incl. front.] a; *B* Wright &
Hasty [1846?]. same collat.; *B* S. C. Fuller 1846. a
Contains, among other narratives and captivities, the experiences of John Colter, discoverer of
the Yellowstone and first white entrant into Wyoming. For another book entitled *Indian atrocities*,
see Knight, John, and Slover, John.

Indian atrocities . . . *See Indian anecdotes and
barbarities . . .*

Indian battles, captivities and adventures.   23
N Y 1855. D 408 a

Indian battles, murders, seiges [*sic*] and forays in
the southwest . . . *See* Wales, G., and Roberts, M.

Indian missions in the United States . . . *Phil*
1841. *See* De Smet, Pierre-Jean.

Indian (the) of New England. *See* Barrat, Joseph.

Indian raid of 1818 . . . *Topeka* 1879. O   24
58 a

Indian trade; from the Detroit Gazette . . . *See*
Crooks, Ramsay.

Indian treaties and laws . . . relating to Indian
affairs . . . *Wash* 1826. *See* Hamilton, Sam'l. S.

INDIAN TERRITORY
Manners (The), customs . . . of the civilized Indians
of the Indian territory. *See* Boudinot, Elias C.

Proceedings of the convention to consider   25
the opening of the Indian territory *K C* 1888. O 80 aa

INDIANA
History of the regulators of Northern Indiana.
See Mott, M. H.

Letters of Decius to the members of the   26
Indiana territory . . . *Louisv* 1805. 16° 44 aa
First Louisville imprint. Attributed to John
Randolph.

The state of Indiana delineated. *See* Colton,
J[oseph] H.

Thoughts on the destiny of man . . . by the   27
Harmony Society of Indiana. *Harmony* 1824. O
[2] 96 b IndS NYP
—Ger. ed., "Gedanken über die Bestimung [*sic*]
des Menschen . . .," *Harmony* 1824. O aa
Only book printed in English by this Rappite
community. It outlines the principles and objects
of that society.

View of the title to Indiana . . . *See* Wharton,
Sam'l.

INDIANAPOLIS   28
Historical sketch of Indianapolis. [*Indp* 1857].
O 45 caption t.only aa

Indianapolis directory . . . ; or, Indianapolis   29
as it is in 1855. *Indp* 1855. O 264 map pls aa
First directory of this city.

INDIANS
Indians (The): or narratives of massacres . . .
See Bevier, Abraham G.

Report on Indians taxed and not taxed. See
Donaldson, Thos. C.

INFLUENCE   30
Influence de la révolution de l'Amérique sur
l'Europe. *Amst* 1786. O 48 [1] a

INFORME   31
Informe dado a las cameras generales . . . por los
diputados . . . Escalante y Gaxiola. *Cosala* 1827.
O 22 [24] aa
First book printed at Cosala. Sonora and Sina-
loa having been united into the single Estado de
Occidente, an agitation to re-separate the two is
here opposed by Sonora's representatives.

Informe de la Comisión Pesquisidora de la   32
frontera del noroeste . . . *Mex* [1875]. Q 669 aa
—enl. ed. *Mex* 1877. Q 760 aa
—Eng. tr. *N Y* 1875. O [8] 3–443 3maps aa
The 1877 edition included the earlier *Informe
. . . de la frontera del norte*. In that complete form
is covered depredations on Mexican property by
Apaches and Navajos from New Mexico and Arizona and by Mexicans and Texans operating from

the Rio Grande to the Nueces, often with unblushing official connivance. For report of the U.S. committee *see Texas frontier troubles.*

Informe de la Comisión Pesquisidora de la 33 **frontera del norte** . . . *Mex* 1874. Q 124 [incl front wrap] map aa
—rptd. *Monterrey* 1877. aa
Cattle rustling on the Texas-Mexico border.

INGALLS, ELEAZER S. 34
Journal of a trip to California . . . across the plains in 1850–51. *Waukegan Ill* 1852. O 51 + 3adv-p d AA G Pn S Y [all cops loc]

[INGERSOLL, CHARLES], 1805-82 35
A letter to a friend in a slave state. *Phil* 1862. O 60 + cov.t. 49copies on L.P. a

INGERSOLL, C[HARLES] J., 1782-1862 36
A discourse concerning the influence of America on the mind . . . *Phil* 1823. O 67 a
—Eng. [and best] ed to which was added Flower's "English settlements in the Illinois." *L* 1824. O b

INGERSOLL, CHARLES J., 1782-1862 37
Historical sketch of the second war between the United States . . . and Great Britain . . . [Ser. 1 & 2]. *Phil* 1845–52. O 4v: [6] 13–515; [8] 17–317; [6] 9–422; [4] 7–374 aa

INGERSOLL, CHARLES J., 1782-1862 38
Recollections . . . Vol.I[all]. *Phil* ptd. 1861, pub. 1886. O [10] 17–458 a

INGERSOLL, CHESTER 39
Overland to California in 1847. *Chi* 1937. D [4] 7–50 [2] a 350cops ptd.
First separate printing of these letters as published in a Joliet newspaper, 1847–8.

INGERSOLL, JARED 40
Letters relating to the stamp-act. *N Hav* [1766]. O [6] 68 aa

INGHAM, GEORGE T. 41
Digging gold among the Rockies . . . Leadville, Black hills and the Gunnison country . . . *Phil* Hubbard [1880]. D 508 front. 28pls a
—rptd. *Phil* Edgewood Pub. Co. [1882]. D 452 incl.front. & pls]
—anr. ed. *Phil* Hubbard 1888.

INGHAM, HARVEY 42
The northern border brigade [in Iowa]. [*Des M* 1926]. O 97 a

INGHAM, HARVEY 43
Ten years on the Iowa frontier . . . [*Des M* 1915]. O 46 lvs. [incl.front.] a

[INGLIS, CHARLES] 44
Case of Major John André . . . candidly represented, with remarks . . . *N Y* 1780. Q 28 b JCB [only cop kn, with some pp in proof-sheet form] suppressed by Clinton before being completed in published form.

[INGLIS, CHARLES] 45
Letters of Papinian: in which the conduct . . . of the American congress are examined. *N Y* 1779. 16° [6] 130 aa
—anr. issue, same impr. & date. O [8] 86 a
—Eng. ed. *L* 1779. O [6] 86 [1] a

[INGLIS, CHARLES] 46
The true interest of America impartially stated, in . . . strictures on a pamphlet intitled Common sense. *N Y* 1776. Nearly all copies destroyed. b
—other eds.: *Phil* 1776. O 71; ed. 2, same impr., date & collat. aa
Ablest Tory reply to Paine's *Common sense.*

[INGLIS, CHARLES]? 47
A vindication of the Bishop of Landaff's [*sic*] sermon from the . . . reflections contained in Mr. William Livingston's Letter to His Lordship . . . *N Y* 1768. O [8] 82 a
Inglis was royalist rector of Trinity Church, New York.

[INGRAHAM, EDWARD D.] 48
A sketch of the events which preceded the capture of Washington . . . *Phil* 1849. O [4] 66 map some L.P. copies, on blue handmade paper a

[INGRAHAM, JOSEPH H.] 49
The south-west. *N Y* 1835. D 2v: [12] 294; [12] 276 aa

[INGRAHAM, JOSEPH H.] 50
The sunny south; or, the southerner at home . . . *Phil* 1860. D 526 + 18adv-p a
Detailed portrayal of life on tobacco, cotton and sugar plantations in ante-bellum Mississippi. This New Englander thought slavery a henevolence.

INGRAHAM, JOSEPH W. 51
A manual for . . . visiters [*sic*] to the falls of Niagara . . . *Buf* 1834. 18° 72 a
For another 1834 guide, claimed to be the first, *see* Parsons, Horatio A.

INGRAHAM, PRENTISS 52
Wild Bill . . . *N Y*, Beadle, 1891. O 30 a

INMAN, E., ed. 53
Stories of Hatfield, the pioneer . . . his experience in the wilderness of east Tennessee, Kentucky and southern Indiana. *New Albany Ind* 1889. D 278 port a
—ed. 2, same impr. & collat. 1890.

INMAN, HENRY, ed.   54
Buffalo Jones' forty years of adventure . . .
Topeka 1899. O [12] 469 43pls aa
—anr. ed. *L* 1899. same collat. a
Authoritative plains narrative.

INMAN, HENRY, and CODY, WILLIAM F.   55
The Great Salt Lake trail. *N Y* 1898. O [14] 529
map 8pls a bdg. 1, blue clo.; bdg 2, brown or
green clo a
—rptd. *Topeka* 1899; 1914.

INMAN, HENRY   56
In the van of empire; sketches and anecdotes of
western adventure. *K C* 1889. D 122 aa

INMAN, HENRY   57
The old Santa Fé trail . . . *N Y* 1897. O [18]
494 + 3adv-p map 9pls aa
—anr. issue, same impr., date & collat. a
—rptd., same impr. & collat., 1898; 1899.
—anr. ed. *Topeka* 1916. same collat., except for
omission of $^1/_2$ t. & substitution of a different port.

INMAN, HENRY   58
Stories of the old Santa Fé trail. *K C* 1881. D [8]
287 aa
—anr. issue [priority undetermined] on thinner
paper, with 291p of text aa
—rptd. "Tales of the trail," *Topeka* 1898. D [8]
280 a

INNIS, HAROLD A.   59
The fur trade of Canada, *Tor* 1927. O 172 fold.
tab a
—enl.ed. "The fur trade in Canada," *N Hav* 1930.
O [14] 444 map 2pls a
—rptd *Tor* 1953

INNIS, H[AROLD] A.   60
Peter Pond, fur trader and adventurer. *Tor* 1930.
O [12] 153 fold map a

INQUIRIES
Inquiries of an emigrant. *See* Pickering, Joseph.

Inquiries respecting the history [etc.] of the
Indians . . . *See* Cass, Lewis.

INQUIRY   61
Inquiry (An) into the condition and prospects of
the African race in the United States . . . By an
American. *Phil* 1839. D 214 a

Inquiry (An) into the nature and causes of the
present disputes . . . [1768]. *See* Franklin, Benj.

Inquiry (An) into the nature and results of   62
the anti-slavery agitation . . . Part I. [all]. By a
citizen of Alabama. *Mobilo* 1851. O 50 cover t.
only a

Inquiry (An) into the present state of the   63
British navy . . . with reflections on the late war
with America . . . By an Englishman. *L* 1815. O
166 a

INTEREST
Interest (The) in slavery of the southern non-
slaveholder . . . *See* De Bow, James D. B.

Interest (The) of Great Britain considered . . .
See Jackson, Richard.

Interest (The) of the merchants and manu-   64
facturers of Great Britain in the present contest with
the colonies . . . *L* 1774. O [2] 50 a
—Am. ed. *B* n.d. D 20

INTERESTING . . .
Interesting detail of the operations of the American fleet in the Mediterranean . . . *See* Eaton, Wm

Interesting narratives and discoveries, in-   65
cluding Maurice Griffith's Discovery of a nation of
Welshmen in the interior of America . . . *Shrewsbury Eng* 1817. O 64 aa

INTERIOR CAUSES   66
Interior causes of the war: the nation demonized
and its President a spirit-rapper. By a citizen of
Ohio. *N Y* 1863. O 115 a

INTRODUCTION
Introduction to the history of America. 1787.
See M'Culloch, John.

IONIA COUNTY [MICH.]   67
History and directory of: *Grand Rapids* Dillen-
back [1872]. O 195 a

IOWA   68
A description of (central) Iowa with especial reference to Polk county and Des Moines . . . *Des M*
1858. D 32 aa

The emigrant's guide to Iowa, Wisconsin   69
and Minnesota. . . . *St P* 1857. 16° 182 [2] + 8adv-p
aa

History of (western) Iowa its settlement   70
. . . *Sioux City* 1882. O 571 [incl.preliminary blank
l.] a

De Hollanders in Iowa. Brieven uit Pella,   71
van een Gelderschman. *Arnhem* 1858. D [4] 7–189
2pls aa

Northern Iowa. By a pioneer. *Dubuque*   72
Emig. Assoc. 1858. O 40 map 2pls aa
—ed. 2, same impr., date & collat. some copies
carry Nonpareil Co. on t-p a

IRBY, RICHARD   **73**
Historical sketch of the Nottoway Grays, afterwards Company G, 18th Virginia . . . *Rich* 1878. O 49 a

IRELAND (JAMES) . . . pastor of the   **74**
Baptist church . . . Virginia.
The life of: *Winchester* 1819. D 232 a

IRELAND, JOSEPH N.   **75**
Records of the New York stage, 1750–1860. *N Y* 1866. O 2v: [4] 663; [2] 746 aa 263copies issued [63 on L.P.]

IRIARTE (FRANCISCO).   **76**
Manifiesto que . . . dirije el congresso de Occidente sobre la conducta politica del ciudano: . . . *Concepcion de Alamos* 1829. O 32 b
The unionist-controlled legislature of the state of Occidente decreed Gov. Iriarte's removal because he advocated a re-separation of that state into Sinaloa and Sonora. On appeal the Mexican Congress declared this decree invalid.

IRONS, CHARLES D., comp.
Guide and directory of the Truckee basin . . . *See* Edwards, W. F., pub.

IRVING, JOHN B.   **77**
A day on the Cooper river. *Charleston S C* 1842. D [4] 83 aa
—enl. ed. *Columbia* 1932. O [16] 220 [1] port fold. map a

[IRVING, JOHN B.]   **78**
The South Carolina Jockey Club. *Charleston* 1857. O 48 211 pl aa

IRVING, JOHN TREAT   **79**
Indian sketches . . . during an expedition to the Pawnee tribes. *Phil* 1835. D 2v: [4] 9–272; [2] 5–296 a
—Eng. ed.—and best—with "contents" added, *L* 1835. O 2v: [12] 273; [8] 301 a

IRVING, THEODORE   **80**
The conquest of Florida . . . *Phil* 1835. D 2v: 290; 302 a
—rptd., in 1v, *N Y* 1851; 1857; 1869. D 457
—Eng. ed. *L* 1835. D 2v: [12] 296; [8] 280
Compiled from Herrera, Garcilaso de la Vega and the narrative of the gentleman of Elvas.

IRVING, WASHINGTON   **81**
Astoria. *Phil* 1836. O 2v: 285; 279 + 8 adv-p. map [earliest issue has map in vol. 1, no copyright notice on verso of that t-p & signature numeral [1] at bottom of p.5] aa
—Eng. ed. *L* 1836. D 3v: [2 16] 317; [10] 320; [8] 294 a
—Fr. tr. *P* 1839. O 2v
—Ger. & Dutch trs. 1837.

Classic account of the first American attempt at settlement on the Pacific coast, 1811—initial action towards substantiating our claim to Oregon—including the earliest extended relation of Wilson P. Hunt's overland expedition from St. Louis to that settlement.

IRVING, WASHINGTON   **82**
Biography of James Lawrence, late a captain in the navy . . . *New Brunswick* 1813. 18° 244 port aa

[IRVING, WASHINGTON]   **83**
A history of New York . . . *N Y* 1809. D 2v: [24] 268; [2] 258. fold.pl[folding to the left, not vertically] c AA N NYP Y
—ed. 2, with some changes, *N Y* 1812. D 2v: 292; 248. port pl a
—ed. 3, *Phil* 1819. D 2v: 296; 265. port pl
—Eng. ed. *L* 1809. D 2v
—many other Am. & Eng. eds., also several European trs.
—best ed., *N Y* Grolier Club 1886. O 2v pls aa 175copies ptd.

IRVING, WASHINGTON   **84**
Life of George Washington . . . *N Y* 1855–9. O 5v: I,(1855), [16] 504; II, (1855), [12] 518 + errata l.; III, [1856], [14] 523 + inserted slip; IV, [1857], [10] 518; V, (1859), [12] 456. 12maps 8pls facs [all vols. carry on copyright p. name of the stereotyper Trow] aa
—rptd. same collat. & impr. 1856–60. a
—anr. ed., with add. pls, *N Y* 1856–9. Q 5v
—reissued in pts, "subscription ed.," tall O, *N Y* 1857–61. aa
—Eng. ed. *L* Bohn 1855–9. D 5v a
—anr. Eng. ed. *L* Murray 1856–9. D 5v
—many later eds., incl. Dutch & Ger. trs.

IRVING, WASHINGTON   **85**
The Rocky mountains . . . adventures in the far west. [From Capt. Bonneville's papers and other sources]. *Phil* 1837. D 2v: 248; 248. 2maps aa rptd *Phil* 1843 a
—anr ed "Adventures of Captain Bonneville," *N Y* 1847. same collat. a
—Eng. ed. "Adventures of Capt. Bonneville," *L* 1837. D 3v: [4] 303; [4] 292; [4] 302
—Fr. tr. *P* 1837. O 2v in 1
—Ger. tr. 1837.
—Dutch tr. 1838.
—many later eds.
Explorations and fur-trade operations from Green river to Salt Lake and Walla Walla, 1832–5, including the first account of the trapping expedition over the Sierras to California, led by "Joe" Walker.

IRVING, WASHINGTON   **86**
A tour on the prairies. *Phil* 1835. D 274 + 12adv-l. a

—issue 2, differs from issue 1 in having the words "No. 1" added to paper label, and in being ptd on whiter paper.
—Eng. ed., *L* 1835, preceded Am. ed. D [14] 336 a
—Fr. tr.: 1835; 1845.
—Dutch tr. *Amst* 1835. O [12] 206 eng.t. port
—Ger tr. 1835.

ISBELL, F. A.   **87**
Mining and hunting in the far west. *Middletown Conn* [1870]? O 41 b G NYP Y
—rptd. *Burlingame Calif* 1948. O 36 port a 200 copies ptd.

ISELIN, ISAAC   **88**
Journal of a trading voyage around the world, 1805–08 . . . [*N Y ca* 1897]. O 110 aa small ed.
Visited California, Hawaii, etc.

ISHAM, G. S.   **89**
Guide to California and the mines . . . from a journal kept . . . in a journey to that country in 1849–50. *N Y* 1850. D 32 dd AA Y [only cops loc]

ISRAEL, RABBI BEN [pseud.]   **90**
The books of the chronicles of the land of Georgia . . . *Rome Ga* 1872. O 68 a

ITHACA AND ITS ENVIRONS.
Views of: By an imperial observer. *See* Southwick, Solomon.

IVANSHINSTOV, N.   **91**
Obozrienie Russikh krugosvietnykh puteshestvii. *St Ptbg* 1850. O 306 map 17 tabs b only 25copies ptd.
—anr. ed. same impr. 1872. O a
Review of Russian voyages, including those of Kotzebue, Krusenstern, Lisianski, *et al.*

IVES, JOSEPH C.   **92**
Report upon the Colorado river of the west . . . H.Exec.Doc.90. *Wash* 1861. Q 5pts in 1: 131 3maps 25pls; 14; 154 6pls; 30; 6 [32] a
—anr. issue, Sen.Exec.Doc., same date. Q 367 3maps 31pls

IVINS, VIRGINIA W.   **93**
Pen pictures of early western days. [*Keokuk*] 1905. O 157 [incl.front.] aa
—rptd., same impr. & collat. 1908. a
Describes overland trip to California with her husband in 1853.

IVINS, VIRGINIA W.   **94**
Yesterdays . . . [*Keokuk* 1908]. O 107 front. a
Reminiscences of Keokuk [founded by her uncle], of Ft. Edward, now Warsaw, Illinois [commanded by her father], and to other river towns in that area.

IZARD, GEN. GEORGE   **95**
Official correspondence . . . relative to the military operations of the American army . . . on the northern frontier . . . 1814–15. *Phil* 1816. O [8] 152 errata slip aa

[IZARD, RALPH]   **96**
An account of a journey to Niagara . . . in 1765 . . . *N Y* 1846. O 30 a

IZARD (MR. RALPH), of South Carolina.   **97**
Correspondence of: 1774–1804. Vol. I [all]. *N Y* 1844. D [14] 389 [2] port a

IZLAR, WILLIAM V.   **98**
A sketch of the war record of the Edisto Rifles. 1861–1865. *Columbia* 1914. D 168 a

J

J., A., and A., R.
A narrative . . . *See* Jones, Absalom, and Allen, Richard.

J., S. L.
Life in the south . . . *See* Hopley, Catherine C.

J., W.   **1**
Perils, pastimes, [etc.], of an emigrant in Australia, Vancouver's island, and California. See Bayswater, J. W.

JACK, O. G., comp.   **2**
A brief history of Muscatine [Iowa] . . . *Muscatine* 1870. O 80 2 errata slips aa

JACKSON, A. P., and COLE, E. C.   **3**
Oklahoma! . . . History and guide to the Indian Territory . . . *K C* [1885]. D 150 + 2adv-p map [not in all copies] aa

JACKSON (ANDREW).
Biographical sketch of the life of: *See* Walsh, Robert, Jr.

JACKSON (MAJOR GENERAL ANDREW).
Brief sketch of the life, character . . . of: *See* Hill, Isaac.

JACKSON (GENERAL [ANDREW]).   **4**
The case of the six mutineers, whose conviction and sentence were approved of by: . . . *Alb* 1828. O 32 a

JACKSON (ANDREW). 5
Civil and military life of: By an American officer. *N Y* 1825. O 359 a

JACKSON (GEN. ANDREW) and 6
CALHOUN (JOHN C.)
Correspondence between: on the subject of the course of the latter, in the deliberations of the cabinet of Mr. Monroe, on the occurrences in the Seminole war. *Wash* 1831. O 52 aa

[JACKSON, ANDREW]
Essays on the spirit of Jacksonism... *See* McKenney, Thos. L.

[JACKSON, ANDREW]
The Jackson wreath... *See* Walsh, Robt., Jr.

JACKSON (GENERAL ANDREW). 7
Memoirs of: and [his] public acts in Florida. *Bridgeton N J* 1824. O 40 a

JACKSON (GENERAL ANDREW). 8
Memoirs of:... By a citizen of western New York. *Auburn* 1845. O 270 a

JACKSON, (ANDREW).
Memoirs of:... compiled by a citizen of Massachusetts. *See* Smith, Jerome V. C.

JACKSON, (ANDREW).
Memoirs of the illustrious citizen and patriot:
... By a citizen of Hagers-Town, Md. *See* Waldo, Saml. P.

JACKSON (GEN. ANDREW). 9
Memoirs of:... with the letter of Mr. Secretary Adams, in vindication of the execution of Arbuthnot and Ambrister... *N Y* 1824. O 40 a
—anr iss, same date & collat Bridgeton, N. J.

JACKSON (MAJ. GEN. ANDREW). 10
Memorial of: *Wash* 1820. O 61 a
Elaborate defence of his conduct in Florida.

JACKSON (LE GÉNÉRAL [ANDREW]).
Notice biographique sur: *See* Walsh, Robt., Jr.

JACKSON (GENERAL [ANDREW]). 11
Official records... of the proceedings of the court martial which tried, and the orders of: for shooting the six militia men... *Wash* 1828. O 32 a
—rptd. several times, same yr.

JACKSON (GENERAL [ANDREW]). 12
The presidential election... relating to the Seminole war and the vindication of: By Philo-Jackson. *Frankf & Louisv Ky* 1823–4. O 6 ser.: 35; 28; 48; 54; [8] 24; 47 a
Defends Jackson's Florida invasion and extols his desire to expand national territory to Oregon.

JACKSON (ANDREW) [Kentucky slave]. 13
Narrative... of:... his life while a slave...
Syracuse 1847. D 120 a

JACKSON, FRANCIS 14
A history of the early settlement of Newton...
Massachusetts... *B* 1854. D 556 map port a
—rptd. later in exact facs.

JACKSON, GEORGE 15
Sixty years in Texas... [*Dallas* 1908] O [8] 322 [incl pls] + errata aa
—ed. 2, same impr & date O [10] 384 incl pls a

JACKSON, HALLIDAY 16
Civilization of the Indian natives... conduct of William Penn... *Phil* 1830. O 120 a

JACKSON, H[ENRY] W. R. 17
Confederate monitor and patriot s friend...
Atlanta 1862. D 120 aa

JACKSON, H[ENRY] W. R. 18
Historical register, and Confederate's assistant to national independence... *Augusta Ga* 1862. D 48 aa

JACKSON, H[ENRY] W. R. 19
The southern women of the second American revolution... *Atlanta* 1863. O 120 [2] aa

[JACKSON, ISAAC R.?] 20
A sketch of the life and public services of William Henry Harrison. *N Y* 1836. O 32 a
—rptd. *Phil* 1836. O 36
—other eds.: *Lex* 1836; *N Y* 1839; *Harrisburg* 1840; *Hart* 1840; *Det* 1840.
—anr. ed., with adds., *Columbus* 1840. O 50 a

[JACKSON, JAMES] 21
The letters of Sicilius, to the citizens of Georgia on the... late sale of western lands... [*Augusta*] 1795. O [10 letters] 66 b GaU
—some copies have 11 letters [81. p.]; others, 12 letters [94 p.] b BA

JACKSON (JAMES W.) 22
The life of: the Alexandria hero, the slayer of Ellsworth, the first martyr in the cause of southern independence... *Rich* 1862. O 48 aa

[JACKSON, JONATHAN] 23
Thoughts upon the political situation of the United States... with some observations on the constitution... *Worc* 1788. O 209 a
Attributed also to George R. Minot and to James Sullivan.

JACKSON (JOSEPH H.) 24
A narrative of the adventures... of: in Nauvoo. Disclosing... Mormon villainy *Warsaw, Ill* 1844. D 32 dd ChiH G [all located]

—anr ed. same impr 1846. D 36 b AA Y
—rptd. with historical introduction by Karl Yost. *Morrison, Ill* 1960. D [12] 32 200cops ptd a

JACKSON, MARY A.   **25**
Life and letters of General Thomas J. Jackson ... *N Y* 1892. O [18] 479 5pls a
—enl. ed. "Memoirs of Stonewall Jackson," *Louisv* [1895]. Q [24] 647 pls a

[JACKSON, RICHARD]   **26**
The interest of Great Britain considered, with regard to her colonies ... *L* 1760. O [2] 58 aa
—rptd. Dub 1760. O 46 a
—ed. 2, *L* 1761. O [2] 58
—Am. eds.: *Phil* 1760. O 47; *B* 1760. O 56 [5] aa
Franklin probably helped in preparing this work; the Boston edition names him as author. Written in reply to Townshend, Charles, *Remarks on the Letter addressed to two great men.*

JACKSON, SHADRACH   **27**
Life of Logan Belt ... desperado of southern Illinois ... *Cave-in-Rock* 1888. O 153 a

JACKSON ("STONEWALL").
A biographical sketch. By the author of "Life in the south." *See* Hopley, Cath. C.

JACKSON ("STONEWALL").
A complete biographical sketch of: *See* Hallock, Chas.

JACKSON, (STONEWALL).
The life of: ... By a Virginian. *See* Cooke, John E.

JACKSON (LIEUT. GEN. T. J.)
The life of: By an ex-cadet. *See* McCabe, James D.

JACKSON (STONEWALL).
Sketches of: *See* Hallock, Chas.

JACKSON, W. H., and LONG, S. A., comps.   **28**
The Texas stock directory; or book of marks and brands. Vol.I[all]. *San Antonio* 1865. D 402 [50] + 50 adv-p b G
Supplements covering all Texas counties were planned but that for Victoria Co. was all to appear [same inprint, 1866, 61 p.]

JACKSON, WILLIAM, 1737-1795 ed.
The constitutions of the several independent states. *See* that title, of which it is the second [and best] English edition.

JACKSON, WILLIAM, 1783–1855   **29**
A lecture on rail roads. *B* Crocker & Brewster, 1829. O 32 a
—rptd. *B* Bowen same date. D 36
—eds. 3 & 4, same impr., date & collat.

One of the earliest treatises on the subject, issued prior to the completion of any American railway.

JACKSON COUNTY, ILLINOIS.
Historical sketches of: 1882. *See* Newsome, E.

JACKSON COUNTY, IOWA.
Gazetteer and directory of: ... *See* Owen Publishing Co.

JACOB, J[OHN] G.   **30**
Brook county ... W. Va. *Wellsburg* 1882. D 194 14adv-p aa

JACOB, J[OHN] G.   **31**
The life and times of Patrick Gass ... *Wellsburg Va* 1859. D 280 4pls aa

JACOB, JOHN J.   **32**
A biographical sketch of ... Capt. Michael Cresap. *Cumberland Md* 1826. D 124 b LC N NYP Y
—rptd., with adds., *Cin* 1866. Q 158 [23] some copies issued without the 23p. Boyer "Journal." a
Defense of Cresap from Jefferson's charges against him in the Logan affair.

JACOB, T. O.   **33**
Reminiscences of the Army of Northern Virginia ... *Forsyth Ga* 1871. O 32 + wraps [cov.t. only] aa

JACOB, UDNEY H.   **34**
Extracts from the peacemaker. *Nauvoo* 1842. D 37 c

JACOBS (REV. BELA).   **35**
Memoir of: ... from his letters and journals, by his daughter. *B* 1837. D 305 port a

JACOBS, [REV.] BELA   **36**
A voice from the west ... report of his tour ... *B* 1833. O 28 aa
Visited Ohio, St. Louis, Kaskaskia and Vincennes.

JACOBS (ORANGE).   **37**
Memoirs of: ... incidents of a life of eighty years ... fifty-six ... in Oregon and Washington. *Seattle* 1908. O 234 port a
Went overland to Oregon in 1852.

JACOBS, THOMAS J.   **38**
Scenes ... and adventures in the Pacific ocean ... during the cruise of the Margaret Oakley, under Capt. Benjamin Morrell. *N Y* 1844. D 372 map 4pls aa

JACOTOT, PROSPER   **39**
Voyage d'un ouvrier dans la vallée du Mississippi ... *Dijon* 1888. O 30 a

JACQUEMIN, [NICOLAS]   **40**
Mémoire sur la Louisiane . . . *P* 1803. D [4] 68 aa
First separate publication; originally appeared in a twenty-four volume *Collection de pièces curieuses* . . . 1752.

JAMES, EDWIN [ed.]   **41**
Account of an expedition . . . to the Rocky mountains . . . [exploring the headwaters of the Platte and the courses of the Arkansas and Canadian rivers]. *Phil* 1823. O 2v: [11] 503; [6] 442 [98] + atlas Q 4 2maps chart 8pls b AA N NYP Y
—rptd., ed. Thwaites, *Clev* 1905. O 4v a
—Eng. ed., omitting some scientific data, *L* 1823, O 3v: [7] 344; [7] 356; [7] 347, map chart 8pls b
Notable government expedition [commanded by Maj. Stephen H. Long], supplementing earlier discoveries of Pike and of Lewis and Clark, and pronouncing the plains region as nothing but a desert, incapable of cultivation! The atlas volume of the original edition is dated 1822.

JAMES, EDWIN [ed.]   **42**
Narrative of the captivity and adventures of John Tanner . . . during thirty years' residence . . . [among the Chippewa, Ottawa and Ojibwa tribes], *N Y* 1830. O 426 port b
—Eng. ed. *L* 1830, same collat. aa
—Fr. tr. omitting vocabs. but with add. notes, *P* 1835. O 2v: [44] 355; [4] 416 a
—Ger. tr. omitting vocabs. *Leip* 1840. D [16] 328 a
Minute, vivid, but not altogether trustworthy, account of all phases of Indian life.

JAMES (FRANK).
The trial of: *See* Miller, Geo., Jr.

JAMES, GEORGE W.   **43**
Indian blankets and their makers. *Chi* 1914. O [18] 213 74pls[some col.] a

JAMES, GEORGE W.   **44**
The wonders of the Colorado desert . . . *B* 1906. O 2v: [44] 270; [14] 271–547. 3maps 33pls a
—rptd., same impr. & collat., 1907.
—anr. ed. *B* 1911. O [50] 547 maps & pls

JAMES, J. A. & U. P., pubs.
James's rail road and route book for the western and southern states. *See* Griswold, J.

JAMES (CAPT. JASON W.)   **45**
Memorable events in the life of: [*Roswell, N Mex*? 1911]. D 150 port a
Companion volume to item below, covering boyhood, civil war and ranger activities, ranching, etc.

JAMES, CAPT. JASON W.   **46**
Memoires and viewpoints. *Roswell N M* 1928. D 183 a

Buffalo hunting; ranching on the Rio Grande; with Johnston's Utah expedition in 1858; etc.

JAMES (JESSE, and FRANK).   **47**
The life and daring adventures of: . . . with exploits of the Younger brothers. Written by "one who dares not disclose his identity." *Phil* [1883?]. O 19–96 aa

JAMES, JESSE E.   **48**
Jesse James, my father . . . *Independence Mo* 1899. D 194[incl.ports] a
—rptd. *Clev* [1906]. O 189
Probably ghost-written by A. B. McDonald.

JAMES, THOMAS   **49**
Three years among the Indians and Mexicans. *Waterloo Ill* 1846. O [4] 130 dd G MoH Y
—rptd. with notes by Walter B. Douglas. *St L* 1916. O [4] 316 + adv-p map 12pls aa 365cops ptd
—anr ed. *Chi* 1953. 16° [38 incl front & facs] 297 [incl 2maps and 2 pls] a
One of the earliest narratives of the fur-trade; covering experiences on the upper Missouri, in 1809, and an expedition to Santa Fe, in 1821. Written from James' dictation by Nathan Niles, who, resenting local newspaper criticism, destroyed nearly all copies.

[JAMES, THOMAS H.]   **50**
Rambles in the United States [etc.], with a short account of Oregon . . . *L* Clarke 1846. D [8] 259 pl a
—anr. issue, pub. Ollivier, same collat. & date.
—ed. 2, *L* Ollivier 1847. same collat.
This Republic portrayed as "a living falsehood," its citizens "gasconading boasters," its future "inevitable ruin."

JAMES, U[RIAH] P. [comp.]
River guide . . . *See* Cumings, Sam'l.

JAMES, W[ILL] S.   **51**
Cowboy life in Texas. *Chi* 1893. D [2] 9–213 [incl.pls] aa
—anr. issue, [probably the first] "27 years a mavrick[sic], or life on a Texas range," *Chi* n.d. [1893]. a
—rptd. same impr. [1898], with fewer ills.

JAMES, WILLIAM   **52**
A full . . . account of the military occurrences of the late war between Great Britain and the United States. *L* 1818. O 2v: [32] 476; [2] 582 [16]. 4maps a

JAMES, WILLIAM   **53**
An inquiry into the merits of the . . . naval actions, between Great-Britain and the United States . . . *Halifax Canada* 1816. O [6] 102 3tabs aa
—expanded ed. "A full . . . account of the . . . naval occurrences . . .," *L* 1817. O [16] 528 216 [16] 3pls a
—anr ed. *L* 1818. O 2v

JAMES, WILLIAM D.   54
A sketch of the life of Brig.-Gen. Francis Marion
. . . *Charleston S C* 1821. O 182 [39] b NYP Y
—rptd. *Marietta Ga* 1948. O same collat a

JAMES, WILL[IAM R.]   55
Cowboys north and south. *N Y* 1924. O [18 incl
front] 217 [incl pls] a
First and best of his many books.

JAMESON, MRS. [ANNA B.]   55a
Winter studies and summer rambles . . . *L* 1838.
D 3v: [14] 315; [6] 341; [6] 356 a
—Am. ed. *N Y* 1839. D 2v: [10] 9–341; [4] 339
—Ger. tr. *Braunschweig* 1839. D 3v:
Almost half of this work is devoted to the
authoress' travels through Michigan.

JAMIESON, MILTON   56
Journal and notes of a campaign in Mexico . . .
Cin 1849. O 105 errata lf b LC

JAMISON, JAMES C.   57
With Walker in Nicaragua; or reminiscences of
an officer of the American plalanx. *Columbia Mo*
1909. O 181 3ports a
Best eye-witness account of Walker's bid for
empire, by one of his most dependable officers.

JAMISON, MATTHEW H.   58
Recollections of pioneer and army life [including
trip to Pike's peak]. *KC* [1911]. O [8] 7–363 front a

JANESVILLE CITY DIRECTORY . . .
1859–60
See Brigham, Alasco D.

JANSON, CHARLES W.   59
The stranger in America . . . observations made
during a long residence in that country . . . *L* 1807.
Q [22] incl eng-t 500 + 6adv-p plan 9col pls b AA
N Also issued with tinted pls aa
—rptd. *N Y* 1935. O [30] 502 [2] pls a
Petulant view of U.S. life.

JAQUES, MRS. MARY J.   60
Texan ranch life . . . *L* 1894. O [12] 363 12pls aa

JAQUITH (JAMES).   65
The history of: . . . n.p. [1818]. O 32 aa
—ed. 3, n.p. 1830. O 36 aa
—ed. 4, n.p. 1831. O 34 a
Includes his adventures as a schoolteacher in
Kentucky and Indiana.

JARDINE, L. J.   66
A letter from Pennsylvania to a friend in Eng-
land: containing . . . information with respect to
America. *Bath Eng* 1795. O [4] 31 aa
Recommends Pennsylvania above all.

JARVIS, N[ATHAN] S.   67
An army surgeon's notes of frontier service,
1833–48. [Repr. from "Journal of Service Institution."] n.p. [1907?]. O 8 12 12 10 20 16 fold.map
capt.t.only a

[JARVIS, RUSSELL]   68
A biographical notice of Com. Jesse D. Elliot
. . . *Phil* 1835. D 480 a
Defends Elliott's conduct as Perry's second in
command at the battle of Lake Erie.

JARVIS, SAMUEL F.   69
A discourse on the religion of the Indian tribes
. . . *N Y* 1820. O 111[incl.tab] a

JAY, JOHN   70
Correspondence . . . Ed. by H. P. Johnston. *N Y*
[1890–93]. O 4v: [24] 461; [14] 452; [26] 489; [22]
532. a 750sets ptd.

JAY'S (MR. [JOHN]) TREATY.
Features of: *See* Dallas, Alex. J.

JAY, WILLIAM   71
Life of John Jay . . . *N Y* 1833. O 2v: [8] 520;
[4] 502. port a

JEFFERSON, H. E.   72
Oklahoma: the beautiful land . . . *Chi* 1889. D
[4] 9–202 a

JEFFERSON, T. H.   73
Accompaniment to the map of the emigrant
road from Independence to San Francisco . . .
N Y 1849. D 11 map[on 4sheets] dd N Pn [only
cops loc]
—rptd. [*S F* 1945]. O 25 map[on 4sheets] aa 300
copies ptd.

JEFFERSON, THOMAS   74
An appendix to the Notes on Virginia relative to
the murder of Logan's family. *Phil* 1800. O 51
map aa
—ed. 2 [with Sappington's testimony added]. O 58
map aa

JEFFERSON (THOMAS).
Defence of the character of: . . . By a Virginian.
See Tucker, Geo.

JEFFERSON (THOMAS).
A defence of the measures of the administration
of: By Curtius. *See* Taylor, John, of Va.

JEFFERSON (THOMAS) and   75
CABELL (JOSEPH C.)
Early history of the University of Virginia, as
contained in the letters of: . . . *Rich* 1856. O [36]
528 a

JEFFERSON AND MADISON. 76

A letter, containing ... observations on mankind and the ... administrations of: By a farmer. *Morris-Town* 1810. D 37 a

JEFFERSON (THOMAS). 77

A letter to: ... By Junius Philaenus. *N Y* 1802. O 64 a

Probably by the printer, P. R. Johnson

JEFFERSON (THE HON. THOMAS).

Memoirs of: ... *See* Carpenter, Stephen C.

[JEFFERSON, THOMAS] 78

Notes on ... Virginia. [*P*] 1782 [ptd 1785]. O [2] 391 fold tab c JCB N NYP 200 copies ptd: from a few p52–54 were replaced with new sheets giving changed text beginning on p52, line 8: "A second opinion, etc."; to other copies was added, from time to time, one, two or three appendices,— on a Va. constitution, on a money unit, on religious freedom—which give additional value to copies containing them. Original uncorrected copies have p.51–4, 167–8, 181–2, & 183–4 in uncancelled state. c
—Fr. tr. and 1st pub'd ed., "Observations sur la Virginie," *P* 1786. O [12] 390 + 2 errata lists[one covering $^1/_4$ p, the other $2^1/_2$ p] fold map[eng. by Neele] tab aa
—Eng. ed. and 1st pub'd ed. in that language, *L* 1787. O [4] 382 map tab aa
—Am. ed.: *Phil* 1788. O [4] 244 fold sheet aa
—Am. ed. 2, *Phil* 1788. O [4] 336 a
—rptd. 1792. a
—anr. ed. 2, *Phil* 1794. O [4] 336 map & tab
—anr. ed. *Balt* 1800. O 194 [2] 53 + tab
—rptd. same year, with add. of 21p on Jefferson's religious principles
—other eds. [all 1801, and all with map & port]: *N Y* O 392 port map tab; *Newark*; *B*
—anr. ed. [with Jefferson's corrections on Logan affair], *Phil* 1801. O [4] 436 56 map port view a
—later eds.: *B* 1802; *Trenton* 1803 [1st ed. announcing app. on t-p]; *N Y* 1804; *Phil* 1812; *Trenton* 1812; *Phil* 1815; *Phil* 1825; *B* 1829; *B* 1832.
—best. ed. [with adds. incl. author's corrections intended for an ed. never pub'd] *Rich* 1853. O [8] 275 map 4pls on 3 sheets fold sheet a
—Ger. ed. "Beschreibung von Virginien," *Leip* 1789.

JEFFERSON'S (MR.) NOTES ON VIRGINIA.

Observations upon certain passages in: *See* Rogers, Nicholas.

JEFFERSON (THOMAS).

The pretensions of: to the Presidency examined ... *See* Smith, Wm. L.

[JEFFERSON, THOMAS] 79

A summary view of the rights of British America

... By a native [etc.]. *Williamsbg* Rind [1774]. D 23 b NYH PhilL
—rptd. *Phil* 1774 aa; *Bklyn* 1892; *N Y* 1943 a
—Eng. ed., with adds., *L* 1774. Q [16] 5–44 a

Submitted to the Virginia convention with the idea of its being sent as a petition to the King; it was deemed too strong to be sent, but some copies were printed by members.

[JEFFERYS, THOMAS] 80

The conduct of the French with regard to Nova Scotia ... *L* 1754. O [2] 77 aa
—Fr. tr. *L* 1755. D [16] 281 a

Contains much on the other British colonies in America.

JEFFERYS, THOMAS, eng. 81

A general topography of North America ... *L* Sayer & Jefferys 1768. F [4] 93maps b
—re-issued, "The American atlas ...," *L* Sayer & Bennet 1775. F [4] 30maps[on 49 sheets] b Y
—other eds.: *L* Sayer 1776. F [4] 30maps [on 49sheets] b H NYP SeattleP Y; *L* Sayer & Bennet 1778. same collat.; *L* 1782. b
—Fr. ed. "Atlas amériquain septentrional," *P* 1778. F 26maps pl b

Number of maps varies; some English editions have thirty maps on forty sheets.

[JEFFERYS, THOMAS]? 82

The great probability of a north west passage; deduced from observations on the letter of Admiral de Fonte ... *L* 1768. Q [24] 154 3maps b N NYP OreH Y

Ascribed also to Theodore S. Drage [or Swindrage]. The authenticity of Fonte's Spanish voyage to the northwest coast is as questionable as the earlier one by Maldonado, but led to great exploring activity in that region by English, French and Spanish.

JEFFERYS, THOMAS 83

The natural and civil history of the French dominions in ... America ... *L* 1760. F 2pts in 1: [8] 168; [4] 246 + duplicate starred p. 129–138 in pt.I 18maps & plans correction slip at p.80, pt.2 b AA MH N NYP Y
—rptd., same collat., *L* 1761. b

Additional information concerning the capture of Quebec, received after printing Part I, necessitated the insertion of the starred duplicate pages.

[JEFFERYS, THOMAS] eng. 84

The North-American pilot ... Pt.I[for Newfoundland, etc.], Pt.II [for New England, New York, etc.]. *L* Sayer & Bennett 1775. F 2v: [8]; [2]. 35maps b
—rptd., same impr. & collat. 1777–8. b
—other Eng. eds.: *L* 1799; 1783; 1784; 1789; 1795. aa

—new ed. *L* Laurie & Whittle 1799–1800. F 2v: [2]; [6]. 45maps aa
—rptd. 1806–09. a
—Fr. tr. "Pilote américain," *P* 1778. F [4] eng.t. 20maps aa
—rptd. *P* [1792]. a

JEFFERYS, THOMAS
Voyages from Asia to America . . . *See* under Müller, Gerhard F., *Nachrichten von Seereisen* . . .

[JEFFREY, J. K.]   85
The Territory of Wyoming; its history [etc.]. *Laramie* 1874. O 84 [incl front wrap] b AA Hn NYP Y
First book printed at Laramie.

JEFFRIES, EWEL   86
A short biography of John Leeth . . . his travels and sufferings among the Indians . . . *Lancaster O* 1831. D 33 dd WisH WRH [only copies known]
—rptd., ed. Butterfield, *Cin* 1883. O 90 + 8adv-p a 143 copies ptd; ed. Thwaites, *Clec* 1904. O 70 a
Captured by Delaware Indians in Ohio in 1772, during Dunmore's war, Leeth remained in captivity until 1790.

JEFFRIES (T[HOMAS] F.)   87
The book of sunshine; or the life and travels of: . . . through Virginia . . . [to Ark., Mo., Kas. & Neb.]. *Balt* 1861. D 177 aa

JEMISON (MRS. MARY).
A narrative of the life of: *See* Seaver, James E.

[JENINGS, EDMUND]   88
A plan for settling the unhappy dispute between Great Britain and her colonies . . . *L* 1775. D 16 b
—ed. 2, n.p. 1776. D 26 b JCB NYP

[JENINGS, EDMUND]   89
A translation of the Memorial to the sovereigns of Europe upon the present state of affairs, between the old and the new world . . . *L* 1781. O [2] 45 aa
—Fr. ed. "Pensées sur la revolution de l'Amérique-Unie . . .," *Amst* [1780]. O [22] 50 aa
—rptd. same impr. [1781]. O [18] 52 a

JENKINS, A. O.   90
The Olives' last round up. [*Loup City, Neb.* 1930] D 81 aa
Cattle rustlers and murderers in Texas, Nebraska and Colorado.

[JENKINS, GRIFFIN]   91
A brief vindication of the purchassors against the proprietors, in a Christian manner. *N Y* 1745–6. D [11] 37 c Hn NYP [of 3copies located]
Relates to the New York-New Jersey boundary dispute and land-titles in the Newark region.

JENKINS, H. M.   92
Historical collections relating to Gwynedd . . . Montgomery county [Pa.]. *Phil* 1884. O 400 12pls a

JENKINS (JAMES).   93
Autobiography of: *Oshkosh* 1889. O [4] 7–110 a
Includes accounts of trading voyages along the California coast, in the thirties.

JENKINS, JEFF   94
The northern tier, or, life among the homestead settlers. *Topeka* 1880. D 205 aa

JENKINS, THOMAS J.   95
Six seasons on our prairies and six weeks in our Rockies . . . *Louisv* 1884. D 218 [2] aa

JENKINS, WARREN   96
The Ohio gazetteer . . . First revised edition. *Columbus* [1837]. D [24] 51–546 map a
—other eds., same impr.: 1839. same collat.; 1841. D [24] 51–578 map
Intended as a continuation of John Kilbourne's *Ohio gazetteer*, the 1833 edition of which had been revised anonymously by Jenkins.

JENKS, J. W. P.   97
Hunting in Florida in 1874. n.p. [1884?]. O 70 fold.map a

JENNESS, JOHN S.   98
Notes on the first planting of New Hampshire . . . *Portsmouth* 1878. O 91 2maps a

JENNINGS, DAVID
An abridgment of the Life of . . . Cotton Mather. *See* Mather, Samuel, *The life of . . . Cotton Mather.*

JENNINGS, LOUIS J.   99
Eighty years of republican government in the United States. *L* 1868. D [16] 288 a
—ed. 2, same impr., date & collat.
—Am. ed. *N Y* 1868. same collat.

JENNINGS, N[APOLEON] A.   100
A Texas ranger. *N Y* 1899. D [12] 321 aa
—rptd. *Dallas* [1930]. D 287 a
—anr ed *Austin* [1959] D [12 incl front] 321 3pls a

JENNINGS, SAMUEL   101
The state of the case . . . betwixt the . . . Quakers, in Pennsilvania . . . and George Keith . . . *L* 1694. D [6] 80 b

JENSEN, J. MARINUS   102
Early history of Provo, Utah [*Provo*] 1924. O 414 a

[JENYNS, SOAME]   103
The objections to the taxation of our American

299

colonies . . . briefly considered. *L* 1765. Q 20 aa
—ed. 2, same impr. & date. Q 23 a
For reply *see* Otis, James; *Rights of British colonies.*

JEROME, CHAUNCEY   104
History of the American clock business . . . *N Hav* 1860. D 144[incl. port] a

JERVEY, THEODORE D.   105
Robert Y. Hayne and his times. *N Y* 1909. O [20] 555 a

JESUIT   106
[Jesuit Relations]. Original French editions issued annually by Cramoisy at Paris, in duodecimo form, 1633–1673. Those published after 1654, having more U.S. interest, are listed below, with no attempt at discriminating between variant issues.
—for 1653–54, by Le Mercier. 1655. [4] 176 Le Moine's trip to Iroquois country. b Hn MinnU N
—for 1655–56, by de Quen. 1657. [6] 168 Missionary visits to northern N.Y. b Hn MinnU N
—for 1656–57, by Le Jeune. 1658. [12] 211 Iroquois missions. b Hn MinnU N
—for 1657—58, by Ragueneau. 1659. [8] 136 One of the rarest of the series. d Hn JCB N
—for 1660–61, by Le Jeune. 1662. [8] 213 [3] Iroquois affairs. b H Hn N
+for 1661–62, by Lalemant. 1663. [8] 118 [2] Indian customs. b Hn MinnU N
—for 1662–63, by Lalemant. 1664. [16] 170 Iroquois hostilities. The only volume of this series with $^1/_2$–t. c Hn MinnU N
—for 1663–64, by Lalemant. 1665. [8] 176 Iroquois troubles. b Hn MinnU N
—for 1664–65, by Le Mercier. 1666. [12] 128 plan. Iroquois affairs. b Hn MinnU N
—for 1665–66, by Le Mercier. 1667. [8] 48 [16] Expedition against Mohawks. b Hn MinnU
—for 1666–67, by Le Mercier. 1668. [8] 160 Mission of Allouez to Lake Superior region. b Hn MinnU
—for 1668–69, 1670. [2] 150 Iroquois missions b Hn MinnU
—for 1669–70, by Le Mercier. 1671. 102 blank lf before and after pagination. Letters from Green Bay, Sault Ste. Marie and the Illinois country. c Hn MinnU N
—for 1670–71, by Dablon. 1672. [16] 192 map [first one showing Lake Superior]. c Hn MinnU N
—for 1671–72, by Dablon. 1673. [16] 264 map [same as in preceding vol] c Hn MinnU N

Jesuit Relations and allied documents . . .   107
Ed by R. G. Thwaites. *Clev* 1896–1901. O 73v. maps pls 750sets ptd d
—rptd. *N Y* 1959. O 73v bound in 36v maps pls c
A monumental editorial achievement. Contains all reports, official and unofficial, made by members of this missionary order, on their activities in

North America from 1601 to 1791. In all, 238 pieces are given in their original French, Latin and Italian texts, with English translations.
For other collected editions see Martin and de Montezon, *Relations des Jesuites* and Rochemonteix, Camille de.

JEVNE and ALMINI [pubs.]   108
Chicago illustrated. *Chi* 1866–7. obl. F 52lvs of letter press 52tinted pls d ChiH G LC NYP
Originally issued in 13parts.

JEWELL, HORACE   109
History of Methodism in Arkansas. *Little Rock* 1892. O [16] 445 a

JEWELL, M. H. [pub.]   110
. . . first annual directory of the city of Bismarck, Dakota . . . with a review of early frontier life . . . *Bismarck* 1879. D 144[incl. prelim. lf of adv.] b G Hn NDH
—anr. issue with unnumb lf between p. 40 and 41 and photo. view of Bismarck pasted on inside cover. b NDH
First non-legal book printed in North Dakota.

JEWITT, JOHN R.   111
Journal kept at Nootka sound . . . *B* 1807. 16° 48 b
—rptd. *N Y* 1812. a
—anr. ed. *B* 1931. 16° front. 100copies ptd.
First printed account of a remarkable captivity among natives of the Northwest coast. For a later account, based on this *Journal*, but so amplified as to be considered a different book, *see* Alsop, Richard.

JOBLIN, M[AURICE] and Co., pubs.   112
Cincinnati past and present; or its industrial history . . . in the life-labors of its leading men. *Cin* 1872. Q 433 127actual photos aa

JOBLIN, M[AURICE] and Co., pubs.   113
Cleveland [Ohio], past and present . . . sketches of pioneer settlers . . . *Clev* 1866 O [6] 500 3views 81 ports[all actual photos] aa
—rptd. 1869 same collat a

JOBLIN, M[AURICE] and Co., pubs.   114
Louisville past and present . . . *Louisv* 1875. Q [4] 357 54ports [actual photos] aa

JOCKNICK, SIDNEY   115
Early days on the western slope of Colorado . . . *Denver* 1913. D 384 + inserted typed lf at p322 25pls aa

[JÖRG, EDUARD]   116
Briefe aus den Vereinigten Staaten [written from a German settlement at Highland, Ill.] *Leip* 1853. D 2v in 1: [8] 274; [8] 358 a

JOGUES, ISAAC   **117**
Narrative of a captivity among the Mohawk Indians, a description of New Netherland in 1642–3, and other papers. Ed., with memoir of Jogues, by John G. Shea. *N Y* 1856. O 69 a
—rptd. 1857.
First printing of four letters written in 1643 and 1644. Issued also in *New York Historical Collections*, series 2, volume 3, pages 173–219. Jogues returned as a missionary to these Indians and met martyrdom at their hands.

JOGUES, ISAAC   **118**
Novum Belgium: description de Nieuw Netherland. *N Y* 1862. O 44 map a 100 copies ptd
—Eng. tr. by John G. Shea + Fr. text, *N Y* 1862. Q [2] 54 map view 2ports 4 l. of facs 100copies ptd.
First printing of a 1646 manuscript. One of the earliest descriptions of New York City.

JOHANET, EDMOND   **119**
Un Francais dans la Floride . . . *Tours* 1889. O 240 a

JOHANNOT? [JOHANNOT?]
See **JOHONNET, JACKSON**

JOHNS, JAMES   **120**
A brief sketch . . . of . . . Huntington [Vt.]. *Huntington* 1861. D 44 aa

JOHNS (MRS. JANE).
A narrative of the life and sufferings of: *See* Welch, Andrew.

[JOHNSON, A. S.?]   **121**
Memoirs of a nullifier . . . *Columbia S C* 1832. O [2] 110 aa some cops on L.P.
—anr. ed., with adds., *N Y* 1860. D
Ascribed also to Dr. Thomas Cooper.

[JOHNSON, ADAM R.]   **122**
The partisan rangers of the Confederate . . . army. *Louisv* 1904. O [14] 476 65pls a
Includes his adventures in West Texas from 1854 to 1860 as Indian fighter, surveyor and overland mail agent, as well as the cavalry operations of his Confederate brigade.

JOHNSON, ALLEN   **123**
Stephen A. Douglas . . . *N Y* 1908. O [10] 503 a

JOHNSON, AMANDUS   **124**
The Swedish settlements on the Delaware, 1638–1664. [*Phil*] 1911. O 2v: [20] 466; [12] 467–880. 6maps 88pls aa
—rptd. in one vol. *Phil* 1915 a

[JOHNSON, ANNA C.]   **125**
The Iroquois . . . *N Y* 1855. D 317 8pls a

JOHNSON, BENJAMIN F.   **126**
Why the "Latter Day Saints" marry a plurality of wives . . . answer to an attack . . . *S F* 1854. O 23 aa

JOHNSON, CAPT. CHARLES   **127**
A general history of the robberies . . . of the most notorious pyrates . . . *L* Rivington 1724. O [22] 17–320 3pls aa
—ed. 2, enl., "A general history of the pyrates . . .," *L* Warner 1724. O [20] 17–427 3pls aa
—rptd. *Dub* 1725. D [8] 248 front. a
—ed. 3, with v.2 added, *L* 1725–[1726]. O 2v: [20] 17–427 + 18p between p416–417; [14] 413 + 3adv-p 3pls fold.map [in v.2 of some copies] b
—ed. 4, *L* 1726. same collat. b
—rptd. *L* 1727. b
—anr. ed. *L* 1734. F [2] 486 26pls b
—rptd., same impr. & collat., 1736 aa
—Dutch tr. *Amst* 1725. O 2v 7pls aa
—Fr. tr. *Utrecht* 1725. D 315; *L* 1726. D [56] 382 [2] aa
Author's name said to be a pseudonym for Daniel Defoe. For a condensation, *see History and lives of . . . notorious pirates.*

JOHNSON, C[HARLES] B.   **128**
Letters from the British settlement in Pennsylvania . . . *Phil* 1819. 16° [12] 25–192 map aa
—rptd. "Letters from North America," *Phil* 1821. D [12] 185 map a
—Eng. ed. *L* 1819. 16° 186 + 6adv-p map
Written to discourage emigration to Birkbeck's "fever prairies" or to other trans-Alleghany colonies.

JOHNSON, CHARLES G.   **129**
The Territory of Arizona . . . history . . . *S F* 1869. F 3pts[paged continuously] 32 3mounted photos b B Hn S

JOHNSON, DON CARLOS   **130**
A brief history of Springville, Utah . . . *Springville* 1900. O [6] 124 errata 1f front. aa

[JOHNSON, EDWARD]   **131**
A history of New-England . . . 1628-1652. *L* 1654. smQ [4] 240 c AA JCB N
—rptd. *Andover* 1867. O front 260 cops ptd [50 on L.P.] a
First general history of this colony. Has been erroneously attributed to Thos. Hooker. Unsold sheets of the original edition were used by the publisher to form the third part of *America painted to the life*, by Gorges, *q.v.*

JOHNSON, EDWIN F.   **132**
Navigation of the lakes . . . to the seaboard and to the Mississippi, and relation of the former to the lines of railway . . . to the Pacific. *Hart* 1866. O 48 a

JOHNSON, EDWIN F. 133
Railroad to the Pacific . . . *N Y* 1854. O 166
2maps 8pls a
First edition in book form, but styles itself 2nd
edition, having previously appeared in a periodical. Favors the Northern route and predicts a great
future for the Columbia River region.

JOHNSON, ELIAS 134
Legends . . . of the Iroquois . . . and history of
the Tuscarora Indians. *Lockport N Y* 1881. O 234
[incl.front.] a

JOHNSON, GEORGE W. 135
Jottings by the way . . . *St George Utah* 1882.
16° 64 b Y
Mostly rhymed Mormon history, but with
prose autobiography.

JOHNSON (SIR JOHN). 136
Orderly book of: during the Oriskany campaign.
1776–7. Ed. W. L. Stone. *Alb* 1882. Q [60] 130 [4]
139–256 [2] 257–273 a

JOHNSON, JOHN, Indian agent 137
Recollections of sixty years. *Dayton* 1915. O
78 a

JOHNSON, JOHN, 1829–1907 138
The defense of Charleston harbor . . . 1863–5.
Charleston 1890. O 2v in 1: 276; 176. 48maps &
pls a

JOHNSON (JOHN W.) 139
Life of: *Biddeford* 1861. 16° 152 b
Includes his Indian captivity.

JOHNSON, JOSEPH 140
Traditions and reminiscences of the . . . revolution in the south . . . *Charleston S C* 1851. O [8]
592 3maps pl aa

JOHNSON, MRS. LAURA W. 141
Eight hundred miles in an ambulance. *Phil* 1889.
D 131 a
Life in Wyoming army posts and Indian agen-
cies.

JOHNSON. OVERTON, and WINTER, 142
WILLIAM H.
Route across the Rocky mountains . . . *Lafayette Ind* 1846. O 152 d N Pn Y
—rptd. *Princeton* 1932. D a
Describes the 1843 Oregon migration, the Oregon region and California. In historical importance
one of the greatest of early overland narratives.
Error in chapter heading [p. 26, line 3] corrected.

JOHNSON, PHIL
Life on the plains . . . *See* Post, Chas. C., *Ten
years a cowboy.*

[JOHNSON, REVERDY] 143
Remarks on popular sovereignty, as maintained
and denied respectively by Judge Douglas, and
Attorney-General Black. *Balt* 1859. O 40 a

JOHNSON, R[OBERT] G. 144
A historical account of the first settlement of
Salem in West Jersey . . . *Phil* 1839. 18° 173 a
First local history of this state.

JOHNSON, ROBERT U., and 145
BUELL, CLARENCE C., eds.
Battles and leaders of the civil war . . . by Union
and Confederate officers. *N Y* Century [1887– 9].
Q 4v: [24] 750; [20] 760; [20] 752; [20] 829 [pagi-
nat. of each vol. includes front. & initial blank
lf] aa
—rptd. *N Y* 1956, O 4v maps pls
Original "subscriber's edition" was in thirty-
two parts.

[JOHNSON, SAMUEL] 146
The false alarm. *L* Cadell 1770. O 53 a
—ed. 2, same impr., date & collat.
For replies to this defense of the Ministry, *see
The constitution defended*; *see* also *Johnson,
Samuel. A letter to:*

[JOHNSON, SAMUEL] 147
Hypocrisy unmasked; or, a short inquiry into
the religious complaints of our American colonies
. . . *L* 1776. D 24 aa
—eds. 2 & 3, same impr., date & collat. a
Defends the Quebec Bill against colonial objections.

JOHNSON (SAMUEL). 148
A letter to: *L* 1770. O 54 a
Refutation of Johnson's *The false alarm.*

JOHNSON (DR. SAMUEL).
A letter to: . . . *L* 1775. *See* Towers, Jos.

[JOHNSON, SAMUEL] 149
Taxation no tyranny; an answer to the Resolutions and address of the American congress. *L*
1775. O [4] 91 + blank lf aa
—eds. 2, 3 & 4. same impr., date & collat. a

JOHNSON (SAMUEL). 150
Taxation tyranny. Adressed to: *L* 1775. O
80 aa

JOHNSON, SIDNEY S. 151
Some biographies of old settlers . . . Vol.I [all].
Tyler Tex 1900. O 400 a

JOHNSON, SID[NEY] S. 152
Texans who wore the gray. Vol I [all] n.p., n.d.
O 407 a

JOHNSON (MRS. SUSANNAH). 153
A narrative of the captivity of: *Walpole N H*
1796. D 144 b N NYP AA
—ed. 2, *Windsor Vt* 1807. same collat. a
—ed. 3, enl., *Windsor* 1814. D 178
—other Am. eds.: *Lowell* 1834. 16° 150; *N Y* 1841.
16°; and others.
—Eng. eds., variant titles: *Glasg* 1797. D 72; *Newcastle* [1797]. same collat.; *Ayr* 1802. D 24 aa
Captured by Indians in New Hampshire, in
1754, she spent four years, in their hands and in
those of the French, before regaining her freedom.

JOHNSON, THEODORE T. 154
Sights in the gold region and scenes by the way.
N Y 1849. D [12] 278 aa
—ed. 2, enl. *N Y* 1850. D [12] 324 map 7pls a
—ed. 3, with app. of Oregon material and new t.
"California and Oregon, or sights in the gold
region [etc.]," *Phil* 1851. D [12] + 24adv-p map
6pls aa
—ed. 4, *Phil* 1853. same collat 6pls but no map
[though t-p calls for one] a
—rptd.: still as ed.4, *Phil* 1854. 1pl no map; same
1857; again 1865. a
—Eng. ed. *Dub* 1850. D 308 a
One of the earlier accounts of the gold fields.
The 3rd, and best, edition contains Thurston's information on the emigrant trail to Oregon and
particulars of the march to Oregon made in 1849,
by the Mounted Rifles.

JOHNSON (SIR WILLIAM) 155
An account of conferences . . . between: and the
chief sachems . . . of the Mohawks, Oneidas . . .
L 1756. O [14] 3–77 b N JCB NYP
Held with the object of restraining the Six Nations from participating with western tribes in
French-inspired attacks on Pennsylvania and Virginia settlements.

JOHNSON, WILLIAM 156
Sketches of the life . . . of Nathanael Greene . . .
Charleston S C 1822. Q 2v: [12] 516; [2] 476
[1] + 11p Appendix[not in all copies] port map
7plans aa

JOHNSON, W[ILLIAM] A. 157
The history of Anderson county, Kansas. [*Garnett*] 1877. O 289 a

JOHNSTON (CHARLES). 158
A narrative of the incidents attending the capture . . . of: *N Y* 1827. D 264 a

JOHNSTON, DAVID E. 159
Four years a soldier. *Princeton W Va* 1887. D
447 a
—rptd. "The story of a Confederate boy . . .,"
[*Port Ore* 1914]. D [14] 379 pls

JOHNSTON, DAVID E. 160
A history of the Middle River new settlements
. . . *Huntington, W. Va.* 1906. O 500 [31] a

JOHNSTON, MRS. ELIZABETH 161
Recollections of a Georgia loyalist. Ed. A. W.
Eaton. *N Y* 1901. D 224 7pls a

[JOHNSTON, F., and HAMILTON, 162
W.] eds.
The Washingtoniana; containing a sketch of
[his] life . . . *Lancaster* 1802. O 320 [78] blank 1f
401–441 port a

JOHNSTON, F[REDERICK] 163
Memorials of old Virginia clerks . . . *Lynchburg*
1888. D 405 [20] 3ports a

JOHNSTON, GEORGE 164
History of Cecil county, Maryland . . . *Elkton*
1881. O [12] 548 [12] fold-map aa

JOHNSTON, JAMES F. W. 165
Notes on North America . . . *Edin* 1851. D 2v:
[16] 415; [12] 512. map a
—Am. ed. [from Eng. sheets], *B* 1851. same collat.

JOHNSTON (GENERAL JOSEPH E.). 166
Correspondence between the President [Davis]
and: . . . *Rich* 1864. O 64 a

JOHNSTON, JOSEPH E. 167
Narrative of military operations . . . *N Y* 1874.
O 602 + 6adv-p 6maps 15pls a

JOHNSTON (JOSEPH E.) and 168
BEAUREGARD (G. T.)
Official reports of: on the battle of Manassas . . .
Rich 1862. O 144 aa
—anr iss, same impr and date O 115 aa

JOHNSTON, JOSEPH E. 169
Report of his operations in the department of
Mississippi and East Louisiana . . . *Rich* 1864. O
213 a

JOHNSTON (JOSEPH E.) et al. 170
Reports of the Secretary of War, with reconnaissances of routes from San Antonio to El Paso, by:
. . . [Sen. Exec. Doc. 64]. *Wash* 1850. O 250 2maps
72pls]nos 2, 21 & 39 not issued]. aa
Contains, among other reports, R. B. Marcy's
[on his route from Ft. Smith to Santa Fe] and J. H.
Simpson's [on his Navajo country expedition],
q.v. for separate printings.

JOHNSTON, JOSIAH S. [ed.] 171
First explorations of Kentucky . . . *Louisv* Filson
Club 1898. Q [22] 222 2pls map a
First complete printing of Thomas Walker's
1750 journal; also Gist's 1751 journal.

[JOHNSTON, RICHARD M.]   172
Georgia sketches . . . [*Augusta Ga*] 1864. O 114
aa only 3cops loc.

JOHNSTON, WILLIAM G.   173
Experiences of a forty-niner . . . *Pitt* 1892. O 390
port 13pls [some copies contain a blue-print map
and an extra port., both issued later for insertion]
b N Y small ed. ptd.
—rptd. "Overland to California . . .," *Oakland*
1948. Q map a
Overland narrative, in diary form, of the first
emigrant train entering California in 1849.

JOHNSTON, WILLIAM J.   174
Sketches of the history of Stephenson county,
Ill . . . *Freeport* 1854. D 102 aa
Second Illinois county history.

JOHNSTON, WILLIAM P.   175
The life of Gen. Albert Sidney Johnston . . .
N Y 1878. O [18] 755 + 4adv-p port 8 pls a

JOHONNET [JOHONNOT] (JACKSON).   176
The remarkable adventures of: . . . who served
. . . in the expedition under General Harmar . . .
Containing . . . his captivity, sufferings, and escape
from the Kickapoo Indians. *B* 1793. O 16 b
—other 1793 eds. [among which no priority is
established]: *Keene* D 12; *Newburyport* D 12;
Newburyport O 30; *Prov* O 15; *Windsor* O 16;
Concord aa
—rptd.: *Walpole* 1795. D 12; *Salem* 1802. O 20;
anr. *Salem* ed. n.d. [1802]. O 20; *Greenfield* 1816.
D 24 aa
Flimsy conjectures of a Lexington Kentucky
edition of 1791 may be dismissed, but this dubious
narrative occupied eight pages of Beer's 36-page
Almanac, Hartford [1792], which may be reckoned
its first appearance in book form.

JOLIET, ILLINOIS.   177
Progress, resources . . . of . . . : *Joliet* 1856. O
40 aa

JOLLIVET, [ADOLPHE]   178
Documents Américai· s. Annexion du Texas
[etc.]. *P* 1845. O 40 aa
—[ser. 2] "Annexion du Texas. Nouveaux documents Américains," *P* 1845. O 55 a
—[ser.3] "Documents Américains. Les États-Unis
. . . et l'Angleterre [etc.]," *P* 1845. O 74 a

JOLLIVET, [ADOLPHE]   179
Plan de colonization [au Texas] . . . *P* 1842.
O 32 aa

JOLY DE ST. VALIER [le sieur]   180
Exposé ou examen des operations des ministres
en Angleterre depuis le commencement de la

guerre contre les Américains jusqu'ici . . . *L* n.d.
Q [4] 59 aa
—rptd. *L* 1781. D 82 aa
—Eng. tr. *L* 1781. O [8] 111 aa

JOLY DE ST. VALIER [le sieur]   181
Exposé ou examen . . . [Pt.2 of above]. *Amst*
1781. O [10] 52 aa
This French officer offered his services to the
British and retaliated, for being snubbed, by these
vindictive attacks. His books were banned and he
himself imprisoned for some time.

JOLY DE ST. VALIER [le sieur]   182
Histoire raisonnée des operations . . . de la dernière guerre . . . *Liege* 1783. O [12] 236 + 10p
suppl in some copies aa
Emphasizes French naval operations.

JOLY DE ST. VALIER [le sieur]   183
Mémoire du: ou exposé de sa conduite avant et
depuis qu'il a quitté la France pour venir offrir ses
services a sa Majesté le Roy d'Angleterre . . . *L*
1780. O [4] 67 a
—ed. 2, *L* 1780. O 93

JONES, A[BNER] D.   184
Illinois and the west . . . *B* 1838. 16° [8] 13–256
map aa 500 cops ptd

JONES, ABSALOM, and ALLEN,   185
RICHARD
A narrative of the proceedings of the black
people . . . in Philadelphia . . . *Phil* 1774. O 28 aa

JONES, A[DOLPHUS] E.   186
Extracts from the history of Cincinnati . . . *Cin*
1888. O 133 11maps & views a

JONES, ALEXANDER   187
The Cymry of '76; or, Welshmen and their de-
scendants of the American revolution . . . *N Y* 1855.
O [4] 132 errata a

JONES, ALEXANDER   188
Historical sketch of the electric telegraph . . .
N Y 1852. O [14] 3–194 a

JONES, ALFRED E.   189
The old silver of American churches . . . *Letchworth Eng* 1913. F [6 9–88] 566 [2] 145 116ills on
16pls aa 500 cops ptd

JONES, ANSON   190
Letters, relating to the history of [Texas] annexation. *Galv* 1848. unbound sheets D 30 aa few
cops kn
—rptd., with same impr. and collat., but ptd.
actually at *Phil* in 1852. Only difference between
the two eds. is that the repr. was issued with wraps.

JONES, ANSON   **191**
Memoranda [etc.] relating to the republic of Texas . . . *N Y* 1859. O [2] 648 + 4adv-p port aa

[JONES, BENJAMIN W.]   **192**
Under the stars and bars; a history of the Surry light infantry . . . *Rich* 1909. D [14] 297 aa

JONES, REV. CHARLES C., 1804–63   **193**
The religious instruction of the negroes in the United States. *Sav* 1842 D [14] 277 a
—rptd. *Sav* 1855 16° 132
—abr ed *Richm* [ca 1862] D 25

JONES, CHARLES COLCOCK, JR.   **194**
Antiquities of the southern Indians . . . *N Y* 1873. O [16] 532 30pls aa

JONES, CHARLES COLCOCK, JR.   **195**
The dead towns of Georgia. *Savannah* 1878. O 263 5plans a 250 copies issued as a separate from v. 4, *Ga. Hist. Soc. Colls.*

JONES, CHARLES COLCOCK, JR.   **196**
Hernando de Soto. The adventures encountered and the route pursued . . . *Sav* 1880. O 42 [2] port a

JONES, CHARLES COLCOCK, JR.   **197**
Historical sketch of the Chatham Artillery . . . *Alb* 1867. O 240 3maps a some copies on L.P.

JONES, CHARLES COLCOCK, JR.   **198**
Historical sketch of Tomo-Chi-Chi, Mico of the Yamacraws. *Alb* 1868. O 133 a

JONES, CHARLES COLCOCK, JR.   **199**
The history of Georgia. *B* 1883. O 2v: [16] 556; [16] 540 19maps and pls aa
Most scholarly history of the colonial and revolutionary periods of this state.

JONES, CHARLES COLCOCK, JR., et al   **200**
History of Savannah, Ga. *Syracuse* 1890. O 655 21ports aa

JONES, CHARLES COLCOCK, JR.   **201**
The life . . . of Commodore Josiah Tattnall. *Sav* 1878. O [10] 225 [4] port a

JONES, CHARLES COLCOCK, JR.,   **202**
and DUTCHER, SALEM
Memorial history of Augusta, Georgia . . . *Syracuse* 1890. O 512 57 10ports aa

JONES, CHARLES COLCOCK, JR.   **203**
Monumental remains of Georgia. Pt. I [all]. *Savannah* 1861. O 119 map 250copies ptd]of which 100 were on medium L. P. & 35 on larger L. P.] aa

JONES, CHARLES COLCOCK, JR.   **204**
Reminiscences of the last days . . . of General Henry Lee. *Alb* 1870. Q 43 port a

JONES, CHARLES COLCOCK, JR.   **205**
The siege of Savannah in December 1864 . . . *Alb* 1874. Q [10] 184 errata slip a some copies on L. P.

JONES, CHARLES COLCOCK, JR., ed.   **206**
The siege of Savannah in 1779 as described in two . . . journals of French officers in the fleet of d'Estaing. *Alb* 1874. Q 70 [7] map a 100 copies ptd [not all had the 7-p. index]
For original editions *see* Estaing. Also *see* Hough, F. B.

JONES, D[ANIEL] W.   **207**
Forty years among the Indians . . . *S L C* 1890. O 400 [incl — in some only — port] a
—rptd. *LA* 1960. O 380

JONES, DAVID   **208**
A journal of two visists made to . . . Indians on the west side of the . . . Ohio . . . *Burl N J* [1774]. O 96 dd AA G JCB N NYP
—rptd., with notes, *N Y* 1865. O [12] 5 127 a 250 copies ptd [50 on L.P.]
A missionary's account of the Delaware and Shawnee tribes in 1772. Thomas Hutchins and George Rogers Clark were his travelling companions on the Ohio.

JONES, EDWARD A.   **209**
The loyalists of Massachusetts. *L* 1930. Q [24] 342 55 pls. [on 28 sheets] à

JONES, [MISS] ELECTA F.   **210**
Stockbridge, past and present; or, records of an old mission station. *Springfield Mass* 1854. D 275 a
Practically a history of the Mohegans.

[JONES, EPAPHRAS]   **211**
On the ten tribes of Israel, and the aborigines of America . . . *New Albany Ind* 1831. O 32 aa

JONES, EVAN ROWLAND   **212**
Lincoln, Stanton and Grant . . . *L* [1875] O [12] 342 port. a

[JONES, G. D.]   **213**
Life and adventures in the South Pacific. *N Y* 1861. D 361 [incl. 21pls] front. a
Whaling experiences, etc.

JONES, GEORGE, of Eng.   **214**
An original history of ancient America . . . identity of the aborigines with the people of Tyrus and Israel . . . *L* 1843. O [20] 462 a
—eds. 2 & 3, same impr., date & collat.
Curious attempt to prove that America was discovered 1824 years before Columbus.

JONES, HENRIETTA C.   215
Sketches from real life. [*Watertown N Y*]
[1897?]. D 239 port a
Illinois and California interest.

JONES, HUGH   216
The present state of Virginia... *L* 1724.
O [12] 152 b AA H N NYP
—rptd. *N Y* 1865. D [14] 152 some copies on
L. P. a; *Chapel Hill* 1956. D [14] 295
Interesting and highly important.

JONES, IGNATIUS, pseud.
See Worth, Gorham A.

JONES, J. W. C.   217
The Elkhorn valley [Neb.]; its climate, soil...
West Point Neb 1880. O 54 map a

JONES, JAMES ATHEARN   218
A letter to an English gentleman, on the...
calumnies on America, by British writers...
Phil 1826. O 46 aa

[JONES, JAMES ATHEARN]   219
Tales of an Indian camp... *L* 1829. O 3v:
[36] 312; [6] 336; [4] 341 aa
—ed. 2, with new introd. & au. named, "Traditions of the North American Indians...,"
same impr. & date. O 3v: [30] 312; [6] 336; [4]
341. 6pls [some copies of this ed. carry the 34p.
introd. of ed. 1, others carry both introds.] aa
—anr. ed. forms vols. 24–26 of "The new British
novelist," *L* [1830]. O 3v aa
—Ger. ed. abr., "Sagen der... Indianer,"
Altenburg 1837. 16° [2] 346 pl a

JONES, J[OHN] B[EAUCHAMP]   220
A rebel war clerk's diary. *Phil* 1866. O 2v:
392; 480 aa
—rptd. *N Y* 1935. O 2v a

JONES, J[OHN] B[EUACHAMP]   220a
The war-path: a narrative of adventures...
Phil 1856 D 335 aa rptd 1858 **a**
—rptd. "Wild western scenes; or, the white spirit
of the wilderness...," *Rich* 1863. D [4] 123 aa
Second series of title immediately following.

JONES, J[OHN] B[EAUCHAMP]   221
Wild western scenes; a narrative of adventures... *Balt* 1841. O 6pts: 247[incl. 6 pls] b
—anr. ed. *N Y* 1841. D same paginat. aa
—ed. 2, au. not named, *Phil* 1845. D 247 a
—anr. ed., au. given as Luke Shortfield, *Phil* 1849.
D 270
—rptd.: 1851; 1856; 1859; 1865; 1869.
—Eng. eds.: au. given as Luke Shortfield, *L* 1850;
Dub 1850. a
Fiction interwoven with a slender historical
thread.

JONES, REV. JOHN G.   222
Concise history of the introduction of Protestantism into Mississippi and the southwest. *St L*
1866. D 257 aa

JONES [COMMODORE JOHN PAUL].   223
An account of...: from a manuscript, written
by himself. *Phil* 1806. O 37 a

JONES (JOHN PAUL).
Echt verslag der voornaamste Levens bijzonder-
heden van: *See* Smart, Theophilus, of which
this is the Dutch translation.

[JONES, JOHN PAUL]   225
The interesting life, travels, voyages and daring
engagements of that celebrated and justly notorious pirate Paul Jones... *L* 1802. O 36 front aa
—rptd. "The life and history...," *L* 1803. O 32
front. a
—rptd. in Eng. many time, sometimes with t.
altered to "Life and history of Paul Jones," "The
life and exploits of the celebrated pirate Paul
Jones," "The life, voyages and sea battles of
that celebrated pirate Paul Jones," etc. a
—Am. eds. *N Y* 1807. D 36; *Hudson N Y* 1809.
16° 46; *Alb* 1809. 24° 96; *N Y* 1809. 16° 36;
N Y 1809. 24° 108; *Alb* 1813. same collat.; *Phil*
1812. D 36 pl; *Hart* 1818. 16° 60; *N Y* 1823. D
28 pl a
—several Am. reprints, most of them dropping
"pirate" from the t.

JONES (the chevalier JOHN PAUL...)   226
Life and character of: *Wash* 1825. O 387 port a

JONES (JOHN PAUL).
Life and correspondence of: *See* Sands, Robt. C.

JONES ([JOHN] PAUL).
The life of: from... documents in the posses-
sion of John Henry Sherburne... *See* Disraeli,
Benj.

JONES (REAR-ADMIRAL JOHN PAUL).   227
Life of:... from his original journals... *Phil*
1845. D 399 a
—rptd., same impr.: 1847; 1853; 1858; 1869.

JONES ([JOHN] PAUL).   228
Mémoires de: *P* 1798. 16° [24] 244 port aa
This translation of the manuscript *Journal*
presented to Louis XVI by Jones was made by
his secretary, Benoit-André.

JONES (REAR-ADMIRAL [JOHN]   229
PAUL).
Memoirs of:... from his original journals...
Edin 1830. D 2v: [12] 331; [4] 341. port a
—rptd. *L* 1843. D same collat.

JONES (COM. JOHN PAUL).
Narrative of the adventures of an American navy officer who served . . . under: *See* Fanning, Nathaniel.

**JONES (the unparalled and celebrated   230
COMMODORE [JOHN] PAUL).**
A narrative of: Tr. from a manuscript written by himself. n.p. n.d. D 23 a

JONES [JOHN] PAUL   231
Jones, [John] Paul, ou prophéties sur l'Amérique, l'Angleterre . . . [*Basle ca* 1781]. O 120 aa

JONES, J[OHN] WESLEY
Amusing . . . adventures of a California artist . . . *B* 1854. *See* Phillips, Geo. Spencer.

JONES, JONATHAN H.   232
A condensed history of the Apache and Comanche Indian tribes . . . *San Antonio* 1899. O 235 [incl. illus.] aa
—rptd., as by Lehmann, Hermann, "Nine years among the Indians," *Austin* [1927]. D [10] 235 pls a
Based chiefly on information supplied by Lehmann.

JONES [JOSEPH] of Virginia.   233
Letters of: 1777–1787. Ed. W. C. Ford. *Wash* 1889. O [14] 157 a 250copies ptd.
Relate to Southern military operations and to Virginia politics following peace.

JONES, JO[SEPH] SEAWELL   234
A defence of the revolutionary history of . . . North Carolina . . . *B* 1834. D [12] 343 a

[JONES, JOSEPH SEAWELL]   235
The mommoth humbug; or, the adventures of Shocco Jones, in Mississippi . . . *Knoxv* 1842. D 54 a

JONES, J[OSEPH] SEAWELL   236
Memorials of North Carolina. *N Y* 1838. O 87 a

JONES, NATHANIEL V   237
A reply to "Mormonism unveiled." *Calcutta* 1853. O 120 b. H [of 3 cops loc]

JONES, PETER   238
History of the Ojebway Indians . . . *L* 1861. O [8] 278 16pls errata slip a
—rptd. same collat. *L* [1862?].

JONES, S[AMUEL]   239
Pittsburgh in . . . eighteen hundred and twenty-six . . . with a directory . . . *Pitt* 1826. D 153 pl + 9adv-l. aa

JONES, SHOCCO [pseud]
The mammoth humbug . . . *See* Jones, Jos. Seawell.

JONES, JUDGE T. E.   240
Leaves from an argonaut's note book . . . *S F* 1905. D 304 7pls a
Most of the edition burned.

JONES, THOMAS A.   241
J. Wilkes Booth . . . his sojourn in southern Maryland after the assassination . . . *Chi* 1893. D 126[incl.pls] aa

**JONES (COMMODORE THOMAS AP.   242
CATESBY).**
Proceedings of a court martial on: . . . Ex. Doc. 45. *Wash* 1851. O 400 aa

JONES (THOMAS H.)   243
The experiences of: who was a slave . . . *Worc* 1849. O 48 a
—other eds.: *B* 1850; *Springfield* 1854; *Worc* 1857; *B* n.d.
—anr. ed. "Experience . . . of Uncle Tom Jones . . .," *B* 1855. O 54 front.

JONES, U[RIAH] J.   244
History of the early settlement of the Juniata valley . . . *Phil* 1856. O 380 14pls a
—rptd. *Harrisburg* 1889. O 429[incl.pls]; again [1940]. O 440 pls

JONES, WILLIAM A.   245
Report upon the reconnaissance of northwestern Wyoming. *Wash* 1874. O [6] 210 49 sheets of fold.plans a
—ed. 2, t. changed, " . . . including Yellowstone park . . .," *Wash* 1875. O [6] 331 49sheets of fold.plans, 6 pls. fold map

[JONES, WILLIAM B.]   246
Wonderful curiosity; or a correct narrative of the celebrated Mammoth Cave . . . *Russellville* 1844. D 67 a

JONES, WILLIAM CAREY   247
Letters . . . on the subject of land titles in California. *S F* 1860. O 31 b LC Y

JONES, WILLIAM CAREY   248
Report on . . . land titles in California . . . *Wash* 1850. O 60 b N
—anr. ed., in "Report of the Secretary of the Interior," *Wash* 1850. O 136 map b
—rptd. *S F* [1852]. O 55 b

JONNY-CAKE LETTERS
See Hazard, Thomas R.

JORDAN, A. C., and CO., publishers   249
The Norfolk directory. *Norfolk* 1806. D 82 aa

JORDAN, SAMUEL   250
The restorer of the Union . . . to its original purity . . . *Augusta Ga* 1866. O 171 a

JORDAN, THOMAS, and PRYOR, J. P.   251
The campaigns of Lieut.-Gen. N. B. Forrest . . .
N O 1868. O [18] 17–704 6maps 6pls a

JORDAN, THOMAS   252
The south; its products . . . *Edin* 1861. O 23 a

JORDAN, WILLIAM C. [of the 15th Ala].   253
Some events and incidents of the civil war.
Montg 1909. O 142 a

JOSSELYN, JOHN   254
An account of two voyages to New-England
. . . *L* 1674. D [8] 282 [incl. advs] c JCB N NYH
—ed. 2, *L* 1675. same collat b MassH.
—rptd. *B* 1865. Sm Q [12] 211 250 cops ptd a
Visited here in 1638–9, and in 1663–71.

JOSSELYN, JOHN   255
New England's rarities discovered . . . *L* 1672.
D [6, incl blank initial lf] 114 [3] pl b H Hn N
—ed. 2, same impr & collat 1675. b JCB
—rptd. *B* 1865. Sm Q [8] 169 250 cops ptd a

JOURNAL
Journal d'un officier de l'armée naval en Amérique en 1781 & 1782. *See* Grasse, comte de

Journal d'un voyage fait dans l'intérieure de
l'Amérique . . . *See* Anburey, Thos.

Journal [A] of a tour from Boston to Savannah
. . . *See* Nason, Danl.

Journal of a tour in the "Indian territory,"
N Y 1844. *See* Harris, N. Sayre.

Journal of a voyage between China and   256
the northwest coast. *N Y* 1868. O 40 a

Journal of a wanderer . . . residence in   257
India and six weeks in North America. *L* 1844. D
[18] 250 port a

Journal of an excursion to the United   258
States and Canada . . . By a citizen of Edinburgh.
Edin 1835. D [8] 168 [4] a
Relates largely to New York state.

Journal of an expedition . . . under the   259
command of . . . Francis Nicholson . . . for the
reduction of Port Royal . . . *L* 1711. Q 24 b

Journal of the congress of the four south-   260
ern Governors . . . with the Five Nations of Indians,
at Augusta, 1763. *See* under Augusta.

Journal [A] of the expedition up the river   261
St. Lawrence . . . By the sergeant major of Gen.
Hopson's grenadiers. *B* 1759. 16° 24 b LC
—Fr. tr. [*Quebec* 1855]. O 16 a

Journal [A] of the march of a party of pro-   262
vincials from Carlisle to Boston, and Quebec . . .
Glas 1776. D 36 b

Journal of the proceedings of the Con-   263
gress held at Philadelphia, September 5, 1774.
Phil Bradford 1774. O [4] 132 b IndU JCB NYP
[only cops loc]
—rptd. with adds, same impr. but erroneously
dated "DCC, LXXIV." O [4] 132 [2] 133–144 aa
—anr. issue, same, but dated correctly. aa
For later curtailed editions, *see Extracts from
the votes and proceedings . . . Sept. 5, 1774.*

Journal of the proceedings of the Con-   264
gress, held at Philadelphia, May 10, 1775. *N Y*
1775. O [4] 140 aa
—anr. ed. *Phil* 1775. O [4] 239 aa
—Eng. ed. *L* 1776. O [2] 200 aa
For curtailed edition *see Extracts from the
votes and proceedings . . . May 10th, 1775.*

Journal of the proceedings of the south-   265
western convention . . . at the city of Memphis.
Memphis 1845. O 127 aa

JOUTEL, HENRI   266
Journal historique du dernier voyage que feu
M. de La Sale fit . . . *P* 1713. D [34] 386 map
b H N NYP Y
—Eng. tr. *L* 1714. O [32] 205 [5] map b AA Hn
NYP Y
—anr. issue, identical, but dated 1715. b
—anr. issue, made from same sheets with changed
t-p, *L* 1719. [map apparently not inserted in all
copies] b N
—Am. ed. *Chi* Caxton Club 1896. O [42] 231 map
a 203 copies ptd.
—rptd. *Alb* 1906. [8] 258 map front a
—Sp. tr., with notes, "Diario historico . . .,"
N Y 1831. D 156 aa
Most reliable eye-witness account of La Salle's
two-years wanderings in Texas. The map, based
on La Salle's Mississippi explorations, was the
first accurate delineation of that river.

JOUVÉ, E[UGENE]   267
Voyage en Amérique. *Lyon* 1853–5. O 2v: 434;
533 a

[JUDAH, THEODORE D.]   268
Report of the chief engineer of the Central
Pacific Railroad Company of California, on his
operations in the Atlantic states. *Sacr.* 1862 O 30
map b
Efforts, in Washington, etc., securing the grant
for this transcontinental line.

[JUDAH, THEODORE D.]   269
Report . . . on the preliminary survey of the

Central Pacific Railroad of California . . . [*Sacr*?
1861]. O 36 b
—anr. ed *Sacr* 1863. O 56 errata map aa

[JUDAH, THEODORE D.] 270
Report . . . upon recent surveys . . . of the
Central Pacific Railroad of California. *Sacr* 1863.
O 26 aa
—anr. ed. n.p. Dec 1864. O 32 aa

JUDD. A. N. 271
Campaigning against the Sioux . . . from a diary
kept during one of three expeditions . . . under
General Alfred Sully in 1863–4–5 . . . [*Watsonville
Calif* 1906]. Q 47 port b Hn N Y only 40copies ptd.

JUDD, H. O. 272
Look within for fact and fiction . . . *Macon Ga*
1864. D 204 aa

JUDD, SILAS 273
A sketch of the life and voyages of Capt. Alvah
Judd Dewey . . . *Chittenango N Y* 1838. D 114 aa
Dewey participated in Mina's filibustering
expedition into Texas.

JUDGES AND CRIMINALS . . .
History of the Vigilance committee of San
Francisco . . . *See* Gray, Henry M.

JUDSON, PHOEBE N. G. 274
A pioneer's search for an ideal home . . .
Bellingham Wash 1925. D 309 [5] [incl. front.] aa
Describes her trip across the plains in 1853 and
experiences on Puget sound.

JUGEMENT 275
Jugement rendu par le conseil de guerre [on
trial of De Grasse *et al* for misconduct in West
Indian naval operations]. *L'Orient* [1784]. SmF
[2] 37 b

JÜNEMANN, FRIEDRICH 276
Rathgeber und Wegweiser für Auswanderer . . .
nach den Vereinigten Staaten . . . *Vienna* 1849.
O [14] 146 a

JULIUS, N[IKOLAUS] H. 277
Nordamerikas sittliche Zustände . . . *Leip* 1839.
O 2v: [28] 514; [12] 502 [2] map 67tabs 15fold
pls of architecture and music. aa
Study of our early social problems, crimes and
punishments.

JUSTESEN, PETER 278
Two years adventures of a Dane in the California gold mines. *Gloucester* 1865. D 78 b

JUSTICE [THE] 279
Justice [The] and necessity of taxing the American colonies demonstrated . . . *L* 1766. O 36 +
4adv-p a

Justice [The] and necessity of the war 280
with our American colonies considered. n.p.
[1775]. O [2] 50 a

JUSTIFICATION 281
Justification de la résistance des colonies
américaines aux oppressions du gouvernement
britannique . . . *Leyden* 1776. O 30 a

K

K., J. M.
Neuste . . . Nachricht . . . *See* Kramer, Johann
M.

K., O
Het Waere Onderscheyt tusschen Koude en
warme Landen . . . *see* Keye, Otto

KAEMPFFERT, WALDEMAR 1
A popular history of American inventions.
N Y 1924. O 2v: [16] 577; [14] 457 [incl. fronts] a

KALAMAZOO. 2
Celebration of the settlement of: *Kalamazoo*
1855. D 72 aa

KALAMAZOO COLLEGE.
An episode in the history of: *See* Stone, Mrs.
Lucinda H.

KALIFORNIEN (DAS GOLDLAND) 3
Mit Berücksichtigung der Auswanderung dort-
hin . . . *Rorschach* 1849. 16° 30 aa

KALIFORNIENS . . .
Kaliforniens Gold-und-Quecksilber-District . . .
See Gerstäcker, Friedrich.

KALIFORNII (OPIS) POD 4
WZGLEDEM . . .
Cracow 1850. D 31 aa
First Polish account of the gold discovery.

KALM, PEHR [PETER] 5
En resa til Norra America . . . *Stockh* 1753–61,
D 3v: [24] 484 [12]; [2] 526 [26]; [2] 538 [14].
view b
—Ger. ed. "Beschreibung der Reise . . .," *Göttin-
gen* 1754–64. O 3v: [18] 568; 592; [4] 648. 9pls aa

—Dutch ed. "Reis door Noord Amerika," *Utrecht* 1772. Q 2v: [18] 233; [12] 240 [8] map 4pls some copies on L.P. aa

—Eng. ed. "Travels into North America . . .," *Warrington Eng* 1770–*L* 1771. O 3v: [24] 400; 352; [8] 310 [14]. map[not in all copies] 6pls b H N

—anr. issue, identical, but v.I has impr. *L* 1771. b

—Eng. ed. 2, *L* 1772. O 2v: [4, 3–12] 414; [4] 423 [8]. map 6pls aa

Most trustworthy description of Swedish settlements in 18th century Delaware, New Jersey and Pennsylvania. For French trans. *See* Rousselot de Surgy.

KAMTSCHATKA
Kamtschatka and the Kurilski islands . . . History of: *See* Krasheninnikov, Stefan P.

[KANE, MRS. ELIZABETH D.]   6
Twelve Mormon homes visited . . . on a journey through Utah . . . *Phil* 1874. O [4] 158 aa

KANE, PAUL   7
Wanderings of an artist among the Indians of North America . . . *L* 1859. O [18] 455 [8] map 8col pls b

—Fr. tr. *P* 1861. 18° [7] 273 a

—Ger. tr. *Leip* 1862. O [12] 225 4col pls

—Dan. tr. *Copenh* 1863. O 344

Travels largely confined to Canada but visits to Wisconsin and Oregon and account of the murder of Dr. Whitman are included.

KANE, THOMAS L.   8
The Mormons . . . *Phil* 1850. O 84 aa

—ed. 2, with postcript [of 7p] and Lat. quot. on t-p, *Phil* 1850. O 92 aa

Most sympathetic Gentile appraisal of Mormon conduct. Kane describes their trek to Utah in which he participated.

KANSAS   9
A description of Kansas: *B* 1854. D 28 a

Facts . . . about Kansas: *Lawrence* 1870.   10
O 64 [incl. front wrap] map pl a

The grim chieftain of Kansas: . . . By one who knows. *See* Fish, Reeder McCandless.

Guide map of the best . . . cattle trail to the Kansas Pacific Railway. *See* Weston, W.

Guide to the new gold region of western Kansas and Nebraska. *See* Oliver, John W.

Handbook of southern Kansas . . . *Chi*   11
1886. O 38 a

Industrial resources of western Kansas . . . *See* Elliott, R. S.

Kansas guide [The] . . . *Ottawa Kas* 1871.   12
O 62 [2] a

A manual of south-eastern Kansas: her   13
counties, cities . . . *Lawrence* 1872. O 64 a

Military history of Kansas regiments   14
during the war. *See* Burke, W. S.

Organization . . . of the Emigrant Aid Company: also a description of Kansas. *See* Webb, Thos. H.

Public documents of . . . Kansas. For the   15
year 1862. *Lawrence* 1862. O 88 a

The reign of terror in Kansas. *See* Briggs, Chas. W.

Report of . . . commissioners for the investigation of [Kansas] election frauds . . . *See* Adams, H. J.

Six months in Kansas. By a lady. *See* Ropes, Mrs. Hannah A.

KANSAS CITY, Mo.   15a
Kansas city illustrated . . . *K C* [1877?] Q 24 40views aa

KAPP, FRIEDRICH   16
Geschichte der deutschen Einwanderung in America. Vol.I(all]. *N Y* 1867. O [8] 410 map a

—rptd. *Leip* 1868. O [8] 370 [30] map

—other eds.: *N Y* 1869; abr., *N Y* 1884.

KAPP, FRIEDRICH   17
Geschichte der Sklaverei in den Vereinigten Staaten . . . *N Y* [1860]. O [10] 516 map a

—rptd. *Hamburg* 1861.

KAPP, FRIEDRICH   18
Die Sklavenfrage in den Vereinigten Staaten. *Göttingen* 1854. 16° [6] 185 pl a

KATE, HERMANN F. C. TEN   19
Reizen en onderzoekingen in Noord-Amerika. *Leyden* 1885. O [10] 464 [1] map 2pls a

KEATING, WILLIAM H. [comp.]   20
Narrative of an expedition to the source of St. Peter's river [etc.] under the command of Stephen H. Long . . . *Phil* 1824. O 2v: [14] 9–439; [6] 5–459. map 15 pls aa

—Eng. ed. *L* 1825. O 2v: [16] 458; [6] 248 [156]. map 8pls 3tabs aa

—rptd., t. changed. same collat., *L* 1828. a

—Ger. ed. "Forschungsreise in dem nordlichen Theile der Vereinigten Staaten . . .," *Jena* 1826. O 238 a

Cited as Long's *Second expedition;* for his *First expedition See* James, Edwin.

KECKLEY, ELIZABETH   **21**
Behind the scenes . . . *N Y* 1868. D [12] 17–371 port. + 8adv.-p a
Account of the family life of the Lincolns by the White House dress-maker. Ghost-written by Hamilton Busbey.

KEELER, WILLIAM J.   **22**
Notes to accompany Keeler's Map of the U. S. . . . from the Mississippi river to the Pacific ocean. *Wash* 1867. Q 30 aa
—rptd., same impr. 1868. O 30 a
The map—*National map of the United States*—folding to quarto, with page of text, was issued separately, Washington 1867, and reprinted, folding to 16mo, 1868. The western part was the best at the time.

KEEMLE, CHARLES, comp.   **23**
The St. Louis directory, for . . . 1836–7 : . . . with a sketch of the city . . . *St L* 1836. D [10] 47 b
—same, for 1838–9, *St L* 1838. D [14] 67 [3] aa
—same, for 1840–1, *St L* 1840. D [12] 84 aa

KEENE, RICHARD R.   **24**
A letter of vindication to . . . Colonel Monroe, President of the United States . . . [*Phil*] 1824. O 47 aa
—Eng. ed. *L* 1824. O 86 aa
Keene, the first American promised land for bringing settlers to Texas, was accused of being a party to Burr's conspiracy; of his *Memoria*, published at Madrid in 1815, only one copy is known.

KEES, JOHN W., pub.   **25**
Directory of . . . Springfield [O.] . . . containing . . . a brief history . . . *Springfield*. 1852. D [2] 7–221 map 2pls aa
First directory of this city; the history is by R. C. Woodward.

KEGLEY, F[REDERICK] B.   **26**
Virginia frontier . . . 1740–1783. *Roanoke* 1938. Q [36] 786 9maps a

[KEILEY, ANTHONY M.]   **27**
Prisoner of war, or five months among the Yankees . . . *Rich* [1865]. O 120 a
—enl. ed. "In vinculis; or, the prisoner of war . . .," *N Y* 1866. D 216 [Some copies have Petersburg impr.] a
Either this or Pollard's *Observations in the north* was the last book printed in the Confederacy.

KEILY, P. T., comp.   **28**
Pierre city directory. [*Pierre* 1883]. D 44 aa

KEILY, RICHARD   **29**
A brief descriptive . . . sketch of Georgia . . . *L* 1849. O 32 map aa

KEIM, DE BENNEVILLE R.   **30**
Our Alaskan wonderland . . . *Wash* [1898]. D 352 map 2pls a

KEIM, DE B[ENNEVILLE] R.   **31**
Sheridan's troopers on the borders . . . *Phil* 1870. O 308 8pls a
—rptd. same impr. & collat.: 1885; [1889].

KEITH, CHARLES P.   **32**
The provincial councillors of Pennsylvania . . . 1733–1776. *Phil* 1883. O [14] 142 [2] 476 a

KEITH, GEORGE   **33**
A journal of travels from New-Hampshire to Caratuck [N.C.] . . . *L* 1706. Q [4] 92 b AA H LC NYP

[KEITH, GEORGE]   **34**
New England's spirit of persecution transmitted to Pennsylvania . . . *Phil* 1693. Q [2] 38 dd AA PaH
—Eng. ed. "The tryals of Peter Boss, George Keith, *et al* . . ." *L* 1693. Q 34 d
There is reason to believe that the original edition, in spite of its Philadelphia imprint, may have actually been printed by Bradford in N.Y. after his removal there; if so, it is one of the earliest books to have been printed in that city.

KEITH (CAPT. THOMAS).   **35**
Struggles of : . . . including the manner in which he, his wife and child were decoyed by Indians; their temporary captivity . . . *L* Tegg [1808?]. D 28 fold. front.[counted as 4p. in collat.] aa
—oth eds.: *Edin* 1813. D; *L* [1825]. D
Fictitious. *See* also Smith, Sarah.

KEITH, SIR WILLIAM   **36**
The history of the British plantations . . . Pt. I [all]. Containing the history of Virginia . . . *L* 1738. Q [8] 187 2maps b
Based largely on Beverley's history.

KELEHER, WILLIAM A.   **37**
The fabulous frontier. Twelve New Mexico items. *Santa Fe* [1945]. O [12] 317 11pls aa 500 cops ptd.

KELEHER, WILLIAM A.   **38**
Maxwell land grant . . . *Santa Fe* [1942]. O [14 incl. front.] 168 8pls aa

KELL, JOHN McI.   **39**
Recollections of a naval life . . . *Wash* 1900. O 307 port a

KELLER, G. R., and McCANN, J. M.   **40**
Sketches of Paris [Ky.] . . . *Paris* 1876 O 46 a

KELLER, GEORGE   **41**
A trip across the plains, and life in California. [*Massillon O* 1851]. O 58 dd AA G Hn Y [of 7cops loc]

KELLETT, ALEXANDER   **42**
A pocket of prose and verse . . . *Bath Eng* 1778. 18° [4] 283 c BM N NYP [only known copies] —ed. 2, "The mental novelist . . .," *L* 1783. 16° [4] 283 aa
Includes narrative of David Menzies' captivity among Georgia Cherokees, unquestionably authentic.

KELLEY, HALL J.   **43**
A general circular to all persons of good character who wish to emigrate to the Oregon territory, embracing some account of . . . the country . . . *Charlestown Mass* 1831. O 28 b AA N NYP OreH Y
Earliest Oregon colonization scheme.

KELLEY, HALL J.   **44**
A geographical sketch of . . . Oregon . . . *B* 1830. O 80 tab map[first of Ore. to be ptd] c N NYP WashU Y
—ed. 2, enl., *B* [1830]. same collat. with 28-p Appendix added b G NYP Y

KELLEY, HALL J.   **45**
A history of the settlement of Oregon and the interior of upper California . . . *Springfield Mass* 1868. O [17] 128 d H WashU Y
—anr. issue, same date & impr. O [18] 7 128 d G LC NYP
Supplements his 1852 *Narrative of events* . . . ; a dangerously convincing facsimile has appeared, evidently with the deliberate attempt of deceiving. Buyers should examine the paper carefully by daylight.

KELLEY, HALL J.   **46**
A narrative of events and difficulties in the colonization of Oregon, and the settlement of California . . . *B* 1852. O 92 c G H OreH Y

KELLEY, WILLIAM D.   **47**
A history of Kansas City, Missouri . . . *K C* 1873. O 67 map a

KELLOGG (GEO[RGE] J.)   **48**
Narative [*sic*] of: 1849 to 1915 . . . [*Janesville Wis* 1915]. O [2] 38[incl.wraps] port cov.t.only aa
Includes his 1849 California overland diary.

KELLOGG, MRS. HARRIET S.   **49**
Life of Mrs. Emily J. Harwood, *Albuquerque* 1903. D [8 incl.front. 28] 152 150–373 [8] aa
Printed at the mission press. For another account of the work done by Mr. and Mrs. Harwood in New Mexico, *See* Harwood, Rev. Thomas.

KELLOGG, LOUISE P.   **50**
The British régime in Wisconsin . . . *Madison* 1935. O [18] 361 8pls 2maps a

KELLOGG, LOUISE P.   **51**
The French régime in Wisconsin . . . *Madison* 1925. O [16] 474 30maps & pls a

KELLOGG, LOUISE P.   **52**
Frontier advance on the upper Ohio, 1778–9. *Madison* 1916. O 509 map 6pls a

KELLOGG, LOUISE P.   **53**
Frontier retreat on the upper Ohio, 1779–1781. *Madison* 1917. O 549 2maps 7pls a

KELLOGG, MERRITT C.   **54**
Notes concerning the Kelloggs. *Battle Creek* 1927. O 116 port a
Contains account of an 1859 California overland.

[KELLS, CHARLES E.]   **55**
California, from its discovery . . . with a brief description of the gold region . . . *N Y* 1848. D 32 b LC

KELLY, CHARLES, and HOWE,   **56**
MAURICE L.
Miles Goodyear; first citizen of Utah, trapper, trader and California pioneer. *S L C* 1937. O 152 [7] [incl. front]. 9pls aa 350 cops ptd.

KELLY, CHARLES   **57**
Old Greenwood . . . trapper . . . *S L C* 1936. O 128[incl. initial blank lf.] [5] 350copies ptd. aa

KELLY, CHARLES   **58**
The outlaw trail . . . "Butch" Cassidy and his wild bunch. *S L C* 1938. O 339 pls aa
—ed 2 *N Y* 1959. D [10] 374 1 pls a
Includes other spectacular bandits infesting the mountains of Colorado, Utah and Wyoming.

KELLY, CHARLES   **59**
Salt desert trails. A history of the . . . early trails . . . seeking a shorter road to California. *S L C* 1930. O 178[incl. pls & 2 initial blank lvs] [6 incl. initial blank lf] a

KELLY, E. S.   **60**
Condensed sketch of . . . California, San Francisco and Oakland. *Oakland* 1879. D 46 a

KELLY [EBENEZER BERIAH]   **61**
Kelly [Ebenzer Beriah]: an autobiography. *Norwich Conn* 1856. D 100 a
Experiences of an American sailor impressed into British naval service.

KELLY, FANNY [WIGGINS]   **62**
Narrative of my captivity among the Sioux . . . *Cin* 1871. D 285 12pls a

—rptd. *Hart* 1871. same collat.; *Phil* 1872; *Hart* 1872; 1873.
—anr. ed. *Tor* 1872. D 304 2pls
—ed. 2, *Chi* 1880. D 285 12pls
—ed. 3, *Chi* 1891. D 285 port

KELLY, GEORGE FOX   **63**
Eight months in Washington; or, scenes behind the curtain . . . n.p. 1863. O 38 b LC
—ed. 2, with app., same date. n.p. O 51 b
Investigation into California land frauds.

KELLY, GEORGE F[OX]   **64**
Land frauds of California . . . [Santa Rosa?] 1864. O 37 b LC Y [of a few copies known]
Sensational charges of how legitimate pre-emptors were, through conniving courts and government officials, deprived of legal rights.

KELLY, J. WELLS [comp.]   **65**
First directory of Nevada Territory, containing . . . a historical sketch [etc.]. *S F* 1862. O [18] 266 b BP NevH Y
—2nd directory, *Virginia Nev* [*S F* ptd] 1863. O 486 + advs b Hn
Earliest book on Nevada, preceded only by De Groot's 1860 pamphlet on the Washoe mines.

KELLY, L[EROY] V.   **66**
The range men. The story of the ranchers and Indians of Alberta. *Tor* 1913. O 468 pls aa
Though chiefly an account of the cattle trade in the Canadian prairie provinces, includes Montana affairs.

KELLY, WAYNE S.   **67**
Lariats and chevrons; or, Corporal Jack Wilson . . . *Guthrie* 1905. D 620 port a [Fiction]

KELLY, WILLIAM   **68**
An excursion to California . . . With a stroll through the diggimgs . . . *L* 1851. D 2v: [10] 342; [8] 334 + 2adv-p aa
—rptd. in 2 separate v. ["Across the Rocky Mountains" and "A stroll through the diggings."] *L* 1852. 16° a
Made the trip from Westport to Weber Creek, in 1849.

KEMBLE [FANNY]   **69**
Kemble [Fanny] in America: or the journal of an actress reviewed . . . By an English lady, four years resident in the United States. *B* 1835. O 48 a
For the *Journal* referred to, *See* Butler, Frances A.

KEMBLE, FRANCES A.   **70**
Journal of a residence on a Georgian plantation . . . *L* 1863. D [8] 434 + 32adv-p, dated Jan. 1863 a

—Am. ed. *N Y* 1863. D 337 + 10adv-p issue 1: "about" repeated, line 6, p314

[KEMP, FRANCIS A. VAN DER]   **71**
Verzameling van stukken tot de dertien Vereenigde Staaten . . . betrekkelijk. *Leyden* 1781. O [48] 300 [2] aa

KENDALL (AMOS).   **72**
Autobiography of: . . . Ed. by William Stickney. *B* 1872. O [10] 700 port 2pls facs a

KENDALL, AMOS   **73**
Life of Andrew Jackson . . . *N Y* 1843–4. O 288 a [Issued also in 7nos.]

KENDALL, EDWARD A.   **74**
Travels through the northern parts of the United States . . . *N Y* 1809. O 3v: [12] 330; [6] 309; [6] 312 aa

KENDALL, GEORGE W.   **75**
Narrative of the Texan Santa Fe expedition. *N Y* 1844. D 2v: [2] 405; [12] 11–406. map 5pls aa
—ed. 7, with 2 extra chaps, and part of Thomas Falconer's diary, relating to this ill-fated undertaking. *N Y* 1856. D 2v: [18] 13–452; [14] 11–442. map 5pls b
—other 2v eds.: *L* 1844; *L* 1845; *N Y* 1846; *N Y* 1847; *N Y* 1850; *N Y* 1857. aa
—several later 1v. Eng eds: *L* 1847. 16° [4] 599; *Bristol* n.d. a

KENDALL, GEORGE W.   **76**
The war between the United States and Mexico . . . *N Y* 1851. F [4] 52 12col.pls map b N NYP Y
The fine plates by Carl Nebel were produced at Paris, the text printed in New Orleans, the book bound and sold by Appleton in New York.

KENDERDINE, THADDEUS S.   **77**
California revisited, 1858–1897. *Newtown Pa* 1898. O 310 a

KENDERDINE, THADDEUS S.   **78**
A California tramp . . . or, life on the plains and in the golden state thirty years ago . . . *Newtown Pa* 1888. O 416 aa
Crossed by the southern route.

KENNAWAY, SIR JOHN H.   **79**
On Sherman's track; or, the south after the war. *L* 1867. O [10 incl. front.] 320 3pls a

KENNEBECK CLAIMS (THE).   **80**
Statement of: . . . *B* 1786. sm Q 29 a
Favorable report by a committee of the Massachusetts Assembly on claims of the Plymouth Company.

[KENNEDY, ARCHIBALD]   **81**
The importance of gaining . . . the friendship of the Indians to the British interest . . . *N Y* 1751. O 31 c AA NYP
—Eng. ed., with 8-p. letter, by Franklin?, added, *L* 1752. O [2] 46 b N Y

[KENNEDY, ARCHIBALD]   **82**
Observations on the importance of the northern colonies under proper regulations. *N Y* 1750. O [4] 36 aa
Advocates colonial union and alliance with the Iroquois to thwart French aggressions from Canada. In 1754 a convention at Albany considered his plan.

[KENNEDY, ARCHIBALD]   **83**
Serious considerations on the present state of affairs of the northern colonies. *N Y* 1754. O [24] aa
—anr. ed. *Phil* 1754 aa
—rptd. *N Y* 1756. a
—Eng. ed., au. named, *L* [1754]. O 24 aa

KENNEDY JAMES   **84**
Probable origin of the American Indians . . . *L* 1854. O [2] 42 a
—enl. ed. "Ethnological . . . essays," *L* 1855. O 3pts in 1 : 42; 57; 30 100 copies ptd. aa

KENNEDY, JOHN [comp.]   **85**
Iowa City directory . . . for 1857. Containing a history [etc.]. *Iowa City* [1857]. D [36] 47 aa
First directory and first history of this city.

[KENNEDY, JOHN P.]   **86**
The border states; their power and duty . . . [*Balt* 1861]? O 46, $^1/_2$ t.only a
—anr. ed., au. named, *Phil* same date. O 47

KENNEDY, JOHN P.   **87**
Memoirs of the life of William Wirt . . . *Phil* 1849. O 2v: 417; 451. port facs aa
—rev ed Phil 1850. D 2v a
—many later eds.

KENNEDY, LIONEL H., and   **88**
PARKER, THOMAS
An official report of the trial of sundry Negroes, charged with an attempt to raise an insurrection in . . . South Carolina . . . *Charleston* 1822. O [2] 188 [14] aa

KENNEDY, P[ATRICK]   **89**
An answer to Mr. Paine's Letter to Gen. Washington . . . *L* 1797. O [2] 55 a
—eds. 2 & 3, same date.
—Am. ed. *Phil* 1798. O [2] 42

[KENNEDY, PHILIP PENDLETON]   **90**
The Blackwater chronicle . . . an expedition

into the land of Canaan, in Randolph county, Virgiania . . . *N Y* 1853. D [2] 223 + 16 adv-p front a
Frequently attributed to the author's brother, John P. Kennedy.

KENNEDY (WILLIAM) et al.   **91**
Correspondence . . . of: showing the danger of emigrating to Texas . . . *L* 1841. O [2] 48 map aa

KENNEDY, WILLIAM   **92**
Texas . . . rise, progress . . . *L* 1841. O 2v: [52] 378; [6] 548. 2maps 2 charts aa
—ed. 2, same collat., 1841. aa
—anr. ed. *Ft Worth* 1925. O 939 2maps a
—rptd., in pt., "Texas: its geography . . .," *N Y* 1844. O [10] 118
—Ger. tr. *Frankf* 1845. O 212 map; anr. Ger. ed., same impr., 1846. O 180 map a
Paints a favorable picture of Texas, and may have hastened English recognition of her independence.

KENNEY, MARTIN M.   **93**
An historical . . . sketch of Austin county, Texas. *Brenham* [1876]. O 25 cover. t only aa

KENRICK, JOHN   **94**
Horrors of slavery. *C* 1817. D 59 a

KENT, L. A.   **95**
Leadville in your pocket: the city and the mines . . . *Denver* 1880. O 198 + 11adv-p a

KENT COUNTY, MICHIGAN.   **96**
History and directory of: . . . *Grand Rapids* 1870. O 319 + 12 inserted adv-p a

KENTOUKEY.
Voyage au: Par M . . . *See* Marechal, Pierre S.

KENTUCKE.
Origine et progres de la mission du: *See* Badin, Stephen T.

KENTUCKY   **97**
The constitution . . . for the state of Kentucky [and] brief commentary . . . *Fleminsburg Ky* [ca 1820]. O 24 b

A description of Kentucky: 1792. *See* Toulmin, Harry.

First explorations of Kentucky 1898. *See* Johnston, Josiah S.

Guide des emigrants francais dans les   **98**
états de Kentucky et Indiana . . . *P* 1834. O 66 aa
—rptd. same impr. 1835. O 55 a

The hunters of Kentucky. *See* Bilson, B.

314

The passenger: or a religious ramble through Kentucky and Ohio. *See* Campbell, John P.

Proceedings of the convention establishing **99** provisonal [Confederate] government of Kentucky. *Augusta Ga* 1863. O 39 b LC [only copy known]

De Zegepraal van het Katholyke Geloof, **100** ter beschaming van ongeloof ... of Verhaal van de uitbreiding in Kentucky. Uit eeneen eigenhandigen Brief van den eerw. Heer Neerinckx ... *Amst* 1819. O [6] 48 aa

KEOKUK CITY DIRECTORY, for 1856–7. *See* Clemens, Orion.

KER, HENRY   101
Travels through the western interior of the United States ... *Elizabethtown N J* 1816. O 372 aa iss 2 376 p.a.
Probably mendacious; but certainly readable.

KER (JOHN).   101a
The memoirs of: *L* 1726–7. O 3v: [16] 180 [4]; [10] 184 [6]; [2] 221 157 [2] + 16adv-p. map port aa
—ed. 2, same impr., date & collat. a
—ed 3, *L* 1727. O 3v in 2: [16] 180 [4]; [10] 184 [6]; [10] 221 160 [16] a
—Dutch tr. *Rotterdam* 1727. O 3 v map port
—Fr. tr. *Rotterdam* 1726–8. O 3v: 302; 228; 308. map port
Volume II largely devoted to French encroachments in the Mississippi Valley, etc.

KERCHEVAL, SAMUEL   102
A history of the valley of Virginia. *Winchester* 1833. D [6] 9–486 aa
—ed. 2, some adds., some omissions, *Woodstock Va* 1850. O 347 a
—ed. 3, *Woodstock* 1902. O 403
One of the best collections on early border wars; as it should be, being largely pirated from Doddridge.

KERGUÉLEN-TRÉMAREC, YVES   103
J. DE
Relation des combats ... de la guerre maritime de 1778 entre la France et l'Angleterre ... *P* 1796. O 403 aa
—rptd. *P* 1801. O 401 a

[KERN, EDWARD M.]   104
A transcript of the Fort Sutter papers ... [*N Y* 1921]. F 722 b N NYP Y 20copies ptd.
Edited by Semour Dunbar from the manuscript papers, reports, etc., kept during Kern's administration of Fort Sutter, in 1846 and 1847.

KERN COUNTY, CALIFORNIA.   105
History of: ... *SF* 1883. F 226 pls b B CalS

[KERR, WILLIAM S. R., Marquess   106
of Lothian]**
The Confederate secession. *Edin* 1864. D [8] 226 a

KESSINGER, L[AWRENCE]   107
History of Buffalo county, Wisconsin. *Alma Wis* 1888. O [16] 656 port map a

[KESTER, JESSE Y.]?   108
The American shooter's manual ... *Phil* 1827. D [4] 9–249 [2] + 3adv-p 3pls Issue 1 has "ribbon" misspelled, p235 b AA NYP
—issue 2 aa
—ed. 2, *Phil* [1827]. aa
First American sporting book.

KETCHAM (COL. JOHN).   109
Reminiscences of: [Indian captivity in 1792 and other adventures in Ind. and Mich.] Ed. by T. M. Hopkins. *Bloomingt, Ind.* 1866. O 22+wraps b

KETCHUM, WILLIAM   110
An authentic ... history of Buffalo ... *Buf* 1864–5. O 2v: [16] 432; [8] 443. 2maps a

KETELTAS, ABRAHAM   111
God arising and pleading his people's cause; or, the American war ... shewn to be the cause of God ... *Newbury-Port* 1777. O 32 b BA MassH

K[EYE], O[TTO]   112
Het Waere Onderscheyt tusschen koude en warme Lande ... *Hague* [1659]. Q [20] 178 b 2cops loc
—ed.2, "Beschryvinge van het Heerlijcke ..." Q [12] 178 [4] b
—Ger. Tr. "Kurtzer Entwurff von Neu-Niederland und Guajana ..." *Leip* 1672. Q [20] 144 [7] b H N NYS
This "True difference between cold and warm lands" emphasizes the superiority of the warm country [Guiana] over the cold [New Netherlands].

KEYES, BENJAMIN F.   113
Historical memorandum ... of West Boylston, Massachusetts ... *Worc* 1861. D [8] 84 a

KEYES, ELISHA W.   114
A reminiscent history of ... Lake Mills, Jefferson County [Wis.]. n.p. [1894]. O 55 a

KEYES, E[RASMUS] D.   115
Fifty years' observation of men and events ... *N Y* 1884. D [8] 515 + 4adv-p a
—rptd. same impr. & collat. 1885.

KEYES, JAMES   116
Pioneers of Scioto county, Ohio. *Portsmouth* 1880. O [4] 122 a

KEYES, WILLIAM   117
History of Quincy, Illinois ... n.p. [1862].
O 105 a

[KHELIEBNIKOV, KIRIL T.]   118
Zhiznepisanie Aleksandra Andreevicha Bara-
nova glavnago pravitelia rossiskikh kolonii v
Amerikie. *St Ptbg* 1835. O [12] 209 b NYP WashU
Biography of A. A. Baranov, founder of the
Russian colonies on the northwest coast of Amer-
ica where he spent twenty-eight years.

KICKAPOO INDIANS (THE).   119
Life ... among: By Texas Jack. *N Hav* n.d.
Q 176 a

KIDD (CAPT. WILLIAM).   120
The arraignment, tryal ... of: ... *L* Nutt
1701. F 60 b JCB NYP
—abr. ed. *L* Robinson 1703. D [27] aa

KIDD (CAPT. [WILLIAM]).
A full account of the actions of ... : By a
person of quality. *See* Mitchell, Dr. John, *A full
account* ...

KIDD (CAPT. [WILLIAM]).
A full account of the proceedings in relation to:
See Mitchell, *Dr.* John.

KIDDER, ALFRED V.   121
An introduction to the study of south-western
archaeology ... *N Hav* 1924. Q [8] 151 50pls a
—rptd. same impr., date & collat.

KIDDER, DANIEL P.   122
Mormonism ... *N Y* 1842. 16° 342 a
—rptd., same impr. & collat.: 1845; 1852.

KIDDER, FREDERIC   123
The expeditions of Capt. John Lovewell ...
B 1865. Q 138 [1] map 200copies ptd [35 on
L.P.] aa

KIDDER, FREDERIC   124
History of the First New Hampshire Regiment
in the ... revolution. *Alb* 1868. O [6] 184 a
Probably the only history of a Revolutionary
regiment.

KIDDER, FREDERIC, comp.   125
Military operations in eastern Maine ... during
the revolution ... from the journals and letters
of Colonel John Allan ... *Alb* 1867. O [12]
5-336 map a

KIDDER, REUBEN   126
The life and adventures of John Damen, the
murderer of Frederick Nolte, etc. *Jeffersonville,
Ind.* 1821. O 108 b IndU LC [only cops loc]

KIDWELL, MR. [ZEDEKIAH]   127
Report on the impracticability of building
a railroad ... to the Pacific ... *Wash* 1856. O
30 fold.map a

KILBOURN, JOHN   128
Columbian geography; or, a description of the
United States ... *Chillicothe* 1815. O 228 b

KILBOURN, JOHN   129
The Ohio gazetteer ... *Columbus* 1816. 16°
[8] 13–166 aa
—ed. 2, rev., 1816. D 114 aa
—8 other eds. by 1831 a.
—ed. 11, rev. & enl. "by a citizen of Columbus,"
Columbus 1833. 16° [48] 65–512 map a
—for continuation, *See* Jenkins, Warren.

[KILBOURN, JOHN]   130
Public documents concerning the Ohio canals
... comprising a complete official history ...
Columbus 1828. O [4] 304 [2] aa
—anr. issue, enl., *Columbus* 1832–3. O [4] 452
[28, 55] aa

KILBOURNE, DAVID W.   131
Strictures, on Dr. I. Galland's pamphlet, entitled, "Villainy exposed" ... *Fort Madison Ia*
1850. D 24 aa
First imprint of this city. For pamphlet attacked. *See* Galland, Isaac.

KILBOURNE, PAYNE K.   132
A biographical history of the county of Litchfield, Connecticut ... *N Y* 1851. D 413 4pls a
—rptd., enl. to 730p, *N Y* 1881. O

KILBOURNE, PAYNE K.   133
Sketches ... of the town of Litchfield, Connecticut ... *Hart* 1859. O [8] 17–264 map 11pls a

KIMBALL, CHARLES P. [comp.]   134
The San Francisco directory. *S F* 1850. 24°
136 [incl.advs] d B G H [of 5cops known]
—rptd. with 3 additional p. of "omitted names,"
[*S F ca* 1869] a
—anr. ed. *S F* [1890]. To "omitted names" those
of 2 Donahoes added.
First real directory of this city, preceded only
by two business directories.

KIMBALL (HEBER C.)
Journal of: *See* Thompson, Robt. B.

[KIMBALL, HORACE]   135
The naval temple ... battles fought by the
navy of the United States ... *B* 1816. O 258
21pls [incl. eng-t] a
—ed. 2, same impr., date & collat.
—anr. ed. 2, same impr. & date O 322 7pls.

—rptd. "American naval battles . . .," *B* 1831. O 278 [2] 21pls; *B* 1836; *B* 1837; *B* 1840.
—other eds. "Naval battles of the United States . . .," *B* 1857. O 279 20pls; same impr. & collat. 1858.
Attributed also to B. Badger, publisher of the first edition.

KIMBALL, MARIA B.   **136**
My eighty years [in Texas, New Mexico and Nebraska]. *B* 1934. O 103 3pls a

KIMBALL, M[ARIA] B.   **137**
A soldier-doctor of our army. *N Y* 1917. D [14] 192 + lf [colophon] 17pls a
Served thirty years on the frontier, from Dakota to New Mexico.

KIMBALL, [SIDNEY] FISKE   **138**
Domestic architecture of the American colonies . . . *N Y* 1922. F [20] 314 a
—rptd. same impr. & collat. 1927.

KIMBALL, SOLOMON F.   **139**
Thrilling experiences. *S L C* 1909. 16° 157 port aa
Indian fighting, etc., by Heber Kimball's son, in Utah and Idaho.

KIMBALL & JAMES' . . . DIRECTORY   **140**
Kimball & James' business directory for the Mississippi valley . . . *Cin* 1844. O [8] 546 4pls a

[KIMBER, EDWARD]   **141**
The history of the life and adventures of Mr. [Peter? or Thomas?] Anderson . . . in Europe and America. L 1754. D [2] 288 b JCB N NYP Y
—other eds.: *Dub* 1754. D 154 a; *Berwick* 1782. D 243 front; *L* n.d. [ca. 1790]; *Glas* 1799. D 243 aa
Supposedly compiled from Anderson's papers, tells of his being kidnapped in England, sold to a Maryland planter and later serving as a ranger against the Indians. If not authentic, it is the first work of fiction with an American setting.

[KIMBER, EDWARD, alias G. L.   **142**
CAMPBELL]
Itinerant observations in America . . . *Savannah* 1878. O 64 a 250 copies issued as a separate from v.4, *Ga. Hist. Soc. Colls.*

[KIMBER, EDWARD]   **143**
A relation . . . of a late expidition to the gates of St. Augustine. By a gentleman . . . *L* 1744. O 36 b LC N NYP Y
—rptd., with notes, *B* 1935. O [8] 36 [2] port facs 250 copies ptd. a

[KIMYSER, ARNOLD]   **144**
Ontdekking van 't geheel . . . Deel des Aardkloots America, Spaansche, Engelsche, Fransche . . . *Dordrecht* 1782. O [16] 198 [18] aa

Description of all North America, with emphasis on the new United States.

[KING, CAMERON H.]   **145**
Resources of Yuma county, Arizona . . . *Yuma* 1888. O 43 a

KING, CAMERON H.   **146**
Southern Arizona. *Phoenix* 1887. O 26 a

KING, CHARLES   **147**
The Fifth Cavalry in the Sioux war . . . *Milw* 1880. O [8] 134 b N
Narrative of service in the Big Horn and Yellowstone campaigns.

KING, CLARENCE   **148**
Mountaineering in the Sierra Nevada. *B* 1872. D [6] 292 a
—anr. issue, identical, except no pub's monogram on t-p recto and stereotyper's notice on t-p verso added.
—rptd.: *B* 1874. D 308 2maps; *N Y* 1879 same collat.
—Eng. ed., from sheets of Am. 1st ed., *L* 1872.
—anr. Eng. ed., same impr. & date, but ptd. in Eng.

KING, EDWARD   **149**
The great south . . . *Hart* 1875. O 806 map 4pls a
—Eng. ed. "The southern states . . .," *L* 1875. same collat.

KING, FRANK M.   **150**
Longhorn trail drivers . . . [*L A*] 1940. O 272 [incl.front.] a 400 copies ptd.

KING, FRANK M.   **151**
Wranglin' the past. [*L A* 1935]. O 244 port a 500copies ptd. [300 signed]
—rev. ed. [*Pasadena* 1946]. O 248[incl. front.] 8 pls

KING, (JAMES, of Wm.)
A true . . . history of the assassination of: [1856]. *See* Fargo, Frank F.

KING, RUFUS [pub.]   **152**
Directory of . . . Milwaukee, for 1848-9, with a sketch of the city . . . *Milw* 1848. D 204 map aa
Second Milwaukee directory and first to contain a map. For first directory, *see* McCabe, Julius P. B.

KING, THOMAS BUTLER   **153**
Report on California. *Wash* 1850 O 32 aa
—ed.2, and best. Same impr and date. O 72 errata lf aa
—unauthorized ed. "California: the wonder of the age". *N Y* 1850. O 34 a
—Ger. tr. *see* Fleischmann, Carl L., "Neuste officielle Berichte . . ."

This report to the government by the Collector of Customs at San Francisco gave Washington its first official information on the gold strike.

[KING, THOMAS BUTLER]   154
First annual report to the Directors of the Southern Pacific Railroad ... with notes on the advantages of the route ... *N Y* 1856. O 71 aa

KING, V. O.   155
The battle of San Jacinto ... *Austin* 1878. O 45 aa

KING, WILLIAM L.   156
The newspaper press of Charleston, S. C. ... *Charleston* 1872. D [12] 192 a

KING'S MOUNTAIN.
Battle of: *See* Shelby, Isaac.

KING'S MOUNTAIN.   157
Celebration of the battle of: ... *Yorkville S C* 1855. O 108 a

KINGDOM, WILLIAM   158
America and the British colonies ... comparative advantages ... *L* 1820. O [8] 360 a
—ed. 2, same date & collat.
Decides that the United States has less to offer than Canada.

KINGMAN (HENRY).   159
The travels and adventures of: in search of Colorado and California gold, 1859–65. *Delavan Kas* 1917. O [2] 68 port 6pls aa

KINGMAN, JOHN   160
Letters written ... on a tour to Illinois and Wisconsin ... 1838. *Hingham* 1842. D 48 b G N NYP Y [cf 5cops kn]

[KINGSBURY, GAINES P.]   161
Journal of the march of a detachment of dragoons, under the command of Colonel Dodge ... 1835. [*Wash* 1836]. Sen. Ex. Doc. 209. O 38 2maps aa
—anr. issue [H.R. 181], same impr. & date O 37 2maps aa
Another journal of the same expedition—by Lt. T. B. Wheelock—occupied pages 73–93, Senate Executive Document I, Washington 1834. aa

KINGSBURY, HARMON   162
The immigrant's good Samaritan. *N Y* 1848. 16° 117 a

[KINGSBURY, WIILLIAM G.]   163
A brief description of western Texas ... [with a report of the Stock-raising, Association]. *San Antonio* 1873. O 64 [incl wraps] aa

[KINGSFORD, WILLIAM]   164
Impressions of the west and south ... *Toronto* 1858. O 83 a

KINGSLEY, PROFESSOR [JAMES L.]   165
A sketch of the history of Yale college ... *B* 1835. O 48 a

[KINGSLEY, VINE W.]   166
Reconstruction in America. *N Y* 1865. O [2] 134 a

[KINGSLEY, Z.]   167
A treatise on the patriarchal, or cooperative system of society ... under the name of slavery ... n.p. [Tallahassee?] 1828. O 23 aa
—ed. 2, n.p. 1829. O 16 a
—ed. 3, n.p. 1833. O 22
—ed. 4, n.p. 1834. O 24

KINGSTON, JOHN   168
The life of General George Washington. *Balt* 1817. 16° 228 port a
See Condie, Thomas, of whose biography of Washington this is a shameless plagiarism.

KINO, EUSEBIO F.   169
Historical memoir ... of the beginnings of California, Sonora, and Arizona ... Tr. by H. E. Bolton. *Clev* 1919. O 2v: 379; 329. 7 maps & pls incl. in paginat. aa 750 cops ptd
—rptd. *Berkeley* 1948. O 2v in 1 a
First publication of the original Jesuit manuscript; of grave value on the eary southwest.

KINZIE, MRS. JULIETTE A. [McGILL]   170
Narrative of the massacre at Chicago ... *Chi* 1844. O 34 front. c LC N Y
—rptd *Chi* 1914 a
Most notable historical narrative from Chicago's pioneer press; based on conversations with Mrs. Helm and other survivors.

KINZIE, MRS. JULIETTE A. [McGILL]   171
Wau-Bun, the "Early Day" in the north-west ... *N Y* 1856. O 498 6pls aa
—ed. 2, same sheets with new t-p, *Chi* 1857. a
—rptd. *Phil* 1873; *Chi* Rand, 1901; *Chi* Caxton Club 1901; Menasha Wis 1930; *Chi* Lakeside 1932. O [28] 453 map 18 pls.

KIP, LAWRENCE   172
Army life on the Pacific ... *N Y* 1859. D 144 a
Best account, by a participant, of the 1858 campaign against the northwestern tribes.

[KIP, LAWRENCE]   173
The Indian council in the valley of the Walla-Walla. *S F* 1855. O 32 b only 25 copies printed G H NYP OreH Y
—rptd. *Eugene Ore* 1897. O 28 a

[KIP, LEONARD]   **174**
California sketches, with recollections of the gold mines. *Alb* 1850. D 57 aa
—rptd. *L A* 1946. O [16] 58[incl.blank 1f] 8pls errata slip 775copies[25signed] a

[KIP, LEONARD]?   **175**
The Volcano diggings . . . By a member of the bar. *N Y* 1851. 16° 131 + 12adv.-p a

KIP, WILLIAM I.   **176**
The early Jesuit missions in North America . . . *N Y* 1846. D 2v: [18] 135; [6] 19–321 [20] + 4adv-p map a. Also 2v. in 1
—rptd., same collat., 1847.
—best ed., with index, *Alb* 1866. D [16] 325 map
—rptd. *Alb* 1873. same collat.
—Eng ed. *L* 1847 D 2v

[KIP, WILLIAM I.]   **177**
A few days at Nashotah [mission]. *Alb* 1849. O 31 a

[KIPPIS, ANDREW]   **178**
Considerations on the provisional treaty with America . . . *L* 1783. O [4] 164 a
—ed. 2, cor., same impr. & date. O [2] 94
Attributed also to Richard Price. Defends the proposed terms and British wisdom in discontinuing hostilities.

KIPPIS, ANDREW   **179**
The life of Captain James Cook . . . *L* 1788. Q [16] 627 port aa
—other 1788 Eng. eds.: *Dub* O [16] 527; *Basel* O 2v a
—many Eng. reprints
—Fr. tr. *P* 1789. O 2v: [44] 388; [4] 420; same impr. & date. Q 546
—Ger. tr. *Hamburg* 1789. O 2v: 284; 301. port
Later editions entitled *A narrative of the voyages . . . performed by . . . Cook. With an account of his life . . .*

KIRCHOFF, THEODORE   **180**
Californische Kulturbilder. *Cassell* 1886. O 376 a

KIRCHOFF, THEODORE   **181**
Reisebilder und Skizzen aus Amerika . . . *Altoona* 1875–6. O 2v: 440; 426 a
Travelled from Texas to Oregon in 1867, visited the Idaho mines, etc.

KIRKHAM, GAWIN   **182**
A holiday tour in America . . . *L* [1884]. O 59 a
Went West as far as Denver.

[KIRKLAND, MRS. CAROLINE M.]   **183**
Forest life . . . *N Y* 1842. D 2v: 250; 234 a
—Eng. ed. *L* 1842. D 2v: [16] 302; [4] 320

—anr. Eng. ed. "The emigrant's home; or, real life in the west," *L* 1848. 32° 276
— *L* 1852. 16°

[KIRKLAND, MRS. CAROLINE M.]   **184**
A new home, who'll follow? or glimpses of western life. *N Y* 1839. D 317 a
—ed. 2, *N Y* 1840. D 2v
—ed. 3, same impr. 1841. D 298
—ed. 4, *N Y* 1850. D
—ed. 5, *N Y* 1855. D
—Eng. ed. "Montacute, or the new home . . .," *L* 1840. D 2v
—anr. Eng. ed., under original t., *L* 1842; *L* 1844 16°

KIRKLAND, MRS. C[AROLINE] M.   **185**
Western clearings . . . *N Y* 1845. D [10] 238 a
—rptd., same impr.: 1846; 1848.

KIRKLAND, JAMES   **186**
Chicago massacre of 1812. *Chi* 1893. O 221 a
Gives Mrs. Heald's narrative differing from Mrs. Kinzie's account [which followed the Helm tradition].

KIRKLAND, THOMAS J., and   **187**
KENNEDY, ROBERT M.
Historic Camden [S. C.] . . . *Columbia* 1905–26. O 2v: 424; [8] 486. 3fold.maps 40 pls & plans a

KIRKPATRICK, A. Y.   **188**
The early settlers' life in Texas . . . *Hillsboro Tex* [1909]. D 107 a

KIRKUP, THOMAS, ed.   **189**
A memoir of Duncan Wallace . . . his voyages . . . *Newcastle Eng* 1862. D [10] 210 port aa
Includes semi-piratical activities in the Gulf of Mexico in 1820 and later service in the United States Navy during which the Louisiana and Texas coasts were surveyed.

KIRKWOOD, JAMES P.   **190**
Report of the chief engineer upon the preliminary surveys. [Contained in the first annual report of the Board of Directors of the Pacific Railroad]. *St L* 1851. O 70 fold. map 12charts & tabs aa
First annual report of the first chartered Pacific railroad, now the Missouri Pacific.

KIRSTEN, A.   **191**
Skizzen aus den Vereinigten Staaten . . . *Leip* 1849. D [22] 375 a
—rptd: *Leip* 1851; 1854.

[KIRTLAND, JOHN T.]   **192**
The life of Commodore Edward Preble. n.p. [*ca* 1807]. O 30 port [$^1/_2$ t. only] a

KISSINGER, L.   **193**
History of Buffalo county [Wis.]. *Alma Wis*
1888. D 656 map port a

KITTLITZ, FRIEDRICH H. VON   **194**
Denkwürdigkeiten einer Reise nach dem russi-
schen Amerika . . . *Gotha* 1858. O 2v: [16] 384;
[4] 464. 4pls aa
For an earlier narrative of this voyage *See*
Litké, Fedorem P.

KITTLITZ, FRIEDRICH H. VON   **195**
Vierundzwanzig Vegetations . . . *Siegen* 1844–5.
F 2v: [one of text, one of 24pls] aa
—Eng tr, "Twenty-four views of the vegetation
of the coasts and islands of the Pacific . . ."
L 1861. Q [10] 68 24pls aa
For other delineations of scenery, etc., made by
Baron Kittlitz on the coasts of northwest America,
while with Litke's 1826–9 expedition, *see* Litke,
Fedorem P.

KLAUPRECHT, EMIL   **196**
Deutsche Chronik in der Geschichte des Ohio-
Thales, [etc.]. *Cin* [1864]. O 198 a
Important material on the early settlement of
Ohio, Klauprecht wrote also a semi-fictionized
narrative of life in the west, entitled *Cincinnati,
oder Gehimnisse des Westens*, Cincinnati, 1854.

[KLAUSING, ANTON E.] tr.   **197**
Geschichte der englischen Kolonien in Nord-
amerika . . . *Leip* 1775–6. 16° 2v: [16] 452; [8]
424 [8]. map aa
Published to give Germans a background of the
Revolution. For original English edition *See History
of the British dominions in North America* . . .

KLEE, FREDERICK   **198**
Amerika isoer i den nyeste Tid, en historisk-
statistik haanbbog. *Copenh* 1837–1839. O [10]
482 aa

KLEINKNECHT, CONRAD D.   **199**
Zuverläsige Nachricht . . .: Nachrichten von
den . . . Colonisten Georgiens zu Eben-Ezer . . .
Augsburg 1749. O [36] 216 [16]; 376 [56] front aa

KLERK, J. DE   **200**
Van den oorspronk en der Kracht der Vooroordeelen, door J. T. Als mede een Koort Uyt-
treskel uyt de Aanteykeninge van de Baron de
Lahontan, rakende de Zeden, 't Geloof, en 't
verstant van de Wilden tot Canada . . . *Amst*
1710. D 52 b
—rptd. *Amst* 1723. D 39 aa

KLINCKOWSTROM, AXEL L.   **201**
Bref om de Förenta Staterna författade under
en resa till Amerika. *Stockh* 1824. O 2v: [4 10]
242 errata lf tab; [8] 274–275 277–496 errata

lf + Atlas F 6 maps & plans 10pls. 2lvs [one
describing a pl, the other listing pls] c N NYP Y
[The 3 eng. titles are counted in the 19pls listed
in the Atlas volume)].

KLONDIKE   **202**
Facts for Klondikers . . . *Seattle* 1898. O 40 a

Guide, map and history of the Klondyke   **203**
. . . **gold fields.** *Chi* L. M. Lord & Co. n.d.
D 46 map a

Guide to the Klondike and the Yukon gold   **204**
fields . . . *Seattle* 1897. D 115 a

Klondike and all about it. By a practical mining
engineer. *See* Carey, T. J.

The official guide to the Klondyke country   **205**
. . . *Chi* Conkey 1897. D 296 front. 7maps a

KLOPFER, EMIL   **206**
Travel, reminiscences and experiences. *Alameda*
1894. D 264 aa
Covers California and Oregon.

KNAPP, H[ORACE] S.   **207**
A history . . . of Ashland county, Ohio . . .
Phil 1863. O 550 pl a

KNAPP, H[ORACE] S.   **208**
History of the Maumee valley . . . *Toledo* 1872.
O [6] 667 26pls a

KNAPP, N. M.   **209**
Historical sketch of Scott county, Illinois . . .
Winchester Ill 1876. O 36 aa

[KNAPP, SAMUEL L.]   **210**
Extracts from a journal of travels . . . con-
sisting of an account of Boston . . . *B* 1818.
D 124 a

[KNAPP, SAMUEL L.]   **211**
Memoirs of General Lafayette. With an account
of his visit to America . . . *B* 1824. D 264 port a

KNICKERBOCKER, DIEDRICH
A history of New York . . . *See* Irving, Washington.

[KNIGHT, HENRY COGSWELL]   **212**
Letters from the south and west. By Arthur
Singleton [*pseud.*] *B* 1824. O 159 a

KNIGHT, JOHN   **213**
The emigrant's best instructor. [cov.t.] Im-
portant extracts from . . . letters: written by
Englishmen, in the United States. [regular t.]
Manch Eng 1818. O 72 aa
—ed. 2, same collat., *L*[1818]. aa

KNIGHT, DR. [JOHN], and   **214**
SLOVER, JOHN
Narratives of a late expedition against the Indians . . . the barbarous execution of Col. William Crawford and the wonderful escape of Dr. Knight and John Slover from captivity. *Phil* 1773[error for 1783]. 16° 38 dd PittU [only copy known]
—issue 2, date corrected to 1783. dd N PaU [only copies known]
—anr. ed., t. slightly altered and captivity of Mrs. Scott added, *Andover* Ames & Parker [1799?]. 16° 46 d AA NYP WisH
—anr. ed. "Remarkable narrative . . .," [*Leominster*] Chapman Whitcomb [1800?]. D 24 c AA
—anr. ed. "Indian atrocities . . .," ed., with adds., by H. H. Brackenridge, *Nashv* 1843. D 96 b Hn N NYP
—rptd. *Cin* 1867. D 72 500 copies[75 on thick paper] a
For interest and importance, in Ohio valley history of the period, comparable only to Filson's *Kentucky* and the narratives of Matthew Bunn and Col. James Smith.

KNIGHT, LUCIAN L.   **215**
Georgia's landmarks, memorials and legends. *Atlanta* 1913–14. O 2v: [16] 1065; [14] 1190. 54pls aa

KNIGHT, LUCIAN L.   **216**
Remisniscences of famous Georgians . . . *Atlanta* 1907–8. D 2v: [22] 763; [20] 723. 33pls errata slip in v.I a

KNIGHT, MADAM [SARAH K.]   **217**
The private journal of a journey from Boston to New York . . . 1704. *Alb* 1865. Q 92 a 350copies ptd [50 on L.P.]
—rptd: *N Y* [1869]; *Norwich* 1901; *B* 1920.
For first edition, *see* following entry.

KNIGHT (MADAM [SARAH K.) and   **218**
BUCKINGHAM (THE REV. MR.)
The journals of: . . . *N Y* 1825. D 129 aa
See preceding entry for later editions of the Knight *Journal.*

KNIGHT, THOMAS, and   **219**
GREENE, NANCY L.
Country estates of the Blue Grass. [*Clev*] 1904. Q 200[incl.pls] a

[KNOX, GEN. HENRY]   **220**
A plan for the general arrangement of the militia of the United States. [*N Y* 1786]. O 34 a
—rptd. *N Y* 1790. F 26
Advocating military service for all men over eighteen and under sixty-five.

KNOX, J. A., and PRATT, J. G.   **221**
All about the Klondike gold miners. *N Y* 1897. D 59 a

KNOX, CAPT. JOHN   **222**
An historical journal of the campaigns in North-America, 1757–1760. *L* 1769. O 2v: [16] 405 [2]; [2] 465 [2]. map 2ports b AA JCB N NYP Y
—rptd. *Tor* Champlain Soc 1914–16. O 3v aa 520copies ptd.
Reliable, full and interesting.

KNOX, JOHN J.   **223**
A history of banking in the United States. *N Y* 1900. O [24] 880 pls a
—rev. ed. *N Y* 1903. O [22] 880 pls

[KNOX, WILLIAM]   **224**
An appendix to The present state of the nation . . . *L* 1769. O 62 a
—anr. issue, with app., same impr. & date. O 68
Attempt to answer Burke's *Observations on a late State of the nation.*

[KNOX, WILLIAM]   **225**
The claim of the colonies to an exemption from internal taxes imposed by . . . parliament . . . *L* 1765. O [2] 46 a

[KNOX, WILLIAM]   **226**
The controversy between Great Britain and her colonies reviewed . . . *L* 1769. O [4] 207 [55] aa
—*Dub* 1769. same collat. a
—Am. ed. *B* 1769. O 100 a
Ascribed also to Thomas Whately, M. P. and former secretary to Lord Grenville, but probably by Knox, who was Under Secretary of State for America at this time.

[KNOX, WILLIAM]   **227**
The present state of the nation . . . its trade finances . . . *L* 1768. Q 48 + 4adv-p a
—rptd.: same impr. & date: O 100; O 155; 1769. O [4] 9–107
—anr. ed. *Dub* 1768.
This defense of Grenville's ministry and of American taxation has been erroneously ascribed to Thomas Whately and to Grenville himself. For answer *see* Burke, Edmund, *Observations* . . .

KNOXVILLE   **228**
The half-century of Knoxville: . . . *Knoxv* 1842. O 106 aa

Knoxville directory . . . 1859–60. *Knoxville*   **229**
1859 O 87 72 aa
First directory of this city.

KOB, KARL F.   **230**
Wegweiser für Ansiedler im Territorium Kansas ... *N Y* 1857. O 42 + 6adv-p a

KOBER (GEORGE M.)   **231**
Reminiscences of: ... Vol. I[all]. *Wash* 1930. O [24] 403 a
Includes his western experiences as an army surgeon.

KOCH, ALBERT C.   **232**
Description of the Hydrarchos Harlani ... a gigantic fossil reptile ... in the state of Alabama ... *N Y* 1845. O 16 a
—ed. 2, same impr. & date. O 24
—Ger. tr. *Dresden* [1845?]. O 32

KOCH, ALBERT C.   **233**
Description of the Missourium, or Missouri leviathan ... its supposed habits and Indian traditions ... *L* 1841. O 24 aa
—Am. ed., probably has priority, *St L* 1841 O 16 aa
—Am. ed. 2, enl., *Louisv* 1841. O 20 a
—anr. ed. [called "ed. 5, enl."] *Dub* 1843. O 28
—Ger. trs.: *Magdeburg* 1844. O pl; *Berlin* 1845. O 8pls a

KOCH, ALBERT C.   **234**
Reise durch einen Theil der Vereinigten Staaten ... 1844–6. *Dresden* 1847. O [4] 162 2pls aa
Chiefly in central west and south.

KOCH, F[RIEDRICH] C. L.   **235**
Die deutschen Kolonien in der Nähe des Saginaw-Flusses ... *Braunschweig* 1851. O 48 map aa

KOCH, F[RIEDRICH] C.L.   **236**
Die Mineral-Regionen der obern Halbinsel Michigan's [N.A.] am Lake Superior und die Isle Royale ... *Göttingen* 1852. O 248 map aa

KOCH, J. G. F.   **237**
Versuch eines Kriegs-Rechts der Negern in Afrika und der Indianer in Amerika. *Tübingen* 1781. O 86 aa
—rptd., same impr. & collat. 1786. a

[KOCHERTHAL, JOSHUA], tr.   **238**
Ausführlich- und umständlicher Bericht von der berühmten Landschaft Carolina ... *Frankf* 1709. O 80 map aa
Abridged German version of John Lawson's *New voyage to Carolina* ... for a complete translation. *See* Visher, Edward.

[KÖHLER, CARL]   **239**
Briefe aus Amerika für deutsche Auswanderer ... *Darmstadt* 1852. D [6] 234 5pls aa
—ed. 2, enl., same impr., 1854. D [8] 288 6pls a
—ed. 3, same impr. & collat. 1856.

KÖPFLI & SUPPIGER (FAMILIE).   **240**
Reisebericht der: nach St. Louis ... und Gründung von New-Switzerland im Staate Illinois. *Sursee* 1833. 16° [6] 235 [2] front. b
—ed. 2, same impr. & date. 16° [8] 298 [2] front. map b N NYP

KÖRNER, GUSTAV [P].   **241**
Beleuchtung des Duden'schen Berichtes über die westlichen Staaten ... *Frankf* 1834. O 62 fold.map a

KÖRNER, GUSTAV [P.]   **242**
Das deutsche Element in den Vereinigten Staaten ... 1818–1848. *Cin* 1880. O 461 errata, 1f a
—ed. 2, *N Y* 1884. O 468

KÖRNER (GUSTAVE [P.])   **243**
Memoirs of: *Cedar Rapids* 1909. O 2v: [16] 628; [12] 768. 2ports aa

KOHL, J[OHANN] G.   **244**
Die beiden ältesten General-Karten von Amerika ... *Weimar* 1860. F [10] 186 2maps a

KOHL, J[OHANN] G.   **245**
Geschichte der Entdeckung Amerika's von Columbus bis Franklin ... *Bremen* 1861. O [8] 454 a
—Eng. ed. "A popular history of discovery of America ...," *L* 1862. D 2v: [10] 275; [6] 284. errata 1f; rptd. *L* 1865.

KOHL, J[OHANN] G.   **246**
History of the discovery of ... the coast of Maine ... *Port Me* 1869. O [14] 9–535 22maps a [In Maine Hist. Soc. Colls.]

KOHL, J[OHANN] G.   **247**
Kitschi-Gami, oder Erzählungen vom Obern-See ... *Bremen* 1859. O 2v in 1: [8] 328; [2] 272 aa
—Eng. ed. "Kitchi-Gami. Wanderings round Lake Superior," *L* 1860. O [12] 428 + 32adv-p aa

KOHL, J[OHANN] G.   **248**
Reisen in Canada, und durch die Staaten von New-York und Pennsylvanien ... *Stuttgart* 1856. O [4] 576 a
—Eng. tr. *L* 1861. O 2v: [10] 346; [4] 358. diag a

KOHL, J[OHANN] G.   **249**
Reisen im Nordwesten der Vereinigten Staaten ... *N Y* 1857. O [6] 534 aa
—anr iss undated, same collat, bears impr *St L* & *Neustadt*. a
—ed 2, with map & 11pls added, *N Y* 1858. O same paginat. aa

KONSAG, FERNANDO   **250**
Konsag, Fernando ... visitador de las misiones de Californias. Carta del: à los padres

superiores de . . . Nueva-España. [*Mex* 1748].
Q 43 capt.t.only c H JCB NYP Y
Gives a biography of Father Antiono Tempis, early California missionary.

KOOTENAI GUIDE 251
Kootenai guide . . . to the mining camps of British Columbia and Klondike. *Rossland Can* 1898. D 78 map a

KORDUL, A. 252
Der sichere fuhrer nach und in Texas . . . *Rottwel am Neckar* 1846. 16° [8] 394 [4] aa

KORT EN BONDIGH VERHAEL . . . 253
Amst, Benjamin, 1667. Q 256 map 3pls b NYP
—iss. 2, same impr. date and collat but with no map and only 1 pl a
—Fr. tr. "Description exacte . . ." *Amst* 1668. a
Best contemporary account of the war between England, France and Holland in which the latter country lost New Amsterdam.

KORTE BESCHRIJVINGE 254
Korte Beschrijvinge der Vereenigde Staten . . . *Nijmegen* 1847. D 47 a

KOSTERING, J. F. 255
Auswanderung der sachsischen Lutheraner im Jahr 1838 ihre Niederlassung in Perry-Co., Mo. *St L* 1866. 16° [24] 279 aa

KOTTENKAMPF, FRANZ 256
Geschichte der Colonization Amerikas . . . *Frankf* 1850. O 2v: [8] 606; [4] 459 a

KOTTENKAMPF, FRANZ 257
Der Unabhängigkeitskampf der spanisch-amerikanischen Colonien. *Stuttgart* 1838. O [10] 459 a
Supplementary volume to Ernst Münch's *Allgemeine Geschichte der neusten Zeit*, giving account of the acquisition of Florida, etc.

KOTZEBUE, OTTO VON 258
Entdeckungs-Reise in die Süd-See und nach der Berings-Strasse . . . 1815–18. *Weimar* 1821. Q 3v: [26] 168; 176; 240. 6maps 2tabs 20pls [19col] b
—issue on L. P. d
—rptd. *Hannover* 1821. O 2v; *Vienna* 1825, O 3v b
—Eng. tr "A voyage of discovery into the South sea and Beering's straits . . ." *L* Longman 1821 O 3v: [16] 358; [4] 434; [4] 442. 7maps 9pls [8 col] b N Y
—rptd. *L* Phillips 1821. O 2pts in 1 4maps 8pls[2col] a
—Dutch tr. *Amst* 1822. O 3v maps pls a
—Rus. tr "Poutechestvïe v ïoujenoï okean. Voyage dans l'ocean de sud et au detroit de Bering . . ." *St Petersb* 1821-3. O 3v + atlas [of 2maps] F aa

Important Russian explorations of the northwest and California coasts. For another narrative of this voyage *See* Choris, Louis.

KOTZEBUE, OTTO VON 259
Puteshestvie vokrug svieta . . . na voennom shliupie Predpriiatii . . . 1823–6. *St Ptbg* 1828. O [8] 200 4maps aa
—Ger. tr "Neue Reise um die Welt . . . 1823–26," *Weimar* 1830. O 2v: [24] 191; 172 [34]. 3maps [on 2 sheets] 2col pls aa
—Dutch tr. Haarlem 1830. O 2v: [8] 254; [6] 274 [1]. 3maps 2 pls aa
—Eng tr "A new voyage round the world . . ." *L* 1830. D 2v: [8] 341; [6] 362. port 3maps pl b
—Swed tr *Stockh* 1830. O 394 pl a
Describes a lengthy stay at the Russian California settlement at Ft. Ross.

KOWALSKI, HENRI 261
À travers l'Amérique . . . *P* 1872. O [12] 268 a

KRACKENFUSS, ABRAHAM 262
Münchausen in California . . . *Bremen* 1849. D [6] 73 a
Wail from the victim of a fraudulent California mining project.

[KRAITSIR, CHARLES V.] 263
The Poles in the United States . . . *Phil* 1837. 16° [8] 196 a

K[RAMER], J[OHANN] M. 264
Neuste und richtigste Nachricht von der Landschaft Georgia . . . *Göttingen* 1746. O 88 aa

KRASHENINNIKOV, STEFAN P. 265
Opisanie zemli Kamchatki sochinennoe . . . *St Ptbg* 1755. O 2v: fold.pls & maps b
—rptd. *St Ptbg:* 1786; 1818-19. aa
—Dutch tr. *Amst* 1770. O [6 3-14] 384 [14] 3pls eng.t. a
—anr. issue, with *Haarlem* impr.
—Eng. tr., abr. by Grieve, "The history of Kamtschatka . . ." *Gloucester* 1764. Q [8] 280 [8] 2maps 7pls [on 5 sheets] aa
—Fr. tr., from abr. Eng. tr., *Lyons* 1767. D 2v: [16] 327; [8] 359. 2maps [sometimes joined together] a
—anr. Fr. tr., unabr. from Russian original, *Amst* 1770. D 2v: [20] 439; [4] 493. map [on2 sheets] 7pls [on 4 sheets] aa
—Ger. tr., from abr. Eng. ed., by Köhler, *Lemgo* 1766. Q [16] 344 4maps 3pls aa
—rptd. same impr. 1789, same collat aa
Contains one of the earliest descriptions of Russian America and the Kurile Islands.

KRESS, BRIG. GEN. JOHN A. 266
Memoirs. [*N Y* 1936]. O 51 front. a
Author was stationed at Ft. Vancouver in the early 'seventies.

KRETSCHMER, KONRAD   267
Die Entdeckung Amerikas... *Berlin* 1892.
Q [24] 471 + Atlas F [6] 40col.pls aa

KROEBER, ALFRED L.   268
Hand book of the Indians of California. *Wash*
1925. O [18] 995 fold.map[in pocket] 10 other
maps 73pls[on 38sheets] aa
—rptd. *Berkeley* [1953] O a

KRUEGER, M[AX]   269
Pioneer life in Texas; an autobiography...
[*San Antonio ca* 1930]. O [6]13–226 [2] port a

KRUSENSTERN, ADAM J. VON   270
Atlas de l'océan Pacifique... *St Ptbg* 1824–7.
F [12] 34maps b
—ed. 2, same impr. 1827 [ptd 1838?]. F [16]
34maps b Y
For explanatory volumes on this *Atlas, see*
below *Beytrage zur hydrographie* ...

KRUSENSTERN, ADAM J. VON   271
Beyträge zur Hydrographie der grössern
Ozeane als erläuterungen zu einer Charte...
Leip 1819. Q 248 map aa
—Rus. tr. *St Ptbg* 1823. Q 2v + suppl [*St Ptbg*
1826. Q] 3v in all b
—Fr. tr "Recueil de mémoires hydrographiques
... d'explication a l'Atlas de l'océan Pacifique,"
St Ptbg 1824–7. Q 2v + "supplemens" *St Ptgb*
1835. Q 172 map 3v in all b
Both Russian and French editions should
preferably be accompanied by the folio *Atlas de
l'ocean Pacifique*, entered separately above.

KRUSENSTERN, ADAM J. VON   272
Poutechestvie vokroug svéta. Voyage autour du
monde... 1803–1806. *St Ptbg* 1809–12–14. Q 3v;
1010 + F atlas [of 105pls] 1814. d Y
—Ger. tr "Reise um die Welt..." *St Ptbg*
1810–12–13–14. Q 3v + F atlas [of 105pls]
c N NYP Y
—rptd. *Berlin* 1811–12. 16° 2v in 3 map 14
pls aa
—Dutch tr "Reise om de Wereld...," *Haarlem*
1811–15. O 4v map pls aa
—Eng. tr. *L* 1813. Q 2v: [40] 314; [10] 404. 1f of
binding directions map 2pls b N NYP Y
—Fr. tr. *P* 1821. O 2v: [12] 418; [4] 531 + F
atlas [4p 30maps & pls] b
—Ital. tr. *Milan* 1818. 16° 3v a
First Russian voyage around the world; of
great value for the Northwest coast. For other
official accounts by co-commanders, *see* Lisianskii,
and Langsdorff.

KU-KLUX-KLAN   273
Horrible disclosures. A full and authentic exposé
of the Ku-Klux-Klan. *Cin* 1868. O 9–109 a

The masked lady of the White House: or   274
the Ku-Klux-Klan... startling exposure... of
this extensive secret band. *Phil* [1868]. O 19–62 a

The oaths, signs, ceremonies and objects   275
of the Ku-Klux-Klan... By a late member. *Clev*
1868. D 30 aa

The terrible mysteries of the Ku-Klux-Klan...
By Scalpel, M. D. *See* Dixon, Edw. H.

KÜNZEL, HEINRICH   276
Obercalifornien... *Darmstadt* 1848. D [4] 41
map aa
First German pamphlet promoting California
emigration.

KURNBERGER, FERDINAND   277
Der Amerika-Müde... *Frankf* 1885. O [4] 504 a
—ed. 2, *Leip* [1889?]. 16° 580
Reactions towards American life by a dis-
gruntled visitor.

KUNSTMANN, FRIEDRICH   278
Die Entdeckung Amerikas. *Munich* 1859. Q [4]
151 + Atlas F [4] 13col.maps b BP N NYP Y
Six of the maps, from an unpublished manuscript of the sixteenth century, give details of the
California coast; another, done in 1592, shows the
coasts of Florida, Virginia, etc.

KUNZE, JOHANN C.   279
Eine Aufforderung an das Volk Gottes in
Amerika zum frohen Jauchzen und Danken...
Phil 1784. D 101 aa

KURTH, GODEFROID   280
Sitting Bull. *Brus* 1879. O 305 cov-t only
[separate from *Revue Générale*] aa

KURZ (RUDOLPH F.)   281
The journal of:... among fur traders... on the
Mississippi and upper Missouri rivers, 1846–52.
Wash 1937. O 382 382 48pls aa

KURZGEFASSTE... NACHRICHTEN   282
Kurzgefasste historisch-geographische Nach-
richten von den englischen Kolonien in Nord
Amerika... *Hamburg* 1778. D 31 a

KUTCHERA, E. E.   283
Briefe eines Deutschen aus Nord-Amerika au
seine freunde. *Saaz* 1837. D [24] 163 aa
Describes trip through western New York,
Ohio and Indiana.

KUYKENDALL, W[ILLIAM] L.   284
Frontier days... n.p. [*Denver?*] 1917. D 251
port a
Personal narrative, by the presiding judge at
the trial of Wild Bill Hickok's assassin, of life
in the West after the Civil War.

L

L., M[ONS.] DE
Histoire impartiale des évenemens . . . de la dernière guerre . . . *See* Longchamps, Pierre de.

L., B. V.   **1**
Die Glaubwürdigkeit von Maldonados nordwestlicher Schiffahrt. *Gotha* 1712. O 52 a

L., D.
California. *See* Lancelot, D.

L., D.   **2**
The diggers' handbook and truth about California. *Sydney* 1849. O 110 a
It has been suggested that these initials [D. L.] stand for Damned Liar; possibly by D. Lancelot, *q.v.*

L. T. D.
A peep at the western world. *See* Laudoin, Thomas D.

LA BORDE, M[AXIMILIAN]   **3**
History of the South Carolina College . . . to 1857. *Columbia* 1859. O 464 a
—ed. 2, brought to 1865, *Charleston* 1874, O [44] 596

LA BREE, BEN, ed.   **4**
The Confederate soldier in the civil war, 1861–65. *Louisv* 1895. F 480 col.front. aa
—rptd, same impr. & collat., 1897, aa; *N Y* 1959 a

LA CARRIÈRES, A. C. DE   **5**
Voyage aux pays aurifères, Afrique, Mexique, Californie . . . *P* [1855]. O [4] 328 12pls aa

LACHAPELLE, A[LFRED] DE, ed.   **6**
Le comte de Raousset-Boulbon et l'expédition de la Sonore. *P* 1859. D [2] 318 [2] map port aa

[LACOCK, ABNER]   **7**
Great national object. Proposed connection of the eastern and western waters, by a communication through the Potomac country. [*Wash* 1822]. O 38 aa
Project was to connect the Delaware and Ohio rivers by a series of canals. Lacock was one of the commissioners appointed to survey the Potomac and the ninety-two page *Report* of that Commission sometimes accompanies the above.

LACOSTE, AUGUSTE   **8**
Californiae. Fragments . . . d'un voyage autour du monde. *P* 1849. O 32 aa

LACY, MARY   **9**
The female shipwright; or, life and extraordinary adventures of Mayr [*sic*] Lacy . . . *Phil* 1814. D 35 fold.pl a

[LADD, WILLIAM]   **10**
A letter to Aaron Burr . . . on the . . . baneful effects of duels. *N Y* 1804. O 32 a

LADE (CAPITAINE ROBERT).   **11**
Voyages du: en l'Afrique, l'Asie et l'Amerique . . . *P* 1744, D 2v: [18] 370; [2] 400 [last p. numb. erroneously 360] 2maps aa
—anr. ed. *Amst* 1784. O 591 2maps a
—rptd., *P* 1810 O [16] 599 2 maps
Purports to be a translation by Abbé Prevost from the English, but no English edition known. Contains a long account of affairs in the infant colony of Georgia, probably translated from some English work.

LÀDRON DE GUEVARA, ANTONIO   **12**
Noticias de los poblados, y tratos de que se componen el Nuevo Reyno de Leon, provincia de Coaguila, Nueva Estremadura, y provincia de las Texas . . . [*Mex*?] 1739. F 32 c JCB
—rptd., with changes, [*Mex*] same date. F 36 c Hn JCB
Mercilessly critical of missionaries and governing authorities, military and civil, in the northern frontier region.

LADUE, JOSEPH   **13**
Klondyke facts . . . *N Y* [1897]. 0 205 18maps & pls a
—anr. issue, same collat. & date, *Mont*
By a pioneer Alaskan, the founder of Dawson.

LADUE, JOSEPH   **14**
Klondyke nuggets . . . *N Y* [1897]. O 92 + 4 adv-p a

LAFAYETTE (MARIE J. P. R. Y. GILBERT DE MOTIER) marquis de   **15**
Mémoires, correspondance . . . du: . . . *P* 1837–8. 0 6v: [12] 495; [4] 504; [4] 520; [6] 449; [4] 545; [4] 814 map & port [in some cops] aa
—rptd. *Brus* 1837. 16° 12v aa
—anr. issue, same impr. & date. O 2v [14] 526; [4] 575 a
—Eng. tr. [first 3v only] *L* 1837. O 3v: [16] 469; [8] 480; [8] 497. port a
—Am. ed. [first vol. only] *N Y* 1837. O [24] 552 port

LA FAYETTE (GENERAL).   **16**
Memoirs of: embracing details of public and private life . . . *Hart* 1825. D 455 a
—rptd. *N Y* 1825. D port

LA FAYETTE (THE MARQUIS DE).   17
Memoirs of the military career of: . . . *B* 1824.
O 56 a

LAFAYETTE (GEN.)   18
Memoirs of: with an account of his tour through
the United States . . . *B* 1825. O 24 a

LAFAYETTE.
Memoirs of: with an account of his visit to
America. *See* Knapp, Saml. L.

LA FAYETTE (MARQUIS DE).   19
Vie privée . . . du: . . . *P* 1790. O 88 port a
A scurrilous lampoon.

LA FAYETTE (LE MARQUIS DE).   20
Vie publique et privée de: [*P*] 1791. O 69 a

LA FAYETTE (GENERAL).   21
Visit of: to Louisiana . . . By a citizen of New
Orleans. *N O* 1825. D 86 a
—Fr. tr. *N O* 1825. D pl

LAFAYETTE (GÉNÉRAL).
Voyage du: aux États-Unis . . .
See Barbaroux, Chas. O., and Lardier, J. A.

LAFITAU, P. [JOSEPH FRANCOIS]   22
Moeurs des sauvages Amériquains . . . *P* 1724.
Q 2v: [22] 610 [2]; [12] 490 [41], map 42pls b
—rptd: *P* 1724, D 4v: [24] 256; [8] 296; [12] 248;
[8] 196 [66]. map 42pls; *Amst* 1730, D 4v; *P* 1733,
Q 2v [32] 616; [48] 694 [89] map 16 pls; *P* 1734,
D 4v in 2 aa
—Dutch ed. "De Zeden der Wilden van Amerika,"
Hague 1731, F 2v in 1: [58] 555 [for 560] map 42
pls; *Amst* 1751, F 2v in 1 [28] 300; [4] 260 42pls
map b
Comprehensive and meticulous information on
the Iroquois and other northern tribes acquired by
a long residence among them.

LAFITTE.   23
The memoirs of: . . . *Prov* 1826. 16° 125 port aa

[LA HARPE, BERNARD DE]   24
Journal historique de l'établissement des Francais à la Louisiane . . . *N O* [*P* ptd] 1831. O [4]
412 aa
Chief authority for the period covered, 1698–
1723; it and the *Memoires* of Dumont de Marigny
serve as sequels to Joutel's *Journal*. La Harpe was
pseudonym for Chevalier de Beaubien.

LAHONTAN, BARON   25
Nouveaux voyages . . . [together with vol. II,
"Mémoires . . . ou la suite des voyages . . .,"] dans
l'Amérique Septentrionale . . . *Hague* Frères l'Honoré 1703. 16° 2v: [22] 279; 220 [16]. 3maps
[2fold.] 22pls 4fronts. [same 2 in each vol.] t-p of

each vol. in red & black, with "angel" vignette b
Clem N NYP
—issue 2, t-p of each vol. in red & black, with
small "scroll" ornament, text re-set, maps & pls
re-eng. 16° 2v: [24] 279; 220 [17]. 3maps[2fold. but
smaller than those in issue 1] 22pls front.[one only
and only in vol.I] b
—issue 3, t-p of each vol. in black, maps & pls
re-eng. & improved, with ornament on t-pp
changed to a "globe." Collates same as issue 2, but
some copies contain an extra pl. at p211, vol.I
[same subject and differing but slightly from one
at p14] b
—anr. ed., re-set in larger type, *Hague* Frères l'Honoré 1704. D 2v: [20] 280; 222 [18] 3maps 23 pls
[incl.front.to vol.I] aa
—"seconde edition, revuë, corrigée, & augmen-
tée," including "Dialogues" [issued as a part of a
separate vol.III with former eds.,] *Hague* Jonas
l'Honoré 1705. 16° [18 incl.eng.t.] 376; 336[incl.
initial blank] 3maps [two fold.] 24pls aa
—anr. issue, pub. by Francois l'Honoré, identical
except for t-p and the omission of one pl. from
vol.I[i.e., the pl. of a globe and a bird found at p. 1
of the Jonas l'Honoré ed.] aa
—rptd., same collat. as the Jonas l'Honoré ed. of
1705, *Hague* Delo 1706.   aa
—anr. ed. *Hague* Delorme 1707–08. 16° 2v: [18]
354 [12]; [2] 239. 3fold.maps 21pls [incl.front. to
vol.I]
—anr. ed. *Hague* Frères l'Honoré 1709. 16° 2v:
[20] 280; 222 [18]. 3maps[2fold.] 23pls [incl.front.
to vol. I] aa
—anr. ed. *Hague* Delorme 1712. 16° 2v: [18] 354
[12]; [2] 239. 3maps 19pls [no front.to vol.I in only
copy located, but perhaps one should be there] aa
—rptd. same impr. 1715. 16° 2v: [18] 280; 222
[18]. 3maps 23pls[incl.front. to vol.I] aa
—anr. ed. calling itself "seconde edition, revuée
. . .," *Amst* Francois l'Honoré 1728. 16° 2v: [18]
408; [2] 238. 3maps[2fold.] 23pls[incl.front. to
vol.I] aa
—tptd. same impr. 1741. 16° 2v in 3: [vol.I, "Voyages . . ."; vol.II, "Suite de voyages . . ."; vol.III]
"Mémoires de l'Amérique . . ."] [10] 188 [4]; [6]
220; [2] 237. 3maps[2fold.] 24pls[incl.front. to
vol.I] aa
—Dutch ed., abr. "Van den oorspronk en de
kracht der Vooroordeelen, door J. T. Als mede een
kort Uyttreksel uyt de Aanteykeninge van de
Baron de Lahontan . . .," *Amst* 1710. D 52 a
—rptd., t. altered, n.p. 1723. O 29 29–39 a
—anr. ed., complete, with add. notes, "Reizen van
den Baron van La Hontan . . .," *Hague* 1739. D
2v [vol.II entitled "Gedenkschiften van het Noor-
delyk Amerika . . ."]: [14] 190 193–281 [3] 281–
582; [2] 8 5-552. 2fold.maps 16 pls aa
—Eng. ed. "New voyages to North Amerika . . .,"
L 1703. O 2v: [24] 280[ending with what seems an
incompleted Index (letter "T"), and a superfluous
catch-word "The" at foot of that page]; [2] 302 +

adv-l. [13]. 4maps[3fold.] 20pls[incl.front. to vol. II] Inasmuch as t-p of vol.I calls for only 23maps & pls, and as so many copies of vol.II lack front. it is a fair assumption that some copies were issued without it. b Clem JCB NYP Y
—Eng. ed. 2, *L* 1735. [vol.I pub. either by Bonwicke or Osborn; vol.II pub. by Walthoe, Bonwicke, Osborn, *et al*] O 2v: [24] 280; 304. 4maps [2fold.] 16pls[incl.front.to vol.II] b
—anr. issue, both vols. pub. by Brindley, same impr., date & collat. [t-pp in vol.I of all 1735 London eds. call erroneously for 23maps & pls] b
—Ger. tr., abr., *Hamburg* 1709. D [12 incl.double-p.t.] 459 small fold.map aa
—anr. Ger. ed., complete, same impr. 1711. D [24 incl.double-p.t.] 753 fold.map aa
—Ital. tr.[of vol.I only], *Milan* 1831. D 2v: 216; 202 a
  The two volumes—*Voyages* and *Memoires*—were apparently, in early editions, sold both separately and in sets. This explains the frequent appearance of individual volumes and of sets not uniform and often with different imprints and dates. As collectors today insist on the set form, the work is here so treated. What constitutes a third volume, but of no historical significance and not generally found with the others, is entered separately, below, under *Suplement.*
  Lahontan's narrative, of considerable value when confined to his actual sojourneyings in the Lake region, was unfortunately disfigured by his inserting an account of a pretended trip west of the Mississippi, about as convincing as the legends of the sea-serpent.

LAHONTAN (BARON).   26
  Suplement aux Voyages du: ou l'on trouve des dialogues curieux entre l'auteur et un sauvage . . . aussi plusieurs observations faites par le même auteur, dans ses voyages en Portugal . . . Tome troisieme. *Hague* Honoré 1703. 16° [16] 222 2fold. maps 4pls b BM JCB NYP
—reissued, from same sheets, with new t., "Suite du voyage . . .," [omitting words "Tome troisieme"], same collat., *Amst* la veuve de Boetman 1704. aa
—anr. issue, identical, with different t., "Dialogues de . . . Lahontan et d'un sauvage . . .," same impr. date & collat. a
—anr. ed., "Dialogues . . .," called "Tome troisieme." *Hague* Delorme 1708. 16° [18] 1–174 blank, l. 177–374 fold.pl a
—anr. ed., "Suite du voyage . . .," *Amst* la veuve de Boetman 1728. 16° 257 2fold.maps 4pls[one fold.] a
—anr. ed. "Dialogues," ed. Chinard, *Balt* 1931. O [4] 272 + colophon, a
  From this volume the portion devoted to his "Dialogues"—a diatribe against Christianity—was included in both English editions and in the 1705 French editions. Most later French editions

were, along with his European travels, issued separately as entered above. French editions of all three volumes were, after 1704, so changed and polished as to verify the suspicion that editorial work on them was done by the apostate monk, Nicolas Guedeville. Some authorities even believe him to have been the veritable author of the "Dialogues."

LAKE, STUART N.   27
  Wyatt Earp, frontier marshal. *B* 1931. D [14] 392 15pls 10facs [issue 1, "belly" misspelled, p54 line 18] a

LAKE ERIE
  Lake Erie and the Hudson river. Remarks on the importance of the contemplated grand canal, between:
  See Williamson, Hugh.

  **A view of the Grand Canal, from Lake Erie   28
  to the Hudson river** . . . *N Y* 1825. D 28 a

LA MADELÈNE, JOSEPH H. DE   29
COLLET, baron de
  Le comte de Raousset-Boulbon: sa vie et ses aventures . . . see Madelène, Henry

[LAMAR, J., and O'FARRELL, J.]   30
  Report on the Mendocino Indian war. [*Sacr* 1860]. O 75 aa

LAMAR, JAMES S.   31
  Recollections of pioneer days in Georgia. [*Wash* 1916]. O 64 a 200copies ptd.

LAMAR, L[UCIUS] Q. C.   32
  Speech on the state of the country . . . *Atlanta* 1864. O 30 a

LAMAR (MIRABEAU B.)   33
  Address of: to the citizens of Santa Fe. *Austin* [1841] O 14 + blank lf. b S TxU [of 5 known cops]
—Sp. ed. with adds. "Proclama . . ." same impr [1841] O 14; 11–47 c S TxU [of 4 known cops]
  Friendly but ineffective blandishments of this romantic poet-statesman, intended to induce New Mexico to enter into the Texas fold; resulting only in the humiliating surrender of the Santa Fe expedition.

LAMAR (MIRABEAU B.)   34
  Letter of: on the subject of annexation . . . *Sav* 1844 O 48 aa

LAMB, E. J.   35
  Memories of the past . . . [*South Bend*] 1906. D 257 5pls a
  Life in Iowa, Kansas and Colorado in the forties and fifties.

LAMB, R[OGER]   **36**
An . . . authentic journal of occurences during
the late American war . . . *Dub* 1809. O [28] 5–438
tab [at p. 158] aa
Originally issued in 11 parts.

LAMB, R[OGER]   **37**
Memoir of his own life . . . *Dub* 1811. O 296 aa

LAMBERT, EDWARD R.   **38**
History of the colony of New Haven . . . *N Hav*
1838. D 216 3maps 11pls a

LAMBERT, GUILLAUME   **39**
Voyage dans l'Amérique . . . *Brus* 1855. O 320
+ atlas[of 32pls] fold.map aa
Investigation into American manufacturing
methods by a Belgian industrialist.

LAMBERT, JOHN.   **40**
Travels through Canada and the United States,
1806–1808. *L* 1810. O 3v: [24] 496; [10] 494; [6]
506. 18maps & pls[some col] b
—ed. 2, *L* 1813. O 2v: [36] 544; [8] 532. 18 maps &
pls aa
—ed. 2, cor., same collat., *L* 1814. aa
—ed. 3, cor. & improved, same collat., *L* 1816. aa

LAMBERTIE, CHARLES DE   **41**
Le drama de la Sonora . . . M. le comte de
Raousset-Boulbon et M. Charles de Pindray. *P*
1855. O 320 aa

LAMBERTIE, CHARLES DE   **42**
Voyage pittoresque en Californie et au Chili. *P*
1853–4. O [12] 310 aa

LAMBOURNE, ALFRED   **43**
An old sketch book. *B* [1892]. F 17 18pls b Y
—rptd. "The old journey," *S L C* [1897]. D 53
18pls a
Sketches of historic spots on the Mormon trail
by an artist who crossed the plains in 1867.

LAMBOURNE, ALFRED   **44**
Scenic Utah. *N Y* 1891. F [28, 44] 20pls aa

LAMBRECHTSEN VAN RITTHEM,   **45**
N[ICHOLAS] C.
Korte Beschrijving van de Ontdekking en der
verdere lotgevallen van Nieuw-Nederland. *Middel-
burg* 1818. O [6] 102 map some copies on thick
paper aa

LAMECH and AGRIPPA
Chronicon Ephratense. *See* Gass, Jacob, and
Miller, Johan P.

LAMON, WARD H.   **46**
The life of Abraham Lincoln . . . *B* 1872. O [16]
547 15pls 3facs a

Slightly unfavorable but important delineation;
ghost-written, from Lamon's material, by Chauncey F. Black.

LA MOTTE MINES . . . IN MISSOURI.   **47**
Observations on: n.p. Royston & Brown [1839].
O 32 fold.map aa

LAMSON, J.   **48**
Round Cape Horn . . . from Maine to California
. . . 1852. *Bangor* 1878. D 156 a

LANCASTER, ALBERT B.   **49**
Quatre mois au Texas. *Brus* 1886. O [18] 250 a
—anr ed, *Mons* 1887. O 351 front

LANCASTER, DANIEL   **50**
The history of Gilmanton [N.H.] . . . *Gilmanton*
1845. O [8] 13–304 map a

LANCASTER, ROBERT A.   **51**
Historic Virginia homes and churches. *Phil* 1915.
Q [18] 527 aa

LANCASTER [PA.]   **52**
**Minutes of conferences, held at Lancaster [Pa.]
in August 1762.** With . . . several tribes of northern
and western Indians. *Phil* 1763. F 36 c PhilL

**A narrative of the late massacres in Lancaster
county [Pa.].** *See* Franklin, Benj.

A treaty, held at . . . Lancaster [Pa.] . . .   **53**
with the . . . Six Nations, in June 1744. *Phil* 1744.
F 39 b N Y
—rptd., with adds., *Wmsbg* [1744]. O [12] 79 b
—Eng ed *L* 1744. aa

[LANCELOT, D.]   **54**
California. n.p. 1869. 16° cover-t. & following
erratic paginat.: 9–62; 65–68; 71; 72; 77–90;
93–96; 99; 100; 103; 104; 107; 108; 111–116;
121–134; 137–160; 163–178; 181–184; 189–200;
205–208. map 4pls aa

LAND
Land-und Seereisen eines St. Gallischen Kan-
tonbürgers nach Nordamerika . . .
See Buechler, Johann U.

LANDAIS, PIERRE DE   **55**
A memorial, to justify [his] conduct during the
late war. *B* 1784. Q 115 aa

LANDAIS, PIERRE DE   **56**
The second part of the memorial to justify [his]
conduct, during the late war. *N Y* [1785]. Q 52 a
Dismissed from the navy for questionable conduct as captain of the frigate "Alliance" when Paul
Jones fought the "Serapis." In the same year and
place was published, in eighteen pages, *Charges
and proofs respecting the conduct of Peter Landais.*

LANDER, FREDERICK W.   57
Additional estimates of the Fort Kearney, South Pass . . . wagon road . . . [*Wash* 1861]. O 27 a

LANDER, FREDERICK W.   58
Maps and reports of the Fort Kearney, South Pass, and Honey Lake wagon road . . . H.Exec. Doc.64 [*Wash* 1861]. O 39 a only 250copies ptd.
No maps accompanied this report as published.

LANDER, FRED[ERICK] W.   59
Report of the reconnaissance of a railroad route from Puget sound via the South pass to the Mississippi . . . [House Ex. Doc. 129, vol. 3]. [*Wash* 1856]. O 56 b S USGeolSurv Y [only copies known]
Intended to accompany the octavo series known as *Pacific railroad explorations, q.v.,* but, being issued a year later, not found ordinarily with sets of that series. Two copies exist of an earlier [1854? or 1855?] thirty-page edition without title-page giving the introductory portion only. The *Report* itself was included in the quarto edition of the *Pacific railroad explorations.*

LANDOLPHE (CAPITAINE [JEAN F.])   60
Memoires du: . . . ses voyages . . . aux deux Amériques . . . *P* 1823. O 2v: 350; 500.map 2pls a

LANDRIN, H[ENRI]   61
De l'or. *P* 1851. D [28] 300 a

LANDRUM, J[OIIN] B. O.   62
Colonial and revolutionary history of upper South Carolina . . . *Greenville S C* 1897. D [16] 360 7pls a

LANDRUM, J[OHN] B. O.   63
History of Spartanburg county, South Carolina . . . *Atlanta* 1900. O [8] 739 a
—rptd. [1954]

LANDVERHUIZING . . .   64
Landverhuizing naar de Vereenigde-Staten . . . *Bergen* 1853. O 112 a

LANE ([GOV.] JOSEPH).   65
Biography of: By "Western" [pseud.]. *Wash* 1852. O 40 aa
—anr. issue, *pseud.* "A Westerner," same impr. date & collat. a
Authorship has been ascribed to Robert Dale Owen.

LANE (GOV. JOSEPH).   66
Life of: by a resident . . . *Port Ore* 1873. O 63 errata lf a

LANE (LUNSFORD)   67
.The narrative of: . . . purchase of himself and family from slavery and his banishment . . . for the

crime of wearing a colored skin. *B* 1842. 16° 54 a
—other eds.: same impr. & collat. 1845; 1848.

LANE, MRS. LYDIA S.   68
I married a soldier. *Phil* 1893. D 214 a
—ed. 2, *N Y* 1910. same collat.
Life in Texas and New Mexican army posts.

LANE (WALTER P.)   69
The adventures and recollections of: . . . containing sketches of the Texian . . . wars. *Marshall Tex* 1887. D [4] 114 port b
—rptd. same impr. [1928]. D 180 port a

LANG, HERBERT O., ed.   70
History of the Willamette valley . . . *Port Ore* 1885, roy O 902 [13] 6pls facs errata slip a

[LANG, HERBERT O.], ed.   71
A history of Tuolumne county, California. *S F* 1882. O [14] 510 [48] 12ports b B G

LANG, JOHN D., and TAYLOR, SAMUEL   72
Report of a visit to some of the tribes . . . west ot the Mississippi river. *Prov* 1843. O 47 a
—anr. ed., priority not established. *N Y* 1843. O 34 a

LANG, COL. W. W.   73
The resources . . . of Texas. n.p. 1881. O 62 fold.map pl a
—anr. issue—without map & pl

LANG, WILLIAM W.   74
A paper on the resources . . . of Texas . . . [*N Y* 1881] O 22 [incl wraps] aa
—ed. 2, with adds [*N Y* 1881] O 31 a
—enl. ed. "The resources . . . of Texas" [*N Y*] n.d. O 62 map and pl [in some cops]

LANGDON, SAMUEL   75
Government corrupted by vice . . . sermon preached the 31st day of May, 1775. *Watertown* 1775. D 29 aa
Describes the battles at Lexington and Concord.

LANGE, HENRY   76
Atlas von Noord America nach den neusten Materialen . . . *Braunschweig* 1854. Q [8] 28 18maps[many on the west] aa
For another edition see Andree, Karl

LANGFORD, ELLA M.   77
Johnson county, Arkansas . . . *Clarksville Ark* 1921. O 210 a

LANGFORD, NATHANIEL P.   78
Vigilante days and ways. The pioneers of the Rockies . . . *B* 1890. O 2v: [26] 426; [16] 486 + 6adv-p 15 pls aa
—rptd. *N Y* 1893, same collat. a
—oth eds: *Chi* 1912., O 554 15pls; *Missoula* 1957. O

LANGMAN, CHRISTOPHER, et al **79**
A true account of the voyage of the Nottingham-Galley . . . to New-England, near which she was cast away on Boon-Island, by the captain's obstinacy . . . with an account of the falsehoods in the captain's Narrative . . . *L* 1711. O [8] 36 b
For the captain's narrative, *see* Dean, Captain John.

[LANGRISHE, SIR HERCULES] **80**
Considerations on the dependencies of Great Britain . . . *L* 1769. O 92 a
Advocates that the Colonies be taxed, but only after their representation in Parliament.

LANGSDORFF, GEORGE H. VON **81**
Bermerkungen auf einer Reise um die Welt 1803–07. *Frankf* 1812. Q 2v: [26] 304 [30]; 336 [20]. 2ports 44pls b
—rptd., same impr. 1813. D 2v aa
—Dutch tr. "Reis rondom de Wereld," *Amst* 1813–19. O 4v 13pls[incl.eng.t.] a
—Eng. tr. *L* 1813–14. Q 2v: [24] 362 [6]; [8] 386 [6]. map 21pls b N NYP
—Am. ed., abr., *Carlisle Pa* 817. O 617 [17] pl aa
—anr. ed. [Calif.section only] *S F* 1927. O [14] 158 [2] map pls 260copies ptd. a
Account of Alaska, the Aleutians, California etc., by the naturalist with Krusenstern.

LANGSTON, MRS. CAROLYNE L. **82**
History of Eastland county, Texas. *Dallas* 1904. D 220[incl.pls] a

[LANGWORTHY, EDWARD] **83**
Memoirs of the life of the late Charles Lee . . . second in command in the service of the United States . . . during the revolution . . . *L* 1792. O [12] 439 a
—rptd. *Dub* 1792. same collat.; with new t., *L* 1797. O [12] 446
—Am. ed. *N Y* 1792. D [8] 284 a
—rptd. *N Y* 1793. same collat
—anr. Am. ed., t. altered, *N Y* 1813. D 352
Said to have been edited by Thomas Paine, under the direction of Langworthy.

LANGWORTHY, FRANKLIN **84**
Scenery of the plains, mountains and mines; or a diary kept upon the overland route to California. *Ogdensburgh N Y* 1855. D 324 aa
—rptd. *Princeton* 1932 D [18] 592 4 pls a

LANGWORTHY, LUCIUS H. **85**
Dubuque; its history [etc.]. *Dubuque* [1855]. O 82 aa
By a pioneer who came to the Dubuque lead mines in 1827.

LANIER, SIDNEY **86**
Florida: its scenery, climate and history . . . *Phil* 1876. D 336[incl.pls] a
—ed. 2, same impr. n.d.

LANMAN, CHARLES **87**
Adventures in the wilds of North America . . . *L* 1854. D 300 a
—rptd. *L* 1863.
—Am. ed., enl., "Adventures in the wilds of the United States . . .," *Phil* 1856. O 2v: [16] 514; [2] 517 [2] 12 pls
—Eng. ed. *L* 1856. same collat.
—Eng. ed. 2, *L* 1859. same collat.
This collective edition contains several of the author's earlier separate publications, with new material added.

LANMAN, CHARLES **88**
Haw-Ho-Noo; or, records of a tourist. *Phil* 1850. D [8] 13–266 a

LANMAN, CHARLES **89**
Letters from the Alleghany mountains . . . *N Y* 1848. D 198 a
—rptd., same impr. & collat. 1849.

LANMAN, CHARLES **90**
A summer in the wilderness; embracing a canoe voyage up the Mississippi and around lake Superior. *N Y* 1847. D 208 + 8adv-p a
—re-issued, with new t-p, "A canoe voyage up the Mississippi . . .," same collat., impr. & date.

LANMAN, JAMES H. **91**
History of Michigan . . . *N Y* 1839. O [16] 398 map a
—rptd. *N Y* 1841. 16° [2] 7–269; *N Y* 1842; *N Y* 1843; *N Y* n.d.
First—and on the early period still the best—history of the state.

LANNING, JOHN T. **92**
The Spanish missions of Georgia. *Chapel Hill* [1935]. O [16] 321 a

LA PÉROUSE, JEAN F. G. DE **93**
Voyage . . . autour de monde . . . redigé par M. L. A. Milet-Mureau . . . *P* [1797]. Q 4v: [4] 72 346 port; [4] 398; [4] 422; [4] 309 + atlas F [2] 69maps & pls b NYP Y
—anr. ed. *P* 1798. O 4v: [72] 368; [4] 414; 316 [178]; [4] 328 + atlas F with port & 69maps & pls b
—anr. ed. *L* 1799. Q 2v: [52] 539; [8] 522 [18]. 70maps & pls aa
—Eng. eds. O: *L* Stockdale 1798, 2v 51 maps & pls; *L* Johnson 1798, 3v 45 maps & pls; rptd. 1799; *L* Johnson 1799, 2v + atlas F; *L* Lackington 1807, 3v + atlas; *L* Johnson 1807, 3v + atlas [of 36 maps & pls] aa
—best Eng. ed. *L* Robinson 1799. Q 2v: [20] 539 port; [8] 531 [14] + atlas F [2] 69maps & pls [some copies carry impr. of printer, Hamilton] b Y
—abr. eds.: *L* 1798. O; *Edin* 1798. O 336 map 3pls; with adds., *B* 1801. D [16] 336 a
—Dutch tr. *Haarlem* 1799. O
—Ger tr Berlin 1800. O 2v: 358; 344 map a
—Swed. tr. *Stockh* 1798. O

—Ital. tr. *Milan* 1815. D 4v: [2] 236; 294; 271; 297 [28] map 16pls

First visit of a foreigner to missionary establishments in Upper California.

LAPEYROWSE, S. DE   **94**

Misères oubliées (Californie, 1850–3); aventures et souvenirs d'un chercheur d'or. *P* 1886. 16° 303 a

LAPHAM, INCREASE A.   **95**

The antiquities of Wisconsin . . . [*Wash* 1855]. Q [12] 95 map 55pls a

—anr. issue, same collat. *N Y* 1855.

LAPHAM, INCREASE A. [ed.]   **96**

A documentary history of the Milwaukee and Rock river canal. *Milw* 1840. O 154 aa

LAPHAM, INCREASE A.   **97**

A geographical and topographical description of Wisconsin, with brief sketches of its history . . . *Milw* 1844. 16° 256 map[with 1844 copyr] aa

—ed. 2, *Milw* [ptd *N Y*] 1846. D 202 + 6adv-p map[dated 1845] a

First bound book printed in Milwaukee.

LAPHAM, INCREASE A., et al   **98**

A paper on the . . . Indians of Wisconsin . . . *Milw* 1870. O 27 map aa

LAPHAM, WILLIAM B.   **99**

Centennial history of Norway . . . Maine . . . *Port* 1886. O [16] 659 36ports 9pls a

[LARIMER, GEORGE W.]   **100**

Hints and information for the use of emigrants to Pike's Peak . . . *Leavenworth* 1860. O 15 b KasH Y [of 5 cops loc]

Ascribed also to Samuel A. Drake, who may have had a hand in it, but the information was probably supplied by Larimer.

LARIMER, MRS. SARAH L.   **101**

The capture and escape; or, life among the Sioux. *Phil* 1870. D 252 5pls aa

—rptd. *Phil* 1871. same collat. a

LARIMER (GENERAL WILLIAM H. H.)   **102**

Reminiscences of: . . . *Lancaster* 1918. O 256 [incl.initial blank, 1.] + 10 inserted pp 15pls fold.tab b G N NYP

Larimer was among the earliest Pike's Peak adventurers, and one of the founders of Denver.

LARIMER COUNTY . . . ASSOCIATION   **103**

Larimer county stock grower's association. Stock brands published by: *Ft Collins* 1885. 16° 36 + 8blank lvs. & 1-p.index b G

LARKIN, STILLMAN C.   **104**

The pioneer history of Meigs county, Ohio. *Columbus* 1908. D 208 a

LARNED, MAJOR   **105**

Diary of a first trip to the Pacific ocean. [*N Hav* 1884?] O 74 aa

LA ROCHEFOUCAULD-LIANCOURT,   **106**
FRANCOIS ALEXANDRE FRÉDÉRIC,
duc de

Voyage dans les États-Unis . . . 1795–7. *P* [1799]. O 8v: [24] 365; [6] 349; [6] 384; [6] 349; [6] 400; [6] 336; [6] 336; [4] 244. 3maps & pls 9tabs aa

—rptd. *P* 1800. aa

—Eng. tr. *L* 1799. Q 2v: [24] 642 [12]; [2] 686 [9] + extra starred p321–364. 3maps 6tabs b LC NYP

—anr ed. same impr & date. O 4v 3maps 9tabs aa

—rptd. *L* 1800. O 4v: [24] 591 [16]; [2] 523 [16]; [2] 717 [22]; [2] 610 [8]. 3maps 9tabs; *L* 1803. same collat. aa

—Ger. tr. *Hamburg* 1799. O 3v: [8] 774; [6] 588; [20] 629 aa

LAROQUE (FRANCOIS A.)   **107**

. . .Journal of: from the Assiniboine to the Yellowstone, 1805. *Ottawa* 1910. O [2] 82 aa

—anr. issue [in Fr.], same impr. 1911. O [2] 87 a

First printing of the day-by-day journal of the first white man, after Verendrye, to visit the Big Horn country and the Crow Indians; first authoritative account of that tribe.

LARPENTEUR, CHARLES

Forty years a fur trader . . . *See* Coues, Elliott.

[LA SALLE, JEAN CAVELIER DE]   **108**

Relation du voyage . . . par feu M. Robert Cavelier, sieur de la Salle, pour découvrir . . . l'embouchure du fieuve de Missisipy. *N Y* 1858. D 54 [2] a 100copies ptd.

First printing of this account of La Salle's last voyage, written by his brother, who accompanied him. Supplements Joutel's narrative of the same event. For English translation see Shea, John G. *Early voyages.*

LA SALLE (NICOLAS DE).   **109**

Relation of the discovery of the Mississippi . . . from the narrative of: . . . *Chi* Caxton Club 1898. O [10] 3–69 a

Translation of account, contained in Margry's *Découvertes . . .*, of La Salle's discovery of the Mississippi. The author was not a relative of the explorer.

LA SALLE ([ROBERT] CAVELIER DE).   **110**

'Relation of the discoveries and voyages of: *Chi* Caxton Club 1901. O [8] 301 a 225copies ptd.

First published, in French, in Margry's six-volume *Découvertes . . .*, from an anonymous manuscript. This, the first separate edition, gives both French and English texts. It was the official account sent to the Ministry of the Marine; if not by La Salle himself, it was probably inspired by him. Hennepin's plagiarisms from it in his 1797 *Nouvelle découverte*, indicate that he had access to the manuscript.

LA SALLE [TEX.] 111
A statement indicating . . . advantages of the proposed city of: . . . *N O* 1848. O 35 map aa

LASLEY, M. E. A. 112
Across America, in the only house on wheels . . . *N Y* 1898. D 158 [2] a
—rptd. *N Y* 1899. same collat.
—anr. ed. *N Y* 1901. D 176

LAST SPIKE 113
Last spike (The), 1850–1883; a historical . . . review of the industries . . . of Oregon and Washington . . . *Port Ore* 1883. O 112 5pls a
Commemorates completion of the Northern Pacific Rail Road.

LATE OCCURRENCES 114
Late occurrences (The) in North America, and policy of Great Britain, considered. *L* 1766. O [2] 42 a
Conciliatory policy urged. Ascribed to Edmund Jenings.

LATE REGULATIONS
Late regulations (The) respecting the British colonies . . .
See Dickinson, John.

LATHAM, HENRY 117
Black and white. A journal of a three month's tour in the United States. *L* 1867. O [12] 304 errata slip map a

LATHAM, H[IRAM] 118
Trans-Missouri stock raising . . . *Omaha* 1871 O 88 [incl wraps] map b
Written to promote Union Pacific interests but constitutes the first survey of the cattle industry.

LATHROP, GEORGE 119
Memoirs of a pioneer . . . *Lusk, Wyo* [ca 1917] D 34 aa
—ed 2, same impr [1929]. 16° 30 2pls wrap-t only a
—enl ed, with Luke Vorhees' "Recollections" added. *Phil* 1927. O 32 [blank lf] 32 port a

LATHROP, J. S. 120
Champaign county, [Ill.] . . . with history . . . *Chi* 1871. D 456 aa

[LATHROP, JOHN] 121
A compendious history of the late war . . . 1811–1815. *B* 1815. O 32 aa

Expansion of material forming appendix to his *Discourse, delivered in Boston, April* 13, 1815. *See also A compendious account of the most important battles, etc.*

LATHROP, JOHN 122
Innocent blood crying from the streets of Boston . . . *L* 1770. Q 22 b
—Am. eds.: *B* 1771, O 21 b; *B* 1778, O 24 aa
Sermon preached at Boston the Sunday following the massacre.

LATHROP, JOHN 123
The present war unexpected, unnecessary and ruinous . . . *B* 1812. O 42 a

LATOUR, A[RSÈNE] LACARRIERE 124
Historical memoir of the war in West Florida and Louisiana in 1814–15. *Phil* 1816. O [20] 264 [190] port + atlas[of 8maps & plans] aa
Chief authority, well documented, on these operations. Portrait evidently not issued in all copies.

[LATROBE, BENJAMIN] 125
A succinct view of the missions established . . . by the Church of the Brethren, or Unitas Fratrum. *L* 1771. O [4] 3–32 + 1adv-p aa
—anr. ed., with adds., *L* 1774. O 32 33 aa

LATROBE (BENJAMIN H.) 126
The journal of: . . . *N Y* 1905. O [42] 269 26pls a

LATROBE, CHARLES J. 127
The rambler in North America. *L* 1835. D 2v: [12] 321;]8] 336 + adv-p a
—ed. 2, *L* 1836. Same collat. with map [dated 1836] added. aa
—Am. ed. *N Y* 1835. D 2v: [7] 14–243; [4] 9–242. a

LATROBE, JOHN H. B. 128
The first steam boat voyage on the western waters . . . *Balt* 1871. O 32 a

LATROBE, JOHN H. B. 129
The history of Mason and Dixon's line . . . [*Phil*] 1855. O 52 a

LATTA, ROBERT R. 130
Reminiscences of pioneer life [in Iowa, etc.] *K C* 1912. O 186 pl a

LATTER-DAY SAINTS. 131
Minutes of a conference of: at Great Salt Lake, Aug. 28, 1852. *S L C* 1852. O 48 b Y

LATTIMORE, S. C. 134
Incidents in the history of Dublin [Texas]. *Dublin* 1914 D 66 + errata slip port a

LATTIN, M. DE PUY 135
Twenty years a gold hunter . . . on the deserts and mountains of Arizona, California and Nevada. *Commerce* 1915. O 160 port a

L[AUDOIN], T[HOMAS] D. 136
A peep at the western world . . . *L* 1863. D [6] 126 a

LAUNAY DE VALÉRY, CORDIER DE 137
Tableau topographique et politique de la Sibérie, de la Chine, de la zone moyenne d'Asie et du nord de l'Amérique. *Berlin* 1806. Q [2] 130 400 copies ptd. aa

LAURE (LE PERE AUGUSTINE) 138
Laure (Le Pere Augustine) de la Compagnie de Jesus, missionaire aux montagnes Rocheuses. *Brus* 1895. O 48 aa
Worked with Father Cataldo among the Indians of Washington, Idaho, etc.

LAURENS, HENRY
Correspondence . . . *See* Moore, Frank, *Materials for history* . . .

[LAURENS, HENRY]? 139
Extracts from the proceedings of the court of Vice-Admiralty in Charles-Town, South-Carolina; in the cause, George Roupell . . . v. the ship Ann and goods . . . *America* 1768. Q [4] 20 c AA PhilL NYP Y
—ed. 2, with adds., *Charlestown S C* 1769. F [4] 64 c NYP

LAURENS (COLONEL JOHN). 140
The army correspondence of: . . . 1777–8 . . . *N Y* Bradford Club 1867. O 250 port a 80copies
For another edition see next entry.

LAURENS (COLONEL JOHN).
A succinct memoir of the life . . . of: *See* Simms, Wm. G.

LAURIDSEN, PETER 141
Vitus J. Bering og de Russiske opdagelsesrejser . . . 1725–1743. *Copenh* 1885. D [4] 210 4maps pls tab a
—Eng. ed., with author's rev., "Vitus Bering; the discoverer of Bering strait . . .," *Chi* 1889. D [16] 223 2maps a

LAUSSAT, PIERRE C. DE 142
Mémoires sur ma vie . . . *Pau* 1831. O 638 + errata lf Y only a few copies ptd. for the family d
Laussat officiated in taking over Louisiana from Spain and in transferring it to the United States.

LAUT, AGNES C. 143
The blazed trail of the old frontier. *N Y* 1926. O [12 incl.front.] 271 map 33pls a also 200signed copies

LAUTS, [GERARD] 144
Brieven van eenen Duitschen land verhuiser, van daar naar Wisconsin. n.p. [1848]. O 36 a

LAUTS, G[ERARD] 145
Kalifornia . . . *Amst* 1849. O [8] 40 aa

LAUZUN ([ARMAND L. DE GONTAUT], le duc de). 146
Mémoires du: *P* 1822. O [24] 399 aa
—ed 2, same impr & date 16° 2v a
—anr ed, [1st complete] *P*, Poulet-Mallassis, [May] 1858. D [56] 330 [2] aa
—rptd. [Oct.] same impr & date D [68] 411 aa
—anr ed, *P*, Didot, 1862. D [4] 435 [2] a
—1st illus ed, *P* 1880. O [48] 268 a
—Eng. tr. calling itself ed 2 [being transl of Fr ed 2?] *L* 1822. D [10] 211 aa
—anr ed, *L* [1928]. O [12] 253 a
—Am ed, *N Y* 1912. D [12] 364 a
Describes in detail his years of romantic indiscretions at the debauched French court—including a torrid affair with Marie Antoinette—as well as his valiant services under Rochambeau in Connecticut, New York and at Yorktown. He later attained high rank in the French revolutionary army but was "railroaded" to the guillotine, where he died like a man in 1793. His MS *"Mémoires"* were discovered about 1820 and written copies circulated, to the consternation of many of the great French families, through whose wealth and influence publication in its scandalous entirety was probably prevented at the time. A rumored uncensored printing [of 1821] may be dismissed from consideration until a copy is found. The suppressed portions were first restored in the two Paris editions of 1858.

LAVAL, [ANTOINE F.] DE 147
Voyage de la Louisiane . . . *P* 1728. Q [24] 304; 96; 191 [8]. 20maps & diagrams 11 tabs b
Report, by the scientist of the expedition, under command of Valette-Laudun, sent in 1720 by the French government to examine the Florida and Louisiana coasts. For another and more interesting narrative of this expedition see Vallette-Laudun.

LAVAYSSIEU, M. 148
Un missionaire en Californie. *Limoges* [1853?]. D 120 pl a

LA VERENDRYE (PIERRE GAULTIER DE VARENNES, sieur de). 149
Journals and letters of: and his sons . . . Ed. L. J. Burpee. *Toronto* Champlain Soc. 1927. Q [24] 548 [11] 7maps 500 copies ptd. aa
First complete edition of these reports of explorations made from Lake Superior to the Rockies, 1730–51.

LAW, (HR. [JOHN], of Lauriston)   **150**
Aanmerkingen over den Koophandel en het Geldt; door den; . . . beschryvinge van Louisiana . . . *Amst* 1721. D [12] 320 map port a

LAW (THE GREAT MR. [JOHN],   **151**
of Lauriston).
The memoirs, life and char. .ter of: . . . by a Scots gentleman. *L* 1721. O [16] 44 aa
—ed. 2, same impr. & date. aa
According to the preface, the author was a Mr. Gray, who spent some time in Louisiana.

LAW (JOHN, of Lauriston).
A sketch of the life of: By I. P. W. *See* Wood, John P.

LAW, JUDGE JOHN   **152**
Address . . . before the Vincennes Historical . . . Society [on the early settlement of Vincennes]. *Louisv* 1839. O 48 map aa
—rptd., with adds., "The colonial history of Vincennes," *Vincennes* 1858. O [8] 157 a

LAW, WILLIAM   **153**
A discourse . . . before the Georgia Historical Society [on settlement of that state] . . . *Sav* 1840. O 43 a

[LAWRENCE, A. B., and   **154**
STILLÉ, C. J.] eds.
Texas in 1840; or, the emigrant's guide . . . By an emigrant . . . with an introduction by A. B. Lawrence. *N Y* 1840. D 275 [incl. front.] aa
—re-issue, "Texas in 1842," *N Y* 1842. Same collat. aa
—anr. ed. "A history of Texas, or the emigrant's guide . . ." *N Y* 1844. D [2] 7–275 front. aa
—rptd., same collat., 1845. a
The frontispiece—colored in some copies—is the earliest view of Austin. For German book based on it, see Scherpf. G. A.

LAWRENCE (JAMES).
Biography of: late a captain in the navy . . . *See* Irving, Washington.

LAWSON, JOHN   **155**
A new voyage to Carolina . . . *L* 1709. Q [6] 258 + adv-l. map pl b AA NYP Y some copies on L. P.
—anr. ed. "The history of Carolina . . .," *L* 1714. same collat. b N LC
—rptd. *L* 1718. same collat. b NYP Y
—Am. eds. *Raleigh* 1860. D 390 aa; *Charlotte* 1903. O [16] 171 map a; *Rich* 1937, O [32] 259 map 7pls aa; *Rich* 1951 a
—Ger. ed. "Allerneuste Beschreibung der . . . Carolina in West-Indien . . .," *Hamburg* 1712. D [14] 365 [3] map pl aa
—rptd., with 30p. added, 1722. D [14] 396 [4] map pl aa

Lawson was unfortunate; burned alive by Tuscarora Indians in 1711, his book, in 1737, was issued by an Irish bookseller and attributed to John Brickell. For another German translation (abridged), *see* Kocherthal, Joshua.

LAY, BENJAMIN   **156**
All slave-keepers that keep the innocent in bondage, apostates, etc. *Phil*, ptd [by Franklin?] for the author, 1737 D 271[6] dd PhilL Y [of 3copies known]
Pioneer American abolition work; by an unlettered eccentric. Probably edited by Franklin.

LAY, JAMES H.   **157**
A sketch of the history of Benton County, Missouri. *Hannibal* 1876. O 76 aa

LAY, WILLIAM, and HUSSEY, CYRUS M.   **158**
A narrative of the mutiny, on board the ship Globe . . . in the Pacific . . . *New-London* 1828. O 168 aa
—rptd. "True history . . .," *Southport Wis* 1848. O 125 5pls no perfect cop kn
—anr. ed. [*N Y* 1900]. O a

LAYTON (GROVENOR I.)   **159**
Two eras in the life of . . .: who was lynched by the vigilance committee, at Sonora . . . California . . . *N O* 1853. O [2] 11–40 [incl. illus.] b Hn NYH [only cops loc]

LAZAREV, ANDREI P.   **160**
Plavanie vokrug svieta na shliupie Ladogie v 1822–24 . . . [Voyage round the world in the sloop Ladoga . . .] *St Ptbg* 1832. O 275 map aa

LEA, ALBERT M.   **161**
Notes on Wisconsin Territory . . . *Phil* 1836. D 53 map b G LC WisH Y
—rptd *Ia C* 1935. a
Written with particular reference to the recently attached District of Iowa, it constitutes the first book on that state.

LEA, TOM, and HERTZOG, CARL   **162**
Calendar of twelve travellers through the Pass of the North. *El Paso* 1946. O 34 365 cops ptd a
—rptd in smaller format for school use.

LEACH, A[DONIRAM] J.   **162a**
Early day stories; the overland trail . . . *Norfolk Neb.*[1916]. O 244 [incl. front.] 7pls aa
—rptd., identical, except "2nd edition" on t-p a

LEACH, A[DONIRAM] J.   **163**
A history of Antelope county, Nebraska. *Oakdale* [ptd *Chi*] 1909. D [6] 262 aa

LEACH, M. L.   **164**
A history of the Grand Traverse region. *Traverse City, Mich* 1884. Q 60 capt-t only a

LEADVILLE . . .
Leadville . . . the most wonderful mining camp
. . . *See* Loomis, John L.

LEAKE, ISAAC Q.   **165**
Memoir of the life . . . of General John Lamb.
Alb 1850. O [10] 432 4maps port a
—rptd., same collat., *Alb* 1857.

[LEAR, TOBIAS]   **166**
Observations on the river Potomack. *N Y* 1793.
O 29 plan of Washington eng. by Hill [probably
not issued with all copies] b AA LC VaU[no plan]
—ed. 2, *N Y* 1794. O 30 plan aa
—rptd *Balt* 1940. O 24 [incl front]
—Dutch tr. *Amst* [1799?]. D 32 a
Ascribed also to Andrew Ellicott. First book on
the nation's capital city.

LEARNED, JOSEPH D.   **166a**
A view of the policy of permitting slaves in the
states west of the Mississippi . . . *Balt* 1820. O 47 a
Concludes that the Federal government had no
right to interfere; prohibition or extension of
slavery must be decided by the states.

LEAVENWORTH . . . DIRECTORY
Leavenworth city directory . . . for 1859–60 . . .
See Sutherland, James.

LE BEAU (C[LAUDE]).   **167**
Avantures du: . . . parmi les sauvages de l'Amérique . . . *Amst* 1738. 16° 2v: [14] 370 [6]; [2]
430 [6]. map 6pls aa
—several Ger. trs., variant titles: *Erfurt* 1752. D
2v map pls; rptd. 1756; *Frankf* 1752. O 2v 6pls;
Leip 1752. O; rptd. 1794. a
Considered a basically veracious narrative by
competent authorities, though somewhat romanticised and with much borrowing from the work of
Father Lafitau, *q. v.*

[LE BLANC, JEAN B.]   **168**
Le patriote anglois, ou reflexions sur les hostilités
que la France reproche à l'Angleterre . . . *Geneva*
1756. D [16] 158 [2] b N NYP
Purports to be the translation of an English
book, but an original work, largely devoted to
American affairs.

[LEBOUCHER, ODET-JULIEN]   **169**
Histoire de la dernière guerre, entre la Grande-
Bretagne, et les États-Unis . . . *P* 1787. Q [36] 357
[3] 7maps 2fold.tabs aa
—rptd. *P* 1788. O 2v: [32] 168; 200. 2tabs a
—anr. ed., with adds., *P* 1830. O 2v: [70] 326 port;
[4] 336 facs + atlas of maps a
—Sp. tr. *Alcala* 1793. Q 2v: 162; 194 a
Best French chronicle of the Revolution; particularly valuable on naval affairs. Ascribed incorrectly to both Pierre and Jonathan Boucher.

LEBROCQUY, AUGUSTE   **170**
Le fondateur des missions du Missouri central.
Vie du R. P. Hélias d'Huddeghem . . . *Ghent* 1878.
O 8 [incl port] 324 aa
His Missouri activities extended from 1838 to
1865.

LEBRUN, MME. CAMILLE [pseud.]
Trois mois à la Louisiane. *See* Guyot, Pauline.

LECLERC, FRÉDÉRIC   **171**
Le Texas et sa révolution . . . *P* 1840. O 104 map
aa
—Eng tr Houst, 1950. Q 150 map 500 cops ptd a
By a French physician who visited Texas in
1838.

LE CLERCQ, CHRÉTIEN   **172**
Premier établissement de la foy dans la Nou-
velle France . . . *P* [A. Auroy] 1691. D 2v: [28] 559;
[2] 454 [wrongly numbered 458] dd N JCB Hn
—anr. iss. "Établissement de la foy . . ." au's
initials only [P.C.L.C.], 20-p catalogue added at
end of v2 dd NYP
—rptd. "Histoire des colonies françoises . . ." *P*
[T. Amaulry] 1692. Collat indentical except dedication to Frontenac omitted from prelim pp of vol 1
dd NYP
—Eng. tr. by Shea. *N Y* 1881. O 2v: 410 [2]; 356
map pls aa
Written by a Recollect missionary so hostile to
his Jesuit co-workers that Frontenac himself is
supposed to have collaborated. However, that it
was suppressed is not substantiated. Supremely
important historically for its details on La Salle's
activities in Illinois and for supplying the first
printed account of his epochal voyage down the
Mississippi.
A map, by Rouillard dated 1691, is found in a
few copies of the early editions; it was probably not
issued with them.

LECLERCQ, JULES J.   **173**
Une été en Amérique . . . *P* 1877. D [4] 414 [2]
16 pls a
Travelled West to the Rockies.

LE CONTE (JOSEPH).   **174**
The autobiography of: *N Y* 1903. D [18] 337
8pls a Also 500 cops on L. P.

LE CONTE, JOSEPH   **175**
A journal of ramblings through the high Sierras
of California . . . *S F* 1875. O 103 9pls only a few
copies ptd aa
—rptd: *S F* 1900; *S F* 1930 a

LE CONTE, JOHN L.   **176**
Notes on the geology of the survey for the exten-
sion of the Union Pacific railway . . . *Phil* 1868.
O 76 map a

LECOUVREUR, FRANK 177
From East Prussia to the Golden Gate . . . *N Y* 1906. O 355 map 20pls a

LEDERER (JOHN). 178
The discoveries of : . . . from Virginia, to the west of Carolina . . . *L* 1672. D [8] 27 map dd H JCB LC N
—rptd : *Cin* 1879; *Roch* 1902. O 30 map a
First eye-witness description of the valley of Virginia.

[LE DUC, WILLIAM G.] 179
Minnesota year book for 1851 . . . *St P* [ptd. *N Y*] [1851]. D 52 + advs[10p in some, 14 and 18p in other copies] errata lf map aa
—same, for 1852, *St P* [1852]. D [18] 17–98 front aa
—same, for 1853, *St P* [1853]. D 37 [17] map aa

LEDYARD (JOHN). 180
The adventures of a Yankee; or, the singular life of : . . . *B* 1831. D 90 aa

[LEDYARD, JOHN] 181
A journal of Captain Cook's last voyage to the Pacific . . . 1776–1779 . . . narrated from the original ms. of Mr. John Ledyard. *Hart* 1783. D 208 map[usually missing] d NYP OreH WashU Y
Evans states that this was first issued in two parts, in June and July. First American book describing the northwest coast. Probably based on Ledyard's recollections, but many sections show unblushing theft from John Rickman's account published at London in 1781; Ledyard himself would not have stooped to this practice, which indicates that another hand prepared the book for publication. *See* also Sparks, Jared, *Life of John Ledyard.* The rare map differs from the one in Rickman only in a decorative border added to its *cartouche.*

[LEDYARD, L. WOLTERS] 182
Gypsy days in Colorado, California, Florida . . . *B* 1890. sm Q [4] 179 26copies ptd. aa
Wagon trips made in the 'seventies.

[LEE, ARTHUR] 183
An appeal to the justice . . . of the people of Great-Britain, in the present disputes with America. *L* 1774. O [4] 63 a
—ed. 2, *L* 1775. O 68
—ed. 3, same impr. & date. O 32
—ed. 4, *L* 1776. O 46
—Am. ed. [called ed. 4], au. named, *N Y* 1775. O 32
Attributed also to Lord Chatham, Franklin and Richard Glover.

[LEE, ARTHUR] 184
An essay in vindication of the continental colonies, from a censure of Mr. Adam Smith . . . with some reflections on slavery . . . *L* 1764. O 46 a
—anr. ed. same impr., date & collat.

Smith referred to "nations of heroes [Negroes] subjected to the refuse of the jails of Europe [American colonists]."

LEE, ARTHUR 185
Extracts from a letter . . . in answer to a libel published in the Pennsylvania Gazette . . . by Silas Deane. *Wmsbg* 1779. O 31 aa
—rptd. *Phil* 1780. Q 74 aa
First enunciation of accusations—now believed doubtful—against Deane, Lee's fellow-Commissioner to France.

LEE, ARTHUR 186
Observations on certain commercial transactions in France . . . *Phil* 1780. Q 51 a
Denounces Franklin's conduct as Commissioner to France.

[LEE, ARTHUR] 187
The political detection; or, the . . . tyranny of administration . . . *L* 1770. O [2] 151 a

[LEE, ARTHUR] 188
A second appeal to the justice and interests of the people, on the measures respecting America. *L* 1775. O 90 + 2adv-p a

[LEE, ARTHUR] 189
A speech intended to have been delivered in the House of Commons, in support of the petition from the General Congress at Philadelphia . . . *L* 1775. O [4] 67 aa

[LEE, ARTHUR] 190
A true state of the proceedings in the parliament of Great Britain, and in . . . Massachusetts Bay relative to . . . granting of the money of the people . . . in the House of Commons, in which they are not represented . . . [*L* 1774]. F 24 capt. t. only b NYP
—Am. ed. *Phil* 1774. O 39 aa
Written by Lee from notes supplied by Franklin.

LEE, B[ENJAMIN] F. 191
The story of my life. [*Paonia Colo* 1907]. O [2] 49 + wraps port 2ms slips inserted wrap.t.only a
Chiefly Colorado interest.

LEE ([MAJ. GEN.] CHARLES).
Memoirs of the life of the late : . . . *See* Langworthy, Edw.

LEE (MAJOR GENERAL [CHARLES]). 192
Proceedings of a general court martial . . . for the trial of : *Phil* 1778. F 62 c Hn Y only 100copies ptd.
—rptd. : *Cooperstown N Y* 1823, O 134 a; *N Y* 1864, O 239 a

[LEE, MAJ. GEN. CHARLES] 193
Strictures on . . . A friendly address to all reasonable Americans . . . *Phil* 1774. O 15 aa

—rptd., same collat 1775: *Newport*; *Prov*; *N Lond* a

—other 1775 eds.: [*N Y*] D 12; [B] O 20, *Phil* O 25 a

—anr. ed., incl. with Henry Barry's "The general attacked by a subaltern," *q. v.*

For pamphlet attacked, *see* Cooper, Myles. For reply to Lee, *see* Barry, Henry.

[LEE, CHARLES] of Va.   **194**
Defence of the alien and sedition laws . . . *Phil* 1798. O 47 a

LEE, CHARLES H.   **195**
The long ago . . . pioneer days in the Red river valley . . . *Walhalla N. D.* 1898. O [2] 76 a

LEE, CHAUNCEY   **196**
The American accomptant . . . *Lansingburgh* 1797. D 297 [16] front aa
First book to adopt the dollar sign.

LEE, DANIEL, and FROST,   **197**
JOSEPH H.
Ten years in Oregon. *N Y* 1844. D 344 map a
—2nd issue, with sub-title: "Containing account of journey with Capt. Wyeth."

LEE, E. G.   **198**
The Mormons, or, knavery exposed . . . *Frankford* [*Phil*] 1841. O 24 pl b Hn Y
—rptd Derby 1852 a

LEE, EDMUND F.   **199**
Notes on the Mammoth Cave. *Cin* 1835. 24° 30 map[not in all copies] a

LEE, F[RANK] D., and AGNEW, J. L.   **200**
Historical record of the city of Savannah. *Sav* 1869. D [12] 212 [48] 3maps 3pls a

[LEE, HANNAH F.]   **201**
The Huguenots in France and America . . . *C* 1843. D 2v: [20] 336; [6] 302 a
—ed. 2, same impr., date & collat.

LEE, GEN. HENRY   **202**
Memoirs of the war in the southern department . . . *Phil* 1812. O 2v: [4] 423; [4] 486. 2ports a
—rptd. *Wash* 1827. O 466
—anr. ed., ed. R. E. Lee, *N Y* 1869. O 620 11maps & pls—also a few copies on L. P., signed a—also, same impr. & collat., 1870.

[LEE, GEN. HENRY?]   **203**
Plain truth: addressed to the people of Virginia [*Rich* 1799]. 16° 56 capt.t.only aa

LEE, MAJ. HENRY, JR.   **204**
The campaign of 1781 in the Carolinas . . . *Phil* 1824. O [2] 511 [47] a

Here the son of "Light Horse" Henry Lee resents the slurs on his father contained in William Johnson's *Life of Greene* and attacks the credibility of that work.

LEE, MAJ. H[ENRY], JR.   **205**
Observations on the writings of Thomas Jefferson, with particular reference to the attack they contain on the memory of the late Gen. Henry Lee *N Y* 1832. O 237 + adv-lf a
—ed. 2, ed. Chas. C. Lee, *Phil* 1839. O [22] 5–262 + 2adv-p errata slip
The original edition was suppressed and most copies destroyed.

LEE, MAJOR HENRY, JR.   **206**
A vindication of the character . . . of Andrew Jackson . . . *B* 1828. O 51 a

LEE, JESSE   **207**
A short history of the Methodists in the United States. *Balt* 1810. 16° 366 [10] a
First history of this sect.

LEE (JOHN D.)   **208**
Journals of: 1846–7 and 1859. Ed. Chas. S Kelly *S L C* 1938. Q 244 [7] map 13pls 250copies ptd. aa
Records events connected with the 1847 migration, the Mountain Meadows massacre, etc.

[LEE, JOHN D.]   **208a**
The Lee trial. An exposé of the Mountain Meadows massacre. *S L C* 1875. O 64 aa
—rptd. "Life and confessions . . .," *Phil* 1877. O 36 a
—anr. issue, "Life, confessions and execution . . .," same impr. & date. O 48
—anr. ed. "Mountain Meadows massacre . . .," *Phil* [1882]. O 64 pls

LEE (JOHN D.)   **209**
Mormonism unveiled; or, the life and confessions of: . . . *St L* 1877. O 390[incl. front.] + adv-p 13 pls a
—issue 2, with app. added, same impr. & date. O 406[incl.front.] + adv-p 13pls
—rptd.: *St L* 1881, O 413[incl.front.] 13pls; *St L* 1882; *St L* 1891. same collat.

LEE, JOHN H.   **209a**
The origin and progress of the American party in politics; embracing . . . the Philadelphia riots in . . . 1844 . . . *Phil* 1855. D 264 a

LEE, L. P.[ed.]   **210**
History of the Spirit Lake massacre . . . and of Miss Abigail Gardiner's [*sic*] three month's captivity among the Indians . . . *New Britain Conn* 1857. O 48 a
For later amplification *see* Sharp, Mrs. Abbie [Gardner].

LEE, LEROY M. 211
The life and times of the Rev. Jesse Lee. *Rich* 1848. O 517 a
—other eds., same date & collat.: *Louisv: Charleston S C*; also *Wash* 1856.

LEE, NELSON 212
Three years among the Camanches . . . containing a detailed account of his captivity [etc.]. *Alb* 1859. D 224 2pls[incl. port-title] b
—anr. issue, identical, but without port-title b
—anr. ed. *Troy* 1871. D 240 aa
—rptd *Norman Okla* 1957

[LEE, RICHARD H.] 213
An additional number of letters prom [*sic*] the federal farmer to the republican; leading to a fair examination of the . . . government proposed by the late convention . . . [*N Y*] 1788. O 41–181 aa
Sequel to, and paged continuously with, his *Observations*, below.

LEE, RICHARD H. 214
Life of Arthur Lee . . . *B* 1829. O 2v: 431; 399 a

LEE, RICHARD H. 215
Memoir of the life of Richard Henry Lee . . . By his grandson. *Phil* 1825. O 2v: 299; [2] 238. port a

[LEE, RICHARD H.] 216
Observations leading to a fair examination of . . . government proposed by the late convention . . . *N Y* 1777 [error for 1787]. O 40 a
—issue 2, cor. dated aa
—rptd., by order of a society of gentlemen, same impr., date & collat. aa
A leading attack on the proposed Constitution. Lee feared the proposed government would degenerate into a bureaucracy, eventually into an aristocracy; he favored the individual states occupying the status of practically independent republics, loosely joined for such conveniences as foreign affairs, defense and coinage.

LEE (ROBERT E.)
The early life, campaigns . . . of: By a distinguished southern journalist. *See* Pollard, Edw. A.

LEE (GENERAL ROBERT E.) 217
Report of: and subordinate reports of the battle of Chancellorsville . . . *Rich* 1864. O 144 [6] aa

LEE (GENERAL ROBERT E.) 218
Report of: of operations at Rappahonnock bridge . . . *Rich* 1864. O 61 a

LEE, ROBERT E. 219
Reports of the operations of the Army of Northern Virginia from June 1862, to . . . Dec. 13, 1862. *Rich* 1864. O 2v: 627; 602 aa

LEE, SUSAN P. 220
Memoirs of William Nelson Pendleton. *Phil* 1893. O 490 port aa
Only biography of Lee's artillery chief.

[LEE, WILLIAM, American consul 221
at Bordeaux]
Les États-Unis et l'Angleterre, ou souvenirs et reflexions . . . *Bordeaux* 1814. O 346 [4] a
Maintains that the current war, provoked by England, would be won by the United States, whose cause was that of all continental Europe.

LEE (WILLIAM) [of England]. 222
The true and interesting travels of: . . . *York Eng* [ca 1782]. D 32 [incl. cover & col. front.] c GaU [only copy known]
—rptd. *L* [1808]. D 40 [incl. cover & front.] b LC Y
Came to America in 1768 and travelled through the back settlements as far south as Georgia, where he remained two years.

LEE COUNTY [ILL.] 223
Recollections of the pioneers of: *Dixon* 1893. O 583[incl.pls] aa

LEECH (SAMUEL). 224
Thirty years from home . . . the experience of: who was for six years in the British and American navies . . . *B* 1843. 16° 305[incl. front.] a
—rptd. *B* 1844. same collat.
—Eng. ed. *L* 1845.
—other Am. eds.: *B* 1847; *B* n.d.

LEEDS, DANIEL 225
News of a trumpet sounding in the wilderness . . . *N Y* 1697. D [16] 151 d Hn PaH
Severe attack upon Philadelphia Quakers by a former member of that sect.

LEEPER, DAVID R. 226
The argonauts of 'forty-nine . . . recollections of the plains and the diggings . . . *So Bend* 1894. O 146 [16] errata slip aa
—rptd. *Columbus O* 1950. O a

LEESON, M[ICHAEL] A. 227
Documents and biography pertaining to the settlement . . . of Stark County, Illinois . . . *Chi* 1887. Q 708 aa

[LEESON, MICHAEL A.] ed. 228
History of Montana, 1739–1885. *Chi* 1885. Q 1367 map many pls aa

[LE FEBRE, H. B.] 229
The "Soapy" Smith tragedy. *Skagway* 1907. obl Q 24 2pls a
Stirring events on the Alaska frontier in 1898, final killing of Smith and dispersal of his outlaw gang.

LEFFERTS, CHARLES M.   **230**
Uniforms of the American, British, French and
German armies in the... revolution. Ed. by
Alexander J. Wall. *N Y* 1926. Q [8] 289 port 50col.
pls 500copies ptd. aa

LEFRANC, ÉMILE   **231**
La vérite sur l'esclavage et l'union aux États-
Unis. *N O* 1861. O [2] 227 a

LEFTWICH, W. M.   **232**
Martyrdom in Missouri... *St L* 1870. D 2v:
436; 445. port a

LEGARD, A[LLAYNE] B.   **233**
Colorado. *L* 1872. D [4] 170 a

LEGENDS
Legends of a log-cabin. By a western man. *See*
Gilman, Chandler R.

LEGGETT (MAJOR ABRAHAM).   **234**
The narrative of: of the army of the revolution
... *N Y* 1865. O [2] 72 port a

LEGION...
  Legion (The) of liberty!... *N Y* 1842. 16°   **235**
[208] map pl a
Some copies of this and later editions were
issued with next entry, intended as a continuation.

  Legion (The) of liberty. Remonstrance...   **236**
to the Texas rebellion... *Alb* 1843. D variously
paged: [60], [64], [72] and [168] a
—ed. 2, with adds., *N Y* 1843. D 371
Many later editions, some entitled "The anti-
Texass[*sic*] legion," some issued with entry next
above, of which it was a continuation.

LEHMANN, HERMANN
Nine years among the Indians. *See* under Jones,
Jonathan H.

LEIDING, HARRIETTE K.   **237**
Historic houses of South Carolina. *Phil* 1921.
O [20] 318 map 100 views [on 78 sheets] aa

[LEIGH, BENJAMIN W.]   **238**
The letters of Algernon Sydney in defence of
civil liberty... *Rich* 1830. O [8] 50 55–65 a

[LEIGH, SIR EGERTON]?   **239**
Considerations on certain political transactions
of the province of South Carolina... *L* 1774. O
[4] 83 b
This analysis of colonial discord—possibly by
William H. Drayton—elicited *An answer to Considerations on certain political transactions...*, *q.v.*

LEIGH, SIR EGERTON   **240**
The man unmasked: or, the world undeceived,
in the author of... "Extracts from the procee-

dings of the... court of Vice-Admiralty in Charlestown, South Carolina"... *Charleston S C* 1769.
O 154 44 16 [1] c AA BA NYP PhilL

LEIGH, FRANCES [BUTLER]   **241**
Ten years on a Georgia plantation since the war.
L 1883. O [12] 347 a
By the daughter of Fanny Kemble.

LEIGH, WILLIAM R.   **242**
The western pony. *N Y* Huntington press [1933].
Q 116 [2] 7col.pls[incl. extra signed pl laid] aa 100
cops ptd
—rptd. *N Y* Harper [1935]. same collat., but no
extra pl a

LEISTE, CHRISTIAN   **243**
Beschreibung des Brittischen Amerika zur
Ersparung der englischen Karten. Nebst einer Spe-
cial-Karte der mittleren... Colonien. *Daselbst*
1778. D [30] 571 map aa
—anr. ed. *Braunschweig* 1778. same collat. aa

LELAND, ALONZO   **244**
New map of the mining regions of Oregon and
Washington... with a sketch of the mines...
S F 1863. O 22 + adv-l. fold.map b B Y [only
copies known]

[LELAND, CHARLES G.]   **245**
Ye book of copperheads. *Phil* 1863. O [2] 25pls a

LELAND, CHARLES G.   **246**
The Union Pacific railway, or, three thousand
miles in a railway car. *Phil* 1867. O 95 aa

LELAND, JOHN   **247**
The Virginia chronicle... *Norfolk* 1790. 16°
45 [3] aa
—anr. ed. *Fredkbg* 1790. O 46 [2] aa
A seven-page poem, with same title, but a different work, was issued by this author at Norfolk the
previous year.

LELAND, JOHN A.   **248**
A voice from South Carolina. *Charleston* 1879.
O 231 a

LELEWEL, JOACHIM   **249**
Géographie du moyen âge. *Brus* 1850–2-7. O 3v
& Epilogue [i.e., 4v]: [20 136] 186; [4] 243; [4] 220
112; [4 8] 308. 18maps & pls + atlas obl. Q [18] 16
30 49sheets of maps b N Y

[LE MASCRIER, L'ABBÉ JEAN B.] ed.   **250**
Mémoires historiques sur la Louisiane...
depuis l'année 1687... composés sur les mémoires
de M. Dumont, par M. L. L. M. *P* 1753. D 2v:
[14] 261; [4] 338. map 4illus [on 2pls] 5plans [on
4pls] b BA MH N NYP Y
—Ger tr Stuttg 1756 a

Carries the history of this colony from La Salle's death, 1687, to 1740. Written by the Abbé Le Mascrier from the MS. memoir of an officer resident there for 25 years; hence the Dumont must have been Dumont de Montigny and not George Marie Butel-Dumont, to whom it is usually ascribed.

LEMLEY (JOHN).   **251**
Autobiography . . . of: *Rockford Ill* 1870. O 64 a [called ed. 2, but first in book form]
—complete ed. *Rockford* 1875–8. D 400 port
—rptd. *Alb* 1885–6. D
Mid-western experiences, 1852–1868.

LEMMON, D. F.   **252**
The ancient capital of Indiana: Corydon . . . *New Alb* 1891. O 47 pls a

LE MOINE, J. M.   **253**
Le massacre au Fort George. La mémoire de Montcalm vengée . . . *Quebec* 1864. D 91 a
Contemporary documents proving Montcalm guiltless in this matter.

LEMON, J. R.   **254**
Hand book of Marshall county [Ky.]. *Benton Ky* 1894. O 160 port a

LEMON, JOHN J., pub.   **254a**
The Northfield tragedy, or the robber's raid . . . *St Paul* 1876. D 95 8pls b KCU [only cop loc].

LENDRUM, JOHN   **255**
A concise . . . history of the American revolution . . . *B* 1795. D 2v: 13-344; [8] [8] 13–412 a
—ed. 2, *Phil* 1795.
—rptd. *Trent* 1811. D 2v: [2] 415; [8] 228. 2maps
—anr. ed., with omissions, *Exeter* 1836. 16° 2v

LENNOX, MARY, pseud.
Ante bellum; southern life as it was. *See* Cook Mrs. Mary L. (Redd).

LE NOIR [JEAN].
The democrat; or, intrigues and adventures of: . . . *See* Pye, Henry J.

LENOX, EDWARD H.   **255a**
Overland to Oregon . . . history of the first emigration . . . in 1843. *Oakland* 1904. O [10] 69 port map a

LENZ, T. W.   **256**
Reise nach Saint Louis am Mississippi . . . *Weimar* 1838. D [12] 251 a
Author spent fourteen months in Illinois and Missouri.

LEON COUNTY, FLORIDA: **256a**
A descriptive pamphlet. *Tallahassee* 1881. O 32 a

[LEONARD, CHARLES C.]   **257**
History of Pithole . . . *Pithole City Pa* 1867. 16° 106 + 8adv-p. aa
Early times in the oil region. Pithole had, during its boom, 16,000 people; it exists no more.

[LEONARD, DANIEL]   **258**
Massachusettensis . . . [*B* 1775]. O 118 b AA NYP
—rptd., in part, "The present political state of . . . Massachusetts-Bay . . .," *N Y* 1775. O [2] 86 aa
—anr. *N Y* ed. "The origin of the American contest . . .," same date & collat. aa
—Eng. ed., all of the letters, "Massachusettensis . . .," *L* 1776. O [8] 118; 3 other Eng. eds., same yr. a
Most influential early Tory attempt to defend England's conduct. Ascribed at the time to Jonathan Sewall. For later edition, *see* Adams, John, *Novanglus* . . .

[LEONARD, DANIEL]?   **259**
Strictures . . . upon the three executive departments of the . . . United States . . . n.p. 1792. O 32 a

LEONARD, DAVID A.   **260**
An oration . . . on the late acquisition of Louisiana. *Newport* 1804. O 30 a

[LEONARD, H. L. W.]   **261**
Oregon Territory . . . [cover t.: History of Oregon Territory . . .] *Clev* 1846. D [4] 88 dd G Y [of 3 copies known]

LEONARD, JOHN W.   **262**
The gold fields of the Klondike . . . *Chi* 1897 D 216 front. map a
—Eng. ed., same collat. *L* [1897].

LEONARD, LEVI W.   **263**
The history of Dublin, N. H. . . . *B* 1855. O [8] 433 map 25ports a
—enl. ed., same impr. 1920. O [26] 1018 pls

LEONARD, ZENAS   **264**
Narrative of adventures. *Clearfield Pa* 1839. O [4] 87 dd N AA Y About 200 cops ptd.
—anr. ed. same impr. [*ca* 1885]. O 106 [3] a
—rptd: with notes by W. F. Wagner, *Clev* 1904. O 317 map 5pls aa; *Clearfield* 1908, a; *Norman Okla* [1954], O [36] 172 5 pls
Completely trustworthy account of Rocky Mountain trapping, 1831–7, including experiences with Walker's expedition from Salt Lake to California, 1833, of which it is the chief first-hand authority.

LEONHART, RUDOLPH   **265**
Erinnerungen an Neu Ulm . . . in Minnesota, 1862. *Pitt* 1880. O 46 + cov.t. a

LE PAGE DU PRATZ, [ANTOINE S.]   266
Histoire de la Louisiane . . . *P* 1758. D 3v: [16]
359 incl.errata; [4] 441; [4] 454 [incl 3adv-p] map
plan 40pls aa
—Eng. tr. [abr.] *L* 1763. D 2v: [4, 50, 8] 368; [8]
272. 2maps b
—new ed. *L* 1774. O [8, 36] 387 2maps aa
—anr. issue differs only in having prelim. pp. [2,
36] aa
—Am. ed. "An account of Louisiana . . .," *Newbern* 1804. 18° [4] 272 118 [2] b N
—anr. ed., with index, "The history of Louisiana
. . .," *N O* 1947. O [26] 376 a
Relation, based on a residence from 1718 to
1734, valuable for showing French claims to
southern territory east of the Mississippi and for
particulars concerning Indian nations there.

LE ROUGE, GEORGES L., pub.
Atlas amériquain septentrional . . . *P* 1778. *See*
Jefferys, Thos., *A general topography.*

LE ROUGE, GEORGES L.
Pilote américain . . . *See* Jefferys, Thos., *The
North American pilot.*

LE ROUGE, GEORGES L.   267
Recueil des plans de l'Amérique Septentrionale.
P 1755. Q [2] 19maps 2pls eng t b

LE ROY (BILLY), the Colorado bandit
See Daggett, Thos. F.

LESLIE (FRANK) AND WIFE.   268
A full account of: *Virginia City Nev* 1878. O 24
aa
Probably suppressed for its scandalous details.

LESQUEREUX, LEO   269
Lettres écrites d'Amérique, destinées aux émigrants. *Neuchatel* 1849–50. O [2] 116 aa
—rptd. with suppl. dated 1854–5, *Neuchatel* 1851
O 258 a
—anr. ed. *Neuchatel* 1853. O [4] 300

LESSEPS (BARON JEAN B. B. DE).   270
Journal historique du voyage de: . . . employé
dans l'expédition de . . . La Perouse . . . *P* 1790.
O 2v: [14] 280; [4] 380 [6]. 2 maps pl aa
—Eng. ed. "Travels in Kamtschatka . . . 1787–8,"
L 1790. O 2v: [16] 283; [8] 408. map aa
—Dutch tr. *Utrecht* 1792. O 2v a
—Ger. tr., by Forster, *Berlin* 1791. O 304
—anr. Ger. tr., by Villaume, *Riga* 1791. D 2v in
1 map

LESTER, C[HARLES] EDWARDS   271
Sam Houston and his republic. *N Y* 1846. O 208
port[not in all copies] aa
—anr. ed., no au. named, "The life of Sam Hous-

ton . . ." *N Y* 1855. D 402 [incl. port and 10 maps
& pls]
—rptd Phil 1867.

**LESTER, JOHN C., and   272
WILSON, D. L.**
Ku Klux Klan. Its origin, growth and disband-
ment. *Nashv* 1884. D 117 aa
—rptd. *N Y & Wash* 1905. D 198 [10] 10 pls a
Lester was one of the ten founding fathers of
this order.

L'ESTRANGE, HAMON   273
Americans no Jewes, or improbabilities that the
Americans are of that race . . . *L* 1652. smQ [4]
80 b JCB N NYP
Disputes conclusions in Thorowgood's *Jewes in
America* [*q.v.*]

L'ESTRANGE, W. D.   274
Under fourteen flags . . . life and adventures of
Brigadier-General Mac Iver . . . *L* 1884. D 2v in 1:
[10] 260; [6] 251. port aa
—rptd. *L* n.d. D 344 a
In addition to exploits in India, Europe, Cuba
Mexico and the Argentine, there is a lengthy but
dubious account of cavalry services by this Scotch
soldier of fortune under Stonewall Jackson and
"Jeb" Stuart.

LETCHER, MONTGOMERY E.   275
Wonderful discovery! . . . exploration of the
celebrated Mammoth cave . . . *N Y* 1839. D 24 a

LETTER . . .   276
**Letter (A) addressed to two great men [i.e. Pitt
and the Duke of Newcastle], on the prospect of
peace; and on the terms to be insisted on . . .** *L*
1760. O [4] 56 a
—ed. 2, same impr., collat. & date
—anr. ed. *Dub* 1760. O 42
—Am. eds.: *B* Fowle & Draper 1760, O 43; *B*
Mecom 1760, O 55 a
Attributed to John Douglas, William Pulteney
and Junius. For *Remarks* [on this *Letter*], *see*
Townshend, Charles.

**Letter (A) from a merchant in London to his
nephew in North America . . .** *See* Tucker, Josiah

**Letter(A) from a merchant in . . . London,   277
to . . . W . . . P . . ., Esq.; upon the affairs and commerce of North America . . .** *L* 1757. D 98 a

Letter (A) from a Russian sea-officer . . . *See*
Müller, Gerhard F.

**Letter (A) from a Virginian to the members of the
Congress to be held at Philadelphia . . .** *See* Boucher, Jonathan.

Letter (A) from an officer retired, to his   278
son in parliament. *L* 1776. O [4] 38 a
—rptd. *Edin* same date. D [4] 30
Urges vigorous prosecution of the war.

Letter from Britannia to the King. *L* 1781.   279
O 61 a

Letter (A) from Freeman of South Carolina, to
the deputies . . . *See* Drayton, Wm. H.

Letter (A) on American history. *See* Reed,
Wm. B.

Letter (A) to a friend in a slave state. By a citizen
of Pennsylvania. *See* Ingersoll, Chas.

Letter (A) to a friend in the country, on the late
expedition to Canada . . . 1712. *See* Dummer
Jeremiah.

Letter (A) to a great M . . .r, on the pros-   280
pect of a peace . . . *L* 1761. O [4] 148 aa
Argues that Louisiana and the Ohio country
would be of more economic and tactical value than
Canada.

Letter (A) to a member of Congress; respecting
the alien and sedition laws. *See* Tucker, St. Geo.

Letter (A) to a member of Parliament, on   281
the importance of the American colonies . . . *L* 1757.
O 24 aa

Letter (A) to a member of Parliament on   282
the present unhappy dispute . . . *L* 1774. O [2] 47 a
Upholds the supremacy of Parliament.

Letter (A) to a member of Parliament,   283
wherein the power of the British legislature, and the
case of the colonists, are . . . considered. *L* 1765.
O [2] 30 a
Supports parliamentary claims, but questions
the wisdom of the Stamp Act.

Letter to a member of the general assembly of
Virginia, on the . . . late conspiracy of the slaves . . .
See Tucker, St. Geo.

Letter (A) to a noble lord concerning the late
expedition to Canada . . . 1712. *See* Dummer
Jeremiah.

Letter (A) to a young officer. By an officer of the
British army. *See* Drewe, Maj. Edward.

Letter (A) to an English gentleman on the libels
and calumnies on America . . . *See* Walsh, Robt.

Letter (A) to an honourable Brigadier-   284
General, commander in chief . . . in Canada. *L* 1760.
O [4] 32 aa

Attack on Lord George Townsend's conduct
after his succession to Wolfe. Attributed to General
Charles Lee, to Thomas Pownall and to "Junius." Answered by Edward Thurlow, *q.v.*

Letter (A) to . . . John Wesley occasioned by his
Calm address . . . *See* Evans, Caleb.

Letter to . . . the Duke of N[ewcastle] on   285
the present crisis in the affairs of Great Britain.
L [1761]. O 48 a
Suggests attacking New Orleans and securing
Louisiana.

Letter (A) to the English nation, on the   286
present war with America; with a review of our
military operations . . . impossibility of reducing
the colonies and the folly of continuing the contest
. . . By an officer returned from that service. *L*
1777. O [4] 59 aa

Letter (A) to the gentlemen of the com-   287
mittee of London merchants, trading to North America . . . *L* 1766. O 30 a
Points out the damage to British trade which
will result from the Stamp Act and other colonial
restrictions.

Letter (A) to the noblemen . . . who have   288
addressed His Majesty on the subject of the American rebellion. *Y* 1776. O 37 a
The colonies must be kept in subjugation.

Letter (A) to the people of America, lately printed
at New York . . . *See* Galloway, Jos.

Letter (A) to the people of England on   289
the necessity of putting an immediate end to the war
. . . *L* 1760. O [2] 54 a

Letter (A) to the people of England on the present
situation . . . *See* Shebbeare, John.

Letter (A) to the people of Great-Britain   290
in answer to that published by the American Congress. *L* 1775. O 59 a

Letter (A) to the Right Honourable Lord   291
M. . . ., on the affairs of America. From a member
of Parliament. *L* 1775. O 38 a

LETTERA   292
Lettera di un missionario sulla schiavitù domestica degli Stati Confederati di America. *Rome*
1864. 16° 83 aa

LETTERS
Letters addressed to the hon. George Poindexter
. . . By Castigator & Philo-Castigator. *See* Mar-
schalk, Andrew.

Letters and dissertations on various subjects . . .
See Crowley, Thos.

Letters from America, 1776–1779 . . . of   293
Brunswick, Hessian and Waldeck officers . . . Tr. by
R. W. Pettingill. *B* 1924. O [26] 281 a 450copies
ptd.

Letters from North America. *See* Moor, Rev.
Allen P.

Letters from the south . . . *See* Paulding, James K.

Letters from the United States, exhibiting   294
the working of democracy therein for the last twenty
years. By an Anglo-American . . . *L* 1844. O 59 a

Letters lately published . . . on the subject of the
present dispute with Spain, under the signature of
Verus. *See* Webb, Francis.

Letters (The) of a British spy. *See* Wirt, Wm.

Letters of Papinian . . . *See* Inglis, Chas.

Letters of the southern spy. *See* Pollard. Edw. A.

Letters (The) of Veritas . . . *See* Richardson,
John.

Letters of Verus . . . *See* Yrujo y Tacon, Carlos M.

Letters on American affairs. n.p. [1769].   295
O 48 a

Letters on emigration. By a gentleman lately
returned from America. *See* Hodgkinson, John.

Letters on the condition of the African race in the
United States. By a southern lady. *See* Schoolcraft
Mrs. Henry R.

Letters (The) on the . . . naval war with America
which appeared . . . under the signature of Nereus.
See Croker, John Wilson.

Letters on the present disturbances in Great
Britain and her American provinces. *See* Ramsay,
Allan.

Letters on the subject of southern wrongs and
remedies. *See* Robertson, John.

Letters to a nobleman on the conduct of the war
in the middle colonies. *See* Galloway, Jos.

Letters to an officer, stationed at an   296
interior post [Michilmackinac] . . . *L* 1773. 16° [6]
111 aa ed 2 "Reciprocal love . . ." *L* 1779. aa
Fiction; and of no historical interest. Author
was a Capt. Phillips.

Letters to the citizens of the United States. [capt
t.] [signed Germanicus]. *See* Randolph, Edmund.

Letters written in London by an American   297
spy, 1764–5. *L* 1786. D [22] 167 aa
—rptd. *L* 1791. D a

LETTRE
Lettre à Napoléon III sur l'esclavage aux états du
sud, par un Créole de la Louisiane. *See* Musson,
Eugène.

Lettre de Mr. . . . à Mr. S. B. . . . au sujet des
troubles qui agitent . . . l'Amérique Septentrionale.
See Pinto, Isaac de.

Lettre d'un officier de la marine Russienne . . .
See Müller, Gerhard F.

LETTRES   298
Lettres curieuses sur l'Amérique Septentrionale,
Canada. *P* 1845. D [22] 264 a
Includes 17th century letters on the Mississippi.

Lettres d'un membre du Congress amériquain, à
divers membres du Parlement . . . *See* Vincent, N.

Lettres edifiantes . . . des missions etran-   299
gères par . . . missionaires de la Compagnie de
Jesus. *P* [1702?]–1776. D 34v maps pls b NYP
—anr. ed., arranged systematically, *P* 1780–83.
D 26v[27 when the 56 maps & pls are bound in
separate vol.] aa
—rptd. *Toulouse* 1810–11. D 26v & O vol of maps
& pls aa
—other Fr. eds.: *P* 1808–09. O 8v; *Lyons* 1819, O
14v 50maps & pls; *P* 1824–26, O 8v; *P* 1838–43,
Q 4v: [12] 820; [4] 807; [4] 844; [4] 723; *P* 1861,
O 3v: *Toulouse* 1870, D 26 v; *P* 1875–77, O 4v
—Eng. eds. *See* "The travels of several learned
missioners . . .," and Lockman, John, "Travels of
the Jesuits."
—Ger. tr., with adds., *see* Stöcklein, Jos.
—Ital. tr. *Milan* 1825–29. O 6v
—Sp. tr. "Cartas edificantes . . .," *Madrid* 1753–
57. O 16v 23 pls b
Includes reports covering New York, Ohio,
Michigan, Illinois, Wisconsin and the southwest.
Of the original edition, some of the earlier volumes
were reprinted; no volumes were issued between
1758 and 1773.

[LETTS, J. M.]   300
California illustrated . . . By a returned Californian. *N Y* Holredge 1852. O 224 48 pls aa
—anr. issue, au. named, *N Y* Young. aa
—rptd. 1853. aa
—anr. ed. "Pictorial view of California," *N Y*
Bill 1853. aa
Number of plates vary in copies of all issues but
48 is the proper complement.

LEVASSEUR, AUGUSTE   301
Lafayette en Amérique . . . ou journal d'un

voyage aux États-Unis. *P* 1829. O 2v: [8] 509; [4] 632. map 11pls[t-p calls for 12, but only 11 issued] aa

—rptd. *Brus* 1829. D 3v a

—Eng. tr. *Phil* 1829. D 2v: [6] 9–227; [4] 9–265 aa

—anr. issue, *N Y* 1829. D 2v: 227 [2]; 284 [2] a

—Ger. tr. *Naumburg* 1829. O 870 [2] port a

—Dutch tr. *Zutphen* 1831. O 2v port a

LEVEANS, H. C., et al   302
History of Copper county, Missouri. *St L* 1876. O 231 errata lf a

[LEVER, W. H.], pub.   303
History of Sanpete and Emery counties, [Utah]. *Ogden* 1898. O 681 [2], incl pls. a

LEVINGE, R[ICHARD] G. A.   303a
Echoes from the backwoods; or sketches of trans-Atlantic life. *L* 1846. D 2v: [18] 294; [6] 258 + 14adv-p. 6pls a

—several later eds.: 1847; 1849; 1859; 1860.

LEVY, DANIEL   304
Les Francais en Californie . . . *S F* 1884. O [10] 373 aa

—rptd. *S F* 1885. a

LEWIS AND DRYDEN'S . . . HISTORY
Lewis and Dryden's marine history of the Pacific northwest . . . *See* Wright, Edgar W.

LEWIS, ALONZO   305
History of Lynn. *Lynn* 1829–30. O 260 4ports a

—ed. 2, with adds., *B* 1844. O 278 2pls

—best ed., with adds. by James R. Newhall, *B* 1865–92. O 2v

LEWIS (ANDREW).   306
The orderly book of that portion of the American army . . . under: . . . *Rich* 1860. O [16] 100 100copies[10 on L. P.] a

LEWIS, CATHERINE   307
Narrative of some of the proceedings of the Mormons . . . *Lynn* 1848. O 24 b 4 cops loc

—rptd. same impr. 1853. O 16 aa

LEWIS, CHARLES E.   308
Two lectures on a short visit to America. *L* 1876 O 106 [1] + errata slip a

Penetrated as far as Chicago.

LEWIS (DAVID).   309
The confession . . . of: . . . celebrated counterfeiter and robber . . . *Carlisle Pa* 1820. D 62 aa

—rptd. *Newville Pa* 1890. O 84 a

LEWIS, FREEMAN, and VEECH, JAMES
The Monongahela of old . . . *See* Veech, James.

LEWIS, GEORGE   310
Impressions of America and the American churches . . . *Edin* 1845. D [8] 432 a

LEWIS (MRS. HANNAH).   311
Narrative of the captivity and sufferings of: and her three children, who were taken prisoners by the Indians, near St. Louis, on the 25th May, 1815 . . . *B* 1817. D 24[incl. pl] aa

—ed. 2, same collat., *B* 1817. aa

—ed. 3, same collat., *B* 1818. aa

—anr. ed. *B* 1821. a

For a later distortion of this questionable narrative, *see* similar title under Lewis, Mrs. Jane; for note as to authorship, *see* Hall, Misses Frances and Almira.

LEWIS, HENRY   312
Das illustrirte Mississippithal . . . vom Wasserfalle zu St. Anthony an bis zum Golf von Mexico . . . *Dusseldorf* [1854–8]. Q 431 79 cold pls, incl. pictorial $\frac{1}{2}$ t. [t-p calls for 80 pls, which no. was arrived at by counting as 2pls the double-p. view of New Orleans. dd LC N NYP Pn

—rptd. *Leip* 1923. large O [22] 431 2ports eng.t. 78 col.pls aa

—Eng. tr. [*see* note below]. *Phil.* 1845 a

Originally issued in 20 installments, consequently bound copies vary in the matter of placing plates. Some plates having titles in English are explainable as being strays from the simultaneously begun, but not completed, English version apparently abandoned after the third installment, as no more parts have been located; these parts end at page 76 and contain 12 plates. Some copies of the German edition carry, in place of the undated title-page [with its misleading indication that the text descriptions were both written and translated by Douglas], a corrected one dated 1858 in which he is credited only with being the translator.

[LEWIS, HENRY C.]   313
Odd leaves from the life of a Louisiana "swamp doctor." *Phil* Carey & Hart [1843]. D [10] 21–203 pls a

—rptd. *Phil* [1846]: 1850; 1852.

—anr. ed., together with John S. Robb's "Streaks of squatter life," *Phil* Peterson [1858]. O 2v in 1: [8] 21–203; 187. 14pls [incl.eng.t.]

LEWIS, J. C.   314
Black Beaver, the trapper . . . n.p. [1911]. O 58 a

LEWIS, J[AMES] O.   315
The aboriginal port-folio. *Phil* 1835. F 10nos. [t-p with no. 10] 72col.ports[in ordinary copies, but some copies contain 77, and a few have 80] c

—bound form, *Phil* 1835-6. b AA N NYP Y

—ed. 2, *Phil* 1836. b NYP Y

Three leaves of *Advertisement* were issued with the original parts and constitute, with title leaf, all the text material that appeared.

LEWIS (MRS. JANE).   316
Narrative of the captivity and . . . escape of: . . . who, with a son and daughter . . . and an infant babe, were made prisoners . . . by a party of Indians . . . commanded by Black Hawk . . . [*N Y*] 1833. O 24[incl. front.] cov.t.only a
—rptd. *N Y* 1834. same collat.
Cf. a similar title under Lewis, Mrs. Hannah, of which this is probably a garbled version; the date of capture is advanced seven years to take advantage of current interest in Black Hawk's activities.

LEWIS (MERIWETHER) and   317
CLARK (WILLIAM).
History of the expedition under: 1804–5–6. [Prepared for publication, from material supplied by the explorers, by Nicholas Biddle, not by Paul Allen who is named as editor]. *Phil* 1814. O 2v: [28] 470; [9] 522. 5charts map[not issued with all copies] bds. dd S calf c N NYP Y Less than 2000 cops ptd
—abr. ed., with introd. added, *N Y* 1842. 16° 2v: [6] 372;[10] 9–396. map 5charts pl a
—Eng. eds., some omissions, prcf. by Thomas Rees added: *L* 1814, Q [24] 663 map 5charts[on 3 sheets] b; rptd. *L* 1815, O 3v: [28] 411; [12] 434; [12] 394. map 5charts; same, *L* 1817. aa
—Irish ed. *Dub* 1817. O 2v: [38] 588; [18] 3–643. map 5charts pl b N Issued also in 42 pts, wraps. c NYP Y
—many later Am. eds., the most scholarly being that ed. by Coues, annotated and indexed, *N Y* 1893. O 4v 2ports 8maps same, on L.P. aa
—Ger. tr. *Weimar* 1814. O 362 map aa
—Dutch tr. *Dordrecht* 1816–18. O 3v: [32] 308; [8] 390; [8] 335. map aa
First authorized and complete account of the most important western exploration and the first of many overland narrative to follow.

LEWIS (CAPTAIN MERIWETHER)   318
and ORDWAY (SERGEANT JOHN).
Journals of: . . . 1803–1806. Ed. by M. M. Quaife. *Madison* 1916. O 444 3maps 7pls 3 facs a

LEWIS, [MERIWETHER], and   319
CLARK, [WILLIAM]
Message of the President [Jefferson] . . . communicating discoveries . . . by Captains Lewis and Clark, Dr. Sibley and Mr. Dunbar . . . *Wash* 1806. O 171 [7] map [in some copies] 2tabs. Issued by both House and Senate; House issue—possibly earlier—states "Read and ordered to lie on the table"; the other issue reads "Printed by order of the Senate." dd G Y copies without map c
—with t. altered. *Natchez* 1806. O 64 64–127 127–166 159–177 c N Y [of 5 cops loc]

—with app. omitted, *N Y* 1806. O 128 fold. tab b Y
—with title altered, *L* 1807. O [24] 17–116 fold. tab aa
Though meager in information on Lewis and Clark, this was the first book giving any of their activities. The map, by Nicholas King, who is also supposed to have prepared this material for publication, was of the lower trans-Mississippi, drawn from Dunbar's survey, and is found in only a few copies. The Sibley-Dunbar descriptions of the Texas-Louisiana frontier gave the first formal and satisfactory picture of the southern portion of the Louisiana Purchase.

LEWIS, [MERIWETHER], and   320
CLARK, [WILLIAM]
Original journals . . . Ed. by Thwaites. *N Y* 1904–05. O 8v [incl.atlas of 56 maps & pls on 62sheets] b N NYP Y
—also issued on L.P. Q 15v 200sets, each on Jap. vell. & on Van Gelder paper c Y
—50 sets on Imperial Jap. paper c G
—rptd. *N Y* 1960. 8v b 750 sets ptd
The most elaborate work on this expedition.

LEWIS (MERIWETHER) and
CLARK, (WILLIAM).
Die Reisen du: *See* below, *Travels of Lewis and Clark* . . .

LEWIS, [MERIWETHER], and   321
CLARK, [WILLIAM].
Travels of: . . . compiled from various authentic sources . . . *Phil* 1809. D 300 map 5pls aa
—same, with slight omissions & no pls, *L* 1809. O [9] 309 map aa
—anr. ed. "Journal . . ." *Dayton O* 1840. D 240 [incl. 3 pls] a
—Ger. trs. [abr.]: *Libanon* [*sic*] *Pa* 1811, D 60 4pls c; *Frederick Md* 1811, D 64 c NYP; *Frederick* 1812, D [t-p calls for port, but none issued] b NYP
Unauthorized or "counterfeit" edition—culled from Jefferson's message, Carver, Mackenzie, and Gass. *See* also Fisher, William.

LEWIS, SETH   322
Abolitionism reviewed . . . n.p. n.d. D [2] 76 a

[LEWIS, MRS. THOMAS B.]   323
What I have saved from the writings of my husband. *S F* 1874. O 64 59 a
Mining experiences, Indian wars, etc., in Montana and elsewhere.

LEWIS, VIRGIL A.   324
History of West Virginia. *Phil* 1889. O [16 incl. front.] 19–744 3ports a

LEWIS, JUDGE WILLIAM   325
Biographical sketch of . . . Sam Houston . . . *Dallas* 1882. O 92 a

LEWIS, WILLIAM S.   326
The story of early days in the Big Bend country. *Spokane* 1926. O 35 2pls a 205 copies ptd.

LEYDEN, JAMES A.   327
Historical sketch of the Fourth infantry . . . *Ft. Shoreham, Ida.* 1891. O 20 + wraps aa

LEZAY-MARNEZIA, CLAUD   328
FRANCOIS ADRIEN, marquis de
Lettres écrites des rives de l'Ohio. *P* [1801?]. O [8] 144 b IndH LC NYP
Suppressed because of its denunciation of the French government. The author contemplated establishing a French colony in Ohio, but negotiations with the Scioto Company fell through and he returned to France after a year's residence in Pennsylvania.

[L'HÉRITIER, LOUIS F.]   329
Le Champ-d'Asile: tableau topographique et historique du Texas . . . *P* 1819. O [24] 247 b
—anr. issue, same collat., except has 8 additional prelim. p. *P* 1819. b
—ed. 2, same collat. as preceding, but with fold. map added, *P* 1819. aa
For similar book see Hartman and Millard.

LIBERTY (THE)   330
Liberty (The) and property of British subjects asserted . . . *L* 1726. O 39 a
Complaints by a Charlestonian against the policy of Carolina's proprietary government.

LIEBER, FRANCIS, ed.   331
Letters to a gentleman in Germany, written after a trip from Philadelphia to Niagara. *Phil* 1834. O 356 a
—rptd. "The stranger in America . . .," *Phil* 1835. O 356
—Eng. ed. *L* 1835. D 2v: [8] 301; [6] 310

LIENHARD, HEINRICH   332
Californien, unmittelbar vor nach der Entdeckung des Goldes . . . *Zurich* 1898. O 318 port a
—Eng. tr.[in part], "A pioneer at Sutter's fort," *L A* 1941. O [28] 291 6pls
In Sutter's employ, 1847.

LIES, EUGENE   333
Landed estates of California pioneers. *S F* 1863. O 27 a

LIFE
Life and adventures in the South Pacific. By a roving printer. *See* Jones, G. D.

Life and manners in the United States. By a traveller. *See* Dwight, Theo.

Life in the south . . . By a blockaded British subject . . . *See* Hopley, Cath. C.

Life in the west; back-wood leaves and   333a
prairie flowers . . . *L* 1842. D [12] 363 3pls a
—ed. 2, same collat., *L* 1843.
The anonymous author's travels extended to western New York, Michigan, Illinois and Wisconsin.

Life on the lakes . . . *See* Gilman, Chandler R.

LIGERET DE CHAZY, MME.   334
ELÉONORE
Les créoles, réponse à Mme. de Grandfort. [*N O* 1855?]. D 42 a

LILLIE, GORDON W. ["PAWNEE   335
BILL"], and TUCKER, J. B.
Condensed topographical handbook of the Cherokee strip . . . *Arkansas City Kas* 1892. O 50 b

LILY (THE) AND THE TOTEM . . .
See Simms, Wm. G.

LINCOLN (ABRAHAM): A STUDY.
Liv 1865. *See* Young, Rob't.

LINCOLN, ABRAHAM   336
Lincoln (Abraham) as attorney for the Illinois Central . . . [*Chi* 1905]. Q 38 port facs a

[LINCOLN, ABRAHAM]   337
The assassination and history of the conspiracy . . . *Cin* Hawley & Co. [1865]. O [12] 21–163 aa

LINCOLN (ABRAHAM) and   338
DOUGLAS (STEPHEN A.)
Debates between: . . . *Columbus* 1860. O 268 [8, incl final blank lf] 268 aa
—issue 1: no rule immediately above pub's impr. on copyr. p., no advs, "2" at bottom of p. 17
—several later issues, same yr., most desirable being state 5 of ed. 3, with letter from Douglas objecting to the publisher's alterations of his words. aa
Historically the most important series of American political debates.

LINCOLN, ABRAHAM
Gettysburg address. *See* Everett, Edward, *An oration* . . .

LINCOLN (PRESIDENT) and   339
BALDWIN (COL. JOHN B.)
Interview between: . . . [concerning Ft. Sumter's evacuation]. *Staunton Va* 1866. O 28 a

LINCOLN (ABRAHAM).   340
Das Leben von: . . . *Chi* 1860. D 108 b ChiH IllH [only copies known]

LINCOLN (ABRAHAM).
Life of: [*Chi* 1860]. *See* Scripps, John L.

LINCOLN (ABRAM [sic]).   341
The life, speeches [etc.] of: . . . With a sketch of the life of Hannibal Hamlin . . . *N Y* 1860. D 117 port aa
—anr. issue, *B* 1860. a
Styled the "Wigwam Edition," this was the first life of Lincoln in book form.

LINCOLN (ABRAHAM) and
HAMLIN (HANNIBAL).
Lives and speeches of: 1860. *See* Howells, Wm D.

LINCOLN (ABRAHAM).
A memoir of: *L* 1861. *See* Black, Rob't.

LINCOLN (PRESIDENT).   342
The terrible tragedy at Washington: assassination of: . . . *Phil* Barclay 1865. O [2] 21–30 [2] 39–52 [2] 61–74 [2] 85–98 101–116 a
—enl. ed. "The great conspiracy . . .," *Phil* 1866. O 201

LINCOLN (ABRAHAM).   343
Trial of the assassins . . . for the murder of: *Phil* Barclay [1865]. O [6] 21–102 aa
—anr. issue, illus. of execution moved to p96

LINCOLN (ABRAHAM).   344
The trial of the assassins [etc.] for the murder of: . . . *Phil* Peterson [1865]. O [2] 15–203 + 7adv-p aa
—anr. issue, enl. to 210p t-p of some copies has "alleged" before the word "assassins."

LINCOLN (MRS. [ABRAHAM]).
Behind the seams; by a nigger woman who took in work from: . . . *See* Ottolengual, D.

[LINCOLN, LEVI]   345
A farmer's letter to the people. *Phil* 1802. O 95 a
—anr. ed. "Letters to the people. By a farmer," *Salem* same date. O 102

LINCOLN, SOLOMON, JR.   346
History of . . . Hingham. *Hingham* 1827. D 183 a

LINCOLN, WALDO   347
History of the Lincoln family . . . *Worcester Mass* 1923. O [10] 718 illus some copies have errata l., issued later, inserted after prelim. pages a

LINCOLN, WILLIAM S.   348
Alton trials . . . *N Y* 1838. D 158 front a

[LIND, JOHN]?   349
An answer to the declaration of the American Congress. *L* 1776. O [20] 137 aa
—rptd., with omissions, first pub. ed., *L* 1776. O 132; 4 other eds., same yr. a
—anr. ed. *Dub* 1777. O [8] 88
—Fr. tr. *L* 1777. O [7] 124 [4]; *Hague* 1777. O 205

This was in reply to *A declaration by the representatives of the united colonies . . . seting* [sic] *forth the causes . . . of their taking up arms*, published at Philadelphia, 1775, *q.v.* For similar reply, *see* Dalrymple, Sir John, *The rights of Great Britain asserted . . .*

[LIND, JOHN]?   350
An Englishman's answer to the address from the delegates, to the people of Great-Britain . . . *N Y* 1775. O [2] 26 aa
—rptd., in several eds., *L* 1776; *Dub* 1777.
This was a reply to *The twelve united colonies, by their delegates in Congress; to the people of Great-Britain*, published at Philadelphia, New York and Newport the same year.

[LIND, JOHN]   351
A letter to the . . . Earl of Abingdon . . . *L* 1778. O [12] 86 a
Upholds the Earl's reply to Burke's Letter to the sheriffs of Bristol.

[LIND, JOHN]   352
Remarks on the principal acts of the thirteenth parliament . . . Vol. I[all]. *L* 1775. O [20] 500 a
—Ger. ed. "Anmerkungen über die vornehmsten Acten . . .," *Braunschweig* 1778. O 334
Defends the stand taken by Parliament to coerce the colonies, but offers a plan of reconciliation.

[LIND, JOHN]?   353
Three letters to Dr. Price, containing remarks on his Observations on the nature of civil liberty . . . and the justice and policy of the war in America. *L* 1776. O [22] 163 a

LINDSAY, WILLIAM   354
View of America . . . *Hawick Eng* 1824. D 104 a

LINDSEY, CHARLES   355
The prairies of the western states . . . *Tor* 1860. D 100 a
Native prejudice, aggravated by the fact that his tour was made during a business depression caused by the 1857–8 speculation mania, combined to give this Canadian observer a dim view of Wisconsin, Iowa and Illinois.

LINDSEY, DOUGLAS   356
Alaska; a complete . . . guide . . . *Stockton* 1897. O 24 map a

LINDSLEY, AARON L.   357
Sketches of an excursion to southern Alaska. [*Port Ore* 1879?]. O 73 a

LINDSLEY, JOHN B.   358
The military annals of Tennessee . . . *Nash* 1886. O 910 2pls a

LINFORTH, JAMES [ed.]   **359**
Route from Liverpool to Great Salt Lake valley
... *Liv* 1855. Q [8] 120 map 30pls b AA N NYP Y
—anr. issue, in 15 monthly pts, dated 1854–5, t-p
& contents with last pt, a slip "Notice to subscribers" in pt. 1. d
One of the most elaborately and beautifully
illustrated of western books. A large portion of the
edition was water-damaged while in transit to New
York. In some copies of the map Utah counties are
hand-colored.

LINGENFELTER, L.   **360**
History of Fremont county [Ia.]. *Hamburg Ia*
[1876]. 24° 62 aa
—rptd.: *St Joseph Mo* 1877. D 28; *Hamburg*
1935. aa

LINN, E[LIZABETH] A., and   **361**
SARGENT, N[ATHAN]
The life and ... services of Dr. Lewis F. Linn
... *N Y* 1857. O 441 2pls a
Senator from Missouri; largely instrumental in
securing occupation of Oregon and its territorial
establishment.

LINN, JOHN B.   **362**
Annals of Buffalo valley [Pa.]. *Harrisburg* 1877.
O [2] 621 map 2pls a

LINN, JOHN J.   **363**
Reminiscences of fifty years in Texas. *N Y* 1883.
D 369 errata slip port 4 pls [incl a view erroneously
captioned "The Alamo" cor. to "Goliad" by an
inserted overlay caption] aa
—rptd. *Austin* 1935. O 369 pls a

LINN, LEWIS F.   **364**
Report of the ... committee on the occupation
of Oregon Territory. [Sen. Doc. 470]. *Wash* 1838.
O 23 2maps aa
Asserts United States' rights to the region and
urges its occupation.

[LINN, WILLIAM]   **365**
Serious considerations on the election of a president ... *N Y* 1800. O 36 a
—rptd., same date, *Trenton*. O 31
Jefferson shown unworthy of Christian support.

LINN, WILLIAM A.   **366**
The story of the Mormons. *N Y* 1902. O 637 a
—rptd. same impr. & collat. 1923.

LIPPARD, GEORGE   **367**
Adventures of the Texas rangers in the Mexican
war ... *N Y* 1849. D 136 a

LIPPARD, GEORGE   **368**
Washington and his generals; or legends of the
revolution. *Phil* 1847. O [4] 538 [27] a

—several reprints, some with t. shortened to
"Legends of the revolution."

LIPPITT (FRANCIS J.)   **369**
Reminiscences of: *Prov* 1902. O 122 port a
Coming to San Francisco with a military organization in 1847, Lippitt was the first commandant
of the Presidio; later practised law there and was a
leading spirit in the 1856 vigilance committee.

LIPSCOMB, W[ILLIAM] L.   **370**
A history of Columbus, Mississippi. *Birm* 1909.
O 167 pls a

LISBON.   **371**
Two very circumstantial accounts of the late
dreadful earthquake at: ... to which is added an
account of the late earthquake in Boston. Ed. 2.
B 1756. O 32 aa
The first edition did not include the Boston
quake.

LISIANSKII [LISIANSKY],   **372**
IURIIA [UREY]
Puteshestvie vokrug svieta v 1803–6 godakh ...
na korablie Nevie ... *St Ptbg* 1812. Q 581 + F
atlas 14maps 3pls b Y
—Eng. ed. "A voyage round the world ... in the
ship Neva ...," *L* 1814. Q [24] 388 8maps 6pls b
N NYP WashU Y
Highly important work on Sitka, Kodiak and
other parts of the northwest coast. The author,
commanding the "Neva," accompanied the great
Russian expedition under Krusenstern.

L'ISLE (HERRN [GUILLAUME] VON).
Erklarung der Charte von neuen Entdeckungen
welche gegen norden des Suder-Meers durch den:
See Buache, Philip, *Explication de la carte ...*

LIST (A)   **373**
**List (A) of ... His Majesty's land forces in North
America** ... [*N Y* Gaine 1761]. D 36 c NYP

List (A) of the general and staff officers   **374**
... serving in North America, under ... Clinton.
N Y 1779. O 65 b

LITKÉ [LÜTKÉ], FEDOREM   **375**
[FREDERIC] P.
Chetyrekratnoe puteshestvie v sievernyi Leodo-
vityi Okean ... ago na voennom brigie Nova
Zemlia, v 1821–24. [Four voyages to the Arctic
ocean ... in the brig Nova Zembla]. *St Ptbg* 1828.
Q 2v in 1: 581 37 maps & pls b Y

LITKÉ [LÜTKÉ], FEDOREM   **376**
[FREDERIC] P.
Puteschestvie vokrug svieta sovershennoe po
povelieniiu Imp. Nikolaia I, na voennom shliupie
Seniavinie v 1826–9 ... *St Ptbg* 1834–5–6. Histor-

ical section [Q 3v: 294; 282; 270. 6pls 25views + atlas F 38 3maps 51pls]. Nautical section [Q 356 + atlas F [12] 11 maps & plans 32views] dd N Y

—Fr. ed. "Voyage autour du monde . . . sur la corvette le Seniavine . . . Partie Historique," *P* [1835–6]. O 3v: [30] 410 [4]; [6] 388 [2]; [14] 352. 3maps plan plate + atlas [of 38 p 3maps 51pls] F d NYP Y

—Fr. tr. "Partie nautique," *St Ptbg* 1836. O [14] 344 [2] 10maps 6pls c

This Russian government expedition was designed to survey the new regions described by Bering and Kotzebue on the northwest coast, Bering's sea and the coastal islands. The plates, drawn by Kittlitz and engraved by Englemann, are the most graphic and beautiful portrayals of scenery and humanity ever made of this region. For another account of this voyage *see* Kittlitz.

LITTELL, WILLIAM   377
An epistle . . . to the people of the realm of Kentucky . . . *Frankfort Ky* 1806. D 40 b ChiU WisH

This satire on certain public agitations was reprinted in his *Festoons of fancy*.

LITTELL, WILLIAM   378
Festoons of fancy . . . *Louisv* 1814. O [2] 180 c ChiU G NYP Y

The first humorous book produced West of the Alleghanies.

LITTELL, WILLIAM   379
Political transactions in and concerning Kentucky, from the first settlement . . . *Frankf Ky* 1806. O 81 [66] b AA KyH LC NYP

LITTLE, GEORGE, and   380
MAXWELL, JAMES R.
A history of Lumsden's Battery, C. S. A. *Tuskaloosa* n.d. [1905] O 70 front. a

LITTLE, JAMES A.   381
Biographical sketch of Feramorz Little. *S L C* 1890. O 191 a
Had charge of the overland mail service from Laramie to Salt Lake, 1851–3.

LITTLE, JAMES A.   382
From Kirtland to Salt Lake City. *S L C* 1890. O 260 aa
Overland trail events, 1846–1852.

LITTLE, JAMES A.   383
Jacob Hamblin: a narrative of . . . experience as a frontiersman . . . *S L C* 1881. D 140 + 4 adv-p a
—ed. 2, same impr. 1909.

LITTLE, JAMES A.   384
What I saw on the old Santa Fé trail . . . *Plainfield Ind* [1904]. D [2] 127 front aa

LITTLE, JOHN B.   385
The history of Butler county, Alabama . . . 1815–1885. *Cin* 1885. D 256 map 7ports a

LITTLE, JOHN P.   386
Richmond, the capital of Virginia: its history. *Rich* 1851. O 102 pls a

LITTLE, LUCIUS P.   387
Ben Hardin: his times and contemporaries. *Louisv* 1887. O [22] 640 front a

[LITTLE, OTIS]   388
The state of trade in the northern colonies . . . *L* 1748. D 84 aa
—Am. ed. *B* 1749. D 43 a

LITTLE, WILLIAM   389
The history of Warren [N. H.] . . . *Concord* 1854. D 140 a 250copies ptd.
—enl. ed. *Manchester* 1870. O 592 pls

LITTLE PLAIN ENGLISH [A]
Little plain English (A) . . . By Peter Porcupine. *See* Cobbett, Wm.

LITTLEFIELD, GEORGE E.   390
Early Boston booksellers, 1642–1711. *B* Club of Odd Volumes 1900. O 256 15pls a 150copies ptd.

LITTLEFIELD, GEORGE E.   391
Early schools and schoolbooks of New England. *B* Club of Odd Volumes 1904. O 354[incl. pls & facs] front. a 167 copies ptd.

LITTLEJOHN, F[LAVIUS] J.   392
Legends of Michigan and the old northwest . . . *Allegan Mich* 1875. O 566 a

LIVERMORE, SAMUEL T.   393
A condensed history of Cooperstown . . . *Alb* 1862. D 276 a
See also Cooper, James Fenimore.

LIVERMORE, SAMUEL T.   394
History of Block Island . . . *Hart* 1877. D 371 a
This miniature democracy existed for 200 years without printing press or lawyers.

LIVINGSTON, EDWARD   395
Address to the people of the United States on the measures . . . with respect to the batture at New Orleans . . . *N O* 1808. O [50] 50 15 [30] 68 [75] a

LIVINGSTON, EDWARD   396
An answer to Mr. Jefferson's justification of his conduct in the case of the New-Orleans batture. *Phil* 1813. O [12] 187 2 maps a

LIVINGSTON (EDWARD, ESQ.)
Examination of the claims of the United States and of the pretensions of: to the batture [at New Orleans]. *See* Thierry, J. B. S.

LIVINGSTON (EDWARD)   397
A letter to: ... on the speech delivered by him at Washington, at the late celebration of the 8th of January, 1815. *Natchez* 1828. O 24 aa

[LIVINGSTON, PHILIP]   398
The other side of the question; or, a defence of the liberties of North-America. In answer to [Myle Cooper's] Friendly address to all reasonable Americans ... *N Y* 1774. O 30 + adv-l. aa
—anr. issue has impr. "America"

[LIVINGSTON, ROBERT R.]   399
Examination of the treaty ... between the United States ... and Great Britain. *N Y* 1795. O 96 a
Ascribed also to Stephen Higginson, and to Alexander Hamilton.

LIVINGSTON, WILLIAM   400
A letter to the ... Bishop of Landaff [*sic*]; occasioned by some passages in his ... sermon ... in which the American colonies are loaded with ... reproach. *N Y* 1768. O [4] 25 a
—rptd. *B* same date. O 26
—Eng. ed. *L* same date. O 31
—Dutch tr. *Utrecht* 1774. O [4] 34

[LIVINGSTON, WILLIAM]   401
A review of the military operations in North America; from the commencement of the French hostilities on the frontiers of Virginia ... *L* 1757. Q [4] 144 b N NYP Y
—rptd., with adds. [incl. Washington's journal of his 1754 Ohio expedition], *Dub* 1757. O 276 aa
—Am. eds.: *New England* [i.e. *N Hav*] 1758, Q 98 b AA NYP N; *N Y* 1770, O 170 b AA NYP Y
Contemporary authority on the Lake George campaign of 1755 and vindication of Gen. Shirley's measures. Attributed also to the New York historian William Smith, who probably assisted in its preparation.

LIVIUS (PETER).   402
The memorial of: one of His Majesty's council for ... New Hampshire ... n.p. 1773. O [2] 50 b JCB LC [of 3copies located]
Relates to his controversy with Gov. Wentworth *in re* New Hampshire grants.

LLANDAFF, JOHN [EWER], Bishop of   403
A sermon preached before the ... Society for the Propagation of the Gospel in Foreign Parts, on February 20; 1767. *L* 1767. O 26 aa
—Am. ed. *N Y* 1768. O 18

The colonists were incensed at being characterized as "infidels and barbarians." For replies *see* Livingston, William, and Chauncy, Charles.

LLOYD, B[ENJAMIN] E.   404
Lights and shades in San Francisco. *S F* 1876. O 523 pictorial t. pls a

[LLOYD, CHARLES]   405
The conduct of the late administration examined ... *L* 1767. O 160 [2] 54 a
—rptd. *B* 1767. O 107.
—ed. 2, with adds., *L* 1767. O 166 [2] 54
—anr. ed., with 2 other tracts, "Three tracts on the conduct of the late and present administrations ...," *L* 1767. O 3pts in 1: 160 [2] 54 + 2adv-p; [2] 74 + 2adv-p; [2] 45 + 3adv-p
Famous defense of the Stamp Act, written by Lord George Grenville's secretary. Attributed also to Lord Temple, to Charles Jenkinson, Earl of Liverpool, and to Grenville himself. For reply *see Grenville, George, A letter to:*

LLOYD, JAMES T.   406
Steamboat directory, and disasters on the western waters ... *Cin* 1856. O 326 aa
—issue 2, *Cin* 1856. O 331 aa
—anr. ed. n.p. n.d. [*Phil* 1856?]. O 223 a
—anr. ed. n.p. n.d. [*Cin* 1856?]. O 279 a
Best historical and statistical treatment on the early period of inland steam navigation.

LLOYD, THOMAS, reporter   407
Debates of the convention, of ... Pennsylvania, on the Constitution, proposed for the government of the Union States ... Vol.I[all]. *Phil* 1787. O 148 [3] aa
—rptd. same impr. & collat. 1788. a
Contains only arguments favoring adoption. The Federalists were able to prevent publication of a projected second volume giving anti-constitution views.

LOBDELL [LUCY A.], the female hunter. 408
Narrative of: *N Y* 1855. D 47 aa

LOBE, GUILLAUME   409
Divorce imminent de la Confederation Nord-Americaine. *Amst* 1850. O 46 a

LOBENSTINE [WILLIAM C.]   410
Extracts from the diary of: 1851–8 ... n.p. [1920]. O [16] 101 pl facs a
Describes his 1851 overland trip to California and life in the mines.

LOCKARD, FRANK M.   411
History of the early settlement of Norton county, Kansas. *Norton* [1894]. O 294[incl. port] a

LOCKE, JOHN L.   412
Sketches of the history pf Camden, Maine . . .
Hallowell 1859. D [12] 267 errata lf a

LOCKE, MRS. MARY   413
In far Dakota. *L* 1890. 16° [6] 152 a

LOCKMAN, [JOHN]   414
Travels of the Jesuits into various parts of the
world . . . *L* 1743. O 2v: [32] 488; [10] 508 +
2adv-p. 6maps & pls aa
—ed. 2, 1743, same collat., with 19p. index added aa
—ed. 2, cor. with add. of 24p. [on Sp. settle-
ments], *L* 1762; rptd. 1767. aa
Translation [abridged] of the first ten volumes
of *Lettres Edifiantes*, containing particulars by
Picolo on California missions, etc.

LOCKWOOD, FRANK C.   415
The Apache Indians. *N Y* 1938. O [18] 348
2maps pls a

LOCKWOOD, FRANK C.   416
Arizona characters . . . *L A* 1928. D [16] 230 pls a

LOCKWOOD, FRANK C.   417
Pioneer days in Arizona . . . *N Y* 1932. O [16]
387 a

LOCKWOOD, JAMES D.   418
Life and adventures of a drummer-boy; or,
seven years a soldier. *Alb* 1893. D 191 front. a
Includes campaigns in Wyoming after the Civil
war.

LOCKWOOD, LUKE V.   419
Colonial furniture in America. *N Y* 1901. Q [20]
352 [incl.pls] 12pls [each with lf of letterpress] a
—enl. ed. *N Y* 1913. Q 2v: [20] 534; [18] 307.
2fronts. aa
—rptd. *N Y* 1926. Q 2v aa
—Eng. ed. *L* 1902. same collat. as Am. 1st ed. a

LOCKWOOD, R. A.   420
The Vigilance committee of San Francisco.
S F 1852. O 48 aa
Bitter denunciation of this extra-judicial body.

LODGE, HENRY C.   421
Life and letters of George Cabot. *B* 1877.
O [12] 615 a
—ed. 2, *B* 1878. O [12] 617

LÖHER, FRANZ VON   422
Aussichten für gebildete Deutschen in Nord-
Amerika . . . *Berlin* 1853. O [6] 92 a

LÖHER, FRANZ VON   423
Geschichte und Zustande der Deutschen in
Amerika. *Cin* 1847. O [16] 544 a
—ed. 2, *Göttingen* 1855. O [16] 544

LÖHER, FRANZ VON   424
Land und Leute in den alten und neuen Welt . . .
Göttingen 1855–8. O 3v: [4] 283; [4] 281; [4] 292 a
—rptd. in part, "Reiseskizzen . . .," *Berlin* n.d.

LOEHR, CHARLES T.   425
War history of the old First Virginia regiment
. . . *Rich* 1884. O 87 a

LÖWENSTERN, ISIDORE   426
Les États-Unis et la Havane . . . *P* 1842. O [12]
372 a

LÖWIG, GUSTAV   427
Die Freystaaten von Nordamerika . . . *Heidelb*
1833. O [10] 264 a

[LOFFT, CAPEL]   428
Observations on Mr. Wesley's second Calm
address, and . . . on other writings upon the
American question . . . . *L* 1777. D 124 a

[LOFFT, CAPEL?]   429
A view of the several schemes with respect to
America . . . *L* 1775. O 55 a
—rptd. *L* 1776. O [4] 55 errata slip
Reviews suggested plans for ending Revolution,
and favors one abandoning taxation.

LOGAN, MRS. INDIA W. P.   430
Kelion Franklin Peddicord of Quirk's scouts,
Morgan's Kentucky cavalry, C.S.A. *N Y* 1908.
O 170 a

LOGAN, JAMES   431
Notes on a journey through Canada, the United
States [etc.]. *Edin* 1838. O [12] 259 map a
Severely critical in tone.

LOGAN, JOHN   432
The western wood pecker . . . journal of a
journey . . . from Georgetown, D. C., to the
Miami . . . and back again. *Georgetown* 1818.
D 38 c LC WRH

LOGAN, JOHN H.   433
A history of the upper country of South Carolina . . . Vol. I [all.] *Charleston S C* 1859. D [4,
7–12] 521 aa

LOGAN, OLIVE   434
Before the footlights and behind the scenes:
a book about "the show business" . . . *Phil* 1870.
O 612 24pls a

LOGAN (JUDGE STEPHEN T.)   435
Memorials of the life and character of: *Springfield Ill* 1882. O 87 port aa
Logan was Lincoln's law partner from 1841 to
1844, and, as a delegate to the Chicago convention,
was helpful in securing his nomination for the
Presidency.

LOMAS, THOMAS J. 436
Recollections of a busy life . . . [including an 1864 wagon trip to California]. [*Cresco, Ia* 1923] D 220 port aa

[LOMBARD, A.] 437
The "high private" . . . exciting history of the New York Volunteers, including the mysteries and miseries of the Mexican war. Part I[all]. *N Y* 1848. D 60 port a

LONDON
A letter from a merchant in London to his nephew in North America. *See* Tucker, Josiah.

A letter from a merchant of the city of 438 London to the R . . .t H . . . ble W . . . P . . . upon the affairs . . . of North America . . . *L* 1757. O 98 a

A letter to a gentleman in London from Virginia. *See* Randolph, Peyton.

LONDONIO, CARLO G. 439
Storia delle colonie Inglesi in America, dalla loro fondzazion, fino allo stabilimento della loro *in* dependenza. *Milan* 1812–13. O 3v: [10] 299; *335*; 382 [2] a

LONG (GREEN H.) 440
The arch fiend: or the life, confession and execution of: . . . *N Y* 1851. O 32 [incl.front]
—anr. ed., same collat., *Little Rock* [ptd Buffalo, *N Y*] 1852. aa
Long, associated with the "Banditti of the West," had sixteen murders to his credit. For his lady friend, *see* Fitz-James, Zillah.

LONG, H. C. 441
The condition and prospects of Cairo City [Ill.]. *N Y* 1850. O 26 a

LONG, J. V. 442
Report of the first general festival of the . . . Mormon Battalion. *S L C* 1855. O 39 b

LONG (JACK); OR SHOT IN THE EYE.
See Webber, Chas. W.

LONG, JOHN 443
Voyages and travels of an Indian interpreter and trader . . . *L* 1791. Q [14] 295 map aa
—Am. eds.: ed. Thwaites, *Clev* 1904, O; *Chi* Lakeside 1922, 16° a
—Fr. tr. *P* [1794]. O [40] 320 map a
—rptd., same collat., *P* 1810
—Ger. trs.: *Hamburg* 1791. O [24] 334 [2] map; *Berlin* 1792, O [8] 88, 176 map pl a

LONG, MORRIS 444
Historical sketch of Warner, N. H. *Concord* 1832. O 26 a
—rptd. 1870. 30copies ptd.

LONG, STEPHEN H. 445
Voyage in a six-oared skiff to the falls of St. Anthony in 1817. *Phil* 1860. O 88 map a

LONG ISLAND MISCELLANIES
By Rusticus, Gent. *See* Furman, Garrett.

LONG ISLAND.
Remarks upon Gen. Howe's account of his proceedings on: *See* Mauduit, Israel.

[LONGCHAMP, FERDINAND]? 446
Asmodée à New-York; revue critique des institutiones politiques et civiles de l'Amérique . . . *P* 1868. O [4] 503 a
—Eng. tr. *N Y* 1868. D 378

[LONGCHAMPS, PIERRE DE] 447
Histoire impartiale des evenemens . . . de la dernière guerre . . . *P* 1785. D 3v: 558; 523; [2] 620 aa
—anr. ed., *Amst* 1785. same collat a
—ed. 2, *P* 1787. D 3v: [116] 446; 511; 607
—ed 3, *Amst* 1787. same collat
—anr ed 3, *P* 1789. D 3v
Largely devoted to military operations in America.

[LONGSTREET, AUGUSTUS B.] 448
Georgia scenes . . . *Augusta Ga* 1835. D 235 b N NYP Y
—ed. 2, *N Y* 1840. D 214 + 36adv-p 12 pls aa
—rptd: 1843; 1848; 1845; 1850; 1858; 1859.
—anr. ed. *Macon Ga* 1864. O 239 aa

[LONGSTREET, AUGUSTUS B.] 449
A voice from the south . . . *Balt* 1847. O 72 aa
—anr. ed., identical, but calling itself "eighth edition" on cover-t., same impr., date & collat.

LONGSTREET, HELEN D. 450
Lee and Longstreet at high tide . . . *Gainesville Ga* [ptd *Phil*] 1904. O 346 12 pls 3facs a
—ed. 2 1905

LONGSTREET, JAMES 451
From Manassas to Appomattox . . . *Phil* 1896. O [20] 11–690 44maps & pls facs[on 2lvs] aa
—rptd. 1903. O 698 maps pls a
—anr. ed. with index *Bloomington Ind.* 1960. O [30] 692 33 maps and pls a

LONGSWORTH (BASIL N.) 458
Diary of: covering the period of his migration from Ohio to Oregon. *Denver* 1927. O 43 + index [pasted on inner back wrap].

LONN, ELLA 459
Reconstruction in Louisiana . . . *N Y* 1918. O [8] 538 a

LOOK BEFORE YOU LEAP   **460**
Look before you leap . . . hints to such artizans
. . . as are desirous of emigrating to America . . .
L 1796. O 144 aa
—ed. 2, same impr. & date. O 144 [24] a
—ed. 3, same impr., date & collat.
Designed to halt British emigration. Probably
edited by William Cobbett, who was later to
make the leap here warned against.

[LOOMIS, AUGUSTUS W.]   **461**
Scenes in the Indian country. *Phil* [1859]. 16°
283 3pls aa

LOOMIS, CHESTER A.   **462**
A journey on horseback through the great
west, in 1825 . . . *Bath N Y* [182–?]. O 27 a

[LOOMIS, JOHN L.]   **463**
Leadville . . . the most wonderful mining
camp . . . *Colorado Springs* 1879. O 44 aa

LOOMIS, LEANDER V.   **464**
A journal of the Birmingham [Iowa] Emi-
grating Company . . . to Sacramento . . . 1850
S L C 1928. O [14] 198 map 17pls a

LOPEZ URAGA (CORONEL JOSÉ)   **465**
Sumaria mandada formar a pedimento del: . . .
en la que se comprueba la conducta militar que
observó en las acciones de guerra dadas á las
tropas de los Estados-Unidos . . . en los puntos
de Palo Alto y Resaca . . . *Mex* 1846. O 40 aa

LORAIN, JOHN   **466**
Hints to emigrants, or a comparative estimate
of the advantages of Pennsylvania, and of the
western territory . . . *Phil* 1819. 16° [2] 144 a
Discredits Birkbeck's Illinois settlement.

[LORD, DANIEL]   **467**
The effect of secession upon the commercial
relations between the north and south . . . *N Y*
1861. O 72 map a
—ed. 2, same impr. & date.
—Eng. ed. *L* 1861. O

LORD, MRS. ELIZABETH   **468**
[LAUGHLIN]
Reminiscences of eastern Oregon. [incl. an 1850
overland trip]. *Port Ore* 1903. O 155 14pls aa

LORD, JOHN K.   **469**
The naturalist in Vancouver Island and British
Columbia . . . *L* 1866. O 2v: [16 incl. front.] 358;
[10 incl.front.] 375. 9pls a
Narrative by the naturalist of the British
Boundary Commission, appointed in 1857 to
fix the line between the United States and Canada
from the coast to the Rockies.

[LORIMER, JOHN]   **470**
An account of the surveys of Florida . . . *L*
1790. Q [4] 27 chart aa

LORING, CHARLES G.   **471**
Memoir of . . . William Sturgis. *B* 1864. O [2]
64 a
Contains accounts of two fur-trading voyages,
in 1798, to the Northwest coast.

LORING, ISRAEL   **472**
Two sermons . . . at Rutland, Sept. 8th, 1723.
After the Indians had . . . killed the Reverend
Mr. Joseph Willard, with two of Mr. Joseph
Steven's children, and captivated the other two.
B 1724. O [4] 44 b AA BP

LORING (MAJOR GENERAL   **473**
[WILLIAM W.])
Report of: . . . the battle of Baker's creek . . .
Rich 1864. O 29 a

LOS ANGELES
**Eine Blume aus dem goldenen Lande oder: Los
Angeles.** *See* Salvator, Ludwig L.

An historical sketch of Los Angeles County.
See Warner, Juan J., et. al.

History of Los Angeles County 1880. *See* Wilson,
John A.

Pocket guide of Los Angeles . . . Ed. by G. B.
G. *See* Griffin, Geo. B.

LOSKIEL, GEORGE H.   **474**
Geschichte der mission der evangelischen
Brüder unter den Indianern . . . *Barby* 1789. O
[16] 784 aa
—issue 1, only 6 lines of errata. aa
—issue 2, errata fills whole page. aa
—Swed. ed. "Historiske Beskrifning . . .," *Stockh*
1789. O [22] 872 [2] aa
—rptd. same collat. & impr. 1792 a
—Eng. tr "History of the mission of the United
Brethren . . .," *L* 1794. 0 3pts in 1: [12] 159;
234; 233 [22]. map aa
—abr. eds.: *L* 1838, 16° [6] 316; *L* 1840, same
collat.
Official account of work among the Indians on
the New York, Pennsylvania and other frontiers,
1735–87. The English edition omits naming some
former antagonists who had later become friendly.

LOSSING, BENSON J.   **475**
The life and times of Philip Schuyler. *N Y* 1860.
O 504 2pls a
—ed. 2—and best—*N Y* [1872]–1873. O 2v: 504;
548. 2ports

LOSSING, BENSON J.   **476**
A pictorial description of Ohio . . . *N Y* 1849.
O 131 front. map aa

LOSSING, BENSON J.   **477**
The pictorial field-book of the revolution . . .
N Y 1851–2. O 2v: [2] 576 [16]; [18] 9–880 [35].
2fronts. a
—ed. 2, *N Y* 1855. O 2v: 783; 772
—rptd. several times.
Originally issued in 30 numbers, June 1, 1850—
December 1, 1852.

LOSSING, BENSON J.   **478**
The pictorial field-book of the war of 1812 . . .
N Y 1868. O [4] 1084 col.front. a
—rptd., same impr. & collat., 1869.
First issued in 12 parts.

LOST PRINCIPLE
Lost principle (The); or the sectional equilibrium . . . By "Barbarossa." *See* Scott, John.

LOTGEVALLEN . . .   **479**
Lotgevallen van een Zwitsersch landverhuizer
op zijne reise naar Noord-Amerika . . . 1816–
1818. *Haarlem* 1819. O [14] 222 [2] aa
This Swiss investigator spent considerable time
in Louisiana, Kentucky and Ohio.

LOTHIAN, THE MARQUESS OF
The Confederate secession. *See* Kerr, Wm. S. R.

LOTHROP, J. S., comp.   **483**
Champaign county [Ill.] directory, 1870–71,
with history . . . *Chi* 1871. O 456 fold.map a

LOTTO, FRANK   **484**
Fayette county, [Texas]: her history . . . *Schu-
lenburg* 1902. O [16] 424 front. ports a

LOUAILLIER (LOUIS).   **485**
The appeal of: against the charge of high trea-
son . . . *N O* 1827. O 28 a
Imprisoned by Jackson on the charge of
mutiny and endeavoring to surrender New
Orleans to the British.

LOUBAT, JOSEPH F.   **486**
Medallic history of America. *N Y* 1878. F
478 87pls aa

LOUDON, ARCHIBALD   **487**
A selection of . . . narratives, of outrages
committed by the Indians, in their wars with the
white people . . . *Carlisle Pa* 1808–1811. D 2v:
[12] 5–355; [4] 13–369 c AA LC N Y
—ed. 2, *Harrisburg* 1888. D 2v: [12] 301; 357
b 100 copies ptd
Vol. II of the original edition of this most
desirable of 19th century books on border wars

is paged erratically, and, being printed three
years later, is generally lacking.

LOUDON, J. B.   **488**
A tour through Canada and the United States
. . . *Coventry Eng* 1879. D 132 port a

LOUGHBOROUGH, J[OHN]   **489**
The Pacific telegraph and railway . . . *St L*
1849. O [22] 80 2maps c G LC StLP Y

LOUIS, D. [pseud.]
Washington und die nordamerikanische Revolution. *See* Gosch, Josias L.

LOUISBOURG.   **490**
An accurate journal . . . of the proceedings of
the New-England land-forces, during the late
expedition . . . to the time of the surrender of:
Oxf 1746. O 40 b AA H

LOUISBOURG.   **491**
An authentic account of the reduction of: . . .
By a spectator. *L* 1758. O 60 aa

LOUISBOURG.   **492**
Lettre d'un habitant de: contenant une relation
. . . de la prise de l'Isle-Royale par les Anglais.
Quebec [ptd. *P*] 1745. D 81 b Clem JCB
—Eng. tr. *Tor* 1897. O 74 a
Surreptitiously issued with false imprint, this
[the only unofficial French account of the siege
of Louisbourg] is highly critical of French colonial
policy.

LOUISIANA   **493**
An account of Louisiana: being an abstract of
documents . . . *Phil* 1800. D 48 + tab b NYS
—other 1803 eds.: *Phil* D; *Wilm Del* D 76;
Alb; *Carlisle*. a
—1804 eds.: *Prov* O 72; *L* O 42 tab
See below for *Appendix* to this work. For other
1803 editions, *see* below *A topographical and
statistical . . . account* . . . The entry immediately
following is an entirely different work. Compiler
of this *Account* was probably John Sibley.

An account of Louisiana: exhibiting a compendious sketch . . . *Newbern* 1804. Entirely different
from preceding entry. *See* under Le Page du
Pratz on whose work this book—by F. -X. Martin
—was largely based. For Martin's extended
History of Louisiana, see under his name.

Address of the citizens of Louisiana: to   **494**
the people of the United States. *Wash* 1872.
O 30 a

An address to the government of the United
States, on the cession of Louisiana.
See Brown, Chas. Brockden.

Appendix to An account of Louisiana: 495
being an abstract of documents . . . [*Wash* 1803].
O 99 tab a
—rptd. *Phil* 1803. O 90 tab
—anr. issue, O 77
For *Account*, to which this was an appendix,
see above, No. 493.

Ausführliche historische und geogra-   496
phische Beschreibung des an dem grossen Flusse
Mississipi . . . gelegenen herrlichen Landes Louisiana. *Leip* 1720. D [6] 102 map b N NYP Y

Biographical memoirs of Northwest Loui-   497
siana. *Nashv* 1890. Q 708 pls aa

Documents relating to the purchase and   498
exploration of Louisiana . . . *B* 1904. O [4] 45
189 76 [2] map 2ports a 550 copies ptd.

Documents relative to Louisiana and   499
Florida. [*Wash ca* 1833]. O 26 [capt.t.only] a

Guide and directory for the state of   500
Louisiana and the cities of New Orleans and
Lafayette . . . *N O* 1838. D 384 map 13pls aa
The third New Orleans directory. For the
second *see* under New Orleans.

Historical epitome of . . . Louisiana.   501
N O [*ca* 1840]. D 372 map 13pls a

Information respecting a demand made by   502
the Spanish government for a surrender of part
of the state of Louisiana. *Wash* 1816. O 23 a
Remonstrance by Luis de Onis against American filibustering expeditions into Texas, with
Monroe's unsympathetic reply.

Interesting account of the project of   503
France respecting Louisiana. By a French coun-
sellor of state. *Martinsburg, Va.* 1803. 16° [2] 48 aa
A review of Charles Brockden Brown's *An
address . . . on the session of Louisiana, q.v.*

The laws of the Territory of Louisiana: 504
. . . *St L* 1808. O 376 [58] c G LC
First book printed west of the Mississippi.

Memorial . . . by the inhabitants of Loui-   506
siana to the Congress of the United States [against
its division into two Territories]. *Wash* 1804. O
140 aa

Military record of Louisiana. *See* Bartlett,
Napier.

Observations on the . . . claims of Ameri-   507
can citizens to lands in . . . Louisiana and Mississippi derived from grants under the former British
province of West Florida . . . *L* 1818. O 23 aa

Pictures of the "peculiar institution" as it   508
exists in Louisiana and Mississippi. By an eye-
witness. *B* 1850. D 24 a

The present state of the country [etc.]   509
of Louisiana . . . By an officer at New Orleans to
his friend at Paris . . . Translated from the French
originals . . . by the Hon. Capt. Aylmer . . . *L*
1744. O 55 + 5adv-p b LC N NYP Y
—ed. 2, *L* 1744. aa
—Fr. ed. "Lettre d'un officier de la Louisiane
. . .," *N O* [ptd in Holland] 1764. D [2] 90 aa
The manuscript was part of the booty secured
by the capture of a French ship. Authorship
ascribed to J. P. Gougon de Grondel; he describes
the entire Mississippi basin from Canada to the
Gulf.

Reflections on the cession of Louisiana   510
to the United States. By Sylvestris. *Wash* 1803.
O 27 aa
Possible author: Joseph Locke, but generally
ascribed to St. George Tucker, or to William
Stedman.

Remarks on a dangerous mistake made as
to the eastern boundary of Louisiana. *See* Vaughan,
Benj.

Schilderung von Louisiana. *See* Berquin-Duvallon.

Sketches of life and character in Louisiana.
See Whitaker, John S.

A summary description of the lead mines in
upper Louisiana. *See* Austin, Moses.

A topographical and statistical account   511
of the province of Louisiana . . . compiled by
different individuals . . . and from the documents
communicated to Congress by the President. *Balt*
1803. 24° [8] 13–80 fold. tab. a
—anr. ed. *Hagerstown Md* 1803. O 80 + tab
—other eds., *see* above, "An account of Louisiana,
being an abstract of documents . . ."

Travels in Louisiana and the Floridas. *See*
Berquin-Duvallon.

View of the political and civil situation of   512
Louisiana . . . By a native. *Phil* 1804. O 36 b
AA NYH
For original French ed. *see* No. 514.

LOUISIANE (LA)   513
Apercu topographique de la Louisiane: . . .
P 1816. D 24 a

Les émigrés francais dans la Louisiane.
See Postl, Karl.

Esquisse . . . de la situation de la Loui-   514
siane. *N O* 1804. O 46 b NYP Y [of 3copies
known]
   Review of the first year of American rule, by
a New Orleans resident. For English translation
see No. 512.

Journal d'un voyage à la Louisiane. Par M . . .,
Capitaine de vaisseau du Roi. *See* Valette-
Laudun.

Journal historique de l'établissement des Francais à la Louisiane . . . *See* La Harpe, Bernard de.

Lettre d'un officier de la Louisiane 1764. *See*
No. 509.

La Louisiane ensanglantée. *See* Champigny,
Jean.

Mémoire sur la Louisiane . . . par Jacquemin.
See Jacquemin, Nicolas.

Mémoires sur Louisiane [la] et la Nouvelle
Orleans. . . . *See* Wante, Chas. Etienne P.

Notice sur l'état actuel de la mission de   515
la Louisiane. *P* 1820. O [2] 58 b
—new ed., enl., *Lyon* 1822. O 67 b
—anr. ed. *Turin* 1822, D 65; *Avignon* 1824,
D aa
   Catholic activity under Bishop Du Bourg
whose diocese embraced the Ohio, Mississippi
and Missouri valleys. For an amplified German
version, *see* under *Luisiana, Berichte über die
Mission von* . . .

Relations de la Louisiane . . . *Amst* 1720. *See*
Tonti, Henri de, *Dernieres decouvertes* . . .

Voyage à la Louisiane . . . 1794–1798 . . . Par
B . . . D . . . P [1802]. *See* Baudry de Lozieres.

LOUISVILLE
Louisville directory [The] . . . 1832. *See* Otis,
Richard W., *pub.*

Louisville past and present. 1875. *See* Joblin,
M., and Co.

LOUNSBERRY, CLEMENT H.   516
   Early history of North Dakota . . . *Wash* 1919.
roy O [16] 647 70pls a

[LOUVET DE COUVRAY, JEAN B.]   517
   The interesting history of the Baron de Lovzinski,
with a relation of . . . occurrences in the life of . . .
Count Pulaski . . . *Hart* 1800. 16° 142 [2] aa
—anr. ed. *N Y* 1807. 16° 108 a
   Translation of a part of this author's *Chevalier
de Faublas.*

[LOUVET DE COUVRAY, JEAN B.]   518
   Love and patriotism! Or, the . . . adventures of
M. Duportail, late major-general in the armies
of the United States . . . with many surprising
incidents in the life of the late Count Pulaski.
Phil 1797. D 120 port aa
—rptd. *B* 1799, D 59; *B* 1800, same collat.;
N Hav 1813, 16° 107; *B* 1825. a
   Translation of a part of this author's *Chevalier
de Faublas.*

LOUYSIANE [LA].   519
   Mémoire des habitans et négocians de: sur le
evenement du 29 Octobre 1768. n.p. n.d. O 90 aa

LOVE (NAT).   520
   The life and adventures of: . . . known in the
cattle country as "Deadwood Dick" . . . *L A* 1907.
O 162 port aa
   Flimsy fabric of a fertile imagination.

LOVE, ROBERTUS   521
   The rise and fall of Jesse James . . . *N Y* 1926.
O [10] 445 front. a

LOVEJOY (ELIJAH P.)
   The martyrdom of: . . . By an eye-witness. *See*
Tanner, Henry.

LOVEJOY, JOSEPH C., and OWEN   522
   Memoir of . . . Elijah P. Lovejoy . . . murdered
. . . at Alton . . . *N Y* 1838. D 382 a

LOVELL (GENERAL).   523
   Correspondence between the [Confederate]
War department and: relating to the defences of
New Orleans . . . *Rich* 1863. O 123 aa

LOVING, GEORGE B.   524
   Stock manual . . . of western and northwestern
Texas . . . *Ft Worth* 1881. D 274 [incl advs] aa

LOVZINSKI (THE BARON DE).
   The interesting history of: *See* No. 517.

LOWDERMILK, WILLIAM H.,   525
   History of Cumberland [Md.] . . . *Wash* 1878.
O 496 [60] 3pls maps aa

LOWE, PERCIVAL G.   526
   Five years a dragoon ('49 to '54) . . . *K C* 1906.
D [2] 418 port a

LOWELL, DANIEL W., & CO. [comp.] 527
   Map of the Nez Perces and Salmon river gold
mines . . . *S F* 1862. 16° 24 map d AA G Ind U N
Pn Y [all loc].

[LOWELL, JOHN]   528
   The Antigallican; or, the lover of his own country . . . *Phil* 1797. O 2 pts [22 nos.] in 1: 82; 84 a

[LOWELL, JOHN] 530
The diplomatick policy of Mr. Madison unveiled . . . [B? 1809?]. O 55 capt.t.only a
—rptd. n.p. [1810]. O 52 capt.t.only
—Eng. ed. "The diplomatic policy . . .," L 1810. O 78

[LOWELL, JOHN] 531
The impartial inquirer . . . examination of the conduct of the president . . . to which is added some reflections upon the invasion of the Spanish territory of West Florida. By a citizen of Mass. B 1811. O 96 a

[LOWELL, JOHN] 532
The New England patriot . . . comparison, of the . . . Washington and Jefferson administrations . . . B 1810. O [2] 148 [12] a

[LOWELL, JOHN] 533
Perpetual war, the policy of Mr. Madison . . . B 1812. O 119 a
—rptd. B 1813. O 78

[LOWELL, JOHN?] 534
Thoughts in a series of letters, in answer to a question respecting the division of states. n.p. [1813]. O 24 a

[LOWELL, JOHN] 535
Thoughts upon the conduct of our administration . . . more especially . . . concerning the attack on the Chesapeake. B 1808. O 28 a

LOWERY, WOODBURY 536
The Spanish settlements within the present limits of the United States, 1513–1574. N Y 1901-05. O 2v: [14] 515; [22] 500. 2pls 6maps [2fold.] aa

LOWIE, ROBERT H. 537
The Crow Indians. N Y [1935]. O [22] 350 7pls a

LOWMAN, HOVEY E. 538
Narrative of the Lawrence massacre [etc.]. Lawrence 1864. O 96 + ? No complete copy known. c

LOWRY (JEAN). 539
A journal of the captivity of: . . . taken by the Indians . . . in Pennsylvania . . . Phil 1760. O 31 c PhilL [only copy known]

LOWRY, ROBERT, and McCARDLE, WILLIAM H. 540
A history of Mississippi . . . Jackson 1891. O [12] 5–648 + 4dupl. pp aa
—ed. 2 identical but with errata lf. aa

LOWRY, THOMAS 541
Personal reminiscences of Abraham Lincoln. L 1910. O 32 port 100copies aa
—rptd. Minneap 1929. a

LUBBOCK (FRANCIS R.) 542
Six decades in Texas; or, memoirs of: . . . Austin 1900. O [16] 685 20 pls a

LUCAS (C., ESQ.) 543
A letter from the town of Boston, to: including a short narrative of the massacre perpetrated there . . . Dub rptd. by Tho. Ewing n.d. O 56 b
Only edition recorded.

LUCAS, CHARLES 544
To the people of Missouri Territory . . . exposition of the late difference between John Scott and himself. St L 1816. O 24 aa

LUCAS, C[ORYDON] L. 545
The Milton Lott tragedy . . . in Boone county [Ia.] . . . Madrid Ia. [1905]. O [2] 24 a

[LUCAS, DANIEL B.] 546
Memoir of John Yates Beall: his life . . . Montr 1865. O [8] 297 port a

LUCAS, DANIEL B. 547
Nicaragua: war of the filibusters . . . Rich1896. D 216 map 2pls a

LUCAS (ELIZA). 548
Journal and letters of: Wormsloe Ga [Phil ptd] 1850. Q 31 19 copies ptd[6 on special paper] aa

LUCAS, FREDERIC W. 549
The annals of the voyages of Nicolo and Antonio Zeno . . . and the claim . . . to a Venetian discovery of America. L 1898. Q [14] 234 18maps & pls a

LUCAS (HON. J[OHN] B. C.) 550
Letters of: from 1815 to 1836. Comp. by his grandson. St L priv. ptd. 1905. O 324 [2] port aa
Valuable contribution to early St. Louis history.

LUCAS, ROBERT 551
Journal of the war of 1812, during the campaign under . . . Hull. Iowa City 1906. Q [10] 103 front. map 2facs a 400copies ptd.

[LUCATT, EDWARD] 552
Rovings in the Pacific . . . with a glance at California. By a merchant . . . L 1851. D 2v: [12] 352; [12] 372. 4col pls aa

LUCE, EDWARDS S. 553
Keogh, Commanche and Custer. n.p. 1939. O 127 small edition. aa

LUCY, ERNEST W. 554
The Molly Maguires of Pennsylvania . . . L [1882]. O [4] 152 a

LUDECUS, EDUARD   555
Reise durch... Tumalipas, Coahuila und
Texas im Jahre 1834. *Leip* 1837. O [20] 356 aa

LUDLOW, N[OAH] M.   556
Dramatic life as I found it... with an account
of the rise and progress of the drama in the west
and south... *St L* 1880. O [20] 733 aa

LUDLOW, WILLIAM   557
Report of a reconnoissance from Carroll,
Montana... to the Yellowstone national park
... *Wash* 1876. Q 145 3maps 2pls a

LUDLOW, WILLIAM   558
Report of a reconnaissance of the Black hills
of Dakota... *Wash* 1875. Q 121 3maps pl a
—anr. ed. same impr & date O 124 3maps pl
Expedition was commanded by Custer.

LUDVIGH, SAMUEL [G.]   559
Licht- und Schattenbilder republikanischer Zustande; skizzirt während seiner Reise in den Vereinigten Staaten. *Leip* 1848. O [8] 344 a
—rptd, same collat *N Y* 1848.
Observations, in Teutonic amplitude, on the
Central West and South.

LÜDER, A[UGUST] F.   560
Statistische Beschreibung der Besitzungen der
Holländer in Amerika. *Braunschweig* 1792. O 230
aa

LÜTKÉ, FREDERIC P.
See Litké, Fedorem [Frederic] P.

LUFF (ELDER JOSEPH).   561
Autobiography of: one of the twelve apostles of
the Reorganized Church... of Latter Day Saints.
Lamoni Ia 1894. O [12] 377 3pls a

LUGRIN, CHARLES H.   562
Yukon gold fields... [*Victoria Can* 1897] D 32
map aa

LUISIANA.   563
Berichte über die Mission von: Gesammelt von
U. R. und R. W. *Mainz* 1821. O 73 aa
See, under Louisiane, *Notice sur l'etat actuel
de la mission...*, of which this is an amplified
version.

LUKE, L. D.   564
A journey from the Atlantic to the Pacific
coast by way of Salt Lake City... *Utica* 1884.
O 79 aa

[LUMEN, DR.]   566
Les matinées de Beaucaire ou recits d'une

promenade sur l'Illinois... *Avignon* 1874. 24°
288 a

LUMPKIN, WILSON   567
The removal of the Cherokee Indians from
Georgia... 1827–41... *Wormsloe Ga* 1907. O 2v:
369; 328. 2ports a 500copies ptd.

[LUMSDEN, JAMES]   568
American memoranda... during a short tour
in... 1843. *Glas* 1844. O [4] 60 a

LUNDY (BENJAMIN).
The life, travels... of: *See* Earle, Thomas.

[LUNDY, BENJAMIN]   569
The origin and true causes of the Texas insurrection... [*Phil* 1836]. O 32 [capt. t. only] aa
—enl. ed. "The war in Texas... By a citizen of
the United States," *Phil* 1836. O 57 a
—anr. ed., enl., *Phil* 1837. O 64
First to ascribe this war to a slave-holding
conspiracy.

LUSHINGTON, S[TEPHEN] R.   570
The life and services of Lord Harris... in
America... *L* 1840. O [16] 551 [incl. map &
port] + 8adv-p a
—ed. 2, rev., same impr. 1845. D [24] 388
Harris served throughout the revolutionary
war.

LUTTIG, JOHN C.   572
Journal of a fur-trading expedition on the upper
Missouri. 1812–13. *St L* 1920. O 192 [incl.initial
blank l.], map 4pls 365copies ptd. aa
Important account, by a clerk of the Missouri
Fur Company, of one of Manuel Lisa's earliest
expeditions.

LUTYNES, GOTTHILFF N.   573
Etwas über gegenwärtigen Zustand der Auswanderungen... im... Pennsylvanien... *Hamburg* 1796. D 23 aa

LYELL, CHARLES   574
A second visit to the United States [in 1845].
L 1849. D 2v: [12] 368; [12] 386 a
—ed. 2, same impr, date & collat
—anr ed. 2, same impr & collat 1850.
—Am ed, *N Y* 1849. D 2v: 273; 287
—Ger tr, *Braunschweig* 1851. O 2v

LYELL, CHARLES   575
Travels in North America, 1841–2. *L* 1845.
D 2v: [16] 316; [8] 272. map 6pls a
—Am. ed. *N Y* 1845. D 2v: [12] 251; [6] 231 +
10adv-p. map 6pls[one incl. in paginat.]
—rptd. *N Y* 1852. D 2v: *N Y* 1856. D 2v
—Ger. tr. *Halle* 1846. D [12] 396 2maps 9pls

LYFORD, WILLIAM G.   **576**
The western address directory . . . with historical [etc.] sketches . . . of the principal cities and towns of the Mississippi valley. *Balt* 1837. D 468 aa

LYKKEJAEGER, HANS, [pseud.]
Luck of a wandering Dane. *See* Smith, Andrew M.

LYMAN, ALBERT   **577**
Journal of a voyage to California, and life in the gold diggings . . . *Hart* 1852. D 192 [incl. front. and view] b

LYMAN, GEORGE D.   **578**
John Marsh, pioneer. *N Y* 1930. O [14] 394 17pls a
—also ltd. ed. of 150copies, with 4facs added

LYMAN, H. H.   **579**
Memoirs of an old homestead. *Oswego* 1900. D 180 a

LYMAN, GENERAL PHINEAS   **580**
General orders [at Ft. Edward in 1757]. Ed. by W. C. Ford from the original MS. *N Y* 1899. D 150 facs a 250copies ptd.

LYMAN, T. P. H.   **581**
The life of Thomas Jefferson . . . *Phil* 1826. O 111 a

[LYMAN, THEODORE]   **582**
The diplomacy of the United States . . . from . . . 1778 . . . *B* 1826. O [12] 380 [2] a
—ed. 2, with adds., *B* 1828. O 2v: [12] 470; [12] 517

LYNCH, JAMES   **583**
With Stevenson to California, 1846. [n.p. 1896]. No t-p. D 65 100 copies ptd. aa

Personal narrative of the Conquest and the Gold Rush.

LYNCH, JAMES D.   **584**
The bench and bar of Mississippi. *N Y* 1881. O 539 12ports correction slip at p. 536 a

LYNCH, JAMES D.   **585**
The bench and bar of Texas. *St L* 1885. O 610 8ports a

LYNCH, MRS. MARTHA C. M., ed.   **586**
Reminiscences of Adams, Jay and Randolph counties, Ind. [cover-t. only]. [*Decatur Ind* 1896]. D 352[incl. advs.] 13ports a

LYNCH, PATRICK, Bishop of Charleston   **587**
Lettera . . . sulla schiavito domestica degli Stati Confederati. *Rome* 1864. O 83 aa

LYNCHBURG [VA.]
Sketches and recollections of: By the oldest inhabitant. *See* Cabell, Margaret C.

LYON, IRVING W.   **588**
The colonial furniture of New England . . . *B* 1891. Q [12] 285 pls aa
—new ed. *B* 1924. Q [4 3–11] 285 pls

LYON COUNTY, [KANSAS].   **589**
A memorial to pioneers of: 1855–1875. *Emporia* [1876]. O 62 aa

LYONS, ESTHER, comp.   **590**
Glimpses of Alaska . . . views . . . of Alaska and the Klondike district. From photographs by Veazie Wilson. *Chi* 1897. obl D 96 pls a
First white woman over Chilkoot pass.

[LYONS, JAMES]   **591**
Four essays on the right . . . of secession by southern states. *Rich* 1861. O 56 aa

M

M . . . (COMTE).
Mémoires du: . . . *P* 1827. *See* Moré, Chas. Albert, Chevalier de Pontgibaud, Comte de.

M., A.   **1**
Reflections on the American contest . . . *L* 1776. O [8] 50 a

M., J.
Le voyageur américain. *See* Mandrillon, Joseph.

M., L. B. DE   **2**
Coup d'oeil sur l'etat actuel des Etats-Unis . . .

et sur les evénemens qui s'y préparent. *P* 1834. O 160 aa

M., P. J.
Aanmerkingen over den Koophandel . . . *See* Law, John.

M., W. T.   **3**
Reminiscences of a trans-atlantic traveller . . . 1831–2. *Dub* 1835. D [8] 188 aa
Visited Virginia, Michigan, etc.

MAAS, OTTO, ed.   **4**
Viajes de misioneros Franciscanos á la conquista del Nuevo México. *Seville* 1915. O 208map a

MABLY, L'ABBÉ [GABRIEL BONNOT] DE   5
Observations sur le gouvernement... des
États-Unis... *Amst* [some cops bear Hamburg
impr] 1784. D [2] 213 aa
—rptd.: same impr., date & collat.; *Dub* 1785,
D [8] 277; *Amst* 1790, D [2] 213; *P,* 1791. D [4]
199 a
—Dutch tr. *Amst* 1785. O
—Eng. tr. *Amst* 1784. 16° [24] 122
—anr. issue, same collat. *L* 1784. aa
—anr. Eng. tr: *L* 1784, O [4] 280; *Dub* 1785,
O [4] 250 a

McADAM, R[EZIN] W.   6
Chickasaws and Choctaws... *Ardmore Okla*
1891. O 67 a

McADAM, REZIN W., and   7
LEVI, S. E., comps.
Directory of Oklahoma City... [*Okla C* 1889].
O [2]? 36 b OkH[only copy located, probably
lacks t-p]

McAFEE, ROBERT   8
McAfee, Robert, the pioneer and the first
commodore of three principal rivers of the west.
n.p. [1888?]. D 194 a

[McAFEE, ROBERT B.]   9
History of the late war in the western country
... *Lex* 1816. O [8, incl blank lf after t-p] 534
[2] aa
—rptd. *Bowling Green* O [1919]. O 591 a
For scope and authenticity rivalled only by
Dawson's *Life of Harrison.* Material was supplied
by two of the ablest commanders, Harrison and
Shelby.

McALEENAN, JOSEPH   10
Leaves from a Wyoming diary. *N Y* 1914. Q
51 30copies ptd. aa

McALEENAN, JOSEPH   11
A trip through Yellowstone park and an elk
hunt in Wyoming. [*N Y* 1913]. obl O 69 24pls
small ed.ptd. aa

McALLISTER, J[OSEPH] T.   12
Virginia militia in the revolutionary war. *Hot
Springs Va* [1913]. O 337 a

McALPINE (J[OHN]).   13
Genuine narratives, and concise memoirs...
of: from... his emigration from Scotland, to
America, 1773... till December 1779, *Greenock*
1780. D 63 b N NYP PhiL
—anr. issue, same impr. & date. D 67 b AA
—rptd. n.p. 1788. 16° 72 b

McARTHUR, MRS. HARRIET [NESMITH] 14
Recollections of the Rickreall [Ore.]. *Port*
1930. O 24 4pls a

MACAULAY, CATHERINE   15
An address to the people of England... on
the present important crisis... *L* 1775. O 29 a
—3 other eds., same yr.
—Am. ed. called ed. 3, *N Y* 1775.

MACAULEY, JAMES   16
The natural... history of ...New York,
N Y 1829. O 3v: [24] 540; [14] 459; [16] 452 a
Of little authority.

[McBRIDE, JAMES]   17
Naval biography... of the most distinguished
officers of the American navy... *Cin* 1815. D
[8] 296 a
—rptd. *Pitt* 1815. 16° 144
—anr ed *Cin* 1815. D [8] 296

McBRIDE, JAMES   18
Pioneer biography... of Butler County, Ohio.
Cin 1869–71. O 2v: [16] 352; 288. port a
Some copies on L. P. aa
Important material on the settlement of the
Miami country and early Indian troubles.

[McCABE, JAMES D.]   19
Fanaticism, and its results: or, facts versus
fancies. *Balt* 1860. O 36 a

[McCABE, JAMES D.]?   20
The grayjackets and how they lived... *Rich*
[1867]. O 574 16 maps & pls a some copies have
Phil impr.

[McCABE, JAMES D.]   21
The life of Lieut. Gen. T. J. Jackson. By an
ex-cadet. *Rich* 1863. O 128 a
—ed. 2, enl., "The life of Thomas J. Jackson,"
Rich 1864. O 196.

McCABE, JULIUS P. B. [comp.]   22
Directory of... Detroit... Containing an
epitomized history [etc.]. *Det* 1837. D 115 + 40
adv-p [in front]. b AA BurtH Clem N
First Detroit directory.

McCABE, JULIUS P. B. [comp.]   23
Directory of... Lexington [etc.] *Lex* 1838.
D [32] 136 aa
First separate Lexington directory, preceded
only by lists in almanacs for 1806 and 1819.

McCABE, JULIUS P. B. [ed.]   24
Directory of... Milwaukee [for 1847–8], con-
taining an epitomized history [etc.]. *Milw* 1847.
D 148 + 92adv-p aa
First directory of this city. The second *Direc-
tory,* 1848, contained a map, see Milwaukee.

McCABE, JULIUS P. B. [comp.]   25
A directory of the cities of Cleveland [etc.]
for 1837–8: comprising historical and descriptive

sketches . . . *Clev* 1837. D [42] 144 b AA LC WisH Y
First Cleveland directory; also its first history.

McCAIN, CHARLES W.   **26**
History of the S. S. "Beaver" . . . *Vancouver Can* 1894. D 99 6pls & copper medal [made from portion of this ship] a

McCAIN, JAMES R.   **27**
Georgia as a proprietary province . . . *B* [1917]. O 357 a

McCALEB, WALTER F.   **28**
The Aaron Burr conspiracy . . . *N Y* 1903. O [20] 377 a
—enlgd ed *N Y* 1936. O 318.

[McCALL, ANSEL J.]   **29**
Pick and pan. Trip to the diggings in 1849 . . . By an argonaut. *Bath N Y* 1883. O 46 b NYP Y

McCALL, GEORGE A.   **30**
Letters from the frontiers . . . during a period of thirty years' service in the army . . . *Phil* 1868. O 539 aa

McCALL, COL. [GEORGE A.]   **31**
Reports in relation to New Mexico. [Sen. Ex. Doc. 26]. *Wash* 1851. O 23 a

McCALL, H. G.   **32**
A sketch . . . of the city of Montgomery . . . its history, etc. *Montg* 1885. O [2] 64 a

McCALL, HUGH   **33**
The history of Georgia . . . *Savannah* 1811–16. O 2v: [8] 376; [8] 424 a
—rptd., with adds., *Atlanta* 1909. O 2v in 1: [10] 565 port
First history of this state; written by a Revolutionary officer and pioneer from personal knowledge and MS. sources no longer extant. Sabin erroneously collates the original edition as having a map.

McCALLA, WILLIAM L.   **34**
Adventures in Texas . . . *Phil* 1841. 16° [10] 13–199 aa

McCARTHY, CHARLES H.   **35**
Lincoln's plan of reconstruction. *N Y* 1901. O [24] 531 aa

MACARTNEY, CLARENCE E. N.   **36**
Lincoln and his generals. *Phil* Dorrance [1925]. D 226 ports a
—rptd. same impr. [1926].

McCARTY, WILLIAM, ed.   **37**
Geographical memoir upon Upper California.
By John C. Fremont. [With extracts from Hakluyt, etc.]. *Phil* 1849. O 80 aa

[McCARTY, WILLIAM]   **38**
History of the American war of 1812 . . . *Phil* 1816. D 252 7pls map [dated 1814] a
—ed. 2, same collat., impr. & date
—ed. 3, same collat., etc. 1817.
—Ger. tr. *Reading Pa* 1817. D 273 7pls

M'CHESNEY, JAMES   **39**
An antidote to Mormonism . . . *N Y* 1838. D 60 [4] a

McCLELLAN, ELIZABETH   **40**
Historic dress in America, 1607–1870. *Phil* [1904–10]. Q 2v: 407; 458. 2fronts. [other pls incl. in paginat.] aa
—anr. ed., same impr. & collat., [1917]. a
—rptd. "History of American costume . . .," *N Y* 1937. Q 661 pls .

McCLELLAN, HENRY B.   **41**
The life and campaigns of . . . J. E. B. Stuart . . . *B* 1885. O [18] 468 port 7maps aa
—rptd. t. changed *Bloomingt* 1958 a

McCLINTOCK, JOHN S.   **42**
Pioneer days in the Black Hills . . . *Deadwood* [1939] O [14] 336 pls aa

McCLINTOCK, JOHN N.   **43**
History of New Hampshire . . . *B* 1888. O 698 [20] 38pls a

McCLINTOCK, WALTER   **44**
Old Indian trails . . . *B* 1923. O [12] 336 28pls a
—Eng. ed. same date & collat. *L*

McCLINTOCK, WALTER   **45**
The old north trail; or, life . . . of the Blackfeet . . . *L* 1910. O [26] 540 map 9pls tab a

McCLUNG, JOHN A.   **46**
Sketches of western adventure . . . *Maysville Ky* 1832. D 360 aa
—anr. issue, same sheets, with impr. *Phil* aa
—other eds.: *Cin* 1832, D 321; 1836; 1837; 1838; 1839; 1851; *Dayton* 1844; 1847; 1852; 1854; with adds., *Covington* 1872, D [30] 398 11pls; *Louisv* 1879 a

McCLUNG, JOHN W.   **47**
Minnesota as it is in 1870 . . . [*St P*] 1870. D 299 + 67adv-p map 4pls a

McCLUNG, ZARAH   **48**
Travels across the plains in 1852. *St L* 1854. D 34 [incl.front wrap.] dd StLMercL [only known copy]

McCLURE, ALEXANDER K.   **49**
Three thousand miles through the Rocky mountains. *Phil* 1869. D [14] 456 3pls a

McCLURE (DAVID).   **50**
Diary of: 1748–1820. *N Y* 1899. O [8] 219 port a 250copies ptd.
Travelled over the Alleghanies to Pittsburgh and Ohio, in 1772.

MC CLURE, DAVID, and   **51**
PARISH, ELIJAH
Memoirs of . . . Eleazer Wheelock . . . *Newburyport* 1811. O 336 port a

M'CLURE, GEORGE   **52**
Causes of the destruction of the American towns on the Niagara frontier . . . *Bath N Y* 1817. D 72 aa
Severely critical of the conduct of 1813 operations.

McCLURE, M. L.   **53**
Major Andrew Drumm, 1828–1919. [*K C*? 1919]. O 41 pls a
Sketch of a prominent figure in the early cattle trade.

McCLURE, W. T.   **54**
The battle of Hickory Point . . . *Holton, Kas.* [1895] O 44 a

McCOLLUM, WILLIAM S.   **55**
California as I saw it . . . and incidents of travel by land and water. *Buf* 1850. O 72 dd CalH NYP Y [of 6 copies known]
—rptd *Los Gatos Calif* 1960. O 219 map 750 cops ptd a
One of the most authentic contemporary narratives of California in the first year of the gold rush.

McCOMB (DAVID B.)   **56**
Answers of: with an accompanying letter of General Lafayette. *Tallahassee* 1827. O 478 aa
Answers to inquiries [concerning Florida's desirability for settlement] submitted by Lafayette in behalf of intending Swiss immigrants.

McCOMBER, F.   **57**
The Temecula valley, etc. [Calif] . . . *Murrieta* 1888. O 16 [8] a

McCONKEY, MRS. HARRIET E.   **58**
[BISHOP]
Dakota war whoop; or, Indian massacres and war in Minnesota. *St P* 1863. D [8] 13–304 6ports aa
—rev. & enl. ed. *St P* 1864. D [14] 17–429 [incl. 10pls] port a

McCONNELL, H. H.   **59**
Five years a cavalryman . . . on the Texas frontier . . . *Jacksboro Tex* 1889. D 319 a

McCONNELL, J. I.   **60**
Yolo county, California, resources . . . *Woodland Calif* 1887. O 96 aa

M'CONNELL, MATTHEW   **61**
An essay on the domestic debts of the United States . . . *Phil* 1787. O [6] 90 a

McCONNELL, WILLIAM J.   **62**
Early history of Idaho . . . *Caldwell* 1913. O 420 2pls a

McCORKLE, JOHN   **63**
Three years with Quantrell. *Armstrong Mo* n.d. [*ca* 1914]. O 157 11pls aa

McCORMICK (the late COLONEL   **64**
HENRY).
Across the continent in 1865. As told in the diary of: *Harrisburg* 1937. O 49 aa
—ed. 2 same impr. & collat 1944 a

McCORMICK, RICHARD C.   **65**
Arizona: its resources and prospects. *N Y* 1865. O 22 map a
—anr. ed. *Phil* 1865. O 24 map a

[McCOY, ALEXANDER W.], et al.   **66**
Pioneering on the plains . . . Journey to Mexico in 1848, the overland trip to California. [cover t.] [*Kaukauna Wis* 1924]. O 60 [4] port aa

[McCOY, ISAAC]   **67**
The annual register of Indian affairs within the Indian . . . territory. [No. I]. *Shawanoe Mission Kas* 1835. O 48 aa
—No. II, same impr. 1836. O 88 aa
—No. III, same impr. 1837. O 81 aa
—No. IV, *Wash* 1838. O 96 aa
The first number was the first English book printed in Kansas. All were gratuitously circulated.

McCOY, ISAAC   **68**
History of Baptist Indian missions . . . *Wash* 1840. O [8] 611 aa
Based on 20 years of personal experience among the Ottawas, Pottawatomies and Miamis, this is one of the most valuable contributions ever made to the subject of Indian life and characteristics.

McCOY, ISAAC   **69**
Periodical account of Baptist missions within the Indian territory, for . . . 1836. No. I. [all] *Shawanoe Mission Kas* 1837. O 52 capt. t. b G
Only a few copies known in original wrappers; the front wrapper constituted the title page.

McCOY, ISAAC   **70**
Remarks on the practicability of Indian reform.
B 1827. O 47 aa
—ed. 2, with appendix added *N Y* 1829. O 72 aa
One of the earliest suggestion for a reservation
on which to colonize and educate Western
Indians.

[McCOY, ISAAC]   **71**
Remove Indians westward... *Wash* [1829].
O 23 aa
—anr. issue, [also a House Doc.], appended to
McLean's Report, same date. O 48 aa
Written after a personal tour of inspection of
the country proposed.

McCOY, JOSEPH G.   **72**
Historic sketches of the cattle trade... *K C*
1874. O [6] 428 + 24adv-p port view[opposite
p416] b G LC NYP Y
—rptd: in facs., *Wash* 1932: *Columbus* O 1951.,
O 427; *Glendale* 1940. a
The outstanding authority on the early phases
of this industry, by one of its pioneer operators.

McCRADY, EDWARD   **73**
The history of South Carolina... *N Y* 1897–
1902. O 4v: [10] 762; [28] 847; [34] 899; [28]
787. 13maps aa
Vol. I, Under proprietary government, 1670–
1719; vol. II, Under royal government, 1719–
1776; vols. III and IV, In the revolution, 1775–
1783.

McCUE, JAMES   **74**
Twenty-one years in California. Incidents in
the life of a stage-driver... *S F* [1878?]. O 30
port aa

[McCULLOCH, HENRY]   **75**
A miscellaneous essay, concerning the courses
pursued by Great Britain, in... her colonies...
L 1755. O [2] 134 aa

[McCULLOCH, HENRY]   **76**
Proposals for uniting the British colonies on
the continent of America... *L* 1757. O [8] 38 aa
Early fore-shadowing of what was to come,
written by a one-time North Carolinian.

[McCULLOCH, HENRY]   **77**
The wisdom and policy of the French... With
some observations in relation to the disputes...
between the English and French colonies in
America. *L* 1755. O [2] 133 aa

[M'CULLOCH, JOHN]   **78**
Introduction to the history of America...
Phil 1787. D 208 map[showing western country
with divisions suggested by Jefferson] b AA
LC Y

—rptd. "A concise history of the United States
...," *Phil* 1795. D 244 [map called for not issued]
aa
—later eds.: 1797; 1813.
First American history text book, and first
appearance of the Federal Constitution in book-
form.

[McCULLOH, JAMES H., JR.]   **79**
Researches on America... *Balt* 1816. O [8]
131 a
—enl. ed., au. named, *Balt* 1817. O 220 a
—best ed., with adds., "Researches... concerning
the aboriginal history of America," *Balt* 1829.
O 535 map aa

McCUTCHEN, HENRY G.   **80**
History of Scott county, Arkansas. [*Little Rock*
1922]. D 74 a

McDANIELD, H. F., and TAYLOR, N. A.   **81**
The coming empire; or two thousand miles in
Texas on horseback. *N Y* [1877]. D 389 a
—rptd., with adds., *Dallas* [1936]. D [12] 383

McDONALD, FRANK V., ed.   **82**
Notes... to a biography of Richard Hayes
McDonald... Vol. 1[all]. *C* 1881. F [26] 29–95
[119] 34pls b N NYP 150copies ptd.
His overland journey to California and life
there.

McDONALD, JOHN   **83**
Biographical sketches of General Nathaniel
Massie, General Duncan McArthur, Captain
William Wells and General Simon Kenton...
Cin 1838. D [6] 267 aa
—rptd. *Dayton* 1852. a
The author knew personally all of these border
Indian fighters and participated in many of the
events described.

McDONALD, JOSEPH L.   **84**
Hidden treasure, or fisheries around the northwest coast. *Gloucester Mass* 1871. O 110 [2] +
10adv-p aa

McDONALD, WILLIAM   **85**
Notes by a pioneer of 1851. n.p. [1914]. O 30 a
With John Work in the Northwest.

[McDONALD, WILLIAM N.]   **86**
The two rebellions; or, treason unmasked.
Rich 1865. D 144 aa
The two rebellions referred to were John
Brown's attempt and the more successful plot
here attributed to Seward and Greeley.

McDONALD, WILLIAM N.   **87**
A history of the Laurel brigade... *Balt* 1907.
O 499 aa

McDONNELL, WILLIAM   **88**
Pioneers of Marion county, Iowa . . . *Des M* 1872. O 340 aa
First history of this county.

M'DOUGALD (ELIZABETH).   **89**
The life, travels . . . of: who, attired as a man, travelled over the principal p‹ ›t of the United States . . . in pursuit of her husband . . . *Prov* 1834. D 24 port a
While stalking her prey from Ohio to Missouri, she served two years as a soldier at the frontier forts, Gratiot and Gibson.

M'DUFFIE, JOHN   **90**
The Oregon crisis, containing a geographical description of . . . Oregon . . . the emigrant's route across the Rocky Mountains . . . review of the British and American claims . . . [wrapper title] *Salem Ore* 1848. O 24 d Y [only cop kn]

McELRATH, THOMSON P.   **91**
The Yellowstone valley . . . *St P* 1880. D 138 + 3adv-l. fold.map a

McELROY, JOHN M.   **92**
Abby Byram and her father, the Indian captives. *Ottumwa* 1897. O 65 a
The Byrams were Pennsylvanians captured by Senecas in 1779.

McEVOY & BOWRON, pub.   **93**
General city directory . . . of Alton for 1858 . . . also . . . historical sketch . . . *Alton* 1858. D 156 pls aa

Mac FADDEN, HARRY A.   **94**
Rambles in the far west . . . *Hollidaysburg Pa* [1906]. O [8] 278 42pls a

McFARLAND, DAVID F.   **95**
Notes on the history of New Mexico. *Wash* 1877. O 28 a

McFARLAND, WILLIAM   **96**
Browne's western calendar; or, the Cincinnati almanac, for . . . 1806. *Cin* [1805] 16° 36 b LC MassH [of 3 perfect cops loc].
First non-legal Cincinnati imprint.

McGARRAHAN, WILLIAM   **97**
The history of the McGarrahan claim. [*S F* 1875]. O 411 aa

McGARRAHAN . . . MEMORIAL   **98**
McGarrahan [The William] memorial . . . *S F* 1870. O 270 map aa

McGAW, JAMES F.   **99**
The impressed seaman; life on board a British man-of-war. *Mansfield O* 1857. O 82 a

M'GAW, JAMES F.   **100**
Philip Seymour, or, pioneer life in Richland County, Ohio . . . *Mansfield O* 1858. O 296 + 2adv-p 2pls aa
—issued also in 3pts, wraps aa
—rptd: 1883, O 432 a; *Mansfield* 1902, O 319
Fictionized narrative purportedly based on fact.

McGEE, MAJOR JOSEPH H.   **101**
Story of the Grand river country . . . *Gallatin Mo* [1909]. O 67 port aa
Twenty pages describe his 1850 trip to California; also much on early Missouri.

McGLASHAN, CHARLES F.   **102**
History of the Donner party: a tragedy of the Sierras. *Truckee Cal* [1879]. O 193 b N
—ed. 2, with pls added, *S F* 1880, rptd. often a
Best account of the most harrowing of all overland disasters.

McGOWAN, EDWARD   **103**
Narrative . . . including a full account of the author's adventures and perils while persecuted by the . . . Vigilance committee of 1856. *S F* 1857. D 240 b G NYP
—rptd. *S F* 1917. O 240 port a 200copies ptd. aa
—rptd: 1927, D; *Oakl* 1946, O [14] 207 2facs a

MACGREGOR, JOHN, 1797–1857   **104**
The progress of America, from the discovery by Columbus to . . . 1846. *L* 1847. O 2v: [16] 1520; [8] 1334 [84] a
Includes four chapters of California, nine on the disputed Oregon country, others on early voyages to the Northwest coast, the fur trade and commerce over the prairies with Santa Fe.

MACGREGOR, JOHN 1825–92   **105**
Our brothers and cousins; a summer tour in Canada and the United States. *L* 1859. D [20] 156 pl a

MacGREGOR, WILLIAM L.   **106**
San Francisco . . . in 1876. *Edin* 1876. O 71 pls aa
—anr. issue, without pls aa

[McGUIRE, MRS. JOHN P.]   **107**
Diary of a southern refugee during the war. *N Y* 1867. D 360 a
—ed. 2, same impr. & collat. 1868.
—ed. 3, *Rich* 1889.

McHENRY, GEORGE   **108**
The cotton trade: its bearing upon the prosperity of Great Britain . . . considered in connection with . . . Negro slavery in the Confederate States. *L* 1863. O [72] 292 a
—ed. 2, same impr. & date. O
Written to influence British recognition for the Confederacy.

McHENRY, GEORGE   **109**

The position and duty of Pennsylvania . . . with sketches of the commercial . . . history of the late American union. *L* 1863. O [4] 91 a

This Pennsylvanian—a Confederate agent in London—urges his State to join the Confederacy; New Jersey and the West would follow, leaving New York and abolition New England in cheerless isolation.

[McHENRY, JAMES]   **110**

The wilderness; or Braddock's times . . . *N Y* 1823. D 2v: [2] 288; 292 aa

—rptd. *Pitt* 1848. D 2v: 229; 230 a

—anr. ed., same sheets with new t-p, *Pitt* 1876. D 2v in 1 same collat.

—Eng. ed. "The wilderness; or the youthful days of Washington," By Solomon Second-sight, *L* 1823. D 3v: [2] 292; [2] 286 [1]; [2] 300 aa

—Ger. ed. "Die Wildniss . . .," *Vienna* 1829. 16° 3v in 1: [2] 159; [2] 168; [2] 164

McILHANY, EDWARD W.   **111**

Recollections of a '49er . . . across the plains, and life in the . . . gold fields. *K C* 1908. D 212 [incl. 2pls] a

M'ILVAINE, WILLIAM   **112**

Sketches of scenery and notes of personal adventure, in California and Mexico. *Phil* 1850. O 44 17pls[incl. eng.t.] b N NYP Y

—rptd. *S F* Grabhorn 1951. F [12] 79, incl 16 pls a 400 cops ptd

The lithograph views of San Francisco and Sacramento are among the earliest drawn "on the spot."

McINTIRE [OR McINTYRE] JAMES   **113**

Early days in Texas . . . *K C* [1902]. D 229 16pls aa

Reminiscences of an old faro dealer.

McINTOSH, JOHN   **114**

The discovery of America . . . and the origin of the . . . Indians. By J. Mackintosh [sic]. *Tor* 1836. O 152 a

—enl. ed. "The origin of the . . . Indians . . .," *N Y* 1843. O 311[incl. pls]

—many reissues.

MACK, EFFIE M.   **115**

Nevada, a history . . . *Glendale* 1936. O 495 map facs diag a also 250copies on fine paper

MACK (SOLOMON [maternal grand-   **116**
father of Joseph Smith, the prophet]).

A narraitive [sic] of the life of: . . . *Windsor* [1811?]. D 48 b NYP Y

Gives his experiences in the Revolution and in the French and Indian war.

MACKAY, ALEXANDER   **117**

The western world; or, travel in the United States . . . *L* 1849. D 3v: 340; 321; 374. map a

—ed. 2, *L* 1849. D 3v 2maps

—ed. 3, *L* 1850. D 3v 2maps

—ed. 4, *L* 1850. D 3v 2 maps; ed 5 *L* 1851

—Am. ed. *Phil* 1849. D 2v: 312; [4] 13–316

—Ger. tr. [by O. L. Heubner], *Leip* 1855. O 4v: [8] 328; [4] 330; [4] 316; [8] 343. tab.

—anr. Ger. tr. [M. Heine], *Leip* 1861. O 1006 4pls

Judicious commentary based on extensive travels.

MACKAY, CHARLES   **118**

Life and liberty in America . . . *L* 1859. D 2v: [8] 344; [4] 336. 10pls a

—ed. 2, same date, impr. & collat.

—Am. ed. *N Y* 1859. D 413 [incl 10 pls].

McKAY (DARING DONALD).

See Edwards, T. A.

MacKAY (LIEUT. HUGH),   **119**
of General Oglethorpe's regiment.

A letter from: . . . *L* 1742. O 39 b

Corrects misconceptions concerning the futile expedition against St. Augustine.

Mac KAY, MALCOLM S.   **120**

Cow range and hunting trail. *N Y* 1925. D [16] 243 24pls a

McKAY, RICHARD C.   **121**

Some famous sailing ships and their builder, Donald McKay. *N Y* 1928. O [28] 395 10col.pls a Also L.P. issue of 250copies.

Practically a history of the packet and clipper ship era.

McKAY, R[OBERT] H.   **122**

Little pills . . . experiences of . . . a medical officer on the frontier . . . *Pittsburg Kas* 1918. O 127[incl. initial blank, 1.] 3pls a

MacKAY, SAMUEL   **123**

Apercu topographique de la Virginie . . . *P* 1816. D 24 a

Mac KEAN, WILLIAM   **124**

Letters home, during a trip to America, 1869. *Paisley Scotland* 1875. D 240 3pls a

Describes conditions throughout the country as far West as Michigan, Ohio, Indiana and Illinois.

McKEE, JAMES C.   **125**

Narrative of the surrender of . . . U. S. forces at Fort Fillmore, N. M., in July, 1861 . . . *Prescott* 1878. D 15 + cover t. aa

—ed. 2, rev., *N Y* 1881. D 30 [incl. wraps] a

—ed. 3, *B* 1886. O 32 2maps a 300 cops ptd

—rptd, with adds *Houston* 1960 D 64

[MacKELLAR, PATRICK]   **126**
A short account of the expedition against Quebec . . . in 1759 . . . *L* [1848]. O 20 fold. plan aa
Has also been ascribed to Major Moncrief.

McKENNA, JAMES A.   **127**
Black Range tales . . . adventures in the southwest. *N Y* 1936. O [16] 301 5pls

[McKENNEY, THOMAS L.]   **128**
Essays on the spirit of Jacksonism, as exemplified in its deadly hostility to the Bank of the United States . . . *Phil* 1835. O 151 a

M'KENNEY, THOMAS L., and   **129**
HALL, JAMES
History of the Indian tribes . . . *Phil* [Biddle] 1836, 1838, 1844. F 3v: [6] 204; [2] 237; [4] 196 [2] + 21p.listing subscribers. 120 col.pls map d NYP Y
—anr. ed. *Phil* 1837–38–44. same collat. but textual changes made in describing the altered front. of v.I c AA NYP
—anr. ed. *Phil* [Greenough] 1838–42–44. b N NYP Y
—rptd. *Phil* [Rice] n.d. same format & collat. b
—Eng. ed. v.I [all], *L* 1837. 30col.pls aa
—octavo eds., with textual adds., [all *Phil* 3v 120col.pls]: 1848–49–50 b 1854; 1855; 1858; 1865; 1870, aa; *Edin* 1933, aa
Mostly the work of King, these are the most colorful portraits of Indians ever executed. Originally issued in twenty parts [in nineteen]; but few sets were retained in that impracticable form. The original oil paintings of which the plates were copies were all destroyed in the 1865 Smithsonian fire.

McKENNEY, THOMAS L.   **130**
Memoirs, official and personal; with sketches of travels among the . . . Indians . . . *N Y* 1846. O 2v in 1: [8] 17–340; [6] 9–136. 13pls[one col]facs a
—ed. 2, *N Y* 1846. O 2v in 1: [14] 17–340; [6] 9–136. 13pls facs a
—ed. 3, "Sketches of travels . . .," *N Y* 1854. same collat.

McKENNEY (COL. [THOMAS L.])   **131**
Reports and proceedings of: on . . . his recent tour among the southern Indians . . . *Wash* 1828. O 37 a

McKENNEY, THOMAS L.   **132**
Sketches of a tour to the lakes [etc.]. *Balt* 1827. O 494 27pls [of which, in some copies, 18 are cold] aa

MACKENZIE, ALEXANDER   **133**
Voyages from Montreal . . . to the frozen and Pacific oceans. With . . . account of . . . the fur trade . . . *L* 1801. Q [12 132] 412 errata lf 3maps port b

—ed. 2, *L* 1802. O 2v: [14] 290; 332. port 3maps [in some copies, bound separately] aa
—anr. ed. *L* 1803. O a
—Am. ed. *N Y* 1802. O [10] 94 296 map a
—anr. ed. *Phil* 1802. O 2v: [14 126] 114; 115–392. port 3maps a
—rptd: *N Y* 1803, D 437 map; *N Y* 1814, O [14 126] 392 port 3maps a
—Fr. tr., with add.notes, *P* 1802. D 3v: [24] 309; [4] 420; [47] 388 3map port tab a
—Ger. tr. *Hamburg* 1802. O [10] 585 map port a
—Rus. tr., *see* Berkh, Vasilii N., "Puteshestvie . . ."
First crossing of the continent from ocean to ocean by a white man. The narrative portion was prepared for publication by William Combe from Mackenzie's notes. The account of the fur trade—first ever published—is attributed to Roderick Mackenzie. For pirated edition, *see* Maclauries, Mr.

MACKENZIE, ALEXANDER S.   **134**
The life of Oliver Hazard Perry. *N Y* 1840. 16° 2v: [14] 322; 270. port a
—rptd., same impr. & collat., 1841.

MACKENZIE, ALEXANDER S.   **135**
The life of Paul Jones. *B* 1841. 16° 2v: [12] 260; [10] 308 a
—rptd., same collat., *N Y* 1845; *N Y* 1848.
—Eng. ed., with omissions, au. named as Edward Hamilton, *Aberdeen* 1848. D 304
—anr. Am. ed., under same pseud., *Phil* 1858. D

MACKENZIE, ALEXANDER S.   **136**
Life of Stephen Decatur . . . *B* 1846. O [14] 433 a some copies on L. P.

MACKENZIE, E[NEAS]   **137**
An historical . . . view of the United States . . . *Newcastle Eng* 1819. O [16] 9–712 9maps & pls a
—ed. 2, same impr., date & collat.

MACKENZIE, RODERICK   **138**
Strictures on . . . Tarleton's History of the campaigns of 1780 and 1781 . . . *L* 1787. O [10] 186 errata lf aa

MACKENZIE, WILLIAM L.   **139**
Sketches of Canada and the United States *L* 1833. D [24] 504 aa

McKIM, RANDOLPH H.   **140**
A soldier's recollections. *N Y* 1921. O 362 a

McKINSTRY, WILLIAM C.   **141**
The Colorado navigator . . . *Matagorda Tex* 1840. D [4] 23 c LC S

MACKINTOSH, J[OHN]
The discovery of America . . . and the origin of the North American Indians. *See* McIntosh, John.

[McKNIGHT, CHARLES]   **142**
Old Fort Duquesne . . . *Pitt* 1844. O 79 aa
—enl. ed., au. named, t. altered, *Pitt* 1873. D 501
7pls a
Romance, subordinated to historical facts,
concerning this region in 1754.

McKNIGHT, CHARLES   **143**
Our western border . . . *Phil* 1875. O [12] 756
15pls a
—rptd., same impr. & collat. 1876.
—oth eds: *Phil* 1880; *Chi* 1902.

McKNIGHT, CHARLES   **144**
Simon Girty: "the white savage" . . . *Cin* [1880].
O 442 a

McKNIGHT, GEORGE S.   **145**
. . . Travels from Perrysburg to California.
Perrysburg O 1903. O 28 Edition suppressed,
because of typographical errors. aa
Describes overland trip through Texas to
Mazatlan, Mexico, and by steamer to San
Francisco.

M'KONOCHIE, CAPTAIN   **146**
A summary view of the . . . commerce of the
principal shores of the Pacific . . . *L* 1818. O [22]
366 map a
Plan for British commercial domination;
California and the Northwest coast included.

McLAUGHLIN, JAMES   **147**
My friend the Indian. *B* 1910. O [14] 418 16pls a
—impression 2, same date & collat.

MACLAURIES, MR.   **148**
A narrative, or journal of voyages and travels
through the north-west continent of America . . .
L 1802. D [4] 91 pl c N NYP WashS Y
Obvious piracy from Alexander Mackenzie's
Voyages. possibly perpetrated by the editor of
that work, William Combe.

MACLAY, EDGAR S.   **149**
A history of American privateers. *N Y* 1899.
O [40] 519 15pls a
—Eng. ed. same collat *L* 1900

MACLAY (SAMUEL).   **150**
Journal of: while surveying the west branch of
the Susquehanna . . . in 1790. *Williamsport* 1887.
O 63 a

MACLAY, WILLIAM   **151**
Sketches of debate in the first Senate of the
United States, 1789–91. *Harrisburg* [1880]. O [18]
357 port a
—rptd., with adds., "Journal . . .," *N Y* 1890. O
[16] 438 port; *N Y* 1927. O [22] 429 port.

Of these proceedings—held behind closed doors
and never printed—this private diary is the chief
source of information.

McLEAN, MR. [WILLIAM?]   **152**
McLean, Mr., from the committee on Indian
affairs, made the following report . . . [H. Doc. 87].
Wash 1829. O 48 a
Contains Isaac McCoy's report *Remove Indians
westward, q.v.*

McLEAN (JAMES).   **153**
Seventeen years history of the life . . . of: an
impressed American . . . *Hart* 1814. D 24 a

MACLEAN, J[OHN] P.   **154**
An historical account of the settlements of
Scotch Highlanders in America . . . *Clev* 1900.
O 459 + inserted l. after p 416 a

[McLENNAN, JOHN]   **155**
Notes of a winter trip to Cuba and back by
way of the Mississippi. *Montr* 1867. D 54 aa

McLEOD, REV. ALEXANDER   **156**
Negro slavery unjustifiable . . . *N Y* 1802.
O 42 a
—Eng. ed. *Glas* 1804. O 35

M'LEOD (ALEXANDER).   **157**
Trial of: for the murder of Amos Durfee; and
as an accomplice in the burning of the steamer
Caroline . . . *N Y* 1841. O 32 a
—enl. ed. *Wash* same date. O 416 [Vol 2, Gould's
"Stenog. Reporter"] aa

McLEOD, DONALD   **158**
A brief review of the settlement of Upper
Canada . . . with a brief sketch of the campaigns
of 1812–13–14 . . . *Clev* 1841. D 144 149–292 aa
Includes details of the rebellion of 1837 and
the organization, within Ohio and New York,
of a patriot army for the invasion of Canada.

McLEOD, DONALD   **159**
History of Wiskonsan . . . *Buff* 1846. 16° [2]
7–310 map 4pls some copies issued with map only;
others with pls, but no map b

MACLURE, WILLIAM   **161**
Observations on the geology of the United
States . . . *Phil* 1817. O 127 [2] fold.map [first geo-
logical map of this country] fold.pl aa

MACLURE, WILLIAM   **162**
Opinions on various subjects . . . *New Harmony,
Ind* 1831. O 2v in 1: [4] 480; 481–592 aa
—iss. 2, identical with above, except paginat of
v2 continues from 592 through 640, text ending
there in middle of sentence. aa

—iss. 3, —of Vol I only—identical with the two other issues of that Vol but with add of 3p of contents, carrying paginat to 483 a.

All 3 issues of Vol I were evidently formed of the same sheets and all bear 1831 date. Issue 3 has the sheets considerably trimmed and has discarded the uncompleted portion of Vol II, with the obvious intention of making it serve as a uniformly sized companion for a contemplated smaller type, complete Vol II [next entry].

MACLURE, WILLIAM   **163**
Opinions on various subjects . . . Vol II. *New Harmony* 1837. O [8] 556 aa

MACLURE, WILLIAM   **164**
Opinions on various subjects . . . Vol III *New Harmony* 1838. O [6] 320 aa

[MACLURE, WILLIAM]   **165**
Suite des observations sur la géologie des États-Unis . . . n.p. [1811]. O 32 map a

M'MAHON, JOHN V. L.   **166**
An historical view of the government of Maryland . . . Vol. I[all]. *Balt* 1831. O [16] 539 a

McMAHON, T. W.   **167**
Cause and contrast: an essay on the American crisis. *Rich* 1862. O [16] 192 a
Southern political philosophy explained and defended.

McMASTER, GUY H.   **168**
History of the settlement of Steuben county . . . *Bath N Y* 1853. D [4] 318 a
—rptd. *Roch* 1893. D 300copies

McMASTER, S. W.   **169**
60 years on the upper Mississippi . . . *Rock Island* 1893. D [4] 300 aa
Printer's foreword is dated Galena 1895.

McMECHEN, EDGAR C.   **170**
Life of Governor [John] Evans, second territorial governor of Colorado. [*Denver* 1924]. D [10] 224 16pls a

McMECHEN, JAMES H.   **171**
Legends of the valley. *Wheeling* 1874. 16° 58 a
—ed. 2, "Legends of the Ohio valley," same impr. & collat., 1877.
—anr. ed. same impr. 1878. 16° 104
—ed. 3, *Wheeling* 1881. 16° [6] 5–110

McMORRIES, EDWARD Y.   **172**
History of the First . . . Alabama . . . Infantry. *Montg* 1904. O 142 a

McMURRAY, W. J.   **173**
History of the Twentieth Tennessee regiment. *Nash* 1904. O 520 ports a

McMURTRIE, HENRY   **174**
Sketches of Louisville [Ky.] and its environs . . . *Louisv* 1819. O [8] 255 map tab aa
First history of this city and first important book printed there.

[McNAMARA, JOHN J.]   **175**
In perils by mine own countryman. Three years on the Kansas border. *N Y* 1856 D 240 a

McNEIL, SAMUEL   **176**
. . . Travels in 1849, to, through and from the gold regions, in California. *Columbus* 1850. O 40 c AA NYP S Y [of 5cops loc]
—rptd. [*N Hav* 1958] 300 cops ptd

McNEMAR, RICHARD   **177**
The Kentucky revival, or, a short history of the late extraordinary out-pouring of the spirit of God, in the western states . . . *Cin* 1807. D 120 aa
—other eds.: *Alb* 1808. D 142; *Pittsfield* 1808 aa
—rptd. *N Y* 1846 a

McNEMEE, ANDREW J.   **178**
"Brother Mack" the frontier preacher . . . *Port* [1924]. D 79 a
Reminiscences of early days in Oregon, from 1845.

MACOMB, CAPT. J[OHN] N.   **179**
Report of the exploring expedition from Santa Fe . . . to the junction of Grand and Green rivers . . . in 1859 . . . *Wash* 1876. Q [8] 152 22pls [11 in color] map a
Publication of this report was intended for 1861, but the Civil War compelled a delay of fifteen years.

McPHERSON, EDWARD   **180**
The political history of the United States during the period of reconstruction . . . *Wash* 1871. O [10] 648 a
—ed. 2, *Wash* 1875. same collat.
—ed. 3, same impr. & collat. 1876; rptd. 1880.

[MACPHERSON, JAMES]   **181**
A short history of the opposition during the last session of Parliament. *L* 1779. O [6] 58 a
—eds. 2, 3, 4 & 5, same impr., date & collat.
—other eds.: n.p. n.d.; *Dub* 1779
Attributes successes of Americans to the encouragement given them by Whig members. Attributed also to Edward Gibbon.

McPHERSON, W[ILLIAM]   **182**
Homes in Los Angeles, city and county . . . *L A* 1873. D 74 + 25adv-p fold.map a
First "boom" pamphlet for Southern California.

MACPHERSON'S DIRECTORY   **183**
Macpherson's directory for . . . Philadelphia . . . *Phil* Oct. 1, 1785. O [4] 159 b AA NYP
First American city directory.

MACRAE, DAVID   **184**
The Americans at home . . . *Edin* 1870. D 2v:
[24] 332; [6] 408 a
—rptd: *Glas* 1874 D; 1885, D 488
—Am. ed *N Y* 1952. D 606
Spent much time in the South, interviewing
various Confederate leaders, and went West to
Illinois, Iowa and Missouri.

McREE, GRIFFITH J.   **185**
Life . . . of James Iredell . . . *N Y* 1857–8, O 2v:
[8] 570; [8] 605. 2pls facs aa
—rptd. *N Y* 1883–5. O 2v aa

McREYNOLDS, ROBERT   **186**
Thirty years on the frontier . . . *Colorado
Springs* 1906. D [8] 256 11pls a

M'ROBERT, PATRICK   **187**
A tour through part of the north provinces of
America . . . *Edin* 1776. O 64 b H NYP
—rptd. [*Phil* 1935] O 47

McSHERRY, JAMES   **188**
History of Maryland . . . *Balt* 1849. O 405 5pls a
—ed. 2, rev., same impr. & date. O [12] 3–405
5pls
—new ed., continued, *Balt* 1904. O 437 front.

McSHERRY, JAMES   **189**
Père Jean; or the Jesuit missionary . . . *Balt*
1847. D [2] 256 2 pls a
—anr. ed. "Father Laval; or the Jesuit missionary", *Balt* 1860. 16° 214[incl.front]
Account of Father Isaac Jogues' labors among
the Mohawks, his captivity and martyrdom.

McSHERRY, RICHARD   **190**
Essays and lectures on . . . the early history of
Maryland . . . *Balt* 1869. O [6] 125 a

[McSPARRAN, JAMES]   **191**
America dissected . . . true account of all . . .
colonies . . . Published as a caution to unsteady
people . . . tempted to leave their native country.
Dub 1753. O [2] 48 aa
Author spent thirty-six years as a missionary
in Rhode Island.

McWHORTER, LUCULLUS V.   **192**
The border settlers of northwestern Virginia,
1768–95. *Hamilton O* 1915. O 509 aa

McWHORTER, LUCULLUS V.   **193**
Tragedy of the Wahk-shum; prelude to the
Yakima Indian war, 1855–6 . . . *Yakima Wash*
[1937]. O [2] 44 [1] 9pls a

McWILLIAMS, JOHN   **194**
Recollections . . . experiences in California . . .
Princeton, 1919 O [6] 186 port aa

Describes his overland trip to Oregon in 1849
and life in the mines.

MACY, OBED   **195**
The history of Nantucket . . . with the rise . . .
of the whale fishery . . . *B* 1835. O [10] 300 map pl a
—ed. 2, *Mansfield* 1880. D 213 map pl

MACY, WILLIAM H.   **196**
There she blows! or, the log of the Arethusa.
B 1877. D [8] 320 pls a
—rptd., t.slightly altered, *B* 1889, same collat.

MADDOX, JOHN, pub.   **197**
The Richmond [Va.] directory . . . for . . . 1819
Rich 1819. O 76 + 12 unpaged pp and 1f betw
pp 40–41 b
First directory of this city.

MADELÈNE, HENRY DE LA   **198**
Le comte Gaston de Raousset Boulbon; sa vie
et ses aventures. *Alencon* 1856. D 162 aa
—ed. 2, *P* 1859. same collat. a
—enlgd ed *P* 1876. D [12] 323 a
The audacious dream of the conquest of Sonora
and the mines of Arizona; extinguished only by
two ill-starred expeditions and a final firing squad.

[MADISON, JAMES]
The diplomatick policy of Mr. Madison unveiled . . . By a Bostonian. *See* Lowell, John.

[MADISON, JAMES]   **199**
An examination of the British doctrine which
subjects to capture a neutral trade not open in
time of peace. [*Phil* 1806]. O [6] 204 a
—ed. 2, *L* 1806. O [2] 200

[MADISON, JAMES]   **200**
Letters of Helvidius . . . on the President's
proclamation of neutrality. *Phil* 1796. O 48 a

MADISON (MR. [JAMES]).
Perpetual war, the policy of: . . . By a Yankee
farmer. *See* Lowell, John.

MADISON (JAMES).   **201**
The republican crisis . . . exposition of the
political Jesuitism of: . . . By an observant citizen
. . . *Alexandria* 1812. O 56 a

MADISON (JAMES).   **202**
Selections from the private correspondence of:
. . . *Wash* 1853. Q [4] 3–419 aa

MADISON COUNTY [IND.]   **203**
History of: *Chi* 1880. O 128 a

MADISON COUNTY [MONT.]   **204**
Resources of: *Virginia City* [ptd *S F*] 1872.
O 60 aa

MADISON [WIS.]
Madison [Wis.] directory ... **1855.** *See* Seymour, Wm. N., comp.

Madison, the capital of Wisconsin; its   205
progress, capabilities and destiny. *Madison* 1855.
O 48 a
For similar title, *see* Draper, Lyman W.

Statistics of Dane county, Wisconsin, with a
business directory ... of Madison: 1851. *See* Dane
county, Wisconsin.

MADOX, D. T.   206
Late account of the Missouri Territory ...
Paris Ky 1817. O [10] 66 c G LexP WisH [only
cops kn]
—rptd. n.p. [1921] O 56. a
First extended description, by an American
citizen, of upper Louisiana after its acquisition
from France.

MADRAY, MRS. I. C.   207
A history of Bee county, Texas. *Beeville* 1939.
O [4] 135 cov.t.only a

MAES, CAMILLUS P.   208
The life of Rev. Charles Nerinckx: with a
chapter on the early Catholic missions of Kentucky ... *Cin* 1880. O [18] 635 port a

MAFFITT, JOHN N.   209
A plea for Texas ... *Nashv* 1836. D 24 aa

MAGAZINE [THE] OF TRAVEL ...
See Travels in the two hemispheres.

MAGILL, JOHN   210
The pioneer to the Kentucky emigrant ...
Frankf 1832. D 84 b Filson Club NYH PittU
[only cops known]
—rptd. *Lex* 1942. O [14] 82 [2] a
From this pamphlet Lewis Collins took, without
acknowledgment, considerable material for his
Historical sketches of Kentucky.

MAGOFFIN, SUSAN S.   211
Down the Santa Fé trail and into Mexico ...
N Hav 1926. O [26] 294 map 7pls aa

MAGOUN, F. ALEXANDER   212
The frigate Constitution ... *Salem* 1928. F
[18] 154 [1] 31pls 16plans also 97copies on L.P. aa

MAGOUN, GEORGE F.   213
The west: its culture and its colleges ...
Davenport 1855. O 35 a

MAGRUDER (ALLAN B.)   214
A letter from: ... to his correspondent in ...
Virginia. *N O* 1808. O 26 d LC

This, together with Magruder's 1803 ... *Reflections* [next entry], gives the earliest detailed
account of the newly purchased lower Louisiana
Territory by a U.S. citizen.

MAGRUDER, ALLAN B.   215
Political, commercial and moral reflections on
the late cession of Louisiana. *Lex* 1803. O 150
d G LC WisH Y

MAGRUDER, JOHN B.   216
Report of his operations on the Peninsula ...
Rich 1862. O 46 aa
—anr. ed., same date & collat., *Mobile* a

MAGUIRE, H[ORATIO] N.   217
The Black hills and American wonderland
Chi 1877. Q 35 c Y
—anr. issue, called "People's ed.," [in "The
Lakeside Library," v.IV, no.82, *Chi* 1877]. b N
The same author's twenty-page duodecimo,
The Black hills of Dakota, [*Chicago* 1879], is an
entirely different book.

MAGUIRE, H[ORATIO] N.   218
The coming empire ... the Black Hills, Yellowstone and Big Horn regions. *Sioux C* 1878. D 177
+ 12 adv-p map 7pls b G H MontH

[MAGUIRE, H[ORATIO] N., and   219
HORN, HENRY]
Historical sketch and essay on ... Montana ...
Helena 1868. O 168 [cover t. only] c G H LC
MontH Y.
—rptd. "Pioneer directory, etc." same impr. &
collat [1869] b

[MAGUIRE, HORATIO N.]   220
New map and guide to Dakota and the Black
hills. *Chi* [1877]. O 86 + 4adv-p 2maps b G
LC Y

MAGUIRE, JOHN F.   221
The Irish in America. *L* 1868. O [18] 653 a
—Am. ed. *N Y* 1868. D [14] 653

MAHIN, JOHN [comp.]   222
Muscatine city directory ... for 1856: containing a history [etc.]. *Muscatine* 1856. D [4 40] 5–33
[inserted slip] 34–80 aa
First history and first directory of this city.

MAHONING VALLEY (THE).   223
Historical collections of: ... Vol.I [all]. *Youngstown* 1876. O 524 map a

MAILHE, M. [J.B.]   224
Discours ... sur la ... importance de la revolution ... dans l'Amérique ... *Toulouse* 1784.
O 40 a

MAILLARD, N. DORAN   225
The history of the republic of Texas . . . *L* 1842.
O [24] 512 map aa
An antidote to the pro-Texan history of another
Englishman, William Kennedy.

MAINE
**An address to the inhabitants of the district of
Maine** . . . By one of their fellow citizens. *See*
Davis, Daniel.

A description of the situation . . . of certain   226
tracts of land in the district of Maine. n.p. [1793].
Q 44 a
Probably by Benj. Lincoln.

Documents relating to the Maine boun-   227
dary . . . *Wash* 1838. O 494 map a

Documents relating to the north eastern   228
boundary of . . . **Maine.** *B* 1828. O 275 a

The seventeenth jewel, of the United   229
States . . . in the latitude and longitude of Maine . . .
n.p. 1797. D 35 a

MAJOR, RICHARD H.   230
The true date of the English discovery of the
American continent . . . *L* 1870. Q 26 a
Analyzes the claim for a 1494 voyage and con-
cludes that the first Cabotian voyage was in 1497.

MAJOR, RICHARD H.   231
The voyages of the Venetian brothers Zeno . . .
in the fourteenth century. *L* Hakluyt Soc. 1873.
O [104] 64 4maps a
—rptd., in part, *B* 1875. O 20 map 100copies ptd.
Attempt to establish the authenticity of the Zeno
account.

MAJORS, ALEYANDER   232
Seventy years on the frontier . . . *Chi* 1893. D
325[incl. front. & pls] + 2adv-p
—rptd., without illus., *Denver* n.d.

MAKEMSON, W. K.   233
Historical sketch of first settlement . . . of Wil-
liamson county [Tex.] *Georgetown, Tex.* [1904?].
D 26 a

MALANGUEULÉ.   234
Relations diverses sur la bataille du: gané par
les Francois sous M. de Beaujeau . . . sur les Anglois sous M. Braddock . . . *N Y* 1860. O [16] 9–91
port 100copies ptd. aa

MALASPINA, ALEJANDRO   235
Viage . . . alrededor del mundo por las corbetas
Descubierta y Atrevida . . . 1789 á 1794. *Madrid*
1885. Q [32] 682 [10] map port 6pls aa
First printing of the official account of this

scientific expedition which made extensive explo-
rations along the California and northwest coasts·
It was edited from Malaspina's papers by Pedro de
Novo y Colson. For an earlier publication by a
subaltern *see* Viana, Francisco Javier de. Also *see*
Suria, Thomas.

MALARTIC (LE COMTE DE   236
MAURÈS DE).
Journal des campagnes au Canada de 1755 a
1760 par: . . . *Dijon* [some cops carry Paris impr]
1890. O [26] 370 [2] errata lf port 4maps a
First publication of this day-by-day diary. Kept
by one who served with distinction throughout the
French war.

MALET, WILLIAM W.   237
An errand to the south in the summer of 1862.
L 1863. 16° [8] 312 pl a

MALÉZIEUX, ÉMILE   238
Souvenirs d'une mission aux États-Unis . . . *P*
1874. O [2] 175 7maps & pls a
Informal account of travels from coast to coast
while gathering material for his official report.

MALÉZIEUX, ÉMILE   239
Travaux publics des États-Unis . . . *P* 1873. sm
F [4] 572 + Atlas[of 61fold.pls] a
Formal report of his investigation of American
public works and engineering methods.

MALLINSON, MRS. FLORENCE L.   240
My travels and adventures in Alaska . . . *Seattle*
1914. D 200 10pls a

MALONE, JAMES H.   241
The Chickasaw nation . . . [*K C ca* 1919]. O [8]
175 a
—enl. ed. *Louisv* 1922. O [30] 537 3maps 10 pls

MALSEN, A. VAN   242
Achttal Brieven uit de Kolonie Hollande in
Amerika [i.e. in Michigan]. *Zwijndrecht* 1848.
D 50 aa

[MALTBY, WILLIAM J.]   243
Captain Jeff; or, frontier life in Texas with the
Texas rangers . . . *Colorado Tex* 1906. O 166[incl.
port] 2pls aa
—ed. 2, same impr. & date. O 204 [incl.port] 2pls
By a companion of Big Foot Wallace in expeditions against the Comanches and Kiowas, 1850–
1875.

MAMMOTH CAVE
Rambles in the Mammoth Cave . . . By a visitor.
See Croghan, John.

**Wonderful curiosity; or, a correct narrative of the
celebrated Mammoth Cave** . . . *See* Jones, Wm. B.

[MANCUR, JOHN H.]   244
   Tales of the revolution . . . *N Y* 1835. 18° 216 a
—rptd., same impr. & collat.: 1839; 1841; 1844;
1858.

MANDAT-GRANCEY, EDMOND, baron de   245
   La brèche aux buffles. [Un ranch francais dans
le Dakota]. *P* 1889. D [16 [incl initial blank lf] 292
[incl. front wrap] + 12adv-p 6double-p.pls aa
—ed. 2, *P* [1893]. same collat. a

MANDAT-GRANCEY, EDMOND, baron de   246
   Dans les montagnes Rocheuses. *P* 1884. D [4]
314 [4] map 9pls aa
—ed. 2, same collat., *P* 1889. a
—rptd. *P* 1894.
—Eng. tr. "Cow-boys and colonels; narrative of a
journey across the prairie and over the Black
Hills of Dakota," *L* 1887. D [12] 352 pls a
—rptd: *N Y* [1887]; *L* [1888]

[MANDRILLON, JOSEPH]   247
   Précis sur l'Amérique Septentrionale . . . *Amst*
1782. O 164 a
   Included with the author's French translation
of Cluny, Alexander, *The American traveller, see*
below [No. 249].

[MANDRILLON, JOSEPH]   248
   Le spectateur américain . . . *Amst* 1784. O [16]
128, 307, 91 [4] map tab aa
—ed. 2, *Amst* 1785. O [20] 519 map tab a

M[ANDRILLON], J[OSEPH], tr   249
   Le voyageur américain . . . traduit de l'Anglois.
Augmenté d'un Précis sur l'Amérique septentrionale . . . *Amst* 1782. O [8] 189, 166 map 3tabs
aa
—rptd. same impr 1783. O [8] 264 map 3tabs a
   This translation of Alexander Cluny's *The
American traveller* [*q.v.*], with additions, is often
confused with Mandrillon's own *Le spectateur
américain.*

MANFORD, ERASMUS   250
   Twenty-five years in the west. *Chi* 1867. D [2]
359 a
—rptd., same collat. & impr.: 1868; 1870
—rev. ed.: *Chi* 1872, O 375 port; 1873; 1885

MANGOLD, F.   251
   Der feldzug in Nord-Virginien in August 1862.
Hannover 1881. O [12] 335 3maps a

MANGOURIT ([MICHEL ANGE   252
BERNARD DE]).
   Mémoire de: Addresses des municipalités . . . de
l'état de la Caroline du Sud . . . *P* [1795]. Q 32 aa
   Mangourit when consul at Charleston became
embroiled with Genet's activities, was recalled to
France and published this exoneration.

[MANHEIM, FREDERICK]   253
   Affecting history of the dreadful distresses of
Frederick Manheim's family . . . *Exeter* 1793. D
66 [incl. blank, l. before t-p] b AA N
—anr. ed. *Phil* 1794. O 48 front. aa
—other eds.: *Newport* Farnsworth [1798? 1799?];
Stonington Conn 1799; [*Leominster*] C. Whitcomb
[1800?]; *Phil* 1800; *Bennington* 1802. aa
   All of above editions of this brief narrative are
padded to book size by including the similar narratives of Massy Herbeson, Peter Wilkinson, Johonnet, *et al.* Manheim had his twin 16-year old
daughters burned by Indians before his eyes.

MANLEY, JOHN, ed.   254
   Original portraits and biographies of the old
pioneers . . . of Cattaraugus county [N.Y.]. *Little
Valley N Y* 1857. O 136 8ports a
—rptd., same impr. 1858. O 140 8ports

MANLY, WILLIAM L.   255
   Death valley in '49 . . . *San José* 1894. O 498
[incl. initial blank & port] 3pls aa
—rptd.: ed. Quaife, *Chi* 1927, 16° [24] 307 map
pl; *Santa Barbara* [1929], D map; *L A* 1949
   Classic account, by a survivor, of dire sufferings
endured by an emigrant party on a short-cut from
Salt Lake City to California through the valley
called ever after by this fearful name.

MANN, A[MBROSE] DUDLEY   256
   Die Nordamericanischen Freistaaten . . . *Bremen* 1845. O [8] 326 a

[MANN, HERMAN]   257
   The female review: or, memoirs of an American young lady . . . a continental soldier . . . By
a citizen of Massachusetts. *Dedham* 1797. D 264
[incl. subscribers' list] port aa
—rptd. *B* 1866. Q 267 port 250copies ptd. [a few
on L. P.] a
   Exploits—not too credible—of Deborah Sampson in the Revolution; that she actually served,
under the name of Robert Shurtleff, is, however, a
matter of indisputable record.

MANN, JAMES   258
   Medical sketches of the campaigns of 1812, 13,
14 . . . *Dedham* 1816. O 318 a

MANN, WILLIAM   259
   Emigrant's complete guide to the United States
. . . *L* 1850. D 72 a

MANNING (EDWARD C.)   260
   Biographical, historical . . . selections by: *Cedar
Rapids* 1911. O 194 [2] pls a

MANNING, WENTWORTH   261
   Some history of Van Zandt county, Texas. Vol.I
[all]. *Des M* [1919]. O 220 a Most of edition burned.

MANRING, BENJAMIN F.   262
Conquest of the Coeur d'Alenes . . . *Spokane*
Graham [1912]. D 280 map 21pls facs a

MANSFIELD, EDWARD D.   263
Exposition of the natural position of Makinaw
City, and . . . the surrounding country. *Cin* 1857.
O 48 2maps aa

MANSFIELD, EDWARD D.   264
Memoirs . . . of Daniel Drake . . . with notices
of the early settlement of Cincinnati. *Cin* 1855. D
408 port a

MANSFIELD, EDWARD D.   265
Personal memories . . . 1803–1843. *Cin* 1879.
D [8] 348 a

[MANSFIELD, JOHN B.] ed.   266
History of the great lakes. *Chi* Beers & Co 1899.
Q 2v: [16] 928; [4] 1108 [incl.pls] 5 double-page
maps aa

MANTE, THOMAS   267
The history of the late war in North America . . .
L 1772. Q [12] 542 18maps & plans errata, lf. c
N NYP Y
Best contemporary chronicle of this war; inclu-
ding detailed accounts of the frontier campaigns
under Washington, Braddock, Amherst, Brad-
street, Bouquet, *et al.*

MANUAL-GUIDE
Manual-guide des voyageurs aux États-Unis . . .
See Fernagus de Gelone.

MANYPENNY, GEORGE W.   268
Our Indian wards. *Cin* 1880. O [26] 436 a

MANZANEDA Y ENCINAS, DIEGO   269
M. B. DE
Sermon que èn las solemnes honras celebradas
en obsequio de los predicadores apostolicos . . .
Garces [*et al*] . . . *Madrid* 1819. Q 94 b G JCB
NYP TxU Y [only cops loc]
First printing of this important historical dis-
course which supplements Arricivita's *Cronica
serafica* [*q.v.*] in furnishing information on the
work of eighteen Franciscan missionaries in
Arizona, New Mexico, Sonora and Texas in the
late eighteenth century.

[MARBAULT, M. DE?]   270
Essai sur le commerce de Russie, avec l'histoire
de ses découvertes. *Amst* 1777. D 300 map aa
Pays considerable attention to discoveries and
trade between Kamschatka and America.

MARCEL, GABRIEL   271
Reproductions des cartes & de globes relatifs à
la découverte de l'Amérique, du XVIe au XVIIIe
siècle. *P* 1894. F 2v: [text 146p., atlas 40maps] aa

Complete in itself, but formed a portion of
Schefer and Cordier, *Recueil de voyages* . . .

MARCH   272
March (The) of the First . . . Regiment of Colorado Volunteers . . . *Denver* 1863. O 40 + 4adv-p
b S

MARCHAND, ÉTIENNE
A voyage round the world . . . 1790–2. *See*
Fleurieu, Charles P. C.

MARCOU, JULES   273
Esquisse d'une classification de chaines de montagnes d'une partie de l'Amérique du Nord. *P*
1855. O 24 2fold.maps a

MARCOU, JULES   274
Geology of North America . . . with two . . .
reports on the prairies of Arkansas and Texas, the
Rocky mountains of New Mexico, and the Sierra
Nevada of California. *Zurich* 1858. Q [8] 144
10maps & pls aa
—Fr. tr., *Geneva* 1858, a
First detailed geological map of the country
west of the 100th meridian.

MARCY, RANDOLPH B.   275
Border reminiscences. *N Y* 1871. D 396 [incl.
front. & pls] a
—rptd. same impr. 1872.

MARCY, RANDOLPH B.   276
Exploration of the Red river of Louisiana . . .
[Sen. Exec. Doc. 54]. *Wash* Armstrong 1853. O
[16] 320 65pls[botanical pl. 18 not issued] + 2maps
[in separate vol.] a
—rptd. [for Sen.], *Wash* Tucker 1854. [16] 310
otherwise same collat.
—rptd. [H. R.], *Wash* Nicholson 1854. [16] 286 +
blank l. otherwise same collat.

MARCY (CAPT. [RANDOLPH B.])   277
Message of the President . . . communicating
. . . the report and maps of: of his explorations of
the Big Wichita . . . [Sen. Exec. Doc. 60]. *Wash*
1856. O 48 map a

MARCY, GEN. RANDOLPH B.   278
Outline description of the posts . . . in the . . .
departments of the United States. *Wash* 1872. Q
324 [printed on one side of leaves]. aa

MARCY, RANDOLPH B.   279
The prairie traveller. A hand-book for overland
expeditions . . . *N Y* 1859. 16° 340[incl. front. &
10pls] map aa
—rptd., with adds., *N Y* 1861. 16° 381[incl. pls]
map a
—Eng. ed., with notes by R. F. Burton, *L* 1863.
16° [16] 251 map
—anr ed *Denver* 1959 map.

MARCY, RANDOLPH B.   **280**
Thirty years of army life on the border . . . *N Y* 1866. O 442 [incl. pls] a

[MARÉCHAL, PIERRE S.]   **281**
Voyage au Kentoukey, et sur les bords du Gene-sée . . . Par M . . . *P* 1820. O [4] 244 map b
—rptd., same collat., *P* 1821. aa
Ascribed also to Mme. V. Lamothe; who-ever wrote it borrowed heavily from Filson's great book and from Bridel's *Le pour et le contre.*

MARESTIER, [JEAN B.]   **282**
Mémoire sur les bateaux à vapeur des États-Unis . . . *P* 1824. Q [4] 291 + atlas F 2 [17fold.pls] b BN N NYP

MARGINALIA
Marginalia; or gleanings from an army note book. By "Personne." *See* Fontaine, Felix G. de.

MARGRY, PIERRE, ed.   **283**
Découvertes et établissements des Francais dans l'ouest et dans le sud de l'Amérique Septentrionale (1614–1754) . . . *P* Jouaust 1876–7–8, 1880–3–6. O 6v: [4] 619; [4] 618 [2]; [4] 656; [4] 654 [2]; [4] 698 [2]; [4] 760. 4ports b AA N NYP
—anr. ed. *P* Maisonneuve 1879–1881–1888. O 6v: [36] 619; [4] 618 [2]; [4] 656; [76] 654 [2]; [164] 698 [2]; [24] 760. 2maps 3ports facs b G JCB NYP Y
Reports, journals and letters, many here first printed, illuminating French explorations and Indian trade, from Canada to the Gulf, from the St. Lawrence to the Rockies.

MARGRY, PIERRE, ed.   **284**
Relations et mémoires inédits pour servir a l'histoire de la France dans les pays d'outre-mer . . . *P* 1867. O [8] 376 aa

MARIGNY, BERNARD   **285**
Reflexions sur la campagne du général André Jackson en Louisiane . . . *N O* 1848. O 51 aa

MARIGNY, BERNARD   **286**
Reflexions sur la politique des États-Unis . . . *N O* 1854. O 96 aa
—Eng. tr. "Thoughts upon the foreign policy of the United States . . .," same impr. & date. O 82 [2] aa

MARIN COUNTY, CALIF.
History of: *see* Munro-Fraser, J. P.

MARION HORNETS   **287**
Marion Hornets (the), Co. H., 7th Regt., Fla. Vols . . . Adventures of: *Knoxv* 1863. O 24 aa

MARIS, MARTIN   **288**
Souvenirs d'Amérique. Relations d'un voyage au Texas et en Haiti. *Brus* 1863. D 135 a

MARIS, OMER   **289**
Sketches from Alaska. *Chi* 1897. O 63 a

MARJORIBANKS, ALEXANDER   **290**
Travels in South and North America. *Edin* 1852. D 486 a
—rptd. *L* 1853; *Edin* 1854.
—best ed. *L* 1854. D [14] 480 pl. Am eds: *N Y* 1853; 1854.

MARKHOV, ALEKSANDR   **291**
Russkie na Vostochnom Okeanie. Vostochnaia Sibirj. Rossiiskiia vladieniia v Amerikie. Ryt dika-rei. Kaliforniia. Proekt Krugosvietnoi torgovoi ekspeditsii. [The Russians on the Pacific ocean. Eastern Siberia. Russian possessions in America. Condition of the natives. California. Plan for a trading expedition round the world]. *Moscow* 1849. O 148 c N
—ed. 2, enl., *St Ptbg* 1856. O 263 aa

MARKS, ALFRED   **292**
On to Klondike! and the . . . gold discoveries . . . [*N Y* 1898]. D 62 a

MARKS (DAVID).   **293**
Memoirs of the life of: . . . Ed. by Mrs. Marilla Marks. *Dover N H* 1846. O 516 port a
Itinerant Free Will Baptist preacher.

MARLETTE, S.   **294**
Report on the northern boundary survey . . . *Sacr* 1855. O 98 aa

[MARLOW, GEORGE and CHARLES]   **295**
Life of the Marlows. *Ouray Colo* [1892]. D 182 front. b
—rptd., same impr., n.d. O 100 a
Five respected, but nomadic, brothers, caught in a conspiracy concocted by a Texas sheriff, had to shoot it out with the county's entire male population. Only the two writing the story survived.

MARQUETTE (R. PÉRE JACQUES).   **296**
Récit des voyages . . . du: en l'année 1673 . . . [*Alb* 1855]. D [10] 169 [2] map facs a

MARQUEZ, JOSÉ A.   **297**
Recuerdos de viaje a los Estados-Unidos . . . *Lima* 1862. O [6] 136 a

MARRANT (JOHN).
A narrative of the Lord's wonderful dealings with: *See* Aldridge, Wm.

[MARRIOTT, JAMES]   **298**
Mémoire justificatif de la conduite de la Grande Bretagne, en arrêtant les navires étrangers . . . destinées aux insurgens de l'Amérique. *L* 1779. Q [8] 60 aa
—rptd. *L* 1804. O [10] 106 a

Refers to Holland's conduct in supplying munitions to America.

MARRYAT, FRANK [FRANCIS S.]   299
Mountains and molehills . . . *L* 1855. O [12] 443 + 24adv-p 8col.pls aa
—Am. ed. *N Y* 1855. D 393 front a

MARRYAT, [FREDERICK]   300
A diary in America, with remarks on its institutions. [Part I]. *L* 1839. D 3v: [4] 321; [4] 319; [4] 312 a
—Am. ed. *Phil* Carey & Hart 1839. D 2v: 242; 228
—one vol. eds., all in 1839; *P*; *N Y*; *Phil*

MARRYAT, [FREDERICK]   301
A diary in America. Part II. *L* 1839. D 3v: [4] 304; [4] 293; [4] 362. 2maps a
—rptd. *L* 1840.
—Am. ed. *Phil* 1840. D [2] 300

MARRYAT, FREDERICK   302
Narrative of the travels and adventures of Monsieur Violet, in California, Sonora and western Texas. *L* 1843. O 3v: [8] 312; [4] 318; [4] 299. map aa
—issue 2, title [a cancel] reading: "Travels and romantic adventures among the Snake Indians, etc." a
—Am. eds.: *N Y* 1843, O 133; same impr. & date, Q 77 a
Incredible adventures of an imaginary Frenchman borrowed from various sources. Other one volume editions were published at Leipzig in 1843, at Paris in 1844 and at London in 1849; a French translation, in two volumes at Paris 1845.

[MARRYAT, JOSEPH]   303
Concessions to America, the bane of Britain . . . *L* 1807. O 63 a

MARRY-IT, CAPTAIN, C. B.   304
[COMMON BLOAT]
Lie-ary in America . . . *B* 1840. 18° 36 a

[MARSCHALK, ANDREW]   305
Letters addressed to the hon. George Poindexter, one of the judges of the Mississippi Territory: on the subject of British claims, and his attack on the liberty of the press. By Castigator & Philo-Castigator. *Washington Miss Terr* 1814. D 34 [2] b PaH [only copy known]
—ed 2, with adds. [*Washington Miss*? 1815?]. D 100 + ? b no complete copy known

MARSH, JAMES B.   306
Four years in the Rockies; or, the adventures of Isaac P. Rose . . . as a hunter and trapper . . . *New Castle Pa* 1884. D 262 port b MontH N NYP Y
—rptd., without port, *Columbus O* 1951. a

Rose was a member of Wyeth's expedition and trapped with all the famous mountain men, Bridger, Carson, Meek, Sublette, *et al.*

MARSH, ROBERT   307
Seven years of my life . . . *Buff* 1848. D 207 aa
Narrative of one of the eighty-two Americans who joined in the Canadian rebellion of 1836, were tried and exiled to Van Dieman's Land.

MARSHALL, ALEXANDER J.   308
Five chapters of an unpublished "Book for the times" . . . demonstrating who were the true authors of the civil war. *Rich* 1863. O 40 [cov-t] aa

MARSHALL (MRS. ANN J.).   309
The autobiography of: . . . *Pine Bluff Ark* 1897. D 232 errata slip a
Missionary teacher among Cherokees and Creeks, from 1846.

MARSHALL (CHRISTOPHER).   310
Passages from the remembrancer of: *Phil* 1839. D 124 [16] errata slip a
—anr. ed. "Passages from the diary of: . . .," vol. 1, 1774–7 [all], *Phil* 1839–48[i.e., 1849]. D 174 [19] errata slip
—rptd., with adds., "Extracts from the diary of: . . ., 1774–81," *Alb* 1877. O 330
Reliable contemporary authority on the Revolution in Pennsylvania.

MARSHALL, EDWARD C.   311
History of the United States Naval Academy . . . *N Y* 1862. O 156 2pls a

MARSHALL, HUMPHREY   312
An address to the people of Kentucky. *Phil* 1796. O 48 aa

MARSHALL, HUMPHREY   313
The history of Kentucky: including an account of the discovery, settlement [etc.]. *Frankf* 1812. O [8] 407 b
—ed. 2, enl. *Frankf* 1824. O 2v: [8 48] 465 [8]; [6] 524 aa
Most valuable early Kentucky history, with the fullest treatment of border wars and massacres. Rafinesque's *Ancient annals of Kentucky* was inserted in Vol I of the 1824 edition.

MARSHALL, HUMPHREY   314
Self-defence. The spurious message, or fraud exposed: . . . *Lex* 1840. O 66 aa
Substantiates charges against Isaac Shelby which had been brought out in his [Marshall's] *History of Kentucky* and attacks the spurious documents in Mann Butler's *History* . . .

MARSHALL, JOHN   315
Expediency of accepting from Connecticut juris-

diction of the territory west of Pennsylvania . . .
Phil 1800. O 31 a

MARSHALL, JOHN   **316**
A history of the colonies planted by the English
on the continent of North America . . . *Phil* 1824.
O [16] 9–486 a
A revision of the introductory portion of the
author's *Life of Washington.*

MARSHALL, JOHN   **317**
The life of George Washington . . . *Phil* 1804–7.
O 5v: [24] 488 [45]; [8] 560 [72]; [8] 580 [28];
[3–8] 626 [1] 16; [8] 780 [36] + Q atlas [22p + 10
maps]. port aa
—rptd., same impr. 1805–7. O 5v: [22] 460 [43];
[8] 516 [67]; [8] 528 [28]; [3–8] 568 [16]; [8] 780
[36] + 0 atlas [10maps]. port a
—abr. Am. eds.: O 2v: *Phil* 1832; 1836; 1840. [In
1832 an atlas, with eng.t. & 10 maps was issued
for owners of these eds.]
—Eng.—and best—ed. *L* 1804–7. Q 5v: [32] 458;
[8] 541; [8] 470; [8] 589; [8] 670. 10maps 6pls aa
—rptd., same impr. & date. O 5v: [36] 576; [8]
634; [8] 570[error for 572]; [8] 684; [8] 844. 10maps
6pls a
—Fr. tr. *P* 1807. O 5v + Q atlas [of 16maps & pls]
—Dutch tr. *Haarlem* 1805–9. O 10v + Q atlas [of
16maps & pls] a
—Ger. tr. *Hamburg* 1805–6. O 4v

MARSHALL (MR. CHIEF JUSTICE   **318**
[JOHN]).
Opinion of the Supreme Court of the United
States by: . . . in the case of Samuel A. Worcester
. . . *versus* the State of Georgia . . . *Wash* 1832.
O 39 a
—anr. ed. same impr. & date. O 20
Reviews the whole history of our Indian treaties.

MARSHALL, ORSAMUS H.   **319**
Historical writings, relating to the early history
of the west. *Alb* 1887. sm Q [24] 500 map port a

MARSHALL, ORSAMUS H.   **320**
The Niagara frontier. [*Buf* 1865]. O 46 a
—rptd. *Buf* 1866; 1881.

MARSHALL, THOMAS M.   **321**
History of the western boundary of the Louisiana purchase . . . *Berkeley* 1914. O [14] 266
30maps[on 19sheets] a

MARSHALL, WILLIAM I.   **322**
Acquisition of Oregon, and the long suppressed
evidence about Marcus Whitman. *Seattle* 1911.
O 2v: [2] 450; 368. port aa
—rptd. Seattle 1911. O 2v
Elaborate monograph, based on twenty-five
years' research, annihilating the myth that Whitman saved Oregon.

MARSILLAC, J.   **323**
La vie de Guillaume Penn . . . contenant l'his-
toire des premiers fondemens de Philadelphie . . .
P 1791. O 2v: 264; 294 a
—Ger. tr. *Strassburg* 1798. O

MARSTON, ANNA L., ed.   **324**
Records of a California family. Journals and
letters of Lewis C. Gunn and Elizabeth Le Breton
Gunn. *San Diego* 1928. O [12] 3–283[incl.map]
15pls [pl facing p. 267 often missing] aa 300copies
ptd.

MARTELS, HEINRICH VON   **325**
Briefe über die westlichen Theile der Vereinigten
Staaten . . . *Osnabruck* 1834. O 195 map aa

MARTHA'S VINEYARD.
Sketches of: . . . *See* Devens, Saml. A.

MARTIAL ACHIEVEMENTS   **326**
Martial achievements (The) of Great Britain and
her allies . . . 1799–1815. *L* Jenkins [1815]. Q [14]
122 53col.pls[incl.eng.t.] b LC NYP

MARTIN, CHARLES I   **327**
History of Door county, Wisconsin. *Sturgeon
Bay* 1881. D [10] 136 port a Inserted in some copies
is an extra lf [p100 $^1/_2$ & 100 $^3/_4$]

[MARTIN, CHARLES L.]   **328**
A sketch of Sam Bass, the bandit. *Dallas* 1880.
O 152 + 3adv-p [1 at front, 2 at rear] 4pls b LC
—rptd. *Norman, Okla* [1956] D [24] 166 a

MARTIN, EDWARD, ed.   **329**
The Watsonville [Calif.] directory . . . [no t-p].
[*Watsonville* 1873]. D 64 + 22adv-p a
Chiefly a history of the region, only five pages
being occupied by the directory.

MARTIN, FELIX   **330**
Le R. P. Isaac Jogues . . . *Queb* 1874 D a
—Eng. tr. *N Y* 1885. D 263 map port
—eds 2 & 3, same impr & collat n.d.

[MARTIN, FELIX, and MONTEZON,   **331**
F. DE] eds.
Mission du Canada. Relations inédites . . . *P*
1861. D 2v: [40] 356; [2] 384. 2maps a

MARTIN, FRANCOIS-XAVIER   **332**
The history of Louisiana . . . *N O* 1827–9. O 2v:
[84] 364; [16] 429. aa
—rptd., with adds., *N O* 1882. O [38] 469 [16] port
plan facs aa

MARTIN, FRANCOIS-XAVIER   **333**
The history of North Carolina. *N O* 1829. O 2v:
[12] 326 + blank l. [114 + blank lf after p70]; [4]
412 aa

[MARTIN, FRANCOIS-XAVIER]   334
The independent citizen . . . majesty of the
people asserted against the usurpations of the
legislature of North Carolina . . . [Newbern
1787]. Q [2] 21 aa

MARTIN, GEORGE W.   335
The first two years of Kansas . . . Topeka 1907.
O 30 a

MARTIN, JACK   336
Border boss; Captain John R. Hughes—Texas
ranger. San Antonio 1942. D [16] 236 front. a

MARTIN, JOHN A.   337
Military history of the Eighth Kansas . . . Infantry. Leavenworth 1869. O 112 aa

MARTIN, JOHN H.   338
Columbus, Georgia . . . history . . . Columbus
1874–5. D 2v in 1[paged continuously] 362 aa

MARTIN, JOHN HILL   339
Historical sketch of Bethlehem, Pennsylvania.
Phil 1872. O [4] 3–191 port a 150copies ptd.

MARTIN, JOSEPH   340
A new and comprehensive gazetteer of Virginia
and the District of Columbia . . . Charlottesville
1835. O 636 map a
—rptd., same impr. & collat. 1836
—anr. ed. "A comprehensive description of Virginia . . . ," Rich n.d. same collat.

[MARTIN, JOSEPH P.]?   341
A narrative of some of the adventures . . . of a
revolutionary soldier. Hallowell 1830. D 213 aa
Experiences from Long Island to Yorktown.

MARTIN, LUDWIG   342
Der nordamerikanische Freistaat Texas . . .
Heilbronn 1847. D [8] 55 map aa
—rptd., same collat., Wiesbaden 1848. a

MARTIN, LUTHER   343
The genuine information . . . relative to the proceedings of the general convention . . . at Philadelphia . . . Phil 1788. O [8] 93 b AA BA NYP
Contained also in Yates, Robert, Secret proceedings . . . q.v.

MARTIN (MRS. MARIA).   344
History of the captivity and sufferings of: who
was six years a slave in Algiers . . . B 1807. O 72 pl a
—rptd. Brookfield 1818. 16° 125

MARTIN (COL. WILLIAM).   345
The self vindication of: against certain charges
. . . made against him by Gen. Andrew Jackson
. . . in relation to . . . transactions in the campaign
against the Creek Indians . . . Nash 1829. O 48 a

MARTIN, WILLIAM T.   346
History of Franklin county [O.]. Columbus
1858. O [6] 450 7pls a

MARTIN COUNTY   347
Martin county and other border counties of
southern Minnesota and upper Iowa. L [1876].
O 47 map a

MARTINEAU, HARRIET   348
Retrospect of western travel. L 1838. D 3v: [8]
318 [2]; [6] 292; [6] 294 a
—Am. ed. N Y 1838. D 2v: [6] 13–276; 239
—oth. Am. eds: Cin 1838, D 2v: 278; 252; N Y
1942, D 2v

[MARTINEAU, HARRIET]   349
A review of [her] work on "Society in America."
B 1837. O 54 a
Attributed to James Boyle and to—Wilkes.

MARTINEAU, HARRIET   350
Society in America. L 1837. D 3v: [19] 364; [6
incl blank lf] 369; [6 incl blank lf] 365 aa
—ed 2 same impr & collat a
—Am. ed. N Y 1837. D 2v: [20] 395; [4] 420
—Fr. tr.: Brus 1836. 16° 3v: rptd. 1838; P 1837 2v;
P 1839. O 2v
—Ger. tr. Cassell 1838. 2v in 1

MARTINELLI, VINCENZIO   351
Istoria del governo d'Inghilterra e delle sue
colonie in India, e nell' America . . . Florence
1776. O [8] 164 aa
—ed. 2, Pescia 1777. O [8] 190 a

MARTÍNEZ CARO, RAMON
See Caro, Ramon M.

[MARTINEZ DE YRUJO Y   352
TACON, CARLOS]
Communications concerning the agriculture and
commerce of America . . . [incl 2 papers on La.] L
1800. O [8] 120 aa
See Strickland, William, of Yorkshire, whose
Observations this supplements.

[MARTYN, BENJAMIN]   353
An account showing the progress of the colony
of Georgia . . . L 1741. F [2] 71 b
—anr. ed. L 1741. F [6] 68 b
—Am. ed. Annap 1742. Q [6] 56 aa
One of several replies to Tailfer's True and
historical narrative . . .

[MARTYN, BENJAMIN]   354
An impartial enquiry into the state and utility of
the province of Georgia. L 1741. O [4] 104 aa
Attributed also to John Percival, Earl of
Egmont.

[MARTYN, BENJAMIN]   355
A new and accurate account of . . . South Caro-
lina and Georgia . . . *L* 1732. O [4] 76 b
—anr. issue, identical, but with new t-p, *L* 1733. b
—Ger. ed. "Neuste und richtigste Nachricht von
der . . . Georgia . . .," *Göttingen* 1746. O 88 aa
Attributed also to General Oglethorpe, in whose
interest it was published.

[MARTYN, BENJAMIN]   356
Reasons for establishing the colony of Georgia
. . . *L* 1733. Q 39 map pl aa
—anr. issue, with adds. Q 48 map pl aa
—ed. 2, au. named, *L* 1733. Q 48 map pl a

MARTYRS
Martyrs to the revolution in the British prison
ships . . . *See* Taylor, George, of Pa.

MARVIN, FREDERIC R.   357
Yukon overland; the gold-digger's handbook.
Cin 1898. D 170 + 4adv-p map 18pls a

MARYLAND
**An address to the people of Maryland on the
origin . . . of French aggression . . .** *See* Dennis,
John.

An answer to the queries on the proprie-   358
tary government of Maryland . . . By a friend to
Maryland. [*Phil*?] 1764. O [2] 160 aa
Authorship has been variously ascribed to James
Tilghman, Secretary Calvert and Benjamin
Franklin.

Papers relating chiefly to the Maryland   359
line during the revolution. Edited by Thomas Balch.
Phil Seventy-Six Soc. 1857. O [4] 219 a 150 cops
ptd

**Personal reminiscences of a Maryland soldier in
the war between the states.** *See* Booth, George W.

**Political schemes . . . addressed to the citizens of
Maryland.** *See* Hanson, Alex. C.

The present state of Maryland. By the   360
delegates of the people. *Balt* ptd., *L* rptd. 1787. O
28 + 2adv-p a

A relation of Maryland. *N Y* 1865. Q [8]   361
103 map a 250copies [50 on L.P.] some copies
issued without the charter.
Reprint of the third publication on Maryland,
issued at London 1635, square 16mo, pages [2] 56,
25, map. b

A relation of the colony of the Lord Baron   362
of Baltimore, in Maryland . . . [*Wash* Force 1846].
O 47 a
—anr. ed., same collat., *Balt* 1847.

A relation of the successefull beginnings   363
of the Lord Baltemore's plantation in Mary-land.
[*Alb* 1865]. Q [2] 24 a 150copies[30 on L.P.]
Partial reprint of a sixteen-page tract published
at London 1634, in quarto, the earliest publication
on Maryland, aside from a 1633 eight-page tract.
Written either by Andrew White or Lord Baltimore.

Secret correspondence illustrating the   364
condition of affairs in Maryland. *Balt* 1863. O 42 a
Letters—captured by Stonewall Jackson from
Banks—from Union informers concerning southern sympathizers in Maryland.

[MASERES, FRANCIS]   365
Considerations on the expediency of admitting
representatives of the American colonies into the
. . . House of Commons. *L* 1770. O [2] 41 aa

[MASERES, FRANCIS]   366
A fair account of the late unhappy disturbance
at Boston . . . extracted from the depositions . . .
made concerning it . . . *L* 1770. O 28 [31] b H
Justifies the Boston massacre on the grounds
that the British soldiers were provoked to it; the
Tory reply to the patriot faction's *Short narrative
of the horrid massacre, see* under Boston.

[MASERES, FRANCIS]   367
Occasional essays on various subjects, chiefly
political and historical . . . *L* 1809. O [16] 607 a

MASON (JEREMIAH).   368
Memoir and correspondence of: . . . *C* 1873.
O [8] 467 port aa
—enl. ed. *K C* 1917. O [16] 491 ports a

MASON, MAJ. JOHN   369
A brief history of the Pequot war . . . *B* 1736.
D [18] 22 d AA N NYP Y
—rptd. *N Y* 1869. O 20 a
Written by a leading participant; most reliable
contemporary account.

MASON, JONATHAN, JR.   370
An oration . . . to commemorate the bloody
tragedy of the fifth of March, 1770. *B* 1780. Q 28 aa

MASON, DR. PHILIP   371
A legacy for my children . . . his autobiography
. . . *Cin* 1868. O 610 port aa
Settled in Indiana in 1816. Describes trips made
in the '50s and '60s, throughout Michigan, Wis-
consin, Iowa and Nebraska.

MASON (RICHARD LEE)   372
in the pioneer west, 1819.
Narrative of: *N Y* [1915]. O 74 port a 160 copies
ptd[10 on Jap. vell.]

MASON, Z. H.   373
A general description of Orange County [Fla.]
. . . *Orlando* [1881]. O 56 map a

MASSACHUSETTENSIS . . .
See Leonard, Danl.

MASSACHUSETTS   374
The book of the general lawes and libertyes concerning the inhabitants of the Massachusetts . . .
C 1660. F [2] 88 [8] dd AA MH NYP
—rptd. with revisions. *C* 1672. F [2] 170 [27] fold
tab d AA MH
—Eng. ed. *L* 1675. F same collat b AA JCB
—anr. ed. *B* 1887. a
Earliest Massachusetts laws of which there
exists a copy. Of an earlier printing—*Cambridge*
1649—no copy has survived.

A brief state of the services and expences   375
[*sic*] of . . . Massachusett's Bay in the common
cause. *L* 1765. O 24 a

The case of the provinces of Massachusetts-Bay
and New York respecting the boundary line . . .
See Hutchinson, Thomas.

A collection of original papers relative to the
history of the colony of Massachusetts-Bay. *See*
Hutchinson, Thos., *The history of Massachusetts-
Bay* . . .

A conference between the commissaries   376
of Massachusetts-Bay and the commissaries of
New-York [concerning boundary line]. *B* 1768. Q
[2] 26 [2] b NYP

A journal of a young man of Massachusetts. *See*
Waterhouse, Benj.

Life and adventures of Robert, the hermit   377
of Massachusetts who has lived 14 years in a cave,
secluded from human society . . . *Prov* 1829. 16°
36 a
Unusual narrative of a fugitive slave.

Massachusetts or the first planters of New-
England. *See* Scottow, Joshua.

A narrative of the planting of the Massachusetts
colony . . . *see* Scottow, Joshua.

The origin of the American contest . . . or, the
present political state of the Massachusetts-Bay.
See Leonard, Danl.

Papers relating to the public events in   378
Massachusetts preceding the . . . revolution. *Phil*
Seventy-Six Soc. 1856. O [4] 199 aa

The present political state of Massachusetts-Bay
. . . By a native of New England. *See* Leonard,
Danl.

The proceedings of the General assembly   379
. . . of Massachusetts-Bay relating to the Penobscot
expedition . . . *B* 1780. Q 29 c AA N

The report of the Lords committees, ap-   380
pointed to enquire into the several proceedings in the
colony of Massachusett's Bay . . . *L* 1774. F [2] 35 a
—anr. ed., same impr. & date. O 62

A short view of the history of . . . Massachusetts
Bay. *See* Mauduit, Israel.

A speech intended to have been spoken on the bill
for altering the charters of . . . Massachusett's Bay.
See Shipley, Jonathan.

A speech never intended to be spoken, in   381
answer to A speech intended to have been spoken on
the bill for altering the charter of . . . Massachuset's
Bay. *L* 1774. O [4] 34 [1] aa
—rptd., same impr. & date. O [14] 35 a

Statistical tables relating to Massachusetts.   382
Worc 1839. 32° 32 map a

MASSEY, S[TEPHEN] L.   383
James' Traveler's companion . . . *Cin* 1851. 16°
224 2 maps b

MASSIE, JAMES W.   384
America: . . . illustrated by incidents of travel
. . . from . . . Maine to the Mississippi. *L* 1864.
O [8] 472 map a

MASSON, L[OUIS] F[RANCOIS] R.   385
Les bourgeois de la Compagnie du Nordouest
. . . *Quebec* 1889–90. O 2v: [10] 154 415; [6] 499.
map b N NYP Y rptd *N Y* 1960. aa
Includes many journals and narratives of early
Indian traders in the lake region, Rockies and
Upper Missouri.

[MATHER, COTTON]   386
Decennium luctuosum . . . occurences, in the
long war . . . with the Indian salvages . . . 1688–
1698. *B* 1699. D 254 [1] d NYP

MATHER (COTTON).   387
The diary of: 1681–1724. *B* 1911–12. O 2v: [28]
604; [16] 860. fold.map port facs aa

MATHER, COTTON   388
Duodecennium luctuosum. The history of a long
war with Indian salvages . . . *B* 1714. D [2] 30 c
AA MH NYP

Recapitulation of New England Indian wars, from 1702 to 1714; continuing the author's *Decennium luctuosum* [covering wars from 1688 to 1698].

[MATHER, COTTON]   389
Humiliations follow'd with deliverances... from the hands of cruel Indians... *B* 1697. D 72 c Hn
Includes the famous five-year captivity of Hannah Dustin [here spelled Swarton].

MATHER, COTTON   390
India Christiana. A discourse, delivered unto the Commissioners, for the Propagation of the Gospel among the... Indians... *B* 1721. D [4] 94[p52–55 on double-pages] + errata slip b AA BP H NYP Y

MATHER, COTTON   391
Magnalia Christi Americana... ecclesiastical history of New England... 1620–1698. *L* 1702. F 7bks in 1: [28 incl. initial blank l.] 38; [2] 76; [2] 238; [2] 125–222; 100; [2] 88; 118 + 4adv-p[in some copies 2] map b AA N NYP Y some copies ptd on L. P. copies containing 2errata l. have had them inserted as they were not issued with the book, but were ptd later, in *B* c AA
—Am. eds.: *Hart* 1820, O 2v: 573; 595 a; *Hart* 1853–5, O 2v: [43] 13–626; 682 port; *Hart* 1870, O 2v port a
Most famous 18th century American book.

MATHER, COTTON   392
Memorable providences, relating to witchcrafts... in New-England... *B* 1689. D [10] 75, 21, 40 [2] 14 d AA JCB
—Eng. ed. "Late memorable providences..." *L* 1691. D [22] 144 b BP
—rptd. "Memorable providences..." *Edin* 1697. D [6] 102 a Hn JCB [of 4 cops loc]

MATHER, COTTON   393
Parentator. Memoirs of remarkables in the life and death of... Dr. Increase Mather. *B* 1724. D [26] 239 [5] port b AA N NYP Y
—anr. ed. *B* 1741. O 256 aa
—Eng. ed. abr., with new pref., no au. named, "Memoirs of... Reverend Increase Mather...," *L* 1725. O [8] 88 port aa

[MATHER, COTTON]   394
Pietas in patriam: the life of... Sir William Phips... governour in chief of... Massachuset-Bay... *L* 1697. D [12] 110 [8] + 2 adv-p b Hn JCB N
—rptd "The life of Sir William Phips". *N Y* 1929. O [12] 208 [2] a

MATHER, COTTON   395
The present state of New-England... *B* 1690. D [2] 52 b Hn JCB Y

MATHER, COTTON   396
The short history of New-England... *B* 1694. D 68 d AA JCB [only cops loc]

[MATHER, COTTON and INCREASE]   397
Some few remarks, upon a scandalous book... by one Robert Calef... *B* 1701. O 72 b AA NYP

MATHER, COTTON   398
The triumphs of the reformed religion... life of the renowned John Eliot... *B* 1691. O [10] 152 b AA Hn
—Eng. ed. "Life... of John Eliot". *L* 1691. O [6] 3–138 aa
—rptd. *L* 1694. D [8] 168 + 4adv-p aa

MATHER, COTTON   399
The wonders of the invisible world... the operations of the devils, etc. *B* 1693. D [32] 152,8 17–32 dd AA JCB
—Eng. ed., with subtitle: "An account of the tryals of... witches, lately executed in New England..." *L* 1693. smQ [4] 98 [so numbered but really 106] + 2adv-p c Hn NYP
—Eng. eds. 2 & 3: somewhat abr, same impr & date. b
—rptd. *L* 1862. D [16] 291 a
First lengthy account of the judicial murders of so-called Salem witches, written approvingly by the most learned New England Puritan of his age; the classic example of religious frenzy sanctifying intolerance and delusion.

MATHER, INCREASE   400
A brief history of the war with the Indians in New-England... *B* 1676. D [6] 52; 8 [4] 26 dd AA JCB Y
—Eng. ed. *L* 1676. D [8] 52 [8] c H JCB LC N
—rptd. "The history of King Philips' war..." *B* 1862. Q 281 2ports fldg chart 261 cops ptd of which 11 were on L. P. a
Titles of both early editions call for *An earnest exhortation* but that portion was not included in the English issue.

MATHER, INCREASE   401
Cases of conscience concerning evil spirits... witchcrafts, etc. *B* 1693. D [6] 67 [7] c AA NYP
—Eng. ed. [as part of "A further account of the tryals of the New England witches..."] *L* 1693. O [2] 10, [4] 40 [6] b AA H JCB

MATHER, INCREASE   402
An essay for the recording of illustrious providences... memorable events... especially in New-England. *B* 1684. D [22] 372 [9] d AA N Y
—anr. ed., same date & collat, ptd at *B* to be sold in *L* c JCB NYP
—rptd. "Remarkable providences..." *L* 1856. D [38] 262 port a
First New England book to discuss witchcraft.

MATHER, INCREASE
A further account of the tryals of the New-England witches ... See above, "Cases of conscience".

[MATHER, INCREASE]   404
The life ... of ... Mr. Richard Mather ... C 1670. Q [4] 38 port [first one eng in America] b BP MassH
—rptd. Dorchester 1850. D a

MATHER, INCREASE   405
A relation of the troubles ... in New-England, by reason of the Indians there ... B 1677. smQ [6] 76; [6] 19 d JCB NYP N
—anr. iss. has only 4prel p in pt 2 ["Historical discourse"] d MassH
—rptd. "Early history of New England" Alb–or– B 1864. Q 309 port a

MATHER, JAMES   406
Two lectures, delivered at Newcastle-upon-Tyne, on the constitutions and republican institutions of the United States ... Newcastle-upon-Tyne 1840. D [10] 90 [2] a

MATHER, MOSES   407
America's appeal to the impartial world ... Hart 1775. O [72] b AA BA NYP Y

MATHER (MR. RICHARD).
The life ... of: See Mather, Increase.

[MATHER, SAMUEL]   408
An attempt to shew, that America must be known to the ancients ... B 1773. O 35 aa

MATHER, SAMUEL   409
The life of ... Cotton Mather ... B 1729. O [8] 6, 10, 186 aa
—Eng. ed., abr. by David Jennings. L 1744. D [16] 143 a
—rptd. Leeds 1802; Edin 1822.

MATHEWS' ... TRIP TO AMERICA.
Sketches of: ... See Smith, James.

MATHEWS, ALFRED E.   410
Canyon City, Colorado ... N Y 1870. Q 24 map 5col pls b

MATHEWS, ALFRED E.   411
Gems of Rocky mountain scenery ... N Y 1869. Q 23 lvs 20pls b LC

MATHEWS (ALFRED E.)   412
Interesting narrative; being a journal of the flight of: from the state of Texas ... across the states of Louisiana, Arkansas and Missouri. [New Philadelphia O] 1861. O [2] 7–34 [2] b LC S

MATHEWS, ALFRED E.   413
Pencil sketches of Colorado. N Y 1866. obl F 16 front. 23col.pls c G NYP Y

MATHEWS, ALFRED E.   414
Pencil sketches of Montana. N Y 1868. Q [6] 95[incl. 31pls front.] d G MontH NYP WashU Y

MATHEWS, EDWARD J.   415
Crossing the plains ... in '59. n.p. [1930?]. 16° 91 aa

MATHEWS, LOIS K.   416
The expansion of New England ... to the Mississippi river, 1620–1865. B 1909. O [16] 304 27maps a

MATHEWS, MARY McN   417
Ten years in Nevada ... Buf 1880. O 343 [incl front] 2ports aa

MATSON, N[EHEMIAH]   418
Map of Bureau county, Illinois, with sketches of its early settlement. Chi 1867. Sm O 88 8pls 26maps aa
—ed 2, same impr, date & format, 108 8pls 26maps a
The larger map, alone, of which the 26 sections were embodied here, was issued at Chicago in 1858.

MATSON, N[EHEMIAH]   419
French and Indians of Illinois river. Princeton Ill 1874. D 5–260 a
—ed. 2, same impr. & date. D [10 incl.final blank l.] 15–270

MATSON, N[EHEMIAH]   420
Memories of Shaubena ... Chi 1878. D [8] 17–269[incl.pls] front. a
—ed. 2, Chi 1880. D 7–252[incl.front & pls]
—ed. 3, Chi 1882. D [4] 13–252[incl.front. & pls]

MATSON, N[EHEMIAH]   421
The pioneers of Illinois ... Chi 1882. D [2] 11–306 port a

MATSON, N[EHEMIAH]   422
Reminiscences of Bureau county, Illinois ... Princeton Ill 1872. O 2pts in 1: [10] 15–212[incl. final blank l.]; [8] 232–406 front. & 15pls all incl. in paginat. a rptd., 1937 200 cops.

MATTHES, BENNO   423
Reise-Bilder. Bilder aus Texas. Dresden 1861. D [8] 104 a

MATTHEWS, FREDERICK C.   424
American merchant ships. Salem 1930–31. O 2v: [16] 400; [12] 359. 47pls Also 97 copies on L.P., Q 2v aa

Supplements *American clipper ships* by Howe and Matthews.

MATTHEWS, LYMAN   **425**
History of . . . Cornwall, Vermont. *Middlebury* 1862. O 356 8pls a

MATTHEWS, SALLIE R.   **426**
Interwoven, a pioneer chronicle [of Texas ranch life]. *Houst* 1936. D [12] 234 port aa

MATTHEWS, WASHINGTON   **427**
Navajo legends . . . *B* 1897. O [8] 299 map 7pls a

MATTHEWS, W[ILLIAM] B.   **428**
The settlers' map and guide book. Oklahoma . . . *Wash* 1889. O 66 [incl front wrap] map aa
—anr. ed., with app., *Wash* dated 1889[but actually 1890]. O 84 map slip of commendation inserted at t-p [cover-t.reads *Topeka* 1890]. aa

[MAUDE, JOHN]   **429**
Visit to the falls of Niagara, in 1800. *L* 1826. O [18] 313 [27] + [in some copies 16p, not issued until later and inserted] 8pls aa 300copies[50 on L. P.]

[MAUDUIT, ISRAEL]   **430**
Remarks upon Gen. Howe's Account of his proceedings on Long Island . . . *L* 1778. O [4] 54 aa
—ed. 2, same impr., date & collat. a

[MAUDUIT, ISRAEL]   **431**
A short view of the history of . . . Massachusetts Bay . . . *L* 1769. O [2] 71 a
—ed. 2, with charter added, *L* 1774. O [4] 93
—ed. 3, with adds., *L* 1774.
—ed. 4, t.altered, with 1764 conference between Grenville and colonial agents added, *L* 1776. O [2] 100
Strives to prove that this colony's charter was not exempt from Parliamentary authority.

[MAUDUIT, ISRAEL]   **432**
Some thoughts on the method of improving . . . the advantages which accrue to Great-Britain from the northern colonies. *L* 1765. O [4] 23 a

[MAUDUIT, ISRAEL]   **433**
Strictures on the Philadelphia mischianza or triumph upon leaving America unconquered . . . *L* 1779. O [4] 42 aa
—Am. ed. *Phil* 1780. O 22 a
The strictures are directed principally against Gen. Howe's conduct.

[MAUDUIT, ISRAEL]   **434**
Three letters to Lieutenant-General Sir William Howe. *L* 1781. O [4] 44 41-48 map a
Not to be confused with this author's *Three letters to Lord Viscount Howe* . . .

[MAUDUIT, ISRAEL]   **435**
Three letters to Lord Viscount Howe . . . *L* 1780. O [4] 47 a
—ed. 2, with adds., *L* 1781. O 48 map
Attributed also to Joseph Galloway. Highly critical of both Admiral and General Howe.

[MAULE, THOMAS]?   **436**
Tribute to Caesar . . . with some remarks on the . . . expedition against Canada . . . [*Phil* 1715?]. sm Q [6] 29 d NYP PaH
The "tribute" was the tax levied for this expedition.

MAUN-GWU-DAUS.   **437**
An account of the North American Indians, written for: . . . *Leicester Eng* 1848. O 24 aa
—Am. ed., t. altered, *B* 1848. a

MAURELLE [or MOURELLE],   **438**
FRANCISCO A.
Journal of a voyage in 1775, to explore the coast of America, northward of California . . . [*L* 1781]. Q [10]3–67 map c B G LC
—Am. ed. *S F* 1920. Q [12] 121 port 2maps aa 230copies ptd.
This translation of a Spanish MS. formed part of Daines Barrington's *Miscellanies* [*q.v.*]. Only a few copies were issued [previously?] in this separate form. Maurelle was pilot on the expedition under Heceta and Quadra, which followed that under Perez, of 1774; these were the earliest Spanish voyages to Alaska, and of them this is the only contemporary account.

MAURY (MRS. BETTY H.)   **439**
The Confederate diary of: . . . *Wash* 1938. O [4] 102 port a 25copies ptd.

MAURY, DABNEY H.   **440**
Recollections of a Virginian in the Mexican, Indian and civil wars. *N Y* 1894. O [12] 280 port a
—Eng. ed same sheets *L* 1894
—eds 2 & 3, same collat *N Y* 1894.

MAURY, RICHARD L.   **441**
A brief sketch of the work of Matthew Fontaine Maury . . . 1861–1865. *Rich* 1915. D 36 a

MAURY, SARAH M.   **442**
An Englishwoman in America. *L* 1848. O [4 118] 251 [2] 204 [2] + 16p of reviews a
—rptd. *L* 1856. O 576

MAVERICK (MARY A.)   **443**
Memoirs of: ed. R. M. Green. *San Antonio* 1921. O 136 16pls a
First woman from the States to settle in San Antonio. In first issue line 5 of p. 63 continued on line 24 p. 69.

MAXIMILIAN, prinz zu Wied-Neuwied   443a
Reise in das innere Nord-America, 1832–4. *Coblenz* 1839–41. Text: Q 2v: [16] 654 [2]; [24] 688 [2]. plan[of Ft. Clark, etc.] key-pl["Lithographie der 21sten Tafel"] & fold. tab[of temperatures], the latter two probably sent to subscribers, after pub., to be inserted in vol.II at p. 686 & 688, are frequently lacking. Pls: 43 large-size pls & 38 small-size vignettes, sometimes all bound in one vol., F, with t-p, sometimes in 2v[large ones in F, vignettes in Q]; these pls differ from those in the English and French eds. in not containing any English letterpress. A map [completed after the German ed. was pub.] is found inserted, generally in the Atlas, but often in vol.II of the text, just as the key-pl and temperature chart are often found in the Atlas instead of in the text. With all pls col. dd N NYP
—Eng. tr., much abr. & without pls, *L* 1839. O 2v a
—most complete Eng. tr., omitting all vocabularies, *L* 1843. Q [12] 520 map + Atlas[same pls as in Fr. ed.]. With all pls col. dd N NYP Y
—Fr. tr., omitting most of the vocabularies, *P* 1840–41–43. O 3v: [6] 383; [6] 487; [14] 410 map + Atlas[of same 81pls as in Ger. ed., but all on folio sheets and with titles in Ger., Fr. & Eng.] With all pls col. dd N NYP Y
—Am. ed., ed. by Thwaites, *Clev* 1906. O 3v + Atlas F [map & 81 black & white pls] a
The same atlas—issued in Paris—was used with all of the above editions. It came with all plates uncolored, with some only colored and with all colored. In the latter state, as originally issued, with the last name of the artist—Charles Bodmer—stamped in blind on each of the forty-eight large plates, this work is the most beautiful, faithful and vivid ever produced depicting western plains and Indians. In 1844 a London engraver, Lumley, reproduced the atlas, even to its title-page, but the inferiority of its plates and the absence of Bodmer's stamp make it readily distinguishable. At Leipsic, early in the 20th century, plates were re-issued [with brief letterpress descriptions] in an edition of 100 copies from the original plates under the title *Nord-Amerika in Bildern*; some of these are found finely colored, but none were so issued.

MAXWELL, A[RCHIBALD] M.   444
A run through the United States ... *L* 1841. D 2v: [22] 310; [12] 261. 2ports a

MAXWELL, HU   445
History of Tucker county, W. Va. *Kingwood W Va* 1884. O 574 28pls a

MAXWELL, JOHN   446
The American patriot and hero ... memoir of ... General Washington ... [*Lancaster Pa*] 1785 [error for 1795]. D 94 [error for 64] errata lf b
One of the earliest biographies of Washington.

MAXWELL, THOMAS   447
Tuskaloosa [Ala.] ... its history ... *Tuskaloosa* 1876. O 86 aa

MAY, CHARLES   448
The pioneers of Nashville ... *Nashv* 1880. 16° 157 a

MAY, ENOCH   449
The olio ... Also some of the exploits of Walker, May, Ringgold, Sackett, and others, in Texas and Mexico. *Indp* 1846. D 144 aa

MAY (COLONEL JOHN).   450
Journal and letters of: relative to two journeys to the Ohio country ... 1788–9. *Cin* 1873. O 160 a

MAYER, BRANTZ   451
Tah-Gah-Jute, or Logan and Captain Michael Cresap ... *Balt* 1851. O 86 + errata lf a
—enl. ed. t. slightly altered, *Alb* 1867. O [14] 204
Refutes Jefferson's accusations against Cresap.

MAXHEW, EVPERIENCE   452
Indian converts ... lives ... of the Christianized Indians of Martha's Vineyard ... *L* 1727. O [24] 310 + advs aa

MAYNARDE, THOMAS   453
Sir Francis Drake, his voyage, 1595 ... *L* Hakluyt Soc 1849. O [10] 65 [12] a

MAYO, ROBERT   454
Political sketches of eight years in Washington ... *Balt* 1839. O [14] 216 facs a
Part I [all published] of a virulent attack on Jackson's administration.

MAZZEI (FILIPPO).   455
Memorie della vita e delle peregrinazioni del: ... *Lugano* 1845–6. 16° 2v: [4] 547; 352 aa
—Eng. tr *N Y* 1942 O [16] 447 2pls a
Significant autobiography by an intimate of Adams, Franklin and Jefferson and an active co-worker with them in the revolutionary movement.

[MAZZEI, FILIPPO]   456
Recherches historiques et politiques sur les États-Unis. *P* 1788. O 4v: [20] 384; [4] 259; [4] 292; [4] 366 aa
The author, Italian by birth, lived in Virginia near his friend Thomas Jefferson, who may have assisted in this work.

MAZZUCHELLI, SAMUELE   457
Memorie istoriche ed edificanti d'uno missionario apostolico ... *Milan* 1844. O 364 3maps front. b S WisH
—Eng. tr., with adds., *Chi* 1915. O [26] 375 2maps 2pls + extra half t. not incl. in paginat. a

Missionary labors in Iowa, Wisconsin and Michigan from 1830.

[MEAD, BRADOCK]   458
Remarks in support of the New chart of North and South America . . . *L* 1753. Q [6] 3-48 map[on 6 sheets]dated 1753 b H N Y
—anr. issue, map undated b
One of the earliest English treatises on the Russian discoveries on the Northwest coast, and the first book to give Bering's name to the straits separating Asia and America; notable, too, for exposing the cartographical errors made by Buache and Delisle in accepting Fonte's fictions.

MEAD, DANIEL M.   459
A history of . . . Greenwich [Conn.]. *N Y* 1857. D [8] 13-318 a
—best ed. *N Y* 1911.

MEAD, EDWARD C.   460
Historic homes of the south-west mountains of Virginia. *Phil* 1899. O 275 map 23 pls a 750copies ptd.

MEAD, WHITMAN   461
Travels in North America. *N Y* 1820. O 2pts in 1 [all]: 160 aa
Title page calls for a third part, which was not included.

MEADE, BISHOP [WILLIAM]   462
Old churches, ministers and families of Virginia. *Phil* 1857. O 2v: 490; 496. 22pls aa
—rptd., same impr. & collat.: 1861; 1878; 1889; 1897. a
—later eds. omitted pls, but incl. 114-p index, by Wise.

MEADER, J. W.   463
The Merrimack river . . . towns along its course . . . *B* 1869. O 307 map a

MEAGHER (GOV. THOMAS F.)   464
Lectures of: . . . Comp. John P. Bruce. *Va C Mont* 1867. O 104 b Mont H Y [of 4 cops loc]

MEALEY, TOBIAS G.   465
. . . Journal . . . during a 175 days sailing voyage . . . from Maine to California, 1849–50. *Minneap* 1904. O 60 a

MEARES, DIXON, PORTLAK   466
(DEN KAPITAINEN)
Reisen nach der nordwestlichen Küste von Amerika von: *Nurnberg* 1795. O 440 aa

MEARES, JOHN   467
An answer to Mr. George Dixon . . . In which the remarks of Mr. Dixon . . . are fully considered and refuted. *L* 1791. Q 32 b

For work answered and rejoinder made to this reply, *see* Dixon, George

MEARES, JOHN   468
. . . Memorial [on capture of his ships at Nootka]. [*L* 1790]. F 31 tab capt.t.only b JCB WashU
—anr. ed. *L* 1760 [i.e. 1790]. O [2] 65 b
—rptd. *L* 1810. O aa
—Am. ed. *Port* 1933. O [16] 93 300 cops ptd a
This was included in the author's *Voyages . . .*, *see* below.

MEARES, JOHN   469
Voyages . . . to the north west coast of America, 1788–9. *L* 1790. Q [20 96] 372 [108] port 26 maps & pls [in some cops an extra pl., of the Philippines, at p. 17] b N NYP Y
—anr. ed. *L* 1791. O 2v: [84] 363; [4] 332 [63]. port 13maps & pls tab aa
—Fr. tr. *P* [1794]. O 3v: [24] 391; [4] 386; [2] 372. port & Q atlas 27maps & pls aa
—Ger. tr: *Berlin* 1791; 1796.
—Ital. trs.: *Naples* 1796. O 4v map 12pls 7 charts [on 6 lvs] aa; *Florence* 1796 O 4v map 22pls aa *Turin* 1797 a, Swed. tr. [abr.] *Stockh* 1797; Rus. tr. St *Ptbg* 1797.
Pioneer English voyage to this coast, supplying the chief basis to British claims to Oregon. Spanish pretensions to territory beyond California were relinquished in the treaty following England's remonstrance over the seizure of Meare's ships, anchored off Nootka.

MEASE, JAMES   470
A geological account of the United States. *Phil* 1807. 16° 496 [14] 5pls a

MEASE, JAMES   471
The picture of Philadelphia . . . *Phil* 1811. D [12] 376 pl a
—anr. ed. "Picture of Philadelphia for 1824," containing adds. to 1811 ed., *Phil* 1823. D 72 85–96 [4 3–12] 358 3pls
—rptd. *Phil* 1831. D 2v: [12] 358; [8] 128. pls

MECKLENBURG COUNTY [N.C.]   472
The declaration of independence by the citizens of: on . . . the twentieth day of May, 1775 . . . *Raleigh* 1831. O 32 aa

[MEDINA, ANTONIO DE]   473
Memoria presentada al soberano congresso mexicano por el Secretario de Estado . . . *Mex* 1822. O 29 fold chart b
Includes account of California, the earliest printed in the Mexican Republic.

MEEK, ALEXANDER B.   474
The claims and characteristics of Alabama history . . . *Mobile* 1858. O 65 aa

MEEK, A[LEXANDER] B.   475
Romantic passages in southwestern history . . .
N Y 1857. D 330
—3 other eds., same collat. & date, some with
Mobile impr.

MEEK, A[LEXANDER] B.   476
The southwest: its history . . . *Tuscaloosa* 1840.
O 40 aa
Relates to the Alabama-Mississippi-Louisiana
region.

MEEKER, EZRA   477
Pioneer reminiscences of Puget sound, the tragedy of Leschi . . . *Seattle* 1905. O [20] 554 25pls
2facs a

MEEKER, EZRA   478
Washington Territory west of the Cascade
mountains . . . *Olympia* 1870. O 52 [24] + 6adv-p
b G NYP PortOreL WashU Y
—rptd. [1920]. O 52
A large part of the edition was bought up by Jay
Cooke in the interest of the Northern Pacific R. R.
It was the first description of this Territory printed
within its confines.

MEEKER, JOSEPHINE
The Ute massacre! *See* that title.

MEGINNESS, JOHN F.   479
Biography of Francis Slocum . . . her captivity
. . . *Williamsport Pa* 1891. O 238 [12] 6pls a

MEGINNESS, J[OHN] F.   480
Otzinachson; or, a history of the West Branch
valley of the Susquehanna . . . *Phil* 1857. O 518
15pls a
—rev. ed. [calling itself V. I] *Williamsport Pa* 1889.
O 702 [5]

MEIGS, CHARLES D.   481
A biographical notice of Daniel Drake . . . *Phil*
1853. O 38 aa

MEIGS (RETURN J.)
An appeal to the people: or, an exposition of the
official conduct of: . . . *See* Hart, Wm.

MEIGS, MAJOR RET[URN] J.   482
A journal of occurrences . . . in the detachment
commanded by . . . Arnold . . . n.p. n.d. [1776]
sm Q 11 b MH.
—anr. ed. "Journal of the expedition against Quebec . . .," *N Y* 1864. O 57 port a

MEIGS, WILLIAM M.   483
The life of John Caldwell Calhoun. *N Y* 1917.
O 2v: 456; [8] 7–478. 12pls a
—rptd. *N Y* [1925?]. O 2v

MEIN, JOHN, and FLEEMING, JOHN   484
Register for New England . . . *B* [1767]. 18° 92
[4] a

[MEIN, JOHN]   485
Sagittarius's letters and political speculations . . .
B 1775. O [2] 127 aa
A Tory publication emphasizing the rebellious
conduct of the New England Puritan element.

[MEIN, JOHN]   486
A state of the importations from Great-Britain
into the port of Boston . . . *B* 1769. Q [4] 130 aa

MELBOURN (JULIUS).   487
Life and opinions of: with sketches of . . .
Thomas Jefferson, John Quincy Adams, *et al.*
Syracuse. 1847. D 239 pl a

MELINE, JAMES F.   488
Two thousand miles on horseback. Santa Fe and
back . . . *N Y* 1867. D [10] 317 map a
—rptd., same impr. & collat. 1868.

MELISH, JOHN   489
A description of the roads in the United States
. . . *Phil* 1814. D [11] 82columns[i.e., 41p] a
—rptd. 1815. D [12] 88 columns[i.e., 44p] 89–97.
—anr. ed. "The traveller's directory through the
United States; being a complete list of the . . .
roads," *Phil* 1819. D 102 2maps.
—rptd. 1822. D [20] 183 2maps; *N Y* 1825. D [20]
194 2maps

MELISH, JOHN   490
A geographical description of the United States
. . . *Phil* 1815. D 32 3maps a
—enl. ed., "A geographical description of the
United States, with the contiguous British and
Spanish possessions," *Phil* 1816. O 182 errata-l.
5maps
—ed. 2, *Phil* 1816. O 182 5maps
—ed. 3, *Phil* 1818. O 186 4maps
—new ed. *Phil* 1822. O [4] 491 [15] 12maps [of 14
listed]
—rptd.: *N Y* 1826, O 497 [15] 12maps; *Phil* 1850
Issued to accompany Melish's *Map of the United
States*, which was sold separately and accompanied
none of the editions. This large map [35″ × 57″]
was the first presenting the entire country, from
coast to coast, and the first to show South Pass. *cf.*
below, *A statistical account* . . .

MELISH, JOHN   491
Information and advice to emigrants . . . *Phil*
1819. 16° [8] 144 2maps a

MELISH, JOHN   492
A military and topographical atlas of the United
States . . . *Phil* 1813. O [6] 3–34; 3–18; 3–29; 44
8maps & plans aa

—rptd. *Phil* 1815. same collat., except 12 maps & plans a

MELISH, JOHN   **493**
A statistical account of the United States . . . *Phil* 1814. D 32 a
—rptd. "A statistical view of the United States . . .," *Phil* 1822. D 45; *N Y* 1825. D 41
—for enl. eds., *see* above, *A geographical description*, [*etc.*]. *cf.* also the two entries immediately below

MELISH, JOHN   **494**
The traveller's directory through the United States: consisting of a geographical description . . . *Phil* 1814. D 2pts in 1: [4] 32; 82 aa
—other *Phil* eds. with maps: 1815; 1816; 1818; 1819. D 134 + 14p calendar 4single sheet maps [and, in special pocket-form copies, 2 extra fold. maps] aa
—anr. ed. *Phil* 1822. D [20] 183 2fold.maps a
—new ed., enl., *N Y* 1825. D [20] 194 2 maps

[MELISH, JOHN]   **495**
The traveller's manual; and description of the United States . . . *N Y* 1831. D 498 [15] a
—other eds.: "The North American tourist . . .," *N Y* 1840. D [10] 506 12maps 5 views; *N Y* 1841; also an undated ed. to which some authorities give precedence on the belief of its having appeared in 1839, but maps in all three eds. bear 1840 dates

MELISH, JOHN   **496**
Travels in the United States . . . 1806–7 and 1809–11 . . . *Phil* 1812. O 2v: [24] 444; [10] 492. 8maps & plans 2tabs errata 1f aa
—rptd., same collat., 1815. a
—anr. ed. with adds. *Phil* 1818. O 648 8 maps & plans 2tabs
—Eng. eds: all dated 1818, same collat.: *L*; *Belf*; *Dub* aa
—Ger. eds: *Weimar* 1819, 16° [18] 378 9maps *Leip* 1821. a

MELLEN, GEORGE W. F.   **497**
An argument on the unconstitutionality of slavery . . . *B* 1841. D 440 a

MELLICK, ANDREW D.   **498**
The story of an old farm, or life in New Jersey in the eighteenth century . . . *Somerville N J* 1889. O [26] 743 4pls a

MELLON (THOMAS)   **499**
Mellon (Thomas) and his times. *Pitt* 1885. O [2] 648 [8] pls aa

MELODY, G[EORGE] H. C.   **500**
Notice sur les Indiens Ioways . . . venu des plaines du Haut-Missouri . . . *P* 1845. D 24 8pls aa
These were the Indians exhibited by George Catlin.

MELSHEIMER, F[REDERICK] V.   **501**
Tagebuch von der Reise der Braunschweigischen auxiliär Truppen von Wolfenbüttel nach Quebec . . . *Minden* 1776. 16° 40 32 b H

MELVILLE, HERMAN   **502**
Israel Potter: his fifty years of exile. *N Y* 1855. D 276
—issue 1, perfect type, top of p113 a
—Eng. ed., same date, but issued 2weeks later, *L*
For earlier form, *see* Trumbull, Henry.

MELVIN, JAMES   **503**
A journal of the expedition to Quebec . . . under . . . Arnold. *N Y* 1857. O [8] 30 a some copies on L. P.
—rptd. *Phil* 1864. O [8] 34 120 copies [20 on L. P.]
—anr. ed., with adds., *Port Me* 1902. Q 90 port 250 copies ptd.

[MEMMINGER, CHRISTOPHER G.]   **504**
The book of nullification . . . *Charleston S C* 1830. O 31 a
Satirizes the movement.

MEMMINGER, C[HRISTOPHER] G.   **505**
Lecture . . . showing African slavery to be consistent with the moral and physical progress of a nation. *Augusta Ga* 1851. O 25 a

[MEMMINGER, CHRISTOPHER G.]   **506**
The mission of South Carolina to Virginia. *Balt* [1861]. O 34 a
—anr. ed. n.p. n.d. same collat.

MÉMOIRE
Mémoire contenant les précis des faits . . . *See* Moreau, Jacob N.

Mémoire historique sur la négociation de   **507**
la France et de l'Angleterre, depuis de 26 Mars 1761 jusqu'au 20 Septembre de la même année . . . *P* 1761. O [6] 197 some copies on L.P. aa
—oth eds: *L* 1761, Q 60; *Amst* 1761, D [6] 160 aa
—Eng. tr. "An historical memorial . . .," *L* 1761. O 64 aa
Preliminaries to the definitive treaty of 1762, ending the French and Indian war. Editorship has been ascribed to Jean F. de Bastide and to the Duke de Choiseul.

Mémoire justificatif de la conduite de la Grande Bretagne . . . *See* Marriott, James.

Mémoire justificatif pour servir de réponse . . . *See* Gibbon, Edw.

MÉMOIRES   **508**
Mémoires des commissaires du roi et de ceux de sa majesté britannique, sur les possessions . . . en Amérique . . . *P* 1755–7. Q 4v: [84] 181 61 [108]

120; [14] 646; [16] 319; [32] 654. 2maps [vol.IV
generally lacking] c AA JCB NYP N TorP Y
—anr. ed. *P* 1756. D 6v: [8] 321; [6] 363; [6] 278;
[8] 331; [10] 335; [22] 438. map aa
—other Fr. eds.: *Amst* 1755, D 3v; *Copenhagen*
1755, D 3v aa
—Eng. ed., in part, "The Memorials of the English
and French commissaries . . .," *L* 1755. Q [4] 520 aa
—anr. issue, same impr. & date. Q [4] 771 map aa
—anr. ed. "All the Memorials of the courts of
Great Britain and France . . .," *L* 1756. Q 2pts in
1: [2] 349; [2] 188. 2maps[on 1 sheet] aa
Presents the conflicting claims of the two nations
concerning the Ohio and Mississippi valleys, etc.,
and includes Washington's 1754 Journal and Braddock's letters which had fallen into French hands
after his 1755 defeat. The most important contemporary source on the origins of the old French
War. *See* note to Moreau, Jacob N., *Mémoire* . . .
Volume four, issued only in the original edition,
gives *in extenso* English and French arguments
concerning Cabot's 1497 voyage.

**Mémoires et observations . . . sur la situation des
pays septentrionaux de l'Asie et de l'Amerique.**
1765. *See* Engel, Samuel.

Mémoires sur l'Amérique et sur l'Afrique   509
. . . *P* 1752. Q 58 a

MEMOIRS
**Memoirs, extracts of speeches, diary of a journey
to America** . . . *See* Freer, R. L.

Memoirs of a nullifier . . . By a native of the
south. *See* Johnson, A. S.

Memoirs of an American lady. *See* Grant, Mrs.
Anne.

Memoirs of an unfortunate young nobleman . . .
See Annesley, James.

**Memoirs of the principal transactions of the last
war between the English and the French in North
America** . . . *See* Alexander, Wm.

MEMORANDA
Memoranda of the experience . . . of a Universa-
list preacher. *See* Rogers, Wm.

MEMORANDUMS . . .
Memorandums . . . respecting plunder taken
after a siege . . . *See* Clinton, Sir Henry.

MEMORIA
**Memoria de las proporciones naturales de las
provincias internas occidentales** . . . *See* Riézo, Juan
M., Velasco, J. Francisco, *et al.*

**Memoria presentada a los dos camaras del Con-
greso** . . . *See* Alaman, Luis.

**Memoria presentada al soberano congresso
mexicano** . . . *See* Medina, Antonio de.

**Memoria que el Secretario de Estado y del
Despacho de Relaciones Exteriores e Interiores.**
See Alaman, Lucas.

MEMORIAL
Memorial (A) containing a summary view of
facts . . . *See* Moreau, Jacob N., *Mémoire contenant les précis des faits* . . .

Memorial (The) of Common-Sense, upon   510
the present crisis between Great-Britain and America . . . *See* Cartwright, John.

Memorial to the Senate and House of Repre-   511
sentatives, in Congress . . . [capt. t.] n.p. n.d. [*Chi*
1848]. O 42 a
—rptd. *Alb* 1848. O 46
For cause of this remonstrance *see Chicago.
Proceedings of the harbor and river convention.*

MEMORIALS (THE)
Memorials (The) of the English and French
commissaries . . . *See Memoires des commissaires
du roi* . . .

MEMORIALS   512
**Memorials presented to the Congress of the Uni-
ted States** . . . by the different societies instituted
for promoting the abolition of slavery . . . *Phil* 1792.
O [4] 31 a

MEMORIES OF THE SOUTHERN STATES.
See Collins, Eliz.

MEN AND MANNERS IN AMERICA.
See Hamilton, Thos.

MENDELL and HOSMER, MISSES   513
Notes of travel and life . . . *N Y* 1854. D 288 a

MENDELSSOHN-BARTHOLDY, ERNST   514
Von New-York nach San Francisco. Flüchtige
Reiseskizzen. [*Leip* 1869]. O [2] 192 aa

MENDOCINO COUNTY, CALIFORNIA.   515
History of: *S F* 1880. O 676 pls b B CalS N

MENDOCINO INDIAN WAR (THE).
Report . . . on: *See* Lamar, J., and O'Farrell, J.

MENEFEE, C[AMPBELL] A.   516
Historical . . . sketch book of Napa, Sonoma,
Lake and Mendocino counties, California. *Napa
City* 1873. O 356[i.e. 358] 14pls a

[MENTELLE, MME. WALDEMARD]   517
Voyages, adventures, etc., of the French emigrants . . . *Lex, Ky* 1800. D [12] 26 aa

MENZEL, GOTTFRIED   **518**
Die Vereinigten Staaten... mit besonderen Rücksicht auf deutsche Auswanderung... *Berlin* 1853. O [8] 364 a
Menzel had pastorates at Friedrichsburg and New Braunfels, Texas, 1849–1851.

MENZIES, ARCHIBALD, JR, 1754–1842 **519**
Journal of Vancouver's voyage... *Victoria Can* 1923. O [20] 171 2maps 11pls 2 facs[on 3 l.] a

MENZIES, ARCHIBALD, SR.   **520**
Proposal for peopling His Majesty's colonies on the continent of America. [*Perth* 1763]. O 44 a

MERCED COUNTY, CALIFORNIA.   **521**
History of:... *S F* 1881. F 232 pls b B Hn

MERCER, A[SA] S.   **522**
The banditti of the plains... [*Cheyenne* 1894]. O [2] 139 b N NYP WashU Y
—oth. eds.: re-written by John Mercer Boots, "The Powder river invasion," *L A* [1923], D 146 a; *Sheridan, Wyo* 1930 D a
—anr. ed., illus. by Parker, *S F* Grabhorn 1935. O [14] 136 aa
Basic authority on the Johnson County war [between big cattle interests, supported by Wyoming officials, and independent ranchers]. Most copies burned by interested authorities; others bought up and destroyed by individuals whose relatives were unfavorably mentioned.

MERCER, A[SA] S.   **523**
Big Horn county, Wyoming... *Hyattville Wyo* [1906]. D 115 8pls aa

MERCER, ASA S.   **524**
Material resources of Linn county, Oregon... *Albany Ore* 1875. O 72 aa

MERCER, A[SA] S.   **525**
The material resources of Marion county, Oregon, with... business directory. *Salem* 1876. O [4] 80 fold.map + double-p. tab aa

MERCER, A[SA] S.   **526**
Washington Territory; the great north-west... *Utica* 1865. O 38 b N WashU Y.
—rptd. *Seattle* 1939. O 54 a 350copies ptd. a

[MERCER, CHARLES F.]   **527**
An exposition of the weakness... of the government of the United States. [*Rich*?] 1845. D 380 a
—Eng. ed., t. altered, *L* 1863. 16° [14] 17–382
Bitter attack on the Constitution and the way it was working; soon suppressed by its repentant author.

MERCER, JESSE   **528**
A history of the Georgia Baptist Association. *Wash Ga* 1836. D 419 aa
—rptd. same impr. 1838. a

MERCER, PHILIP   **529**
The life of the gallant Pelham. *Macon Ga* [1929]. D 180 a
—rptd. n.d. D 1000cops ptd.

MERCER, W. T., ed.   **530**
The fall of Oswego, August 14, 1756... from the papers of Colonel Mercer, commanding the British forces... *Reading Eng* 1873. O 32 a

MEREDITH, EDMUND A.   **531**
Essay on the Oregon question... *Montr* 1846. O 43 a

[MEREDITH, SIR WILLIAM]   **532**
Historical remarks on the taxation of free states ... *L* 1778. Q [2] 82 b AA N NYP Y
Only thirty copies issued of this refutation of British claims that historical precedents warranted colonial taxation.

MERENESS, NEWTON D.   **533**
Maryland as a proprietary province. *N Y* 1901. O [22] 530 a

MERENESS, NEWTON D. [ed.]   **534**
Travels in the American colonies. *N Y* 1916. O [6] 693 a
Collection of eighteen previously unpublished travel journals, some highly interesting.

[MERIWETHER, MRS. ELIZABETH A.]   **535**
Facts and falsehoods concerning the war on the south. *Memphis* [1904]. O [10] 271 a
References to a suppressed 1866 edition of Herndon's biography–depicting Lincoln's unsavory character and differing entirely from the 1889 issue—gave birth to a troublesome and wholly false bibliographical myth.

MERK, FREDERICK, ed.   **536**
Fur trade and empire. George Simpson's journal ... in the course of a voyage from York factory [to the Columbia river]... 1824–5. *C* 1931. O [380] 370 map a

MERKELEY (CHRISTOPHER).   **537**
Biography of:... by himself. *S L C* 1887. D 46 a
Adventures of a Mormon in Missouri, Illinois and the far West.

MERLE, J. A.   **538**
De l'emigration aux États-Unis... *Geneva* 1849. O 46 map a

MERRICK, GEORGE B.   **539**
Old times on the upper Mississippi . . . *Clev*
1909. O 323[incl. 16pls] map pl aa

MERRIFIELD, EDWARD   **540**
The story of the captivity . . . of Luke Swetland
. . . *Scranton* 1915. D 68 a small ed.
Amplification of Swetland's own narrative, *q. v.*

MERRILL, ELIPHALET and   **541**
PHINEHAS
A gazetteer of . . . New Hampshire . . . *Exeter*
1817. O 218 [13] a
First gazetteer of this state.

MERRILL, GEORGIA D.   **542**
History of Carroll county, New Hampshire. *B*
1889. O [14] 987 map pls a
—rptd. 1891 O

MERRILL, J[AMES] W.   **543**
Yellow Spring and Huron [in Des Moines
county, Ia.] . . . *Mediapolis* 1897. O 433 [incl.front.]
+ inserted l. at p420 2fold. maps 13pls a

MERRILL, JOHN L.   **544**
History of Acworth, N. H. . . . *Acworth* 1869.
O 306 56pls a

MERRILL, O. N.   **545**
True history of the Kansas wars, and their
origin [etc.]. *Cin* 1856. O 56 port 3col pls b

MERRITT, CAPT. W[ILLIAM] H.   **546**
Journal of events . . . on the Detroit and Niagara
frontiers, during the war of 1812. *St Catherines
Canada* 1863. O 82 aa

MERWIN, H.   **547**
An historical sketch of Leavenworth, with a
directory of the city . . . *Leavenworth* 1870. O 184 aa

MESA COUNTY, COLORADO.   **548**
History and business directory of: . . . *Grand
Junction* 1886. O [4] 93 pls a

MESERVE, FREDERICK H.   **548a**
Historical portraits and Lincolniana. Index of a
part of the collection [of the author]. *N Y* 1915.
Q [12] 143 a

MESERVE, FREDERICK H.   **549**
Lincolniana. Historical portraits and views
printed . . . from original negatives [etc.]. *N Y* 1915.
Q 104 369photos[108 of Lincoln] 16copies c IllH.

MESERVE, FREDERICK H.   **550**
The photographs of Abraham Lincoln. *N Y* 1911.
Q 110 130 mounted photos 100 copies c AA IllH
—suppl. No. 1, *N Y* 1917. Q 7 7photos aa
—suppl. No. 2, *N Y* 1938. Q 7 7photos aa

MESSAGE   **551**
Message from the President . . . transmitting . . .
such further information, in relation to our affairs
with Spain, as . . . is not inconsistent with the public
interest to divulge. *Wash* 1819. O 215 a
Documents concerning troubles resulting from
Jackson's high-handed conduct in Florida.

Message from the President . . . transmit-   **552**
ting the correspondence between this government
and that of Great Britain, on the subject of the
claims . . . to the territory west of the Rocky mountains. *Wash* 1828. O 77 aa

Message from the President . . . transmit-   **553**
ting the correspondence with the British government, in relation to the boundary of the United
States on the Pacific ocean. *Wash* 1826. O 26 a

Message (A) of the President . . . relative   **554**
to France and Great-Britain . . . December 5, 1793
. . . *Phil* 1793. O 102 [2] 116 32 [4] 12 36 4 a
—Eng. ed. [omitting documents], *L* 1794. O 103
First of many presidential messages to Congress.
It presents the official version of the Genet affair.

Message of the President . . . relative to   **555**
the affairs of the United States on the Mississippi
. . . *Phil* Ross [1798]. O 91 a

Message of the President . . . to explain   **556**
the . . . failure of the United States on the northern
frontier, Feb. 2nd 1814. *Wash* 1814. O 115 114 fold
tab a
—rptd. *N Y* 1814. O [2] 65; *Alb* 1814. 16° 175

Message of the President . . . transmitting   **557**
. . . documents . . . from a secret agent of the British
government, employed . . . to destroy the union . . .
Wash 1812. O 50 a *see* also Seaver, Eben.

MESSITER, CHARLES A.   **558**
Sport and adventure among the . . . Indians [in
Mont., Neb., Texas, etc] . . . *L* 1890. O [18] 368[incl.
pls] a

METCALF, ANTHONY   **559**
Ten years before the mast . . . How I became a
Mormon . . . [*Malad City Ida ca* 1880]. O [2] 81
b LC Y[only copies located].

METCALF, SAMUEL L.   **560**
A collection of . . . narratives of Indian warfare in
the west . . . *Lex* 1821. O 270 errata slip b KyH N Y
This compilation, seeking to preserve for posterity early border narratives, has become almost as
rare as the originals themselves.

METHODIST CONFERENCES (THE).   **561**
Minutes of: annually held in America . . . 1773–
1794. *Phil* 1795. 16° 214 aa

METHVIN, J. J.   562
Andele, or the Mexican-Kiowa captive . . .
Louisv 1899. D 184 a
—ed. 2, *Louisv* 1899. same collat

[METLAR, GEORGE W.]   563
Northern California, Scott and Klamath rivers
. . . By a practical miner. *Yreka* 1856. D 24 b

MEXICAN
Claims of Mexican citizens against the United
States for Indian depredations . . . *See* Gomez del
Palacio, Francisco.

Complete history of the late Mexican   564
war . . . *N Y* 1850. D 128 pls a

The Mexican cordillera. By Cincinnatus. *See*
Wheat, Marvin T.

Mexican treacheries and cruelties. By a volunteer
returned from the war. *See* Allen, Lieut. G. N.

MEXICANA   565
Mexicana (la Republica) y los Estados-Unidos
. . . Tratado de paz . . . entre: [in Eng. & Span.]
Queretaro 1848. O 28 27 b
—anr. ed., with emendations *Mex* 1848 O 55 aa
—U.S. ed. "The treaty between the United States
and Mexico . . ." [*Wash* 1848]. O 384 Sen. ex. doc.
52 aa abr ed. O 74 a
Treaty of Guadeloupe Hidalgo, ending the
Mexican war and adding to our national domain
Ariz., Calif. and New Mex.

MEXICO.
Camp life of a volunteer. A campaign in Mexico
. . . By "One who has seen the elephant." *See*
Scribner, Benjamin F.

A campaign in Mexico. "By one who was thar."
See Scribner, Benjamin F.

The conquest of Mexico! An appeal to the   566
citizens of the United States, on [its] justice and
expediency . . . *B* 1846. O 32 map a

Message from the President [Jackson] . . .   567
concerning the fur trade, and inland trade to
Mexico. [Sen. Ex. Doc. 90] *Wash* 1832. O 86 aa
Among the several communications on the
subject suggested by the title is Joshua Pilcher's
report.

Mexico en 1847: Contiene una relacion de   568
las revoluciones . . .desde que comenzó la guerra
contra los Estados-Unidos . . . *Mex* 1847. Q 40 aa

Mexico in 1842. *N Y* 1842. *See* Folsom, George F.

Mexico versus Texas . . . By a Texian. *See*
Ganilh, Anthony.

Official despatches . . . . connected with the Commission to . . . mark the boundary between the
United States and Mexico. *See* Bartlett, John R.

Recollection of Mexico and the battle of   569
Buena Vista. *B* 1871. O 27 a

Reminiscences of a campaign in Mexico.
See Robertson, John B.

Sketches of the campaign in Northern Mexico . . .
By an officer . . . *See* Giddings, Maj. L.

Sketches of the war in Northern Mexico   570
with pictures of life . . . *N Y* 1848. 16° 75 b

The statistical account of Mexico. *See* Villa-
Señor y Sanchez, Joseph A.

The treaty between the United States and Mexico
. . . [*Wash* 1848]. *See* No. 565, above.

MEYER, BALTHASAR H., ed.   571
History of transportation in the United States
before 1860. *Wash* 1917. O [12] 678 a

MEYER, CARL   572
Nach dem Sacramento . . . *Aarau* 1855. D [4]
366
—Eng. tr. *Claremont Cal* 1938. O 2v 450cops ptd.

MEYER (GEORGE).   573
Autobiography of: Across the plains with an ox
team in 1849 . . . *Shenandoah Ia* 1908. O 29[incl.
front.] aa

MEYERS, AUGUSTUS   574
Ten years in the . . . army. *N Y* 1914. O [6] 356 a
iss 1 has gilt top
Campaigning on the Nebraska-Dakota frontier,
1855–60.

MEYERS, R[OBERT] C. V.   575
Life and adventures of Lewis Wetzel. *N Y*
[1883]. D 414[incl.front.] 3pls a
—anr. issue, same collat. *Phil* [1883].
—rptd.: *Phil* 1889, same collat; *Phil* 1890. a

MICHAELER, KARL   576
Historisch-Kritischer Versuch über die ältesten
Volkerstamme, und ihre Wanderungen nebst wei-
terer Verpflanzung nach Amerika. *Vienna* 1801–
02. D 5v a

MICHAËLIUS, JONAS D.   577
The first minister of the Dutch Reformed Church
in the United States. *Hague* [1858]. O 25 aa
—rptd., in Dutch & Eng., *Amst* 1883. a
—anr. ed. "Manhattan in 1628 . . .," *N Y* 1904.
Q [14] 204 [2] [incl.front.] pls 225 copies ptd.[50
on Jap.P.]

Contains the first printing in separate form of a letter of 1628 giving the first description of New York City.

MICHAUX (ANDRÉ).   578
Journal of: 1787–1796. [*Phil* 1889]. O [4] 145 aa
Separate printing from American Philosophical Society Proceedings, volume 26; text in French, notes in English. Informative diary of travels to remote settlements of the South and West, made obviously in behalf of Genet's filibusting scheme against Spanish possessions.

MICHAUX, F[RANCOIS] A.   579
Voyage à l'ouest des monts Alléghanys . . . *P* 1804. O [10] 312 map aa
—rptd., same collat., 1808. a
—Eng. tr., by Lambert, *L* Mawman 1805. O [16] 350 + 2adv-p map a
—Eng. ed. 2, *L* Crosby 1805. O [12] 294 a
—anr. Eng. tr. *L* Phillips 1805. O 96 map a
—Ger. tr. *Weimar* 1805. O [14] 250 map a

MICHIGAN   580
Appeal by the convention of Michigan . . . in relation to the boundary question between Michigan and Ohio. *Det* 1835. O 176 aa

Des auswanderers Wegweiser nach . . .   581 Michigan. *N Y* 1849. O 31 a

The emigrant's guide to . . . Michigan. [1849]. *See* Thomson, E. H.

Historic and scientific sketches of Michi-   582 gan . . . *Det* 1834. D 215 aa

De Toestand der Hollandische Kolonisa-   583 tie in den Staat Michigan . . . *Amst* 1849. O 39 2maps a

MICISSIPI.   584
Journal de la guerre du: . . . 1739–1740. Par un officier de l'armée . . . *N Y* 1859. D 92 a 100 copies ptd.
Diary of an expedition against the Chickasaws, under Bienville. Written by M. de Nouailles.

MICKLE, ISAAC   585
Reminiscences of old Gloucester . . . [N. J.]. *Phil* 1845. O [4] 98 errata lf pl a

MIDDLE LINE (THE)   586
Middle line (The): or, an attempt to furnish some hints for ending the differences . . . between Great Britain and her colonies. *Phil* 1775. D 48 a
Probably by Richard Wells.

[MIDDLETON, H.]   587
Economical causes of slavery in the United States, and obstacles to abolition. *L* 1857. O [4] 56 a

MIDDLETON, JOHN W.   588
History of the regulators and moderators and the Shelby county war in 1841 and 1842, in the republic of Texas . . . *Ft Worth* 1883. O 40 a
—rptd. same collat. [*Austin* 1926]

[MIFFLIN, WARNER]   589
A serious expostulation with the members of the House of Representatives . . . *Phil* 1793. D 24 a
—rptd., same impr. & date. D 16
—other eds.: *New Bedford* 1793. D 16; *Poughkeepsie* 1794. D 24
Plea for slavery abolition.

MIGNARD, JACQUES   590
Appercu [*sic*] des crimes commis par les Anglo-Américains envers les Francais. *P* [1800]. O 52 a
Furious excoriation of everything English or American.

MIGNARD, JACQUES   591
Quelques escrocs Anglais démasqués, ou les deserts de l'Amerique du Nord . . . tels qu'ils sont. *P* [1797–8]. O 52 aa
Exposé of the Scioto Company land fraud.

MILAM [pseud.]
Texas . . . *See* Thompson, Henry.

MILBERT, J[ACQUES G.]   592
Itinéraire pittoresque du fleuve Hudson et des parties latérales . . . *P* 1828–9. Q 2v: [40] 246 [2]; [4] 257 [2] + atlas F [2] map 54pls c AA BA NYP Y
—some cops have only 53pls b

MILES (GEN. NELSON A.)   593
Annual report of: commanding the Department of the Pacific. *S F* 1889. O 74 a

MILES (GEN. [NELSON A.])   594
Official report of: commanding the Department of Arizona. [*L A*] 1888. O 40 cover t. only a

MILES (GENERAL NELSON A.)   595
Personal recollections . . . of: . . . *Chi* 1896. O [8] 590[incl. pls]
—issue 1, rank on front.port given as "General" aa
—issue 2, [identical except rank on port cor. to "Maj. Gen."] a
—ed. 2, same impr. & collat., 1897, with p.591 [a pl.] added a

MILES, W. H., and BRATT, JOHN   596
Early history and reminiscence of Frontier county, Nebraska. *Maywood Neb* 1894. D [2] 39 aa

MILES, WILLIAM   597
Journal of the sufferings . . . of Capt. Parker H. French's overland expedition to California. *Chambersburg Pa* 1851. O 24 dd AA G Hn [of 7 known copies]
—rptd. *N Y* 1916. O 26 a 250cops ptd

Followed the southern route, via San Antonio and El Paso to the Gila river and San Diego. First gold-rush expedition across Texas.

MILET [or MILLET], PIERRE   598
Relation de sa captivité parmi les Onneiouts [Oneidas] en 1690–1. *N Y* 1864. D [5] 9–56 a 100copies ptd.
—Eng. tr. *N Y* 1888. O 18 a
—rptd. *Chi* 1897. D [4] 7–72 75copies ptd.
First printing of one of the earliest accounts of the Five Nations.

MILFORT, LE CLERC   599
Mémoire ou coup-d'oeil rapide sur . . . mon séjour dans la nation Crëck . . . *P* [1802]. O [4] 332 b N NYP Y
—Eng trs: *Chi* 1956, 16° [4 56] 257 map; *Kenesaw Ga* 1959, D [20] 230 map a
Narrative of an extraordinary French adventurer among the Upper Creeks, somewhat—but not entirely—invalidated by its extravagant romanticism.

MILITARY HISTORY (THE)   600
Military history (The) of Great Britain, for 1756–7. Containing a letter from an English officer . . . taken prisoner at Oswego [etc.] *L* 1757. O 125 plan b LC

MILITARY POSTS
Military posts—Council Bluffs to the Pacific . . . *See* Pendleton, N. G.

MILLER, ANDREW   601
New states and territories . . . [*Keene N H*] 1819. 24° 96 fold.tab c AA LC N Y
—anr. issue, [*Keene* 1819]. O 32[incl.tab] c AA ChiH WisH
Priority between these issues not established, but probabilities favor the octavo.

MILLER, BENJAMIN S.   602
Ranch life in southern Kansas and the Indian Territory . . . *N Y* 1896. D 164 port aa

MILLER, E[LIJAH]   603
The history of Page county, Iowa . . . *Clarinda* 1876. D 100 + 17adv-p and inserted lf after p. 98 map aa

MILLER, FRANCIS W.   604
Cincinnati's beginnings . . . chiefly from hitherto unpublished documents. *Cin* 1880. D [10] 235 pl a

MILLER (BISHOP GEORGE).   605
Correspondence of: with the northern islander. n.p. [*ca* 1900]. O 50 capt.t.only a
All of these letters were written from St. James, Michigan, in 1855.

MILLER, GEORGE, JR.   606
The trial of Frank James for murder . . . *K C* [1898]. D 348 pls a

MILLER, J. M.   607
Recollections of "a pine knot" in the lost cause . . . *Greenwood Miss* [1899]. O 56 a

MILLER, "JOAQUIN" [CIN-   608
CINNATUS H.]
Life amongst the Modocs . . . *L* 1873. O [8] 400 a
—Am. ed., "Unwritten history . . .," *Hart* 1874. O 445 24pls a
—rptd. variously entitled "Paquita, the Indian heroine," and "My own story," *Hart* 1881; *Chi* 1890.

MILLER, "JOAQUIN" [CIN-   609
CINNATUS H.]
Memorie and rhyme . . . *N Y* 1884. D 237 a

MILLER, REV. JOHN   610
A description of . . . New York. *L* 1843. O [4] 44 + advs [4] 21–116 6pls a
—rptd. *N Y* 1862. O 127 6plans 50copies on L. P.; *Clev* 1903. O 400copies ptd.
Miller resided in New York from 1693 to 1695.

MILLER, LEWIS B.   611
A crooked trail . . . *Pitt* [1908]. O 184 aa
—rptd. *B* [1911]. O 413 front a
A thousand mile horse-back trip along the Texas frontier.

MILLER, LEWIS B.   612
Saddles and lariats . . . *B* [1912]. O 285 front a
—rptd. *B* [1917].

MILLER, LINUS W.   613
Notes of an exile to Van Dieman's Land: comprising incidents of the Canadian rebellion in 1838. *Fredonia N Y* 1846. D [12] 378 a

MILLER, MARK   614
The Racine register, business directory . . . *Racine* [1849]. D 84 + 34adv-p aa
Contains an historical sketch.

MILLER, REUBEN   615
James J. Strang weighed in the balance of truth and found wanting . . . *Burlington Ia* 1846. O 24 d ChurchL[S L C] only 2copies known
Exposé by a disillusioned "Strangite".

MILLER, STEPHEN F.   616
The bench and bar of Georgia . . . *Phil* 1858. O 2v: 483; 454 aa

MILLER, STEPHEN F.   617
Memoir of Gen. David Blackshear . . . *Phil* 1858. O [4] 355–483, 133–157 a

Separate printing from *The bench and bar of Georgia*, with introduction and muster rolls added.

MILLER, SUSAN G.   **618**
Sixty years in the Nueces valley . . . *San Antonio* [1930]. O [10] 374 maps pls a

MILLER, WILLIAM H.   **619**
The history of Kansas City . . . *K C* 1881. O [6] 5–264 map a

MILLIGAN, JACOB   **620**
The Charleston directory and revenue system. *Charleston S C* 1790. O [2] 56 b
—contd. annually for some yrs.

[MILLIGEN, GEORGE]   **621**
A short description of . . . South Carolina . . . *L* 1770. O 96 aa

MILLISON, D. G., pub.   **622**
Topeka city directory . . . [with an historical sketch]. *Topeka* 1868. O [2] 19–26 25–145 aa
First directory of this infant municipality.

MILLS, ANSON   **623**
My story. *Wash* 1918. D 412[incl. maps & pls] errata slip a
—ed. 2, with adds., *Wash* 1921. D 431
Service in Arizona, at Ft. Bridger and with Crook's 1876 Sioux campaign.

MILLS, ROBERT   **624**
The American pharos, or light-house guide . . . also a general view of the coast, from the St. Lawrence to the Sabine. *Wash* 1832. O 184 aa

[MILLS, ROBERT]   **625**
[Atlas of . . . South Carolina. *Balt* 1825.] F [4] 29maps b AA N Y
—rptd., same collat: *Phil* 1826; *Phil* [1838]. aa
—anr. ed. *Columbia S C* 1937. F [8] 29maps 350 copies ptd. aa

MILLS, ROBERT   **626**
Memorial, submitting a plan for a new roadway, with the operation of steam carriages, for a commercial highway to Oregon and California. *Wash* 1846. O 27 map a

MILLS, ROBERT   **627**
Statistics of South Carolina . . . *Charleston* 1826. O [8] 17–782 [48] map[not in all copies] aa
Intended as a companion volume for his *Atlas*, above.

MILLS, ROBERT   **628**
A treatise on inland navigation. *Balt* 1820. O 104 [4] map aa

MILLS, SAMUEL J., and   **629**
SMITH, DANIEL
Report of a missionary tour . . . west of the Allegheny mountains . . . *Andover* 1815. O 64 aa
Best first-hand account of Illinois in its territorial period.

MILLS, T. B.   **630**
Handbook to New Mexico. *Las Vegas* 1879. O 38 map aa

MILLS, T. B.   **631**
New Mexico. San Miguel county, illustrated . . . *Las Vegas* 1885. O 52 map a

MILLS, W. JAY   **632**
Historic houses of New Jersey. *Phil* 1902. O [16] 13–348 19 pls a
—anr. issue, identical except for Ins. Co. adv. on cover.

MILLS, WILLIAM W.   **633**
Forty years at El Paso . . . [*El Paso*, ptd. *Chi* 1901]. D 165 [incl.front.] a

MILMINE, GEORGINE   **634**
The life of Mary Baker G. Eddy . . . *N Y* 1909. O [14] 495 25pls aa
Miss Milmine assembled the facts; the actual writer was Willa Cather.

MILNER, JOE E., and FORREST,   **635**
EARLE R.
California Joe, noted scout and Indian fighter. *Caldwell Ida* 1935. D 396 27pls a

[MILNOR, WILLIAM]   **636**
An authentic historical memoir of the Schuylkill Fishing Company . . . *Phil* 1830. O [8] 127 58 5pls aa
—rptd. *Phil* 1889. O 446 pls a
Founded in 1732, this is the oldest sporting club in the world. Includes, with separate title, *Memoirs of the Gloucester . . . club.*

MILWAUKEE   **637**
Directory . . . : for 1848–9, with a sketch of the city . . . *Milw* King 1848. O 204 map aa
Second directory of this city; for the first, *see* McCabe, Julius, F. B.

MINER, CHARLES   **638**
History of Wyoming [Valley] . . . *Phil* 1845. O 488 [2] 104 2maps 2pls a
—anr. ed. *Phil* 1846

MINER'S (THE) OWN BOOK.   **639**
S F 1858. O 32 b G NYP Y issue 1 has inverted woodcut on p23 iss. 2 aa
—rptd. *S F* 1949. O 50 a 500copies ptd. a
Probably by Jas. M. Hutchins.

MINNEAPOLIS DIRECTORY   640
Minneapolis directory for . . . 1865–6 . . . *Minneap* 1865. D 99 aa 1 cop loc.

MINNEHAHA COUNTY, DAKOTA.
History [etc.] of: *See* Ellis, Frankwill.

MINNESOTA   641
Annals of the Minnesota Historical Society.
Four annual nos. *St P* 1850–53. O 4v: 32; 183; 64; 72 aa
—rptd., in combined form, *St P* 1856. O 158 5pls a
The Society's activities went into eclipse in 1856; on resumption of operations sixteen years later, the above material was reissued as volume I of their *Collections.*

A guide for emigrants to Minnesota. By   642
a tourist. *St P* 1857. D 24 map aa

The guide to Minnesota . . . *St P* 1868.   643
D 81 + 14 adv-p a

The immigrants' guide to Minnesota in   644
1856. By an old resident. *St Anthony* [ptd in *N Y*] 1856. D 127 map a

Minnesota als eine Heimat für Einwan-   645
derer . . . n.p. 1864. O 59 [36 8] a
—anr. issue. O 59 [25]

Minnesota gazeteer and business direc-   646
tory, for 1865 . . . *St P* 1865. O 399[incl.advs] aa
First state directory.

Minnesota guide (The) . . . *St P* 1869. D   647
94 [3] a

Minnesota messenger (The), containing   648
sketches of the rise and progress of Minnesota . . . *St P* 1855. O 78[incl.advs] b G

Minnesota year book for 1851. [Same for 1852— and for 1853]. *See* Le Duc, W. G.

Rise and progress of Minnesota territory.   649
St P 1855. O 64 b
—rptd. 1865. a

Rural sketches of Minnesota . . . *See* Hamilton, H. W.

Wanderings in Minnesota during the Indian troubles of 1862. *See* Scantlebury, Thos.

MINOT, GEORGE R.   650
Continuation of the history of . . . Massachusetts Bay, from 1748 . . . *B* 1798–1803. O 2v: 304; 222 a
Continues Hutchinson's history of this province to 1765

MINOT, GEORGE R.   651
The history of the insurrections in Massachusetts . . . *Worc* 1788. O 192 aa
—ed. 2, *B* 1810. same collat. a
—ed. 3, *B* 1840.
Shay's rebellion, etc.

MINUTES   652
Minutes of the proceedings of the convention of delegates from the abolition societies . . . *Phil* 1794. O 30 a
—same, 2nd convention, *Phil* 1795. O 32
—con., to over 20 conventions, 1796–1830.

MIRABEAU, HONORÉ G. R, comte de   653
Considerations sur l'ordre de Cincinnatus . . . *L* 1784. O [12] 385 [3] anr. iss. O [12] 203 aa
—rptd.: *L* 1785; *L* 1788. a
—Eng. tr., with omissions, *L* 1784. O [12] 203 a
—anr. ed. *L* 1785. O [12] 284
—Am. ed. *Phil* 1786. O [4] 68 a
—rptd. n.p. n.d. O [4] 82

MIRANDA'S EXPEDITION.
A general account of: . . . *See* Sherman, John H.

MIRANDA'S ATTEMPT
Miranda's attempt to effect a revolution in South America . . . History of: *See* Biggs, James.

MIRICK, B. L.   654
The history of Haverhill. *Haverhill Mass* 1832. D 277 pl a
The poet Whittier assisted in the preparation of this work.

MISCEGENATION
Miscegenation: the theory of the blending of the races . . . *See* Croly, David G.

MISCELLANEOUS ESSAY (A)
Miscellaneous essay (A), concerning the courses pursued by Great Britain, in . . . her colonies . . . *See* McCulloch, Henry.

MISCELLANIES; BY AN OFFICER . . .
See De Peyster, Arent S.

MISSISSIPPI   655
An address to the people of the Mississippi territory showing the . . . expedience of dividing the Territory preparatory to the formation of two states . . . By Tempus Nunc. *Natchez* 1816. D 48 b PaH Y

Chronicles of the fire-eaters of the tribe   656
of Mississippi. By Seraiah the scribe. *Brandon Miss* 1853. O 38 aa

The commerce and navigation of the valley of the Mississippi. *See* Allen, Thos.

Documents relating to the improvement of   657
the navigation of the Mississippi River *N O* 1837.
O 82 [12] map aa

An estimate of commercial advantages by way
of the Mississippi and Mobile rivers . . . *See* Cox,
Zachariah.

A full and impartial account of the Com-   658
pany of Mississippi . . . projected and settled by Mr.
Law . . . to which are added, a description of the
country and a relation of the first discovery of it
. . . *L* 1720. O [4] 64 73–79 b LC N NYP Y
Principal English promotion tract for Law's
Mississippi Bubble; text in both English and
French. For a similar German work, *see Histori-
sche und geographische Beschreibung des an dem . . .
Mississippi.*

History of the upper Mississippi valley.
See Winchell, N. H., *et al.*

An impartial enquiry into the right of   659
the French king to the territory west of the great
river Mississippi . . . a vindication of the English
claim to the whole continent . . . *L* [1762]. O [2] 58
b BA N Y

A journey on the Mississippi river . . .   660
a lecture . . . *Phil* 1847. O 24 a

Mississippi navigator (The); revised and   661
corrected. *Phil* Bradford 1815. D pls Sabin 49528
See Cramer, Zadok. A doubtful edition.

Mississippi question (The) fairly stated . . . By
Camillus. *See* Duane, Wm.

Mississippi river (The) from St. Louis to   662
the sea. *St L* 1892. obl F [8] 42maps a

Nine years of Democratic rule in Mississippi. *See*
Van Winkle, H. E.

Notes on the navigation of the Mississippi   663
. . . by a gentleman of talents and observation . . .
Frankfort Ky 1803. D 56 c WisH[only copy known]

Le nouveau Mississippi, ou les dangers d'habiter
les bords du Scioto . . . *See* Roux, Sgt.-Maj.

Official proceedings of the Mississippi   664
valley railroad convention . . . *St L* [1852]. O 64
+ cover t. tab a

Opening of the Mississippi or two year's campaigning in the south-west . . . *See* Driggs, Geo. W.

Remarks on the western states . . . or the   665
valley of the Mississippi . . . *L* 1839. O 45 aa

Mississippi river (The), from St. Paul to New
Orleans . . . *See* Harthill, A.

Some considerations on the consequences   666
of the French settling colonies on the Mississippi . . .
L 1720. O [4] 60 map b N NYP Y
—rptd. *Cin* 1928. O 51 map a
Probably by James Smith of Carolina.

Tales of travel west of the Mississippi. *See* Snelling, Wm. J.

View of the valley of the Mississippi . . . *See*
Baird, Rob't.

Vue de la colonie espagnole du Mississippi . . .
See Berquin-Duvallon.

MISSOURI
Brief narrative of incidents in the war in Missouri.
See Painter, Henry M.

Life and scenery in Missouri. *See* O'Hanlon, John.

Outline descriptions of the posts in the   667
military division of the Missouri . . . *Chi* 1872.
D 130 [2] fold.map, inserted slip showing distances
aa

Outline descriptions of the posts in the   668
military division of the Missouri . . . *Chi* 1876. D 157
fold.map 120pls aa

Proceedings of a convention . . . for pro-   669
motion of internal improvements within . . . Missouri *St L* 1836. O 30 aa

Rebel invasion of Missouri and Kansas. . . . *See*
Hinton, Richard J.

Table of distances in the Department of   670
Missouri embracing the Districts of Kansas, Upper
Kansas, New Mexico and Indian Territory. *Leaven-
worth* 1868. O 28 [4] b

MITCHEL, MARTIN, and   671
OSBORN, JOSEPH H.
Geographical . . . history of the county of Winnebago [Wis.]. *Oshkosh* 1856. D 120 + 7adv-p
12pls aa

MITCHEL, MARTIN   672
History of the county of Fond du Lac, Wis . . .
Fond du Lac 1854. D 96 aa

MITCHELL, COLIN, et al   673
Mitchell, Colin, *et al*, versus the United States.
Record in the case of: . . . *Wash* 1831. Q 736 b
NYP
—anr. ed. "Exposition . . . of the title . . .," *Wash*
1834. O aa

Appellants claimed a million and a quarter acres in Florida—acquired under the original Panton, Leslie 1783 Spanish grant, confirmed in 1806 and 1811—and the presentation of their case involved an elaborate account of Florida's complicated history and Indian trade, from the Revolution to American accession.

MITCHELL, DAVID W.   **674**
Ten years in the United States . . . L 1862. D [12] 332 a
Favorable account of the South and its peculiar institution.

MITCHELL, FRANCES L.   **675**
Georgia land and Georgia people. [Atlanta 1900]. D [30] 495 a

[MITCHELL, JOHN]   **676**
The contest in America between Great Britain and France. By an impartial hand . . . L 1757. O [2, 50] 17–244 aa
Ascribed also to Oliver Goldsmith.

[MITCHELL, JOHN]   **677**
A full account of the proceedings in relation to Capt. Kidd . . . L 1701. sm Q [8] 51 b
—ed. 2, same impr. & date O 40 [1] aa
—rptd. "A full account of the actions of . . . Capt. Kidd. With the proceedings against him . . .," Dub 1701. O [4] 42 aa
Defends the Earl of Bellomont from charges of being implicated in Kidd's piracies. Ascribed also to Lord Somers and to Lord Halifax.

MITCHELL, JOHN   **678**
A map of the British and French dominions in North America . . . L pub. by au. & sold by And. Miller 1755. F 8sheet maps in col. [extended would be 55" × 77"] b N Y
—anr. issue, identical except Miller is cor. to Millar and map cold in outline b
—rptd. Amst Covens & Mortier [ca 1756]. F only 4sheet maps aa
Most comprehensive, detailed and accurate map of North America produced up to its time.

[MITCHELL, JOHN]   **679**
The present state of Great Britain and North America . . . L 1767. O [24] 364 aa

MITCHELL, JOSEPH   **680**
The missionary pioneer . . . life . . . of John Stewart . . . N Y 1827. 16° 96 b
—rptd. N Y 1918. same collat. a
Stewart founded the Sandusky Wyandotte mission.

MITCHELL, NAHUM   **681**
History of . . . Bridgewater [Mass.]. B 1840. O 402 a
—rptd. Bridgewater 1897. O 430

MITCHELL, MRS. REBECCA   **682**
Historical sketches . . . of eastern Idaho. [Idaho Falls 1905]. O 96 port a

MITCHELL, GOV. ROBERT H.   **683**
First annual message to the legislative assembly of the Territory of New Mexico. Santa Fe 1867. O 31 aa
Describes territorial conditions just after the Civil War.

MITCHELL, SAMUEL A.   **684**
An accompaniment to [his] reference and distance map of the United States . . . Phil 1834. D 324 a
—rptd.—5 eds.—from 1835 to 1845.
—Ger. eds.: "Die Vereinigten Staaten . . .," Phil 1846. O; Phil 1849. O

[MITCHELL, SAMUEL A.]   **685**
Accompaniment to Mitchell's new map of Texas, Oregon and California . . . Phil 1846. 18° 34 map aa
—anr. issue, 46p. map aa
—rptd. Oakland 1948. O [6] 47 map pl a

MITCHELL, SAMUEL A.   **686**
Compendium of the internal improvements of the United States . . . Phil 1835. 24° 84 [4] fold. map[in some copies] a
—rptd., same impr. & collat. 1838.

[MITCHELL, SAMUEL A.]   **687**
Description of Oregon and California: embracing an account of the gold regions . . . Phil 1849. 18° 76 map b N Y

MITCHELL, SAMUEL A., pub.   **688**
Geographical description of . . . Texas; also of . . . Oregon and upper California. Phil 1846. D 62 map aa

[MITCHELL, SAMUEL A.]   **689**
Illinois in 1837; a sketch . . . Phil 1837. O 144 map a issue 1 has word "animals" misspelled on t-p; this was corrected in issue 2. a
—anr. issue, with cover t. "Illinois in 1837 & 8 . . .," Phil 1838. same collat.
—abr. ed. "Sketches of Illinois . . .," Phil 1838. O 32 map
—Eng. ed. "The far west; a sketch of Illinois . . .," Bolton-le-Moors 1842. D no perfect copy known aa

MITCHELL, SAMUEL A.   **690**
The principal stage, steamboat and canal routes in the United States . . . Phil 1834. 16° 96 a
—continued as "Traveller's guide . . .," Phil [1836]. 16° 74 [4] map; rptd. several times
—reissued as "New traveller's guide . . .," Phil 1849. 16° 128 map; Phil 1857. 16° [32] 122 2maps
The 1834 edition was the first containing text; the map alone, however, was issued under both of above titles in 1832, 1833 and 1835.

MITCHELL, W. H. 691
Dakota county [Minn.]: its past and present . . .
Minneap 1868. D [6] 162 + 8adv lvs 2pls aa
First history of the second Minnesota settlement.

MITCHELL, W. H., and STEVENS, J. H. 692
Geographical . . . history of the county of Hennepin [Minn.] *Minneap* 1869. 16° 149 + 25adv-p
errata lf aa
First history of the first Minnesota settlement.

MITCHELL, W. H. 693
Geographical . . . history of the county of Olmstead [Minn.] . . . *Rochester Minn* [1866]. 16° 121 aa

MITCHELL, W. H. 694
Geographical . . . sketch of . . . Goodhue county
[Minn.]. *Minneap* 1869. D 191 aa

MITCHELL, W. H., and CURTIS U. 695
Geographical . . . sketch of . . . Wabasha county
[Minn.] . . . *Rochester Minn* 1870. 16° 164 a

MITCHELL, W. H., and CURTIS, U. 696
Historical sketch of Dodge county, Minn.
Rochester Minn 1870. D 124 + errata p & 11adv-p a

MITCHELL, W. H. 697
History of Steele county [Minn.]. *Minneap* 1868.
D 97 + 10 adv-1. aa

MITCHELL, WESLEY C. 698
A history of the greenbacks. *Chi* 1903. O [16]
577 a
—rptd *Chi* 1960. O 608

MITCHELL, REV. WILLIAM 699
Personal reminiscences . . . circuit riding . . . in
the early days of Illinois. *Arcola Ill* 1897. D 85 a

MITCHELL [SOUTH DAKOTA]. 700
The city of: and the country tributary thereto.
Mitchell 1887. O [4] 82 a

MITCHENER, C. H. 701
Ohio annals . . . events in the Tuscarawas and
Muskingum valleys . . . *Dayton* 1876. O [8] 358 a

MITCHILL, SAMUEL L. 702
The life, exploits . . . of Tammany, the famous
Indian chief . . . *N Y* 1795. O 36 port [in some
copies, but probably not issued with the pamphlet] a
Spurious biography of a mythical character.

[MITCHILL, SAMUEL L.] 703
The picture of New York . . . *N Y* 1807. 16° [8]
224 map aa
—rptd. [1828]. 16° [8] 492 7 pls
Inspired Irving's burlesque *Knickerbocker
history.*

[MITCHILL, SAMUEL L.] 704
A tour through part of Virginia in the summer
of 1808 . . . *N Y* 1809. O 31 aa
—rptd. *Belf* 1810. D 63
Attributed also to Joseph Caldwell and to T.
Caldwell.

MITE (A) CAST INTO THE TREASURY.
See Benezet, Anthony.

MITTELBERGER, GOTTLIEB 705
Reise nach Pennsylvanien . . . 1750 . . . *Stuttgart*
1756. D [8] 120 aa
—rptd. *Frankf* 1756. same collat. aa
—Eng. tr. *Phil* 1898. D 129 facs a
The author taught school in this State.

MOBILE
The chase of the rebel steamer . . . Oreto . . . into
the bay of Mobile by the . . . steam sloop Oneida . . .
See Preble, Geo. H.

Mobile directory . . . for 1837. *Mobile* 706
1837, D [10] 75 76 a

Mobile directory . . . 1839. *See* Fay T. C.

MODERN VIEW (A) 707
Modern view (A) of the thirteen United States
. . . settlement . . . cities . . . *L* D. Walker [1784].
O [2] 101 aa

MODEST ENQUIRY (A) 708
Modest enquiry (A) into the grounds . . . of a late
pamphlet, intituled, A memorial of the present
deplorable state of New-England. By a disinterested
hand. *L* 1707. O [2] 30 b AA JCB N
Defends Governor Dudley from charges levelled
against him in the pamphlet answered.

Modest enquiry into the nature and necessity of a
paper currency. *See* Franklin, Benj.

MODOC INDIANS (THE). 709
Message from the President [Grant] . . . relative
to the war with: [Ex. Doc. 112]. *Wash* 1873. O
330 a

MÖLLER, JOACHIM VAN 710
Auf nach Alaska; ein Führer fur Wagemutige.
Charlottenburg 1897. D 208 [incl 2adv-p and colophon map a

MÖLLHAUSEN, BALDUIN 711
Die in Texas und Virginien gelegenen, der Londoner allgemeinen Auswanderungs- und Colonisations-Gesellschaft gehörigen Landerein . . . *Berlin* 1850. O 55 2maps aa

MÖLLHAUSEN, BALDUIN 712
Reisen in die Felsengebirge Nord-Amerikas bis

zum Hoch-Plateau von Neu-Mexico . . . *Leip* [1860?] O 2v: [16] 455 + adv-p; [10] 406. map facs 12col pls aa
—oth. eds. *Jena* 1861. O 2v in 1: [26] 861 map 12pls aa; *Leip* O 2v aa
—Swed. tr. "Resor . . .," *Stockh* 1867. O 2v map 6pls a
   Narrative—never translated into English—of the Ives Colorado River expedition of 1857–8.

MÖLLHAUSEN, BALDUIN   713
   Tagebuch einer reise vom Mississippi nach den Küsten der Südsee. *Leip* 1858. Q [28] 496 map 14pls[13col] b
—anr. issue, same impr. & date. Q 2v: [10] 222; [20] 223–496. map 14pls aa
—rptd. 1858. O 2v map 13col.pls a
—ed. 3, 1860. O [16] 492 map
—Danish tr. "Vandringer, etc." *Copenhagen* 1862. O [16] 476 map 9pls a
—Dutch ed. "Reis van den Mississippi . . .," *Zutphen* 1858–9. O 2v [20] 358 [4]; [4] 370 [14] 3fold. maps & pls a
—Eng. ed. "Diary of a journey from the Mississippi to the coasts of the Pacific . . .," *L* 1858. O 2v: [32 incl prelim blank lf] 352; [12] 397 + adv-l. map 19pls[some col]
   Experiences and observations of the author while with the Whipple expedition, of which his is the best account.

MÖLLING, PETER A.   714
   Reise-Skizzen in Poesie und Prosa. Gesammelt auf einer siebenmonatlichen Tour durch die Vereinigten Staaten . . . *Galv* [1859?]. O 384 9pls a

MOEN, C. G. DE   715
   De Toestand der Hollandische Kolonisatie en den Staat Michigan. *Amst* 1849. O 39 2maps a

MOFFETTE, JOSEPH F.   716
   The territories of Kansas and Nebraska. *N Y* 1855. 18° 84 + 36adv-p 2maps b AA Hn N Y
—anr. ed. 1856, only 24adv-p; one of the maps, now dated 1856, contains add.matter aa
   Some of the information was secured from Peter Sarpy, one of the pioneer traders on the upper Missouri.

MOHR, EDUARD   718
   Reise-und-Jagd-Bilder aus der Südsee, Californien . . . *Bremen* 1868. D [4] 112 a

MOKLER, ALFRED J.   719
   History of Natrona county, Wyoming . . . *Chi* 1923. O [16] 477 [incl.pls] aa

MOMBERT, JACOB I.   720
   An authentic history of Lancaster county . . . Pennsylvania. *Lancaster* 1869. O [8] 617 [175] 8maps a

MONDOT, ARMAND   721
   Histoire des Indiens des États-Unis . . . *Montpellier* 1858. O [4] 352 4pls a
—anr. issue, same collat. & date, with *P* impr.
   Condensation of the first three volumes of Schoolcraft.

MONETTE, JOHN W.   722
   History of the discovery and settlement of the valley of the Mississippi . . . *N Y* 1846. O 2v: [24] 567; [16] 595. 3maps 4plans 2pls aa
—rptd., same collat., *N Y* 1848. aa

MONKS, WILLIAM   723
   History of southern Missouri and northern Arkansas . . . *West Plains Mo* 1907. D 247 [incl front]

MONROE, PRES. JAMES   724
   Message . . . at the first session of the eighteenth Congress. [And] Documents . . . [Sen. Ex. Doc. 1]. *Wash* 1823. O 2pts in 1: 16; 206. 26fold.tabs b AA NYP
   In addition to containing the notable first enunciation of the "Monroe Doctrine", one of the accompanying documents gives General Gaines' report on the upper Missouri campaign against the Arikaras.

MONROE'S EMBASSY
   Monroe's embassy . . . in relation to our claims to the navigation of the Mississippi . . . *See* Brown, Chas. Brockden.

MONROE (JAMES).   725
   A narrative of a tour . . . by: through the northeastern and north-western departments of the Union . . . *Phil* 1818. D 228 [36] a
   Not to be confused with a more general, and less military, account of this same tour, *q.v.* under its author, Samuel P. Waldo.

MONROE (COLONEL JAMES).
   Observations to shew the propriety of the nomination of: . . . By a South-Carolinian. *See* Pinckney, Chas.

[MONROE, JAMES?]   726
   Observations upon the proposed plan of federal government . . . *Petersburg* 1788. Q 64 [2] aa

MONROE'S VIEW
   Monroe's View of the conduct of the Executive. Scipio's reflections on: *See* Tracy, Uriah.

MONROE, JAMES   727
   A view of the conduct of the Executive, in the foreign affairs, etc. *Phil* 1797. O [60] 407 a
—Eng. eds. with omissions: ed. 1, *L* 1797. O [8] 117; ed. 3, same impr. & date O [16] 117

Issued in reply to criticisms on Monroe's French mission contained in Robert G. Harper's *Observations on the dispute between the United States and France*; Monroe, in turn, blames Washington.

MONTAGU, LORD ROBERT   727a
A mirror in America. *L* 1861. O 108 a

MONTAGUE, E. J.   728
A directory, business mirror, and historical sketches of Randolph County [Ill.] . . . *Alton* 1859. 16° 246 aa

MONTAGUE, PHIL. S.   729
Ready reference and hand book of the Klondike . . . gold fields. *S F* [1897]. O 58 map a

MONTAGUE, WILLIAM L.   730
Illinois and Missouri state directory . . . *St L* 1854. O 504 a

MONTAGUE COUNTY [TEXAS].   731
History of: [By Mrs. W. R. Potter] *Austin* n.d. D [8] 191 a

MONTANA
Brand book Montana Stock Growers'   731a
Association. [*Helena* 1885]. D 147 b
—same for 1886. *Chi* 1886. D 213 b
—others followed annually.

Eastern Montana in a nut shell . . . *Bozeman* 732
1879. D 40 a

Facts about Montana territory and the way to get there. *See* Boyce, James R.

Historical sketch and essay on the resources of Montana . . . *See* Maguire, H. N., and Horn, Henry

History of Montana. *Chi* 1885. *See* Leeson, Michael A.

Montana territory. History and business directory. 1879. *See* Warner, F. W.

A record of the stock brands . . . of   732a
Montana territory. [*Va City* 1872] D 4 b MontH
—rptd. *Helena* 1876. D 45 aa

MONTANUS, ARNOLDUS   733
De nieuwe en onbekende Weereld: of Beschryving van America en't Zuid-Land. *Amst* 1671. F [8, incl eng-t] 585 [27] 54maps & pls [with large fldg map signed by Schagen] b Hn JCB
—iss. 2, identical with iss 1 except port of the Prince of Nassau is omitted & fldg map is either unsigned or signed by Meurs. b
—Eng. tr. *See* Ogilby, John
—Ger. tr. *See* Dapper, O

For beauty and wealth of copperplates comparable only to De Bry. Some cops of the Dutch original edition were on L.P.

MONTCALM, marquis de   734
Lettres . . . a messieurs de Berryer & de la Molé. [Fr. & Eng. on opposite pages]. *L* 1777. O [2] 56 aa
Parkman proved these letters to be forgeries.

[MONTEIRO, ARISTIDES]   735
War reminiscences . . . *Rich* 1890. D 208 front. errata lf a Small ed.
—ed 2, same impr & date D 238 + inserted pink lf a

MONTEITH, JOHN B.   736
The status of young Joseph and his band of Nez Perce Indians . . . *Port Ore* 1876. O 49 a

MONTÉMONT, ALBERT   737
De l'Oregon et de la Californie . . . *P* 1846. O 23 a
Compilation, chiefly from Duflot de Mofras.

MONTEREY   738
Hand book to Monterey and vicinity. Containing a brief . . . history . . . *Monterey* 1875. 16° 128 aa

History of Monterey county, California   739
[*S F*] 1881. F 188 pls c B CalS

Taking possession of Monterey. Message   740
of the President . . . in reply to the resolution . . . calling for information in relation to the taking . . . of Monterey by Thomas Ap. Catesby Jones. [House Ex. Doc. 156]. [*Wash* 1843]. O 117 aa
Presents the Government's story of the conquest of California. Said to have been suppressed.

MONTGOMERY, CORA
Eagle pass. *See* Cazneau, Mrs. Wm. L.

MONTGOMERY, CORINNE
Texas and her presidents. *See* Cazneau, Mrs. Wm. L.

MONTGOMERY, ELIZABETH   741
Reminiscences of Wilmington [Del.] . . . *Phil* 1851. O [12] 7–367 4pls a
—rptd. *Wilm* 1872. O 310
Nearly all of the original edition burned.

[MONTGOMERY, DR. JAMES]   742
Decius's letters on the opposition to the new constitution in Virginia, 1789. *Rich* [1789]. O [2] 134 b
—ed. 3, with adds., *Rich* 1818. O [2] 36 aa
Attributed also to John Nicholas.

MONTGOMERY, M. W.   743
History of Jay county, Ind. *Chi* 1864. D 288 map a

[MONTGOMERY, SIR ROBERT]　　744
A description of the golden islands, with an account of the undertaking . . . of making a settlement there . . . *L* 1720. O 45 b GaU
These were islands on the Georgia coast, included in the proposed Margravate of Azilia.

MONTGOMERY, SIR ROBERT　　745
A discourse concerning the design'd establishment of a new colony to the south of Carolina . . . *L* 1717. O [2] 30 [3] plan c N NYP [the 3-p Appendix is not found in all cops]
—rptd. *Tarrytown* [1915] Q 36 pl a
Earliest project for a settlement in Georgia on the coast islands and between the Altamaha and Savannah rivers, to be called the Margravate of Azilia.

MONTGOMERY
City directory and history of Montgomery, Ala. 1878. *See* Beale and Phelan.

Journal of the Southern Rights conven-　746 tion, held in . . . Montgomery [Ala.]. *Montg* 1851. O 40 a

Montgomery directory . . . 1859–60.
See Turnbull, M. S.

MONTIGNY, [JEAN FRANCOIS] DE, et al　747
Relation de la mission du Mississippi . . . en 1700. *N Y* 1861. D 66 [2] a 100 copies ptd.
Contains St. Cosme's narrative of his work among the Indians in the upper Mississippi valley.

[MONTLEZUN, baron de]　　748
Souvenirs des Antilles: Voyage en 1815 et 1816, aux États-Unis. *P* 1818 O 2v: [8] 406; [4] 590 aa
For his later visit to the United States, *see* next entry.

[MONTLEZUN, baron de]　　749
Voyage . . . de New-Yorck à la Nouvelle-Orléans . . . *P* 1818. O 2v: [4] 374; [4] 408 aa
Bitterly satirical views of republican society by a Parisian aristocrat who maintains that the sale of Louisiana to the United States by "a miserable Corsican" should be annulled, as a fraud on the French nation, and the province restored to France.

MONTULÉ, EDOUARD DE　　750
Voyage en Amérique . . . *P* 1821. O 2v: [10] 466; [8] 448 + atlas Q [map 58pls] b H IndU NYP Y
—Eng. tr. [of portion relating to North America] *L* 1821. O 102 6pls a
—anr. Eng. tr. *Bloomington Ind* 1951. O 197 map 17pls
Describes his steamboat trip up the Mississippi and Ohio. The plates are highly interesting.

MOODY, JAMES　　751
Narrative of his exertions . . . in the cause of government, since . . . 1776. *L* 1782. O 59 aa
—ed. 2—and best—with adds., *L* 1783. O [4] 57 [7] aa
—Am. ed. *N Y* 1865. O 98 4ports 100 copies ptd a
Services of a New Jersey Tory as a British scout and spy.

[MOOERS, J. H.]　　752
Sioux Falls, the queen city of South Dakota . . . *Sioux Falls* 1889. O 32 a

MOONEY, THOMAS　　753
Nine years in America. *Dub* 1850. D 154 a
—ed. 2, same impr., date & collat.

[MOOR, REV. ALLEN P.]　　754
Letters from North America . . . *Canterbury* 1855. D [4] 72 small ed. ptd. a
Visited Maine, Connecticut and west to Illinois and Wisconsin.

MOORE, ALBERT B.　　755
Conscription and conflict in the Confederacy. *N Y* 1924. O [14] 367 a

MOORE, CHARLES B.　　756
Town of Southold, Long Island . . . *N Y* 1868. obl Q 145 a

MOORE, CLEON　　757
Epitome of the life of . . . John Brown . . . his attack on Harper's Ferry . . . *Point Pleasant W Va* 1904. O 22 port a

MOORE (DANIEL . . . collector of . . .　758
customs at Charles-Town).
A representation of facts relative to the conduct of: . . . *Charleston S C* 1767. F [8] 3–43 c BM 2copies located

MOORE, EDWARD A.　　759
The story of a cannoneer under Stonewall Jackson . . . *N Y* 1907. D 215 15pls a

MOORE (POST-CAPTAIN E[DWIN] W.)　760
A brief synopsis of the doings of the Texas navy under . . . : *Wash Tex* 1847. O 32 aa

MOORE (POST-CAPTAIN EDWIN W.)　761
Documents relative to the dismissal of: from the Texian navy. [*Wash Tex* 1847?]. O 29 aa

[MOORE, POST-CAPTAIN EDWIN W.]　762
To the people of Texas. [A documented appeal, vindicating his conduct, as commander of the Texas navy, against Sam Houston's insensate charges]. [*Galveston* 1843] O 204 [incl blank prelim lf] caption title only. c S TxU [of 4 known cops]

MOORE, FRANCIS 763
A voyage to Georgia . . . *L* 1744. O 108 [2] b AA GaU N NYP Y

MOORE, FRANCIS, JR. 764
Map and description of Texas . . . *Phil* 1840. 16° 144 front.[not in all copies] 8pls fold.map b
—ed. 2, "Description of Texas," *N Y* 1844. 16° [2] 144 no map or pls aa

MOORE, FRANCIS M. 765
A brief history of the missionary work in the Indian Territory . . . *Muskogee* 1899. O 227 aa

MOORE, FRANK, ed. 766
Diary of the American revolution . . . *N Y* 1860–59. O 2v: 528; 559. 6maps 12pls a
—anr. issue, both vols. dated 1860.
—rptd., same collat. & impr. 1863.
—anr. ed., on L.P., with pls on India paper, same collat. *N Y* 1865. 100copies a
—other eds.: *Hart* 1875. O 1084 pls; 1876.

MOORE, FRANK, ed. 767
Material for history printed from original manuscripts. Series I, Laurens correspondence. [all]. *N Y* Zenger Club 1861. Q [4] 9–240 port 250 copies ptd a

MOORE, GEORGE 768
Journal of a voyage across the Atlantic . . . *L* priv. ptd. 1845. D [8] 96 aa

MOORE, H. JUDGE 769
Scott's campaign in Mexico . . . *Charleston S C* 1849. D [12] 234 aa
Narrative of an eye-witness; remarkable for credit given Santa Anna.

MOORE, HORATIO N. 770
Life . . . of Gen. Anthony Wayne . . . *Phil* [1845]. 18° 208[incl.pls] a

MOORE, HORATIO N. 771
The life . . . of Gen. Francis Marion . . . *Phil* 1845. D [2] 7–210 7pls a
—other eds., same impr. & collat., n.d.; 1855.

MOORE HUGH 772
Memoir of Col. Ethan Allen . . . *Plattsburgh* 1834. D 252 a

MOORE, J. H. 773
The political condition of the Indians . . . of the Indian Territory. *St L* 1874. O 62 aa

MOORE, JAMES, M. D. 774
Kilpatrick and our cavalry . . . from the beginning of the rebellion to the surrender of Johnston. *N Y* 1865. D [14 incl.port] 26–245 12pls a

MOORE, JOHN WHEELER 775
History of North Carolina . . . *Raleigh* 1880. O 2v: [21] 495; 530 b
—rptd. *Raleigh* 1900, same collat a

MOORE (MISS MADELINE). 776
A wonderful . . . narrative of the adventures of: who, in order to be near her lover, joined the army, was elected Lieutenant and fought in West Virginia. *Phil* Barclay [1862]. O 40 a
Sheer romance, factually worthless.

MOORE, M[AURICE] A. 777
The life of Gen. Edward Lacey . . . in South Carolina during the revolution. *Spartanburg* 1859. O 32 aa

MOORE, S. S., and JONES, T. W. 778
The traveller's directory . . . from Philadelphia to New York . . . *Phil* 1802. O [6] 52 38maps[on 22 l.] aa
—ed. 2, same impr. 1804. O [4] 37 [19] 38maps[on 22 l.] a
One of the earliest guides.

[MOORE, WILLIAM] 779
The crisis. To be continued weekly during the present bloody civil war in America. [*L*] 1775–6. F 91nos[paged continuously] 574 & broadside Declaration of Independence for July 4, 1776 b NYP
—Am. eds.: *Newport* [1775], O 9nos[caption titles, paged continuously] 72; *Hart* 1775 D 6 nos.only 48 p; *N Y* 1776, D 28nos [paged continuously] 236 aa
Violent censure of the British ministry's American policy; Thomas Paine probably borrowed this title when he launched a similar series. One extra number was issued, August 9, 1775, called "The Crisis. Extraordinary."

[MOORE, WILLIAM H.] 780
Startling incidents . . . of Osawotomy Brown's . . . movements at Harper's Ferry. *Balt* 1859. O 72 a

MOOREHEAD, WARREN K. 781
The American Indian in the United States . . . 1850–1914. *Andover* 1914. O 440 2maps 9pls a

MOOREHEAD, WARREN K. 782
The stone age in North America . . . *B* 1910. O 2v: [12] 458 [1]; [8] 418. 20pls aa

MOOREHEAD, WARREN K. 783
Stone ornaments used by Indians . . . *Andover* 1917. O [4] 10–458 + adv-p 10pls aa

MOOSO (JOSIAH). 784
The life and travels of: . . . A life on the frontier among Indians and Spaniards . . . *Winfield Kas* 1888. O 400 port aa

MORAN, THOMAS

The Yellowstone national park . . . *See* Hayden, Ferdinand V.

MORAVIANS (THE).

Historical sketch of the church and missions of: *See* Reichel, Edw. H.

[MORDECAI, SAMUEL]   **785**

Richmond in by-gone days . . . *Rich* 1856. 16° 321 [incl initial blank 1f] a

—ed. 2, with adds., "Virginia, especially Richmond, in by-gone days . . .," *Rich* 1860. 16° 359

—rptd *Rich* [1946] D 362

MORÉ, [CHARLES ALBERT, CHEVA-   **786**
LIER DE PONTGIBAUD] comte de.

Mémoires du: . . . *P* 1827. O [4] 319 front. aa

—rptd. *P* 1898. O [6] 343 5pls a

—Eng. ed. "A French volunteer of the war of independence (the Chevalier de Pontgibaud)," *P* 1897. O [12] 209 port

—ed. 2, *P* 1898, t. slightly altered. same collat.

—Ger. ed. "Denkwuerdigkeiten des Grafen von M . . .," *Dessau* 1829. 16° [6] 258

The original Paris edition was printed by Honoré Balzac.

[MOREAU, JACOB N.] comp.   **787**

Mémoire contenant les précis des faits . . . pour servir de réponse aux Observations envoyées par les Ministres d'Angleterre, dans les cours de l'Europe. *P* 1756. Q [6] 198 c H NYP Y

—other Fr. eds.: *P* 1757, D [12] 275; *P* 1756, D [8] 292; *P* 1757, same collat; *P* 1758 aa

—Eng. ed. "The conduct of the late ministry . . .," *L* 1757. O [6] 320 b N NYP

—rptd. under t. "The mystery revealed; or, truth brought to light . . . By a patriot . . .," *L* 1759. O [2] 319 b N Y

—Am. eds. "A memorial containing a summary view of facts . . .," *Phil* 1757, O [6 incl. $^1/_2$ t. probably added later] 338 b AA NYP Y; *N Y* 1757, O [4] 190 b AA N NYP Y

France had issued a *Memorial* to the world presenting her side of the dispute with England; England replied with her *Observations* [on that *Memorial*]; this *Mémoire* is in rebuttal and embodied papers taken from Washington on his surrender of Ft. Necessity, which, it was claimed, proved him to have practically murdered Jumonville, *cf.*, *Reasons humbly offered* . . .

MOREAU DE SAINT-MÉRY,   **788**
MÉDÉRIC L. É.

Extrait d'un ouvrage manuscrit intitulé: Lettres d'un francais voyageur à un de ses amis en France. *Phil* [1798]. O 45 aa

MORECAMP, ARTHUR, *pseud.*   **789**

Live boys in the Black hills . . . adventure during a second trip over the great Texas cattle trail . . . among the miners . . . *B* 1880. D 363 a

—ed 2 *B* [1880] D 364 + 4adv-p [2 front, 2 rear]

MORECAMP, ARTHUR, *pseud.*   **790**

Live boys; or Charley and Nasho in Texas . . . their life on the great Texas cattle trail . . . *B*[1878]. D 308 [12] 11–308 + 10adv-p 6pls aa

Author of this earliest authentic, though fictionalized, cowboy narrative was Thomas Pilgrim, who wrote under pseudnym shown.

MOREHEAD, JAMES T.   **791**

An address in commemoration of the first settlement of Kentucky. *Frankfort* 1840. O 181 aa

MORFI, JUAN A.   **792**

History of Texas, 1673–1779 . . . *Albuquerque* Quivira Soc 1935. O 2v: 242; [6] 243–496 map 4pls 500 copies ptd. aa

First complete publication in any language of this contemporary manuscript; most complete history of Spanish Texas in its early period. Portions only were given in a 1932 San Antonio ed.

MORFIT, HENRY M.   **793**

The political, military and civil condition of Texas. [H. Doc.35]. *Wash* 1836. O 34 a

Report on the new republic made by an investigator for the United States.

MORGAN, A. W., & CO., pub.   **794**

San Francisco directory . . . *S F* 1852. O 174 b Hn Soc. of Calif.Pioneers

MORGAN, A[LBERT] T.   **795**

Yazoo, or the picket line of freedom in the south. *Wash* 1884. O [6] 9–512 a

MORGAN, GEORGE H.   **796**

Annals . . . of Harrisburg . . . *Harrisburg* 1858. D 400 a

MORGAN, [MRS.] GERTRUDE: **797**

or, life and adventures among the Indians of the far west. *Phil* Barclay [1866? 1876?]. O 40 a Unadulterated fiction.

MORGAN, JAMES M.   **798**

Recollections of a rebel reefer . . . *B* 1917. O [22] 492 18pls a also a special issue of 200copies, with leather label and g.t. aa

MORGAN, JOHN   **799**

A discourse upon the institution of medical schools in America . . . *Phil* 1765. D [36] 63 b

MORGAN, JOHN, et al   **800**

Four dissertations on the reciprocal advantages of a perpetual union between Great Britain and her American colonies . . . *Phil* 1766. O [18] 12 [2] 112 a

—Eng. ed. *L* same date. O

MORGAN, JOHN 801
A vindication of his public character in the station of . . . physician in chief of the American army . . . *B* 1777. O [44] 158 a

MORGAN, LEWIS H. 802
The American beaver . . . *Phil* 1868. O 330 map 23pls a

MORGAN, LEWIS H. 803
Ancient society . . . *N Y* 1877. O [16] 560 a
—rptd., same impr. & collat., 1878.

MORGAN, LEWIS H. 804
League of the . . . Iroquois. *Roch* 1851. O [18] 477 map 21pls fold. tab aa
—anr. ed. *N Y* 1901. O 2v: [24] 338; [4] 332 2maps 33pls 300 sets ptd [30 on Jap. vell.] aa
—rptd.: *N Y* 1904, O 2v in 1; *N Y* 1922 a

MORGAN, MRS. MARTHA M., ed. 805
A trip across the plains in . . . 1849 . . . *S F* 1864. D 31 & cover t. dd CalS Hn H S Y [only copies known]
Written from the journal kept by the writer's husband. For another book by this authoress, *see* Graham, Mrs. Martha M.

MORGAN, RICHARD P. 806
Report of the survey of the route of the Galena and Chicago Union Rail Road . . . *Chi* 1847. O 28 map aa anr. iss t. shortened no impr a
For annual reports *see Galena and Chicago Union Railroad.*

MORGAN (WILLIAM).
Confession of the murder of: *See* Valance, Henry L.

MORGAN (WILLIAM). 807
A narrative of the facts . . . relating to the kidnapping . . . of: [*Batavia N Y* 1827]. O 36 aa
—anr. ed., with trials added, *Brookfield Mass* 1827. D 84 aa
—ed. 3, *Roch* 1828. D 72 a
—Ger. tr. n.p. 1828. 16° 80 a

MORGAN (CAPT. WILLIAM). 808
The trial of James Lackey, Isaac Evertson and others for kidnapping: *N Y* 1827. O 24 a

MORI, ARINORI 809
Life and resources in America . . . *Wash* 1871. D 404 [1] port a

MORINEAU, AUGUSTE DE 810
Essai statistique et politique sur les États-Unis. *P* 1848. F [6] 5–39 port 27tabs a

MORISON, GEORGE 811
An interesting journal of occurrences during the expedition to Quebec under Arnold. *Hagerstown* 1803. D 66 b
—rptd. *Tarrytown* 1916. O 44 a

MORISON, SAMUEL E. 812
The maritime history of Massachusetts . . . *B* 1921. O [18] 402 48pls a
—L.P. issue. Q same paginat. 60pls 385 copies ptd.
First issue has reading, on page 150, "scared codfish."

[MORMON]
A book of commandments, for the government of the Church of Christ . . . 1833. *See* Smith, Joseph.

Constitution of the State of Deseret, with 813
a journal of the convention which formed it and the
proceedings of the legislature consequent thereon.
Kanesville Iowa 1849. O 16 dd G H[of 4copies known]
—anr. ed., with laws passed by the legislature from Nov. 12, 1849 to March 28, 1850, [*S L C* 1850?]. O 34 capt.t.only c G H

Document containing the correspondence 814
[etc.] in relation to the disturbances with the Mormons . . . *Fayette Mo* 1841. O [4] 163 c LC MoH NYP Y

Life among the Mormons and a march to their Zion . . . By an officer . . . *See* Waters, Wm. E.

Mormon fanaticism exposed. *See* Parsons, Tyler.

Mormonism exposed: in which is shown . . . *See* Sunderland, La Roy.

Mormons (The); or, knavery exposed . . . 815
Frankfort Pa 1841. O 24 aa
The Kirtland period of the Saints.

Mormons (The): or Latter Day Saints. With memoirs of the life . . . of Joseph Smith . . . *See* Mayhew, Henry.

Mormons (The). The dream and the re- 816
ality . . . *L* 1857. 16° [8] 92 a

Some account of the so-called Church of 816a
the Latter-Day Saints. *L* 1852. 18° 24 a

Twelve Mormon homes . . . *See* Kane, Mrs. Elizabeth D.

MORPHIS, J[AMES] M. 817
History of Texas . . . *N Y* 1874. O [8] 601 [incl advs] map a
—rptd., same impr. 1875, same collat

MORRELL, BENJAMIN 818
A narrative of four voyages, to the South sea,

north and south Pacific . . . 1822–31. *N Y* 1832. O [8] 492 + 4adv-p port aa
—rptd., same impr.: 1841; 1853. a
Includes visit to the Northwest coast and a long stay in California, in 1825.

MORRELL, Z. N.   **819**
Flowers and fruits from the wilderness; or thirty-six years in Texas . . . *B* 1872. D 386 aa
—ed. 2, rev., *B* 1873. D 386 port a
—ed. 3, with sub-t. "forty-six years in Texas," *St L* 1882. D 412 port a
—rptd. *Dallas* 1886. D 426 port a
Corner-stone narrative of early Texas.

MORRILL, EDMUND N.   **820**
History and statistics of Brown county, Kansas . . . *Hiawatha* 1876. D 82 aa
—ed. 2, "History of Brown county . . .," *Hiawatha* 1876. aa

MORRIS, B. F.   **821**
Historical sketch of Rising Sun, Indiana . . . *Cin* 1858. O 31 a

MORRIS (COMMODORE CHARLES).   **822**
The autobiography of: *Annap* 1880. O 111 front. a
—anr. issue, same date & collat., *B*

MORRIS (DRAKE).   **823**
The travels of . . .: *L* 1755. D [20] 328 aa
—ed. 2, same impr., date & collat. a
—rptd., "Interesting narrative . . .," *L* 1797. D [16] 198 a

MORRIS, EASTIN   **824**
The Tennessee gazetteer . . . And a condensed history [etc.]. *Nashv* 1834. D [4] 116 178 [18] aa

[MORRIS, GOUVERNEUR]   **825**
An answer to War in disguise . . . *N Y* 1806. O 76 a
—rptd. *L* 1806. same collat.
More probably by Rufus King.

MORRIS (GOUVERNEUR).   **826**
The diary and letters of: Ed. A. C. Morris. *N Y* 1888. O 2v: [16] 604; [12] 630. 2ports a

MORRIS, GOUVERNEUR   **827**
A diary of the French revolution. Ed. Beatrix C. Davenport. *B* 1939. O 2v: [46] 618; [8] 652 16 pls. a

[MORRIS, GOUVERNEUR]   **828**
Notes on the United States . . . *Phil* 1816. O 48 a

[MORRIS, GOUVERNEUR]   **829**
Observations on the American revolution . . . *Phil* 1779. O [4] 122 a
—ed. 2, *Prov* 1780. O 126

MORRIS, MARGARET   **830**
Private journal kept during a portion of the revolutionary war . . . *Phil* priv. ptd. 1836. sm Q 31 aa
—rptd. *N Y* 1865. Q [4] 36 50copies ptd [only 12 with t-p & pref] a

MORRIS, MAURICE O'C.   **831**
Rambles in the Rocky mountains . . . *L* 1864. O [8] 264 a

MORRIS, [BISHOP] T[HOMAS] A.   **832**
Miscellany . . . *Cin* 1852. D 390 port a
—rptd., same collat., *Cin* 1853; *Cin* 1854.
Includes a 46-page account of a trip through Missouri and Arkansas to Austin, Texas, in 1841–2; also an 1844 trip to Tahlequah.

MORRIS, CAPT. THOMAS   **833**
Miscellanies in prose and verse. *L* 1791. O [8] 64 [4] 67–181 port d N NYP PittU.
Valuable source on Pontiac's conspiracy.

[MORRIS, WILLIAM W.]   **834**
Considerations on . . . annexing the province of Texas to the United States. *N Y* 1829 O 40 b TxU Y

MORRISON, ADÈLE SARPY   **835**
Memoirs. *St L* 1911. O [10] 206 [2] 5pls aa 100copies ptd.
By the daughter of Jean Baptiste Sarpy, partner in the American Fur Company and Nebraska pioneer.

MORRISON, ANDREW   **836**
The industries of Dallas . . . *Dallas* 1887. O 136 a

MORRISON, M. V. B.   **837**
The orphan's experience: or, the hunter and trapper . . . in the southern states . . . Also . . . trapping expeditions on the plains of the great west . . . *Des M* 1868. O [12] 204 aa

MORRISON (WILLIAM, the Rocky   **838**
mountain trapper).
Horrible and awful developments from the confession of: . . . *Phil* 1853. O 32 b G
Lots of blood and thunder; quite incredible; equally rare.

MORSE, JEDIDIAH   **839**
The American gazetteer . . . *B* 1797. O [8] 619 7maps a
—abr. ed. *B* 1798. D 388 map
—ed. 2, enl., *Charlestown* 1804. O [6] 628 6maps
—ed. 3, rev., *B* 1810. O 600 2maps
—Eng. ed., with adds., calling itself 2nd ed., *L* 1798. O [8] 634 7maps
—later Am. eds., "The traveller's guide; or pocket

gazetteer,": *N Hav* 1823. 16° 324 map; *N Hav* 1826. D

This formed Vol. I of his *Universal gazetteer,* 1810.

MORSE, JEDIDIAH   **840**
The American geography, or, a view of the present situation of the United States ... *Elizabeth Town N J* 1789. O [12] 534 [4] 2maps aa
—ed. 2, *L* 1792. O [16] 536 2maps a
—ed. 3, *Dub* 1792. O same collat a
—new ed., enl., *L* 1794. Q [12] 715 3maps Of this best ed. a few copies were issued with 25maps [earliest separate dated ones of the various states] aa
—anr. ed. *Edin* 1795. 7maps a
—Fr. tr. Tableau ... des États Unis ... *P* 1795. O 2v 2maps a

MORSE, JEDIDIAH   **840a**
Annals of the American revolution ... *Hart* 1824. O [4] 400 [50] 6pls a

MORSE, JEDIDIAH   **841**
A description of the ... Georgia Western Territory ... *B* 1797. D 24 map aa
Separate printing from author's *American gazetteer.*

MORSE, JEDIDIAH   **842**
Geography made easy ... for the use of schools in the United States. *N Hav* Meigs, etc. [1784]. D 215 2maps b
—cd. 2, calling itself "An abridgment of The American geography," *B* 1790. D 322 8maps
—22 reprs. issued by 1820.
First American school geography and first American book describing the western country. Later expanded into his *American geography* of 1789 and *American gazetteer* of 1797.

MORSE, JEDIDIAH   **843**
A report ... on Indian affairs, comprising a narrative of a tour ... for the purpose of ascertaining ... the actual state of the Indian tribes ... *N Hav* 1822. O 96 400 errata 1f map port a

MORSE, JEDIDIAH and R. C.
The traveller's guide; or, pocket gazetteer. *See* above under *The American gazetteer.*

MORSE, JOHN F., and   **844**
COLVILLE, SAMUEL
Illustrated historical sketches of California ... No.I[all]. *Sacr* 1854. O 46 [8] front. b N

MORTIMER, GEORGE   **845**
Observations ... during a voyage to the islands of Teneriffe ... Owhyhee, the Fox islands on the northwest coast of America ... *L* 1791. Q [16] 72 2maps pl c JCB N NYP Y
—rptd. *Dub* 1791. O [14] 119 b
—Dutch tr. *Leyden* 1793. O aa

Early British investigation into the possibilities of fur-trading on the northwest coast. For German account of this voyage *see* under Portlock and Mortimer, *Reisen an die Nortvestkuste von Amerika* ...

[MORTIMER, J.]   **846**
La sécession aux États-Unis et son origine ... *P* 1861. O 30 a

MORTON, CAPITAIN   **847**
Californien das neue Goldland ... Nach dem Englischen ... *Grimma* 1849. 16° [6] 5–77 map b NYH S
Apparently no English edition exists.

[MORTON, CHARLES]?   **848**
A vindication of New-England, from the vile aspersions ... by a late address of a faction there ... n.p. [1688?] Q 27 b AA Clem
Ascribed also to Increase Mather, who probably had a hand in its preparation.

MORTON, JOHN W.   **849**
The artillery of ... Forrest's cavalry. *Nashv* 1909. O 374 10pls a

MORTON, OREN F.   **850**
A history of Pendleton county, West Virginia. *Franklin* 1910. O [8] 493 map 10 pls a

MORTON, NATHANIEL   **851**
New Englands memoriall ... *C* 1669. smQ [12] 198 [10] dd H LC N
—ed. 2, with adds by Josiah Cotton. *B* 1721. D [10] 248 [2] b
—ed. 3, *Newport* 1772. O [8] 208 [8] aa
—oth. eds: *Plymouth* 1826, D [12] 204; *B* 1826, O 481 [2] map; *B* 1855, O [24] 515 2pls a
One of the earliest secular products of the Cambridge press and the first strictly historical book published in New England.

MORTON, SAMUEL G.   **852**
An inquiry into the distinctive characteristics of the aboriginal race of America. *Phil* 1840. O 37 a
—rptd. *B* 1842. same collat.
—ed. 2, *Phil* 1844. O 48

MORTON (CYRUS).   **853**
Autobiography of: *Omaha* 1895. O 46 port b G
Includes trips from Nebraska to Colorado and Montana gold regions.

MOSBY (JOHN S.)   **854**
The memoirs of: *B* 1917. O [22] 414 fold. map 16pls a

MOSBY'S COMMAND.
Reminiscences of his capture and escape ... by a member of: *see* Rahm, Frank H.

MOSER, JOHANN J.   **855**
Nord-Amerika nach den Friedensschlüssen vom Jahr 1783 . . . *Leip* 1784–5. O 3v: [16] 840; [4] 682; [2] 598 [24]. map a
First comprehensive analysis of this republic of states.

MOSES, JOHN   **856**
Illinois, historical . . . *Chi* 1889–92. O 2v: [4] 9–552 + 6adv-p; [10] 553–1316 + 2adv-p. 52pls aa
—ed. 2, enl., *Chi* 1895. O 2v: 1419, pls

MOSGROVE, GEORGE D.   **857**
Kentucky cavaliers in Dixie . . . *Louisv* 1895. O 265 22pls errata slip aa
—rptd. *Jackson Tenn* 1957.

MOTA PADILLA, MATIAS A. DE LA   **858**
Historia de la conquista de la Nueva-Galicia. *Guadalajara* 1855–6. O 3v: b
—best ed. *Mex* 1870–[72]. Q [20] 524 [10] 3pls 4fold.tabs aa
—rptd. *Guadalajara* 1920. Q 555 [10] a
Written originally in 1742 and first printed as shown, in 1855–6, from an untrustworthy manuscript and containing 1265 errors, that edition was pronounced by the Mexican Geographical Society as "non-existent," to be replaced by the 1870 version. Most comprehensive early chronicle of the interior states of Mexico, including Arizona, New Mexico and Texas. It is also a recognized authority on both the Coronado expedition and the Cabeza de Vaca incident.

MOTT, FRANK L.   **859**
A history of American magazines, 1741–1905. *C* 1938-1957. O 4v: [20] 848; [18] 608; [16] 649; [20] 858. 92pls aa

[MOTT, M. H.]   **860**
History of the regulators of northern Indiana . . . *Indp* 1859. O 67 b G IndS LC N [only cops loc]
Operations of organized counterfeiters, horse-thieves and murderers who ravaged this region from 1835 until dispersed in 1858 by outraged citizens.

MOULTON, JOSEPH W.   **861**
New York 170 years ago . . . *N Y* 1843. O 24 pl a

MOULTON, JOSEPH W.   **862**
A view of the city of New Orange (now New York), as it was in . . . 1673. *N Y* 1825. O 40 pl a

MOULTON (WILLIAM).   **863**
A concise extract, from the sea journal of: . . . *Utica* 1804. O 159 aa
Voyage was from New London to the Pacific, 1799–1804. First book printed at Utica.

MOULTRIE, A.   **864**
An appeal to the people on the conduct of a certain public body in South-Carolina, respecting Col. Drayton and Col. Moultrie. *Charleston* 1794. O 28 aa

MOULTRIE, WILLIAM   **865**
Memoirs of the American revolution . . . as it related to . . . Carolina, and Georgia . . . *N Y* 1802. O 2v: 506[incl. port]; 446 [2] aa
—rptd. *N Y* 1805. same collat. aa

MOUNTAIN MEADOWS   **866**
History of the Mountain Meadows massacre . . . account of the trial . . . and execution of John D. Lee . . . [*S F*] Spalding & Barto 1877. O 32 port a

Message of the President communicating   **867**
information in relation to the massacre at Mountain Meadows . . . [Sen. Exec. Doc. 42]. [*Wash* 1860]. O 139 a
A fifty-one-page House Document 78, issued the same year, differed in contents. *See* also Carleton, James H., and Cradlebaugh, John.

MOUNTAINEER (THE).
See Speece, Conrad.

MOUNTGOMERY, SIR ROBERT
See Montgomery.

MOUSTIER, ELEONORE-FRANCOIS-   **868**
ELIE, comte de
Observations . . . sur l'affaire du Scioto. *P* 1790. O 25 aa

MOWRY, SYLVESTER   **869**
The geography and resources of Arizona and Sonora. *Wash* 1859. O 48 errata slip aa
—anr. ed. enl. *S F* 1863. O [6] 3–124 map errata slip aa
—ed. 3, rev. t. altered *N Y* 1864. D 251[incl. pl] a

MOWRY, SYLVESTER   **870**
Memoir of the proposed Territory of Arizona. *Wash* 1857. O 30 b
Most important Arizona historical document of the period, and the first book relating exclusively to that Territory. A map lithographed in Cincinnati, intended to accompany this *Memoir* but probably not issued with it, is found inserted in some copies.

MUDD, NETTIE   **871**
The life of Dr. Samuel A. Mudd. *N Y* 1906. O 326 port 6pls aa
—enl ed *Marietta Ga* 1955. O 361 a

MUDD (DR. SAMUEL A.)   **872**
Testimony for the prosecution [etc.] in the case of: charged with conspiracy to assassinate the President . . . *Wash* 1865. O 311 aa

MUDGE, ZACHARIAH A.   **873**
The missionary teacher: a memoir of Cyrus Shepard, embracing a brief sketch of the . . . Oregon mission. *N Y* 1848. 16° 221 [incl.front.] + adv-p aa
—rptd., same collat.: *N Y* n.d.; *N Y* 1853. a
Shepard crossed the plains with Wyeth in 1834. *Cf.* Perkins, H. K. W., *Sketches of mission life . . .*

[MÜLLER, GERHARD F.]?   **874**
Lettre d'un officier de la marine Russienne . . . concernant la carte des nouvelles découvertes au nord de la mer du Sud, et la mémoire . . . publie par M. de Lisle à Paris . . . *Berlin* [1753]. Q 60 b
—Eng. tr., abr., with observations by Arthur Dobbs added, *L* 1754. O [2] 84 b Hn JCB Y
—Ger. tr. *Berlin* [1753?]. 16° 54 aa
Important work on efforts to discover a passage from the Pacific to the Atlantic, containing account of Bering's second voyage. *See* also No. 875, below, and Buache, Philip, *Explication de la carte . . .* Wickersham gives name of the Russian officer as Sven Waxel, Bering's second in command who brought back from the American coast the few survivors of his expedition.

MÜLLER, GERHARD F.   **875**
Nachrichten von Seereisen und zur See gemachten Entdeckungen, die von Russland aus längs den Küsten des Eismeeres und auf dem östlichen Weltmeere gegen Japan und Amerika geschehen sind, zur Erlauterung einer bei der Academie der Wissenschaften verfertigten Land-karte. [Vol. III, Pt. 1, *Sammlung russischer Geschichte*, issued at *St Ptbg* 1758, in 4vols.]. O 304 b NYP Y
—rptd. 1759. aa
—Eng. ed. by Thomas Jefferys, "Voyages from Asia to America for completing the discoveries of the north west coast of America . . .," *L* 1761. Q [52] 76 4maps[on 3 sheets] b N NYP WashU Y
—Eng. ed. 2, enl. with index added *L* 1764. Q [8] 120 4maps [on 3sheets] b
—Fr. ed. "Voyages et découvertes faites par les Russes le long des côtes de la mer glaciale . . .," *Amst* 1766. D 2v: [12] 388; [4] 207 [22]. map aa
—rptd. 1768. same collat. aa
Most important contemporary account of Bering's discoveries, by a scientist attached to his second expedition. *See* also, No. 874 above, *Lettre d'un officier de la marine . . .*

MÜLLER, J.   **876**
Das goldland Californien . . . *Leitmoritz* 1850. 16° 84 6pls[on 3sheets] aa

MÜLLER, JOHANN J.   **877**
Extract aus unsers Conferenz-Schreibers . . . gehalten in Germantown . . . *Phil* B. Franklin 1742. Q 2pts: [2] 93–102; [2] 105–120 b NYP Y

For earlier Moravian conferences, of which these were continuations [and from which these were continued in pagination], *see Authentische Relation von dem Anlass . . .*

MÜLLER, M. G. P.
Voyages et découvertes faites par les Russes . . . *See* No. 875 above.

MÜLLER, S.
Voyages from Asia to America . . . *See* No. 875, above.

MÜNCH, FRIEDRICH   **878**
Der Staat Missouri . . . *N Y* [1858]. D 237 2maps a
—rptd. *Bremen* 1866. D map
—ed. 2, *N Y* 1875. O 181 map 4pls

MUHLENBERG, HENRY A.   **879**
The life of Major-General Peter Muhlenberg . . . *Phil* 1849. D 456 port a

MUIR, JOHN   **880**
The mountains of California. *N Y* 1894. D [4 9–14] 381 front. a

MULFORD, AMI F.
Fighting Indians in the 7th United States Cavalry . . . *Corning N Y* 1878. 16° 223 b G Y
—ed. 2, same impr., [*ca* 1930] D 155 a

MULFORD, ISAAC S.   **881**
Civil and political history of New Jersey. *Camden* 1848. O 500 a
—rptd., t. lengthened, *Phil* 1851. same collat.

MULFORD, PRENTICE   **882**
Prentice Mulford's story . . . *N Y* 1889. D 300 + adv p a
—rptd. [*Oakl* 1953] a
Embraces his life in California in the '50's and '60's, including a ten-month whaling voyage.

MULLAN (LT. (JOHN)).   **883**
Letter from the Secretary of War transmitting the report of: in charge of the construction of a military road from Ft. Benton to Ft. Walla-Walla . . . [H. Exec. Doc. 44]. *Wash* 1861. O 171 map aa

MULLAN (CAPTAIN JOHN).   **884**
Letter of the Secretary of War, transmitting . . . the report and maps of: . . . of his operations . . . in the construction of a military road from Fort Walla-Walla . . . to Fort Benton . . . Sen.Exec. Doc. 43. [*Wash* 1863]. O [2] 363 errata 1f 4maps 10pls aa
—anr. issue, same impr., date & collat., with t., "Report on the construction of a military road . . ." aa

MULLAN, JOHN   885
Miners' and travelers' guide to Oregon, Washington, Idaho, Montana, Wyoming and Colorado. *N Y* 1865. D 153 map aa

MULLETT, J. C.   886
A five years whaling voyage. *Clev* 1859. D 68 aa
Visited Hawaii and the N. W. coast.

MULLINS (LIEUTENANT COLONEL   887
HON. THOMAS).
General court martial for the trial of: [for misconduct in the attack on New Orleans]. *Dub* 1815.
O [4] 83 aa

MUMEY, NOLIE   888
Calamity Jane . . . her life and adventures . . .
Denver 1950. O 146 port map and 2 facs. pamphlets [in rear pocket], aa 200 cops ptd.

MUMEY, NOLIE   889
The life of Jim Baker . . . trapper, scout, guide
and Indian fighter . . . *Denver* 1931. O [4 incl.
front.] 234 map b 250copies ptd.

MUMEY, NOLIE   890
Creede. History of a Colorado . . . mining town.
Denv 1949. O [16] 185 3maps pls 500cops ptd a

MUMEY, NOLIE   891
History of the early settlements of Denver . . .
Glendale 1942. O 213 map aa

MUMEY, NOLIE   892
The Teton mountains . . . *Denv* 1947. O 462 pls
700 cops ptd aa

MUNGER, JAMES F.   894
Two years in the Pacific . . . being a journal of . . .
events peculiar to a whaling voyage. *Vernon N Y*
1852. O 80 b LC N Prov L Victoria [only cops loc]

MUNRO, ROBERT [pseud.]
A description of the Genesee country . . . *See*
Williamson, Chas.

[MUNRO, WILFRED H.]   895
Tales of an old sea port . . . sketch of the history
of Bristol, Rhode Island . . . *Princeton* 1917. O [4]
292 4pls a
Includes particulars of John D'Wolf's voyage to
the Northwest coast, 1804–08. For original
account, *see* D'Wolf, John.

[MUNRO-FRASER, J. P.]   896
History of Marin county, Calif . . . *S F* 1880.
Q 516 pls b B CalS Hn

MUNRO-FRASER, J. P.   897
History of Solano county [Calif.]. *Oakland*
1879. Q 503 pls b

MUNSELL, JOEL   898
The annals of Albany. *Alb* 1850–9. D 10v [Cont.
as] Collections on the history of Albany. *Alb*
1865–71. O 4v In all, 14v maps & pls aa
—ed. 2, ["Annals" only] *Alb* 1869. D 10v aa
Volume one of the *Annals* has no pages 27–36.
Of the *Collections*, 50 copies were on large paper.

MURAT, PRINCE [NAPOLÉON]   899
ACHILLE
Esquisse morale et politique des États-Unis . . .
P 1832. 16° [32] 389 a
—Eng. ed. "A moral and political sketch of the
United States . . .," *L* 1833. D [40] 402 map
—Eng. ed. 2, "The United States . . .," *L* 1833. D
same collat.
—Am. ed. "America and the Americans," *N Y*
1849. D [4] 260
—rptd. *Buf* 1851.
—Ger. ed. "Briefe über den moralischen . . .
Zustand der Vereinigten Staaten . . .," *Braunschweig* 1833. O
—Dutch tr. *Zalt-Bommel* 1834. O 2v: [16] 173; 177
Praises American institutions—even slavery—
but is critical of the wide-spread religious hypocrisy.

MURAT, PRINCE [NAPOLÉON]   900
ACHILLE
Exposition des principes du gouvernement . . .
en Amerique. *P* 1833. O [32] 414 tab a
—Ger. ed. "Darstellung der Grundsätze der republikanischen Regierung . . . in Amerika . . .,"
Braunschweig 1833. D [30] 325

MURAT, PRINCE [NAPOLÉON]   901
ACHILLE
Lettres sur les États-Unis . . . *P* 1830. D [4] 155 a
—Swed. ed. "Karakteristik öfver Förente Staterna," *Stockh* 1831. O
Contains four of the ten letters later issued as
Esquisse . . . des États-Unis, see above.

MUREL (JOHN A.)
A history of the detection . . . of: . . . *See* Walton, Augustus Q.

MURIETA (JOAQUIN), the brigand chief.   902
The life of: *S F* 1859. O 72 9pls by Nahl c B S
—rptd. *S F* 1861. b one cop kn
—anr. ed. *S F*, Grabhorn, 1932. Q [10] 116 [4]
front, fold facsm aa 400 cops ptd
For edition of which this is a spurious version,
See Ridge, John R.

MURIETA (JOAQUÍN) . . .
The life and adventures of: . . . By Yellow Bird.
See Ridge, John R.

MURIETA (JOAQUÍN) . . .
The life of: *See* Dewitt, Robt. M.

MURPHY, D. F.   903
The Jeff Davis piracy case . . . trial of William Smith for piracy, as one of the crew of the Confederate privateer, the *Jeff Davis*. *Phil* 1861. O [4 incl.front cov.] 7–100 a
The United States got its verdict of guilty, of course, and, of course, it was rendered barren when the Confederacy threatened reprisals.

MURPHY, HENRY C.   904
Henry Hudson in Holland . . . objects of the voyage which led to the discovery of the Hudson river. *Hague* 1859. O 72 port a
—rptd., same impr., 1909. O [12] 150

MURPHY, HENRY C., ed.   905
Journal of a voyage to New York and a tour in several . . . American colonies, in 1679–80, by Jaspar Dankers and Peter Sluyter. Trans.from the original manuscript. *Bklyn* 1867. O [8 48] 440 12pls a

MURPHY, HENRY C.   906
The voyage of Verrazano . . . *N Y* 1875. O 206 5maps a

MURPHY, J. W.   907
Outlaws of the Fox river country [Mo.] . . . *Hannibal* 1882. O 138 aa
Lurid narrative of midwestern crime, comparable to Bonney's classic *Banditti of the prairies*.

MURPHY, JOHN M., comp.   908
Oregon business directory and . . . gazetteer. *Port Ore* 1873. O 382 5pls aa

MURPHY, JOHN M., comp.   909
Oregon hand-book and emigrant's guide. *Port Ore* 1873. O 136 4pls tab a

MURPHY, JOHN M., and   910
HARNED [comp.]
Puget Sound business directory and guide to Washington Territory, 1872, comprising a correct history [etc.]. *Olympia* [1872]. O 72 [116] + 6adv-p b

MURPHY (TIMOTHY).
Life and adventures of: . . . *See* Sigsby, Wm.

MURRAY, ALEXANDER H.   911
Journal of the Yukon, 1847–8. Ed. L. J. Burpee. *Ottawa* 1910. O [2] 125 map 14pls plan a
—Fr. tr., same impr. & collat., except paginat. runs to 138
First detailed account of the Yukon region.

MURRAY, AMELIA M.   912
Letters from the United States . . . *L* 1856. D 2v: [12] 320; [10] 318. map a
—Am. ed. *N Y* 1856. D 402

MURRAY, CHARLES A.   913
Travels in North America . . . including a summer residence with the Pawnee tribe . . . *L* 1839. O 2v: [16] 473; [12] 372 2pls[omitted in all later eds.] a
—eds. 2 & 3, both D 2v, *L* 1841; *L* 1854.
—Am. ed. *N Y* 1839. D 2v: 324; [8] 13–247
Best account of the Pawnees while yet uncontaminated by whites.

MURRAY, HUGH   914
Historical account of discoveries and travels in North America. *L* 1829. O 2v: [12] 530; [12] 556 [1] map a

MURRAY (JAMES) [of N. Y.]   915
Letters of: *B* 1901. O [14] 324 [2] 13pls & facs a

MURRAY, REV. JAMES   916
An impartial history of the present war in America . . . *L* & *Newcastle Eng* [1778–80]. O 3v: [4] 573; 576; 332[unfinished & ending abruptly]. 31pls & maps [only 28 in some cops] issue 1 of v.1 has Address to King, dated July 29, 1778 b NYP Y
—later issues of v.I have Address dated later aa
—other eds. of vols. 1&2: *Newcastle* 1779; 1781; 1782; 1784; n.d. Each: O 2v: [4] 573; 576. map 23ports aa
—Am. ed. "An impartial history of the war in America," *B* 1781–82–84. O 3v: [4] 445; 448; 190 [unfinished]. 3plans 12pls c AA H
The original edition of vols. 1 and 2 was issued in 24 parts. Volume 3, entitled *Short account of commotions in America*, is seldom found with the other vols.

MURRAY, REV. JAMES   917
A short account of the commotions in America . . . *Newcastle Eng*. 1780. O 332[ending abruptly] 6pls
This constitutes an unfinished volume III of *An impartial history . . .*, *see* above, original edition.

MURRAY, MRS. LOIS L.   918
Incidents of frontier life . . . *Goshen Ind* 1880. D 274 2ports a
Narrative of eighteen years of life in Cotton Wood valley, Kansas. Scarce but uninspiring.

MURRAY, NICHOLAS   919
Notes . . . concerning Elizabeth-Town. *Elizabeth-Town N J* 1844. D 166 front. a
—rptd. *N Y* 1941. D [18 incl.front.] 174

[MURRAY, WILLIAM VANS]   920
Political sketches . . . *L* 1787. O [8] 96 a

MURRELL (JOHN A.)   921
Life and adventures of: . . . *Phil* 1845. 0 126 port aa
—rptd. *N Y* 1847. same collat a

MURSINNA, FRIEDRICH S. 922
Geschichte der Entdeckung von Amerika. *Halle* 1795. D [8] 400 a

MUSCATINE CITY DIRECTORY . . . 1856.
See Mahin, John.

MUSKINGUM (THE) . . . 923
Message from the President . . . transmitting information in relation to certain Christian Indians . . . on: *Wash* 1823. O 58 a
Documents—by Heckewelder and De Schweinitz—on Moravian missions in Ohio.

MUSSEY, OSGOOD 924
Review of Ellwood Fisher's lecture, on the North and the South. *Cin* 1849. O 98 [2] a

[MUSSON, EUGÈNE] 925
Lettre à Napoléon III sur l'esclavage aux états du sud . . . *P* 1862. O [8] 160 a
—Eng. tr. *L* 1862. O [4] 160

MUYBRIDGE, [EADWEARD] 926
Panorama of San Francisco . . . [*S F* 1877]. Q 12photos cover t.only b LC
—rptd. *S F* [1896?]; 1911. a

MY FIRST TRIP TO AMERICA. 927
By the rambling reporter of the Glasgow "Herald." *Glas* 1866. D 319 port a
Fine account of a war-worn South just after hostilities ended.

MYERS, ALBERT C. 928
Immigration of the Irish Quakers into Pennsylvania, 1682–1750. *Swarthmore* 1902. O [22] 477 pls a

MYERS, FRANK 929
Soldiering in Dakota . . . 1863–4–5. *Huron S D* 1888. D 60 b
—rptd. *Pierre* 1936. O 48

MYERS, FRANK M. 930
The Comanches: a history of White's battalion, Virginia cavalry . . . *Balt* 1871. O 400 aa
—rptd. *Marietta Ga* 1956, same collat

MYERS, HARRY M., and WILLIAM A. 931
Back trails. [Experiences in Alaska and California]. *Lapeer, Mich* [1933]. D [8] 269 500cops ptd a

MYERS, J. C. 932
Sketches on a tour through the northern and eastern states . . . *Harrisonburg Va* 1849. 16° 476 a

MYERS (CAPT. JOHN). 933
Life, voyages and travels of: . . . exhibiting a most instructive description of the northwest trade. *L* 1817. O 410 [8] b

MYRAND, ERNEST 934
Sir William Phips devant Québec: histoire d'un siège. *Quebec* 1893. O 428 errata lf 7maps & pls a

MYRICK, HERBERT 935
Cache la Poudre . . . a tenderfoot in the days of Custer. *N Y* 1905. Q [14] 19–202 map pls (one col) a
—Ltd iss on L.P. same collat but with 6 col pls 500cops aa

MYRTHE, A. T. [*pseud.*]
Ambrosio de Letinez, etc. *See* Ganilh, Anthony.

MYRTLE, MINNIE [pseud.]
The Iroquois . . . *See* Johnson, Anna C.

MYSTERY
Mystery (The) revealed; or, truth brought to light . . . By a patriot . . . *See* Moreau, Jacob N., *Mémoire contenant les précis des faits . . .*

N

N., J. C.
See No. 3, below.

N., N. 1
America . . . more especially . . . provinces which are under the dominion of the King of Spain. *L* 1655. D [14] 484, errata lf map c N
—rptd. *L.* 1657. b
Contains one of the earliest descriptions of California. Attributed to Thos. Peake.

N., S. VON 2
Mein Besuch Amerikas im Sommer 1824 . . . *Aarau* 1827. D 251 + cov.t. a
Travelled widely throughout Ohio and Indiana.

NAAUWKEURIGE BESCHRYVING 3
Naauwkeurige Beschryving van Noord-America . . . *Dordrecht* 1780. 16° 207 pl a
—rptd. same collat; *Amst.* 1783; *Rotterdam n. d.*

NACHRICHTEN
Nachrichten und Erfahrungen über die Vereinigten Staaten . . . Von einem Rheinländer. *See* Gottlieb, G. A.

NAGEL, RUDOLF 4
Geschichtliche Entwicklung der nord-amerikanischen Union . . . *Leip* 1854. O [6] 130 a
Includes California, Texas and other parts of the West.

[NAIRNE, THOMAS] 5
A letter from South Carolina ... by a Swiss gentleman ... *L* 1710. O 63 c JCB N
—ed. 2, *L* ptd for Smith 1718. O 56 b
—anr. issue, *L* Clarke 1732. O 63 b
One of the best early accounts of this province. Attributed also to Jean Pierre Purry, but it is more likely that it was to him this letter was sent. Indians burned Nairne at the stake in 1715.

NAPA
Handbook and directory of Napa, Lake, 6
Sonoma and Mendocino counties, California. ...
S F 1874. Q 296 maps aa

History of Napa and Lake counties, 7
California ... *S F* 1881. O [16] 600; 291 pls b

Illustrations of Napa county, California ...
See Smith, Clarence, and Elliott, W. W.

NAPEY, H. 8
The Harrisburg business directory ... with a sketch of its ... settlement. n.p. 1842. O 64 map a

NAPTON, WILLIAM B. 9
Over the Santa Fé trail, 1857. *K C* 1905. D 99 aa
Includes his trip into the upper Missouri country in 1858.

NARET, EDWARD 10
History of the French settlers at Gallipolis in 1791. *Cinc* [1890]. O 41 a

NARRAGANSET CHIEF (THE) 11
Narraganset chief (The), or the adventures of a wanderer. *N Y* 1832. D 195 a

NARRATIVE
Narrative (A) of a light company soldier's service ... during the late American war ... *See* Byfield, Shadrach.

Narrative of a voyage to the Spanish 12
main, in the ship "Two Friends" ... *L* 1819. O [16] 328 errata slip b
—rptd., same impr. & collat., 1827 aa
Almost entirely devoted to events in Florida during its last days under Spain, including the best narration of Captain McGregor's filibustering seizure of Amelia Island, account of Seminole Indians, etc.

Narrative (A) of some of the adventures ... of a revolutionary soldier. *See* Martin, Joseph P.

Narrative of the adventures of an American navy officer ... *See* Fanning, Nathaniel.

Narrative (A) of the capture of the ... 13
brig Vixen ... By one of the Vixen's crew ...
N Y 1813. D 35 aa

Narrative (A) of the horrid massacre by the 14
Indians of the wife and children of the Christian hermit, a resident of Missouri ... *St L* 1840. O 24 [incl. front.] aa
James B. Taylor was the unfortunate hermit's name.

Narrative of the missions to the new 15
settlements [and] Continuation of the Narrative ... according to the appointment of the General Association of ... Connecticut. *N Hav* 1794. O 2v: [2] 17; 32 aa
—rptd.: 1795; 1797.

Narrative of the negotiations occasioned by the dispute between England and Spain ... *See* Burgess, Sir James B.

Narrative (A) of the proceedings ... con- 16
cerning the lands to the westward of Connecticut river, lately usurped by New-Hampshire ... *N Y* 1773. F 28 [34 lvs] b AA H NYP
Usually bound with its appendix volume, *A state of the right of the colony of New-York with respect to its eastern boundary on Connecticut river . . .*, see under Duane, James.

Narrative respecting the conduct of the British ... *See* Wilmer, James.

Narrative (A) shewing the promises made to the officers of the ... continental army ... *See* Hill, Mark L.

NASH, CHARLES E. 17
Biographical sketches of Gen. Pat Cleburne and Gen. T. C. Hindman ... *Little Rock* 1898. D 300 aa

NASH (SOLOMON), a soldier of 18
the revolution.
Journal of: ... *N Y* 1861. O 65 3pls a

NASHOTAH [WIS.]
A few days at: *See* Kip, Wm. I.

[NASON, DANIEL] 19
A journal of a tour from Boston to Savannah ... to New Orleans and several western cities ...
L 1849. 16° 114 aa

NATION'S PERIL (THE) 20
Twelve years' experience in the south ... the Ku Klux Klan ... *N Y* 1872. O 144 a

NATIONAL PORTRAIT GALLERY (THE)
National portrait gallery (The) of distinguished Americans. *See* Herring, James, and Longacre, James B.

NATIONAL RAILROAD 21
CONVENTION (THE).
Proceedings of: ... *St L* 1850. O 98 aa

NAUMANN, JAKOB   22
Nordamerika, sein Volksthum und seine Institutionen . . . *Leip* 1848. O [8] 414 aa
—anr. ed. "Reise nach den Vereinigten Staaten . . .," *Leip* 1850. O [6] 390 a

NAUVOO.   23
Manifestations et addresses par les Icariens de: au fondateur d'Icarie. *P* 1856. O 35 a

NAVAL
Naval atalantis (The) . . . By Nauticus, Junior. *See* Harris, Jos.

Naval battles (THE) of the United States . . . *See* Kimball, Horace.

Naval biography: . . . most distinguished American naval heroes . . . *See* Mc. Bride, James.

Naval monitor . . . By an officer. *See* Claxton, Christopher.

Naval monument (The) . . . *See* Bowen, Abel.

Naval temple (The) . . . *See* Kimball, Horace.

[NAVARRE, ROBERT]?   24
Journal of Pontiac's conspiracy, 1763. [*Det* 1912]. O [4] 7–243 3facs a
First separate printing of an original diary kept during the siege of Detroit; gives both French and English texts.

NAVARRO, FERNANDO   25
Memoria sobre la poblacion del . . . Nueva España. *Mex* 1820. O 23 chart aa

NAVIGATOR (THE) . . .
Pitt 1804. *See* Cramer, Zadok.

NEAL, DANIEL   26
The history of New-England . . . *L* 1720. O 2v: [20] 330; [4] 331–712 [15]. map aa
—ed. 2, with adds., *L* 1747. O 2v: [16] 392; [4] 380 [15] aa
Based chiefly on Mather's *Magnalia* and Old-mixon's *British empire in America*.

NEBRASKA   27
Brownville and Nemeha county in 1859. Containing a short historical sketch [etc.]. *Brownville* 1859. 16° 99[incl. advs] aa

Guide, gazetteer and directory of Nebraska   28
. . . *Omaha* 1872. O 210 map aa

Nebraska City directory, for 1870. Con-   29
taininga historical . . . sketch of the city . . . *Neb City* 1870. O 152 [incl. advs] + unnumb adv-pp interspersed. [Probably not ptd at Nebraska City]. aa

Nebraska: a sketch of its history. *See* Smith, C. C.

Pioneer sketches, Nebraska and Texas. *See* Straley, Wm. Wilson.

NEBROFF, JOHANNES   30
Geschichte de ersten deutschen Evangelisch-Lutherischen Synode in Texas. *Chi* 1902. O 360 a

NECESSITY   31
Necessity (The) of repealing the . . . Stamp-act . . . *L* 1766. O 46 + 2adv-p aa
—Am. ed. *B* 1766. O 31 a

NEEDLES, EDWARD   32
An historical memoir of the Pennsylvania Society, for pomoting [*sic*] the abolition of slavery . . . *Phil* 1848. D 116 a

NEESE, GEORGE M.   33
Three years in the Confederate horse artillery. *N Y* 1911. O [8] 3–362 a

NEGRO SLAVERY   34
Negro slavery; or, a view of some . . . features of that state of society . . . in the United States . . . *L* 1823. O 118 a
—rptd. several times.

NEILL, EDWARD D.   35
Dahkotah land and Dahkotah life . . . *Phil* 1859. O [4] 49–239 + 4adv-p a

NEILL, EDWARD D.   36
Early settlement of Virginia . . . *Minneap* 1878. O 47 a

NEILL, EDWARD D.   37
The English colonization of America during the seventeenth century. *L* 1871. O [12] 352 a

NEILL, EDWARD D.   38
The Fairfaxes of England and America in the seventeenth and eighteenth centuries . . . *Alb* 1868. O 234 a

NEILL, EDWARD D.   39
The founders of Maryland. *Alb* 1876. O 193 a

NEILL, EDWARD D.   40
The history of Minnesota . . . *Phil* 1858. roy O 628 3maps a 100copies on L.P., with 45pls.
—ed. 2, same impr. 1873. roy O [52] 49–758 4maps 3ports
—ed. 3, *Minneap* 1878. O 778 10 [4] 14 4, maps & pls
—ed. 4, *Minneap* 1882. O [52] 49–928 [10 16 4] 6maps 8ports tab

NEILL, EDWARD D.   41
History of the Virginia company of London . . . *Alb* 1869. O [16] 432 port a

NEILL, EDWARD D.   **42**
Materials for the future history of Minnesota ... *St P* 1856. O 142 [17] front. a

NEILL, EDWARD D.   **43**
Pocahontas and her companions ... *Alb* 1869. Q 32 port a

NEILL, EDWARD D.   **44**
Terra Mariae; or, threads of Maryland colonial history. *Phil* 1867. D [8] 260 a

NEILL, EDWARD D.   **45**
Virginia Carolorum ... 1625–1685 ... *Alb* 1886. O 447 a

NEILL, EDWARD D.   **46**
Virginia vetusta, during the reign of James the first ... *Alb* 1885. O [16] 216 a

NEILSON, PETER   **47**
Recollections of a six years residence in the United States ... *Glas* 1830. D [8] 358 [4] a

NEILSON, PETER, ed.   **48**
Zamba; life and adventures of an African Negro king, and his experience of slavery in South Carolina. *L* 1847. O 258 port a
Unconvincing English abolition propaganda.

NELL, WILLIAM C.   **49**
The coloured patriots of the ... revolution ... *B* 1855. D 396 2pls facs a

NELL, WILLIAM C.   **50**
Services of colored Americans, in the wars of 1776 and 1812. *B* 1851. O 24 a
—ed. 2, *B* 1852. O 40
—rptd. *Tor* 1854. D 32

NELSON, WILLIAM   **51**
Notes toward a history of the American newspaper. Vol.I [all]. *N Y* 1918. O [6] 644[incl. initial blank lf] a 150copies ptd [45 on fine paper]

NEPTUNE AMERICO-SEPTENTRIONAL   **52**
Neptune Americo-Septentrional ... depuis le Groenland ... jusques et compris le Golfe du Mexique ... *P* [1778–80]. F [2] 18maps b
—anr. issue, same impr. & date. 25maps [on 31 l.] b N NYP
Published for use of the French navy in the Revolution.

NERINCKX (CHARLES).   **53**
Nagelaten Brief van: in leven missionaris in Kentucky ... *Hague* 1825. D [10] 66 aa

[NETTLE, GEORGE]   **54**
A practical guide for emigrants to North America ... *L* 1850. O [8] 7–57 map aa

NEU ENGLAND.   **55**
Vertrauliche briefe, aus Kanada und: vom J. 1777 und 1778 ... *Göttingen* 1779. O 84 aa
Letters written by German officers serving in America.

NEU-GEFUNDENES EDEN   **56**
Neu-Gefundenes Eden ... Bericht von Süd und Nord Carolina, Pensilphania, Mary Land & Virginia ... *Truck* 1737. D [16] 288 map b JCB
Embodies result of two trips through these regions.

NEUE NACHRICHTEN
Neue Nachrichten von denen ... Insuln in der See zwischen Asien und Amerika ... *See* Schulze, Johann L.

NEUESTE EISENBAHN POST   **57**
Neueste eisenbahn post und kanal-karte fur Reisende in den Vereinigten Staaten ... Canada, Texas ... *Hamburg* 1853. D 32 [10] map aa
—rptd. *Bamberg* 1855 a

NEUSTE KUNDE VON AMERIKA.   **58**
Weimar 1815–16. O 2v: 610; 648 aa

NEVADA
The bonanza mines of Nevada: ... *See* Dewey, Squire P.

Cattle brands ... Nevada ...   **59**
Reno 1885. D 85 [4] b

First directory of Nevada territory. *See* Kelly, J. Wells.

History of Nevada. *Oakland* 1881. *See* Angel, Myron.

History of Nevada county, California ...   **60**
Oakl 1880. Obl F [6] 11–234 pls map b B Hn

Nevada, Grass valley and Rough and Ready directory ... *See* Brown, Nat. P., and Dallison, John K., pubs.

Second directory of Nevada territory. *See* Kelly, J. Wells.

The silver districts of Nevada: *N Y* 1865. *See* Blatchly, A.

The silver mines of Nevada: *N Y* 1864.   **61**
O 76 [2] map aa
—rptd. *N Y* 1865. same collat. a

The wonders of Nevada ... and how to get   **62** to them. *Virginia City* 1879. 16° 32 aa

[NEVILL, SAMUEL]?   **63**
The history of North America, from the first

discovery . . . By Sylvanus Americanus. Vol. I
[all]. *Woodbridge N J* 1760. O [4] 284 b NYP
PaH

NEVINS, ALLAN   **64**
Fremont, the west's greatest adventurer . . .
N Y 1928. O 2v: [12] 344; [10] 345–738. errata
slip 64pls a

NEW   **65**
**New and complete history (A) of the British
empire in America.** *L* [1756–8]. O 3v: [46] 402;
496; 272. 10maps&pls b
Issued first in 56 monthly parts and never
completed, hence last page of volume three ends
abruptly.

**New and impartial collection (A) of interesting
letters, from the public papers** . . . *See* Almon,
John, *A collection of interesting, authentic papers* . . .

New crisis (The). By an old Whig. *N Y*   **66**
1810. O 96 a

New empires in the northwest. *See* Quigg,
Lemuel E.

New gospel of peace . . . *See* White, Rich. G.

NEW ALBION.
A description of the province of: *See* Plantagenet, Beauchamp.

NEW BRITTAINE.
The discovery of: *See* Bland, Edward.

NEW ENGLAND
A declaration of the . . . martyrdom of the . . .
Quakers, in New-England: *See* Burrough, Edward.

The deplorable state of New-England: . . . **1708.**
See Holmes, Alex.

A history of New-England . . . *L* 1654. *See*
Johnson, Edward.

A memorial of the present deplorable state   **67**
of New-England . . . **by the male-administration of
their present Governour** . . . by Philopolites. [*L*]?
1707. Q [4] 41 b BM
For similar pamphlet, *see* Holmes, Alexander,
The deplorable state of New England. Both have
been ascribed to Cotton Mather.

New England patriot (The) . . . *See* Lowell, John.

New England Primer (The).   **68**
Of ed 1 [*B* 1690?] and of ed 2 [*B* 1691] no cops kn
—ed. 3, *B* 1727. 24° 80 dd NYP [only cop kn]
—oth early 18th cent *B* eds: 1735; 1737; 1738;
1746 [of each one cop kn] dd

—later 18th cent *B* eds: 1750; 1761; 1762; 1763;
1767. ea d
—oth 18th cent eds: *N Y* 1750 [one cop kn] d;
Germantown 1754, c; *Phil* 1757, c; *B* 1770, b;
B 1773, b; *B* 1774, b; *B* 1778, b; *B* 1780, b
A combined speller, reader and religious catechism, this was the first school book printed in the
colonies.

New-England's ensigne . . . *See* Norton, Humphrey.

New England's spirit of persecution . . . *See*
Keith, George.

Records of the council for New England. *See*
Deane, Chas.

**The revolution in New England justified, and
the people there vindicated** . . . *See* Rawson,
Edward, and Sewall, Saml.

A short account of the province of New   **69**
England . . . : *L* [1774]. O 32 a

The state of religion in New-England . . .   **70**
Glas 1742. O 44 a
—enl. ed., with Whitefield's "Reply . . .," same
impr. & date. D [20] 112 [4]
—Am. ed. *B* 1743.

The traveller's guide in New England.   **71**
N Y 1823. 16° 94 a

A vindication of New-England: *see* Morton,
Charles.

NEW HAMPSHIRE
Notes . . . during an excursion to . . . New
Hampshire. By a gentleman of Boston. *See* Hale,
Nathan.

A public defence of the right of the New-   **72**
Hampshire grants . . . **to associate together and form
themselves into an independent state** . . . *Dresden
N H* 1779. 16° 56 [4] c Hn JCB NYP

NEW-HAVEN'S SETTLING   **73**
New-Haven's settling in New-England . . . *L*
1650. Q [2] 81 dd AA NYP [of 4 cops in America]
—rptd *Hart* 1858. Q a
First book on this colony.

NEW-JERSEY   **74**
An abstract . . . of some . . . testimonys from the
inhabitants of New-Jersey: . . . *L* 1681. smQ 32 dd
BM Hn JCB [of 5 cops loc]

An account of the college of New-Jersey: . . . **75**
Woodbridge 1764. O 47 pl aa

An advertisement concerning the province 76
of East New-Jersey: . . . *Edin* 1685. smQ [2]
22 dd Hn JCB NYP [only cops loc]

A brief of the claim, on the part of the 77
province of New-Jersey: . . . for settling the boundary line, between . . . New-Jersey, and . . . New-
York. [*N Y* 1769]. F [44] b NYP VtS

A concise view of the controversy between the
proprietors of East and West-Jersey . . . *See*
Cowell, Ebenezer.

A letter from New Jersey . . . By a gentleman
. . . *See* Thompson, Thos.

The memorial of the council of proprietors 78
of the eastern division of New Jersey . . . with
documents (in support of their title to the lands in
controversy between . . . New York and New
Jersey) . . . [*N Y* 1755]. F 118 b NYP

The model of the government of East New-
Jersey: . . . *See* Scott, George.

The petitions and memorials of the pro- 79
prietors of West and East-Jersey, to the legislature
of New Jersey . . . *N Y* [1784]. O 76 + errata lf at
p72 map aa
—ed. 2, *N Y* [1785]. O 96 + errata lf at end map aa

Proposals for traffick and commerce . . . in 80
New-Jersey: . . . By Amicus Patriae. [*N Y*] 1718.
Q 24 b NYH NYP

A short state of the proceedings of the pro- 81
prietors of East and West Jersey relative to the
line of division between them . . . *N Y* 1775. O
23 aa

NEW LONDON, WIS. 82
Sketches of the early history . . . of: . . . *New
London* 1857. D 31 aa

NEW LYME, OHIO.
Condensed history of: *See* Phillips, B. F.

NEW MEXICO
Address to the inhabitants of New Mexico and
California. . . . *N Y* 1849. *See* Burnett, Peter H.

The emigrant's guide to: New Mexico, California, and Oregon. *See* Disturnell, John.

An illustrated history of New Mexico. 83
Chi Lewis 1895. Q 672 37pls aa

Land claims in the Territory of New 84
Mexico: . . . [H. R. 457, 35th Cong.] *Wash* 1858.
O 326 aa

A political problem: New Mexico and the New
Mexicans. *See* Ruffner, Ernest H.

Report of the Secretary of War, communicating
. . . Colonel [George A.] McCall's reports in
relation to New Mexico. *See* Mc Call, Geo A.

Table of distances for troops in New 85
Mexico. *Santa Fe* 1878. O 27 a

NEW MIRROR
New mirror (The) for travellers; and guide to
the Springs. By an amateur. *See* Paulding, James K.

NEW ORLEANS 86
Battle of New Orleans: or, Jackson's victory.
By a citizen of Baltimore. *Balt* 1825. 16° 36 a

A faithful picture of the political situation of
New Orleans . . . *See* Workman, James.

Historical sketch book and guide to New Orleans and environs. *See* Coleman, Wm. H.

New Orleans as it is: its manners and 87
customs . . . By a resident. *Utica* 1849. O 79 b
AA LaU
—rptd., same collat., [*N O?*] 1850. b LC

New Orleans directory for 1835. [*N O* 88
1834]. D [7–19] 216 [22] aa
This city's 2nd directory; its 1st appeared in
1822.

New Orleans sketch book (The). *See* Wharton,
Geo. M.

Notes of conversations with a volunteer officer . . .
on the passage of the forts below New Orleans.
See Taylor, G. C.

Proceedings of the court of inquiry relative 89
to the fall of New Orleans. *Rich* 1864. O 206 aa

Remarks on the late infraction of treaty at
New Orleans. By Corialanus. *See* Smith, Wm.
Stephens.

A short review of the late proceedings at New
Orleans: . . . By Agrestis. *See* Allston, Jos.

NEW STATES 90
New states (The) . . . history . . . of North
Dakota, South Dakota, Montana and Washing-
ton. *N Y* 1889. O 72 + 6adv-p fold.map a

New states (The), or a comparison of the 91
wealth . . . of the northern and southern states . . .
to expose the injustice of erecting new states at
the south. By Massachusetts. *B* 1813. O 36 a

NEW TRAVELS
New travels among the Indians . . . taken partly from the communications . . . of Captains Lewis and Clark . . . *See* Fisher, Wm.

New travels to the westward, or unknown parts of America. *See* Decalves, Don Alonso.

NEW VOYAGES AND TRAVELS . . .
See Phillips, Sir Richard.

NEW YORCK   92
New Yorck à la Nouvelle-Orleans. Examen . . . d'un ouvrage intitulé: Voyage . . . de: où l'on réfute les calomnies . . . sur les Américains . . . et les réfugiés francais . . . *P* 1818. O [4] 23 aa

NEW YORK   93
An account of the soil [etc.] of the lands . . . in the back parts of New York and Pennsylvania. And particularly of the lands in the . . . Genesee tract . . . [*L*] 1791. sm F [2] 37, 4, 39–45 2maps b only 3 cops loc
—Ger. ed. "Bericht über den Genesee-Distrikt . . .," n. p. 1791. O 32, 8, 8 aa
—anr. Ger. ed. "Kurze Beschreibung . . .," *Bremen* 1792. O aa
Refers to the unfortunate land speculation of Robert Morris. *See* also *Genesee tract (The)* . . .

An address to the people of . . . New-York: shewing the necessity of . . . amendments to the constitution proposed for the United States. *See* Smith, Melancthon.

An argument delivered on the part of New-   94
York: at the hearing before His Majesty's commissioners . . . to settle . . . the boundary line, between . . . New York and New-Jersey. [*N Y*?] 1769. Q [2] 80 b BP NYP

Asmodée à New-York: revue critique des institutiones politiques et civiles de l'Amérique . . . *See* Longchamp, Ferdinand.

A brief topographical . . . manual of the state of New York: *See* Goodenow, Stirling.

The charter of the city of New-York: *N Y*   95
Bradford [*ca* 1720]. F 11 d Hn
—anr. ed. n.p. [*ca* 1730]. O 96 c
—anr. ed. [known as "Montgomeries charter"], *N Y* Zenger 1735. F 52 b AA BA NYP

The citizens directory and strangers guide through the city of New York: *See* Stanford, Thos. N.

A clear and concise statement of New-York   96
and the surrounding country. containing . . . account of . . . impositions . . . upon British emigrants. *L* [1819?]. D 30 a
—Am. ed. *N Y* 1819. D

A concise description of the city of New York. *See* Stanford, Thos. N.

The cries of New York. *See* Wood, Saml. S.

An Englishman's sketch-book; or, letters   97
from New York. *N Y* 1828. D [2] 195 aa

Glimpses of New York City. By a South Carolinian. *See* Bobo, Wm. M.

A journal of the proceedings in the detection of the conspiracy . . . for burning the city of New York. *See* Horsmanden, Daniel.

A letter from a gentleman of . . . New-York   98
concerning the troubles . . . in that province . . . in the late happy revolution. *N Y* 1698. Q 24 c Hn NYP

A letter from an officer at New-York: to a   99
friend in London. *L* 1777. O [2] 81 aa

A letter to the people of America, lately printed at New York: now re-published by an American . . . *See* Galloway, Jos.

Minutes of the trial . . . of certain persons   100
in the province of New York: charged with . . . a conspiracy against . . . the Congress and the liberties of America. *L* 1776. O [4] 45 b Hn N NYP Y
—rptd., with slightly altered t., *Phil* 1865. O [18] 112 [2] a 250copies ptd[25 in F, 75 in Q] aa
The famous "Hickey Plot" [to kidnap Washington] in which were implicated Governor Tryon, the Mayor of New York, and one of Washington's life-guards, Hickey, who was executed.

New York directory . . . 1786. *See* Franks, David.

New York directory . . . 1789. *N Y*   101
Hodge, Allen & Campbell 1789. D 144 map b AA NYP Y
The third directory of this city; for two earlier ones *see* Franks, David.

Papers concerning the boundary be-   102
tween . . . New York and New Jersey. Ed. H. B. Dawson. *Yonkers* 1866. O [8] 159 a

Papers relating to an act of the Assembly of the province of New-York: for encouragement of the Indian trade . . . *See* Colden, Cadwallader.

The picture of New York. *See* Mitchill, Sam'l L.

Proceedings of the congress at New York: 103
[in 1765]. *Annap* 1766. F 28 b LC
—anr. ed, *Phil* 1767. aa
—rptd., same impr 1813. a
—Eng ed, [*L*] 1767. O [2] 37 b N NYP

The declaration of rights and grievances recorded by this "Stamp Act Congress" forshadowed the Declaration of Independence.

Public documents relating to the New York canals . . . *See* Haines, Chas. G.

Review of the trade and commerce of New   104 York: from 1815 . . . By an observer. *N Y* 1820. O 43 a

A serious appeal to . . . **the legislature of   105 New York: on the subject of a canal communication between the** . . . **lakes and the** . . . **Hudson.** By a friend to his country. n.p. 1816. O 37 a

Sketches of the character of the New-York   106 press. By O. P. Q. *N Y* 1844. O 47 a

A state of the right of the colony of New-York: with respect to its eastern boundary . . . *See* Duane, James.

Statistical tables of the state of New   107 York . . . *N Y* 1828. D 24 a

A statistical . . . **view of the state of New   108 York.** *Roch* 1846. 16° 71 + 9adv-p a

The traveller's guide through the state of   109 New York, Canada, etc. . . . *N Y* 1836. 18° 71 + adv-p front. 2maps plan a

NEWARK.   110 Directory of: for 1835-6. With an historical sketch . . . *Newark* 1835. D [24] 102 a First Newark directory.

NEWCOMB., REV HARVEY   111 The North American Indians . . . *Pitt* [1835]. 18° 2v: 169; 169 a Limited chiefly to missionary aspects.

NEWCOMB, JAMES P[EARSON]   112 History of secession times in Texas and journal of travel from Texas . . . to California . . . *S F* 1863. O [4] 12 [2] 33 aa

NEWCOMB, REXFORD   113 Old Kentucky architecture. *N Y* 1941. F 22 130pls on 65 lvs front. a

NEWCOMER, ARMOUR   114 Cole's cavalry in the Shenendoah valley . . . *Balt* 1895. O 165 front a

NEWELL, C[HESTER]   115 History of the revolution in Texas . . . *N Y* 1838. D [4, 7–10] 215 map aa —rptd. *Austin* 1935. D 215 map

[NEWHALL, FREDERIC C.]   116 With General Sheridan in Lee's last campaign. *Phil* 1866. D [2] 235 [2] map port a

NEWHALL, JOHN B.   117 The British emigrant's "hand book," and guide to the new states . . . Illinois, Iowa and Wisconsin . . . *L* 1844. D 100 [incl front wrap] aa

NEWHALL, JOHN B.   118 A glimpse of Iowa in 1846, or the emigrant's guide and territorial directory . . . *Burlington* 1846. D 80 c No perfect copy known, though 600 cops were ptd —ed. 2, with state constitution added and word "territorial" [in sub-t.] changed to "state." *Burlington* [ptd *St L*] 1846. D [4] 9–106 + 6adv-p c G NYP WisH —anr. issue, same date, *St L* D 106 + 6adv-p b N

NEWHALL, JOHN B.   119 Sketches of Iowa, or the emigrant's guide. *N Y* 1841. 16° 252 map aa

NEWHOUSE, S[EWELL]   120 The trapper's guide . . . and narratives of trapping and hunting excursions . . . *Wallingford Conn* 1865. O 118[incl.port] a —ed. 2, same impr. 1867. O 216 port 31pls —ed. 3, *N Y* 1869. O 32pls The second edition first included Henry Thacker's narrative of three hunting expeditions, in 1844–1845, to the Chicago region.

NEWMAN, ALFRED   121 Ups and downs . . . with incidents of travel and adventure . . . 1855–62. *L* 1868. D 83 a

NEWMAN, JOHN B.   122 Texas and Mexico in 1846 . . . *N Y* 1846. O 32 map aa

NEWMARK, HARRIS   123 Sixty years in Southern California . . . 1853–1913. *N Y* 1916. O [30] 688 33pls a also L.P. issue of 50copies aa —ed. 2, same impr. 1926. O [36] 688 pls a —rptd. *B* 1930. O [36] 744 43pls

NEWSOM, J. A.   124 The life . . . of the wild and modern Indian. [*Okla C* 1923] O [6] 219 front a

[NEWSOME, E.]   125 Historical sketches of Jackson County, Illinois . . . *Carbondale* 1882. O 138 a —ed. 2, 1894. O 233 a

NEWSON, THOMAS M.   126 Drama of life in the Black hills. *St P* 1878. O 90 a

NEWSON, T[HOMAS] M.   127
Thrilling scenes among the Indians . . . Custer's
last fight . . . *Chi* 1884. D 241 8pls a
—rptd. same impr. & collat: 1888; 1889.

NEWTON, J[AMES] H., ed.   128
History of the Pan-handle [W.Va.] . . . *Wheeling*
1879. Q 450 [34] 2maps 2pls facs aa

NEWTON, J[AMES] H., ed.   129
History of Venango county [Pa.] . . . *Columbus
O* 1879. Q 651 47pls[some double] on 33 l. a

NEWTON (JOHN MARSHALL).   130
The memoirs of: [*Cambridge N Y*]1913. O [2]
91 7pls a
Includes his overland trip to California and
experiences there from 1850 to 1952.

NEZ-PERCE INDIANS.
The status of young Joseph and his band of:
See Wood, H. Clay.

NIAGARA
**An account of a journey to Niagara, Montreal
and Quebec.** *See* Izard, Ralph.

**Facts relative to the campaign on the Niagara
in 1814.** *See* Ripley, Eleazer W.

A guide to travelers visiting the falls of Niagara.
By a resident . . . *See* Parsons, Horatio A.

A summer month; or, recollections of   131
a visit to the falls of Niagara and the lakes. *Phil*
1823. D [8] 250 a

Visit to the falls of Niagara in 1830. *See*
Maude, John.

NICAISE, AUGUSTE   132
. . . Une année au désert; scènes et récits du
far-west américain. *Chalons* 1864. D [4] 115
[unp] c Hn Y [of 4copies known]
There were some copies at the printers in
1916; all went when the Germans sacked Chalons. Nicaise crossed the plains to Ft. Walla
Walla in 1858.

NICELY, W[ILSON] S.   133
Facts for emigrants. A description of twenty-
six counties of south-west Missouri . . . *St L*
1867. D 72 aa

NICELY, WILSON [S.]   134
The great southwest, or plain guide for emigrants and captitalists. *St L* 1867. D 115 + 9adv-p
map a

NICHOLAS (GEORGE) of Kentucky.   135
Correspondence between: and . . . Robert G.
Harper . . . *Lex* 1799. O 26 [8] a

NICHOLAS (GEORGE) of Kentucky.   136
A letter from: to his friend in Virginia . . .
Lex 1798. O 42 b AA N NYP
—rptd. *Phil* 1799. O 39 aa
Justifying Kentucky's resolutions opposing the
Alien and Sedition laws. The friend mentioned
was Thos. Jefferson.

NICHOLAS (GEORGE).   137
Observations on a letter from: . . . to his
friend in Virginia . . . By an inhabitant of the
north-western territory. *Cin* 1799. O [2] 46 b
BA BP OHP [only cops loc]

NICHOLAS, GEORGE   138
To the citizens of Kentuckty. [capt. t.] [*Lex*?
1798]. D 42 b Hn[only copy known]

[NICHOLAS, ROBERT C.]   139
Considerations on the present state of Virginia
examined. [*Wmsbg*] 1774. O 43 d LC NYP
—rptd., with adds., *Metuchen N J* 1919. a 65copies
ptd.
For pamphlet to which this replies *see* Randolph, John.

NICHOLL, EDITH M.   140
Observations of a ranchwoman in New Mexico.
L 1898. D [8] 271 pls
—Am. ed. *Cin* 1901. D [6] 260

NICHOLLS, JOHN ASHTON   141
Letters from America. Ed. by his mother.
n.p. 1862. O 418 a
Observations on an extensive tour, including
Minnesota, Illinois, Ohio, Louisiana, etc.

NICHOLS, G. W.   142
A soldier's story of his regiment [61st Ga.].
Jesup Ga [1898]. D [2] 291 [2] a

NICHOLS, JOSEPH   143
Condensed history of the construction of the
Union Pacific R. R . . . *Omaha* 1892. D 192 aa

NICHOLS, THOMAS L.
Forty years of American life. *L* 1864. O 2v:
[12] 408; [12] 368 aa
—ed. 2, *L* 1874. D [16] 509 a
—Am. ed. *N Y* [1937] O 421
By a New Englander, who, believing it uncon-
stitutional to compel the South to remain in the
Union, expatriated himself.

[NICHOLSON, C. A. P.]   144
Life of General Lewis Cass, comprising . . . services in the north-west . . . *Phil* 1848. D 210 2ports a

NICHOLSON (FRANCIS . . . Governor   145
of South Carolina).
An apology or vindication of: from . . . aspersions cast on him by some of the members of the
Bahama-Company. *L* 1724. O 62 b Hn JCB Y

[NICHOLSON, JOHN]?   146
A view of the proposed constitution . . . compared
with the present confederation. *Phil* 1787. O [37] aa

NICHOLSON (THOMAS).   147
An affecting narrative of the captivity . . . of:
. . . among the Algerines . . . *B* 1816. D 24 port aa
—rptd. B [1818] aa

[NICKLIN, PHILIP H.]   148
Letters descriptive of the Virginia Springs . . .
Phil 1835. 16° 100 + 4adv-p map aa
—ed. 2, enl., same impr., 1837. D 248 map pl
—ed. 3 *N Y* 1844 D

[NICKLIN, PHILIP H.]   149
A pleasant peregrination through the prettiest
parts of Pennsylvania. *Phil* 1836. O 148 a
—ed. 2, with 8 add letters *Phil* 1837 D 248 map

NICOL (JOHN, mariner).   150
The life and adventures of: *Edin* 1822. D [10]
215 port b
—rptd. *N Y* [1937]. O [10] 245[incl.front] a
Accompanied Portlock to the Northwest Coast.
Probably edited by John Howell.

[NICOLAY, CHARLES G.]   151
The Oregon Territory; a geographical . . .
account . . . *L* Knight 1846. 16° 226 2maps
[one fold.] a
—anr. issue, bound with *The backwoods of
Canada* . . .
—ed. 2, with suppl. [on Brit. Columbia] *L* Hodson
1860. 16° 237 2maps [one fold.]
—rptd. *L* Renny 1886. 16° [8] 157 2maps pl
For similar title, but entirely different work,
issued same year by Nattali, *see Oregon Territory
(The)* : *consisting of a brief description* . . .

NICOLET, J[OSEPH] N.   152
Report . . . to illustrate a map of the hydro-
graphical basin of the upper Mississippi . . . [Sen.
Doc. 237]. *Wash* 1843. O 170 map aa
—anr. issue [H.R. Doc. 52] *Wash* 1845. same
collat., but smaller map a

NIEU-NEDER-LAND
Vertoogh van: *see* Donck, Adriaen van der.

NIEUW NEDERLANTS   153
GELEGENTHEIT, ETC.
Kort verhael van: . . . [*Amst*] 1662. Q [8] 84
c Hn JCB NYP
—rptd. "Zeekere vrye-voorlagen . . ." same impr
& collat 1663, b JCB
Favorable account of New Netherland's fitness
for colonization.

NIEUW YORK
Herinnerigen eener Reize naar: *See* Brauw, J. de.

NIKKANOCHEE (OSCEOLA).
A narrative of the early days and reminiscences
of: . . . *See* Welch, Andrew.

NILES, HENRY C.   153a
History of Douglas County, Illinois . . . *Tuscola
Ill* 1876. O 79 aa

NILES, H[EZEKIAH]   154
Principles and acts of the revolution . . . *Balt*
1822. O [8] 495 a

[NILES, HEZEKIAH]   155
Things as they are, or Federalism turned inside
out . . . *Balt* [1809] .O 75 a

NILES, JOHN M.   156
History of South America and Mexico . . .
[with] a geographical and historical view of
Texas [by L. T. Pease] . . . *Hart* 1837. O 2v in 1:
370; 230 5maps & pls aa
—oth eds, 1838; 1839; 1843; 1844. a
The 1837 edition was the first to include the
Texas portion. An 1827 edition, published at
New York as *A view of South America and
Mexico*, is purposely omitted here.

NILES, JOHN M.   157
The life of Oliver Hazard Perry . . . *Hart* 1820.
D 376 3 pls a
—ed. 2, enl., *Hart* 1821. D 384 5pls

NIMMO, JOSEPH   158
Letter . . . transmitting a report . . . in regard
to the range and ranch cattle traffic . . . [H. R.
Doc. 267]. [*Wash* 1885]. O 200 4maps no t-p aa
—anr. ed. issued by Senate aa
—anr. ed. [occupying p95–294 of "Report on
Internal Commerce,"]*Wash* 1885. O 562 5maps aa
—anr. issue, *Wash* 1885. O 200 + wraps fold.
map[only one issued, though 4 called for] a
—rptd. *N Y* 1961
Contributed to by cattle experts, statistically
documented, the unrivalled source for the period.

NISBET, COL. JAMES C.   159
Four years on the firing line. *Chattanooga*
[1914]. D [4] 445 port aa

[NISBET, RICHARD]   160
Slavery not forbidden by Scripture . . . By a
West-Indian. *Phil* 1773. O (6) 30 a
This defense of slavery was aroused by Ben-
jamin Rush's *An address . . . upon slavekeeping*.
For Rush's reply, *see* his *A vindication of the
Address* . . .

NIXON, PAT[RICK] I.   161
The medical story of early Texas, 1528–1855.
[*Lancaster Pa*] 1946. O [16] 507 ports a

NOAH, MORDECAI M.   162
Discourse on the evidences of the American
Indians being the descendants of the lost tribes
of Israel . . . *N Y* 1837. O 40 a
—Ger. tr. *Altoona* 1838. 18° [2] 54

NOAILLES, AMBLARD M. R. A.,   163
vicomte de
Marins et soldats francais en Amérique . . .
(1778–83). *P* 1903. O [8] 440 7ports 2fold. maps a
—ed. 2, same impr., date & collat.

NOBLE, JOHN   164
Instructions to emigrants . . . account of the
United States . . . *B* [Eng] 1819. O [6] 112 errata 1.
map tab aa

NOEL, BAPTIST W.   165
Freedom and slavery in the United States . . .
L 1863. 16° [4] 242 a

NOEL, BAPTIST W.   166
The rebellion in America. *L* 1863. D [20] 494 a
— Dutch ed. "De Opstand in Noord-Amerika,"
Kampen 1864. O 2v

NOEL, THEO[PHILUS]   167
A campaign from Santa Fé to the Mississippi
. . . a history of the old Sibley brigade . . . 1861–4.
Shreveport 1865. O 152 fold. tab d Duke N TxU
[only cops loc]

NOLAN, PHILIP   168
Description of Texas. *Natchez* 1799. 16° map
dd no perfect copy known
First non-legal book printed in Mississippi and
first book on Texas printed in the United States.

NOLTE, VINCENT   169
Fünfzig Jahre in beiden Hemisphären . . .
Hamburg 1853. O 2v: [24] 391; [16] 241 facs aa
—ed. 2, same impr 1854. D2v; [18] 323; [14] 360 aa
—Eng. tr. "Fifty years in both hemispheres"
N Y 1854. D [22] 11–226 218–476 a
—Eng. ed 2 *L* 1854 D 484

NOMBELA Y TABARES, JULIO   170
La fiebre de riquezas. Siete años en California
. . . *Madr* 1871–2. O 2v: 547; 580 20pls aa

NOOTKA SOUND
An authentic statement of all the facts relative
to Nootka Sound . . . *See* Etches, John C.

A continuation of an authentic statement of all the
facts relative to Nootka Sound. *See* Etches, John C.

Official papers relative to the dispute   171
between . . . Great Britain and Spain, on the
subject of the ships captured in Nootka Sound . . .
L Debrett [1790]. O [8] 100 b H PortOreL Y ˙

NORD-AMERIKA   172
Nord-Amerika [Das] historisch und geogra-
phisch Beschrieben . . . *Hamburg* 1777–8. 16° 4v:
[32] 160; 192; [8] 179; [2] 126. map port a

Nord-Amerika in Bildern oder eine Auswahl von
Ansichten der interessantesten Gegenden . . . *See*
note to Maximilian, Prinz zu Wied.

Nordamerika, oder neuestes Gemälde   173
der nordamerikanischen Freistaaten. Von einem
Würtemberger . . . *Tübingen* 1818. 16° [10] 166 a

NORDENSKIÖLD, G[USTAV E. A.]   174
The cliff dwellers of the Mesa Verde, southwestern Colorado . . . *Stockh* [1893]. F [8] 174
[16] map port 61pls [34 of which are accompanied
by explanatory text of one lf each] aa
—anr. issue, same impr. & date, in Swedish
F [6] 194 [4] map 17pls aa

NORDENSKIÖLD [NILS] A. E.   175
Fascimile-atlas to the early history of cartography . . . *Stockh* 1889, F [10] 141 51pls[con-
taining 170maps] b N NYP
—anr. issue, same impr & date, in Swedish. b

NORDENSKIÖLD, [NILS] A. E.   176
Periplus; an essay on the early history of
charts . . . *Stockh* 1897. F [10] 208 60pls [con-
taining 234maps] b N NYP

NORDHOFF, CHARLES   177
The communistic societies of the United
States . . . *N Y* 1875. O 440 [incl. front] + 7adv-p
map 15pls tab a

NORDHOFF, CHARLES   178
The cotton states in the spring and summer of
1875. *N Y* 1876. O 112[incl. front cover] a
Honest report on reconstruction conditions
made to the New York Herald.

NORGATE, E[LIAS]   179
Mr. John Dunn Hunter defended . . . *L* 1826.
O 38 a

NORMAN, B[ENJAMIN] M.   180
New Orleans and environs . . . *N O* 1845. 24°
223 + blank leaves for memoranda front. a

NORMAN, JOHN, pub.   181
The Boston directory . . . *B* 1789. 16° 56 plan
errata lf b AA
—rptd., *B* 1852. D 63 a
First Boston directory; no others published
until 1796.

NORRIS (ISAAC).   182
The journal of: . . . during a trip to Albany in
1745 . . . *Phil* 1867. Q [4] 31 a 80copies ptd

NORRIS, J[AMES] W.   18 [3]
A business advertiser and general directory
of . . . Chicago, for 1845–6 . . . Chi 1845. D [2]
156 [12] pl b ChiH MH N
—for 1847–8, Chi 1846. D 104 + 36adv-p b
ChiH LC
—for 1848–9, Chi 1848. D 132 [28] b ChiH[only
copy known]

NORRIS, J[AMES] W.   184
Business directory . . . of Chicago, for 1846.
Chi 1846. D 64 b AA ChiH N
Second Chicago business directory.

NORRIS, J[AMES] W.   185
General directory [etc.] of . . . Chicago, for
1844, with a historical sketch . . . Chi 1844. D
[2] 116 wraps c AA ChiH G NYP
—anr. issue, clo., with 2adv-lvs. before t-p and
binder's adv-slip c
Chicago's first real city directory, preceded only
by an incomplete 6-page list of businessmen
appended to The laws and ordinances of Chicago,
1839, q. v.

NORRIS, J[AMES] W., and   186
GARDINER, G. W.
Illinois annual register, and western business
directory . . . Chi 1847. O 120 36 [12] b G LC
Embraces a complete account of the Mormons
in Illinois.

[NORRIS, JOHN]   187
Profitable advice for rich and poor. In a
dialogue . . . between James Freeman, a Carolina
planter, and Simon Question . . . containing a
description . . . of South Carolina . . . L 1712.
D 110 + 2adv-p b

NORTH, F. A.   188
The hand-book of Sedalia . . . history, etc.
Sedalia, Mo. 1882. O 245 map a

NORTH, JAMES W.   189
The history of Augusta [Me.] . . . Augusta 1870.
O [12] 990 2maps 28pls[incl.fold. panorama] a

[NORTH, LORD]   190
The history of Lord North's administration.
Pt. 1[all.] L 1781 .a
—rptd. Dub 1783. O [8] 183
—complete ed. "A view of the history of Great-
Britain during the administration of Lord North,"
L 1782. O 2pts in 1: [4] 170; 169–412 Sabin mentions prt., but all copies do not have it a
—anr. ed. Dub 1782. O 2pts in 1: [2] 184; [8]
185–427
—Fr. ed., tr. by Hilliard d'Auberteuil, with large
adds., "Histoire de l'administration de Lord
North . . .," L & P 1784. O 2v: [20] 276; [4] 180
[80]. map aa

—Sp. tr. [from Fr. ed.], Madrid 1806. 16° [14] 402
Animadversions on the feeble showing of the
British army in America in spite of great expend-
itures.

NORTH, LORD, et al.
Het Oor in het Kabinet. Of geheime zamen-
spraaken tusschen: . . . Betreffende den Toestand
van Amerika. See Cerisier, Antoine M., Le
destin de l'Amérique . . .

NORTH (the Right Honble. LORD).   191
Letter to: to which is added a petition . . . in
favour of the colonies. L [1776] .O 28 a

NORTH (LORD).   192
Nathan to: . . . L 1780. O [4] 59 a
Venomous upbraiding of this minister.

NORTH (LORD).
A view of the history of Great Britain during
the administration of: See above, The history of
Lord North's administration, No. 190.

NORTH, THOMAS   193
Five years in Texas; or, What you did not hear
during the war . . . Cin 1870 D 231 a
—rptd., Cin 1871. same collat.

NORTH   194
North-American and West-Indian gazetteer
(The) . . . L 1776. D [30] 218 [2] 2maps aa
—ed. 2, same impr. & collat. 1778 a

North-American atlas (The) . . . 1776. See Faden,
Wm.

North-American pilot (The) . . . See Jefferys,
Thos.

North American tourist (The). See Melish,
John, The traveller's manual . . .

North and south. Impressions of northern   195
society upon a southerner . . . N Y 1853. D 35 a

NORTH CAROLINA   196
An adress to the people of North Carolina on the
evils of slavery. By the friends of liberty . . .
Greensborough 1830. 16° [2] 68 [1] a

A continuation of the . . . differences . . . in the
province of North Carolina. See Husband, Harmon.

An impartial relation of the . . . cause of the
recent differences . . . in the province of North
Carolina. See Husband, Harmon.

Information concerning the province of   197
North Carolina. By an impartial hand. Glas 1773.
O 32 a

The swamp outlaws; or the North Carolina 198
bandits . . . *N Y* 1873. O 84 a
Lurid crimes by this band of monsters which
terrorized the Cape Fear region.

NORTH DAKOTA
Wam-Dus-Ky . . . record of a hunting trip to
North Dakota . . . *See* Tuttle, J. H.

NORTH EASTERN
North-eastern boundary (The) of the United
States. *B* 1832. *See* Davies, C. Stewart.

NORTH RIVER (THE).   199
Sketches of: *N Y* 1838. D 119 map a

NORTHERN TOUR (A) TO SARATOGA.
See Gilpin, Thos.

NORTHERN TRAVELLER
Northern traveller (The); . . . routes to Niagara
. . . *See* Dwight, Theo.

NORTHFIELD TRAGEDY (THE) . . .
See Lemon, John J.

NORTHROP, N. B.   200
Pioneer history of Medina County [O.].
Medina 1861. 16° 224 a
Medina was one of the earliest counties formed
from the Western Reserve.

NORTHWEST COMPANY OF
CANADA (THE).
On the origin and progress of: *See* Atcheson,
Nathaniel.

NORTON, A[NTHONY] BANNING   201
A history of Knox county, Ohio . . . *Columbus*
1862. O 424 4pls a

NORTON, CHARLES   202
Der treue Führer des Auswanderers nach den
Vereinigten Staaten . . . Texas [etc.]. *Regensburg*
1846. D 2pts in 1 : 142 [2]; 120. map aa
—ed. 2, same impr. & collat. 1848. aa
—rptd., same collat., 1850 a
Relates chiefly to Texas, but has chapters on
Oregon and the Midwestern states.

NORTON, DAVID   203
Sketches of . . . Old Town [Me.]. *Bangor* 1881.
O 152 a

NORTON, HARRY J.   204
A bird's-eye view of the Black hills . . . mining
region. *N Y* 1879. O 32 [incl. advs] b

NORTON, HARRY J.   205
Wonder-land illustrated; or, horseback rides
through Yellowstone . . . Park. *Va City* [1873].
D 132 18pls map aa

[NORTON, HUMPHREY]   206
New-England's ensigne . . . account of the
sufferings sustained by us [i.e. the Quakers] in
New-England . . . *L* 1659. SmQ [4] 121 b Hn
NYP

NORTON, JOHN   207
The heart of New-England rent . . . a brief
tractate concerning the doctrine of the Quakers,
the destructive nature thereof, to religion, etc.
C 1659. D [2] 58 dd JCB MassH
—Eng. ed., *L* 1660. D [4] 83 c BP NYP
Some cops of Eng. ed have pagination extended
to 96 by add. of *Matter coming from New-England
since this book was printed.* d

[NORTON, JOHN]   209
The redeemed captive . . . a narrative of the
taken [*sic*] and carrying into captivity the Reverend Mr. John Norton . . . *B* 1748. O 40 d AA N
—issue 2, word "taking" on t-p correctly spelled
d Y
—anr. ed., with notes, "Narrative of the capture . . . of Fort Massachusetts by the French and
Indians . . .," *Alb* 1870. Q 51 a 100 copies ptd.

NORTON (COL. L[EWIS] A.)   210
Life and adventures of . . . by himself. *Oakland
Cal* 1887. D 492 port a

NOTA ESTADISTICA [TEXAS, ETC.]   211
Mex 1826. D 99 b

NOTES
Notes of a tour in North America in 1861 . . .
See Fergusson, James.

Notes of a western hunting trip. *Easton* 212
1875. O 39 pl b

Notes of a winter trip . . . *See* McLennan, John.

Notes on political economy as applicable to the
United States. By a southern planter. *See* Ware,
N. A.

Notes on the origin and necessity of slavery.
See Brown, Edw.

Notes on the United States. *See* Morris, Gouverneur.

Notes upon Canada and the United States . . .
By a traveller. *See* Todd, Henry C.

NOTICE SUR LA RIVIERE ROUGE.
Montr 1843. *See* Taché, Alex.

NOTIONS OF THE AMERICANS.
Picked up by a travelling bachelor. *See* Cooper,
James F.

NOTT, MANFORD A.   **213**
Across the plains in '54 . . . n.p. n.d. [1905].
D 2pts in 1: [4] 232 [incl. blank l. before 2nd
t-p] port aa
Called second edition on title, but apparently
the first in book form. Almost all copies destroyed
in the 1906 San Francisco fire.

NOUVELLE FRANCE [LA]
Estat present de l'eglise et de la colonie de la
Nouvelle France. *See* St. Valier, Jean B. de.

Recueil de pièces sur la negociation entre   **214**
la Nouvelle France et la Nouvelle Angleterre. Ès
années 1648 et suivantes. *N Y* 1866. sm O 62 [1]
a 100copies ptd.

Relation de ce qui s'est passé . . . aux missions
des pères de la Compagnie de Jésus en la Nouvelle
France. For listing of those volumes [issued
annually in Paris under this title from 1632 to
1672] which contain sufficient United States
material for inclusion here, *see Jesuit relations.*

NOUVELLE ORLEANS (LA).
Relation du voyage des dames religieuses
Ursulines de Rouën à : . . . *See* Hachard, Marie M.

NOVA SCOTIA.
The conduct of the French with regard to : . . .
See Jefferys, Thos.

NOVO Y COLSON, PEDRO DE   **215**
Historia de las exploraciones articas . . . en
busca del paso del nordeste . . . *Madrid* 1880.
F [14] 260 map port aa
—ed. 2, same impr. & collat. 1882 a

NOVO Y COLSON, PEDRO DE   **216**
Sobre los viajes apocrifos de Juan de Fuca y de
. . . Maldonado . . . *Madrid* 1881. Q 223 a

NOWLIN, WILLIAM   **217**
The bark covered house . . . pioneer life in . . .
Michigan. *Det* 1876. D 250 [incl. prelim blank lf]
6pls b N
—rptd., ed. Quaife, *Chi* 1937. a
Best picture of pioneer Michigan.

NOYES, ALVA J.   **218**
In the land of Chinook; or, the story of Blaine
county. *Helena Mont* [1917]. O 152 24pls a

NOYES, ALVA J.   **219**
The story of Ajax: life in the Big Hole basin.
Helena 1914. O [8] 158 13pls aa
First autobiography published in Montana;
by a settler of 1860.

NOYES, DAVID   **220**
The history of Norway [Me.] . . . *Norway* 1852.
O 216 a

NOYES, JOHN H.   **221**
History of American socialisms. *Phil* 1870. O
[6] 678 a

NUCKOLLS, B. F.   **222**
Pioneer settlers of Grayson County, Virginia.
Bristol 1914. O 206 a

NUECES AND THE RIO GRANDE.
Appeal to the people . . . between: *See Texas.
An appeal, etc.*

NUEVA-ESPAÑA   **223**
Instruccion para formar una linea . . . de quince
presidios sobre las fronteras de las provincias
internas de . . . Nueva-España y nueva reglamento . . . *Mex* 1771. F [2] 80 c B JCB
This Mexican reglamento was superseded by
the official Spanish one issued at Madrid, 1772,
q.v. For the earliest *Reglamento see* Acuña, Juan de.

Real ordenanza para el establecimiento . . .   **224**
de intendentes de exército y provincia en el reino de
la Nueva-España. *Madrid* 1786. F [62] 410 b NYP
Sometimes bound with *Leyes de la recopilacion
de Indias*, containing 68 leaves and index of
24 pages.

Reglamento . . . para los presidios que se   **225**
han de formar en la linea de frontera de la Nueva-
España. *Madrid* 1772. Q [4] 122 d JCB N
—rptd., *Mex* 1773, Q [2] 132 b B NYP; *Madrid*
1822, Q c
—other eds.: n.p. n.d. *ca* 1810–25? O [2] 46 b;
Monterrey 1827, O [2] 54 a; *Mex* 1834, F 30 b
Includes the military establishments in New
Mexico and Texas. For the first of such *Regla-
mentos, see* Acuña, Juan de. *See* also Rivera,
Pedro de, and, above, *Instruccion* . . .

NUEVO ALMADEN   **226**
Nuevo Almaden en la alta California. Algunas
declaraciones en el asunto de: *Mex* 1859. O 36 aa

NUEVO MEJICO.   **227**
Leyes del Territorio de: [in Spanish and
English]. [*Santa Fe* 1846]. O 115 dd Y
This fundamental work, erecting the conquered
region into a part of the United States, defining
its powers, etc., was written by Colonel A. W.
Doniphan, promulgated by General Stephen W.
Kearny and is cited as the "Kearny Code."

NUGENT, H. P.   **228**
A letter to . . . William C. C. Claiborne, gov-
ernor of the Territory of Orleans . . . *N O* 1808.
Q 52 b LC NYH

NUTTALL, THOMAS   **229**
A journal of travels into the Arkansa Territory
. . . [with observations on the Chickasaw, Cherokee
and Osage Indians inhabiting the prairie country

traversed]. *Phil* 1821. O [12] 9–296 map 5pls b
—rptd., ed. Thwaites, *Clev* 1905. O [8] 11–366
[incl. map & pls]

NUTTING, WALLACE 230
Furniture of the Pilgrim century, 1620–1720.
B [1921]. Q [12] 587 a
—enl. ed. *Framingham Mass* [1924]. Q 716

NYE, WILLIAM F., tr. 231
Sonora; its extent . . . *S F* 1861. D 190 a
Abridged translation of the Spanish work by
José F. Velasco, *q. v.*

NYE-STARR, KATE 232
A self-sustaining woman; or, the experience of
seventy years. *Chi* 1888. D 161 [incl. port] b
G Y [only cops loc.]
Account by the sister of Governor Nye of
Nevada of her 1862 trip west and life in Carson
City.

NYSTEL, OLE T. 233
Lost and found, or, three months with the
wild Indians . . . *Dallas* 1888. D 26 + wraps and
inserted $^1/_2$ lf of certification aa
—rptd. *Keene, Tex* 1930. D 52

O

OAKES, WILLIAM 1
Scenery of the White mountains. *B* [1848].
F [4] 4 16pls[sometimes colored, each with ac-
companying lf of explanatory text] b AA H
N NYP Y with uncold pls aa

OAKLAND [CALIF.]
Directory of . . . : 1869. *See* Stillwell, B. F.

OATES, WILLIAM C. 2
The war between the Union and the Confederacy . . . *N Y* 1905. O 808 13pls aa
—rptd., same impr. & collat., 1906.

O'BEIRNE, H[ARRY] F. 3
Leaders and leading men of the Indian Terri-
tory. Vol.I, Choctaws & Chickasaws [all pub.].
Chi 1891. O 320 [6] 7pls aa
—anr. ed. "The Indian Territory, its chiefs . . .,"
St L 1892. O [8] 15–485[incl.pls] a

[O'BEIRNE, THOMAS L.?] 4
A candid and impartial narrative of the transactions of the fleet under Lord Howe . . . *L* 1779.
O 44 aa
—ed. 2, rev., *L* [1779]. O 58 plan aa
Vindication of Lord Howe. O'Beirne was
chaplain of the fleet.

OBJECTIONS
Objections (The) to the taxation of our Ameri-
can colonies . . . briefly considered. *See* Jenyns,
Soame.

OBREGON, BALTASAR DE 5
Historia de los descubrimientos antiguos y
modernos de la Nueva España . . . *Mex* 1924. O
[26] 304 [19] 4facsms 4maps aa
—Eng. tr, *L A* 1928. O 351 a
Written in 1584 by this conquistador and first
native Mexican historian but here first published.
Covers all sixteenth century conquests and explorations in Arizona, New Mexico and Texas.

O'BRYAN, WILLIAM 6
A narrative of travels in the United States . . .
Shebbear [*L* ptd] 1836. D 419 port aa
By the founder of the "Bryanite" religious sect.
He travelled through Pennsylvania and spent
some time in Ohio. Most of the edition was
destroyed at a printer's fire.

OBSERVATIONS 7
**Observations d'un hiomme impartial sur la
Lettre de Mr . . . à Mr. S. B. . . .** *L* [ptd Holland?]
1776. O 65 a
Defence of colonies against the *Lettre* of
Isaac Pinto, *q.v.* For answer to Pinto's *Seconde
lettre, see* under that author.

Observations impartiales d'un vrai Hollandois . . .
See Cerisier, Antoine M.

**Observations leading to a fair examination of
the . . . government proposed by the late convention . . . in a series of letters from the federal
farmer to the republican.** *See* Lee, Rich H.

Observations occasion'd by reading a 8
**pamphlet . . . concerning the currencies of the
British plantations . . .** *L* 1741. O 23 a

Observations on a late pamphlet, entitled, 9
"Considerations upon the order of the Cincinnati"
. . . evincing the . . . propriety of that . . . institution. By an obscure individual. *Phil* 1783. O 28
+ 4adv-p a
—rptd. *Hart* 1784. O 22
For pamphlet attacked, *see* Burke, Aedanus.
The "obscure individual" was possibly Stephen
Moylan, one of the founders of this society.

Observations on a late State of the nation . . .
See Burke, Edmund.

Observations on government. By a farmer of
New Jersey. *See* Stevens, John.

Observations on the American revolution . . . *See* Morris, Gouverneur.

Observations on the . . . conduct of the French . . . 1755. *See* Clarke, Wm.

Observations on the debates of the American congress . . . By Peter Porcupine. *See* Cobbett, Wm.

Observations on the importance of the northern colonies . . . *See* Kennedy, Archibald.

Observations on the impressment of Ame-   **9a** rican seamen by . . . Great Britain . . . By a citizen of Baltimore. *Balt* 1806. O 60 a

Observations on the late popular measures. By a tradesman. *See* Drinker, John.

Observations on the North American Land   **10** Company . . . *L* 1796. O [2] 149 a
This Company controlled six million acres in the South, in Pennsylvania and in Kentucky.

Observation on the present state of the waste lands of Great Britain . . . *See* Young, Arthur.

Observations on the proposed constitution for the United States . . . *See* Lee, Richard H.

Observations on the reconciliation of Great-Britain and her colonies . . . *See* Green, Jacob.

Observation on the Review of the con-   **11** troversy between Great Britain and her colonies. *L* 1769. O [2] 43 a

Observations on the slavery of the Afri-   **12** cans . . . *N Y* 1814. D 23 a

Observation upon the proposed plan of federal government . . . By a native of Virginia. *See* Monroe, James.

Observations upon the railway of the   **13** western and southern states. *Cin* 1850. O 28 aa

Some observations on the . . . Indian natives of this continent. See Benezet, Anthony.

OBSERVATOR'S TRIP   **14**
Observator's trip (The) to America, in a dialogue [with] his countryman Roger. [*Phil*] 1726. 16° 45 b BM

O'CALLAGHAN, E[DMUND] B. tr.   **15**
A brief . . . narrative of the hostile conduct of the barbarous natives towards the Dutch. *Alb* 1863. O 48 a 50copies ptd.

O'CALLAGHAN, E[DMUND] B.   **16**
The documentary history of the state of New York. *Alb* 1849–51. O 4v: [8] 787; [8] 1212; [8] 1215; [32] 1144. 28maps & pls a
—anr. ed. same impr. 1850–51. Q 4v: 536; [8] 711; [6] 748; [24] 700. 78maps & pls

O'CALLAGHAN, E[MUND] B.   **17**
History of New Netherland . . . *N Y* 1846–8. O 2v: 493; 608. 2maps 2pls 2facs a
—ed. 2, *N Y* 1855. O 2v

OCCASIONAL
Occasional essays on various subjects, chiefly political and historical. *See* Maseres, Francis.

Occasional reflections on the importance of the war in America . . . *See* Williamson, Peter.

OCEAN TO OCEAN.
The Pacific railroad . . . *See* Carrington. Mrs. Henry B.

OCEOLA NIKKANOCHEE.
A narrative of the early days . . . of: By his guardian. *See* Welch, Andrew.

OCHS, JOHANN R.   **18**
Americanischer Wegweiser oder Kurtze . . . Beschreibung der Engelischen Provintzen in Nord America, sonderlich aber der Landschafft Carolina . . . *Bern* 1711. D 102 map b JCB

O'CONNELL, REV. J[EREMIAH] J.   **19**
Catholicity in the Carolinas and Georgia . . . *N Y* [1879]. O 647 [incl.front] port a

O'CONNOR, JOHN   **20**
Wanderings of a vagabond . . . *N Y* 1873. D 492 aa
Lively narrative of a gambler who plied his profession on steamboats and in various southern cities.

[O'CONNOR, THOMAS]   **21**
An impartial and correct history of the war between the United States and Great Britain . . . *N Y* 1815. D 304 pl a
—ed. 2, rev., *N Y* 1815. D 312 pl
—ed. 3, *N Y* 1816. D 336 pl
—ed. 4, *N Y* 1817. D 336 3pls
—Eng. ed. *Belf* 1816. D 300

ODELL, JAMES [pub.]   **22**
Dayton directory . . . To which is prefixed a sketch of the history of the city. *Dayton* 1850. D 120 map aa
For separate edition of the *History see* Curwen, Maskell C.

ODENEAL, T. B.   **23**
The Modoc war . . . origin . . . *Port Ore* 1873. O 56 aa

ODÉRAHI, HISTOIRE AMÉRICAINE.
See Palisot de Beauvois.

ODIN (MGR. JEAN-MARIE).
Vie de: *See* Bony, Monsieur.

O'DONOVAN, JEREMIAH   **24**
A brief account of the author's interview with his countrymen... during his travels through various states of the Union in 1854–5. *Pitt* 1864. D 382 aa
Went west to St. Louis, Nauvoo and Galena.

OEHLER (ANDREW).   **25**
The life, adventures... of:... [*Trenton*] 1811. D 226 aa
Narrative of a restless adventurer who operated throughout the southern states from Charleston to New Orleans.

OFFICIAL DOCUMENTS   **26**
Official documents relative to the operations of the British army in the reduction of the Canadas under... Wolfe, Amherst... *Phil* 1813. O 29 2maps aa

OFFICIAL REPORTS   **27**
Official reports of battles, embracing the defence of Vicksburg... and the attack upon Baton Rouge... *Rich* 1863. O 170 aa

Official reports of battles [evacuation of   **28** Little Rock, Look Out mountain, etc.]. *Rich* 1864. O 72 aa

Official reports of battles [evacuation of   **29** Pensacola Navy yard, etc.]. *Rich* 1864. O 562 aa

Official reports of battles [from Seven   **30** Pines to Chickamauga]. *Rich* 1862. O 571 a

Official reports of battles [Ft. McAllister,   **31** Fayette C. H., Seven Pines, Stone River]. *Rich* 1864. O 98 a

Official reports of battles [operations in   **32** northwest Va.]. *Rich* 1864. O 96 [2] a

Official reports of battles. Published...   **33** at Richmond... *N Y* 1863. O 578 port aa

[OGDEN, AARON]   **34**
Concerning steam boats. Documents without comments. n.p. [1818]. O 25 a

OGDEN, GEORGE W.   **35**
Letters from the west... and a residence of two summers in... Ohio and Kentucky... *New Bedford* 1823. D 126 b AA N Y
—anr. issue, same sheets with *Exeter* impr. b

OGDEN, H[ENRY] A., illustrator   **36**
The army of the United States. *N Y* [1888]. F 43 lvs. 44 col.pls aa
—best ed. "Uniform of the army and navy...," *Akron & N Y* 1889. F 2v: 242 103col. pls b
—enl. ed. *N Y* [1907]. F [77] 70col.pls b
—Eng. ed. [army only] *L* 1960. F 44 cold.pls aa

OGDEN, JOHN C.   **37**
An excursion into Bethlehem & Nazareth, in Pennsylvania... *Phil* 1800. D [2] 168 aa
—rptd., same impr. & collat. 1805.

[OGDEN, JOHN C.]   **38**
A tour through Upper and Lower Canada. *Litchfield* 1799. 16° 119 a
—ed. 2, au. named, *Wilm Del* 1800. D 117 a
Includes description of Detroit, Mackinac and Ft. Miami.

[OGDEN, PETER S.]?   **39**
Considerations on the Indian trade... *Det* 1821. O 15 10 b

OGG, FREDERIC A.   **40**
The opening of the Mississippi; a struggle for supremacy... *N Y* 1904. O [12] 670 5maps a

OGILBY, JOHN   **41**
America... the latest and most accurate description of the new world, etc. *L* ptd by the author, 1671. F [10 incl eng-t] 675 54maps & pls. Some cops were on L.P.
—iss. l, has eng on p200 and pl "Arx Carolina". c
—iss. 2, no eng on p 200 and map of Carolina replaces the pl "Arx Carolina". b
—ed. 2, title slightly altered. *L*, ptd by Johnson for the author M.D.C.LXX [this puzzling date should obviously have an added digit, for printing was undoubtedly subsequent to 1671]. F [6] 629 maps & pls. b Sabin 50088 credits Harvard with a copy of this "freak" ed. Another copy is owned by a St. Louis collector.
Though a mere translation of Montanus [*q.v.*] Ogilby unblushingly claims authorship and never mentions Montanus. Piracy at this period was not confined to the high seas.

OGILVIE, WILLIAM   **42**
Lecture on the Yukon gold fields. *Victoria Can* 1897. O 32 a

OGLE COUNTY, ILL.
Sketches of the history of: *See* Boss, H. R.

OGLETHORPE (GENERAL [JAMES]).   **43**
Appendix to the report of the [S. C. Assembly] committee... to enquire into the causes of the disappointment... in the late expedition against St. Augustine, under...: *L* 1743. O [4] 79 b

This appendix—containing vouchers—was included in the Charleston edition of the *Report*, but not in the London edition, which requires it for completion. *See* below, No. 45.

OGLETHORPE (GENERAL [JAMES]).   44
An impartial account of the late expedition against St. Augustine under: *L* 1742. O 68 map c AA BA GaU NYP
For reply to this criticism of Oglethorpe's conduct, *see* Cadogan, George. For another account *see* Kimber, Edward.

OGLETHORPE (GENERAL [JAMES]).   45
The report of the committee, of both houses of Assembly of . . . South-Carolina, appointed to enquire into the causes of the disappointment . . . in the late expedition against St. Augustine, under the command of: *Charles-Town S C* 1742. F 108 + app 52 [1] map c N NYP[only 2copies known]
—rptd., without app. *L* 1743. O [4] 112 b GaU N [for scparatcly ptd. Appendix completing this ed. *see* No. 43].

[O'HANLON, JOHN]   46
Life and scenery in Missouri. Reminiscences of a missionary priest. *Dub* 1890. 16° [12] 292 + 4adv-p. a

O'HANLON, J[OHN]   47
The Irish emigrant's guide for the United States. *B* 1851. 16° 224 aa

OHIO
The advantages of a settlement upon the Ohio. *See* Wharton, Sam'l.

An adventure on the banks of the Ohio: . . . story of Mrs. Eliza Williamson . . . *See* Farnesworth, Frederick.

Articles of an association by the name of   48 the Ohio company: *N Y* 1787. O 45 b MH NYP WisH
An earlier tract of twelve pages, same title, was issued at Worcester, 1786. c

A concise view of the State of Ohio: . . .   49 *L* 1825. O 30 aa
Emigration tract, with no historical significance.

Description abrégé du territoire . . . au sud de l'Ohio. *See* Smith, Daniel.

Facts and observations, respecting the country granted . . . by the Six United Nations . . ., on the south-east side of the river Ohio. *See* Wharton, Sam'l.

An historical account of the expedition against Ohio Indians. *See* Smith, [*Provost*] Wm.

Laws of the Territory of the United States   50 north-west of the Ohio: . . . by the Governour and Judges, in their legislative capacity . . . *Cin* Maxwell 1796. O 225 dd IndH NYP JCB [of 5perfect copies known]
—rptd. in facs, *Cin* [*ca* 1890]. a
—anr. ed. *Wash* 1891.
Cited as the *Maxwell Code*, this first collection of N. W. territory laws was the first book printed in Ohio or anywhere in the Northwest Territory. Of a separately printed *Table of Contents*, of the same year, no copy is known.

A letter to a friend, giving a concise . . . account . . . of the Ohio defeat. [etc.]. *See* Chauncy, Chas.

Ohio and Mississippi navigator [The] . . . *See* Cramer, Zadok.

Ohio navigator [The] . . . account of that   51 . . .. river from its head . . . From the journals of gentlemen . . . who have frequently navigated it. *Washington* [*Ky*?] 1798. No copies now known.
Evans cites two editions as published that year. These predecessors to his *Navigator* may have caused Cramer to style the first of his series, in 1802, as "third edition."

Ohio railroad guide [The] . . . *Cin* 1852.   52 D 96 map a
—enl. ed. *Columbus* 1854. D [6] 135 32pls

Ohio valley historical miscellanies . . . *See* Espy, Josiah.

Prospectus pour l'établissement sur les ri-   53 vieres d'Ohio et de Scioto . . . [*P* de Prault 1789–90]. Q [2] 16, 14 [3] map tab aa
Glowing account of an Ohio Eden, circulated in France by the Scioto Company, which lured 500 emigrants to their ruin; probably written by Joel Barlow and William Playfair.

Public documents concerning the Ohio Canals . . . *See* Kilbourn, John.

Railroad from the banks of the Ohio river: 54 to the tide waters of the Carolinas and Georgia. *Cin* 1835. O 30 a

Report of proceedings in Ireland relative to the church in Ohio: *See* West, G. Montgomery.

Three days on the Ohio river. *See* William, Father.

Topographical description of Ohio, Indiana . . . and Lousiana. By a late Officer in the U.S. Army. *See* Cutler, Jervis.

Traveler's guide to and through Ohio. 55
N Y 1833. O 24 map a

OJIBBEWAY INDIANS 56
Ojibbeway Indians (the) now on a visit to
England. A short history and description of:
L 1844. D 30 [incl. front.] + 6adv-p a
By Charles Stuart.

O'KELLY, PATRICK 57
Advice and guide to emigrants . . . to the
United States. *Dub* 1834. D 96 [2] a

OKLAHOMA CITY.
Directory of Oklahoma City. [1889]. *See* Mc
Adam, Rezin W., and Levi, S. E.

The first eight months of Oklahoma City. By
Bunky. *See* Geffs, Irvin.

OLD, R. O. 58
Colorado . . . history, geography . . . *L* [1869].
O 64 map aa
—rev. ed. *L* 1872. O 95 map a

OLD BLOCK'S SKETCH BOOK . . .
See Delano, Alonzo.

OLD FOX (AN) TARR'D AND FEATHER'D
See Toplady, Augustus M.

OLD MAN'S STORY 59
Old man's story (The) of old times . . . *Adrian
Mich* 1855. O 38 port aa

OLD SOLDIER'S STORY (THE) . . .
See Fairbanks, Chas.

OLDFIELD, J. 60
"'Tother side of Ohio," or a review of a "Poem
in three cantos." *Hart* 1818. D 40 a

[OLDMIXON, JOHN] 61
The British empire in America . . . *L* 1708.
O 2v: [40] 412; [2] 382 [32]. 8maps aa
—ed. 2, cor. & enl., but with some omissions,
L 1741. O 2v: [36] 567; [2] 478. 8maps aa
—Ger. tr. *Hamburg* 1715. O [28] 879; *Lemgo*
1744. Q 2v: [36] 706; [2] 709–1254 [22]. 8maps
13pls; *Sorau* 1761, Q front 3maps a
—Dutch tr: *Amst* 1721. Q 2v: [26] 300; [2] 327
[14], 8maps 5pls; *Amst* 1727, Q 2v same collat.

OLDMIXON, CAPT. [JOHN W.] 62
Transatlantic wanderings; or, a last book at
the United States. *L* 1855. 16° [4] 189 a
Uncomplimentary portrayal of the American
scene, with visits to Pittsburgh, Cincinnati, New
Orleans, Mobile, Pensacola, etc.

OLDYS, FRANCIS [pseud.]
The life of Thomas Pain [*sic*] . . . *See* Chalmers,
Geo.

OLIPHANT, EDWARD 63
The history of North America . . . *Edin* 1800.
O 408 map aa
—ed. 2, same impr. 1801. a
Largely an unblushing piracy from Jedidiah
Morse's *History of America*.

OLIPHANT, LAURENCE 64
Minnesota and the far west . . . *Edin* 1855.
O [14] 306 + 16 adv-p map 7pls a

OLIVÁN REBOLLEDO, JUAN DE 65
Informe juridico al Rey . . . [*Madrid* 1724].
F 50 lvs. b JCB
Answers certain complaints against the *Audiencia* of Mexico, of which the author was a member.
Contains his plan, as governor of the "Pais de
los Texas", to erect there a province to be named
"Nuevas Philipinas," with its boundaries described.

OLIVER (ANDREW). 66
Proceedings of His Majesty's Council of the
province of Massachusetts-Bay, relative to the
deposition of: . . . *B* 1770. F [2] 33 b AA BA
NYP Y
Oliver's deposition claimed the British soldiers
were justified in shooting the Boston citizens.

OLIVER, BENJAMIN L. 67
The rights of American citizens; with a commentary on state rights . . . *B* 1832. O 411 a

OLIVER, DAVID D. 68
Centennial history of Alpena county, Michigan.
Alpena 1903. O 186 [2] port a

[OLIVER, JOHN W.] 69
Guide to the new gold region of western
Kansas and Nebraska. *N Y* 1859. D 32 map dd
AA G [of 5copies known]

OLIVER, PETER 70
The Puritan commonwealth. An historical
review of the Puritan government in Massachusetts . . . *B* 1856. O [12] 502 + 4adv-p at front a

OLIVER, WILLIAM 71
Eight months in Illinois . . . *Newcastle Eng*
1843. D [10] 142 b Duke G Y
—rptd. *Chi* 1924. O 260 a

OLLIFFE, CHARLES 72
Scènes américaines: dix-huit mois dans le
nouveau monde. *P* 1852. D [14] 320 2pls a
—ed. 2, with 7 chaps. added, *P* 1853. D [16] 344
2pls
—rptd. *Brus* 1853. D [14] 298 2pls

Extensive travels in the Central West and South; concluded that the slaves' condition was superior to that of any laborer in the world.

OLLIVANT, J. C. 73

A breeze from the great Salt Lake; or, New Zealand to New York ... *L* 1871. O 176 map a

OLMSTED, DENISON 74

Memoir of Eli Whitney. *N Hav* 1846. O 80 2pls a

Revolutionized fire-arms manufacturing; his cotton gin, increasing in ten years our annual cotton export from two hundred thousand to forty-one million pounds, sounded the death knell to peaceful emancipation.

OLMSTED, FRANCIS A. 75

Incidents of a whaling voyage ... *N Y* 1841. D 360 12pls aa

One of the earliest accounts of the sperm-whale industry.

OLMSTED, FREDERICK L. 76

The cotton kingdom ... *N Y* 1861. D 2v: [8] 376; [4] 404. map a

—rptd. *N Y* 1862. same collat.

—Eng. ed. "Journeys ... in the cotton kingdom ...," *L* 1861. same collat.

Condensation of his three separately published Journeys, the most minute study of the antebellum south.

OLMSTED, FREDERICK L. 77

A journey in the back country ... *N Y* 1860. D [16] 11–492 a

—rptd. *N Y* 1861. same collat.; *N Y* 1863. same collat.

—Eng. ed. *L* 1860. same collat.

—new ed. *N Y* 1907. O 2v: [18] 281; [6] 284 [4]

OLMSTED, FREDERICK L. 78

A journey in the seaboard slave states ... *N Y* 1856. D [6, 9–16] 724 + 4adv-p] map pl a

—rptd.: same collat. *N Y* 1859; *N Y* 1861

—Eng. ed. *L* 1856. D

—new ed. *N Y* 1904. O 2v: [42] 418; [4] 412. port

OLMSTED, FREDERICK L. 79

A journey through Texas ... *N Y* 1857. D [36] 516 map pl a

—rptd. *N Y* 1860. same collat.

—Ger. tr. *Leip* 1857. O [20] 286

—Eng. ed. *L* 1859 D

OLMSTED, JOHN 80

A trip to California in 1868. *N Y* 1880. 16° 131 a

OLSHAUSEN, THEODOR 81

Geschichte der Mormonen ... *Gottingen* 1856. O [4] 244 a

OLSHAUSEN, THEODOR 82

Die Vereiningten Staaten von Amerika ... *Kiel* 1853–5. O 3pts in 2v: [8] 427; [18] 190 [10] 201. 9maps & pls[on 7 sheets] b

Vol. I, Das Mississippi-Thal; Vol. II, pt. 1, Der Staat Missouri, pt. 2, Der Staat Iowa. No more issued.

OMAHA DIRECTORY ... 1866

See Collins, Chas., comp.

O'MEARA, JAMES 83

Broderick and Gwin. The most extraordinary contest for a seat in the Senate of the United States ever known. *S F* 1881. 16° [10] 254 a

[O'MEARA, JAMES] 84

The vigilance committee of 1856 ... *S F* 1887. D 57 aa

—rptd. *S F* 1890 [date on wrap] a

OMWAKE, JOHN 85

The Conestoga six-horse bell teams of ... Pennsylvania. *Cinc* 1930. Q 163 pls a

ON THE FRONTIER

On the frontier, or, scenes in the west. *See* Pearson, C. H.

ON THE PAST RELATIONS 86

On the past relations between Great Britain and the United States. *L* 1813. O 59 a

ON THE TEN TRIBES

On the ten tribes of Israel, and the aborigines of America ... By a Bible professor. *See* Jones, Epaphras.

ON THE ... PAY-ROLL

On the "White Pass" pay-roll ... *See* Graves, S. H.

ONDERDONK, HENRY, JR. 87

Annals of Hempstead [*L.I.*] ... *Hempstead* 1878. O 107 a

ONDERDONK, HENRY, JR. 88

The barbarous capture and death of Gen. Nathaniel Woodhull ... *N Y* 1848. D 52 a

ONDERDONK, HENRY, JR. 89

Documents ... to illustrate the revolutionary incidents of Queens county [N. Y.]. Ser. I & II. *N Y* [& *Hempstead*] 1846–84. D 2v: 264; 70 map a

ONDERDONK, HENRY, JR. 90

Queens County [N. Y.] in olden times ... *Jamaica N Y* 1865. Q [2] 122 a

ONDERDONK, HENRY, JR. 91

Revolutionary incidents of Suffolk and Kings counties [N. Y.] ... *N Y* 1849. D 268 map a

—rptd. 1866.

ONDERDONK, JAMES L. 92
Idaho; facts ... *S F* 1885. O 150 aa

O'NEALL, JOHN B. 93
The annals of Newberry [S. C.] ... *Charleston S C* 1859. D 413 [8] port a
—enl. ed., with pt. 2 [by J. A. Chapman], *Newberry* 1892. O 816 [8] port aa
—rptd. 1949, same collat

O'NEALL, JOHN B. 94
Biographical sketches of the bench and bar of South Carolina. *Charleston S C* 1859. O 2v: [32] 431; [4] 614 [1] tab 3facs a

ONEER, P. I. [pseud.]
The early pioneers of the west. *See* Gregg, Wm. J.

ONEIDA COMMUNITY 95
Oneida community (The) ... its ideas ... *Wallingford Conn* 1865. O 32 pl a

O'NEIL, NEAL J. 96
The guide to Texas ... *Dub* 1834. O [12] 176 map b
—rptd., "Observations ... on Texas, etc." *L* 1834. O aa

O'NEILL, JOHN 97
Northern Nebraska as a home for immigrants. *Sioux City* 1875. O 108 fold.map b G Y
Account of the Platte River and Black Hills country, written from investigations made while seeking a site for an Irish colony.

ONIS, LUIS DE 98
Memoria sobre las negociaciones entre Espana y los Estados-Unidos, que dieron motivo al tratado de 1819 ... *Madrid* 1820. Q 2pts in 1: [8] 108 [2] 70 [1]; 213 map b NYP Y
—rptd.: *Mex* 1820, Q [6] 60 [72] map; *Mex* 1825, same collat. *Mex* 1826 aa
—Eng. tr.: [*Wash*] 1821, O 152; *Balt* 1821, same collat. aa
Official correspondence concerning the Floridas and the disputed western boundary of Louisiana.

ONIS, (LOUIS DE, Minister from Spain) 99
and ADAMS (JOHN QUINCY ...)
Official correspondence between: in relation to the Floridas and the boundaries of Louisiana ... *L* 1818. O 130 b

ONKEN, OTTO, illustrator
Western scenery ... *See* Wells, Wm.

ONSTOT, T[HOMAS] G. 100
Pioneers of Menard and Mason counties ... including personal reminiscenes of Abraham

Lincoln ... *Forest City Ill* 1902. O 400 [incl. prelim blank lf] aa
Almost the entire edition burned.

ONTDEKKING VAN 'T GEHEEL ...
See Kimyser, Arnold.

OPIE, JOHN N. 101
A rebel cavalryman. *Chi* 1889. O 336 a

ORACLE
Oracle (The) of liberty, and mode of establishing a free government. By Hermes. *See* Rodney, Caesar A.

ORATION
Oration (An), upon the beauties of liberty, or the essential rights of the Americans. *See* Skillman, Isaac.

ORCUTT, SAMUEL, and 102
BEARDSLEY, AMBROSE
The history of ... Derby, Connecticut ... *Springfield Mass* 1880. O [2 98] 844[incl. illus] 21pls a

ORD, GENERAL E[DWARD] O. C. 103
... Annual report ... [*San Antonio* 1880]. D 94[incl. 5blank p] capt.t.only a

ORD, GENERAL E[DWARD] O. C. 104
Report ... relative to ... protection of the Texas frontier. *San Antonio* 1879. D [6] 28 [4] fold.tab a

OREGON
An account and history of the Oregon Territory ... *See* Wilkes, Geo., *The history of Oregon*, of which this is a garbled reprint.

Correspondence relative to the negotiation 105 of the question of the disputed right to the Oregon Territory: ... *L* 1846. F [4] 71 a

Description of Oregon and California. 1849. *See* Mitchell, Sam'l. A.

Excursion to the Oregon. *See* Townsend, John K.

The extent and value of the ... rights of the Hudson's Bay Company in Oregon. *See* Coxe, Rich'd S.

Historical sketches of the Catholic church in Oregon ... *See* Blanchet, Francis N.

Inside history of the Oregon Central Rail- 106 road Companies. *Port* 1869. O 39 a

Memorial of the legislative assembly of 107 Oregon: relative to their present situation ... [H Misc. Doc. 98] *Wash* 1848. O 36 a

Submitted by Joe Meek; includes account of the Whitman massacre. For another similar memorial, *See* Thornton, James Q.

Message from the President . . . commu- 108 nicating information relative to Indian hostilities in . . . Oregon and Washington. [H. Exec. Doc. 93]. *Wash* 1856. O 144 a

Notice sur le territoire et sur la mission 109 de l'Oregon. *Brus* 1847. D 180 [map called for, but apparently not issued] a

Oregon and the Pacific northwest . . . *Port* [ca 1879]. *See* Davidson, I. G.

Oregon controversy [The] reviewed . . . By 110 a friend of the Anglo-Saxons. *N Y* 1846. O 54 b N OreH Y

Oregon-gebiet [Das], der Rechtstitel der 111 Vereinigten Staaten klar und unbestreitbar . . . *Bremen* 1846. O 114 a
On the title to the Oregon country, with official correspondence, British and American.

Oregon question [The]. *See* Senior, Nassau W.

Oregon territory [The]; a geographical [etc.] account . . . *See* Nicolay, Chas. G.

Oregon territory . . . and the claims of the United States. *See* Leonard, H. L. W.

Oregon territory [The], consisting of a 112 brief description . . . *L* Nattali 1846. 16° 78 map a
The anonymous author had probably been a Hudson's Bay employee. For an entirely different work of similar title, issued by Knight the same year, and, like it, frequently bound with Mrs. Traill's *The backwoods of Canada*, *See* Nicolay, Charles G.

Oregon: the claim of the United States 113 . . . as stated in the letters of . . . Calhoun and . . . Buchanan . . . *L* 1846. O [4] 55 16 a

Rambles in the United States . . . with a short account of Oregon: . . . By Rubio. *See* James, Thos. H.

Report of the Adjutant General of Oregon: for . . . 1856–6. *See* Reed, Cyrus A.

Report on the territory of Oregon: by a 114 committee, appointed at a meeting of the citizens of Columbus . . . *Columbus O* 1843. O 22 map[possibly not issued with all copies] c NYP WashU Y
Earliest attempt at a guide for Oregon emigrants.

Sketches of mission life among the Indians of Oregon: *See* Perkins, H. K. W.

Statement . . . in relation to the Indian war 115 claims of: Oregon and Washington. [*Salem Ore* 1857?]. O 67 aa

Statement of facts relating to incorpo- 116 ration . . . of the Oregon Central Railroad Company. *Port* 1868. O 38 a

Tracts on the Oregon question. By an 117 American. *N Y* 1846. D 52 a

Traveler's guide and Oregon railroad gazetteer. *See* Samuel, Leo.

OREGONIAN . . . ADVOCATE 118
Oregonian, and Indian's advocate . . . Vol. I, 11monthly nos.[all]. *B* Oct. 1838–Aug. 1839. O 352 map tab b NYP OreH SeattleP Y
This periodical was continued as *Oregon Weekly Times* from 1853 to 1858.

O'REILLY, GOV. ALEXANDER 119
Le procès qui a été fait à cause du soulévement . . . dans cette colonie . . . [*N O*? 1769?]. O 32 b B

O'REILLY, HARRINGTON 120
Fifty years on the trail . . . *L* 1889. D [16 incl. front.] 382 + 32adv-p a
—ed. 2, same impr. & collat. 1890.
—rptd. same impr. & collat. 1891.
—Am. ed., from sheets of *L* ed. 1, *N Y* 1889.
—Fr. tr. *P* 1889. D 348
Life story of Johnny Nelson, white renegade with the Sioux, adopted by Spotted Tail, married to Red Cloud's sister, army scout, trapper and colossal liar.

[O'REILLY, HENRY] 121
Notices of Sullivan's campaign, in . . . western New York . . . *Roch* 1842. D 192 pl aa

O'REILLY, HENRY 122
Settlement in the west. Sketches of Rochester; with . . . notices of western New-York . . . *Roch* 1838. D [4] 17–336 starred p337–338 337–416 map 43pls a
Enlarged from the author's sixteen-page pamphlet of 1835 entitled *Rochester in* 1835. Correct spelling of his name is said to be O'Rielly.

ORIGIN 123
Origin [The] and progress of the present difficulties between the United States and Great Britain . . . By a citizen of Otsego County. *Utica* 1809. D 24 a

Origin (The) of the american contest. *See* Leonard, Dan'l., *Massachusettensis*.

OROZCO Y BERRA, MANUEL 124
Apuntes para historia y geografia de California, Nueva Mexico, Nutka, y Arizona. *Mex* 1881. O 502 a

ORR, GEORGE   125
The possession of Louisiana by the French, considered as it affects the interests of . . . Great Britain, America [etc.]. *L* 1803. O 45 aa

ORR, N. M.   126
The city of Stockton . . . *Stockton* 1874. O 64 [2] aa

[ORTEGA, JOSÉ]   127
Apostolicos afanes de la Compaña de Jesus . . . por un Padre de la misma sagrada religion de su provincia de Mexico. *Barcelona* 1754. Q [12] 452 [10] b N NYP Y
—rptd. with new t-p, "Historia del Nayarit, Sonora, Sinaloa, y ambas Californias," *Mex* 1887. D [10] 564 [6] aa
—anr. ed., with original t., *Mex* 1944. O [24] 446 [2]
Includes much on the movements and discoveries of the missionary priests Kino and Consag in Arizona and California.

[ORTON, A. R.], pub.   128
The Derienni; or, land pirates of the isthmus . . . *N O* 1853. O 44 pl b NYP

OSAGE CAPTIVE (THE LITTLE).
See Cornelius, Elias.

OSAGE CITY [KAS.]
Directory of: 1887. *See* Black, Amos, and White, V.

OSAGES
Histoire de la tribu des Osages . . . Par M. P. V. *See* Vissier, Paul.

Six Indiens rouges de la tribu des Grands   129
Osages: arrivés du Missouri au Havre . . . *Brus* 1827. 16° [4] 28 pl aa
—ed. 2, enl., *Havre* [1827]. O [4] 28 aa
—ed. 3, *P* 1827. D 36 front aa

OSGOOD, ERNEST S.   130
The day of the cattleman . . . *Minneap* 1929. O [14] 283[incl. front] 14pls & maps aa
Significant study into the expansion of the range cattle industry into the northern plains, from the late sixties to the early nineties.

OSGOOD, HERBERT L.   131
The American colonies in the seventeenth century. *N Y* 1904–07. O 3v: [32] 578; [20] 490 + 2adv-p; [22] 551 a
—rptd.: *N Y* [1930], O 3v; *Gloucester* 1957, O 3v
Awarded the Loubat accolade in 1908 as the best work on early American history published in five years.

OSGOOD, HERBERT L.   132
The American colonies in the eighteenth cen-

tury. *N Y* 1924. O 2v: [32] 552; [24] 554; [28] 580; [24] 582 aa

OSHKOSH   133
Biographical and statistical history of Oshkosh [Wis].: . . . *Oshkosh* 1867. O 76 aa

Oshkosh city directory . . . 1868. *See* Thomas, James M.

Oshkosh city directory . . . Containing   134
. . . history . . . *Oshkosh* 1872. O 306 map 2pls aa

[OSSOLI, SARAH M.]   135
Summer on the lakes, in 1843. *B* 1844. D [4] 256 7pls aa issued also without the pls a
—Eng. ed. *L* 1861. 16° 360

OSTERMAYER, H.   136
Tagebuch einer Reise nach Texas. *Biberach* 1850. O 200 2pls b

O'SULLIVAN, MICHAEL   137
The history of Franklin county [Neb.]: its settlement, [etc.]. *Lincoln* 1873. O 74 a

[OSWALD, ELEAZER]   138
Letters of "Franklin," on the conduct of the executive, and the treaty . . . with the court of Great Britain. *Phil* 1795. O 56 a
Attributed also to Alex. J. Dallas.

OSZWALD, H. FR.   139
Californien und seine Verhaltnisse . . . *Leip* 1849. 16° 130 map aa

OSZWALD, H. FR.   140
Der Deutsche in Californien . . . *N Y* 1853. O 130 a

OTERO, MIGUEL A.   141
My life on the frontier . . . 1864–1897. *N Y* 1935 & *Albuquerque* 1939. O 2v: [10] 293; [14] 306 aa
—both vols also iss in ltd form, sgd and with pls added

OTERO, MIGUEL A.   142
The real Billy the Kid . . . *N Y* 1936. O [20] 200 8pls aa
Portrays this controversial sinner as more sinned against than sinning.

OTHER SIDE
Other side (The) of the question; or, a defence of the liberties of North-America . . . *See* Livingston, Philip.

[OTIS, HARRISON GRAY]   143
Letters developing the character . . . of the Hartford convention. *Wash* 1820. D 43 a
—enl. ed. "Letters in defence of the Hartford convention . . .," *B* 1824. O [8] 103

OTIS (HARRISON GRAY).   **144**
Resistance to laws of the United States, considered in four letters to: . . . By Leolin. *B* 1811. O 24 a
Attributed also to James T. Austin.

[OTIS, JAMES]   **145**
Brief remarks on the defence of the Halifax libel, on the British-American-colonies. *B* 1765. Q 40 a
An intemperate reply to Martin Howard's answer to Otis' earlier *Vindication, see* below.

[OTIS, JAMES]   **146**
Considerations on behalf of the colonists. In a letter to a noble lord. *L* 1765. O [2] 52 aa
—ed. 2, same impr., date & collat. a

OTIS, JAMES   **147**
The rights of the British colonies asserted and proved. *B* 1764. O [80] aa
—rptd. *L* 1765; *L* 1766; both: O 120 a
Of great influence on colonial thought concerning the constitutionality of being taxed without representation. It answered the Tory pamphlet by Soame Jenyns *q.v.*

[OTIS, JAMES]   **148**
A vindication of the British colonies . . . *B* 1765. O 32 aa
—Eng. ed. *L* 1769. O [4] 48 a
—anr. Eng. ed., same impr. & date. O [4] 58
Reply to Martin Howard's *Letter from a gentleman at Halifax* . . ., a twenty-two-page pamphlet answering Samuel Hopkins' *The rights of the colonies examined.*

OTIS, JAMES   **149**
A vindication of the conduct of the House of Representatives . . . *B* 1762. O 53 aa
This defence of the legislative body, in refusing to provide payment for the Governor's use on the ground that that body only could originate taxes, was the source of all subsequent colonial argument in the controversy with England.

OTIS, RICHARD W. [pub.]   **150**
The Louisville directory, for . . . 1832. *Louisv* 1832. 16° 198 b AA N
Louisville's first directory, containing its history by Mann Butler.

OTTAWA RIVER (THE).   **151**
Minutes of debates in council on the banks of: *Phil* 1792. O [6] 5–22 b LC NYP
—rptd. *Balt* 1800. O 23 aa
This fictitious account of a conference of Indian chiefs after their defeat of St. Clair's army was an attack on the "lawless ambition" of the Ohio land companies.

OTTER, WILLIAM   **152**
History of my own times. *Emmitsburg Md* 1835. 16° 357 a

OTTO, W. T.   **153**
Authentic . . . information on the origin . . . of the Indian hostilities on the frontier. *Wash* 1867. O 128 a
Covers the Fetterman massacre and other events on the Bozeman Trail.

[OTTOLENGUAL, D.]   **154**
Behind the seams; by a nigger woman who took in work from Mrs. Lincoln and Mrs. Davis. *N Y* 1868. O 23 + cov.t. aa
Parody on Keckley's *Behind the scenes.*

OUR   **155**
Our cruise in the Confederate States' war steamer "Alabama." The private journal of an officer. From a supplement to the South African Advertiser and Mail. Cape Town, Saturday, September 19, 1863. [*L* 1863?]. O 64 aa

Our forefathers; their homes. By the author of "Carolina in the olden time." *See* Poyas, Mrs. Eliz. A.

Our friends the Coeur d'Alene Indians. *See* Palladino, Lawrence B.

Our great indian war. The miraculous lives of Mustang Bill and Miss Marion Fannin . . . *See* Decker, Wm. R.

Our south and her future. By a southerner   **156**
. . . *Augusta Ga* 1862. D cover-t. 34 [2] a

OUSELEY, WILLIAM G.   **157**
Remarks on the statistics and political institutions of the United States . . . *L* 1832. O [16] 208 a
—Am. ed. *Phil* 1832. O 226

OUTLAW BROTHERS (THE) . . .
By the author of "Billy Le Roy, the Colorado bandit." *See* Daggett, Thos. F.

[OVERTON, JOHN]   **158**
A vindication of the measures of the President and his commanding generals, in the . . . Seminole war. *Nashv* [1819]. O 122 [incl. errata] b BP N [of 3copies known]
—*Wash* 1819. O 133 a
Defends Jackson's Florida invasion as attacked in chairman Abner Lacock's *Report of the Select Committee of the Senate* . . .

OVIEDO Y VALDES, GONZALO F. DE   **159**
Historia general y natural de las Indias, islas y tierra-firme del mar océano . . . *Madrid* 1851–5.

Q 4v: [112] 632 [2]; [8] 511 [2]; [8] 651 [2]; [8] 619 [2]. 15pls b N NYP Y

Contains so much material not included in the original Spanish editions of his *Natural hystoria* [1526] and his *Historia general* [1535], that it may be properly included in this compilation as a new work.

OWEN, DANIEL E.   **160**

Old times in Saco... *Saco Me* 1891. O [12] 172 8pls a

OWEN, G., comp.   **161**

Salt Lake City directory... [*N Y*]1867. O [4] 135 aa [Said to have been suppressed by the Church]. First directory of this city. For the second, *see* Sloan, E. L.

OWEN (JAMES TUDOR).   **162**

The life and travels of:... *L* Fisher [1801?]. D 42[incl.front.] aa

Highly improbable adventures, containing a captivity by Indians during the Revolution.

OWEN (MAJOR JOHN, pioneer of   **163**
the northwest).

The journals and letters of:... *N Y* 1927. O 2v: [20] 346; [4] 367 2maps 30pls a 50 copies on L.P. [of 550 ptd.] aa

OWEN (MRS. NARCISSA).   **164**

Memoirs of: [*Wash* 1907]. O 126[incl. illus] a

By the widow of Colonel Robert L. Owen, U. S. Agent to the Oklahoma Cherokees, and next to Ross in influence with that nation.

OWEN, RICHARD E., et al.   **165**

Report on the mines of New Mexico. *Wash* 1865. O 59 cov.t.only aa

OWEN, ROBERT   **166**

[His] Opening speech, and his reply to the Rev. Alex. Campbell... also [his] Memorial to the Republic of Mexico and a narrative of the proceedings thereon, which led to the promise... to place a district... along the whole line of frontier bordering on the United States, under [his] jurisdiction... *Cin* 1829. O 226 [2] aa

Abortive scheme for an independent Texas to be established under a new moral system of government and guaranteed by Mexico.

OWEN (ROBERT).

Life of: 1866. *See* Packard, Fred. A.

OWEN (ROBERT).   **167**

Life of: written by himself... *L* 1857-8. O 2v: [44] 390 [1]; [16, 38] 358 [1] aa

OWEN, ROBERT   **168**

Two discourses on a new system of society... *L* 1825. O 36 aa
—Am. eds.: *Pitt* 1825, O 36; *Louisv* 1825; *Phil* 1825. O 52 a

OWEN PUBLISHING CO.   **169**

... Gazetteer and directory of Jackson county, Iowa... history... *Davenport* 1878. O 308 [incl. paste-down end pages front & rear] + adv-pp. interspersed throughout aa

OWENS, GEORGE, comp.   **170**

A general directory... of the principal towns in the upper country, embracing a portion of California; together with... information concerning Idaho Territory. *S F* 1866. O 171 map aa

OWENS, GEORGE [pub.]   **171**

Idaho directory, including... towns in Boise, Owyhee and Altruras counties, with a brief account of each place... [*SF*? 1864?]. O [2] 56 [2] b LC [only copy known]
—enl. ed., "A general directory... of... towns east of the Cascade mountains," *S F* 1865. O 210 map b PortOreL Y

OWENS, JAMES B.   **172**

The right, causes and necessity for secession [*Apalachicola*? 1861] O 32 aa

OWYHEE COUNTY, IDAHO.   **173**

Historical descriptive and commercial directory of: *Silver City* 1898. O 140 16 [4] 28pls a

OZANNE, T. D.   **174**

The south as it is... *L* 1863. D [6] 306 a

P

P., ABBÉ J.

Vie de Monseigneur Dubuis... *See* Perrichon, Abbé J.

P..., J...

The life of General James Wolfe... *See* Pringle, John.

Pxxxx, M.

Discours sur les avantages... de la découverte de l'Amérique. *See* Chastellux, Francois J.

P., S. F.   **1**

Stepping westward. *Nashua N H* [1878]. O 79 a

PACIFIC (THE).   2
Outline descriptions of the military posts in the Department of : *S F* 1879. D 104 68 maps & pls a

PACIFIC RAILROAD
First annual report of . . . the Pacific railroad. *See* Kirkwood, James P.

Report of the Secretary of War on . . .   3
Pacific railroad explorations. H.Exec.Doc.129. *Wash* 1855. O 43 a
This report—Document 129— summarizing the several surveys was accompanied by nine other reports, all bearing that same document number. For information on these separate reports, *see* entries under the various explorers: I, Humphreys, Andrew A.; II, Stevens, Isaac A.; III & IV, Beckwith, Edward G.; V, Whipple, Amiel W.; VI, Pope, John; VII, Parke, John G.; VIII, Williamson, R. S.; IX Lander, Fred'k W.
This document was originally issued as an entity, bound in two volumes of text, together with a third volume containing eleven maps and profiles [on fourteen sheets]. Of a contemplated third volume of text, only one report—that of Frederick W. Lander, *q. v.*—was issued in 1856, bearing the same document number. Of it only two copies are known; hence a complete set of the octavo edition, with all ten reports and the maps, is not easily assembled. A set will have enhanced value if accompanied by the huge folding map made by Warren, engraved by Siebert, and issued at Washington in 1857, both separately and with the quarto edition of the reports; it was the best cartographical work on the West up to its time and some copies were colored.
In 1855–1860 all of above reports, elaborately illustrated and with considerable additions, appeared in quarto form—12 volumes in 13—as House Executive Document 91, serials 791-801, and House Executive Document 56, serials 1054–1055. A Senate issue [Executive Document 78, serials 758–768, and Executive Document 46, serial 992] differed only in the matter of arrangement.

PACIFIC WAGON ROADS
Pacific wagon roads [*Wash* 1859]. *See* Campbell, Alex. H.

PACIFICUS.
Letters of: *See* Hamilton, Alex.

[PACKARD, FREDERICK A.]   4
Life of Robert Owen. *Phil* 1866. D 264 a
—ed. 2, same impr. 1868. D [2] 264

PACKARD, JASPER   5
History of La Porte County, Indiana . . . *La Porte* 1876. D 467 map aa

PACKARD, WELLMAN, and LARISON, G.   6
Early emigration to California. *Bloomington Ill* 1928. O 23 3ports a 30copies ptd.

PADDOCK, B[UCKLEY] B.   7
Early days in Fort Worth . . . [*Ft. Worth*?] n.d. O 36 a

PADDOCK B[UCKLEY] H.   8
A history of central and western Texas. *Chi* 1911. Q 2v: [2] 451; [2] 452–897 aa

[PAGE, FREDERIC B.]   9
Prairiedom; rambles and scrambles in Texas . . . By a Suthron. *N Y* 1845. D 166 fold. map aa
—ed. 2, with "Southron" spelling on t-p. same impr 1846. D 166 [incl map] aa

PAGE, KARL G.   10
Darstellung der burgerlichen Verhaltnisse in den Freistaaten von Nordamerika . . . *Bautzen* ptd for subscribers only, n.d. [*ca* 1830]. D 110 aa

PAGE'S BATTERY   11
Page's battery, or Morris artillery . . . Army Northern Virginia. Sketch of: By one of the company. *N Y* 1885. D 82 [2] aa

PAGÈS, [PIERRE MARIE F.]   12
vicomte de
Nouveau voyage du monde . . . 1788–89–90. *P* 1797. O 3v 6pls aa
Visited the eastern states, Florida and Louisiana. No English translation of these travels has appeared.

PAGÈS, [PIERRE MARIE F.]   13
vicomte de
Voyages autour du monde . . . 1767–1776. *P* 1782. O 2v: 432; 272. 10maps & pls aa
—rptd. *Berne* 1783. O 3v in 1: [8] 199; [2] 166; 219 [incl 2 fold tabs] a
—Dutch tr. *Rotterdam* 1784. Q [18] 261 a
—Eng. tr. *L* 1791. O 2v: [14] 289; [4] 261 [error for 257] + 3adv-p aa
—rptd. *Dub* 1791. O [16] 437 a
—Eng. ed. 2—& best—with v. 3 added [voyages of 1773 & 1776], *L* 1792–3. O 3v: [20] 300; [12] 268; [22] 303. 2tabs[one fold.] aa
—Ger. tr. *Frankf* 1786. O [10] 716 7maps a
Describes a 1767 horse-back journey across Texas, from Natchitoches to the Rio Grande. The 1791 English editions included only the voyages from 1767 to 1771.

PAINE, ALBERT B.   14
Captain Bill McDonald, Texas ranger . . . *N Y* 1909. O 448 8pls facs a First bdg. gilt-stamped.

PAINE, ALBERT B.   15
Thomas Nast: his period and his pictures. *N Y* 1904. O [22] 584 [20] port a

[PAINE, THOMAS]   16

The American crisis. Regular series consisted of Nos. I to XIII, issued at *Phil*, except No. V [ptd at *Lancaster*]. Nos. 1–1V [I777]; Nos. V–VII [1778]; Nos. VIII–IX [1780]; Nos. X–XII [1780]; No. XIII [1783]. Two supernumerary Nos. [XIV–XV] followed in 1783, the latter No., through error dated 1793. A "Crisis extraordinary," [really No. 10] issued in 1780, completes the set as originally pub., in 15pts b Y
—collected eds.: *L* [1788]; O [2] 293 aa; rptd 1796 a
—Am. ed.: contained in "Writings," *Alb* [1792]. *see* below
—Fr. tr. *P* 1791. O

Of the original thirteen numbers, probably only the first five were issued in pamphlet form, the others appearing only in newspapers.

[PAINE, THOMAS]   17

Common sense . . . *Phil* Bell 1776. O [4] 80 b AA Hn NYP PaH Y
—rptd., same yr., *B*; *N Y*; *Phil*, Bell; *Norwich*; *Prov*; *Salem* a
—ed. 2, with "large additions," *Phil* Bell 1776. O 2pts in 1: [4] 80; [2] 81–148 a
—ed. 3, further enl. with "A dialogue between the ghost of General Montgomery . . .," *Phil* Bell 1776 O 3pts in 1: [8] 80; [2] 81–148; [2] 16 b BA N NYP Y
—new ed., with adds., *Phil* Bradford [1776]. O [6] 50 aa
—rptd.: *Lancaster* [1776], O 63; *Newburyport* [1776]; *Phil* Bradford 1776, O [6] 99 a
—anr. ed. "Thoughts on the present state of American affairs: extracted from . . . 'Common sense'," [with] "large additions . . ." *Newport* 1776. O 2pts in 1: 31; [2] 33–70 [2] a
—Eng. eds.: *L* 1776, O [6] 54; *Edin* 1776, D [6] 99; *Newcastle* 1776, O 131; and several later *L* eds. a
—Fr. trs.: *Rotterdam* 1776; *P* 1791; *P* 1793, O [8] 119 a

This first appeal for separation from England, issued in January, really paved the way for the July Declaration of Independence. *See* also *Large additions to Common sense*. Most English editions deleted the many aspersions on King and Government.

[PAINE, THOMAS]   18

Dissertations on government, the affairs of the bank . . . *Phil* 1786. O [2] 53 aa

This defence of the Bank of North America is a different work from his *Dissertations on first principles of government* . . .

[PAINE, THOMAS]   19

Dissertations on first principles of government . . . *P* [1795]. O 32 issue 1 has "stands" [for "all men"], p. 25, line 9, paragraph 2 aa
—ed. 2, same impr. n.d. O 40 a
—anr. ed. *L* [*ca* 1796]. O 31

PAINE (THOMAS).   20

An impartial sketch of the life of: . . . *L* 1792. O 48 port a

PAINE, THOMAS   21

La justice agraire opposée a la loi. *P*, Ragalou 1797. O 44 aa
—anr. ed, *P* [1797]. O 22 a
—Eng tr, "Agrarian justice" *L*, Parsons, [1797]. O 38 aa
—rptd, *L* 1797. O 50; *L*, Williams, 1797. O 20
—Am. eds, *Phil*, Folwell, [1797]. O 32; *Balt* 1797. O 34 2adv-p

Advocates what now seems a mild social security plan: every citizen at 21 years to receive from government $75 to start him in life; when 50 years old he would be paid $50 annually for life.

PAINE, THOMAS   22

Large additions to Common sense. *Phil* Bell 1776. O [2] 81–147 aa
—rptd. *B* 1776. O 44; *Newport* 1776. O [2] 33–70 [2]
—Eng. ed. "Additions to Common sense," *L* 1776. O 47

Paine was not the author of these *Additions*; they were gathered from various sources by Bell to make his edition 3 larger than the enlarged edition issued at Philadelphia by Bradford, to whom Paine had turned after his estrangement from Bell. Some copies were issued separately— and paged, as shown in above Philadelphia and Newport editions, to permit their being bound with the first and second editions of *Common sense, see* above.

PAINE, THOMAS   23

Letter to . . . Dundas. *L* Parsons 1792. O 24 a
—anr. ed., possibly the earlier, *L* Society for Promoting, etc. 1792. O 16
—anr. ed. *L* Ridgway 1792. O 24

PAINE, THOMAS   24

Letter to George Washington . . . *Phil* 1796. O [2] 76 + adv-l. aa
—anr. issue, same impr. & date. D 64 aa
—rptd: *Balt* 1797, O 36; *N Y* 1802, O 34; *Balt* 1802, O 44 a
—Eng. eds.: *L* 1797[ptd variously by Eaton, Symonds, & Williams]; *Dub* 1797, O 48 a

For reply *see* Horry, Chas. L. P.

PAINE, THOMAS   25

Letter . . . to the Abbé Raynal on the affairs of North-America . . . *Phil* Aitken 1782. O [4] 77 aa
—ed. 2, same impr., date & collat. but pub. by Steiner. a
—rptd: *B* 1782; *Trenton* 1782.
—Eng. eds.: *L* Dilly 1782, O [8] 76; *L* Stockdale

1782, O [2] 83; *Dub* 1782, O [8] 76; and others.
—Fr. tr. n.p. 1783. O [12] 124 a
—oth. Fr. eds.: "Remarques sur les erreurs . . .
de . . . Raynal," *Amst* 1783, O 126; *Brus* 1783, O

PAINE, THOMAS   **26**
A letter to the Earl of Shelburne, on his speech
. . . respecting the acknowledgement of American
independence. *L* 1783. O [2] 28 a
—other eds.: *L* Ridgeway 1791. O 58 port; *L*
Jordan 1791. O 28; *Dub* 1791. O 48
This was No. 12 of *The American crisis*, as
published in a Philadelphia newspaper in 1782;
there was no separate American edition.

PAINE (THE INFAMOUS TOM).
A letter to: *See* Cobbett, Wm.

PAINE, (THOMAS).   **27**
A letter to: in answer to his scurrilous epistle . . .
to Washington . . . By an American citizen.
N Y 1797. O 24 a

PAINE, THOMAS   **28**
Letters addressed to the addressers of the late
proclamation . . . *L* Jordan 1792. D 40 a
—ed. 2, *L* Symonds, same date. D 78 [2]
—Am. ed. *Phil* 1793. D 43 [4]
This attack on the evils of English government
is practically a third part of his *Rights of man.*

PAINE (THOMAS).   **29**
Letters from: . . . to the citizens of the United
States on his arrival from France. *Wash* 1802.
O 34 aa
—anr. ed., same impr. & date. O 40 a
—anr. ed., same impr. & date. O 50
—anr. ed., *N Y* 1802. O 24
—same impr. & date. O 32
—Eng. eds, with adds.: *L* 1804, O [10] 70; *L*
1817; *L* 1819.

PAIN[E] (THOMAS).
The life of: . . . *See* Chalmers, George.

PAINE (THOMAS).
The life of: . . . by Peter Porcupine. *See* Cobbett, Wm.

[PAINE, THOMAS]   **30**
Public good . . . examination into the claim
of Virginia to the vacant western territory . . .
Phil 1780. O 38 aa
—anr. ed. *Alb* Webster [1792]. D 41 a
—Eng. ed. *L* 1817 O 35 a

PAINE, THOMAS   **31**
The rights of man . . . an answer to Mr. Burke's
attack on the French revolution. *L* Johnson
1791. O [2] 158 b AA BM [of a few cops kn]
—anr. issue, with pref. added, *L* Jordan same
date. O [2] 6–162 aa

—later Jordan eds., same date, all O [10] 7–171 a
—Am. eds., 1791: *Balt* D 88; *Bennington* O 86;
Bost D 79; *Carlisle* O 90; *Phil* O [4] 100; *Phil* O 105 a
—Fr. ed. "Droits de l'homme," *P* 1791. O [12] 227

PAINE, THOMAS   **32**
Second part of The rights of man. *L* ptd. by
Chapman, but sheets acquired by Jordan 1792.
O [16] 178 aa
—rptd. 8 times 1792.
—anr. ed. "Rights of men . . .," *L* Parsons 1792.
D 81
—Am. ed. *N Y* 1742 [error for 1792]. D 164 aa
—other Am. eds: 1792: *B* D [10] 108; *Phil* O 96 a
—Fr. tr. *P* 1792. O [24] 224
For what may be considered a third part, *see*
above *Letters addressed to the addressers . . .*

[PAINE, THOMAS]
Thoughts on the present state of American
affairs: extracted from . . . "Common sense."
See, above, *Common sense.*

PAINE (THOMAS).   **33**
The works of: *Phil* 1797. O 2v: [8] 391; [6]
368 148 a

PAINE (THOMAS).   **34**
The writings of: *Alb* [1792]. O [7 sections
separately paged] 517 a
—ed. 2 [9 sections] *Alb* [1792] O 623 a

PAINE'S . . . LETTER
Paine's [Thomas] Letter to Gen'l. Washington.
A five minutes answer to: . . . *See* Horry, Chas.
L. P.

[PAINTER, REV. HENRY M.]   **35**
Brief narrative of incidents in the war in Missouri . . . *B* 1863. O 28 a

PAINTER, ORRIN C.   **36**
William Painter and his father, Dr. Edward
Painter [Indian agent to the Omahas, 1869–73],
sketches and reminiscences. *Balt* 1914. Q 153 a
About 40 pages on the artist and photographer
Wm. H. Jackson, who married Dr. Painter's
daughter.

PALAIRET, J[EAN]   **37**
Description abrégée des possessions angloises
et francoises du continent septentrional de
l'Amerique . . . *L* Nourse 1755. O 62 aa
—rptd. *L* 1756. O 72 aa
—Eng. tr: *L* Haberkorn 1755, O 72; ed. 2,
same impr. & date. O 70 b
—Dutch tr. *Amst* 1755. O 72 aa. Ger. tr. Leip
1755 D 12 aa
The large folding map [pirated from John
Mitchell's English one] of which this was an explanation, found inserted in some copies of the French
and English editions, was published separately.

**[PALISOT DE BEAUVOIS, AMBROISE   38
M. F. J., [baron de]**
Odérahi, histoire américaine . . . une peinture
fidelle des moeurs des habitants de l'intérieur de
l'Amérique septentrionale . . . *P* [1801]. D [10]
261 a
—Ger. tr *Berl* 1803
—Sp. tr. *Madr.* 1804 D 288
Originally issued in this author's *Veilées
américaines*, next entry, but may not have been
written by him.

**[PALISOT DE BEAUVOIS, AMBROISE   39
M. F. J., baron de**
Veilées américaines. ed. 2. *P* 1796. D 3v: 192;
202; 196. 3pls a

PALLADINO, LAWRENCE B.   40
Indian and white in the northwest . . . *Balt*
1894. O [26] 411 map 90pls 55ports aa
—ed. 2, rev. & enl., *Lancaster Pa* 1922. O [20]
512 pls a
History of all missions in the region—among
the Blackfeet, Piegans, Cheyennes and Crows,
and in the white settlements of Montana.

[PALLADINO, LAWRENCE B.]   41
Our friends the Coeur d'Alene Indians. *St
Ignatius, Mont* 1886. O 22 + wraps aa

PALLISER, JOHN   42
Exploration—British North America. *L* 1859–
65. F 4v: "Papers" 64 8maps & pls on 12 sheets;
"Further papers" 75 3maps; "Journal, reports
. . ." 325; "Index and maps" [3] 5 maps c G Y

PALLISER, JOHN   43
Solitary rambles . . . of a hunter in the prairies.
L 1853. O [6] 326 front eng t-p 6pls + adv-l. aa
—anr. ed. entitled "The Solitary hunter . . ." *L*
1856. D [16] 234 7pls
—rptd: *L* 1857; *L* 1860 a
—Am. ed. *N Y* De Witt [1860?] O 100 a

PALMER (BENJAMIN F., privateersman).   44
The diary of: *N Hav* 1914. O [10 15–22] 274,
pls a 102copies ptd.

PALMER, BENJAMIN M.   45
A vindication of secession and the south . . .
Columbia S C 1861. O 46 aa

PALMER, H. E.   46
The Powder river Indian expedition, 1865.
Omaha 1887. O 59 aa
—rptd., with adds., same impr. 1902 a

PALMER, JOEL   47
Journal of travels over the Rocky mountains,
to the mouth of the Columbia. *Cin* 1847. D
[8] [9]–189 errata slip wraps, dd calf d AA N Pn

—other issues, some with 2, some with 4, prelim.
p. causing paginat. hiatus. Possibly such issues
were printed earlier, but collectors prefer the
completed form. Slight textual changes were made
on p. 31 and 121, first reading on p. 31, 7th line
from bottom is "sandy"—not "grassy"; on p.
121, 4th line from bottom: "The Company own
from six to eight mills above the fort." c Y
—anr. issue, with date 1847 on t-p changed in
ink to 1848. [This alteration of the final numeral
was done by Palmer himself to make his unsold
copies sell better in 1848]. b to some copies of
this ed. was added John T. Hughes' "California."
—other eds. 1850; 1851; 1852. aa
—rptd., ed. Thwaites, *Clev* 1906. O 312+5adv. p. a
Most reliable of the early guides to Oregon;
in addition, the best narrative by a participant in
the overland migration of 1845, which more than
doubled the population of Oregon.

PALMER, JOHN, 1650–1700   48
The present state of New-England impartially
considered . . . [*B* 1689]. SmQ 44 d LC MassH
—Eng ed. "An impartial account of the state
of New England . . ." *L* 1690. SmQ 40 b Hn
JCB LC N
For an answer to this defense of Andros *see*
Rawson, Edward, and Sewall, Samuel.

PALMER, JOHN [fl. 1818]   49
Journal of travels in the United States . . . *L*
1818. O [8] 456 map[col, in some copies] aa
—Dutch tr. *Haarlem* 1820. O 318 map a
—Ger. tr. [*Jena* 1819] O [2] 201–406

PALMER, LYMAN L.   50
History of Napa and Lake counties [Calif.]
. . . *S F* 1881. Q 891 68ports aa

PALMER, ROBERT H.   51
A voyage around Cape Horn. *Phil* 1863. O
31[incl. cover-t.] aa
Includes account of the discovery of Humboldt
Bay.

PALMER, SARAH L.   52
Six months among the secessionists . . . *Phil*
1862. O 40 a
—rptd. *N Y* 1863. O

PALMER, THOMAS H. ed.   53
The historical register of the United States . . .
1812–15. *Wash* and *Phil* 1814–16. O 4v: [10] 164,
226; [4] 132, 351; [6] 246 [2] 328; 136, 354 a
—ed. 2, same impr. & dates. O 4v

PALMER, WILLIAM J.   54
Report of surveys . . . for a route extending the
Kansas Pacific railway to the Pacific ocean.
Phil 1869. O [6+inserted lf] 250 3maps[in some
copies only one] profile aa

A few special copies contained, in addition to the maps, twenty photographic views along the explored route. b

PALOÚ, FRANCISCO **55**
Noticias de la Nueva California. *S F* 1874. O 4v: [20] 270; 301; 315; 253. 19pls c 100 copies ptd N NYP Y
—Eng tr. ed. by Bolton "Historical memoirs of new California" *Berkeley* 1926. 4v aa
Compiled before 1784; first published at Mexico, in 1856, as a part of an extensive historical series.

PALOÚ, FRANCISCO **56**
Relación historica de la vida y apostolicas tareas del . . . Fray Junipero Serra, y de las misiones que fundó en la California septentrional . . . *Mex* 1787. Q [28] 344 pl map[with no descriptive words on space showing the ocean] c JCB N Y
—issue 2 of map had words "Mar Pacifico" added c NYP
Eng. trs.: *S F* 1874. b; *S F* 1884, O 156 port errata slip a; *Pasadena* 1913, O [34] 338 map 2pls; *S F* 1934, O 124 maps & pls
Most extensive early work on Upper California.

PAMPHLET **57**
Pamphlet (The), entitled, "Taxation no tyranny" candidly considered . . . *L* [1775]. O [4] 132 a
—issue 2, same impr. & date, has errata added on last p.

PANET, JEAN C. **58**
Journal du siége de Québec en 1759. *Montr* 1866. O 24 a
For similar titles *see* under Quebec.

PANZACOLA. **59**
Diario de las operaciones de la expedicion contra la Plaza de: . . . baxo las ordenas del . . . Bernardo de Galvez. [*Madrid*? or *Havanna*? 1781?]. Q 48 b N NYP
—rptd Madr 1959. Q 96 3maps 200 cops ptd a
Account of Galvez's capture of Baton Rouge, Natchez, Mobile and Pensacola, resulting ultimately in Florida being ceded by England to Spain.

PAPERS **60**
Papers relating to America, presented to the House of Commons. *L* 1810. O [8] 178 [4] a
Relate largely to the "Leopard" and "Chesapeake" affair.

Papers relating to the action between . . . **61** sloop Little Belt, and . . . frigate President . . . *L* 1811. O [12] 21 a

PARADÈS (ROBERT, comte de). **62**
Mémoires secrets de: . . . n.p. 1789. O 188 a
—Eng. tr. *L* 1791. O
Operations in England during the Revolution of a French spy transmitting information on military and naval movements.

PARALLEL **63**
Parallel (A) between the . . . revolution in England of 1688, and the American revolution of 1860–61, by a gentleman of Mississippi. *Meridian* 1864. O 41 a

PARAMORE, H. H. **64**
The practical guide to . . . Klondike gold fields. *St L* 1897. D 64 map 12pls a

[PAREDES, M.] **65**
Proyectos de leyes sobre colonizacion y comercio en el estado de Sonora. *Mex* 1850. O 24 fold. map b LC Y
These laws and plans cover the author's colonization project in present Arizona.

PARISOT, PIERRE F., and SMITH, C. J. **66**
History of the Catholic church in . . . San Antonio . . . *San Antonio* 1897. O 218 a

PARISOT, PIERRE F. **67**
The reminiscences of a Texas missionary. *San Antonio* 1899 D 227, inc. port [5] a

PARGELLIS, STANLEY **68**
Lord Loudoun in North America. *New Haven*, 1933. O [6] 399 2maps a

PARGELLIS, STANLEY, ed. **69**
Military affairs in North America, 1748–1765; selected documents from the Cumberland papers in Windsor Castle. *N Y* [1936] O [32] 514 maps a

PARK, ROBERT E. **70**
Sketch of the Twelfth Alabama Infantry. *Rich* 1906. O 106 a

PARK, SAMUEL **71**
Notes on the early history of Union township, Licking county, Ohio. *Terre Haute O* 1870. O 56 a

PARKE, JOHN E. **72**
Recollections of seventy years, and historical gleanings of Allegheny, Penna. *B* 1886. O [12] 385 port a

PARKE, JOHN G. **73**
Report of explorations for that portion of a railway route . . . between . . . the Rio Grande and . . . the Gila. [*Wash* 1855]. O 53 a
For series [House Executive Document 129] of which this formed a part, and which contained a map and a profile relating to this report, *see Pacific railroad explorations.*

PARKER, A[MOS] A.   **74**
Trip to the west and Texas . . . *Concord N H*
1835. D 276 2pls a
—ed. 2 [and best] *Concord & B* 1836. D 380
[incl. 2pls] map[not in all copies] front. a

PARKER, B. G.   **75**
Recollections of the Mountain Meadows
massacre . . . *Plano Calif* 1901. D 31 port b Y

PARKER, EDWARD L.   **76**
The history of Londonderry . . . N. H. *B* 1851.
D [56] 358 [1] map 7pls a

PARKER, GRANVILLE   **77**
The formation of . . . West Virginia . . . *Wellsburg* 1875. O [10] 482 a

PARKER, J. M.   **78**
An aged wanderer . . . a cowboy on the western
plains . . . *San Angelo, Tex* n.d. O 32+wraps port
[on verso of front wrap] aa
—rptd, "The poor orphan boy . . ." n.p. n.d. D 40
front a

PARKER, JAMES M., pub.   **79**
San Francisco directory . . . *S F* 1852. O 20
20 [4] 31–106 12 107–114 13–32 21–48 [1] map pl a

PARKER, JAMES W.   **80**
Narrative of adventures . . . during a frontier
residence in Texas. *Louisv* 1844. D 95 36 d N NYP
—rptd. 1845 c; anr. repr. 1848 b
A separately-paged "Narrative" by his daughter,
Mrs. Rachel Plummer, giving details of her
captivity among the Comanches, is included and
was undoubtedly printed at the same time; in her
preface she alludes to an earlier edition, of which
no copy is known, unless that statement refers to
the 1838 pamphlet listed below under Plummer,
Clarissa.

PARKER, NATHAN H.   **81**
Illustrated handbook of the great west . . .
N Y 1869. O 162 3maps a

PARKER, [NATHAN H.]?, &   **82**
HUYETT, [D. H.]?
The illustrated miner's handbook . . . to Pike's
Peak . . . *St L* 1859. D [4] 7–76 + 36adv-p 6pls
2maps dd H Y
—rptd. *Denver* 1950.

PARKER, N[ATHAN] H.   **83**
Iowa as it is in 1855 . . . *Chi* 1855. D 264 map
2pls a
—rptd. "Iowa as it is in 1856," *Chi* 1856. 2issues
[of 264 & 282p] map pls
—abr. ed. "The Iowa handbook for 1856 . . ."
B 1856. D 188 map
—rptd. "The Iowa handbook for 1857," *B* 1857.
same collat.

PARKER, NATHAN H.   **84**
The Kansas and Nebraska hand-book for
1857–8 . . . *B* 1857. D 189 map a

PARKER, NATHAN H.   **85**
The Minnesota hand book for 1856–7 . . . *B*
1857. D 160 [incl adv-p] map a

PARKER, NATHAN H.   **86**
Missouri as it is in 1867 . . . *Phil* 1867. O 458 pl a

PARKER, NATHAN H.   **87**
The Missouri hand-book . . . *St L* 1865. D 162
2maps a

PARKER, NATHAN H.   **88**
Stranger's guide to St. Louis . . . *St L* 1867.
D 58 + advs fold.map pl a

PARKER, [SAMUEL]   **89**
Journal of . . . tour beyond the Rocky mountains, 1835–7. *Ithaca* 1838. D 371 pl map [earliest
showing accurately the Oregon interior] aa
—rptd. *Auburn* 1838; *Ithaca* 1840; and later.
—Eng. ed. *Dub* 1840. D 209; *Edin* 1841. O 78 a
—Ger. tr. *Dresden* 1840. D
Parker accompanied a fur-trading party, in 1835,
from Council Bluffs to Walla Walla.

PARKER, THOMAS   **90**
A history of Farmington, Maine . . . *Farmington*
1846. O 136 a
—ed. 2, enl., same impr. 1875. O 120

PARKER, W[ILLIAM] B.   **91**
Notes taken during the expedition commanded
by Capt. R. B. Marcy, through unexplored Texas.
Phil 1856. D [12] 9–242+6 adv.p. aa

PARKER, WILLIAM H.   **92**
Recollections of a naval officer [in the United
States and Confederate navies] 1841–1865. *N Y*
1883. D [16] 372 a

PARKER, WILLIAM T.   **93**
Annals of old Fort Cummings, New Mexico,
1867–8. *Northampton* 1916. O [2] 56 port pls a
—suppl. to above [on Apache war], same impr.
[1925]. O 28 [4] port pl

PARKER, WILLIAM T.   **94**
Personal experiences among our . . . Indians,
from 1867 to 1885. *Northampton* 1913. O 232
5pls a
—suppl. to above, same impr. 1918. O 46 pls
The author served in Kansas, Colorado, New
Mexico and Texas.

PARKHURST (JACOB).   **95**
Sketches of the life and adventures of: . . .
sufferings of the early pioneers along the Ohio . . .

Newcastle Ind 1842. 16° 28 c N[only copy known]
—rptd. *Knightstown Ind* 1893. 16° 55 port aa
Served in Harmar's Ohio campaign of 1790 and barely escaped with his life.

PARKINSON, RICHARD   96
The experienced farmer . . . *Phil* [save for t-pp ptd in London] 1799. O 2v: [20] 275; [2] 292 b
—Eng. ed. "The experienced farmer's tour in America." *L.* Stockdale, 1805. O 2v in 1: [12] 735 aa
—Eng. ed.2, "A tour in America . . ." *L* Harding, 1805. O 2v: [8] 319; [8] 320–735 aa

PARKMAN, FRANCIS   97
The California and Oregon trail . . . *N Y* [March] 1849 1000 copies ptd. Bound either in one vol. brown cl. or in 2 pts wraps. D 448 [incl. front. & eng. t]+6 adv. p [numbered, at front, pp 1 & 2, at end, pp 3–6] cl. b Y wraps c Y
—some copies of Mch. ptg were sent in sheets to Eng. and were there issued with new t.p. giving *N Y* & *L* impr. b
—later Am. bdg. of Mch. ptg., brown or bluish-purple cl., final advs. increased to p. 10 [i.e. pp. 3–10] aa
—anr. bdg. of this ptg., dark brown cl., omits frontis., eng. t. and all final adv's. This "freak" variant was probably one of the 6 special copies sent by the pub. to Parkman. b
—2nd ptg. *N Y* [early Apr.] 1849 500 copies, blue or bluish-gray cl., same collat. as Mch. ptg., but no front advs., 7 adv. p. at end, numbered 1 to 8 [error for 7], worn type on pp. 436 & 437 aa
—3rd ptg. *N Y* [late Apr.] 1849 1000 copies, bluish-purple cl., same collat. as 2nd ptg. but no printers impr. on verso of t.p. and words "see p. 290" added to frontis. aa
—ed 3 *B* 1852. D 448 a
—ed 4 rev. with shortened t. "The Oregon trail" *B* 1872. D [12] 381 a
—anr. ed., with Remington ills. *B* 1892 O [16] 411 9 pls. aa
—anr. ed. with ills by Remington & Wyeth. *B* 1925 O 975 copies. a
—same, trade ed., omitting the 5 Remington pls.

PARKMAN, FRANCIS   98
The discovery of the great west. *B* 1869. O [24] 425 map a
—anr. ed., same collat., *B* 1870. also 75copies on L. P.
—ed. 11, rewritten to incorporate Margry's new findings, "La Salle and the discovery of the west," *B* 1879. O [28] 483 2maps
Part three in the series on France and England in North America. *See* next entry.

PARKMAN, FRANCIS   99
France and England in North America. *B* 1865–92. O 9v Pt.1, "Pioneers of France in the

new world," 1865. [24] 420 2maps port; Pt. 2, "The Jesuits in North America," 1867. [92] 463 map; Pt.3, "The discovery of the great west [entered separately, above]; Pt.4, "The old regime in Canada," 1874. [16] 448 map; Pt.5, "Count Frontenac and New France," 1877. [4 7–16] 463 map; Pt.6, "A half century of conflict," 1892. 2v 3 maps; Pt. 7, "Montcalm and Wolfe," 1885. 2v map 2pls 75 copies of each on L.P. ea. a

PARKMAN, FRANCIS   100
History of the conspiracy of Pontiac . . . *B* 1851. O [24] 630 4maps aa
—rptd. *B* 1866. same collat. also 75 copies on L.P. a

PARKMAN CLUB PAPERS.   101
Complete set [of 17monographs on early Wisconsin, etc.] in 18pts. *Milw* 1896–7. O 2v: [4] 264; 244 aa
Title-page is dated 1896–1897, although part one appeared in 1895.

PARLEMENT [LE]   102
Parlement (Le) de Paris établi au Scioto, sur les bords de l'Oyo. *P* 1790. O 60 b Y

PARR, L. L.   103
Sketch of the life of "Dick" Parr in the far west . . . chief of scouts, Indian interpreter and guide during the Indian campaign of 1868–9 . . . [*N Y* 1901]. D 62[incl. 9pls] aa

PARRISH, JOHN   104
Remarks on the slavery of the black people . . . *Phil* 1806. O [4] 66 a
Abolition argument that "a house divided against itself cannot stand; neither can a government or constitution."

PARSONS, GEORGE F.   105
The life and adventures of James W. Marshall, the discoverer of gold in California. *Sacr* 1870. 16° 188 port aa
—rptd. *S F* Grabhorn 1935. D [16] 145 port 3 pls 500 copies ptd. a

[PARSONS, HORATIO A.]   106
A guide to travelers visiting the falls of Niagara. [*Buf* 1834?] D 12 a
—ed 2, enl, au named, same impr 1835. 18° 96 2plans [on 1 sheet] a
—anr ed, "The book of Niagara Falls" same impr 1836.
—rptd. often
Said to be the first guide to this resort; but *see* Ingraham, Joseph W., for another of same date.

[PARSONS, THEODORE, and   107
PEARSON, ELIPHALET]
A forensic dispute on the legality of enslaving the Africans . . . *B* 1773. O 48 a

[PARSONS, TYLER]   108
Mormon fanaticism exposed ... *B* 1841. O
102 [1] a
—rptd., same impr. 1842 .

PARSONS, USHER   109
The life of Sir William Pepperrell ... only
native of New England who was created a baronet ... *B* 1855. O [12] 352 map port a
—ed. 2, same impr. & collat., 1856.
—ed. 3, same impr. & date. O [16] 356 map 2pls

PARSONS, WILLIAM B.   110
The gold mines of western Kansas. *Lawrence*
1858. D [4] 45+3adv-p c G LC[only known copies]
—enl. ed. "The new gold mines [etc.]," *Cin* 1859.
D 63+advs[8p in some and 13p in others] b
Pn KasH NYP Y
—anr. ed., *Cin* [1860?], with fold.map by Pearman
added. c
Earliest known guide book to the Pike's Peak
mines.

PARTISAN LEADER (THE) ...
See Tucker, Nathaniel Beverley.

PARTON, J[AMES]   111
The life ... of Aaron Burr ... *N Y* 1858. O
706 2ports a
—enl. ed. *N Y* 1864. D 2v: [22] 443; [12] 431.
2ports
—rptd. often.

PARTON, JAMES   112
Life of Andrew Jackson ... *N Y* 1860. O 3v:
[30, 2, 30] 636; 672; 734 4ports a
—rptd. same impr. & collat. 1861.

PARTON, JAMES   113
The life ... of Benjamin Franklin. *N Y* 1864.
D 2v: 627; 707. 4ports a
—anr. ed. *N Y* 1865. O same collat. 100 copies ptd
—rptd. *B* 1867. D same collat.

PARTON, JAMES   114
Life of John Jacob Astor ... *N Y* 1865. D
[6] 13–121 a

PASQUIN, ANTHONY pseud.
The Hamiltoniad: or, an extinguisher for the
royal faction of New-England ... *See* Williams,
John.

PASTORIUS, FRANCIS D.   115
Umständige geographische Beschreibung der
zu allerletzt erfundenen ... Pensylvaniae. *Frankf*
1700. D [12] 140 b N NYP PhilL Y
—rptd., same impr. 1704. D [12] 140 [4] map aa
For supplement, sometimes bound with this,
see under German edition of Thomas, Gabriel, *An
historical account of Pensilvania*.

PATE, HENRY C.   116
John Brown ... *N Y* 1859. O 48 a

PATRIOTE ANGLOIS (LE) ...
See Le Blanc, Jean B.

PATTEN, EDMUND   117
A glimpse at the United States ... *L* 1853.
O 109 8pls a

PATTERSON, A. W.   118
History of the backwoods; or, the region of the
Ohio ... *Pitt* 1843. O [12] 5–311 map b BP N
NYP Y
One of the best compilations of frontier
narratives.

PATTERSON, D. C., ed.   119
Centennial history and directory of La Porte
City ... Iowa ... *La Porte City* 1876. O 15lvs
[incl.wraps] wrap.t.only aa

PATTERSON, J. B. ed.   120
Life of ... Black Hawk ... dictated by himself.
Cin 1833. D 155 b AA IH N NYP
—other eds.: *B* Abbott 1834, D 155 port; *B* Russell
1834, same collat., but different port; *Cooperstown*
1842, D no port; with adds., *Oquawka Ill* 1882,
D 208 3pls; *Chi* 1916, 16°; *Champaign Ill* 1955 ea a
—Eng. ed. *L* 1836. D 185 port a
—Dutch tr. *Leeuwarden* 1847. D a

PATTERSON, LAWSON B.   121
Twelve years in the mines of California ...
C 1862. 16° 108 a

PATTERSON (SAMUEL).   122
Narrative of the adventures and sufferings of:
... *Rhode Island* 1817. D 114 aa
—issue 2, *Palmer Mass* 1817. D 144 aa
—ed. 2, enl. *Prov* 1825. 16° 164 aa ·
Compiled by Ezekiel Terry. Patterson made
three voyages to the Northwest coast.

PATTIE, JAMES O.   123
Personal narrative ... during an expedition
from St. Louis through the vast regions between
that place and the Pacific ocean ... Ed. by
Timothy Flint. *Cin* [John H. Wood] 1831. O
300 5pls dd AA G Hn IndU Y
—re-issued, from unsold sheets of above, with
new t-p, *Cin* [E. H. Flint] 1833. [In this issue are
found 4 variant copyright readings, viz: by
Wood in 1831, by Wood in 1833, by Flint in
1831, by Flint in 1833]. c G NYP Y
—for pirated issue *see* Bilson, B., *Hunters of
Kentucky*.
—other eds.: ed. Thwaites, *Clev* 1905, O 382
[incl. pls. & final blank lf+adv.p; ed. Quaife,
Chi 1930, 16° a

Second overland journey to California, first over the route taken, with adventures incredible had they not been substantiated by later investigations.

PAUER, FRIEDRICH   **124**
Texas: ein sichrer Fuehrer für Auswanderer . . . *Bremen* 1846. D 200 b

PAUER, FRIEDRICH   **125**
Die Vereinigten Staaten . . . nach erfolgtem Anschuss der Republik Texas . . . *Bremen* 1847. O 256 aa

PAUL (MRS. ALMIRA).   **126**
The surprising adventures of: who . . . served as a common sailor . . . *B* 1819. 16° 24 a

PAUL, HILAND   **127**
History of Wells, Vermont. *Rutland* 1869. D 154 a

PAUL, HIRAM V.   **128**
History of . . . Durham, N. C. *Raleigh* 1884. O 256 map ports a

[PAUL, VINCENT DE]   **129**
Relation de ce qui est arrivé à deux religeux de la Trappe pendant leur séjour aupres des sauvages. *P* 1824. D 168 b
Valuable account of missionary work in Louisiana, Illinois, etc. ,1805–1812.

PAUL-JONES
Paul-Jones, ou prophéties sur l'Amérique . . . *See* Jones, Paul.

PAUL WILHELM FRIEDRICH,   **130**
DUKE OF WÜRTTEMBURG
Reise in Nordamerika . . . 1822–4. *Mergentheim* 1828. O c Hn StuttgartL Y [all located]
—ed. 2, "Erste reise . . ." *Stuttg* 1835. O [6] 394 map [not in all cops] errata lf b Hn G LC NYP Y
—Eng. tr. *Pierre, S. D.* 1941. [v19 Hist Colls] O a
Ascended the Missouri to Council Bluffs, visiting the Pawnees Osages and Otoes. His diaries on his second trip, in 1830 [to the Yellowstone], and on his third trip, in 1850–51 [to California], have never appeared in print.

PAULDING, HIRAM   **131**
Journal of a cruise . . . among the islands of the Pacific ocean . . . in pursuit of the mutineers of the whaleship Globe . . . *N Y* 1831. D 258 map aa

[PAULDING, JAMES K.]   **132**
John Bull in America; or, the new Munchausen. *N Y* 1825. D [18] 226 a
—ed. 2, same impr. & date
—Eng. ed. *L* 1825. D [20] 327
Satire on English observers.

[PAULDING, JAMES K.]   **133**
Letters from the south . . . 1816. *N Y* 1817. D 2v: 254; 260 a
—rptd. *N Y* 1835. D 2v: 224; 212

[PAULDING, JAMES K.?]   **134**
The new mirror for travellers; and guide to the Springs. *N Y* 1828. D 292 a

PAULDING, JAMES K.   **135**
Slavery in the United States. *N Y* 1836 16° 312 a
Slavery defended by a New Yorker.

[PAULDING, JAMES K.]   **136**
The United States and England: . . . reply to the criticism on Inchiquin's letters . . . *N Y* 1815. O 115 a

PAULISON, C. M. K.   **137**
Arizona. The wonderful country. *Tucson* 1881. D 31 aa

PAULLIN, CHARLES O.   **138**
Atlas of the historical geography of the United States. *Wash* 1932. F [20] 162 [4incl. blank lf.] numerous maps[many col.]on 121 sheets a

PAULLIN, CHARLES O.   **139**
The battle of Lake Erie . . . *Clev* 1918. O 222 a 150copies ptd.

PAUSCH (CAPTAIN GEORG).   **140**
Journal of: . . . during the Burgoyne campaign. Tr. & ed., W. L. Stone. *Alb* 1886. Q [14] 186 [incl. pls] a
First printing of this manuscript.

[PAUW, M. CORNEILLE DE]   **141**
Defense des Recherches philosophiques sur les Américains. *Berlin* 1770. D 256 a
—rptd., same impr. & collat.: 1771; 1772.
For work to which this replies, *see* Pernety, Antoine J. D.

[PAUW, M. CORNEILLE DE]   **142**
Recherches philosophiques sur les Américains . . . *Berlin* 1768–9. D 2v: [24] 326 [26] tab; [2] 366 [32] tab a
—many later eds., to which were added vol. 3 [containing Pernety's critical "Dissertation" on this work, together with de Pauw's "Defense"]
—Eng tr, abr, "General history . . ." *Rochdale* 1806 aa

PAVIE, THÉODORE   **143**
Scenes et recits des pays d'outre-mer. *P* 1853. D [8] 472 a

PAVIE, THÉODORE   **144**
Souvenirs atlantiques; voyage aux États-Unis et au Canada. *Angers* 1832. O [8] 550 [2] a

—rptd. with adds., *P* 1833. O 2v in 1: [8] 350 [2]; [4] 354 [2]

—Ger. tr "Atlantische Erinnerungen . . .," *Braunschweig* 1834. 16° 2v: 274; 276

Extensive travels throughout the east and central west, reaching Louisiana and Texas.

PAWNEE INDIANS (THE). A SKETCH.
See Dunbar, John B.

PAXSON, FREDERICK L.   **145**
History of the American frontier, 1763–1893 . . . *B* 1924. O [20] 598 11maps a

PAXTON, J. D.   **146**
Letters on slavery . . . *Lex Ky* 1833. D [8] 207 a

PAXTON, JOHN., ed.   **147**
Elisha Franklin Paxton. Memoir and memorials. [*N Y*] 1905. O 114 port a Small ed.
General Paxton was on Stonewall Jackson's staff.

PAXTON, JOHN A. [ed.]   **148**
The St. Louis directory . . . with descriptive notes on St. Louis, [etc.]. *St L* 1821. D [6]; [48]; [14] [38] map d G MoSH Y
The first directory of this city.

PAXTON, PHILIP [pseud.]
A stray Yankee in Texas. *See* Hammett, Samuel A.

PAXTON, WILLIAM E.   **149**
History of the Baptists of Louisiana. *St L* 1888. D 622 port a

PAXTON, W[ILLIAM] M.   **150**
Annals of Platte county, Missouri, *K C* 1897. O 1182 port a

PAXTON-MEN (THE).
Conduct of: . . . 1764. *See* Barton, Thos.

PAYNE, E. W.   **151**
South-western brand-book . . . *Medicine Lodge* [Kas] 1884. D 3–88 aa
For 1883 edition *see South-western brand book*.

[PAYNE, J.]   **152**
French encroachments exposed; or, Britain's original right . . . *L* 1756. O 44 map a

[PAYSON, GEORGE]   **153**
Golden dreams and leaden realities. By Ralph Raven. *N Y* 1853. D 344 a
—rptd. "Romance of California," *N Y* 1854.

[PAYSON, GEORGE]   **154**
The new age of gold; or, the life and adventures of Robert Dexter Romaine. *B* 1856. D 403 a

PAYSON, PHILLIPS   **155**
A memorial of Lexington battle . . . A sermon preached at Lexington, on the nineteenth of April, 1782. *B* 1782. O 24 a

PEABODY, ALFRED   **156**
The early days and rapid growth of California. *Salem* 1874. O 32 a

PEARCE, STEWART   **157**
Annals of Luzerne county [Pa.] . . . *Phil* 1860. O [4] 554 a
—ed. 2, with adds., same impr. & date. O 564 map 33pls

PEARESON, P[HILIP] E.   **158**
Sketch of . . . Judge Edwin Waller . . . early Texas revolution . . . *Galveston* 1874. O 25 a

PEARL (THE) OF GREAT PRICE.
See Smith, Jos.

PEARSE (JAMES).   **159**
A narrative of the life of: . . . particularly of five years residence in . . . Mississippi and Louisiana . . . *Rutl* 1825. D 144 aa

[PEARSON, C. H.]   **160**
On the frontier, or, scenes in the west. *B* [1864]. 16° [4] 7–320 2pls a

PEARSON, CAPT. D[ANIEL] C.   **161**
Notes on the Platte-Dakota campaign. n.p. [1896]. O 24 a

PEARSON, JOHN   **162**
Notes . . . during a journey in 1821 . . . from Philadelphia to the neighborhood of lake Erie . . . *L* 1822. O 72 aa

PEARSON, JONATHAN   **163**
Contributions for the genealogies of the county of . . . Albany. *Alb* 1872. O [2] 182 a

PEARSON, JONATHAN   **164**
Early records of . . . Albany . . . *Alb* 1869. O [8] 528 a

PEARSON, JONATHAN   **165**
Contributions to the genealogies . . . of the first settlers of . . . Schenectady . . . *Alb* 1873. Q 324 aa
—enl. ed. "A history of the Schenectady patent . . ." *Alb* 1883. Q 466 28maps & pls. Also 50 copies on L.P., with add. illus. aa
Well documented and authoritative.

PEASE, JOHN C., and   **166**
NILES, JOHN M.
A gazetteer of . . . Connecticut and Rhode Island . . . *Hart* 1819. O [8] 390 2maps 2 ports a

PEASE & COLE, pubs   **167**
Complete guide to the gold districts of Kansas and Nebraska . . . *Chi* 1859. D 20+wraps map c G WisH [only copies located]
—rptd. *Chi* 1936 .a

PECK, JEDIDIAH   **168**
The political wars of Otsego . . . *Cooperstown* 1796. O 122 [5] a

[PECK, JOHN M.]   **169**
"Father Clark"; . . . sketches and incidents of Rev. John Clark. By an old pioneer. *N Y* 1855. D 287 front.[not issued in all copies] a
—rptd. *N Y* 1868.

PECK, JOHN M.   **170**
A gazetteer of Illinois . . . *Jacksonville* 1834. 16° [8] 376 a
—ed. 2, same impr., date & collat.
—ed. 2, rev., *Phil* 1837. 16° [12] 328

PECK, JOHN M.   **171**
A guide for emigrants; containing sketches of Illinois, Missouri and adjacent parts. *B* 1831. 16° 336 maps a
—rptd., same collat., *B* 1835.
—enl. ed. [incl. also O., Ind., Mich., Wis. and Ark.], "A new guide for emigrants," *B* 1836. 16° [8] 5–374+6 adv-p
—ed. 2, *B* 1837. 16° 381+2adv-p
—rptd. *B* 1843.
—other eds.: *B* 1844, 16° 394; *Cin* 1848, 16° 381

PECK, JOHN M.   **172**
The traveller's directory for Illinois . . . *N Y* 1839. O 220 map[by Peck & Messinger] a
—rptd., same collat., *N Y* [1840].
Utilizes much material used in his *Gazetteer of Illinois.*

PECKARD, P.   **173**
Memoirs of the life of Mr. Nicholas Ferrar. *Cambridge.* Eng. 1790. O [16] 316 fold.tab port a
—abr. ed. *L* 1833. D
Contains valuable data on the London Virginia Company and court intrigues concerning it.

PEEK, PETER V.   **174**
Inklings of adventure in the campaigns of the Florida Indian war . . . *Schenectady* 1846. O 72 b LC [of 2 cops loc]

PEEP (A) INTO THE PAST.
By the ancient lady, of Charleston. *See* Poyas, Mrs. Eliz. A.

PEET (FREDERICK T.)   **175**
Civil war letters . . . of: *Newport* 1915. Q 285 50cops ptd a

PEET, FREDERICK T.   **176**
Personal experiences in the civil war. *N Y* 1905. Q 107 50cops ptd aa

PEIRCE, BENJAMIN   **177**
A history of Harvard University . . . to the . . . revolution. *C* 1833. O [20] 316 159 2pls a
—rptd., same impr. & date, without pls

PEIRCE, EBENEZER W.   **178**
Indian history . . . *No. Abington* 1878. D [14] 261 11pls a

PEIRCE (HENRY A.)   **179**
Biography of: *S F* 1880. O 24 port a
Made trading voyages to California and the Northwest coast from 1825 to 1849.

PEIRCE, PARKER I.   **180**
The adventures of "Antelope Bill" in the Indian war of 1862. [*Marshall, Minn* 1898] D 244 b LC N
Also includes later activities in the Montana gold regions.

PELET DE LA LOZÈRE, COMTE   **181**
[P. J. C.]
Lafayette en Amérique et en France. *P* 1867. D [4] 210 [1] a

PELET DE LA LOZÈRE, COMTE   **182**
[P. J. C.]
Précis de l'histoire des États-Unis . . . *P* 1845. O [4] 550 [1] a

PELLETREAU, WILLIAM S.   **183**
Early New York houses . . . *N Y* 1900. Q 10pts 243 pls a 350copies ptd[25 on Jap. P.]
—rptd., same impr., 1909.

PELLETREAU, WILLIAM S.   **184**
History of Putnam county [N. Y.]. *N Y* 1866 O 777 a
—rptd. *N Y* 1886

PELTON, JOHN C.   **185**
Life's sunbeams and shadows . . . Vol. I [all]. *S F* 1893. O 260 2pls a
Along with poetical effusions contains account in prose of Frank Pixley's trip to California and Pelton's establishing the first San Francisco school in 1849.

[PELTON, JOHN C.]   **186**
Origin of the free public schools of San Francisco. *S F* 1865. O 129 a

PELZER, LOUIS   **187**
The cattlemen's frontier . . . *Glendale Calif* 1936. O 351[incl.front. & pls] a

PELZER, LOUIS   188
Marches of the dragoons in the Mississippi valley . . . *Iowa City* 1917. O [10] 282 a

PEMBER, PHOEBE Y.   189
A southern woman's story. *N Y* 1879. O 192 a

PEMBERTON, E[BENEZER]   190
A sermon . . . at the ordination of Mr. David Brainerd . . . *B* 1744. Q [8] 39 a
Contains Brainerd's narrative of his 1743–4 missions among the Indians, as well as an account of Azariah Horton's similar work in Long Island.

[PEMBERTON, ISRAEL, et al]   191
An address to the inhabitants of Pennsylvania by those freemen . . . now confined in the Mason's lodge . . . *Phil* 1777. O [4] 52 a
—rptd. *N Y* same date. O 43
—Eng. eds.: *L* 1777, D 46; *Dub* same date. O 32
These Quakers were imprisoned for security reasons by the Revolutionary Council of Pennsylvania.

[PEMBERTON, ISRAEL]   192
Several conferences between . . . Quakers in Pennsylvania and the deputies from the Six Indian Nations . . . *Newcastle Eng* 1756. O 28 b LC N NYP

PEMBERTON, THOMAS   193
An historical journal of the American war . . . *B* 1795. O [2] 206 aa
First appearance was in the Massachusetts Historical Society Collections, 1793.

PEN KNIFE SKETCHES . . .
See Delano, Alonzo.

PEÑA Y PEÑA, D. MANUEL DE LA   194
Communicacion circular estendio en el año de 1845 sobre la cuestion de pax o guerra . . . *Queretaro* 1848. O 44 aa
A Mexican objection to this war.

PENA Y REYES, JUAN   195
ANTONIO DE LA
Derrotero de la expedición en la provincia de los Texas . . . que passa à executar . . . D. Joseph de Azlor . . . *Mex* 1722. F 31lvs [incl 4 plans] dd Hn JCB G Y
First book relating solely to Texas and the chief source on this expedition sent to protect Spanish missions in that province from French attacks.

PENDER, ROSE   196
A lady's experience in the wild west [from California and Texas to Wyoming and Dakota]. *L* [1889]. O [8] 80 a
Unflattering picture of an un-heroic West.

PENDERGRAST, GARRETT E.   197
A physical and topographical sketch of the Mississippi Territory, lower Louisiana, and a part of West Florida . . . *Phil* 1803. O 34 b AA LC NYP
Based on the author's own travels and on information contributed by William Dunbar.

[PENDLETON, EDMUND]   198
The crisis; or nullification unmasked. n.p. [1832]. O 35 a
—anr. iss. has no sub-t.

[PENDLETON, NATHANIEL G.]   199
Military posts—Council Bluffs to the Pacific . . . [H.R. Rep. 830, Sess. 2, 27th Cong.]. *Wash* 1842. O 64 map aa
—anr. issue, with extract from Wilkes added [H.R. Doc, 31, Sess.3, 27th Cong.], *Wash* 1843. O 78 map aa

PENGRA, B. J.   200
Report of . . . surveys and progress of construction of the Oregon central military road. *Eugene* 1865. O 63 b B G Y [all cops known]
—rptd. *Wash* 1868 O 19 aa

PENHALLOW, SAMUEL   201
The history of the wars of New-England . . . *B* 1726. O [8] 135 c AA N NYP
—rptd. *Cin* 1859. Q 138 [36] a some copies issued without the app. ["A history of the Pequot war . . .," *q.v.* under Gardiner, Lion]
Best early summary of New England's Indian troubles.

PENINGTON, JOHN   202
An examination of Beauchamp Plantagenet's Description of the province of New Albion. *Phil* 1840. O 33 a
The pamphlet examined, referring to a royal grant of land in Delaware, New Jersey, and Long Island, was published at London in two editions, 1648 and 1650. *See* No. 415, below.

PENN, WILLIAM [pseud.]
Essays on the present crisis in the present condition of the . . . Indians. *See* Evarts, Jeremiah.

PENNINGTON, MRS. R. E.   203
The history of Brenham and Washington county . . . *Houston* 1915. O 123 a 100copies ptd.

PENNSYLVANIA
An address to the inhabitants of Pennsylvania by those freemen . . . now confined in the Mason's lodge . . . *See* Pemberton, Israel.

An answer to an invidious pamphlet, intituled A brief state of the province of Pennsylvania . . . *See* Cross, Henry.

A brief state of the province of Pennsylvania in a letter from a gentleman . . . *See* Smith, [*Provost*] Wm.

A brief view of the conduct of Pennsylvania for 1755 . . . *See* Smith, *Provost* Wm.

Brief view of the system of internal improvement of . . . Pennsylvania. By a Pennsylvanian. *See* Carey, Mathew.

Continuation of the account of the Pennsylvania hospital . . . *See* Franklin,Benj., *Some account* . . .

Early history of western Pennsylvania . . . *See* Rupp, I. Daniel.

An explanation of the map which delineates that part of the Federal lands, comprehended between Pennsylvania west line, the rivers Ohio and Sioto, and lake Erie. *See* Cutler, Manasseh.

An historical account of . . . canal navigation in Pennsylvania. *See* Smith, *Provost* Wm.

An historical review of the constitution   204 and government of Pennsylvania . . . *L* 1759. O [26] 444 aa
—rptd. *Phil* 1812. O a
Attributed to Benjamin Franklin, who must have had a hand in it.

History of Pennsylvania Hall. *See* Webb, Saml.

An important statement . . . relative to the   205 invalidity of the pretensions formerly made upon the Pennsylvania lands: by the unincorporated companies of Connecticut claimants . . . *Lancaster* 1801. O 40 aa

Letters from a farmer in Pennsylvania to the inhabitants of the British colonies. *See* Dickinson, John.

Memoirs of a life, chiefly passed in Pennsylvania . . . *See* Graydon, Alex.

A memorial of the case of the German emigrants settled in Pennsylvania . . . *See* Franklin, Benj.

The planter's speech to his neighbors . . . of Pennsylvania, East and West Jersey [etc.]. *See* Tryon, Thomas.

A pleasant peregrination through . . . Pennsylvania. *See* Nicklen, Philip H.

Remarks on the New essay of the Pennsylvania Farmer . . . *See* Gray, John.

Report of the legislative committee . . .   206 to enquire into the causes of the disturbances at the seat of government, Dec. 1838. *Harrisburg* 1829. O 163 a
The "Buckshot War," resulting from party clashes, during which the Legislature was dispersed, local business suspended and the militia called out.

Several conferences between . . . Quakers in Pennsylvania and the deputies from the Six Indian Nations . . . *See* Pemberton, Israel.

Some account of the Pennsylvania Hospital . . . *See* Franklin, Benj.

A true and impartial state of . . . Penn-   207 sylvania. *Phil* 1759. O [8] 3–173 [35 incl.adv-p] aa
This defense of Quaker assemblymen, from accusations made in William Smith's *Brief state* and *Brief view*, may have been written by Franklin, but more likely by Jos. Galloway.

The true policy of . . . Pennsylvania regar-   208 ding the land of her citizens. By one of the people. n.p. 1818. O 35 a

PENNSYLVANIE (LA)
Description du sol . . . de cette portion des Etats-Unis, située entre la Pennsylvanie, les rivieres de l'Ohio & du Scioto, & le lac Erie. *See* Cutler, Manasseh, *An explanation of the map* . . .

Histoire naturelle et politique de la Pennsylvanie. *See* Rousselot de Surgy, Jacques P.

Recüeil de diverses pièces, concernant la   209 Pensylvanie. *Hague* 1684. D 118 dd Hn JCB LC N [only perfect cops loc]

Voyage dans la haute Pennsylvanie . . . *See* Crevecoeur, Michel-Guillaume Saint Jean de.

PENNSYLVANIEN (OBER-).
Reise in: und im Staate Neu York . . . *See* Crevecoeur, Michel-Guillaume Saint Jean de.

PENNSYLVANISCHE NACHRICHTEN . . .
See Zinzendorf, Nicolaus Ludwig.

PENNY (JOSHUA).   210
The life and adventures of: . . . who was impressed into the British service . . . *N Y* 1815. O 60 aa

PENNYPACKER, SAMUEL W.   211
Annals of Phoenixville [Pa.] . . . *Phil* 1872. O 295 map 4pls a

PENNYPACKER, SAMUEL W.   212
Historical and biographical sketches. *Phil* 1883. O 416 a

PENNYPACKER, SAMUEL W.   213
The settlement of Germantown, Pennsylvania, and the beginning of German emigration to North America. *Phil* 1899. O [8] 310 port a 300 cops ptd

PENOBSCOT.
The siege of: by the rebels . . . *See* Calef, John.

PENROSE, ELDER CHARLES W.   214
The Mountain Meadows massacre. Who were guilty of the crime? *S L C* 1884–5. D 104 a
—rptd. same impr. 1899. D 108

PENROSE, JOHN   215
Life of Sir Charles Vinicombe Penrose and Capt. James Trevenen. *L* 1850. O 301 2ports a
Trevenen accompanied Cook on his third voyage and witnessed his death.

PENSÉES
Pensées sur la revolution de l'Amérique-Unie . . . *See* Jenings, Edmund, *A translation of the Memorial to the sovereigns of Europe* . . .

PENSILVANIA.
News from: . . . By the author of the Pilgrim's progress. *See* Bugg, Francis.

PENSILVANIE (LA).   216
Etat présent de: . . . [*P*?] [1756]. D 128 map aa
Abridged translation of William Smith's *A brief view of the conduct of Pennsylvania* . . ., and his *A brief state of the province of Pennsylvania* . . ., with additions by the translator, Abbé Jean Ignace de la Ville.

PENSYLVANIA.   217
. . . Reasons why the lands . . . of the southern boundary line of: . . . should be separated from Virginia. [*L* 1770]. O 26 a

PEORIA.   218
A descriptive account of . . . Peoria combining a sketch of its early history . . . *Peoria* 1859. O 32 aa

Peoria directory . . . 1844. *See* Drown, S. De Witt, comp.

PEPIN (FRANCOIS).   219
A narrative of the life . . . of: *Det* 1854. 16° 76 port a
Describes life in Detroit, from 1840.

PEPPER, GEORGE W.   220
Personal recollections of Sherman's campaigns in Georgia and the Carolinas. *Zanesville* 1866. O 522 a
One of the best narratives by a Union soldier.

[PEPPERELL, SIR WILLIAM]   221
An accurate journal . . . of the proceedings of the New-England land-forces, during the late expedition against the French settlements on Cape Breton . . . *Exeter Eng* 1746. O 40 b AA LC JCB
—rptd. "Accurate account of the taking of cape Breton . . .," *L* 1758. O b JCB

PEPPERRELL [sic] (SIR WILLIAM) et al.   222
A conference held at St. George's . . . between: and the Indians of the Penobscott tribe . . . *B* 1753. Q 26 c AA N NYP

PERCEVAL, DEAN   223
A thousand miles in a canoe . . . from Denver . . . to Leavenworth . . . 1867. *Bushnell Ill* 1880. D 60 aa

[PERCEVAL, JOHN, EARL   224
OF EGMONT?]
Faction detected, by the evidence of facts . . . parties at home, and affairs abroad. *L* 1742. O 175 aa
—eds. 2,3,4 & 5, same impr., date & collat. a
—anr. ed. *Dub* 1743. O [2] 170 + adv-lf
Attributed also to William Pulteney. For a reply, *see A defence of the people* . . . For other titles by Perceval see Egmont.

PERCH, PHILEMON [pseud.]
Georgia sketches . . . *See* Johnston, Richard M.

PERCY, ADRIAN   225
Twice outlawed . . . history of Ed. and Lon Maxwell, alias the Williams brothers . . . *Chi* 1884. D 194 a
—rptd., same impr. & collat., [1890].
These outlaws operated in northern Illinois, Wisconsin and Minnesota.

PÉREZ DE LUXÁN, DIEGO   226
Expedition into New Mexico made by Antonio de Espejo, 1582–3 . . . *L A* Quivira Soc 1929. O 143 18pls 500copies ptd. aa

PERIER, M[ONS.] DU [pseud.]
A general history of all voyages . . . *See* Bellegarde, L'Abbé Jean B. M. de.

PERIER, M[ONS.] DU [pseud.]
Histoire universelle des voyages . . . *See* Bellegarde, L'Abbé Jean B. M. de.

PERILS
Perils, pastimes, and pleasures of an emigrant in New Zealand, Vancouver's island and California. *See* Bayswater, J. W.

PERINE (MISS).   227
The pathetic narrative of: . . . in the present Florida war . . . *Phil* Gill [1841]. O 28 2pls aa

PERIODICAL SKETCHES
Periodical sketches by an American patriot. *See* De Witt, Charles G.

PERKINS, G. W.   **228**
Historical sketches of Meriden. *W. Meriden*
1849. D 117 map a

PERKINS, MRS. GEORGE A.   **229**
Early times on the Susquehanna. *Binghamton*
1870. D 288 [2] a
—ed. 2, same impr., 1906. O [28] 285

[PERKINS, H. K. W.]?   **230**
Sketches of mission life among the Indians of
Oregon. *N Y* 1854. 16° 229[incl. front. & 4pls] +
4adv-p aa
—rptd., same impr. & collat., n.d. a
Ascribed also to Zachariah A. Mudge, *q.v.*;
whoever the editor, the narrative was obviously
that of Jason Lee.

PERKINS, JAMES H. [ed.]   **231**
Annals of the west . . . *Cin* 1846. O [20] 592
2maps a
—rptd., same collat., 1847.
—ed. 2, rev. by J. M. Peck, *St L* 1850. O [24] 808
—anr. ed. *St L* 1851. O 818
—ed. 3, publisher [James R. Albach] named as
compiler, neither Perkins nor Peck being mentioned, *St L* 1852. O 818
—enl. ed., Albach given as compiler, *Pitt* 1856. O
1016
—rptd., same collat., 1857; 1858.
Albach was the actual compiler; Perkins the
competent editor.

PERKINS (JAMES H.)   **232**
The memoir and writings of: Ed. William H.
Channing. *B* 1851. D 2v: [12] 527; [8] 502. port a
—anr. issue, same collat. *Cin* 1851.

PERKINS, MARY E.   **233**
Old houses of . . . Norwich, Connecticut, 1660–
1800. *Norwich* 1895. sm Q 621 map pls a

PERKINS (NATHAN E.)   **234**
Events and travels of: 1824–1887. *Camden* 1887.
D 490 port a
Describes two overland trips to California, expe-
riences there and in Colorado, Nevada, Utah and
elsewhere.

PERKINS, SAMUEL   **235**
General Jackson's conduct in the Seminole war
. . . *Bklyn* 1828. O 39 a

PERKINS, SAMUEL   **236**
A history of the . . . events of the late war . . .
N Hav 1825. O [12] 9–512 a
—enl. ed. "Historical sketches of the United
States" *N Y* 1830.
—rptd. 1835

PERLOT, JEAN N.   **237**
Vie et aventures d'un infant de l'Ardenne. *Arlon*
[*Belgium*] 1897. O 546 [10] port aa

Only narrative by a California gold-seeker from
Belgium; based on letters written from the mines,
1851–1857.

[PERNETY, ANTOINE J. D.]   **238**
Dissertation sur l'Amérique et les Américains,
contre Les recherches philosophiques de Mr. de
P[auw]. *Berlin* [1769]. D [8] 239 a
—rptd., same collat. & impr.: 1770; 1772.
Disputes de Pauw's attempt to prove America's
natural inferiority to other parts of the world.

[PERNETY, ANTOINE J. D.]   **239**
Examen des Recherches philosophiques sur
l'Amérique, et de Défense de cet ouvrage. *Berlin*
1771. D 2v: [20] 318 [1]; [20] 604 a
De Pauw had replied to Pernety's *Dissertation*
and this is Pernety's rejoinder.

PÉRON (CAPITAINE [FRANCOIS]).   **240**
Mémoires du: sur ses voyages aux côtes d'Afrique . . . aux côtes nord-ouest de l'Amérique . . . *P*
1824. O 2v: [10] 328; [4] 359. 6maps & pls b N
NYP
Spent several months on the northwest coast in
1796, and coasted south as far as Monterey on the
"Otter," first American ship to enter California
waters.

[PERRICHON, ABBÉ J.]   **241**
Vie de Monseigneur Dubuis l'apôtre du Texas.
Lyons 1900. O [12] 304 a
Dubuis was the second bishop of Texas.

[PERRIE, GEORGE W.]   **242**
Buckskin Mose; or, life from the lakes to the
Pacific . . . Ed. C. G. Rosenberg. *N Y* 1873. D 285
12pls + 3adv-p aa
—rptd. 1890. D 288 port a

PERRIN, WILLIAM H.   **243**
The pioneer press of Kentucky. *Louisv* Filson
Club 1888. Q 93 4pls facs a

PERRIN DU LAC, [FRANCOIS MARIE]   **244**
Voyage dans les deux Louisianes, et chez les
nations sauvages . . . en 1801–03 . . . *P* 1805. O [16]
479 map & pl[these probably not issued in all
copies] b IndU N
—anr. issue, probably the first, same collat., but
map on bluish paper and with *Lyons* impr. b
—Eng. tr. abr. *L* 1807. O 106 [2] aa
—Ger. tr.: *Leip* 1807, O 2v: [10] 206; [6] 122. map
pl; *Vienna* 1807, O 364 [5] map pl aa
Important for details concerning the early fur
trade with the Indians on the upper Missouri, but
that information was probably obtained from
Pierre Menard at St. Louis and there is little doubt
that Du Lac lied like a horse-thief in claiming to
have gone on a trading expedition up the Missouri.
The map is the best of that region published at the
time.

PERRINE, HENRY E.   **245**
A true story of some eventful years in grandpa's life . . . *Buf* [1885]. O 303 map pl aa
Includes journal of his 1849 trip to California, life in the mines, etc.

PERROT, NICOLAS   **246**
Memoire sur les moeurs, coustumes et religion des sauvages de l'Amérique Septentrionale. Ed. by R. P. J. Tailhan . . . *Leip & P* 1864. O [8] 342 [43] aa
First printing of a manuscript narrative written [ca 1700] by an Indian trader long active in the region of the Great Lakes. Some copies were on Large Paper; a few on Extra Large Paper, in quarto. For English version see Blair, Emma H.

PERRY, DAVID   **247**
Recollections of an old soldier . . . of the French and revolutionary wars. *Windsor Vt* 1822. O 55 b AA LC

PERRY, J[OHN] A.   **247a**
Thrilling adventures of a New Englander . . . in Cuba, Mexico and California. *B* 1853. O 96 b G
Chiefly of California interest.

PERRY (the late COMMODORE O. H.)   **248**
and ELLIOTT (CAPT. J. D.)
Documents in relation to the differences . . . between: *Wash* 1821. O 38 a
—rptd. *B* 1834. O 36

PERRY (the late COMMODORE   **249**
OLIVER H.) and ELLIOTT (CAPT. JESSE D.)
A review of a pamphlet purporting to be Documents in relation to the differences . . . between: By a citizen of Massachusetts. *B* 1834. O 55 a

PERRY (OLIVER H.), of Cleveland . . .   **250**
Hunting expeditions of: *Clev* 1899. O [8] 246 [2] 3pls 100copies ptd. b
Contemporary accounts, here first printed, of hunting expeditions in Ohio and Michigan, 1836 to 1855.

PERRY, WILLIAM S., ed.   **251**
Historical collections relating to the American colonial church. Vols. I to IV [all]. [*Hart*] 1870–78. Q 5v in 4: [18] 585; [24] 607; [26] 720; [12] 370 [2] 151 250copies ptd. aa
Intended to be in ten volumes, covering all colonies, but only these five, covering Virginia, Pennsylvania, Massachusetts, Maryland, and Delaware, were done. Each of these was issued separately, with special title-pages, as *Papers* . . . see next entry.

PERRY, WILLIAM S., ed.   **252**
Papers relating to the history of the [Episcopal] church in Virginia, Pennsylvania, Massachusetts, Maryland and Delaware. *Hart* 1870–78. O 5v a

Also issued with title *Historical collections relating to the American colonial church*, see No. 251, above.

PERSONAL NARRATIVE   **253**
Personal narrative of events by sea and land: 1800–1815. By a captain of the [British] navy. *Portsmouth* [*Eng*] 1837. 16° [8] 186 pls map a

PERVOE MORSKOE
Pervoe morskoe pouteshestvie Rossiian predpriniatoe . . . *See* Berkh, V. N.

PETER, ROBERT   **254**
A brief sketch of the history of Lexington, Kentucky . . . *Lex* 1854. O 24 a

PETER, ROBERT   **255**
History of Fayette county, Kentucky . . . *Chi* 1882. Roy O 905 pls aa

PETERS, DEWITT C.   **256**
Life . . . of Kit Carson . . . from facts narrated by himself. *N Y* 1858. O [4] 534 + 6adv-p 10pls aa
—rptd., with slight changes, and add.pls, *N Y* 1859; *N Y* 1860. a
—anr. ed., considerably enl., *Hartford* 1873. O 604 35pls
Dedication in the first edition—"to Col. Ceran St. Vrain"—reads in later editions, "to the companions of Kit Carson." *See* also Carson, Christopher.

PETERS, HARRY T.   **257**
America on stone: . . . a chronicle of American lithography. *Garden City* [1931]. Q 415 [2] 154pls [18col.] a 751copies ptd. aa

PETERS, HARRY T.   **258**
California on stone. *Garden City* 1935. F [8] 3–227 [2] 112 pls a 501copies ptd. aa

PETERS, HARRY T.   **259**
Currier & Ives: printmakers to the American people. *Garden City* 1929–31. Q 2v: 332 [1]; 404 [1]. 319pls[on 204sheets] 6-p. facs catalogue inserted in vol.I b AA N NYP 501copies ptd.
—rptd. *Garden City* 1942. Q [20] 41 192numb.pls [on 96sheets] some col. a

PETERS (HUGH).
An historical . . . account of: *See* Harris, Wm.

PETERS, RICHARD, reporter   **260**
The case of the Cherokee nation against the state of Georgia . . . *Phil* 1831. O [8] 286 a

PETERS, SAMUEL   **261**
A history of the Rev. Hugh Peters. *N Y* 1807. D [6] 155 port a

[PETERS, SAMUEL A.]   262
A general history of Connecticut . . . *L* 1781. O
[10] 436 + 2starred p. between p2 & 3 b JCB N
NYP Y
—ed. 2, *L* 1782. same collat. aa
—Am. eds., with adds.: *N Hav* 1829, D 405 8pls;
N Y 1877, D 285 a
Mobbed in Connecticut for his Tory activities,
Peters fled to England and, in retaliation, wrote
this false and vicious misrepresentation of that
commonwealth. Included were the *Blue laws of the
New Haven colony*, manufactured by his animos-
ity, but still swallowed as true by many people.

PETERSEN, WILLIAM J.   263
Steamboating on the upper Mississippi . . . *Iowa
City* 1937. O 576 aa

PETERSON, EDWARD   264
History of Rhode Island. *N Y* 1853. O [16] 370
eng.t. 7pls a

PETERSON, FREDERICK A.   265
Military review of the campaign in Virginia and
Maryland . . . in 1862. Parts I & II. *N Y* 1862–3.
O 2pts: 55; 69 a

PETIT-THOUARS, ABEL-AUBERT DU   266
Vie, lettres, mémoires . . . d'Aristide-Aubert du
Petit-Thouars . . . precédés d'un precis de la guerre
que la France a eu avec l'Angleterre de 1778 à 1783
. . . [*P*] n.d. O [44] 232 aa
—anr. ed *P* 1822. O [44] 404 6pls aa
Another volume was planned but never issued;
however, the revolutionary services of this officer
in the French fleet are here completely covered.

PETIT-THOUARS, ABEL-AUBERT DU   267
Voyage autour du monde . . . *P* 1840–43. O 4v:
[8 44] 402; [8] 464; [8] 490; [8] 178. 7tabs + atlas
F [4] tabs maps 68pls c NYP Y
Most important book on California during its
Mexican regime. In addition to these four volumes
of narrative, with *Atlas pittoresque*, there were six
other volumes covering data on botany, zoology,
etc., gathered on this voyage, with an *Atlas hydro-
graphique* [2pages, 19maps on 16 sheets].

PETTIJOHN (JONAS).   268
Autobiography . . . and various reminiscences
of the life of: among the Sioux . . . *Clay Center
Kas* 1890. D 104 aa
Experiences, in the 'thirties and 'forties, from
Missouri to Minnesota.

PETTIS, GEORGE H.   269
Frontier service, or a history of Company K,
First Infantry, California Volunteers. *Prov* 1885.
D 54 + errata 1f 250 copies ptd. aa
—rptd. "The California column . . .," *Santa Fe*
1908. D 45 capt.t.only a

PETTIS, GEORGE H.   270
Kit Carson's fight with the Comanche and
Kiowa Indians, at the Adobe Walls . . . *Prov* 1878.
O 44 aa
—rptd. *Santa Fe* 1908. O 35[incl.front] a

PETTIT, EBER M.   271
Sketches in the history of the underground railroad . . . *Fredonia N Y* 1879. O 174 port a

PETTY, A. W. M.   272
A history of the Third Missouri cavalry [Feder-
al] . . . *Little Rock* 1865. O 111 aa

PETZHOLDT, JULIUS   273
"Das Buch der Wilden" im Lichte französischer
Civilisation . . . *Dresden* 1861. O 16 8pls aa
—eds. 2 & 3, same impr., date & collat. a
—Fr. tr. *Brus* 1861. O 16 8pls
Attacks the authenticity of Abbé Domenech's
Manuscrit pictographique . . ., q. v.

PEUPLE [LE] INSTRUIT . . .
See Shebbeare, John, *A fourth letter to the people
of England.*

PEUPLE [LE] JUGE . . .
Peuple (Le) juge, ou considérations sur lesquelles le peuple anglois pourra décider . . . *See Reasons humbly offered, to prove . . .*

PEVERELLY, CHARLES A.   274
The book of American pastimes . . . history of
the principal base-ball, cricket . . . clubs of the
United States. *N Y* 1866. D [4] 556 4pls a

PEYTON, JOHN L.   275
The adventures of my grandfather . . . *L* 1867.
O [10] 249 port + 4adv-p aa

PEYTON, JOHN L.   276
The American crisis; or, pages from the note-
book of a state agent during the civil war . . . *L*
1867. O 2v: [12] 340; [6] 329. port a
Valuable contribution to the history of the Confederate struggle for foreign recognition.

PEYTON, JOHN L.   277
History of Augusta county, Virginia. *Staunton*
1882. O [8] 388 [9] port a
—rptd.: same impr., 1918; *Bridgewater* 1953, O
428 a

PEYTON, JOHN L.   278
Memoir of John Howe Peyton . . . *Staunton Va*
1894. O [2 6] 3–297 a

PEYTON, JOHN L.   279
Memoir of William Madison Peyton, of Roa-
noke . . . *L* 1873. O [8] 392 aa

PEYTON, JOHN L.   280
Over the Alleghanies and across the prairies . . .
L 1869. D [16] 377 + 2adv-p aa
—ed. 2, same collat., 1870. a

PEYTON, JOHN L.   281
A statistical view of . . . Illinois . . . *Chi* 1855.
D 48 aa

PEYTON, JOHN L.   282
Suggestions on railroad communication with
the Pacific . . . *Chi* 1853. O 32 b ChiH LC

PFEIFFER, GEORGE   283
An eulogium to the memory of General George
Washington. *Natchez* 1800. D 38 aa one cop loc

PHELAN, JAMES   284
History of Tennessee . . . *B* 1888. O [6] 478
map a
—rptd., same impr. 1889.

[PHELPS, ———]?   285
The rights of the colonies, and the extent of the
legislative authority of Great Britain, briefly stated
. . . *L* 1769. O [4] 20 a

PHELPS (ALONZO), the Rob Roy of   286
the Mississippi.
Confession of: *Jackson* 1834. O 50 aa

PHELPS, JOHN S.   287
Visit to the Territory of New Mexico [and "Are-
zonia"]. *Quincy Ill* 1859. O 27 aa

PHELPS (CAPTAIN MATTHEW).
Memoirs and adventures of: . . . *See* Haswell,
Anthony.

PHELPS, NOAH A.   288
A history of the copper mines . . . at Granby,
Conn . . . *Hart* 1845. O 34 aa
—enl ed, "History of Simsbury, Granby and Canton" [Conn] . . . same impr and date O [4] 9–176 a
Both editions contain account of the 1707 Indian
captivity of Daniel Hayes.

PHELPS, RICHARD H.   289
Newgate of Connecticut . . . *Hart* 1844. O 24 a
—ed. 2, same impr., date & collat.
—ed. 3, same impr. & date. O 33
—enl. ed. "A history of Newgate . . .," *Alb* 1860
Q 151 port 300copies ptd, 10 on L.P.
—anr. ed. "Newgate of Connecticut . . .," *Hart*
1876. O [6] 13–117 4pls

[PHELPS, WILLIAM D.]   290
Fore and aft; or, leaves from the life of and old
sailor. By "Webfoot." *B* 1871. D 359 aa
Author came to California in 1840, was active
n the "Bear Flag Revolution" and his unpreten-

tious narrative is a basic source on that event and
on Hudson's Bay Co. operations in California.
Only a few copies had been issued when fire
destroyed the plates.

PHELPS & ENSIGN [pubs.]   291
Traveller's guide through the United States . . .
N Y 1838. 16° [2] 53 map aa
—rptd. same collat. 1839; 1843; 1844. a
—reissued, "Phelps' traveller's guide," *N Y* 1847.
16° 70 map
—other eds., same collat., pub. Thayer & Ensign:
1848; 1850; 1851; 1853.

PHILADELPHES.   292
Mémoires du cercle des: Vol. I [all]. *Port-au-
Prince* 1788. O 264 [8] b H NYP

PHILADELPHIA   293
The cries of Philadelphia. *Phil* 1810. 32° 36 aa

Full . . . account of the late awful riots in   294
Philadelphia. *Phil* [1844]. O 60 [2] 36 pl aa
—rptd., same impr., 1848. 16° 96 10pls aa
Disturbances in the "city of brotherly love,"
between Irish Catholics and members of the Native
American party, resulting in many deaths and
colossal property damage.

Philadelphia directory (The) . . . 1791.
See Biddle, Clement.

Philadelphia directory . . . 1793. *See* Hardie,
James.

Philadelphia in 1824 . . . complete guide   295
for strangers . . . *Phil* 1824. 18° [12] 238 + 16adv-pp.
and errata slip map 2plans pl a

Philadelphia in 1830-1 . . . *Phil* 1830. D   296
288 map pl a

**Plain truth: or, serious considerations on the pre-
sent state of Philadelphia** . . . By a tradesman . . .
See Franklin, Benj.

A plan of Philadelphia. Or the stranger's   297
guide . . . *Phil* 1832. 16° 54 [38] a

Proceedings of the national convention   298
held at Philadelphia . . . [*Phil* 1856]. O 101 aa
First Republican party convention, in which
Lincoln's name was offered as candidate for Vice
President.

Reise von Hamburg nach Philadelphia.   299
Hannover 1800. 16° 208 a

Sketches of the higher classes of colored   300
society in Philadelphia. By a southerner. *Phil* 1841.
D 116 a

The stranger's guide to . . . Philadelphia   301
and adjoining districts. *Phil* 1828. 24° 38 10 map pl a

Strictures on the Philadelphia mischianza. *See*
Mauduit, Israel.

Strictures upon the Declaration of the Congress
at Philadelphia. *See* Hutchinson, Thos.

Thoughts on emigration, in a letter from a gentleman in Philadelphia. *See* Cooper, Thos.

The treaty held with the . . . Six Nations at   302
Philadelphia in July 1742. *Phil* 1743. F 25 b NYP Y
—Eng. ed., with adds., *L* n.d. O [14] 37 aa

Views in Philadelphia. *See* Childs, C. G.; also
Wild, J. C.

PHILADELPHUS, THEOPHILUS [pseud.]   303
A sequel to Common sense: or the American
controversy considered in two points of view
hitherto unnoticed . . . ed. 2, enl. *Dub* 1777. O 78 aa

PHILIPPI, FERDINAND   304
Geschichte der Vereinigten Freistaaten . . .
Dresden 1826. 16° 3v: [10] 112; [6] 106; [8] 162 a

[PHILIPS, GEORGE]   305
Travels in North America. *Dub* Bentham 1822.
16° [2] 9–184 5pls a
—other eds.: *Dub* Jones 1824, 16° 180; *Dub*
Smith 1824, same collat.; *Dub* Hardy n.d. same
collat.; *L* 1831, 16° [2] 168 5pls a
Imaginary experiences of an imaginary Irishman
with the Lewis and Clark expedition, etc.

PHILLIPPO, JAMES M.   306
The United States and Cuba. *L* 1857. D [12]
476 a

[PHILLIPS, B. F.]   307
Condensed history of New Lyme, Ohio. *Jefferson O* 1877. D 60 a

PHILLIPS, MRS. CATHERINE C.   308
Cornelius Cole, California pioneer . . . *S F* 1929.
Q [8] 379 27pls a 250copies ptd.

PHILLIPS, MRS. CATHERINE C.   309
Coulterville chronicle: the annals of a . . .
mining town. *S F* Grabhorn 1942. O [10] 275
23pls a 500 cops ptd

PHILLIPS, MRS. CATHERINE C.   310
Jessie Benton Fremont: a woman who made
history. *S F* 1935. O [8] 344 347–361 front. 2facs a

PHILLIPS, [MRS.] CATHERINE C.   311
Portsmouth plaza. The cradle of San Francisco.
S F 1932. sm Q [14] 464 front. a

PHILLIPS, D. L.   312
Letters from California. *Springfield Ill* 1877.
O [8] 171 a

[PHILLIPS, EDWIN D.]   313
Texas and its late military occupation and evacuation. *N Y* 1862. O 35 a

[PHILLIPS, GEORGE SEARLE]   314
Transatlantic tracings; or, sketches of persons
and scenes in America. *L* 1853. 16° 337 port a

[PHILLIPS, GEORGE SPENCER]   315
Amusing . . . adventures of a California artist,
while daguerreo-typing a continent. *B* 1854. D 92
b AA G N Y

PHILLIPS, HENRY   316
Historical sketches of the paper currency of the
. . . colonies. [And] Continental paper money.
Roxbury 1865–6. sm Q 2v: [4] 233; 264 a 303copies
ptd[50 on L.P. & 3 on Whatman paper]

PHILLIPS, P[HILIP] L.   317
The first map and description of Ohio . . . by
Manasseh Cutler. *Wash* 1918. Q 41 fold.map a
200copies ptd.

PHILLIPS, P[HILIP] L.   318
The first map of Kentucky, by John Filson
Wash 1908. Q 22 fold.map a 200copies ptd.

PHILLIPS, P[HILIP] L.   319
Notes on . . . Bernard Romans. *Deland Fla*
1924. O 128 [6] facs + Atlas F [2maps in 13sec-
tions] 325copies ptd. aa
Atlas volume was sold separately.

PHILLIPS, P[HILIP] L.   320
The rare map of the northwest . . . by John
Fitch. *Wash* 1916. Q 43 fold.map a 200 copies ptd.

PHILLIPS, P[HILIP] L.   321
The rare map of Virginia and Maryland, by
Augustine Herrman . . . *Wash* 1911. Q 23 fold.
map a 200copies ptd.

[PHILLIPS, SIR RICHARD] ed.   322
A collection of modern and contemporary
voyages and travels . . . *L* 1805–10. O 11v[some-
times bound in 6] maps pls b
Contains fifty-four narratives, some of United
States interest, with separate title-pages and
paginations.

[PHILLIPS, SIR RICHARD] ed.   323
New voyages and travels . . . *L* [1819–23]. O 9v
maps pls b
Contains sixty-five narratives, some of United
States interest, with separate title-pages and
paginations.

[PHILLIPS, SIR RICHARD]   **324**
A view of the character . . . of the North-Americans . . . *Phil* 1810. D [2] 39 3pls aa

PHILLIPS, ULRICH B.   **325**
American Negro slavery . . . *N Y* 1918. O [12] 529 + fold tab a

PHILLIPS, ULRICH B., ed.   **326**
Florida plantation records . . . *St L* 1927. O [10] 596 map 5pls a

PHILLIPS, ULRICH B.   **327**
A history of transportation in the eastern cotton belt to 1860. *N Y* 1908. D [18] 405 3maps a

PHILLIPS, ULRICH B.   **328**
The life of Robert Toombs. *N Y* 1913. O [12] 281 port a

PHILLIPS, ULRICH B., ed.   **429**
Plantation and frontier documents, 1649–1863 . . . *Clev* 1909. O 2v: 275; 279 aa [150sets ptd. as separate from "The documentary history of American industrial society"]

PHILLIPS, WILLIAM [A.]   **330**
The conquest of Kansas, by Missuori and her allies . . . *B* 1856. D 414 a

PHILLIPSON (WILLIAM M.)   **331**
The life and voyages of: . . . *Sonora Calif* 1924. O [6] 9–114 a 200copies ptd.

PHILO-JACKSON [pseud.]
The presidential election . . . *See* under Jackson, Gen. Andrew.

PHILOPATRIOS [pseud.]   **332**
Some observations on the two campaigns against the Cherokee Indians . . . *Charlestown* 1762. O 88 tab b Y
Defense of the conduct of the regiment of South Carolina Rangers against imputations made by Col. Grant, commanding the expedition.

PHINNEY, ELIAS   **333**
History of the battle at Lexington . . . *B* 1825. O 40 a
—rptd. *B* 1875. same collat.

PHOCION.
A letter from: . . . *See* Hamilton, Alex.

PHOTOGRAPHIC SKETCH BOOK
Photographic sketch book of the war. *See* Gardner, Alex.

PIATT, EMMA C.   **334**
History of Piatt county [Ill.] . . . [*Chi* 1883]. Q 643 map a

PICK AND PAN.
Trip to the diggings in 1849 . . . By an argonaut. 1883. *See* McCall, A. J.

PICKELL, JOHN   **335**
A new chapter in the early history of [George] Washington, in connection with the . . . history of the Potomac Company. *N Y* 1856. O [12] 17–178 a

PICKERING, JOSEPH   **336**
Emigration, or no emigration . . . narrative of the author . . . *L* 1830. D [12] 132 a
—new ed. "Inquiries of an emigrant . . .," *L* 1831. D [16] 132 + 18adv-p
—anr. ed. *L* 1832. D [16] 208 map
—Ger. tr., "Führer für Auswanderer nach Amerika." *Potsdam* 1832 D

PICKERING, OCTAVIUS, and UPHAM,   **337**
CHARLES W.
The life of Timothy Pickering . . . *B* 1867–73. O 4v: [20] 549; [20] 509; [4] 499; [4] 512. 2ports 2pls 2facs a

PICKERING (COLONEL [TIMOTHY]).   **338**
A letter from: containing a narrative of the outrage committed on him in Wyoming; with an account of the controversies respecting the lands claimed by . . . Pennsylvania and Connecticut . . . [*Salem* 1819]. O 39 aa

PICKERING, TIMOTHY   **339**
Letters addressed to the people . . . on the conduct of . . . the American government, towards Great Britain and France. *L* 1811. O 168 a
—rptd. same impr. & collat. 1812
—Am. ed. "Political essays . . . ," *Canandaigua* 1812. D 215
A collected edition formed from several of his American pamphlets. The Canandaigua edition was the first bound book printed in western New York.

PICKERING (MR. [TIMOTHY]).   **340**
Letters from: to the Chevalier de Yrujo [Spanish Minister to the United States]. n.p. [*Phil*?] 1797. O 37 aa
For reply to this attack on Spanish diplomacy, *see* Yrujo y Tacon, Carlos M.

[PICKERING, TIMOTHY]   **341**
Review of the administration of the government of the United States; since the year ninety-three . . . *B* 1797. O 87 a
Correspondence between Secretary of State Pickering and the French minister Adet.

PICKERING, TIMOTHY   **342**
A review of the correspondence between the Hon. John Adams . . . and the late Wm. Cunningham . . . 1803–1824. *Salem* 1824. O [4] 197 a
—ed. 2, same impr. & date. O [4] 140

PICKERING'S . . . LETTER 343
Pickering's (Mr. [Timothy]) letter, on the subject of the embargo. Some remarks and extracts, in reply to: *N Hav* [1808]. O 24 [capt.t.] aa
Pickering's Letter [16p.] was published at Boston, 1808, and reprinted many times that year. It was the first of many New England pamphlets opposing the Embargo Act.

[PICKERSGILL, LIEUT. RICHARD] 344
A concise account of voyages for the discovery of a north-west passage . . . *L* 1782. D [28] 69 b JCB NYP ProvArchVictoria Y

PICKETT, ALBERT J. 345
Eight days in New Orleans . . . [*Montg*] 1847. O 40 a

PICKETT, ALBERT J. 346
History of Alabama, and incidentally of Georgia and Mississippi . . . *Charleston* 1851. D 2v: [20] 377; [8] 445. map 3plans 8pls aa
—eds. 2 & 3, same collat. and yr. aa
—anr. ed. *Sheffield Ala* 1896. O 669 port a
—rptd., with adds. & index, *Sheffield* 1896. O 773 port a
—anr. ed., same collat., *Birm Ala* 1900. a
Essential work on the deep south.

PICKETT, ALBERT J. 347
Invasion of the territory of Alabama by . . . Spaniards, under Ferdinand de Soto . . . *Montg* 1849. O 41 aa
Prospectus of his *History of Alabama.*

[PICKETT, JAMES C.] 348
The memory of Pocahontas vindicated against the erroneous judgement of the Hon. Waddy Thompson . . . *Wash* 1847. O 39 a

PICTET DE ROCHEMONT, 349
C[HARLES]
Tableau de la situation actuelle des États-Unis d'après . . . les meilleurs auteurs américains. *P* 1795. O 2v: 360 [2]; 340 [2]. 2maps a

PICTURE
Picture of slavery in the United States . . . *See* Bourne, Geo.

PICTURESQUE VIEWS 350
Picturesque views of American scenery. *Phil*, Thomas, 1819. F 116 18col-pls [incl eng-t] b
—ed 2, *Phil*, Carey, 1820. F 116 20col-pls [incl eng-t] b

PIDGEON, WILLIAM 351
Traditions of De-coo-dah, and antiquarian researches . . . *L & N Y* 1853. O 334 map fold.pl a
—rptd., same collat., but no map: *N Y* 1854; *N Y* 1858.

PIÈCES OFFICIELLES
Pièces officielles . . . relatives a la négociation qui a eu lieu . . . sur les differens . . . *See* Talleyrand, Mons.

PIERCE, DR. A. C. 352
A man from Corpus Christi; or, adventures of two bird hunters and a dog in Texan bogs. *N Y* 1894. O 257 O [4] 257 + 16adv-p a

PIERCE, GEORGE F. 353
Incidents of western travel . . . *Nashv* 1857. D 249 port aa
—rptd. 1859. D same collat. a

PIERCE, HENRY H. 354
Report of an expedition from Fort Colville to Puget sound . . . *Wash* 1883. O 25 map a

PIERCE, JOSIAH 355
A history of . . . Gorham, Maine. *Port* 1862. O 240 a

PIERCE, M[ARIS] B. 356
Address on the present condition . . . of the aboriginal inhabitants of America . . . [*Buf*] 1838. O 16 a
—ed. 2, *Phil* 1839. D 24

PIERCE, W. H. 357
Thirteen years of travel and exploration in Alaska. *Lawrence Kas* 1890. D 224 a
One of the earliest accounts of gold discovery on the Yukon, by a pioneer of 1886.

PIERCE COUNTY, WIS. 358
First annual review of: . . . *Prescott Wis* [1856]. D 46 + cover t. aa

PIERCY, FREDERICK
Route from Liverpool to Great Salt Lake valley. *See* Linforth, James.

PIERSON, HAMILTON W. 359
Jefferson at Monticello . . . *N Y* 1862. O 138 pl 8facs a

PIERZ [or PIRC], FRANZ 360
Die Indianer in Nord-America . . . *St L* 1855. D 130 [2] aa

PIETAS IN PATRIAM: [life of Sir Wm. Phips]
See Mather, Cotton.

PIGMAN (WALTER G.) 361
The journal of: [from Ohio to California, in 1850]. *Mexico Mo* 1942. O [10] 82 port a 200copies ptd.

PIKE (ALBERT). 362
Letter of: to the Choctaw people. *Wash* 1872. O 26 [14] a

455

Discusses his participation in securing collection of their claims.

PIKE, ALBERT   363
Letters to the people of the northern states, on the Nebraska and Kansas act, and southern slavery . . . *Wash* 1856. O 40 a

PIKE (ALBERT).   364
Message of the President [Davis], and report of: of the results of his mission [as Commissioner of the Confederate States to the Indian Nations]. *Rich* 1861. O 38 a

PIKE, ALBERT   365
Prose sketches and poems, written in the western country. *B* 1834. D 200 b AA N NYP Y
Includes a graphic 80-page narrative of a trip over the southwestern prairies to Santa Fe, made by Aaron Lewis, in 1831. Pike's own narrative covers his trip to Santa Fe the same year, trapping adventures in the Comanche country and Colorado and return to Arkansas, in 1832.

PIKE, ALBERT   366
State or province? Bond or free? [*Little Rock* 1861]. O 40 aa
Advocates secession for Arkansas. One copy known has a 23-page appendix.

PIKE, ALBERT   367
Treaty . . . at the North Fork village in the Creek nation, on the 12th day of July, 1861. [*Rich*? 1864]. D 25 aa

[PIKE, ALBERT]   368
Treaty with the Cherokees. October 7th, 1861. [*Rich*? 1862?]. O 26 [capt.t.only] b H LC Y
The fateful instrument joining this Nation to the Lost Cause; one of the few treaties made by the Confederate States.

PIKE, [JAMES], corporal   369
The scout and ranger: . . . adventures . . . as a Texas ranger in the Indian wars . . . *Cin* 1865. O [12] 19–394[incl.24pls] port with hair parted on the left errata lf b
—iss 2 no errata lf hair in port parted on right aa

PIKE, JAMES S.   370
First blows of the civil war. The years of preliminary conflict. *N Y* [1879]. O [14] 526 a

PIKE, JAMES S.   371
The prostrate State: South Carolina under Negro government. *N Y* 1874. D 279 + 8adv-p a
—rptd. *N Y* [1935]. O 279 front.
—Dutch tr. *Doesborgh* 1875. O [4] 296

PIKE, ZEBULON M.   372
An account of a voyage up the Mississippi . . . 1805–1806 . . . [*Wash*? 1807?] O 68 map [possibly not issued with all copies] made by Nicholas King d AA G; *sans* map c B NYP Y
Generally thought to have been compiled [from Pike's MS journal] by Dr. Samuel L. Mitchill, but more probably the work of Nicholas King. For another account of this Pike exploration, see *The political cabinet.*

PIKE, ZEBULON M.   373
An account of expeditions to the sources of the Mississippi and through western parts of Louisiana . . . 1805–07. *Phil* 1810. O [8] 106 [10] 107–278 [4] 66 53 87 4maps 2charts port 3tabs b
—best issue, with maps & charts in separate 4° atlas b N NYP
—Eng. ed., with slightly altered t. & some scientific data omitted, *L* 1811. Q [20] 436 2maps aa
—rptd. *Denver* 1889. Q 394 3pls 4maps a
—best ed., ed. by Coues, with copious notes *N Y* 1895. O 3v: [8 114] 356: [6] 357–856; [6] 857–955. port 7maps facs also 150 sets on L.P. aa
—Ger. tr. Weimar 1813. O [16] 556 map 536 map tab a
—Dutch tr *Amst* 1812. D 2v: 3map 2 tabs aa
—Fr. tr. *P* 1812. O 2v: [16] 368; 374 map [on 3 sheets] a
First government exploration of the Southwest. For his *Arkansaw journal,* see Hart, Stephen H., and Hulbert, Archer B.

PIKE'S PEAK.
Hints and information for the use of emigrants to: *Leavenworth* 1860. *See* Larimer, George W.

PILGRIMAGE (A) OVER THE PRAIRIES.
See Ruysdale, Philip.

PINAL COUNTY, ARIZONA.   374
Resources of: *Florence* Ariz 1889. O 23 4pls fold.map a

PINCKNEY, CHARLES   375
Observations on the plan of government submitted to the federal convention . . . *N Y* [1787]. sm Q 27 aa
This speech, made before the Constitutional Convention, furnishes the only contemporary clue to the much discussed Pinckney plan for a Federal Constitution.

[PINCKNEY, CHARLES]   376
Observations to shew the propriety of the nomination of Colonel James Monroe, to the presidency . . . *Charleston S C* 1816. O 52 a

PINCKNEY, CHARLES   378
Three letters written . . . under the signature of a South Carolina planter . . . *Phil* 1799. O [2] 65 a
—rptd. *Charleston S C* 1799. O [2] 69
On unlawful seizure of American vessels by British cruisers, etc.

PINCKNEY, JAMES D.   379
Reminiscences of Catskill [N. Y.]. *Catskill* 1868.
O 79 a

[PINCKNEY, THOMAS]   380
Reflections, occasioned by the late [Negro] disturbances in Charleston. *Charleston S C* 1822.
O 30 a

PINE, GEORGE W.   381
Beyond the west . . . two years travel . . . on the plains, in the Rocky mountains . . . *Utica* 1870. D 444 6pls aa
—ed. 2 enl., same impr. 1871. D 483 a
—oth. eds: *Utica* 1873; Buff 1873.

PINE, GEORGE W.   382
Two wonders of the world [Yosemite, etc.] *N Y* 1870. 16° 78 aa

PINO, PEDRO BAUTISTA   383
Exposicion sucinta . . . de la provincia del Nuevo México . . . *Cadiz* 1812. O 48 [3] map b G TxU JCB
—rptd. with Barreiro's Ojeada sobre Nuevo-México, ed. by Escudero, with adds., [under title "Noticias historicas . . . de la antigua provincia del Nuevo-México,"] *Mex* 1849. O [6] 98 [4] map b G
Pino, supplemented by Barreiro, is the chief source on New Mexico's last years as a Spanish province and of her beginnings as a Mexican state. *See* Barreiro for original edition of his book. The 1849 edition treats fully the trade, developed after Pino's time, between Santa Fe and the United States.

[PINTO, ISAAC DE].   384
Lettre de Mr. . . . : à Mr. S. B[arretts] au sujet des troubles qui agitent . . . l'Amérique Septentrionale. *Hague* 1776. O 29 aa
—Eng. ed., with his second letter added, "Letters on the American troubles . . .," *L* 1776. O [4] 89 aa

PINTO (MR. [ISAAC] DE).   385
Nouvelles observations sur la seconde lettre de: . . . *L* [ptd Holland?] 1776. O 60 a
For same author's reply to Pinto's first *Lettre*, see *Observations d'un homme impartial* . . .

PINTO (MR. J.[i.e., ISAAC] DE).   386
Réponse de: aux Observations d'un homme impartial, sur sa Lettre à Mr. S. B. . . ., au sujet des troubles qui agitent . . . l'Amérique Septentrionale. *Hague* 1776. O 60 a

PINTO (M[ONS. ISAAC DE]).   387
Seconde lettre de: à l'occasion des troubles des colonies . . . *Hague* 1776. O 90 [2] a
—Eng. ed., *see* above "Lettre . . ."

PIONEER . . .
Pioneer and personal reminiscences. *See* Crary, C. G.

Pioneer days in the southwest. *See* Hart, John A.

Pioneer life in the west . . . adventures of   388
Boone, Kenton, *et al. Phil* 1858. D 332[incl. pls] a
—rptd., same impr. & collat. 1860

PIONEERING ON THE PLAINS . . .
See McCoy, Alex. W., *et al.*

PIRATE'S OWN BOOK (THE) . . .
See Ellms, Chas.

PIRTLE, ALFRED   389
The battle of Tippecanoe. *Louisv* Filson Club 1900. Q[20] 158 7pls plan a

PISANI, FERRI
Lettres sur les États-Unis . . . *See* Ferri-Pisani.

PITEZEL, JOHN H.   390
Lights and shadows of missonary life . . . during nine years spent in the region of lake Superior. *Cin* 1857. D 431 4pls a
—rptd. same impr.: 1859; 1860 a
—new ed., with adds., *Cin* 1883. D 468 4pls[incl. in paginat.] port

PITHOLE, [Pa.]
History of: by "Crocus." *See* Leonard, Chas. C.

PITKIN, TIMOTHY   391
A political and civil history of the United States . . . *N Hav* 1828. O 2v: 528; [12] 9–539. port a
—rptd., same impr. & collat. 1831.

PITKIN, TIMOTHY   392
A statistical view of the commerce of the United States . . . *Hart* 1816. O [12] 407 [20] a
—ed. 2, with adds., *N Y* 1817. O [12] 445 [8]
—anr. ed., enl., *N Hav* 1835. O [16] 600

PITMAN, BENN [reporter]   393
The assassination of President Lincoln and the trial of the conspirators . . . *Cin* 1865. O 421 [2] pl a
Officially expurgated transcript.

PITMAN, BENN [reporter]   394
The trials for treason at Indianapolis, disclosing the plans for . . . a north-western confederacy . . . *Cin* 1865. O 340 + 16adv-p front. pl a

PITOU, LOUIS-ANGE   395
Voyage à Cayenne, dans les deux Amériques . . . *P* 1805. O 2v: 312; 404. 2pls a
—ed. 2, *P* 1807. O 2v: [12] 5–60, 312; [12] 404. 2pls
—Ger. tr. *Leip* 1805. O [6] 391 2pls; *Leip* 1838.

Exiled to Cayenne, in 1797, he was pardoned in 1801 and returned to France via the United States.

PITTMAN, PHILIP   396
The present state of the European settlements on the Mississippi . . . *L* 1770. Q [8] 99 8maps & plans c N NYP Y
—rptd. *Clev* 1906. O 165[incl.facs] 6maps + 8 adv-p 500 cops ptd a
Extremely thorough description—in point of time the second English—of the western country under British occupation.

PITTS, J[AMES] R. S.   397
Life and confession of the . . . outlaw James Copeland . . . [*Hattiesburg, Miss*] 1858. D 237 [incl. front wrap.] aa
—ed. 2, "Life and career of . . . James Copeland . . . *Jackson, Miss* 1874. O 220 a
—rptd. *Hattiesburg* [1909] O 237
Written by the sheriff who hanged this southern land pirate.

PITT'S ADMINISTRATION (MR.)
An appendix to the Review of: *See* Almon, John

PITT'S ADMINISTRATION (MR.)
A review of: *See* Almon, John.

PITTSBURGH   398
Address of a committee appointed by the citizens of Pittsburgh . . . on the . . . railroad from the western termination of the Pennsylvania canal to the Ohio canal. *Pitt* 1832. O 24 b

Documents relative to a communication   399 between Pittsburgh and the Ohio canal. *Pitt* 1833. O [32] 27 fold.map a

A full account of the great fire at Pitts-   400 burgh . . . *Pitt* 1845. O 52 [14] a

Pittsburgh directory for 1815. *See* Riddle, James M., pub.

PLACER.   402
Directory of the county of Placer . . . history . . . *S F* 1861. O 208 b Hn

History of Placer county, California *Oakl*   403 1882. Q 416 pls b B Hn N

Placer county [Calif.] business and official   404 directory . . . historical sketches . . . *Auburn Calif* 1875. O 136 aa

PLACERVILLE [CALIF.]   405
Directory of: . . . containing a history . . . *Placerville* 1862. D 128 aa

PLACERVILLE AND SACRAMENTO RAILROAD (THE).
Report of the chief engineer on the survey of: *See* Bishop, Francis A.

PLAIN   406
Plain and seasonable address (A) to the freeholders of Great Britain, on the present posture of affairs in America. *L* 1766. O [2] 21 a
Denunciation of both Pitt and America.

Plain English, [pseud.] A letter to the   407 King. [*L* 1778]. O [38] 53 a
Defends revolting colonies and thinks they cannot be subdued.

Plain facts: . . . examination into the rights of the Indian nations . . . *See* Wharton, Sam'l.

Plain letter (A) to the common people of England and Wales . . . *See* Tucker, Josiah.

Plain question (The) upon the present   408 dispute with our American colonies. *L* 1776. D 24 a
—eds. 2 & 3, same impr., date & collat.
—anr. ed., same date & collat. *Dub*
Rebellion against a benevolent Parliament pronounced unreasonable.

Plain sense, on national industry . . .   409 *N Y* 1820. O 51 a

Plain sense, or sketches of political   410 frenzy and federal fraud and folly. *Wash* 1803. O 40 a

Plain truth: addressed to the inhabitants of America . . . By Candidus. *See* Smith, *Provost* Wm.

Plain truth: or, a letter to the author of Dispassionate thoughts on the American war . . . *See* Galloway, Jos.

PLAN   411
Plan einer geregelten deutschen Auswanderung und Ansiedelung in den Vereinigten Staaten . . . *Darmstadt* 1848. O 48 a

Plan (A) for settling the unhappy dispute between Great Britain and her colonies. *See* Jenings, Edmund.

Plan (A) for the . . . militia of the United States. *See* Knox, Henry.

Plan of association of the North American   412 Land Company. *Phil* 1795. D 25 a
—Eng. ed. *L* 1795.
See also Observations on the North American Land Company,

Plan (A) of reconciliation between Great Britain and her colonies . . . *See* Ramsay, Allan.

Plan (A) of reconciliation with America; consistent with the dignity . . . of both countries. *See* Cawthorne, J.

Plan of re-union between Great Britain and her colonies. *See* Pulteney, Wm.

Plan of the new constitution of the United   413
States . . . *L* 1787. O [2] 30 + 8adv-p a
—new ed., cor., *L* 1791. O
—ed. 2, cor., same impr. 1792. O 32
—Am. eds., *see* "Constitution for the United States of America . . ."

Plan (A) to reconcile Great Britain and   414
her colonies, and preserve the dependency of America. *L* M.DDC.LXXIV[error for 1774]. O [16] 40 a

[PLANTAGENET, BEAUCHAMP]   415
   A description of the province of New Albion. *L* 1648. smQ 32 dd H LC JCB N
—ed. 2, *L* 1650. smQ [8] 24 d Hn
This vast plantation, described as "in North Virginia", lay really in Delaware, New Jersey and Long Island.

PLANTER
   Planter (The): or, thirteen years in the south. By a northern man. *See* Brown, David.

PLASBERG, C. L.   416
   Californië. Beschrijving van dat land. *Arnhem* 1849. O 38 aa

PLATT, P. L., and SLATER, N.   417
   Traveler's guide across the plains . . . *Chi* 1852. 16° 64 map dd Only one perfect cop known.

PLATTE VALLEY (THE GREAT).
   Incidents of a trip through: *See* Seymour, Silas.

PLAYFAIR, ROBERT   418
   Recollections of a visit to the United States . . . 1847–8–9. *Edin* 1856. D [8] 266 a
—rptd. 1859. same collat.

PLEA   419
   Plea [A] for the Indians. *Phil* 1838. O 29 port a
—rptd. [*Hart ca* 1845].
For similar title, *see* Beeson, John.

Plea [A] for the poor soldiers. By a citizen of Philadelphia. *See* Webster, Pelatiah.

Plea of the colonies [The], on the charges brought against them . . . *See* Williamson, Hugh.

PLEAS, ELWOOD   420
   Henry County [Ind.]; past and present . . . *New Castle Ind* 1871. 16° [4] 148 errata slip 2pls a

PLEASANTS, W[ILLIAM] J.   421
   Twice across the plains, 1849, 1856. *S F* 1906. D 160 b G LC

PLEMPEL, CHARLES A.   422
   The Klondyke gold fields . . . *Balt* 1897.D 63 a

PLIMPTON, FLORUS B.   423
   The lost child . . . narrative of the loss and discovery of Casper A. Partridge among the Menominee Indians . . . *Clev* 1852. D 79 [cover t. only] b AA N NYP

PLUMAS, LASSEN & SIERRA   424
COUNTIES, CALIFORNIA . . .
   Illustrated history of: *S F* 1882. Q 507 map pls aa

PLUMBE, JOHN   425
   Memorial against Mr. Asa Whitney's railroad scheme. [*Wash* 1851]. O 48 map[issued in only a few copies] b G
—ordinary copy without map a

PLUMBE, JOHN   426
   Sketches of Iowa and Wisconsin . . . *St L* 1839. D [6] 5–103 map d G NYP WisH Y
—rptd *Ia City* 1948 a
Covers Iowa only; Wisconsin part was planned but never appeared.

PLUMMER (MRS. CLARISSA).   427
   Narrative of the captivity of: [by Texas Comanches]. *N Y* 1838. O 24 [incl. front.] b AA N NYP
—ed. 2, *N Y* 1839, same collat. b
For similar narratives ascribed to Mrs. Caroline Harris, Mrs. Jane Adeline Wilson and Mrs. Sarah Ann Horn, *see* those entries. *See* also Parker, James W.

PLYMOUTH COMPANY   428
   An answer to the Remarks of the Plymouth Company . . . on the Plan and extracts of deeds published by the proprietors of the township of Brunswick . . . and also the boundaries of the Plymouth company's tract upon Kennebeck-River are . . . ascertained. *B* 1753. Q 33 aa

   A defence of the Remarks of the Plymouth   429
Company on the Plan . . . published by the proprietors . . . of the township of Brunswick . . . *B* 1753. Q 50 aa
   The *Remarks on the plan*, here defended, had been issued by the Plymouth Company, at Boston, same year, in an eight-page tract. For the claims of the Brunswick proprietors, *see* above, *An answer to the Remarks of the Plymouth company* . . .

POCAHONTAS.
The memory of: vindicated against the erroneous judgement of the Hon. Waddy Thompson . . . By a Kentuckian. *See* Pickett, James C.

POE, JOHN W. 430
The true story of the death of "Billy the Kid" . . . *L A* 1922. D 30 a 305copies[55 si ꓭned by printer] —rptd., "The death of Billy the Kid," *B* 1933. D [42] 60 + pls

POINDEXTER [THE HON. GEORGE] . . .
Letters addressed to: *see* Marschalk, Andrew.

POLARI, CONSTANT, [pseud] 431
Herinneringen eener Reize naar Nieuw York . . . 1831–2. *See* Brauw, J. de.

POLES [THE] IN THE UNITED STATES.
See Kraitsir, Chas. V.

[POLETICA, PIERRE] 432
Apercu de la situation interieure des États-Unis . . . *L* 1826. O [10] 164 a
—Eng. tr. *Balt* 1826. O [8] 163
Attributed also to Paul Svin'in.

POLICY 433
Policy (The) of the nation, particularly as it respects a navy, in the present crisis . . . *N Y* 1814, O 55 a

POLIGNAC, CAMILLE A. J. M., 434
prince de
L'union américaine après la guerre. *P* 1866. O 48 a

POLITE TRAVELLER 435
Polite traveller (The): . . . a modern view of the thirteen United States . . . *L* [1783]. 18° 144 map a

POLITICAL 436
Political cabinet (The). *B* 1806–07. O 2v in 1; 96; 80 b N NYP Y
These appendices—twenty-two in number—to the *Monthly Anthology* [vols III and IV] contain material on the Lewis & Clark expedition and a narrative of Pike's expedition up the Mississippi.

Political, commercial, and statistical 437 sketches of the Spanish empire in both Indies; reflections on the policy proper for Great Britain . . . and a view of the political question between Spain and the United States respecting Louisiana and the Floridas, with the claims of Great Britain . . . to the commercial navigation of the Mississippi . . . *L* 1809. O [4] 156 a

Political detection [The];)or, the . . . tyranny of administration . . . letters signed Junius Americanus. *See* Lee, Arthur.

Political essays . . . *See* Galt, John M.

Political essays concerning the present state of the British empire . . . *See* Young, Arthur.

Political establishments [The] of the 438 United States . . . **in a candid review of their deficiencies** . . . By a fellow citizen. *Phil* 1784. O 28 a

Political intolerance . . . **exemplified in a 439 recent removal from office** . . . By one of the American people. *B* 1801. O 36 a
Laudatory defence of Winthrop Sargent, just removed as Governor of Mississippi Territory.

Political mirror [The]; or review of 440 Jacksonism . . . *N Y* 1835. D [16] 316 a

Political mirror [A]; or . . . review of the 441 present reign. With . . . list of the ships . . . destroyed since the commencement of hostilities. *L* 1779. O [2] 67 aa

Political opinions; particularly respecting 442 the seat of federal empire . . . the utility . . . of erecting the great city in the centre of the states . . . By a citizen of America. n.p. 1789. D 72 a

Political reconciling-pamphlet, or patriotic 443 address to all the people in North America . . . *Stamford Conn* 1813. 16° [6] 3–50 a

Political reflections on the late colonial governments . . . By an American. *See* Galloway, Jos.

Political reflections on the royal, proprietary, and charter governments of the American colonies . . . *See* Galloway, Jos.

Political reformer (The) . . . *See* Forrest, Michael.

Political sketch [A] of America. *Edin* 444 1808. O 87 a

Political sketches . . . By a citizen of the United States. *See* Murray, Wm. Vans.

Political truth . . . **with an inquiry into the truth of the charges** . . . **against Mr. Randolph.** *See* Randolph, Edmund.

POLITICKS
Politicks (The) and views of a certain party displayed. *See* Smith, Wm. Loughton.

POLITIEK VERTOOG . . .
See Goens, R. M. van.

POLITIQUE DANOIS (LE).
See Hübner, Martin.

POLK, JAMES K.   **445**
Diary... 1845–1849. Ed. M. M. Quaife. *Chi* 1910. O 4v: [32] 498; [6] 494; [6] 508; [6] 462. 4pls facs aa

[POLK, JAMES K.]   **446**
Message of the President... to the two houses of Congress [including official announcement of the California gold discovery]. Ex. Doc I, 2" Sess. 30th Cong. *Wash* 1848. O 1275 maps aa

[POLK, JAMES K.]   **447**
Message of the President [with documents covering California affairs from May 1846 to January 1850]. Exec. Doc. 17, Session 1, 31st Congress. *Wash* 1850. O 976 7maps a

POLK (DR. J[EFFERSON] J.)   **448**
Autobiography of:... *Louisv* 1867. D 254 [1] port aa
Men and manners in Kentucky, 1835–1866.

POLLARD, EDWARD A.
Black diamonds gathered in the darkey homes of the south. *See* "The southern spy," below, of which it is an enlarged edition.

POLLARD, EDWARD   **449**
The first year of the war... *Rich* 1862. O [8] 17–374 aa
—cor. ed. *Rich* 1862. O [2] 389 ports
—anr. iss. O 406
—rptd: *N Y* 1863, O [6] 360 [2] map & 3 ports; *N Y* 1864, O [6] 389 map 3ports; *N Y* 1865, same collat., but port of Jackson added.
—Eng. eds: *L* Stevens 1863, O [10] 360 [2] map 4ports; *L* Philip 1863, D [16] 354
—anr. ed. "Southern history of the great civil war ...," *Tor* 1863. O 383

POLLARD, EDWARD A.   **450**
The key to the Ku Klux... n.p. n.d. D 32 a

POLLARD, EDWARD A.   **451**
The last year of the war. *N Y* 1866. O 363 4ports a
Only a small edition, and no reprint, was issued of this final volume, the publisher almost immediately bringing out the 4 series complete in 2 volumes; *see* below, *Southern history of the war.*

POLLARD, EDWARD A.   **452**
Lee and his lieutenants... *N Y* 1867. O 851 7pls a
—rptd., same impr. & collat. 1868.
—anr. ed. "The early life, campaigns... of Robert E. Lee; with... deeds of his companions in arms," *N Y* 1870. O [26] 33–851 6pls

[POLLARD, EDWARD A.]   **453**
Letters of the southern spy, in Washington and elsewhere. [*Balt* 1861]. D 92 [3] aa

—rptd., au. named, with 3add. letters, "The southern spy. Letters on the policy and inauguration of the Lincoln war," *Rich* 1862. 16° 108 a
—ed. 3 same impr. & date D 118

POLLARD, EDWARD A.   **454**
Life of Jefferson Davis, with a secret history of the southern confederacy... *Phil* [1869]. O [8] 536 port a

POLLARD, EDWARD A.   **455**
The lost cause... *N Y* 1866. O 752 6pls a
—enl. ed., same impr. 1867. O [2] 762 map 6pls
—rptd., same impr. & collat. 1868.
—Fr. tr., with notes by tr., *N O* 1867. Q 420 [3] 3maps 8pls

POLLARD, EDWARD A.   **456**
The lost cause regained. *N Y* 1868. D 214 a

POLLARD, EDWARD A.   **457**
Observations in the north: eight months in prison and on parole. *Rich* 1865. O 142 a
Last book published during the Confederate regime, with the possible exception of Keiley's *Prisoner of war.*

POLLARD, EDWARD A.   **458**
The rival administrations: Richmond and Washington in December, 1863. *Rich* 1864. O [8] 32 aa
Part only of his *Third year of the war,* [*q. v.*] Attacks Lincoln's inhumanity and Davis' political ineptitude.

POLLARD, EDWARD A.   **459**
The second battle of Manassas... *Rich* 1862. O 48 aa

POLLARD, EDWARD A.   **460**
The second year of the war. *Rich* 1863. O [10] 17–326 iss 2 has cov. t. dated 1864 aa
—rptd. *N Y* 1863. O [10] 17–386 map 5 ports; also *N Y* 1864 & 1865. same collat.

POLLARD, EDWARD A.   **461**
The seven days battles... *Rich* 1862. O 45 aa
—anr. issue, same date & collat., *Charleston.* a

POLLARD, EDWARD A.   **462**
Southern history of the war. *N Y* 1866. O 2v: 676; 644. 20ports a
—rptd., same date & impr. O 2v in 1: [2] 657; [2] 5–598 [2] 20ports

[POLLARD, EDWARD A.]   **463**
The southern spy, or curiosities of slavery in the south... *Wash* 1859. D 72 a
—rptd., au. named, "Black diamonds gathered in the darkey homes of the south," *N Y* 1859. D [14] 17–122
—anr. ed. *N Y* 1860. D 155
See also, above, No. 553

POLLARD, EDWARD A.   464
The third year of the war. *N Y* 1865. O 391 +
3adv-p 5ports aa
—rptd. *N Y* 1866. same collat. a
—Eng. ed. "The war in America, 1863–64," *L*
1866. D [16] 407
Owing to lack of paper in the Confederacy, there
was no complete Richmond ed ion of this title;
for a portion only, *see* above, *The rival administra-*
tions . . .

POLLEY, J[OSEPH] B.   465
Hood's Texas brigade . . . *N Y* 1910. O 347 25pl sa

POLLEY, J[OSEPH] B.   466
A soldier's letters to charming Nellie . . . *N Y*
1908. O 317 16pls a

POLLOCK, J. M.   467
The unvarnished west: ranching as I found it.
L [1911]. O [8] 253 pls a

POMFREY, J. W.   468
A true disclosure . . . of the Knights of the Golden Circle . . . *Cin* [186–?]. 16° [6] 47 a

PONTGIBAUD, Chevalier de
See Moré, Chas. A.

PONTIAC'S CONSPIRACY.
Journal of: *See* Navarre, Robert.

PONTING (TOM CANDY).   469
Life of: [*Decatur Ill* 1907]. D 102 + wraps
2ports b G 25copies ptd.
—rptd., same collat. & impr., also n.d. [but done
1908]. 25copies ptd[13 in wraps, identical with ed.
1;12 bd. in clo] b Y
——anr. ed. *Evanston Ill* 1952. D [16] 133 4ports
a 500copies ptd.
Ponting was prominent in the western cattle
trade from 1848 to 1900; in 1854 he took Texas
longhorns to New York.

POOLE, CAPT. D[E WITT] C.   470
Among the Sioux of Dakota . . . *N Y* 1881. D
235 a
Author was Indian Agent at the Whetstone
Sioux Reservation in the 'sixties and a prominent
figure in military events on the Dakota-Wyoming-
Montana frontier.

POOR, HENRY V.   471
History of the railroads and canals of the United
States . . . Vol. I [all]. *N Y* 1860. O [8] 632 [3]
2maps[sometimes bound separately] a

[POOR, HENRY V.]   472
Influence of the railroads of the United States
in the creation of its commerce and wealth. *N Y*
1869. O 43 a

POOR, HENRY V.   473
The Pacific railroad. The relations . . . between
it and the Government . . . *N Y* 1871. O 55 a
—abr. ed. *N Y* 1879. O 16

POOR, JOHN A.   474
English colonization in America. A vindication
of the claims of Sir Ferdinando Gorges, as the
father of English colonization . . . *N Y* 1862. O
144 a

POORE, BEN: PERLEY [ed.]   475
The conspiracy trial for the murder of the Presi-
dent . . . *B* 1865. D 3v: 480; 552; 552 c G IaU IH
NYP
—anr. issue, in 10pts, wraps c IH
Only unexpurgated transcript.

POPE, JOHN, of Va.   476
A tour through the southern and western territories . . . *Rich* 1792. O 105p & errata 1f dd N
StLMerc [only perfect cops kn]
—rptd., with index added, *N Y* 1888. O 104 [4] this
repr. was made from a cop having only 104 p. Its
pub, on discovering this, printed p. 105 and it is
inserted in some cops.

POPE (GEN. [JOHN]).   477
Official communications from: . . . concerning
Indian affairs. *St L* 1865. D 30 a
Minnesota uprising, etc.

POPE, CAPTAIN JOHN   478
Report of exploration of a route for the Pacific
railroad . . . from the Red river to the Rio Grande.
[*Wash* 1855]. O 324 a
For series [House Executive Document 129] of
which this formed a part, and which contained a
map belonging to this report, *see Pacific railroad*
explorations.

POPE, [CAPTAIN] JOHN   479
Report of an exploration of the Territory of
Minnesota. *Wash* 1850. O 56 map a

POPE, WILLIAM F.   480
Early days in Arkansas . . . *Little Rock* 1895.
D 330 16pls a

POPPLE, HENRY   481
A map of the British empire in America . . . *L*
Austen [1732]. F contents 1f 20 sectional maps &
key map [Issue with maps colored preferred] b
JCB N NYP Y
—anr. ed. *L* 1733 b
—rptd. *Amst* Covens & Mortier [*ca* 1735]. F
6maps[incl. general or key map] some copies have
add.sheet[of 4views] b
Best map of the country at this date; the first
large-scale one done in the colonial period. Some
English editions give engravers as Toms and

Searle, others name Toms only; later ones, printed for Jefferys and Faden, give Kitchin as engraver. The Amsterdam issue was incorporated into Delisle's *Atlas nouveau* . . .

PORCHER, FRANCIS P.   482
Resources of the southern fields and forests . . . *Charleston S C* 1863. O [26] 601 aa
—anr. ed. *Rich* same date. O [26] 601 aa
—new ed. enl., *Charleston* 1869. O [16] 733 + 22adv-lvs a

PORCUPINE, PETER [pseud]
See Cobbett, Wm.

PORTER, CHARLES T.   483
Review of the Mexican war . . . *Auburn N Y* 1849. D 220 a

PORTER (CAPTAIN DAVID).   484
Journal of a cruise made to the Pacific ocean, by: in the . . . frigate Essex . . . 1812–1814 . . . *Phil* 1815. O 2v[generally bound in 1v]: [6] 263; [2] 169. 14maps & pls aa
—ed. 2, with adds., *N Y* 1822. O 2v: [76] 246; [4] 256. map port 7pls fold.tab aa
—Eng. ed., abr., "A voyage to the south seas . . .," *L* 1823. O [2] 126 map 2pls a
—Ital. tr. *Milan* 1820. D 3v 2maps 11pls a

PORTER, DAVID T.   485
Memoir of Commodore David Porter . . . *Alb* 1875. O [12] 427 port 25pls a

PORTER, EDWIN H.   486
The Fall river tragedy: a history of the Borden murders . . . *Fall River* 1893. O [4] 3–312 pls a
The perfect crime, committed by a girl; all the world believed her guilty, but it couldn't be proved.

PORTER, JACOB   487
Topographical description and historical sketch of Plainfield . . . Massachusetts. *Greenfield* 1834. O 44 port a

PORTER, MRS. LAVINIA H.   488
By ox team to California . . . in 1860. *Oakland* 1910. O [12] 139 port b 50copies ptd G NYP Y

PORTER, WILLIAM D.   489
State sovereignty and the doctrine of coercion . . . *Charleston S C* 1860. O 36 a

PORTER, WILLIAM S.   490
Historical notices of Connecticut. 2nos. [all]. *Hart* 1842. O 2v: 24 12; 13–48 a

PORTER, WILLIAM T., ed.
The big bear of Arkansas . . . *See* Thorpe, Thos. B.

PORTER, WILLIAM T., ed.   491
A quarter race in Kentucky . . . *Phil* 1847. D 203[incl. pls] aa
—rptd., same impr. 1850.
Ascribed to Geo. W. Harris.

PORTILLO, ESTEBAN, ed.   492
Apuntes para la historia antigua de Coahuila y Texas. *Saltillo* [1886]. D 482 [2] aa

PORTLAND [ORE.] DIRECTORY . . .   493
Port McCormick 1863. O 133 b
First Portland directory.

[PORTLOCK, NATHANIEL, and   494
DIXON, GEORGE]
An abridgement of Portlock and Dixon's voyage round the world. *L* Stockdale 1789. O 272 map pl aa
—rptd. *Dub* 1789. O 144 a
—Am. ed. "Voyage of Captains Portlock and Dixon to King George's sound . . .," *Phil* 1803. D 120 a
—Dutch ed. "Reis naar de noord-west Kust . . .," *Amst* 1795. Q [16] 265 [1] map 9pls
—Ger. tr. *Berlin* 1789. O 159

PORTLOCK, NATHANIEL, and   495
MORTIMER, GEORGE
Reisen an die Nortvestkuste von Amerika . . . *Berlin* 1796. O [8] 384 8maps & pls aa

[PORTLOCK, NATHANIEL, and   496
DIXON, GEORGE]
A voyage round the world . . . in the King George, commanded by Captain Portlock; and the Queen Charlotte, commanded by Captain Dixon . . . *L* 1789. O [6] 144 150–151 pl b NYP Y
Preface signed C. L.

PORTLOCK, NATHANIEL   497
A voyage round the world . . . particularly to the north-west coast of America . . . 1785–1788. *L* 1789. Q [12] 384 [40] 20maps & pls aa some copies have bird pls col. b
—Ger. tr., ed. J. R. Forster, *Berlin* 1790. Q [30] 314 map 11pls aa

PORTRAIT [A]   498
Portrait (A) of the evils of democracy . . . *Balt* 1816. O 101 a

PORY'S . . . DESCRIPTION   499
Pory's (John) lost description of Plymouth colony . . . *B* 1918. O [24] 65 2 fold. maps 4pls a 350 copies ptd.
First printing of a manuscript which antedated Bradford's *History*.

POSITIVELY TRUE.
A dialogue . . . *See* Van Dusen, Increase McG.

POST, C[HARLES] C.　　　　　　　**500**
Ten years a cowboy. *Chi* 1886. D [6] 17-358
14pls aa
—anr. issue, au. named as Tex Bender, *Chi* 1886.
same collat. aa
—anr. issue, au. given as Post, with 113-p. addenda
by Bender, same impr. & date. 18pls [4repeated] aa
—rptd., au. named as Post, with adds. by Tex
Bender, *Chi* 1887. D [6] 17–471 18pls [4 being
repeated] a
—anr. ed., au. given as Phil Johnson, t. changed to
"Life on the plains . . .," *Chi* 1888. same collat. as
ed. 1 a
—anr. ed., no au, given, with t. "Oklahoma boo-
mers life" *Chi* 1889. D [8] 358 a
—other *Chi* eds., with and without the adds.,
under variant authorship—Post, Bender, Johnson:
1890; 1893; 1895; 1896; 1897; 1899.
A cowboy autobiography preceded only by that
of Siringo.

POST (CHRISTIAN F.)　　　　　　**501**
The second journal of: . . . *L* 1759. O 67 b JCB
N NYP Y
Successful attempt of this Moravian missionary
to win over Indians on the Ohio from French to
British interests. For his first journal *see* Thomson,
Chas., *An enquiry* . . .

[POSTL, KARL]　　　　　　　　**502**
Das Cajütenbuch oder nationale Charakteristi-
ken . . . *Zurich* 1841. 16° 2v: [2] 300; [10] 421 aa
—rptd.: *Stuttgart* 1846; 1847 2v in 1 a
—Am. ed. "The cabin book; or, sketches of life in
Texas," *N Y* 1844. O [4] 155 a
—rptd. "Life in Texas," *Phil* 1845.
—Eng. eds: different tr. from Am. ed., *L* 1850;
L 1852. D [6] 296 8pls

[POSTL, KARL]　　　　　　　　**503**
Les émigrés francais dans la Louisiane (1800–
1804). *P* 1853. 16° [6] 194 [1] a
Translation of four fictional sketches in his
Lebensbilder aus beiden Hemisphären.

[POSTL, KARL]　　　　　　　　**504**
Life in the new world; or sketches of American
society. *N Y* [1842]. O 340 aa
—also issued serially, 5pts in 7nos aa
—ed. 2, same collat, *N Y* [1844] a
Translation of five sketches in his *Lebensbilder
aus beiden Hemisphären*, Zurich 1834–7, 6 volumes;
later issued at Stuttgart in 5 volumes, with title
slightly changed, 1843 and 1846.

[POSTL, KARL]　　　　　　　　**505**
Nathan der Squatter-Regulator, oder der erste
Amerikaner in Texas . . . [*Geschienen* 1837]. O [2]
451 aa

[POSTL, KARL]　　　　　　　　**506**
Die Vereinigten Staaten von Nordamerika nach
ihrem politischen . . . Verhältnisse betrachtet. Von
C. Sidons. *Stuttgart* 1827. O 2v: [10] 206; [4] 247 aa
—Dutch tr. *Leeuwarden* 1828. O a
—Eng. tr. [of v. I] "The United States . . . as they
are," *L* 1827. O [12] 242 [2] aa
—rptd. 1828. a
—Eng. tr. [of v. II] "The Americans as they are;
described in a tour through the valley of the Mississippi," *L* 1828. D [14] 218 [4] aa

POSTON, CHARLES D.　　　　　**507**
The Arizona election . . . *N Y* 1865. O 72 aa

POTE (CAPTAIN WILLIAM, JR.)　　**507a**
The journal of: during his captivity in the French
and Indian war . . . *N Y* 1896. O [40] 223 9maps &
pls + fold.map in separate vol. a 375copies ptd.[25
on Jap. P.]

POTENT ENEMIES [THE] OF AMERICA
See Benezet, Anthony.

POTIEKHIN, V.　　　　　　　　**508**
O byvshem Rossa, zaselenii na beregakh verkh-
nei Kalifornia. *St Ptbg* 1859. O 48 aa
Account of the Fort Ross Russian settlement in
California.

POTOMACK (RIVIER).
Beschryving der: *See* Lear, Tobias.:

POTTER, C[HANDLER] E.　　　　**509**
The history of Manchester . . . New Hampshire
. . . *Manchester* 1856. O [14] 67 764 46pls a

POTTER, ELISHA R.　　　　　　**510**
The early history of Narragansett . . . *Prov* 1835.
O [20] 316 a

[POTTER, ELIZA]　　　　　　　**511**
A hairdresser's experience in high life. *Cin* 1859.
D [4] 11–294 a

POTTER (ISRAEL R.)
Life and remarkable adventures of: . . . *See*
Trumbull, Henry.

POTTER, JACK M.　　　　　　　**512**
Cattle trails of the old west. *Clayton New Mex*
1935. O 40 fold.map aa
—rev. ed., same impr. [1939] D 87 map

POTTER, JACK M.　　　　　　　**513**
Lead steer, etc. *Clayton, N Mex* 1939. O [18]
13–116 7pls a

POTTER (THEODORE E.)　　　　**514**
The autobiography of: [*Concord N H* 1913].
O [12] 228 3ports a
Describes his 1852 overland trip to California,
adventures as a filibuster with Walker, etc.

[POTTER, WOODBURNE]   515
The war in Florida ... its causes [etc.]. By a
late staff officer. *Balt* 1836. D [8] 184 3maps &
plans aa
Unsparingly critical of Jackson, Jesup and the
Secretary of War.

POUCHOT, [FRANCOIS]   516
Mémoires sur la dernière guerre de l'Amérique
Septentrionale, entre la France et l'Angleterre ...
Yverdon 1781. D 3v: [42] 184; [4] 308; [4] 398.
3maps c H N NYP Y
—Eng. tr. by F. B. Hough, with notes, *Roxbury*
1866. O 2v: [4] 268; 283. 21maps & pls 200 copies
ptd[of which 50 were in Q and 7 were on Whatman
paper] aa
Contemporary authority of the first importance
from the French point of view; Capt. Pouchot
commanded forts Niagara and Lévis.

[POULLIN DE LUMINA]   517
Histoire de la guerre contre les Anglois ...
Geneva 1759 60. O 2v: [24] 244; [28] 211 aa
Contains account of Washington's operations
on the Ohio, and accuses him of assassinating
Jumonville.

POUSSIN, GUILLAUME T.   518
Chemins de fer américains ... *P* 1836. Q [20]
271 map 7pls a
—ed. 2, *Brus* 1836. Q 124 map 7pls
—Ger. tr. *Regensburg* 1837. O [20] 408 map pl
Supplements the author's *Travaux d'améliorations intérieures, see* below, No. 521

POUSSIN, GUILLAUME T.   519
De la puissance américaine. *P* 1843. O 2v: [28]
554; [12] 428, map a
—ed. 2, *P* 1843. O 2v same collat.
—ed. 3, *P* 1848. O 2v: [4] 492; [4] 448
—Eng. tr. "The United States; its power ...,"
Phil 1851. O [24] 33–488

POUSSIN, GUILLAUME T.   520
Question de l'Oregon ... *P* 1846. O 100 a

POUSSIN, GUILLAUME T.   521
Travaux d'améliorations intérieures ... par le
gouvernement ... des États-Unis. *P* 1834. Q [32]
364 + atlas F [4] 10pls a

POWELL, C. FRANK   522
Life of ... Zachary Taylor ... *N Y* 1846. O 96
port a
—enl. ed. *N Y* 1847. O 121 port

POWELL, CUTHBERT   523
Twenty years of Kansas City's livestock trade
... [*K C* 1893]. O 345 aa
In the first issue author's name is not on spine.

POWELL, FRED W.   524
Hall Jackson Kelley, prophet of Oregon. *Port
Ore.* 1917. O 185 port 3maps & plans a 100copies
ptd.
Separate from *Oregon Historical Quarterly.*

POWELL, H. M. T.   525
The Santa Fé trail to California ... Ed. D. S.
Watson, *S F* Grabhorn [1931]. Q [16] 272 18maps
& pls b N NYP Y 315 copies ptd [15 with col.
pls]
Day-by-day journal from Illinois, via Santa Fe,
to San Diego.

POWELL, JOHN J.   526
Nevada: the land of silver. *S F* 1876. O [7] 306
+ 6adv-p errata slip a

POWELL, JOHN W.   527
Canyons of the Colorado. *Meadville Pa* 1895.
Q 400 + adv-p front. 10fold.pls aa
First complete narrative; his earlier reports were
largely devoted to scientific data.

POWELL, JOHN W.   528
Exploration of the Colorado river ... 1869–
1872. *Wash* 1875. Q [10 7–11] 291 2maps [on 1
sheet] 80 views [on 68 sheets] a

POWELL, J[OHN] W.   529
Report of explorations in 1873 of the Colorado
of the west ... *Wash* 1874. O 36 a

POWELL, WILLIAM H.   530
A history of the ... Fourth Regiment of Infantry ... *Wash* 1871. O 215 aa

POWELL, WILLIS J.   531
A brief sketch of ... Santa-Anna ... *St L* 1844.
D 36 aa only 1 cop loc

POWER, JOHN C.   532
History of the early settlers of Sangamon
county, Illinois ... *Springfield* 1876. O 798 map
2ports aa

POWER, TYRONE   533
Impressions of America ... 1833–1836. *L* 1836.
O 2v: [16] 440; [6] 408. 2pls a
—Am. ed., cor. by au., *Phil* 1836. D 2v: [8] 13–262
[2]; 219
—ed. 2, same date, impr. & collat.
The author's full name was William Gratton
Tyrone Power.

POWER (THE)   534
Power (The) and grandeur of Great-Britain,
founded on the liberty of the colonies ... *Phil*
1768. O 22 aa
—rptd. *N Y* same date. O 24 aa

POWERS, GRANT   535
Historical sketches of the . . . Coos country [N. H.]. *Haverhill N H* 1841. D 240 a
—rptd., same impr. & collat. 1880.

POWERS, JULIUS H.   536
History and reminiscences of Chickasaw county, [Iowa]. *Des M* 1894. O 332 port a

POWERS, STEPHEN   537
Afoot and alone; a walk from sea to sea by the southern route . . . *Hart* 1872. O [6] 11–327 12pls + adv-p a
—ed. 2, same impr. 1884.
Vivid narrative of a pedestrian pilgrimage of 3500 miles from Carolina to California.

POWESHIEK COUNTY, IOWA.   538
A descriptive account . . . *Montezuma Ia* 1865. O 38 aa

[POWNALL, THOMAS]   539
The administration of the colonies. *L* 1764. O [2] 131 a
—ed. 2, enl., au.named, *L* 1765. O [28] 202 [60]
—ed. 3, further enl., *L* 1766. O [28] 202 60 [52]
—ed. 4, *L* 1768. O [32] 318 [73]
—ed. 5, with Pt. 2 added, but omitting "Considerations on . . . Parliament's right of taxing the colonies," which appeared in eds. 3 & 4, *L* 1774. O 2v: [20] 288; [12] 308
—ed. 6, *L* 1777. same collat.
Suggests the formation of a union of the thirteen colonies.

[POWNALL, THOMAS]   540
Considerations on the points lately brought into question as to the . . . right of taxing the colonies . . . *L* 1766. O [2] 52 a
Included also as an appendix in the third and fourth editions of *The administration of the colonies, see* above, No. 539

POWNALL, T[HOMAS]   541
A memorial addressed to the sovereigns of America . . . *L* 1783. O [6] 139 aa
Foresees the wisdom of supplanting the original government, under the Articles of Confederation, by a more centralized form.

[POWNALL, THOMAS]   542
A memorial . . . to the sovereigns of Europe, on the present state of affairs between the old and new world. *L* 1780. O [10] 127 aa
—ed. 2, same impr. & collat. 1781. a
—Fr. tr. *L* 1781. O 6 [8] 82
—rptd., same impr. 1782. O [4] 8 [8] 82
For an unauthorized transliteration, *see* Jenings, Edmund, *A translation of the Memorial* . . .

POWNALL, THOMAS   543
A topographical description of . . . parts of

North America . . . contained in the (annexed] map of the middle British colonies. *L* 1776. F [6] 46 [16] map b N NYP Y There were 2printings, identical, of 1000copies each, some on L.P.
—rev. ed. *Pitt* 1949. Q [16] 235 2maps front. 3facs a
An improved version of Lewis Evans's *Map* and *Analysis* of 1755. Contains the first printing of the first of Gist's *Journals* and of Gordon's *Journal of an expedition to the Illinois.* Some copies were issued on L.P., with map colored. Pownall uses *verbatim*, without quotation marks, the Preface of Evans's *Analysis*, which indicates his anonymous authorship of that preface.

POWNALL, THOMAS   544
Two memorials, not originally intended for publication . . . *L* 1782. O [4] 58 errata slip a
Outlines a plan for a truce and eventual peace with the colonies, submitted earlier in the war to the British ministry, but never acted upon.

POWYS (MR. [THOMAS?]).   545
Letter to: on the independency of America. By a man of candor . . . *L* 1778. O 44 a

[POYAS, MRS. ELIZABETH A.]   546
Carolina in the olden time. *Charleston* 1855. D [4] 202 a

[POYAS, MRS. ELIZABETH A.]   547
Days of yore; or shadows of the past. Parts I & II. *Charleston S C* 1870. D 2v: [4] 43; 44 a

[POYAS, MRS. ELIZABETH A.]   548
Our forefathers; their homes . . . *Charleston S C* 1860. D 172 a

[POYAS, MRS. ELIZABETH A.]   549
A peep into the past. *Charleston S C* 1853. D 238 a

PRACTICAL GUIDE (A)
Practical guide (A) for emigrants to North America . . . By a seven years' resident . . . *See* Nettle, Geo.

PRAIRIE VERSUS BUSH . . .
See Cook and Sargent, pubs.

PRAIRIEDOM
Prairiedom; rambles and scrambles in Texas . . . *See* Page, Frederic B.

PRASLOW, DR. J.   550
Der Staat Californien in medicinisch-geographischer Hinsicht. *Göttingen* 1857. O [6] 66 a
—Eng. tr. *S F* 1939. O [18] 86 [2] facs 250 cops ptd.

PRATT, ENOCH   551
A comprehensive history . . . od Eastham, Wellfleet and Orleans . . . Mass. *Yarmouth* 1844. O [8] 180 a

PRATT, GEORGE W.   552
An account of the British expedition above the
highlands of the Hudson river and . . . the burning
of Kingston in 1777. *Alb* 1861. Q 73 a 50copies ptd.

PRATT, [JOHN J.], and HUNT,   553
[HENRY J.?]
Guide to the gold mines of Kansas . . . *Chi*
1859. O 70 [10] map c N WisH Y [of 4copies
known]

PRATT, JULIUS H.   554
Reminiscences . . . [with the narrative of a sea
trip to California in 1849.] n.p. 1910. D [10] 287
9pls a

PRATT, PARLEY P.   555
An appeal to the inhabitants of . . . New York.
Milw [1841?]. O 24 [incl. cover t.] b Y
—anr. ed. *Nauvoo* [1841?]. O [2] 40 aa

PRATT (PARLEY P.)   556
The autobiography of: *N Y* 1874. D 502 [10]
6pls a

PRATT, PARLEY P.   557
An exile of Missouri. *Nauvoo* [1844]. O 40 b

PRATT, PARLEY P.   558
History of the late persecution . . . by the state
of Missouri upon the Mormons . . . *Det* 1839. D
40 no copy located c
—rptd. *Mexico N Y* 1840. D 40 b WisH
—enl. ed. with adds., "Late persecution . . .," *N Y*
1840. 16° 216 a

PRATT, PARLEY P.   559
Mormonism unveiled. *N Y* 1838. O 47 a
—rptd. several times, same impr., date & collat.

PRATT, PARLEY P.   560
Scriptural evidences in support of polygamy.
S F 1856. O 24 a

PRATT'S . . . GUIDE   561
Pratt's river and railroad guide . . . *N Y* [1848]
16° 119 aa

[PRAY, ISAAC C.]   562
Memoirs of James Gordon Bennett and his
times. *N Y* 1855. D [6] 15–488 port a

PREBLE (COMMODORE EDWARD).
The life of: *See* Kirtland, John T.

[PREBLE, GEORGE H.]   563
The chase of the rebel steamer . . . Oreto . . .
into the bay of Mobile, by the . . . steam sloop
Oneida . . . *C* priv. ptd. 1862. O 60 a
—anr. ed., *C* Farnham 1862. O 48

PREBLE, GEORGE H.   564
The first cruise of the . . . frigate Essex, with a
short account of her origin and subsequent career
until captured by the British, in 1814 . . . *Salem*
1870. O [2] 108 a

PREBLE, GEORGE H.   565
Our flag; origin and progress of the flag of
the United States . . . *Alb* 1872. O [12] 11-535
14pls a
—ed. 2, rev., "History of the flag . . .," *B* 1880.
O [22] 815 port 10pls
—rptd. *B* 1893; O; *Phil* 1917, O 2v

PRÉCIS   566
Précis historique de la révolution des États-Unis
. . . *Ghent* [1782?]. O [4] 3–28 a

Précis politique sur l'origine de la guerre   567
des Américains . . . *L* 1783. D 39 a

Précis sur l'Amérique . . . *See* Mandrillon, Jos.

PRELIMINARY ARTICLES   568
**Preliminary articles [The] of peace between Great
Britain, France, Spain and the United States** . . .
**signed at Versailles, 20th January, 1783. Authentic
copies of:** *L* 1783. O 32 a
—anr. ed., t. slightly altered, *L* 1783. O 28

Preliminary articles of peace, between His   569
**Britannick Majesty, the most Christian king, and
the Catholick king, signed at Fontainebleau, the 3rd
day of November, 1762.** *L* 1762. Q 23 a
For final terms, signed at Paris, the following
year, *see The definitive treaty* . . .

[PRENTISS, CHARLES]   570
The life of the late Gen. William Eaton . . . from
his correspondence . . . *Brookfield* 1813. O 448
port a
Though published at the expense of the son-in-
law of this unstable adventurer, none of his frailties
—vanity, arrogance, intemperance, connection
with Burr's conspiracy—are concealed.

[PRENTISS, GEORGE L.]   571
A memoir of S. S. Prentiss. *N Y* 1855. D 2v: 382;
581 a
—rptd., same impr. 1856; 1858.

PRENTISS (S. S.)
A memoir of: Edited by his brother. *See* Prentiss, Geo. L., above.

[PRESCOTT, BENJAMIN]   572
A free and calm consideration of the unhappy
misunderstanding . . . between the Parliament of
Great-Britain, and these . . . colonies . . . *Salem*
1774. O 52 aa

PRESCOTT, GEORGE F.
The Lee trial! An exposé of the Mountain Meadows massacre . . . *S L C* 1875. *See* Lee, John D.

PRESENT   573
Present claims [The] and complaints of America briefly . . . considered. *L* 1806. O [16] 48 a

Present ctisis (The) with respect to Amer-   574
ica, considered . . . *L* 1775. O [2] 46 a

Present hour (The). *L* 1782. O [2] 41 a   575

Present [The] state of Great Britain and North America . . . *See* Mitchell, John.

Present state [The] of his Majesties . . . territories in America. *See* Blome, Richard.

Present state [The] of liberty in Great   576
Britain and her colonies. By an Englishman. *L* 1769. O 32 a

Present state [The] of North America . . . *See* Huske, John.

Present state [The] of the British empire . . . *See* Goldsmith, J.

Present state of the nation. *See* Knox, Wm.

PRESTON, THOMAS L.   577
Historical sketches . . . *Rich* 1900. O [2] 7–170 port a

PRESTON, WALTER W.   578
History of Harford county, Maryland . . . *Balt* 1901. O 360 [19] port 5pls a

PRESTON, LT. COL. WILLIAM   579
Journal in Mexico . . . 1847–8. *P* n.d. Q 48 small ed. aa

PREVOST (MR. [J. B.])   580
Message from the President [Monroe] . . . communicating the letter of: . . . relating to an establishment made at the mouth of the Columbia river. *Wash* 1823. O 65 tab aa

PREVOST (SIR GEORGE).
The letters of Veritas . . . containing a succinct narrative of the military administration of: *see* Richardson, Major John.

PREVOST (the late LIEUTENANT-GENERAL SIR GEORGE).
Some account of the public life of: . . . *See* Brenton, E. B.

PRICE, EBENEZER   581
A chronological register of Boscawen . . . New-Hampshire . . . *Concord* 1823. O 116 a

PRICE, GEORGE F.   582
Across the continent with the Fifth Cavalry . . . *N Y* 1883. O 706 4ports aa
—rptd. *N Y* 1960, same collat a

PRICE, RICHARD   583
Additional observations on the nature . . . of civil liberty, and the war with America . . . *L* 1777. O [16] 176 a
—ed. 2, with suppl., *L* 1777. O [16] 176 [36] fold. tab
—rptd. *Dub* 1777. O [24] 260
—ed. 3, *L* 1778. O [22] 176
—later eds. entitled "Two tracts on civil liberty . . ."
—Am. ed. *Phil* 1778. O 122
—Dutch ed. *Leyden* 1777. O 58 106

PRICE, RICHARD   584
The general introduction and supplement to the two tracts on civil liberty . . . *L* 1778. O [28] 181–216 fold.tab a
—ed. 2, *L* 1778. O [32] 36 fold.tab
—Am. eds.: *Phil* 1778. O 27; same impr. & date. O [2] 15
Supplements the author's *Additional observations* . . .

PRICE (the REV. DR. [RICHARD]).
A letter to: wherein his Observations on the nature of civil liberty . . . are candidly examined . . . By a lover of peace . . . *See* Stewart, James, of London.

PRICE, RICHARD   585
Observations on the importance of the American revolution . . . *L* 1784. O [2] 110 + 2adv-p a
—rptd., with adds., *L* 1785. O [8] 156
—anr. ed. *Dub* 1785. O [8] 156
—Am. ed. *B* 1784. O 88
—rptd. *N Hav* 1785. O 65[i.e. 87]; *Trenton* 1785. O 88; *Bennington* 1785. O 84
—Am. ed. 2, *Phil* 1785. O [2] 60 [2]; and 3 other eds. by 1820.
Price, intimate friend of Franklin, was the most influential British advocate of American independence.

PRICE, RICHARD   586
Observations on the nature of civil liberty . . . and the justice and policy of the war with America . . . *L* 1776. O [8] 128 a
—rptd., in at least 13 other eds., same yr.
—Am. eds.: *Phil* 1776. O 71; *B* 1776. same collat; *N Y* 1776. O 107; *Charleston S C* 1776. O [8] 104
—Fr. tr. *Rotterdam* 1776. O [6] 48
—Ger. tr. *Braunschweig* 1777. O 108; *Leip* 1777.

PRICE (DR. [RICHARD]).
Remarks on a pamphlet . . . by: intitled [*sic*], Observations on the nature of civil liberty . . . *See* Ferguson, Dr. Adam.

PRICE (DR. [RICHARD]).
Three letters to: containing remarks on his Observations ... By a member of Lincoln's Inn ... *See* Lind, John.

PRICE'S NOTIONS
Price's (Doctor) notions of the nature of civil liberty ... contradictory to reason ... *See* Gray, John.

PRICE'S THEORY
Price's (Dr.) theory and principles of civil liberty ... Observations on: *See* Goodricke, Henry.

PRICE, SIR ROSE L.   587
A summer on the Rockies. *L* 1898. D [10] 279 map 2pls a

PRICE, SAMUEL W.   588
The old masters of the bluegrass. *Louisv* Filson Club 1902. Q [18] 181 15pls a

PRICE, REV. T.   589
A narrative of the adventure and escape of Moses Roper, from American slavery. *L* 1837. 16° 108 a
—rptd., same impr., date & collat.
—Am. ed. *B* 1838. 18° 89
—rptd., same impr. & date. D [8] 72

PRICE, T. M.   590
An historic narrative of the bear flag revolution. n.p. [*ca* 1912?]. O 23 [cover t. only] a

PRICE, WILLIAM T.   591
Historical sketches of Pocahontas county, W. Va. *Marlinton* 1901. O [6] 622 [3] 2pls a

PRIEST, JOSIAH   592
American antiquities ... *Alb* 1833. O 400 map 2pls a
—eds. 2 & 3, same impr., date & collat.
—rptd. several times.

PRIEST, JOSIAH   593
The captivity ... of Gen. Freegift Patchin ... among the Indians under Brant ... *Alb* 1833. D 50 pl b NYP [of 4 cops loc]
—ed. 2, *Lansingburg* 1841. aa

PRIEST, JOSIAH   594
A copy of the grants to the Van Renssaeler and Livingston families ... with a history of the settlement of Albany ... *Alb* 1844. O 32 b

PRIEST, JOSIAH   595
The Fort Stanwix captive ... adventures of Isaac Hubbell among the Indians ... from the lips of the hero himself. *Alb* 1841. O [32] b N NYP Y 600 cops ptd.

PRIEST, JOSIAH   596
History of the early adventures of Washington among the Indians of the west. *Alb* 1841. O 64 aa

PRIEST, JOSIAH   597
The Low Dutch prisoner ... capture of Frederick Schermerhorn ... by a party of Mohawks ... *Alb* 1839. O 32 b LC N
—anr. issue, "The Low Dutch boy ...," same date & collat., *N Lond* aa

PRIEST, JOSIAH   598
Slavery, as it relates to the Negro ... with strictures on abolitionism. *Alb* 1843. D 340 a
—rptd., same impr. & collat. 1844; 1845.
—ed. 5, enl. "Bible defence of slavery ...," *Glasgow Ky* 1852. O [10] 3–569 8

PRIEST, JOSIAH   599
Stories of early settlers in the wilderness ... *Alb* 1837. O 40 front. aa

PRIEST, JOSIAH   600
Stories of the revolution ... *Alb* 1836. O 32 pl aa
—ed. 2 same impr & collat a
—rptd., same collat., *Alb* 1838.

PRIEST, JOSIAH   601
A true narrative of David Ogden among the Indians ... *Lansingburgh* 1840. O 32 front aa
—rptd., same impr. & collat., 1841. aa
—anr. ed. *Essex Junct.* 1929 a

PRIEST, JOSIAH   602
A true story of the ... adventures and sufferings of Matthew Calkins ... never before published, [etc.]. *Lansingburgh* 1832. O 40 b
—other eds., same impr. & collat.: 1833; 1840; 1841. aa
Includes also captivity of Gen. Patchin and other material.

PRIEST, WILLIAM   603
Travels in the United States ... *L* 1802. O [12] 214 front. aa

PRIESTLY, HERBERT I., ed. & tr.   604
The Luna papers: documents relating to the expedition of Don Tristán de Luna y Arellano for the conquest of La Florida, 1559–61. *Deland Fla* 1928. O 2v: [64] 272; [16] 384. 7 pls map 360copies ptd. aa

PRIESTLY, JOSEPH   605
Letters to the inhabitants of Northumberland [Pa.] and its neighborhood ... Pts. I & II. *Northumberland* 1799. O 2v: [4] 48; 42 [1] aa
—rptd., with added letter on Liancourt's travels in the U. S., *Phil* 1800. O [6] 96 a
—ed. 2, same impr. & collat. 1801.

PRIESTLY (JOSEPH).   **606**
Memoirs of: written by himself: with a continuation ... by his son ... *Nothumberland Pa*
1806. O 2v: [12] 336; [6] 337–824 [10] errata slip
errata lf aa
—Eng. ed. *L* 1806–7. O 2v: [12] 469[for 481];
482–824. 2errata lvs [in some copies a 10-p bibliog.
added to v.2] aa

[PRIETO, GUILLERMO]   **607**
Viaje á los Estados Unidos. *Mex* 1877–8. O 3v:
[10] 625 [2]; 593 [2]; 532 [2]. 30pls aa
—Eng. tr. of a portion only, *S F* 1938. Q [24] 91
3pls a 650 cops ptd
Sketches of most of our large cities, including
San Francisco.

PRIME, NATHANIEL S.   **608**
A history of Long Island ... *N Y* 1845. D [12]
420 map a

[PRIMM, WILSON]   **609**
Report of the celebration of the anniversary of
the founding of St. Louis ... *St L* 1847. O 32 aa

PRINCE, FREDERIC   **610**
The story of Fort Hill ... previous to the settlement of Auburn ... *Auburn N Y* 1859. O 50 a

PRINCE, L. BRADFORD   **611**
Historical sketches of New Mexico ... *N.Y. &
K C* 1883. D 327 a
—ed. 2 *K C* 1883

PRINCE, L. BRADFORD   **612**
New Mexico's struggle for statehood ... *Santa
Fe* 1910. O 128 [2] front. a

PRINCE, L. BRADFORD   **613**
Spanish mission churches of New Mexico ...
Cedar Rapids 1915. O 374[incl. pls] + adv-p a

PRINCE, THOMAS   **614**
Annals of New England. Vol.II, 3nos. [all]. *B*
[1755]. D 96 b AA H MH
For vol. I, *see* below *A chronological history of
New England*, No. 615.

PRINCE, THOMAS   **615**
A chronological history of New-England ...
Vol. I [all]. *B* 1736. D [42] 104 [2] 254 aa
—complete ed., with v.2 added, *B* 1826. O 2v in 1:
439 a
—ed. 3, sheets of 1826 ed., with new t. & adds., *B*
1852. O [18] 3-12, 5–439 7pls[14 in some of the 30
copies issued] a
Though merely a skeletonized register of historical fragments, our most scholarly colonial work.
For volume two, *see* above, No. 614.

[PRINCE, THOMAS?]   **616**
The vade mecum for America: or a companion

for traders and travellers ... *B* 1731. D [8] 220 aa
—rptd.: same impr. & collat, 1732; 1733, aa

PRINCETON, ILLINOIS.
Sketches of the early settlement ... of: *See*
Smith, Isaac B.

PRINCIPLES
**Principles [The], history, and use, of air-balloons
... *See* Blanchard, Jean Pierre.**

Principles of law and government ... the   617
justice and policy of the present war ... *L* 1781.
Q 2pts: [6] 202; [2] 127 [1] a
Defense of the colonies, probably written by
Franklin's friend, David Williams.

PRINDLE, CYRUS   **618**
Memoir of the Rev. Daniel Meeker Chandler
... missionary among the Indians, at Kewa-we-
non, and Sault St. Marie ... *Middlebury Vt* 1842.
D 114 a

[PRINGLE, EDWARD J.]   **619**
Slavery in the southern states. *C* 1852. D [2] 53 a
—ed. 2, same impr., date & collat.
—ed. 3, au. named, *C* 1853. same collat.

PRINGLE, J. J.   **620**
Twenty years of snipe-shooting ... *N Y* 1899.
O [12] 324 pls aa

[PRINGLE, JOHN]   **621**
The life of General James Wolfe ... *L* 1760. Q
[4] 24 aa
—Am. eds., same date: *B* O 36; *Portsmouth* O 24 aa.
Ascribed also to John Penrose.

PRISONER OF WAR
Prisoner of war, or five months among the Yan-
kees ... By A. Rifleman, Esq.... *See* Keiley,
A. M.

[PRITTS, JOSEPH]   **622**
Incidents of border life ... *Chambersburg* 1839.
O 491 5pls aa
—issue 2, enl. to 507p with 6pls aa
—ed 2, *Lancaster* 1841. O 491 front.
—other eds.: *Chambersburg* 1841, O 511 7 pls;
Lancaster 1842, O 491 7pls a
—anr. ed., with adds. & omissions, and differently
arranged, "Mirror of olden time border life ...,"
Abingdon Va 1849. O 700 13pls[17 in a few copies]
aa
—Ger. tr. "Abentheuerliche Ereignisse aus dem
Leben der ersten Ansiedler an den Grenzen der
mittleren und westlichen Staaten ...," *Chambersburg* 1839, O 537 front; *Lancaster* 1842, O 537 7pls a

PRIVATE (THE) IN GRAY ...
By a private. *See* Smith, Wm. Calvin.

PROCEEDINGS 623
Proceedings of the American Equal Rights Association..., N. Y., May 9th & 10th, 1867. *N Y* 1867. O 80 a

Proceedings (The) of the Executive of the 624 United States respecting the insurgents. *Phil* 1795. O 130 aa

Proceedings of the Republican national 625 convention... *Chi* 1860. O 153 a

PROCTOR, GEORGE H. 626
The fishermen's memorial... containing a list of vessels and their crews, lost from the port of Gloucester, 1830–1873. *Gloucester* 1873. O [4] 172 a

PROCTOR, GEORGE H. 627
The fishermen's own book... men and vessels lost from... Gloucester, 1874–1882. *Gloucester* [1882]. O [2] 274 3pls a

PROFITABLE ADVICE
Profitable advice for rich and poor. In a dialogue between James Freeman, a Carolina planter, and Simeon Question... *See* Norris, John.

PROMINENT FEATURES 628
Prominent features of a northern tour... *Charleston S C* 1822. D 48 aa

PROOFS
Proofs that Great Britain was successful against each of her numerous enemies... *See* Barrington, Daines.

PROPHETICK DISCUSSION (THE).
See Strang, James J.

PROPHETS (THE)
Prophets (The); or, Mormonism unveiled... *See* Belisle, Orvilla S.

PROPOSALS 629
Proposals for a plan towards a reconciliation... with the thirteen provinces of America... By one of the publick. *L* 1778. O [8] 41 a

Proposals for carrying on an effectual war 630 in America, against the French and Spaniards... *L* 1702. sm Q 24 aa
These prophetic suggestions were pretty much carried out in the French war fifty years later.

Proposals for uniting the English colonies on the continent of America... *See* McCulloh, Henry.

Proposals to amend and perfect the policy 631 of the government of the United States... n.p. 1782. D 36 a

PROPOSITION (A) 632
Proposition (A) for the present peace and future government of the British colonies in North America. *L* [1775]. O [6] 54 a

PROSCH, CHARLES 633
Reminiscences of Washington Territory... *Seattle* 1904. O 128 2pls port a

PROSCH, THOMAS W. 634
David S. Maynard and Catherine T. Maynard... two of the Oregon immigrants of 1850. *Seattle* [1906]. O 80 2ports a

PROSCH, THOMAS W. 635
McCarver and Tacoma. *Seattle* 1906. O [8] 198 2pls a

PROSE AND POETRY 636
Prose and poetry of the live stock industry. Vol.I [all]. *Denver & K C* [1905]. Q [4] 7–757 10ports c LC G NYP Y
—rptd. *N Y* 1959. Q aa

PRO-SLAVERY ARGUMENT (THE)
Pro-slavery argument (The); as maintained by... distinguished writers of the south. *See* Harper, William C., *et al.*

PROSPECT
Prospect (The) before us... *See* Callender, James T.

Prospect (The) before us, or, strictures on 637 the late message of the President of the United States... *Charleston S C* 1832. D 24 a

Prospect (A) of the consequences of the 638 present conduct of Great Britain towards America *L* 1776. O 98 + 2adv-p a

PROTEST
Protest against the bill to repeal the American Stamp act. *See Correct copies of the two protests...*

PROUD, ROBERT 639
The history of Pennsylvania... *Phil* 1797–8. O 2v: 508: 373 [146]. map port aa

PROVIDENCE STATE (THE). 640
A historical account of: *Prov* 1868. D 297 a 200copies ptd.

PROVIDENTIAL ASPECT
Providential aspect... of the existing crisis. *See* Bridge, Isaac.

PROVISIONAL... CONSTITUTIONS 641
Provisional and permanent constitutions... with the acts... of the first session of the provisional congress, of the Confederate States. *Montg* 1861. O 160 a

—anr. ed. *Rich* 1861. O 159 [some copies of this ed. have the acts of the 2nd & 3rd sessions of the provisional congress bound in]

PROWE, A.   **642**
John Osawatomie Brown, der Negerheiland ... *Braunschweig* 1876. O 148 a

PRUDHOMMEAUX, JULES J.   **643**
Histoire de la communauté icarienne. *Nîmes* 1906. O [28] 484 a

PRUDHOMMEAUX, JULES J.   **644**
Icarie et son fondateur. Étienne Cabet ... *P* 1907. O [40] 688 2maps 12pls facs a
—rptd. same impr. & collat. 1926.

PUBLIC GOOD
Public good ... examination into the claim of Virginia to the vacant western territory. *See* Paine, Thos.

Public good without private interests ... *See* Gatford, Lionel.

PUCKETT, J[AMES] L., and ELLEN   **645**
History of Oklahoma and Indian territory and homeseeker's guide. *Vinita* 1906. O 152 [incl. wraps & pls] a

[PUELLES, JOSE MARIA]   **646**
Informe ... sobre limites de la provincia de Tejas con la de la Luisiana. *Zacatecas* 1828. O [6] 38 d B G Hn S Y [of 7cops loc]
Study of the conflicting claims concerning the Louisiana-Texas boundary by a resident of Nacodoches.

PUGET SOUND ... DIRECTORY
Puget Sound business directory ... 1872. *See* Murphy and Harned.

PULASKI VINDICATED ...
See Bentalou, Paul.

PULSZKY, FRANCIS and THERESA   **647**
White, red and black; sketches of society in the United States ... *L* 1853. D 3v: [12] 288; [6] 344; [6] 281 + 6adv-p a
—Am. ed. *N Y* 1853. D 2v: [4, 7–12] 331; 342
—Ger ed. *Kassell* 1853. O 5v [bd in 2v.]

[PULTENEY, WILLIAM]   **648**
Plan of re-union between Great Britain and her colonies. *L* 1778. O [16] 211 a

[PULTENEY, WILLIAM]   **649**
Thoughts on the present state of affairs with America ... *L* 1778. O [4] 100 a
—eds. 2, 3 & 4, same impr.: and date
—rptd. *Dub* 1778.

—ed. 5, with Franklin letter dated 1778 added, *L* 1778. O [4] 111

PUMPELLY, RAPHAEL   **650**
Across America and Asia ... and ... a residence in Arizona ... *N Y* 1870. O [16] 454 4maps 12pls a
—eds. 2 & 3, rev., same impr., date & collat.
—enl. ed. "My reminiscences," *N Y* 1918. O 2v: [14] 438; [14] 439–844 9maps 59pls

PUNDERSON (MR. EBENEZER]).   **651**
The narrative of: ... drove [*sic*] away by the rebels in America ... *L* 1776. D 24 aa
—rptd. "Mr. Punderson's narrative," [*L* 1780]. D 12 a

[PURMANN, J. G.]   **652**
Sitten und Meinungen der Wilden in America. *Frankf* 1777–81. D 4v: [8] 503; [4] 476; 461; 461. 44pls aa
—rptd. *Vienna* 1790. D 4v 44pls aa
Compiled from Charlevoix, Garcilasso de Vega, *et al*

PURRY, JEAN P.   **653**
Memoire ... sur l'état présent de la Caroline ... *L* 1724. Q 11 d JCB only a few copies known
—Eng. ed. "Memorial ... upon the present condition of Carolina ...," *L* 1724. O 11 d BM only 2copies known
—rptd. *Augusta Ga* 1880. O 24 250 copies ptd. a
—Fr. ed. 2, enl. "Description abrégée de l'état présent de la Caroline ...," *Neufchâtel* [1730?]. O 36 d GaU [only copy known]
—Ger. ed. "Kurze Nachricht ...," *Leip* 1734. O aa
The Swiss author settled 600 of his countrymen at Purrysburg, S. C.

PURVIANCE (ELDER DAVID).   **654**
The biography of: ... With a historical sketch of the great Kentucky revival. By Elder Levi Purviance. *Dayton* 1848. D 304 [incl. port] a
—rptd., with adds., [*Lenoir City Tenn* 1940]. D 278 port
Travelled in Kentucky, Ohio, Indiana and Tennessee from 1790 onward.

PURVIANCE, ROBERT   **655**
A narrative of events ... in Baltimore Town during the revolutionary war ... *Balt* 1849. D [4] 231 a

PUSEY, WILLIAM A.   **656**
The wilderness road to Kentucky. *N Y* [1921]. Q [14, incl init blank lf & front] 131 [14] [incl.pls] 2fold.maps a

PUTESHESTVIE
Puteshestvie Kapitana Billingsa ... i plavaniye Kapitana Galla ... *See* Sarychev, Garvrilla A.

PUTNAM, A. W.   657
History of middle Tennessee . . . *Nashv* 1859. O
668 3maps 10pls aa
Authoritative account of pioneer times in the
old Southwest.

PUTNAM, GEORGE P.   658
American facts . . . *L* 1845. D 292 map 4 ports
[only 3 in some copies] a

[PUTNAM, HENRY]   659
A description of Brunswick [Me.] . . . *Brunswick* 1820. O 28 a
—ed. 2, with adds., same impr. 1823. D 39

PUTNAM (GENERAL ISRAEL).   660
The interesting life and adventures of: . . . to
which is added the singular case of Dr. Menzies . . .
taken prisoner by the Cherokee Indians . . . *L*
[1800?]. D 24 b N
—rptd. *Falkirk* 1817. same collat. aa

PUTNAM, REV. J. W.   661
Minesota [*sic*]: a description . . . presenting
prospects for . . . organization into a new territorial
government . . . *Galena Ill* [1849?]. O 27 b NYS?
First book written in Minnesota.

PUTNAM (GEN. RUFUS).   662
Journal of: . . . in New York . . . 1757–60. *Alb*
1886. Q 115 [incl.port] a 100 ptd.

PUTNAM (RUFUS).   663
The memoirs of: and . . . papers . . . Ed. by
Miss Rowena Buell. *B* 1903. O 443 a

PUTNAM, RUFUS   664
Pioneer record . . . of the . . . settlement of
Fayette county, Ohio. *Cin* 1872. O 120 errata-lf a

[PYE, HENRY J.]   665
The democrat; or, intrigues and adventures of
Jean Le Noir . . . *NY* 1795. D 2v: [12] 136; [4] 162 aa

Q

QUAIFE, MILO M.   1
Chicago and the old northwest, 1673–1835 . . .
Chi [1913]. O [8] 480 map 10pls a

QUAIFE, MILO M., ed.   2
The development of Chicago, 1674–1914. *Chi*
Caxton Club 1916. O [6] 290 4pls a 175 copies ptd.

QUAKERS   3
An humble apology for the Quakers . . . to which
are added observations on a new pamphlet, intituled
A brief view of the conduct of Pennsylvania . . . *L*
1756. D 39 b NYP

A serious address to such of the people called
Quakers as profess scruples relative to the present
government . . . By a native of Philadelphia. *See*
Grey, Isaac.

QUANTRELL   4
Quantrell, the terror of the west. By Allouette.
N Y 1865. D 59 aa

QUEBEC   5
An accurate and authentic journal of the siege of
Quebec 1759. By a gentleman . . . *L* 1759. O [2]
44 b H JCB NYP
—anr. ed. *Quebec* 1790. O 2pts[Eng. & Fr.] in 1v:
34; 34 aa

Accurate journal of the siege of Quebec.   6
By a gentleman in an eminent position on the spot.
Dub 1759. D 341 aa

Annales de la Propagation de la Foi pour . . .
Québec. *See* below No. 8.

Journal of the march of a party of provincials   7
from Carlisle to Boston, and from thence to Quebec
. . . *Glas* 1776. D 36 b
Attributed to Sergeant William McCoy.

Journal of the principal occurences during the
siege of Quebec . . . *See* Shortt, W. T. P.

Notice sur les missions du diocèse de Québec   8
. . . secourues par l'Association de la Propagation
de la Foi. [Later nos. entitled "Rapport sur les missions . . .,"] *Québec* 1839–74. D 21nos b NYP Y
Published annually, from January 1839 to June
1843, then [except for No. 16, March 1864] every
other year to May 1874. Contains valuable reports
on missions in the Oregon country. Concurrently
with these Quebec *Rapport*(s) ran a Montreal
series [*see Rapport*]. The two were continued, in a
single series, *Annales de la Propagation de la foi
pour . . . Québec et de Montréal*, 141 numbers,
Montreal, 1877–1923, value: b

Rapport sur les missions du diocèse de Québec
See above *Notice* . . . No. 8.

Relation de ce qui s'est passé au siège   9
de Québec . . . par une religieuse . . . [*Québec* 1840].
O 24 8 8 a
—anr. ed. [*Québec*] 1855. 16° 24 pl
—rptd. n.p. n.d. 16° 24 [16]
—Eng. ed. "Siege of Quebec in 1759," [*Québec*
1858] D 20 pl

A short account of the expedition against Quebec
. . . By an engineer . . . *See* MacKellar, Patrick.

A short authentic account of the siege of Quebec. By a volunteer . . . *See* Thompson, James.

Siège de Québec en 1759 . . . *Quebec* 1836.   **10**
O 41 a
Different book from *Relation . . . par une religieuse*, above, No. 9. For still another *see* Panet, Jean C.

The siege of Quebec . . . *See* above *Relation de ce qui s'est passé au siege* . . . No. 9

QUELQUES CONSIDÉRATIONS
Quelques considérations sur l'Amérique; par un vieux philanthrope. *See* Carlet, Jos. A.

QUENTIN, KARL   **11**
Reisebilder und Studien aus dem Norden der Vereinigten Staaten . . . *Arnsberg* 1851. O 2pts in 1: [8] 152; [6] 210 a

QUESTION (THE)   **12**
Question (The) answered: or, how will nullification work? . . . *Charleston S C* 1832. O 23 a

QUICKFALL, BOB G.   **13**
Western life and how I became a bronco buster. *L* n.d. D 96 [incl. front covert] front a

[QUIGG, LEMUEL E.]   **14**
New empires in the northwest . . . *N Y* [1889]. O 84 a

QUIGG, MATTHEW [comp.]   **15**
Atchison city directory . . . for 1865 . . . and sketch of the city . . . [*Atchison* 1864?] D 126 aa

QUINCY, JOSIAH   **16**
The history of Harvard university. *C* 1840. O 2v: [24] 612; [16] 728 [1]. 3pls a
—rptd. *B* 1860. O 2v

QUINCY, JOSIAH   **17**
Memoir of the life of Josiah Quincy, Jr. . . . 1744–1775. *B* 1825. O [8] 498 a
—ed. 2, enl., *B* 1874. O [16] 431 2facs
—ed. 3, same collat. & impr., 1875.
One of the early opposers of British aggression. Includes his journal on a visit to Carolina in 1773 and another on his stay in London, 1774–5.

QUINCY, JOSIAH, JR.   **18**
Observations on . . . the Boston Port-Bill . . . *B* 1774. Q [2] 82 a
—rptd. *Phil* 1774. O 60
—Eng. ed. *L* 1774. O [6] 80

[QUINER, EDWARD B.]   **19**
The city of Watertown, Wisconson: its . . . advantages . . . *Watertown* 1856. D 24 fold. map aa

QUINLAN, JAMES E.   **20**
A history of Sullivan county, N.Y. . . . *Liberty N Y* 1873. O 700 aa

QUINLAN, JAMES E.   **21**
Tom Quick, the Indian slayer . . . *Monticello N Y* 1851. 16° 264 aa
—rptd. "The original life of Tom Quick . . .," *Deposit N Y* 1894. a

QUINTUS, J.   **22**
De Hollander in Amerika. Leerwijze der Engelsche Tal, door H. P. . . . *Buf* 1848. D [4] 77 a

R

R., C. H.
Incidents of travel in the southern states and Cuba . . . *See* Rogers, Carlton H.

R., I.
A lady's ranche life in Montana. *See* Randall, Isabelle.

R., J.   **1**
The portfolio; or a view of the manners and customs of various countries . . . *L* 1812. O 2v: 116; 146 aa
Vol. II gives this officer's experiences in the Revolution, from 1777 to the Yorktown surrender.

RACINE
Racine register . . . [1849]. *See* Miller, Mark.

Early days at Racine, Wisconsin . . . By an outsider. *See* Hurlburt, S. S.

RADEBAUGH, RANDOLPH F.   **2**
Tacoma, the western terminus of the Northern Pacific Railroad. *Tacoma* 1887. O 43 maps & pls. a

RADFORD, B. J.   **3**
History of Woodford county [Ill.]. *Peoria* 1877. O 78 a

RADGES, SAMUEL   **4**
Biennial directory of Topeka . . . with a history . . . *Topeka* 1870. O 278 a
Second directory of this city.

RADICAL (THE)
Radical (The): and advocate of equality . . . *See* Brown, Paul.

RADICALISM   **5**
Radicalism *vs.* liberty of the press. An account by the editors of the Memphis "Avalanche" of their incarceration by Judge Hunter of the carpet bag criminal court of Memphis for contempt. *Memphis* 1868. O 79 a
In a all-time high of vituperative abuse, "his Honor" is characterized as: "a petty-tyrant, cowardly poltroon, giddy bigoted fool, insatiable harpy, slimy reptile, sneaking informer, bankrupt brass-band swindler, mangy cur, hybrid hippo-graff, slabsided champion of radicalism, contemptible whangdoodle wallowing in the sewers of party filth, the most loathesome blotch that ever polluted the bench, gangrened with corruption, rancid with rascality and feculent with all that is vile; lies buzz in swarms around his mouth like summer flies on kitchen garbage; he is steeped so deep in infamy that if the genius of gravitation descended with the velocity of a sunbeam, it could never even reach him," etc. The "Avalanche" was appropriately named.

RADISSON (PIERRE ESPRIT).   **6**
Voyages of: . . . his travels . . . 1652–1684. Ed. Gideon D. Scull. *B* Prince Soc 1885. Q [8] 385 250copies ptd. aa
—rptd. same collat. *N Y* 1943. a
First printing of these famous journals. Radisson and Groseilliers were the first Europeans to see the upper reaches of the Mississippi. They probably got to the Missouri.

RAFINESQUE, C[ONSTANTINE] S.   **7**
The American nations . . . *Phil* 1836. D 2v in 1: [4] 260; 292. [maps & pls called for but not issued] aa

RAFINESQUE, CONSTANTINE S.   **8**
Ancient annals of Kentucky. *Frankf Ky* 1824. O [4] 39 aa
—anr. issue [omitting 2 tabs] inserted in v.I, Marshall's *History of Kentucky*. [2] 39 aa

RAFINESQUE, C[ONSTANTINE] S.   **9**
The ancient monuments of . . . America. ed. 2, enl. *Phil* 1838. O 28 a
Called second edition, having previously in the year appeared in a magazine. It embodies much material used in his *Ancient annals of Kentucky,* above.

RAFINESQUE, C[ONSTANTINE] S.   **10**
Ichthyologia Ohiensis, or natural history of the fishes inhabiting the river Ohio . . . *Lex* 1820. O 90 [incl.front wrap.] b AA N NYP Y [of 10copies known]
—rptd., with adds., *Clev* 1899. O 175 a 250 copies ptd

RAFINESQUE, C[ONSTANTINE] S.   **11**
A life of travels and researches in North America and south Europe . . . *Phil* 1836. D 148 aa

RAFINESQUE, C[ONSTANTINE] S.   **12**
Western Minerva or American annals . . . *Lex* 1821. O 88 b Phila Acad of Sciences [only cop kn] —rptd. *N Y* 1949.

RAFN, CHARLES C.   **13**
Antiquitates americanae, sive scriptores septentrionales rerum ante-columbianarum in America . . . *Copenh* 1837. Q [46 incl. eng. t.] 479 [6], 18 maps pls & facs. eng.t. aa
—anr. issue, with Fr. t., *Copenh* 1845. Q [4] 24 [42] 479 [6] 18maps, pls & facs aa
—abr. issue, same impr. & date. Q [24] 200 2maps aa
The pioneer investigation into the Norse discoveries, with original sagas included.

RAFN, CHARLES C.   **14**
Supplement to the Antiquitates americanae . . . *Copenh* 1841. O 27 2maps 7pls a

[RAHM, FRANK H.]   **15**
Reminiscences of his capture and escape . . . by a member of Mosby's command . . . *Rich* 1895. O [4] 48 incl cov-t a

RAHT, CARLYSLE G.   **16**
The romance of Davis mountains and Big Bend country . . . *El Paso* [1919]. O [6] 381 map 13pls aa
A history of the region between the Pecos and the Rio Grande.

RAINE, WILLIAM MacL., and   **17**
BARNES, WILL C.
Cattle. *N Y* 1930. O [14] 340 9pls a
—rptd. t. altered *N Y* n.d.

RAINEY, GEORGE   **18**
The Cherokee strip. *Guthrie* 1933. D [10] 504 a
Enlarged from his thirty-page pamphlet of similar title, published at Enid, 1925. aa

RAINEY, THOMAS C.   **19**
Along the old trail. Vol.I [all]: Pioneer sketches of Arrow Rock [Mo.] and vicinity. *Marshall Mo* 1914. D 94 2ports a also 50 signed copies. aa

RALEIGH (SIR WALTER) and   **20**
SMITH (CAPT. JOHN).
The lives of: with an account of the Governors of Virginia . . . By a Virginian. *See* Caruthers, Wm. A.

RALFE, J[AMES]   **21**
The naval chronology of Great Britain . . . 1803–1816 . . . *L* 1818–19 O 12parts d; anr ed *L* 1820. roy. O 3v: [12] 288; [2] 284; [2] 318. 60 col. pls port b BP N NYP Y

RAMBLER [THE]   **22**
The rambler, or a tour through Virginia, Ten-

nessee, Alabama, Mississippi and Louisiana . . . By a citizen of Maryland. *Annap* 1828. D 42 b G LC

RAMBLING RECOLLECTIONS
Rambling recollections of a trip to America. *See* Smith, T.

RAMEAU, MR. [E.]   23
Notes historiques sur la colonie Canadienne de Detroit . . . *Montr* 1861. 16° 68 a

RAMEZAY ([JEAN B. N. ROCH] Sieur de).   24
Mémoire du : commandant à Québec, au sujet de la reddition de cette ville . . . 1759. *Quebec* 1861. O [4] 84 38 a

RAMOS DE ARÍZPE (MIGUEL).   25
Idea general sobre la conducta politica de: . . . *Mex* 1822. O 59 b
Of California, New Mexico and Texas interest.

RAMOS DE ARÍZPE, MIGUEL   26
Memoria . . . presénta á el augusto Congreso, sobre el estado . . . de la provincia de Coahuila y las del nuevo reyno de Leon, nuevo Santander y los Texas . . . *Cádiz* 1812. sm Q 60 b Y
—rptd. *Guadalajara* 1813 b
—Eng. ed. "Memorial on the natural, political . . . State of Coahuila . . .," *Phil* 1814. O 47 b B H NYP Y
Presented to the Spanish National Cortes in which Arízpe was representing Coahuila. He was expelled from that body and banished because of the accusations of government corruption contained in this memorial.

[RAMSAY, ALLAN]   27
An historical essay on the English constitution . . . Wherein the right of parliament, to tax our distant provinces, is explained . . . *L* 1771. O [8] 210 a

[RAMSAY, ALLAN]   28
Letters on . . . disturbances in Great Britain and her American provinces. *Rome* 1777. O 40 aa
—rptd, *L* 1777. O 40 a

[RAMSAY, ALLAN]   29
A plan of reconciliation between Great Britain and her colonies . . . By which the rights of Englishmen are preserved to the inhabitants of America . . . *L* 1776. O [4] 60 aa

[RAMSAY, ALLAN]   30
A succinct review of the American contest . . . *L* [1782]. Q [2, 5–8] 35 aa

[RAMSAY, ALLAN]   31
Thoughts on the origin and nature of government. Occasioned by the late disputes between Great Britain and her colonies. *L* 1769. O 64 a

RAMSAY, DAVID, of Scotland   32
Military memoirs of Great Britain, or, a history of the war, 1755–1763. *Edin* 1779. O [16] 7–473 12ports a

RAMSAY, DAVID, of S. C.   33
A chronological table of the principal events . . . in the English colonies, now United States. From 1607, till 1810 . . . *Charleston S C* 1811. O 54 [2] a

RAMSAY, DAVID, of S. C.   34
The history of South Carolina . . . *Charleston* 1809. O 2v: [12] 478; [4] 602. 2maps aa
—rptd. *Newberry S C* 1858. O 2v in 1: [8] 274; 307. 2maps a

RAMSAY, DAVID, of S. C.   35
The history of the American revolution. *Phil* 1789. O 2v: [6] 359; [6] 360 a
—other Am. eds.: *Trenton* 1811. O 2v; *Lex* 1815. O 2v
—Eng. ed. *L* 1791. O 2v: [14] 360; [6] 360. 2errata lvs
—other Eng. eds., all O 2v: *L* 1793; *Dub* 1793; *Dub* 1795.
—Ger. tr. *Berlin* 1794–5. 18° 4v
—Dutch tr. *Campen* 1792–4. O 4v

RAMSAY, DAVID, of S. C.   36
The history of the revolution of South-Carolina, from a British province to an independent state. *Trenton* 1785. O 2v: [20] 453; [20] 574. 5maps aa
—Fr. tr.[by Lefort] *L & P* 1787. O 2v [30] 521; [4] 675 5maps
—anr. Fr. tr. [by Mirabeau], with adds., *P* 1796. O 4v [bd in 2v] maps
Copyright granted by Congress April 20, 1789; first ever obtained.

RAMSAY, DAVID, of S. C.   37
History of the United States . . . 1607-1808. *Phil* 1816–17. O 3v: [28] 418; [8] 445; [56] 368 [86] a
—ed. 2, rev., *Phil* 1818. O 3v: [8] 5–462; 492; [8] 5–498. map

RAMSAY, DAVID, of S. C.   38
The life of George Washington . . . *N Y* 1807. O [8] 376 port[eng. by Leney] a
—ed. 2, *B* 1811. D [8] 371 port
—anr. issue of ed. 2, same impr. & date. D [8] 442 port
—ed. 3, *Balt* 1814. D [8] 442 port
—ed. 4, *Balt* 1815. D [8] 13–266 6pls
—ed. 5, same impr. & collat. 1818.
—several later Am. eds.
—Eng. ed. *L* 1807. O [8] 464 port[eng. by Heath]
—Fr. tr. *P* 1809. O [28] 472 port[eng. by Macret]
—Sp. tr. *N Y* 1825. 18° 2v: [8] 277; 238 [2]
—rptd. *Barcelona* 1842. O 2v
—anr. Sp. tr. *Phil* 1826. D 270

RAMSAY, DAVID, of S. C.   39
An oration, on the cession of Louisiana . . .
Charleston S C 1804. D 27 a

RAMSAY, DAVID, of S. C.   40
A sketch of the soil, climate . . . of South-Carolina. *Charleston* 1796. O [4] 30 3tabs aa

RAMSAY, T. N.   41
Sketches of the great battles in 1861 . . . *Salisbury, N.C.* 1861. O 32 aa

RAMSDELL, CHARLES W.   42
Reconstruction in Texas. *N Y* 1910. O 324 a

RAMSEY, ALBERT C.
The other side [etc.]. *See* Alcarez, Ramón.

RAMSEY, J[AMES] G. M.   43
The annals of Tennessee . . . *Charleston* 1853.
O [16] 744 map plan aa
—anr. issue, *Phil* 1853, same collat. aa
—rptd: same collat, 1860; with index added
Kingsport 1926.

[RAMSEY, JAMES G. M.]?   44
Tales of the revolution. By a young gentleman
of Tennessee. *Nashv* 1833. D 179 aa

RANCK, GEORGE W.   45
Boonesborough; its founding . . . *Louisv* Filson
Club 1901. Q [12] 286 map 16pls a

RANCK, GEORGE W.   46
History of Lexington, Kentucky. *Cin* 1872. O
[6] 428 pl aa

RANCK, GLENN N.   47
Pictures from northwest history. [*Vancouver
Wash* 1902]? O 38 a
—enl. ed. "Legends . . . of northwest history . . .,"
same impr. [1914]. O 152 map 13pls

RANDALL, HENRY S.   48
The life of Thomas Jefferson. *N Y* 1858. O 3v:
[24] 645; [12] 694; [12] 731. 2ports 2pls 7facs a
—rptd. *Phil* 1863. O 3v

[RANDALL, ISABELLE]   49
A lady's ranche life in Montana. *L* 1887. O [8]
170 + 2adv-p a

RANDALL, ORAN E.   50
History of Chesterfield . . . N. H. . . . . *Brattle-
boro Vt* 1882. O [6] 9–525 map port a

RANDALL, THOMAS E.   51
History of the Chippewa valley [Wis.] . . . *Eau
Claire* 1875. O 207 a

RANDEL, JOHN, JR.   52
Description of a direct route for the Erie canal
. . . *Alb* 1822. O 72 a
—rptd., same impr., 1836. O

[RANDOLPH, EDMUND], 1753–1813   53
Letters to the citizens of the United States. [capt.
t.]. [*Phil* 1794]. O 77 errata slip a
Includes remarks on the whiskey insurrection
and the Society of the Cincinnati.

[RANDOLPH, EDMUND], 1753–1813   54
Political truth . . . with an inquiry into the truth
of the charges . . . against Mr. Randolph. *Phil*
1796. O 44 a

[RANDOLPH, EDMUND], 1753–1813   55
A vindication of Mr. Randolph's resignation . . .
Phil 1795. O 104 errata lf a
—issue 2, re-set, with cor. made, & containing a
lf inserted after t-p
—new ed., with pref. by Daniel, *Rich* 1855. O [12]
82
The author had resigned from Washington's
cabinet under fire, suspected of aiding French
intrigue.

RANDOLPH, EDMUND, 1819–61   56
Address on the history of California . . . *S F*
1860. O 72 2maps a
—rptd., without maps, n.p. 1860. O 42
—anr. ed., "An outline of the history of California
. . ." *S F* 1861 O 42
—rptd. *S F* 1868 O

[RANDOLPH, JOHN]   57
Considerations on the present state of Virginia.
[*Wmsbg*] 1774. O 24 d MH NYP [only cops kn]
O 83
—rptd., with adds., *Metuchen N J* 1919. O 83
63copies ptd. a
Plea for conciliation with England; for reply see
Nicholas Robt C.

RANDOLPH, JOHN   58
Randolph (John) abroad and at home . . . By
Julius. *Wash* 1828. O 29 a
—eds. 2 & 3, same impr. & date.
For sustained vituperation unexcelled by Amer-
ican pamphleteers.

[RANDOLPH, PEYTON]   59
A letter to a gentleman in London, from Virginia. *Wmsbg* 1759. O 28 aa

RANDOLPH, THOMAS J., ed.   60
Memoir, correspondence . . . from the papers of
Thomas Jefferson. *Charlottesville Va* 1829. O 4v:
[10] 466; [4] 500; [4] 519; [4] 532. port 4facs a
—ed. 2, *B* 1830. O 4v
—Eng. ed. *L* 1829. O 4v: [10] 464; 496; 521; 552.

RANKIN, ADAM   61
A review of the . . . revival in Kentucky . . . *Lex* 1802. 16° 144 a
—other eds.: *Pitt* 1802; [*Lex*?] 1803. O 70

RANKIN, JOHN   62
Letters on American slavery . . . *B* 1833. 18° 118 a
—ed. 2, *Newburyport* 1836. same collat.
—3 later eds.

RANKIN, M. WILSON   63
Reminiscences of frontier days, including . . . account of the Thornburg and Meeker massacre. *Denver* [1938]. O [10] 140 front. aa

RANKIN, MELINDA   64
Texas in 1850 . . . *B* 1850. D 199 a
—rptd: *B* 1852; with t. "Twenty years among the Mexicans" *Cin* 1875.

RAPELJE, GEORGE   65
A narrative of excursions . . . in America, Europe . . . *N Y* 1834. O 416 port a

RAPPORT   66
Rapport de l'Association de la Propagation de la Foi. *Montr* 1839–46. D 46nos. c AA N Y
For note on concurrent *Rapport(s)* issued at Quebec and later continuation, *see Québec. Notice sur les missions* . . .

RATHBUN, JOHN C.   67
History of Thurston county, Washington. *Olympia* 1895. O 131 a

RATHBUN (JONATHAN).   68
Narrative of: with . . . accounts of the capture of Groton Fort . . . by the British forces under . . . Benedict Arnold. [*N Lond*? 1840]. D [2] 80)a

RATIFICATIONS (THE)   69
Ratifications (The) of the new foederal constitution . . . with the amendments proposed . . . *Rich* 1788. D 32 a

[RAUDOT, ANTOINE DÉNIS]   70
Relation par lettres de l'Amérique Septentrionale, 1709–1710. Ed. by Camille de Rochemonteix. *P* 1904. O [64] 221 a
These hitherto unpublished letters, on French activities in the Upper Mississippi and Lake regions, etc., were erroneously attributed by the editor to Antoine Silvy or, possibly, Moreau de Nautour.

RAUM, JOHN O.   71
The history of New Jersey . . . *Phil* 1877. O 2v: 450 [incl. front.]; 496 front. a

RAUM, JOHN O.   72
History of . . . Trenton, New Jersey. *Trenton* 1871. O [12] 448 map 3pls a

RAUMER, FRIEDRICH VON   73
Die Vereinigten Staaten . . . *Leip* 1845. D 2v: [24] 553; [12] 541. map 4tabs aa
—rptd. *Phil* 1846. O 2v in 1: [8] 223 tab a
—Dutch tr. *Deventer* 1849. O 2v: [12] 324; [6] 344, tab a
—Eng. tr. "America and the American people," *N Y* 1846. O 512 tab a
Travelled South to Charleston and West to St. Louis and Chicago.

RAVEN, RALPH, [pseud.]
Golden dreams and leaden realities. *See* Payson, Geo.

[RAVESIES, PAUL]   74
Scenes and settlers of Alabama. By Sub Rosa. [*Mobile* 1886?] O 120 [incl advs] a

RAVOUX, AUGUSTIN   75
Reminiscences, memoirs . . . *St P* 1890. O [10] 223 3ports aa
—Fr. ed., with adds., "Mémoires, reminiscences . . .," *St P* 1892. O [12] 257 3ports a
Ravoux came to Minnesota in 1840: as missionary to the Sioux from 1840 to 1876 his operations covered the vast region between Dubuque and Ft. Pierre.

[RAWLE, FRANCIS]   76
Ways and means for the inhabitants of Delaware to become rich . . . *Phil* 1725. 16° 66+adv-p c NYP PhilL PaH Y
—rptd. *Phil* 1878. O [2] 65 a
First American book on which Franklin worked.

RAWLE, WILLIAM   77
A view of the constitution of the United States . . . *Phil* 1825. O [8] 5–347 a
—ed. 2, *Phil* 1829. O 349
First authoritative interpretation, in which was admitted the abstract right of state secession. These views exerted a profound influence on Southern political thought.

RAWLINS, CHARLES E.   78
American dis-union: constitutional or unconstitutional? A reply to Mr. James Spence . . . *L* 1862. D [12] 228 a

[RAWSON, EDWARD, and SEWALL, SAMUEL]   79
The revolution in New England justified . . . from the aspersions . . . by Mr. John Palmer . . . *B* 1691. SmQ [6] 48 d Hn JCB NYP
—rptd. title altered. *B* 1773. O 59 b
For tract complained of *see* Palmer, John, *An impartial account* . . . Authorship of this piece has been ascribed to both Increase Mather and Sir Edmund Andros, but "To the Reader" bears initials "E. R. and S.S."

RAY, P[ERLEY] ORMAN   80
The repeal of the Missouri compromise...
Clev 1909. O 315 a

RAYMOND, DANIEL   81
The Missouri question. *Balt* 1819. O 39 a

RAYMOND, DANIEL   82
Thoughts on political economy... *Balt* 1820.
O [4] 470 aa
—ed. 2, "The elements of political economy,"
same impr. 1823. O 2v: [2] 418; [2] 438
First systematic work on this subject by an
American.

RAYMOND, DORA R.   83
Captain Lee Hall of Texas. *Norman, Okla.*
1940. O [14] 352 map 17pls a

RAYNAL, ABBÉ GUILLAUME T. F.   84
A philosophical and political history of the
British settlements and trade in North America.
Edin 1776. D 2v: 240; 231 a
—rptd. *Aberdeen* 1779. D 2v in 1: [12] 336
—anr. ed., to which was added "History of the
present war," *Edin* 1779. D [12] 410
The *History*, added to the 1779 Edinburgh edition and apparently not by Raynal, was one of the
earliest histories of the Revolutionary movement.

RAYNAL, L'ABBÉ GUILLAUME T. F.   85
Révolution de l'Amérique. [unauthorized ed.]
L [ptd. *Geneva*?] 1781. D [16] 171 a
—rptd., same date & impr. D [16] 183 port
—other issues, same impr. & date, with variant
paginat.
—[authorized ed.] *P* 1782. O 122
—[unauthorized Eng. tr.] *L* 1781. D [16] 181+
2adv-p
—rptd. same date & impr. D [4] 199; *Dub* 1781,
16° [20] 244
—[authorized Eng. tr.] *Edin* 1782. D [6] 162; anr.
ed., same impr. & date, D [8] 191
—Am. eds.: *B* 1781; *N Y* 1781; *Phil* 1782; *Salem*
1782; *Norwich* 1782.
—Dutch tr. *Amst* 1781. Ger tr *Berl* 1786 O
Intended to supplement the author's earlier
history of European trade in the two Indies. An
enterprising printer secured the manuscript and
without consent issued simultaneous English and
French editions.

RAYNAL, L'ABBÉ GUILLAUME T. F.   86
The sentiments of a foreigner on the disputes
of Great-Britain and America. Tr. from French.
Phil 1775. O 28 aa
—Eng. ed. *Belf* 1775. O

RAYNAL, ABBÉ GUILLAUME T. F.   87
Tableau et révolutions des colonies angloises...
Amst 1781 D 2v: [4] 273; [4] 270 a
—rptd., *P* 1783, same collat.

RAYNOLDS, WILLIAM F.   88
Report on the exploration of the Yellowstone
... [Sen. Exec. Doc. 77]. *Wash* 1868. O [2] 174
map a
A four-page preliminary report was issued in
Senate Executive Document 1, 1860; the Civil
War prevented earlier publication in this com-
pleted form.

REA, D. B.   89
Sketches from Hampton's cavalry. *Columbia
S C* 1864. O 158 aa

READ, BENJAMIN M.   90
Historia ilustrada de Nuevo Mexico... *Santa
Fe* 1911. O 616[incl. pls] a
—Eng. tr., same impr. [*ca* 1912]. O 812 [incl.
advs & pls] aa 500 cops ptd

READ, GEORGIA W., and   91
GAINES, RUTH, eds.
Gold rush: the journals... of J. Goldsborough
Bruff, 1849–51. *N Y* 1944. O 2v: [88] 630; [8]
631–1404. 21pls[others incl. in paginat.] aa
—rptd. *N Y* 1949. O 2v in 1 [72] 794 a
Most elaborate of overland narratives.

READ, J. A., and D. F.   92
Journey to the gold diggins. *Cin* 1849. oblong
D 63 b N
—anr. issue, same collat. *N Y* n.d. [1849]
—rptd. *S F* Grabhorn 1950 a
One hundred and twelve caricature illustrations
of various phases of life to and at the mines.

READ, JOHN M.   93
A historical inquiry concerning Henry Hudson
... *Alb* 1866. O [8] 5–209 pl a
—Eng. ed., abr. *Edin* 1883. O 88

READ, WILLIAM T., ed.   94
Life and correspondence of George Read, a
signer of the Declaration of Independence...
Phil 1870. O 575 port a

REAGAN, JOHN H.   100
Memoirs, with special reference to secession
and the civil war. *N Y* 1906. O 351 5pls aa

REASONS   101
**Reasons humbly offered, to prove, that the letter
printed at the end of the French memorial of justification, is a French forgery** ... *L* 1756. O [2] 61 aa
—Fr. tr. by Edmond J. Genet, "Le peuple juge, ou
considérations sur lesquelles le peuple anglois
pourra décider si la lettre...," [*P*]? 1756. D [10]
160 a
Relates to the Ohio expedition. *Cf.* Moreau,
Jacob N., *Memoire contenant les précis des
faits*..., in which the questionable letter appeared.
Reasons humbly offered... has been ascribed to
John Shebbeare.

Reasons why the British colonies . . . should not be charged with internal taxes by . . . parliament . . . *See* Fitch, Thos.

REAVIS, L[OGAN] U[RIAH]   **102**
The life and military services of Gen. William Selby Harney . . . *St L* 1878. O [2] 477 3pls aa

[REAVIS, S. A.], comp.   **103**
The Hillsboro and Hill county [Texas] directory . . . *Hillsboro* 1884. O 92 a

REBELLION (THE)
Rebellion (The): its consequences . . . By Investigator. *See* Barker, Jacob.

RECHERCHES . . .
Recherches historiques . . . sur les États-Unis. Par un citoyen de Virginie. *See* Mazzei, Filippo.

Recherches philosophiques sur les Américains . . . Par Mr. de P . . . *See* Pauw, M. Corneille de.

RECIPROCAL LOVE . . .
See Letters to an officer . . .

RÉCIT FIDELE . . .
See Chalesme, M. de

RECK ([PHILIPP G. F.] VON).   **104**
An extract of the journals of: . . . *L* 1734. O [4] 72 b GaU N NYP
Account of the bringing over and settling in Georgia of the 1733 Salzburger colony.

RECK, PHILIPP G. F. VON   **105**
Kurz gefasste Nachricht von dem Etablissement derer salzburgischen Emigranten zu Ebenezer in . . . Georgien . . . *Hamburg* 1777. D 44 aa

RECOLLECTIONS
Recollections of rambles in the south. *See* William, Father [*pseud.*]

Recollections of the United States army . . . By an American soldier . . . *See* Gordon-Miller, William L.

RECONSTRUCTION IN AMERICA.
B a member of the New York bar. *See* Kingsley, Vine W.

RECOVERY (THE)   **106**
Recovery (The) of America demonstrated to be practicable . . . By the author . . . *L* 1782. O [4] 7–26 a

RECUEIL   **107**
Recueil d'arrests [*sic*] et autre pieces pour l'etablissement de la Compagnie d'Occident . . . *Amst* 1720. D 2pts in 1: [2] 100; 253. map 3pls aa

Part two [containing Crozat's concession, etc.] sometimes accompanies *Relations de la Louisiane*, *q.v.*

Recueil d'edits. déclarations et arrêts . . .   **108**
concernant l'administration de la justice, et la police des colonies francaises de l'Amerique . . . *P* 1744. D 220 b

Recueil d'estampes representant les differents evenemens de la guerre qui a procuré l'independance aux États-Unis . . . *See Collection d'estampes . . .*

Recueil de reglemens, concernant le com-   **109**
merce des isles et colonies francoises de l'Amérique. *P* 1744. D [24] 531 b

Recueil de reglemens, edits, déclarations   **110**
et arrêts, concernant le commerce, l'administration de la justice et la police des colonies francaises de l'Amérique . . . avec le Code noir et l'addition au dit code. *P* 1745. D [16] 357 b
—new ed. *P* 1765. D 2v: 301; [2] 193 b
This work superseded the two earlier colonial regulations, shown above: *Recueil d'edits . . .* and *Recueil de reglemens, concernant . . .*

Recueil des loix constitutives des colonies   **111**
angloises, confédérées sous la dénomination d'États-Unis . . . les actes d'independance, de confédération . . . *Phil & P* [ptd *P*] 1778. D [12] 370 aa
—anr. ed., "En Suisse," same date & collat. aa
First collected edition, compiled by Regnier. For later editions *see Constitutions of the several independent states . . .*

REDFIELD (LEVI).   **112**
A true account of . . . occurences in the life of: *Norwich Conn* [1798]. 16° 24 aa
—anr. ed., no priority established, *Brattleborough* [1798]. D 12 aa

[REDFIELD, WILLIAM C.]   **113**
Sketch of the geographical rout [*sic*] of a . . . railway . . . to connect the canals and navigable waters of New York, Pennsylvania, Ohio, Indiana, Illinois, Missouri [etc.]. *N Y* 1829. O 16 map aa
—ed. 2, enl. *N Y* 1830. O 48 map aa
Prospectus on the initial part of a grandiose project to extend rail lines eventually from the Atlantic to the Pacific.

REDFORD, A. H.   **114**
The history of Methodism in Kentucky [to 1832]. *Nash* 1868–70. D 3v: 479; 512; 554. 4pls a

REDFORD, A. H.   **115**
Western cavaliers . . . history of the Methodist Episcopal church in Kentucky . . . 1832–1844. *Nash* 1875–6. D 552 a
May be considered a fourth and concluding volume of the preceding item.

REDICK-LE-MAN, JOHN   **116**
A detection of the conduct ... of Messrs.
Annan and Henderson ... *Balt* [1765]. D [48]
48 errata lf b only 1 cop loc
First Baltimore imprint.

REDMOND, PAT. H.   **117**
History of Quincy [Ill.], and its men of mark ...
Quincy 1869. 16° 302 a

REDNITZ, L.   **118**
Getreuste und zuverlassigter Wegweisser und
Rathgeber zur Reise nach und in Amerika und
Californien ... *Berlin* 1852. D [8] 151 aa

REDPATH, JAMES   **119**
Echoes of Harper's Ferry ... *B* 1860. D 514 a

REDPATH, JAMES, and HINTON,   **120**
RICHARD J.
Hand-book to Kansas Territory and the Rocky
mountains' gold region. *N Y* 1859. 16° 178+adv-
pp[varying no. in different copies] 2maps aa
—rptd. 1954 a

REDPATH, JAMES   **121**
The roving editor: or, talks with slaves in the
southern states. *N Y* 1859. D [16] 349 2pls a
Vitriolic abolition propaganda.

REDSECKER, JACOB H.   **122**
Across the continent ... *Lebanon Pa* [1879?].
D 98 a

REED AND CADWALADER   **123**
PAMPHLETS (THE).
A reprint of: [*Phil* ptd. *Alb*] 1863. O [4] 82
44 12 a 199 copies ptd.
For original editions *see* Cadwalader, John, and
Reed, Joseph.

[REED, CYRUS A.]   **124**
Report of the Adjutant General of Oregon
for ... 1865–6. *Salem* 1866. O 353 errata slip aa

REED, EMILY H.   **125**
Life of A. P. Dostie; or, the conflict in New
Orleans. *N Y* 1868. D 375 port a

REED, ISAAC   **126**
The Christian traveller ... including nine
years, and eighteen thousand miles. *N Y* 1828.
16° 243 b IndU IH KyU N
Observations, on people, manners and conditions in frontier Indiana, Illinois and Kentucky,
by an intelligent itinerant preacher. Portions
were included in his *The youth's book*, Indianapolis, 1840 [16° 230 pages].

REED, J. W.   **127**
Map and guide to the Kansas gold fields.
N Y 1859. D 24 map dd S Y [only copies known]
—rptd. *Denv* 1960. same collat

REED, JOHN   **128**
An explanation of the map of the city ... of
Philadelphia. *Phil* 1774. Q 24 [8] 23 [9] a
—rptd. *Phil* 1844.
The map [17 ³/₄" × 29"] was issued separately.

REED, JONAS   **129**
A history of Rutland ... Massachusetts ...
Worc 1836. D 168 plan a
—new ed., with suppl. to 1879 by Daniel Bartlett,
Worc 1879. D 194 errata slip map

REED, JOSEPH   **130**
Remarks on a late publication in the Independ-
ent gazetteer ... *Phil* 1783. O 72 errata slip aa
Denial of charges that the author, Washington's
Adjutant General, became disaffected after the
battle of Trenton. For answer to this denial *see*
Cadwalader, John.

REED, NATHANIEL   **131**
The life of Texas Jack ... *Tulsa* [1936] O 55
[incl front wrap] a

REED, PARKER McC   **131a**
History of Bath, Maine ... *Port Me* 1894. O
526 port a

REED [SILAS].   **132**
Report of: [on his five personal investigations
into Wyoming's potential resources]. *Wash* 1871.
O 46 aa

REED, WALLACE P.   **133**
History of Atlanta ... *Syracuse* 1889. O 2pts
in 1 : 491; 211. 46ports aa

REED, WILLIAM   **134**
Life on the border [of northern New York],
60 years ago. *Fall River* 1882. D 120 a

REED, WILLIAM B.   **135**
A lecture on the romance of American history
... *Phil* 1839. 16° 46 a

[REED, WILLIAM B.?]   **136**
A letter on American history. *Phil* priv. ptd.
1847. O 39 a

REED, WILLIAM B.   **137**
Life and correspondence of Joseph Reed ...
Phil 1847. O 2v: 437; [4] 9–507. port a

REES, O. VAN   **138**
Geschiedenis der Nederlandsche Volksplan-
tingen in Noord-Amerika ... *Te Tiel* 1855. O [2]
162 [2] a

REES, WILLIAM   **139**
Description of ... Keokuk ... *Keokuk* 1854.
O 24[incl.covers] aa
—rptd., t. & text slightly altered, same impr.
1855. O [4] 24 + wraps aa
—ed. 2 1856 aa

REES, WILLIAM   **140**
The Mississippi bridge cities, Davenport,
Rock Island and Moline ... *Rock Island* [ptd
Cin] 1854. O 32[incl.front.] + 4adv-p at front aa

[REESE, LISLE, ed].   **141**
South Dakota guide [A]. [*Pierre*] 1938. D [24]
441 map [in rear cover] 64pls [on 32 sheets] aa

REEVES, ARTHUR M., ed.   **141a**
The finding of Wineland the good. The history
of Icelandic discovery in America ... *L* 1895. Q
[72] 205 port facs a
Most satisfactory English presentation of
Norse discoveries.

[REEVES, JOHN]   **142**
Two tracts, shewing, that Americans born be-
fore the Independence, are ... not aliens ... *L*
1814. O [8] 65 [2] 34 a
—ed. 2, au. named, *L* 1816. same collat; except
that it has 12 prelim pp.

REFLECTIONS   **143**
**Reflections and suggestions on the present state
of parties.** By an old Clay Whig. *Nash* 1856. O
88 a

**Reflections moral and political on Great Britain
and her colonies.** *See* Wheelock, Matthew.

Reflections offertus aux capitalistes de l'Europe
... *See* Van Pradelles, Capt.

Reflections on government, with respect   **144**
to America ... *L* 1776. O 32 a

Reflections on our present critical situation. **145**
In a letter from a landed proprietor. *L* 1777.
O 33 a
Peace with America essential to the interests
of England.

Reflections on the conservatory elements   **146**
of the American republic. By a lady. *Chillicothe*
1842. O 55 a

Reflections on the inconsistency of man   **147**
... **exemplified in the practice of slaverny in the
United States.** *N Y* 1796. O 27 a

Reflections on the most proper means of   **148**
reducing the rebels ... By an officer who served
in the last war in America. *L* 1776. O 39 aa

Reflections on the present combination of   **149**
the American colonies against the ... **authority of
the British legislature** ... By a real friend to legal
liberty ... *L* 1777. O [4] 100 aa

**Reflections on the present state of the American
war** ... *See* Hampson, J.

Reflections on the proposition to commu-   **150**
**nicate, by a navigable canal, the waters of Chesa-
peake with those of Delaware bay** ... *Annap*
[1797]. O 50 a

**Reflections on the rise and progress of the
American rebellion.** *See* Wesley, John.

Reflections on the rise, progress ... **of the present
contentions with the colonies.** By a freeholder.
See Erskine, John.

Reflections on the state of affairs in the   **151**
south ... n.p. [*Wash*?] *ca* 1833. O 31 a

Reflections on the state of parties. *See* Champion, J.

REFLEXIONS   **152**
Reflexions on representation in parliament ...
L 1766. O 46 a
Advocated more equal representaion, extending
even to American colonies.

**Reflexions politiques sur la guerre actuelle
de l'Angleterre avec ses colonies** ... *See* Le
Trosne, G.-F.

REFUTATION
Refutation [A] of the calumnies ... **against the
southern and western states** ... By a South-
Carolinian. *See* Holland, Edwin C.

**Refutation [A] of the Letter to an Honble.
Brigadier-General** ... **in Canada.** By an officer.
See Thurlow, Ed.

REGAN, JOHN   **153**
The emigrant's guide to the western states ...;
or, backwoods and prairies. *Edin* Oliver & Boyd
[1852]. D [14] 9–408 front [called ed.2 on t-p
because previously issued in the columns of the
Ayrshire Advertiser] aa
—ed. 2, enl., "The western wilds ...; or, backwoods and prairies," *Edin* Menzies, etc. 1859.
same collat. aa
This Scotsman, who came to Illinois in 1842,
gives one of the most entertaining accounts of
pioneer life in the Upper Mississippi Valley.

REGNAULT-WARIN, [JEAN]   **154**
Histoire du ... Lafayette en Amérique ... *P*
1832. O [40] 373 a

REGULATIONS   **155**
Regulations for the uniform and dress of the Army
of the United States ... *Wash* 1851. D 28 a
—ed. 2, *Phil* [1851]. F 12 25chromo-lith pls aa
—anr. ed. *Phil* 1882. F 6p 19pls[10col.] aa
—oth. eds. *Phil*1888, F 25pls [12 col.]; *Wash* 1889,
F 44col pls aa

Regulations for the uniform and dress   **156**
of the Marine corps ... *Phil* [1859]. Q 9 16pls
[some col.] aa

Regulations for the uniform and dress of   **157**
the ... Navy. [*Wash* 1841]. D 17 3pls a
—rev. ed. *Wash* 1866. O 16 29pls aa
For later regulations *See Uniforms* ...

Regulations for the uniform ... of the   **158**
Navy and Marine corps ... *Phil* 1852. Q 16 15pls
[13col.] aa

Regulations governing the uniform of ...   **159**
officers, warrant officers and enlisted men ...
Wash 1886. O 26 p 52col.pls aa

Regulations lately made concerning the colonies
... *See* Whately, Thos.

[REICHEL, EDWARD H.]   **160**
Historical sketch of the church and missions
of the ... Moravians. *Bethlehem* 1848. D 93 a

REICHEL, LEVIN T.   **161**
The Moravians in North Carolina: an authentic
history. *Salem N C* 1857. D [4] 13–206 a

REICHEL, WILLIAM C., ed.   **162**
Memorials of the Moravian church. Vol. I
[all]. *Phil* 1870. O [15] 19–366 errata slip a

REID, A[LEXANDER] J.   **163**
The resources ... of the lower Fox river valley
[Wis.]. *Appleton Wis* 1874. O 56 2maps 3pls a

REID, ARTHUR   **164**
Reminiscences of the revolution, or Le Loup's
bloody trail ... *Utica* 1859. O 31 a

REID, HIRAM A.   **165**
History of Pasadena ... *Pasadena* 1895. O 675
2maps aa

REID, H[UGO]   **166**
Sketches in North America ... *L* 1861. D 320 a
—rptd. "American crisis ...," *L* 1862. D
Favored English recognition of the Confederacy.

REID, HUGO [J.]   **167**
Account of the Indians of Los Angeles county.
Salem 1885. O [2] 33 pl a
—rptd. *L A* 1926. O [4] 70
Reid's book was written in 1852.

REID, J. M.   **168**
Sketches and anecdotes of the old settlers ...
Keokuk 1876. O 177 + 16adv-p aa
Mormon troubles, etc., in the 'forties.

REID, JESSE W.   **169**
History of the Fourth Regiment S. C. Volun-
teers ... *Greenville S C* 1892. O 143 [incl. front[a

[REID, JOHN] pub.   **170**
The American atlas; containing the following
maps ... *N Y* 1796. F [2] 20maps [and, in some
copies, add. unlisted plan of Washington] b AA
N NYP Y
—anr. issue, undated, same collat. aa
Accompanied the 1796 edition of Winterbotham's *Historical ... view of the United States*,
but also sold separately. The second purely
American atlas of the United States, preceded
only by Carey's 1795 atlas, *q.v.*

REID, JOHN, and EATON, JOHN H.   **171**
The life of Andrew Jackson ... *Phil* 1817. O
425 port 4maps aa
—ed. 2, Reid's name as co-author omitted, *Phil*
1824. O 468 port[different from one in ed.1] a
—rptd. without port, *Cin* 1827. D 454
—ed. 3, *Phil* 1828. D 335 port.; rptd. same impr.
& collat. 1839.
—Ger. tr. *Reading Pa* 1831. D 419 map port

REID, JOHN C.   **172**
Reid's tramp ... through Texas, New Mexico,
Arizona, Sonora and California ... *Selma Ala*
1858. O 237 d AA Hn N NYP Y
—rptd. *Austin* 1935. O 245 a
Important early account of the Gadsden Purchase; includes adventures with Crabb's filibusters.

REID, RICHARD   **173**
Historical sketches of Montgomery county
[Ky.]. [cover-t.] *Mt Sterling* 1882. D 69 a
—rptd. same collat. *Lex* 1926.

REID, SAMUEL C.   **174**
History of the wonderful battle of the brig-of-
war General Armstrong with a British squadron
at Fayal, 1814. *N Y* 1833. 16° 46 a

REID, SAMUEL C.   **175**
The scouting expeditions of McCulloch's Texas
rangers ... *Phil* 1847. D [10] 251 12pls plan aa
—rptd. Phil 1848; 1859; 1860; *Austin* 1935. a
Adventures in the Mexican war and in border
campaigns against Comanches.

REID, WHITELAW   **176**
After the war: a southern tour ... *Cin* 1866.
D 589+6adv-p 7pls aa
—Eng. ed. *L* 1866. same collat. a
Best portrayal of conditions in the war-torn
South.

REIERSEN, J[OHAN] R.   177
Veiviser for norske emigranter til de forenede nord-amerikanske stater og Texas . . . *Christiania* 1844. O [30] 166 b Y

REIGART, J. FRANKLIN   178
The life of Robert Fulton . . . *Phil* 1856. O 297 26pls[some col.] a

REISE   179
Reise [Die] nach Amerika, und das leben in den Vereinigten Staaten . . . *Frankf* 1855. O 165 a

Reise (Eine), um die Welt, von Westen   180
nach Osten durch Siberien und das stille und atlantische Meer. *Aschaffenburg* n.d. O 136 map 2pls aa

REISEN
Reisen durch Amerika . . . Aus dem Französichen, 1783. *See* Cluny, Alex.

Reisen durch einige französische, eng-   181
lische, hollandische, spanische, Besitzungen in der neuen Welt . . . *Leip* 1789. D 230 a

Reisen eines Schweizers in . . . Kolonien von Amerika . . . *See* Girod-Chantrans, Justin.

Reisen im Inneren von Nordamerika . . . *See* Anburey, Thos.

REISS, N.   182
Excursion à New York en 1850. *Brus* 1851. D 96 a

REISTER, J. T.   183
Sketches of Colorado . . . from personal observations . . . *Macon Mo* 1876. 16° 62 [incl.initial blank lf] aa

REITER, ERNST A.   184
Schematismus der deutschen katolischen Geistlichkeit in den Vereinigten Staaten . . . *Cin* 1870. O [8] 252 [2] a

REJON (MANUEL C.)   185
Justificazion de la conducta de: . . . *N O* 1846. Q 35 a

REJON, MANUEL C.   186
Observaciones . . . contra los tratados de paz, firmados en la ciudad de Guadalupe . . . *Queretaro* 1848. D 62 [2] b B LC NYP Y
Spirited attack on the terms of the treaty of peace with the United States.

RELACION   187
Relacion de las causas que influeron en los desgraciados sucesos del dia 20 de Agosto de 1847. *Mex* 1847. O 36 aa

Relacion del viage hecho por las goletas Sutil y Mexicana . . . *See* Galiano, Dionisio Alcala.

RELATION
Relation de ce qui est arrivé à deux religeux de la Trappe . . . *See* Paul, Vincent de.

Relation d'un voyage en Afrique et en Amérique, par Madame xxxxx. *See* Uitenhage de Mist, Mlle. van.

Relation d'une traversée faite en 1812 d'Angleterre en Amérique. *See* Becours, Mich. V.

RELATIONS   188
Relations des Jésuites . . . Publié sous les auspices du gouvernement canadien. *Quebec* 1858. Q 3v: 43 relations paged separately, with index added aa
Reprints Biard's relation of 1611, a relation of 1626, and the regular series of 41 relations issued annually from 1632 to 1672. The four preliminary pages to Biard's relation are often lacking as they were printed after volume one was completed. The 1665 relation contains a folding map.

Relations diverses sur la battaile du   189
Malangueulé . . . 1755 . . . *N Y* 1860. D [16] 9–52 port a 100 copies ptd.
Nine documents relating to Fort Duquesne affairs and Braddock's defeat.

REMARKABLE SHIPWRECKS . . .   190
Hart 1813. D 384+subscriber's names, p373–419 a

REMARKS
Remarks on a late pamphlet entitled Plain truth. *See* Dickinson, John.

Remarks on a pamphlet . . . "A Dissertation on the political union and constitution of the . . . United States." By a Connecticut farmer. *See* Sherman, Roger.

Remarks on African colonization and the   191
abolition of slavery. By a citizen of New England. *Windsor Vt* 1833. O 48 a

Remarks on slavery in the United States . . . *See* Sewall, Saml.

Remarks on the conduct of opposition   192
with regard to America . . . *L* 1777. O [4] 42 a
Intemperate defense of all measures of Parliament.

Remarks on the different opinions relative   193
to the American colonies. *L* 1776. O 44 a
—ed. 2, same impr., date & collat.

Remarks on the embargo law. By Civis.   194
N Y 1808. O [2] 41 a

Remarks on the Indians ... *See* Bannister, Saxe.

Remarks on the Letter address'd to two great
men ... *See* Townshend, Chas.

Remarks on the Letters from an American
farmer. *See* Ayscough, Sam'l.

Remarks on the moral and religious char-   195
acter of the United States ... By Observer.
Colchester 1831. O 64 a
  Denies its existence.

Remarks on the nature and extent of liberty ...
See Blacklock, Thos.

Remarks on the ordinance of nullification   196
... By a South-Carolinian. *Charleston* 1833. O 71 a

Remarks on the policy and practice of the   197
United States and Great Britain in their treatment
of the Indians. *B* 1827. O 78 a

Remarks on the policy of recognizing the   198
independence of the southern states ... By Nemo.
L 1863. O 31 a

Remarks on the principal acts of the thirteenth
parliament ... By the author of Letters concerning
the present state of Poland. *See* Lind, John.

Remarks on the proposed plan of a federal
government ... By Aristides. *See* Hanson, Alex. C.

Remarks on the Review of the controversy
between Great Britain and her colonies ... *See*
Bancroft, Edw.

Remarks on the western states ... or valley   199
of the Mississippi ... *L* 1839. O 45 a

Remarks upon a letter ... in the London   200
Chronicle ... containing an Enquiry into the
causes of the failure of the late expedition against
Cape Breton ... *L* 1757. O 30 a

Remarks upon slavery ... *See* Hobby, Wm. J.

REMEMBRANCER (THE)
  Remembrancer (The); or impartial repository
of public events, from 1775 to 1784. *See* Almon,
John.

REMER, JULIUS A.   201
  Amerikanisches Archiv. *Braunschweig* 1777–8.
O 3v: [16] 268 [3]; [8] 294 [4]; [24] 335 aa
  Revolutionary affairs in America. More vol-
umes were planned, but never published.

REMINGTON, CYRUS K.   202
  The ship-yard of the Griffon ... *Buf* 1891. O 78
[2] [incl.maps & pls] a

REMINGTON, FREDERIC   203
  Crooked trails. *N Y* 1898. O [8] 151 49pls aa
—rptd. same collat. & impr. 1899; [1923] a

REMINGTON, FREDERIC   204
  Done in the open. *N Y* Russell 1902. obl F
90[incl.pls]
—issue 1, au's first name spelled "Frederick" on
front cover, caption for pl. "Caught in the Circle" ptd. in blue & red aa
—ltd. issue, leather bdg. 250copies, signed aa
—rptd., same date, *N Y* Collier. F a

REMINGTON, FREDERIC   205
  Drawings. *N Y* Russell 1897. obl F [6] 61 pls aa
—ltd. issue, leather bdg. 250 copies, proof print
signed b
—rptd., same impr. & collat., 1898; 1800.

REMINGTON, FREDERIC   206
  Frontier sketches. *Chi* [1898]. Q 7 15pls aa

REMINGTON, FREDERIC   207
  Pony tracks ... *N Y* 1895. O [10] 269 [incl.
pls] front. + adv-lf aa
—rptd. *Columbus O* 1951. O a

REMINGTON, FREDERIC   208
  The way of an Indian. *N Y* Duffield 1906. D
252 14pls issue 1: bd. in red clo., yellow lettering
on both covers, "Duffield" at foot of spine,
numeral on p9 aa

REMINISCENCES
  Reminiscences of America in 1869. By two
Englishmen. *See* Rivington, Alexander, and Har-
ris, W. A.

  Reminiscences of the French war. *See* Rogers,
Robt., *Journals*.

  Reminiscences of the Indians. *See* Washburne,
Cephas.

  Reminiscences of travel, 1852–65. *See* Clark,
Austin S.

REMOVE INDIANS WESTWARD ...
  See McCoy, Isaac.

[REMSBURG, GEORGE J.]   209
  Life of Charley Reynolds, Custer's chief of
scouts. [*Potter Kas* 1914–15]. O 40 capt. t.only
Proof sheets of the series of 20 articles as pub.
in the "Weekly Kansan." aa
—rptd. *K C Mo* 1931. D 88 [2] [incl.port] 175
copies ptd. a

REMY, JULES   **210**
Voyage au pays des Mormons... *P* 1860.
O 2v: [88] 432; [8] 544. map 10pls aa
—Eng. ed. "Journey to Great-Salt-Lake City."
L 1861. O 2v: [34] 508; [8] 606 map 10pls aa

RENICK, WILLIAM   **211**
Memoirs, correspondence and reminiscences.
Circleville O 1880. O [6] 115 port erratum slip b
Renick owned, in 1853, the first drove of Texas
cattle brought to Illinois; his article reprinted
herein [on cattle and cattle trade of the West]
appeared first in Nimmo's *Report* of 1860.

RENO (JOHN).   **212**
Life and career of:... by himself. *Indianap*
1879. D 108 pls a
Operations in Missouri and the West by a
criminal history immortal, the first train robber
in the world.

RENSEIGNEMENTS   **213**
Renseignements sur la partie des États-Unis...
la plus favorable aux agriculteurs... *P* 1834. O
30 a

RENVILLE, MRS. MARY BUTLER   **214**
A thrilling narrative of Indian captivity.
Minneap 1863. O 52 b Y [of 2 cops loc]

REPLY (THE)   **215**
Reply (The) of a gentleman... upon the im-
portant contest between Great Britain and
America. *L* 1775. O 39 errata slip a

RÉPONSE
Réponse aux... questions... sur les États-
Unis... par un habitant de la Pennsylvanie.
See Bonnet, Abbé J. E.

REPORT   **216**
Report of the committee relative to excitements
on the part of British subjects, of the Indians, to
commit hostilities against the United States...
Wash 1812. O 43 a

Report of the Lords Commissioners for Trade
and Plantations on the petition of... Thomas
Walpole [*et al*] for a grant of lands on the river
Ohio... *See* Walpole, Thos.

Report of the Secretary of the Treasury... on
the subject of manufactures... 1791. *See* Hamilton, Alex.

Report [A] on barracks and hospitals... *See*
Billings, John S.

Report on hygiene of the... army... [Surgeon
General's circulars nos. 4 & 8]. *See* Billings,
John S., *A report*...

REPORTS
Reports of the committee of investigation sent
in 1873 by the Mexican government to the frontier
of Texas... *See Informe de la Comisión*...

Reports of the operations of the Army of Northern Virginia, from June... to Dec. 1862. *Rich*
1864. *See* Lee, Robert E.

REPUBLIC (THE)
Republic (The) of the United States; its duties
... Embracing also a review of the late war
between the United States and Mexico... *See*
Capen, Nahum.

RESEARCHES ON AMERICA...
By an officer... *See* McCulloh, James H., Jr.

RESISTANCE   **217**
Resistance no rebellion: in answer to Dr. Johnson
"Taxation no tyranny," *L* 1775. O [4] 35 a

Resistance no rebellion. In which the   **218**
right of a British parliament to tax the American
colonies, is fully considered and found unconstitutional... [*L*] ptd for N. Mand 1775. D [2] 65 a

RESULT   **219**
Result of the deliberations of the federal convention... Sept. 17, 1787. [*Phil* 1787]. O 15 b
One of the earliest printings of the constitution,
accompanied by Washington's circular letter of
transmission to the states. For other editions,
see under *Constitution of the United States.*

RETORT, JACK [pseud.]
A humble attempt at scurrility... *See* Franklin,
Wm.

RETROSPECTIVE VIEW (A)
Retrospective view (A) of the causes of the
difference between Great Britain and her colonies
... *See* Simpson, Wm.

RETURN   **220**
Return of the whole number of persons within...
the United States... *Phil* Child & Swaine 1791.
O 56 [some copies signed by Secy. of State
Jefferson] b AA N Y
—anr. ed. *Phil* Gales [1798?]. O 56 aa
—rptd. *Wash* 1802. O 52 aa
—Eng. ed. *L* 1793. O 56 aa
First census, taken pursuant to act of March 1,
1790 [not 1791, as on title-page of first edition].

Return of the whole number of persons   **221**
within the... United States. [2nd census]. [*Wash*
1801]. F [4] 34 [36] + add. starred p. 12 aa
—anr. ed. *Wash* 1802. O [4] 9–88 fold. tab a
For later enumerations *see Census of the
United States.*

REVELATIONS
Revelations: a companion to the "New gospel of peace . . ." *See* White, Rich. G.

REVERE, JOSEPH W.   222
A tour of duty in California . . . *N Y* 1849. D [12] 305 map 6pls aa
—rptd. "Naval duty in California," *Oakland* 1947. a
Description of the gold fields and authoritative particulars on the California conquest.

REVERIES   223
Reveries d'un Suisse, ayant pour but la réconciliation entre l'Angleterre et ses colonies. *L* [*Amst?*] 1781. O 40 a

REVIEW
Review of the administration of the government of the United-States; since the year ninety-three . . . *See* Pickering, Timothy.

Review of the constitution proposed by   224
the late convention at Philadelphia. By a federal republican. *Phil* 1787. O 39 b

Review of the controversy between feder-   225
alists and republicans. *Phil* 1800. O 50 a

Review (A) of the military operations in North America. *See* Livingston, Wm.

Review (A) of the question, In whom has   226
the constitution vested the treaty power? . . . By a senator of the United States. *Phil* 1796. O 36 a

Review (A) of The rector detected, or, the colonel reconnoitred. Pt. I [all]. *See* Camm, John.

Review (A) of the revenue system . . . By a citizen. *See* Findley, Wm.

Review of the slave question. By a Virginian. *See* Harrison, Jesse B.

REVIEWERS (THE)   227
Reviewers (The) reviewed, or British falsehoods detected by American truths. *N Y* 1815. D 72 a

RÉVOIL, BÉNÉDICT H.   228
Chasses et pêches de l'autre monde. *P* 1856. 16° 320 a
—anr. ed. [in part], enl., "Chasses dans l'Amérique du Nord," *P* 1861. D [12] 326
—anr. ed. [in part], enl., "Pêches dans l'Amérique du Nord," *P* 1863. D [4] 320
—Eng. tr. [by the "Chronicler"], "Shooting and fishing in . . . North America," *L* 1865. D 2v: [20] 291; [6] 279
—Eng. tr. [by W. H. D. Adams], "The hunter and trapper in North America," *L* 1874. D 393 [incl.front]

REVOLUTION (THE) IN 1782   229
Impartially considered. *L* 1782. O 35 a

REVUELTAS, J. C.   230
Articulos en defensa de los creditos de la frontera contra los Estados-Unidos del Norte por depredaciones de las tribus barbaras. *Mex* 1857. O 28 a

REY, WILLIAM   231
L'Amérique protestante: notes et observations d'un voyageur. *P* 1857. D 2v: [8] 326 [1]; [4] 371 a

REYNAL, RAFAEL, ed.   232
Viage por los Estados Unidos . . . *Cin* 1834. 24° [6] 164 7pls aa
Describes his trip up the Mississippi to Louisville, Cincinnati, Pittsburgh and the East.

REYNOLDS, BERNARD.   233
Sketches of Mobile . . . *Mobile* 1868. O [2] 80 aa

REYNOLDS (CHARLEY).
Life of: *See* Remsburg, Geo J.

REYNOLDS, JOHN   234
"The balm of Gilead." An enquiry into the right of American slavery. *Belleville Ill* 1860. O 48 b B N NYP

REYNOLDS, JOHN   235
Friendship's offering. A sketch of . . . Dr. John Mason Peck. *Belleville Ill* 1858. D 34 b ChiH G IH

REYNOLDS, JOHN   236
My own times . . . [*Belleville*] 1855. D 600 [23] port b of 400 cops ptd 300 burned in the first Chicago fire.
—ed. 2, *Chi* 1879. O [22] 396 port a
Best picture of Illinois pioneer life.

REYNOLDS, JOHN   237
The pioneer history of Illinois . . . *Belleville* 1852. D 348 aa
—ed. 2, with index, *Chi* 1887. O [8] 17–459 10ports plan a

REYNOLDS, JOHN   238
Sketches of the country on the northern route from Belleville, Illinois, to . . . New York, and back by the Ohio valley. *Belleville* 1854. D 264 b N NYP WisH

REYNOLDS, JOHN G.   239
A conclusive exculpation of the marine corps in Mexico . . . *N Y* 1853. O 124 a
—anr. issue, *Wash* same date. O
Answer to allegations made by Lieut. Devlin in *The marine corps in Mexico.*

REYNOLDS, JOHN S.   240
Reconstruction in South Carolina . . . *Columbia* 1905. O [4] 522 port aa

REYNOLDS, SAMUEL   **241**
A history of the city of Williamsburgh [N. Y.].
Williamsburgh 1852. D 137 [4] a

REYNOLDS, STEPHEN   **242**
The voyage of the New Hazard to the northwest coast, Hawaii and China, 1810–13. *Salem*
1938. O [22] 158 [2 l.] 12pls[on 6 sheets] a 600
copies ptd.[100 on special paper]

REYNOLDS, LIEUT. W. D.   **243**
The rebel fiend; or, the scout of secession . . .
historical romance . . . embracing passages . . .
in the varied career of . . . Parson Brownlow.
Also . . . heroism . . . of his . . . daughter. *Phil*
Reichner n.d. [1862?]. O [2] 21–49 a
—rptd. "Miss Martha Brownlow; or the heroine
of Tennessee . . .," au. given rank of Major,
Phil Barclay [1863]. same collat.
—Ger. tr., same impr., date & collat.

[REZANOV, COUNT NICOLAI P.]   **244**
The Rezanov voyage to Nueva California.
The report . . . with notes . . . by Thomas C.
Russell . . . *S F* 1926. O [12] 104 [1] 5pls aa
260copies ptd.
A translation of a part of the second volume
of P. Tikhmenev, *Rossisko-Amerikanskoi Kompanii*,
St. Petersburg, 1863—giving Rezanov's report.

RHODE ISLAND
Rhode Island and Providence Plantations.
Records of the colony of: *See* Bartlett, John R.

RHYS, HORTON   **245**
A theatrical trip for a wager through Canada
and the United States. *L* 1861. O 140 5pls a

[RICE, DAVID]   **246**
Slavery inconsistent with justice and good
policy. *Lex* 1792. 16° 34 a
—rptd. *Phil* 1792.
—other eds.: *L* 1793; *N Y* 1804; *N Y* 1812.
Kentucky's first protest against slavery delivered in a speech before that state's constitutional
convention.

RICE, HARVEY   **247**
Incidents of pioneer life in the . . . western
reserve. *Clev* 1881. D 300 a

RICE, JOHN H.
A system of modern geography . . . for use in
the Confederate States . . . *Atlanta* 1862. Q 91 aa
A geography *sans* maps, no facilities being
available for making them; but conditions and
resources of the South, "studiously concealed by
every Yankee work," are amply presented.

RICHARDS, FRANKLIN D., comp.   **248**
Latter Day Saints in Utah. Opinion of Judge

Z. Snow upon the official course of Brigham
Young . . . *Liv* 1852. O 24 aa

RICHARDS, GEORGE H.   **249**
Memoir of Alexander Macomb . . . *N Y* 1833.
D 130 a
By an artillery officer serving under Macomb.

[RICHARDS, ROBERT] pseud.   **250**
The California Crusoe; or the lost treasure
found. A tale of Mormonism. *L* 1854. 18° [4]
162 pl aa
—rptd. *L* 1858. a
Completely fictitious, even to the pseudonym.

RICHARDS (STEPHEN DEE).   **251**
Life and confession of: the murderer of nine
persons . . . [*Lincoln Neb* 1879]. D 72 aa

RICHARDS, WILLIAM C., ed.   **252**
Georgia illustrated . . . *Penfield Ga* 1842. Q [6]
44 13pls[incl. eng. t.] aa
Originally issued in 5parts, 1841–2.

RICHARDSON, ALBERT D.   **253**
Our new states and territories . . . notes of a
recent tour . . . *N Y* Beadle [1866]. O 80 [incl.front
wrap] a

RICHARDSON, D.   **254**
Texas as seen in 1870 . . . *Shreveport* 1870.
O 48 a

RICHARDSON, HESTER D.   **255**
Side-lights on Maryland history . . . *Balt* 1913.
O 2v: [22] 460; [12] 498. 2errata-lvs 102pls a

[RICHARDSON, MAJ. JOHN]?   **256**
The letters of Veritas . . . a succinct narrative
of the military administration of Sir George
Prevost . . . *Montreal* 1815. O 157 aa
Severely critical of Prevost's conduct as British
commander in the War of 1812. Ascribed also
to Stephen Sewell.

RICHARDSON, MAJ. JOHN   **257**
Wacousta; or, the prophecy . . . *L* 1832. D
3v: [4] 280; [2] 332; [2] 371 aa
—ed 2, *L* 1839. same collat a
—Am ed, *Phil* 1833. D 2v: 264; 274 a
Fiction; but gives good account of Pontiac's
attempt on Detroit.

RICHARDSON, MAJ. [JOHN]   **258**
War of 1812. First series [all.] [*Brockville*]
1842. O [8] 182 aa
—rptd. *Tor* 1902. O [60] 320 32pls 1100 copies
ptd.[100 with some pls col.] a

RICHARDSON, SIR JOHN, et al.   **259**
The zoology of Captain Beechey's voyage . . .

1825–1828. *L* 1839. Q [12] 180 4maps [on 3sheets] 44col.pls b LC NYP Y

RICHARDSON, N. S.   **260**
Historical sketch of Watertown [Conn.] . . .
N Hav 1845. D 48 a
—enl. ed. *Waterbury* 1858. D 72

RICHARDSON, RUPERT N., and   **261**
RISTER, CARL C.
The greater southwest . . . from the Spanish conquest to the twentieth century. *Glendale, Cal.* 1934. O 506 6maps a

RICHARDSON, W., and D., [comps.]   **261a**
Galveston directory for 1859–60; with a brief history . . . *Galv* 1859. O 92 map aa

RICHARDSON (WILLIAM H.)   **262**
Journal of: a private soldier in Col. Doniphan's command. *Balt* 1847. D 84 c G Hn LC Y
—ed. 2, *Balt* 1848. D 96 3pls facs aa
—ed. 3, same collat., *N Y* 1848. rptd: 1849; 1850. aa

RICHMOND, C. W., and   **263**
VALLETTE, H. F.
A history of the county of Du Page, Illinois . . .
Chi 1857. D [4] 6–212 aa

RICHMOND, WILLIAM   **264**
A discourse . . . with referenec to the mission . . . through the valley of the Mississippi . . . 1829–30.
L 1830. O [8] 31 a

RICHMOND, INDIANA
Annals of pioneer settlers on the Whitewater and its tributaries, in the vicinity of Richmond, Ind. By a native. *See* Wasson, John M.

Directory of Richmond, Indiana: with a   **265**
historical sketch. By John T. Plummer . . . *Richmond* 1857. O 168 map a

RICHMOND, VA   **266**
A concise statement of the awful conflagration of the theatre, in . . . Richmond, [Va] [*Phil*?] 1812.
O 36 aa

Richmond during the war . . . By a Richmond lady. *See* Brock, Sallie A.

Richmond Howitzers in the war . . . *See* Daniel, Frederick S.

Richmond in by-gone days. *See* Mordecai, Samuel.

The seven days' battles in front of   **267**
Richmond: . . . Rich 1862. O 45 aa
—anr. iss. with *Charleston* impr aa

The stranger's guide . . . for Richmond: . . . **268**
offices of the Confederate . . . government . . . [*Rich*]
1863. 16° 31 aa

RICHTER, GUSTAV   **269**
Der Nordamerikanische Freistaat Wisconsin.
Wesel 1849. O 32 map aa

RICHTER, KARL E.   **270**
Reisen nach Nordamerika und zurück in den Jahren 1835 bis 1849. Zugabe: Ein brief aus Californien von Moritz A. Richter . . . *Leip* 1852. 16°
2v: [8] 374; [6] 3–271 [1] aa

RICHTHOFEN, FERDINAND,   **271**
baron von
The Comstock lode: its character . . . *S F* 1866.
O 83 a

RICHTHOFEN, FERDINAND,   **272**
baron von
Explorations in the iron fields of Sierra county [Calif.]. n.p. [1867]. O 31 fold.map a

RICHTHOFEN, WALTER,   **273**
baron von
Cattle-raising on the plains . . . *N Y* 1885. D [8]
102 + 6adv-p a
The Baron was a leading cattleman of Colorado and father of Germany's famous flyer.

RICKETSON, DANIEL   **274**
The history of New Bedford. *New Bedford* 1858.
D 412 a

RICKETTS, WILLIAM P.   **275**
Fifty years in the saddle. *Sheridan Wyo* 1942.
O [12] 198 pls a

[**RICKMAN, JOHN**]   **276**
Journal of Captain Cook's last voyage to the Pacific . . . 1776–1780. *L* 1781. O [50] 388[error for 396] map 5pls b N NYP
—ed. 2, *L* 1781. O [52] 404 map 5pls aa
—rptd. *Dub* 1781. same collat. as ed. 1, with final p. correctly numb. aa
—new ed. *L* 1785. O [66] 376 map 10pls aa
—Am. ed. ["By an officer on board the Discovery,"—au.unnamed] *Phil* 1783. O [2] 9–96 99–230
+ 2adv-p b JCB LC
—Fr. tr. *P* 1782. O [10] 508 map pl; *Versailles* 1783, O [64] 454 a
—Ger. tr: *Beri* 1781 map pl; *Leip* 1790. O 2v aa
First published account of Cook's third and last voyage, preceding the official publication three years. Map is substantially same as in the narrative attributed to John Ledyard, and the texts of the two accounts are quite similar, hence some authorities attribute this book to Ledyard, However, the text shows that its anonymous author was origi-

nally on the "Discovery" and not transferred to the "Resolution" until 1777, whereas Ledyard was on the latter throughout the voyage. The American edition, with title-page copying almost exactly that of William Ellis's account of this voyage, has been erroneously ascribed to that officer.

[RICKMAN, THOMAS C.] 277
Emigration to America candidly considered . . . *L* 1798. O [8] 62 [2] a
Condemnatory.

RICKMAN, THOMAS C. 278
The life of Thomas Paine . . . *L* 1819. O [16] 278 port a
Attempts to vindicate Paine from the earlier unfriendly biographies by George Chalmers and James Cheetham.

RIDDLE, JAMES M., pub. 279
Pittsburgh directory for 1815. *Pitt* 1815. 16° 156 chart b AA LC Y
First directory of this city. The second was issued in 1819. For the third, *see* Jones, Samuel.

[RIDGE, JOHN R.] 279a
The life and adventures of Joaquin Murieta, the . . . California bandit. By Yellow Bird. *S F* 1854. O 91 2pls d S [of 3 cops known]
—For an anonymous, unauthorized plagiarism [what might be considered a spurious ed. 2] see "Murieta (Joaquin) The brigand chief . . ." *S F* 1859.
—ed. 3, [so styled in recognition of the above plagiarized version, but actually ed. 2] author's name disclosed and text somewhat enlarged. *S F* 1871. O 82 aa
—rptd. together with Sawyer's "Career of Tiburcio Vásquez . . ." *S F* 1874–75. O 2pts in 1 : 82; 85–98 b.
—Sp. tr. *San Antonio* [1885?] Q 59 aa
First biography of this sanguinary villain, the flimsy, romanticized base on which has been built an apparently enduring hero myth.

RIDGELY, DAVID 280
Annals of Annapolis . . . *Balt* 1841. O [16] 13–283 front a

RIDINGS, SAM P. 281
The Chisholm trail . . . *Guthrie* [1936]. O [12] 591[incl. front.] map aa

RIDLEY, BROMFIELD L. 282
Battles and sketches of the Army of Tennessee. *Mexico Mo* 1906. O 662 [10] map 8 pls errata slip a

RIDLON, G. T. 283
Saco valley [Maine] settlements and families . . . *Port* 1895. Q [14] 1250 68pls a
For the 1200 copies of this most ambitious of all local histories two tons of paper were required.

RIEDESEL, FRIEDRICH A., and FREDERICA C. L. 284
Auszüge aus den Briefen und Papieren des: . . . Ihre beyderseitige Reise nach America . . . [*Berlin* 1800]. O [2] 386 260 copies [60 on fine paper] b BP LC NYP
—rptd. "Die Berufs-Reise nach America . . .," *Berlin* 1800. D [10] 352 [incl eng t-p] aa
—ed. 3, *Berlin* 1801. D [10] 352 eng.t. a
—Dutch tr. *Haarlem* 1802. O [8] 220 [2]
—Eng. tr., with about 40p. omitted, as indelicate, and some adds., "Letters and memoirs relating to the war of American independence . . .," *N Y* 1827. D 323 a
—best—complete—Eng. tr. "Letters and journals . . .," tr. Wm. L. Stone, *Alb* 1867. O 235 3pls a Also 50 copies on L. P. aa
Larger portion of the letters was by the wife. For other Riedesel material *see* Eelking, Max von.

RIES, JULIUS 285
Schilderungen des Treibens im Leben und Handel in den Vereinigten Staaten und Havanna . . . *Berlin* 1840. O [10] 236 [2] a

RIETTI, J. C. 286
Military annals of Mississippi . . . Vol. I [all]. n.p. [1896?]. D 196 aa

[RIÉZO, JUAN M., VELASCO, J. FRANCISCO, et al] 287
Memoria de las proporciones naturales de las provincias internas occidentales . . . *Mex* 1822. O 62 b
Report by delegates from Sonora to the commissioners of the Mexican constitution, including account of present Arizona and New Mexico.

RIGGS, STEPHEN R. 288
Mary and I. Forty years with the Sioux. *Chi* Holmes [1880]. D [20] 388 3ports [on 2 pls] a
—rptd. *B* [1887]. D 437 3ports

RIGGS, STEPHEN R. 289
Tah-Koo Wah-Kan; or, the gospel among the Dakotas. *B* [1869]. D [36] 491 5pls a
Describes Sioux life and polytheistic worship.

RIGHT 290
Right (The) and practice of impressment, as concerning Great Britain and America, considered. *L* 1814. O [2] 68 a

Right (The) of the British legislature to 291 tax the American colonies vindicated . . . *L* 1774. O [4] 48 41–50 a
—ed. 2, with adds., same impr. 1775. O 88
Attributed to Samuel Johnson but more probably by John Gray.

Right (The) of the British legislature to   292
tax the colonies considered, in a letter to . . . Lord
North. *L* [1774]. O 24 a
Attributed to John Gray.

RIGHTS
Rights (The) of colonies examined. *See* Hopkins,
Steph.

Rights (The) of Great Britain asserted against
the claims of America . . . *See* Dalrymple, Sir John.

Rights (The) of Parliament vindicated, on   293
occasion of the late stamp-act . . . *L* 1766. O 44 aa

Rights (The) of the British colonies consid-   294
ered. The administration and regulation of the
colonies exploded . . . *L* [1765]. O [6] 3–91 errata
slip a
Defence of colonial rights, highly critical of the
pamphlets of Grenville and Pownall.

Rights (The) of the colonies, and the extent of the
legislative authority of Great-Britain, briefly stated
. . . *See* Phelps,—.

Rights (The) of the English colonies . . .   295
stated and defended . . . *L* 1774. Q [2] 51 a

RIKER, JAMES   296
The annals of Newtown, in Queens county, New
York. *N Y* 1852. O [6] 3–437 2maps port[in some
copies] a

RIKER, JAMES   297
Harlem: its origin and early annals . . . *N Y*
1881. O [14] 636 map a
—rptd. 1904.

RIKER, JOHN F.   298
Journal of a trip to California. [*Urbana* O 1855]?
O 32 capt.t.only dd G Y [only cops loc]

RILEY, BENJAMIN F.   299
History of Conecuh county, Alabama . . . *Columbus Ga* 1881. D [12] 233 a

RILLIET DE CONSTANT, M[ONS.   300
LOUIS]
Extraits de correspondance d'un colon américain sur la colonie suisse à Highland, près de Saint-Louis [in Madison county, Ill.]. Pt.I[all]. *Berne*
1849. D 54 tab map aa

RINFRET, RAOUL   301
Le Yukon et son or. *Mont* [1898]. D 89 a

RING, WILLIAM B.   302
A guide to mechanics . . . wishing to emigrate
to the United States . . . *L* [1837]. D 24 cov. t.
only aa

RINGGOLD, CADWALADER   303
A series of charts . . . embracing surveys of the
. . . entrance to the bay of San Francisco . . . *Wash*
1851. O 44 6maps 8pls a
—rptd. 4 times, same impr.: 1851 and 1852.
Some copies are accompanied by a separately
printed undated fifteen-page pamphlet. *Correspondence to maps and charts of California.*

RINGWALT, J[OHN] L.   304
Development of transportation systems in the
United States. *Phil* 1888. Q 398 48pls aa

[RIPLEY, ELEAZER W.]   305
Facts relative to the campaign on the Niagara in
1814. *B* 1815. O 48 [4] fold.tab a
Vindicates the conduct of this general at Lundy's
Lane.

RIPLEY, MRS. ELIZA [M.]   306
Capture . . . of Richmond. *N Y* 1907. O 31 a

RIPLEY, MRS. ELIZA M.   307
From flag to flag; a woman's experience in the
south during the war . . . *N Y* 1889. D 296 a

RIPLEY, MRS. ELIZA [M.]   308
Social life in old New Orleans . . . *N Y* 1912. O
[12] 332 8pls + 2adv-p a

RIPLEY, EZRA, et al   309
A history of the fight at Concord . . . *Concord*
1827. O 60 a
—ed. 2, same impr. 1832. O 40

RIPLEY, BRIGADIER GENERAL   310
R[OSWELL] S.
Report of operations from August 21 to September 10, 1863 . . . *Rich* 1864. O 42 aa

RIPLEY, R[OSWELL] S.   311
The war with Mexico. *N Y* 1849. O 2v: [2] 13–
524; 650 14 plans a

RIPLEY, THOMAS   312
They died with their boots on. *N Y* 1935. O [22]
285 + adv-p 8ports a

RISE   313
Rise (The) and progress of . . . abolitionism . . .
Alexandria La 1840. O 23 a

Rise (The), progress, and present state, of   314
the dispute between the people of America, and the
administration. By the bishop of—. *L* [1775?]. D 56
front. a
Contains account of the fight at Concord. Attributed to William Jackson, Bishop of Oxford,
but more probably by Rev. Wm. Jackson, an
Irish revolutionary who defended the American
revolt.

RISHEL, C. D., ed.   315
The life and adventures of David Lewis, the robber and counterfeiter, the terror of the Cumberland valley. *Newville Pa* 1890. O 84 a

RISLER, JEREMIAS   316
Leben August Gottlieb Spangenbergs, Bischofs der Evangelischen Brüder-Kirche ... *Barby* 1794. D [20] 516 a
—Fr. tr. *Neuchatel* 1835. O
Includes his missionary travels from Pennsylvania to Georgia.

RISLEY'S AUS AMERICA
Risley's Aus America ... panorama des Mississippi flusses. *See* Smith, John R., *Descriptive pamphlet* ...

RISTER, CARL C.   317
Southern plainsmen ... *Norman, Okla.* 1938. O [18] 290 map pls a

RISTER, CARL C.   318
The southwestern frontier, 1865–1881 ... *Clev* 1928. O 336 [incl double-p map] a

RITTENHOUSE, RUFUS   319
Boyhood life in Iowa forty years ago ... *Dubuque* 1880. O 23 a

RITTER, ABRAHAM   320
History of the Moravian church in Philadelphia ... *Phil* 1857. O [20] 17–282 [2], 21 pls a

RITTER, ABRAHAM   321
Philadelphia and her merchants ... *Phil* 1860. O 223 20pls&plans

RIVERA, PEDRO DE   322
Diario. Y derrotero de lo caminado, visto y obcervado en el discurso de la visita general de precidios ... en las provincias ynternas de Nueva España ... *Guatemala* 1736. F [2] 76 c B N NYP
General Rivera's inspection tour of presidios in the frontier provinces included those of New Mexico and Texas; his description of the people, settlements, etc., is of high value. *Cf.* Acuña, Juan de, and *Nueva España.*

RIVERS, WILLIAM J.   323
A chapter in the early history of South Carolina. *Charleston S C* 1874. O 110 a
A continuation of his 1856 *History.*

[RIVERS, WILLIAM J.]   324
A sketch of the history of South Carolina to ... 1719 ... *Charleston S C* 1856. O 470 errata slip aa
—rptd. *Charleston* 1857. a

[RIVERS, WILLIAM J.]   325
Topics in the history of South-Carolina. *Charleston* 1850–53. D 2v: 60; [4] 61–96 a

RIVERSIDE [CALIF.]   326
History and directory of: By A. A. Bynon & Son. *Riverside* 1893. O 152 189 [incl. advs] a

RIVES, WILLIAM C.   327
History of the life and times of James Madison. *B* 1859–68. O 3v: [22] 660; [22] 658; [26] 639 a
Due to the author's death an intended fourth volume never appeared.

[RIVINGTON, ALEXANDER, and   328
HARRIS, W. A.]
Reminiscences of America in 1869. *L* 1870. D [20] 332 a

[RIVINGTON, JAMES] pub.   329
A list of the officers ... serving under ... General Sir Guy Carleton ... *N Y* 1783. O 98 [4] c NYH

RIVORS, [C.]   330
A full and authentic account of the murders of James King, of Wm., *et al.* The execution of James P. Casey, *et al. Roch* 1857. O 64 aa
For similar title, *see* Fargo, Frank F.

RIVOT, LOUIS E.   331
Notice sur le lac Supérieur ... *P* 1857. O [4] 112 pl a

RIVOT, LOUIS E.   332
Voyage au lac Supérieur. *P* 1855. O [4] 156 3maps aa

ROA BÁRCENA, JOSÉ M.   333
Recuerdos de la invasion Norte-Americana, 1846–8. *Mex* 1883. O [8] 866 aa

ROACH, LIEUT. ALVA C.   334
The prisoner of war and how treated. Containing a history of Col. Streight's expedition to the rear of Bragg's army ... *Indp* 1865. D 244 a
—rptd., same impr. & collat., 1887.

[ROBB, JOHN S.]   335
Streaks of squatter life, and far-west scenes ... *Phil* 1847. D 187 9pls aa
—rptd., same impr. & collat., 1849; [1858]. a
—anr. ed. "Western scenes ...," *Phil* [1858?]. same collat.
For another reprint, *see* Lewis, Henry C.

ROBBINS (REV. AMMI R.),   336
a chaplain in the American army.
Journal of: in the northern campaign of 1776. *N Hav* 1850. O 48 a

ROBBINS, THOMAS   337
An historical view of the first planters of New England. *Hart* 1815. 18° 300 a
—rptd., same impr. & collat. 1843.

ROBERT, T.   338
A narrative of the life of the Reverend Mr. George
Whitefield . . . with the history of his travels . . .
L J. Bunyan [1770?]. D [4] 259 a

ROBERTS, CAPTAIN [pseud.]
Never caught . . . blockade-running during the
American civil war . . . *See* Hobart-Hampden,
Augustus C.

ROBERTS, DAN[IEL] W.   339
Rangers and sovereignty. *San Antonio* 1914. D
[10] 15—190 port a
Reminiscences of a Ranger captain.

ROBERTS, MRS. D[ANIEL] W.   340
A woman's reminiscences . . . in camp with the
Rangers. *Austin Tex* [1928]. O 64 6pls a

ROBERTS, DE WITT C.   341
Southern sketches . . . *Jacksonville* 1865. 16°
142 a

ROBERTS, JAMES   342
The narrative of: a soldier under Gen. Washing-
ton, and under Gen. Jackson . . . *Chi* 1858. O 32 aa
Unconvincing reminiscences of a centenarian
Negro; issued obviously as anti-slavery prop-
aganda.

ROBERTS, JOHN M., ed.
Autobiography of a revolutionary soldier. *See*
Collins, James.

ROBERTS (CAPT. LEMUEL).   343
Memoirs of: . . . as a continental soldier . . . as
prisoner . . . *Bennington Vt* 1809. O 96 aa

ROBERTS, ORAN M.   344
A description of Texas . . . *St L* 1881. O [12]
17–133 14maps & pls aa

[ROBERTS, ROBERT E.]   345
Sketches of the city of Detroit . . . *Det* 1855.
O 63 aa

ROBERTS, S.   346
To emigrants to the gold region . . . *N Hav* 1849.
O 32, 12 c

ROBERTS, W. H.   347
Northwestern Washington: its soil, climate . . .
Port Townsend 1880. D 52 fold. map b Y

ROBERTS, WILLIAM   348
An account of the first discovery and natural
history of Florida . . . *L* 1763. Q [10] 102 7maps &
pls b AA H N NYP Y
A timely book, issued immediately after the cession of this colony from Spain to England, to satisfy
British curiosity concerning the territory acquired.

ROBERTS, W[ILLIAM] MILNOR   349
Special report of a reconnoissance of the route
for the Northern Pacific railroad between lake Superior and Puget sound . . . [*Phil*? 1869]. O 51 [4] a

ROBERTSON, ARCHIBALD, Lieut. general   350
Robertson, Archibald, Lieut. General . . . ; his
diaries and sketches in America, 1762–80. Ed. by
H. M. Lydenberg. *N Y* 1930. sm Q [12] 300 [2]
63maps & pls a

ROBERTSON (GEORGE).   351
Outline of the life of: written by himself . . . *Lex
Ky* 1876. O 210 port a
Primitive Kentucky described by one of her
ablest sons.

ROBERTSON, GEORGE   352
Scrap book on law and politics, men and times.
Lex Ky 1855. O 402 a

ROBERTSON, JAMES   353
A few months in America . . . *L* [1855]. D 230 [9] a

ROBERTSON, JAMES A., ed.   354
Louisiana under the rule of Spain, France and
the United States . . . *Clev* 1911. O 2v: 376; 391
maps & plans aa

[ROBERTSON, JOHN]   354a
Letters on . . . southern wrongs and remedies.
Rich 1861. O 60 + cover t. aa

[ROBERTSON, JOHN B.]   355
Reminiscences of a campaign in Mexico; by a
member of "The Bloody-First" . . . *Nashv* 1849.
D 288 front. map aa

ROBERTSON, W., and W. F.   356
Our American tour . . . from the Atlantic to the
Golden Gate . . . *Edin* 1871. O 148 pl a

ROBERTSON, W. G.   357
Recollections of early settlers of Montgomery
co. [Ala.] . . . *Montg* 1892. 16° 157 a

ROBERTSON, WILLIAM   358
The history of America. [Books I to VIII, covering discovery and Spanish conquests]. *L* 1777. Q
2v: [24] 488; [4] 536 [20] pl 4maps a
—continued, posthumously, in Books IX to X
[covering early histories of Va. & New Eng.], *L*
1796. Q [8] 249
—complete ed., all 10 books, called 8th ed., *L*
1800–01. D 3v: [42] 417; [4] 458; [2] 438. 11pls a
—anr. ed. [continued by David McIntosh through
the revolution], *Edin* 1817. Q 588 [4] 3maps 12pls
—Am. eds: *N Y* 1798, O 2v: 512; 512 [30]; *Phil*
1812, O 2v: [12] 532; 514
Most highly regarded secondary source of its
time; now entirely superseded.

ROBERTSON, WYNDHAM 359
Oregon ... with a statement of the claims of
Russia, Spain, Great Britain, and the United
States. *Wash* 1846. O [8] 5–203 [24] map b N NYP
OreH Y

ROBIDOUX, MRS. ORRAL M. 360
Memorial to the Robidoux brothers ... *K C*
1924. O 311[incl.front.] map 16pls aa

ROBIN, L'ABBÉ 361
Nouveau voyage dans l'Amérique ... *Phil & P*
1782. D [10] 222 a
—anr. issue, same date & impr. D 192
—anr. ed., same impr., 1783. D [8] 224
—anr. ed. *Phil* [ptd. *P*] 1783. D 192
—Eng. tr: by Freneau, *Phil* Bell 1783, O 112 aa;
B 1784. O 96 aa
—Dutch tr. *Amst* 1782. O [8] 284 [2] map
—Ger. tr. *Nurnberg* 1783. O 176

ROBIN, C[LAUDE] C. 362
Voyages dans l'intérieur de la Louisiane, de la
Floride Occidentale ... *P* 1807. O 3v: [16] 346;
[4] 511; [12] 551. map plan port aa
—Ger. tr. *Berlin* 1808–9, O 3v: *Vienna* 1811, O
2v a
Robin witnessed at New Orleans and at Nachi-
toches, the transfer of Louisiana to the United
States; he gives a most ample description of Loui-
siana's Western interior and of Spanish Texas.

[ROBINSON, ALFRED] 363
Life in California: during a residence of several
years ... By an American. *N Y* 1846. D [14] 341
9pls aa
—rptd. 1849. aa
—Eng. ed., omitting the 2nd pt. [Boscana's account of Cal. Indians] and all pls. *L* 1851. D 182
[incl. initial blank lf] + 10adv-p
—rptd. with add. reminiscences and port., *S F* 1891,
O 284; 1897; 1925. O [28] 316 [2] pls 250copies ptd.
Useful authority on the period covered and one
of the first accounts of California in English by a
resident. The author came to the province in 1829
and married into the prominent De Guerra family.

ROBINSON, CONWAY 364
An account of discoveries in the west until 1519,
and of voyages to and along the Atlantic coast,
1520–73. *Rich* 1848. O [16] 491 a

ROBINSON, FAYETTE 365
An account of the organization of the army of
the United States; with biographies ... *Phil* 1848.
D 2v: 352; [10] 334. 36 ports a

ROBINSON, FAYETTE 366
California and its gold regions ... *N Y* 1849.
O 138 + 6adv-p map b
—anr. issue, with app.added, 144p. map b

A view of San Francisco is sometimes found,
inserted, but was not issued with the book.

ROBINSON, DR. J. H. 367
Silver-Knife: or, the hunters of the Rocky
mountains. *B* Hotchkiss, 1850. O 103 aa
—anr. ed. *B* 1854. D 168
—rptd. *B* Gleason 1864. Q

ROBINSON, JACOB S. 368
Sketches of the great west. A journal of the
Santa-Fe expedition. *Portsmouth N H* 1848. 18°
71 b AA G LC [of 4cops loc]
With Doniphan to Santa Fe and operations in
the Navajo country.

ROBINSON, JOHN, and DOW, 369
GEORGE F.
The sailing ships of New England. Ser. 1, 2 & 3.
Salem 1922–4–8. O 3v: 66 [2] 182 pls; 52 [2] 209
pls; 46 [2] 216 pls aa
—L P iss b

ROBINSON, JOSEPH W. 370
History of Kansas, and railroad and steamboat
sketches ... *Phil* 1857. D 74 [22] b G KasH [only
copies known]

ROBINSON, J[OSEPH] W. 371
Railroad and steamboat sketches between New
York and Kansas. [*Phil*? 1859?]. D 22 + cover. t.
b H NYP Y

[ROBINSON, MATTHEW, BARON 372
ROKEBY]
Considerations on the measures ... with respect
to the British colonies ... *L* [1774]. O [4] 160 aa
—to later issues of ed. 1, errata lf added a
—ed. 2, *L* [1774]. O [4] 176 [45]
—ed. 3, *L* [1774]. same collat.
—rptd. *Bath* [1776].
—Am. eds: *B* 1774 [3 eds.]. O [64]; *Hart* 1774,
same collat.; *N Y* 1774, O [2] 73; *Phil* 1774, O 60
Strongly critical of Lord North's policy, and
also of Franklin's conduct. The *Appendix*, added
to edition two, was issued separately at Philadelphia, 1775, in a octavo of 19 pages.

[ROBINSON, MATTHEW, BARON 373
ROKEBY]
A further examination of our present American
measures ... *Bath Eng* 1776. O [6] 3–256 a

ROBINSON, MATT[HEW], BARON 374
ROKEBY
Peace the best policy or reflections upon the
appearance of a foreign war ... *L* 1777. O [4] 112 a
—ed. 2, same impr. & date. O [2] 59

ROBINSON, T. H. 375
America's alpine region ... *Newville, Pa* 1875.
O 54 a

[ROBINSON, MRS. THÉRÈSE L. VON J.]   **376**
Aus der Geschichte de ersten Ansiedelungen in den Vereinigten Staaten. *Leip* 1845. O 191 a

[ROBINSON, MRS. THÉRÈSE L. VON J.]   **377**
Geschichte der Colonization von Neu-England . . . 1607–92. *Leip* 1847. O [18] 710 map a
—Eng. tr. *L* 1851. D 2v: [14] 381; [4] 407

ROBINSON, W. A.   **378**
A business directory of Grand Rapids . . . [with historical sketch]. *Chi* 1856. O 56 aa

ROBINSON, W[ILLIAM] D.   **379**
Memoir . . . to persons of the Jewish religion in Europe, on the subject of emigration to . . . one of the most eligible parts of the United States . . . *L* 1819. O 40 a
Advocates settling on the Upper Mississippi or the Missouri. This Arcadian dream was never realized.

ROBINSON, WILLIAM D.   **380**
Memoirs of the Mexican revolution . . . *Phil* 1820. O [36] 396 a
—Eng. ed. *L* 1821. O 2v: [56] 328; [8] 389 [3] map port aa
—Dutch tr. *Haarlem* 1823. O [48] 414 port
—Ger. tr. *Hannover* 1824. O
—Sp. tr. *L* 1824. O [54] 336 + 16adv-p map port
Chief contemporary authority on the audacious filibustering expedition against Mexico under Mina, launched with a handful of men, through Texas in 1817. Notable also for its advocacy of a communication between the Atlantic and Pacific via Nicaragua.

ROBLES, MANUEL   **381**
Memoria del secretario de estado y del despacho de guerre y marina. *Mex* 1852. O 118 [57] fold. map a
Includes material on the boundary between Mexico and the United States, the Gadsden Purchase territory, etc.

ROBLES, VITO A.   **382**
Coahuila y Texas en la epoca colonial. *Mex* 1938. O [12 incl. front wrap.] 752 [1] 8maps[7 fold.] 9pls[3 col.] a
—also issued in 100copies, signed

ROBUCK, J. E.   **383**
My own personal experience . . . in the Confederate army; appending a history of the . . . Ku Klux Klan . . . *Birm Ala* 1911. O 136 port a

ROCHAMBEAU ([JEAN B. D. DE VIMEUR comte de]).   **384**
Mémoires militaires, historiques . . . de: *P* 1809. O 2v: [16] 437; [4] 395 aa
—rptd. *P* 1824. O 2v aa
—Eng. tr. [in part.], *P* 1838. O [6] 114 aa

ROCHE, ALFRED R.   **385**
A view of Russian America in connection with the present war. *Montr* 1855. O 70 b LC PortOreL Y
Views with alarm the probable purchase of Alaska by the United States and suggests that Canada, now that England is at war with Russia, take armed possession.

ROCHEMONTEIX, CAMILLE DE   **386**
Les Jesuites et la Nouvelle-France au XVIIe siècle. *P* 1895. O 3v: [68] 488; [2] 536; [4] 694. 3maps 8ports aa
Thorough, but biased narrative of missionary activities and exploring enterprise throughout the Lake region and the Mississippi valley.

ROCHEMORE [LE FEU SR. DE].   **387**
Mémoire concernant: . . . ordonnateur a la Louisiane. Contre le Sieur de Kerlerec, gouverneur de la même colonie . . . *P* 1765 Q 160 [9] 14 a
Rochemore had charge, under Kerlerec, of all French trading stations and forts from Pittsburgh to New Orleans.

ROCHESTER, [N.Y.]   **388**
Life in Rochester. By a resident citizen. *Roch* 1848. O 100 aa

Rochester in 1827. *See* Hawley, Jesse.

ROCK, JAMES L., and SMITH, W. I.   **389**
Southern and western Texas guide . . . *St L* 1878. O 282 map port a

ROCK, MARION T.   **390**
Illustrated history of Oklahoma. *Topeka* 1890. O [12] 278[incl. 2 lvs of illus] 99pls aa
Most of the edition burned. Some copies were printed on cheap, thin paper and bound in wrappers.

ROCK ISLAND.   **391**
A directory of . . . : for 1856–7 . . . *Rock Island* 1856. D 114 aa
Some copies, bound with Davenport and Moline directories of the same year. *See* Fleming and Torrey.

Rock Island and its surroundings. *See* Bross, Wm.

ROCKFELLOW, JOHN A.   **392**
Log of an Arizona trail blazer. *Tucson* [1935] O [16] 201 pls a

ROCKWELL, M. E.   **393**
Home in the west . . . *Dub* 1858. D 24 aa

ROCKWELL, WILLIAM S.   **394**
The Oglethorpe Light Infantry . . . *Sav* 1894. O 36 errata slip port aa

ROCQUE, JEAN and MARY ANN
A set of plans and forts in North America. *See*
Andrews, P. and John.

RODENBOUGH, THEO. F.   395
From everglade to canyon with the Second Dragoons . . . *N Y* 1875. O [14] 17–562 + 4adv-p
2maps 8pls a

[RODNEY, CAESAR A.]   396
The oracle of liberty, and mode of establishing a
free government. *Phil* 1791. O 39 a

RODRIQUEZ, A. DE   397
Calendario para 1849: breve resena historica de
. . . la rebelion de la colonia de Tejas. *Mex* 1849.
D 72 2pls aa

RODRÍGUEZ, JOSÉ M.   398
Memoirs of early Texas. *San Antonio* 1913. O 76
[incl. front.] 100copies ptd. aa

RODRIQUEZ, JOSÉ POLICARPO   399
Rodriguez (José Policarpo), the old guide . . .
Indian fighter . . . *Nashv* [ca 1897]. D 121 front. aa

RODRIQUEZ DE SAN MIGUEL, JUAN   400
Documentos relativos al fondo piadoso de missiones para conversion . . . de los numerosas tribas
de las Californias. *Mex* 1845. O 60 b

ROE, MRS. ELIZABETH A.   401
Aunt Leanna, or, early scenes in Kentucky. *Chi*
[ptd. *Auburn N Y*] 1855. D [12] 281 aa
Describes the emigration and settlement of Col.
Matthew Lyon and family, early advocates of
emancipation.

ROE, MRS. ELIZABETH A.   402
Recollections of frontier life [in Ky., Neb. &
Ill.]. *Rockford* 1885. O 295 2ports aa
This daughter of the Kentucky colonist, Colonel
Matthew Lyon, gives the best account by any
woman of the hardships and perils of backwoods
life.

ROE, MRS FRANCES M.   403
Army letters from an officer's wife. *N Y* 1909.
D [10] 387[incl. 10pls] front. a

ROEBUCK, J. E.   404
My . . . experience . . . in the Confederate army.
Birmingh 1911. O 136 port a

[ROEBUCK, JOHN]   405
An enquiry, whether the guilt of the present civil
war, ought to be imputed to Great Britain or America. *L* 1776. O [2] 69 aa
—anr. issue, [*L* 1776]. O 61 a
—new ed. *L* 1776. O [2] 73

Attributes everything to America's folly and
ingratitude.

RÖMER, FERDINAND   406
Die Kreidebildungen von Texas und ihre Orga-
nischen Einschlüsse . . . *Bonn* 1852. Q [8] 100 11pls aa
First treatise on Texas geology.

RÖMER, FERDINAND   407
Texas. Mit besonderer Rücksicht . . . *Bonn* 1849.
O [16 incl. errata lf] 464 fold.map [first geological
map of this state] b N NYP Y
—Eng. tr. *San Antonio* 1935. O [12] 301 map a
Römer was the father of Texas geology.

ROESLER, CORPORAL J. N.   408
Army sketches. *Cin* 1862. obl. F 20 lith. pls[of
army life & operations] b

ROFF, JOE T.   409
A brief history of early days in north Texas and
the Indian Territory. [*Allen Okla*] 1930. D 40 a

ROGER, R. C.   410
My wife and I . . . *S F* 1871. O 440 50 copies
ptd. aa
Narrative of California life in the 'fifties.

[ROGERS, CARLTON H.]   411
Incidents of travel in the southern states and
Cuba . . . [in 1856]. *N Y* 1862. D [2] 320 a

[ROGERS, GEORGE?]   412
Memoranda of the experience . . . of a Univer-
salist preacher. *Cin* 1845. D 400 a
Fine picture of frontier travel, social conditions
etc., in the West and South.

ROGERS, HOWARD S.   413
History of Cass county, Michigan . . . *Cassopo-
lis* 1875. O 406 a

ROGERS, JOHN   414
The biography of Elder J. T. Johnson. *Cin* 1861.
D 408 port a
His life in Kentucky before 1800, and travels
throughout the South and Central West.

ROGERS, JUSTUS H.   415
Colusa county [California]; its history . . . *On-
land* 1891. O 474[incl.front.] fold.map 59pls aa
Includes sketches of Bidwell, Larkin, Ide and
Lassen, and the autobiography of Major Stephen
Cooper, who crossed the plains in 1846, became
Alcalde of Sonoma and was the man who first
wrote President Polk of the gold discovery.

[ROGERS, NICHOLAS?]   416
Observations upon certain passages in Mr. Jef-
ferson's Notes on Virginia . . . *N Y* 1804. O 32 a
Ascribed also to Clement C. Moore.

ROGERS (RANSFORD). 417

An account of the beginning, transactions and discovery of: who seduced many by pretended hobgoblins and apparitions, and thereby extorted money from their pockets . . . [Elizabeth-town?] 1792. D 28 aa

—rptd. "The wonderful history of the Morristown ghost . . .," ed. David Young, *Newark* 1826. 24° 76 a

—anr. ed., with app., "Original history of the Morristown ghost!" *Morristown* 1876. D [4 incl. cover-t.] 41[incl. blank lf]

ROGERS, ROBERT 418

A concise account of North America . . . also of the interior or westerly parts . . . *L* 1765. D [8] 264 b

—rptd. *Dub*: 1769; 1770. aa

Based largely on personal knowledge, this was the first geographical account of the American interior after England had wrested it from France, and, aside from those by Pittman and Hutchins, the most accurate of the period.

ROGERS (MAJOR ROBERT). 419

Journals of: during the late war . . . *L* 1765. O [8] 236 + 4adv-p b AA N NYP Y

—rptd.: [with "Bouquet expedition"] *Dub* 1769, D [10] 218 [20] 99; *Dub* 1770, same collat. aa

—Am. ed. "Reminiscences of the French war," with adds., but "Journals" condensed, *Concord N H* 1831. D 276 port of Stark[not in all copies] a

—rptd.: 1860; 1877.

—best Am. ed., ed. with notes by Hough, *Alb* 1883. O 297 map aa 100copies ptd.

In these military journals Rogers describes visits to the shores of lakes Erie and Huron, and a trip from Detroit to the Delaware villages on the Muskingum and to Pittsburgh.

ROGERS, THOMAS J., comp. 420

A new American biographical dictionary . . . confined exclusively to those who signalized themselves . . . in the revolutionary war . . . *Easton Pa* 1813. D [6] 424 [4] a

—ed. 2, same impr. 1823. D 352

—ed. 3, same impr. 1824. O 504

—ed. 4, *Phil* 1829. D [4] 400 5ports

—anr. ed. "Lives of the departed heroes . . .," *N Y* 1834. D

ROGERS, WOODES 421

A cruising voyage round the world . . . *L* 1712. O [22] 428 56 [14] 5maps b

—ed. 2, cor. 1718. O [20] 428 57 [7] 5maps + 8adv-p aa

—rptd. 1726, same collat. but 2pls added aa

—Fr. trs., with adds.: *Amst* 1716 D 2v 7maps 16pls[incl. 2eng. t-p]; 3v. 1723; 3v. 1725. aa

—Dutch tr. *Amst* 1715. Q [8] 14 438 [8] 9maps & pls a

—Ger. tr., abr, *Frankf* 1769. D [16] 216 8pls a

Accounts of this richly rewarded buccaneering expedition were written by commanders of both ships, Rogers and Edward Cooke. The California coast was visited.

ROLES, JOHN 422

Inside views of slavery on southern plantations . . . *N Y* 1864. O 47 a

ROLLE (DENYS). 423

The humble petition of: setting forth the hardships . . . which have attended him in his attempts to make a settlement in East Florida . . . [*L* 176–?]. O 85 47 pl fold.sheet b

Rolle purchased an extensive tract, to which he brought 1000 colonists. On the complete collapse of his project, he worked his way back to England and submitted this plea to the privy council.

ROLPH, THOMAS 424

A brief account . . . made during a visit to the West Indies, and a tour through the United States . . . *Dundas Canada* 1836. O 272 [21] errata slip aa

—ed. 2, "A descriptive . . . account of Canada . . .," *L* 1842. O 300 a

ROMAINE (ROBERT DEXTER) [pseud.]

The new age of gold; or, the life and adventures of: *See* Payson, Geo.

ROMANCE 425

Romance of Indian history . . . incidents in the early settlement of America. *N Y* [*ca* 1850]. D 24 a

Contains Adam Poe captivity, etc.

ROMANS, BERNARD 426

A concise natural history of East and West Florida . . . Vol. I. [all]. *N Y*, for the author, 1775. O [14] 175 178–342 [2] 90 [3] front. eng. dedication lf. 3maps 6pls fold.tab dd AA N NYP VaU

—ed. 2, *N Y* Aitken 1776. Made from sheets of ed. 1, omitting the 3maps, part of prelim. matter and app. O [4] 175 178–342 dedication lf 6pls tab b AA N

Romans, who spent several years in Florida, gives a valuable description of the country and its natives. The title page calls for 12 plates and 2 whole-sheet maps, but ordinary copies contain only the 9 maps and plates shown. Perhaps the other 5 maps and plates were to accompany a second volume, proposed but never issued. The only known copies of these original 2 maps are in the Pennsylvania Historical Society; but some copies have, inserted, reprints of them made later in Londen.

ROMSPERT, GEORGE W. 427

The western echo . . . *Dayton* 1881. D 406 [incl. port] a

RONAN, PETER 428

Historical sketch of the Flathead . . . nation . . . *Helena* [1890]. O [4] 80 3pls a

RONDTHALER, EDWARD   429
Life of John Heckewelder. *Phil* 1847. D 149 +
2adv-p port a

ROOSEVELT, THEODORE   430
Hunting trips of a ranchman . . . *N Y* 1885. Q
[18] 318 20pls a 500copies ptd. "Medora ed." aa
—trade ed., same impr. 1886. O [16 incl. front.]
348 + 3adv-p a

ROOSEVELT, THEODORE   431
The naval war of 1812 . . . *N Y* 1882. O [18]
498)aa
—ed. 2, same impr. & date. O a
—seven other eds. before 1902.

ROOSEVELT, THEODORE   432
Ranch life and the hunting trail . . . *N Y* Century Co. [1888]. F [8] 186 2pls Binding 1: coarse
light tan buckram, stamped in green & gold;
binding 2: smooth brown linen, stamped in brown
& gold aa
—some copies carry *L* impr. a
—rptd., with 12 add.illus., *N Y* 1896.
—other eds.: *N Y* 1899; *N Y* 1901.

ROOSEVELT, THEODORE   433
The winning of the west. *N Y* 1889–1894–1896.
O 4v: [16] 352; [4] 427; [6] 339; [8] 363. 4maps
Issue 1 has "diameter," last word, pl 60, vol.I. aa
—issue 2, "diameter" cor. to "circumference" a
—best ["Alleghany"] ed. *N Y* 1900. O 4v: [20] 352;
[10] 427; [12] 339; [14] 363. 5maps 153pls a
—anr. issue, ["Boone ed."], p. of Ms inserted,
same impr., date & collat. 200copies aa

ROOT, FRANK A., and   434
CONNELLEY, WILLIAM E.
The overland stage to California . . . *Topeka*
1901. O [18] 630 + adv.p map front. aa
—rptd. *Columbus* O 1950. O, same collat a

ROOT, HENRY   435
Personal history and reminiscences . . . 1845–
1921. *S F* 1921. O [6] 134 port a Not over 100
copies ptd.
Informative on early California railroads.

ROOT, RILEY   436
Journal of travels . . . to Oregon . . . [with a
description of California . . . and its gold mines].
Galesburg Ill 1850. O 143 c AA G IndU Y
—rptd. Oaki 1955. O a
One of the best overland journals, one of a few
covering 1848, one of the earliest describing the
California gold-fields, which he reached from Oregon, May 1849.

ROOT, W. D.   437
Sandusky in 1855; with historical sketches of the
region and a directory . . . *Sandusky* 1855. D 151 aa

ROQUEFEUIL, CAMILLE DE   438
Journal d'un voyage autour du monde . . . 1816–
1819. *P* 1823. O 2v: [50] 344; [4] 407. 2maps b N
NYP Y
—Eng. tr. abr. *L* 1823. O 112 a
—Am ed. [Calif portion only] *L A* 1954 200 cops
ptd a
—Ger. ed. "Reise um die Welt . . .," *Jena* 1823.
O [2] 396 a
Visited California and the northwest coast, in
1816–17.

ROSA, GABRIELE   439
Constantino Beltrami, da Bergamo. Notizie . . .
dedicate alla Societá di Minnesota. *Bergamo* 1865.
Q 134 port aa

ROSA, GABRIELE   440
Della vita e degli scritti di Constantino Beltrami
. . . scopritore delle fonti del Mississippi. *Bergamo*
1861. O 34 a

ROSA, LUIS DE LA   441
Impresiones de un viage de México á Washington . . . *N Y* 1849. O 54 a
—rptd. same collat *N Y* [1854]

ROSE, MRS. S. E. F.   442
The Ku Klux Klan or invisible empire. *N O*
1914. D 84 pls a

ROSE, VICTOR M.   443
Life and services of General Ben McCulloch.
Phil 1888. O [6] 25–260 2 ports aa
—rptd. *Austin* 1958. a
Most famous Texas ranger.

ROSE, VICTOR M.   444
Ross' Texas brigade . . . *Louisv* 1881. O 185
2pls aa

ROSE, VICTOR M.   445
Some historical facts in regard to the settlement
of Victoria, Texas. *Laredo Tex* [1883]. O 216 aa

[ROSE, VICTOR M.]   446
The Texas vendetta; or, the Sutton-Taylor feud.
N Y 1880. D 69 [incl front wrap] b TxS

ROSEN, PETER   446a
Pa-Ha-Sa-Pah, or the Black hills of South Dakota . . . *St L* 1895. O [14] 645 + adv-l. 27 pls aa
By a missionary in that region from 1882 to
1889.

ROSIER, ELLIK   447
The emigrant's friend in Canada . . . *Glas* 1834.
D 81 map a
—rptd. *L* 1839.
Contains information on Midwestern states.

ROSS, ALEXANDER   **448**
Adventures of the first settlers on the Oregon . . .
L 1849. D [16] 352 + 16adv-p map col front. [in
few copies] b NYP Y no front. aa
—Am. ed., ed. Thwaites, *Clev* 1904. O 332 [incl
map & facs.] + 4 adv. p a

ROSS, ALEXANDER   **449**
Fur hunters of the far west. *L* 1855. D 2v: [15]
333; [8] 262 + 2adv-lvs port pl map b
—Am. ed., abr., ed. Quaife, *Chi* 1924. 16° a

ROSS, CAPT. C.   **450**
The earthquake at New Madrid . . . *Cin* 1847.
O 24 aa

ROSS, C. P., and ROUSE, T. L.   **451**
Early day history of Wilbarger county, Texas.
Vernon 1933. O 208 a

ROSS, EDMUND G.   **452**
History of the impeachment of Andrew Johnson
. . . [*Santa Fe*] 1896. O [4] 180 aa
By the Kansas senator who with two other heroic
Republicans defied party dictation and voted a
pivotal "Not Guilty." Political oblivion naturally
followed.

ROSS, FITZGERALD   **453**
A visit to the cities and camps of the Confederate States. *Edin* 1865. O [10] 300 map aa
—rptd. *N Y* 1958. O 262 a

ROSS GEORGE M. VON   **454**
Des Auswanderer's Hand-buch . . . *Elberfeld*
1851. D [12] 509 a

ROSS, GEORGE M. VON   **455**
Der Nordamerikanische Freistaat Texas . . .
Rudolstadt 1851. O [2] 85 map aa

ROSS, HARVEY L.   **456**
The early pioneers and pioneer events of . . .
Illinois . . . *Chi* 1899. O [12] 199 port aa
Ross knew Lincoln intimately at New Salem; he
takes issue with many of Herndon's statements
concerning Lincoln's early life.

ROSS, JAMES, and GARY, GEORGE   **457**
From Wisconsin to California, and return . . .
Madison Wis 1869. O 132 aa

ROSS, JAMES   **458**
Life and times of Elder Reuben Ross. *Phil*
[1882]. D 427 2ports a
Pioneer conditions and early Indian troubles in
northeast Tennessee.

ROSS, JOEL H.   **459**
What I saw in New-York; or, a bird's-eye view
of city life. *Auburn* 1851. D 326 pl a
—ed. 2, same impr. & collat., 1852.

ROSS (JOHN, principal chief of the   **460**
Cherokee nation).
Letter from: . . . regarding the Cherokee affairs
with the United States . . . [*Wash* 1836]. O 31 a

ROSS (JOHN, principal chief of the   **461**
Cherokee nation).
Letter from: to a gentleman of Philadelphia [i.e.,
Job R, Tyson]. [*Phil* 1838]. O 40 a

ROSS, MRS. WILLIAM P.   **462**
The life and times of Hon. William P. Ross. *Ft
Smith* 1893. O [22] 272 port a

ROSSI, LOUIS   **463**
Six an en Amérique: Californie et Orégon.
[*Brus*] 1863. O 322 [2] 2maps aa
—ed. 2, *P* 1863. same collat. aa
—anr. ed., same impr. & collat., entitled "Souvenirs d'un voyage en Orégon et en Californie,"
1864. a
This missionary priest went to Washington Territory with Bishop Blanchet in 1856 and was later
assigned to northern California and Nevada.

ROSSIGNON, JULES   **464**
Guide pratique des émigrants en Californie . . .
P 1849. 16° 108 aa

ROTHERT, OTTO A.   **465**
A history of Muhlenberg county, Kentucky.
Louisv 1913. O [18] 496 front aa

ROTHERT, OTTO A.   **466**
The outlaws of Cave-in-Rock . . . *Clev* 1924. O
364[incl.10maps & pls] a

ROTTERMUND, COMTE DE   **467**
Report on the exploration of lakes Superior and
Huron. [*Tor* 1856]. O 24 a

ROTTERMUND, COMTE DE   **468**
Second rapport sur l'exploration des lacs Supérieur et Huron. *Tor* 1857. O 50 a

ROUBY, JULES   **469**
Guide américain. *P* 1859. 16° 248 a

ROUHAUD, HIPPOLYTE   **470**
Les régions nouvelles . . . au nord de l'Océan
Pacifique. *P* 1868. O [10] 404 a
Embraces accounts of Oregon, California and
Texas.

[ROUSSELOT DE SURGY,   **471**
JACQUES P.] tr.
Histoire naturelle et politique de la Pennsylvanie
. . . Traduite de l'Allemande . . . P[ar] M. D[e]
S[urgy]. *P* 1768. D [20] 372 [4] map aa
Translations from travel narratives written by
Kalm and Mittelberger.

ROUTES
Routes and tables of distances . . . in the Traveller's guide . . . *See* Davison, Gideon M.

[ROUX, SERGEANT-MAJOR]   472
Le nouveau Mississipi, ou les dangers d'habiter les bords du Scioto, par un patriote voyageur. *P* Jacquemart 1790. D 44 aa
—anr. issue, *P* Jacob-Sion 1790. O [6] 44 aa
Adverse report on the Ohio lands of the Scioto Company.

ROUX DE ROCHELLE, JEAN B. G.   473
États-Unis . . . *P* 1837. O [6] 400 [2] map 96pls aa
—rptd., same impr. & collat.: 1838; 1839; 1845; 1853.
—Ital. ed. "Stati Uniti d'America . . .," *Venice* 1839. O 416 pls
—Sp. tr. *Barcelona* 1841. O [4] 79pls
By the French Minister to this country, 1829–1831. French editions formed part of *L'univers*.

ROVINGS IN THE PACIFIC . . .
By a merchant . . . 1851. *See* Lucatt, Edw.

ROWAN (ARCHIBALD H.)   474
Autobiography of: *Dub* 1840. O [16] 475 port a
Exiled for conspicuous activities as an Irish political leader, Rowan spent the years 1795 and 1796 at Philadelphia and Wilmington.

ROWLAND, DAVID S.   475
Historical remarks . . . a sermon . . . wherein are represented, the . . . dispensations of . . . providence to the people . . . in the rise and progress of the present war . . . *Prov* [1779]. O 35 aa

ROWLAND, KATE M.   476
The life of Charles Carroll of Carrollton . . . *N Y* 1898. O 2v: [22] 400; [6] 487. 7pls pedigree tab a

ROWLAND, KATE M.   477
The life of George Mason, 1725–1792. *N Y* 1892. O 2v: 400; 475. fold.tab port aa
—rptd. 1898. a

ROWLANDSON (MRS. MARY).   478
The sovereignty & goodness of God . . . narrative of the captivity and restauration of: . . . *C?* or *B?* 1682? SmQ [6] 73? [only 4 lvs exist of this ed. 1, hence description given is conjectural; it may have appeared both separately and with a 2nd part, a sermon by the captive's husband, "The possibility of God's forsaking a people . . ." same impr. & date, pp. [6] 22 dd
—ed. 2, with the sermon included, *C* 1682. SmQ [6] 73; [6] 22 dd [3 cops loc (of iss. 1, with "edition" misspelled "addition",) at BM & BostP, and

of iss. 2, with that spelling corrected, at BostP]
—Eng. ed. "A true history of the captivity . . . of Mrs. Mary Rowlandson . . ." with sermon incl. *L* 1682. SmQ [6] 46 d Hn N Y [of 12 cops loc]
—18th cent Am reprs: *B* 1720, D 80 c LC [of 3 cops loc]; *B* 1770, D 60 a; *B* 1771, D 60; *B* 1773, O 40; *N Lond* 1774, O 48; *B* 1791, D 40; *Amherst, N.H.* [1792], D 64; *B* 1794, D 57; *Amherst* [1795], D; n.p. n.d., D 54; *Haverhill* 1796, D
—later Am reprs: *B* 1800, 16°; *B* 1805, D 36; *Lancaster*, Mass. 1828, 16°; and a few others
First printed account of a New England Indian captivity.

[ROY, JUST J. E.]   479
Les aventures d'un capitaine francais . . . au Texas. *P* 1858. D 191[incl.front.] a
—rptd. *Tours* 1860. D 185 pl
—oth. Fr. eds: 1862; 1864; 1866; 1868; 1872; and later
—Eng. tr. *N Y* [1876?]. D 180 pl
Fictionalized, but reasonably authentic, account of the French settlement at Champ d'Asile.

ROY, WILLIAM L.   480
A new work: the emigrant's guide to the United States . . . *N Y* 1850. 16° 72 a

ROYALL, MRS. ANNE   481
The black book . . . continuation of travels in the United States. *Wash* 1828–9. D 3v: 184 205–329; 396; 235 b AA LC N
Volume III, an afterthought, is seldom found with the other two of this title, which is a continuation of her *Sketches of history* . . .

ROYALL, MRS. ANNE   482
Letters from Alabama . . . *Wash* 1830. O 232 [6] a
Covers years 1817–1822, the early, less bitter period of her life.

ROYALL, MRS. ANNE   483
Mrs. Royall's southern tour, or second series of The black book. *Wash* 1830–31. O 3v: 169 [12]; 218; 148 179–218; 247 aa
The last of the author's travel series.

ROYALL, MRS. ANNE   484
. . . Pennsylvania, or travels continued . . . *Wash* 1829. D 2v: 276, 273 [24] aa
This was a continuation of *The black book*, above.

[ROYALL, MRS. ANNE]   485
Sketches of history, life and manners in the United States. By a traveller. *N Hav* 1826. D [4] 13–356, 359–392 front aa
First publication of this nation's most eminent literary virago and most uncommon scold.

ROYCE, C[HARLES] C.　　　　486
John Bidwell, pioneer . . . a biographical sketch. *Chico Calif* 1906. O 66 [incl.pls] facs a
—enl. ed. [to which is added Bidwell's "Addresses, reminiscences . . .," dated 1907]. *Chico* 1906–07. O 2v in 1: [2] 66; [4] 293 map pls 100copies ptd. aa

ROYCE, JOSIAH　　　　　　487
California, from the conquest in 1846 . . . *B* 1886. D [16] 513 map + 6adv-p a
—rptd. same impr. 1888.

ROZIER, FIRMIN A.　　　　　488
History of the early settlement of the Mississippi valley. *St L* 1890. O 337[incl. front.] 13pls a

RUBESAM, EM FRED　　　　489
Grenzerleben: Bilder und Skizzen aus dem "Wilden-Westen." *Chi* 1892. O 167 aa
Service with Texas Rangers and in a Comanche uprising of 1858.

RUBIO, pseud.
Rambles in the United States . . . *See* James, Thos. H.

RUCKER, GEN. D[ANIEL] H.　　　490
Lists of distances between . . . western forts and . . . points along the various overland trails. *Wash* 1868. D 121 aa

RUDO ENSAYO . . .
See Smith, Buckingham, *ed.*

RÜHL, KARL　　　　　　　491
Californien . . . Mit Verücksichtigung der Minen-Regionen der benachbarten Staaten und Territorien. *N Y* 1867. O [8] 283 2maps aa

RUFFIN, EDMUND　　　　　492
Agricultural, geological and descriptive sketches of lower North Carolina [etc.]. *Raleigh* 1861. O 296 aa
By the "Father of modern scientific agronomy" and radical advocate of State's Rights.

RUFFIN, EDMUND　　　　　493
Anticipations of the future . . . as lessons for the present . . . *Rich* 1860. D [10] 416 aa
A series of letters from an English resident in the United States that would appear in the London "Times", 1864–70. Under Seward, who followed Lincoln, South Carolina secedes in 1867 and is joined by sister states; war, following the first armed clash in Charleston harbor, lasts one year and a ruined and disrupted North recognizes Southern independence. An ingenious effort, this, to awaken the South to the inevitability of sectional war and the advisability of immediate secession. Ruffin fired the first shot of the Civil war, at Ft. Sumter; after Appomattox and the collapse ef

his anticipated Confederacy he triggered another shot — into his own brilliant but erratic brain.

RUFFIN, EDMUND　　　　　494
The political economy of slavery; or, the institution considered in regard to its influence on public wealth and . . . welfare. [*Wash* 185–?]. O 31 a

[RUFFNER, ERNEST H.]　　　495
A political problem: New Mexico and the New Mexicans. By an officer of the army. [*Leavenworth*? 1876]. O 31 + cov.t. aa

[RUFFNER, HENRY]　　　　496
Address to the people of West Virginia; shewing that slavery is injurious to the public welfare . . . *Lex., Va.* 1847 O 40 aa
—rptd. *Louisv* 1847. O 32; also [*Bridgewater Va* 1933].

RUGER (GEN. THOMAS H.)　　497
Report of: [to the Adj. Gen. of the Army] . . . [*S F* 1891]. 16° 120 lvs b G
Includes reports of various subordinate officers, all concerning the Messiah Craze, death of Sitting Bull, etc., each separately paged.

RUMPLE, JETHRO　　　　498
A history of Rowan county, N. C. *Salisbury N C* 1881. 24° [8] 508 [10] slip inserted at p505 aa
—rptd., same impr., n.d.; *Salisbury* 1916; *Raleigh* 1929. a
One of the most admirable of Southern local histories.

RUMSEY, JAMES　　　　　499
A plan, wherein the power of steam is fully shown, by a new constructed machine for propeling [*sic*] boats . . . [*Winchester*? 1788]. Q 20 [2] no t-p only a few copies ptd b AA
—rptd. "A short treatise on the application of steam, whereby is clearly shewn . . .," *Phil* 1788. O 26
—issue 1, word "cheap" misspelled on t-p b
—issue 2, spelling corrected. aa
—anr. ed. dated *Phil* 1788, but ptd. *ca* 1850. same collat. a
Earliest work on steam navigation.

[RUNCKLER, SEB.]　　　　500
Handbuch für meine Freunde in den Districten von Canajohary und Palatine, an der Mohawk-Rivier . . . *Phil* 1794. D [6] 40 aa

RUNNELLS, E[LIZA] B.　　　501
A journal of facts, descriptive of scenes and incidents in Maryland, Pennsylvania and New-Jersey . . . *Phil* 1839. D 40 a

RUNNELS, M[OSES] T.　　　502
History of Sanbornton, N. H. *B* 1882. O 2v: [30] 570 [10]; [14] 1022. 2maps 43pls a

[RUNNION, JAMES B.]   **503**
Out of town . . . account of the suburban towns . . . of Chicago. *Chi* 1869. O 64 + 2 initial adv-l. map a

RUPP, I[SRAEL] DANIEL, ed.   **504**
A collection of . . . thirty thousand names of . . . immigrants in Pennsylvania, 1725–1776 . . . *Harrisburg* 1856. D [24] 368 aa
—anr. issue, identical except for additional "Remarks on the origin of surnames," with separate t. & 37p aa
—ed. 2, enl., *Phil* 1876. D [10] 495 + 23 adv-p 8pls[on 4 l.] a
—rptd. same impr. & collat. [1898].

[RUPP, ISRAEL DANIEL]   **505**
Early history of western Pennsylvania, and of the west, and of western expeditions and campaigns, 1754–1833. By a gentleman of the bar . . . *Pitt* 1846. O 352 406 [10] 2 maps aa
This historical treasure-house includes the journals of Bouquet, Croghan, Post, etc.

RUPP, I[SRAEL] DANIEL   **506**
The geographical catechism of Pennsylvania and the western states . . . *Harrisburg* 1836. D [4] 384 aa
—rptd., same collat., *Phil* 1837. a

RUPP, I[SRAEL] DANIEL, ed.   **507**
He pasa ekklesia. An original history of the religious denominations . . . in the United States . . . *Phil* 1844. O 734 a
Separate histories of the various churches written by members; that of the Mormons by Joseph Smith.

RUPP, I[SRAEL] DANIEL   **508**
The history . . . of Dauphin, Cumberland, Franklin, Bedford, Adams and Perry counties [Pa.]. *Lancaster* 1846. O [2, 5–12] 25–605 4pls a
—ed. 2, with Somerset, Cambria and Indiana counties added, same impr. 1848. O 660 10 pls

RUPP, I[SRAEL] DANIEL   **509**
History of Lancaster county [Pa.] *Lancaster* 1844. D 524 5pls fold.tab a
—other eds., same impr. & date, contain 528p & 531p

RUPP, I[SRAEL] DANIEL   **510**
History of Northampton, Lehigh, Monroe, Carlson and Schuylkill counties [Pa.]. *Lancaster* 1845. O [16] 568 5pls a
—anr. issue, same impr. & date. O 550 5pls

RUPP, I[SRAEL] DANIEL   **511**
History . . . of Northumberland, Huntington, Mifflin, Centre, Union, Columbia, Juniata and Clinton counties, Pa. . . . *Lancaster* 1846. O 556 4pls a
—anr. ed., same impr. 1847. O 568 8pls

RUPP, I[SRAEL] DANIEL   **512**
History of the counties of Berks and Lebanon. *Lancaster* 1844. O 512 3pls a

RUPP, I[SRAEL] DANIEL   **513**
History of York county [Pa.]. *Lancaster* 1845. O [8] 525–750 a
Usually found with Rupp's *History of Lancaster county*, but some copies issued separately.

RUPPIUS, OTTO   **514**
Der prairie-teufel. *St L* 1859. D 311 4cops loc aa
—rptd, same impr [but printed in Berlin] 1861. D [2] 295 aa
Fictional account of adventures on a trading expedition to Santa Fe. Author lived for several years in St Louis.

RUSCHENBERGER, WILLIAM S. W.   **514a**
A voyage round the world . . . 1835–7. *Phil* 1838. O 559 + 12adv-p a
—best ed., "A narrative of a voyage round the world," *L* 1838. O 2v: [8] 450; [8] 472. 4pls aa
Contains account of a visit to California. The Philadelphia edition prints some aspersions on the British, omitted in the London issue.

RUSH, BENJAMIN   **515**
An account of the life . . . of Christopher Ludwick . . . Baker-General . . . during the revolutionary war. *Phil* 1831. D 61 a
First appearing in a periodical in 1801, this is the first edition in book form.

RUSH, BENJAMIN   **516**
An account of the manners of the German inhabitants of Pennsylvania. Ed. I. D. Rupp. *Phil* 1875. 16° 72 port a
Written in 1789, but here first printed.

RUSH, BENJAMIN   **517**
An address to the inhabitants of the British settlements in America, upon slave-keeping. *Phil* 1773. O [2] 30 a
—rptd., same date: *N Y* O 36; *B* .O [2] 30
—anr. ed., *Norwich* 1775. O 24
—ed. 2, with adds., *Phil* 1773. O [2] 28 + adv-l + "Observations, &c." 54p some copies of this ed. 2 have slightly altered t-p

RUSH, BENJAMIN   **518**
Observations upon the present government of Pennsylvania . . . *Phil* 1777. O [24] some copies have a 4-line errata on p24 a
—rptd. *Phil* 1783. O

RUSH, BENJAMIN   **519**
A vindication of the Address, to the inhabitants of the British settlements, on the slavery of the negroes in America, in answer to a pamphlet

entitled "Slavery not forbidden by Scripture . . ." *Phil* 1773. O 54 a

Included with some editions of Rush's *An address . . .*

RUSH, CHRISTOPHER   520
A short account of the rise . . . of the African Methodist Episcopal church in America . . . *N Y* 1843. 16° 117 a

RUSH, OSCAR   521
The open range . . . [*Denv* 1930] D 110 [incl front] a
—enl. ed. *Caldwell, Ida* 1936. D 263 [incl. front] Of this ed 10 cops were signed & numbered.

RUSH, RICHARD   522
Memoranda of a residence at the court of London. *Phil* 1833. O 460 a
—ed. 2, enl., same impr. & date. O [12] 9–501
—Eng. ed., t. slightly different, *L* 1833. O [18] 420
—Eng. ed. 2, same impr. & date. O
Above constituted the first series, covering the years 1817 to 1819. For second series *see* following entry. Together they present the diplomatic maneuvers concerning the conflicting claims to Oregon and the adjustment of a Northwestern boundary line. English editions of both series probably have priority.

RUSH, RICHARD   523
Memoranda of a residence at the court of London . . . from 1819 to 1825. Including negotiations on the Oregon question . . . *Phil* 1845. O [12] 640 a
—Eng. ed., t. slightly altered, *L* 1845. O 2v: [15] 392; [7] 326
—anr. Eng. ed., styled ed. 3, ed. Benj. Rush, with adds., *L* 1872. O [36] 595 port

RUSHTON, EDWARD   524
Expostulatory letter to George Washington . . . on his continuing to be a proprietor of slaves. *Liv* priv. ptd. 1797. D 24 aa
—Am. eds: *Lex* 1797, D 16 aa; *B* 1831, O 8 a

RUSO D'ERES (CHARLES DENNIS).   525
Memoirs of: *Exeter N H* 1800. D 176 b AA BA Hn JCB N
Captivity of 11 years among Canadian Indians; authentic in the main, but not in all details.

RUSSELL, CHARLES M.   526
Back-trailing on the old frontier. *Great Falls* 1922. large O [4] 56 14pls a

RUSSELL, CHARLES M.   527
Good medicine. *Garden City* 1929. O 162 [2] 2pls[incl. one separate extra] ltd. ed. of 134copies, bound in ³/₄ blue buckram, vell. sides aa
—trade ed., brown buckram, same impr. & collat., except supplementary pl used as end papers, 1930.

[of this ed. 59copies in blue buckram for presentation] a

RUSSELL, C[HARLES] M.   528
More rawhides. *Great Falls Mont* 1925. Q [4, incl init blank lf] 60 aa
—rptd. *Pasadena* 1946 a

RUSSELL, CHARLES M.   529
Pen sketches. [*Great Falls* 1899]. F 50 [incl 12 pls] cover t. only b
—issue 2, identical except that vignette of camp scene above pub's.impr. on fly lf has been replaced by buffalo skull. aa
—ed. 2, same collat., but no titles on pls aa
—ed. 3, same collat., but pub's. name on cover stamped in gold aa

RUSSELL, C[HARLES] M.   530
Rawhide Rawlins stories. *Great Falls Mont* 1921. Q [4] 60 aa
—later printings shown on t-p
—rev. ed., with biog. added, [*Pasadena* 1946]. Q

RUSSELL, CHARLES M.   531
Studies of western life. *N Y* Albertype Co [1890]. obl O clo. 24 l. [incl. 12pls] letterpress describing each pl on separate sheet, except in case of pl. no. 1 a
—issue 2, identical except letter-press, relating to pl. 1, added to verso of t-p
—anr. ed., with pub. given as J. L. Robbins Co *Spokane* [1919?]. obl Q wraps 26[incl. 12pls] letterpress for each pl. on verso of preceding pl. aa
—rptd. [*Helena Mont* B. R. Roberts *ca* 1929]. a
First book devoted to illustrations of cowboy life.

RUSSELL, CHARLES M.   532
Trails plowed under . . . *N Y* 1927. O [22] 211 10pls[some col] a

RUSSELL, CHARLES T.   533
The history of Princeton [Mass.] *B* 1838. O [8] 130 a

RUSSELL (DAVID).   534
Autobiography of: . . . his travels, romantic adventures . . . *B* 1857. D 372 5pls a

RUSSELL, J[OHN], JR.   535
The history of the war, between the United States and Great-Britain . . . *Hart* 1815. O 472 a
—ed. 2, same impr. & date. O 402

RUSSELL, M[ORRIS] C.   536
Uncle Dudley's odd hours; western sketches, Indian trail echoes . . . *Lake City Minn* 1904. O 256 [incl.port] a
Uncommon; uncommonly uninteresting.

RUSSELL, OSBORNE   537
Journal of a trapper; or, nine years in the Rocky mountains: 1834–1843 . . . [*Boise* 1914]. O 105 b 100 copies ptd G NYP OreH WashU Y
—ed. 2, with adds., *Boise* [1921]. O [18] 149 a
—best ed. *Port* 1955 O [20] 180 [15] facs 21 maps & pls
The fur trade in its most colorful period.

[RUSSELL, ROBERT W.]   538
America compared with England, with the social effects of their respective governments, and the mission of democracy. *L* 1848. D [24] 289 a
—rptd., au.named, same impr. & collat., 1849.
By an Ohio social philosopher; with critical remarks on Trollope, Hall and other English observers and a study of various American communal experiments.

RUSSELL, WILLIAM   539
The history of America . . . *L* 1778. Q 2v: [4] 596; 630 [2]. 51maps & pls aa
—rptd. *L* 1780. same collat. a
—Ger. tr. *Leip* 1779–80. O 4v: [14] 782; [6] 752 [7]; [4] 660; [4] 480 [34]. 4maps 4ports a

RUSSELL, WILLIAM H.   540
My diary north and south. *L* 1863. D 2v: [16] 424; [12] 442. map aa
—Am. eds.: *B* 1863, D [22] 602; *N Y* 1863, O 225 port; *Tor* 1863, D [22] 602; abr ed *N Y* 1954. a
—Ger. tr. *Altona Ger* 1864 2v

RUSSELL, WILLIAM H.   541
Pictures of southern life, social, political and military. *N Y* 1861. D 143 a

[RUSSELL, WILLIAM H. C.]   542
Running the blockade. *L* 1863. D 315 a

[RUSTON, THOMAS]   543
Remarks on Lord Sheffield's Observations on the commerce of the American states. *L* 1784. O [1] 51 a

RUTER, P. S.   544
Reminiscences of a Virginia physician. *Louisv* 1849. D [4] 278 a

RUTHERFURD, JOHN   545
The importance of the colonies to Great Britain . . . *L* 1761. O 46 aa

RUTHERFURD (THE LATE MAJOR JOHN).   546
Narrative of: *Berwick-upon-Tweed* [1878] D 45 b LC [only cop loc in Am.]
—rptd. [in "The siege of Detroit"] *Chi* 1958. 16°
Served at Ft. Detroit, in 1763, and suffered a short captivity among Pontiac's Indians.

RUTLEGE [pseud.]   547
Separate state secession practically discussed . . . [*Edgefield S C*] 1851. O 42 a
—rptd., same impr. [1860?]. O 38

RUTTENBER, E[DWARD]   548
History of . . . Newburgh [N. Y.]. *Newburgh* 1859. O [12] 322 [10] 3pls a Issued originally in 10pts
—rptd. 1875

RUTTENBER, E[DWARD] M.   549
History of the county of Orange [N.Y.] . . . *Newburgh* 1875. O 424 [1] 4maps 17pls a
—rptd., with adds., *Phil* 1881. O [12] 820 pls

RUTTENBER, E[DWARD] M.   550
History of the Indian tribes of Hudson's river . . . *Alb* 1872. O 415 5ports[not issued in all copies] aa *Sans* ports a

RUTTENBER, E[DWARD] M.   551
Obstructions to the navigation of Hudson's river . . . *Alb* 1860. sm Q [10] 210 map a 110copies[10 on L. P.] aa

RUTTER'S . . . QUARTERLY   552
Rutter's political quarterly: devoted to unearthing the sanctimonious political rats of the south . . . *Memphis* 1870. O 56 a

RUXTON, GEORGE F. [A.]   553
Adventures in Mexico and the Rocky mountains. *L* 1847. D [8] 332 aa
—anr. issue, same impr. & date, in wraps. D 2v aa
—rptd. *L* 1849; 1861. a
—Am. eds: *N Y* 1848; 1860. D 312 a

RUXTON, GEORGE F. [A.]   554
Life in the far west. *Edin* 1849. D [16] 312 aa
—ed. 2, *Edin* 1851. D [14] 289 a
—rptd. *Edin* 1854; 1861; 1868; 1869.
—Am. eds: *N Y* 1849; 1855. D 235 + 4adv-p
—Ger. tr.: *Dresden* 1852; *Leip* 1852

RUXTON, G[EORGE] F. [A.]   555
The Oregon question . . . *L* 1846. O 43 c G Y
Obviously prepared and printed for government officials only; it leaves little doubt that Ruxton's trip to the West was undertaken, to some extent, as that of a secret agent, to report on the military situation there in the event that the Oregon controversy ended in war.

[RUYSDALE, PHILIP]   556
A pilgrimage over the prairies. *L* 1863. O 2v in 1: [2] 298; [2] 313 [wrongly numb. 216] 6pls aa
A romance, incorporating an 1825 trip to the Rockies and the Wind River Blackfeet.

[RYAN, JOHN G.]   **557**
The life and adventures of Gen. W. A. C. Ryan
... *N Y* 1876. 16° 256 aa
Includes his 1866 Montana adventures.

RYAN (GEN. W. A. C.)
The life ... of: By an old comrade. *See* Ryan,
John G., above.

RYAN, WILLIAM R.   **558**
Personal adventures in ... California ... *L*
1850. D 2v: [12] 348; [2] 414. 23pls aa
—rptd., same collat., *L* 1852. aa
—Dutch tr. *Haarlem* 1850. O 2v: [12] 308; [8] 325.
10pls a
Both text and illustrations are among the best
of the period.

RYE, EDGAR   **559**
The quirt and the spur ... *Chi* [1909]. D 363
[incl. 10pls] front. a

RYERSON, [ADOLPHUS] EGERTON   **560**
The loyalists of America ... *Tor* 1880. O 2v:
[28] 517; [28] 490. port a
—ed. 2 same impr & date
Standard Canadian study of Loyalist persecutions.

[RYNNING, OLE]   **561**
Sandfaerdig beretning om Amerika ... *Chris-
tiania* 1839. O 39 aa
—Eng. tr. "True account of America". Minneap
1920.
Advice to Norwegian immigrants.

S

S. ..., (A.)
A narrative of the official conduct of: *See*
Stokes, Anthony.

S., J. L.
Neue Nachrichten von denen neuentdekten Insuln ... *See* Schulze, Johann L.

S., M. D.
Histoire ... de la Pennsylvanie ... *See* Surgy,
Jacques P. Rousselot de.

S., S. S.
Two hundred years ago; or, a brief history of
Cambridgeport and East Cambridge. *See* Simp-
son, S. S.

S., T.
A cool reply to A calm address ... *See* Stanley,
Thos.

SABIN, EDWIN L.   **1**
Kit Carson days (1809–1868). *Chi* 1914. O [15]
669 many maps & pls a
—ed. 2, same collat., 1919.
—new ed. *N Y* 1935. O 2v: [16] 488; [12] 489–996
[1] a Also 200 cops, signed aa

SABIN, EDWIN L.   **2**
Wild men of the wild west ... *N Y* [1929]. D
[14] 363 pls a

SABINE, LORENZO   **3**
The American loyalists, or biographical sketches ... *B* 1847. O [8] 733 a
—enl. ed. "Biographical sketches of loyalists ...,"
B 1864. O 2v: [12] 608; [2] 600

SABINE, LORENZO   **4**
Notes on duels and dueling ... *B* 1855. D [8]
394 a
—ed. 2, same impr. 1856. D [8] 426
—ed. 3, same impr. & collat. 1859.

SACHOT, OCTAVE L. M.   **5**
Récits de voyages. Les grandes cités de l'Ouest
... *P* 1874. D 344 7pls a
—ed. 2, *P* 1874 D 337

SACHOT, OCTAVE L. M.   **6**
La Sibérie orientale et l'Amérique russe ... *P*
1875. O [6] 370 [1] map a
—rptd. *P* 1883. D [6] 266 [2] map

SACHSE, JULIUS F.   **7**
The German pietists of provincial Pennsylvania.
Phil 1895. O [18] 504 3maps pl a 500copies ptd.

SACHSE, JULIUS F.   **8**
The German sectarians of Pennsylvania ... *Phil*
1899–1900. O 2v: [22] 506; [16] 535. 55pls 350
copies ptd. aa

SACRAMENTO ILLUSTRATED ...
See Barber and Baker, pubs.

SACRAMENTO COUNTY,   **9**
CALIFORNIA.
History of: ... *Oakl* 1880. Obl F [8] 11–294
pls b
—rptd. *Berkeley* 1960. F 500 2maps pls

SADDLEBAGS, JEREMIAH [pseud.]
Journey to the gold diggins. *See* Read, J. A.,
and D. F.

SAFFELL, W[ILLIAM] T. R.   **10**
Records of the revolutionary war ... *N Y* 1858.
D 554 + 12adv-p a
—rptd: *Phil* 1860; *Balt* 1894.

[SAFFORD, A[NSON] P. K.]   **11**
Resources of Arizona Territory ... *S F* 1871.
O 31 aa
—rptd., "The Territory of Arizona ...," *Tucson*
1874. O 38 cov.t.only a

SAFFORD, WILLIAM H.   **12**
The Blennerhasset papers ... *Cin* 1861. O 665
4pls a
—rptd., same collat., 1864.

SAFFORD, WILLIAM H.   **13**
The life of Harman Blennerhassett ... *Chillicothe* 1850. D 239 pl a
—rptd., same collat. but pl omitted: *Cin* 1853;
1861.

SAGATOO, MRS. M. A.   **14**
Wah-sash-kah-moqua, or thirty-three years
among the Indians. *B* 1897. D 140 a
By a Boston girl who lived with the Chippewas
in Michigan and married two of them.

[SAGE, BERNARD J.]   **15**
Davis and Lee; a protest ... *L* 1865. O 80 a
—Am. ed. "Davis and Lee: a vindication of the
southern states ...," *N Y* 1866. O 80

[SAGE, RUFUS B.]   **16**
Scenes in the Rocky mountains ... By a New
Englander. *Phil* 1846. D 303 map b AA G Hn
NYP Y
—ed. 2, same collat., but no map, au. named, *Phil*
1847. a
—anr. ed. *Phil* 1854. D [6 incl. eng. t. 10] 13–304 +
blank l. + 24adv-p 11pls
—other eds: 1855; *B* 1857; 1858; 1859; 1860.
Intelligent narrative of extensive travels from
the Platte to the Arkansas, including the best contemporary account of Snively's abortive land-
pirate expedition. Sage's map seems not to have
been completed until after many copies of the early
issues in wrappers had been distributed. Collectors, however, insist on its presence. In the earliest
issue the following pages were numbered on the
inner margin: 77–88, 270, 271, 302.

SÂGEAN (MATTHEW).   **17**
The original manuscript account of the King-
dom of Aacaniba, given by the affidavit of: ... *L*
1755. F [4] 10 [text in Fr. & Eng.] b G N
—anr. ed., Fr. text only, "Extrait de la relation des
avantures et voyage ...," *N Y* 1863. O 32 a some
copies on L. P.
From a manuscript dictated by this imposter in
1701, in which he claims to have gone far west of

the Mississippi, in about 1680, at the head of a
party sent out from Illinois by Tonty; on the faith
of this relation France erected its Mississippi Company.

SAGEN
Sagen der nordamerikanischen Indianer. *See*
Jones, James Athearn.

SAGINAW VALLEY (THE).
Indian and pioneer history of: ... *See* Thomas,
James M., and Galatian, A. B.

SAGITTARIUS'S LETTERS ...
See Mein, John.

SAGRA, RAMÓN DE LA   **18**
Cinco meses en los Estados-Unidos ... *P* 1836.
O [40] 437 a
—Fr. tr: *P* 1837, O [28] 458 [1] 4pls; *Brus* 1837.
D 484
A study of social and industrial conditions by a
Spanish scientist.

SAINT-AMANT, PIERRE CHARLES DE   **19**
Guide pour les voyageurs ... à travers l'isthme
d Peanama ... *P* 1853. D 108 [incl. 6adv-p]
map a
Chiefly a re-writing of the introductory chapters
of the author's *Voyages en Californie et dans
l'Oregon*, next entry.

SAINT-AMANT, PIERRE   **20**
CH[ARLES] DE
Voyages en Californie et dans l'Oregon ...
1851–1852. *P* 1854. O [52] 651 2maps aa
Most comprehensive and reliable French
description of the Pacific coast at this time. Not to
be confused with the author's previous 48-page
pamphlet, *Voyage en Californie*, [1851] which is
chiefly devoted to his journey from France to the
Golden State.

ST. ANTHONY AND MINNEAPOLIS.   **21**
Historical sketch of St. Anthony and Minneapolis ... *St. Anthony* 1855. D 24 + 4 adv-p map
errata slip aa

Sketch of St. Anthony and Minneapolis *St*   **22**
Anthony 1857 D 32 errata slip map aa
A 15-page pamphlet with similar title was
published at Philadelphia in 1856.

ST. AUGUSTINE
A relation ... of a late expedition to the gates of
St. Augustine ... *See* Kimber, Edw.

St. Augustine: sketches of its history ...   **23**
By an English visitor. *N Y* 1869. 16° 62 fold.view
[59" in length] a

**ST. CLAIR (MAJOR GENERAL   24
[ARTHUR]).**
A narrative of the manner in which the campaign against the Indians . . . was conducted by: . . . *Phil* 1812. O [20] 274 + 20p of subscriber's names [some copies have 24] and errata lf. aa
Attempt to vindicate his surprise and rout by Ohio Indians.

**ST. CLAIR (MAJOR GENERAL   25
[ARTHUR]).**
Proceedings of a general court martial . . . for the trial of: *Phil* 1778. F 52 plan c AA N NYP
Best contemporary account of the forced American abandonment of Ft. Ticonderoga in 1777.

ST. CLAIR PAPERS (THE).   26
The life . . . of Arthur St. Clair . . . with his correspondence and other papers. Ed. by William Henry Smith. *Cin* 1882. O 2v: [12] 609; [4] 649 + 8adv-p. map 2ports a

ST. CLAIR, HENRY, comp.   27
The United States criminal calendar . . . *B* 1832. D [2] 5–356 13pls a
—rptd. same impr. & collat: 1833; 1835.
—anr. ed., comp. by P. R. Hamblin, "United States criminal history," *Fayetteville N Y* 1836. D 560 other eds: *N Y* 1840; *B* 1840.

ST. CLAIR COUNTY, ILLINOIS.
History of: 1876. *See* West, Edw. W.

ST. EUSTASIUS.   28
Authentic rebel papers seized at: 1781. *L* 1781. Q [8] 23 aa
These papers—perhaps less authentic than claimed—relate to economic conditions in the colonies, particularly those in the South.

ST. GEORGE'S   29
St. George's in the county of York. A conference held at: on the twentieth day of September . . . 1753, between Sir William Pepperrell, et al . . . to treat with the eastern Indians . . . *B* 1753. Q 26 b AA N NYP

ST. GERMAIN, ALFRED H.   30
A voyage to California . . . *Tor* 1853. D 24 b

ST. JOHN, J. HECTOR [pseud.]
Letters from an American farmer. *See* Crevecouer, Michel-Guillaume Saint Jean de.

ST. JOHN, JOHN R.   31
A true description of the Lake Superior country . . . *N Y* 1846. D [2] 118 2maps aa

[ST. JOHN, PERCY BOLINGBROKE]?   32
A hunter's experiences in the southern states . . . *L* 1866. D [6] 359 + 32adv-p aa

Under the same pseudonym — Captain Flack — appeared several other fictionalized "westerns" by this author, in the same period: *The prairie hunter*; *The Texan ranger*; *The Texan rifle hunter*; *The wigwam in the wilderness*.

ST. LOUIS   33
History of St. Louis . . . *St L* 1854. O 48 map [showing routes west] 2pls aa
Probably by William M. McPherson.

**Proceedings of the national railroad con-   34
vention . . . in St. Louis.** 1849. *St L* 1850. O 98 aa
First convention of national nature; assembled when the California gold discovery made evident the need for transcontinental communication.

Railroad from St. Louis to San Francisco   35
B 1849. O 24 a
P. P. F. De Grand's plan to complete the undertaking in four years.

Report of the celebration of the anniversary of the founding of St. Louis . . . *See* Primm, Wilson.

St. Louis business directory, for 1847; con-   36
taining the history of St. Louis . . . *St L* 1847. D 176 b only 1 cop loc.

St. Louis directory and register. *St L* 1821.   37
O [4] 100 [2] d G MoH Y
Including, as it does, an historical sketch, this is both the first directory and the first historical work printed west of the Mississippi.

Thoughts about the city of St. Louis. *See* Hogan, John.

**The western metropolis; or St. Louis in   38
1846.** *St L* W. D. Skilman 1846. D 161 fold. plan a
—rptd., same collat. & impr., 1847.

ST.-MÉMIN, M[ONS. FEVRET] DE
The St.-Mémin collection of portraits . . . *See* Fevret de St.-Mémin, Charles B. J.

ST. PAUL, HENRY   39
Our home and foreign policy. [*Mobile*] 1863. O 23 aa
Dream of an imperial Confederacy: French alliance, control of Central America and the Mexican Gulf.

ST. PAUL . . . DIRECTORY   40
St. Paul city directory for 1856–7. *St P* Goodrich & Somers 1857. D [8] 194 [4] [incl. advs] map aa
First city directory of this city.

[ST. VALIER, JEAN B. DE]   41
Estat present de l'eglise et de la colonie française dans la Nouvelle France. *P* 1688. O [2] 268 c JCB MinnU N

—iss. 2., "Relation des missions de la Nouvelle France", with slight textual changes, same impr, date & collat b JCB MinnU
—rptd. *Queb* 1856. O [10] 102 a

Describes a survey of the extensive territory of the Quebec bishopric to which St. Valier had been appointed; with account of the Indian nations and their relation to white settlers. Indicative of keen rivalry between Dutch and French fur traders, he relates that, when at Mackinac, that post narrowly escaped capture by an invading armed force from Albany.

[SAINT-VICTOR, JACQUES B. M. B.,   42 comte de]
Lettres sur les États-Unis . . . *P* 1835. O 2v: [14] 355; [4] 359 a
—Ger. tr. *Berlin* 1835. O 2v: [16] 293; [24] 372 a

Valuable study of American life by a royalist with little sympathy for democratic institutions.

[SAINTE-CROIX, GUILLAUME E. J. G.   44 DE CLERMONT-LODÈVE, baron de]
De l'état et du sort des colonies . . . avec observations sur . . . la conduite des Anglois en Amérique. *Phil* [probably ptd at *P*] 1779. O [14] 336 a
—anr. issue, same date & collat., carries impr. *Yverdon*
—Ital. tr. *Phil* 1780. O 278 tab

SALA, GEORGE A.   45
My diary in America . . . *L* 1865. O 2v: [10] 424; [6] 425 a
—ed. 2, rev., same impr. & date. O 2v

[SALAZAR, JOSEPH DE]   46
Crisis del Ensayo a la historia de la Florida. *Alcala* 1725. Q 55 aa

For work here attacked—but without disturbing its scholarly reputation—*see* Barcia, *Ensayo chronologico* . . .

SALAZAR YLARREGUI, JOSÉ   47
Datos de los trabajos . . . por la Comision de Limites Mexicana en la linea que divide esta republica de la de los Estados Unidos . . . *Mex* 1850. O [2] 123 2maps b AA Hn N NYP Y

Day-by-day report of the Mexican Boundary Survey, printed prior to the American report, and the earliest detailed account of the region.

SALE, EDITH T.   48
Colonial interiors, second series. *N Y* 1930. Q 15 front. 159pls on 81 lvs. a

SALE, EDITH T.   49
Interiors of Virginia houses of colonial times . . . *Rich* 1927. O [24] 503[incl.pls] a

SALE, EDITH T.   50
Manors of Virginia in colonial times. *Phil* 1909. O [2] 310 49pls aa

SALE, EDITH T.   51
Old time belles and cavaliers. *Phil* 1912. O [2] 285 51pls a

SALEM WITCHCRAFT.
Records of: . . . *See* Woodward, Wm. Elliot.

[SALES, LUIS]   52
Noticias de la provincia de Californias . . . *Valencia* 1794. 16° 3pts in 1: 104; 96; 104. 2fold. tabs b N NYP Y
—Eng. tr. "Observations on Calif," *L A* 1956. a

This book, which contains interesting material on the Nootka embroglio and Martinez's capture of Colnett, is said to have been suppressed. It was the only work on California written by a Dominican.

SALLEY, ALEXANDER S.   53
The history of Orangeburg County, S. C. . . . *Orangeburg* 1898. O [8] 572 map port a

[SALPOINTE, JOHN B.]   54
A brief sketch of the mission of San Xavier del Bac . . . *Tucson* 1880. O [2] 22 aa some cops carry *S F* impr.

SALPOINTE, JOHN B.   55
Soldiers of the cross. Notes on the ecclesiastical history of New-Mexico, Arizona and Colorado. *Banning Calif* 1898. O [15 incl.front.] 299 [2] 19pls aa
—anr. issue, same sheets, with Appendix No. 7 [8 unnumb p] added in 1900. aa

SALTIEL, EBENEZER H., and   56 BARNETT, GEORGE
History and business directory of Cheyenne and guide to the mining regions of the Rocky mountains . . . *Cheyenne* [ptd *Omaha*?] n.d. [1868]. O 113[incl. cover t.] + fold.adv-sheet c Y[only copy known]

[SALVATOR, LUDWIG L.]   57
Eine Blume aus dem goldenen Lande oder Los Angeles. *Prague* 1878. D [12] 257 front. 12pls aa
—Eng. ed. "Los Angeles in the sunny seventies . . .," *L A* 1929. a 900 cops ptd.

SALZBACHER, JOSEPH   58
Meine Reise nach Nord-Amerika . . . *Vienna* 1845. O [12] 480 [14] map aa

SAMPSON (ABEL).   59
The wonderful adventures of: . . . Ed. by Edmund H. Kendall. *Lawrence Mass* 1847. O 91 [4] a
Privateering in the war of 1812, etc.

SAMPSON, M. B.   60
Slavery in the United States . . . *L* 1845. O [8] 88 a

SAMPSON (WILLIAM).   **61**
Memoirs of: . . . adventures in various parts of
Europe . . . and a few observations on the state of
manners . . . in America. *N Y* 1807. O [12] 448 a
—ed. 2, rev., *Leesburg Va* 1817. O 432 port
—Eng. ed. *L* 1832. 18° [32] 292 port

SAMS, CONWAY W.   **62**
The conquest of Virginia . . . [1584–1624]. *Nor-*
folk [& *N Y*] 1916–29–39. O 3v: [30] 547; [52] 174
171–916 + explanatory lf after p132; [16] 824.
14fold,maps 172 pls aa

SAMUEL, L[EO] pub.   **63**
Traveler's guide and Oregon railroad gazetteer.
[*Port Ore* 1872]. D 96 tab aa

SAMWELL, DAVID   **64**
A narrative of the death of Captain James Cook;
to which are added some particulars concerning
his life . . . *L* 1786. Q [4] 34 b NYP Y
—Fr. tr. *P* 1786. O 56 + advs aa

SAN BENITO COUNTY, CALIFORNIA.   **65**
History of: . . . *S F* 1881. F 188 pls b Hn CalS

SAN BERNARDINO COUNTY   **65a**
History of San Bernardino country, California . . .
S F 1883. F [6] 17–204 b B Hn

Illustrated description of San Bernardino **66**
county, California. *San Bernardino* 1881. O 34 a

SAN DIEGO   **67**
Descriptive, historical . . . information relative to
. . . San Diego [*San Diego*] 1874. O 52 22 photo.
views on 7 lvs. aa

History of San Diego and San Bernardino   **68**
counties[*Calif.*] . . . *S F* 1883. F 204 pls b CalS Hn

SAN FELIPE DE AUST[I]N.   **69**
Journal of the consultation held at: October . . .
1835. *Houston* 1838. O 54 b Hn NYP Y

SAN FRANCISCO
Judges and criminals . . . History of the Vigilance
comittee of San Francisco. 1858. *See* Gray, Henry
M.

Manuel of the corporation of the city of   **70**
San Francisco . . . *S F* 1852. O [50 6 9–16] 261
2maps b LC NYP Y
—anr. issue, same impr. & date. O [16] 96 aa
—anr. ed. *S F* 1853. O [16] 261 2maps aa

Mysteries and miseries of San Francisco.   **71**
By a Californian [—Garrett?]. *N Y* [1853]. O [2]
7–208 b
—rptd. *N Y* Dick & Fitzgerald, n.d. a

Origin of the free public schools of San Fran-
cisco. *See* Pelton, John C.

The Presidio of San Francisco . . . [*Wash* 1874].
See Elliott, Geo. H.

Public schools of San Francisco. John C.   **72**
Pelton's course in regard to same unmasked. *S F*
1865. O 129 a
See Pelton, John C., for his claims.

SAN JACINTO.   **73**
A detailed account of the battle of: . . . *N O*
1836. D 34 c NYH [only cop. loc.]

SAN JOAQUIN   **74**
An illustrated history of San Joaquin county,
California. *Chi* 1890. Q 666 pls aa

San Joaquin county, California. Its favour- **75**
able location . . . *Stockt* 1887. O 130 map a

SAN JUAN [COLO.]   **76**
San Juan [Colo.], its past and present . . .
Denver 1876. D 93[incl.advs] a

SAN LUIS OBISPO COUNTY [CALIF.]
History of: *See* Angel, Myron.

SAN MATEO COUNTY, CALIFORNIA.   **77**
History of: . . . *S F* 1883. Q 322 pls b B CalS

SAN SALVADOR, AUGUSTIN P. F.   **78**
Los Jesuitas quitados y restuidos al mundo.
Historia de la antigua California. *Mex* 1816. D 214
[10] a

SANBORN, KATE   **79**
Old time wall papers . . . *Greenwich Conn* 1905.
Q 16 116 [2] 62pls 1050copies ptd. [75 on Jap.
Paper] a

SAND CREEK MASSACRE (THE).   **80**
Report of the Secretary of War, communicating
. . . evidence . . . taken by a military commission,
ordered to inquire into: [*Wash* 1865]. Sen. Exec.
Doc. 26. O 228 a
This investigation required seventy-six days of
testimony.

SANDBURG, CARL   **81**
Abraham Lincoln: the prairie years. *N Y* [1926].
O 2v: [16] 480; [6] 482. 2fronts. 22 pls[with illus on
both sides] L. P. issue, signed, of 260 sets b AA
12copies of v.I contained error "ears [for "eyes"],
p175, line 9
—trade issue, ptd later, same yr., same collat. a

SANDBURG, CARL   **82**
Abraham Lincoln: the war years. *N Y* [1939–

40]. O 4v: [32] 660; [12] 655; [14] 673; [12] 515. 64pls L. P. issue of 525 sets b
—trade issue, same yr. a
—rptd., with "Prairie years," in the "Sangamon ed." *N Y* 1940. O 6v

SANDER, CONSTANTIN   83
Der Amerikanische Bürgerkrieg... *Frankf* 1863. O 121 a
—enl. ed. "Geschichte des vierjährigen Bürgerkrieges...," same impr. 1865. O [16] 587 3maps
—anr. ed. vol. I[all], same impr. 1876. O [16] 792 7maps & plans

[SANDERS, DANIEL C.]   84
A history of the Indian wars... particularly in New England. *Montp Vt* 1812. 16° 319 aa
—ed. 2, with adds. & omissions; *Roch* 1828. D 180 [incl. front. & pl] 185–196 aa
—anr. ed. *Roch* 1893. D 196 2pls a
The sensitive author, chagrined over some scornful critique of his book, strove to suppress the 1812 edition.

SANDERS, JOHN   85
A centennial address relating to the early history of Schenectady... *Alb* 1879. O [14] 346 3 ports a

SANDERS, [CAPT.] JOHN   86
Memoir on the military resources of the valley of Ohio... *Pitt* 1845. O 19 a
—anr. ed., with adds. *Wash* 1845. O 24

SANDERSON, GEORGE   87
A brief history of the early settlement of Fairfield County [O.]... *Lancaster O* 1851. O 32 view a

SANDERSON, JOHN, ed.   88
Biography of the signers to the declaration of independence. *Phil* 1820–27. O 9v: [4] 224 [43]; [6] 250; [2] 310; [6] 288 + errata slip; [2] 382; [2] 354; [2] 343; [2] 348; [2] 339. 31ports 4 lvs. of facs a some copies on L.P. aa
—ed. 2, enl. *Phil* 1828. O 5v: [22] 397; [6] 435; [6] 391; [6] 372; [6] 386. 31ports 4 lvs of facs; rptd. *Phil* 1831. a
—abr.ed. in 1v, ed.Conrad, O: 1846; 1848; 1852.
For a later work, based on this, *see* Brotherhead, William.

SANDFAERDIG
Sandfaerdig beretning om Amerika... *See* Rynning, Ole.

SANDFORD, ADAM C.   89
My recollections of eighty years of a strenuous life. *Port Ore* [1910?]. O 96 map pls tab a

SANDS, FRANK   90
A pastoral prince. The history and reminiscences of J. W. Cooper. *Santa Barbara* 1893. D [16] 190[incl.front.& 3pls] aa

Thrilling account of early California. Cooper helped drive the first drove of sheep across the plains.

[SANDS, ROBERT C.] ed.   91
Life and correspondence of John Paul Jones... *N Y* 1830. O 556 port errata slip a

SANDUSKY [OHIO].   92
Directory of: for 1858–9. *Sandusky* 1858. D 162 front. aa
Includes a twenty-six page historical sketch.

SANFORD, A.   93
Treason unmasked... origin... of the Knights of the Golden Circle... *Albion N Y* 1863. 16° 42 a

SANFORD, EZEKIEL   94
A history of the United States before the revolution. *Phil* 1819. O [192] 342 a

SANFORD, MRS. NETTIE   95
Central Iowa farms and herds. *Newton Ia* 1873. O [6] 125 a

SANFORD, MRS. NETTIE   96
History of Marshall county, Iowa. *Clinton Ia* 1867. D [8] 158 + 10adv-p front. lf. of ports a

SANPETE AND EMERY COUNTIES [UTAH].
History of: *See* Lever, W. H.

[SANTA-ANNA, ANTONIO LÓPEZ DE]   97
Detalle de las operaciones ocurrida en la defensa de la capital de la republica, atacada por el ejercito de los Estados-Unidos. *Orizava* 1847. O 54 aa
—anr. ed. *Mex* [1847?]. O 48 aa

SANTA-ANNA, ANTONIO LÓPEZ DE   98
Manifiesto que de sus operaciones en la campaña de Tejas... *Vera Cruz* 1837. Q 108[incl. cover-t.] aa
Official report on the San Jacinto campaign.

SANTA BARBARA   99
All about Santa Barbara. *Santa Barbara* 1878. O 100 8 photos [on 5 pls] aa
—anr. iss. no. pls. a

History of Santa Barbara and Ventura   100 counties, California ... *Oakl* 1883. Q 415; 496 pls b B Hn

Sketch of the history of Santa Barbara. *See* Huse, Chas. E.

SANTA CLARA COUNTY, CALIFORNIA.   101
History of... *S F* 1881. Q 798 pls b N

SANTA CRUZ COUNTY, CALIFORNIA.   101a
Illustrations... of its scenery... with historical sketch. *S F* 1879. F [4] 102 [6] pls b B CalS

SANTA FÉ   **102**
The conquest of Santa Fé . . . by the military
forces of the United States; with . . . a history of
Colonel Doniphan's campaign . . . By a Captain
of Volunteers. *Phil* 1847. O 48[incl. cov.t. &
t.] b

Message from the President . . . trans-   **103**
mitting information relative to the . . . imprisonment
of certain American citizens at Santa Fé. *Wash*
1818. O 23 aa

SANTLEBEN, AUGUST   **104**
A Texas pioneer . . . *N Y* 1910. O 321 aa

SAN XAVIER DEL BAC.
A brief sketch of the mission of: *See* Salpointe,
John B.

SARGENT, GEORGE B.   **105**
Lecture on the "West" . . . *Davenport Ia* 1858.
O 27 a

SARGENT, GEORGE B.   **106**
Notes on Iowa. *N Y* 1848. 18° 74 map b
—rptd. *N Y* 1849. same collat. aa

[SARGENT, JOHN O.]   **107**
. . . General Hazen . . . reviewed. *N Y* 1874. O
32 aa

SARGENT, MARTIN P.   **108**
Pioneer sketches . . . *Erie Pa* 1891. D 512 aa
Early Pennsylvania oil operations.

SARGENT, WINTHROP, [1753–1820]   **109**
Diary during the campaign of 1791. *Wormsloe
Ga* [*Phil* ptd] 1851. Q 59 2pls aa 46 copies ptd.
Highly important account of St. Clair's disas-
trous defeat, kept by his Adjutant General. The
brutal truth on the Pearl Harbor of 1791.

SARGENT (WINTHROP) [1753–1820].   **110**
A letter from: to Dr. Benjamin Smith. *Cin* 1794.
Q 39 2pls aa

SARGENT (WINTHROP) [1753–1820].   **111**
Papers in relation to the official conduct of: . . .
governor of the Mississippi Territory . . . [*Wash*
1801]. O 29 aa
—rptd. *B* 1801. O 64 aa
Justifies his conduct from Claiborne's accusations which had brought about his removal by
Jefferson.

SARGENT, WINTHROP, ed. [1825–70]   **112**
The history of the expedition against Fort Du
Quesne, in 1755 . . . *Phil* 1855. O 423 10pls a
—rptd. *Phil* 1856. same collat.
Best account of the Braddock disaster.

SARGENT, WINTHROP, [1825–70]   **113**
The life and career of Major John André . . . *B*
1861. D [16] 471 map port a 75copies ptd on L.P.
in O.
—rptd. "The life of Major John André . . .," *N Y*
1871. D [16] 478 map 2ports
—enl. ed. *N Y* 1902. O 558 map 75 L.P. copies

SARYCHEV, GARVRILLA A.   **114**
Atlas [in Russian] of the northern part of the
Pacific ocean. *St Ptbg* 1826. Q 33 double-sheet
maps aa

[SARYCHEV, GARVRILLA A.]   **115**
Puteshestvie flota Kap.Sarycheva po siev.-
vostochnoi chasti Sibiri, Ledovitom moriu i
vostoch, okeanu v prodolzhenie osjmi liet pri
geogr. i astron. morskoi eksped. byvshei pod
nachalj. flota Kap. Billingsas 1785–93 g. [Voyage
to N. E. Siberia, the Arctic and Pacific oceans, on
an 8-year geographical and astronomical expedition under Capt. Billings]. *St Ptbg* 1802. Q 2v: [20]
187 [3]; [4] 192. tab + atlas F 53 maps & pls d
N NYP Y
—Dutch ed. "Reis in het . . . Siberien . . .," *Amst*
1808. O 2v: [32] 190; [10] 334 map tab 14pls aa
—Eng. ed., with vocabularies omitted, "Account
of a voyage of discovery . . .," *L* 1806–7. O 2v: 70;
82. 5pls aa
—Ger. ed., with vocabularies omitted, "Achtjah-
rige Reise im . . . Siberien auf dem Eismeere und
dem nordostlichen Ozean," *Leip* 1805–06 O 2v
[24] 190; [12] 196 map 14 pls b
Account by the surveyor on this official expedition, sent out by Catherine II, on which Alaska and
the Aleutians were first carefully charted. For
another account, by the secretary, *see* Sauer,
Martin.

[SARYCHEV, GARVRILLA A.]   **116**
Puteshestvie Kapitana Billingsa . . . i plavaniye
Kapitana Halla . . . *St Ptbg* 1811. Q [6] 191 3maps
3pls aa
Voyages made by Billings and Hall to the Alas-
kan coast, etc.

SAUER, MARTIN   **117**
An account of a geographical, [etc.], expedition
to the northern parts of Russia . . . and of the
islands in the eastern ocean, stretching to the American coast. Performed by Commodore Joseph Billings . . . 1785–94. *L* 1802. Q [26] 332 [58] map
14pls aa
—Fr. tr.—and best ed.—*P* [1802]. O 2v: [26] 385;
[4] 418 + atlas Q [of 2p & 15maps & pls] aa
—Ger. tr. *Berlin* 1802. O [4] 334 map 2pls
—rptd. *Weimar* 1803. O [14] 296 map a
—Ital. tr. *Milan* 1816. 16° 2v: [30] 288; 324. 8pls
[6 col]
For another account of, and note on, this
voyage, *see* Sarychev, Gavrilla A., No. 115, above.

SAUNDERS, ARTHUR C.   **118**
The history of Bannock county, Idaho. *Pocatello* 1915. O 143 a 100 cops ptd, 700 burned.

SAUNDERS, JAMES E.   **119**
Early settlers of Alabama. Pt.I[all]. *N O* 1899. O 530 [24] aa

SAVAGE, EDWARD H.   **120**
A chronological history of the Boston watch and police . . . *B* 1865. O 396 a
—ed. 2, rev., same impr. & date. O 408 port
—rptd. "Police records and recollections . . .," *B* [1873]. O 400 [2] 9pls

SAVAGE, I. O.   **121**
A history of Republic county [Kas.]. *Topeka* 1883. O 112 map pl a
—enl. ed., to 1901, *Beloit Kas* 1901. O 323 map 34pls

SAVAGE, JAMES, 1767–1845   **122**
Memorabilia; or, recollections . . . *Taunton Eng* 1820. O [8] 328 a
—rptd., same impr. & collat., 1822.

SAVAGE, JAMES, 1784–1873   **123**
A genealogical dictionary of the first settlers of New England . . . *B* 1860–2. O 4v: [16] 516; [4] 599; [4] 664; [6] 714 aa
—index to above, by O. P. Dexter, *N Y* 1884. O 38 a

SAVAGE, JAMES W., BELL, JOHN T., et al   **124**
History of . . . Omaha . . . *N Y & Chi* 1894. Q [16] 699 54ports a

SAVAGE, WILLIAM   **125**
Observations on emigration to the United States . . . *Y* 1819. O 66 a

SAVANNAH
Census of Savannah [Georgia] . . . **1848.** *See* Bancroft, Jos.

Directory of . . . **Savannah for 1849.** *See* Galloway, David H., comp.

Savannah directory . . . *Sav* Purse 1866. **126**
O 200 aa
First "post-bellum" directory of Savannah.

SAVARDAN, AUGUSTIN   **127**
Un naufrage au Texas . . . *P* 1858. D [4] 344 aa
Best account of Victor Considerant's ill-fated socialistic colony at Reunion, written by its physician.

SAVERY (WILLIAM).
A journal of the life, travels . . . of: *See* Evans, Jonathan.

SAVVAGE (JEHAN).   **128**
Memoire du voiage en Russie fait . . . par: suivi de l'expedition de Fr. Drake en Amérique . . . *P* 1855. 16° [10] 30 a

SAWYER, EUGENE T.   **129**
The life and career of Tiburcio Vasquez, the Californian bandit and murderer . . . [*San José* 1875]. O 48 pls aa
—rptd. *Oakland* 1944. O [10] 92 front 500copies ptd. a
Best biography of this outlaw; written by a local journalist who attended his trial and interviewed him at length.

SAWYER, GEORGE S.   **130**
Southern institutes . . . with notes and comments in defence . . . *Phil* 1858. O 393 a
—rptd., same impr. & collat., 1859.

SAWYER, JAMES A.   **131**
Report on the wagon road from Niobrara to Virginia City. [H. Doc. 58]. *Wash* 1866. O 32 a
A train of eighty wagons, convoyed by less than one hundred and fifty men, was shown to be an irresistable temptation to the hostile Indians of this region.

SAWYER, JOSEPH D.   **132**
Washington, *N Y* 1927. O 2v: [20 incl. front.] 640; [10] 619 a
Contains 1500 illustrations, including 250 portraits of Washington.

SAWYER, LORENZO   **133**
Way sketches . . . incidents of travel across the plains . . . *N Y* 1926. O 126 port a 35copies were on L. P. aa

SAXE-WEIMAR-EISENACH, duke of
Reise . . . durch Nord Amerika. *See* Bernhard, Karl, Duke of Saxe-Weimar-Eisenach.

SAXON, ISABELLE, pseud.
Five years within the Golden Gate. *See* Sutherland, Mrs. Redding.

SAXTON, CHARLES   **134**
The Oregonian; or history of the Oregon Territory. No. 1 [all]. *Wash* 1846. D 48 [2] map[called for on t-p]not issued c N NYP Y

SCAMEHORN, GEORGE N.   **135**
Behind the scenes; or, Denver by gaslight. *Denver* 1894. O 80[incl.pls] aa

SCAMMON, CHARLES M.   **136**
The marine mammals of the north-western coast . . . with an account of the American whale-fishery. *S F* 1874. Q 319 [5] 27pls b

SCANLAND, JOHN M.   137
Life of Pat F. Garrett and the taming of the
border outlaw . . . *El Paso* 1908. O [2] 42[incl.pls] b
G NYP 4copies known
—rptd. *Col Spqs* 1952

[SCANTLEBURY, THOMAS]   138
Wanderings in Minnesota during the Indian
troubles of 1862. *Chi* 1867. O [2] 32[incl.wraps] b
G MinnH[only copies known]

SCARBOROUGH, KATHERINE   139
Homes of the cavaliers. *N Y* 1930. O [16] 392
pls a
Maryland architecture.

SCENES IN THE INDIAN COUNTRY.
Phil [1859]. *See* Loomis, Augustus W.

SCENES IN THE ROCKY MOUNTAINS.
Phil 1846. *See* Sage, Rufus B.

SCENOGRAPHIC AMERICANA . . .   140
L 1768. F 4 28pls d AA
—anr. issue, with Fr. text, same impr., date &
collat. aa

SCHABELSKI, ACHILLE   141
Voyage aux colonies russes de l'Amérique . . .
1821–1823 . . . *St Ptbg* 1826. O [6] 106 aa

SCHARF, J[OHN] THOMAS   142
The chronicles of Baltimore . . . *Balt* 1874. O
[8] 756 a Also 50 L. P. cops aa
—enl. ed. "History of Baltimore, city and county
. . .," *Phil* 1881. O 947 map pl

SCHARF, J[OHN] THOMAS, ed.   143
History of Delaware. *Phil* 1888. Q 2v: [10] 610
[33] errata slip; [8] 611–1358. 157pls facs aa

SCHARF, J[OHN] THOMAS   144
History of Maryland . . . *Balt* 1879. O 3v: [16]
556; [14] 635; [16] 782 [38]. 26maps & pls aa
Most valuable history of this state.

SCHARF, J[OHN] THOMAS, and   145
WESTCOTT, THOMPSON
History of Philadelphia, 1609–1884. *Phil* 1884.
O 3v: [10] 852 [4]; [6] 853–1702; [6] 1703–2399.
5fold.maps 108pls facs a

SCHARF, J[OHN] THOMAS   146
History of Saint Louis city and county . . .
Phil 1883. Q 2v: [12] 988; [4] 989–1943. 2maps
162pla aa

SCHARF, J[OHN] T[HOMAS]   147
History of the Confederate States navy . . . *N Y*
1887. O 824 42pls aa
—ed. 2 *Alb* 1894 a

SCHARF, J[OHN] THOMAS   148
History of western Maryland . . . *Phil* 1882. Q
2v: [8] 13–788; [4] 789–1560. map 109pls tab aa

SCHARMANN, H[ERMANN] B.   149
. . . Landreise nach Californien . . . [*N Y* 1905?].
16° 125 port aa
—Eng. ed. "Overland journey to California . . .,"
[*N Y* 1918]. 16° 114 port 50copies ptd. aa

SCHEER, FREDERICK   150
A letter on the effects of the California gold
discoveries. *L* 1852. O 38 a

SCHEIBERT, J[USTUS]   151
Der Bürgerkrieg in den nordamerikanischen
Staaten . . . *Berlin* 1874. O [4] 182 map 4 pls a
—Fr. tr. *P* 1876. O [6] 320 map 4pls

SCHEIBERT, JUSTUS   152
Sieben monate in den Rebellen-Staaten . . .
1863. *Stettin* 1868. O [6] 126 5maps and plans aa
—Eng. tr. *Tuscaloosa* 1958. O 166 map
The author served in the Confederate army.

SCHEIBERT, JUSTUS   153
Das Zusammenwirken der Armee und Marine.
Eine Studie illustriert durch den Kampf um den
Mississippi, 1861–3. *Rathenow* n.d. O [6] 64 [4]
7maps aa

SCHENCK, DAVID   154
North Carolina . . . 1780–81. *Raleigh* 1889. O
498[incl.front.] map 2pls a

SCHENECTADY DIRECTORY . . . 1841–2 154a
Schenectady 1841. D 46 a

SCHÉRER, JEAN-BENOIT   155
Recherches historiques et géographiques sur le
nouveau-monde. *P* 1777. O [16] 352 map 8pls a
Exposition of the similarity of Asiatic language
with that of the Northwest coast tribes.

SCHERMERHORN, JOHN F., and   156
MILLS, SAMUEL J.
A correct view of that part of the United States
. . . west of the Alleghanies . . . *Hart* 1814. O
52 a

SCHERPF, G. A.   157
Entstehungsgeschichte und gegenwärtiger Zu-
stand des neuen, unabhängigen, amerikanischen
Staates Texas. *Augsburg* 1841. D [8] 154 2maps aa
Based on Lawrence, A. B. "Texas in 1840".

SCHICKSALE [DIE]   158
Schicksale (Die) und Abenteuer der aus Sachsen
nach Amerika ausgewanderten Stephanianer. Ihre
Reise nach St. Louis . . . *Dresden* 1839. D [8]
124 aa

SCHIEL, J[AMES]   159
Reise durch die Felsengebirge und die Hum-
boldtgebirge nach dem Stillen Ocean. *Schaffhau-
sen* 1859. D [2] 139 errata l. b Hn NYP Y
—Eng. tr. *Norman* Okla 1950 O 114
Account of Beckwith's Pacific Railroad exploration, from Salt Lake to California, written by
the geologist of the expedition.

[SCHIRACH, G. B. VON]   160
Historisch-statistische Notiz der gross-brittanischen Colonien in America... *Frankf* 1776. D
96 aa
—anr. ed. *Hanover* 1776. D

SCHLÄGER, E[DUARD]   161
Die sociale und politische Stellung der Deut-
schen in den Vereinigten Staaten... *Berlin* 1874.
D [4] 50 a

SCHLAGINTWEIT, ROBERT VON   162
Californien. Land und Leute. *Cologne* 1871. D
[16] 380 port a
—Dutch tr. *Deventer* 1873. O [12] 243 front.

SCHLAGINTWEIT, ROBERT VON   163
Die Mormonen... *Cologne* 1874. O [16] 292 a
—ed. 2 same impr. 1878. O 318

SCHLAGINTWEIT, ROBERT VON   164
Neue Pfade vom Missouri-Strom zum stillen
Meere... *Cologne* 1883. O 42 2maps a

SCHLAGINTWEIT, ROBERT VON   165
Die Pacific-Eisenbahnen... *Cologne* 1870. D
[14] 203 map front. tab a
—Am. ed., same collat. & date, *N Y*

SCHLAGINTWEIT, ROBERT VON   166
Die Prairien des amerikanischen Westens...
Cologne 1876. D [12] 202 front. a

SCHLATTER, MICHAËL   167
Getrouw Verhaal van den waren toestant der
meest herderloze Gemeentens in Pennsylvanien...
Amst 1751. Q [22] 56 aa
Describes the author's visit to Pennsylvania and
adjacent states while on a mission to the churches
there. *See* also Harbaugh, H.

SCHLESINGER, ARTHUR M.   168
The colonial merchants and the American revolution. *N Y* 1917. O 631 a
—anr. ed., same impr. 1918. O 647

SCHLIEBEN, WILLIAM E. A. VON   169
Atlas von Amerika. *Leip* 1830. F [4] 54 [2] 30
maps aa

SCHMIDT, CARL   169a
Dies Buch gehört dem deutschen Auswanderer

... Beschreibung der Vereinigten Staaten...
Leip 1853. O [10] 333 map a

SCHMIDT, CARL E.   170
A western trip... to the Yellowstone Park...
[*Det* 1904]. Q 90 28photo views[some col.] aa

SCHMIDT, FRIEDRICH   171
Versuch über den politischen Zustand der Vereinigten Staaten... *Stuttgart* 1822. O 2v: [16] 585;
[12] 663. 14charts 20pls aa
Unfavorable observations, based on four years
of residence, done with Teutonic thoroughness.

SCHMÖLDER, B.   172
Neuer praktischer Wegweiser für Auswanderer
nach Nord-Amerika in drei Abtheilungen. Erste
Abtheilung... Oregon und Californien und Allgemeines über das Mississippi-und Missouri-Thal...
Mainz 1848. O [6] 120 port 3maps plan 3pls b
—ed. 2, same collat. but no maps in most copies,
1849. b NYP PortOreL Y
—Eng. tr. [in part]. *See* "California. Emigrant's
guide to: By a traveller [etc.]."
Schmölder reached California, overland, before
the gold discovery, with a plan for colonizing Sutter's property.

SCHMÖLDER, B.   173
Neuer praktischer Wegweiser... Zweite Abtheilungen... Die mittlern Staaten... Missouri,
Iowa, Wiskonsin, Illinois [etc.] *Mainz* 1848. O 152
map b
—ed. 2, *Mainz* 1849. O 154 no map in most copies,
which is then generally replaced with view of St.
Louis, but some copies have both map and view aa

SCHMÖLDER, B.   174
Neuer praktischer Wegweiser... Die Dritte
Abtheilung... Congress-Landes in Iowa...
Mainz 1849. O 106 map b Y
Usually found bound with the 1849 editions of
Parts I and II. A 3rd edition was issued at Mainz in
1855. [O [8] 120 84–154 map 4 pls]

SCHÖPF, JOHANN D.   175
Beyträge zur mineralogischen Kenntniss des
östlichen Theils von Nordamerika und seiner Ge-
bürge. *Erlangen* 1787. O [12] 194 [2] b
First consequential work on American geology.

SCHÖPF, JOHANN D.   176
Reise durch einige der mittlern und südlichen...
Staaten nach Ost-Florida... *Erlangen* 1788. O
2v: [24] 644 [2]; [40] 352 map aa
—issue 1, on thick paper.
—issue 2, on thinner paper.
—Eng. ed. "Travels in the Confederation...,"
Phil 1911. D 2v: [10] 426; [4] 344. port 2facs aa
First notable 18th century account of the United
States by a German traveller.

SCHOLTE, HENRY P.   177
Eene Stem uit Pella, Iowa . . . *Amst* 1848. O [4]
63 2pls a
—ed. 2, same impr. & date
Appendix relates to Dutch settlements in Michigan. There was an abridged German version of
sixteen pages.

SCHOLTE, HENRY P.   178
Tweede Stem uit Pella, Iowa . . . *Bosch* 1848.
O 35 2pls a

[SCHOLTE, HENRY P.]   179
Wegwijzer en raadgever voor landverhuizers
naar Noord-Amerika, inzonderheid naar de weste-
lijke staten: Ohio, Michigan, Indiana, Illinois,
Missouri, Wisconsin en Jowa [i.e. Iowa]. *Zwijndrecht* 1846. D [4] 64 [2] aa
This political exile from Holland, after extensive
investigations throughout the central West, founded Pella, Iowa.

SCHOOLCRAFT, HENRY R.   180
Algic researches . . . inquiries respecting the
mental characteristics of the North American Indians. First series [all]. *N Y* 1839. D 2v: [2] 5–248;
[4] 9–244 + 18adv-p aa
—anr. ed., with omissions and adds., "The myth
of Hiawatha . . .," *Phil* 1856. D [24] 13–343
Algic was Schoolcraft's term for Algonquin.

SCHOOLCRAFT, HENRY R.
The American Indians. *See* below, *Oneöta* . . .

SCHOOLCRAFT, HENRY R.   181
Annual report of . . . Indian affairs for Michigan. *Det* 1840. O 28 aa

SCHOOLCRAFT, HENRY R.   182
A discourse . . . on the anniversary of the Historical Society of Michigan. *Det* 1830. O 44 aa

SCHOOLCRAFT, HENRY R.   183
Historical . . . information respecting the . . .
Indian tribes . . . *Phil* 1851–7. Q 6v: v.I, [2, 18] 13–
568 eng.t. 76maps & pls; v.II, [24] 17–608 eng.t.
78pls[incl. 2 unnumb. pls of Cherokee alphabet];
v.III, 635 eng.t. 42 pls[numb. 1–21, 25–45]; v.IV,
[26] 19–668 eng.t. 41pls; v.V, 712[incl. eng.t.] 33
maps & pls[numb. 1–8, 10–36]; v.VI, [28] 25–756
port 57pls[some duplicating pls in previous vols.]
3tabs b N NYP Y
—rptd., with shortened t., "Information respecting . . .," *Phil* 1853–57. Q 6v: same collat. b AA
NYP
—cheaper ed., smaller size and omitting v.VI[the
general history or prelim. resumé], *Phil* 1853–6.
5v aa
—anr. ed., with slight changes and indexes added
to first 5vols., "Archives of aboriginal knowledge,"
Phil 1860. Q 6v: [28] 13–575; [24] 17–614; 642;

[26] 19–674; 718; [28] 25–756. port 5eng.t. 328
maps & pls aa
—for condensed ed., *see* Drake, Francis S.

SCHOOLCRAFT, HENRY R.
The Indian in his wigwam. *See* below, *Oneota* . . .

SCHOOLCRAFT, HENRY R.   184
Inquiries respecting the history . . . of the Indian
tribes . . . [*Wash* 1847]. Q 55 caption t.only aa
—anr. ed. [separate printing from v.I of au's. "Historical and statistical information . . ."] *Phil* 1851.
Q paged 523–568

SCHOOLCRAFT, HENRY R.   185
Journal of a tour into the interior . . . from Potosi . . . towards the Rocky mountains, 1818–19.
L 1821. O 102 fold.map aa
This constituted a part of this author's *A view of
the lead mines . . .*, but was not included in that
work as published.

SCHOOLCRAFT, HENRY R.   186
Narrative journal of travels through the northwestern regions . . . *Alb* 1821. O 419 [4] eng. t. map
7pls errata slip aa
—rptd. [in part] in "Summary narrative . . .,"
below.

SCHOOLCRAFT, HENRY R.   187
Narrative of an expedition through the upper
Mississippi to Itasca lake . . . *N Y* 1834. O [2] 308
5maps aa
—rptd. [in part] in "Summary narrative . . .,"
below.
On this trip was discovered what later proved
to be the real source of the Mississippi.

SCHOOLCRAFT, HENRY R.   188
Oneóta, or the red race of America. *N Y* Bur-
gess, Stringer 1844–5. O 8nos[of 64p each] aa
—re-issued, bound form, "Oneóta, or characteristics of the red race . . .," *N Y* Wiley & Putnam
1845. O [6] 5–512 aa
—and. ed., wraps, "The red race of America,"
[cover t. "The Indian in his wigwam . . .,"], *N Y*
Graham 1847. O 418 [incl. front & rear wraps]
2pls a
—anr. issue, bound form, "The Indian in his wigwam . . .," *N Y* Graham 1848. O 416 [incl. front.]
2pls[different from those in 1847 ed.] some copies
of this issue carry Dewitt & Davenport's *N Y*
impr.; others the *Buf* impr. of Derby & Hewson
—rev. & enl. ed. "The American Indians . . .,"
Auburn 1850. O 495 [incl. front. & 7pls]
—rptd., same collat., *Buf* 1851; *Roch* 1851.
—anr. ed. "Western scenes and reminiscences
. . .," *Auburn & Buf* 1853. O [6] 495 6pls
Issuing a book under 5 different titles within 10
years is an unparalleled Protean feat—even for
Schoolcraft.

SCHOOLCRAFT, HENRY R. 189
Outlines of the life . . . of Gen. Lewis Cass. *Alb* 1848. O 64 a

SCHOOLCRAFT, HENRY R. 190
Personal memoirs of a residence of thirty years . . . on the American frontiers . . . *Phil* 1851. O [48] 17–703 port[not issued in all copies] aa *sans* port a

SCHOOLCRAFT, HENRY R.
The red race of America. *See* above, *Oneóta* . . . No. 188

SCHOOLCRAFT (HENRY R.) 191
Report of: [on the N. Y. Indians] . . . contained in "Communication from the [N. Y.] Secretary of State." Sen. doc. 24. [*Alb* 1846]. O 286 a
—rptd., with list of contents added, "Notes on the Iroquois . . .," *N Y* 1846. O [8] 286
—enl. ed., re-written, *Alb* 1847. O [16] 498 + 12adv-p 2col ports

SCHOOLCRAFT, HENRY R. 192
Summary narrative of an exploratory expedition to the sources of the Mississippi . . . in 1820 . . . completed, by the discovery of its origin in Itasca lake, in 1832 . . . *Phil* 1855. O [20] 17–596 2maps pl a
—rptd., without maps, + pl, same impr. & date.
A fusion of his 1821 and 1834 *Narratives*, with some additions.

SCHOOLCRAFT, HENRY R. 193
Travels in the central portions of the Mississippi valley . . . *N Y* 1825. O [4] 459 5maps & pls aa
Describes a trip, with Gen. Cass, via the Wabash and Ohio to Illinois and Missouri, returning via the Mississippi and Illinois rivers to Peoria and Chicago.

SCHOOLCRAFT, HENRY R. 194
A view of the lead mines of Missouri . . . and other sections of the western country. *N Y* 1819. O 299 3pls aa
—anr. ed. with changes, "Scenes and adventures in the . . . region of the Ozark mountains of Missouri and Arkansas . . .," *Phil* 1853. O 256 + 36 adv-p 3pls a

SCHOOLCRAFT, HENRY R.
Western scenes and reminiscences. *See* above, *Oneota* . . .

[SCHOOLCRAFT, MRS. HENRY R.] 195
Letters on the condition of the African race in the United States. *Phil* 1852. O 34 a

SCHOONOVER, T[HOMAS] J. 196
The life . . . of Gen'l. John A. Sutter. *Sacr* 1895. 16° [8] 136 port a
—enl. ed., same impr. 1907. D 312 [3] errata slip port

SCHORI, P. 197
Das Neuste aus dem Staate Ohio . . . *Berne* 1834. 16° [6] 100 map aa

SCHREIBEN 198
Schreiben des Evangelisch-Lutherisch und Reformirten Kirchen-Rathes, wie auch der Beamten der teutschen Einwohner der Provinzen von Neu-York und Nord-Carolina. *Phil* 1775. 16° 40 aa
The Philadelphia Germans here go on record officially as favoring the Revolutionnary cause, and ask their New York and North Carolina brethren to fall in line.

SCHREIBEN
Schreiben eine russichen Officier von der Flotte . . .
See Lettre d'un officier de la marine russienne . . .

SCHREYVOGEL, CHARLES 199
My bunkie and others . . . *N Y* 1909. obl F [8] 36pls aa

[SCHRÖTER, JOHANN F.] 200
Algemeine Geschichte der Länder und Völker von America . . . *Halle* 1752–3. Q 2v: [46] 688; [22] 905 [63]. 68maps & pls aa
Chiefly a compilation, from Lafitau, Charlevoix and others.

SCHÜTZ, KUNO D. VON 201
Texas. Rathgeber für Auswanderer nach diesen Lande. *Wiesbaden* 1846. D [8] 232 map aa
—rptd. same impr. 1847. D 260 map a

SCHULTZ, CHRISTIAN 202
Travels on an inland voyage through . . . New York, Pennsylvania, Virginia, Ohio, Kentucky . . . Tennessee [etc.]. *N Y* 1810. O 2v: [18] 207; [8] 224. port 2pls 4[in some copies 5]maps aa
Best description of this region at the period.

SCHULTZ, JAMES W. 203
My life as an Indian . . . *B* 1907. D [16] 3–426 16pls a

SCHULTZ, JAMES W. 204
William Jackson, Indian scout . . . *B* 1926. D [6] 201 4pls a

SCHULTZ, J[OHN] H. S. 205
Die deutsche Ansiedelung in Texas . . . *Bonn* 1845. O 60 aa
—rptd. *Wiesbaden* 1846. O a

SCHULZE, JOHANN L., ed. 206
Nachrichten von den vereinigten deutschen Evangelisch-Lutherischen Gemeinen in Nord-America, absonderlich in Pennsylvanien . . . *Halle* 1787. Q 2v: [14] 700; [12] 701–1518 [20] aa
—rptd. *Allentown Pa* 1886–95. O 2v a
Collection of reports of Lutheran missionaries.

[SCHULZ[E], JOHANN L.]   207
Neue Nachrichten von denen neuentdekten In-
suln in der See zwischen Asien und Amerika . . .
Hamburg 1776. D [2] 173 aa
On this study of the Russian discoveries, Aleu-
tian Islands, etc., was largely based William Coxe's
Account . . ., *q.v.* It has been ascribed also to
J. A. Schlozer.

SCHULZE, W.   208
Reise-und Lebens-bilder aus Neuholland, Neu-
seeland, und Californien. *Magdeburg* 1853. O 144 aa
—enl. ed. same impr. & date O 167 aa

SCHURICHT, HERRMANN   209
History of the German element in Virginia. *Balt*
1898–1900. O 2v: 160 [8]; 239 [5]. port with lf of
letterpress a

SCHURZ (CARL).   210
The reminiscences of: *N Y* McClure 1907–08. O
3v: [8] 405; [10] 443; [10] 486. 96pls a
—Ger. tr. "Lebenserinnerungen . . .," *Berlin* 1906–
12. O 3v [vol.I preceded *N Y* ed. of that vol., being
tr. from McClure's magazine, in which it ran
serially, beginning in 1906].
In another printing of Vols. 1 and 2 of the N.Y.
edition pagination differs throughout from collation given above.

SCHURZ, CARL   211
Report on the states of South Carolina, Georgia,
Alabama, Mississippi and Louisiana; also the
report of Lieut. Gen. Grant on the same subject.
[*Wash* 1865]. O 108 a
Contained in Executive Document 2, *Message
of the President.*

SCHUYLER, GEORGE W.   212
Colonial New York . . . *N Y* 1885. O 2v: [12]
509; [4] 539 a

SCHUYLER, MAJOR GENERAL   213
[PHILIP].
Proceedings of a general court martial . . . for
the trial of: *Phil* 1778. sm F 62 b Hn NYP

SCHUYLKILL . . . COMPANY (THE)
Schuylkill Fishing Company (the). An authentic
historical memoir of: . . . By a member. *See* Milnor, Wm.

SCHWAB, JOHN C.   214
The Confederate States of America . . . a financial and industrial history. *N Y* 1901. O [12] 332
tab aa
—rptd. same collat *N Hav* 1913. a

SCHWARTZ, J. L., ed.   215
Briefe eines Deutschen aus Kalifornien . . .
Berlin 1849. D [4] 54 a

SCIOTO   216
Lettre écrite par un Francais emigrant sur les
terres de la Compagnie du. [*P* ? 1790]. O 27 aa

Observations generales . . . sur l'affaire du Scioto.
See Barlow, Joel.

Le parlement de Paris établi au Scioto. *See* Parlement, No. P–102

SCOBLE, JOHN   217
Texas: its claims to be recognized as an independent power . . . *L* 1839. O 56 b LC NYP S

SCOTT (THE DRED) CASE.
Historical and legal examination of that part of
the decision . . . in: which declares the unconstitutionality of the Missouri compromise act . . . *See*
Benton, Thos. H.

SCOTT (DRED) versus SANFORD   218
(JOHN F. A.)
A report of the decisions of the Supreme Court
. . . in the case of: *N Y* 1857. O 393–633 a
—anr ed. *Wash* 1857. O 239

SCOTT, EBEN G.   219
Reconstruction during the civil war . . . *B* 1895.
D [10] 432 a

SCOTT, EDWIN J.   220
Random recollections of a long life, 1806–1876.
Columbia S C 1884. D [2, 6] 3–216 a

SCOTT (MRS. FRANCES).   221
A true [etc.] narrative of the . . . captivity of:
eds. 1 & 2 [possibly ptd at *B* 1785 by E. Russell, in
about 15p.] No copies known
—ed. 3, with Capt. Stewart's captivity added, *B*
E.Russell 1786. D 24 c MH [of 2 perfect copies
known]
—rptd. *B* 1788. b
—other eds. "A remarkable narrative . . .," *Newbypt* 1789. 32° 14 b; *Newbypt* [1799]. aa; [*Leominster*] Whitcomb [*ca* 1810]; *Leominster* S. Wilder
1811; *Leominster* J. Wilder 1811. Ea aa
Captured in Virginia by Indians [who killed her
husband and children], Mrs. Scott soon escaped
and finally, after much suffering, reached a white
settlement.

(SCOTT [or SCOT], GEORGE)   222
The model of the government of . . . East-
New-Jersey . . . *Edin* 1685. D [8] 272 in iss 1 last
paragraph on p 37 begins "I find removal";
in iss 2 it begins "Where people find" c H N
NYP
Contains many letters from early settlers.

SCOTT, HARVEY W., ed.   223
  History of Portland, Oregon . . . *Syracuse* 1890.
Q 651 69ports facsims table aa
  First full-scale history of this metropolis.

SCOTT, HERVEY   224
  A complete history of Fairfield county, Ohio . . .
Columbus 1877. O [10] 304 4pls a

SCOTT, JAMES   225
  Recollections of a naval life. *L* 1834. O 3v: [12]
312; [6] 324; [6] 372 aa
  Vol 3 almost entirely devoted to this officer's
service under Sir Peter Parker in the war of 1812.

SCOTT, JAMES L.   226
  A journal of a missionary tour . . . *Prov* 1843.
D [8] 203 aa
  Valuable description of the country from Penn-
sylvania to Iowa and Wisconsin.

SCOTT, J[ESUP] W.   227
  A presentation of causes tending to fix . . . the
future great city of the world in the central plain of
North America . . . *Toledo* 1868. O 28 a
—ed. 2, same impr. 1876. O 41
  Centre of world commerce, once at London,
now at New York, by 1968 at some city on the
Great Lakes.

SCOTT (JOB).   228
  Journal of the life, travels, and gospel labours of
. . .: *N Y* 1797 D [14] 360 a
—rptd. *Wilm. Del.* 1797 D [12] 324
—Eng. ed. L. 1797 D [14] 354
—3 other Eng. eds. 1798: *L*; *Warrington*; *Dub.*
  Visited almost every part of the then United
States.

SCOTT, JOE M.   229
  Four years service in the southern army. *Mul-
berry, Ark* 1897. D 74 aa

SCOTT, JOHN, of Ind.   230
  The Indiana gazetteer . . . *Centreville* 1826. 16°
143 [2] c N LC WisH Y
—ed. 2, *Indp* 1833. D [4] 200 tabs aa
—ed. 3, ed. by E. Chamberlain, *Indp* 1849. O 440

[SCOTT, JOHN] of Ky.   231
  Encarnacion prisoners; comprising an account
of the march of the Kentucky cavalry from Louis-
ville to the Rio Grande . . . By a prisoner . . .
Louisv Prentice & Weisinger 1848. O 96 b
—anr. issue [priority undetermined], au. named,
"Encarnacion, or the prisoners in Mexico . . .,"
Louisv Monsarrat & Co 1848. O 123 b

SCOTT, JOHN, of Va.   232
  Letters to an officer in the army, proposing constitutional reform in the Confederate government
. . . A supplement to "The lost principle." *Rich*
1864. O 82 aa

[SCOTT, JOHN] of Va.   233
  The lost principle; or the sectional equilibrium
. . . *Rich* 1860. O 266 a

SCOTT, MAJ. JOHN, of Va.   234
  Partisan life with . . . Mosby. *N Y* 1867. O 492
[incl. prel blank lf wrp 2 ports facs.] a
—Eng. ed., same date & collat., *L*

SCOTT, JOSEPH   235
  A geographical description of . . . Maryland and
Delaware . . . *Phil* 1807. 16° [2] 191 2maps a

SCOTT, JOSEPH   236
  A geographical description of Pennsylvania . . .
Phil 1806. 16° 147 map a

SCOTT, JOSEPH   237
  The United States gazetteer . . . *Phil* 1795. D [8]
286[unpaged] 19maps aa
—rptd. [maps only] as "An atlas of the United
States," *Phil* 1796. D cover t. 19 maps a
—rev. & enl. ed., "A geographical dictionary of
the United States . . .," *Phil* 1805. O [4] 584[un-
paged] map
  First gazetteer of the United States; in its 1796
form, the first national atlas.

SCOTT, NANCY N., ed.   238
  A memoir of Hugh Lawson White . . . *Phil* 1856.
O [10] 455 port a

SCOTT, SAMUEL   239
  Map of the Black hills. *Custer* 1897. D 40 map aa

SCOTT, REV. WILLIAM A.   240
  My residence in and departure from California.
[*P* 1861]. O 31 a
  Sermons against the Vigilantes brought such
threats as to compel his departure.

SCOTT, WILLIAM W.   241
  A history of Orange county, Virginia. *Rich* 1907.
O 292 map 18pls a

SCOTT (LIEUT.-GENERAL [WINFIELD]).   242
  Memoirs of: . . . by himself. *N Y* 1864. D 2v:
[24] 330; [4] 331–653. 2ports a
—rptd., same impr. & collat. 1865.
  Of the 1864 edition, a special large paper edition
of 250 copies was issued in one volume, royal
octavo.

SCOTT (MAJOR GENERAL WINFIELD).   243
  Official list of officers who marched with the
army under the command of: from Puebla upon
the City of Mexico . . . *Mex* 1848. obl Q 24 2errata
slips plan aa
  Printed on the occupying army's own press.

SCOTT (GENERAL) AND HIS STAFF.
  See Conrad, Robert T.

[SCOTTOW, JOSHUA]   244
A narrative of the planting of the Massachusets
colony . . . *B* 1694 . . . O [4] 77 d JCBMassH
—ed. 2, title altered *B* 1696. D [2] 56 d H JCB N
Ascribed also to Gov. Thos. Dudley, a letter
from him being included.

[SCOVILLE, JOSEPH A.]   245
The old merchants of New York. 5 series. *N Y*
1863–4–9. D 5v: 472; 406; 351; 255; 304. aa
—rptd. *N Y* 1870. D 5v in 3: [6] 9–472; [6] 9–406
[2] 5–255; [4] 9–351 [2] 5–308 a
—anr. ed., same collat. 1872, with map & 11pls
added

[SCRIBNER, BENJAMIN F.]   246
Camp life of a volunteer. A campaign in Mexico
. . . *Phil* 1847. O 75[incl. front. & cover-t.] a
—rptd. "A campaign in Mexico. By one who was
thar," *Phil* 1850. Same collat.

[SCRIBNER, J. P.]   247
Laconia: or legends of the White mountains. By
an old mountaineer. *B* 1856. D 489 a

[SCRIPPS, JOHN L.]   247a
Life of Abraham Lincoln. [capt. t.]. [*Chi* 1860].
O 32, advs, p. 32, in double columns c IH Y
—issue 2, identical except advs, p. 32, in one
column covering whole p. b IllH N
—anr. ed. [*N Y* Greeley 1860]. aa
—rptd. [*Det*] 1900. O 85 [2] port 245 copies aa
Most authentic of Lincoln campaign biographies.

SCRIPPS, JOHN L.   248
The undeveloped northern portion of the American continent. *Chi* 1856. O 24 [incl. wraps] aa

SCUDDER (WILLIAM).   248a
The journal of: . . . taken captive by the Indians
at Fort Stanwix . . . 1779 . . . [*N Y*?] for the au.
1794. D 250 d NYH [only copy known]
Only edition of one of the most authentic and
detailed of narratives by captives of the French and
Indian war.

[SEABROOK, WHITMARSH B.?]   249
An appeal to the people of the northern and
eastern states on . . . negro slavery in South Carolina. *N Y* 1834. O 27 a
—rptd., same impr. 1838. O 24

SEABROOK, WHITMARSH B.   250
A concise view of the critical situation . . . of the
slave-holding states . . . *Charleston S C* 1825. O
29 a
—ed. 2, same impr. & date. O 31

SEABROOK, WHITMARSH B.   251
A memoir on the origin, cultivation and uses of
cotton . . . *Charleston S C* 1844. O [4] 62 [1] a

[SEABURY, SAMUEL]   252
The congress canvassed: or, an examination into
the conduct of the delegates, at . . . Philadelphia,
Sept. 1, 1774. [*N Y*] 1774. O 28 aa
—Eng. ed. *L* 1775. O [4] 59 aa

[SEABURY, SAMUEL]   253
Free thoughts on the proceedings of the Conti-
nental Congress . . . By a farmer . . . [*N Y*] 1774.
O 31 [last p. wrongly numb 29] aa
—anr. issue, *N Y* 1774. O 24 aa
—Eng. ed. *L* 1775. O [4] 50 a
This was answered by Alexander Hamilton's
Full vindication of . . . Congress, q.v.

[SEABURY, SAMUEL]   254
A view of the controversy between Great-Bri-
tain and her colonies. *N Y* 1774. O 37 + 2adv-p[in
some copies] aa
—Eng. ed. *L* 1775. O [4] 90 a
Reply to Hamilton's *Full vindication of . . . Con-
gress.* All of these Tory pamphlets, issued as by A.
W. Farmer [i. e., A Westchester farmer], have been
also variously ascribed to T. B. Chandler, Charles
Inglis and Isaac Wilkins. Seabury was undoubt-
edly their author, aided some by Wilkins. For
Hamilton's rejoinder, *see* his *The Farmer refuted
. . . Seabury was the pre-eminent exponent of
Tory thought in America.

SEALSFIELD [OR SEATSFIELD], CHARLES
See Postl, Karl, for whom this was a pseudonym.

SEAMAN, E. F.   255
Memoirs of Commodore Stephen Decatur . . .
Lebanon L 1820. 16° 72 a

SEAMAND, WILLIAM G.   256
Map of the Wood river, Saw Tooth and Smoky
mining districts, Idaho Territory. *Bellevue Idaho*
[ptd. *Chi*] 1881. 16° 15 + 11 adv-p map aa

SEARIGHT, THOMAS B.   257
The old pike. A history of the national road . . .
Uniontown Pa 1894. O 384 pl a

SEASONABLE ADVICE   258
Seasonable advice to the members of the British
parliament concerning conciliatory measures with
America . . . *L* 1775. O [8] 38 a

SEAT, W. H.   259
The Confederate States . . . in prophecy. *Nashv*
1861. D 144 a

SEATTLE
**Business directory of . . . Seattle for the year 1876
. . . See** Ward, Kirk C.

Report of the chief engineer of the Seattle   260
**and Walla Walla Railroad and Transportation
Company** . . . *Seattle* 1874. O 48 map aa
First book printed in Seattle.

Residence and business directory of . . . **261**
Seattle for 1882 . . . sketch of the settlement . . .
Seattle Elliott & Sweet [1882]. O 88 [10] aa
Third Seattle directory. For the earlier two, *see*
Ward, Kirk C., and Choir, Melody.

SEAVER, EBEN, ed. **262**
Documents from Henry, the British spy! [*B*
1812]. O 22 + blank lf a
John Henry, Canadian adventurer in British
employ, met with some success in fomenting New
England disaffection towards the war. Chagrined
by a niggardly reward, he sold his documents to
President Madison.

SEAVER, JAMES E. **263**
A narrative of the life of Mrs. Mary Jemison . . .
taken captive by the Indians in . . . 1755 [etc.].
Canandaigua N Y 1824. 16° 189 some copies have
no copyr. on verso of t-p, others have separate
copyr. leaf [either pasted down on that p. or
bound in after it] b AA N NYP Y
—abr. ed. "Interesting narrative of Mary Jemison," [capt.t.] [*Buf* 1834]. D 36 a
—rptd. *Roch* 1840; 1841; *Utica* 1842, D 32 fold. pl
—anr. ed. enl. by E. Mix, "Deh-he-wa-mis; or a
narrative of the life of Mary Jemison . . .," *Batavia
N Y* 1842, 16° 192 a; ed. 2, same impr. & collat.,
1842; ed. 3, same impr. & collat., 1844.
—anr. ed., ed. L. H. Morgan, "Life of Mary Jemison: Deh-he-wä-mis," *N Y* & *Auburn* 1856. D 312
[incl. front. & 5pls]
—rptd., same collat., *N Y* 1859; *N Y* 1860.
—most complete ed., ed. W. P. Letchworth, *Buf*
1877, D [4] 7–303 9pls a; rptd., same collat., 1880.
—Eng. eds.: *Howden* 1826, 16° 180 aa; *L* 1827, 16°
180; *Otley* 1842, 16° 192; *Devon* 1847, 16° 184. a
One of the most authentic and interesting of
captivity narratives, told by one who spent a long
life among the Senecas and was the first white
woman to descend the Ohio.

SEAVER, WILLIAM **264**
A historical sketch of the village of Batavia.
Batavia 1849. O 56 a

SÉCESSION (LA)
Sécession (La) aux États-Unis et son origine. Par
un journaliste americaine. *See* Mortimer, J.

SECESSION **265**
Secession: considered as a right . . . By a gentleman of Mississippi. *Jackson* 1863. O 45 a

SECOND
**Second appeal (A) to the justice and interests of
the people, on the measures respecting America.**
See Lee, Arthur.

Second crisis (The) in America, or . . . **266**
view of the peace lately concluded between Great

Britain and the United States . . . By a citizen of
Philadelphia. *N Y* 1815. O 87 a

**Second protest against the bill to repeal the Amer-
ican Stamp act.** *See Corrct copies of the two
protests* . . .

SECRET WORKES (THE) OF A **267**
CRUEL PEOPLE . . .
L 1659. SmQ [2] 26 b
Tract, by Geo. Fox, *et al*, upbraiding the New
England church hierarchy for its persecutions of
Quakers.

SECRETS OF THE AMERICAN BASTILE.
See Winder, Wm. H.

SEDGLEY, JOSEPH **268**
Overland to California in 1849. *Oakland* 1877.
O 66 b N NYP Y

SEDGWICK (GEN. JOHN). **269**
Correspondence of: *N Y* 1902–3. O 2v: [16]
188; 244 aa 300cops ptd.

SEELY, O. C. **270**
Oklahoma illustrated . . . *Guthrie* 1894. O 229 +
23adv-p pls aa

SEEMAN, BERTHOLD C. **271**
Narrative of the voyage of H. M. S. Herald . . .
1845–51 . . . *L* 1853. O 2v: [16] 322; [8] 302. map
2pls aa
—Ger. tr. *Hannover* 1853. O 2v: [12] 335; [6] 294.
4pls aa
Visited San Francisco, Monterey and San Diego
just after the Conquest; later coasted North to
Bering's Strait.

SEGAR (LT. NATHANIEL). **272**
A brief narrative of the captivity . . . of: taken
prisoner by the Indians . . . during the revolutionary war. *Paris Me* 1825. D 36 c AA H Y
—rptd.: 1911; 1940.
Written by Rev. Daniel Gould from Segar's
dictation.

SEGUIN (JOHN N.) **273**
Memoirs of: from . . . 1834 to the retreat of
Generall Woll from . . . San Antonio in 1842. *San
Antonio* 1858. O 32 b TxU[of 2 copies known]

SELKIRK, THOMAS DOUGLAS, **274**
earl of
A sketch of the British fur trade in North America . . . *L* 1816 O [6] 130 aa
—Fr tr. *Montr* 1819 O 116 + lf aa

SELL, JOHANN J. **275**
Versuch einer Geschichte des Negersclavenhan-
dels . . . *Halle* 1791. O [10] 246 [2] aa

SELLERS, WILLIAM W.   **276**
A history of Marion county [S. C.]. *Columbia* 1902. O [10] 647 port a
—rptd. *Marion* 1956, same collat.

SELLON, C. J.   **276a**
A review of the commerce . . . of Galesburg, Illinois . . . and sketches of the first settlement of the town. *Galesburg* 1857. O 62 aa

[SEMERIA, GIOVANNI B.]   **277**
Sketches of the life of the Very Rev. Felix de Andreis . . . with a sketch of the progress of the Catholic religion in the United States. *Balt* 1861. D 276 port a

SEMINOLE
An authentic narrative of the Seminole   **278**
war . . . *Prov* 1836. O 24 pl b AA Y
—anr. issue, *N Y* 1836. same collat. b NYP Y
—ed. 2, *Prov*, same date & collat. b
—anr. ed. "A true and authentic account of the Indian war in Florida . . .," *N Y* 1836. O 28 pl b N
—ed. 2, same impr., date & collat. aa
No priority is yet established between the Providence and New York editions.

A concise narrative of the Seminole cam-   **279**
paign. By an officer . . . *Nashv* 1819. D 41 b BA LC NYP

Debate in the House of Representatives   **280**
. . . on the Seminole war. *Wash* 1819. O [4] 591 a

Message of the President . . . transmitting   **281**
copies of documents . . . in relation to the Seminole war . . . *Wash* 1818. O 165 a

Report of the select committee of the   **282**
Senate relative to the Seminole war . . . [*Wash* 1819]. O 40 a
Attacks Jackson's Florida invasion and suggests that President Monroe be impeached.

Reports detailing the hostilities and outra- **283**
ges committed by the Seminole Indians in Florida. *Wash* 1850. O 173 a

Sketch of the Seminole war . . .   **284**
By a lieutenant [etc.]. *Charleston S C* 1836. D [6] 312 aa

SEMMES, RAPHAEL   **285**
The cruise of the Alabama and the Sumter . . . *L* 1864. D 2v: [16] 411; [12] 436. 7pls a Issued July
—ed. 2, same date, impr. & collat. Issued Sept.
—abr. ed. "The log of the Alabama and Sumter," *L* 1864. D [12] 297; *L* 1865
—Am. ed. *N Y* 1864. D 2v in 1: 328 port
—Fr. tr. *P* 1864. D [6] 471 front.
—Ger. tr. *Zwolle* 1864–5. O 2v

SEMMES, RAPHAEL   **286**
My adventures afloat . . . cruises and services in the "Sumter" and "Alabama." *L* 1869. O 2v in 1: [2] 444; [2] 445–833. map 10pls a
—Am. ed. "Memoirs of service afloat during the war between the states," *Balt* 1869. O [6] 11–833 map 10pls a
—other eds., "Service afloat . . .," " . . .," *Balt* 1887; *L* 1887; *N Y* n.d.

SEMMES (RAPHAEL) THE PIRATE.   **287**
N Y 1865. 18° 105 a

SEMMES, RAPHAEL   **288**
Service afloat and ashore during the Mexican war. *Cin* 1851. D [12] blank l. 7–480 map 6pls a
—rptd., somewhat abr. "The campaign of Gen. Scott . . .," *Cin* 1852. D 367 map

SEMPLE, ROBERT B.   **289**
A history of the rise and progress of the Baptists in Virginia. *Rich* 1810. O [8] 446 [1] a
—enl. ed., same impr., 1894. O [10] 536 port

[SENIOR, NASSAU W.]   **290**
The Oregon question. n.p. n.d. O 28 a

SENTER (ISAAC).   **291**
The journal of: . . . on a secret expedition against Quebec under . . . Arnold. *Phil* 1846. O 40 a

SENTER (NATHANIEL G. M.)   **292**
A vindication of the character of: against the charge of being a spy and traitor . . . *Hallowell Me* 1815. O 64 a

SEPARATE STATE SECESSION . . .   **293**
[*Edgefield, S. C.*] 1851. O 42 a

SEQUEL   **294**
Sequel to the Counsel for emigrants . . . *Aberdeen* 1834. D 72 map aa
See also Counsel for emigrants.

SEQUOYAH.   **295**
Constitution of the state of: [capt.t.]. *Muskogee* "Phoenix" 1905. O 68 map aa
—issue 2, p68 not numb. & printer's name at foot of that p aa
—unofficial ed. [*Guthrie* 1905]. O 50 a
—anr. ed. *Wash* 1906. O 87 map
Proposed state advocated by Indian Territory citizens, who wanted statehood separate from Oklahoma.

SERIES
Series (A) of answers to certain popular objections, against separating from the rebellious colonies . . . *See* Tucker, Josiah.

SERIOUS 296

Serious address (A) to the rulers of America, on the inconsistency of their conduct respecting slavery: forming a contrast between the encroachments of England on American liberty, and American injustice in tolerating slavery. [Signed "A farmer."]. *Trenton* 1783. O 22 a
—Eng. eds. *L* 1783. O 24; [*Liv*] 1784. O 22
Ascribed to Anthony Benezet.

Serious considerations on several important subjects . . . *See* Benezet, Anthony.

Serious considerations on the election of a president . . . *See* Linn, Wm.

Serious considerations on the present state of affairs of the northern colonies. *See* Kennedy, Archibald.

Serious expostulation (A) with the members of the House of Representatives . . . *See* Mifflin, Warner.

[SERLE, AMBROSE] 297

Americans against liberty . . . [their] designs and conduct . . . tend only to tyranny and slavery . . . *L* 1775. O 64 aa
—ed. 2, enl., *L* 1776. O 44 a
—ed. 3, same impr. & date. O 48

SESHERRE-DESCOSSAS, M. DE 298

Cours des trois premiers fleuves des États-Unis . . . *Angouleme* 1855. D [8] 230 a
The Mississippi, Ohio and Red rivers described, both in prose and verse.

SET OF PLANS AND FORTS . . .
See Andrews, P. and John.

SETON, JULIA M. 299

The Indian costume book. *Santa Fe* 1938. O [24] 212 [8] 68pls [all incl in paginat] 500cops ptd, of which 100cops are signed and have 21 of the plates hand-colored. aa

SEVILLE, WILLIAM P. 300

Narrative of the march of Co. A. Engineers, from Fort Leavenworth . . . to Fort Bridger . . . 1858. *Wash* 1912. O [2] 46 a

[SEWALL, JONATHAN] 301

A cure for the spleen . . . a conversation on the times . . . [*B*] 1775. O 32 b JCB NYP
—ed. 2, "The Americans roused, in a cure for the spleen . . .," *N Y* [1775?]. O 32 aa
Political grievances of the colonies ridiculed in this Tory tract.

SEWALL, OLIVER 302

History of Chesterville, Maine. *Farmington* 1875. O 96 a

SEWALL, RUFUS K. 303

Ancient dominions of Maine . . . *Bath* 1859. O 366 9pls a

SEWALL, R[UFUS] K. 304

Sketches of St. Augustine . . . *N Y* 1848. D 69 + 11adv-p 6pls aa
—ed. 2, *Phil* 1849. D 100 6pls a
Most copies of the first edition have pages 39–40 deleted.

SEWALL (SAMUEL) [1652–1730]. 305

Diary of: 1674–1729. *B* 1878–82. O 3v: [10 9–40] 532; [6 4 4 7–132] 462; [6] 572. port errata slip aa
—rptd. *N Y* 1961 3v a
Most valuable American diary of the 18th century. Constitutes volumes 5, 6 and 7, Massachusetts Historical Society Collections, series 5.

[SEWALL, SAMUEL] 1757–1814 306

Remarks on slavery in the United States . . . *B* 1827. O 28 a

SEWARD, WILLIAM 307

Journal of a voyage from Savannah to Philadelphia . . . *L* 1740. O [8] 88 aa
Seward accompanied Whitefield on his 1740 trip.

SEXAGENARY

Sexagenary (The); or, reminiscences of the . . . revolution. *See* Bloodgood, Simeon De Witt.

SEXTON, GEORGE 308

A portraiture of Mormonism . . . *L* 1849. D 113 aa

SEYBERT, ADAM 309

Statistical annals . . . of the United States . . . 1789–1818. *Phil* 1818. Q [28] 803 a
—Fr. tr. *P* 1820. D [16] 455 69tabs[on 24sheets]
Especially useful on early financial history.

SEYD, ERNEST 310

California and its resources . . . *L* 1858. O [4] 168 2maps 22pls [on 18sheets] aa

SEYMOUR, CHARLES 311

Historical address . . . in La Crosse . . . *La Crosse* 1877. O 32 a

SEYMOUR, E[PHRAIM] SANFORD 312

Emigrant's guide to the gold mines of upper California. *Chi* 1849. O 104 map c B NYP [only copies known]
The extreme rarity of this *Guide* suggests its possible suppression; perhaps because of Henry I. Simpson having published one with the same title in 1848, *q.v.*

SEYMOUR, E[PHRAIM] S[ANFORD]   313
Sketches of Minnesota . . . with incidents of travel in that Territory . . . *N Y* 1850. D 281 [6] map a

SEYMOUR, FREDERICK H.   314
A canoe trip . . . from Lake Huron to Lake Erie. *Detroit* [1880]. 16° 104 front a

[SEYMOUR, SILAS]   315
Incidents of a trip through the great Platte valley, to the Rocky mountains . . . *N Y* 1867. D 129 port a
—ed. 2, same impr., date & collat.

SEYMOUR, SILAS   316
A reminiscence of the Union Pacific Railroad . . . *Quebec* 1873. O 74 pls a

SEYMOUR, SILAS   317
Union Pacific railroad. Report of the consulting engineer on the location between Omaha City and the Platte valley . . . *N Y* 1865. O 10 [38 2] 2maps cov.t.only a
—issue 1 has p8 & 29 of suppl. pp. misnumb.
—issue 2, mispaging cor.

SEYMOUR, CAPT. W. D.   318
Journal of a voyage round the world. *Cork* 1877. D [8] 169 port aa
Includes trip from Chicago to California, via the Platte valley and Utah.

SEYMOUR, WILLIAM N., comp.   319
Directory of Galena, Illinois. *Galena* [possibly ptd. Chi] 1847. D 72 b ChiH N [only cops loc] b
First directory of this city.

SEYMOUR, WILLIAM N., comp.   320
Madison [Wis.] directory . . . *Madison* 1855. 16° 192 + 64adv-p map aa
First directory of this city, with historical sketch.

SHAFFNER, TAL[IAFERRO] P.   321
The war in America . . . *L* [1862]. D [6] 418 map a

SHAFFORD (JOHN CONRAD).   322
Narrative of the . . . life of: . . . *N Y* 1840. O 24 [incl.front.] aa
—rptd., same collat. & impr., 1841. a
Contains account of the Indian captivity of his daughter, Ellen.

SHAFTER, EDMUND F., ed.   323
Voyages of the Northmen to America . . . *B* Prince Society 1877. sm Q 162 a

SHALER, WILLIAM   324
Journal of a voyage between China and the north-western coast of America. *Phil* 1808. O 38 aa
—anr. ed. *Claremont Cal* 1935. O 108 map 700 cops ptd a

SHALL THE FREEDMEN   325
Shall the freedmen be admitted to the right of suffrage. By a member of the Richmond bar. *Augusta Ga* 1865. O 133 a

SHALLENBERGER, MRS. E. H.   326
Stark County [Ill.] and its pioneers. *Cambridge Ill* 1876. O 328 aa

SHANNON, FRED A.   327
The organization and administration of the Union army, 1861–5. *Clev* 1928. O 2v: 323; 348 a

SHARAN (JAMES).   328
The adventures of: . . . during his voyages and travels in the four quarters of the globe . . . *Balt* 1808. D 225 [14] aa
Includes account of his overland trip from New Orleans to Niagara. Authenticity questionable.

SHARLAND, GEORGE   329
Knapsack notes of . . . Sherman's grand campaign through . . . Georgia . . . *Springfield Ill* 1865. O 68 a

SHARP, MRS. ABBIE [GARDNER]   330
History of the Spirit Lake massacre. *Des M* 1885. D [4] 312 pls a
For abbreviated earlier version *see* Lee, L. P. There were numerous later editions.

SHARP, GRANVILLE   331
A declaration of the people's natural right to a share in the legislature . . . the fundamental principle of the British constitution . . . *L* 1774. O 32 a
—Am. eds., same date: *Phil O* 21; *N Y O* 16; *B O* 22
—enl. ed. *L* 1774. O [44] 244
—ed. 2, *L* 1775. O [44] 244 [some copies have index carrying paginat. to 279]
A powerful influence in determining colonial resistance.

SHARP (JAMES MEIKLE).   332
Brief account of the experiences of: [*Saticoy Calif*?] 1931. D 72[incl. 2ports] + preliminary blank lf aa
Describes his 1852 trip to Oregon.

SHARP, LEANDER J.   333
Vindication of . . . the late Col. Solomon P. Sharp, from the calumnies published . . . since his murder, by . . . Beauchamp. *Frankfort Ky* 1827. O 140 b ChiU KyH
All but 25copies were destroyed by the Sharp family.

SHATTUCK, LEMUEL   334
A history of . . . Concord [Mass.] . . . *B* 1835.
O [8] 392 map aa

SHAVER, LEWELLYN A.   335
A history of the Sixtieth Alabama Regiment . . .
Montg 1867. O 111 front. aa

SHAW, ALBERT   336
Icaria; a chapter in the history of communism.
N Y 1884. D [10] 219 aa
—Ger. tr. *Stuttgart* 1886. O [8] 139 a
Best study of Cabet's experiment in rational
democratic communism.

SHAW, CHARLES   337
A topographical . . . description of Boston . . .
B 1817. D 312 8pls a

SHAW (ELIJAH).   338
A short sketch of the life of: who served for
twenty-two years in the navy . . . *Roch* 1843. 16°
87 a
—ed. 3, *Roch* 1845. 16° 63

SHAW, J. HENRY   339
Historical sketch of Cass county, Illinois.
Beardstown 1876. O [2] 54 aa few cops kn

SHAW, REV. JAMES, of Ireland   340
Twelve years in America . . . *L & Dub* 1867. D
[16] 440 map front. a
—ed. 2, same sheets, with 2pls added & new t-p
pasted over the old t-p, "American resources . . .,"
L & Dub 1867.
Resided chiefly in Illinois.

SHAW, REV. JAMES, of Kansas   341
Early reminiscences of pioneer life in Kansas.
[*Atchison* 1886]. D 238[incl. port] a

SHAW (JAMES C.)   342
Pioneering in Texas and Wyoming. Incidents in
the life of: *Orin, Wyo.* [1931] D 43 b
—rptd. "North from Texas . . ." *Evanston, Ill.*
1952. O [14] 111 map port a

SHAW, JOHN   343
A ramble through the United States . . . *L* 1856.
O [2] 370 pl errata slip a

SHAW, JOHN ROBERT   344
Shaw (John Robert, the well-digger) . . . A narrative of the life and travels of: *Lex* 1807. D 180
[incl. subscribers' list] 6pls b BA N TennS Y
This curious autobiography of an eccentric character was the earliest original work of a literary
nature produced and written west of the Alleghanies.

SHAW, JOSHUA   345
Picturesque views of American scenery. 3pts

[all]. *Phil* [1820–21]. F [21 lvs.] 51 col. pls[incl.eng.
t.] dd PhilL
—issue 2—of pt. 1 only, *Phil* 1829. F 20col.pls c

SHAW, JOSHUA   346
United States directory for . . . travellers and
merchants . . . *Phil* [1822]. 16° [10] 156 + 40adv-p a

SHAW, LUELLA [C.]   347
True history of some of the pioneers of Colorado
. . . *Hotchkiss* [ptd *Denver*] 1909. D [2] 269 12pls a

SHAW, PRINGLE   348
Ramblings in California . . . *Toronto* [ca 1856–
60]. D 239 a
Experiences, in the Yuba district, both as miner
and local magistrate.

SHAW, R[EUBEN] C.   349
Across the plains in forty-nine. *Farmland Ind*
1896. D 200 port aa
—rptd. *Chi* Lakeside series 1948. 16°

SHAW, S. C.   350
Sketches of Wood county, western Virginia . . .
Pt. I [all]. *Parkersburg* 1878. O 60 a

SHAW, WILLIAM   351
Golden dreams and waking realities . . . adven-
tures of a gold-seeker in California . . . *L* 1851.
D [12] 316 + 16adv-p a

SHAWANGUNK.   352
Sketch of an Indian irruption into the town of:
in 1780. n.p. [1823?]. O [2] 7–35 a

SHAWNEE . . . KANSAS   353
Directory of Shawnee. Wakaunsee and Osage
counties, Kansas . . . *Topeka* 1887. O 155 a

Historical sketch of Shawnee county, Kan-   354
sas 1876. *See* Giles, Frye W.

SHEA, J[OHN] C., ed.   355
. . . The only true history of Quantrell's raid . . .
K C 1879. O 27 aa

SHEA, JOHN G.   356
The bursting of Pierre Margry's La Salle bubble.
N Y 1879. O 24 a
Discredits Margry's claim that La Salle ante-
dated Marquette and Joliet in descending the Mis-
sissippi.

SHEA, JOHN G.   357
Discovery and exploration of the Mississippi
valley: with the original narratives of Marquette,
et al. N Y 1852. O [80] 268 map facs aa
—anr. issue [v. IV of French, B. F., *Historical
collections of Louisiana*].
—ed. 2, same collat., *N Y* 1853. a
—rptd. *Alb* 1903. O 267 map port 500 cops ptd a

SHEA, JOHN G.   358
Early voyages up and down the Mississippi . . .
Alb 1861. sm Q [10] 7–191 100 copies ptd [a few on
L. P.] aa
—rptd. *Alb* 1902. a

SHEA, JOHN G.   359
The hierarchy of the Catholic church in the
United States . . . and a brief history of the church
. . . *N Y* 1886. O 402 a

SHEA, JOHN G.   360
A history of the Catholic church within the . . .
United States. *N Y* 1886–92. O 4v: [22] 9–663 [2];
[4] 11–695 [2]; 732; [34] 23–727. maps & pls aa
rptd. *N Y* 1961. 4v a
Vol. I, In colonial days; vol. II, Life and times of
[Bishop] Carroll; vol. III, From 1808 to 1843; vol.
IV, From 1843 to 1866.

SHEA, JOHN G.   361
History of the Catholic missions among the Indian tribes . . . 1529–1854. *N Y* 1855. D 514 + 10
adv-p eng. t. 5ports 4 pp of facms. a
—rptd. often
—Ger. tr. *Wurzburg* [1858?]. D 668 6pls

SHEA, JOHN G., and MCGEE,   362
THOMAS D.
Die Katholische Kirche in den Vereinigten Staa-
ten . . . *Regensburg* 1864. O [16] 518 a

SHEA, JOHN G.   363
Perils of the ocean and wilderness; or, narratives of shipwreck and captivity . . . from early
missionary annals. *B* Donahue [1856]. D 206 a
—anr. ed., same impr. & collat., 1857.

SHEA, JOHN G., ed.   364
Relations diverses sur la battaile du Malangueulé [i.e., Monongahela] . . . *N Y* 1860. O [16]
9–51 front. a 100copies ptd.

SHEAFER, P[ETER] W., et al, eds.   365
Historical map of Pennsylvania. Showing the
Indian names . . . *Phil* 1875. O 26 [1] map a

[SHEBBEARE, JOHN]   366
An answer to a pamphlet, call'd The conduct of
the ministry impartially examined . . . *L* 1756. O
100 aa
Relates largely to disputes with France over the
Ohio country.

SHEBBEARE (DR. [JOHN]).
An appendix to a letter to: . . . By a doctor of
laws. *See* Baillie, Hugh.

SHEBBEARE, J[OHN]   367
An essay on the origin . . . of national society; in
which the principles . . . contained in Dr. Price's

Observations . . . are . . . refuted: together with a
justification of the legislature, in reducing America
to obedience by force . . . *L* 1776. O [4] 212 a

[SHEBBEARE, JOHN]   368
A fourth letter to the people of England. On the
conduct of the M - - - - rs . . . since the first differences on the Ohio . . . *L* 1756. O [4] 111 aa
—ed. 2, same impr., date & collat.
—anr. ed., same impr. & date. O [2] 49
—Fr. ed., tr. Edmond J. Genet, "Le peuple instruit
. . .," [P?] 1756. O [24] 212 [8]
—rptd. *Vienna* 1757. Q 55
Highly critical of the Ministry's futile policy in
checking French encroachments. For reply, *see
Full and particular answer* . . .

SHEBBEARE, JOHN   369
A letter to the people of England on the present
situation and conduct of national affairs. Letter I.
L 1755. O [2] 58 aa
—ed. 2, same impr., date & collat. a
—3 other eds., *L* 1756.
Shebbeare issued, in all, seven *Letters*, of which
the *First* and *Fourth* have been selected for inclusion here, as being more concerned with American
affairs. This first *Letter* blames Braddock's failure
to Quaker influence persuading the Ministry to
send the expedition from Virginia rather than from
Pennsylvania. *See* also *Reasons humbly offered*,
probably by him.

SHECUT, J[OHN] L. E. W.   370
Medical and philosophical essays. Containing . . .
historical and other sketches of the city of Charleston . . . *Charleston S C* 1819. O [8] 260 [2] pl a

SHEEDY (D.)   371
Autobiography of: *Denver* [1922]. O 61 a

SHEFFIELD, EARL OF
Observations on the commerce of the American
states . . . *See* Holroyd, John B.

SHEFFIELD'S . . . OBSERVATIONS
A brief examination of Lord Sheffield's observations . . . *Phil* 1791. *See* Coxe, Tench

Remarks on lord Sheffield's observations . . . by
an American. *See* Ruston, Thos.

SHELBURNE (THE RIGHT HONOUR-   372
ABLE THE EARL OF).
A letter to: on . . . the principles which have
actuated the opposition to the measures of the
administration in respect to America. *L* 1776. O
28 a

[SHELBY, ISAAC]   373
Battle of King's mountain. To the public. n.p
[1823?]. D 24 b AA LC NYP Y

SHELDON, MRS. E[LECTRA] M.   374
The early history of Michigan . . . *N Y* 1856. O
409 4ports a
—rptd. *N Y* 1874.
Based largely on unpublished manuscripts concerning Jesuit missions among the Indians, etc.

SHELDON, HEZEKIAH S.   375
Documentary history of Suffield [Mass.], 1660–
1749. *Springfield* 1879–88. O [4] 343 2plans a 250
copies ptd.

SHELDON, MARK   376
An autobiographical sketch. *S F* n.d. [1913] O
[2] 120 port aa
Account of mining experiences, etc., by a California pioneer of 1851.

SHELDON, REV. STEWART   377
Gleanings by the way . . . *Topeka* 1890. O 262 a
His 1849 trip to California and later missionary
labors in Colorado, Dakota and Missouri.

SHELDON, WILLIAM   378
Mormonism examined: or was Joseph Smith a
divinely inspired prophet? . . . [*Broadhead Wis*]
n.d. 16° 184 aa

SHELEKHOV, GRIGORII I.   379
Rossiiskago kuptsa imenitago . . . [The voyage
of Grigorii Shelekhov, Russian merchant, in the
year 1783, from Okhotsk over the eastern ocean to
the American shores . . .] *St Ptbg* 1791. D [4] 76
map pl c N Y
—anr. ed., with sequel [expedition under Izmailov
and Bocharov made to same region in 1788–9]. *St
Ptbg* 1793. D 2v in 1: 172 map c
—rptd. 1812. D 2v in 1: 172; 90 pl c Y
—Ger. ed. by J. Z. Logan, "Erste und Zweyte
Reise . . . nach den Kusten von Amerika . . . 1783–
9," *St Ptbg* 1793. O 2pts in 1: 104 b NYP Y
—Eng. tr. [1783 voyage only], in vol. 2, "Varie-
ties of literature," *L* 1795. O 42 aa
Shelekhov established the first permanent Russian settlement on the northwest coast, from which
evolved the great Russian-American fur-trading
monopoly.

SHELLEY, JOE   380
Western wilds of America . . . [*Brussels* 1888].
O 20 + cov.t. aa
Five years with Texas Rangers and scout for
General Ord.

[SHELTON, FREDERICK W.]   381
The Trollopiad; or travelling gentleman in
America: a satire. *N Y* 1837. D 151 a

SHELTON, WILLIAM H.   382
The Jumel mansion. *B* 1916. O [12] 257 33pls
a 750copies ptd.
Most famous American residence, aside from
Mt. Vernon, still standing.

SHELVOCKE, GEORGE   383
A voyage round the world by way of the great
South sea . . . 1719–1722 . . . *L* 1726. O [44] 468
map[on 2sheets] 4pls b
—ed. 2, rev. 1757. O [12] 476 map 4pls aa
—ed. 3, 1767. a
—Ger. tr. *Bremen* 1787. O 407 a
Of his visit to California Shelvocke gives an interesting account, including particulars of finding
gold. For another narrative of this voyage *see*
Betagh, William.

SHEMELIN, FEDOR   384
Zhurnal pervago puteshestviia Rossiian vokrug
zemnago shara . . . [Journal of the first Russian
voyage around the globe]. *St Ptbg* 1816–18. Q 2v
in 1: [112] 168; [2] 428 [2] b

SHEPARD, A. K.   385
The land of the Aztecs . . . *Alb* 1859. D 209 a
Contains meager Texas and Arkansas material.

SHEPARD (ELIHU H.)   386
The autobiography of: . . . *St L* 1869. O 275
2ports a

SHEPARD, ELIHU H.   387
The early history of St. Louis and Missouri . . .
St L 1870. O 170 a

SHEPHERD, J[OSEPH] S.   388
Journal of travel across the plains to California
. . . *Racine* 1851. O 44 d Pn[only known copy]
—rptd. *Placerville* 1945. O 45 250copies ptd[12 in
cl. bdg.] a

SHEPHERD, WILLIAM   389
Prairie experiences in handling cattle and sheep
. . . *L* 1884. O [6] 266 + 40adv-p map 8pls a
—Am. ed. *N Y* 1885. D 215[incl. front.]

SHEPPARD, GEORGE   390
New homes in Minnesota, Northern Dakota,
Montana, *etc. Liv* 1881 O 36 fold map a

SHERBURNE (ANDREW).   391
Memoirs of: a pensioner of the navy of the revolution. *Utica* 1828. D 262 [1] a
—rptd. *Prov* 1831. D 312 front.

SHERBURNE (CAPT. JACOB).   392
A narrative of . . . the life and adventures of: . . .
in the merchant service . . . *Castine Me* 1829. D
96 aa

SHERBURNE, JOHN H.   393
Life . . . of the Chevalier John Paul Jones . . .
Wash 1825. O 364 port a
—ed. 2, *N Y* 1851. O [16] 9–408 port facs
—Eng. ed. *L* 1825. D [12] 320
—Dutch tr. *Groningen* 1829. O port

SHERIDAN, PHILIP H.   **394**
Outline descriptions of military posts in the division of the Missouri. *Chi* 1872. D 131 maps a
—rptd. *Chi* 1876.
For 1870 edition, *see* Hartsuff, George L.

SHERIDAN, P[HILIP] H.   **395**
Record of engagements with hostile Indians . . . 1868–82 . . . *Chi* 1882. O 120 aa
—rptd., *Wash* same date. O 112 a
Official compilation covering the bloodiest years of western warfare.

SHERIDAN, LIEUT. GEN. P[HILIP] H.   **396**
Report of an exploration of parts of Wyoming, Idaho and Montana . . . *Wash* 1882. O 69 map 2diags a

SHERIDAN (P[HILIP] H.) and   **397**
SHERMAN (W[ILLIAM] T.)
Reports of inspection made by: . . . of the country north of the Union Pacific railroad. *Wash* 1878 O 110 10maps 5pls a

SHERIDAN (GENERAL [PHILIP H.])
With: in Lee's last campaign. By a staff officer. *See* Newhall, Frederic C.

SHERIDAN'S . . . SQUAW SPY   **398**
Sheridan's [General] squaw spy and Mrs. Clara Blynn's captivity among the wild Indians of the prairies . . . *Phil* 1869. O [2] 19–80 + 2adv-p 5pls [4 incl. in paginat.] aa
—Ger. ed. "General Sheridan's Indianer-Kundschafterin . . .," same impr. [1869]. O a
Two utterly incredible narratives.

SHERMAN (ELEAZER).   **399**
The narrative of: . . . *Prov* 1832. 16° 263 a
Describes his travels south to Georgia, plantation life there, etc.

[SHERMAN, JOHN H.]   **400**
A general account of Miranda's expedition . . . *N Y* 1808. O 120 aa

[SHERMAN, ROGER?]   **401**
Remarks on a pamphlet . . . "A dissertation on the political union and constitution of the . . . United States . . ." [*N Hav*?] 1784. O 43 a
The pamphlet referred to was by Pelatiah Webster, *q.v.*

SHERMAN (GEN. SIDNEY).   **402**
Defence of: against the charges made by Gen. Sam Houston . . . *Galv* 1859. O 29 + adv-p aa
—rptd. *Houston* 1885. O 35
Claims that Houston's popularly accepted account of San Jacinto was a tissue of lies.

SHERMAN, GEN. WILLIAM T.   **403**
Official account of his . . . march through Georgia and the Carolinas . . . *N Y* 1865. O 214 a

SHERMAN, GEN. WILLIAM T. and   **404**
SACKETT, GEN. D. B.
Protection of the routes across the continent . . . from molestation by hostile Indians. *Wash* 1867. O 55 a

SHERWELL, SAMUEL   **405**
Old recollections of an old boy [including his 1864 overland trip]. *N Y* 1923. O 271 port aa

SHERWIN, W[ILLIAM] T.   **406**
Memoirs of the life of Thomas Paine . . . *L* 1819. O [8] 232 [48] port a

SHERWOOD, ADIEL   **407**
A gazetteer of . . . Georgia. *Charleston* 1827. 16° 143 aa
—ed. 2, *Phil* 1829. 16° 300 errata-lf map plan aa
—ed. 3, enl., *Wash* 1837. D [4] 344 maps a
—anr. issue with pp: [4] 356
—ed. 4, rev. *Macon* 1860. D 209 map
—rptd. *Athens Ga* 1939. D 143 map

SHERWOOD, J. ELY   **408**
California: her wealth and resources . . . *N Y* 1848. O 40 b NYP S Y
One of the earliest publications evoked by the gold discovery but giving chiefly information already published in the President's message and other official reports.

SHERWOOD, J. ELY   **409**
The pocket guide to California, sea and land route. *N Y* 1849. O 72 + 4adv-p map b NYP S Y
—later issues include advs at rear carrying paginat. to 80 in some copies, to 98 in others. b

SHERWOOD, SAMUEL   **410**
The church's flight into the wilderness . . . observations on scripture prophecies: shewing that sundry of them relate to Great-Britain and the American colonies . . . *N Y* 1776. O 54 aa

SHERWOOD, SAMUEL   **411**
A sermon . . . in which the principles of . . . good government are established . . . and some doctrines advanced . . . by New England tories, are considered and refuted . . . *N Hav* [1774]. O 82 a

SHIELDS, GEORGE O.   **412**
Battle of the Big Hole . . . *Chi* 1889. D 120 + 4adv-p 8pls a

SHIELDS, GEORGE O.   **413**
The blanket Indian of the northwest. *N Y* 1921. O 322 32pls a 500copies ptd.

SHIELDS, JOSEPH D.   **414**
Life, and times of Seargent Smith Prentiss. *Phil* 1883. O 442 port a
—rptd., same impr. & collat., 1884.

SHILOH OR THE TENNESSEE CAMPAIGN.
By a comrade . . . *See* Worthington, Thos.

SHINN, CHARLES H.   **415**
Graphic description of Pacific coast outlaws . . . [*S F* 1887] D 32 port a

SHINN, CHARLES H.   **416**
Mining camps: a study of American frontier government . . . *N Y* 1885. D [11] 316 + 8adv-p aa
—rptd. *N Y* 1948. D [26] 292 [9] a

SHINN (CAPT. JONATHAN).   **417**
The memoirs of: *Greeley Colo* 1890. D 88 [incl wraps] b N Y small ed.
Pioneer experiences in the upper Mississippi country, Iowa, Nebraska and Colorado.

SHINN, JOSIAH H.   **418**
Pioneers and makers of Arkansas . . . Vol. I [all]. n.p. n.d. [*Little Rock* 1908]. O 423 a

SHIPHERD, JACOB R., comp.   **419**
History of the Oberlin-Wellington rescue . . . *B* 1859. O [8] 280 a
One of the most famous fugitive slave affairs.

[SHIPLEY, JONATHAN]   **420**
A speech intended to have been spoken on the bill for altering the charters of . . . Massachusett's Bay. *L* Cadell 1774. O [8] 36 a
—rptd. several times, same impr., collat. & date
—Am. eds., all 1774; *B* Edes & Gill. O 24; *B* Greenleaf. O 12; *Hart*; *N Y*; *Lancaster*; *Newport*, Q 20; *Phil*, Bradford, O [6] 29; *Phil*. Towne, O 18; *Salem*, Hall, Q 16; *Salem*, Russell, O 16 a
Deplores Britain's uncompromising colonial measures.

SHIPMAN, DANIEL   **421**
Frontier life; or, fifty-eight years in Texas . . . [*Houston* 1879]. O [8] 403 port aa

SHIPMAN, MRS. O. L.   **422**
Taming the Big Bend . . . [*Austin*? 1926]. O [8] 215 fold.map 4pls aa
History of West Texas from El Paso to Fort Clark.

SHIPP, BARNARD   **423**
The history of Hernando de Soto and Florida . . . 1512–1586. *Phil* 1881. O [12] 689 2maps pl a
Based entirely on accounts by participants, as given by Garcilasso de la Vega, etc.

SHIRLEY (MAJOR GEN. [WILLIAM]).
The conduct of: . . . *See* Alexander, Wm.

SHIRLEY [GEN. WILLIAM].   **424**
A letter from: . . . to his grace the Duke of Newcastle: with a journal of the siege of Louisbourg . . . *L* 1746. O 32 aa
—rptd. *L* 1748. same collat. aa
—Am. eds.: *B* Draper [1746], Q 31 a; *B* Rogers & Fowle 1746, O 16; *N Y* 1746, O 20   aa

SHIRLEY LETTERS
Shirley letters (The) from the California mines. *See* Clappe, Louise Amelia Knapp Smith.

SHIRREFF, PATRICK   **425**
A tour through North America . . . *Edin* 1835. O [12] 473 a

SHOEMAKER, FLOYD   **426**
Missouri's struggle for statehood. *Jefferson City* 1916. O 383 20pls aa

SHOEMAKER, R. M.   **427**
Reports of . . . surveys for the Union Pacific railway from Fort Riley to Denver. *Cin* 1866. O 27 2maps b Pn Y [of 3 cops loc]

SHORT, RICH   **428**
Travels in the United States . . . Ed. 2. *L* [1834]. D 24 [cov.t. only] aa
With his manifest antipathy to this country, one wonders at his making three trips here; one of these extended to Michigan. No earlier edition is recorded.

SHORT   **429**
Short account (A) of the naval actions of the last war . . . By an officer. *L* 1788. O [8] 148 fold.sheet aa
—ed. 2, *L* 1790. O 147 fold.sheet a
Sneers for the enemy, praise for British valor; even the fight with the "Serapis" by "the desperate English outlaw Paul Jones," is a British victory.

Short address (A) to the government . . . **on the present state of affairs.** By a member of parliament. *See* Bacon, Anthony.

Short and friendly caution (A) to the good   **430**
people of England . . . *L* 1766. O [4] 20 a
Contends that the Stamp Act must be continued.

Short (A) and interesting account of Amer-   **431**
ica. By English settlers. *Chester Eng* 1835. 16° 56 a

Short and thrilling narrative of . . . **inci-**   **432**
dents . . . **in the** . . . **war of 1812–14.** *Norway Me* 1853. O 62 a

Short appeal (A) to the people of Great 433 Britain; upon the unavoidable necessity of the present war with our disaffected colonies . . . *L* 1776. O 24 aa
—ed. 2, same impr., date & collat. a
Support of ministerial policy, probably by Samuel Johnson.

Short history (A) of the conduct of the 434 present ministry, with regard to the American stamp act. *L* 1766. O 24 aa
—ed. 2, same impr., date & collat. a

Short history (A) of the opposition. *See* Macpherson, James.

Short ravelings from a long yarn.
See Taylor, Benjamin F.

Short stories and reminiscences of the 435 last fifty years. By an old traveller. *N Y* 1842. D 2v: 226; 220 aa
Spent much time on the Ohio and Mississippi, from Cincinnati to Natchez and New Orleans.

SHORTFIELD, LUKE [pseud.]
Wild western scenes . . . *See* Jones, John Beauchamp.

SHORTT, WILLIAM T. P., ed. 436
Journal of . . . the siege of Quebec . . . 1775-6 . . . By an officer [Sir J. Hamilton?]. *L* 1824. O [16] 112 aa

SHOURDS, THOMAS 437
History and genealogy of Fenwick's colony. *Bridgeton N J* 1876. O 554 [2] 14pls errata slip a

SHRIVER, JAMES 438
An account of surveys . . . relative to the projected Chesapeake and Ohio, and Ohio and Lake Erie canals. *Balt* 1824. O 116 2maps aa

SHUCK, OSCAR T., comp. 439
The California scrap-book . . . *S F* 1869. O 704 a

SHURTLEFF, NATHANIEL B., ed. 440
Records of the colony of New Plymouth . . . [1633–1692]. *B* 1855–61. roy O 12v in 10 aa
Volumes 1–6, Court orders; vol. 7, Judicial acts; vol. 8, Miscellaneous records; vols. 9–10, Acts of Commissioners; vol. 11, Laws; vol. 12, Deeds.

SHURTLEFF, NATHANIEL B., ed. 441
Records of the Governor and Company of het Massachusetts Bay . . . [1626–1686]. *B* 1853–4. Q 6v: [16] 479; [12] 344; [18] 510; [12] 578; [10] 647; [12] 615 aa

SIATKA, STANISLAW 442
Krotkie Wspomnieinie o Zyciu i Dzialalnosci Ks. M. Wincentego Barzynskiego . . . [Short mem-

oirs from the life . . . of the Rev. M. Vincent Barzynski]. *Chi* 1901. O 65 a
Pastor of Polish churches in Texas and at Chicago.

SIBBALD, GEORGE 443
Notes . . . on the pine lands of Georgia . . . To which is added a geographical sketch . . . *Augusta Ga* 1801. O 71 b
—anr. issue, identical except for add. of a postscript [6 lvs] b
—rptd. *N Y* 1917 Q 66 a

SIBLEY'S . . . EXPEDITION 444
Sibley's [Henry Hastings] Indian expedition, during the summer of 1863 . . . Journal of: *Winona* 1864. O 52 b

SIBLEY (HENRY HASTINGS). 445
The unfinished autobiography of: . . . Ed. by T. C. Blegen. *Minneap* 1932. O [6 incl. front.] 78 a 200copies ptd.

SIBLEY, JOHN L. 446
A history of . . . Union [Me.] . . . *B* 1851. D [14] 540 port a

SIDDONS (MISS LEONORA). 447
The female warrior . . . adventures of: who joined the Texas army . . . and fought in the battle of San Antonio. *N Y* 1843. O 23 pl aa
—ed. 2, *N Y* 1844. same collat. aa
—rptd. *N Y* [1847], same collat. a
Unquestionably fictitious.

SIDNEY, ALGERNON [pseud.]
See Granger, Gideon.

SIDNEY, EDWARD W. [pseud.]
The partisan leader; a tale of the future. *See* Tucker. Nathaniel Beverley.

SIDONS, CHARLES [pseud.]
Die Vereinigten Staaten . . . *See* Postl, Karl.

[SIEBERT, JOHN] comp. 448
Columbus business directory for 1843-4. *Columbus* 1843. D 201 aa
—anr. ed. "Directory of . . . Columbus for . . . 1848," comp. named, *Columbus* 1848. D 264 a
Both editions contain historical sketch.

SIEBERT, WILBUR H. 449
Loyalists in East Florida, 1774–1785 . . . *Deland Fla* 1929. Q 2v: [14] 264; [10] 432. 6maps & pls facs 350copies ptd. aa

SIEBERT, WILBUR H. 450
The underground railroad . . . *N Y* 1898. O [26] 478 fold.map pls a
—rptd. same impr. & collat. 1899.

SIGNS 451
Signs of the times; or, reflections on nullification. By a citizen of Abbeville. *Columbia* 1831. O 32 a

[SIGOURNEY, MRS. LYDIA H.] 452
Sketch of Connecticut forty years since . . . *Hart* 1824. D [2] 278 a

[SIGSBY, WILLIAM] 453
Life and adventures of Timothy Murphy . . . from the commencement of the revolution . . . *Schoharie N Y* 1839. O 32 b NYP
—rptd. 1863. same impr. O 23 aa
—anr. ed. *Middleburgh N Y* 1912. O 32 a
Murphy was a Mohawk Valley patriot scout.

SIGÜENZA Y GÓNGORA, CARLOS DE 454
Descripcion, que de la Vaia de Santa Maria de Galve (antes Pansacola) de la Movila, y rio de la Palicada, en la costa septentrional del seno Mexicano, hizo: . . . yendo para ello en compañia de Don Andres de Pes . . . [*Mex ca* 1700?]. F 32 lvs [capt.t. only] d JCB[only copy known]
Account of an exploring voyage from Vera Cruz to Pensacola and the Mississippi made in 1693 under the command of Admiral Pez. Wagner says publication date may have been 1719.

SIGÜENZA Y GONGORA, CARLOS DE 455
Mercurio volante con la noticia de la recuperacion de las provincias del Nuevo Mexico . . . *Mex* 1693. O [2] 18 numb lvs. c Hn JCB TxU
—Eng. tr. *L A* [Quivira Soc.] 1952. O 136 11pls fold map a
Best contemporary chronicle of the 1692 reconquest of New Mexico by Diego de Vargas, based on that commander's report to the Spanish viceroy.

SIKES, WILLIAM W. 456
A midsummer's ride on the great lakes. *Chi* 1864. O 30 a

SILINGSBY, MAURICE 457
Buckskin Joe; or, the trapper's guide. *N Y* [1879] O 300 aa

SILLIMAN, AUGUSTUS E. 458
A gallop among American scenery . . . *N Y* 1843. 16° [8] 267 a
—rptd., with adds., *N Y* 1881. D 345 pls

[SILLIMAN, BENJAMIN] 459
Remarks made on a . . . tour, between Hartford and Quebec . . . *N Hav* 1820. D 407 eng.t. 9pls a
—ed. 2, with adds., *N Hav* 1824. D [10] 9–443 eng.t. 9pls
—Eng. ed., au. named, "A tour to Quebec . . .," *L* 1822. O [8] 128 2pls [containing 4 views] a

SILVERSMITH, JULIUS 460
The new northwest . . . *Cheyenne* [but ptd *Chi*]

1869. O cover t. 72 + 12adv-p[4 at front, 8 at back] map b Y [of 2copies known]
—anr. ed. *Omaha* [*Chi* ptd] 1869. O 32 aa
One of the earliest accounts of Wyoming, published just after its Territorial creation.

SILVY, ANTOINE
Relation par lettres de l'Amérique Septentrionale . . . *See* Raudot, Antoine Denis.

SIMCOE, JOHN G. 461
A journal of the operations of the Queen's Rangers . . . *Exeter Eng* [1787]. Q [8] 184 [48] 10maps d AA H N NYP
—Am. ed. *N Y* 1844. O [20] 13–328 10maps. Also 25 copies on L. P. with maps col. aa

[SIMCOE, JOHN G.] 462
Remarks on the travels of the Marquis de Chastellux . . . *L* 1787. O [4] 80 aa
—Am. ed. *Phil* 1787. O [2] 89 aa
Defends Arnold's treason, hence authorship has been erroneously attributed to that renegade.

SIMMONDS, FLORA E. [pub.] 463
A complete account of the John Morgan raid . . . n.p. [*Louisv?*] 1863. 32° 94 aa
—anr. issue, same date. 108 aa

SIMMONS, JAMES 464
The history of Geneva, Wisconsin . . . *Geneva* 1875. O 101 a

SIMMONS, N[OAH] 465
Heroes and heroines of the Fort Dearborn massacre . . . *Lawrence Kas* 1896. O 75 2pls a
Story of Corporal John Simmons, who, with one of his children, was killed in this affair; his wife with her remaining child—one of the first white children born in Chicago—escaped after wandering a thousand miles.

[SIMMS, JEPTHA R.] 466
The American spy; or, freedom's early sacrifice. *Alb* 1846. O 63 a
—ed. 2, same impr. & collat. 1857. Also 28copies on L.P. a
The story of Nathan Hale.

SIMMS, JEPTHA R. 467
History of Schoharie county, and border wars of New York . . . *Alb* 1845. O 672 front. [facs & 3pls incl. in paginat.] a
—best ed., enl. & re-written, "The frontiersmen of New York," *Alb* 1882–3. O 2v: 713; 760. port aa

SIMMS, JEPTHA R. 468
Trappers of New York . . . *Alb* 1850. D 280 4pls a
—ed. 2, *Alb* 1851. D 287 2pls
—other *Alb* eds., same collat.: 1857; 1860; 1871.
—rptd. *St. Johnsville* 1935. D 300

SIMMS, WILLIAM G.   469
The geography of South Carolina . . . *Charleston*
1843. D 192 map a

SIMMS, WILLIAM G.   470
The history of South Carolina . . . *Charleston*
S C 1840. O [2] 355 a some copies on L. P.
—ed. 2, *Charleston* 1842. D 345
—rev. ed.: *N Y* 1860, D [8] 437; *Charleston* 1860;
N Y 1866. same collat.

SIMMS, W[ILLIAM] G.   471
The life of Captain John Smith . . . *N Y* Cooledge [1846]. D [4] 379 eng.t. 13pls a
—rptd. many times.

SIMMS, WILLIAM G.   472
The life of Francis Marion. *N Y* 1844. D [4] 9–
349 eng. t. 11pls a
—rptd. *N Y* 1845.

SIMMS, W[ILLIAM] G.   473
The life of Nathanael Greene . . . *N Y* Cooledge
1849. D 393 eng.t. 13pls a
—rptd.: same impr. 1858; 1861.

[SIMMS, WILLIAM G.]   474
The lily and the totem, or, the Huguenots in
Florida. *N Y* 1850. D [12] 470 a
—ed. 2, same impr., date & collat.
—ed. 3, "The Huguenots in Florida . . ." *N Y*
1854.

[SIMMS, WILLIAM G.]   475
Sack and destruction of the city of Columbia, S.
C. . . . *Columbia* 1865. O 76 aa
—rptd. Oglethorpe Univ. 1937. D 106
After selling about 100 of the 5000 copies print-
ed, most of those remaining were destroyed.
Simms was an eye-witness of the holocaust
described.

[SIMMS, WILLIAM G.]   476
Slavery in America . . . brief review of Miss
Martineau on that subject. *Rich* 1838. O 84 aa
—anr. issue, t.slightly altered, au. named, Charleston, 1838 a

[SIMMS, WILLIAM G.]   477
South Carolina in the revolutionary war . . . By
a Southron. *Charleston S C* 1853. D [4] 177 a

[SIMMS, WILLIAM G.]   478
Southern passages and pictures. *N Y* 1839. D
[14] 228 a

[SIMMS, WILLIAM G.]   479
A succinct memoir of the life . . . of Colonel
John Laurens . . . *Williamstadt* 1867. O 250 a
For original edition, *see* Laurens, Col. John,
The army correspondence of:

[SIMMS, WILLIAM G.]   480
Views and reviews in American literature, history and fiction . . . [2 series]. *N Y* 1845. D 2v: [8]
238; [4] 184 aa
—Eng. ed. [ser. 1 only] *L* 1846. D a

SIMON, MRS. BARBARA ANNE   481
The hope of Israel; . . . evidence that the aborigines of the western hemisphere are descended
from the ten missing tribes of Israel. *L* 1829. O [8]
328 a

SIMON, MRS. BARBARA ANNE   482
The ten tribes of Israel . . . identified as the aborigines of the western hemisphere. *L* 1836. O [40]
370 2pls a

SIMONDS, T. C.   483
History of South Boston, formerly Dorchester
Neck, now ward II of . . . Boston. *B* 1857. D 331
2plans 4pls a

SIMONIN, L[OUIS L.]   484
La Californie. [*P* 1860]. 16° 40 a

SIMONIN, LOUIS L.   485
Une excursion chez les peaux-rouges. *P* 1868. O
73 aa

SIMONIN, L[OUIS] [L.]   486
Le grand-ouest des États-Unis . . . *P* 1869. D
[8] 364 map a
—Ital. tr. *Milan* 1876 D maps
Letters written on trips to Dakota and the far
West made in 1859 and in 1867–8.

SIMONIN, L[OUIS L.]   487
L'homme américain. Notes sur les Indiens . . .
P 1870. O 30 2maps a

SIMONIN, L[OUIS L.]   488
Le mineur de Californie. *P* 1866. 16° 52 a

SIMONIN, LOUIS L.   489
Le monde américain . . . *P* 1876. O [8] 395 +
4adv-p a
—ed. 2, *P* 1877. D [6] 445 [2] 24pls

SIMONIN, LOUIS L.   490
Le pays lointains . . . *P* 1867. 16° [8] 350 a
Includes a visit to California.

SIMPSON, ALEXANDER   491
The Oregon Territory. Claims thereto of England and America considered . . . *L* 1846. O
60 aa

SIMPSON, ELIZABETH M.   492
Bluegrass houses and their traditions. *Lex* 1932.
O [12] 408[incl.pls] a

SIMPSON, ELIZABETH M.   **493**
The enchanted Bluegrass . . . *Lex* 1938. O [12] 313 [incl.pls] a
Sequel to preceding work.

SIMPSON, SIR GEORGE   **494**
California, its history . . . *Cin* 1848. D 120 aa
—other eds., same impr. O 144: 1849; 1850. aa

SIMPSON, SIR GEORGE   **495**
Narrative of a journey round the world, 1841–2. *L* 1847. O 2v: [12] 438 + 24adv-p; [7] 469. port map aa
—Am. ed., title altered. *Phil* 1847. O 2pts in 1v: 273; [2] 17–230 a
—anr. ed. [in part], "Narrative of a voyage to California ports . . .," *S F* 1930. Q 250 copies ptd. a

SIMPSON, HENRY   **496**
The lives of eminent Philadelphians . . . *Phil* 1859. O 993 44ports a Some copies on L.P. in Q. aa

SIMPSON, HENRY I.   **497**
The emigrant's guide to the gold mines . . . *N Y* 1848. O 30 + 2adv-p map [not issued with all copies] c H N NYH NYP S Y

SIMPSON, JAMES H.   **498**
Journal of a military reconnaissance, from Santa Fe . . . to the Navajo country. *Phil* 1852. O 140 + 32adv-p map 72pls[some col.] nos. 2, 21 & 39 not issued aa
First separate printing; somewhat amplified from its first appearance as a part of Joseph E. Johnston's *Reconnaissance*, 1850, *q.v.*

SIMPSON, CAPT. [JAMES H.]   **499**
Report and map of wagon road routes in Utah Territory. [*Wash* 1859]. Sen Doc 40 O 84 map a

SIMPSON (LIEUTENANT [JAMES H.])   **500**
Report from the Secretary of War, communicating . . . the report of the . . . route from Fort Smith . . . to Santa Fe . . . made by: [Sen. Exec. Doc. 12]. *Wash* 1850. O 25 4maps a
—anr. issue, [H. R. Exec. Doc. 45] to which is added Marcy's report, *Wash* 1850 O 89 map 2pls aa

SIMPSON, COL. JAMES H.   **501**
Report of explorations across the great basin of . . . Utah for a direct wagon-route . . . *Wash* 1876. Q 518 25maps & pls a
This route, explored in 1859, shortened the distance to California by 250 miles; it was adopted by the overland mail, pony express and telegraph. The report was submitted in 1861, but publication had to be deferred because of the Civil War. Portions, however, appeared in the author's *The shortest route to California*, see below.

SIMPSON (LIEUT. COL. JAMES H.)   **502**
Report of: . . . on the change of route west from Omaha . . . proposed by the Union Pacific . . . *Wash* 1865. O 70 [2] map a

SIMPSON (LIEUT. COL. JAMES H.)   **503**
Report of: on the Union Pacific railroad . . . *Wash* 1865. O [4] 161 4maps a
—rptd., same impr. & collat. 1866.
This report, dated November, includes the author's September report, listed above . . . *On the change of route west from Omaha.*

SIMPSON, J[AMES] H.   **504**
The shortest route to California . . . *Phil* 1869. O 58 map a
See note to his author's *Report of explorations across the great basin of . . . Utah*, above.

[SIMPSON, S. S.]   **505**
Two hundred years ago; or, a brief history of Cambridgeport and East Cambridge . . . *B* 1859. sq 18° 111 pl a

SIMPSON, STEPHEN   **506**
The lives of George Washington and Thomas Jefferson . . . *Phil* 1833. D [6] 389 port a

[SIMPSON, WILLIAM]?   **507**
A retrospective view of the causes of the difference between Great Britain and her colonies . . . [*L* 1783]. O [8] 126 a

SIMS, A. D.   **508**
A view of slavery, moral and political. *Charleston S C* 1834. D 34 a

SIMS, DR. J. MARION   **509**
The story of my life. *N Y* 1884. D 471 + 8adv-p
—rptd.: same impr. & collat. with port added 1885; 1886 a
—ed. 2, *N Y* 1889. D 471 port

SIMS, WILLIAM   **510**
Kansas: Auskunft über seinen Ackerbau, Gartenbau . . . *Topeka* 1884. O 60 fold.map pls a

SINGLETON, ARTHUR [pseud.]
Letters from the south and west. See Knight, Henry Cogswell.

SINGULARITY (THOMAS).   **511**
Novelettes of a traveller; or odds and ends from the knapsack of: . . . *N Y* 1834. D 2v: 228; 203 aa
—Eng. ed. "Sketch of the life of Thomas Singularity . . .," *L* 1835. D [8] 123 a
Adventures of a roving South Carolina printer who served in the war of 1812, etc.

SIOUX FALLS.
Sioux Falls, the queen city of South Dakota . . . *See* Mooers, J. H.

SIOUX INDIANS (THE).   512
Military expedition against: *Wash* 1876. [Ho.
Doc. 184] O 63 aa
Custer fight, etc.

SIPES, WILLIAM B.   513
The Pennsylvania railroad . . . *Phil* 1875. roy O
[4] 281 3pls a

SIPMA, S. A.   514
Belangrijke Berigten uit Pella, Iowa. n.p. 1849.
O 44 a
Same author issued in 1848 an 18-page *Brief van
Land . . . naar Pella.*

SIRINGO, CHARLES A.   515
A cowboy detective . . . *Chi* 1912. D 519 9pls aa
—rptd. *N Y* [1912] D 2v ["A cowboy detective",
"Further adventures of a cowboy detective"]:
paged continuously. aa
—anr. ed. *Santa Fé* 1914. D aa
By court action Siringo was forced to abandon
his intended title ["Pinkerton's cowboy detective"],
to refer throughout only to a fictitious "Dickinson
Detective Agency" and to its clients under fictitious names.

SIRINGO, CHARLES A.   516
History of Billy the Kid. [*Santa Fe* 1920].
D 142 aa

SIRINGO, CHARLES A.   517
Riata and spurs . . . *B* 1927. O [16] 276 16pls aa
—rev. ed., with many suppressions, *B* [1927]. O
[16] 261 + inserted lf between p260 & 261 pls

SIRINGO, CHARLES A.   518
A Texas cow-boy . . . *Chi* Umbdenstock 1885.
D 316[incl.front. & eng.t.] port b
—anr. ed. with 31–p addenda *Chi* Siringo & Dobson 1886. D 347 8pls aa. Sheets of this ed. were
acquired by Rand. McNally and issued by them
sans date [1886] aa
—anr. ed., *Chi* Rand McN. [1886]. D [4] 9–316
[31] 8pls aa
—oth. eds. *Chi* Eagle Pub Co: 1890; 1892; 1893 a
—rptd. under t. "Lone Star cowboy . . .," *Santa
Fe* 1919. D [8] 290 a
—anr. issue, same impr. & date. D [8] 291
—anr. ed. *N Y* [1950]. O 198
The first—and best—cowboy autobiography.

SIRINGO, CHARLES A.   519
Two evil isms: Pinkertonism and anarchism.
Chi 1915 D [4] 109 + adv-p front. aa
Rather libellous account of his twenty-two years
detective operations against cattle-rustlers, mining
swindlers, etc. The greater portion of the edition
was destroyed by the Pinkertons on a court decree.

SISKIYOU COUNTY, CALIFORNIA.   520
History of: *Oakl* 1881. Q 218 map pls b B CalS

SITGREAVES, LORENZO   521
Report of an expedition down the Zuni and Colorado rivers. [Sen. Exec. Doc. 59]. *Wash* Armstrong 1853. O 198 map 23views &c. [no pl. 14, pl.
23 sometimes unnumb.] 6animal pls 5bird pls [no
pl.2] 21 reptile pls[no pl.12, but pls 10 & 13 are
repeated] 3fish pls 21botanical pls[one not listed] a
—rptd. [Sen. Exec. Doc. unnumb.], *Wash* Tucker
1854. same collat., except as to reptile pls, where
no. 12 replaces one of the 2pls numb. 10

SITTEN
Sitten und Meinungen der Wilden in America.
See Purmann, J. G.

SIX MOIS CHEZ LES SAUVAGES.   522
Par un missionaire. *Limoges* [*ca* 1855]. O 191
front. aa
Apparently written in the eighteenth century.

SKETCH   523
**Sketch (A) of the claims of sundry . . . citizens
on the government . . . for indemnity, for depredations . . . by the French . . .** *Bult* 1826. O 145 a
—rptd. *Wash* 1836. O 109
Possibly by Robert Purviance, but more probably by Jas, H. Causten.

**Sketch of the geographical rout[*sic*] of a . . .
railway . . . to connect the canals and navigable
waters of New York,** Pennsylvania, Ohio [etc.].
See Redfield, Wm. C.

**Sketch (A) of the geography and present   524
state of the united territories of North America . . .**
Phil 1805. O 57 aa

**Sketch (A) of the internal conditions of the 525
United States . . . By a Russian.** *Balt* 1826. O 163 a

**Sketch (A) of the origin and progress of the 526
causes which have led to the overthrow of our union.**
By a man who has been an actor in many scenes
. . . *Wash* 1861. O 33 aa

**Sketch (A) of the politics, relations . . .   527
of the western world . . . intended to demonstrate
the necessity of a grand American confederation . . .**
Phil 1827. O 200 a

SKETCHES
Sketches and incidents; or, a budget from the
saddle-bags of a superannuated itinerant. *See*
Stevens, Abel.

Sketches by a traveller. *See* Holbrook, S. B.

Sketches from the civil war. By V. Blada. *See*
Volck, Adalbert J.

**Sketches from the study of a superannuated itiner-
ant** . . . *See* Stevens, Abel.

Sketches of celebrated murderers and **528** pirates . . . *B* [1854]. O 95 + covers aa

Sketches of French and English politicks **529** in America . . . By a member of the old Congress. *Charleston S C* 1797. O [2] 65 a

Sketches of history, life and manners in the United States. By a traveller. *See* Royall, Anne.

Sketches of scenery and manners in the United States. By the author of the "Northern traveller." *See* Dwight, Theo.

Sketches of the war between the United States and the British Isles. 1815. *See* Williams, Sam'l.

SKIDMORE, THOMAS **530** The rights of man to property . . . *N Y* 1829. D 406 [2] aa Wealth to be equally divided, with its equal transmission to later generations on the maturity of each individual. An early Townsend plan.

SKIFF, V[ERNON] W., pub. **531** The Springfield [Ill.] almanac, directory and business advertiser, for 1845. *Springfield* 1845. 16° 128 [2] 129–130 3plans aa First directory of this city.

[SKILLMAN, ISAAC] **532** The American alarm . . . for the rights, and liberties, of the people. *B* 1773. O 4pts in 1: 35; 8; 9; 16 aa Ascribed also to John Allen.

SKILLMAN, ISAAC **533** An oration, upon the beauties of liberty, or the essential rights of the Americans . . . *B* 1773. O 31 aa —ed. 2, same impr., date & collat. a —ed. 3, *N Lond*, same date. O 23 —ed. 4, with adds., *B* same date. O 80 —rptd. *Hart* 1774. O; *Wilm Del* 1775. O

SKILLMAN, W[ILLIAM] D. [comp.] **534** The western metropolis; or Saint Louis in 1846. *St L* 1846. 18° 161[incl.inital blank lf] map b H N NYP

SKINNER, J[OHN] E. H. **535** After the storm; or Jonathan and his neighbours in 1865–6. *L* 1866. D 2v: [16] 312; [6] 370 a

SKIPWITH, H. **536** East Feliciana [La.], past and present. *H O* O 1928. 38 a

SKIRVEN, PERCY G. **537** The first parishes of . . . Maryland . . . *Balt* [1923]. O [14] 181 [21] fold.map 56pls a

SKIRVING, J. **538** Descriptive of Fremont's overland route to Oregon and California . . . [*L ca* 1850]. D 48[incl. wrap.t.] aa Ussued when Skirving was exhibiting his panorama of this route.

SLAFTER, EDMUND F. **539** Sir William Alexander and American colonization . . . *B* Prince Soc. 1873. Q [10] 283 map port 160copies ptd[10 on L.P.] aa

SLAFTER, EDMUND F. **540** Voyages of the northmen to America . . . *B* Prince Soc. 1877. Q 162 2maps pl aa 210copies ptd [10 on L.P.]

SLANEY, ROBERT A. **541** Short journal of a visit to Canada and the states . . . *L* 1861. D [2] 73 a

SLATER, N[ELSON] **542** Fruits of Mormonism . . . *Coloma Calif* 1851. D [2] 94 c AA NYP Y Blanket arraignment of Utah Mormons. One of the earliest English books printed in California.

SLAUGHTER, LINDA W. **543** The new northwest . . . advantages of Bismarck and vicinity . . . *Bismarck* 1874. O 24 c LC MinnH —rptd. *N Y* [1959]. O [2] 24 a Earliest North Dakota pamphlet.

SLAUGHTER, PHILIP **544** A history of Bristol parish [Va.]. *Rich* 1846. O 51 pl a —ed. 2, same impr. 1879. D [20] 237 front.

SLAUGHTER, PHILIP **545** A history of St. George's parish [Va.]. *N Y* 1847. O 62 pl a —rptd., with adds., *Rich* 1890. D 78 pl

SLAUGHTER, PHILIP **546** A history of St. Mark's parish [Va.]. *Rich* 1877. D [10] 200 errata slip map a —rptd., same impr. 1879. —for enl. ed., *see* under Green, Raleigh T.

SLAUGHTER, PHILIP **547** The history of Truro parish in Virginia. *Phil* [1908]. D 164 [6] a

SLAUGHTER, PHILIP **548** Memoir of Col. Joshua Fry . . . Washington's senior in command of Virginia forces . . . *Rich* [1880]. O [6] 113 [2] a

SLAUGHTER, PHILIP **549** A sketch of the life of Robert Fairfax . . . with an

account of Jackson's . . . Valley campaign. *Rich* 1864. D 48 a
—rptd. [*Balt*] 1878. D [10] 72 port
Above editions are styled "second" and "third" editions. First appearance was probably in some periodical.

SLAUGHTER, PHILIP   **550**
The Virginian history of African colonization. *Rich* 1855. O [16] 116 a

SLAVERY
Essays on Slavery . . . By Vigornius, *et al. See* Worcester, Samuel M.

Slavery; a treatise showing that slavery   **551**
is neither a moral, political or social evil. By a Baptist minister. *Penfield Ga* 1844. O 40 a

Slavery in America . . . By a South Carolinian. *See* Simms, Wm. G.

Slavery in the southern states. By a Carolinian. *See* Pringle, Edw. J.

Slavery inconsistent with justice. By Philanthropos. *See* Rice, David.

Slavery not forbidden by Scripture . . . By a West-Indian. *See* Nisbet, Richard.

SLEEPER, JOHN, and HUTCHINS,   **552**
J. C., comps.
Waco and McLennan county, Texas . . . *Waco* 1876. O [2] 171 pl aa

SLEIGH, W. W.   **553**
Abolitionism exposed! . . . injurious to the slaves . . . destructive to this nation, and contrary to the . . . commands of God. *Phil* 1838. O 93 a

SLENDER, ROBERT
Letters on various . . . subjects . . . *See* Freneau, Philip.

SLIGHT, BENJAMIN   **554**
Indian researches; or, facts concerning the North American Indians . . . *Montr* 1844. D 179 + 12adv-p a

SLOAN, EDWARD L.   **555**
Salt Lake City directory and business guide, for 1869. *S L C* [probably ptd in Chi] 1869. O 53–219 map view aa
For earlier directory, printed in New York, *see* Owen, G.

SLOAN, JOHN A.   **556**
Reminiscences of the Guildford Grays, Co. B, 27th N. C. Reg't. *Wash* 1883. O [6] 130 a

SLOAN, WALTER B., pub.   **557**
History and map of Kansas and Nebraska. *Chi* 1855. D [6] 9–144 map c KasH
—anr. issue [probably the first] *Chi* same date. D [6] 9–80 [incl. wraps]. map c N Y
—anr. iss., same collat Galesburg 1857. D [4] 9–80 b

SLOCUM, CHARLES E.   **558**
The history of the Maumee river basin . . . *Defiance O* [1905]. Q 638 [20] a

SLOCUM, JOHN, comp.   **559**
An authentic narrative of the life of Joshua Slocum . . . revolutionary services . . . *Hart* 1844. D 105 [incl. front. & 6pls] a

SMALL, FLOYD B.   **560**
Autobiography of a pioneer . . . 1867–1916. *Seattle* 1916. D 106 a
Adventures with buffalo, cattle and outlaws.

SMALLEY, EUGENE V.   **561**
History of the Northern Pacific railroad. *N Y* 1883. O [26] 5–437 6maps[1in pocket] 48pls a
some copies on L.P.

SMART, STEPHEN F.   **562**
. . . Colorado Mining Camps . . . [guide to Leadville, Ten Mile, California Gulch . . .] *K C* 1879. O 56 2maps aa

SMART, STEPHEN F.   **563**
Colorado tourist . . . *K C* 1879. O 72 map aa

SMART, THEOPHILUS   **564**
Authentic memoirs of Capt. Paul Jones, the American corsair . . . *L* 1779. O 40 port b
—Dutch tr. "Echt verslag, etc." *Amst* 1780. port a

SMEAD, W. H.   **565**
Land of the Flatheads . . . *St P* [1905]. O 142 a

SMEDLEY, WILLIAM   **566**
Across the plains in '62. [*Denver* 1916]. O [2] 56 map port small ed. ptd. aa

SMET, PIERRE-JEAN, DE
See De Smet, Pierre-Jean.

SMETHURST, GAMALIEL   **567**
A narrative of an . . . escape out of the hands of the Indians . . . Likewise a plan for reconciling the differences between Great Britain and her colonies. *L* 1774. O 48 c N

SMILEY, JEROME C.   **568**
History of Denver . . . *Denver* 1903. Q 978 a
Also a limited & signed ed aa

535

SMITH, ABNER C. 569
A random historical sketch of Meeker county Minnesota. *Litchfield Minn* 1877. sq D [4] 160 [2] map aa

SMITH (MR. ADAM). 570
An essay in vindication of the continental colonies of America. From a censure of: in his Theory of moral sentiments ... By an American. *L* for the author 1764. O 46 aa
—anr. issue, same collat. & date, pub. by Becket. aa
Smith had characterized the colonists as "the refuse of the jails of Europe."

SMITH, ALICE R. and D. E. H. 571
The dwelling houses of Charleston ... *Phil* 1917. O [6 incl.front.] 389[incl.pls] aa
Of the 1000 copies printed many were destroyed in the publisher's fire.

[SMITH, ANDREW M.] 572
Luck of a wandering Dane. *Phil* 1885. D [2] 130 aa

SMITH, ASHBEL 573
Notice sur la géographie du Texas ... [*P* 1844?]. O 24 a

SMITH, ASHBEL 574
Reminiscences of the Texas republic ... *Galv* 1876. O 82 100 copies, unbound in sheets aa
—rptd. in facs., bound in wraps, [Austin] n.d.a.

[SMITH, AUGUSTIN S.] 575
A vindication of the recent ... policy of the state of Georgia ... *Athens Ga* 1827. O [10] 9–90 a

SMITH, BUCKINGHAM [ed.] 576
Coleccion de varios documentos para la historia de la Florida y tierras adyacentes. Tomo I [all]. *L* [1857]. Q [8] 208 port[not issued with all copies] aa 500 cops ptd.
Among. the 33 documents assembled are many of the highest importance on De Soto, Coronado, Cabrillo and other early explorers in the southern portions of the present Republic, from the Atlantic to the Pacific.

SMITH, BUCKINGHAM 577
An inquiry into the authenticity of documents concerning a discovery in North Amercira claimed to have been made by Verrazzano. *N Y* 1864. Q 31 map a 120copies ptd.

SMITH, BUCKINGHAM, ed. 578
Rudo ensayo, tentativa de una prevencional descripcion geografica de la provincia de Sonora ... *St Augustine* [ptd. *Alb*] 1863. Q [10] 208 160 copies ptd[a few on L. P.] aa
—Eng. tr., Cath. Hist. Soc., 1896. a
—rptd. *Tucson* 1951. 500copies ptd.

First printing of a manuscript compiled in 1762 by an unknown missionary. Valuable for light thrown on the Apache and other tribes of Arizona and New Mexico.

SMITH, BYRON 579
Reminiscences of a Confederate prisoner ... *Jackson, Miss* 1910 O 42 a

[SMITH, C. C.] 580
Nebraska; a sketch of its history ... *Neb City* 1870. O 31 a

SMITH, CHARLES, 1768–1808 581
The American war ... 1775–1783. *N Y* 1797. O 183 7plans port pl b AA BA NYP Y
A re-publication of articles on this war [based on information supplied by Gates and Steuben] which appeared serially in Smith's *Military repository*, 1796–7. Some copies have 8 plans and 2 plates.

SMITH, CHARLES J. 582
Annals of the town of Hillsborough ... N. H. ... *Sanbornton N H* 1841. O 72 a

SMITH, CHARLES K. 583
Three years in North America ... *Glas* 1858. 16° [8] 112 128 a

SMITH, [CLARENCE] & ELLIOTT, 584
[WALLACE W.] pubs.
Illustrations of Napa county, California, with historical sketch. *Oakland* 1878. Q [4] 28 2maps 68pls b

SMITH, D. N. [pub.] 585
Gold in the Black Hills ... *Burlington Ia* 1876. O 40 + adv-p map b Y

SMITH, D. P. 586
Company K, 1st Alabama regiment. *Prattville Ala* 1885. O 135 [10] aa

[SMITH, DANIEL] 587
A short description of the Tennassee government ... to accompany ... a map ... *Phil* 1793. O 26 b AA N WisH
—anr. ed. "A short description of the State of Tennassee ...," *Phil* 1796. D 36 b AA N MH b
—anr. issue, with spelling "Tennessee" on t-p, *Phil* 1796. D 44 b
—anr. ed. *N Y* 1797. D aa
—Fr. ed. "Description ... du territoire ... au sud de l'Ohio," [*P* ca 1793–6?]. O 28 aa
No map issued with the pamphlet, but one by Smith, engraved by Scott, was sold separately; copies of it appeared also in Carey's American edition of Guthrie's *Geography*. The *Description* was the first account of this Territory. *Cf. Tennessee. A short description of the situation ... and history of:*

SMITH, DELAZON 588
A history of Oberlin, or new lights of the west ... [cover t. "Oberlin unmasked"] *Clev* 1837. D 82 aa
The college is said to have bought and destroyed many copies of this scurrilous pamphlet.

SMITH, EDWARD, M. D. 589
Account of a journey through north-eastern Texas ... *L* 1849. D [6] 5–188 2maps b
—ed. 2, *L* 1852. aa

SMITH, EDWARD M. 590
Documentary history of Rhinebeck ... New York. *Rhinebeck* 1881. O [2] 239 map a

SMITH, MRS. ELIZA R. [SNOW] 591
Biography ... of Lorenzo Snow, one of the twelve apostles of the church of ... Latter-Day Saints. *S L C* 1884. O [16] 581 2ports a

SMITH, FRANCIS H. 592
Discourse on the life ... of Lt. Gen. Thomas J. Jackson ... *Rich* 1863. O 23 aa

SMITH, GAMALIEL E. 593
Journal of the proceedings of the convention ... at Brunswick ... on the separation of Maine from Massachusetts ... *Kennebunk* 1817. D 80 a

SMITH, GEORGE 594
History of Delaware county, Pennsylvania ... *Phil* 1862. O [8] 582 4maps 32 pls a

SMITH, GEORGE A[LBERT] 595
The rise, progress ... of the church of ... Latter Day Saints ... *S L C* 1869. O 49 a
—ed. 2, enl., same impr. 1872. O 71
—Eng. ed. *L* 1873. O

SMITH, GEORGE G. 596
History of Methodism in Georgia and Florida, 1785–1865. *Macon* 1877. D 530 10ports a

SMITH, GEORGE G. 597
The story of Georgia ... *Macon* 1900. O [20] 634 31pls a
—ed. 2, with pref. dated 1901, *Macon* 1900[1904]. O [8 incl.front., l., 9–20] 664 40pls

SMITH, GEORGE W. 598
Incidents of travel ... *Indp* 1855. O 118 b N

SMITH, GUSTAVUS W. 599
Confederate war papers. *N Y* 1884. O 381 3maps port a
—ed. 2, same impr., date & collat.

SMITH, HAMILTON 600
Cannelton, Perry county, Indiana ... its natural advantages ... *Louisv* 1850. O 108 map a

SMITH, REV. HENRY 601
Recollections ... of an old itinerant ... *N.Y* 1848. 16° 352 front a

SMITH, ISAAC 602
Reminiscences of a campaign in Mexico ... *Indp* author 1848. 16° [12] 204 b LC WisH [of 3 cops loc]
—ed. 2, rev. *Indp* Chapmans & Spann 1848. O 116 b IndS LC N NYP Y
Chapters devoted to Price's campaign, Doniphan's march and the conquest of California.

[SMITH, ISAAC B.] 603
Sketches of the early settlement ... of Princeton, Illinois, with a sketch of Bureau county. *Princeton* 1857. D 96 front. aa

SMITH, J. FRASER 604
White pillars ... *N Y* 1941. Q 252[incl. pls] a
—ed. 2, same impr. 1946.
Architecture along the lower Mississippi.

SMITH, J. GRAY 605
A brief historical ... review of east Tennessee ... *L* 1842. O [12] 71 map pl aa
—rptd. in abr. form, *L* 1843. O 24

SMITH (COLONEL JAMES). 606
An account of ... occurrences in the life and travels of: ... *Lex* 1799. O 88 fold pl dd H Hn N NYP
—anr. ed., with account of Smith's second wife, *Phil* 1831. 18° 162 b N NYP Y
—rptd., same collat., *Phil* 1834. aa
—anr. ed. "Life of Colonel James Smith ...," *Phil* 1838. No copy known
—anr. ed., ed. by Darlington, *Cin* 1870. O [12] 190 Also 50 copies on L. P. aa
—rptd: *Cin* 1907, same collat; *Chi* 1948. a
Dynamic activities of an inveterate frontiersman on the borders of Pennsylcania, Ohio and Kentucky, including captivity among the Indians from 1755 to 1759. One of the imperial books on the early Ohio valley.

SMITH, COLONEL JAMES 607
A treatise on the mode and manner of Indian war ... Also—a brief account of twenty-three campaigns ... against the Indians ... since the year 1755 ... *Paris Ky* 1812. O [2] 2–59 dd G MH N [only cops kn]
Free use is made of material in the author's autobiography, above.

[SMITH, JAMES], 1775–1839 608
Sketches of Mr. Mathews' celebrated trip to America ... *L* 1824. D 24 4pls a

SMITH, JAMES W., pub. 609
First directory of Oklahoma Territory ... *Guthrie* [1890]. O [6, incl. 2adv-p] 67–84 33–226

[6adv-p] 225–331 + 3adv-p inserted slip at p33 b
OkH[of 2copies located]

SMITH, JEDEDIAH [S.]
The travels of: *See* Sullivan, Maurice S.

[SMITH, JEROME V. C.]   610
Memoirs of Andrew Jackson ... *B* 1828. 18°
334 port a
—rptd., same impr. & collat., but different port:
1832; 1833; 1834; 1845; 1847; 1850.

SMITH, JOE H.   611
History of Harrison county, Iowa ... *Des M*
1888. O 491[incl.front.] a

SMITH, REV. J[OHN] C.   612
Reminiscences of early Methodism in Indiana
... *Indp* 1879. O [22] 322 a

SMITH (JOHN CALVIN).   613
The autobiography of: ... trip to Missouri in
1816 ... border ruffian war ... *Phil* 1907. D 96 a

SMITH, J[OHN] CALVIN   614
The illustrated hand-book ... for travelers
through the United States ... *N Y* 1846. 16° 233
map pl aa
—rptd., same impr. & collat., 1847. a
—other eds.: same impr., 234p, map & pl: 1848;
1948; 1850.
—anr. ed. "Hand-book for travellers ...," *N Y*
1856. 16° 275 map
—Eng. ed. "The emigrant's hand-book ...," *L*
[1850]. 16° [10] 267 map pl
—rptd., same collat., *Liv* n.d.
—abr. ed. "A new guide for travelers through the
United States ...," *N Y* 1846. 16° 79 map
—rptd., same collat.: 1847; 1848; 1850.

SMITH, J[OHN] CALVIN   615
The western tourist and emigrant's guide, with a
compendious gazetteer ... *N Y* J. H. Colton 1839.
180 map aa
—rptd., same collat., 1840. a
—anr. ed. "The western tourist, or emigrant's
guide ... being an accurate [etc.] description ...,"
[Smith's name not on t-p] *N Y* 1843. 18° 119 map
—rptd., same collat.; 1844; 1845; 1846; 1847.
—other eds., with 89p & map: 1850; 1851; 1853;
1854.
—reissued, "Colton's Traveller and tourist's guide-
book through the western states and territories,"
1855; 1856; 1857.
For other handbooks, essentially the same, *see*
Colton, Joseph H.

SMITH, JOHN JAY, and WATSON,   616
JOHN F.
American historical and literary curiosities ...
[No. 1]. *Phil* 1847. F [6] 74 a

—eds. 2 & 3, same impr., date & collat.
—No. 2, *Phil* 1847. F [4] 74 a
—eds. 4, 5 & 6, containing material in above 2nos.:
N Y 1850; *N Y* 1852; *N Y* 1861.
—ser. 2, *Phil* 1860. F [4] 200 a
—anr. issue with *N Y* impr.

SMITH, JOHN R.   617
Descriptive pamphlet of Smith's leviathan panorama of the Mississippi river ... *Phil* 1848. O 32 b
only onc cop loc.
—anr. ed., with different title, *Phil* 1853. O 32 aa
—Eng. ed., with different title, *L* 1849. O aa
—Ger. tr. *Berlin* 1851, D 32; *Leip* 1851 aa
This moving panorama was 4 miles in length and
depicted the river, in its 4,000 miles, from St. Paul
to the Gulf.

SMITH, JOHN W.   618
History of Macon county, Illinois. *Springfield*
1876. O 304 [4] port a

SMITH, J[OHN] Y.   619
History of Madison [Wis.]. [*Madison* 1866] D
9–78 No t-p a
For book, of which this is a separate printing of
the historical portion, see Suckow, B. W.

SMITH, JOSEPH, D. D.   620
History of Jefferson college: ... *Pitt* 1857. D
433 + 2adv-p port a
—anr. issue, with list of graduates, &c., added,
same impr. & date. D 433 [24] + 2adv-p port

SMITH, JOSEPH, D. D.   621
Old Redstone; or, historical sketches of western
Presbyterianism ... *Phil* 1854. O 459 8pls a

[SMITH, JOSEPH] prophet   622
A book of commandments, for the government
of the Church of Christ. *Zion* [i.e. *Independence
Mo*] 1833. 24° 160 [incomplete, but all ptd] There
were 2 variations of t-p, one without, one with,
ornamental borders. dd G NYP UCHO Y
—rptd.: *S L C* 1884, 18° 96 [inc. front cover] a;
S L C 1903, same collat.; *Lamoni Ia* 1903, 16° 136
[incl. front cover]; *Independence* 1926, 16° 127
First book printed at Independence and the
second publication of the Mormon Church. While
being printed, a Missouri mob attacked the printing office and destroyed nearly all the sheets. For
a later work containing these commandments,
written down from revelations received by Smith,
see below *Doctrines and covenants.*

SMITH, JOSEPH, prophet   623
The book of Mormon ... *Palmyra N Y* 1830. O
588 [2] a Some copies have, inserted, a 4-p. index
["References"] which was ptd. later b N NYP
—ed. 2, with changes, *Kirtland O* 1837. 16° [2]
5–621 aa

—ed. 3, rev., *Nauvoo Ill* [ptd. *Cin*] 1840. 16° [4] 7–573 aa

—anr. issue of this ed. has different set-up of type, at end, carrying text to p. 574. aa Some copies have, inserted, 4 l. of index, ptd. at Nauvoo a little later b

—ed. 4, *Nauvoo* 1842. 16° same collat. a

—Eng. ed., from Am. ed. 2, with index added, *Liv* 1841. 16° [4] 634 637–643 a

—rptd. often in Am. & Eng. and in tr. in many countries.

On this flimsy foundation was reared America's most successful theocracy, its most enduring communal movement. In the first edition only was Smith named as author; in all subsequent ones he is designated as translator. The first edition was also the only one carrying his two-page preface.

SMITH, JOSEPH, prophet, et al   624
Doctrines and covenants of the Church of Latter Day Saints . . . *Kirtland O* 1835. 18° 257 [25] aa

—ed. 2, with adds., *Nauvoo Ill* 1844. 18° 448 aa

—ed. 3, *Nauvoo* 1845. same collat. a

—ed. 4, *Nauvoo* 1846. same collat.

—many later eds.

Contains revelations to Smith as printed in *A book of commandments*, with additions.

SMITH (JOSEPH, JR. [prophet] et al).   625
Document containing the correspondence . . . and the evidence given . . . on tthe trial of: for high treason . . . *Fayette Mo* 1841. O [4] 163 b NYP UCHO Y

—rptd., in part, ["Document showing the testimony . . .," [*Wash* 1841]. O 47 a

SMITH (MR. [JOSEPH]) [prophet].   626
Evidence taken on the trial of: before the municipal court of Nauvoo . . . *Nauvoo* [1843]. O 38 b H Y

The evidence relates to Mormon persecutions in Missouri.

SMITH (JOSEPH [Mormon prophet]).   627
History of: *Liv* [1852]. O 88 no t-p, capt. heading "Supplement to vol. 14 . . . of the . . . Millenial Star." a

(SMITH, JOSEPH) prophet.   628
The pearl of great price . . . Selections from the revelations . . . of: . . . *Liv* 1851. O [8] 56 fold.pl aa

—Am. ed., with adds., *S L C* 1878. O [4] 71 fold. pl a

—many reprints, Eng. & Am., and tr. into several languages

SMITH, JOSEPH, prophet   629
The voice of truth, containing [his] correspondence . . . *Nauvoo* 1844. O 64 b G NYP Y

—rptd. with cover-t. dated, *Nauvoo* 1845. aa

SMITH, JOSEPH A.   630
A pamphlet descriptive of northwestern Iowa and southwestern Minnesota . . . *Spirit Lake Ia* 1874. O 24 + cover-t. a

SMITH, JOSHUA H.   631
An authentic narrative of the causes which led to the death of Major Andrè . . . *L* 1808. O [8] 358 + 2adv-p map 2pls a

—Am. ed. *N Y* 1809. 16° 214 port

SMITH (JOSHUA H.)   632
Record of the trial of: for . . . conspiracy in the treason of Benedict Arnold. *Morrisania N Y* 1866. O [6] 116 a 50copies ptd.

Only separate edition of this trial.

SMITH, JOSHUA TOULMIN   633
The northmen in New England . . . *B* 1839. D [12] 364[incl. chart] 2maps a

—Eng. ed. "The discovery of America by the northmen . . .," *L* 1839. D [12] 344[incl. chart] 2maps 2pls

—Eng. ed. 2, with adds., *L* 1842. D [12] 348 2maps 2pls

SMITH, JUSTIN H.   634
The annexation of Texas . . . *N Y* 1911. O [10] 496 [1] a

—rptd. with cor *N Y* 1941

SMITH, JUSTIN H.   635
Our struggle for the fourteenth colony. Canada and the American revolution. *N Y* 1907. O 2v: [26] 638; [18] 635. 2fronts. a

SMITH, JUSTIN H.   636
The war with Mexico. *N Y* 1919. O 2v: [22] 572; [14] 620. map aa

SMITH, MRS. LUCY   637
Biographical sketches of Joseph Smith, the prophet . . . *Liv* 1853, 18° 298 aa

—rptd. *Plano Ill* 1880. 18° 312 a

—rev. ed. "History of the prophet Joseph . . .," *S L C* 1902. O 296 4ports a

The original edition was condemned in 1865 by the Mormon Church as unauthorized and inaccurate and some copies were destroyed. The 1902 edition was from a revision made by order of Brigham Young in 1876.

SMITH, MARGARET
Leaves from [her] journal . . . *See* Whittier, John G.

SMITH (MRS. MARY).   638
An affecting narrative of the captivity . . . of: . . . rescued from the merciless hands of the savages by a detached party from the army of . . . General Jackson, now commanding at New-Orleans. *Prov*

by L. Scott [1815]. D 24 front. b Hn LC N NYP
—issue 2, omitting the account of Indians killing thirty persons [which followed Mrs. Smith's captivity in issue 1], *Prov* for L. Scott [1815]. D 24 front. b AA
—anr. ed., with "New Orleans" on t-p not hyphenated, *Prov* for L. Scott [1815]. D 24 front. b
—anr. ed., t-p describes General Jackson as "late commanding at New-Orleans," *Prov* for L. Scott [1816?]. D 24 front. b
—other eds.: *Bangor* 1816, D 18; *Wmsbg Mass* 1818, D 24; n. p. [1818?], D 24 b Y

SMITH, MATTHEW H.   639
Twenty years among the bulls and bears of Wall street. *Hart* 1870. O [22] 25–557 + 2adv-p 12pls aa
—rptd., same impr. & collat: 1871; *N Y* 1871. a
—anr. ed., with 1873 crisis added, "Bulls and bears of New York . . .," *Hart* 1874. O [22] 25–576 12pls
—rptd., same impr. & collat. 1875.

[SMITH, MELANCTHON]   640
An address to the people of . . . New-York; shewing the necessity of . . . amendments to the constitution proposed for the United States. *N Y* 1788. O 26 aa
One of the amendments urged, the Bill of Rights, was adopted; another, for a definite limit upon federal taxation, has remained unheeded to this day.

SMITH, M[ICHAEL]   641
A complete history of the late American war . . . Sixth edition, rev. *Lex* 1816. 16° 288 aa
Called "sixth edition," as there had previously appeared five editions of the author's *Geographical view*, the fifth edition of which included a concise sketch of this war, *see* following entry.

SMITH, M[ICHAEL]   642
A geographical view, of . . . upper Canada. And remarks relative to the situation of the inhabitants respecting the war. *Hart*, por [*sic*] the author, 1813. D 107 aa
—ed. 2, enl., *Hart* John Russell 1813. 16° [4] 119
—anr. issue, *N Y* 1813. D 119
—ed. 3, *Trenton* 1813. D 119 pl
—other issues: *Phil*, for the author, 1813, D 120; *Phil*, for Desilver, 1813, same collat.; *N Y* 1813, same collat.
—anr. ed. enl., with a concise history of the war, "A geographical view of the British possessions . . .," *Balt* 1814. 16° 288
The author considered the last entry as being the 5th edition: some copies, sent to Washington, were burned by the British. For a 6th edition, *see* above, *A complete history* . . .

SMITH (M[ICHAEL]).   643
Human sorrow and divine comfort, or a short narrative of the sufferings . . . of: *Rich* 1814. D 38 b Hn[only copy known]
—rptd. *Rich* 1815. aa

—ed. 3, enl. "A narrative of the sufferings in upper Canada . . . and journey to Virginia and Kentucky . . .," *Lex* 1817. 16° 162 b
Another edition, with separate title-page, was issued at Lexington, in 1816, continuously paged, with the author's *Complete history of the late American war, q.v.*

SMITH (MOSES).   644
History of the adventures and sufferings of: . . . *Bklyn* 1812. D [8] 13–124 2pls aa
—rptd. *Alb* 1814. 18° [4] 13–146 [6] 2pls a
One of the few contemporary narratives relating to the Miranda expedition.

SMITH, MOSES   645
Naval scenes in the last war; or, three years on board the frigate "Constitution" . . . *B* 1846. O 50 a

SMITH, NELSON F.   646
History of Pickens county, Ala . . . 1817–1856. *Carrolton Ala* 1856. 16° 272 aa

SMITH, O[LIVER] H.   647
Early Indiana trials; and sketches . . . *Cin* 1858. O 640 port a
—rptd., same impr., date & collat.

SMITH, PHILIP H.   648
General history of Dutchess county [N.Y.] . . . *Pawling N Y* 1877. O [2] 7–507 map 5pls a

SMITH, PHILIP H.   649
Legends of the Shawangunk . . . and its environs . . . historical sketches . . . relating to those portions of the counties of Orange, Ulster and Sullivan . . . *Pawling N Y* 1887. Q [8] 168 8pls a

SMITH, PLATT   650
The Central Pacific railroad . . . *Dubuque* 1859. O 38 map b Y

SMITH, R. F. [ed.]   651
Doniphan county, Kansas, history and directory for 1868-9 . . . [*Wathena*] 1868. O [48, 2] 349 aa

SMITH, R. F.   652
Guide to the southwest along the line of the Missouri, Kansas and Texas Railway. Containing historical sketches . . . *Sedalia Mo* 1871. O 216 map aa

SMITH, RALPH J.   653
Reminiscences of the civil war . . . [*San Marcos Tex* 1911.] O 26 + cov.t. port a

[SMITH, RICHARD PENN]?   654
Col. Crockett's exploits and adventures in Texas . . . written by himself . . . *Phil* 1836. D 216 [incl. 4adv-p at front] port aa
—ed. 6 [probably ed. 2], *Phil* 1837. same collat. a

—rptd. *Cin* 1839. same collat.; *N Y* 1845. D port; *N Y* 1848. D 2pls
—Eng. ed. *L* 1837. D [8] 152
Ingenious pseudo-autobiography, purportedly printed from the manuscript found with the baggage of a Mexican general slain at San Jacinto.

SMITH, ROBERT   655
Railroad to the Pacific. Report from the Committee . . . to whom was referred the memorial of George Wilkes . . . upon the subject of constructing a railroad . . . between . . . the Missouri and the Columbia. [*Wash* 1846]. O 48 aa

SMITH, ROBERT, of Maryland   656
Address to the people of the United States. *Balt* 1811. D 41 a
—rptd., without app., *Lex Ky* same date. O 34; [*Balt* 1811] O
—several other eds.
Concerning his leaving Madison's cabinet over a disagreement on foreign policy.

[SMITH, ROBERT HALL]   657
A series of intercepted letters, captured by the American guard at Tacubaya . . . *Mex* 1847. O 37 aa
—rptd. *N O* 1847. O 32 aa
—ed. 2, enl., au. named, *Columbus O* 1848. O 56 aa

SMITH, ROBERT H[ARDY]   658
An address to the citizens of Alabama on the constitution and laws of the Confederate States. *Mobile* 1861. O 24 aa

SMITH, R[ODERICK] A.   659
A history of Dickinson county, Iowa . . . *Des M* 1902. O 598 port a

SMITH, SAMUEL, L. L. B.   660
A sermon preach'd before the Trustees for Establishing the Colony of Georgia . . . *L* 1733. O 42 map aa
Second official publication of the Georgia Trustees; in it was reprinted their first publication—
Some account of the designs of the Trustees . . .,—
a folio of four leaves, issued the previous year, containing the earliest map of the colony, reproduced here with some changes. This sermon was the first of a long-continued annual series.

SMITH, SAMUEL, 1720–76   661
The history of the colony of . . . New Jersey . . . *Burl* MDCCLXV. O [10] 573 [1] aa 600 cops ptd
—issue 2, identical except date punctuated: M, DCC,LXV aa
—ed. 2 [*Trenton* 1877]. O [16, incl. final blank lf] 574 map a
—rptd., with index added, [*Trenton ca* 1880]. O [16, incl. final blank lf] 602 2maps
—anr. ed., with new t., *Trenton* 1890. O [14] 613 2fold.maps

SMITH (SAMUEL, revolutionary soldier).   662
Memoirs of the life of: . . . from a journal written by himself, 1776–1786. *Middleborough Mass* 1853. D 24 a
—rptd., t. altered, *N Y* 1860. O 41 2pls

SMITH, S[AMUEL] R.   663
The story of Wyoming valley. *Kingston Pa* 1906. O 97 6pls a

SMITH, S[AMUEL] R., ed.   664
The Wyoming valley in 1892. *Wilkesbarre* 1892. sm Q 160 11pls a

SMITH, S[AMUEL] R.   665
The Wyoming valley in the nineteenth century. Vol.I [all]. *Wilkesbarre* 1894. Q 153 8pls a

SMITH (SARAH) AND THE HESSIAN.   666
The thrilling . . . story of: . . . Together with Mr. Keith's captivity among the Indians. *Phil* 1844. O 24 a
—rptd., without Keith's captivity, *Phil* 1845. O 32 [incl. front.]
For original edition of the fictitious Keith captivity, *see* Keith, Capt. Thos.

SMITH, SARAH SAUNDERS   667
The founders of the Massachusetts Bay colony . . . *Pittsfield* 1897. O 372 21pls 3facs plan a

SMITH, MRS. SEBA   668
The western captive; or the times of Tecumseh. *N Y* 1842. Q 48 aa
Captivity of Mrs. Margaret Mason.

SMITH, SIDNEY   669
The setter's new home . . . a guide to emigrants . . . *L* 1849. 16° [2] 106 + 8adv-p aa
—anr. issue, *L* n.d. D [44] 106 a
—enl. ed. [with pt2 on Austria, Africa, etc.], *L* 1850. 16° 2pts in 1: [6, 3–12] 144; [26] 105 a
One of the earliest English emigration manuals to mention California.

SMITH (THE "SOAPY") TRAGEDY.
See Le Febre, H. B.

SMITH, SOL[OMON F.]   670
The theatrical apprenticeship [etc.] of: . . . the first seven years of his professional life . . . *Phil* Carey & Hart 1846. D 216 [incl. front. and illus t-p] 6pls aa
—rptd., same collat., 1847 [illus t-p dated 1848]. a
—anr. ed., no text on p216, otherwise same collat., *Phil* Peterson [1854].
—anr. undated ed. D [2] 7–254 port

[SMITH, SOL[OMON F.]   671
The theatrical journey-work [etc.] of: . . . the second seven years of his professional life . . . *Phil* [1855]. D 254 [incl. front-cover & port] a

SMITH, SOL[OMON F.] **672**
Theatrical management in the west and south for thirty years . . . *N Y* 1868. O 276 + 4adv-p a

SMITH, S[TEPHEN] R. **673**
Historical sketches . . . illustrative of the establishment . . . of Universalism in the state of New York. *Buf* 1843. 18° 249 [1] a
—ser. 2, *Buf* 1848. D 248 a

[SMITH, T.] **674**
Rambling recollections of a trip to America. *Edin* 1875. D [6] 9–55 a

SMITH, JUSTICE [THEOPHILUS W.] **675**
Opinion . . . on Beaubien's claim . . . *Chi* 1837. O 26 b ChiH LC
This case involved land on which Chicago was laid out. First book of a literary nature printed in that city.

[SMITH, THOMAS] of Liverpool **676**
Hints to emigrants . . . with copious extracts from the journal of Thomas Hulme . . . *Liv* 1817. O 37 aa
—ed. 2, enl. & au. named, "The emigrants' guide to the United States . . . including the substance of the journal of Thomas Hulme . . .," *L* 1818. O [4] 52
—anr. iss. *Newcastle* 1818. a

SMITH (REV. THOMAS), of Portland. **677**
Extracts from the journals of: . . . 1720–1788. *Port Me* 1821. D 164 [4] 154 [2] a
—rptd., with journal of Rev. Samuel Deane and other adds., *Port* 1849. O 484 map 3ports
Includes much on Indian wars of New England.

SMITH, T[HOMAS] MARSHALL **678**
Legends of the war of independence, and of the early settlements in the west. *Louisv* 1855. O 397 a

SMITH (THOMAS W.) **679**
Narrative of the life, travels . . . of: *B* 1844. D 233 [7] aa
Eighteen voyages, including seven whaling expeditions to the South Pacific.

SMITH, TRUMAN **680**
Speech on the physical character of the northern states of Mexico [including the disputed territory between the Nueces and the Rio Grande, also New Mexico and Upper California] . . . showing that the present war with Mexico has been prosecuted for objects . . . injurious to the American people. [*Wash* 1848]. O 31 no t-p aa
One of the earliest Congressional utterances on this region.

[SMITH, VENTURE] **681**
A narrative of the life . . . of Venture, a native of Africa . . . resident above sixty years in the United States . . . *N Lond* 1798. O 32 aa
—rptd.: same impr. 1835, D 24; *Middletown* 1897, O 41 a

SMITH, WALKER C. **682**
The Everett massacre: a history of the class struggle in the lumber industry. *Chi* [1918] D 358 a
—rptd. *Chi* [1919?] D [6] 9–302 + 2adv-p.

SMITH, REV. WESLEY **683**
A family history and fifty-two years . . . in Mississippi and Texas. *Nashv* 1898. O 167 [38] a

[SMITH, WILLIAM], provost **684**
An account of the proceedings of the Ilinois and Ouabache Land Companies . . . *Phil* 1796. O [16] 55 b AA G JCB NYP Y
—rptd., with adds., "Illinois" on t-p spelled correctly, *Phil* 1796 [i.e. 1797]. O [16] 55, 8, 8, 7, 7 b JCB N
—anr. issue, paginat. after p. 55 continuous. O [16] 55, 26 aa
—rptd. *Phil* 1803. O [14] 74 a; 1810.
These two companies having acquired land in present Illinois and Indiana, separately, from Indians, merged in 1780 as the United Illinois and Ouabach Land Companies.

SMITH, WILLIAM, provost **685**
Additional discourses and essays . . . *L* 1762. O 112 [21, 39–106] a
Separate printing of new material added to edition two of his *Discourses*, issued for the convenience of owners of edition one of that work.

[SMITH, WILLIAM], provost **686**
A brief state of the province of Pennsylvania . . . *L* 1755. O [2] 45 aa
—ed. 2, same place, date & collat. aa
—rptd.: *Dub* 1755, O 48; *N Y* 1865, O a
—ed. 3, *L* 1756. O 47
Denunciation of Quakers for their attitude concerning frontier defence.

[SMITH, WILLIAM], provost **687**
A brief view of the conduct of Pennsylvania, for . . . 1755; . . . as it affected the general service of the British colonies, particularly the expedition under . . . Braddock . . . *L* & sold by Mr. Bradford in Philadelphia 1756. O 88 a
Sequel to the author's *Brief state of Pennsylvania*. For abridged French translation of both, *see Pensilvanie (la). État présent de:*

SMITH, WILLIAM, provost **688**
Discourses on several public occasions during the war in America . . . *L* 1759. O [12] 246 a
—ed. 2, with adds., t. slightly altered, *L* for A. Miller, D. Wilson, *et al* 1762. O [16] 224 [34 39–160]

—ed. 2, issue 2, *L* for A. Miller, R. Griffiths, *et al* 1762. same collat
—ed. 3 *L* 1769.
For *Additional discourses, see* above.

SMITH, WILLIAM, provost   689
Eulogium on Benjamin Franklin . . . *Phil* 1792. O [4] 40 [6] a
—Eng. ed. *L* 1792. O [4] 39

[SMITH, WILLIAM, provost   690
An examination of the Connecticut claim to lands in Pennsylvania . . . *Phil* 1774. O [2] 93 32 map aa
—anr. issue, with text on p94. O [2] 94 32 map aa
A post-revolution Congress awarded the contested land to Connecticut; from the proceeds of its sale, Connecticut's school fund was established.

[SMITH, WILLIAM, provost, et al]   691
Four dissertations, on the reciprocal advantages of a perpetual union between Great-Britain and her American colonies . . . *Phil* 1766. O [18] 12 [2] 112 aa
—Eng. ed. *L* [1766]. O [10] 12 [2] 112 a
Smith made the presentation address at the delivery of the prize medal. The dissertations were by John Morgan, Stephen Watts, Joseph Reed and Francis Hopkinson.

[SMITH, WILLIAM], provost   692
An historical account of . . . canal navigation in Pennsylvania . . . *Phil* 1795. Q [16] 77 map aa
—anr. issue, with adds., same impr. & date. Q [16] 80 map aa
Ascribed also to Robert Morris.

[SMITH, WILLIAM], provost   693
An historical account of the expedition against the Ohio Indians . . . under the command of Henry Bouquet . . . *Phil* 1765. Q [16] 71 map 2plans c NYP Y
—Eng. ed. *L* 1766. Same collat. with different map and 2pls[by Benjamin West] added. c AA N NYP Y
—rptd., with adds., *Cin* 1868. O [24] 162 map 2plans 2pls a some copies on L.P.
—oth. eds: [with "Rogers' Journals"] *Dub* 1769, D [10] 218 [20] 99; *Dub* 1770, same collat. aa
—Fr. tr., with biog. of Bouquet, *Amst* 1769. O [4 7–16] 147 [10] 2maps 4pls aa
—rptd. *P* 1778. same collat. a
Originally ascribed to Thomas Hutchins, who accompanied this expedition and executed the 2plans; but that the book was prepared by Smith, from Bouquet's notes, has been established. This campaign gave Pontiac's conspiracy its death-blow.

[SMITH, WILLIAM], provost   694
Memorial of the Illinois and Wabash Land Companies. [*Phil* 1797]. O 8 8 7 7 aa
—rptd. *Balt* 1810. O 47 a

This *Memorial* also formed a part of the second Philadelphia edition of this author's *An account of the proceedings of the Illinois and Ouabache Land Companies, q.v.*

SMITH, WILLIAM, provost   695
An oration in memory of General Montgomery, and of the officers and soldiers, who fell with him . . . before Quebec . . . *Phil* 1776. O [6] 44 some copies have errata list on p44 aa
—rptd., same yr.: *N Y* D 36; *Newport* O [2] 30; *Norwich* O 22 aa
—Eng. eds., same yr.: *L* O [4] 36 [2 eds.]; *Newcastle* O 35; *Belf* O 48 a
In making this address before Continental Congress, Smith aroused stupefaction and hostility by suggesting appeasement with England.

[SMITH, WILLIAM]?, provost   696
Plain truth; addressed to the inhabitants of America, containing remarks on . . . Common sense . . . *Phil* 1776. O [8] 84 + 4 adv-p a
—other variant issues, same impr. & date, collate erratically: one paged [6] 9–64 57–64 73–86 79–84; the other paged [6] 9–64 57–64 73–80 73–78 89–96
—ed. 2, possibly precedes last of above variants, *Phil* 1776. same collat. as first of above variants
—new ed., with adds., *Phil* 1776. O [2] 5 64 57 64 73–96 [8] 97–136
—anr. issue, same date & impr., collates: 64 57–64 73–96 [8] 97–136
—Eng. eds.: *L* 1776, O [4] 48; ed. 2, cor., *L* 1776, same collat.; *Dub* 1776, O [4] 44; *L* 1783.
Most famous answer to Paine's advocacy for independence in *Common sense*. Attributed also to George Chalmers, Alexander Hamilton, Joseph Galloway, Charles Inglis, and Richard Wells. Take your choice.

SMITH, WILLIAM, provost   697
A sermon on the present situation of American affairs . . . *Phil* 1775. O [8] 32 a
—other eds., same yr.: *N Y*; *Wilm Del*
—Eng. eds. [of 1775]: *L* [3eds.]; *Bristol* [2eds.]; *Dub*; *Belf*
—Welsh ed. "Pregeth ar Helynt Bressenol America," *Bristol* 1775. O 24

[SMITH, WILLIAM], provost   698
The speech of a Creek-Indian . . . *L* 1754. O 68 b.
—rptd. "Some account of the North-America Indians; their genius . . .," *L* [1754]. O 68 + 2adv-p aa

SMITH, WILLIAM, banker   699
Notes of a short American tour. *Dumfries* 1873. D [4] 3–82 a

SMITH, WILLIAM, of Canada   700
The history of the post office in British North America, 1639–1870. *C* 1920. O [10] 356 3ports a

SMITH, WILLIAM, of Yorkshire   701
A Yorkshireman's trip to the United States and
Canada. L 1892. O [16] 317 + 3adv-p 2ports a

[SMITH, WILLIAM, JR.] historian of N. Y.   702
The candid retrospect: or, the American war
examined . . . Charlestown S C 1780. Q 30 b BM
[only copy known]
—rptd. N Y 1780. sq. D 28 aa
Pleads for compromise and reconciliation.

SMITH, WILLIAM, JR., historian of N. Y.   703
The history of the province of New-York . . . L
1757. Q [12] 255 pl b Hn NYP Y
—untrimmed copy on larger and thicker paper d
Hn N
—ed. 2, omitting dedication & pl, L 1776. O [8]
160 [12] 161–256 [12] 257–334 aa
—Am. ed. [also styling itself ed. 2] Phil 1792. O
276 a
—anr. Am. ed.: Alb 1814, with adds. O 512
—Fr. tr. L 1767. D [4, 7–16] 415 a
First history of New York.

SMITH, MAJ. W[ILLIAM] A.   704
The Anson guards, Company C, Fourteenth
Regiment, North Carolina Volunteers, 1861–5.
Charlotte N C 1914. O [12] 368 10pls aa

SMITH, WILLIAM C.   705
Indiana miscellany . . . Cin 1867. D 304 a

[SMITH, WILLIAM CALVIN]   706
The private in gray . . . [Dallas 1908]. O [4]
7–134 a

SMITH, WILLIAM HENRY 1833–96   707
A political history of slavery . . . N Y 1903. O
2v: [18] 350; [6] 456 port a

SMITH, WILLIAM HENRY, 1833–96, ed.   708
The St. Clair papers . . . Cin 1882. See St. Clair
Papers.

SMITH, WILLIAM HENRY, 1839–1935   709
The history of . . . Indiana . . . 1763–1897. Indp
1897. O 2v: [20] 512; [12] 513–1015. 4maps 28pls a
—rev. ed. Indp 1903. O 2v: [12] 512; [8] 522. 2maps
22pls

[SMITH, WILLIAM L., of S. C.]   710
A candid examination of the objectons to the
treaty . . . between the United States and Great
Britain . . . Charleston S C 1795. O 42 aa 1 cop loc.
—rptd., with added t-p, "The eyes opened . . .,"
N Y 1795. O [2] 43 [2] 5 a

SMITH, WILLIAM L., of S. C.   711
A comparative view of the constitutions of the
several states . . . Phil 1796. Q [10] 9–34 6fold.tabs a
—rev. ed. Wash 1832. O

[SMITH, WILLIAM L.] of S. C.   712
The politicks and views of a certain party displayed. [Phil?] 1792. O 36 aa
Defends Hamilton's financial policies. Ascribed
also to Hamilton.

[SMITH, WILLIAM L.] of S. C.   713
The pretensions of Thomas Jefferson to the Presidency examined . . . [Phil] 1796. O 2pts.: [64];
[2] 42 aa
—rptd. "Phocion's examination of the pretensions
of . . . Jefferson . . .," Phil 1797. a
Oliver Wolcott probably helped in the production of these Federalist pamphlets. For reply see
Federalist (The) containing some strictures . . .

SMITH, W[ILLIAM] L. G.   714
Fifty years of public life. The life and times of
Lewis Cass. N Y 1856. O 781 port a

SMITH, W[ILLIAM] L.G.   715
Life at the south; or "Uncle Tom's cabin" as it
is . . . Buf 1852. D [6] 13–519 7pls a
—Eng. ed. "'Uncle Tom's cabin' as it is; or, life at
the south," L 1852. D

[SMITH, WILLIAM PRESCOTT]   716
A history and description of the Baltimore and
Ohio rail road . . . Balt 1853. O 200 map 6ports a

SMITH, W[ILLIAM] ROY   717
South Carolina as a royal province . . . N Y
1903. O 20 441 + 2adv-p a

SMITH, WILLIAM RUDOLPH   718
Discourse . . . before the State Historical Society
of Wisconson . . . Madison 1850. O 53 a

SMITH, WILLIAM R[UDOLPH]   719
The history of Wisconsin. Vols. I & III [all].
Madison 1854. O 2v: 432; 443 a

SMITH, WILLIAM RUDOLPH   720
Incidents of a journey from Pennsylvania to
Wisconsin . . . in 1837. Ed. J. G. Gregory. Chi [ptd.
Wooster O] 1927. O 82 a 115copies ptd.
—L. P. issue, Wooster O. same date & collat. 35
copies ptd.

[SMITH, WILLIAM RUDOLPH]   721
Observations on the Wisconsin Territory . . . Phil
1838. D [8] 134 map[eng. by Young] b AA N NYP Y
Based on personal investigation; aside from
Lea's Notes, earliest extensive description of Wisconsin. The ten pages on "Iowa Territory" is the
first account of it under that desognation.

SMITH, WILLIAM R[USSELL], of Ala   722
The history and debates of the convention of the
people of Alabama . . . Montg 1861. O 336 339–
464 [12] aa

Principal authority on the momentous secession convention.

SMITH, WILLIAM R[USSELL], of Ala   723
Reminiscences of a long life. Vol. I [all]. *Wash* [1889]. O 376 8ports [of 9 called for, that of Levin Powell not issued] a

[SMITH, WILLIAM STEPHENS]   724
Remarks on the late infraction of treaty at New Orleans. *N Y* 1803. O 44 aa
Relative to Spain's suspension of American right to use this port.

SMITH, Z[ACHARIAH] F.   725
The history of Kentucky... *Louisv* 1886. O [28] 824 2maps 8pls a
—anr. ed., with adds., same impr. 1892. O [32] 916 2maps 8pls
—anr. ed., with add. chap., same impr. 1895. O [32] 848 3pls.
—rptd. *Louisv* 1901. O

SMITHWICK, NOAH   726
The evolution of a state; or, recollections of old Texas days... *Austin* [1900]. D [10] 9–354 5pls a
—rptd. *Austin* 1935, same collat.
After some lawless years, served through the War for Texas Independence and later as a Ranger. He was the blacksmith who forged the knife bearing Colonel Bowie's name.

SMOKY HILL EXPEDITION (THE).
Report and map of the superintendant and engineer of:... *See* Green, H. T., and Tennison, O. M.

SMYLIE, JAMES   727
Review of a Letter from the presbytery of Chillicothe to the presbytery of Mississippi, on the subject of slavery. *Woodville Miss* 1836. D 88 a
Refutation of Ohio's charge that slavery being an accursed thing, all slaveholders were essentially evil and should be denied church membership.

SMYTH, SIR JAMES CARMICHAEL   728
Précis of the wars in Canada, from... 1755 to ... 1814... *L* 1826. O [14] 186 aa
—rptd. *L* 1862. O [4] 7–216 + 4adv-p a

SMYTH (JOHN F. D.)   729
Narrative or journal of: taken prisoner by the rebels in 1775, lately escaped from them... [capt. t.] n.p. n.d. [*N Y*? 1778?]. O 24 b JCB NYP

SMYTH, JOHN F. D.   730
A tour in the United States... *L* 1784. O 2v: [24] 400; [12] 455. 2errata lvs. & 6p. of subscribers aa
—anr. ed. *Dub* 1784. D 2v: [16] 263; [10] 288 aa
—Fr. tr. abr. *P* 1791. 2v: [12] 206; [4] 272 a

SMYTH, PATRICK   731
The present state of the Catholic mission, conducted by the ex-Jesuits in North-America... *Dub* 1788. L 48 a
Arraignment of Bishop Carroll, of Maryland.

SMYTH, THOMAS   732
The battle of Fort Sumter... a discourse... *Columbia S C* 1861. O 37 aa
For similar title, *see* Fort Sumter.

SMYTH, THOMAS   733
The true origin of the Mecklenburg and national declaration of independence... *Columbia* 1847. O 29 a
Argues that both of these instruments were influenced by Presbyterian covenants in Scotland and Ireland.

SMYTHE, HENRY   734
Historical sketch of Parker county and Weatherford, Texas. *St L* 1877. D [8] 476 + 16adv-p at front aa

SNAKE INDIANS (THE).   735
Correspondence relating to the massacre of immigrants by: *Salem Ore* 1854. O 25 b OreH S

SNEDECOR, VICTORIA G.   736
A directory of Green county... embracing... sketch of the early settlement... *Mobile* 1856. O 74 + 24adv-p map[not issued in all copies] aa

[SNELLING, WILLIAM J.]   737
A brief and impartial history of the life and actions of Andrew Jackson... *B* 1831. 16° 216 port a

[SNELLING, WILLIAM J.]   738
Tales of the northwest; or, sketches of Indian life and character. *B* 1830. 16° [8] 288 aa
Based on the author's fur-trapping adventures in the upper Missouri region.

[SNELLING, WILLIAM J.]   739
Tales of travel west of the Mississippi. *B* 1830. 16° [16] 162 map aa
—rptd. *B* 1836. 16° 176 map
First American juvenile book on the trans-Mississippi region, giving account of its early explorers, wild tribes, etc.

SNIVELY, JACOB   740
Field notes of thirteen leagues of land... in Coryell county, Texas. *Wash* 1858. D 155 map aa

SNOW, CALEB H.   741
A history of Boston... *B* 1824–5. O 16pts, paged continuously to 400. [t-p bears date 1825, hence bound copies show that date only] 3maps 17pls aa

—ed. 2, with minor changes, *B* 1828. O 427 3maps 18pls a

SNOW (SAMUEL).   **742**
The exile's return; or narrative of: . . . banished to Van Dieman's Land for participating in the patriot war in Upper Canada, in 1838. *Clev* 1846. O 32 aa

[SNOW, WILLIAM P]   **743**
Southern generals, who they are .· . *N Y* 1865. O [6] 9–474 + 3adv-p 17ports a
—rptd., au. named, with adds., "Southern generals, their lives . . .," *N Y* 1866. O [6] 9-500 + 3adv-p 17ports
—anr. ed., "Lee and his generals," *N Y* 1867. O 500[incl. front.] + 2adv-p 17ports

SNOWDEN, JAMES R.   **744**
The Cornplanter memorial . . . *Harrisburg* 1867. O [2] 115 front. a

SNYDER, JOHN F.   **745**
Adam W. Snyder and his period in Illinois history . . . *Springfield Ill* 1903. D 392 [2] 2pls aa
—rptd. *Virginia Ill* 1906. D 437 5ports a
First edition was rigidly suppressed.

SNYDER, JOHN F.   **746**
Captain John Baptist Saucier at Fort Chartres in the Illinois, 1751–63. *Peoria* 1901. D 93 small ed. aa
—ed. 2, *Springfield Ill* 1919. D a
All known facts concerning the French officer who built this stronghold.

[SÖRGEL, ALWIN H.]   **747**
Für Auswanderungslustige! Briefe eines unter des Mainzer Vereins nach Texas Ausgewanderten . . . *Leip* 1847. D [6] 58 aa

SÖRGEL, A[LWIN] H.   **748**
Neuste Nachrichten aux Texas . . . *Eisleben* 1847. D 38 aa

SOJOURNER TRUTH.
Narrative of: *B* 1850. *See* Gilbert, Olive.

SOLA, A. E. I.   **749**
Klondyke; truth and facts of the new Eldorado. *L* [1897]. O [10] 102 30 maps and pls a

SOLANO COUNTY, CALIFORNIA
History of: *Oakl* 1879. *See* Munro-Fraser, J. P.

SOLDIER'S STORY [A] OF THE WAR . . .
See Bartlett, Napier.

SOLIGNAC, ARMAND DE   **750**
Les mines de la Californie. *Limoges* [1852]. O [8] 12–98 pl aa

SOLMS-BRAUNFELS, CARL, prinz zu   **751**
Texas. Geschildert in Beziehung auf seine geographische, socialen und übrigen Verhältnisse mit besonderer Rücksicht auf die deutsche Colonisation . . . *Frankf* 1846. O [10] 134 4maps b N Y
—Eng. tr. *Houston* 1936. Q [14 incl.port] 141 a 750 copies ptd.
By a leading German colonizer in Texas.

SOLON, OR THE REBELLION OF '61.
By Delphine. *See* Baker, Delphine P.

SOME . . .
Some account of the North-America Indians; their genius . . . *See* Smith, *Provost* Wm., *The speech of a Creek Indian* . . .

Some candid suggestions towards accomo-   **752**
dation of differences with America . . . *L* 1775. O 33 a

Some corrections of "life on the plains". *See* note to Hazen, William B, *"Our barren lands"*.

Some hints to people in power, on the   **753**
present . . . situation of our colonies in North America . . . *L* 1763. O 48 aa

Some observations of consequence . . .   **754**
occasioned by the stamp-tax . . . *Phil* 1768. O 80 a

Some observations on the . . . Indian natives of this continent. *See* Benezet, Anthony.

Some reason for approving of the Dean of   **755**
Gloucester's plan of separating from the colonies . . . *L* 1775. O 32 a

Some strictures on the late occurences in   **756**
North America . . . *L* 1766. O 24 aa

Some thoughts concerning domestic slavery . . . *See* Carey, John L.

Some thoughts on the method of improving . . . **the advantages which accrue to Great-Britain from the northern colonies.** *See* Mauduit, Israel.

SOMERS, ROBERT   **757**
The southern states since the war. *L* 1871. O [12] 286 [2] map a

SOMMER, J[OHANN] G.   **758**
Beschrijving der nieuwe Staten van Amerika . . . *Amst* 1828. O 2v: [10] 360; [6] 298 + 2dv-p 3pls aa
—Ger. ed., "Neustes gemälde von Amerika . . ." *Vienna* 1831–2. O 2v: 312; [6] 442 3pls a

SOMMER, K[ARL] V[ON]   **759**
Bericht über meine Reise nach Texas im Jahre 1846 . . . *Bremen* 1847. D [8] 84 pl a
Usually bound with following entry.

SOMMER, K[ARL] V[ON]   760
Nachtrag zu dem Berichte meiner Reise nach
Texas . . . *Braunschweig* 1847. D [8] 51 a

SOMMER, WILH[ELM]   761
Erindringer fra et ophold i Amerika. *Copenh*
1868. 16° 122 a

SONOMA COUNTY [CALIFORNIA].   762
History of: . . . *S F* 1880. Q [2] 5-717 pls aa

SONORA
Proyectos de leyes sobre colonizacion y comercio
en el estado de Sonora. *See* Paredes, M.

Report of the Sonora Exploring and   763
Mining Co. *Cin* 1856. O 43 4maps 4pls b Hn
NYP
—anr. issue, possibly earlier, ends on p44 & has
only 2maps & 4pls b G
—anr. ed. *Cin* 1857. O 24 map 3pls aa
—abr. ed. n.p. [1857]. Q 4 aa
—same, "2nd Annual Report," *Cin* 1858. O 16 aa
—same, "3rd Annual Report," *N Y* 1859. O 30
5maps & pls b
—same, "4th Annual Report," *N Y* 1860. O 18 aa
These reports, based on surveys made by C. D.
Poston, Herman Ehrenberg, *et al*, presented the
first reliable information on Arizona after the
Gadsden Treaty.

Rudo ensayo, tentativa de una prevencional
descripcion geographica . . . de Sonora. *See* Smith,
Buckingham.

Sonora filibustering expedition. Execution   764
of Col. Crabb and associates. Message from the
President communicating official information and
documents . . . [*Wash* 1858]. O 84 a
Crabb invaded Sonora with a handful of Cali-
fornians, intending to conquer that Mexican state
and annex it to the United States. All fell before a
firing squad.

SORENSEN, ALFRED R.   765
Early history of Omaha . . . *Omaha* 1876. O [4]
248 [incl. advs] front. port a
—rptd., with adds., *Omaha* 1889. O 342[incl.
initial blank lf & advs at end] double-p.pl

SORENSEN, AL[FRED R.]   766
"Hands up!" or the history of a crime. The great
Union Pacific express robbery. *Omaha* 1877. D
[8] 11–139[incl.pls] + 4adv-p b G LC
Most famous exploit of Sam Bass.

SORRELL, G. MOXLEY   767
Recollections of a Confederate staff officer. *N Y*
1905. O 315 port a
—ed. 2, *N Y* 1917. O 309 port

SOTO (HERNANDO DE).   768
Letter of: and memoir of Hernando de Escalante
Fontaneda. Tr. Buckingham Smith. *Wash* 1854.
Q 67 map 100 copies ptd., some on L. P. aa

SOULÉ, FRANK, et al   769
The annals of San Francisco . . . *N Y* 1855. O
824 2maps 6pls aa

SOULÉS, FRANCOIS   770
Histoire des troubles de l'Amérique anglaise . . .
L 1785. O 2v: [8] 335; [2] 12[mispaged 8] 9–224
223–233 [59] a
—enl. - & best - ed. *P* 1787. O 4v: [8] 380 + 3adv-p,
misnumb. 4–6; [4] 365; [4] 420; [4] 272 [43].
3maps aa
—Ger. tr. *Zürich* 1788. O 2v: [16] 510; 520. map a
In its completed form the best French history of
this war; Rochambeau aided in its preparation.

SOUTH   771
South (Our) and her future. By a southerner . . .
Augusta Ga 1862. D 34 [2] cover t. only aa

South (The) alone should govern the south . . .
See Townsend, John.

South [The] and the North . . . reply to   772
Lecture on the North and the South, by Ellwood
Fisher. By a South Carolinian. *Wash* 1849. O 32 a

South by west; or, winter in the Rocky mountains . . . *See* Kingsley, Rose G.

SOUTH CAROLINA   773
Address by the people of South Carolina to the
slave-holding states. *Charleston* 1860. O 50 a

An address to the freemen of . . . **South Carolina.**
By Cassius. *See* Burke, Aedanus.

An answer to Considerations on certain   774
political transactions of the province of South Caro-
lina . . . *L* 1774. O [4] 140 a
For the book eliciting this scurrilous reply, *see*
Leigh, Sir Egerton.

An appeal to the people of the northern and
eastern states on . . . **negro slavery in South Caro-**
lina. By a South Carolinian. *See* Seabrook, W. B.

An appeal to the state rights party of South
Carolina. *See* Calhoun, A. P., *et al*.

Considerations on certain political transactions of
the province of South Carolina . . . *See* Leigh, Sir
Egerton.

The correspondence between the commis-   775
sioners of South Carolina . . . **to the government at**
Washington . . . *Charleston* 1861. O 26 a

Debates . . . in the House of Representati-   776
ves of South Carolina on the constitution framed
for the United States . . . *Charleston* 1788. Q 55 b
BA PhiLL
—rptd., same impr. 1831. O [4] 95 a

A description of South Carolina. . . . *See* Glen,
Dr. James.

Documents ordered by the convention of   777
the people of South Carolina to be transmitted to the
President of the United States . . . *Columbia* 1832.
O 3pts in 1 : [2] 28; 15; 16 a
—anr. issue, "The report, ordinance and addresses
of the convention . . .," same impr., date &
collat.
—anr. ed. "Proceedings of the convention . . .
upon the subject of nullification . . .," *B* 1832. O 52
—anr. ed., with 1833 session added, "Journal of
the convention . . .," *Columbia* 1833.

A full state of the dispute betwixt the   778
Governor and the . . . Assembly . . . of South Carolina . . . [*L*] 1763. sm F [4] 78 a

An historical account of the rise and progress of
the colonies of South Carolina and Georgia . . . *See*
Hewatt, Alex.

Journal of the convention of the people of   779
South Carolina . . . Nov. 19, 1832, and again,
March 11, 1833. *Columbia* 1833. O 131 a
    The convention which in defiance of the Consti-
tution and Acts of Congress adopted the Nullification Ordinance.

Journal of the convention of the people of   780
South Carolina held in 1860–61 . . . with the reports,
resolutions . . . *Charleston* 1861. O 420 [1] aa
—issue 2, with S. C. & C. S. A. constitutions
added, same impr. & date. O 420 [1] 96 aa
    Appended matter of issue two was also publish-
ed separately.

Journal of the state convention of South   781
Carolina . . . *Columbia* 1852. O 45 aa
    Declares that this state has the right—and suffi-
cient cause—to secede from the Federal Union and
that she forbears from exercising such right only
from considerations of expediency. Marks the
evolution of States Rights opinion, from mild
nullification to the final break.

A letter from South Carolina . . . by a Swiss
gentleman . . . *See* Nairne, Thos.

A letter from a freeman of South Carolina to the
deputies . . . at Philadelphia. *See* Drayton, Wm. H.

The mission of South Carolina to Virginia. *See*
Memminger, C. G.

A narrative of the proceedings of the people of
South Carolina in the year 1719 . . . *See* Yonge,
Francis.

A new and accurate account of South Carolina
and Georgia. *See* Martyn, Benj.

Notes on the finances of South Carolina. *See*
Dessausure, Henry W.

Observations on the South Carolina me-   782
morial upon . . . duelling . . . By Postumus. n.p.
1805. D 32 a

The political annals of South Carolina. By a citizen. *See* De Bow, James D. B.

Practical considerations . . . relative to the slave
population of South Carolina. By a South-Carolinian. *See* Dalcho, Frederick.

Proceedings of the meeting of delegates   783
from the Southern Rights Associations of South
Carolina. *Columbia* 1851. O 31 a

A reminiscence of the bold . . . adventures   784
of small scouting parties . . . in South Carolina and
Georgia. *N Y* 1840. O 40 aa
    Extracted from Horry's *Life of Marion, q.v.*

Report of the committee appointed to   785
examine into the proceedings of the people of Georgia, with respect to the province of South-Carolina
and the disputes . . . between the two colonies.
Charles-Town S C 1736. Q 120 [1] b GaU H NYP
—rptd., same impr. & collat. 1737. b

A short description of South Carolina . . . *See*
Milligan, Georges.

A sketch of the history of South Carolina . . . *See*
Rivers, William J.

South Carolina in the revolutionary war . . . By
a Southron. *See* Simms, Wm. G.

South Carolina (The) Jockey Club. *See* Irving,
John B.

Three letters, written . . . under the signature of
a South Carolina planter . . . *See* Pinckney, Chas.

Topics in the history of South-Carolina. *See*
Rivers, Wm. J.

SOUTH-CAROLINIAN (A).   786
Letters by: Sketches of some Virginians. *Norfolk* 1827. 16° 89 a

SOUTH DAKOTA GUIDE (A).
See Reese, Lisle.

SOUTHAMPTON COUNTY [VA.]
Authentic . . . narrative of the tragical scene . . . in: *See* Warner, Saml.

SOUTHERN . . .   787
Southern and south-western sketches. Ed. by a gentleman of Richmond. *Rich* [1853?]. 16° 191 a

Southern business directory (The). *See* Campbell, John P.

Southern generals, who they are. *See* Snow, Wm. P.

Southern history of the war. Official reports   788
of battles as published by order of the Confederate congress . . . *N Y* 1864. O 578 a
For original Richmond editions from which this was compiled, *see Official reports.*

Southern passages and pictures. *See* Simms, Wm. G.

Southern slavery considered on general   789
principles . . . By a North Carolinian. *N Y* 1861. O 24 a
—rptd. twice, same impr., date & collat.

Southern spy (The), or curiosities of slavery in the south . . . *See* Pollard, Edw. A.

Southern state rights, free trade and anti-   790
abolition tract No. 1 [all]. *Charleston S C* 1844. O [2] 40 a

Southern states [The], their present peril . . . *See* Townsend, John.

SOUTHERN PACIFIC
First annual report to the Directors of the Southern Pacific railroad . . . *See* King, Thomas Butler.

SOUTHWEST
South-West (The). By a Yankee. *See* Ingraham, Jos. H.

Southwest historical series. Ed. by Hafen   791
and Bieber. *Glendale Calif* 1931–43. O 12v b N

Southwest revisited . . . letters of the se-   792
cond annual hunting expedition to Missouri, Kansas and the Indian Territory . . . *Easton Pa* [1875]. Q 39 aa

SOUTH-WESTERN BRAND BOOK . . .   793
Medicine Lodge [*Kas.*] 1883. D 3–84 b
Covers S. W. Kansas, Oklahoma and the Texas Panhandle. For 1884 issue *see* Payne, E. W.

[SOUTHWICK, SOLOMON]   794
Views of Ithaca and its environs. *Ithaca* 1835. O 44 a

SOUVENIR   795
Souvenir (The) of the lakes. *Det* 1831. 16° 38 [1] b BP ChiU

Souvenir (A) of the trans-continental   796
excursion. By one of the party. *Alb* 1871. O 92 pl a

SOWELL, A[NDREW] J.   797
Early settlers and Indian fighters of southwest Texas. *Austin* 1900. O [8] 844 12pls aa
Nearly all copies were either destroyed or damaged by fire.

SOWELL, A[NDREW] J.   798
History of Fort Bend county . . . *Houston* 1904. O [12] 373 2 ports Less than 100 copies ptd. aa

SOWELL, A[NDREW] J.   799
Incidents connected with the early history of Guadalupe county, Texas. *Seguin Tex* n.d. 16° 60 aa

SOWELL, A[NDREW] J.   800
Life of "Big Foot" Wallace. *Devine, Tex* 1899. O [4] 124 + wraps aa
—rptd., *Austin* [1957]. O same paginat 9ports [on 5 sheets] 7col-pls a

SOWELL, A[NDREW] J.   801
Rangers and pioneers of Texas . . . *San Antonio* 1884. D [2] 411 aa

SPAFFORD, HORATIO G.   802
A gazetteer of . . . New York . . . *Alb* 1813. O 334 [2] map 2pls a
—enl. ed. *Alb* 1824. O 620 map addenda slip pasted at end
—rptd. *Alb* 1837.
First gazetteer of this state.

SPAFFORD, HORATIO G.   803
A pocket guide for the tourist, along the line of the canals, and the interior commerce of New-York. *N Y* 1824. 18° 72 a
—ed., with adds., *Troy* 1825. 18° 89

SPALDING, ALBERT G.   804
America's national game . . . baseball . . . *N Y* 1911. O [20incl. front.] 542 6pls[5fold.] a

SPALDING, CHARLES C.   805
Annals of the City of Kansas: embracing . . . the trade and commerce of the great western plains . . . *K C* 1858. O 111 7pls c AA N NYP Y
—rptd. [*Columbia Mo* 1950] O 116

SPALDING, REV. H[ENRY] H.   806
The early labors of the missionaries of the American Board of Foreign Missions in Oregon . . . [Sen Exec. Doc 37] *Wash* [1871]. O 81 aa
Baseless and hysterical accusations, against

Jesuit missionaries and Hudsons' Bay Company officials, of their inciting Indian hostilities against American Protestants in Oregon; written in refutation of Brouillet's *Protestantism in Oregon*.

SPALDING, M[ARTIN] J.   **807**
Miscellanea . . . *Louisv* 1855. O 61 [3] 17–639 a
—6 other eds., last in 1885.

SPALDING, M[ARTIN] J.   **808**
Sketches of the early Catholic missions of Kentucky, 1787–1827. *Louisv* 1844. D [16] 308 a
—anr. issue, same collat., *Louisv & Balt* [1844].

SPALDING, M[ARTIN] J.   **809**
Sketches of the life . . . of . . . Benedict Joseph Flaget, first bishop of Louisville. *Louisv* 1852. D 406 port aa
—anr. issue, D 407 port aa
—Ger. tr. abr *Louisv* 1884 a

SPANGENBERG, AUGUST G.   **810**
Leben des Herrn Nicholaus Ludwig . . . von Zinzendorf . . . [*Barby*?] 1772–5. O 8pts: [20] 5–176; [6] 179–393; [4] 395–766; [4] 767–1158; [4] 1159–1602; [4] 1603–1852; [4] 1853–2080; [4] 2081–2258 [104] aa
—Eng. tr. *L* 1838. O [36] 511 port aa
Includes his visit to Pennsylvania and New York.

[SPANGENBERG, AUGUST G.]   **811**
Von der Arbeit der Evangelischen Brüder unter der Heiden. *Barby* 1782. O 168 aa
—Eng. tr. "An account of the manner in which the . . . church of the Unitas Fratrum . . . carry on their missions among the heathen," *L* 1788. O [12] 127 + adv-p aa
—Am. ed. *Phil* 1789.
Work among the Indians from Pennsylvania to Georgia.

SPANGLER (EDWARD).   **812**
Testimony . . . in the case of: tried for conspiracy to murder the president . . . [*Wash* 1865?]. O 66 [2] caption t. only aa

SPANISCHE REICH [DAS] IN AMERIKA.
Sorau 1763. Q 136 aa

SPANISH EMPIRE (THE) IN AMERICA.
Spanish Empire (The) in America . . . *See* Campbell, John.

SPARKS, A. W.   **813**
The war between the states, as I saw it . . . *Tyler Tex* 1901. O [8] 393 port a

SPARKS, JARED, ed.   **814**
Correspondence of the American revolution . . . letters of eminent men to George Washington . . . *B* 1853. O 4v: [8] 549; [4] 554; [4] 560; [4] 555 a 250copies on L. P. aa

SPARKS, JARED, ed.   **815**
The diplomatic correspondence of the revolution . . . *B* 1829–[30]. O 12v aa
—rptd. *B* 1854.
—new ed. *Wash* 1857. O 6v

SPARKS, JARED   **816**
The life of George Washington. *B* 1839. O [20] 562 10pls 2plans 2facs a
—innumerable Am. eds.
—Eng. ed. *L* 1839. O 2v: [12] 486; [8] 500. 2ports
—rptd. 1842.
—Ger. tr. *Leip* 1839. O 2v: [16] 560; [10] 533

SPARKS, JARED   **817**
The life of Gouverneur Morris . . . *B* 1832. O 3v: [12] 520; [6] 531; [4] 520 a
—Fr. tr. *P* 1842. O 2v: [12] 547; [4] 578 [2]

SPARKS, JARED   **818**
The life of John Ledyard . . . comprising selections from his journals, [etc.]. *C* 1828. O [12] 325 aa
—ed. 2, *C* 1829. D [12] 310 a
—Eng. ed. "Memoirs of the life and travels of John Ledyard . . .," *L* 1828. O [12] 428 a
—Eng. ed. 2, au. not named, "Travels and adventures of John Ledyard . . .," *L* 1828. same collat.
—rptd. *L* 1834.
—Ger. tr. *Leip* 1829. O [12] 350 front.

SPARKS, W[ILLIAM] H.   **819**
The memories of fifty years . . . chiefly spent in the southwest. *Phil* 1870. O 489 + 6adv-p a
—ed. 3, same impr. & collat., but port added, 1872.
—ed. 4, *Phil* 1882. O
Apparently there was no 2nd edition.

SPARRMAN, A[NDERS]   **820**
Resa till Goda Hoppsuden . . . *Stockh* 1783, 1802, 1818. O 3v: [16] 766; [12] 180; [4] 234 [4] 2maps, 26pls [incl. 2 clo specimens] c

SPEARS, JOHN R.   **821**
Illustrated sketches of Death valley . . . *Chi* 1892. D 226[incl.pls] a

SPECTATEUR AMÉRICAIN (LE) . . .
Amst 1784. *See* Mandrillon, Jos.

[SPEECE, CONRAD]   **822**
The mountaineer. ed.2[so called because previously ptd. in a periodical]. *Harrisonburg Va* 1818. 16° 240 [2] aa
—rptd. *Staunton* 1823. a

SPEECH
Speech [A] intended to have been delivered in the House of Commons, in support of the petition from the General Congress at Philadelphia. *See* Lee, Arthur.

Speech [A] on some political topics . . . intended to have been delivered in the House of Commons . . . *See* Goodricke, Henry.

Speech (A) to the people of England [on   823 the revolution in America]. *L* 1777. O [4] 34 a

SPEECHES   824
Speeches delivered by several Indian chiefs . . . *N Y* 1810. 16° 24 a
—rptd. same impr. & collat. 1812.

Speeches (The) in . . . **parliament** . . . **by**   825
several of the principal advocates . . . **in favour of the rights of America** [by Governor Johnstone, Mr. Cruger, et al] *N Y* 1775. O 72 a

SPEED, JOSHUA F.   826
Reminiscences of Abraham Lincoln . . . *Louisv* Morton & Co 1884. O 67 aa
—anr. ed., same collat. *Louisv* Bradley & Gilbert 1896. a

SPEED, THOMAS   827
The wilderness road . . . *Louisv* Filson Club 1886. Q 75 map a
First work on the first travel-route to Kentucky.

SPEER, JOHN   828
Life of General James H. Lane, "the liberator of Kansas" . . . *Garden City, Kan* 1896. O 336 pls a
—ed. 2, same impr. 1897. O 352 pls

SPELMAN, HENRY   829
Relation of Virginia. *L* 1872. sq 24° 58 [1] extra t. lf a 100copies ptd.
—anr. issue, without extra t., same impr. & date. Q 20 50copies ptd.
First printing of a 1609 manuscript.

SPENCE, IRVING   830
Letters on the early history of the Presbyterian church in America . . . *Phil* 1838. D 199 a

SPENCE, JAMES   831
The American union . . . with an enquiry into secession as a constitutional right . . . *L* 1861. O [16] 367 a
—eds. 2 & 3, same impr. & collat., 1862.
—ed. 4, rev., same impr. & date. O [16] 392 [1]
—Am. ed., from Eng. ed. 4, *Rich* 1863. D [24] 262
—Fr. tr. *P* 1862. O 434
—Ger. tr. *Leip* 1863. O 272
Most influential pro-Southern English book.

SPENCER, MRS. CORNELIA P.   832
The last ninety days of the war in North-Carolina. *N Y* 1866. D 289 a
—rptd., same impr., date & collat.

SPENCER, ELIHU   833
Pioneers of Outagamie county. *Appleton Wis* 1895. O 303 a

SPENCER, J[OHN] W.   834
Reminiscences of pioneer life in the Mississippi valley . . . *Davenport* 1872. O 73 port[not issued in all copies] aa
—rptd., with adds., "The early days of Rock Island . . .," *Chi* 1942. 16° [20] 315 [incl.front. & pls] a

SPENCER (O[LIVER] M.)   835
Indian captivity: a true narrative of the capture of: by the Indians in the neighbourhood of Cincinnati. *N Y* 1835. 16° 157[incl. 5pls] 4pls[not incl. in paginat.] aa
—anr. ed., probably prior to *N Y* ed., *Wash Pa* 1835. O 56 b N WisH
—other *N Y* eds.: 1836; 1842; 1846; 1847; 1848; 1852; 1854; and others a
—Eng. eds.: *L* 1836, 16° [38] 247; *L* 1842, 16° 282; *L* 1854, 16° [8] 278; *L* 1861, same collat. a

SPENCER, WILLIAM S., comp.
Davenport city directory . . . for 1855–6 . . . *Davenport* [1855]. *See* Davenport.

SPENCER, WILLIAM S., comp.   836
Rock Island directory . . . for 1855–6. *Rock Island* 1855. D 48 [4] preceded by 36adv-p aa
First directory of this city.

SPILMAN, T. E.   837
Semi-centenarians of Butler Grove township, Montgomery county, Ill. Also a brief history of the village of Butler. [*Butler* 1878]. D 143 a

SPLAWN, ANDREW J.   838
Ka-mi-akin, the last hero of the Yakimas. [*Port Ore* 1917]. O [14 incl.front.] 436 [6] a
—ed. 2, [*Port*] 1944. O [16 incl.front.] 500
Indian side of the Northwestern wars of 1855–8.

SPOFFORD, JEREMIAH   839
A gazetteer of Massachusetts . . . *Newburyport* 1828. D 348 map a
—ed. 2, rev., *Haverhill* 1860. 16° [4] 9–372 map

SPOONER, ALDEN   840
Brooklyn directory, for 1822. *Bklyn* 1822. D 71 map aa
First Brooklyn directory.

SPOONER, WALTER W.   841
The backwoodsmen . . . authentic accounts of early adventure among the Indians. *Cin* 1883. O 608 [incl. front. & 25pls] a

SPORTSMAN'S COMPANION (THE)   842
Sportsman's companion (The); or, an essay on shooting . . . By a gentleman who has made shoot-

ing his favourite amusement . . . in Great-Britain, Ireland and North-America. *N Y* 1783. O 90 [2] dd Y [of 2cops loc]
—ed. 2, *Burl N J* 1791. D 90 [2] c AA NYP
—rptd. *N Y* 1930. 200copies ptd. a
—ed. 3, *Phil* [1792]. b
First American work on shooting.

SPOTTS, DAVID L.   843
Campaigning with Custer [in the Washita campaign of 1868-9]. *L A* 1928. O [2] 215 map 13pls a of 800copies ptd., all but about 300 burned.

SPRAGUE, JOHN T.   844
The origin, progress and conclusion of the Florida war . . . *N Y* 1848. O 557 map 10pls aa
—anr. issue, identical, except no pls a

SPRATT, L. W.   845
A series of articles on the value of the Union to the south . . . *Charleston* 1855. O [4] 39 a

SPRENGEL, C. M.
See Sprengel, Matthias C.

SPRENGEL, M[ATTHIAS] C.   846
Allgemeines historisches Taschenbuch oder Abrisz der merkwürdigsten neuen Welt-Begebenheiten enthaltend für 1784 die Geschichte der Revolution von Nord-Amerika von C. M. [sic] Sprengel. [Engraved title reads: "historisch genealogischer Calender . . ."] *Berlin* Haude & Spener [1783]? 24° [2] 74 [6] 182 map 18pls eng. t. aa
—anr. issue, paginat.: [14] 182, otherwise same collat. aa
—anr. iss. paginat: [8] 182 + blank lf, same map & pls
—anr. issue, paginat.: [24] 74 [6] 182 map 18pls eng. t. aa
—rptd. "Geschichte der Revolution von Nord-Amerika," *Frankenthal* 1785. O [12] 272 map a
—same impr. 1788. same collat.
—Swed. tr. "Historia om Förenta Amerikas Sjelfständighet och Frihetskrig mot England . . .," *Örebro* 1810. D 250 2pls
For first edition, *see* below, *Ueber den jetzigen nordamericanischen Krieg.*

[SPRENGEL, MATTHIAS C.?]   847
Briefe den gegenwärtigen Zustand von Nord America. *Göttingen* 1777. D [8] 118 [1] a

SPRENGEL, MATTHIAS C.   848
Geschichte den Europäer in Nordamerica. Vol.I [all]. *Leip* 1782. D [14] 3–244 a

SPRENGEL, MATTHIAS C.   849
Ueber den jetzigen nordamericanischen Krieg . . . *Leip* 1782. O [4] 3–126[incl.tabs] aa
First German history of the Revolution. For later editions, *see* above, *Allgemeines historisches . . .*

SPRING, AGNES W.   850
Seventy years . . . history of the Wyoming Stock Growers Association. n.p. [*Cheyenne*] 1942. O 273 pls [incl fold facsm] a
—100 cops in clo bdg aa

SPRING, GARDINER   851
Memoirs of . . . Samuel J. Mills, late missionary to the southwestern section of the United States . . . *N Y* 1820. O [4] 9–247 a
—ed. 2, *B* 1829. 18° [8] 260
—rptd. *N Y* 1842. D
—Eng. ed., t. altered, *L* 1820. D [12] 214

SPRINGFIELD, ILLINOIS   852
Proceedings and debates of the American convention of cattle commissioners held at Springfield, Illinois. *Springfield* 1869. O 163 a

Springfield [Ill.] city directory . . . for 1855–6. *See* Hall, Edward H., pub.

SPRINGFIELD, MO.   853
Fragments of the early history of Springfield [Mo.]. [*Springfield Mo*] 1908. O 34 a

Springfield [Mo.] city directory for 1873–   854 4. Containing a historical sketch . . . *St L* 1873. O 180 aa

SPRINGFIELD, OHIO   855
Directory of . . . Springfield, Ohio containing . . . a brief history. *Springfield* 1852. 16° 212 aa

Sketches of Springfield [O.] . . . early set-   856 tlement . . . By a citizen. *Springfield* [1852]. 16° 48 [2] + 11adv-lvs a

Sketches of Springfield [O.] in 1856.   857 *Springfield* 1856. D 96 a

SPROAT, GILBERT M.   858
Scenes and studies of savage life. *L* 1868. D [12] 318 + 2adv-p front. aa
Largely concerned with Vancouver Island Indians, but includes account of the massacre of the crew of the "Boston" at Nootka, in 1803.

SPRUNT, JAMES   859
Chronicles of the Cape Fear river. *Raleigh* 1914. O [14] 594 aa
—ed. 2, same impr. 1916. O [12] 732 port 5maps a

SQUIER, E[PHRAIM] G.   860
The ancient monuments . . . of New Mexico and California. *N Y* 1848. O 26 map capt.t. only a

SQUIER, E[PHRAIM] G., and   861
DAVIS, E. H.
Ancient monuments of the Mississippi valley . . . [*Wash* 1848]. F [39] 306 48pls aa

—anr. issue, *N Y*, for the authors, same collat. and date aa

First thorough scientific investigation of the problem of the mound builders.

STACEY (NATHANIEL).   862
Memoirs of the life of: *Columbus Pa* 1850. O [6] 523 front. a

Pioneer life in New England, New York, Pennsylvania and Ohio.

STAEHLIN, [JACOB] VON   863
Das von den Russen in den Jahren 1765, 66, 67 entdekte nordliche Insel-Meer zwischen Kamtschatka und Nordamerika. *Stuttgart* 1774. O [8 incl. blank lf] 40 map aa
—Eng. ed., with adds., "An account of the new northern archipelago . . .," *L* 1774. D [20] 118 + 2adv-p map aa
—anr. issue differs only in having vignette on t-p aa
—Fr. ed. [P 1782]. D 2pts in 1: [2] 60; [2] 96 aa

Geographical information on what was then a little-known region. The map shows Alaska as an island and indicates routes of various eighteenth century expeditions through Bering's straits.

STAFFORD, MRS. MALLIE   864
The march of empire . . . sketches of California history . . . *S F* 1884. D 189 port aa

Went to California with her husband in 1854 and describes life there in the mines; later they went to Colorado.

[STAFFORD, MARSHALL P.]   865
A life of James Fisk . . . *N Y* 1868. D 300 5pls a
—rptd. same collat. & impr. 1871.
—anr. ed., with adds., same impr. 1872. D 325 [16] 6pls

STALKER, BEN   866
Life and adventures of "Buckskin Ben". Twenty years a cowboy. *Columbus* [1906?]. O 32 a

[STAMBAUGH, SAMUEL C.] et al   867
A faithful history of the Cherokee tribe . . . *Wash* 1846. O 40 aa

STAMER, W[ILLIAM]   868
The gentleman emigrant . . . life . . . in Canada, Australia and the United States. *L* 1874. O 2v: [8] 306; [6] 286 a

STANARD, MARY N.   869
Colonial Virginia . . . *Phil* 1917. O [18] 15–376 93pls a

STANART, STEPHEN H., pub.   870
Colorado brand book . . . *Denver* [1887]. D [10 incl.advs] 320 + 2adv-p b N

For earlier issues *see Colorado brand book.*

STANBERY, LON R.   871
The passing of 3D ranch. [Tulsa 1930?] O 92 cov.t. only aa

STANDISH, GEORGE   872
Adventures of a Baltimore trader on the coast of the Pacific. Pt. I[all]. *Phil* 1869. D 87 aa
—rptd. same impr. & collat., 1870. a

[STANFORD, THOMAS N.]   873
The citizens directory and strangers guide through the city of New York . . . Part I [description, history, etc.]. Part II [directory]. *N Y* 1814. 18° 446 2pls aa
—Part I only, issued separately, "A concise description . . .," *N Y* 1814. 18° 69 [incl. front.] map a

STANISLAUS COUNTY, CALIFORNIA.   874
History of: . . . *S F* 1881. F 254 pls b B CalS

STANLEY, CLARK   875
The life and adventures of an American cowboy . . . [*Providence*] 1897. O 42 + ads for snake-oil liniment a
—anr. ed. n.p., n.d. O 78
—new ed. "True life in the far west". Worcester [*ca.* 1898] O 78 [2]

If the medicine this fakir sold was as ineffective as his book the snakes died in vain.

STANLEY, BRIGADIER GENERAL   876
D[AVID] S.
Annual report [as commander of the Department of Texas]. [*San Antonio*?] 1886. D 40 lvs a

STANLEY (MAJOR-GENERAL   877
D[AVID] S.)
Personal memoirs of: *C* 1917. O [2] 271 aa
Services in the Civil war and on the plains.

STANLEY, E[DWARD G. S.] Earl of Derby 878
Journal of a tour in America, 1824–5. [*L*] 1930. O [6] 342 [1] 2fold.maps b 50copies ptd. LC N

This rather unfriendly observer, later England's Prime Minister and translator of Virgil, travelled through Ohio and Kentucky, by river to Natchez and Louisiana and by horseback through the deep South to Charleston.

STANLEY, E[DWIN] J.   879
Life of Rev. L. B. Stateler, or sixty-five years on the frontier . . . *Nash* 1907. D [18] 356 + adv-p 47pls a
—ed. 2, same impr. 1916. D [22] 356 + adv-p 47 pls.

Based on the journals of this pioneer Methodist itinerant in Kansas, Colorado and Montana.

STANLEY, EDWIN J.   880
Rambles in wonderland . . . the Yellowstone . . . *N Y* 1878. D [10] 7–180 + 10adv-p map 12pls a
—rptd., same impr. & collat., 1880.

STANLEY, F. [pseud.]
For books under this name *see* Crocchiola, Father Stanley.

[STANLEY, THOMAS]   881
A cool reply to A calm address . . . by Mr. John Wesley. *L* 1775. D 33 a
—ed. 2, same impr., date & collat.

STANLEY, WILLIAM M.   882
A mile of gold . . . adventures on the Yukon. *Chi* 1898. D 219 map a

STANSBURY, CHARLES F.   883
Klondike, the land of gold . . . *N Y* 1897. D 190 maps pls a

STANSBURY, HOWARD   884
An expedition to the valley of the Great Salt lake . . . *Phil* 1852. O 487 map 57pls + 2 fold.maps [in separate vol.] aa
—anr. issue [Sen. Exec. Doc. 3], "Exploration . . . of the valley . . .," same impr., date & collat., some copies ptd. by Armstrong in *Wash* a
—rptd. *Wash* 1853. [ptd. for H.R.] O 495 same maps & pls, but inferior impressions; anr. ed. *Phil* 1855.
—Eng. ed. *L* 1852. same collat. as *Phill* eds. a
—Ger. tr. *Stuttgart* 1854. sq 16° [8] 293 map a

STANSBURY, P[HILIP]   885
A pedestrian tour of two thousand three hundred miles . . . to the lakes . . . *N Y* 1822. D[12, 8] 13–274 + 6adv-p 9pls a

STANTON, G[ERRIT] S.   886
"When the wildwood was in flower" . . . fifteen years' experience . . . on the western plains. *N Y* [1909]. D 130 a
—rptd., t.slightly altered, same impr. [1910]. D 123 + 2adv-p.

STANTON, IRVING W.   887
Sixty years in Colorado. *Denver* 1922. O [4] 9–320 port aa

STANTON, ROBERT B.   888
Colorado river controversies. *N Y* 1932. O [48] 232 16pls a

STANTON, CAPT. W. S.   889
Tables of distances and . . . routes between the military posts in the Department of the Platte . . . *Omaha* 1877. D 39 + 4adv-p, 3tabs [2fold] b

STAPLES, THOMAS S.   890
Reconstruction in Arkansas. *N Y* 1923. O 451 a

STAPP, WILLIAM P.   891
The prisoners of Perote . . . *Phil* 1845 D 164 aa
—rptd. *Austin* 1935, same collat.

Contains the journal of his captivity as one of the members of the Texas expedition against Mier.

STARBUCK, ALEXANDER   892
History of the American whale fishery . . . *Waltham Mass* 1878. O 768 6pls aa
First appeared as Part IV, *Report of the U. S. Commissioner of Fish and Fishing*, [Washington 1875] aa

STARING, GEORGE E., comp.   893
Helena [Montana] directory . . . history . . . *Helena* 1884. O 116 + 2adv-l. [one front, one rear] aa

STARK, CALEB   894
Memoir . . . of Gen. John Stark . . . *Concord N H* 1860. O 495 port a
—rptd., same impr. 1877. same collat.
First issued with the 1831 Concord edition of Robert Rogers' *Reminiscences of the French war*.

STARK, JAMES H.   895
The loyalists of Massachusetts. *B* 1910. O [12] 509 + 4adv-p fold.map[in pocket] 46 pls a
—rptd., same impr. & collat., n.d.
Courageous portrayal of the Loyalist side of the Revolution.

STARKEY, JAMES   896
Reminiscences . . . Indian depredations. [*StP* 1891] O 25 a

STARR (BELLA), the bandit queen   897
Starr (Bella), the bandit queen, or the female Jesse James. *N Y* 1889. O 64 + 8adv-p b only a few cops kn
—rptd. *Austin* 1960. O [4] 64 + 10 adv-p 12 pls a
Published by the "Police Gazette," hence of dubious authenticity, but the pioneer presentation of a romantic legend.

STARR, EMMET   898
Cherokees "west", 1794–1839. *Claremore Okla* 1910. O 164 [incl. init. blank lf] aa
Largely a reprint of Cephas Washburn's *Reminiscences of the Indians*.

STARR, EMMET   899
Early history of the Cherokees . . . n.p. [*ca* 1917]. D 254 [14] 6maps 26pls[incl. Cherokee alphabet] aa

STARR, EMMET   900
History of the Cherokee Indians . . . *Okla City* 1921. O [4] 11–680 front. aa

STARR, HENRY   901
Thrilling events; life of Henry Starr . . . Cherokee Indian outlaw . . . [*Tulsa*] 1914. D 51 + cov. t. a

STARR, JEREMIAH 902
A California adventure and vision. *Cin* 1864.
16° 102 aa
Experiences of a California miner of 1850
chronicled in both verse and prose.

STARTLING FACTS
Startling facts for native Americans called
"Know nothings . . ." *See* Hutchinson, E.

STARTLING INCIDENTS
Startling incidents . . . of Osawotomy Brown's
. . . movements . . . *See* Moore, Wm. H.

STATE 903
State of the British and French colonies in Amer-
ica . . . *L* 1755. O [2] 150 [misnumb. 190] [map in
some copies] b
Treats of French encroachments on the Ohio,
with notices of Gist's surveys and Washington's
1753 expedition.

State [A] of the importations from Great-Britain
into the port of Boston . . . *See* Mein, John.

State [The] of trade in the northern colonies . . .
See Little, Otis.

State papers, on the negotiations and peace 904
with America, 1814 . . . *L* 1815. O [2] 86 a

STATISTICS
Statistics of the woolen manufactories in the
United States . . . *See* Goulding, John.

STEADMAN, E. 905
A brief treatise on manufacturing in the south.
Clarksville Tenn 1851. O 24 a

STEADMAN, E. 906
The southern manufacturer; showing the advantage of manufacturing the cotton . . . where it is
grown . . . *Gallatin Tenn* 1858. O 84 87–120 [incl.
2illus] a

STEAMBOAT DISASTERS
Steamboat disasters and railroad accidents in
the United States . . . *See* Howland, S. A.

STEARNS, CHARLES 907
The black man of the south, and the rebels . . .
N Y 1872. O 562 8pls a

STEARNS, CHARLES 908
Facts in the life of Gen. Taylor . . . bloodhound
importer . . . slave-holder, and the hero of the
Mexican war!! *B* 1848. D 36 a

STEARNS, CHARLES, ed. 909
Narrative of Henry Box Brown, who escaped
from slavery in a box . . . *B* 1849. D 90 [incl. front.
& covers] a

STEARNS, ISAAC 910
Right and wrong, in Mansfield, Mass . . .
account of the pro-slavery mob . . . *Pawtucket
Mass* 1837. O 61 a

STEARNS, SAMUEL 911
The American herbal, or materia medica . . .
Walpole 1801. D 360 a
First North American herbal.

STEARNS, SAMUEL 912
A short history of the treatment that [he] hath
met with in Massachusetts, since the . . . hostilities
between Great Britain and her colonies . . . by
reason of his loyalty . . . [*Worc*] 1786. D 24 a

STEARNS, WILLIAM 913
A view of the controversy . . . between Great-
Britain and the American colonies. A sermon . . .
Watertown 1775. O 33 aa

STEDMAN, C[HARLES] 914
The history of the origin, progress and termination of the American war. *L* 1794. Q 2v: [16] 399;
[16] 449 [14]. 15maps b
—rptd. *Dub* 1794. O 2v: [12] 446; [2, 5–19] 502
[26] aa
—Ger. tr. *Berlin* 1795. O 2v: [10] 3–504; [2] 564.
3maps a
British history of this war by a participant who
leaned heavily upon *The annual register* but what
contemporary historian didn't?

STEED (THOMAS). 915
The life of: . . . [*S L C* 1935]. O 43 wrap t. only a
Describes his trip, in 1850, from Nauvoo to Salt
Lake.

STEEDMAN, CHARLES J. 916
Bucking the sagebrush . . . *N Y* 1904. D [10]
270 9pls[by Russell] map 3ports aa

STEEL, DAVID 917
Steel's naval remembrancer . . . transactions of
the late war . . . *L* 1784. sm Q [4] 104 [3] a
—rptd., same impr. & collat. 1785.
—anr. ed., same impr. & date, sm Q [2] 96 89–102

STEELE, ASHBEL 918
Chief of the Pilgrims: or, the life and time of
William Brewster . . . *Phil* 1857. O 416 map 7pls a

STEELE, MRS. [ELIZA R.] 919
A summer journey in the west . . . *N Y* 1841. D
[6] 13–278 eng.t. a

STEELE, JAMES W. 920
The Klondike . . . gold fields of Alaska . . . *Chi*
1897. O 80 2 maps aa

STEELE, JAMES W. 921
The Oklahoma opportunity. Opening of the

Kiowa, Comanche and Apache reservations. *Chi* 1900. O 24 map aa

STEELE, JAMES W.   **922**
The sons of the border. *Topeka* 1873. O 260 aa
—ed. 2, "Frontier army sketches," includes 5 new sketches and omits 5 found in ed. 1. *Chi* 1883. D 329 + 6adv-p a
—rptd. "West of the Missouri" *Chi* 1885. D 313.

STEELE, JOHN   **923**
Across the plains in 1850 . . . *Chi* Caxton Club 1930. O [38] 234 map 7pls a 350 cops ptd.

STEELE, JOHN   **924**
In camp and cabin; mining life in California . . . *Lodi Wisc* 1901. O 81 b
—rptd., with Bidwell, "Echoes of the past," *Chi* Lakeside 1928. a

STEELE, JOHN   **925**
The traveler's companion through the great interior. A guide for the road to California . . . *Galena* 1854. 16° 54 d G Hn NYP Y [of 5copies known]

[STEELE, JOSHUA?]   **926**
An account of a late conference on the occurences in America. *L* 1766. O 40 a
Imaginary conference on Parliament's right to tax the colonies.

[STEELE, OLIVER G.]   **927**
The traveller's directory, and emigrant's guide . . . through . . . New York, Ohio, Indiana, Illinois, and . . . Michigan . . . *Buf* 1832. 18° 82 [2] aa 3 cops kn
—anr. ed., enl., "The western guide book . . .," *Buf* 1834. D 90 [2] aa
—rptd. *Buf* 1835. 18° 89 [2] a
—7 other eds., with map added, *Buf* 1836 to 1839 aa
—later eds.: 1843; 1846; [1847]. a
—ed. 16, with app. on Ore. & Calif. routes, *Buf* 1849. 18° 72 2maps b AA
—rptd., same impr. & collat., n.d. aa

STEELE, R. J., et al, [comp.]   **928**
Directory of the county of Placer, for . . . 1861: *see* Placer.

STEELE, W. R., ed.   **929**
The trans-continental. Vol. I[all]. [*N Y*] 1870. Q 12nos. [each 4p] aa

STEELE (ZADOCK).   **930**
The Indian captive . . . narrative of the captivity . . . of: . . . *Montp Vt* 1818. 16° 142 [2] aa

STEINER, BERNARD C., ed.   **931**
A history of the plantation of Menunkatuck and of the original town of Guilford, Connecticut . . . from the manuscripts of the Hon. Ralph Dunning Smyth. *Balt* 1897. O 538 a

STEINER, BERNARD C.   **932**
The life and correspondence of James McHenry . . . *Clev* 1907. O [10] 640 5pls a

STEINERT, W.   **933**
Nordamerika vorzüglich Texas im Jahre 1849. *Berlin* 1850. O [6] 280 [1] aa

STELLER, G[EORG] W[ILHELM]   **934**
Beschreibung von dem lande Kamtschatka . . . *Frankf* 1774. O 384 2maps 13pls b
Steller was one of the scientists accompanying Bering's second expedition.

STELLER, G[EORG] W[ILHELM]   **935**
. . . Reise von Kamtschatka nach Amerika mit . . . Bering. Ein Pendant zu dessen Beschreibung von Kamtschatka. *St Ptbg* 1793. O [4] 3–133 pl b NYP Y
—anr. ed. "Tagebuch seiner Seereise . . .," same impr. & date. O 2pts in 1: [4] 26; [5] 129–236
Most important contemporary account of Bering's second voyage.

STENHOUSE, T[HOMAS] B. H.   **936**
Les Mormons . . . et leurs ennemis . . . *Lausanne* 1854. D [12] 207 a

STEPHANISCHE LANDVERHUIZING (DE).
See Vehse, Karl Eduard.

[STEPHEN, JAMES]   **937**
War in disguise; or, the frauds of the neutral flags. *L* 1805. O [4] 215 a
—ed. 2, same impr. & date. O [8] 252
—two other Eng. eds.
—Am. ed. *N Y* 1806. O [6] 215
—ed. 2, same impr. & date. D [6] 9–228
Defends the illiberal English interpretation of neutral trade and her right to search our ships.

STEPHENS, ALEXANDER H.   **938**
A constitutional view of the late war between the states . . . *Phil* [1868–1870]. O 2v: [6] 3–655; [12] 5–827 [6]. map 16pls facs a
Most elaborate—and best—argument for the constitutional validity of the doctrine of state sovereignty and the right of secession.

STEPHENS, ALEXANDER H.   **939**
The reviewers reviewed; a supplement to "The war between the states" . . . *N Y* 1872. O 273 a

STEPHENS (MRS. ELLEN).   **940**
The cabin boy wife; or . . . surprising adventures of: who . . . made several passages up and down the [Mississippi] river . . . *N Y* 1840. O 24 [incl.front.] a
—rptd., same impr. & collat. 1841.
—anr. ed. "The afflicted and deserted wife . . .," *N Y* 1842. O 18 [incl. front.]
—rptd., same impr. & date. O 24 [incl. front.]

STEPHENS, L[ORENZO] DOW   **941**
Life sketches of a jayhawker of '49 ... [San José] 1916. O 68 6pls 300copies ptd. aa
Travelled to California through Death Valley with Manly.

[STEPHENS, THOMAS] of Ga.   **942**
A brief account of the causes that have retarded the progress of ... Georgia [etc.]. L 1743. O [28] 101 aa
Strictures on Oglethorpe's administration and on tract by author's father, No. 946

STEPHENS, THOMAS, pub.   **943**
Philadelphia directory, for 1796 ... Phil [1795]. D [20] 286 blank lf, 70 + 2adv-p map a
George Washington is listed. The final seventy pages has running title *A short account of Philadelphia*, which may have been also issued separately.

STEPHENS, WILLIAM   **944**
A journal of the proceedings in Georgia [Oct. 20, 1737-Oct. 28, 1741] ... L 1742. O 3v: [2] 480 [15]; [2] 508, 32 [16]; 391 [16] b GaU NYP Y
—rptd. *Atlanta* [1906] Q 2v a
Less than 100 copies seem to have been printed of any of the three volumes of the original edition. Volume 3 usually lacking, as all but 30 copies were destroyed by fire at the printer's; a portion only [p. 348–91] was reprinted, the same year, [see No. 945]. For reprint of appendix to volume 2, *see*, below, *A state of the province of Georgia* ... No. 946

STEPHENS, WILLIAM   **945**
Journal received February 4, 1741, by the Trustees for Establishing the Colony of Georgia. L 1742. O 44 aa
This is a reprint of p. 348–391 of the third volume of *A journal of the proceedings in Georgia*; issued in an edition of 100 copies to counteract the charges against the Trustees made in Tailfer's *A narrative of the colony of Georgia*.

[STEPHENS, WILLIAM]   **946**
A state of the province of Georgia, attested ... L 1742. O [4] 32 aa
Reprint of appendix to volume 2 of his *Journal of the proceedings in Georgia*. Stephens succeeded Oglethorpe as governor of this colony. For strictures on this *see* No. 942, above.

STEPHENSON, GEORGE M.   **947**
The political history of the public lands ... 1840–1862 ... B 1917. O 296 a

STEPHENSON, ISAAC   **948**
Recollections of a long life ... Chi 1915. D [2] 265 6pls a
Early Wisconsin lumbering, shipping and politics.

STEPHENSON, WILLIAM, comp.   **949**
Business directory of Cleveland ... with historical and statistical account. *Clev* 1848. O 224 fold. plan a

STERNE, LOUIS   **950**
Seventy years of an active life. L 1912. O [4] 191 port a small ed.
Helped build the first railroad in Texas, etc.

STEUBEN, FRIEDRICH W. A.   **951**
H. F. VON
Regulations for the order and discipline of the troops of the United States. Part I [all]. *Phil* Styner & Cist 1779. D 154 [9] 8fold.pls aa
—rptd. *Hart* Patten 1782. 16° 96 8pls aa
—anr. issue, *Hart* [1782?]. D 138 [6] 8pls aa
—rptd., same impr. Hudson & Goodwin [1782?]. D 90 [6] 8pls aa
—other eds.: *Phil* 1782, D 78 [4] 8pls; *Hart* Patten [1783], D 108 8pls; *B* 1784; *Phil* 1785, D [4] 151 [8] 8pls; *Phil* 1786, D 143; many later eds. a

[STEVENS, ABEL]   **952**
Sketches and incidents; or, a budget from the saddle-bags of a super-annuated itinerant. *N Y* 1844–[1845]. 16° 2v: 166; 198 a
—other eds., 2v in 1: *N Y* 1846; *N Y* 1847.
—rptd.: *Cin* 1847; *N Y* 1853; *Cin* 1854; *Cin* 1863.
For another edition, with altered title, *see* next entry.

[STEVENS, ABEL]   **953**
Sketches from the study of a superannuated itinerant ... *B* 1851. D 257 a

STEVENS, B[ENJAMIN] F., comp.   **954**
Facsimiles of manuscripts ... relating to America, 1773–1783 ... L 1889–98. F 25v c AA LC N NYP Y 200 sets ptd. [at a price of $ 5,000]
The 2107 facsimiles were issued in twenty-four portfolios; the index volume, added in 1898, collates: [4 7–30] 352 portrait.

STEVENS, CALVIN F.   **955**
A list of the post-offices in the United States ... *N Y* 1808. D [4] 92 a

STEVENS, CHARLES   **956**
Constitutional arguments indicating the rights and policy of the southern states. *Charleston S C* 1832. O 24 a

STEVENS, C[HARLES] A.   **957**
Berdan's United States sharpshooters ... *St P* 1892. O [24] 555 3pls a

STEVENS, HENRY   **958**
Historical ... notes on the earliest discoveries in America. *N Hav* 1869. O 54 6maps 75cops ptd aa

STEVENS, HENRY   959
Sebastian Cabot—John Cabot=0. *B* 1870. 16°
32 a

STEVENS, ISAAC I.   960
Address on the northwest. *Wash* 1858. O 56 aa
Conclusions drawn from the author's several
Pacific railroad surveys.

STEVENS (ISAAC I.)   961
A brief notice of the outrages committed by: . . .
Olympia 1856. O 32 b NYP WashU Y

STEVENS, ISAAC I.   962
Campaigns of the Rio Grande . . . *N Y* 1851. O
108 a

STEVENS ISAAC I.   963
A circular letter to emigrants desirous of lo-
cating in Washington Territory. *Wash* 1858. O
21 aa

STEVENS, ISAAC I.   964
Message of the Governor of Washington Territory, also the correspondence with the Secretary
of War. *Olympia* 1857. O [20] 406 [20] b NYP

STEVENS, I[SAAC] I.   965
Report of exploration of a route for the Pacific
railroad . . . from St. Paul to Puget sound. [*Wash*
1855]. O [12] 600 [15] a
For series [House Executive Document 129] of
which this formed a part, and which contained a
map [in three sheets] relating to this report, *see*
Pacific railroad explorations.

STEVENS, JAMES W.   966
An historical . . . account of Algiers; comprehending . . . detail of events relative to the American captives. *Phil* 1797. D 304 [6] + 2adv-p front.
aa
—ed. 2, *Bklyn* 1800. D 318 [2] + 4p subscriber's
names, front. a

[STEVENS, JOHN] 1749–1838   967
Documents tending to prove the . . . advantages
of rail-ways . . . over canal navigation. *N Y* 1812.
O 43 b AA Hn NYP
—rptd. *N Y* 1852. O [14] 46 aa
First American railroad book.

[STEVENS, JOHN] 1749–1838   968
Observations on government; including . . .
animadversions on Mr. Adams's Defence of the
constitutions . . . of the United States . . . *N Y*
1787. O 56 a
—Fr. ed. with adds. "Examen du gouvernement
d'Angleterre, comparé aux constitutions des États-
Unis . . .," *L* 1789. O [8] 291 a
Attributed also to William Livingston. One of
the earliest works on the Constitution.

STEVENS, JOHN H.   969
Personal recollections of Minnesota . . . *Minn*
1890. O [8] 432 [15] 7pls a

STEVENS, J[OHN] W.   970
Reminiscences of the civil war. *Hillsboro Tex*
1902. O 213 port aa

STEVENS, S[AMUEL] C.   971
Sketch of Dover, N. H. . . . *Dover* 1833. 16° 24 a

[STEVENS, W. H.]   972
Field notes, crossing the prairies from Atchison
. . . to Denver . . . *Phil* 1865. O 21 + wraps c Y
[of 2 cops loc]

STEVENS, WALTER B.   973
Through Texas . . . letters originally printed in
the . . . "Globe-Democrat." [*St L*] 1892. O 108 aa
rptd. 1893 a
Graphic picture of Texas, its cattle industry,
etc.; an interview with a *senora* who nursed Bowie
at the Alamo, and another with the last survivor
of Lafitte's band, a soldier of San Jacinto.

STEVENS, WILLIAM B.   974
A history of Georgia . . . *N Y* 1847–*Phil* 1859.
O 2v: [16] 494, 497–503; [2] 11–524. map 4pls
[fewer in some copies] aa

STEVENS POINT   975
Stevens Point, and the upper Wisconsin. Hand-
book of: . . . *Stevens Point* 1857. 16° 46 + 17adv-p
map a

STEVENSON, DAVID   976
Sketch of the civil engineering of North America . . . *L* 1838. O [4] 7–320 map 2pls 12diagrams a
—ed. 2, *L* 1859. D [14] 218 12pls
—Fr. tr. *P* 1839. O pls

STEVENSON, H.   977
A lecture on Mormonism . . . *Newcastle Eng*
1839. 18° 32 aa

STEVENSON, JOHN   978
Letters in answer to Dr. Price's two pamphlets
on Civil liberty . . . *L* 1778. O [16] 184 a
—ed. 2, *L* 1779. O

STEVENSON (COL. J[ONATHAN] D.)   979
Memorial and petition of: *S F* 1886. O 89 +
10add.p. inserted at center port 3views b G LC
NYP
This petition for a pension for services in the
Mexican war throws light upon the operations of
the petitioner's famous New York regiment.

STEVENSON, ROBERT L.   980
The silverado squatters. *L* 1883. D [8] 254 +
adv-p front. aa
—issue 2, bound in buckram, no adv-p a

Of the first issue, bound in figured cloth, there were two states of advertisements, one dated October, the other, November.

STEVENSON, ROGER 981
Military instructions for officers detached in the field . . . *Phil* 1775. D [16] 232 [4] 12diagrams[7 fold.] aa
First book carrying a dedication to Washington.

STEWARD, REV. JAMES [pseud.]
History of the discovery of America . . . *See* Trumbull, Henry.

STEWART, CATHERINE 982
New homes in the west. *Nashv* 1843. D 198 aa
Travelled in Mich. Ill. and Wis.

STEWART (COMMODORE CHARLES). 983
Biographical sketch, and services of: *Phil* 1838. O [4] 50 2pls a
—Ger. tr. *Phil* 1838. O 54 2pls

STEWART, GEORGE R. 984
Ordeal by hunger: the story of the Donner party. *N Y* [1936]. D [12] 328 12pls a

[STEWART, JAMES] 985
A letter to the Rev. Dr. Price, wherein his Observations on the nature of civil liberty . . . are candidly examined . . . *L* 1776. O 54 a

STEWART, JAMES 986
The total refutation . . . of Doctor Price; or, Great Britain successfully vindicated against all American rebels . . . in a second letter to that gentleman . . . *L* 1776. O [8] 88 a

STEWART, JAMES H. 987
Recollections of the early settlement of Carroll county, Ind. *Cin* 1872. D 372 2ports pl a

STEWART (JOHN).
The missionary pioneer, or a brief memoir of . . .: *See* Walker, Wm.

STEWART, MRS. LILIAN K. 988
A pioneer of old Superior. *B* 1930. D [4] 7–322 a
Story of Charles Kimball.

STEWART, SAMUEL 989
Travels and residence in the free states of America . . . or, the emigrants hand-book. *Belf* 1842. D 24 a

STEWART, W. M. 990
Eleven years' experience in the western states. *L* 1870. D 139 a

[STEWART, SIR WILLIAM DRUMMOND] 991
Altowan; . . . life and adventure in the Rocky mountains. By an amateur traveller. Ed. by J. Watson Webb. *N Y* 1846. D 2v: [4, 3–29] 25–255; 240. aa
Based on this baronet's sporting trips of 1832, 1838 and 1842, but probably actually written by Webb.

[STEWART, SIR WILLIAM DRUMMOND] 992
Edward Warren . . . *L* 1854. O [2] 724 dd G Ind U MoH Y
An atrociously written novel, but notable as incorporating this eccentric sportsman's personal experiences in the Rockies, from 1833 to 1837. Some copies were issued in two volumes, volume two beginning at page 371, preceded by an added title-page.

STEWART, WILLIAM F. 993
Last of the filibusters . . . *Sacr* 1857. O 85 b G LC NYP

STEWART (WILLIAM M.) 994
Reminiscences of: Ed. Geo. R. Brown. *N Y* 1908. O 358 port a

STICKNEY, CHARLES E. 995
A history of the Minisink region . . . in Orange county, N. Y. . . . *Middletown N Y* 1867. O [10] 211 a

STIDGER, FELIX G. 996
Treason history of the . . . Sons of Liberty . . . *Chi* 1903. D 246 [30] front. a

STIERLIN, L. 997
Der Staat Kentucky und die Stadt Louisville . . . *Louisv* 1873. O 234 51 [23] a

STIFF, EDWARD 998
The Texan emigrant . . . *Cin* 1840. O 368 [incl. 2illus] map aa
—enl. ed. "A new history of Texas . . .," *Cin* 1847. O 320, incl front, [16] aa
—anr. issue, *Cin* n.d. O [6 incl. front.] 9–336 [8] aa
—anr. issue, *Cin* 1847. O 246 incl. front. [74] 15 aa
—anr. issue, *Cin* 1847. O 244 incl. front. [74] 17 aa
—other eds.: 1848 [2issues]; 1849; 1857. a
One of the most objective accounts of Texas affairs issued in the days of the Republic, written largely from personal knowledge. Later editions included account of the war between Mexico and the United States.

STILES, EZRA 999
A history of three of the judges of King Charles I . . . secreted and concealed, in Massachusetts and Connecticut . . . *Hart* 1794. D 358 + adv-p errata slip pasted at end of text port 8numb. maps & pls [no No. 7 issued] aa
—issue 2, same collat., but no errata slip a

STILES, EZRA   1000
Literary diary, 1769–1795. Ed. F. B. Dexter.
N Y 1901. O 3v: [4] 665; [4] 573; [6incl.errata l.]
648 6pls a

STILES, HENRY R.   1001
History of ancient Wethersfield, Conn . . . *N Y*
1904. Q 2v: 995; 946 maps & pls a

STILES, HENRY R.   1002
The history of ancient Windsor, Connecticut.
N Y 1859. O [14] 922 2maps 2pls + suppl [*Alb*
1863]. O 134 a
—ed. 2, *Alb* 1863. O 2v: [14] 510; [2] 511–922.
2maps 2pls a
—ed. 3 - and best - *Hart* 1891–2. O 2v: [8] 950;
[10] 867. pls a

STILES, HENRY R.   1003
A history of . . . Brooklyn . . . *Bklyn* 1867–70. O
3v: [8]464;500;[8]501–982. errata l. 66maps & pls a
—also a special ed. of 80copies on thick tinted
paper
—vol. I only, rptd. *Alb* 1869.

STILES, HENRY R., ed.
Letters from the prisons . . . *See* "Account of
the interment . . ."

STILES, ROBERT   1004
Four years under Marse Robert. *N Y* 1903. O
368 a

STILLÉ, CHARLES J.   1005
Major-General Anthony Wayne and the Pennsylvania line . . . *Phil* 1893. O [10] 441 4pls a also
150copies on L.P.

STILLMAN, J[ACOB] D. B.   1006
Seeking the Golden fleece; a record of pioneer
life in California . . . *S F* 1877. O 352 4pls aa

STILWELL, B. F.   1007
Directory of . . . Oakland . . . for 1869. Also a
history of . . . Oakland . . . [*Oakland*] 1869. O 272
fold.map aa
First directory of this city.

STIMSON, A[LEXANDER] L.   1008
History of the express companies: and the origin
of American railroads . . . *N Y* 1858. O cover-t. +
40[incl. illus] a
—ed. 2, same impr. & date. O [8] 287 [incl. illus]
port
—rptd., same impr. & collat. 1859.
—anr. ed. "Express office hand-book and directory . . . being the history of the express business
. . .," *N Y* 1860. O 228 + interspersed adv-pp. aa
—best ed., with adds., "History of the express
business," *N Y* 1881. O [one issue has 468p, anr.
only 388p] 11pls aa

STINSON, H. C., and CARTER, W. N.   1009
Arizona . . . its history, etc. [*L A*] 1891. O 144 aa

STIPES, MILLARD   1010
Fort Orléans on the Missouri: its history . . .
Jamesport Mo 1906. D 67 a

STIPP, G. W.   1011
The western miscellany . . . *Xenia O* 1827. 16°
224 [incl.blank l. before text] d KyH WisH
Contains first separate printing of John Bradford's valuable *Notes on Kentucky*, originally appearing in a Kentucky newspaper, and reprinted by
the Grabhorn Press, San Francisco, 1932. [O
[16] 212 aa]

STIRLING, JAMES   1012
Letters from the slave states. *L* 1857. D [8] 374
map a

STIRLING, PATRICK J.   1013
The Australian and Californian gold discoveries
and their probable consequences . . . *Edin* 1853. D
[4 14] 13–279 diag. a
—Fr. tr. *P* 1853. D [4] 270 [2] pl

STITH, WILLIAM   1014
The history . . . of Virginia . . . *Wmsbg* 1747. O
[8] 256, 247–331 [40] b Hn NYP Y
—issue 2, line omitted above footnotes, p.21 & 27
of app. *Wmsbg* 1747. b AA HN JCB N
—issue 3, paginat. & other errors cor., *Wmsbg*
1747. [probably ptd 1753]. O [8] 304, 295–331
[39] b
—rptd. *N Y* 1865. O [16] 331 [34] a 250 copies ptd.
50 L.P. cops aa
—Eng. ed., sheets of 2nd Am. issue, *L* 1753. aa
—some copies made from sheets of 3rd Am. issue. aa
—index to above, *Rich* 1912. a

STOBO (MAJOR ROBERT).   1015
Memoirs of: *L* 1800. O 78 b JCB PaH
—anr. ed., ed. by N. B. Craig, *Pitt* 1854. 16° [6
incl.front.] 9–92 aa
The two editions were apparently printed from
slightly different manuscript copies.

STOCKELL (CAPT. WILLIAM).   1016
The eventful narrative of: . . . in the land and
naval service, and . . . whale fishery. *Cin* 1840. O
326 [1] 12pls a

STOCKING (ABNER).   1017
An interesting journal of: . . . detailing the
distressing events of the expedition against Quebec
. . . 1775. *Catskill* 1810. 18° 36 b BP[only copy
known]
Day-by-day narrative of Arnold's expedition.

STOCKING, MOSES   1018
History of Saunders county, Nebraska. [*Wahoo*

Neb? 1876]. O 42 + wraps[these are lacking in the only known copy, the front one probably serving as t-p] aa

STOCKTON (COM. ROBERT F.)
A sketch of the life of: *See* Bayard, Saml. J.

STOCKTON   **1019**
Stockton city directory, for . . . **1856** . . . with a historical sketch . . . *S F* 1856. D 96 aa

The Stockton directory, and emigrant's   **1020**
guide to the Southern mines. *Stockton* 1852. D [4] 140 [incl. advs] map b Hn LC

STODDARD, AMOS   **1021**
Sketches . . . of Louisiana. *Phil* 1812. O [8] 172 175–488 aa

STÖCKLEIN, JOSEPH, et al, eds.   **1022**
Allerhand So Lehr-als Geist-reiche Brief,Schrifften und Reis-Beschreibungen, Welche von denen Missionariis der Gesellschafft Jesu . . . *Augsburg* 1726–[1761]. F 5v [vol. V with 1/2 t. only] 29maps 8pls 15tabs b AA JCB NYP
Considered a German translation of *Lettres edifiantes* . . ., but includes much added material. Volume I only was reprinted, in 1728.

S[TOKES] (A[NTHONY]).   **1023**
A narrative of the official conduct of: . . . [*L* 1784]. O 112 b JCB GaU
Stokes was Chief Justice of Georgia under the royal government. His narrative covers the Revolutionary troubles in that province.

STOKES, ANTHONY   **1024**
A view of the constitution of the British colonies in North America . . . at the time the civil war broke out . . . *L* 1783. O [20] 556 a

[STOKES, C.]   **1025**
A few notes respecting the United States . . . *L* 1839. O 23 a

STOKES, I. N. P.   **1026**
The iconography of Manhattan island, 1498–1909. *N Y* 1915–28. Q 6v many pls [some colored] c AA N NYP Y 360sets ptd.
—anr. issue, on Jap. vell. d NYP 42sets ptd.
Most elaborate and comprehensive history of New York City.

STONE, ARTHUR L.   **1027**
Following old trails. *Missoula* 1913. O 304 [incl.pls] front. aa
Little known information on men and events in early Montana.

STONE, ASA   **1028**
Narrative of Amos Dressner; with . . . letters

from Natchez . . . relating to the treatment of slaves. *N Y* 1836. D 42 a

STONE (ELD[ER] BARTON WARREN).   **1029**
The biography of: . . . by himself . . . *Cin* 1847. D [10] 404 port a
—rptd. 4 times by 1853. same collat.

STONE, CHARLES P.   **1030**
Notes on the state of Sonora. *Wash* 1861. O 28 a

STONE, EDWIN M., ed.   **1031**
The invasion of Canada in 1775 . . . *Prov* 1867. Q [8 7–24 48] 47–104 map 2ports tab 2errata slips a
A reprint, on L. P., of R.I. Hist. Colls., v.6.

STONE, EDWIN M.   **1032**
Our French allies . . . in the . . . revolution. *Prov* [1883]. O [32] 632 fold.plan 3pls a

[STONE, WILLIAM H.]   **1033**
Twenty-four years a cowboy and ranchman in southern Texas . . . *Hedrick Okla* [1905]. D 268 [incl. pls] aa few cops kn
—rptd. *Norman, Okla* 1959.

STONE, HENRY L.   **1034**
"Morgan's men". A narrative of personal experiences. *Louisv* 1919. O 36 port a

[STONE, MRS. LUCINDA H.]   **1035**
An episode in the history of Kalamazoo College . . . *Kalamazoo* 1868. D 171 a

STONE, WILLIAM L.   **1036**
The campaign of . . . Burgoyne, and the expedition of . . . St. Leger. *Alb* 1877. D [12] 9–461 fold. map 8pls a

STONE, WILLIAM L., tr.   **1037**
Letters of Brunswick and Hessian officers during the . . . revolution. *Alb* 1891. O [6, 5-10] 9–258 [11] 2pls a
Translated from a contemporary German periodical.

STONE, WILLIAM L.   **1038**
The life and times of Red Jacket . . . *N Y* 1841. O [12 incl. eng. t.] 484 3pls a
—ed. 2, index & memoir of au. added, *Alb* 1866. O 510 5pls 500 copies ptd & 75 on L. P. a

STONE, WILLIAM L. and   **1039**
EDWIN M.
The life and times of Sir William Johnson. *Alb* 1865. O 2v: [16] 9–555; [16] 544. port a Also 50 copies on L. P. aa

STONE, WILLIAM L.   **1040**
Life of Joseph Brant . . . *N Y* 1838. O 2v: [36] 425 [59]; [6, 3–8] 537 [66]. 8pls & plans a

—anr. issue has facs & 10additional supplementary pp. in vol. I
—2 other eds. with same date on t-p, carry on spines later dates [1839 & 1841].
—anr. ed. *Cooperstown* 1841. O 2v: [21 incl. eng. t.] 425 [56]; [10] 537 [66]. 7pls & plans
—rptd. 1844; 1845; 1846; 1847; *Buf* 1851.
—best ed. with index added, *Alb* 1864. O 2v: [5–32] 500; [8] 602 [601–630]. 7pls & plans a 50 copies on L. P. aa
—rptd., same collat., 1865. a
—abr. ed. "Border wars of the American Revolution," *N Y* 1843. 16° 2v: 384; 381 + 1adv-p; frequently reissued.
Best biography of an American Indian.

STORIA
Storia della Rivoluxione dell' America Inglese . . . *See* Dubuisson, Paul U.

STORIES   1041
Stories of the Indians during the revolution . . . *N Y* 1836. O 32 fold.pl a

[STORK, WILLIAM]   1042
An account of East-Florida . . . *L* [1766]. O [6] 90 aa
—ed. 2, with Bartram's journal added, *L* [1766]. O [6] 90 [8] 70 b
—ed. 3, enl., slight change in t., *L* 1769. Q [12] 40 [12] 36 3maps & plans b GaU N NYP Y
—ed. 4, same collat., *L* 1774. aa

STORK, WILLIAM   1043
Extract from the account of East Florida . . . *L* 1766. D [2] 39 aa
Summarizes Stork's *Account of East-Florida*, with the *Observations* of Denys Rolle added.

STORM, GUSTAV   1044
Studier over Vilandsreiserne . . . *Copenh* 1888. O [4] 80 a
—Eng. ed. "Studies on the Vineland voyages . . .," *Copenh* 1889. O [2] 80
Critical investigation, corroborating the authenticity of Icelandic sagas.

STORNOWAY, L.   1045
Yosemite, etc. *S F* 1888. O 98 map a

STORROW, SAMUEL A.   1046
[Narrative of a tour . . . on the shores of lake Superior . . . in a letter to Maj. Gen. Jacob Brown]. No t-p. n.p. [1818?]. O 39 c WisH Y [of 4copies known]

STORY, JOSEPH   1047
Commentaries on the Constitution . . . *B* 1833. O 3v: [26] 494; [2] 555; [2] 776 a
—ed. 2, *B* 1851. O 2v: [20] 734; [2] 632
—ed. 3, *B* 1858. O 2v: [36] 735; [2] 702
—rptd. several times; also tr. into Fr. & Sp.

STORY (THOMAS).   1048
A journal of the life of: . . . *Newcastle Eng* 1747. F [8] 768 8 a
Prominent Pennsylvania Quaker who travelled to various parts of the country.

STOTLER, JACOB   1049
Annals of Emporia and Lyon county, Kansas, 1857–1882 . . . *Emporia* [1898?]. O 100 a

STOUGHTON, JOHN A.   1050
"Windsor farmes" . . . *Hart* 1883 Q [10] 9–150, front., fold. plan, facsims. a

STOUT, F. E.   1051
Rube Burrows; or life, exploits and death of the bold train robber. *Aberdeen Miss* 1890. D 78 aa

STOVALL, PLEASANT A.   1052
Robert Toombs . . . *N Y* [1892]. O [8 7–8] 396 port a

STRACHEY, WILLIAM   1053
The historie of travaile into Virginia . . . Now first edited from the original manuscript. *L* Hakluyt Soc 1849. O [8] 36 [4] 203 map facs 5pls aa

STRAHORN, MRS. CARRIE A.   1054
Fifteen thousand miles by stage . . . *N Y* 1911. O [28] 673 5pls a
—rptd., same collat., 1915.

STRAHORN, ROBERT E.   1055
The hand-book of Wyoming and guide to the Black hills . . . *Cheyenne* [*Chi* ptd] 1877. O 272 [incl.advs.] aa

STRAHORN, ROBERT E.   1056
The resources and attractions of Idaho Territory . . . *Boise* [ptd. at *Omaha*] 1881. O 88 + 8adv-p map a

STRAHORN, ROBERT E.   1057
The resources of Montana Territory . . . *Helena* [ptd *Omaha*] 1879. O 80 [incl 3adv-p] aa
—ed. 2, *K C* 1881. O 205 a

STRAHORN, ROBERT E.   1058
To the Rockies and beyond . . . *Omaha* 1878. O 142 map a
—ed. 2, *Omaha* 1879. O 216 map front.
—ed. 3, *Chi* 1881. O 213 map front.

[STRALEY, WILLIAM WILSON]   1059
Pioneer sketches, Nebraska and Texas. *Hico Tex* 1915. O [6] 58 pls a

[STRANG, JAMES J.]   1060
Ancient and modern Michilimackinac . . . [*St James Mich*] 1854. O cover t. + 48 dd LC WisH Y N 600 cops ptd.

—rptd. same date & collat.[but on paper obviously later], *ca* 1894, aa
—anr. issue, also same date [but later] and with only 40p a
—other eds.: *St Ignace Mich.* 1885, O 52; [Burlington. Wis] 1894, O 48
—rptd. *Maekinac* 1959.

STRANG, JAMES J.   **1061**
The book of the law of the Lord. *St James Mich* [1851]. D 80 dd G Y [only copies known]
—rptd. [*K C* 1927?]. same collat. a
—ed. 2, enl. [*St James* 1856]. D 17–336 Made from salvaged sheets of the book as printed, but awaiting a t-p & Strang's preliminary pages, when a mob destroyed the press c NYP Y
—anr. ed., same sheets with t-p & 6preliminary p.added, n.p. [*ca* 1878]. b There were several issues with this collat., and a later one with t-p & 7preliminary p. [*Lansing* 1890]? aa
—also, n.p. [1920]. D [8] 17–336 aa
Intended by Strang to replace *The book of Mormon* among his schismatic followers.

STRANG, JAMES J.   **1062**
Facts; ancient American records. [*St James Mich*] 1844. O 44 b UCHO

STRANG, JAMES J.   **1063**
The prophetic controversy . . . [*St James Mich* 1855]? O 49 errata lf b
—anr. ed. "The prophetick discussion," [*St. James* 1856]? Q 44 errata lf b
—rptd. n.d. [before 1900]. O 35 pl a
—anr. issue, n.d. O 38
An earlier pamphlet of sixteen pages on this question—as to Strang's right of succession to Smith—entitled *The diamond*—was issued with imprint of Voree, Wisconsin, and date 1848 [probably ptd. at St. James after 1850]. It was reprinted in fifteen pages, and later in twenty pages. aa

STRANGE, JAMES C. S.   **1064**
Journal . . . of the commercial expedition from Bombay to the north-west coast . . . *Madras* 1928. Q 63 map a
First fur-trading voyage to these regions of which an adequate record survives.

STRANGER   **1065**
Stranger, traveller, and merchant's guide through the United States. *Phil* 1825. D [4 7–10] 156 map fold.tab aa

STRANGER'S GUIDE (THE)   **1066**
Stranger's guide (The) through the United States and Canada. *Edin* 1838. 16° 143 3maps a

STRATEN-PONTHOZ, AUGUSTE VAN DER, baron   **1067**
Recherches sur la situation des émigrants aux États-Unis . . . *Brus* 1846. O [8] 158 map aa

—Ger. eds: "Forshungen über der Auswanderer . . .," *Augsburg* 1846, D [8] 196 a; with adds., *see* Berghaus, Heinrich K. W.
—Dutch tr. *Utrecht* 1847. O [4] 124 map
The Baron's two years' tour of investigation carried him through Ohio, Indiana, Michigan, Illinois, Wisconsin, Iowa and Missouri.

STRATTON, R[OYAL] B.   **1068**
Life among the Indians . . . captivity of the Oatman girls among the Apache and Mohave Indians *S F* 1857. D [4] 183 d AA N Y
—ed. 2, new t.: "Captivity of the Oatman girls," *S F* 1857. D 231 b
—rptd. *Chi* 1857. aa NYP Y
—ed. 3, enl. *N Y* 1858. D [2] 5–290 [2] 3pls a
—rptd. *N Y* 1859.
—rptd. *S F* Grabhorn 1935. O [12] 209 pls 550 copies ptd.

STREAKS OF SQUATTER LIFE.
By "Solitaire." *See* Robb, John S.

STRECKFUSS, G. F.   **1069**
Der Auswanderer nach Amerika, oder treue Schilderung der Schicksale . . . *Zeitz* 1837. D [4] 124 a

STRECKFUSS, G. F.   **1070**
Sittengemälde und Landesansichten aus den Vereinigten Staaten . . . *Zeitz* 1837. D [14] 156 a

STREET, FRANKLIN   **1071**
California in 1850 . . . Also . . . description of the overland route, from the Misssouri river to Sacramento . . . *Cin* 1851. D 88[incl. front. and 2 other pls] c N NYP S Y

STREETER, FLOYD B.   **1072**
Prairie trails and cow towns. *B* [1936]. O 236 12pls aa

STREETER, S. F.   **1073**
Papers relating to the early history of Maryland. *Balt* 1876. O 315 a
Contains Capt. Thomas Young's *Relation of a voyage* . . . 1634.

STRICKLAND, W[ILLIAM], of Yorkshire   **1074**
Observations on the agriculture of the United States . . . *L* 1801. O [6] 3–74 a
See also Martinez de Yrujo y Tacon for an auxiliary report.

STRICKLAND, WILLIAM, C. E.   **1075**
Reports on canals, railways . . . *Phil* 1826. oblong F [6] 51 errata slip 72 drawings on 58pls, some fold. b AA NYP Y

STRICKLAND, WILLIAM, C. E., et al   **1076**
Reports, specifications and estimates of public works in the United States . . . *L* 1841. O [4] 168 +

atlas F [4] 31drawings [on 40 sheets] b ColumbiaU
LC

STRICTURES

Strictures on . . . A friendly address to all reasonable Americans . . . *See* Lee, Chas.

Strictures on a pamphlet, entitled, "An examination of the president's reply to the New-Haven remonstrance . . ." *See* Bishop, Abraham.

Strictures [The] on the Friendly address examined . . . *See* Barry, Henry.

Strictures upon the Declaration of the congress at Philadelphia . . . *See* Hutchinson, Thos.

Strictures . . . upon the three executive departments of the . . . United States . . . By Massachutensis. *See* Leonard, Daniel.

STRINGFIELD, THOMAS   1077
Captured by the Apaches . . . *Hamilton Tex* [1911]. O 65 aa

STROBEL, P[HILIP] A.   1078
The Salzburgers and their descendants . . . *Balt* 1855. D 308 2pls a
—rptd. *Athens Ga* 1953. D [8] 318 front.

STROCK, DANIEL   1079
Pictorial history of King Philip's war . . . *B* [ptd *Phil*] 1851. O 448 eng.t. port a
—anr. issue, same date & collat. *Hart*
—rptd. 1852; 1853; 1854.

STRONG (JAMES CLARK).   1080
Biographical sketch of: . . . *Los Gatos Cal* 1910. D [6] 106 [incl.port.] a Small ed.
A Californian of 1850, member of Washington Territory's first legislature and active in Northwestern Indian wars.

STRONG, MOSES M. [comp.]   1081
History of the Territory of Wisconsin . . . *Madison* [1855]. O 637 aa
—rptd. same impr. & collat 1875 a

STRONG, THOMAS M.   1082
The history of . . . Flatbush, in Kings county, Long-Island. *N Y* 1842. D 178 [1] map 5pls a

STRONG, WILLIAM E.   1083
A trip to the Yellowstone . . . *Wash* 1876. Q 143 2maps 7ports 7views b

[STROTHER, DAVID H.]   1084
Virginia illustrated: containing a visit to the Virginia Canaan . . . *N Y* 1857. O [4] 8–300[incl. illus] a
—rptd: *N Y* 1859; 1872; with t. altered *Chapel Hill* 1959.

STROUD, JOSEPH G.   1085
Memoires of old western trails in Texas longhorn days . . . [*Williston N D*] 1932. O [6] 93 [3] a

[STRUBBERG, FRIEDRICH ARMAND]   1086
Amerikanische Jagd-und Reiseabenteuer aus meinem Leben in den westlichen Indianergebieten. Von Armand. *Stuttgart* 1858. O [6] 460 24pls aa
—rptd. "Frontierleben . . .," *Hannover* 1868. 12° 3v aa
—Dutch tr. *Utrecht* 1860. O 2v a
—Eng. tr. "The backwoodsman, or life on the Indian frontier," ed. Wraxall. *L* 1864. D [4] 428 12pls [incl. pictorial t.] aa
—rptd. *L* Ward Lock [*ca* 1880]. D pls
—Am. ed. *B* 1866. D 302 12pls[incl.pictorial t.] a
—Fr. tr. "Mes aventures, etc." *P* 1880 D 2v a
Florid narrative, possibly based on actual experiences in the Rio Grande region.

[STRUBBERG, FRIEDRICH ARMAND]   1087
Bis in die Wildniss. *Breslau* 1858. O 4v: [8] 312; [6] 343; [6] 266; [6] 264 a
Romanticised autobiography.

[STRUBBERG, FRIEDRICH ARMAND]   1088
Friedrichsburg, die colonie des deutschen Fürsten-vereins in Texas. Von Armand [pseud.] *Leip* 1867. D 2v: [14] 244; [8] 236 [1] a

[STRUBBERG, FRIEDRICH ARMAND]   1089
Scenen aus den Kämpfen der Mexicaner und Nordamerikaner. *Breslau* 1859. 16° [4] 288 a
Two tales, based on the author's life in Texas.

STRYKER, WILLIAM S.   1090
The battles of Trenton and Princeton . . . *B* 1898. O [16] 514 [2] 4plans front. a

STUART, MRS. A. H. H. [comp.]   1091
Washington Territory: its soil, climate . . . *Olympia* 1875. O 64 aa

[STUART, ANDREW]   1092
Notes upon the south western boundary line of . . . Lower Canada and New Brunswick, and the United States . . . *Quebec* 1830. O 58 a

[STUART, ANDREW]   1093
Succinct account of the treaties . . . relating to the boundary line between . . . Lower Canada and New Brunswick and the United States . . . [*L* 1838]. O [2] 206 2maps diagram [capt.t.only] aa

STUART, CHARLES B.   1094
The naval and mail steamers of the United States. *N Y* 1853. Q 216 + 22adv-p 35pls a
—ed. 2, same impr. & date. Q 216 [4] + 22 adv-p 36pls
—ed. 3, same collat, with press notices, *N Y* 1855

STUART, CHARLES B.   **1095**
The naval dry docks of the United States, *N Y*
1852. Q [4] 126 94 24pls aa
—ed. 2, same impr. & date. Q [4] 113 84 + 14adv-p
24pls a
—rptd. same impr. 1855. F [12] 9–113 [14] +
adv-p 24pls
—ed. 4, same impr. 1870.

STUART, GRANVILLE   **1096**
Forty years on the frontier . . . *Clev* 1925. O 2v:
272; 265 [incl.pls] aa
—rptd. *Glendale Cal.* 1960. O 2v in 1 a

STUART, GRANVILLE   **1097**
Montana as it is . . . *N Y* 1865. O 175 map[by de
Lacy] dd N Pn Y
The most cherished Montana book. 1500 copies
were printed, of which 300 contained the map,
however all but 150 copies were destroyed by fire.
The correct issue of the map bears copyright date
1865 and was lithographed by Rae Smith; there
were three other issues [all rare]: one lithographed
by Smith but without copyright; another, lithographed by Friedenwald; and a third, engraved in
St. Louis by J. Hutawa.

STUART, JAMES   **1098**
Refutation of aspersions on "Stuart's Three
years in North America." *L* 1834. D 108 a
The aspersions—printed herein—were made by
Major Norman Pringle in an Edinburgh paper;
after Stuart's *Refutation* appeared they were issued
separately, with additions, in a sixteen-page
pamphlet.

STUART, JAMES   **1099**
Three years in North America. *Edin* 1833. D
2v: [10] 496; [8] 580. map a
—ed. 2, rev., *Edin* 1833. D 2v: [12] 526; [8] 544.
map
—ed. 3, same collat., *Edin* 1833.
—Am. ed. *N Y* 1833. D 2v: 334; 337
—Dutch tr. *Gorinchem* 1835–[1836]. O 3v: [16]
404; [8] 382; [8] 386 3eng. t. 2 pls

STUART, JOHN, of Ark   **1100**
A sketch of the Cherokee and Choctaw Indians.
Little Rock 1837. O 42 b JCB GeorgetownU Y
[only cops loc]

STUART, JOHN, of Va.   **1101**
Memoir of Indian wars . . . [*Rich* 1833]. O
35–68 aa
Separate printing from the first and only volume
of the *Virginia Historical Collection*.

STUART, JOSEPH A[LONZO]   **1102**
My roving life . . . *Auburn Calif* 1895. D 2v: [10
incl. 2blank lvs.] 203; [8 incl. 2blank lvs.] 229.
20maps & pls b N Y 50 copies said to have been
ptd.

Includes account of an 1849 overland trip and
life in the California mines.

STUART, ROBERT   **1103**
The discovery of the Oregon trail . . . Ed. Philip
A. Rollins. *N Y* 1935. O [138] 392 10maps & ports aa
—rptd. *N Y* n.d. [1936] a
First English publication of this diary of a trip
from Astoria to St. Louis, in 1812–13, on which
South Pass was discovered and the Oregon Trail
established. A French version, *Voyage de l'em-
bouchére de la Columbia . . .*, appeared in volumes
ten and twelve, *Nouvelles annales des voyages*, 1821.

STUART (WILLIAM) the first . . .   **1104**
counterfeiter of connecticut.
Sketches of the life of: *Bridgeport* 1854. sq 16°
223 port a

STUART-WORTLEY, EMMELINE
See Wortley, Emmeline Stuart.

STUCKLÉ, HENRI   **1105**
Voies de communication aux États-Unis . . . *P*
1847. O [8] 470 [1] map 6tabs aa

STUDER, HERMANN   **1106**
Auswanderung nach hoch-Texas. II Theil.
Zurich 1855. O 32 b [Forms part of the Ger. ed. of
Victor Considerant's "Au Texas," *q.v.*]

STUDLEY, R. P., pub.   **1107**
The Springfield [Mo.] city directory for 1873–4.
Containing a historical sketch . . . *St L* 1873. O
180 aa

STULLKEN, G.   **1108**
My experiences on the plains. *Wichita* 1913. D
36 front. a

STURGES, J. A.   **1109**
Illustrated history of McDonald county, Missouri. [*Pineville*] 1897. D 344 aa
Annals of a community partaking of the lawless
character of the neighboring Indian Territory;
hence distinguished for bank robberies and
murders.

STURGIS, THOMAS   **1110**
Common sense view of the Sioux war . . .
Cheyenne 1877. O 52 aa
—rptd. *Waltham Mass* 1877. O 45 aa

STURGIS, THOMAS   **1111**
The Ute war of 1879 . . . *Cheyenne* 1879. O 26 aa
—anr. issue, without impr. [*Cheyenne* 1879]. aa

[STURGIS, WILLIAM]   **1112**
Examination of the Russian claims to the northwest coast of America. [*B* 1822]. O 31 [capt.t.only] a
Separate printing of an article originally appearing in the *North American Review*.

STURGIS, WILLIAM   **1113**
The Oregon question . . . *B* 1845. O 32 map a
Authoritative review of British and American
claims written by one who as a youth had made
several trading voyage to the Northwest coast.

STURTEVANT, P[ELEG]   **1114**
The Harrisburg directory; with a sketch of [its]
first settlement . . . *Harrisburg* 1839. D 48 aa
First directory of this city.

SUBALTERN (A)   **1115**
Subaltern (A) in America . . . campaigns of the
British army at Washington and New Orleans . . .
Phil 1833. D 266 a
Attributed erroneously to George R. Gleig,
author of a similar work, *A narrative of the cam-
paigns of the British army* . . ., [*q.v.*]

SUBLIME (THE)
Sublime (The) and ridiculous blended . . . *See*
Van Dusen, Increase McG.

SUCCINCT
Succinct review (A) of the American contest . . .
By Zero. *See* Ramsay, Allan.

Succinct view (A) of the missions established . . .
by the Church of the Brethern . . . *See* La Trobe,
Benj.

Succinct view (A) of the origin of our colonies . . .
See Bollan, Wm., *The freedom of speech and
writing* . . .

SUCHARD, PHILIPPE   **1116**
Un voyage aux États-Unis . . . il y a quarante
ans . . . *Neuchatel* 1868. D 231, aa
Travels through Ohio, etc., in 1824, by this Swiss
observer. It appeared originally in German as
"Mein besuch Amerika's . . ." in 1824.

SUCKOW, B. W., comp.   **1117**
Madison [Wis.] directory for 1866, with a history . . . by J. W. Smith. *Madison* 1866. D 175 +
suppl. lf betw. p 78–79 and 23adv-p [7 in front,
16 in rear] aa
For separate printing of history *see* Smith,
John Y.

SUGGS (CAPTAIN SIMON).
Some adventures of: . . . *See* Hooper, Johnson J.

SUITE
Suite des observations sur la géologie des États-
Unis . . . *See* Maclure, Wm.

SULLIVAN, A. M.   **1118**
A visit to the valley of Wyoming, with narrative
of the massacre . . . *Dub* 1865. O 33 4-col pls aa

SULLIVAN, SIR EDWARD [R.]   **1119**
Rambles and scrambles in North and South
America. *L* 1852. D [6] 5–424 errata slip a
—ed. 2, *L* 1853. D 403
Includes his hunting trip in the Sioux country.

SULLIVAN, G. W.   **1120**
Early days in California . . . Vol. I[all]. *S F*
1888. O [8] 7–230 ports a

SULLIVAN, JAMES   **1121**
The history of land titles in Massachusetts. *B*
1801. O 392 aa

SULLIVAN, JAMES   **1122**
The history of . . . Maine. *B* 1795. O [8] 421
map aa
First general history of this state.

SULLIVAN, JAMES   **1123**
Observations upon the government of the
United States . . . *B* 1791. O 55 aa
For reply *see* Ford, Timothy.

[SULLIVAN, JOHN H.]   **1124**
Broncho John . . . first trip up the trail . . . [*Valparaiso Ind* 1905]. D 32 + cover t. a
—anr. ed. "Life and adventures of Broncho John:
his first trip up the trail," [same impr. 1908]. D 24
A drive of five thousand head from San Antonio
to Fremont, Nebraska.

[SULLIVAN, JOHN H.]   **1125**
Life and adventures of Broncho John. His second
trip up the trail. n.p., n.d. D 32 [incl. front wrap] a

[SULLIVAN. JOHN H.]   **1126**
Life and adventures of a cow-boy; or, valuable
hints on raising stock . . . *N Y* [1885?]. D 16 a
—anr. ed. "Life and adventures of the genuine
cowboy," [*N Y*? ca 1900]. D 36 cover t. only
—rptd., t. altered, [*Valparaiso Ind* 1905]. D 40
cover t.only

SULLIVAN, MAURICE S., ed.   **1127**
The travels of Jedediah Smith . . . including the
journal of the great American pathfinder. *Santa
Ana Calif* 1934. O [16] 200 map 12pls aa
First printing of Smith's own account of his
entrance into the fur trade in 1822, his journey up
the Missouri to the Rockies, his trip to Salt Lake
and across the Mojave desert and up the Sacramento in 1827–8.

SULLIVAN, T[HOMAS] R.   **1128**
Letters against the immediate abolition of
slavery . . . *B* 1835. O [4] 51 a

SULLIVAN, W. JOHN L.   **1129**
Twelve years in the saddle . . . on the frontiers of
Texas . . . *Austin* 1909. O [6] 284 13pls aa

Ranger activities against marauders red and white.

[SULLIVAN, WILLIAM]   1130
Familiar letters on public characters, and public events . . . 1783–1815. *B* 1834. O [12] 468 a
—ed. 2, app. omitted, same impr. & date. D [24] 345
—anr. ed., with adds., "The public men of the revolution . . .," *Phil* 1847. O 463 port

SULLIVAN'S CAMPAIGN
Sullivan's campaign, in . . . western New York. Notices of: *See* O'Reilly, Henry.

SUMMARY
Summary observations and facts . . . from late and authentic accounts of Russian and other navigators . . . *See* Travers, De Val.

Summary (A) of the first planting . . . of the British settlements . . . *See* Douglass, Wm.

Summary view (A) of America . . . the result of observations . . . during a journey in the United States. By an Englishman. *See* Candler, Isaac.

Summary view (A) of the rights of British America . . . *See* Jefferson, Thos.

Summary view (A) of the United States   1131
. . . *N Y* 1835. 24° 54 a

SUMMER ON THE LAKES, IN 1843.
See Ossoli, Sarah M.

SUMMER'S VACATION (A)
Summer's vacation (A); or, a trip to the west . . . *See* Kimball, Chas.

SUMMERFIELD, CHARLES, [pseud.]
The desperadoes of the south-west . . .; [also] The lives . . . of the desperadoes of the south-west . . .; [also] The rangers and regulators of the Tanaha . . . *See* Arrington, Alfred W.

SUMMERHAYES, MRS. MARTHA   1132
Vanished Arizona. *Phil* 1908. D 270 22pls a
—ed. 2, *Salem* [1911]. D 319 26pls
—rptd., ed. Quaife, *Chi* 1939. 16°

SUMMERS, LEWIS P.   1133
History of southwest Virginia, 1746–1786, Washington county, 1777–1870. *Rich* 1903. O 921 [incl. 3pls] a
—ed. 2—and best, "Annals . . .," *Rich* 1929. O [10] 1757 3maps pls aa

SUMNER, CHARLES   1134
Speech on the cession of Russian America. *Wash* 1867. O 48 fold.map[not in all copies] a

SUMNER, CHARLES A.   1135
'Cross the plains. A narrative lecture. *S F* [1875]. O 27 2 maps aa

SUMNER, WILLIAM G.   1136
The financier and the finances of the American revolution. *N Y* 1891. O 2v: [10] 309; [8] 330 a
—rptd. *N Y* 1892. same collat.

[SUMNER, WILLIAM H.]?   1137
Address to the reader of the documents relating to the Galveston Bay and Texas land company . . . *N Y* 1831. O 38 69 b G NYP LC Y
See also, Texas. Emigrant's guide to:

SUNDERLAND, LA ROY   1138
Mormonism exposed and refuted. *N Y* 1838. 18° 54 aa
—anr. ed., with longer t. & no. au. named, *N Y* 1842. 16° [4] 3–64 a
This early attack on the Church was answered by Parley P. Pratt's *Mormonism unveiled.*

SUNNY SOUTH [THE]
Sunny south [The]; or, the southerner at home . . . *See* Ingraham, Jos. H.

SUPREMACY (THE)   1139
Supremacy (The) of the British legislature over the colonies, candidly discussed. *L* 1775. O [4] 38 a

SURBY, RICHARD W.   1140
Grierson's raids and Hatch's sixty-four day's march. *Chi* 1865. D 396 9 pls a
—rptd: *Alb* 1866; *Wash* 1897.

SURIA (TOMAS).   1141
Journal of: of his voyage with Malaspina to the northwest coast . . . *Glendale* 1936. O 44 8pls a 100copies ptd.
Translation of an unpublished manuscript. For official account *see* Malaspina.

SURRATT (JOHN H.), the conspirator.   1142
Private journal and diary of: Ed. by Dion Haco. *N Y* Brady [1866]. D [2] 11–104 a
Has all the ear-marks of being bogus.

SUSQUEHANNAH.
A description of the Susquehannah river. *See* Condy, Jonathan W.

Report of sundry commissioners appointed   1143 to view and explore the Susquehannah and Juniata rivers; the river Delaware; the river Schuylkill. *Phil* 1791. O 27 a
For similar work, *see* Howell, Reading.

Susquehanna case (The).   1144
[*Norwich Conn* 1774]. Q 24 aa
Intended to accompany the *Report* of Connecti-

cut commissioners relating to the boundaries between Connecticut and Pennsylvania, published in 1774. This dispute over the Wyoming Valley was later decided in Pennsylvania's favor by the Continental Congress.

Susquehannah title (The) stated and examined . . . *See* Bidwell, Barnabas.

SUTCLIFF, ROBERT   1145
Travels in some parts of North America . . . *York Eng* 1811. D [12] 293 6pls a
—Am. ed. *Phil* 1812. D [10] 289 front.
—Eng. ed. 2, *York Eng.* 1815. D 312 6pls
—anr. Eng. ed. *L* 1817 D 325

SUTHERLAND, [JAMES], and   1146
McEVOY, [HENRY N.], comps.
Atchison city directory . . . for 1859–60. *St L* 1859. O 83 aa
First directory of this city.

SUTHERLAND, JAMES, pub.   1147
Atchison city directory, for 1860–61.*Indp* [1860]. O 98[incl.ads & front.] + adv-p on end sheet [pasted down on recto of rear cover] & adv-card of "Massasoit House" pasted on inserted lf [between p. 16–17 c G KasH Y [of 4copies known]
Contains, in addition to information on this city, a six-page guide to the Colorado gold fields.

SUTHERLAND, [JAMES] & McEVOY,   1148
[HENRY N.], comps.
Kansas City directory . . . *St L* [ptd. *Indp*] [1859]. O [8 11–18] 99 aa

SUTHERLAND, [JAMES]   1149
Leavenworth city directory . . . for 1859–60 . . . and a brief sketch of the city. [*St L* 1859]. O [24] 198 + interspersed adv-pp. aa
—same, for 1860—61, *Leavenworth* [ptd. *Indp* 1860]. O 207 aa
In the 1860 issue, H. M. Moore's sketch of the city was replaced by Ward Burlingame's account of its prospects resulting from Pike's Peak excitement.

[SUTHERLAND, MRS. REDDING]   1150
Five years within the Golden Gate. *L* 1868. D [10] 315 a

SUTHERLAND, THOMAS A.   1151
Howard's campaign against the Nez Perce-Indians, 1877. *Port Ore* 1878. O 48 + 4adv-p b G OreH Y
By Howard's aide-de-camp.

SUTHERLAND, TH[OMAS] J.   1152
Three political letters . . . *N Y* 1840. O 64 aa
Anti-Harrison campaign pamphlet; severely critical of his military operations on the western frontier.

SUTHERLAND, WILLIAM   1153
The wonders of Nevada . . . guide to the great silver mines . . . *Virginia Nev* 1878. D 32 fold.map aa

SUTTER (JOHN A.)   1154
The diary of: *S F* Grabhorn 1932. D [26] 56 [2] 3pls 3facs 500copies ptd. aa

SUTTER, JOHN A.   1155
New Helvetia diary . . . 1845–8. *S F* Grabhorn 1939. Q [28] 138 [8] map 2pls facs aa 950copies ptd.

SUTTER'S . . . SETTLEMENT   1156
Sutter's Fort Ross settlement . . . n.p. [*ca* 1865]. O 32 b

SUTTER COUNTY [CALIF.].   1157
History of: . . . *Oakl* 1879. Obl. F [6] 9–127 pls aa

SVALANDER, CARL E.   1158
Tillförlitliga underrättelser om Nord-Amerikas förenta stater . . . En illustrerad handbok för emigranter . . . *Götheborg* 1853. D [8] 3–168 maps & pls a

SVIN'IN [or SWININ], PAVEL   1159
[PAUL] P.
Opyt zhyvopisnavo puteshestviya po severnoi Amerike . . . *St Ptbg* 1815. 16° [8] 219 6pls[5 fold.] b LC NYP Y
—anr. ed., same impr. 1818. 16° [8] 170 6fold. pls aa
—Dutch tr. *Haarlem* 1818. O [8] 127 aa
—Ger. ed. "Malerische Reise durch Nord-amerika," *Riga* 1816. O [6] 170 aa
—Eng. tr., in part, "Picturesque United States . . .," *N Y* 1930. Q [18] 46 [4] 52pls a
First description of the United States by a Russian traveller; based on wide travels extending from 1811 to 1813.

SWAIN, DAVID L., et al   1160
Early times in Raleigh . . . Ed. by R. S. Tucker. *Raleigh* 1867. D 41 22 [12] + 10 adv-p 3fold.maps a

SWALUE, E[DELHARDUS] B., ed.   1161
Brieven uit en over de Vereenigde Staten . . . *Schoonhoven* 1853. O [14] 304 map 5pls a

SWAN, ALONZO M.   1162
Canton [Ill.]; its pioneers and history . . . *Canton* 1871. O 164 a
By the son of the original proprietor, who laid out the town in 1825.

[SWAN, ELIZA]   1163
An affecting account of the tragical death of Major Swan, and of the captivity of Mrs. Swan . . . *B* [1815]. D 24 b AA LC N Y

SWAN, JAMES G.   **1164**
The northwest coast; or, three years' . . . in Washington Territory. *N Y* 1857. D 435 + 4adv-p map pl aa

SWANTON? or SWARTON?,   **1165**
[MRS.] HANNAH
Swanton? or Swarton?, [Mrs.] Hannah, the Casco captive . . . *B* 1837. 16° 63 aa
—ed. 2, same impr. 1839. 16° 60 a
—ed. 3, same impr. n.d. 16° 72

SWARTZELL, WILLIAM   **1166**
Mormonism exposed . . . a journal of a residence in Missouri . . . *Pekin O* 1840. O 48 b MoH NYP [of 3 copies known]

SWASEY, WILLIAM F.   **1167**
The early days and men of California . . . *Oakland* 1891. O [10] 9-406 port 2pls aa
Authentic memoirs of one who came to California in 1845, worked for Sutter and was with Fremont's little army on its march to Los Angeles.

SWAVING, [JUSTUS G.]   **1168**
Swaving's reizen en lotgevallen . . . *Dordrecht* 1827. O 2v: [32] 314; [6, 9–20] 456 [2] aa
Narrative of personal experiences in America.

SWEARINGEN (GEORGE).   **1169**
Life and confessions of: *Hagerstown* 1829. O 83 plan port aa

SWEDBERG, JESPER   **1170**
America illuminata, skrifwen och utgifwen . . . *Skara* Moeller [1732]. O 163 [5] b N NYP Y
By the father of Emanuel Swedenborg, who, as bishop of the Swedish churches in America, received reports from church leaders on conditions, both civil and ecclesiastical, in Pennsylvania and New Jersey.

SWEDBERG [or SVEDBERG],   **1171**
JOHAN D.
Dissertatio gradualis de Svionum in America . . . *Upsala* [1709]. O [6] 32 b N NYP PaH
On Swedish colonies on the Delaware.

SWEENY, LIEUT. THOMAS W.   **1172**
Military occupation of California . . . [*Wash*] 1909. O 47 map pls aa

SWEET, E. N.   **1173**
History of Cuming county, Nebraska. *Lincoln* 1876. O 52 a

SWEET, GEORGE H.   **1174**
Texas: her early history . . . *N Y* 1871. O 160 [incl. 7adv-p] a

SWEET, WILLIS   **1175**
The mining camps of Leadville and Ten-Mile. *K C* 1879. D 83 map aa

SWETLAND (LUKE).   **1176**
A very remarkable narrative of: . . . *Hart* [1785? 1790?]. O 16 c Y [only known copy]
—anr. ed., with adds., *Waterville N Y* 1875. O 40 12 copies ptd [cover t. only] aa
Captured by Senecas, in Pennsylvania, 1778; rescued by Sullivan's army in 1779. *See* also under Merrifield, Edw.

SWETT, MORRIS   **1177**
Fort Sill: a history . . . *Ft Sill Okla* 1921. O 66 cover t. only aa

SWETT, S[AMUEL]   **1178**
Historical and topographical sketch of Bunker Hill battle . . . [*B* 1818]. D 104 [plan called for not issued] a
—ed. 2, enl., "History of Bunker Hill battle . . .," *B* 1826. O 58 30 map
—ed. 3, same impr. 1827. O 58 34 map [ports called for not issued]

SWETT, S[AMUEL]   **1179**
Notes to his sketch of Bunker-Hill battle. *B* 1825. O 24 a
—eds. 2 & 3, same impr. & date, respectively 30 & 34p., were issued separately and also with eds. 2 & 3 of his larger work.

SWIFT, CHARLES F.   **1180**
History of Old Yarmouth [Mass.]. *Yarmouth Port* 1884. O 281 [2] map 9ports facs a

[SWISHER, MRS. BELLA FRENCH]   **1181**
The American sketch book. *Lacrosse* [& *Green Bay*] 1874–6. O 3v *see* note aa
Started as a monthly, devoted to Wisconsin local history; volume I in six numbers, volume II in three numbers. For volume III *see* next entry. Revived later, and continued for a time, at Austin, Texas.

[SWISHER, MRS. BELLA FRENCH]   **1182**
History of Brown county, Wisconsin. *Green Bay* 1876. O 330 2foldmaps 10pls aa
Complete history of the Green Bay region, next to Mackinac most important point in the old Northwest. Includes reminiscences by the first white child born in Wisconsin. Forms volume III of *The American sketch book*, above.

SWISHER, JAMES   **1183**
How I know . . . adventures in Utah, Arizona, New Mexico and California. *Cin* 1880. O 384 port a

SWITZLER, WILLIAM F.   **1184**
Illustrated history of Missouri . . . *St L* 1879. O [18] 601[incl.pls] a

SYDNEY (ALGERNON) [pseud.]
The letters of: in defence of civil liberty . . . *See* Leigh, Benj. W.

SYKES, C. P.   **1185**
Prospectus and reports of the Calabasas Land and Mining Company . . . Pima county, Arizona Territory. *S F* 1878. O 52 fold.map pls a
Territorial Indian wars, etc.

SYLVESTER, HERBERT M.   **1186**
Indian wars of New England. *B* 1910. O 3v: [6] 5–528; [4] 3–626; [4] 3–703 a

SYMMES, JOHN CLEVES   **1187**
On the first settlement of the Northwest Territory.[*Cin* 1796]. Pamphlet. No copy known Evans 31261 b

SYMMES, JOHN CLEVES   **1188**
To the respectable public. [capt. t.] [*Trenton* 1787]. 24° 30 b AA
—rptd., same yr., 16° 16 aa
First publication concerning the Ohio colony on the Miami.

SYMMES, THOMAS   **1189**
Lovewell lamented . . . sermon occasion'd by the fall of . . . Capt. John Lovewell . . . in the late heroic action at Piggwacket. *B* 1725. O [16] 32 d AA Hn NYP
—ed. 2, with minor changes, "Historical memoirs of the late fight . . .," *B.* same collat. & date. d AA Hn NYP Y

—anr. ed., with textual changes & adds., "The history of the fight of the intrepid Captain John Lovell . . .," *Fryeburg Me* 1799. D 60 b AA H NYP
—other eds., various titles: *Port Me* 1818, D 19 a; *B* 1819, D 12 a; *Concord N H* 1861, sm Q 48 map; *see* also Kidder, Frederic.

SYMMS, T[HOMAS]
A brief history of the battle between Capt. John Lovell . . . and a body of Indians. *See* Symmes, Thos.

SYMONDS, JOHN   **1190**
Remarks upon an essay intituled "The history of the colonization of the free states of antiquity applied to the present contest . . ." *L* 1778. Q [4] 52 a
For work refuted, *see* Barron, William.

SYMONS, JOHN, ed.   **1191**
The battle of Queenston Heights . . . opening of the war of 1812 . . . *Tor* 1859. O 39 front plan a

SYMONS, THOMAS W.   **1192**
Itineraries of route and tables of distances, with a list of posts . . . in the Department of the Columbia. *Vancouver Barracks* 1881. O map 66tabs aa

T

T., J.
Van den oorspronk . . . *See* Klerk, J. de.

TAAFE, G. O'HARA   **1**
Californien som det er. *Copenh* 1869. D 40 a
Information for emigrants to California.

TABOR, SILVER DOLLAR   **2**
Star of blood . . . [story of outlaw Allen Downman]. [Denver 1909]? O 74 a

[TACHÉ, ALEXANDRE?]   **3**
Notice sur la riviere Rouge . . . *Montr* 1843. O 32 aa
Includes account of Blanchet and Demer's trip to Oregon in 1838.

TACUBAYA.
A series of intercepted letters, captured by the American guard at: *See* Smith, Robt. Hall.

TAFT, ALPHONSO   **4**
Lecture on Cincinnati and her railroads. *Cin* 1850. O 52 a

[TAILFER, PATRICK]?   **5**
A new voyage to Georgia . . . By a young gentleman . . . *L* 1735. O [2] 62 b NYP
—anr. issue, identical, but with new t-p, calling itself 2nd ed. *L* 1737. b GaU NYP

TAILFER, PATRICK, et al   **6**
A true and historical narrative of the colony of Georgia . . . *Charles-Town S C* 1741. O [26] 176 b JCB NYP Y
—anr. issue, with date in Roman, M.DCC.XLI, impr. same [but probably ptd at *L*]. O [18] 78 87–118 b
—rptd., undated, impr. given as "*Charles-Town* and sold at *L*" [probably ptd at *L* 1741]. O [18] 112 b
Registers complaints against Oglethorpe's administration urged by the discontented element which had left Georgia and resided in Charleston.

TAIT, J. L.   **7**
A six-months exploration of . . . Texas . . . *L* 1878. O 31 aa

TAIT, J[AMES] S.   **8**
The cattle-fields of the far west . . . *Edin* 1884.
O 71 + 2adv-p b G LC

TALBOT, EDWARD A.   **9**
Five years' residence in the Canadas: including
a tour through part of the United States. *L* 1824.
O 2v: [16] 419; 400. 2pls a
—Fr. tr. *P* 1825. O 3v: [22] 364; [4] 323; [4] 175.
8maps & pls
—rptd. *P* 1833. O 3v: [32] 364; [4] 323; [4] 175.
7maps & pls
—Ger. tr. *Vienna* 1825. O [4] 3–140 3maps & 5pls

[TALBOT, JOHN]   **10**
History of North America; comprising a . . .
view of the United States . . . *Leeds* 1820. O 2v:
[4] 498; [2] 458. 8maps & pls a
—ed. 2, au. named, *Liv* 1821. O 2v same collat.

TALBOT [MARY ANN].   **11**
The life and adventures of: . . . cabin boy and
sailor [including experiences in the U. S. and West
Indies]. *L* 1809. O 60 port aa

TALBOT (SILAS).   **12**
An historical sketch, to the end of the revolu-
tionary war, of the life of: . . . *N Y* 1803. D [10]
147 aa
—Eng. ed. "The life and surprising adventures of
Captain Talbot . . .," *L* [1803?]. D [8] 148 aa

TALBOT (THEODORE).   **13**
The journals of: . . . with the Fremont expedition of 1843 and . . . in Oregon Territory, 1849–
1852. *Port Ore* 1931. O [10] 153 a

TALES
Tales of an Indian camp. *See* Jones, James
Athearn.

Tales of the northwest . . . By a resident beyond
the frontier . . . *See* Snelling, Wm. J.

Tales of the revolution . . . *N Y* 1835. *See* Man-
cur, John H.

Tales of the revolution. By a young gentleman of
Tennessee. *See* Ramsey, James G. M.

TALLENT, MRS. ANNIE D.   **14**
The Black hills . . . *St L* 1899. O [22] 713 50pls aa

TALLEYRAND, CHARLES M.   **15**
Mémoire sur les relations commerciales des
États - Unis avec l'Angleterre . . . *L* 1805. O 48 aa
Points out that the citizens of this country still
remain essentially British; their trade with England
since the Revolution has increased.

TALLEYRAND ([CHARLES M.])   **16**
The whole official correspondence between the
envoys of the American states, and: . . . *L* 1798.
D 57 + 3adv-p a
—Fr. tr. "Pièces officielles . . .," *L* 1798. O 70
Appeared originally in *Message of the president
. . . April 3rd*, 1798, Philadelphia 1798.

TALLMADGE (COL. BENJAMIN).   **17**
Memoir of: *N Y* 1858. O 70 port a
—rptd. *N Y* 1904. O [18] 168 [2] incl.pls 350copies
ptd.

TALLMADGE, OHIO.   **18**
Proceedings in commemoration of the fiftieth
anniversary of the settlement of: with the historical discourses . . . *Akron* 1857. O 111 a

TALVI [pseud.]
See Robinson, Mrs. Therese L. von J.

TANEY, MARY F.   **19**
Kentucky pioneer women. *Cin* 1893. D 99 a

TANGUAY DE LA BOISSIÈRE, C. C.   **20**
Mémoire sur la situation commerciale de la
France avec les États Unis . . . n.p. 1795. Q 82
31tabs 100copies ptd a

TANGUAY DE LA BOISSIÈRE, C. C.   **21**
Observations sur la dépêche écrite . . . par M.
Pickering . . . à M. Pinckney . . . *Phil* 1797. O
50 aa
—Eng. tr. *Phil* 1797. O 50 aa

[TANNER, HENRY]   **22**
The martyrdom of Lovejoy . . . killed by a pro-
slavery mob, at Alton. *Chi* 1881. O [14] 18–234 +
4adv-p 2ports fold.facs a

TANNER, H[ENRY] S.   **23**
An alphabetical index to the four sheet map of
the United States. *Phil* [1839?]. 16° [8] 100 + advs
[paged 3–14] a
This index should be accompanied by the large
map, which was issued separately and carries
various dates, 1829, 1830, 1832, 1834, 1838, 1839.
[ea aa] *see* also No. 28, below.

TANNER, H[ENRY] S.   **24**
The American traveller; or, guide through the
United States . . . *Phil* 1834. 18° 144 map 4plans a
—ed. 2, *Phil* 1836. 18° 144 map 4plans 4pls
—8 other eds. pub. between 1837 and 1846.

TANNER, HENRY S.   **25**
Atlas of the United States . . . *Phil* 1826. F [4]
11maps a
—anr. ed. *Phil* 1835. F [4] 28maps
See below his *A new American atlas . . .*

TANNER, H[ENRY] S.   **26**
A brief description of the canals and railroads
of the United States . . . *Phil* 1834. 16° 31 map a
—anr. ed., same date & impr. 16° 63 map 2pls
—enl. ed. "A description of the canals and railroads . . .," *N Y* 1840. O 272 3maps 2 diagrams

TANNER, H[ENRY] S.   **27**
A geographical, historical . . . view of the central
or middle United States . . . *Phil* 1841. 16° [5]
3–524 4maps a
—ed. 2, same impr., date & collat.

TANNER, H[ENRY] S.   **28**
Memoir on the recent surveys [etc.] in the
United States . . . to accompany his new map . . .
Phil 1829. D [2] 108 + 8adv-p a
—ed. 2, same collat., *Phil* 1830.
Editions of his *Map of the United States* were
issued—to be sold separately—in 1829, 1830, 1832,
1834, 1838, 1839. [ea aa] *see* also No. 23, above.

TANNER, HENRY S.   **29**
A new American atlas . . . *Phil* 1823. F [4] 18
eng.t. 18maps[16 double p. & 2fold.] aa
—some copies issued in 5pts dated 1818–23 have
8 preliminary p.; others issued in 3pts dated 1819–
23 have 10 preliminary p.
—rptd. *Phil* 1825. same collat., but only 2 preliminary p. aa
—anr. ed., same date, impr. & collat., but with
maps dated to 1833; the 18maps are on 42 leaves,
& 6 preliminary p. [incl. eng.t.] a
—anr. ed., same impr. 1839. F [2] 18maps [on
24sheets] a
See above his *Atlas of the United States* . . . No. 25

TANNER, HENRY S.   **30**
A new pocket atlas of the United States . . . *Phil*
1828. 24° [2] 12maps a

TANNER (JOHN).
A narrative of the captivity and adventures of:
. . . *See* James, Edwin.

TARASCON, LOUIS A.   **31**
Republican education, and gradual western
march, of enlightened . . . generations . . . through
their Rocky mountains, to their north-west coasts
on the Pacific . . . *Louisv* 1836. O 24 + 12 lvs
[intended for writing in names of those joining
in this emigration enterprise] dd S Y [only copies
located]
A well considered, detailed plan to organize
large emigrating groups, with which to occupy the
Pacific shores prior to their being grasped by European nations.

TARASCON, L[OUIS] A.   **32**
. . . to his fellow citizens of the United States . . .
N Y 1837. 16° 82 errata slip b N Hn Y

One of the earliest agitations for expansion to
the Pacific and settlement of Oregon. This was an
amplification of his fourteen-page tract, *L. A.
Tarascon, to his friends . . .*, Louisville, 1836;
includes also *Republican education*, above, No.
31.

TARBELL, IDA M.   **33**
The history of the Standard Oil Company. *N Y*
1904. O 2v: [20] 406; [14] 409. 32pls aa
—rptd., same impr. & collat. 1905. a

TARBLE, MRS. HELEN M.   **34**
The story of my capture and escape, during the
Minnesota Indian massacre . . . *St P* 1904. O 65 aa
An outstanding epic of female heroism under
unbelievable ordeals.

TARBOX, INCREASE N.   **35**
Sir Walter Raleigh and his colony in America
. . . *B* Prince Soc 1884. O [8] 329 2pls a 250 cops
ptd.

TARDUCCI, FRANCESCO   **36**
R. deputazione Veneta di storia patria di Gio-
vanni e Sebastiano Caboto. Memorie . . . *Venice*
1892. O [4] 429 a
—Eng. tr. "John and Sebastian Cabot . . .,"
Detroit 1893. O [10] 409 port

TARLETON, SIR BANASTRE   **37**
A history of the campaigns of 1780 and 1781, in
the southern provinces . . . *L* 1787. Q [8] 518 +
2adv-p 5maps b
—rptd. *Dub* 1787. O [8] 533 aa
—ed. 2, *L* 1796. Q [26] 518 5maps aa

TARRANT, EASTHAM   **38**
The wild riders of the First Kentucky [Union]
cavalry . . . [*Louisv ca.* 1894] O [10] 503 front aa

TASISTRO, LOUIS F.   **38a**
Random shots and southern breezes . . . *N Y*
1842. D 2v: [12] 274; [8] 230 + 14adv-p a
—ed. 2, *N Y* 1847. D 2v in 1
Observations on the ante-bellum South while
playing in the theatres of Charleston, Mobile, New
Orleans, Savannah, etc.

TASSÉ, JOSEPH   **39**
Les Canadiens de l'ouest . . . *Montr* 1878. O 2v:
[40] 364; [4] 413. 21pls aa
—eds. 2 & 3, same impr, date and collat. a
—ed. 4, same impr & collat. 1882.
Largely devoted to those conspicuous in the
early settlement of the Western states.

TATHAM, WILLIAM, ed.
Communications concerning the agriculture and
commerce of America. *See* Martínez de Yrujo y
Tacon, Carlos.

TATHAM, WILLIAM   **40**
An historical, etc. essay on the culture and commerce of tobacco. *L* 1800. O [16] 330 4pls aa

TATHWELL, S. L., and MAXEY, H. O.,   **41**
pubs. & comps.
The old settler's history of Bates county, Missouri . . . *Amsterdam Mo* [1897] O 212 + unpaged lf after p.208 33ports map a
—rptd. same impr. & collat [1902]

TATUM, LAWRIE   **42**
Our red brothers and the peace policy of . . . Grant. *Phil* 1899. O 366 16pls a
Most copies destroyed—or damaged—by fire.

TAXATION NO TYRANNY . . .
See Johnson, Samuel.

TAYLOR, BAYARD   **43**
Eldorado; or, adventures in the path of empire . . . pictures of the gold region [etc.]. *N Y* 1850. D 2v: [12] 251; [4] 247 + 45adv-p 8tinted pls aa
—Eng. ed., Am. sheets with new t-p, *L* 1850. aa
—anr. Eng. ed. *L* 1850 16° 2v. in 1: [4] 188; [4] 189–360 a
—ed. 2, *N Y* 1850, same collat.
—ed. 3, *N Y* 1850. 2v in 1 no pls
—Ger. tr. *Weimar* 1851. D [8] 176 2maps pl a
Unexcelled description of California's gold-rush days by a professional traveller and trained observer.

TAYLOR, ALEXANDER S.   **44**
Discovery of California and northwest America . . . *S F* 1853. O 20 + wraps b

[TAYLOR, BENJAMIN F.] ed.   **45**
Short ravelings from a long yarn . . . sketches of the Santa Fé trail. *Chi* 1847. O 64 c ChiH WisH Y
—rptd. *Santa Ana Calif* 1936. D [14] 168 aa
Account of a trading expedition, under Captain Houck, made in 1841.

TAYLOR, CHARLES B.   **46**
Early history . . . of Wilkesville and Salem, Ohio. *Cin* 1874. 16° 89 a

TAYLOR, CAPT. DREW K.   **47**
Thrilling tales of Texas . . . [*Austin*] 1926. O 94 [incl. front] a
Ranger experiences, etc.

TAYLOR, G. of England   **48**
A voyage to North America . . . manner of trading with the Indians . . . From Philadelphia to New Orleans . . . to the Illinois . . . *Nottingham* 1771. O [8] 248 b N NYH
One of the earliest English books advocating prairie settlement.

[TAYLOR, G. C.]   **49**
Notes of conversation with a volunteer officer . . . on the passage of the forts below New Orleans . . . *N Y* 1868. Q [4] 29 100 copies ptd. aa

[TAYLOR, GEORGE, of Pa.]   **50**
Martyrs to the revolution in the British prison-ships . . . *N Y* 1855. D 60 fold.map a
—anr. issue, same impr. & date. D 64 fold. map

TAYLOR, H[ORACE] C.   **51**
Historical sketches of . . . Portland [N.Y.] . . . *Fredonia* 1873. O [2] 5–446 4pls a

TAYLOR, [JACOB N.], and   **52**
CROOKS, [M. G.]
Sketch book of St. Louis. *St L* 1858. D 430 + errata lf 4fold.pls aa

TAYLOR, JAMES B.   **53**
Lives of Virginia Baptist ministers. *Rich* 1837. D 444 a
—ed. 2, enl., same impr. 1838. D 492
A second series was published at Philadelphia in 1859; both series were reprinted at New York in 1860. Continued by George B. Taylor—third, fourth and fifth series—Lynchburg, 1912. [1913], 1915.

TAYLOR, JAMES W[ICKES]   **54**
History of . . . Ohio. First period, 1650–1787. [all]. *Cin* 1854. D 557 a
First history of pre-territorial Ohio, its aborigines, border wars, etc.

TAYLOR, JAMES W[ICKES]   **55**
Alleghania . . . the strength of the Union, and the weakness of slavery in the mountainous districts of the south. *St P* 1862. O [8] 24 a

TAYLOR, JAMES W[ICKES]   **56**
. . . Northwest British America, and its relations to . . . Minnesota. A report communicated to the Legislature . . . by Governor Ramsay and ordered to be printed. *St P* Newson, Moore, Foster & Co. 1860. O 42[incl. map] b G N Y
—anr. issue, *St P* Minnesotian & Times 1860. same collat. b
—anr. ed., possibly the earliest, ptd. as a suppl. to the Journal of the House of Representatives, *St P* Newson, Moore, Foster & Co. 1860. O 54 map [in some copies] b NYP WisH
—anr. ed., giving abstract of above report with considerable adds., "Relations between the United States and Northwest British America," H.Exec. Doc. 146, *Wash* 1862. O 85 map aa
—anr. issue, unnumb.H.Exec.Doc., with t-p added, same impr. & date. O 87 map aa

TAYLOR, JAMES W[ICKES]   **57**
The railroad system of . . . Minnesota . . . *St P* Pioneer Ptg. Co. 1859. O 24 b N Y

—anr. ed. *St P* [G. W. Moore] 1859. O 22 b
Describes the Northwest and proclaims the inevitability of a railroad from St. Paul to Puget Sound.

TAYLOR, JOHN, of Ky.   **58**
A history of ten Baptist churches . . . *Frankfort Ky* 1823. D 300 aa
—ed. 2, *Bloomfield Ky* 1827. D 144 149–304 aa

TAYLOR, JOHN, of Va.   **59**
Construction construed and constitutions vindicated. *Rich* 1820. O [6] 344 aa

[TAYLOR, JOHN] of Va.   **60**
A defence of the measures of the administration of Thomas Jefferson. *Wash* 1804. O 136 a
—rptd. *Prov* 1805. O 88

[TAYLOR, JOHN] of Va.   **61**
An enquiry into the principles and tendency of certain public measures. *Phil* 1794. O [4] 92 a

[TAYLOR, JOHN] of Va.   **62**
An examination of the proceedings in Congress respecting the official conduct of the Secretary of the Treasury [Alex. Hamilton]. n.p. [1793]. O 28 [ptd. in March] a
—anr. issue, n.p. [*Rich*] 1793. [ptd. in Oct.]

TAYLOR, JOHN, of Va.   **63**
An inquiry into the principles and policies of the government of the United States . . . *Fredkbg* 1814. O [2, 5–8] 656 [1] aa
—rptd. 1950.
Presents the contemporary political ideas of the agrarian South.

TAYLOR, JOHN, of Va.   **64**
New views of the constitution . . . *Wash* 1823. O [4] 316 aa

TAYLOR, JOHN, of Va.   **65**
Tyranny unmasked . . . *Wash* 1822. O 349 errata slip aa

TAYLOR, JOSEPH H.   **66**
Beavers—their ways . . . *Washburn N D* 1904. O 178 + 4 pp of reviews 20 pls aa
—ed. 2, enl., same impr. 1906. O 218 26pls a

TAYLOR, JOSEPH H.   **67**
Kaleidoscopic lives. A companion book to Frontier and Indian life. *Washburn N D* 1901. O [4] 113 + 2 pp. of reviews 9pls aa
—ed. 2, enl., *Washburn* 1902. O [4 incl. initial blank lf] 20 20–207 + 4adv-p 31pls a
—rptd., together with his "Sketches of frontier life", same impr. 1932. O 328 a

TAYLOR, JOSEPH H.   **68**
Sketches of frontier and Indian life . . . *Pott-*

stown Pa 1889. O 136 138–200 12pls [3 called for replaced by 3 unlisted] b
—ed. 2, *Washburn N Dak* 1895. O 283 pls aa
—ed. 3, *Bismarck* 1897. O [6] 2–306 pls a
—rptd. [with preceding t.] same impr. 1932

TAYLOR, JOSEPH H.   **69**
Twenty years on the trap line . . . trapping . . . on the great northwestern plains. *Bismarck* 1891. D 154 8pls aa
—anr. issue, same impr. & date. D 173 8pls aa
Companion to his earlier *Sketches of frontier and Indian life*, No. 68.

TAYLOR, LANDON   **70**
The battle field reviewed . . . *Chi* 1881. O [24] 375 2ports a
—ed. 2, enl., *Chi* 1883. O 489 3ports
Pioneer days in Iowa, overland trip from Council Bluffs to Denver, etc.

TAYLOR, LYTTON   **71**
Alaska and the Yukon valley . . . *Nash* 1897. D 124 a

TAYLOR, OLIVER I.   **72**
Directory of . . . Wheeling . . . with a history . . . *Wheeling* 1851. O 112 [62] 2pls a

TAYLOR, GEN. RICHARD   **73**
Destruction and reconstruction . . . *N Y* 1879. O 274 a some cops have *L* impr.
—rptd. *N Y* 1883.

TAYLOR, WALTER H.   **74**
Four years with General Lee. *N Y* 1877. O 199 port a
—rptd. same impr. & collat. 1878.

TAYLOR, WALTER H.   **75**
General Lee; his campaigns in Virginia. *Norfolk* [1906]. O [10] 314 maps aa

[TAYLOR, WILLIAM]   **76**
Will there be war? . . . the proper course to secure . . . Oregon. *N Y* 1846. O 44 aa

TAYLOR, YARDLEY   **77**
Memoir of Loudon county, Virginia. *Leesburg* 1853. O 31 a

TAYLOR (ZACHARY).   **78**
Letters of: from the battle-fields of the Mexican war. *Roch* 1908. Q [26] 194[incl. front.] 4ports facs 300 copies ptd. aa

TAYLOR (GENERAL [ZACHARY]).   **79**
Message of the President . . . transmitting the correspondence with: since the commencement of hostilities with Mexico . . . [*Wash* 1847]. O 454 a

TAYLOR (GEN. [ZACHARY]).   80
A sketch of the life of: . . . *N Y* 1847. O 36 [incl.
wraps] a

TEACH (EDWARD), commonly called   81
black beard . . .
The voyages and adventures of: . . . *Newcastle
Eng* n.d. D 24 a
For similar title *see* Wilkinson, S.

TEATRO   82
Teatro della guerra . . . fra la Gran Bretagne, la
Colonie Unite . . . *Venice* 1781. Q [32] 13–14 [10]
3–8 [2] 11–12 [14] 9–10 [10] 43maps & plans pl b
First atlas on the American Revolution.

TEBIENKOV, CAPT. MIKHAIL D.   83
Atlas siev.-zapadnykb beregov Ameriki . . .
[Atlas of the northwest shores of America, etc.]. *St
Ptbg* 1852. Q [6] 39maps & pls[eng. by a native at
New Archangel] b NYP Y
Should accompany the text volume entered be-
low. Tebienkov was governor of Russian America,
1845–1850, and an eminent surveyor whose charts
for this region were the most correct ever made.

TEBIENKOV, CAPT. MIKHAIL D.   84
Gidrograficheskiia zamechaniis k atlasu siev.-
zapadnykh beregov Ameriki . . . [Hydrographic
notes to the Atlas of the Northwest shores of Amer-
ica]. *St Ptbg* 1852. Q [12] 148 [20] b NYP Y

[TEFFT, B. F.]   85
The far west: its present, past and future. *Indianap* 1845. O 38 a

TEGOBORSKI, LOUIS DE   86
Essai sur les conséquences . . . de la découverte
des gites aurifères en Californie et en Australie.
P 1853. O [14] 199 a

TEHAMA COUNTY, CALIFORNIA.   87
Illustrations . . . of its scenery . . . with historical sketch . . . *S F* 1880. F 166 pls b B Hn

TEICHMANN EMIL   88
A journey to Alaska in . . . 1868. [*L*] 1925. O 272
2ports 100copies ptd. aa

TEJAS   89
Constitucion, leyes . . . de la républica de Tejas.
Houston 1841. O 324 [6] b 1 cop kn.

Dictámen leido . . . sobre la cuestion de Tejas.
See Gorostiza, Manuel E. de.

Expedicion hecha en Tejas. *See* Woll, Adrian.

**Informe . . . sobre limites de la provincia de Tejas
con la de la Luisiana.** *See* Puelles, Jose Maria.

Reflexiones sobre la Memoria del minis-   91
terio de relaciones, en la parte relativa á Tejas *Mex*
1845. 16° 40 b S Y
Because of Texas annexation advocates war on
this country.

**Resumen instructivo, que publica el comisario de
division del exército de operaciones sobre Tejas.**
See Barreiro, Miguel.

La verdad desnuda sobre la guerra de Tejas. 92
Mex 1845 O 42 aa
Answer to *La guerra de Tejas sin mascara*, a 20-
page pamphlet published at Mexico the same year.

TELLO, ANTONIO   93
Libro segundo de la Cronica miscelanea . . . y
descubrimiento del Nuevo México. *Guadalajara*
1890–91. O 2v in 1: [28] 886 [27] b N NYP Y
First printing of a manuscript written in 1650.
Mentions Cabeza de Vaca and explorations by
Coronado and others.

TEMPLE, GEORGE   94
The American tourist's pocket companion; or,
a guide to the springs, and trip to the lakes . . . *N Y*
1812. 18° 114 [30] fold.tab. a

TEMPLE (J.) and WHATELY (W.)   95
A faithful account of the . . . transactions relating to the late affair of honour between: . . . *L*
1774. O 38 b LC NYP Y
Whately accused Temple of obtaining improp-
erly the letters of Governor Hutchinson and
Lieutenant Oliver and sending them to Boston
where their publication incensed the colonists.
Franklin's letter admitting his guilt in the matter
is included.

TEMPLE, J[OSIAH] HOWARD, et al   96
History of . . . Northfield, Mass . . . *Alb* 1875.
O [8] 636 a

TEMPLE, OLIVER P.   97
East Tennessee and the civil war. *Cin* 1899. O
[16] 588 fold.map 6pls aa

TEN DAYS ON THE PLAINS.
See Davies, Gen. Henry E.

TENESLES, NICOLA
The Indian of New England . . . *See* Barrat, Jos.

TENNASSEE GOVERNMENT (THE).
A short description of: *See* Smith, Daniel.

TENNESSEE   98
Address to the republican people of Tennessee.
By the central corresponding committee . . . *Nashv*
1840. O [2pts in 1, paged consecutively] 40 a

Description of improved farms in . . . Ten- 99
nessee. *L* [184–?]. O 58 a

History of Tennessee with histories of 100
Maury [and five other counties]. *Nashv* Goodspeed
1886. O [8] 13–1282 8maps & plans 31pls aa
Other issues differed only in containing supplements covering various other counties; one with
Montgomery and six others, one with Lauderdale
and three others, one with Giles and three others,
one with Gibson and four others and one with all
East Tennessee counties.

A short description of the situation . . . and 101
history of Tennessee n.p. [1810]. D 48 c no perfect
copy known
The first history of this state. *Cf.* Smith, Daniel,
A short description of the Tennassee government . . .

TENNISON, O. M., and GREEN, H. T. 102
Report and map of the superintendant of the
Smoky hill expedition. *Leavenworth* 1861. 16° 19
map dd S Y

TENSAS, MADISON, M. D. [pseud.]
See Lewis, Henry C.

TERNAUX-COMPANS, H[ENRI] 103
Notice sur la colonie de la Nouvelle Suède. *P*
1843. O [4] 30 map a
—Swed. ed. "Underrättelse om den Fordna
Svenska Kolonien . . . Nya Sverige," *Stockh* 1844.
O [2] 41

TERNAUX-COMPANS, H[ENRI], ed. 104
Recueil de pièces sur la Floride . . . *P* 1841. O
[8] 368 + 40adv-p aa
Volume XX of the editor's *Voyages, relations et
memoirs.* Ten of these 16th century pieces had
never been printed.

TERNAUX-COMPANS, H[ENRI], ed.
Relation du voyage de Cibola . . . *See* Castaneda
de Nagera, Pedro de.

TERRELL, JOSEPH C. 105
Reminiscences of the early days of Fort Worth
. . . *Ft Worth* 1906. O [2] 101 aa
Includes narrative of his trip to California in
1852.

TERRY (DAVID S.) 106
Trial of: by the committee of vigilance . . . *S F*
1856. O 75 aa
Most famous Vigilante trial.

[TERRY, EZEKIEL] 107
A sketch of the life and character of Gen.
George Washington . . . *Palmer* E. Terry [1810?].
sq 16° 64 a
—rptd. several times.

TESTMAN, PETER 108
Kort Beskrivelse over de vigtigste Erfaringer
under et ophold i Nord-Amerika og paa flere der-
med forbundne Reiser. *Stavenger* 1839. D 27 aa
—Eng. ed. ". . . Experiences in North America
. . .," *Northfield Minn* 1927. O [8] 60 a

TETLOW, RICHARD-JOHN 109
An impartial sentimental letter, relating to the
. . . dissensions . . . betwixt Old-England and
America . . . *York Eng* 1776. O [2] 35 a

TEXAN REVOLUTION (THE).
See Child, David Lee.

TEXAS 110
Abstract of original titles of record in the Land
Office of Texas. *Houston* 1838. O 182 b NYP
—anr. ed. enl. *Galv* 1852. O 612 [18] aa
—anr. ed., further enl., *Austin* 1860. O [2] 1600 a

An appeal by the people of the state of 111
Texas . . . to the President, for protection against
the incursions of the savages of . . . Coahuila,
Mexico. *Corpus Christi* 1878 O 40 aa

Au Texas . . . Par Col. . . . n.p. [1856]. *See*
Considerant, Victor P.

Auswanderung (Die) der Deutschen nach 112
Texas . . . *Munich* 1844. O 56 aa
Exposes the various schemes for enticing Ger-
mans to Texas.

A brief description of western Texas. *See* Kingsbury, Wm. G.

Captain Jeff; or frontier life in Texas. *See*
Maltby, Wm. J.

Charter of the Texas Western Railroad with . . .
survey of route . . . *See* Gray, A. B.

Comite-Bericht des Vereines zum schutze 113
deutscher Einwanderer in Texas. *Wiesbaden* 1850.
O 47 aa

Communicaciones relativos á la agre- 114
gacion del deparmento de Texas á los Estados-
Unidos . . . *Mex* 1845. O 30 Issued with, and without, heading stating it to be a supplementary No.
of "La Union nacional." aa

Considerations on . . . annexing the province of
Texas to the Unites Stated. By a revolutionary officer. *See* Morris, Wm. W.

Constitution of the republic of Texas . . . 115
Wash 1836. O 24 b AA H
—for later eds., *see* below "Declaration of independence . . ."

For first Constitution of Texas as a Mexican state, *see Coahuila y Tejas.*

Constitution of the state of Texas. *Austin*   **116**
1845. O 32 b Hn S TxU [of 4 perf cops kn]
—same [in Sp.]. O 34 aa
—rptd. [Eng.], *Houston* 1845. O 32 aa

Constitution of the state of west Texas.   **117**
[*Austin* 1868?]. D 36 b G S Y
Constitution of a proposed new state drawn up by a convention of Federal sympathizers who conceived the idea of dividing Texas into two commonwealths.

De landverhuizers naar Texas. *See* Haeberlin, Carl L.

Debates of the Texas convention. *Houston*   **118**
1846. O 759 aa

Declaration of independence . . . and the   **119**
constitution of the Republic of Texas adopted . . .
March 17, 1836 . . . *Columbia* 1837. O [7] 3–19 b
NYH TxU [of 3 cops loc]
—anr. ed. *Houston* 1838. O 32 b LC Y
This constitution for the unestablished republic operated as the instrument of government from 1836 until 1845, when, after annexation to the United States, a state constitution was adopted. For earlier edition *see* above, *Constitution of the Republic* . . . For the constitution of Texas as a Mexican state, *see Coahuila and Texas.*

The emigrant farmer: . . . **advantages of**   **120**
Texas . . . by a practical farmer. *L* n.d. O 24 a

Emigrant's guide to Texas containing . . .   **121**
documents relative to the Galveston Bay and Texas Land Company. *N Y* 1834. D 36 b S [only copy known]
See also Summer, William H.

Emigration to Texas . . . prospectus of the   **122**
advantages offered . . . by the Texas Emigration and Land Company. *L* [1843]. O 24 map a
An earlier English book of eighteen pages with similar title was published at Bath, 1831, and reprinted 1832.

Exposé des éventualités . . . **d'une guerre**   **123**
entre les États-Unis et l'Angleterre, traitant les
questions de l'annexation du Texas . . . par un citoyen de New-York. [*P*] 1845. O cover-t. & 60 aa
Pages 41–60 consist of a supplement; it and the main body [pages 1–40] were apparently each issued separately.

Für Auswanderungslustige! Briefe eines unter des
Mainzer Vereins nach Texas ausgewanderten. *See*
Sörgel, Alwin H.

Geographical description of . . . **Texas** also of . . .
Oregon and upper California. *See* under Mitchell, Saml. A.

Gesammelte Aktenstücke des Vereins zum   **124**
Schutze deutscher Einwanderer in Texas. *Mainz*
1845. O [2]80 [4] map aa
Sketch of the German Emigration Society's Texas activities.

Guide map of the great Texas cattle trail from Red
river crossing to the . . . **Kansas Pacific railway** . . .
K C 1875. *See* Weston, W.

Handbook of northern Texas. *Chi* 1886.   **125**
D 40 aa

L'heroine du Texas ou, voyage de M. G.   **126**
. . . n F . . . n aux États-Unis . . . *P* 1819. O 118 pl b
First Texas novel. For first Texas novel in English *see* Ganilh, Anthony.

Historical . . . **record of the cattle industry** . . . **of**
Texas and adjacent terrirory. *See* Cox, James.

A history of Texas or the emigrant's guide . . .
See Lawrence, A. B.

History of pioneer days in Texas and Oklahoma
. . . *See* Hart, John A.

History of the cattlemen of Texas. *Dallas*   **127**
1914. Q 237 [incl. front] a

Important documents concerning Texas   **128**
and the controversy between General T. J. Cham-
bers and . . . **Wilson and Postlethwaite.** *Natchez*
1836. O 24 b only 1 copy known
—anr. issue, "Documents [etc.], "*Louisv* 1836. O 27 b only 1 copy known

In relation to the claims of the officers of the late
Texas navy. *See* Buchanan, Franklin.

Instruction für deutsche Auswanderer nach   **129**
Texas. *Wiesbaden* 1851. sm F 26 3fold.maps b

Journal of the proceedings of the General   **130**
Council of the republic of Texas held at San Felipe
de Austin, November 14th 1835 [-March 11, 1836].
Houston 1839. O 363 b Hn NYP Y

Journals of the consultation held at San Felipe de
Austin, October 16 [-Nov. 14], 1835. *Houston* 1838.
See San Felipe de Aust[i]n.

Journals of the convention . . . **for** . . .   **130a**
framing a constitution for the state of Texas. *Austin*
1845. O 378 aa
Voted to accept annexation and framed a state constitution.

Letter to the Hon. John C. Calhoun on the annexation of Texas. *See* Hammond, Jabez D.

Letters upon the annexation of Texas ad-   131 dressed to Hon. John Quincy Adams . . . *B* 1845. O 47 a
Attributed to George Edward Ellis.

Mexico versus Texas. *See* Ganilh, Anthony.

Mosquito-Küste (Die) und Texas . . .   132 *Charlottenburg* 1846. D [6] 70 map a

Nathan der Squatter-Regulator, oder der erste Amerikaner in Texas . . . *See* Postl, Karl.

New history of Texas. *See* Stiff, Edw.

Ordinances and decrees of the consulta-   133 tion, provisional government of Texas and the convention, which assembled at Washington [Tex.] March 1, 1836. *Houston* 1838. O 156 [3] b Hn N NYP Y
The three-page index was not issued with all copies.

The origin and true causes of the Texas insurrection. *See* Lundy, Benj.

Origin, principles, and objects of the   134 contest in which Texas is at present engaged. *N Y* 1836. O 56 aa

Proceedings of the general convention of   135 delegates representing the citizens . . . of Texas held at the town of San Felipe . . . *Brazoria* 1832. O 35 c TxS [only cop kn]
Attempt to form a separate Mexican state. A constitution, adopted the following April, was never in operation, and the proposed state was never recognized by Mexico. This was the first popular Texas assembly.

Recollections of western Texas. *See* Wright, Wm., and John W.

Report of the Secretary of State of Texas   136 . . . [Austin] 1839. O 38 aa
Chiefly relating to Indian incursions.

Reports of the Committee of Investigation sent . . . by the Mexican government to the frontier of Texas. *See Informe de la Comision Pesquisidora* . . .

Supplement à l'almanach Icarien . . . rela-   137 tif au Texas. [*P* 1847]. 16° 216 map a

Texas almanac, for 1857, with . . . histori-   138 cal [etc.] sketches. *Galv* Richardson & Co 1856. O 160 + 48adv-p map aa
—contd., annually, to 1873. Issues for 1862–3–4–5 are the most uncommon. aa

This Richardson series has no connection with an earlier *Texas almanac*, of 1853, bearing a New Orleans imprint, nor with J. Burke's *Texas almanac* and *Immigrant's hand book*, issued at Houston from 1865 to 1884. Each issue through 1861 contained a map, except that for 1858.

Texas. An English question. *L* 1837. O   139 40 aa

Texas, and its late military occupation . . . By an officer . . . *See* Phillips, Edwin D.

Texas and Mexico, a few hints to the   140 creditors of Mexico, who hold her . . . bonds . . . in the faith of . . . land pledged by Mexico in Texas. By a Mexican merchant. *L* 1841. O 48 map aa

Texas (Le) en 1845. Castroville, colonie Francaise . . . *See* Castro, Henry.

Texas. Ein handbuch für deutsche Aus-   141 wanderer . . . *Bremen* 1845. O [8] 141 aa
—rptd. same impr. O 60, 34, map 1846 aa

Texas. Evidence in relation to land titles . . .   142 [*Austin Tex* 1840]. D 39 b 150copies ptd.

Texas frontier troubles. *Wash* 1876. O   143 [22] 180 [Report No. 343] aa
Testimony on border cattle thefts submitted by the U. S. investigating committee. For reports made by Mexican investigators see *Informe de la comisión pesquisidora*.

Texas in 1840; or, the emigrant's guide . . . *See* Lawrence, A. B.

Texas question (The) reviewed by an adopted citizen . . . *See* Attellis Santangelo, Gideon de.

Texas sketches of character. *See* Thompson, Henry.

Texas vendetta (The) . . . *See* Rose, Victor M.

Translation of the laws . . . on coloniza-   144 tion . . . in virtue of which Col. Stephen F. Austin, has . . . settled foreign emigrants in Texas . . . *San Filipe* [*sic*] *de Austin* Nov. 1829. D 70 [1] c NYP TxU
—abr. ed. *Columbia* 1837. O 81 b TxU Y
First book printed in Texas; of first importance on the establishment there of the first Anglo-American colony.

A visit to Texas. . . . journal of a traveller   145 . . . *N Y* 1834. D [4] 9–264 [4] map 4pls aa
—ed. 2, with app. on the war, *N Y* 1836. 16° [12] 262 aa
Authorship has been attributed to a Col. Morris and to Dr. M. Fiske.

The war in Texas a review of facts . . . *See* Lundy, Benj.

Western Texas the Australia of America . . . **146**
By a six years' resident. *Cin* E. Mendenhall 1860. D 235 a

THACHER, JAMES   147
American medical biography . . . To which is prefixed a succinct history of medical science in America: *B* 1828. O 2v in 1: 436; 280. 15ports aa

THACHER, JAMES   148
History of . . . Plymouth [Mass.]. *B* 1832. D [12] 382 front. map a
—ed. 2, enl. *B* 1835. D 401 map

THACHER, JAMES   149
A military journal during the . . . revolutionary war . . . *B* 1823. O 603 aa
—ed. 2, rev., *B* 1827. O [8] 11-488 + adv-p a
—other eds. [some entitled "The American revolution . . .,"] *Hart* 1854; *Hart* 1861; *Hart* 1862; *Cin* [1856]; *Cin* 1857]; *N Y* 1857; *Cin* 1859; *N Y* 1860.
—best ed. *Hart* 1862. O [14 incl.front.] 7–618 ports pls a

THACHER, JOHN B.   150
The continent of America: its discovery . . . *N Y* 1896. F [18] 271 18maps 8pls aa 250copies ptd.

THARIN, W. C.   151
A directory of Marengo county . . . embracing . . . a short sketch . . . *Mobile* 1861. O 68 + 26 adv-p aa
Next to Townes *History* of *Marion* Alabama's rarest local history.

[THATCHER, BENJAMIN B.]   152
A retrospect of the Boston tea party . . . memoir of George R. T. Hewes . . . *N Y* 1834. D [2] 206 aa
—rptd., "Traits of the tea party . . ." *N Y* 1835. 16° 265 port a

THAYER, WILLIAM M.   153
The pioneer boy: and how he became President. *B* 1863. D 310 [incl. illus] a
—rptd. often: 1863; 1864; 1865; etc.
—anr. ed., re-written, "From pioneer home to the White House," *Norwich Conn* 1882. D 469 a many reprints
—Eng. ed., styled "second thousand" *L* 1882. D [20] 395 front; many reprints
—Ger. tr. *Gotha* 1886.
—Greek tr. *Athens* 1865.
—Hawaiian tr. *Honolulu* 1868. aa
—Swed. tr. *Stockh* [1887].
First complete biography of Lincoln. The Honolulu edition is the rarest life in a foreign language.

THAYER and ELDRIDGE [pubs.]   154
The life and public services of Hon. Abraham Lincoln . . . and Hon. Hannibal Hamlin . . . *B* 1860. D 128 2ports wraps a
—issue 2, identical except p. nos. at center of pages
—anr. issue, "Wide-Awake Edition," clo. 320p front.

THEATRE (THE)
Theatre (The) of the present war in North America . . . *See* Young, Arthur.

THEOBALD, J.   155
Mormonology . . . *Leicester Eng* [1852]. D 24 [incl.wrap.covers] aa

THÉVENOT, MR. [MELCHISEDÉCH]   156
Recueil de voyages . . . *P* [Michallet] 1681. D: [2] 16; 44; 20; 36; 20; 14; 8; 16 4pls 3maps [incl. first one ever made of the Mississippi]. c ChiH Hn N
—rptd. same printer & collat, 1682. b
—later eds: *P* 1687; 1689. Both made from unsold sheets of the 1682 ed, with those dates and the printer Moette's name superimposed over Michallet's 1682 t-p b
—anr. ed. [Mississippi portion only] *P* 1845. D 43 map. 125 cops ptd for Obadiah Rich. a
Containing, as it does, the first publication of Dablon's account of Marquette's and Joliet's 1673 discovery of the Mississippi, the first edition of Thévenot's *Recueil*, while less rare than Le Clercq's *Premier établissement de la foi* [1691], is of equal importance and enjoys, along with that work, top rank on the subject of early French activities in this region. As collation indicates, the book was printed in 8 sections; binders observed no uniform sequence of arrangement, so copies vary in that respect. A collector's only concern is whether all sections are present.
For a later discovered and somewhat ampler Dablon Ms see Shea, *Discovery, etc.* and Marquette, *Recit.*

THICKNESSE (PHILIP).   157
Memoirs and anecdotes of: . . . [*L?*] 1788–91. O 3v [16 8] 326; [6 4] 3–326; [2 20] 189. port [in v. 3, which v. is usually lacking] b JCB NYP
—rptd. *Dub* 1790. O [12 4] 421 + 3adv-p aa
The author was with Oglethorpe in Georgia, 1735–6.

[THIERRY, J. B. S.]   158
Examination of the claims of the United States and of the pretensions of Edward Livingston, Esq. to the batture [at New Orleans]. *N O* 1808. Q 51 3plans[in some copies] aa
—Fr. tr., same impr. & date. Q 49 a
Reply to Livingston's *Address to the people of the United States.*

THIERSANT, P. DABRY DE   159
De l'origine des Indiens . . . et de leur civilisation. *P* 1883. O [4] 360 a

THINGS
Things as they are . . . notes of a traveller . . .
See Dwight, Theo.

Things as they are, or Federalism turned inside
out . . . *See* Niles, Hezekiah.

THIRTY-SIX YEARS
Thirty-six years of a seafaring life . . . By an old
Quartermaster. *See* Bechervaise, John.

THISSEL, G. W.   160
Crossing the plains in '49 . . . *Oakland* 1903.
D 176 11pls aa

THOM, ADAM   161
The claims to the Oregon Territory considered.
L 1844. D [4] 44 aa
Refutation of American claims.

THOMAS, DAVID   162
Travels through the western country in . . . 1816.
Auburn 1819. 16° [4] 320 errata slip map aa

THOMAS, E.   163
A concise view of the slavery of the people of
colour in the United States . . . *Phil* 1834. 18° [6,
3–4] 7–178 2pls a

THOMAS, E[BENEZER] S.   164
Reminiscences of the last sixty-five years . . .
Hart 1840. O 2v: 300; 300 a

THOMAS, ELIZABETH P.   165
Old Kentucky homes and gardens. *Louisv* [1939].
F [26] 180[incl.pls] a

THOMAS (LIEUT. COL. [FREDERICK]).   166
The trial of: on a charge . . . by Lieut. Col.
Cosmo Gordon . . . *L* 1781. O [2] 118 aa
After the New York court-martial, the two officers fought a duel in New Jersey, and Thomas was
killed. *See* Gordon, Cosmo.

THOMAS, GABRIEL   167
An historical . . . account of . . . Pensilvania, etc.
L 1698. D 2 pts in 1: [8] 56; [12] 34 map dd Hn JCB
—rptd.: *N Y* 1848. D; *Clev* 1903. O
—Ger. tr. [with portion on West-New-Jersey
replaced by anr tract], "Continuatio der Beschreibung der . . . Pensylvaniae . . ." [issued as supplement to Pastorius' "Beschreibung"] *Frankf* 1702.
O [4] 40; [6] 58 map b Hn JCB

THOMAS, ISAIAH   168
The history of printing in America . . . *Worc*
1810. O 2v: 487; 576. 2pls 3facs aa

—ed. 2, with adds., *Alb* 1874. O 2v: [88] 423; [8]
666 [2] 47. port pl aa

THOMAS, REV. J. A. W.   169
History of Marlboro county [S. C.] . . . *Atlanta*
1897. O 292 map port a

THOMAS (QR. M. GEN. JAMES).   170
A brief statement of the transactions . . . of: . . .
on the Niagara frontier, 1812–13. n.p. [1815?].
O 34 [capt.t.] a

[THOMAS, JAMES M., and   171
GALATIAN, A. B.]
Indian and pioneer history of the Saginaw valley
E Saginaw 1866. O 72 104 152 72 aa

THOMAS, JAMES W.   172
Chronicles of colonial Maryland . . . *Balt* [1900].
O [2] 334 fold.map 6pls aa
—rptd. *Cumberland Md* [1913]. O 389 map pls a

THOMAS, JANE H.   173
Old days in Nashville, Tennessee . . . *Nash* 1897.
D 135 port a

THOMAS, JESSE B.   174
Report . . . of the statistics concerning Chicago.
Chi 1847. O 32 aa

THOMAS, JOHN   175
Sketch of the . . . Mormons . . . to which is
added An account of the Nauvoo temple mysteries
. . . by Increase McGee Van Dusen . . . *L* [1850?].
D 24 aa
—anr. ed. *Nottingham* n.d. D 32 a
For other editions of the Van Dusen portion,
see that name.

THOMAS (JOSEPH, the pilgrim).   176
The life of: . . . his trials, travels, etc. *Winchester, Va* 1817. D 372 aa
A frontier gospel ranter who vied with Lorenzo
Dow in wander lust and eccentricity. In two years
he traveled 7000 miles through Tenn., Ky. and
Ohio.

THOMAS, LEWIS A.   177
Report of a . . . survey of a portion of the Central Pacific R. R. route through . . . Nebraska . . .
Dubuque 1857. O 26 map aa

THOMAS, LEWIS F., and WILD, J. C.   178
The valley of the Mississippi illustrated . . . with
historical descriptions. *St L* 1841–[42]. Q 60 [incl.
eng.t.] [6] 61–145 unpaged lf containing note after
p44 34pls[6not numb. & 2pls numb.26] plan dd
ChiH G LC
—rptd. *St. L.* 1948 Q pls. a 300 copies ptd.
Originally issued in nine monthly parts; pt. 3
is accompanied by an "extra" [4pages and plate]

and pts. 8 and 9 [issued together as pt.8] end on page 130, with an unfinished sentence, noting that it would be continued in pt. 10. No pt. 10 was ever issued. The actual final part, No. 9, does not continue the text from page 130, but the pagination is continuous.

THOMAS, PATRICK J. 179
Our centennial memoir ... San Francisco de Assis in its hundredth year ... *S F* 1877. D 192 map pls aa
—ed. 2, "Founding of the missions of California ..." *S F* 1882. D 192 map a

THOMAS, R. 180
An authentic account of the most remarkable events ... *N Y* 1836. D 2v in 1: 298; 359. [incl. pls] a
—rptd., same impr. & collat., 1837.

THOMAS, R. 181
Interesting and authentic narratives of the most remarkable shipwrecks ... *Hart* 1836. D 360 [incl. pls] a
—rptd., same impr. & collat.: 1837; 1839; 1847; 1848.
Some copies issued with his *An authentic account* ..., above.

THOMASON, A. [pseud.]
Men and things in America ... *See* Bell, Andrew

THOMASON, D. R. 182
Hints to emigrants ... to the United States ... *Phil* 1848. 16° 124 aa
—Eng. ed., with adds. on Calif., *L* 1849. 16° [12] 117 [8] aa

THOMASSY, RAYMOND 183
De la Salle et ses relations inédites de la découverte du Mississippi. *P* 1859[date on cover 1860]. O [6] 24 fold.map a

THOMASSY, RAYMOND 184
Géologie pratique de la Louisiane. *N O* 1860. Q [68] 264 5maps 2pls [on 1 sheet] aa
—rptd. *N O* 1860; *P* 1861.
Not confined to geological observations, and contains the first attempt at a bibliography of Louisiana cartography.

THOMES, WILLIAM H. 185
On land and sea, or California in ... 1843–4–5. *B* 1884. D [6] 351 a
Cast in the form of an adventure story, but based on personal experiences; as an authentic picture of California in the early 'forties comparable to Dana's classic narrative.

THOMES, WILLIAM H. 186
The whaleman's adventures in the Sandwich islands and California. *B* 1872. D 444 front. pictorial t. a
—rptd. same impr. & collat., 1874; 5 later eds., 1876–1890.

THOMPSON, BENJAMIN F. 187
The history of Long Island. *N Y* 1839. O 536 2pls a
—ed. 2, enl., *N Y* 1843. O 2v: 512; 554. map 16pls aa
—ed. 3—and best—with adds., *N Y* 1918. O 4v 135 sets aa
—anr. issue in 3v 600 sets aa

THOMPSON, CHARLES 188
Evidences in proof of the Book of Mormon being a divinely inspired record ... *Batavia, N Y* 1841. 16° 256 aa
Brigham Young, objecting to some of its pronouncements, called in all copies owned by the Saints.

THOMPSON, CLARA M. 189
Reconstruction in Georgia ... *N Y* 1915. [6] 5–418 a

THOMPSON, DANIEL P. 190
History of ... Montpelier [Vt.]. *Montpelier* 1860. O 312 port a

THOMPSON, DAVID, of Niagara 191
History of the late war, between Great Britain and the United States ... *Niagara Upper Canada* 1832. 16° 300 aa
—ed. 2, same collat. *Tor* 1845.
One of the earliest books printed in Upper Canada; based on official documents.

THOMPSON, DAVID, 1770–1857 192
Narrative of ... explorations in western America, 1784–1812. *Tor* Champlain Soc. 1916. O [98] 582 [8] 23maps & pls b N NYP Y 550copies ptd.
Most important contribution to Western history and exploration published in the twentieth century. Thompson's operations on the Upper Columbia and Spokane rivers, in 1807, gave color to England's Oregon claims.

THOMPSON, ED[WIN] P. 193
History of the First Kentucky brigade. *Cin* 1868. O 931 2pls aa
—enl. ed. "History of the Orphan Brigade," *Louisv* 1898. O 1104 ports 2col.pls aa

THOMPSON, G[EORGE] A. 194
Handbook to the Pacific and California, describing ... routes ... *L* 1849. 16° [2] 108 port map aa

[THOMPSON, HENRY, of Texas] 195
Texas. Sketches of character, ... *Phil* 1839. 16° 95 b NYH TxU Y

THOMPSON, HUGH B. 196
Directory of the city of Nevada and Grass Valley: containing a history . . . *S F* 1861. O 128 + adv-l. at front b

[THOMPSON, JAMES] 197
A short authentic account of the siege of Quebec . . . *Quebec* 1872. O 48 a

THOMPSON, LIEUT. J[AMES] J. 198
A history of the feud between the Hill and Evans parties of Garrard county, Kentucky . . . *Louisv* [1854]. O 115 map pl b
—rptd. *Cin* [1854]. O 112 a book-list on inside of front wrap, in issue 1; on inside of back wrap, in later issues.
Cover title: *Kentucky tragedy* . . . The youthful author was lynched in Tennessee a few years later for the brutal murder of his mother, sister and brother.

THOMPSON, ROBERT A. 199
Conquest of California . . . *Santa Rosa Calif* 1896. O [2] 33[incl.port] aa

THOMPSON, ROBERT A. 200
Historical . . . sketch of Sonoma county, California. *Phil* 1877. O 104 map + 15adv-p aa

THOMPSON, ROBERT A. 201
The Russian settlement in California . . . *Santa Rosa Calif* 1896. O [2] 34 700copies ptd. aa

THOMPSON, R[OBERT] B., ed. 202
Journal of Heber C. Kimball . . . *Nauvoo* 1840. D 60 b G H Hn Y
—rptd. *S L C* 1882. D 104 a

THOMPSON, THOMAS 203
An account of two missionary voyages . . . one to New Jersey . . . the other . . . to the coast of Guiney. *L* 1758. O [4] 88 aa

[THOMPSON, THOMAS?] 204
A letter from New Jersey, in America . . . *L* 1756. O 26 b N NYP

THOMPSON, [WILLIAM], and WALKER, [JAMES] 205
The Baltimore Town and Fell's Point directory . . . *Balt* [1796]. D 100 aa
First Baltimore directory.

THOMPSON, ZADOCK 206
Appendix to the history of Vermont . . . *Burl* 1853. O 64 map a
Separate publication of additions incorporated in the 1853 edition of his *History*.

THOMPSON, ZADOCK 207
A gazetteer of . . . Vermont . . . *Montpelier* 1824. D 310 [2] map 3pls a

THOMPSON, ZADOCK 208
History of . . . Vermont . . . *Burl Vt* 1833. 16° 252 a
—rptd. *Burl* 1836.
—anr. ed., with new t-p, *Burl* 1858. same collat.

THOMPSON, ZADOCK 209
History of Vermont, natural, civil and statistical . . . *Burl* for the au. 1842. O 3pts in 1: [4] 224; 224; 200 [4]. map a
—issue 2, *Burl* Goodrich, same date & collat.
—anr. ed., same impr. 1853. O 3pts in 1: [6] 224; 200; 5–64 [5]. map

[THOMSON, CHARLES] 210
An enquiry into the causes of the alienation of the Delaware and Shawanese Indians from the British interest . . . with the . . . journal of Christian Frederic Post by whose negotiations, among the Indians on the Ohio, they were withdrawn from the interest of the French . . . *L* 1759. O 184 map b N NYP Y
—rptd. *Phil* 1867. O map a 250 copies ptd. Also 75copies on L.P.
For Post's second journal, *see* under his name.

[THOMSON, E. H.] 211
The emigrant's guide to . . . Michigan. *N Y* 1849. O 47 [text in Ger. & Eng.] a
—Dutch ed. "Gids voor Landverhuizers . . .," *Amst* 1850. O 36

[THOMSON, JOHN], of Va. 212
The letters of Curtius. Addressed to General Marshall. *Rich* 1798. D 40 a
—rptd., with adds., au. named, *Rich* 1804. 16° [14] 78

THOMSON, JOHN L. 213
Historical sketches of the late war . . . *Phil* 1816. D [12] 3–360 [1] 11maps & pls a
—ed. 2, enl., *Phil* 1816. D [4] 368 13maps & pls
—ed. 3, same impr., date & collat.
—ed. 4, *Phil* 1817. same paginat. 2plans
—ed. 5, *Phil* 1818. same paginat. 6pls
—anr. ed. "History of the second war . . .," *Phil* 1848. O 656 pls

THOMSON, MATT 214
Early history of Wabaunsee county, Kansas . . . *Alma, Kas* 1901. O 368 [8] a
—ed. 2, same impr. & collat 1902.

THOMSON, MONROE 215
The golden resources of California . . . *N Y* 1856. O 91 + 4adv.p. a

THOMSON, ORIGEN 216
Crossing the plains . . . to the "far off" Oregon, in 1852 . . . *Greensburg Ind* 1896. D 122 b N

THOMSON, WILLIAM, of Scotland   217
A tradesman's travels in the United States . . .
Edin 1842. D [8] 228 front. a
Travelled through the South and Middle West,
spending considerable time in Ohio.

THOMSON, WILLIAM, of Va.   218
A compendious view of the trial of Aaron Burr
. . . [*Abingdon*, Va., 1807] D 135 b
—rptd, author's name spelled Thompson. *Petersburg*, Va., 1808 D 138 a

THORBURN, GRANT   219
Forty years' residence in America . . . *B* 1834.
D 264 port a
—Eng. eds., with introd. by John Galt: *L* 1834 .D
[12] 280 port; ed. 2, same impr., date & collat.

THOREAU, HENRY D.   220
A week on the Concord and Merrimack. *B* J.
Munroe & Co. 1849. D 413 b N NYP
—issue 2, made up of unsold sheets of issue 1, with
new t-p dated 1862. aa
—new ed., cor., *B* Ticknor & Fields 1868. a
Both issues of the original edition have following
printer's errors: page 120, "work" for "wash";
page 139, "experience" for "expediency"; page
396, last three lines omitted.

THORNE, J.   221
Hanover; or the persecution of the lowly. A
story of the Wilmington [N.C.] massacre. n.p. [*ca*
1899]. O 136 a
The race conflict of November, 1898.

THORNTON, DE MOUNCIE   222
De la Californie et des côtes de l'ocean Pacifique
. . . *P* 1849. 16° 72 map b Hn S

THORNTON (J[ESSY] QUINN).   223
Memorial of: praying for the establishment of a
territorial government for Oregon. [Sen. Misc.
Doc. 143]. *Wash* 1848. O 24 a
For similar memorial, submitted by Joe Meek,
see Oregon. Memorial of the legislative assembly of:

THORNTON, J[ESSY] QUINN   224
Oregon and California in 1848. *N Y* 1849. D 2v:
[10] 13–393; [2] 7–379 + advs map 12pls aa
—rptd., same impr. & collat., but with different
map, 1855; 1864. aa

THORNTON, JOHN   225
Diary of a tour through the northern states . . .
and Canada. *L* 1850. D 120 a

THORNTON, JOHN W.   226
The landing at Cape Ann . . . *B* 1854. O [12] 84
map front. a

THORNTON, WILLIAM   227
Short account of the origin of steamboats . . .
Wash, Elliot, 1814. 16° 20 b LC

—anr. iss, same date, *Wash*, Rapine & Elliot. D
12 b NYP
—rptd. *Alb* 1818. 16° 18 b NYH
Thornton, principal architect of the Capitol
building at Washington, here upholds John Fitch's
claims as the inventor of the steamboat.

THORNWELL, J[AMES] H.   228
The state of the country. *Columbia S C* 1861.
O 32 a
—other eds.: [*N O* 1861]. O 15; t.altered, *N Y*
1861. O 30

THOROWGOOD, THO[MAS]   229
Jewes in America; or, probabilities that the
Americans are of that race . . . *L* 1650. Q [44] 136
[3] b AA Hn N NYP
—rptd. "Digitus Dei, etc." *L* 1652. Q [40] 136 [3] b
First English book advocating this theory.

THOROWGOOD, THO[MAS]   230
Jews in America; or, probabilities that Indians
are Judaical, made more probable . . . *L* 1660. Q
[10] 30 [8] 28, 67 b Hn JCB N
—enl. ed. "Vindiciae Judaecorum . . ." same
impr & date Q [10] 30 [8] 32, 67 b
This second work of the author was intended as
a reply to L'Estrange's *Americans no Jews* [*q.v.*]

THORP, JOSEPH   231
Early days in the west. Along the Missouri 100
years ago. *Liberty* 1924. O 95 a
First printed serially in an 1880 newspaper; it
inspired Emerson Hough's *Covered wagon.*

[THORPE, THOMAS B.]   232
The big bear of Arkansas and other sketches . . .
of characters and incidents in the south and southwest. *Phil* 1845. D 181 eng.t. [pls incl. in paginat].
aa
—rptd. *Phil* 1855. a

THORPE, T[HOMAS] B.   233
The hive of "the bee-hunter" . . . *N Y* 1854. D
312 front. 8pls aa
Hunting adventures in Arkansas and Louisiana.

THORPE, THOMAS B.   234
The mysteries of the backwoods . . . *Phil* 1846.
D 190[incl.front.] 5pls aa

THORPE, T[HOMAS] B.   235
Our army at Monterey . . . *Phil* 1847. O 204
eng.t. map 2 pls a
—rptd., *Phil* 1848.

THORPE, T[HOMAS] B.   236
Our army on the Rio Grande . . . *Phil* 1846. D
300 10pls[incl.eng.t.] a
—anr. issue, omitting official reports; paginat.
ending at p196

THOUGHTS

Thoughts in a series of letters, in answer to a question respecting the division of states. By a Massachusetts farmer. *See* Lowell, John.

Thoughts (The) of a traveller upon our American disputes . . . *See* Draper, Sir Wm.

Thoughts on a question of importance . . . **237** Whether . . . territory acquired by this nation at the late peace, will operate towards the prosperity or the ruin of . . . Great Britain. *L* 1765. O 48 a

Thoughts on American slavery and its   238 proposed remedies. By a northerner. *Hart* 1838. 18° 82 a

Thoughts on emigration . . . and a short account of Kentucky. *See* Toulmin, Harry.

Thoughts on government: applicable to the present state of the American colonies . . . *See* Adams, John.

Thoughts on the increasing wealth . . . **of the United States** . . . *See* Blodget, Saml.

Thoughts on the origin and nature of government. Occasioned by the late disputes between Great Britain and her colonies. *See* Ramsay, Allan.

Thoughts on the present relations and in-   239 terests of the Unites States. *N Y* 1810. O 36 a

Thoughts on the present state of affairs with America. *See* Pulteney, Wm.

Thoughts on the present war. With an im-   **240** partial review of Lord North's administration . . . *L* 1783. O [6] 78 a

Thoughts on the state of the American Indians. By a citizen . . . *See* Wood, Silas.

Thoughts on the subject of naval power in the United States . . . *See* Coxe, Tench.

Thoughts upon the conduct of our administration . . . **more especially** . . . By a friend of peace. *See* Lowell, John.

Thoughts upon the political situation of the United States . . . By a native of Boston . . . *See* Jackson, Jonathan.

Thoughts upon the present contest, be-   241 tween administration, and the British colonies . . . *L* 1775. O 46 a
Possibly by William Smith, [Provost].

## THRALL, HOMER S.			242

A pictorial history of Texas . . . *St L* 1878. O 858 fold.map a
—later eds.: 1879; 1883.
Useful for its biographies; historically a minor contribution.

## THRAN, JAKOB			243

Meine Auswanderung nach Texas . . . *Berlin* 1848. O [10] 121 aa

## THREE			244

Three letters addressed to the public on . . . the nature of a foederal union . . . *Phil* 1783. O 28 a

Three letters to a member of parliament,   245 on the subject of the present dispute with our American colonies . . . *L* 1775. O [4] 74 errata slip a

Three tracts on the conduct of the late and present administrations . . . *See* Lloyd, Chas.

## THRIFT, MINTON			246

Memoirs of Jesse Lee . . . *N Y* 1823. D [8] 360 a

## THRUSTON, GATES T.			247

The antiquities of Tennessee and the adjacent states . . . *Cin* 1890. O [16] 369 21 pls
—ed. 2, enl. 1897, same collat.

## THÜMMEL, A. R.			249

Die Natur und das Leben in den Vereinigten Staaten . . . *Erlangen* 1848. O [8] 521 aa

## [THURLOW, EDWARD]?			250

A refutation of the Letter to an Honble. Brigadier-General . . . in Canada. *L* 1760. O [2] 52 a
—3 other eds., same impr. & date
Defends Gen. Townsend's conduct after succeeding Wolfe.

## [THURSTON, BENJAMIN]			251

An address to the public . . . on the present political state of the American republicks . . . *Exeter* [1786]. O 36 a

## THURSTON, JOHN H.			252

Reminiscences . . . of early days in Rockford. *Rockford* 1891. O 117 port a

## THURSTON, WILLIAM			253

Guide to the gold regions of California. *L* 1849. D 70 [2] map aa

## THWAITES, REUBEN G., and			254
KELLOGG, LOUISE P.

Documentary history of Dunmore's war, 1774 . . . *Madison* 1905. D [28] 472 port 3 maps facs a

THWAITES, REUBEN G., ed.   **255**
Early western travels . . . *Clev* 1904–07. O 31v +
F atlas c N NYP Y
Of the set itself, with volume numbers shown on
spines, 750 cops were published. Volumes were
also issued separately, with no volume numbers on
spines. Contains the travel journals of Bracken-
ridge, Bradbury, Bullock, Croghan, Cuming, De
Smet, Evans, Farnham, Faux, Flagg, Flint,
Flower, Franchere, Gregg, Harris, Hulme, James,
Long, Maximilian, Michaux, Morris, Nuttall, Og-
den, Pattie, Ross, Townsend, Welby, Wood and
Wyeth, with two volumes of index.

THWAITES, REUBEN G., and   **256**
KELLOGG, LOUISE P.
Frontier defense on the Upper Ohio. *Madison*
1912. O [18] 329 fold.map 12pls 2facs a

THWAITES, REUBEN G. [ed.]
Original journals of the Lewis and Clark expedi-
tion. *N Y* 1904–5. *See* Lewis, Meriwether, and
Clark, William.

THWAITES, REUBEN G., and   **257**
KELLOGG, LOUISE P.
Revolution on the upper Ohio . . . *Madison*
1908. D [20] 275 fold.map 9pls a

[TICKELL, RICHARD]   **258**
Anticipation: . . . the substance of His M—y's
most gracious speech . . . on the opening of the
approaching session . . . *L* 1778. O [8] 74 a
—ed. 2, same impr. & date. O 74
—10 other Eng. eds. pub. by 1794.
—Am. eds.: *Phil* 1779, O [6] 33; *N Y* 1779.

[TICKELL, RICHARD]?   **259**
Anticipation: (for the year 1779) . . . substance
of His M . . . y's most gracious speech to both H
. . . s of P . . . l . . . t, on the opening of the approaching session . . . *L* Bladen 1779. O [8] 51 a
—ed. 2, same impr., date & collat.
—anr. issue, "Anticipation continued . . .," *L* for
the editor 1779. O 57
—ed. 2, same impr., date & collat.
Probably by some inferior hack seeking to profit
by letting the public think it the work of Tickell.

TICONDEROGA AND MT.   **260**
INDEPENDENCE.
Orderly book of the northern army, at: 1776–8.
Alb 1859. Q [8] 224 map port a 110 copies ptd]
[10 on L.P.]

TIERNEY, LUKE   **261**
History of the gold discoveries on the South
Platte . . . *Pacific City Ia* 1859. O 27 + 5adv-p d
ColH S [only copies known]
—rptd., with notes, *Denver* 1949. a

TIKHMENEV, P[ETR A.]   **262**
Istoricheskoe obozrienie obrazovaniia Rossiis-
ko-Amerikanskoi Kompanii . . . *St Ptbg* 1861–63.
O 2v: [8] 386 [66]; 389 79 292 [10]. 4maps 4pls aa
History of the Russian American Company. For
English translation of the part relating to Cali-
fornia, *see* Rezanov, Nicolai P.

TIKHMENEV, P[ETR A.]   **263**
Materialy dlia istorii Russikh zaselenii po bere-
gam Vostochaago okeana . . . [Materials for the
history of the Russian settlements on the shores of
the Pacific ocean]. *St Ptbg* 1861. O 4pts in 1: 670 aa

TILDEN, BRYANT P.   **264**
Notes on the upper Rio Grande . . . *Phil* 1847.
O 32 9maps a

TILGHMAN, OSWALD, ed.   **265**
History of Talbot county, Maryland . . . *Balt*
1915. O 2v: [8] 649; [10] 573. 2fronts. aa

TILGHMAN (LIEUT. COL. TENCH).   **266**
Memoir of: . . . *Alb* 1876. Q 179 port some cops
on L.P. a

TILING, MORITZ P. G.   **267**
History of the German element in Texas . . .
Houston 1913. O [8] 225 a

[TILLSON, CHRISTIANA H.]   **268**
Reminiscences of early life in Illinois . . . [*Am-
herst* 1872? 1873?]. O [4] 138 front. 3ports b ChiH
WisH
—rptd. "A woman's story of pioneer Illinois,"
Chi 1919. D [22] 169 2ports a

[TILTON, JAMES]   **269**
The biographical history of Dionysius, tyrant of
Delaware [i.e., George Read]. *Phil* 1788. O 100 a

TIMAEUS, J[OHANN] J. C.   **270**
Nordamerikanischer Staats-Kalender, oder Sta-
tistiches Hand- und Addressbuch der Vereinigten
Staaten . . . *Hamburg* 1796. D [38 incl final blank
lf] 530–540 543–544 2tabs aa

TIMBERLAKE (HENRY).   **271**
The memoirs of: . . . *L* 1765. O [8] 160 front.
map b AA N NYP Y
—rptd.: *Johnson City Tenn* 1927, a 35 copies ptd
on L.P. aa; *Marietta Ga* 1948
—Fr. tr. "Voyages du . . . Henri Timberlake . . .,"
P [1797]. D [10] 188 front. a
—Ger. tr. Gottingen 1767–9. O 328 [10] 329–669 a
Describes travels through Virginia, the Carolinas, Georgia and Tennessee; an important source
on the Cherokee nation and on the little-known
southern phase of the French and Indian war, as
well as the first eye-witness account of the Tenn.
country.

TIMLOW, HERMAN R.   272
Ecclesiastical and other sketches of Southington, Connecticut. *Hart* 1875. O [10] 570 [2] 275 27ports a

TINKHAM, GEORGE H.   273
A history of Stockton [Calif.] . . . *S F* 1880. O [16] 196 203–397 6pls a

TIPPECANOE.   274
Celebration . . . of the twenty-fourth anniversary of the battle of: *Lafayette Ind* 1835. O 24 no t-p aa only 3 cops loc.
First Lafayette imprint.

TITSWORTH, W. G.   275
Outskirt episodes. [*Avoca Ia*, ptd *Des M.* 1927] D 233 port[inserted on t-p] aa
Largely experiences in Wyoming.

TIXIER, VICTOR   276
Voyage aux prairies osages . . . 1839–40. *Clermont-Ferrand* [& *P*] 1844. O 260 [4] 5pls b MoH MinnU N NYP Y
—Eng. tr. *Norman Okla* 1940. O [16] 310 2maps 7pls a

TO THE PEOPLE OF THE UNITED   277
STATES.
British pretensions and American rights. By a citizen of New York. n.p. [1814?]. O [2] 27 a
Reply to *The right and practice of impressment* . . . , [*q.v.*].

TOCQUEVILLE, ALEXIS [C. H.   278
M. CLÉREL] DE
De la démocratie en Amérique. *P* 1835. O 2v: [28] 367; [4] 459. map aa
—ed. 2, same impr. & date. O 2v: [6] 3–387; [4] 447. map a
—many later Fr. eds. before 1840 [when pt. 2 appeared]
—Eng. tr. *L* 1835. O 2v: [44] 334; [8] 462. map a
—Eng. ed. 2, *L* 1836. O 2v: same collat.
—Eng. ed. 3, *L* 1838. D 2v: [36] 302; [8] 325. map
—Am. ed., *N Y* 1838. O [30] 464
—ed. 2, same date, impr. & collat.
—ed. 3, *N Y* 1839. O [16] 455
—rptd., new t. "American institutions . . . ," *N Y* 1845.
—Ger. tr. *Leip* 1836. O 2v
—Sp. tr. *P* 1837. O 2v map

TOCQUEVILLE, ALEIXS [C. H.   279
M. CLÉREL] DE
De la démocratie en Amérique. [2nd pt.] *P* 1840. O 2v[numb III & IV]: [12] 333; [4] 363 aa
—eds. 2 & 3, same impr., date & collat. a
—anr. issue, same date & impr. D 2v[numb I & II]
—anr. ed. *Brus* 1840. D 3v
—anr. issue, *Brus* 1840. 16° 2v

—many later Fr. eds.
—Eng. tr. *L* 1840. O 2v[numb III & IV]: [16] 334; [8] 365
—Am. ed. *N Y* 1840. O [20] 355
Complete editions in English—containing both parts of this classic analysis—were issued at New York in 1841, with many later reprints, American and English.

[TOD, NICHOLAS], pseud.   280
Good humor; or, a way with the colonies . . . *L* for the au. 1766. D [2] 37 aa
—anr. issue, *L* Nicoll 1766. D
Bitter attack on the colonies and their British defenders, Pitt and Wilkes.

[TOD, THOMAS]   281
Consolatory thoughts on American independence . . . *Edin* 1782. O [4] 68 a

TODD, ALBERT   282
The campaigns of the rebellion. *Manhattan Kas* 1884. O 130 errata slip 2maps a

TODD, CHARLES S., and   283
DRAKE, BENJAMIN
Sketches of the . . . services of William Henry Harrison . . . *Cin* 1840. 16° [2] 5–165 a
—anr. ed., enl. by James H. Perkins, *Cin* 1847. 16° 224

[TODD, HENRY C.]   284
Notes upon Canada and the United States . . . *Tor* 1835. O 95 a
—ed. 2, *Tor* 1840. O [8] 3–95 [184] some copies also added an 8–p app., and the 1833 ed. of the au's "Manual of orthoepy," O [4] 104

TODD, REV. JOHN   285
The lost sister of Wyoming . . . *Northampton* 1842. 16° 160 front. a
Narrative of Frances Slocum's remarkable captivity among the Delaware Indians.

TOLL, D[ANIEL] J.   286
Narrative . . . *Schenectady* 1847. O 57 a

TOLMER, J.   287
Scènes de l'Amérique du Nord en 1849. *Leip* 1850. 16° [6] 134 a
Ten letters, chiefly from southern and western cities.

TOME, PHILIP   288
Pioneer life; or, thirty years a hunter. *Buff* 1854. D 238[incl. front.] b N Y

TOMLINSON, ABRAHAM, ed.   289
The miliatry journals of two private soldiers, 1758–1775 . . . *Poughkeepsie* 1855. O 128 a

TOMLINSON, WILLIAM P.   290
Kansas in eighteen fifty eight . . . *N Y* 1859. D
[6] 9–304 a

TOMPKINS, DANIEL A.   291
History of Mecklenburg county [N. C.] . . .
Charlotte 1903. O 2v: [18] 202; [10] 214 [2]. 93pls a

TONER, J[OSEPH] M.   292
The medical men of the revolution . . . *Phil*
1876. O 140 a

TONGUE, JAMES   293
A letter . . . to the people of Maryland, giving a
short account of the country on the south shore of
lake Erie . . . *Wash* 1807. O 32 aa

[TONTY, HENRI DE]?   294
Dernières découvertes dans l'Amérique septentrionale de . . . La Sale . . . *P* 1697. D [4]334[20]
c N NYP MinnU
—In many cops data on pearls given on 2 lvs [pp
185 to 188] were suppressed and those 2 lvs were
replaced by 1 lf in smaller type. c ChiH WisH
MinnU
—anr. ed. [in "Relations de la Louisiane . . ."]
Amst 1720. D 408 map 13pls aa
—Eng. tr. "Account of . . . La Salle's last expedition", with another narrative by Montauban added.
L 1698. O [2] 212, 44 c Clem NYP
Tonty disclaimed authorship of this narrative
but it was probably based on his letters or memoirs with help possibly from Le Clercq's *Premier établissement de la foi* which had appeared in
1691. For an English translation of another Tonty
Memoir see Falconer, *On the discovery of the
Mississippi.*

TONTY (HENRI DE).   295
Relation of: *Chi* Caxton Club 1898. O [10] 122
[2] 194 cops ptd a
First separate printing, in both English and
French, of an actual Tonty narrative which had
previously appeared in Margry's 1879 *Origines
françaises des pays d'outre mer* . . .

TOOLEY, HENRY   296
History of the yellow fever . . . in the city of
Natchez . . . 1823. *Natchez* 1823. O 29 aa
—ed 2, *Wash, Miss* 1823. D 23 a

TOPEKA.
City directory . . . of: 1868. *See* Millison, D. G.
pub.

TOPHAM, EDWARD   297
An address to Edmund Burke, Esq., on his late
letter relative to the affairs of America. *L* 1877.
Q [4] 27 a
—ed. 2, same impr., date & collat.

[TOPLADY, AUGUSTUS M.]   298
An old fox tarr'd and feather'd. Occasioned by
. . . John Wesley's Calm address . . . *L* 1775. D
24 a
—ed. 2, cor., same impr., date & collat.
—rptd. *L* [1775?]. O 16

TOPONCE (ALEXANDER).   299
Reminiscences of: pioneer, 1839–1923. [*Ogden
Utah* 1923]. D 248 14pls a

TOPPING, E. S.   300
The chronicles of the Yellowstone . . . *St P* 1883.
O [4] 246 map 3 pls aa
—rptd. *St P* 1888. same collat. a

TORCH LIGHT (THE).
An examination of the origin [etc.] of the opposition to the administration, and an exposition of
the official conduct of Thomas H. Benton . . . see
Benton, Thos. H.

TORFAEUS, THORMODUS   301
Historia Vinlandiae antiquae . . . *Havniae* 1705.
O [52] 93 [16] b JCB N NYP Y
—rptd., same impr. & collat. 1715. aa
—Eng. tr. *N Y* 1891. O 83 a
Pioneer presentation of Norse claims to Ameri-
can discovery.

TORNEL [Y MENDIVIL], JOSÉ M.   302
Tejas y los Estados Unidos . . . en sus relaciones
con la República Mexicana. *Mex* 1837. O 98 b G
H LC TxU Y

TORRENS Y NICOLAU, FRANCISCO   303
Bosquejo histórico del . . . Junipero Serra . . .
Felanitx 1913. O [16] 227 [4] pls a

TORREY, JESSE   304
A portraiture of domestic slavery . . . *Phil* 1817.
O 94 6pls a
—ed. 2, *Ballston Spa* 1818. D 108 port
—Eng. ed., "American slave trade . . .," *L* 1822.
D 119 5pls

TORREY (WILLIAM).   305
Torrey's narrative; or, the life and adventures
of: . . . *B* 1848. D 300[incl. front. & pls] a
Visited California in 1837.

TORRUBIA, [JOSÉ] GUISEPPE   306
I Moscoviti nella California o sia dimostrazione
verita' del passo all' America . . . scoperto dai
Russi . . . *Rome* 1759. D 83 c N
—rptd. *Venice* 1760. b Hn JCB Y
Traces the early voyages to the Northwest coast,
especially those from Russia, and attempts to
prove that the earliest was made in 1640, a century
prior to Bering.

TOUCHSTONE
Touchstone to the people of the United States, on the choice of a president. *See* Herring, Elbert.

[TOULMIN, HARRY]   **307**
A description of Kentucky . . . [*L*] 1792. O 124 map & descriptive lf between p68 & 69 b H Hn NYP
—rptd. *Lex* 1945. O [14] 120 map a
Probably printed early in 1793, as a letter is included dated Feb. 2, 1793. Though signatures are numbered to follow those in the first part of the item just below, of which it was obviously intended to form a part, separates must have been issued.

[TOULMIN, HARRY]   **308**
Thoughts on emigration . . . and a short account of the State of Kentucky. [*L*] 1792. O 24 124 map & lf. explaining it, both inserted between p68 & 69 b N NYP
The first part—*Thoughts*—may not have been by Toulmin.

TOUR
Tour (A) through part of Virginia. *See* Mitchill, Sam'l L.

Tour through parts of the United States and Canada. By a British subject. *See* Beaufoy, Mark.

TOURIST (THE)
Tourist (The); or, pocket manual for travellers . . . *See* Vandewater, Robt. J.

TOURNÉE
Tournée à la mode dans les États-Unis. *P* 1829. *See* Davidson, Gideon M., *The fashionable tour*, of which this is a translation.

TOUSEY, FRANK   **309**
The life and trial of Frank James. *N Y* 1883. Q 28 a

TOWER, PHILO   **310**
Slavery unmasked . . . *Rochester* 1856. D 432 pl a
The wildest flight of anti-slavery fantasy.

[TOWERS, JOSEPH]   **311**
A letter to Dr. Samuel Johnson, occasioned by his late political publications . . . *L* 1775. O [4] 78 + adv-p a

TOWLE (NANCY).   **312**
Vicissitudes . . . in the experience of: . . . *Charleston S C* 1832. 16° [6 5–12] 5–294 front. aa
—ed. 2, *Portsmouth N H* 1833. D 310[incl. front.] aa
Largely devoted to her life with the Kirtland Mormons.

[TOWN, ITHIEL], ed.   **313**
A detail of some particular services . . . in

America . . . 1776–1779. *N Y* 1835. D [10] 117 aa
Most of the edition burned. Includes a British sailor's journal of operations along the Atlantic coast.

TOWNES, SAMUEL A.   **314**
The history of Marion [Ala.] . . . *Marion* 1844. O 61 b AlaA
First and rarest Alabama local history.

[TOWNSEND, GEORGE A.]   **315**
The life, crime and capture of John Wilkes Booth . . . *N Y* Dick & Fitzgerald [1865]. O [4] 65 aa
—anr. issue. O 80 a

[TOWNSEND, JOHN]   **316**
The doom of slavery in the Union: its safety out of it. *Charleston S C* 1860 O 40 aa
—ed. 2, same impr., date & collat. a
Urges immediate secession if Lincoln is elected.

[TOWNSEND, JOHN]   **317**
The south alone should govern the south . . . [*Charleston S C* 1860]. O 60 aa
—3 other eds., same yr.   a

[TOWNSEND, JOHN]   **318**
The southern states, their present peril, *etc.* *Charleston S C* 1860. O 62 aa

TOWNSEND, JOHN K.   **319**
Narrative of a journey across the Rocky mountains, to the Columbia river . . . *Phil* 1839. O 352 aa
—Eng. ed. "Sporting excursion in the Rocky mountains." *L* 1840. D 2v: [12] 310 + 2adv-p; [12] 312 + 8adv-p 2pls [both incl. in collat.]
—abr. ed. "Excursion to the Oregon," [no t-p] [*ca* 1846]. D 32 a
With Wyeth's second expedition, of 1834. In the English edition, author is given as Townshend.

TOWNSEND, WILLIAM H.   **320**
Lincoln and his wife's home town. *Indp* [1929]. O [16] 11–402 pls a

[TOWNSHEND, CHARLES]   **321**
Remarks on the Letter address'd to two great men . . . *L* 1760. O [2] 38 aa
—rptd. *L* Dodsley [1760]. O 64 a
—ed. 2, same collat., *L* [1760].
—ed. 3, *L* [1760]. O 72
—Am. ed. *B* Mecom [1760]. O 40
Attributed also to William Burke. For the *Letter* referred to, *see* that title. For reply to these *Remarks*, *see* Jackson, Richard, *The interest of Great Britain considered.*

TOWNSHEND, F[REDERICK] TRENCH   322
Ten thousand miles of travel, sport and adventure. *L* 1869. O [14 incl. front.] 275 + 18 adv-p. a

TOWNSHEND, S[AMUEL] NUGENT   323
Our Indian summer in the far west. *L* 1880. Q
123 60photos. b
Southwestern cattle industry, etc.

[TOWSON, NATHAN]   323a
Correspondence . . . [in relation to the capture
of the British brigs Detroit and Caledonia, 1812].
[*Wash?* 1835]. O 46 37–43 a
Cf. similar title on the same affair by Elliott,
Jesse D.

TRACY, J[OSHUA] L.   324
Guide to Missouri and St. Louis . . . historical
sketches . . . *St L* 1871. D 32 2fold. maps a

TRACY, J[OSHUA] L.   325
Guide to the great west . . . *St L* 1870. D 236
[i.e. 224] 215–290 [7] 2maps aa

[TRACY, URIAH]   326
Scipio's reflections on Monroe's View of the conduct of the Executive . . . *B* 1798. O [4] 140 a
—rptd., with adds., title altered, [*Phil* 1798]. O 88
Ascribed also to Alexander Hamilton.

TRACY, WILLIAM   327
Notices of men and events connected with the
early history of Oneida county [N. Y.]. *Utica* 1838.
O 45 errata slip a

TRADE [THE] . . . OF GREAT BRITAIN . . .
Trade [The] and navigation of Great Britain
condidered . . . *See* Gee, Joshua.

TRAIN . . . ROBBERS
Train and bank robbers of the west . . . *See*
Appler, Augustus C.

TRAITÉ   328
Traité d'amitie et de commerce, conclu entre le
roi [of France] et les États-Unis . . . le 6 Février
1778. *P* 1778. Q 23 a
—anr. ed. [capt.t. only], *P* Simon [1778]. Q 8
—Am. ed. "Treaties of amity and commerce, and
of alliance eventual and defensive . . .," *Phil*
Dunlap 1778. Q [4] 3–10 [2] 11–34 b AA Hn NYP
—rptd. *B* 1778. Q [6] 5–6 [1] 7–9 [2] 10–23 a
—anr. ed. *Newbern* 1778.
—other eds., all 1779; *Hart*; *Lancaster* n.d.;
Norwich
—Eng. eds.: *L* 1782. O [2] 40; same impr. &
collat. 1783.

TRAITS
Traits of american-indian life. *See* Finlayson,
Duncan.

Traits of character . . . manifested by the inhabitants of the north-eastern states . . . By Uncle
Daniel, L.L.D. *See* Wrifford, Alison.

TRANCHEPAIN, MÈRE MARIE DE   329
ST. AUGUSTIN
Relation du voyage des premières Ursulines à
la Nouvelle Orléans . . . *N Y* 1859. D 62 [2] 100
cops ptd a
For an earlier printed account of the founding
of New Orleans' first convent school *see* Háchard,
Marie M.

TRANSATLANTIC
Transatlantic rambles . . . By a Rugbaean. *See*
Dixon, —.

Transatlantic tracings . . . *See* Phillips, Geo.
Searle.

TRANSLATION (A)
Translation (A) of the Memorial to the sover-
eigns of Europe upon the present state of affairs
. . . *See* Jenings, Edmund.

TRAVELER AND TOURIST'S GUIDE BOOK.
See Colton, Jos. H.

TRAVELLER'S
Traveller's directory (The), and emigrant's guide
. . . through . . . New York, Ohio . . . *See* Steele,
Oliver G.

Traveller's guide (The) across the plains . . . *See*
Platt, P. L., and Slater, Nelson.

Traveller's guide (The) to America . . .   330
Cork 1818. D 71 a

Traveller's manual (The); and description of the
United States . . . *See* Melish, John.

Travellers' own book (The) . . . *See* De Veaux,
Saml.

Traveller's pocket directory (The) and   331
stranger's guide; exhibiting distances on the principal canal and stage routes . . . in New York . . .
Schenectady 1831. 24° 66 [4] + 33adv-p 4pls aa
—ed. 2, *N Y* 1832. 24° 96 2pls aa
—variant issue of this ed. carries 1833 date on slip
pasted on front cover aa
—ed. 3, *Schenectady* 1833. aa
—rptd., same impr., 1834; 1836. a
Some editions entitled *The western traveler's . . .
directory . . .*

Traveller's register (The) and river and   332
road guide. *Cin* 1846. O 36 map aa
—other eds.: same impr. 1847; 1848. aa

TRAVELS
Travels in America . . . in 1806. *See* Ashe, Thos.

Travels in North America. *Dub* 1822. *See*
Philips, George.

Travels in the two hemispheres. *Det* 1847.   333
O 576 front. aa
—ed. 2, same impr. & collat., 1848.

Contains two important serials: Warren Isham's *Sketches of border life* [describing a railroad survey through Iowa] and Gilbert Hathaway's *Travels in the southwest* [describing life in Arkansas and Texas]. The original plan of m nthly issuance as *The magazine of travel* was apparently abandoned as this work is only known in book form.

Travels (The) of several learned mission-   334
ers of the Society of Jesus . . . *L* 1714. O [16] 336
[12] + 4adv-p 2pls aa

Travels on the western slopes. By Cincinnatus.
See Wheat, Marvin.

Travels through the interior parts of America . . .
By an officer. *See* Anburey, Thos.

Travels through the United States and Canada . . .
L 1828. *See* Blane, Wm. N.

[TRAVERS, DE VAL?]   335
Summary observations and facts . . . from late and authentic accounts of Russian and other navigators, to show the practicability . . . in enterprises to discover a northern passage . . . between the Atlantic and Pacific . . . *L* 1776. Q [2] 29 c N Y
Attributed also to Daines Barrington. Covers geographical discoveries on the North West Coast.

TREADWELL, EDWARD F.   336
The cattle king . . . [biography of Henry Miller, of California]. *N Y* 1931. O [10] 367 4pls a
—rev. ed. *B* [1950] O 286

TREAT (CAPTAIN JOSEPH).   337
The vindication of: against the atrocious calumny . . . in Major General Brown's official report of the battle of Chippeway. *Phil* 1815. O 62 aa

TREATIES   338
Treaties between the United States and . . . Indian tribes . . . 1778–1837. *Wash* 1837. O [2, 5–84] 699 a
—new ed., same impr., date & collat.

TREATISE   339
Treatise (A) on slavery, by an unknown author, of Virginia. n.p. [183–?]. D 40 a

Treatise (A) on the art of flying . . . *N Y*   340
1814. D 64 a
—rptd. same impr. 1816.
First American book on the subject.

Treatise (A) on the patriarchal, or co-operative system of society . . . **under the name of slavery** . . . **by an inhabitant of Florida.** *See* Kingsley, Z.

TREATY   341
Treaty of amity, commerce, and navigation between His Brittanic Majesty, and the United States . . . *Phil* Bache [1795]. O 24 aa
—anr. issue, with motions of Burr and Tazewell added, same impr., n.d. [1795?]. O 27 a
—other 1795 Am. eds: *Bennington* O 35; [*B*] n.d. F 2; *N Y* O 32; *Phil* Neale & Kammerer D 72; *Phil* Tuckniss, with adds., D 283; *Phil* Lang & Ustick O 190 [2] a
—Eng. eds.: *L* Debrett 1795. O 26; same, with adds. O 28; *L* Johnston 1795. Q 33 a

Though the 1783 peace treaty gave the Northwest Territory to the United States, actual possession of strategic posts was not relinquished until after this treaty [Jay's] of 1794.

TREDWAY, THOMAS J.   342
Statistics of the United States . . . for the use of emigrants . . . *L* [1834]. 18° [4] 176 a

TREGO, CHARLES B.   343
A geography of Pennsylvania . . . history . . . of the state; with . . . description of each county . . . *Phil* 1843. D 384 [incl. illus.] map a

TREMENHEERE, HUGH S.   344
Notes on public subjects . . . during a tour in the United States and Canada. *L* 1852. D [8] 320 + 32adv-p map a

TRENHOLM, VIRGINIA C.   345
Footprints on the frontier: saga of the La Ramie region of Wyoming. [*Douglas, Wyo.* 1945] O 384 45maps and pls aa

TRENT (CAPTAIN WILLIAM).   346
Journal of: from Logstown to Pickawillany, 1752. *Cin* 1871. O 117 a
First printing of an unpublished MS. *See* also *Case* [*of William Trent and other traders*].

TRÉNY, M.   347
La Californie dévoilée . . . *P* 1850. O 60 + 2adv-p aa
—eds. 2 & 3, same impr., date and collat.

TREU, GEORG   348
Das Buch der Auswanderung . . . *Bamberg* 1848. O [8] 216 aa
Issued chiefly in the interest of Texas emigration companies.

TREZEVANT, D. H.   349
The burning of Columbia, S. C. . . . *Columbia* 1866. O 30 a
—rptd.: same impr. & date. O 31; *Marietta Ga* 1958 D 39

TRIAL (THE) OF REPUBLICANISM . . .
By Peter Porcupine. *See* Cobbett, Wm.

TRIBUTE TO CAESAR . . .
By Philalethes. *See* Maule, Thos.

TRICOCHE, GEORGES 350
La vie militaire à l'étranger: notes d'un engagé
volontaire au 11e United States Cavalry. *P* [1892].
D 352 a

TRIGGS, J. H. 351
History and directory of Laramie City . . . *Laramie*
1875. O 91 [incl. front wrap] b AA N NYP WisH Y
—rptd. *Laramie* 1955. a

TRIGGS, J. H. 352
History of Cheyenne and northern Wyoming . . .
Omaha 1876. O 144 [incl. advs] map b LC N NYP Y
—rptd. *Laramie* 1955 a

TRIGGS, J. H. 353
A reliable . . . guide to the Black Hills [etc.].
Omaha 1876. O 144 map b LC N WisH
—anr. ed. *Omaha* 1878. b Y
With exception of title and first 16 pages indent-
ical with author's *History of Cheyenne,* above.

TRIOMPHE (LE) DU NOUVEAU MONDE
See Brun, Jean B.

TRIP (A) TO THE UNITED STATES . . .
See Beadle, Chas.

TRIPLER, EUNICE 354
Some notes of her personal recollections. *N Y*
1910. 16° 184 port aa

TRIPLETT, FRANK 355
History . . . of great American crimes . . . *N Y*
1884. O 659 front. a

TRIPLETT, FRANK 355a
The life, times and . . . death of Jesse James.
St L 1882. D [16] 416 Iss l [of May 22]: front of
Jesse returning from a raid, with cpyrt notice on
recto, and illus [of his flight after wrecking a train]
on verso of t-p b
—iss. 2 [pubd between June and Nov.]: bust of
Jesse as front, with cpyrt on verso of t-p b
—iss. 3 [pubd *ca* Nov.]: somewhat enlgd by inclusion of Frank James' surrender in Oct. and an
added pl D [16] 7–426 b
It is alleged that efforts were made to suppress
this biography. The scarcity of all issues tend to
confirm this.

TROBRIAND, PHILIPPE RÉGIS 356
DENIS DE KEREDERN, comte de
Vie militaire dans le Dakota . . . (1867–1869).
P 1926. O [16] 408 port a
—Eng. tr., abr. ed. Quaife, *Chi* 1941. 16°
—anr. tr., complete, *St P* [1951]. O [28 incl. map]
395 12 pls

TROLLOPE, MRS. [FRANCES M.] 357
Domestic manners of the Americans. *L* 1832.
O 2v: [12] 336; [6] 272. 24pls aa
—ed. 2, *L* 1832. D 2v: [12] 304; [8] 304. 24pls a
—eds. 3 & 4, same collat., *L* 1832.
—ed. 5, *L* 1839. 16° [8] 384 port pl
—Am. ed. *N Y* 1832. O [10, 3–8] 25–325 8pls a
—trs.: [Fr.] *P* 1833, 2v: [Ger.] *Kiel* 1835. 3v;
[Dutch] *Harlem* 1833, 2v; [Sp.] *P* 1835, 2v: [24]
312; [4] 331. ea a

TROLLOPIAD (THE) . . .
By Nil Admirari. *See* Shelton, Frederick W.

[TROTTER, ISABELLA S.] 358
First impressions of the new world . . . *L* 1859.
D [12] 308 + 24adv-p map a
Penetrated West to Missouri and liked it all.

TROWBRIDGE, M[ARY] E. D. 359
Pioneer days . . . *Phil* [1895]. D 160 port a
Includes sketchy account of an 1849 overland
trip to California; made by Gershom Day, who
was killed by Indians there in 1852.

TROY DIRECTORY . . . 1829
See Disturnell, John, pub.

TRUE 360
**True constitutional means (The) for putting an
end to the disputes between Great Britain and the
. . . colonies.** *L* 1769. O [2] 38 aa
Offers a "Henry George" solution to the colonial tax problem, substituting, for all others, a
single land tax.

**True interest (The) of America impartially stated,
in . . . strictures on a pamphlet intitled Common
sense.** *See* Inglis, Chas.

**True interest (The) of Great Britain, with respect
to her American colonies . . .** By a merchant of
London. *See* Bacon, Anthony.

True merits (The) of a late treatise . . . 361
intitled Common sense . . . By a late member of the
continental congress . . . *L* 1776. O [8] 44 a

True picture (A) of emigration. *See* Burlend,
Rebecca.

True picture (A) of the United States . . . 362
By a British subject. *L* 1807. O 100 aa
—ed. 2, same date & impr. D 111 a

True sentiments (the) of America. *See* Hollis,
Thos.

**True state (A) of the proceedings in the parlia-
ment of Great Britain . . .** *See* Lee, Arthur.

TRUESDELL, WINIFRED P.   363
Engraved . . . portraits of Abraham Lincoln.
Vol. II [only one pub.]. *Champlain N Y* 1933. O
[14] 241 front. 49photos 225copies, 25 on Jap.
vellum aa
—anr. issue, with 26 prelim. p. aa

TRUMAN, BENJAMIN C.   364
Life, adventures . . . of Tiburcio Vasquez, the
great California bandit . . . *L A* 1874. O 44 [incl.
front.] aa

TRUMAN, BEN[JAMIN] C.   365
Occidental sketches. *S F* 1881. D 228 [incl. prel.
blank lf and final advs.]
Adventures in California, Nevada and Alaska.

TRUMBULL, BENJAMIN   366
A complete history of Connecticut . . . Vol. I
[all]. *Hart* 1797. O [20] 587 map 3 ports a
—rptd. *N Lond* 1798.
—anr. ed., with v. 2 added, *N Hav* 1818. O 2v: 563
[last p. misnumb. 567]; [2] 7–548 port
—rptd. *N Lond* 1898. O 2v front.

TRUMBULL, BENJAMIN   367
A general history of the United States . . . in
three volumes. Vol. 1 [all]. *B* 1810. O [2] 442 a
—issue 2, same impr. & date. O [12] 9-467 errata
slip
—anr. issue, identical with issue 2, but t-p omits
mention of 3vols.
—rptd. *N Y* 1810. O 442

TRUMBULL, BENJAMIN   368
A plea, in vindication of the Connecticut title
to . . . lands, lying west of . . . New-York, *N Hav*
1774. O 102 + errata lf aa
—anr. ed., same impr. & date. O 161 aa

[TRUMBULL, HENRY, senior]?   369
The adventures of Colonel Daniel Boon . . .
Norwich, Conn 1786. 16° 24 d S Y [of 3cops loc]
—rptd, *Windsor* 1793 c
—anr. ed, "Life and adventures of Colonel Daniel
Boon . . ." *Bklyn* 1823. 16° 36 port c AA N NYP
WisH
—oth eds, same collat, with both *Bklyn* & *Prov*
imprints 1824. ea b
—anr. ed, *Louisv* 1932. O 62 a
First separately printed account of Boone, plagiarized from his so-called autobiography incorporated in John Filson's *Kentucke*, of 1784, *q.v.* The
Providence edition and the two Brooklyn editions
were evidently from the same type. Possibly all
were printed in Providence.

[TRUMBULL, HENRY], junior   370
History of the discovery of America . . . By the
Rev. James Steward. *Bklyn* [1802?]. O 176 fold.
front. aa

—anr. iss. au. given as "a citizen of Connecticut,"
Norwich 1810. D 176 fold.pl a
—anr. ed. au.named, same impr. & date. D 184
2pls a
—anr. ed. same impr. 1812. D 184 [8] 2pls
—many later eds., some with t. changed to "History of the Indian wars . . ."
A well-nigh worthless production of a seven-
teen-year old lad which enjoyed wide favor by an
uncritical public.

[TRUMBULL, HENRY], junior, ed.   371
Life and remarkable adventures of Israel R. Pot-
ter . . . soldier in the American revolution . . . *Prov*
Trumbull 1824. D 108 [incl. front.] a
—anr. ed., same impr., collat. & date, but ptd by
Howard, different front. & no errata list on p. 108
[errors having been cor. in text]
Purported autobiography, of dubious authentic-
ity. *See* also another version under Melville,
Herman.

TRUMBULL, H[ENRY], junior   372
Western emigration . . . *B* [1819?]. D 36 front. a
—rptd. *Prov* [1826] 16° 36 front.
Fictitious experiences of a Maine family attempting to make a home in Ohio. Written to discourage emigration.

TRUMBULL, JAMES [pseud.]   373
Life of George Washington . . . *N Y* 1829. 18°
168[misnumb. 166] 3pls aa
Essentially the biography written by Thomas
Condie, with a few additions and a fictitious author
named.

TRUMBULL, JAMES H., ed.   374
The memorial history of Hartford county, Conn.
B 1886. O 2v: [14] 704; [10] 570. 4 maps 67 pls a

TRUTH
Truth is no slander . . . *Natchez* 1827. *See* Clement, Samuel.

Truth is stranger than fiction. New Orleans as it
is . . . By a resident. *See New Orleans as it is* . . .

TRUXTUN (COMMODORE [THOMAS]).   375
Reply of: to an attack made on him in the National Intelligencer . . . *Phil* 1806. O [3] 32 a

[TRYON, THOMAS]   376
The planter's speech to his neighbors . . . of
Pennsylvania [etc.]. *L* 1684. D 73 [incl. initial
blank lf] dd Hn [only cop loc]

TUBBEE, LAAH C. M. E.   377
A sketch of the life of Okah Tubbee . . . of the
Choctaw nation. *Springfield* 1848. D 84 a
—rptd. *Tor* 1852. Q 96
Cf. similar title by Allen, Lewis L.

TUCKER, BEVERLEY
See Tucker, Nathaniel Beverley.

TUCKER, EPHRAIM W.   378
A history of Oregon ... *Buf* 1844. D 84 c B
G LC NYP Y

[TUCKER, GEORGE]   379
Defence of the character of Thomas Jefferson,
against a writer in the New York Review ... *N Y*
1838. O 46 a

TUCKER, GEORGE   380
The life of Thomas Jefferson ... *Phil* 1837. O
2v: [4 9–10 2 11–18 13–20] 9–545 [1]; [2] 526 [1].
port a
—Eng. ed. *L* 1837. O 2v: [22] 612; [10] 588. port

TUCKER, DR. J[OSEPH] C.   381
To the golden goal, and other sketches. *S F* 1895.
D 303 9pls 50copies ptd. aa

TUCKER, JOSIAH   382
Cui bono? or, an inquiry, what benefits can arise
... from the greatest victories, or successes, in the
present war? *Glocester* 1781. O 142 + adv-p a
—ed. 2, with pacification plan added, same impr.
& collat. 1782.
—ed. 3, *L* 1782. O [2, 5–25] 3–142 + adv-p
—Dutch tr. [*Amst* 1781]. O [2] 127
—Fr. trs.: *L* 1782. O [2] 116; *L* 1782. O 95; *Rotterdam* 1782. O [2] 116

[TUCKER, JOSIAH]   383
Dispassionate thoughts on the American war ...
L 1780. O 36 a

TUCKER, JOSIAH   384
Four tracts ... *Glocester* 1774. O [18] 9–216
[36] a
—eds. 2 & 3, same impr. & date. O 224
Contains reprints of his *Letter from a merchant
in London*, and *The true interest of Great Britain*,
see below.

TUCKER, JOSIAH   385
An humble address and earnest appeal ...
whether a connection with, or separation from the
continental colonies of America be most for the
national advantage ... *Glocester* 1775. O 93 +
2adv-p fold.tab. a
—ed. 2, same impr., date & collat.
—ed. 3, *L* 1776. O 94 + 2adv-p fold.tab

[TUCKER, JOSIAH]   386
A letter from a merchant in London to his
nephew in North America, relative to the present
posture of affairs in the colonies ... *L* 1766. O
[4] 55 a
—Dutch trs.: "Verhandeling over het recht van
het Britsche parlement ...," *Utrecht* 1775. O [8]

56; "Onzydidge brief van een voornam Koopman
te London ...," *Utrecht* 1778. O [2] 8 56

TUCKER, JOSIAH   387
A letter to Edmund Burke ... in answer to his
printed speech [on conciliation with America].
Glocester 1775. O 58 + 2adv-p a
—ed. 2, same impr., date & collat.
—anr. ed. *Dub* 1775. O 48

TUCKER (DOCTOR [JOSIAH]).   388
A letter to: on his proposal of a separation between Great Britain and her American colonies.
L 1774. O [4] 36 a
—ed. 2 *L* 1776. O 58

[TUCKER, JOSIAH?]   389
A plain letter to the common people of England
and Wales ... against transporting themselves to
America ... *Bristol* 1783. D 24 a
—anr. ed., possibly the first, *L* 1783. same collat.
Early effort to discourage emigration of British
laboring classes.

TUCKER, JOSIAH   390
The respective pleas ... of the mother country,
and of the colonies ... *Glocester* 1775. O [16]
9–51 + adv-p a
—ed. 2, same impr. 1776. O 60

[TUCKER, JOSIAH]   391
A series of answers to certain popular objections,
against separating from the rebellious colonies ...
Glocester 1776. O [15] 9–108 [5] + 6adv-p a
Advocates granting the colonies independence
and then forming a union between them and
England.

TUCKER, JOSIAH   392
The true interest of Great Britain ... in regard
to the colonies ... *Norfolk Va* 1774. O 66 a
—rptd. with adds., *Phil* 1776. O 66 [6]
—Eng. ed. *L* 1776

TUCKER ([NATHANIEL] BEVERLEY).   393
Address of: to the people of the United States ...
[cover t.only]. *Montr* 1865. 24° 44 b Duke Emory
Indignant denial of accusation made against
himself, Davis and other Confederate leaders of
complicity in Lincoln's assassination and suggests
President Johnson as the likeliest fomentor of
Booth's act.

[TUCKER, NATHANIEL BEVERLEY]   394
The partisan leader; a tale of the future. [*Wash*]
1856. D 2v: [6] 201; [2] 201 b AA N NYP Y
—rptd. *N Y* 1861. D 2v: [2, 5–16] 195; [8] 199–392 a
—anr. issue, *N Y* 1861. D 2v: in 1: [2, 5–16] 195;
196–392 a
—anr. ed. *Rich* 1862. D [8] 220 + 4adv-p aa
—rptd. *N Y* 1863; *N Y* 1933. a

Original edition suppressed on its publication in 1836. Date 1856 was fictitious. A prophetic foretelling of the Civil war.

TUCKER, PATRICK T. 395
Riding the high country. *Caldwell* 1933. D 210 pls Issued also in a ltd and sgd ed of 25cops a

TUCKER, ST. GEORGE 396
A dissertation on slavery; with a proposal for the gradual abolition . . . in Virginia. *Phil* 1796 O [6] 9–106 a
—rptd., *N Y* 1861

[TUCKER, ST. GEORGE?] 397
A letter to a member of Congress; respecting the alien and sedition laws. n.p. [1799]. O 48 capt.t. a
Ascribed also to James Madison.

[TUCKER, ST. GEORGE?] 398
Letter to a member of the general assembly of Virginia, on the . . . late conspiracy of the slaves . . . *Balt* 1801. O 23 a

[TUCKER, THOMAS T.] 399
Conciliatory hints, attempting . . . to remove party-prejudices . . . and proposing a convention by delegates, for the purpose of accommodating our Constitution more perfectly to the principles of equal and permanent freedom: submitted to the consideration of the citizens . . . of South-Carolina *Charleston S C* 1784. Q 34 aa

TUCKERMAN, HENRY T. 400
America and her commentators . . . *N Y* 1864. D [8] 460 a

TUCKERMAN, HENRY T. 401
Book of the artists . . . sketches of American artists, preceded by an historical account . . . *N Y* 1867. Q [12] 7–639 17pls aa also 50copies on L.P.
—ed. 2 *N Y* 1867. front only. a

TUCKERMAN, HENRY T. 402
The life of Silas Talbot . . . *N Y* 1850. 16° [12] 9–137 a
Intended for inclusion in Sparks' series of American biographies, but completed too late.

TUCSON AND SURROUNDINGS. 403
Handbook of: *Tucson* 1880. D [12] 68 map aa

**TUCSON AND TOMBSTONE . . .
"DIRECTORY" 1883.**
See Cobler, Frank, and Swanwick, T. F., comps.

TUDOR, HENRY 404
Narrative of a tour in North America . . . *L* 1834. D 2v: [22] 468; [12] 548 a
Travels extended from Maine to Virginia, Kentucky, Ohio and Louisiana; Americans are defended from Trollopian accusations.

TUDOR, WILLIAM 405
Letters on the eastern states. *N Y* 1820. D [8] 5–356 a
—ed. 2, *B* 1821. O 423

TUDOR, WILLIAM 406
The life of James Otis . . . *B* 1823. O [20] 508 + 2adv-p port pl facs a

TUFTS (HENRY). 407
A narrative of the life, adventures . . . of: . . . *Dover N H* 1807. 16° 366 a
—rptd., t. altered, *N Y* 1930. O [18] 357 4facs
This autobiography of a New England vagabond was ghost-written. Members of the Tufts family destroyed many copies and others went up in the printer's fire.

TULARE COUNTY, CALIFORNIA. 408
History of: . . . *S F* 1883. F 226 pls b Pomona Coll Kern Co. L.

TULLIDGE, EDWARD W. 409
The history of Salt Lake City . . . *S L C* [1883–4]. O 336 3pls aa
—rptd., with adds., same impr. [1886]. O [10] 3–896 28 151 33pls a
—anr. ed., same impr. & date. O [8] 3–896 172 36 33pls

TULLIDGE, EDWARD W. 410
Life of Brigham Young . . . *N Y* 1876. O [8] 458 [81] port a
—ed. 2, same impr., 1877. O [8] 458 [108] port

TULLIDGE, EDWARD W. 411
Life of Joseph [Smith] the prophet. *Plano Ill* 1880. O [12] 827 4ports a

TULLIDGE, EDW[ARD] W. 412
Tullidge's histories, volume II [covering Utah sections, etc., not included in his "History of Salt Lake City . . .,"]. *S L C* 1889. O [6] 440[error for 540] [2] 372 26pls aa

TUMBLETY (T. F.) 413
A few passages in the life of: *Cin* 1866. O 82 a

TUNNARD, W[ILLIAM] H. 414
A southern record. The history of the Third Louisiana Infantry. *Baton Rouge* 1866. D 393 2ports aa

TUOLUMNE COUNTY, CALIFORNIA.
A history of: *See* Lang, Herbert O.

TUPPER, FERDINAND B. 415
Family records; containing memoirs of Major-General Sir Isaac Brock . . . to which are added the life of Te-cum-seh . . . *Guernsey* 1835. O [12] 218 3pls a

—enl. ed. "The life and correspondence of . . . Brock . . .," *L* 1845. D [12] 468
—ed. 2, same impr. 1847. D [12] 492

TURENNE D' AYNAC, GABRIEL L., 416
comte de
Quatorze mois dans l'Amérique du Nord. *P* 1879. D 2v: [6] 390 [2]; [4] 396 [3] map a

TURGOT, [ANNE ROBERT J., 417
baron de l'Aulne]
Mémoire sur les colonies américaines . . . *P* 1791. O 75 aa

TURLAND, EPHRAIM 418
Notes of a visit to America . . . *Manchester* 1877. D [8] 190 a

TURNBULL, M. S., comp. 419
The Montgomery directory, for 1859–60 . . . *Montg* 1859. D 128 aa
First directory of this city.

[TURNBULL, ROBERT J.] 420
The crisis; or, essays on the usurpations of the federal government. *Charleston S C* 1827. O 166 a

TURNER, FREDERICK J. 421
The frontier in American history . . . *N Y* 1920. D [8] 375 a
—rptd., same impr. & collat., 1921; 1923; 1926; 1928; 1950.

TURNER, FREDERICK J. 422
The significance of the frontier in American history. *Madison Wis* 1894. O 34 + cover t. aa
Few copies issued as a separate from Wisconsin Historical Society Proceedings of 1893 [published 1894]. Later amplified into *The frontier in American history*, see above.

TURNER, G[EORGE] 423
Traits of Indian character . . . *Phil* 1836. D 2v: 207; [4] 7–196 a

TURNER, JOHN 424
Pioneers of the west. *Cin* 1903. D 404 a

TURNER (NAT).
The confessions of: *See* Gray, Thos. R.

TURNER, O[RSAMUS] 425
History of the pioneer settlement of Phelps and Gorham's purchase . . . embracing the counties of Monroe, Ontario, etc. to which is added a supplement . . . of the pioneer history of Monroe county . . . *Roch* 1851 O 624 a
—anr. ed., to which is added a suppl. of the history of the counties of Ontario, etc. *Roch* 1852 O [16] 9–588

TURNER, O[RSAMUS] 426
Pioneer history of the Holland purchase of western New York . . . *Buf* 1849. O 666 5maps 9ports 4pls a
—rptd.: same impr. 1850, O 670 5maps 9 ports 4pls; *Rochester* 1851; 1852.

TURNER, T[IMOTHY] G. 427
Gazetteer of the St. Joseph valley [Michigan and Indiana]. *Chi* 1867. O 166 [2] [incl.front. & pl] a

TURNLEY (PARMENAS T.) 428
Private letters of: . . . on the character of the constitutional government of the United States . . . *L* 1863. O [12] 194 aa

TURNLEY, PARMENAS T. 429
Reminiscences . . . *Chi* [1892]. D 448 3pls [and in some copies 3 extra pls inserted] aa
After service in the Mexican war, this West Pointer campaigned for ten years in Nebraska. Dakota and Utah. A leaf of "contents" is sometimes found inserted.

TURPIE, DAVID 430
Sketches of my own times. *Indp* [1903]. D [10] 387 a
Account of life in the southern Indiana backwoods in the thirties, etc., by a United States senator.

TURREAU DE LINIERES, LOUIS M., 431
baron de
Apercu sur la situation politique des États-Unis . . . *P* 1815. O 154 a
Author fought in the Revolution and from 1804 to 1811 was Minister to the United States.

TURRILL, H. B. 432
Historical reminiscences of . . . Des Moines . . . *Des M* 1857. D 144 fold.view + 4pls a

TUSCARORA INDIANS (THE).
A Sabbath among: *See* Duncan, John M.

TUTHILL, FRANKLIN 433
The history of California. *S F* 1866. O [4 7–16] 657 a

TUTTLE, C[HARLES] R. 434
History of Grand Rapids . . . *Grand Rapids* 1874. D 153 a

TUTTLE, EDMUND B. 435
Border tales around the camp fire. *L* 1878. D [18] 243 + adv-l. 5pls aa
—Am. ed., same collat. *N Y & L* 1878. a
These tales—including a fine account of the fall of the Alamo—were told on a surveying expedition from Omaha to the Yellowstone country.

TUTTLE, EDMUND B.   **436**
The boy's book about Indians . . . *Phil* 1873. D 207 7pls a
—rptd., same impr. & collat. 1874.
—Eng. ed. *L* n.d. same collat.
The author, chaplain at several Wyoming army posts, describes the Ft. Kearney, Sweetwater and Plum Creek Indian fights.

TUTTLE, E[DMUND] B.   **437**
The history of Camp Douglas . . . *Chi* 1865. O 51 a

TUTTLE, E[DMUND] B.   **438**
Six months on the plains . . . *Chi* 1868. Q 32 + 20adv-p aa

TUTTLE, EDMUND B.   **439**
What I saw and heard for three years on the plains. *Phil* 1874. D 207 pls a

TUTTLE, J. H.   **440**
Wam-dus-ky: . . . record of a hunting trip to North Dakota . . . *Minneap* 1893. O 178 pls aa 35copies ptd.

TWENTY-FOUR LETTERS   **441**
Twenty-four letters from labourers in America to their friends in England. *L* 1829. O 48 aa
Preface signed Benjamin Smith.

TWENTY THOUSAND MUSKETS!!!
See Allen, Ira.

TWISS, TRAVERS   **442**
The Oregon question examined . . . *L* 1846. O [11] 392 front 2maps aa
—Am. ed. "The Oregon territory, its history [etc.]," *N Y* 1846. D 264 [4] aa

TWITCHELL, RALPH E.   **443**
The leading facts of New Mexican history. *Cedar Rapids* 1911–12. O 2v: [24] 506; [24] 631 pls aa
These volumes gave the state history; three later volumes cover the history of the twenty-six counties. The 5-volume set b

TWITCHELL, RALPH E.   **444**
Old Santa Fe . . . *Santa Fe* [1925]. O 488 [incl. front. & pls] a

TWITCHELL, RALPH E.   **445**
The Spanish archives of New Mexico. [*Cedar Rapids*] 1914. O 2v: [24] 525; [8 incl. final blank l.] 683. 42pls & facs a

TWO
Two letters to a friend, on the present critical conjuncture of affairs . . . *See* Chauncy, Chas.

Two months in the Confederate States . . . By an English merchant. *See* Corsan, W. C.

Two rebellions (The); or, treason unmasked. By a Virginian. *See* McDonald, Wm. N.

Two tracts: information for those who would remove to America . . . *See* Franklin, Benj.

Two tracts, shewing, that Americans born before the Independence, are . . . not aliens . . . By a barrister. *See* Reeves, John.

Two years before the mast. *N Y* 1840. *See* Dana, Richard H.

TWYMAN, R. B. J. [pub.]   **446**
Memphis directory . . . for 1850, with a brief history . . . *Memphis* 1849. O 112 a
First directory—and first historical sketch—of this city.

TYLER, DANIEL   **447**
A concise history of the Mormon Battalion . . . 1846–1847. [*S L C*] 1881. O [4] 3-376 aa
Detailed narrative, by a member, of the memorable march of this organization from Council Bluffs to San Diego. Though dated 1881, internal statements indicate its actual publication in 1882.

TYLER, LYON G.   **448**
The letters and times of the Tylers . . . *Rich* 1884–5, *Wmsbg* 1896. O 3v: [16] 633; [16] 736; [14] 234[actually 240, as 6p are repeated]. 15 pls 3 facs. aa

TYRANNY UNMASKED.   **449**
An answer to . . . Taxation no tyranny [by Samuel Johnson]. *L* 1775. O [4] 90 aa

TYRRELL, JOSEPH B.   **450**
A brief narrative of the journeys of David Thompson in northwestern America. *Tor* 1888. O 29 a

TYSON (ELISHA).
Life of: . . . By a citizen of Baltimore. *See* Tyson, John S.

TYSON, JAMES L.   **451**
Diary of a physician in California . . . *N Y* 1850. O 92 + 4adv-p aa

TYSON, JOB R.   **452**
Discourse on the colonial history of the eastern and some of the southern states. *Phil* 1842. O 64 a

[TYSON, JOHN S.]   **453**
Life of Elijah Tyson, the philanthropist. *Balt* 1825. 16° [8] 142 errata slip port a

Describes his 1803 trip to Ohio with Gerard T. Hopkins. *See* Tyson, Martha E.

TYSON, MARTHA E. [comp.]   **454**
A mission to the Indians . . . to Fort Wayne, in 1804. Written at the time. by Gerard T. Hopkins, with an appendix. *Phil* 1862. 16° 198 aa
Privately printed and never sold. Hopkin's account of his visit to the Miamis and Pottawatomies is interesting and important, but no more so than the additional material, by George Ellicott on the same mission, found in the appendix.

TYSON, PHILIP T.   **455**
Memoir on the geology of California. *Wash* 1850. [Sen. Exec. Doc. 47, 31 Cong., Sess. 1] O [24] 127 37 3maps 10pls aa
—rptd. with introd. "Geology and industrial resources of California . . .," *Balt* 1851. O [34] 127 37 3maps 9pls tab a
Based on a four month's stay in California.

TYSON, ROBERT A.   **456**
History of East St. Louis . . . *E St L* 1875. O 152 fold.map fold.pl aa

U

UDALL and HOPKINS [pubs.]   **1**
Chicago city directory, for 1852–3. *Chi* 1852. D [4adv-p] 294 map[intended for issue with book, but not in all copies as it was not ready in time and had to be supplied later] aa

UDELL, CORNELIUS   **2**
Condensed history of . . . Jefferson [O.] . . . *Jefferson* 1878. D 116 a

UDELL, JOHN   **3**
Incidents of travel to California, across the great plains . . . *Jefferson O* 1856. D 302 errata l. port [not issued in all copies; probably added after some had been distributed] aa
—rptd. *L A* 1946. O [4, 9–20] 88 8pls 775 copies [25signed]

UDELL, JOHN   **4**
Journal . . . during a trip across the plains containing an account of the massacre of a portion of his party by the Mohave Indians, in 1859. *Suisun City Cal* 1859. O 45[incl. cover t.] dd Y[only copy known]
—rptd., *Jefferson O* 1868. O 48 port d AA G Hn Pn WrH
—anr. ed. *L A* 1946. O [4 9–22] 88 7pls a
Udell's party went to southern California via the Santa Fe trail and Albuquerque.

UEBER NORDAMERIKA   **5**
Ueber Nordamerika und Demokratie . . . *Koppenhagen* [ptd *Königsberg*] 1782. D 212 [2] aa

UHDE, ADOLPH   **6**
Die Länder am untern Rio Bravo . . . *Heidelberg* 1861. O [8] 432 map aa
Based on a years' residence in Texas.

[UHLENHUTH, E.]   **7**
Rathgeber für auswanderer nach Californien. *Bremen* 1849. O 84 map b

UHLHORN, JOHN A., comp.   **8**
The Virginia and Truckee railroad directory . . . *S F* 1873. O [52] 416 aa

[UITENHAGE DE MIST, MLLE. VAN]   **9**
Relation d'un voyage en Afrique et en Amérique. *Namur* 1821. Priv.ptd. D 63 aa only 1 cop loc.

UMFREVILLE, EDWARD   **10**
The present state of Hudson's bay . . . *L* 1790. O [12] 128 133–230 + adv-l. pl 2fold. tabs b H N NYP Y
—Ger. tr. *Helmstadt* 1791. O [26] 164 map 2tabs aa
Contains experiences in the lake region, etc.

UNANIMITY   **11**
Unanimity in all parts of the British commonwealth, necessary to its preservation . . . *L* 1778. O [4] 39 a

UNCONNECTED WHIG'S ADDRESS   **12**
Unconnected Whig's (An) address to the public; upon the present civil war . . . *L* 1777. O [4] 80 + errata slip pasted on verso of t. a.

UNDER THE STARS AND BARS . . .
See Jones, Benjamin W.

UNDERWOOD, GEORGE C.   **13**
History of the Twenty-sixth regiment of the North Carolina troops . . . *Goldsboro* [1901]. O [4] 122 [6] pls aa

UNIFORM OF THE ARMY . . .
Phil 1882. *See Regulations for the uniform . . . of the Army . . .*

UNIFORMS FOR THE U.S. NAVY   **14**
Wash 1869. F 12 9pls[8col.] aa
—anr. issue. O 17 no pls a
For earlier works on the subject, *see Regulations . . .*

UNION (THE):   **15**
. . . a condemnation of Mr. Helper's scheme . . .
By one who has considered both sides of the
question . . . *N Y* [1857]. O 32 a

UNION COUNTY, IOWA.   **16**
Centennial sketches of: *Creston* 1876. O 145
map a

UNION PACIFIC RAILROAD CO. (THE).
Report of the organization . . . of: *See* Dix,
John A.

UNITED STATES   **17**
The proceedings of the United States Anti-
Masonic Convention . . . at Philadelphia, September
11, 1830. *Phil* 1830. O 164 [incl. blank lf] aa
—issue 2, identical except no blank lf it being used
as separate t. for Address to the people of the
United States.
Contains report on murder of William Morgan.
For reprints of that report *see* Whittlesey, Frede-
ric, *Abduction and murder of William Morgan.*

United States (The) and Canada, as seen   **18**
by two brothers . . . *L* 1862. D [6] 137 map a

United States (The) and England: . . . reply to
the criticism on Inchiquin's letters . . . *See*
Paulding, James K.

United States register (The) . . . with . . .   **19**
routes . . . *N Y* 1837. D 2pts in 1: 54; 27. [map
mentioned on p2 apparently not issued with the
book] a

UNONIUS, GUSTAF [E. M.]   **20**
Minnen frän en sjuttonärig vistelse i nordvestra
Amerika. *Upsala* 1861-2. O 2v: [8] 424; [8] 621.
8pls aa
—ed. 2, same impr. & collat., 1862. aa
Describes his activities as founder of a Swedish
settlement in Wisconsin, in 1841, and his later
residence in Chicago.

UPHAM, CHARLES W.   **21**
Lectures on witchcraft . . . *B* 1831. 18° [8] 280 a
—ed. 2, *B* 1832. 16° [6] 300 a
—enl. ed. "Salem witchcraft," *B* 1867. Q 2v a
some copies on L. P. aa

UPHAM, CHARLES W.   **22**
The life of Washington . . . *B* 1840. D 2v: 402
[incl. blank lf]; 388 [incl. blank lf] b AA N NYP Y
—issue 2, with 2ports added, same impr. & date.
D 2v: 443; 423. 2ports b
—Eng. eds., from sheets of above issue 2, with new
t-p, *L* 1851 a; *L* 1852.
Both issues of the Boston edition were suppress-
ed, almost at once by court order, as infringing on
Sparks' copyright.

UPHAM, SAMUEL C.   **23**
Notes of a voyage to California via Cape Horn
. . . with scenes in El Dorado . . . 1849–50 . . . *Phil*
1878. O [2] 7-594[incl.pls] 2ports aa
By a pioneer journalist of Sacramento and San
Francisco.

[UPSHUR, ABEL P.]   **24**
A brief enquiry into the true nature . . . of our
federal government . . . *Petersburg Va* 1840. O 132 a
—rptd., with au. named, *Phil* 1863.
—anr. ed. "The federal government . . .," *N Y* 1868.

UPTON, CHARLES E.   **25**
Pioneers of El Dorado. *Placerville* 1906. O [6]
3–201 6pls a

URLSPERGER, SAMUEL   **26**
Americanisches Ackerwerk Gottes . . . *Augsburg*
1754–1755–[1767], Q 5v: [14] 126, 137–174 port;
[26] 175–334, 353–390 [23]; [8] 335–525; [12] 72,
71–80, 83–84; [60] 286 b GaU NYP Y
Continuation of his *Ausführliche Nachrichten* . . .,
see below.

URLSPERGER, SAMUEL   **27**
Der ausführlichen Nachrichten von der König-
lich-Gross-Britannischen Colonie Saltzburgischer
Emigranten in America. *Halle* 1731[i.e. 1735]-
1752. Q 19pts in 3v: v.I, 6pts: [2] 14, 242 + 2adv-
p; [20] 243-574; [18] 575–980; [12] 981–2072; [12]
2073–2312; [28] 2313–2598 [38]. v.II, 7pts: [32]
358 [2]; [52] 361–716 tab; [36] 717–844, 843–1014;
[4] 1015–1270; [24] 1771–1930; [12] 1931–2138;
[12] 2139–2270 [35]. v.III, 6pts: [10] 72 [20] 73–
203; [14] 205–340; [8] 341–436; [12] 437–536; [36]
537–744 [15p wrongly numb. 745–774]; [16] 777–
1004 [18]. map & port in v.I, map & plan in v.III
b GaU H
—rptd., with index: *Halle* 1741; 1746; 1752; Q 3v:
v.I, 6pts; v.II, 7pts; v.III, 6pts b Y
This series of Journals, or annual accounts of the
Salzburger settlements over a long period, issued
originally separately, forms one of the most important sources for the provincial history of Georgia. For a continuation *see* above this author's
Americanisches Ackerwerk . . .

URQUHART, D[AVID]   **28**
Annexation of Texas . . . *L* 1844. O 104 aa

URQUHART, DAVID   **29**
Exposition of the causes and consequences of
the boundary differences between Great Britain
and the United States . . . *Liv* [1839]. Q [8] 5–95
[16] map aa
—rptd. *Glas* 1840. O [16] 5–91 [20] map aa

URQUHART, DAVID   **30**
Reflections and thoughts on things, moral, religious and political. *L* 1844. O [4] 332 [74] aa

Contains his two famous international articles, *Annexation of Texas* and *England in the western hemisphere*.

URREA (JOSÉ).   31
Diario de las operaciones militares de la division que al mando del: hizo la campaña de Tejas. *Victoria Mex* 1838. O 136 c AA B Y
—Eng. tr. Dallas [1928] O [8] 391
Vindication of his conduct attempted by the perpetrator of the Goliad massacre. Cover title differs slightly.

UTAH   32
The crimes of the Latter-Day Saints in Utah. By a Mormon of 1831. [*Cin* 1899]. O 101 a

Utah expedition (The) ... information   33
relative to the military expedition ... H. Exec. Doc. 71. *Wash* 1858. O 215 a
Authoritative reports of General Johnston and his subordinate officers on operations connected with this "Mormon war."

Utah expedition (The) ... **with incidents** of travel on the plains ... *See* Conway, Cornelius.

UTE   34
Letter of the secretary of the Interior ... transmitting ... correspondence concerning the Ute Indians of Colorado. [Sen. Exec. Doc. 31] *Wash* 1880. O 274 aa
White river massacre, captivity of Mrs. Meeker, etc.

**Testimony in relation to the Ute indian   35
outbreak.** *Wash* 1880. O 204 a
Details of the terrible White River massacre, the Meeker captivity, etc.

**Ute massacre (The)! Brave Miss Meeker's   36
captivity!** [etc.]. *Phil* [1879]. O 62 b
—Ger. ed. "Ute Blodbadet ...," *Minneap* n.d. D 54

UTICA   37
Utica directory ... for 1817. *Utica* Williams [1816]. 16° 57 aa
—rptd. [*Utica*] 1920. 16° a
First Utica directory.

Utica directory ... 1828. *See* Harrington, Elisha, pub.

V

V., M. P.
Histoire de la tribu des Osages ... *See* Vissier, Paul.

VAAS, LACHLAN C.   1
History of the Presbyterian Church in New Bern ... and a sketch of the early days ... *Rich* 1866. O 196 a

VADE MECUM (THE) FOR AMERICA.
See Prince, Thos.

VAHL, JENS   2
Alaska: folket og missionen ... *Copenh* 1872. O [6] 108 a

VAIL, A. L.   3
A memorial of James M. Haworth, super intendant of United States Indian schools. *K C* 1886. O 178 aa

VAIL, ALFRED   4
The American electro magnetic telegraph ... *Phil* 1845. O 208 a
—rptd., same impr. & collat. 1847.

VAIL, ALFRED   5
Description of the American electro magnetic telegraph ... *Wash* 1845. O 24 a
—rptd., same impr. & collat. 1847.

VAIL, ALFRED   6
Réponse à quelques imputations contre les États-Unis ... *P* 1837. O 36 a

VAIL, EUGÈNE A.   7
Notice sur les Indiens ... *P* 1840. O 246 map 4pls a

VALANCE, HENRY L., ed.   8
Confession of the murder of William Morgan, as taken down by John L. Emery ... *N Y* 1849. D 24 a

VALE, G[ILBERT]   9
A compendium of the life of Thomas Paine. *NY* 1837. O 32 a
—enl ed "The life of Thomas Paine" ... *N Y* n.d. [*ca* 1839]. O 192 a
—rptd. *N Y* 1841. O 192 29 [2] port

VALE, JOSEPH G.   10
Minty and the cavalry ... in the western armies. *Harrisburg* 1886. O [32] 550 6maps 13ports a

VALERO, FERNANDO   11
Bosquejo de la republica de los Estados Unidos ... *Guatemala* [1830]. 16° 2pts in 1: [4] 81; [2] 37 [2] aa

[VALETTE-LAUDUN, MONS. DE]   **12**
Journal d'un voyage à la Louisiane, fait en 1720. Par M . . ., Capitaine de vaisseau du Roi. *Hague* 1768. D [8] 376 + 3adv-p a
By the commander of the expedition sent to examine the Florida and Louisiana coasts; for scientific results of this voyage, *see* Laval, Antoine Jean de. For earlier appearance of this journal *see* Tonty.

VALLEJO, CALIFORNIA.
The future of Vallejo . . . by Solano. *See* Hittell, John S.

The prospects of Vallejo. *See* Hittell, John S.

The resources of Vallejo. *See* Hittell, John S.

VALLET, EMILE   **13**
Communism. A history of the experiment at Nauvoo of the Icarian settlement. *Nauvoo* [ca 1900]. D 31 a

VALPARAISO, INDIANA.   **14**
History of: . . . By a citizen. *Valparaiso* 1876. O 24 a

VAN BUREN, A. DE PUY   **15**
Jottings of a year's sojourn in the south . . . *Battle Creek* 1859. D 320 aa
Favorable impressions of southern Mississippi registered by a school teacher from Michigan.

VAN BUREN, MARTIN   **16**
Inquiry into the origin and course of political parties in the United States . . . *N Y* 1867. O [10] 436 port a

VAN BUREN (MARTIN).   **17**
Memoir of: . . . By a citizen of New York. *N Y* 1838. O 137 a
—ed. 2, same impr. 1839. O 137 [2]

[VAN CAMPEN, MOSES]   **18**
A narrative of the capture of certain Americans at Westmoreland, by savages . . . *Hart* [1780?]. O 24 c AA N NYP [of 4 copies known]
—rptd. *N Lond* 1784. O 16 b MH [of 2 copies known]
—anr. ed. "A narrative of the Pennsylvania frontier . . .," *Wash* 1838. 16° 10 a
For more extended account of Van Campen's border adventures—including this and another later captivity—*see* Hubbard, John N.

VANCE, ZEBULON B.   **19**
Sketches of North Carolina. *Norfolk* 1875. O 175 a

[VAN CISE, EDWIN]   **20**
The Black Hills of Dakota. *Deadwood* [1881]. O 44 + 10adv-p aa

VAN CLEVE, MRS. CHARLOTTE O. C.   **21**
"Three score years and ten," life-long memories of Fort Snelling . . . [*Minn*] 1888 O 176 port a
Iss 1: copyright notice on slip
—2 other eds., same impr. & collat., by 1895.
Authoress was the first white child born in Wis.

VANCOUVER, GEORGE, and   **22**
BROUGHTON, LIEUTENANT [WILLIAM R.]
A narrative or journal of a voyage . . . to the north Pacific ocean . . . by: *L* 1802. D [4] 80 pl aa
Chap-book version of this voyage.

VANCOUVER, GEORGE   **23**
A voyage of discovery to the north Pacific . . . and round the world . . . *L* 1798. Q 3v: [46] 432 7pls; [10] 504 5charts & pls; [10] 505 [3] 6pls + atlas F [16 charts & pls] c Hn N NYP Y
—new ed. with cor., *L* 1801. O 6v: [28] 33–410 3maps & pls; [2] 418 6pls; [2] 435 pl; [2] 417 3pls; [2] 454 3pls; [2] 412 + 2 adv-p 3pls b
—Fr. tr. by Demeunier and Morellet, *P* [1800]. Q 3v: [4, 3–12] 491 7pls; [6] 516 5charts & pls; [6] 562 6pls + atlas F [4] 16charts & pls b
—rptd. 1803. aa
—anr. Fr. tr., by Henry, *P* [1801]. O 6v 26maps & pls aa
—Swed. tr. *Stockh* 1800. O 2v in 1 map pls a
—Rus. tr. *St Ptbg* 1827–8. O 6v a
—Ger. trs. *Halle* 1789. O 308; *Berlin* 1799–1800. O 2v map 2pls a
Most of the three years occupied was spent on the California and Northwest coasts which were now first accurately charted. Of all modern exploring voyages to the Pacific those of Cook, La Perouse and Vancouver were the most important.

VANDELEUR [or VAN DELURE] (JOHN).   **24**
A history of the voyages and adventures of: Giving an account of his being left on the N. W. coast of America . . . *Montpelier* 1812. 16° 96 b Hn N
—other eds.: *Greenwich Mass* 1812; *Northampton* 1816; *Vergennes* 1827. b
See also below, Nos. 25 and 26.

VANDELEUR (JOHN).   **25**
A narrative of the travels of: on the western continent . . . *Hallowell* 1817. 16° 87 map 4pls b
For other accounts of this 7-year captivity among the Indians, *see* Decalves, Don Alonzo, and Van Leason, James.

VANDELURE (JOHN).   **26**
History of: . . . [*Andover N H* 1819?]. 18° 72 [cap.t. only] b NYP
Abridged by Josiah Wheet.

VAN DE WATER, FREDERIC F.   **27**
Glory-hunter; a life of General Custer. *Indp* [1934]. O 394 2maps 13pls a

[VANDEWATER, ROBERT J.]   **28**
The tourist; or, pocket manual for travellers on the Hudson river . . . *N Y* 1830. 16° 59 map a
—ed. 2, enl., *N Y* 1831. 16° 69 map
—ed. 3, *N Y* 1834. 16° 95 map
—ed. 4, *N Y* 1835. 16° 106 map
—several later eds.

VAN DIEST, P. H.   **29**
The Grand Island mining district . . . Colorado. *Denver* 1876. O 25 fold.map aa

VAN DORN (MAJ. GEN. EARL).   **30**
Proceedings of a court of inquiry . . . on charges preferred against: . . . *Mobile* 1862. O 56 b VaH [of 2cops kn]
—rptd., *Jackson, Tenn* 1955. D 78 map a
The general's conduct at Corinth was vindicated.

[VAN DUSEN, or VAN DEUSEN,   **31**
INCREASE MCG.]
Positively true. A dialogue between Adam and Eve, the Lord and the Devil, called the Endowment: as it was acted . . . in the Nauvoo temple . . . *Alb* 1847. O 24 aa
—rptd. "The sublime and ridiculous blended . . .," *N Y* 1848. O aa
—anr. ed. "Startling disclosures . . .," *N Y* 1849, O 24; *N Y* 1850, O 328 col pls; *N Y* 1852 a
—anr. ed., au. named, "Spiritual delusions . . .," *N Y* 1854. O 64 col.front. 8 col pls
—rptd. same impr. & collat 1855, 1856; 1859.
—anr. ed. *N Y* 1864. O 29 4col.pls

[VANÉECHOUT, ÉDOUARD P.]   **32**
Campagnes et stations sur les côtes de l'Amérique . . . Par L. du Hailly [*pseud*]. *P* 1864. D [4] 295 a

VAN GUNDY, JOHN C.   **33**
Reminiscences of frontier life on the upper Neosho [Kas.] in 1855–6. n.p. [1925]. O 41 a
—rptd. [*Topeka* 1925], same collat.

VAN HORNE, THOMAS B.   **34**
History of the army of the Cumberland . . . *Cin* 1875. O 2v: 454; 478 + atlas [of 22maps] a
—anr. issue, without atlas, same impr. & date. O 2v map

VAN LEASON [or VANLEASON],   **35**
JAMES
A narrative of a voyage . . . to China and . . . the western continent of North-America . . . *Windsor* 1801. O 44 b Y
—rptd. *Ballston Spa* 1816. D 45 aa
For other accounts of this voyage *see* Vandeleur, John, and Decalves, Don Alonso; Van Leason commanded the ship which left Vandeleur on the northwest coast.

[VAN NESS, WILLIAM P.]   **36**
A concise narrative of General Jackson's first invasion of Florida, and of his immortal defence of New Orleans . . . By Aristides. *N Y* 1827. O 40 aa
—ed. 2, *Alb* 1828. O 28 a
—4 other eds. followed within a year or two.
Ascribed also to Samuel Swartout.

[VAN NESS, WILLIAM P.]   **37**
An examination of the various charges . . . against Aaron Burr . . . *N Y* 1803. O 118 + errata lf a
—anr. ed. *Phil* for the au. 1803. O **77** [2issues, p4 in one begins with word "Ready," in the other with "terest"] a
—new ed. n.p. for the au. 1804. O [4] 116
—anr. ed., with adds., *Virginia* 1804. O 59

VAN NESS, MR. [WILLIAM P.]   **38**
MR. CAINES, et al
The speeches at full length of: in the great cause of the People, against Harry Croswell . . . for a libel on Thomas Jefferson . . . *N Y* 1804. O 78 a

[VAN PRADELLES, CAPT.]   **39**
Reflections offertes aux capitalistes de l'Europe, sur les benefices . . . que présente l'achat de terres incultes . . . dans les États-Unis . . . *Amst* 1792 O 42 map tabs aa
Promotion literature for the Holland land company's Genesee tract in Western *N Y*.

VAN RENSSELAER, SOLOMON   **40**
A narrative of the affair of Queenstown, in the war of 1812 . . . *N Y* 1836. D 44[incl. final blank l.] 95 map a

VAN SCHEVICHAVEN, S. R. J.   **41**
De Noord-Amerikaanse Staat Minnesota . . . *Amst* 1872. O 95 map aa

VAN SICKEL, S. S.   **42**
A story of real life on the plains . . . n.p. [1875]. pref. dated at Bull City, Kas. 1875. D 50 b KasH Y[only copies known]
—anr. ed. "Thrilling adventures with the Indians . . .," *Chi* 1876. O 36 aa
—anr. ed. *Topeka* 1877. O 31 aa
—rptd. "Real life on the plains . . .," *Harper Kas* [1885?]. O 50 a
—other eds.: Cedar-Rapids 1892; 1895; 1896. a
An episode in the life of a buffalo hunter; includes account of the Adobe Walls fight.

VAN TRAMP, JOHN C.   **43**
Prairie and Rocky mountain adventures . . . *Columbus* 1858. O 640 61pls some copies carry *St L* impr., with note at bottom of p640 added aa
—rptd. *St L* 1859; and many later eds. a

VAN TYNE, CLAUDE H.   **44**
The loyalists in the American revolution. *N Y* [1902]. O [12] 360 [2] a
—rptd., same collat, N.Y., 1929

[VAN WINKLE, H. E.]   **45**
Nine years of Democratic rule in Mississippi . . . *Jackson* 1847. D [12] 304 a
A Whig editor's bitter criticism of the McNutt regime, its financial policy and repudiation of the State's bond obligations. Ascribed also to Dudley S. Jennings.

VAN WOERT, WILLIAM T.   **46**
Fifteen years of frontier life. *Dubuque* 1870. O 80 c

VAN WYCK, FREDERICK   **47**
Keskachauge, or the first white settlement on Long Island. *N Y* 1924. O [45] 778 6maps 55pls aa said to have been suppressed.

VAN ZANDT, NICHOLAS B.   **48**
A full description of . . . the military lands between the Mississippi and Illinois rivers. *Wash* 1818. O [4] 127 aa some copies accompanied by a map[which was issued separately] b G NYP

VARLE, CHARLES   **49**
A complete view of Baltimore . . . *Balt* 1833. 18mo 166 plan aa
—iss 2, lf of preface replaced by author's note that he is returning to France, 10 lines of errata [3 less than in iss 1] and an added p of adv at end. a
—rptd. same impr. 1838.

VARLE, CHARLES   **50**
Topographical description of the [Va.] counties of Frederick, Berkeley and Jefferson . . . *Winchester* [1810]. O [6] 5–34 [map called for by t-p apparently never issued] aa

VARLO [or VARLEY], C[HARLES]   **51**
The essence of agriculture . . . with the author's . . . tour thro America . . . *L* 1786. O [10] 283 124 aa
—ed. 2, "Miscellany of knowledge . . .," *L* 1792.
For later editions *see* below *Nature displayed* . . .

[VARLO or VARLEY, CHARLES]   **52**
The finest part of America . . . Long Island, in New Albion, lying near New York . . . [*L* 1784?]. O 30 aa
Varlo purchased before the Revolution a third part of what was granted to Lord Plowden, in 1634, as New Albion [embracing Long Island and parts of New Jersey and Maryland] and issued this prospectus of land for sale while in America unsuccessfully prosecuting his legal claim, in 1784-5.

VARLO [or VARLEY], C[HARLES]   **53**
Nature displayed . . . A twelve month's tour through America . . . ed. 3. *L* 1793. O [12] 9–320 aa
—anr. ed., t. slightly altered, *L* 1794. O 320 a
—enl. ed. "The floating ideas of nature . . .," *L* 1796. D 2v: 318[fold.tab at front counted as 4p] [2]; 299 + duplicate p109–134 & app. p325–332 [In some copies p291–299 are bound after app.] aa
For earlier editions *see* above *The essence of agriculture* . . .

VARLO [or VARLEY], C[HARLES]   **54**
A new system of husbandry . . . To which are annexed a few hints . . . for the perusal of the legislators of America . . . *Phil* 1785. O 2v: [20 incl. 10p of subscriber's names] 17–87 98–364; [8] 5–368. fold.tab a
Earlier English editions did not contain the "few hints." Preliminary pages in volume I vary with additional subscriber's lists.

[VAUGHAN, BENJAMIN]   **55**
Remarks on a dangerous mistake made as to the eastern boundary of Louisiana. *B* 1814. O 28 aa

VAUGHAN, W. R.   **56**
The emigrant's guide . . . of the central branch of the Union Pacific . . . *Cawker City Kas* 1878. Q 40 map aa

VAUGHAN, W. R.   **57**
Guide and emigrant's handbook from Kansas City . . . to Cheyenne. *Council Bluffs* 1872. O 160 + 4preliminary adv-p 2maps b Y

VAUGHAN, W. R.   **58**
A pocket account book and diary from Kansas City west . . . *Council Bluffs* 1872. D 72 aa

VAUGHN, JEROME H.   **59**
Resources of Graham county, Arizona. *Solomonville* [ptd at Clifton] 1888. D 31 a

VAUGHN, ROBERT   **60**
Then and now; or, thirty-six years in the Rockies . . . 1864–1900. *Minneap* 1900. O [6] 13–461 front. aa

VAUGONDY, ROBERT DE   **61**
Mémoire sur les pays de l'Asie et de l'Amérique situées au nord de la mer de Sud . . . *P* 1774. Q [8] 32 [4] map b JCB N NYH Y

VAUGONDY, ROBERT DE   **62**
Observations critiques sur les nouvelles découvertes de l'Amiral de la Fuente. *P* 1753. D 23 aa
These "nouvelles découvertes" had been claimed by Font [de Fuente] in 1640; interest in a passage through the northern parts of America between the Atlantic and Pacific was revived when European nations saw commercial adventages in a South Sea trade.

VEECH, JAMES   **63**
Mason and Dixon's line: a history . . . *Pitt* 1857.
O 58 map a

VEECH, JAMES   **64**
The Monongahela of old. [*Pitt* 1857]. O 17–240
[sheets, without t-p & prelim pp and with unfinished text] b suppr before printing was finished
but a few caps of the sheets were given to friends
of the au.
—re-issued, with t.: "The Monongahela of old: or,
history of Fayette County, Pennsylvania. By Freeman Lewis and James Veech," *Pitt* 1860. O [2]
7–240 aa
—anr. issue, completed by Veech's daughter, Mrs.
E. V. Blaine, "The Monongahela of old; or, historical sketches of southwestern Pennsylvania . . .,"
Pitt 1892. O [2] 17–259 a
—rptd., with 2-p pref. added, *Pitt* [1910]. 4pls

VEHSE, KARL EDUARD   **65**
Die Stephan'sche Auswanderung nach Amerika.
Dresden 1840. D [6] 184 + 3adv-p aa
—Dutch ed. [in part[, "De Stephanische Landver-
huizing . . .," *Amst* 1846. O [8] 30 a

VELASCO, J. FRANCISCO   **66**
Noticias . . . del estado de Sonora . . . con los
journados para la bonanza de Alta California, por
D. José Elias. *Mex* 1850. O 350 b G NYP Y
—Eng. tr. [in part], *see* Nye, Wm. F., tr.
—Fr. tr. *P* 1864 a

VENABLE, W[ILLIAM] H.   **67**
Beginnings of literary culture in the Ohio valley.
Cin 1891. O [16] 519 aa

VENEGAS, MIGUEL   **68**
El apostol Mariano representado en la vida del
. . . Juan Maria de Salvatierra . . . conquistador
apostolico de las Californias . . . *Mex* 1754. Q [12]
316 [6] b B N
—Eng. tr. *Clev* 1929. O 350[incl. pls] a

VENEGAS, MIGUEL   **69**
Noticia de la California, y de su conquista tem-
poral, y espiritual . . . *Madrid* 1757. Q 3v: [24] 240;
[8] 564; [8] 436, 4maps c N NYP Y
—Eng. ed., with omissions, "Natural and civil
history of California," *L* 1759. O 2v: [20] 455; [8]
387. map 4pls b N NYP Y
—Fr. tr. of Eng. ed., "Histoire naturelle et civile
de la California," *P* 1766–7. D 3v: [24] 360; [8] 375;
[8] 354 [2]. map aa
—Ger. tr. of Eng. ed., "Natürliche und bürgerliche
Geschichte von Californien," *Lemgo* 1769–[1770].
O 3v in 1: 184; 198; 176. map aa
—Dutch tr. "Natuurlyke en burgerlyke historie
van California," *Haarlem* 1761–[1762]. O 2v: [22]
436; [6] 375. map pl; re-issued, with new t-p, *Amst.*
1777.

First attempt at a history of California. Based,
by the anonymous editor, Father Andrés Marcos
Burriel, on Venegas's 1739 MS., but incorporating
information from other sources. Volume three of
the original Spanish edition contains account of
discoveries on the Northwest coast attacking, as
fictitious, the then accepted voyages of de Fonte
and de Fuca.

VENIAMINOV, IVAN Y.   **70**
Zapiski ob Ostrovakh Unalashkinskago otdiela
. . . [Notes on the islands of the Unalaska archipelago, etc.]. *St Ptbg* 1840. O 3v: [18] 364; [8] 409
[16]; [4] 155. tab b B H Y
Veniaminov was, for 15 years, missionary in the
Alaska region, became Archbishop of Kamchatka,
the Kuriles and the Aleutians and later was known
as Innocent, Metropolitan of Moscow and Kolo-
ma. He also published, same impr. & date, a 44-
page pamphlet on his American church.

VENTURE.
A narrative of the life . . . of: a native of Africa
. . . *See* Smith, Venture.

VEREENIGDE STATEN [DE] . . .   **71**
Tiel 1846. O 32 [2] a
Guide issued to promote emigration to the
U.S.A. from Holland.

VEREINIGTEN STAATEN   **72**
Vereinigten Staaten (Die) . . . im Jahre 1852 . . .
Kiel 1853. D [4] 76 aa

VERGARA (VINCENTE S.)   **73**
Contestacion que da el ciudano: a los articulos
que sobre algunos puntos relativos a la pacifica-
cion de Nuevo Mexico . . . ha publicado en su
contra el teniente coronel D. Cayetano Justiniani.
Mex 1840. O 28 aa

VERGENNES, CHARLES G. DE   **74**
Mémoire . . . sur la Louisiane . . . *P* 1802. O 315
port aa

VERLANGTE
Verlangte (Das), nicht erlangte Canaan bey den
Lust-Gräbern . . . *See* Höen, M. W.

VERMILYA, LUCIUS H.   **75**
The battles of Mexico . . . with a sketch of California. *Prattsville* 1849. D 32 port aa

[VERNON, FRANCIS V.]?   **76**
Voyages and travels of a sea officer. *Dub* 1792.
O [24] 3–306 b Clem N NYP Y
—anr. ed. *L* 1792. O b
Of Nootka Sound interest.

[VERNON, JOSEPH S.]   **77**
Along the old trail . . . *Cimarron Kas* [1910]. O
[4 incl. descriptive lf] 110 113–144 149–166 163–
190 3pls[2col.] a

**VERREAU, L'ABBÉ [HOSPICE   78
A. J. B.], ed.**
Invasion du Canada . . . Vol.I[all]. *Montr* 1873.
O [22] 394 [44] a

VERWYST, CHRYSOSTOM   79
Life and labors of Rt. Rev. Frederic Baraga . . .
Milw 1900. O 476 17pls a

VERWYST, CHRYSOSTOM   80
Missionary labors of . . . Marquette, Menard
and Allouez, in the lake Superior region. *Milw*
1886. D 262 a

VERY, LAWSON   81
Description of the plan of the Falls City [In-
diana], and vicinity [Jeffersonville and New Al-
bany]. *New Alb* 1854. D 21 map 3plans aa

VERZAMELING
Verzameling van stukken tot de dertien Vereenigde Staaten . . . betrekkelijk. *See* Kemp, Francis A. van der.

VESTAL, STANLEY   82
Sitting Bull . . . *B* 1932. D 350 8pls a

VETANCURT, AUGUSTIN DE   83
Chronica de la provincia del Santo Evangelio de
Mexico . . . *Mex* 1697. F [12] 138 [2] 156 b Hn
JCB N NYP
This concluding [fourth] part of title next below
includes much early New Mexican history.

VETANCURT, AUGUSTIN DE   84
Teatro Mexicano . . . los sucesos exemplares,
historicos, etc., del nuevo mundo occidental de las
Indias . . . *Mex* 1698. F 3pts in 1. pt 1: [12] 66;
pts 2 and 3: 168 [2] b JCB N NYP
Part four had appeared the previous year under
title next above.

VIAJE A LOS ESTADOS UNIDOS.
Por Fidel. *See* Prieto, Guillermo.

VIANA, FRANCISCO JAVIER DE   85
Diario del viage explorador de las corbetas . . .
"Descubierta" y "Atrevida" . . . 1789–94. [*Ma-
drid*?] 1849. O 360 a
For a later, official account, *see* Malaspina,
Alejandro.

VIAUD (PIERRE).   86
Naufrage et aventures de: *P et Bordeaux* 1770.
D 340 aa
—oth Fr. eds of 1770: *Bordeaux*, D 144; *Neuchâtel*, D 279 a
—later Fr. eds: *Neuchâtel* 1771; *Bordeaux* 1772;
same impr. 1780; *P* 1797.
—Dutch tr. "Schipbreuk . . ." *Amst* 1771.
—Eng. tr. by Mrs. Griffith [a wretched job]: *L*

1771, D [12] 276 incl pl; *L* 1798, D 112 2pls; *L*
1800, D 88 incl pl aa
—anr. Eng. tr. by a different hand *L* 1814. D a
—Am. eds, tr. by Mrs Griffith: *Phil* 1774, D [12]
144; [4] 108 + 4adv-p pl; *Dover, N.H.* 1799, D [8]
203; *Lewiston, Pa.* 1832, D 252 a
In maritime annals few personal narratives seem
better authenticated than this account of shipwreck
and horrifying sufferings on an island off Florida's
west coast. Appended to the narrative is a certification, by the commanding officer at the British
post at St. Marks, of the rescue of Viaud and the
other two half-dead survivors, effected under his
orders. The name of this officer of the 9th Foot is
found in annual official army lists from 1768 to
1780; in the Revolution he served meritoriously,
and was wounded in Burgoyne's expedition; in
the same regiment was the well-known Sergeant
Lamb who in both of his authoritative books refers
to the Viaud disaster as a reality; it was naturally a
common subject of camp-gossip in the 9th Foot.
Furthermore, Bernard Romans, who lived in Florida for several years shortly after this event, de-
votes to it a page and a half in his great Florida
history and describes his interview with the Indian
interpreter who accompanied the rescue party.
These facts cast grave doubt on the long-accepted
belief that Viaud's voyage was imaginary, that his
narrative was a mere fiction parading as fact: it
may well be that the history of Florida, for its short
period as a British colony, has been unjustly despoiled of an interesting and most unusual episode.

VICTOR, MRS. FRANCES F.   87
All over Oregon and Washington . . . *S F* 1872.
O 368 a
—rptd. *Hart* 1872. same collat.

VICTOR, MRS. FRANCES F.   88
The early Indian wars of Oregon . . . *Salem Ore*
1894. O [14] 719 tab aa

VICTOR, MRS. FRANCES F.   89
The river of the west. Life and adventure in the
Rocky mountains and Oregon . . . *Hart* 1870. O
[2] 602 31pls aa
—rptd. *Hart* 1871. same collat. a
—anr. ed., with adds., "Eleven years in the Rocky
mountains . . .," *Hart* 1877. O 425 156
—rptd. *Hart* 1879; *Hart* 1881; *Columbus O* 1950.

VICTOR, WILLIAM B.   90
Life and events. *Cin* 1859. O 232 + 8adv-p aa
Includes account of Col. Joseph H. Hawkins and
how he aided Austin in financing his Texas colony.

VICTOR, WILLIAM B.   91
Memorial to the legislature of Texas [asking
compensation for aid given to the Austins by their
financial associate, Joseph H. Hawkins]. *Cin* 1859.
O 36 [3] aa

VIELÉ, MRS. [EGBERT L.]   **92**
"Following the drum" ... *N Y* 1858 D 256 a
—rptd. *Phil* [1864]. D [2] 19–262
Experiences of an officer's wife at frontier posts
in Texas.

VIEW
View (A) of North America, in its former happy,
and its present belligerent state ... *See* Walker, Geo.

View of the claims of American citizens ... assumed by the United States, in the Louisiana convention ... By a citizen of Baltimore. *See* Causten,
James H.

View (A) of the controversy between Great-
Britain and her colonies. By A. W. Farmer. *See*
Seabury, Sam'l.

View (A) of the evidence relative to the   **93**
conduct of the American war ... *L* 1779. O [6]
9–154 aa
—ed. 2, same impr. & date. O 154 aa
—ed. 3, enl. & re-arranged, "The detail and conduct of the American war," *L* 1780. O 190 aa
Ascribed to Joseph Galloway.

View (A) of the exertions lately made for   **94**
colonizing the free people of color in the United
States, in Africa, or elsewhere. *Wash* 1817. O 22
[error for 21] a
—rptd., same impr. & date. O 23
—anr. ed., same impr. & date. O 25

View (A) of the proposed constitution ... compared with the present confederation. *See* Nicholson,
John.

View (A) of the relative situation of Great Britain
and the United States ... By a merchant. *See* Bird,
H. M.

View (A) of the several schemes with respect to
America ... *See* Lofft, Capel.

View (A) of the state of parties in the   **95**
United States ... an attempt to account for the
present ascendancy of the French, or Democratic
party, in that country ... By a gentleman ... *Edin*
1812. O 110 a
—ed. 2, with adds., t. slightly altered, *Edin* 1812.
O 167
Attributed to McCormick.

VIEWS
Views and reviews in American literature, history
and fiction ... *See* Simms, Wm. G.

Views of society and manners in America ... By
an English-woman. *See* D'Arusmont, Mme. Fanny
(Wright).

VIGILANCE COMMITTEE [THE] OF 1856.
See O'Meara, James.

VIGNE, GODFREY T.   **96**
Six month's in America. *L* 1832. D 2v: 283; [4]
276. 4pls a
—Am. ed. *Phil* 1833. 16° 209

VIGNOLES, CHARLES [B.]   **97**
Observations upon the Floridas. *N Y* 1823. O
198 erratalf aa
—anr. issue. O 220 erratalf aa
—anr. ed. "The history of the Floridas ...," *Bklyn*
1824. O [4] 7–219 + lf aa
A map—sold separately and issued with none
of the editions—is found, inserted, in some copies.

VILAPLANA, HERMENEGILDO DE   **98**
Vida portentosa del ... Antonio Margil de
Jesus ... *Mex* 1763 O [34] 336 port c JCB LC N
NYP Y
—rptd. *Madr* 1775. O [16] 335 b B NYP
Father Margil's activities in Texas, 1716–1721,
included establishment of three missions in the
Nacodoches area and several years residence in
San Antonio.

VILLAINY EXPOSED ...
See Galland, Isaac

VILLA-SEÑOR Y SANCHEZ,   **99**
JOSEPH ANTONIO
Theátro Americano ... *Mex* 1746–8. F 2v: [20
incl.eng.t.] 382 [10]; [14 incl.eng.t.] 428 [10]. 2 lvs
intended for insertion between p. 232 & 233 of vol.
I are usually found inserted between those pages of
vol.II c JCB N NYP Y
—Eng. ed. "The statistical account of Mexico,"
L 1748. c
Official account of all Mexican provinces, including the frontier ones of California, New Mexico
and Texas, and information on the French trespas-
sers, La Salle and St. Denis.

VILLARD (HENRY).   **100**
Memoirs of: 1835–1900. *B* 1904. O 2v: [12] 394;
[6] 394. 8maps 5pls a

VILLARD, HENRY.   **101**
The past and present of the Pike's Peak gold
regions. *St L* 1860. O 112 + 8adv-p front. 2maps d
AA NYP Y[of 4copies known]
—anr. issue, unsold sheets of above, inserted, as
app., in Hawes, "Missouri state gazetteer," *St L*
[1865]. *See* Hawes, George W., and Co.
—rptd. *Princeton* 1932. 16°

VILLARD, OSWALD G.   **102**
John Brown, 1800–1859 ... *B* 1910. O [16] 738
[2] 19pls a
—rptd.: *N Y* 1929. same collat; *N Y* 1943

VILLARS, MIETTE DE 103
Manuel des émigrants en Californie. *P* 1849. O 40 aa

For another French quide, same date. *See* Rossignon

VILLAVICENCIO, JUAN J. DE 104
Vida y virtudes de . . . Padre Juan de Ugarte . . . missionero de las islas Californias, y uno de sus primeros conquistadores. *Mex* 1752. O [12] 214 [2] c JCB N.

Ugarte worked 30 years among the Indians of lower California and explored the California Gulf to its northern end, the mouth of the Colorado, thus disposing of the erroneous geographical conception of an insular California.

VILLIERS DU TERRAGE, MARC, 105
baron de
La découverte du Missouri et l'histoire du Fort d'Orleans (1673–1728). *P* 1925. O [4] 138 [2] 2maps a 350 cops ptd

First publication of the two journals of Bourgmond describing his 1714 and 1717 trips to the upper Missouri as far as the Cheyenne river. He later established this fórt on the lower Missouri and led expeditions into Kansas.

VILLIERS DU TERRAGE, MARC, 106
baron de
Les dernières années de la Louisiane francaise . . . *P* [1903]. O [10] 468 a

VILLIERS DU TERRAGE, MARC, 107
baron de
L'expédition de Cavelier de la Salle dans le golfe du Mexique . . . *P* 1931. O 235 [2] 2fold.maps a

VILLIERS DU TERRAGE, MARC, 108
baron de
Histoire de la fondation de la Nouvelle Orléans (1717–1722). *P* 1917. Q [16] 130 5pls a

Study of the struggle between France and England for the Mississippi, with much on the Illinois country, Pontiac, etc.

VINAL, WILLIAM 109
A sermon . . . occasioned by the defeat of . . . Braddock . . . *Newport* 1755. Q 25 b AA Hn Y

VINCENT, FRANCIS 110
A history of . . . Delaware . . . Vol. I [all]. *Phil* 1870. O [10] 478 a

Issued also in fifteen parts.

[VINCENT, N.] 111
Lettres d'un membre du Congress amériquain, à divers membres du Parlement . . . *Phil* 1779. O [4] 108 a
—rptd. "L'Amériquain aux Anglois . . .," *Phil* 1781. same collat.

Both editions were probably printed at Paris.

VINDEX 112
Vindex on the liability of the abolitionists to criminal punishment . . . *Charleston S C* 1835. O 31 a

VINDICATION
Vindication (A) of the Address, to the inhabitants of the British settlements, on the slavery of the negroes . . . By a Pennsylvanian. *See* Rush, Benj.

Vindication (A) of the Bishop of Landaff's [*sic*] sermon from the . . . reflections, contained in Mr. William Livingston's Letter to His Lordship . . . By a lover of truth . . . *See* Inglis, Chas.

Vindication (A) of the British colonies, against the aspersions of the Halifax gentleman . . . *See* Otis, James.

Vindication (A) of the measures of the President [etc.], in . . . the Seminole war. *See* Overton, John.

Vindication (A) of the rights of the Americans. 113
L [176–]. O 25 a

VINTON, STALLO 114
John Colter, discoverer of Yellowstone park . . . *N Y* 1926. O 114 map front. a 500 copies ptd.
—L.P. issue of 31 copies aa

VIRGINIA
Address to the convention of . . . Virginia on the subject of government . . . *See* Braxton, Carter.

An address to the people of Virginia respecting the alien and sedition laws. By a citizen . . . *See* Evans, Thos.

Beschrijvinghe van Virginia, Nieuw Nederlandt, Nieuw Engelandt, etc. 115
Amst 1651. smQ 88 map c JCB LC NYP

Assemblage of several previously printed works, including a 1644 treatise on the Mohawks [of the original of which only one copy exists]. In the text is the first engraved view of Fort New Amsterdam.

A brief narrative of the revival of religion 116
in Virginia. In a letter to a friend . . . *L* 1778. D 35 a
—eds. 2 & 3, same impr., date & collat.
—ed. 4, same impr. & collat. 1779.
—anr. ed. 3, same impr. & collat. 1786.

The case of the planters of tobacco in 117
Virginia. . . . to which is added, A vindication . . . *L* 1733. O 64 aa

Considerations on the present state of Virginia. *See* Randolph, John.

Considerations on the present state of Virginia. examined. *See* Nicholas, Robt. C.

Decius's letters on the opposition to the new constitution in Virginia. *See* Montgomery, James.

Exiles in Virginia. *See* Gilpin, Thos.

Histoire de la Virginie. *See* Beverley, Rob't.

The history and present state of Virginia. By a native [etc.]. *See* Beverley, Rob't.

The letter of Appomatox to the people of **118** Virginia . . . on . . . abolition of slavery. *Rich* 1832. O 47 a

Letters descriptive of the Virginia springs . . . By Peregrine Prolix. *See* Nicklin, Philip H.

Letters from Virginia translated from the **119** French. *Balt* 1816. 32° 220 aa
Original work, not a translation; authorship variously attributed to William Maxwell, to J. K. Paulding and to George Tucker, the latter being the likeliest candidate.

A narrative of the Indian and civil wars in **120** Virginia. *B* 1814. O 47 a
—anr. ed. "The history of Bacon and Ingram's rebellion . . .," *C* 1867.
Attributed to Sir William Berkeley and also to a Virginian named Cotton.

Observations upon . . . Notes on Virginia. *See* Rogers, Nicholas.

Plain truth addressed to the people of Virginia. *See* Lee, Henry.

The rambler, or, a tour through Virginia, **121** Tennessee, etc. By a citizen of Maryland. *Annap* 1828. D 46 aa

The resolutions of Virginia and Kentucky **122** penned by Madison and Jefferson; in relation to the alien and sedition laws. *Rich* 1826. O 71 aa
—other eds.: *Wash* 1832, O 82; *Rich* 1835, O 228

A short account of the first settlement of **123** the provinces of Virginia, Md., etc. *L* 1735. Q 22 map by Senex d H LC
—rptd. *N Y* 1922. map a
Most copies of the original edition lack both map and final page [i.e. postscript].

A short collection of the most remarkable passages . . . of the Virginia Company. *See* Wodenoth, Arthur.

Sketch of western Virginia for the use of **124** British settlers . . . *L* 1837. D [8] 118 [6] fold.map a

Sketches of Old Virginia family servants. **125** With a preface by Bishop Meade. *Phil* 1847. 16° 126 a

A tour through part of Virginia in the summer of 1808. *See* Mitchill, Saml. L.

Virginia and Kentucky resolutions of 1798 . . . *See* No. 122.

Virginia and Maryland. Or, the Lord Bal- **126** tamore's printed case . . . *L* 1655. SmQ [2] 52 c H Hn
—rptd. *Wash* 1837. O 47 a
A reply to a 20-p tract of 1653, *The Lord Baltemore's case.*

Virginia doctrines (The), not nullification. **127** By Agricola . . . *Rich* 1832. O 52 a

Virginia illustrated . . . *See* Strother, David H.

Voyage d'un Francois, exilé pour la reli- **128** gion, avec une description de la Virginie et Marilan . . . *Hague* 1687. 16° 140 b LC H JCB
—rptd. *Balt* 1932. O 158 map pls a
—same, Eng. tr. *N Y* 1934. O 190 map pls
One of the best 17th century accounts of the region. Little is known of the author except that his family name was Durand.

VISCHER, EDWARD **128a**
Briefe eines Deutschen aus Californien. *S F* 1873. O 31 + wrap.t. aa
—Eng. tr. *S F* 1940. O a
First separate printing of this account of an 1842 visit to California.

VISCHER, EDWARD **129**
Missions of upper California . . . a supplement to Vischer's Pictorial of California. *S F* 1872. Q 44 [12] 15pls b NYP Y

VISCHER, EDWARD **130**
Sketches of the Washoe mining region. *S F* 1862. Q [24] + portfolio [of 26pls] c Y [of 2copies known]

VISCHER, EDWARD **131**
Vischer's pictorial of California . . . *S F* [1870]. Q [6] 132 + 4p of press notices[inserted in some copies] 6sheets of views. This text v. [usually bound in clo.] is accompanied by a larger sized vol of 100-or 120-mounted views [unbound or bound in ¹/₂ or full mor.] b G
In some copies the plates [photos of drawings] are bound in two volumes. There was also a cheaper octavo edition of the text, containing in end pocket a set of sixty views on six cards of the same octavo size.

VISCHER, EDWARD **132**
Vischer's views of California. The mammoth tree grove . . . *S F* [1852]. Q [4] eng.t. 25 views [on 11 sheets] b Y

[VISSIER, PAUL]   133
Histoire de la tribu des Osages . . . Par M. P. V.
P 1827. O 92 b

[VIZETELLY, HENRY]   134
Four months among the gold-finders of California . . . *L* 1849. O [18] 207 map aa
—ed. 2, same impr., date & collat. a
—Am. ed. *N Y & Phil* 1849. O 94 map
—anr. Eng. ed. *P* 1849. O [4] 136 map
—Dutch tr. *Amst* 1849. O 168 map
—Ger. trs.: *Leip* [&] *Zurich* 1849, D [16] 232 map
with Leip ed.; *Hamburg* 1849.
One of the most remarkable "imaginary voyages"
since Defoe. For French translation *see* Arcis, M.H.

VLEESCHOUWER, LOUIS-J.   135
Stukken en Brokken. *Antwp* 1851. D 312 aa
—ed. 2, same impr. 1914. D 238 a
Describes travels from 1828 to 1834 in the
United States, with residences at Philadelphia,
Charleston and Savannah.

VOCELLE, JAMES T.   136
History of Camden county, Georgia. *Jacksonville* [1914]. D 156[incl.pls] a

VOEU (LA) DE TOUTES LES NATIONS.
See Beaumarchais, Pierre A. C. de.

VOICE
Voice (A) from America to England. By an American gentleman. *See* Colton, Calvin.

Voice (A) from the south . . . *See* Longstreet,
Augustus B.

Voice (The) of truth; or, thoughts on the   137
affair between the Leopard and the Chesapeake. In
a letter from a gentleman at New York . . . *N Y*
1807. O 55 a

VOLCANO DIGGINGS (THE) . . .
By a member of the bar. *See* Kip, Leonard.

[VOLCK, ADELBERT J.]   138
Sketches from the civil war [cov.t.]. *L* [actually
Balt? 1863?]. obl F index lf 30pls b 200copies ptd.
—reissued, "Confederate war etchings," [cov.t.],
n.p. n.d. [*Phil*? 1880? 1890?]. same collat. except
only 29pls 100copies issued. aa
The original issue was probably suppressed by
the author as the caricatures bordered on treason.
The re-issued form was doubtless made up of the
suppressed sheets or printed from the original
copper-plates. One of the plates, "Meeting of the
Southern emissaries and Lincoln," had evidently
been lost in storage, so does not appear in that
issue. Of another supposed issue, with the spurious London imprint, containing fifteen additional plates [forty-five in all], no definite information
is available.

VOLLMER, CARL G. W.   139
Astoria; oder, Reisen und Abenteuer der Astor-
expeditionen. *Leip* [1858]. O [4] 575 a

[VOLLMER, CARL G. W.]   140
Kalifornien och guldfebern . . . *Stockh* [1862].
D 662 8col-pls aa
—Dutch trs, *Amst* 1864. O 2v: 2pls; *Amst* 1865.
O 2v: 2pls a
—Ger. tr., *Berlin* 1863. O [6] 744 8col-pls aa

VOLNEY, C[ONSTANTIN] F., comte de   141
Tableau du climat et du sol des États-Unis . . .
P 1803. O 2v: [24] 300; [4] 301–534 + errata lf
2maps 2pls In some copies the 8-p Miami vocabu-
lary at end of vol. 2 is separately paged, in others it
is paged consecutively with the rest of the text.
Some copies issued on L.P. aa
—rptd.: *P* 1822., O [24] 494 2maps; *P* 1825, O [20]
478 2maps a
—Eng. tr. *L* 1804. O [24 3–6] 504 2maps 2pls a
—Am. ed., somewhat abr., tr. C. B. Brown, *Phil*
1804. O [28] 446 2maps 2pls a
—Ger. tr. "Reisen durch die Vereinigten Staaten
. . .," *Weimar* 1804. O [4 3–8] 283 map a

VOLWILER, ALBERT T.   141a
George Croghan and the westward movement,
1741–1782. *Clev* 1926. O 370 map a

VON DER ARBEIT . . .
See Spangenberg, August C.

VOORHEES, LUKE   142
Personal recollections of pioneer life. *Cheyenne*
[1920]. O 76 port aa
—rptd., with adds., *Phil* 1927. O 76 [32] a
Colorado, Utah, Montana, Wyoming.

VORSTELLUNG   143
Vorstellung der Staatsveränderung in Nord-
Amerika. Ed. 2, with adds. *Bern* 1784. O [8] 352
153–174 a
See Dubuisson, Paul U., *Abrégé de la revolu-
tion* . . .

VOSE, HENRY   144
Topography of . . . Mississippi . . . *Natchez*
1835. O 24 aa

[VOSE, REUBEN]   145
Despotism; or, the last days of the American
republic. *N Y* 1856. D 463 a

VOSE, REUBEN   146
The life . . . of Abraham Lincoln, and Hannibal
Hamlin . . . *N Y* [1860]. 24° 51 [incl. cover t.] 42–
71$^{1}/_{2}$ [blank p] 72–118 + 4adv-p c no comma after
"Hamlin" on t-p LincLife[only copy known] c
—anr. issue, identical except for comma after
"Hamlin." c Hn MH [only copies known]

10,000 copies issued; sickeningly rare; excessively unimportant. A facsimile of issue one was made at Ft. Wayne in 1938.

VOYAGE

Voyage aux États Unis . . . *P* 1834. *See* Davison, Gideon M., *The fashionable tour*, of which this is a translation.

Voyage de l'Amérique . . . *Amst* 1723. *See* Bacqueville de la Potherie.

Voyage d'un Suisse dans différentes colonies d'Amérique . . . *See* Girod-Chantrans, Justin.

Voyage fait . . . **de New-Yorck à la Nouvelle-Orléans** . . . *See* Montlezun, Baron de.

Voyage (A) from the United States to South America . . . *See* Bennett, Thos. H.

Voyage (A) round the world . . . **in the King George, commanded by Captain Portlock** . . . *See* Portlock, Nathaniel, and Dixon, George.

VOYAGES   147

Voyages (The), adventures and discoveries of the following circum-navigators . . . *L* Owen 1758. D [4] 438 a
—rptd., with new t., "A collection of authentic discoveries and entertaining voyages . . .," *L* Knox 1763. front.

Voyages, adventures, etc., of the French emigrants. *See* Mentelle, Mme. Waldemard.

Voyages and travels of a sea officer. *See* Vernon, Francis V.

Voyages dans les parties intérieurs de l'Amérique . . . *See* Anburey, Thos.

Voyages intéressans dans differentes colonies Francaises . . . *See* Bourgeois, Nicolas L.

VRANGEL, FERDINAND P.
See Wrangel.

VRIES, DAVID P. DE   148
Korte historiael . . . van verscheyden voyagiens in . . . Europa, Africa, Asia, ende Amerika . . . *Hague* 1655. SmQ [4] 190 errata lf port c Hn JCB N
One of the earliest and most reliable accounts of Dutch New York; by one of its residents.

W

W., A. O.
Eye witness . . . 1865. *See* Wheeler, A. O.

W., C.
A two years journal in New York . . . *See* Wolley, Chas.

W., T.
A letter to a friend . . . *B* 1774. *See* Chauncy, Chas.

WADDELL, ALFRED M.   1
A colonial officer and his times . . . sketch of Gen. Hugh Waddell, of North Carolina . . . *Raleigh* 1890. O 242 2pls a

WADDELL, JOSEPH A.   2
Annals of Augusta county, Virginia . . . *Rich* 1886. O [8] 374 2maps aa
—anr. ed., same impr., 1888. O [8] 492 2maps a
—ed. 2, enl., *Staunton* 1902. Q[10] 545 2maps a
—also ltd. issue of 100copies aa
—rptd. 1958.
This county, up to 1770, extended from the Blue Ridge mountains to the Mississippi, and embraced present West Virginia, Kentucky, Ohio, Indiana and Illinois.

WADSWORTH, W[ILLIAM]   3
The national wagon road guide . . . to California. *S F* 1858. O 160[incl.front.] map d G Hn Y 4copies known, only two of which have the map

WADSWORTH [OHIO] MEMORIAL   4
Wadsworth [Ohio] memorial . . . with the early history of adjoining townships. *Wadsworth* 1875. D 232 [2] a

WAGNER, MRS. GLENDOLIN D.   5
Old Neutriment . . . *B* [1934]. D 256 27pls a
Biography of Custer's orderly, John Burkman.

WAGNER, HENRY R., ed.   6
California voyages, 1539–1541. *S F* 1925. O 95 [4] a

WAGNER, HENRY R.   7
The cartography of the northwest coast . . . to 1800. *Berkeley* 1937. Q 2v: [12] 270; [6] 271–543 13maps [not incl. in paginat] aa

WAGNER, HENRY R.   8
Juan Rodriguez Cabrillo, discoverer of the coast of California. *S F* 1941. O [2] 95 front. aa

WAGNER, HENRY R.   9
Sir Francis Drake's voyage around the world . . . *S F* 1926. O [12] 543 7maps a
—anr. issue, with 21pls added. 100signed copies aa

WAGNER, HENRY R.   **10**
Spanish explorations in the strait of Juan de Fuca. *Santa Ana Calif* 1933. Q [6] 324 13 maps & charts aa 425 cops ptd.

WAGNER, HENRY R.   **11**
Spanish voyages to the northwest coast . . . *S F* 1929. O [8] 571 port 15maps aa
—ltd ed. aa

WAGNER, MORITZ, and SCHERZER,   **12**
KARL
Reisen in Nordamerika . . . *Leip* 1854. D 3v: [20] 471; [14] 429; [14] 409 aa
Comprehensive, important and unbiased.

[WAGNER, P. W. G.]   **13**
Wanderungen eines Heimathlosen in Nord Amerika . . . *Reading Pa* 1844. 16° 112 aa

WAGSTAFF, A[LEXANDER] E.   **14**
Life of David S. Terry . . . *S F* 1892. O [16] 15–526 5pls aa
Best biography of a violently eccentric Californian.

WAHLSTEDT, JACOB J.   **15**
. . . Iter in Americam . . . *Upsala* [1725]. O [2] 48 aa
University dissertation on Norse voyages to America.

WAIT, BENJAMIN   **16**
Letters from Van Dieman's Land . . . during four years imprisonment for political offences . . . in upper Canada . . . *Buf* 1843. 16° 356 map front. a

WAITZ, THEODOR   **17**
Die Indianer Nordamerica's . . . *Leip* 1865. O [10] 180 a

[WAKEFIELD, EDWARD G.]   **18**
England and America. A comparison . . . *L* 1833. O 2v: [12] 332; [4] 341 a
—Am. ed. *N Y* 1834. O [10] 17–376
An essential supplement to Stuart's *Three years in North America.*

WAKEFIELD, JOHN A.   **19**
History of the war between the United States and the Sac and Fox nations . . . *Jacksonville Ill* 1834. 16° [10] 142 b N NYP Y
—ed. 2, enl. *Cin* 1836. No copy located and publication probably mythical.
—anr. ed., ed. by Stevens, *Chi* Caxton Club 1908. O 225 13pls 203 copies ptd a

WAKEFIELD, J[OSEPHUS]   **20**
History of Waupaca county [Wis.] *Waupaca* 1890. D 219 port a

WAKEFIELD, PRISCILLA   **21**
Excursions in North America . . . *L* 1806. D [12] 420 [4] fold.map a
—ed. 2, same impr. & collat., 1810
—ed. 3, same impr. & collat., 1819.
Flights of imagination by a lady who never saw this country.

WAKEFIELD, SARAH F.   **22**
Six weeks in the Sioux tepees: a narrative of Indian captivity. *Minneap* 1863. O 54 cY[only copy known]
—ed. 2, *Shakopee* 1864. O 64 b N 2copies known

WAKEMAN, EDGAR   **23**
The log of an ancient mariner . . . *S F* 1878. O 378 + 4 adv-p port a
The author came to California in 1849, and spent much of his life in Pacific coastal waters.

WALCOT, JAMES   **24**
The new pilgrim's progress . . . account of Hattain Gelashmin, who was baptis'd . . . by the name of George James . . . with a narrative of his travels among the savage Indians . . . *L* 1748. D [2] 316 a
—ed. 2, same impr. 1749. D [2] 316 + 2adv-p before text
—anr. ed. "The history of the pious Indian convert . . .," *Blackburn* 1792. O 268 a
His travels were among tribes adjacent to South Carolina. Of doubtful authenticity.

WALDO, SAMUEL   **25**
A defence of the title of the late John Leverett, Esq.; to a tract of land in the eastern parts of the province of Massachusetts Bays. [*B*] 1736. F 41 aa

WALDO, S[AMUEL] PUTNAM   **26**
Biographical sketches of distinguished American naval heroes . . . *Hart* 1823. O 392 3pls a

WALDO, S[AMUEL] PUTNAM   **27**
The life . . . of Stephen Decatur . . . *Hart* 1821. D 312 port a
—ed. 2, enl. *Middletown* 1821. D 372 367–378 4pls
—rptd., same impr. & collat. 1822.

WALDO, S[AMUEL] PUTNAM   **28**
Memoirs of Andrew Jackson . . . *Hart* Andrus 1818. 16° 316 aa
—anr. issue, same place, collat. & date, but with impr. of Russell aa
—rptd. same impr. 1819. D 312 a
—several later eds., incl. one with t. "Memoirs of the illustrious . . . Andrew Jackson . . . By a citizen of Hagers-Town, Md.," *Chambersburg* 1828. 16° 306 port

WALDO, S[AMUEL] PUTNAM   **29**
The tour of James Monroe . . . in the year 1817

. . . *Hart* 1818. 16° [12] 288 [last p misnumb 300] port a

—rptd. *Hart* 1819. D 348 port

—ed. 2, *Hart* 1820. same collat.

For another—and more uncommon—account of this tour, *see* under Monroe, James.

[WALES, G., and ROBERTS, M.]   **30**

Indian battles, murders, seiges [*sic*] and forays in the southwest . . . *Nashv* [1853]. O 100 b KyH N

WALGAMOTT, CHARLES S.   **31**

Reminiscences of early days . . . of Snake river valley . . . [*Twin Falls Idaho* 1926–7]. O 2v: [6] 3–128; 128. 2pls aa

—anr. ed. "Six decades back," *Caldwell Idaho* 1936. O 358 31pls a

WALKE, HENRY   **32**

Naval scenes and reminiscences of the civil war . . . on the southern and western borders. *N Y* 1877. O [12] 480 15pls diagram a

WALKER, ADAM   **33**

A journal of two campaigns of the Fourth Regiment of U. S. Infantry, in the Michigan and Indiana Territories . . . 1811–12. *Keene N H* 1816. D 143 b AA N Y

WALKER, CHARLES M.   **34**

History of Athens county, Ohio, [etc.]. *Cin* 1869. O [8] 600 map 5ports a also L. P. copies, in 2v aa

[WALKER, FOWLER]   **35**

The case of Mr. John Gordon, with respect to . . . certain lands in East Florida . . . *L* 1772. Q 32 [42] plan b H NYP

Attempt to establish his title to a large tract south of St. Augustine purchased after 1763 from Spanish owners.

WALKER (COMMODORE [GEORGE]).   **36**

The voyages and cruises of: during the late Spanish and French wars. *L* 1760. D 2v: [20] 240; [4] 312 2maps b JCB NYP

—rptd. *Dub* 1762. D 2v aa

—Am. ed. abr., "An account of the voyages . . . of Capt. Walker . . . ," *B* 1761. D 42 [2] b

—rptd. *L* [1928] O [52] 219 map pls a

Includes operations against Spanish privateers along the Carolina coast.

WALKER, GEORGE, of Philadelphia   **37**

New directions for sailing along the coast of North America . . . *L* 1799. O [4] 48 aa

—rptd. same impr. & collat. 1803; 1804. a

—rev. ed. *L* 1806. O [6] 49

[WALKER, GEORGE] of Scotland.   **38**

A view of North America . . . with the travels and adventures of the author through . . . that continent . . . *Glas* 1781. O 247 b JCB N

WALKER, SIR HOVENDEN   **39**

A journal . . . of the late expedition to Canada . . . *L* 1720. O [4] 304 b

—rptd. "A full account of the late expedition . . . ," *L* n.d. O same collat. aa

Defense by commander of this unfortunate 1711 expedition, which operated from Boston and was of New England instigation.

WALKER (JOSEPH REDDEFORD).

West wind; the life story of: *See* Watson, Douglas S.

WALKER, JUDSON E.   **40**

Campaigns of General Custer, and the . . . surrender of Sitting Bull. *N Y* 1881. O 139 [10] 7pls aa

WALKER (ROBERT J., Governor of   **41**
Kansas Territory).

Inaugural address of: . . . *Lecompton* 1857. D 24 aa

WALKER (MR. [ROBERT J.])   **42**

Letter of: . . . relative to the annexation of Texas . . . *St L* 1844. O 50 aa

—rptd: *Wash* 1844, O 32; *Phil*, same date & collat.

WALKER, DR. THOMAS   **43**

Journal of an exploration into Virginia in . . . 1750. *B* 1888. sm Q 69 front. a

Earliest recorded visit into interior Kentucky by a white man; he preceded Boone by twenty years and named both Cumberland Gap and Cumberland River. For a more complete version of this journal, accompanied by that of Cist, *see* Johnston, Josiah S.

WALKER, W. W.   **44**

First report of the Cedar Rapids and Missouri River railroad . . . *Chi* 1860. O 38 fold.map b Y

Gives tables of distances of various routes to the Pikes Peak gold region, and favors the one surveyed [through the Platte valley via Ft. Laramie].

[WALKER, WILLIAM]   **45**

The missionary pioneer, or a brief memoir of . . . John Stewart . . . founder under God of the mission among the Wyandotts at Upper Sandusky . . . *N Y* 1827. 16° 96 a

—rptd. *N Y* 1918. same collat. a

Ascribed also to Joseph Mitchell, publisher of the book.

WALKER'S TEXAS DIVISION.

The campaigns of: by a private soldier . . . *See* Blessington, Jos. P.

WALL, OSCAR G.   **46**

Recollections of the Sioux massacre . . . *Lake City Minn* 1909. D 282 [3] [incl.pls] front. a

With Marsh at Fort Ridgely in 1862, and with Sibley's 1863 expedition.

WALL, W[ILLIAM] G.   **47**
Wall's Hudson river portfolio. *N Y* [1826?]. Obl
F 21col.pls with letter-press d NYH Y
—rptd., same impr. & collat. 1828. c
—anr. ed. *N Y* 1846. D 32 fold.map[12^1/$_2$″ long ×
6″ high] aa

WALLA-WALLA (THE).
The Indian council in the valley of: *See* Kip,
Lawrence.

WALLACE, DANIEL   **48**
The political life . . . of the Hon. A. Barnwell
Rhett . . . *Cahawba Ala* 1859. O 47 a

WALLACE, DAVID D.   **49**
The life of Henry Laurens . . . *N Y* 1915. O [14]
539 2ports 2tabs a

WALLACE, E. R.   **50**
Parson Hanks. Frontier life in the Panhandle.
Arlington, Tex. 1906. O 162 a

WALLACE, EDWARD J.   **51**
The Oregon question determined by the rules of
international law. *L* 1846. O 39 aa

WALLACE, HENRY   **52**
Uncle Henry's own story of his life . . . *Des M*
1917–18–19. O 3v: 119[incl. initial blank l. & port];
129; [6] 5–114. aa
Reminiscences of pioneer life and travel in Pennsylvania, Ohio, Kentucky and Iowa.

WALLACE, JOHN   **53**
Carpetbag rule in Florida . . . *Jacksonville* 1888.
O 444 port b rptd. 1959 a
By an ex-slave, who served in Florida's post-
bellum legislature.

WALLACE, JOHN W.   **54**
An old Philadelphian, Colonel William Brad-
ford . . . *Phil* 1884. O [14 incl.front.] 5–517 2maps
2pls 3facs 100copies ptd. aa

WALLACE, JOSEPH   **55**
The history of Illinois and Louisiana under the
French rule. *Cin* 1893. O [10] 433 a [many copies
burned]
—ed. 2—and best, with map added, *Cin* 1899.

WALLACE, W[ILLIAM] H.   **56**
Closing speech for the State in the trial of Frank
James . . . *K C* 1883. O 65 a
—anr. ed. *K C* 1884
—rptd., with adds., n.p. [1890?]. D 131

WALLEN (CAPT. H[ENRY] D.)   **57**
Report of: of his expedition . . . from Dalles
City to Great Salt Lake and back . . . [Sen. Ex.
Doc. 34]. [*Wash* 1860]. O 51 map a

WALLER, ZEPHENIAH   **58**
Seven letters from an emigrant . . . containing
remarks on the manners, . . . of the United States.
Diss Eng 1831. O 38 aa

WALLIS, MRS. JONNIE L.   **59**
Sixty years on the Brazos . . . *L A* 1930. O [14]
336 16pls 200copies ptd. aa

[WALN, ROBERT, JR.]   **60**
The hermit in America on a visit to Philadelphia
. . . *Phil* 1819. D [8] 13–216 [3] a
—ed. 2, same impr. and date. D [10] 13–246 [3] 4pls
—ser 2. *N Y* 1821. O 228

WALN, ROBERT, JR.   **61**
Life of the marquis de La Fayette . . . *Phil* 1825.
D [4] 9–380 383–450 3pls a
—anr. issue, same impr. & date. D [4] 9–505 3pls
—ed. 3, same impr. 1826. O 502 3pls
—ed. 4, same impr. 1827. O [20] 11–507 3pls

WALPOLE, FREDERICK   **62**
Four years in the Pacific . . . 1844–1848. *L* 1849.
O 2v: [16] 432; [10] 415. 2pls aa
—rptd., same impr. & collat. 1850. a
Visited Monterey immediately after American
occupation.

WALPOLE, THOMAS, et al.
Considerations on the agreement of the Lords
Commissioners . . . with: *See* Wharton, Sam'l.

WALPOLE (THOMAS, et al.)   **63**
Report of the . . . Commissioners for Trade and
Plantations on the petition of: for a grant of lands
on the . . . Ohio; for the purpose of erecting a new
government . . . *L* 1772. O [2] 108 fold. tab b N
NYP WisH Y
—anr. issue, probably first, *L* [1772]. Q 27 [no t-p] b
Report written by Lord Hillsborough, *Observations* by Samuel Wharton. Only the Revolutionary
war prevented the realization of this scheme of
Walpole, Franklin and other associates for establishing their western colony of Vandalia. This
project for interior expansion was the real beginning of the West. The folding table in the octavo
edition is usually closely trimmed.

WALSH, C. C.   **64**
Early days on the western range. *B* 1917. D 81 a

[WALSH, ROBERT] ed.   **65**
The American register; or, summary review of
history . . . *Phil* 1817. O 2v: [12 incl. 2adv-p 9–40]
450; [36] 464 a

[WALSH, ROBERT] ed.   **66**
The American review of history and politics . . .
Vol. I [all]. *Phil* 1811–12. O [22] 408 112 + 2adv-p
3tabs a
—Eng. ed. *L* 1812. O [4] 366

WALSH, ROBERT   **67**
An appeal from the judgments of Great Britain respecting the United States . . . *Phil* 1819. O [56] 512 a
—ed. 2, same impr., date & collat., but errata slip added
—Eng. ed. *L* 1819. O [56] 505
—ed. 2, same impr. & collat. 1820.

[WALSH, ROBERT]   **68**
Biographical sketch of the life of Andrew Jackson . . . *Hudson N Y* 1828. 16° 65[incl. port] aa
—re-issued, same date, impr. & collat., but with 1832 on front cover a
—rptd. *Bristol R I* 1836. same collat.
—anr. Am. ed., with adds., "The Jackson wreath . . .," *Phil* 1829. O 88 eng.t. port map 4pls 3 l. of music

[WALSH, ROBERT]   **69**
Free remarks on the spirit of the federal constitution . . . respecting the exclusion of slavery . . . *Phil* 1819. O 116 a

[WALSII, ROBERT?]   **70**
A letter to an English gentleman on the libels and calumnies on America by British writers . . . *Phil* 1826. O 43 a

WALTER, GEORGE   **71**
History of Kansas . . . [*N Y* 1854]. D 59 map c Hn KasH
First book on Kansas.

[WALTER, JOHN]   **72**
First impressions of America. *L* 1867. D [4] 131 a

WALTERS, LORENZO D.   **73**
Tombstone's yesterday. *Tucson* 1928. O 293 port aa

WALTHER, C. F., and TAYLOR, I. N.   **74**
The resources . . . of . . . Nebraska. [*Omaha* 1871]. O 27 map aa

WALTHER, F. E., and ROWED, RICHARD   **75**
Texas in sein wahres Licht gestellt . . . *Dresden* 1848. D [2] 70 map plan aa
Immigration pamphlet.

[WALTON, AUGUSTUS Q.]   **76**
A history of the detection . . . of John A. Murel, the great western land pirate . . . [*Lex* 1835]. D 75 b H LC
—anr. ed., au. named, *Athens* Tenn 1835, same collat. aa
—other eds.: n.p. 1835 [2 issues, 84 & 89p]; n.p. 1836 60p; n.p. 1837 Q 86. a
—anr. ed. *Cin* n.d. O [4] 17–84[incl.pls]
For another account of this desperado, *see* Howard, H. R.

WALTON, DANIEL   **77**
The book needed for the times, containing . . . facts from the gold regions [etc.]. *B* 1849. O 32 b Hn Y

WALTON, JOSEPH S.   **78**
Conrad Weiser and the Indian policy of colonial Pennsylvania. *Phil* [1900]. O 420 19pls facs a
The early struggle for the Ohio Valley, in which Weiser played a leading part.

WALTON, J[OSIAH] P., ed.   **79**
Scraps of Muscatine history. [*Muscatine*] 1893. O 112 [erratically paged] a
—anr. iss. 134 [erratically paged] aa

[WALTON, WILLIAM], 1740–1824, ed.   **80**
A narrative of the captivity [etc.] of Benjamin Gilbert and his family . . . *Phil* 1784. O 96 aa
—Eng. ed. *L* 1785. D 124 aa
—rptd. same collat. *L* 1790. aa
—anr. ed. *Phil* 1813. D [2] 7–46 48–82 [2] 89–96 front. a
—ed. 3, rev. & enl., ed. Comly, *Phil* 1848. 16° 240 a

WALTON, WILLIAM, 1843–1915, et al   **81**
The army and navy of the United States . . . *Phil* 1889–95. F 12pts pls aa
—anr. issue, on Jap. Vell. 500sets b
—rev. & enl.ed. *Phil* 1900. F 25pts usually bound in 2v: [6] 130; [8] 74 [2] 204. 50pls, each with a guard-sheet of descriptive letterpress aa

WALTON, WILLIAM M.   **82**
Life and adventures of Ben Thompson, the famous Texan . . . *Austin* 1884. D 229 15pls b
—rptd: *Bandera* 1926; *Austin* 1956. a
A distinguished Texas outlaw.

WALZ, EDGAR A.   **83**
Retrospection. n.p. 1931. O 32 port a
Privately printed reminiscences of New Mexico's Lincoln county war, etc.

WANDELL, CHARLES W.   **84**
History of the persecutions! ! endured by the . . . Latter Day Saints in America. *Sydney N S W* [1852?]. O 64 b G NYP Y

WANDELL, C[HARLES] W.   **85**
Reply to Shall we believe in Mormon? [*Sydney N S W* 1852?]. O 24 [caption t. only] b B Y

WANDERUNGEN
Wanderungen eines Heimathlosen in Nord Amerika . . . *See* Wagner, P. W. G.

WANDERUNGEN EINES JUNGEN NORDDEUTSCHEN . . .
See Delius, Edouard.

WANSEY, HENRY   86
The journal of an excursion to the United States
... *Salisbury* 1796. O [16] 290 [13] view port[letter-
ed "G. Washington, Esq."] aa
—issue 2, port carries different lettering and an
eye-lash is added aa
—ed. 2, "An excursion to the United States ...,"
same impr. 1798. O [12] 270 [14] + errata lf view
port fold-tab aa
—Ger. tr. *Berlin* 1797. O [4] 3–232 view port a

[WANTE, CHARLES ETIENNE P.]?   87
Mémoires sur la Louisiane et la Nouvelle Or-
leans ... *P* 1804. O [8] 176 tab b
Ascribed also to G. Boucher de la Richardière.
The author—whoever he was—travelled exten-
sively throughout the lower Mississippi valley.

WAPPÄUS, J. C.   88
Deutsche Auswanderung und Colonization. *Leip*
1846. O [8] 152 aa
Of 85 pages on American fields for exploitation.
15 are devoted to California and Oregon.

WAR   88a
War (The) ... *N Y* 1813–1817. O 3v: [4] 218;
[4] 210; 72 b AA NYP Y
Originally appeared in weekly parts, June 27,
1812—Sept. 6, 1814. Suspended after publication
of vol. 3, no. 12 at the latter date, and resumed Feb.
24, 1817, after which only two more numbers were
issued. Edited by Samuel Woodworth.

War (The) and its heroes ... Vol. I[all].   89
Rich 1864. O 88 port [2] 17–88 ports a

War in disguise; or, the frauds of the neutral
flags. *See* Stephen, James.

War, or no war? Introduced with a view   90
of the causes of our national decline ... By Ly-
curgus. *N Y* 1807. O 65 a

**War reminiscences by the surgeon of Mosby's
command.** *See* Monteiro, Aristides.

War with America. The crisis of the dis-   91
pute with the United Stat.s ... *L* 1811. O 72 a
—ed. 2, *L* 1812. O

War without disguise; or, the frauds of   92
neutral commerce a justification of belligerent captures ... *America* 1807. O [4] 87 a
Rejoinder to answers, written by Gouverneur
Morris and James Madison, to Stephen's *War in
disguise.*

WARD, ANDREW H.   93
A history of ... Shrewsbury [Mass.] ... *Worc*
1826. O [4] 36 a
—best ed., greatly enl., *B* 1847. O 508 port

WARD, DILLIS B.   94
Across the plains in 1853. *Seattle* [1911]. D [2]
55 port aa
Started from Arkansas, followed the Santa Fe
trail to Colorado, then north to the Overland trail
and Oregon.

WARD, JAMES   95
A history of gold ... probable supplies from
California ... *L* [1853]. D 144 map view aa

WARD, KIRK C. [comp.]   96
Business directory of ... Seattle. Comprising a
history [etc.]. *Seattle* 1876. O 106 b SeattleP
WashU Y
First Seattle directory.

WARD, MINUS   97
Remarks ... relative to a rail-road and locomo-
tive engines to be used upon the same, from Baltimore to the Ohio river. *Balt* 1827. O 50 aa

[WARDEN, DAVID B.]   98
A chorographical ... description of the District
of Columbia ... *P* 1816. D [8] 212 [2] map pl 2
tabs aa

WARDEN, D[AVID] B.   99
A statistical, political and historical account of
the United States ... *Edin* 1819. O 3v: [66] 552; [12]
571; [12] 588 2 maps issue 1, colophon dated 1818 aa
—Fr. tr. *P* 1820. O 5v: [32] 537; [12] 528; [12] 581;
[14] 718; [16] 658 [2] 2 maps pl 2 tabs a
—Ger. tr., abr. *Ilmenau* 1824. O [40] 536

WARDEN, ROBERT B.   100
An account of the private life and public services
of Salmon Portland Chase. *Cin* 1874. O [12] 838
port a
The Chase family objected to some statements
and the publisher suppressed many copies.

WARDER, T. B., and CATLETT, J. M.   101
Battle of Young's branch or Manassas plain ...
Rich 1862. D 157 map[2 in some copies] aa

WARDMAN, GEORGE   102
A trip to Alaska. *S F* 1884. D [4] 237 a

WARE, EUGENE F.   103
The Indian war of 1864 ... *Topeka* 1911. D [12]
601 [incl. front.] aa
—rptd. *N Y* 1960. O 483
Day-by-day occurences in the campaigns around
Forts Kearney and McPherson.

WARE, JOSEPH E.   104
Emigrant's guide to California ... *St L* [1849].
16° 56 map[by Ware] dd G Hn NYH NYP Y [only
cops loc]
—rptd. *Princeton* 1932. 16° [24] 64 map 2 pls a

First adequate guide to California, the first covering the central route in its entirety; no better one was available until 1852.

[WARE, N. A.]   **105**
Notes on political economy as applicable to the United States . . . *N Y* 1844. O [8] 304 a
—Ed. 2, same impr. date & collat.

WARFIELD, J[OSHUA] D.   **106**
The founders of Anne Arundel and Howard counties, Maryland . . . *Balt* 1905. O 544 [56] 2ports aa

WARNEFORD, LIEUT. [pseud.]
Running the blockade. *See* Russell, Wm. H. C.

WARNEFRIED, CARL B. A.   **107**
Pilgerfahrt nach den Vereinigten Staaten . . . *Cologne* 1857. D 480 aa

[WARNER, FRANK W.]   **108**
Montana Territory. History and business directory . . . With a sketch of the vigilantes *Helena* [1879]. O 218 map b
Includes first reprint of Dimsdale's *Vigilantes.*

WARNER, I. W.   **109**
The immigrant's guide . . . *N Y* 1848. D [6] 172 aa

[WARNER, J[UAN] J., et al]   **110**
An historical sketch of Los Angeles county, California . . . *L A* 1876. O 88 aa
—rptd. *L A* 1936. O 159 front.
First history of this county. Includes Dr. J. S. Griffin's overland diary. First issue of the 1876 edition had only 72 pp.

WARNER, M. M.   **111**
History of Dakota county, Nebraska . . . *Lyons Neb* 1893. [7–24] 37–387 a
The author interviewed every local pioneer.

WARNER, MATT   **112**
The last of the bandit riders . . . *Caldwell, Ida* 1940. O 337 pls a
Story of "Butch" Cassidy's "Wild Bunch" told by one of its few survivors.

[WARNER, SAMUEL]   **113**
Authentic . . . narrative of the tragical scene . . . in Southampton county [Va.]. [*N Y*] 1831. O 38 front. aa
Contemporary account of Nat Turner's insurrection.

WARRE, HENRY J.   **114**
Sketches in North America and the Oregon Territory. [*L* 1848] F [4] 5, map 20col. views [on 16sheets] c with pls not col. b N NYP Y

Made, in 1845, when war between England and the United States over the Oregon boundary seemed imminent, this trip by Capt. Warre across the northern Rockies to Puget Sound must have had some military purpose. However, any report of that nature became waste-paper on his return to London, as an amicable adjustment had then been made; but a better fate attended the views he had painted and were here magnificently reproduced; they remain the only western color-plates comparable in beauty to those by Bodmer accompanying Maximilian's *Travels.* The dedication forming prelim. p. 3 and 4 was not issued in all copies.

WARREN, CHARLES   **115**
A history of the American bar. *B* 1911. O [12] 586 a

WARREN, CHARLES   **116**
The Supreme Court in United States history. *B* 1922. O 3v: [18] 540; [12] 551; [12] 532. 16pls a
—rptd., same impr. & collat., 1923.

WARREN [EDWARD]: A NOVEL.
L 1854. *See* Stewart, Sir Wm. Drummond.

WARREN, MRS. ELIZA [SPALDING]   **117**
Memoirs of the west: the Spaldings. [*Port Ore* 1916]. D 153 10pls a
By the first white child born in the Pacific Northwest; an eye-witness, ten years old, of the Whitman massacre.

WARREN, G[OUVERNEUR] K.   **118**
Explorations in the Dacota country . . . *Wash* 1856. O [2] 79 [6] 3maps aa

WARREN, G[OUVERNEUR] K.   **119**
Preliminary report of surveys in Nebraska . . . *Wash* 1859. O 173 fold-map a
First separate printing; it had been included in the 1858 Report of the *Sec'y of War.*

WARREN, G[OUVERNEUR] K.   **120**
Preliminary report of explorations in Nebraska and Dakota . . . *Wash* 1875. O 125 fold-map [same as in 1858 and 1859 eds] inserted in some cops. a
This re-issue of material from above earlier editions was made to meet the interest awakened by the Black Hills gold discovery of 1874.

WARREN, KITTRELL J.   **121**
History of the Eleventh Georgia Volunteers . . . *Rich* 1863. O 58 aa

WARREN, MRS. MERCY   **122**
History of the . . . American revolution . . . *B* 1805. O 3v: [12] 447; [8] 412; [6] 475 aa
First important historical work by an American woman.

WARREN, T. ROBINSON   **123**
Dust and foam; or, three oceans and two continents. *N Y* 1859. D 397 front. a

WARREN, OHIO.   **124**
Minutes . . . of a convention holden at: on the subject of connecting the Pennsylvania and Ohio canals. *Warren* [1833]. O 40 a

WARS (THE) OF AMERICA . . .
See Eggleston, Benjamin.

WASEURTZ, G. M.   **125**
A sojourn in California. *S F*, Grabhorn, 1945. Q [12] 85 [5] 300 cops ptd a

WASH, CAPT. W. A.   **126**
Camp, field and prison . . . *St L* 1870. D 382 a
Describes Confederate prison life at Johnson's Island.

[WASHBURN, CEPHAS]   **127**
Reminiscences of the Indians . . . *Rich* [1869]. D 236 aa rptd. *Van Buren Ark* 1955. II [28] 192
For what is essentially a reprint, *see* Starr, Emmet, *Cherokees west* . . .

WASHINGTON, GEORGE   **128**
America's lecacy [*sic*] being [his] Address, on . . . declining a re-election [together with his Circular letter . . . Farewel [*sic*] orders to the armies] . . . *Hudson* 1797. D 200 aa
—rptd., with some re-arrangement, "America's legacy . . .," *Charleston S C* 1800. D 58 a
Separate printings were made of the *Address* and of the *Circular letter* in the 1797 edition. *See* also Nos. 129 and 149, below.

WASHINGTON (GEN. GEORGE).
Biographical memoirs of the illustrious: . . . *Phil* Charless & Ralston 1800. *See* Condie, Thos.

WASHINGTON (GENERAL GEORGE).
Biographical memoirs of the illustrious: . . . *Phil* Hogan 1808. *See* Corry, John.

WASHINGTON, GEORGE   **129**
A circular letter . . . to the several states, called his legacy, being his last public communication. *Annap* [1783]. D [4] 27 aa
—other 1783 eds.: *Phil* n.d. 16° 52; *Newport* Q 12; *L O* [4] 24 aa
—anr. ed., t. slightly altered, *N Y* 1786; *Phil* 1786; *Phil* R. Smith [1787?]. 16° 52 aa
For another 1783 edition, *see* below, *The last official address* . . .

WASHINGTON, GEORGE   **130**
A collection of the speeches of the president . . . to both Houses of Congress . . . *B* 1796. D 282 + adv-p a

WASHINGTON (GEORGE).   **131**
Diary of: . . . Oct. 1789–March 1790. *N Y* 1858. O [8] 89a 100copies ptd.
First publication of the manuscript.

WASHINGTON (GEORGE).   **132**
The diary of: from 1789 to 1791 . . . Ed. by B. J. Lossing. *N Y* 1860. D 248[incl. front.] a
—anr. ed. *Richmond* 1861. O 248 aa

WASHINGTON, GEORGE   **133**
Epistles, domestic, confidential, and official . . . None of which have been printed in the two volumes published a few months ago. *N Y* 1796. O [16 incl. final blank lf] 303 port aa
—rptd. *L* 1796. O [16] 303 a
First seven letters are Tory forgeries previously printed as *Letters from General Washington to several of his friends . . ., q.v.* For the two-volume work referred to in title, *see* below *Official letters to . . . Congress.*

WASHINGTON (MAJOR GEORGE).   **134**
The journal of: sent by the Hon. Robert Dinwiddie . . . to the commandant of the French forces on Ohio . . . *Wmsbg* 1754. O 28 dd JCB N NYP [of 9cops loc]
—Eng. ed. *L* 1754. O 32 map c JCB N NYP
—rptd. *N Y* 1865. O 46 map a; with adds., *Alb* 1893, O 273 map
Washington's first published work and of great historical significance as being the narrative of England's first move in attempting to wrest the Ohio country from France. In its original form the most desirable eighteenth century American rarity.

WASHINGTON, GEORGE   **135**
Journal of my journey over the mountains; in the northern neck of Virginia . . . 1747–8. *Alb* 1892. Q 144 9maps a
From original MS journal kept by Washington at the age of 16 on a surveying trip.

WASHINGTON, GEORGE   **136**
The last official address . . . to the legislatures of the United States. To which is annexed, A collection of papers relative to half-pay . . . *Hart* 1783. O 48 aa
For other editions of *The last official address, see* above, *Circular letter* . . . This was his famous address on resigning his command of the army.

WASHINGTON (GENERAL [GEORGE]).   **137**
Letters from: to several of his friends in . . . 1776 . . . *L* 1777. O [2] 73 aa
—Am. eds.: [*N Y*] 1778, D [2] 53 b AA N NYP; [*Phil*] 1778, D [2] 53 b; *Phil* 1795, O [6] 9–44 a
These were "spurious letters" fabricated by Loyalists to damage the patriot cause. Probably written by John Randolph, last Royal Attorney General of Virginia. For later edition incorpora-

ting them, *see* above, *Epistles, domestic, confidential, and official* . . . Ascribed also to Rev. John Vardill.

WASHINGTON, GEORGE   **138**
Letters . . . to Arthur Young . . . *L* 1801. O [8] 112 109–172 map aa
—rptd., with "Letters . . . to Sir John Sinclair," *Alexandria* 1803, O 128; *Wash* 1847, Q 198 map 5pls a

WASHINGTON, GEORGE   **139**
Letters to . . . Sir John Sinclair . . . *L* 1800. F [6] 9–52 [4] incl. 2ports & facs a
—rptd., with "Letters . . . to Arthur Young." *See* above under that title.
—other Am. eds.: *Phil* 1839 Q; *Wash* 1844 Q

WASHINGTON, GEORGE   **140**
Letters to Tobias Lear . . . *Roch* 1905. Q [12] 66 [2 unnumb. l.] 73–102 7 pls & facs a 300 copies ptd

WASHINGTON (GEORGE).
The life and memorable actions of: . . . [*Balt* 1800?]. *See* Weems, Mason L.

WASHINGTON (GEN. [GEORGE]).
The life of: . . . also, of the brave General Montgomery . . . *See* below, *A true and authentic history of* . . . *Washington* . . .

WASHINGTON ([GEORGE]).   **141**
Memory of: . . . his life . . . *Newport* 1800. D 252 port a

WASHINGTON, GEORGE   **142**
Official letters to . . . Congress . . . *B* 1795. D 2v: 340; 356. port[not issued in all copies] a
—rptd. *B* 1796. same collat.
—*N Y* 1796. O 2v: 296; [2] 311 no port
—Eng. ed., with add.t-pages, "American state papers," *L* 1795. O 2v: [8] 364; [4] 384. front.[in some copies]
—anr. issue, same impr. & date, without add. t-pages, O 2v: [2 5–8] 364; [2] 384
—Ger. tr. *Leip* 1796. D 2v

WASHINGTON (GEORGE).
A poetical epistle to: . . . *See* Wharton, Chas. H.

WASHINGTON, GEORGE   **143**
The President's address to the people of the United States [announcing his intention of retiring from public life] capt. t. [*Phil* Ormrod Sept. 20, 1796]. O 16 a
+anr. issue, priority undetermined, *Phil* for the proprietors, Sept. 20, 1796. O 16
—ed. 2, same impr. & collat. dated Sept. 22, 1796
—rptd., same year, 28 times in 17 cities, under variant titles ["Legacy of the father of his country," "Columbia's legacy," "President Washington's resignation," etc.]; 3 other eds., 1798.

WASHINGTON (MR. [GEORGE]).
Remarks occasioned by the late conduct of: *See* Bache, Benj. F.

WASHINGTON (GEN. GEORGE).
A sketch of the life and character of: . . . *See* Terry, Ezekiel

WASHINGTON (GEORGE).   **144**
A true and authentic history of: . . . Also, of . . . generals Montgomery and Greene, and . . . La Fayette . . . *Phil* 1790. O 24 a
—anr. issue, 22p.
—anr. ed., omitting sketches of Greene & La Fayette, changed t., *Phil* 1794. 24° 36 2ports

WASHINGTON [GEORGE]
Washington [George] and the generals of the . . . revolution. *See* Griswold, Rufus W.

WASHINGTON [GEORGE]
Washington [George] und die amerikanische Revolution. *See* Gosch, Josias L.

WASHINGTON (GEORGE).
The wilderness; or the youthful days of: *See* McHenry, James.

WASHINGTON'S [GEORGE] JÜNGLINGSJAHRE.
Die Wildniss; oder: *See* McHenry, James.

WASHINGTON, GENERAL GEORGE   **145**
The will of: . . . *Alexandria* 1800. 16° 32 aa
—rptd., same yr.: *Balt*; *B*; *Frederick Town*; *Hudson*; *N Y*; *Phil* [2 issues, by Maxwell, and by Freneau & Paine]; *Port*; *Stonington-Port Conn*; *Worc*; *B* a
—Eng. eds.: *L* Fairburn 1800; same impr. & date, Stower & Hare a

WASHINGTON (GEORGE).   **146**
The writings of: Ed. W. C. Ford. *N Y* 1889. O 14v aa

WASHINGTON'S . . . LETTERS   **147**
Washington's [General] letters to the Marquis de Chastellux. *Charleston S C* 1825. O 35 aa

WASHINGTON'S MONUMENTS   **148**
Washington's monuments of patriotism . . . *Phil* 1800. O 338 [44] port pl a
—rptd., with slight changes, same collat. & impr. 1802. port

WASHINGTON'S . . . LEGACIES   **149**
Washington's political legacies . . . *B* 1800. O 208 + 14p of subscriber's names a
—anr. ed. *N Y* 1800. D 292 + 8p of subscriber's names
—anr. ed. "Legacies of Washington . . .," *Trenton* 1800. 16° 283 port
—Eng. ed. *L* 1801

WASHINGTONIANA   150
Washingtoniana: a collection of papers . . .
Blandford & Petersburg Va 1800. O [16] 96 a

Washingtoniana (The): containing a bio-   151
graphical sketch of the late Gen. George Washington . . . *Balt* 1800. 16° [8] 7–258 271–298 [6] port a
—anr. issue, identical—except for having 7 final p.
[of subscribers]
—rptd. *N Y* 1865. 150copies [50 on L. P.]

Washingtoniana (The); containing a sketch . . .
1802. *See* Johnston, F., and Hamilton, W.

WASHINGTON, D. C.
**Beschryving der Rivier Potomack en der Stad
Washington, [D.C.]** *See* Lear, Tobias.

**An enquiry respecting the capture of Washington
by the British.** By Spectator. *See* Armstrong, John.

**Mysteries of Washington City during . . . the
session of the 28th Congress.** *See* Atwater, Caleb.

**A narrative of the campaigns of the British army
at Washington and New Orleans . . .** *See* Gleig,
Geo. R.

**Observations on the river Potomack, and the
country adjacent, and the city of Washington.** *See*
Lear, Tobias.

**Remarks on a pamphlet, entitled An enquiry
respecting the capture of Washington . . .** *See*
Winder, R. H.

**Report of the committee appointed . . . to   152
inquire into the causes and particulars of the invasion of . . . Washington, by the British . . .** *Wash* 1814.
O 188 201–370 2 tabs a

**A sketch of the events which preceded the capture
of Washington.** *See* Ingraham, Edw. D.

Wanderer in Washington. *See* Watterston, Geo.

Washington directory . . . 1822. *See* Delano,
Judah.

Washington guide (The) . . . 1822. *See* Elliot, Wm.

WASHINGTON TERRITORY
**Map of the Nez Perces and Salmon river gold
mines in Washington territory.** *See* Lowell, Daniel
W., & Co.

**Northwestern Washington its soil, climate   153
. . . [*Port Townsend*] 1880. D 52 map a

Washington Territory and the far northwest . . .
See Ballard, D. P.

[WASSON, JOHN MACAMY]   154
Annals of pioneer settlers on the Whitewater and
its tributaries, in the vicinity of Richmond, Ind . . .
Richmond Ind 1875. O 59 a

[WATERHOUSE, BENJAMIN], ed.   155
A journal of a young man of Massachusetts, late
a surgeon on board an American privateer . . . *B*
1816. D 228 front. aa
—rptd., same date & collat., *Milledgeville Ga* a
—ed. 2, with adds., *B* 1816. 16° 240 front.
—rptd., same date & collat., *Lex Ky*
Author was Dr. Amos G. Babcock.

WATERMAN, G. F.   156
A history of Harrison county, Iowa. *Magnolia*
1868. O 64 aa

[WATERS, WILLIAM E.]   157
Life among the Mormons, and a march to their
Zion . . . *N Y* 1868. D [16] 219 + 2adv-lvs 4pls aa

WATERTON, CHARLES   158
Wanderings in South America, the northwest of
the United States, and the Antilles . . . *L* 1825. Q
[8] 326 front. a
—ed. 2, *L* 1828. O [8] 341 front.
—rptd. several times
—Fr. tr. *Rouen* 1833. O [16] 470 front.

WATERTOWN, WISCONSIN.
City of: *See* Quiner, Edward B.

WATKIN, SIR EDWARD W.   159
A trip to the United States and Canada . . . *L*
1852. D [12] 149 a

WATKINS, C. L.   161
Yosemite valley. *S F* 1863. F map 62pls aa

WATKINS, SAM[UEL] R.   162
"Co. Aytch," Maury Grays, First Tennessee
regiment . . . *Nashv* 1882. O 236 aa
—ed. 2, *Chattanooga* 1900. O 223 a

WATROUS, ANSEL   163
History of Larimer county, Colorado . . . *Ft
Collins Colo* 1911. Q [2] 513 map 46pls a

WATSON, DOUGLAS S.   164
California in the fifties. *S F* 1936. obl F 113
50pls aa. Also 50 cops on L.P.

[WATSON, DOUGLAS S.]   165
West wind; the life story of Joseph Reddeford
Walker . . . *L A* 1934. O [8] 110 [2] map port b
100copies ptd.
Presents all available information on an eminent
figure of the early fur-trade era, the leader, in 1836,
of the first trapping expedition into California over
the Sierras.

WATSON, ELKANAH   166
History of the rise ... of the western canals in
... New York ... *Alb* 1820. O [2] 104 [4] 111–210
[2] 2 maps 2pls 3facs a

WATSON, ELKANAH   167
Men and times of the revolution ... *N Y* 1856.
O 460 a
—ed. 2, *N Y* 1857. O 557 port
—rptd., same impr. & collat, 1861

WATSON, HENRY C.   168
Nights in a block-house; or sketches of border
life ... *Phil* 1852. O 448 aa
—ed. 2, *Phil* 1853. same collat. a
—rptd. *Phil* 1854; 1860; 1863.
Written in fictional form, but primarily an historical presentation.

WATSON, JOHN F.   169
Annals of Philadelphia ... *Phil* 1830. O [12] 740
78 [8] 24pls a
—enl. ed. *Phil* 1844. O 2v: [16] 609; [2, 5–8[567
—other 2v eds.: 1845; 1850; 1856; 1857.
—best ed. *Phil* 1877. O 3v: rptd. 1884.

WATSON, JOHN F.   170
Historic tales of olden time: concerning the
early settlement ... of New York ... *N Y* 1832.
16° 214 10pls a
—enl. ed. "Annals ... of New York ...," *Phil*
1846. O 390 pls

WATSON, JOHN F.   171
Historic tales of olden time: concerning the early
settlement ... of Philadelphia and Pennsylvania.
Phil 1833. D 316 [incl. eng. t-p & front.] 8pls a

WATSON, MRS. MAY M.G., [and]   172
LILLICO, ALEX.
Taft ranch, a history ... n.p., n.d. O 52 [incl.
16adv-p at end] a

WATSON, WILLIAM   173
Life in the Confederate army ... *L* 1887. D
456 a
—Am. ed. *N Y* 1888. same collat.
Narrative of operations in Arkansas and Mis-
souri.

WATSON, WILLIAM J.   174
Journal of an overland trip to Oregon ... 1849.
Jacksonville Ill 1851. O 48 d H [only copy known]

WATSON, WINSLOW C.   175
Pioneer history of the Champlain valley ...
Alb 1863. O 231 227copies ptd. [27 on L.P.]

WATTERSTON, GEORGE   176
A picture of Washington ... *Wash* 1840. 16°
[6] 5–138 4plans a

—rptd., same impr. & date. 18° [2]; 127; same
impr. 1841. 18° [6] 5–131 2plans; "New guide to
Washington," same impr. 1842, D 224 map 17pls
—rptd. 1847–8. D 224 map 17pls

[WATTERSTON, GEORGE]   177
Wanderer in Washington ... *Wash* 1827. 16°
[4] 13–226 a
—ed. 2, with changes, [*Wash*] 1829. D same collat.

WATTS, J., comp.
The museum of remarkable ... events ... *See*
Andros, Thos.

WATTS, JOHN S.   178
Indian depredations in New Mexico. *Wash* 1858.
O 66 aa

WATTS, WILLIAM C.   179
Chronicles of a Kentucky settlement. *N Y* 1897.
O [14] 490 a
A real contribution, in spite of its fictional form,
to the early history of Livingston county.

WATTS, W[ILLIAM] J.   180
Cherokee citizenship ... affairs in the Cherokee
nation ... *Muldrow Okla* 1895. O [2] 144 + wraps
cov.t.only aa

WAUGH (LORENZO).   181
Autobiography of: *Oakland* 1883. D 311 2ports a
—rptd. *S F* 1884.

WAY, W[ILLARD] V.   182
The facts and historical events of the Toledo
war of 1835 ... *Toledo* 1869. O [4] 52 a
Best history of this territorial dispute between
Michigan and Ohio.

WAYLAND, JOHN W.   183
Historic homes of northern Virginia. *Staunton*
1937. Q 625 aa

WAYLAND, JOHN W.   184
A history of Shenandoah county, Virginia.
Strasburg Va 1927. O 874 a

WEAKNESS (THE) OF BRUTUS EXPOSED.
By a citizen of Philadelphia. *See* Webster, Pelatiah.

WEARING OF THE GRAY ...
See Cooke, John E.

WEAVER, BENJAMIN   185
The first settling of Kansas ... [*St Joseph, Mo*
1898] D 41 aa

WEAVER, WILLIAM   186
History of ancient Windham, Connecticut ...
Part I [all]. *Willimantic* 1864. O [8] 112 a

[WEAVER, WILLIAM A.?]   187

Examination and review of a pamphlet . . . circulated by M. E. Gorostiza . . . entitled "Correspondence between the legation . . . of Mexico and the department of state of the United States, respecting the passage of the Sabine, by the troops under . . . General Gaines." *Wash* 1837. O 188 aa

For pamphlet referred to *see* Gaines, el General. Attributed also to Peter Force.

[WEBB, FRANCIS]?   188

Letters lately published . . . on the subject of the present dispute with Spain . . . *L* 1790. O 101 b NYP ProvArchVictoria

First appearance in book form of these eight letters, relating chiefly to the Nootka Sound controversy. Authorship also ascribed to James B. Burges.

WEBB, JAMES WATSON [ed.]

Altowan; . . . life and adventure in the Rocky mountains. By an amateur traveller. *See* Stewart, Wm. Drummond.

[WEBB, SAMUEL] ed.   189

History of Pennsylvania Hall . . . *Phil* 1838. Q 200 3pls a

WEBB (SAMUEL BLACHLEY).   190

Correspondence and journals of: Ed. by W. C. Ford. *N Y* 1893–4. O 3v: [30] 422; [28] 441; [24] 432. 51pls 350sets ptd[100 for sale] aa

WEBB, THOMAS H.   191

Information for Kanzas immigrants. *B* 1854. O 24 aa

—rptd. 13 times by 1857.

[WEBB, THOMAS H.]   192

Organization . . . of the Emigrant Aid Company; also a description of Kansas. *B* 1854. D 22 [2] aa

—ed. 2, same impr. & date. D 24 a

—ed. 3, same impr. & date. D 24 [4]

—10 other eds. followed, some considerably enl.

WEBB, WALTER P.   193

The great plains . . . *B* Ginn [1931]. O [16] 345 [2] 346–525 2maps 8pls [issue 1 has 2 errors in heading of chap. 2] a

—ed. 2 *B* 1936

WEBB, WALTER P.   194

The Texas rangers. *B* 1935. O [18] 584 front. a

Also ltd. ed., signed, of 200 copies aa

WEBBER, CHARLES W.   195

The gold mines of the Gila. *N Y* 1849. D 2v [or 2v in 1]: [8] 134; [4] 135–263 aa

WEBBER, CHARLES W.   196

The hunter-naturalist . . . or wild scenes . . . Vol.

1 [all]. *Phil* [1851]. O 610 eng.t. & 9col.lith.pls [first to appear in an Am. bk] aa

—rptd. same impr. & collat: 1852; 1856; 1859 a

—anr. ed. entitled, "Romance of hunting . . .," *Phil* 1865. O 610 pls

[WEBBER, CHARLES W.]   197

Jack Long; or, shot in the eye. A true story of Texas border life. *N Y* 1846. O 30 a

—rptd. "The shot in the eye . . .," *Elizabethtown N J* 1847. O 24

—Eng. ed. *L* 1853. D

WEBBER, CHARLES W.   198

Old Hicks the guide . . . *N Y* 1848. D 356 + adv-pp aa

—rptd. 1855; 1859; 1868. a

—Eng. ed. "Adventures in the Camanche country." *Glas* 1848. D 299[erroneously paged 296] a

For sequel, *see* above his *The gold mines of the Gila.*

WEBBER, CHARLES W.   199

Tales of the southern border. *Phil* 1852. O 400 6 pls aa

—rptd, same impr. and collat.: 1853; 1856; 1868. a

WEBSTER (DANIEL).   200

Speech of: in reply to Mr. Hayne . . . *Wash* 1830. O 76 aa

—anr. issue, with "reply" misspelled "rely" on t-p, same impr. & date. O 96 aa

—anr. issue, capt.t. only, [*Wash* 1830]. O 35 a

—rptd., same date: *Cin* O 40; *N Y* O 72; *Hart* O; 3 *B* eds. O[one n.d., 40p; one with p. [16] 76; one with adds., O 136p]

Most famous American oration of the nineteenth century, presenting the doctrine of a Union paramount and indissoluble. Hayne's defense of the theory of State sovereinty and the right of nullification—forensically almost its equal—is included in the 136-page Boston edition.

WEBSTER, DELIA A.   201

Kentucky jurisprudence . . . *Vergennes Vermont* 1845. D 84 a

Account of her trial and conviction for inciting a slave to escape to Ohio.

[WEBSTER, GEORGE G.]   202

Journal of the Hartford Union Mining and Trading Company. Printed by J. L. Hall on board the Henry Lee, 1849. D 88 dd B NYH S Y [of a few known copies]

—rptd. with adds., "Around the Horn in '49," [*Hartford? Wethesfield?* 1898]. D [18 incl. 2ports] 252] incl. 25pls] aa

—anr. ed. *S F* Grabhorn 1928. O [18] 5–128 front. 250copies ptd. a

The original edition was largely printed during the voyage and finished in San Francisco harbor.

Usually listed under the printer [Hall], but the journal was written by Webster; it was the first printed narrative of a California gold-seeker and the best record of an argonaut expedition by sea.

WEBSTER, NOAH   **203**
A collection of essays and fugitiv writings . . . *R* 1790. O [16] 414 + 6adv-p a
Early example of phonetic spelling.

WEBSTER, NOAH   **204**
Effects of slavery, on morals and industry. *Hart* 1793. O 56 a

WEBSTER, NOAH   **205**
An examination into the . . . federal constitution proposed by the late convention . . . *Phil* 1787. O 55 aa
Urges adoption of the proposed instrument.

WEBSTER, NOAH   **206**
Miscellaneous papers, on political and commercial subjects . . . *N Y* 1802. O [8] 227 48 a

WEBSTER, NOAH   **207**
Sketches of American policy . . . *Hart* 1785. O 48 a

[WEBSTER, PELATIAH]   **208**
A dissertation on the political union and constitution of the thirteen United States . . . *Phil* 1783. O 47 aa
—rptd. *Hart* 1783. O 30 aa
For an answer *see* Sherman, Roger.

[WEBSTER, PELATIAH]   **209**
An essay on the seat of government . . . *Phil* 1789. O [4] 3–34 a

[WEBSTER, PELATIAH]   **210**
A plea for the poor soldiers . . . *Phil* MDCC LXC[error for 1790]. O 39 aa
—rptd. *N Hav*, same erroneous date. O 33 aa

WEBSTER, PELATIAH   **211**
Political essays . . . published during the American war . . . *Phil* 1791. O [8] 504 a
Collected works of an influential political economist of the period who was often consulted by members of Congress on finance and taxation.

[WEBSTER, PELATIAH]   **212**
The weakness of Brutus exposed . . . in vindication of the constitution proposed . . . *Phil* 1787. D 23 b AA Hn NYP
Reply to objections to the constitution published in a New York newspaper under the pseudonym of Brutus.

WEBSTER, RICHARD   **213**
History of the Presbyterian church in America . . . [1670–1760]. *Phil* 1857. O 720 port a

WEDDELL, ALEXANDER W., ed.   **214**
A memorial volume of Virginia historical portraiture . . . *Rich* 1930. F [32] 556[incl. front.] map 197ports aa 1000 cops ptd [50 in special leath. bdg]

WEED, JOSEPH   **215**
A view of California . . . *S F* 1874. 18° 192 a

WEEDEN, WILLIAM B.   **216**
Economic and social history of New England, 1620–1789. *B* 1890. O 2v: [16] 448; [14] 449–964 a

WEEDON (GENERAL GEORGE).   **217**
Valley Forge orderly book of: . . . *N Y* 1902. O [6] 323 front. plans a 255copies ptd.
First printing of an important manuscript; includes events such as the battles of Brandywine and Germantown.

[WEEMS, MASON L.]   **218**
The life and memorable actions of George Washington . . . [*Balt* Keatinge 1800?]. 16° 96 port b Hn IndU LC MH PaH [only copies known]
—new ed. cor. *Frederick-Town* 1801. D 70 [incl. port] a
—Ger. tr. "Die Lebensbeschreibung und merkwürdige Handlungen von . . . Washington . . .," *Frederick-Town* 1809. D [2] 176 port
—anr. ed., re-written, "A history of the life and death . . . of General George Washington . . .," *George-Town* Green and English [1800?]. O [4] 80 aa
—anr. issue, *Alexandria* [1800]. aa
—ed. 2, *Phil* Bioren [1800?]. O [2] 82 port[in some copies] aa
—ed. 3, same impr. [1800?]. O 84 port[in some copies] aa
—rptd. *Elizabeth-Town* Kollock [1802?]. O 61 port; *Alb* Webster [1802–3?]. D 84 a
—ed. 4, *Alb* Webster [1805–6?]. 16° 152
—ed. 5, improved [one of the improvements being the "cherry-tree" anecdote], "The life of Washington the great . . .," *Augusta Ga* 1806. b NYP [of 3copies known]
—ed. 9, greatly improved, *Phil* 1809. D 228 port 6pls a
—later eds. [in both Eng. and Ger.] too numerous to cite.

WEEMS, M[ASON] L.   **219**
The life of Benjamin Franklin . . . Ed. 5, enl. *Balt* 1820. D 264 port a
For earlier editions, *see* next entry.

WEEMS, MASON L., ed.   **220**
The life of Doctor Benjamin Franklin, written chiefly by himself . . . *Balt* 1815. 16° 264 aa
Called a "new edition" as it was based entirely on the London 1793 *Works* of Franklin [which contained his Autobiography]. After issuing three subsequent editions of this opus, Weems issued a fifth edition, written entirely by himself. *See* above.

WEEMS, M[ASON] L., ed.
The life of General Francis Marion. *See* Horry, Peter.

WEEMS, M[ASON] L.   **221**
The life of William Penn . . . *Phil* 1822. 16° [2] 219 port a

WEGWIJZER
Wegwijzer en raadgever voor landverhuizers naar Noord-Amerika . . . *See* Scholte, Henry P.

WEICHARDT, KARL   **222**
Die Vereinigten Staaten . . . und deren Territorien . . . *Leip* 1848. O [10] 448 map pl a
Also issued in 1848, as Vol. IV of Heinzelmann's *Weltkunde* [1847–1855]

WEIGHTMAN (RICHARD H.)   **223**
Speech of: . . . vindicatory of the course of Governor James S. Calhoun of New Mexico . . . *Wash* 1852. O 29 aa

WEIGHTMAN, RICHARD H.   **224**
To the Congress of the United States, requesting the passage of a bill declaring New Mexico one of the United States . . . *Wash* 1851. O 25 aa

WEIK, JOHANN   **225**
Californien wie es ist oder Handbuch von Californien . . . *Phil & Leip* 1849. 16° 108 + 4adv-p aa

WEILAND, C. F.
Atlas von Amerika . . . *See* Carey, Henry C., and Lea, J., *A complete historical . . . American atlas*, of which this is a translation.

WEIMER, M. D. K.   **226**
True story of the Alaska gold fields. [no t-p]. [ca 1903]. O 312 [33] a
Day-by-day journal of 1898 adventures.

[WEIN, PAUL]   **227**
A concise historical account of all the British colonies in North America. *L* 1775. O [4] 196 tab aa
—rptd. *Dub* 1775. aa
—best ed. *Dub* 1776. D [4] 228 map tab aa

WEISER, CONRAD   **228**
Narrative of a journey . . . from Tulpehocken in . . . Pennsylvania to Onondaga . . . *Phil* 1853. O 33 a

WELBY, ADLARD   **229**
A visit to North America and the English settlements in Illinois . . . *L* 1821. O [12] 224 14pls errata slip[correcting 3 errors] or errata lf [containing also binder's directions] b N NYP Y

[WELCH, ANDREW]   **230**
A narrative of the early days and remembrances of Oceola Nikkanochee . . . Written by his guardian. *L* 1841. O [10] 228 3pls a

This Seminole, nephew of the famous chief, was captured by United States troops and adopted by the author.

[WELCH, ANDREW] ed.   **231**
A narrative of the life and sufferings of Mrs. Jane Johns . . . scalped by Seminole Indians . . . *Charleston S C* 1837. O 29 b H N
—rptd. *Balt* 1837. O 24 b

WELCH, CHARLES A.   **232**
History of the Big Horn basin . . . [*S L C*] 1940. O 276 pls a

WELCH, MRS. EMILY S.   **233**
A biographical sketch; John Sedgewick, Major-General . . . [*N Y*] 1899. O [4] 24 a

WELD, CHARLES R.   **234**
A vacation tour in the United States and Canada. *L* 1855. D [12] 394 map a

WELD, ISAAC   **235**
Travels through . . . North America . . . 1795–1797. *L* 1799. Q [24] 464 + 8adv-p 16 maps & pls erratum slip aa
—ed. 2, same impr. & date. O 2v: [24] 427; [12] 376 + 16adv-p 16maps & pls a
—ed. 3, same impr., 1800. O 2v: [20] 427; [8] 376 + 26adv-p 16maps & pls
—ed. 4, same impr., date & collat. except for omission of adv-pp.
—anr. issue: O [8] 552 8maps & pls
—rptd. *L* 1807. O 2v 16maps & pls
—Fr. tr.: *P* [1800], O 3v: [12] 5–321; 344; [4] 294. 12maps & pls; *P* 1803 a
—Dutch, Ger. & Ital. trs. also appeared. a
Thought Canada preferable to the States.

WELKER, MARTIN   **236**
Farm life in central Ohio, sixty years ago. *Wooster* 1892. D 106 a

WELLARD, JAMES   **237**
Wellard, James, companion of John A. Murrell, the great western land pirate. *Cin* 1855. O 95 aa

WELLES, ALONZO M.   **238**
Reminiscent ramblings. *Denver* 1905. O 459 a
Mining experiences in Colorado, Arizona and New Mexico.

WELLES, C. M.   **239**
Three years' wanderings of a Connecticut Yankee in South-America, Africa, Australia, and California . . . *Hart* 1859. D 358 10pls [incl.eng.t.] a
—anr. ed., same date & collat., *N Y*

WELLES (GIDEON).   **240**
Diary of: *B* 1911. O 3v: [54] 549; [18] 653; [18] 672. 36pls a

Of prime importance on the civil war and reconstruction; one of the great American historical diaries.

WELLINGS, JAMES H. [comp.]   **241**
Directory of . . . Detroit, for 1845 . . . Containing an epitomized history . . . *Det* 1845. D 122 [48] aa
—for 1846. *Det* 1846. D 214 a

WELLINGTON, JOHN L.   **242**
The gold fields of Alaska . . . *Cripple Creek* 1896. O 72 a

WELLS ([CHARLES K.] POLK).   **243**
Life and adventures of: the notorious outlaw . . . written by himself. [*Halls Mo* 1907]. O 259 [incl. front.] a
Feeble "apologia" of a second-rate, highly unsuccessful outlaw who claimed he was a "chum" of Kit Carson, Slade and "Wild Bill"!

WELLS, CHARLES W.   **244**
A frontier life . . . *Cin* [1902]. D 313 a
Life in Nebraska and the Black Hills, in the 'sixties.

WELLS, EDWARD L.   **245**
Hampton and his cavalry in '64. *Rich* 1899. O [4 incl.front.] 429[incl.pls] [14] + 4adv-p a

WELLS, EDWARD L.   **246**
Hampton and reconstruction. *Columbia S C* 1907. O [8] 238 port errata slip a

WELLS, HARRY L., and CHAMBERS,   **247**
W. L.
History of Butte county, California. *S F* 1882. Q 305 pls b B CalS

WELLS, HARRY L.   **248**
Popular history of Oregon . . . *Port Ore* 1889. O 480 4pls facs tabs a

WELLS, JAMES M.   **249**
With touch of elbow . . . narrative of adventure. *Chi* 1909. D [12 incl.front.] 362 15pls a
Cavalry service in the Civil war, preceded by freighting experiences on the plains in the 'fifties.

WELLS, [JOHN G.]   **250**
Pocket hand-book of Iowa . . . history . . . *N Y* 1857. 16° 136 fold.map aa

WELLS, [JOHN G.]   **251**
Pocket hand-book of Nebraska . . . its history . . . *N Y* 1857. D [4] 9–90 + 10adv-p fold.map aa

WELLS, PROCTOR R.   **252**
Memories of early days. *San José* 1904. D 39 port a

[WELLS, RICHARD]   **253**
A few political reflections submitted to the consideration of the British colonies. By a citizen of Philadelphia. *Phil* 1774. O 86 aa

WELLS, ROLLA   **254**
Episodes of my life. [*St L* 1933] O [12] 510 35pls a
Cattle ranching in Kansas, Oklahoma, etc.

WELLS, WILLIAM   **255**
Western scenery, or land and river . . . in the Mississippi valley. *Cin* 1851. Q 54 [incl.wraps] eng.t. 19 col pls c ChiH MoH NYP

WELLS, WILLIAM V.   **256**
Walker's expedition to Nicaragua . . . *N Y* 1856. D [6] 11–316 map port a
—Ger. tr. *Braunschweig* 1857. D [10] 217 map port

WELSH, HERBERT   **257**
The Apache prisoners in Fort Marion . . . Florida. *Phil* 1887. O 62 a

WEMMS (WILLIAM, et al . . .).
The trial of: *See* Hodgson, John.

WENNER, FRED L.   **258**
Home-seeker's guide to Oklahoma . . . *Guthrie* 1900. D 23 aa

WERNER, HERMAN   **259**
On the western frontier with the U. S. cavalry fifty years ago. n.p. [1934]. O 98 port a
The Modoc war, Montana operations, etc.

WERTENBAKER, THOMAS J.   **260**
The planters of colonial Virginia. *Princeton* 1922. O 260 a

WERTENBAKER, THOMAS J.   **261**
Virginia under the Stuarts. *Princeton* 1914. O 271 maps a

WERTH, JOHN J.   **262**
A dissertation on the resources and policy of California . . . *Benicia* 1851. D [8] 87 errata lf. b G LC NYP Y
One of the earliest books on this state written by a resident.

WESLEY, JOHN   **263**
A calm address to our American colonies. *L* 1775. D 23 a
—rptd. often, same yr. [in *L*, *Bristol*, *Dundee*, *Edin*, *Salisbury*].
Essentially a condensation of Samuel Johnson's *Taxation no tyranny.*

WESLEY, JOHN   **264**
A calm address to the inhabitants of England. *L* 1777. D 23 a
—ed. 2, same impr. & date. D 24

[WESLEY, JOHN] ed.   265
An extract from a Reply to the Observations of
Lieut. General Howe on a pamphlet, entitled Let-
ters to a nobleman. *L* 1781. D 104 a

WESLEY, JOHN   266
An extract of . . . Wesley's journal from his
embarking for Georgia to his return to London . . .
Bristol Farley [1739]. O [28] 75 errata slip aa
—4 other eds. by 1775. a
—Am. ed., with European Journals added, v.I
[all], *Phil* 1795. D [2] 316 [2]
His Georgia Journal covers period from October
1735 to February 1738.

WESLEY (THE REV. MR. JOHN).   267
Political empiricism; a letter to: *L* 1776. O 32 a
Defends the colonies from the fallacious reason-
ing in Wesley's *Calm address.*

[WESLEY, JOHN]   268
Reflections on the rise and progress of the American rebellion. *L* 1780. D 96 aa
More probably by Joseph Galloway, from whose
*Historical and political reflections on the rise and
progress of the American rebellion* it doesn't mate-
rially differ.

WESLEY, JOHN   269
Some observations on liberty . . . *Edin* 1776. D
36 a
—rptd. *L* 1776. D 36
Answer to Richard Price's *Observations on . . .
civil liberty.*

WESLEY'S [MR.] SECOND CALM ADDRESS.
Observations on: . . . *See* Lofft, Capel.

[WEST, BECKWITH]   270
Experience of a Confederate States prisoner . . .
an ephemeris regularly kept by an officer of the
Confederate . . . army. *Rich* 1862. O 64 + wraps
b Duke Emory LC

WEST (CATO, et al).   271
Petition of: in behalf of themselves and other
inhabitants of the Mississippi Territory . . . [*Wash*
1800]. O [2] 27 aa

WEST, D. PORTER   272
Early history of Pope County, Arkansas. *Russellville* 1906. O 53 a

[WEST, EDWARD W.]   273
History of St. Clair county, Illinois . . . *Belleville* 1876. O 41 aa

WEST, GEORGE M[ONTGOMERY]   274
The emigrant's companion and guide . . . to the
continent of America . . . especially to the fertile
region of Ohio . . . *Liv* [1830]. D 48 aa

[WEST, GEORGE MONTGOMERY]   275
Report of proceedings in Ireland relative to the
church in Ohio, since the arrival of the Rev. G.
Montgomery West, chaplain to the . . . Bishop of
that diocese . . . *Dub* 1828. D 46 aa
West, a malicious adventurer, insinuated himself
into the Kenyon college enterprise, fomented
rebellion and forced Bishop Chase into resigning
from both college and bishopric.

WEST (HARRIET CLINE).   276
The life and travels of: *Kahoka Mo* 1910. D 177
port a
Of Kansas interest.

WEST, JOHN   277
The Boston directory . . . *B* 1796 D 117 plan
[issued both with the book and separately] a
Boston's second directory.

WEST, JOHN C.   278
A Texan in search of a fight . . . *Waco* 1901. O
189 [incl.port] aa

[WEST, MRS. LUCY BREWER]   279
The adventures of Louisa Baker [alias for Lucy
Brewer] . . . *N Y* [1815]. D 24 port aa
—rptd., same impr. & date. O 36 a
—rptd. "An affecting narrative of Louisa Baker
. . .," *B* 1815, D 24; *Portsmouth N H* 1816, D 24
port a
—con. as "The adventures of Lucy Brewer . . .,"
B 1815. O 36
—rptd. *B* 1816; *B* 1817.
—con. again as "The awful beacon, to the rising
generation . . .," *B* 1816. O [2] 60 port
—complete ed. [containing all of the above 3pts],
"The female marine, or adventures of Miss Lucy
Brewer . . .," n.p. ptd May 30, 1816. 18° 100[incl.
port] aa
—rptd. June 19, 1816. same collat. a
—ed. 2, June 24, 1816. same collat.
—ed. 3, *B* 1817. 18° 90
—rptd. n.p., n.d. D 60
—ed. 4, n.p. 1818. 18° 120 port
Narrative of dubious veracity in which the seduced heroine, after a life of shame, serves for
three years on board the "Constitution."

WEST, ROBERT A., reporter   280
Report of debates in the general conference
of the Methodist . . . church . . . *N Y* 1844. O
240 a
This heated fight on slavery between Northern
and Southern delegates split the Church.

WEST (S[IMEON] H.)   281
Life and times of: *Le Roy Ill* [1908]. O 298 aa
Includes his 1859 overland trip to the Pacific
coast with another, via Panama, in 1852.

WEST POINT.   282
The military academy at: unmasked ... By
Americanus. *Wash* 1830. O 28 a

WEST VIRGINIA.
Address to the people of: By a slaveholder ...
See Ruffner, Henry.

WESTBROOK, G. W.   283
The Mormons in Illinois ... *St L* 1844. D 36 b
IH LC
—for anr. ed., with Hunt's "History of the Mormon war in Missouri," *see* Hunt, James H.

WESTCOTT, J. D.   284
The Everglades of Florida ... *Tallahassee* 1848.
O 141 aa

WESTCOTT, JOHN   285
De Soto in Florida ... route ... *Palatka* 1888.
sm Q 11 6maps a

WESTCOTT, JOHN   286
An exposition of the titles to property in Jacksonville [Fla.]. *Jacksonv* 1869. O 25 a

WESTERLEY [CAROLINE]   287
Westerley (Caroline); or, the young traveller
from Ohio ... letters of a young lady ... to her
sister. *N Y* 1833. 16° 233 front. a
—rptd., same impr. & collat., 1870.
Travelled from Ohio through western New York
to Albany. Written by Mrs. Almira (Hart) Lincoln
Phelps to her sister, the famous Emma Willard.

WESTERN
Western guide book (The), and emigrant's directory ... *See* Steele, Oliver G.

Western industries of America ... *Chi*   288
1879. F 136 [111] a
History of manufacturing throughout the West,
from Ohio to California.

Western march of emigration. *Lancaster Pa* 1874.
O 53 a

Western souvenir (The) ...for 1829.
See Hall, James.

Western tour (A), in a series of letters ... *See*
Heald, Henry.

Western tourist ... *See* Smith, John Calvin.

Western traveller's ... directory. *See The traveller's pocket directory* ...

WESTMORELAND [PA.]
A narrative of the capture of certain Americans
at: ... *See* Van Campen, Moses.

WESTON, D. H.   289
A record of marks and brands. *Helena* 1881.
O 43 aa

WESTON, PLOWDEN C. J., ed.   290
Documents connected with the history of South
Carolina. *L* 1856. Q [8] 5–228 facs a 121 copies
ptd.

WESTON, RICHARD   291
A visit to the United States and Canada ... *Edin*
1836. D [4] 312 a
Visited Pennsylvania, New York, Illinois and
Ohio; a repulsive portrayal of backwood's life.

WESTON, S[ILAS]   292
Life in the mountains: or four months in the
mines of California. *Prov* 1854. O 35 b H Hn N
NYH
—ed. 2, "Four months in the mines of California
...," *Prov* 1854. O 46 [2] b G NYP Y

WESTON, W., ed.   293
Guide map of the best ... cattle trail to the
Kansas Pacific railway. *K C Mo* 1874. O 24 [incl.
wraps] fold.map 4fold.pls b
—rptd., t.altered, same impr., 1875. same collat.,
but no pls aa
A separately printed portion of the next entry.
The R.R. had previously issued such information in an 1871 fold sheet and in a 15–p. 1873
pamphlet. Trails are described from Texas to Abilene and other stations.

WESTON, W., ed.   294
Guide to the Kansas Pacific railway ... from
Kansas City and Leavenworth ... to Denver ...
K C 1872. D 208 + 6 blank lvs for memoranda
inserted between p.96 & 97 16 adv-p 4pls 2fold.
maps[one showing the cattle route from Texas to
Ellsworth] b NYP Y
—2 other issues have different paginat. [one, 204p.,
the other, 216]

WETHERBEE, J[OHN]   295
A brief sketch of Colorado Territory ... *B* 1863.
O 24 b N Y [all cops loc]

WETMORE, ALPHONSO   296
Gazetteer ... of Missouri ... [With appendix
containing "Sketch of mountain life by a trapper,"
etc.] *St L* 1837. O [4] 9–382 front. map aa

WETMORE, MRS. HELEN C.   297
Last of the great scouts: the life story of ...
"Buffalo Bill." [*Duluth* 1899]. O [2 14] 267 19pls a
—rptd. *Duluth* [ptd. *Chi*] n.d. [1899]. O [8 11–14]
296 5pls
—anr. issue, same impr. & paginat., but 16 pls
—anr. issue, same impr. O [14] 296 16pls

WETTE, L[UDWIG] DE   298
Reise in den Vereinigten Staaten und Canada
... *Leip* 1838 O [6, 9–14] 364 aa
—Dutch tr. *Zalt-Bommel* 1839. O 2v: [12] 281;
[8] 296. 2pls a

[WHARTON, CHARLES H.]   299
A poetical epistle to ... George Washington ...
to which is annexed, a short sketch of General
Washington's life ... *Annap* 1779. O 24 b Hn NYH
—Eng. ed. *L* 1780. O 24 port aa
—rptd. *L* 1796. a
—other Am. eds.: *Prov* 1781, Q 24 port; aa;
Springfield 1782, Q 18; *Alb* 1865. 75copies; *B*
1881. a
The biography of Washington—by John Bell—
was the first ever printed, with exception of an
eight-page tract by J. L. A. Roubaud - *A compendious history of George Washington* - published,
without title-page, London, *ca* 1777.

WHARTON, CLARENCE R.   300
Remember Goliad. *Houston* [1931]. O 61 a
100copies ptd.

[WHARTON, GEORGE M.]   301
The New Orleans sketch book. *Phil* 1853. D 8,
[incl. eng.t.] 21–202 front. b
—rptd. *Phil* [1860?]. same paginat. front. 2pls a

WHARTON, JOHN A.   302
Speech in defence of the Hon. S. Rhoads Fisher
... *Houston* 1838. O 53 aa

WHARTON, J[UNIUS] E.   303
History of ... Denver. *Denver* 1866. D 184 b Hn
N NYP Y rptd. *Denv* 1909 a
Rarest of Colorado local histories; first of this
city.

[WHARTON, SAMUEL]?   304
The advantages of a settlement upon the Ohio.
L 1763[error for 1773]. O [4] 44 b JCB N OHP
Refers to a proposed colony—Georgiana?—to
be erected by the Walpole associates west of their
Vandalia project. Attributed also to Bayly, Anselm
Yates.

[WHARTON, SAMUEL]?   305
Considerations on the agreement of the Lords
Commissioners ... with ... Thomas Walpole and
his associates for lands upon the river Ohio ...
L 1774. O [4] 46 b H NYP WisH
Attributed also to Franklin.

[WHARTON, SAMUEL]   306
Facts and observations, respecting the country
granted ... by the Six United Nations ..., on the
south-east side of the ... Ohio; the establishment
of a new colony there; and the causes of the Indian
war ... *L* 1775. O 171 fold. tab c JCB PaH

[WHARTON, SAMUEL]   307
Plain facts: ... examination into the rights of
the Indians nations ... and a vindication of the
grant, from the Six ... Nations, to the proprietors
of Indiana ... *Phil* 1781. O 165 b N NYP WisH Y
Disputes Virginia's claim to territory west of the
Alleghanies where the Walpole interests proposed
establishing their colony of Indiana. Attributed
also to Anthony Benezet and to Benjamin Franklin.

[WHARTON, SAMUEL]   308
View of the title to Indiana ... on the river Ohio
... [*Phil* 1775?]. O 24 d JCB WisH
—anr. ed. *Phil* 1776. O 46 b AA PaH Y
—rptd. *Wmsbg* 1779. Q 8 b
Refers to a tract in present West Virginia where
Thomas Walpole and his associates [including
Franklin] proposed establishing a colony of In-
diana. For an enlarged edition, *see* this author's
Plain facts: ... For another earlier work contain-
ing some of this material *see* Case [*of William
Trent and other traders*]

WHARTON (WILLIAM H.)   309
Address of: delivered in New York ... also,
Address of ... Stephen F. Austin, delivered in
Louisville ... with other documents explanatory
... of the contest in which Texas is at present
engaged. *N Y* 1836. O 56 aa
Stimulated national sympathy for Texas. Con-
tains the first appearance in a book of the 1836
Declaration of Independence.

WHAT
What I have saved from the writings of my
husband. *See* Lewis, Mrs. Thomas B.

What is our situation? and what our prospects?
... By an American. *See* Hopkinson, Jos.

What think ye of the Congress now? *See* Chandler, Thos. B.

[WHATELY, THOMAS]   310
Considerations on the trade and finances of this
kingdom, and on the measures of administration
... *L* 1766. Q 119 a
—ed. 2, same impr., date & collat.
—ed. 3, same impr. 1769. O 239
—rptd. *Dub* same date. O 108
Discusses—and defends—colonial taxation.

[WHATELY, THOMAS]   311
The regulations lately made concerning the colonies ... *L* 1765. O [2] 114 a
Ascribed also to John Campbell and to Lord
George Grenville [who is named as author in the
1775 edition], but probably by Whately, his
secretary.

WHEAT, CARL I.   312
The maps of the California gold region, 1848–

1857 . . . *S F* Grabhorn 1942. F [42] 152 [1] 26maps b N NYP Y 300copies ptd.
—anr. iss. of only 22 cops c.

[WHEAT, MARVIN T.]   313
Travels on the western slopes of the Mexican Cordillera. *S F* 1857. D 438 eng.t. aa
Made several trips through Arizona.

[WHEELER, A. O.]   314
Eye witness; or, life scenes in the old north state, depicting the . . . sufferings of the Unionists. *Russell* 1865. O 276 aa

WHEELER, ALFRED   315
Land titles in San Francisco . . . *S F* 1852. O 127 [2] map b LC

WHEELER, ALFRED, et al   316
Report on the condition of the beach and water lots in . . . San Francisco . . . *S F* 1850. O 104 b B Hn Y

WHEELER, ALFRED, et al   317
Report on the condition of the real estate within . . . San Francisco . . . *S F* 1851. O 156 b B Hn Y

WHEELER, ANDREW C.   318
The chronicles of Milwaukee . . . *Milw* 1861. D 303 a

WHEELER, A[NDREW] C.   319
The iron trail. A sketch of a journey to Colorado. *N Y* 1876. Q 46 a

WHEELER, B. C.   320
Western Colorado and her resources . . . *Aspen Colo* 1891. O 73 + 5adv-pages map a

WHEELER, GEORGE M.   321
Preliminary report concerning explorations . . . in Nevada and Arizona. *Wash* 1872. Q 96 fold. map a
First official exploration of this area, including the Mojave and Death valleys.

WHEELER, HOMER W.   322
The frontier trail . . . narrative of forty three years in the old west . . . *L A* 1923. O [18] 15–334 15pls a
—rptd. "Buffalo days . . .," *Indp* [1925]. O [26] 369 18pls

WHEELER, JOHN H.   323
Historical sketches of North Carolina . . . *Phil* 1851. O 2v in 1: 138; 480. 2 pls a

WHEELER, JOHN H.   324
Reminiscences and memoirs of North Carolina . . . *Columbus* 1884. O [16 74] 478 port aa
—rptd. *Wash* 1885.

A revised form of the biographical section of his *Historical sketches*, above.

WHEELER, OLIN D.   325
The trail of Lewis and Clark, 1804–1904. . . . *N Y* 1904. O 2v: [24] 377; [16] 420 + 4adv-p 4maps 2col.pls a
—rptd. 1913.

WHEELER, THOMAS   326
A thankful remembrance of God's mercy to several persons at Quabaug or Brookfield . . . *C* 1676. SmQ [6] 14 [misnumbered 10] 32 d JCB Y [of 4 cops loc]
Account of the Indian attack on Brookfield and the timely relief of that place by Boston troops under Willard.

WHEELING DIRECTORY . . . 1839
See Bowen, J. B.

WHEELOCK, ELEAZER   327
A brief narrative of the Indian charity-school in Lebanon in Connecticut . . . *L* 1766. O 48 aa
—ed. 2, with app., *L* 1767. O 63 a
—anr. issue, identical except note added at bottom of p. 63
Prepared from Wheelock's *A plain and faithful narrative, see* below. Probably by Nathaniel Whitaker. No. 3 of series.

WHEELOCK, ELEAZER   328
A continuation of the narrative of the Indian charity-school . . . *L* 1769. O [2] 146 aa
Contains letters of Wheelock from Dec. 1766 to Aug. 1768. No. 4 of series.

WHEELOCK, ELEAZER   329
A continuation of the narrative of the Indian charity-school . . . from the year 1768 to the incorporation of it with Dartmouth-College, and removal and settlement of it in Hanover, in the province of New-Hampshire, 1771. n. p. [*N Lond*] 1771. O 61 aa
—issue 2, errata list added to p. 61 a
No. 5 of series.

WHEELOCK, ELEAZER   330
A continuation of the narrative of the Indian charity-school . . . now incorporated with Dartmouth-College . . . [May 1771-Sept. 1772]. *New Hampshire* 1772. O 40 a
—rptd., same collat. & impr., 1773. No. 6 of series.

WHEELOCK, ELEAZER   331
A continuation of the narrative of the Indian charity-school . . . [Sept. 1772–Sept. 1773]. *Hart* 1773. O 68 aa
Contains journal of David MacClure and Levi Frisbie kept on their mission to the Delaware Indians in Ohio. No. 7 of series.

WHEELOCK, ELEAZER　　　332

A continuation of the narrative of the Indian charity-school . . . [Sept. 1773–Feb. 1775]. *Hart* 1775. Q 31 a

—anr. issue, with app. carrying paginat. to 54

Eighth—and last—report of our earliest Indian school, the acorn from which grew Dartmouth College.

WHEELOCK, ELEAZER　　　333

A continuation of the narrative of the state . . . of the Indian charity-school at Lebanon . . . *B* 1765. O 23 aa

—anr. issue, with app., carrying paginat. to 25 a

Covers period from Nov. 1762 to Sept. 1765. No. 2 of series.

WHEELOCK, ELEAZER　　　334

A plain and faithful narrative of the original design . . . and present state of the Indian charity-school at Lebanon, in Connecticut. *B* 1763. O 55 aa

Covers the years 1754–1762. No. 1 of series.

WHEELOCK, HARRISON　　　335

Guide and map of Reese river and Humboldt . . . *S F* 1864. D 43 + 9adv.p dd B Y [only 3 copies known]

The Bancroft copy contains a folding map of these mines published by Wheelock, same place and date; it may have been sold separately, but the book's title induces the belief that the map was issued with it.

[WHEELOCK, MATTHEW]　　　336

Reflections moral and political on Great Britain and her colonies. *L* 1770. O [6] 66 aa

WHICKER, J[OHN] W.　　　337

Historical sketches of the Wabash valley. [*Attica Ind*] 1916. O 159 port a

WHILLDIN, M.　　　338

A description of western Texas . . . *Galv* 1876. D 120 map[on verso of front wrap] 28 pls a

WHIPPLE, A[MIEL] W.　　　339

Report of an expedition from San Diego to the Colorado. Sen.Exec.Doc. 19. *Wash* 1851. O 28 a

First official government survey of Arizona around the junction of the Colorado and Gila rivers.

WHIPPLE, A[MIEL] W.　　　340

Report of explorations for a railway route, near the thirty-fifth parallel . . . from the Mississippi to the Pacific ocean. [*Wash* 1855]. O 154 [8] a

For series [House Executive Document 129] of which this formed a part, and which contained three sheets [of map and two profiles] for this report, *see Pacific railroad explorations.*

WHIPPLE, JOSEPH　　　341

A geographical view of the district of Maine . . . *Bangor* 1816. O 102 aa

—anr. issue, same collat., impr. & date, "The history of Acadie . . . with . . . view of the district of of Maine." aa

WHIPPLE-HASLAM, MRS. LEE　　　342

Early days in California . . . *Jamestown Calif* [1923]. O 34[incl. cover t.] port a

WHIRRY, WILLIAM T.　　　343

The town of Randolph, Columbia county, Wis. Its first settlement . . . *Randolph* 1873. O 24 a

WHITAKER, ARTHUR P., tr.　　　344

Documents relating to the commercial policy of Spain in the Floridas . . . *Deland Fla* 1931. Q [64] 278 7maps & pls a 360 copies ptd.

WHITAKER, ARTHUR P.　　　345

The Spanish-American frontier: 1783–1795 . . . *B* 1927. O [14] 255 3maps a

[WHITAKER, JOHN S.]　　　346

Sketches of life and character in Louisiana . . . By a member of the New Orleans bar. *N O* 1847. O 84 aa

WHITE, ALEXANDER　　　347

The American bloody register:—containing—a true . . . history of the lives . . . of three of the most noted criminals . . . in America. *B* 1784. D 30 [2]

Apparently the first number of a contemplated series; no more appeared.

WHITE, ANDREW　　　348

Narrative of a voyage to Maryland. An account of the colony . . . 1635–77. *Balt* 1874. O 128 a

WHITE, ELIJAH　　　349

A concise view of Oregon Territory. *Wash* 1846. O 72 [2] cover t. only c BA G NYP Y

Describes the initial establishment of organized society in that region. Consists of letters written by White to government authorities at Washington, printed previously in various documents. In issue one, word "honored," bottom of page thirty-nine, is not hyphenated.

WHITE, ELIJAH

Ten years in Oregon . . . *Ithaca* 1848. *See* Allen, Miss A. J.

WHITE, ELIJAH　　　350

Testimonials and records . . . in favor of special action for our Indian tribes. *Wash* 1861. O [4] 84 a

WHITE, FRANCIS　　　351

The Philadelphia directory . . . *Phil* 1785. O [4] 98 [2] b AA NYP PaH

For another Philadelphia directory, same year, *see* Macpherson.

WHITE, REV. GEORGE   352
An accurate account of the Yazoo fraud . . .
Marietta Ga 1852. O 64 aa

WHITE, REV. GEORGE   353
Historical collections of Georgia . . . *N Y* 1854.
O [14] 688 22pls aa
—eds. 2 & 3, with map & some text added, *N Y*
1855. O [20] 688 [41] aa

WHITE, REV. GEORGE   354
Statistics of . . . Georgia . . . *Sav* 1849. O 624
[77] errata 1f map aa

WHITE, GEORGE S.   355
Memoir of Samuel Slater, the father of American manufactures . . . *Phil* 1836. O 448 120 12pls
9plans facs a
—ed. 2, omitting Letter of Secy. of Treas., same
impr. & date. O 448 12pls 9plans facs

WHITE, REV. HENRY   356
The early history of New England . . . *Concord
N H* 1841. D 412 a
—7 eds. by 1843.
—rptd., "Indian battles . . .," *N Y* [1859]. D 412

WHITE (CAPTAIN HUGH A., of   357
the Stonewall brigade).
Sketches of the life of: By his father [Wm. S.
White]. *Columbia* 1864. O 124 a

WHITE, JOHN, of England   358
Sketches from America [including a trip from
Chicago to Cheyenne and Denver]. *L* 1870. O [8]
373 a

WHITE, JOHN, of Gloucester, Mass.   359
New England's lamentations . . . *B* 1734. O [14]
42 10 [2] 15 b AA JCB
—ed. 2, enl., same impr., & date. O [10] 42 10 [2]
15 aa
—Eng. ed. *L* 1735. aa

WHITE, JOHN M.   360
The newer northwest . . . Black hills and Big
Horn mountains . . . *St L* 1894. O 216 photo-
graphic pls a

WHITE, J[OSEPH], 1755–1836   361
An [*sic*] narrative of events . . . in the revolutionary war . . . *Charles-town* [1833?]. sq 18° 30 aa

WHITE (MRS. K.)   362
A narrative of the life, occurrences, vicissitudes
and present situation of: *Schenectady* for the
authoress 1809. 16° 127 [incl. blank 1f] b AA N
NYH NYP

Romantic episodes, including an Indian captivity, all placing severe strain on credulity.

WHITE, OWEN P.   363
The autobiography of a durable sinner. *N Y*
[1942] O [6] 344 [last 3 lvs of iss 1 are integral parts
of the printing] aa
—iss. 2, identical except that last 3 lvs are tipped
in, replacing those that were suppressed. a

WHITE, OWEN [P.]   364
Out of the desert: the historical romance of El
Paso. *El Paso* 1923. O [12] 445 9pls aa
—ed. 2, with biog. & newspaper sections omitted,
same impr. 1924. O 345 23pls a

WHITE, OWEN P.   365
Trigger fingers . . . *N Y* 1926. D [8] 323 a

WHITE, RICHARD EDWARD   366
Padre Junipero Serra and the mission church of
San Carlos del Carmelo. *S F* 1884. D 32 a

[WHITE, RICHARD G.]   367
Book of the prophet Stephen, son of Douglas.
Books I & II. *N Y* [1863–4]. D 2v: 48; 48 a

[WHITE, RICHARD G.]?   368
The new gospel of peace . . . *N Y* [1863–6]. D
4pts: 42; 48; 47; 56 a
—rptd. in 1v. *N Y* 1866. D [26] 643
White disavowed authorship.

[WHITE, RICHARD G.]   369
Revelations: a companion to the "New gospel of
peace . . ." *N Y* Doolady 1863. D 36 a
—anr. issue, same collat. *N Y* Bancker 1863.

WHITE, SAMUEL   370
History of the American troops . . . under the
command of Cols. Fenton and Campbell . . . *Balt*
1829. D 107 [cov.t. only] aa
—rptd., same collat: *Balt* 1830; *Phil* 1831; *Roch*
1896. a

WHITE, WILLIAM   371
A history of Belfast [Me.]. *Belfast* 1827. 16°
120 a

[WHITE, WILLIAM F.]   372
A picture of pioneer times in California . . . By
William Grey [*pseud.*] *S F* 1881. O [7] 677 a

WHITE MOUNTAINS (THE).
Laconia: or legends of: *See* Scribner, J. P.

WHITECAR, WILLIAM B.   373
Four years aboard the whaleship . . . *Phil* 1860.
D 413 a
Sailed from New Bedford.

WHITEFIELD, GEORGE　　　　374

[Journals—and continuations] as follows: [Journal I] . . . London to Savannah. Pt. 1, . . . to Gibralter. Pt. 2 . . . Gibralter to Savannah. Unauthorized ed. *L* Cooper 1738. O 2v: [2] 34; [2] 34 a
—authorized ed.: *L* Hutton 1738. O 2pts in 1: [6] 64, mispaged 56; 5 other Eng. eds. by 1743
—Am. eds.: *Phil* Franklin, pt. 1, 1740, pt. 2, 1739. 24° 2v: 64; 45 c Y; *B* 1740. O 2v: 46 + adv-p; 54 + adv-p
[Journal II] . . . from arrival at Savannah to return to London. *L* 1739. O [4] 38 + adv-p a
—ed. 2, *L* 1739.
—Am. ed. *B* 1741. O 54 + adv-p
[Journal III] . . . from arrival at London, to departure to Georgia. *L* 1739. O 92 a
—anr. issue, same date & impr. O 115
—ed. 2, *L* 1739. O [4] 40; and other eds.
[Journal IV] . . . during the time detained in England. *L* 1739. O [4] 40 a
—3 other eds., same date, impr. & collat.
[Journal V] . . . from embarking after the embargo, to arrival at Savannah. *L* 1740. O 88 a
—ed. 2, same impr., date & collat.
—Am. ed. *Phil* 1740. D 145 + 5adv-p b Y
[Journal VI] . . . after arrival at Georgia, to his second return thither from Pennsylvania. *Phil* 1740. 24° 96 b
—Eng. ed. *L* 1741. O 58 + 2adv-p
[Journal VII], Pt. 1 . . . from Savannah to arrival at Rhode Island. *Phil* 1741. 24° 126 b
—*B* Fowle 1741. a
—other eds. *B* 1741 [various imprints of Fowle, Rogers and Kneeland]. O 96
—Eng. ed., both pts., probably ed. 1, *L* 1741. O [2] 86 b
—ed. 2, *L* 1744. a
[Journal VII], Pt. 2 . . . from leaving New-England . . . to arrival at Falmouth. *B* Rogers 1741. O 48 a
　B Kneeland 1741. 16° 38 [2]
—*Phil* 1741, with adds. 24° 126 b
—Eng. ed, with Pt. 1 - prob. has priority, *L* 1741 O [2] 86 b

In addition to above separate printings of the 9 parts constituting the 7 journals, there were several editions combining several of the parts. All of the Philadelphia editions were printed by Franklin. Complete set of these - 7 journals in 9 parts - b

WHITEFIELD, GEORGE　　　　375
Remarks on the injustice of slavery. *L* 1730. O 42 a

WHITEHEAD, WILLIAM A.　　　　376
Contributions to the early history of Perth Amboy . . . *N Y* 1856. O [8] 428 a

WHITELY, IKE [ISAAC H.]　　　　377
Rural life in Texas. *Atlanta* 1891. O 82 + 2 adv-p. copyright slip. a

WHITEWATER [THE].
Annals of pioneer settlers on . . . *See* Wasson, John Macamy.

WHITFORD, WILLIAM C.　　　　378
Colorado volunteers in the civil war. The New Mexico campaign in 1862. *Denver* 1906. O [4] 9–159 front. a

WHITING, HENRY　　　　379
A discourse . . . on the anniversary of the Historical Society of Michigan. *Det* 1831. O 40 aa

WHITMAN COUNTY [IDAHO] . . .　　　　380
Descriptive pamphlet of: Comp. by Kellogg and Hopkins. *Colfax Ida* 1878. O 32 aa

WHITMER, DAVID　　　　381
An address to all believers in Christ . . . *Richmond Mo* 1887. O 75 aa
Sketch of the part played by the author—one of the three original witnesses to the divine authentication of the Book of Mormon—in the early history of the Church.

WHITNEY, ASA　　　　382
Address before the legislature of Alabama, on his project for a railroad from lake Michigan to the Pacific. [*Wash* 1847]. O 44 2maps aa

WHITNEY, ASA　　　　383
A project for a railroad to the Pacific . . . *N Y* 1849. O [8] 112 2maps aa
Whitney was the first to bombard Congress with plans for a transcontinental railway. His efforts culminated in this matured proposal.

WHITNEY, CASPAR　　　　384
Charles Adelbert Canfield. *N Y* 1930. Q 218 14pls 200copies ptd. [25 in leather] aa
Relates largely to his mining experiences in Colorado and Nevada.

WHITNEY, E. C. and T. H.　　　　385
History and capture of Geronimo and the Apache Indians: [*St Augustine* 1887]. 16° 48 pls b G

WHITNEY, HENRY C.　　　　386
Life on the circuit with Lincoln . . . *B* [1892]. O [8] 601 67pls aa
—rptd. *Caldwell Ida* 1940. O 530 pls a
Intimate account by a fellow lawyer.

WHITNEY, J[OEL] P.　　　　387
Colorado . . . *L* 1867. O 61 2maps a

WHITNEY, J[OEL] P.　　　　388
Silver mining regions of Colorado . . . *N Y* 1865. 16° 107 cov.t.only a
—anr. issue, same impr. & date. O 111
—rptd. *B* 1867.

WHITNEY, J[OSIAH] D.   **389**
The Yosemite book: a description . . . *N Y* ptd.
C 1868. Q 118 2maps 28photo pls only 250copies aa
—anr. ed. "The Yosemite guide-book . . .," *N Y*
1869. O 155 2maps 8pls a
—anr. ed. 1871. 16° 133 2maps
—rptd., same yr., with new maps dated 1872
—new ed. 1874. 16° 186 4maps

WHITNEY (PARKHURST, et al.)   **390**
Trial of: for a conspiracy; the abduction . . . of
William Morgan . . . *Lockport* [1831]. O 63 aa

WHITNEY, PETER   **391**
The history of the county of Worcester . . . Massachusetts . . . *Worc* 1793. O 339 map a

WHITON, JOHN M.   **392**
Sketches of the history of New Hampshire . . .
1623–1833 . . . *Concord* 1834. D 222 a

WHITTAKER, MILO L.   **393**
Pathbreakers and pioneers of the Pueblo region
. . . [*Pueblo Colo*] 1917. O 160 pls aa

WHITTIER, JOHN G.   **394**
Justice and expediency; or, slavery considered
with a view to its rightful . . . remedy, abolition.
Haverhill 1833. O 23 c H Hn NYP

[WHITTIER, JOHN G.]   **395**
Leaves from Margaret Smith's journal . . . 1678–
9. *B* 1849. 16° [6] 224 a

[WHITTIER, JOHN G.] ed.   **396**
Narrative of James Williams, an American slave
. . . *N Y* 1838. 18° 108 port a
—issue 2, period after Williams on t-p, and printer's name on verso of t-p
—ed. 2, *N Y & B*. same collat. & date

WHITTLESEY, CHARLES   **397**
Ancient mining on the shores of lake Superior.
Wash 1863. Q [4] 29 map cov.t.only a

WHITTLESEY, CHARLES   **398**
A discourse relating to the expedition of Lord
Dunmore . . . against the Indian towns upon the
Scioto in 1774. *Clev* 1842. O 33 a

WHITTLESEY, CHARLES   **399**
Early history of Cleveland, Ohio . . . *Clev* 1867.
O [10] 487 6pls diag a some copies on L. P.
Covers the period prior to 1810.

WHITTLESEY, CHARLES   **400**
Fugitive essays . . . relating to the early history
of Ohio . . . *Hudson O* 1852. D 397 a

WHITTLESEY, CHARLES   **401**
A sketch of the settlement . . . of the township of

Tallmadge . . . Summit county, O. *Clev* 1842. 16°
29 a

WHITTLESEY, CHARLES   **402**
Topographical and historical sketch of . . . Ohio.
Phil 1872. O 34 map a

WHITTLESEY, FREDERIC, chairman   **403**
Abduction and murder of William Morgan . . .
Report of a committee appointed by the National
Anti-Masonic Convention . . . at Philadelphia,
September 11, 1830 . . . *Hallowell Me* 1832. O
24 a
—rptd., with different title, [*B*. 1833]. O [2] 18 [5]
For first printing *see United States Anti-Masonic
Convention. Proceedings of:*

WICHITA CITY DIRECTORY . . .
See Emmert, D. B.

WIDENMANN, ED[UARD]   **404**
Die nordamerikanische Revolution und ihre
Folgen . . . *Erlangen* 1826. O [6] 262 a

WIERZBICKI, F[ELIX] P.   **405**
California as it is . . . a guide to the gold region.
S F 1849. O 60 errata 1f dd B N NYH Y
—ed. 2, with adds., *S F* 1849. O [6] 5–76 errata 1f
dd B G NYH Y
—anr. ed. *Launcestown Tasmania* 1850. c
—rptd. *S F* [Grabhorn Press] 1933. O a 500 copies
ptd. aa
—Ger. tr. *Bremen* 1850. c
First California-printed English book of an
original nature; this, with its highly interesting
content, renders it the most important and prized
of all books printed there, with the possible exception of Figueroa's *Manifesto*.

WIGGLESWORTH, EDWARD   **406**
Calculations on American population . . . annual increase . . . *B* 1775. O 24 a
This optimistic Harvard professor envisioned a
population, in 1950, of 320 millions.

WILBARGER, J. W.   **407**
Indian depredations in Texas . . . *Austin* 1889.
O [12] 672 port 38pls[37listed] aa
—ed. 2 same impr. & collat 1890. aa
—anr. ed. *Austin* 1935. O [14] 672 pls a
Most complete of the early compilations on
Texas Indian fights and fighters.

WILBER, C. D.   **408**
The great valleys . . . of Nebraska . . . *Omaha*
1881. O [8] 382 map a
—eds. 2 & 3, same impr. & date.

WILCOX, CADMUS M.   **409**
History of the Mexican war . . . *Wash* 1892. O
[10] 711 29pls 14maps errata 1f a

WILD, J. C., engraver   **410**
Panorama and views of Philadelphia, and its vicinity . . . *Phil* 1838. F [22] 24pls c NYP
—rptd. "Views of Philadelphia," *Phil* 1848. F [24] 20pls b
The 1848 edition omitted the 4 large panoramas, but some copies had the 20 plates in color.

WILD, J. C., engraver
The valley of the Mississippi illustrated . . . *See* Thomas, Lewis F., and Wild, J. C.

WILDER, DANIEL W.   **411**
The annals of Kansas. *Topeka* 1875. O 691 a
—rptd. 1886. O 1196 front.

WILDERNESS [THE]; OR BRADDOCK'S TIMES.
See McHenry, James.

WILEY, [JOHN], and PUTNAM,   **412**
G[EORGE P.], pubs.
Emigrant's guide . . . *L* 1845. 16° 141 aa

[WILHELM, THOMAS]   **413**
Synopsis of the history of the Eighth U. S. Infantry . . . 1838–1871. *David's Island N Y* 1871. D [6] 495 front. aa
—ed. 2, enl., "History of the Eighth U. S. Infantry," [*N Y*?] 1873. O 2v: [14] 5–430; [14] 7–432 [7]. 6maps 11pls aa
An addition to this history was issued, *circa* 1874, without title-page, captioned *Memorandum from the Adjutant's office*, octavo, 117 pages.

WILKES, CHARLES   **414**
Narrative of the United States Exploring Expedition . . . *Phil* ptd for Congress by Sherman 1844. Q 5v: [68] 455 map 8pls; [16] 505 3maps 14pls; [16] 463 11pls; [16] 574 map 16pls; [16] 591 4maps 15pls; + Atlas Q [4] 5maps[2col.] c LC NYP Y 100 sets ptd, 63 of which were given to states and foreign nations and 25 were destroyed by fire
—unofficial ed. *Phil* Lea & Blanchard 1845. same size & collat., except for added ¹/₂ t. in Atlas b BP NYP Y 150 sets ptd
—rptd., in smaller type, *Phil* 1845. large O 5v: [60] 434 map 8pls; [16] 476 3maps 14pls; [16] 438 12pls; [16] 539 map 15pls; [16] 558 4maps 15pls; + Atlas large O [4] 5maps aa
—later eds.—1845, 1849, 1850, 1851 & 1852— omitted lists of illustrations and were not accompanied by Atlas, 11 maps being included, along with 3tabs, in the text vols. a
The first United States scientific expedition by sea. Wilkes sailed along and surveyed the whole Northwest coast and his exploring parties penetrated into the interior at many points. The official edition of the *Narrative* was followed, 1846–1858, by volumes giving scientific data; these were numbered 6 to 17, 20 and 23 [volumes 18, 19, 21, 22 and 24 never issued].

WILKES, CHARLES   **415**
Synopsis of the cruise of the . . . exploring expedition. *Wash* 1842. O 56 map aa
Issued three years before the complete report, with some material not in that work.

WILKES, CHARLES   **416**
Western America, including California and Oregon. *Phil* 1849. O [2, 5–10] 13–130 blank lf [32] 3maps [some copies have 4] aa
—Ger. tr. *Bayreuth* 1850 O 120 3 maps a
Written from material gathered by the author on his famous government exploring expedition of 1832–4, but not included in his official *Narrative*, as this region was not then United States public domain. In a sense it constitutes the first Pacific coast guide; De Smet contributed some geographical information.

WILKES, GEORGE   **417**
The great battle . . . at Manassas . . . *N Y* 1861. D 36 map a

WILKES, GEORGE   **418**
The history of Oregon . . . *N Y* 1845. O 127 [1] map c N NYP Y
—rptd. *Phil* 1849. O b
—Eng. ed., in garbled form, with t. altered & parts re-written [by John H. Bryant?] to support British claims. *L* 1846. 16° [2] 160 [8] b NYH
—Eng. ed. 2, same impr., date & collat. aa
Contains journal of the 1843 emigration expedition to Oregon kept by Peter Burnett, later governor of California.

WILKES, GEORGE   **419**
Project of a national railroad from the Atlantic to the Pacific. [Called "ed.2," as it first appeared in the author's *History of Oregon*]. *N Y* 1845. O 23 + cover-t. b LC N NYP Y pref. of issue 1 is dated June, 1845.
—rptd. "Memorial for . . . railroad to the Pacific." [capt. t.] *N Y* 1846. O 24 b NYP
—ed. 4, "Proposal for . . . rail-road to the Pacific," *N Y* 1847. O 24 + cover-t. map b LC NYP
—enl. ed. "A project . . .," *N Y* 1849. O 112 fold. maps aa
One of the earliest transcontinental agitations; framed while California was still a Mexican province, an Oregon terminus was planned.

WILKESON, SAMUEL   **420**
Notes on Puget sound . . . *N Y*[1870?]. O 47 a
—rptd. [*N Y* 1870]. O 44
—abr. ed. n.p. n.d. O 32

WILKEY, WALTER [pseud.]
Western emigration . . . *See* Deming, Ebenezer.

WILKIE, D[AVID]   **421**
Sketches of a . . . trip to New York and the Canadas. *Edin* 1837. O [6] 294 a

WILKIE, FRANC B.   **422**
The Iowa First. Letters from the war. *Dubuque* 1861. O 114 aa

WILKIE, F[RANC] B.   **423**
Sketches and notices of the Chicago bar . . . Ed. 3. *Chi* 1871. O 90 a
—ed. 4—and best—*Chi* 1872. Q 128 49 photos
No record found of any edition earlier than the third.

WILKINS (LIEUTENANT COLONEL).
A memorial . . . against: . . . *See* Blouin, Daniel.

WILKINS, BEN C.   **424**
Cruise of the "Little Nan"; five hundred miles down the Mississippi . . . *Huron N D* 1886. D 89 pls aa

WILKINSON (ELIZA).
Letters of: . . . *See* Gilman, Mrs. Caroline.

WILKINSON, J. B.   **425**
The annals of Binghamton . . . *Binghamton* 1840. D 256 a
—rptd., with adds., same impr., 1872. D [6] 312

WILKINSON (GENERAL JAMES).   **426**
A brief examination of testimony, to vindicate the character of: . . . *Wash* 1811. O 32 80 b

WILKINSON (GENERAL [JAMES]).   **427**
Debate in the House of Representatives of the territory of Orleans, on a Memorial to Congress respecting the illegal conduct of: *N O* 1807. O 42 [6] b

WILKINSON (GENERAL).   **428**
Memoirs of: Vol. II. *Wash* 1810. O 18 3–99 136 aa
—anr. ed., with add. t-p, "Burr's conspiracy exposed [etc.]," *Wash* 1811. O [6] 3–18 3–99 136 aa
A pre-issue of this volume of his *Memoirs*, circulated to vindicate the author's questionable conduct in the Burr affair.

WILKINSON, [GENERAL] JAMES   **429**
Memoirs of my own times. *Phil* 1816. O 3v: [16] 855 [44]; [4] 578 [260]; [4] 496 [62] 9fold.tabs 3fold.facs + atlas Q [8 p 19maps & plans] b N NYP Y
The atlas must have been sold separately as it seldom accompanies the text volumes.

WILKINSON (BRIGADIER GENERAL JAMES).   **430**
Message from the President . . . communicating . . . information touching the official conduct of: *Wash* 1808. O 30 aa
Another message, communicating further information in eight pages, was issued the same year.

WILKINSON (GENERAL [JAMES]).   **431**
A plain tale . . . justifying the character of: By a Kentuckian. *N Y* 1807. O 24 aa
Possibly by Charles Winterfield.

WILKINSON (GEN. JAMES).   **432**
Report of the committee . . . to inquire into the conduct of: . . . his connection with the agents of Spain . . . his connection with Aaron Burr . . . *Wash* 1810. O 174–217 5 tabs aa

WILKINSON (GENERAL [JAMES]).   **433**
Report of the committee . . . to inquire into the conduct of: *Wash* 1811. O 582[some copies end at p522] 5tabs 2fold.cipher sheets aa

WILKINSON (GEN. JAMES).   **434**
Trial of: . . . at a general court martial . . . at Fredericktown, Md. n.p. [*ca* 1811]. 16° 37 aa
As always, the wiley Wilkinson cheated justice.

WILKINSON, S.
The voyages and adventures of Edward Teach, commonly called Black Beard . . . *B* 1808. D 35 aa
For similar title *see* Teach, Edward.

WILL THERE BE WAR? . . .
By an adopted citizen. *See* Taylor, Wm.

WILLCOX (LIEUT. JOSEPH M.)   **435**
A narrative of the life . . . of: massacred by the Creek Indians . . . *Marietta O* 1816. O 23 b

WILLCOX, R. N.   **436**
Reminiscences. Of California life . . . *Avery O* 1897. D. [2] 290 inserted in some copies is a port [ptd ca. 1901] aa Not over 100 cops ptd

[WILLETT, ELBERT D.]   **437**
History of Co. B., 40th Alabama regiment. [*Anniston* 1902]. O [2] 89 aa

WILLETT, WILLIAM M. [ed.]   **438**
A narrative of the military actions of Colonel Marinus Willet . . . *N Y* 1831. O [6] 5–162 port plan aa
Revolutionary experiences and account of a 1790 visit to the Creek Indians.

WILLETT, WILLIAM M.   **439**
Scenes in the wilderness . . . labours and sufferings of the Moravian missionaries among the . . . Indians. *N Y* 1842. 16° 208 [incl.front.] a
—rptd: *N Y* [1842?]; *N Y* 1851.

WILLEY, SAMUEL H.   **440**
A historical paper relating to Santa Cruz, California . . . *S F* 1876. O 37 a

WILLEY, S[AMUEL] H.   **441**
Thirty years in California . . . *S F* 1879. O 76 a

WILLEY, SAMUEL H.   442
Two historical discourses... *S F* 1859. O
46 a

WILLIAM, FATHER [pseud.]   443
Recollections of rambles in the south. *N Y* 1854.
16° 196[incl.pls] a

WILLIAM, FATHER [pseud.]   444
Three days on the Ohio river. *N Y* 1854. D 60
[incl.pls] aa
—rptd. *N Y* 1857 a

WILLIAMS, AARON   445
The Harmony Society at Economy, Pennsyl-
vania. *Pitt* 1866. 16° 182 a
Includes a chapter on this Society's earlier establishment in Indiana.

WILLIAMS, ALFRED M.   446
Sam Houston and the war... in Texas... *B*
1893. O [10] 405 port map a
—rptd., same impr. & collat. n.d.

WILLIAMS, B. G.   447
Life... of Cornplanter... [*Warren*, Pa.] 1883.
O 42 [2] a

WILLIAMS, MRS. [CATHERINE   448
R. ARNOLD]
Biography of... Brigadier Gen. William Bar-
ton, and... Captain Stephen Olney. *Prov* 1839.
D 312 [incl. front] a

WILLIAMS, CHAUNCEY P.   449
Lone Elk: the life story of Bill Williams, trapper
... *Denver* 1935-6. O 2pts: 50; 35 a 500copies
ptd.

WILLIAMS, EDWARD   450
Virgo triumphans: or, Virginia richly... valued
... especially the south part thereof... Carolina,
and... isle of Roanoak... *L* 1650. D [14] 47 [8]
dd JCB LC N
—ed. 2, with adds, same impr. & date. D [12] 47
[8]; [6] 75 [3] d
—anr. ed. "Virginia... richly valued..." *L* 1651
map added d no cop loc
Promotional literature for luring emigration to
these parts.

WILLIAMS, ELEAZER   451
Life of Te-ho-ra-gwa-ne-gen, alias Thomas Williams... *Alb* 1859. O [cover t. & 4blank lvs] 91 a
200copies
Biography of the son of Eunice Williams—the
Deerfield captive of 1704—prominent in New
York's border wars and the unquestionable father
of the biographer, the unscrupulous "Lost Dauphin" pretender.

WILLIAMS, MRS. ELLEN   452
Three years and a half; or, history of the Second
Colorado. *N Y* [1885]. D [4] 178 + 8adv-p port aa
This civil war outfit operated from New Mexico
to Missouri.

WILLIAMS, GEORGE W.   453
History of the Negro race in America, 1619–
1880... *N Y* 1883. O 2v: [20] 481; [2 14] 611.
front. a
—rptd., popular ed., *N Y* n.d. O 2v in 1front.

WILLIAMS, HENRY L.   454
"Buffalo Bill"... a full account of his adventurous life. *L* 1887. O 192 port a

WILLIAMS, J. C.   455
The history... of Danby, Vermont. *Rutland*
1869. O 393 map a

WILLIAMS (JAMES, [b. 1805] an American slave)
Narrative of: *See* Whittier, John G.

WILLIAMS (JAMES). [b. 1825]   456
Life and adventures of:... *S F* 1873. O 108 aa
—rptd. 3 times by 1874.
Story of a fugitive slave who came to the California mines in 1851.

WILLIAMS, HON. JAMES, d. 1869   457
Letters on slavery... *Nashv* 1861. D [10] 9–321 a
—Eng. ed. "The south vindicated...," *L* 1862.
O [10] 444
—Ger. tr. *Berlin* 1863. O 326

WILLIAMS, HON. JAMES, d. 1869   458
Rise and fall of "The Model Republic." *L* 1863.
O [14] 424 a

WILLIAMS, JESSE   459
A description of the United States lands in Iowa
... *N Y* 1840. 24° 180 + adv-p map b AA N
NYP Y

[WILLIAMS, REV. JOHN] 1664–1729   460
Good fetch'd out of evil: a collection of memorables relating to our captives. [supposed title] [*B*
1706?]. D [2] 46 d only 4 imperfect copies known,
all lacking t-p
—ed. 2, n.p. 1783. Q 34 b AA NYH [only copies
known, both defective]
—for eds. under anr. t., *see* next entry.

WILLIAMS ([REV.] JOHN) [1664–1729]   461
The redeemed captive... remarkable occurrences in the captivity and the deliverance of:...
B 1707. O [6] 104 d AA N NYP [of 4 perfect copies
known]
—ed. 2, with omissions, *B* 1720. O [6] 98 c NYP
[of 2 perfect copies known]
—ed. 3, with adds., *B* 1758. O [8] 104 c N NYP

—ed. 4, *N Lond* T Green [1773]. O 79 b ConnH NYP [only perfect copies known]
—ed. 5, *B* 1774. O 71 b AA N NYP
—anr. ed. 5, *N Lond* T Green [1776]. O 72 aa N NYP Y
—anr. ed. styled "4th ed. with adds.," *Greenfield Mass* 1793. D [6] 154 aa
—anr. ed. styled "6th ed.," *B* 1795. D 132 aa
—ed. 6, with sketch of Deerfield added. *Greenfield Mass* 1800 D 248
—many later eds.

One of the most famous and most popular captivity narratives. Williams, Harvard graduate, in charge of the church at Greenfield when it was attacked by Indians, in 1703, was taken, with others, to Canada, his wife and two of his children being tomahawked on the way. As a powerful picture of Indian cruelty, ranks next to the Rowlandson captivity narrative, published in 1682, *q.v.*

WILLIAMS, JOHN, 1727–98   **462**
An enquiry into the truth of the tradition, concerning the discovery of America, by Prince Madog . . . *L* 1791. O [8] 82 [4] aa

WILLIAMS, JOHN, 1727–98   **463**
Farther observations, on the discovery of America, by Prince Madog . . . *L* 1792. O [10] 52 aa

[WILLIAMS, JOHN] 1761–1818   **464**
The Hamiltoniad: or, an extinguisher for the royal faction of New-England . . . *B* [1804?]. O 104 a

WILLIAMS, JOHN G.   **465**
The adventures of a seventeen-year-old lad . . . *B* 1894. O 308 port a

WILLIAMS, JOHN G.   **466**
A forty-niner's experience in the Klondike . . . *B* 1897. 16° 29 port a

WILLIAMS, JOHN LEE   **467**
The territory of Florida . . . from its first discovery. *N Y* 1837. O 304 map port 2pls aa
—rptd. same collat. 1839. aa

WILLIAMS, JOHN LEE   **468**
A view of West Florida . . . *Phil* 1827. O 178 map aa

WILLIAMS, JOHN S. [ed.]   **469**
The American pioneer . . . sketches relative to the early settlement . . . of the country. *Chillicothe* 1842, *Cin* 1843. O 2v: 448; 480. 21pls aa

Originally issued in 21 monthly numbers; 12 in 11 [vol. I], 10 [vol. II]. Vol. I twice reprinted, *Cincinnati* 1842 and 1844. As a repository of material on Ohio valley pioneer events ranks with Craig's *Olden time.* Earliest state of volume one gives date April 1 [for August 1], page 24, line 11.

WILLIAMS, JOSEPH, of the British army   **470**
Considerations on the American war . . . *L* 1782. Q 31 a
For a different pamphlet with same title, *see Considerations on the American war* . . .

WILLIAMS, JOSEPH, of Ind.   **471**
Narrative of a tour from . . . Indiana to the Oregon Territory . . . 1841–2. *Cin* 1843. O 48 dd G Hn NYH Pn Y [of 6 cops loc]
—rptd. *N Y* 1921. O 95 a 250copies ptd.[12 on L.P.]
Account of the 1841 overland expedition, the first to be made by actual settlers. His return in 1842 was over the southern route via Taos and Bent's Fort.

WILLIAMS, JOSEPH S.   **472**
Old times in west Tennessee . . . *Memphis* 1873. D [4] 295 aa

WILLIAMS, LLEW   **473**
The Dalton brothers in their Oklahoma cave . . . *Chi* [1893] D 234 a

WILLIAMS, MARY A. B.   **474**
Pioneer days of Washburn, North Dakota, and vicinity. [*Washburn* 1936]. O [4] 120 a

WILLIAMS, R. H.   **475**
With the border ruffians: memories of the far west, 1852–68. *L* 1907. O [20] 478 6pls aa
—rptd. *L* 1908. same collat. a
—Am. ed. *N Y* 1907. same collat.
—anr. ed. *Tor* 1919.
After a lurid frontier apprenticeship in Kansas, this young Englishman ranched in Western Texas and served with the Rangers.

[WILLIAMS, ROGER]   **476**
The bloudy tenent, of persecution . . . [*L*] 1644. SmQ [24] 247 c Hn LC N
—anr. iss - prob the 1st - has no errata list and the word "tenent" spelled "tenet". c JCB
In this, his most famous work, Williams insists that freedom of religious thought is a natural right and that church and state should always be separate powers.

WILLIAMS, SAMUEL, 1743–1817   **477**
A discourse on the love of our country . . . *Salem* 1775. O 29 a

WILLIAMS, SAMUEL, 1743–1817   **478**
The natural and civil history of Vermont. *Walpole N H* 1794. O 416 map aa
—ed. 2, enl. *Burlington Vt* 1809. O 2v: 515; 488. map a

[WILLIAMS, SAMUEL], 1786–1859   **479**
Sketches of the war between the United States and the British Isles . . . *Rutland* 1815. O 2v in 1 [4] 496 a

Originally appeared, as the war progressed, in 8 numbers. Attributed also to Gideon M. Davison, one of the publishers.

WILLIAMS, SAMUEL, 1786–1859   480
Two western campaigns in the war of 1812 . . . *Cin* 1870. O 58 aa
Only a few copies printed separately from Robert Clark's *Ohio Valley Historical Series,* in which it formed part of the volume entitled *Miscellanies.*

WILLIAMS, SAMUEL C.   481
Beginnings of west Tennessee . . . *Johnson City Tenn* 1930. O [14] 331 9maps &pls a

WILLIAMS, SAMUEL C.   482
Dawn of Tennessee valley . . . history. *Johnson City* 1937. O [12] 495 9maps and pls a

WILLIAMS, SAMUEL C. [ed.]   483
Early travels in the Tennessee country, 1540–1800. *Johnson City* 1928. O [12] 540 10maps & pls a

WILLIAMS, SAMUEL C.   484
History of the lost state of Franklin. *Johnson City Tenn* 1924. O [14] 371 port aa
—rev. ed. *N Y* 1933. O [20] 378 port a

WILLIAMS, STEPHEN W.   485
American medical biography: or memoirs of eminent physicians . . . principally those who have died since the publication of Dr. Thacher's work . . . *Greenfield Mass* 1845. O 664 errata slip ports a

WILLIAMS, STEPHEN W.   486
A biographical memoir of the Rev. John Williams . . . with a slight sketch of ancient Deerfield . . . *Greenfield Mass* 1837. D 127 a
Based largely on John Williams' *Redeemed captive. q.v.*

WILLIAMS, T[HOMAS] J. C.   487
History of Frederick county, Maryland . . . [*Hagerstown*] 1910. Q 2v: [8] 685; [4] 693-1635. 227 pls a

WILLIAMS, THOMAS J. C.   488
A history of Washington county, Maryland . . . [*Hagerstown*] 1906. Q 2v: 602; [2] 611-1347. pls aa

WILLIAMS, W[ELLINGTON]   489
Appleton's railroad and steamboat companion . . . *N Y* 1847. 16° [2] 236 12 maps [one fold.] aa
—rptd. same impr. & collat 1848 a
—enl. ed. *N Y* 1849. 16° 313 30maps 26 pls

WILLIAMS (WILLIAM), 1763–1824.   490
Journal of the life, travels, . . . of: . . . *Cin* 1828. D 272 a
—rptd. *Dub* 1839. D [10] 195
Travelled extensively through the South and Middle West.

WILLIAMS, WILLIAM [pub.]   491
The Utica directory, for . . . 1817. *Utica* [1816]. D 24 [36] a
First directory of this city.

WILLIAMS AND FULTON COUNTIES [O] 492
History of: . . . *Bryan* 1877. O 14 34 a

[WILLIAMSON, CHARLES]   493
Description of the Genesee country . . . [five letters] *Alb* 1798. Q 37 front. 2maps b AA JCB N NYP Y
—ed. 2, "Description of the settlement of the Genesee country . . .," [eight letters], *N Y* 1799. O 63 map aa
—anr. ed. "A view of the present situation of the . . . Genesee country," *Frederick-Town* 1804. D 23 aa
—anr. ed., under pseud. of Robert Munro, "A description of the Genesee country," *N Y* 1804. O 20 map aa
—anr. ed., with app., [*Balt*] 1804. aa
Ascribed also to Ignatius Davis.

WILLIAMSON, HUGH, of N.C.   494
The history of North Carolina. *Phil* 1812. O 2v: [20] 289; [8] 289. map errata slips pasted on verso of last p. in v.I aa

WILLIAMSON, HUGH, of N.C.   495
Observations on the climate in different parts of America . . . an introductory discourse to the history of North Carolina. *N Y* 1811. O [8] 199 [incl. 2charts] a

WILLIAMSON, HUGH, of N.C.   496
Remarks on the importance of the contemplated grand canal, between lake Erie and the Hudson river. [*N Y?*] 1812. O 31 a

[WILLIAMSON, HUGH?] of Pa.   497
The plea of the colonies, on the charges brought against them . . . *L* 1775. O 47 b
—rptd., same impr. & collat. 1776. aa
—Am. ed. *Phil* 1777. O [8] 38 pl aa

WILLIAMSON, JAMES J.   498
Mosby's rangers . . . *N Y* 1896. O 511 a
—ed. 2, enl. *N Y* 1909. O 554

WILLIAMSON, PETER   499
A brief account of the war in N. America . . . *Edin* [& *L*] n.d. [1760]. O [2] 38 b BP N Y

WILLIAMSON (PETER).   500
French and Indian cruelty; exemplified in the life of: *York* 1757. O [4] 104 b N PittU
—ed. 2, same collat., 1758. b N NYP
—ed. 3, *Glas* 1758. O [4] 112 b
—ed. 4, *L* 1759. O 120 front. aa
—ed. 5, *Edin* 1762. D [6] 120 119–147 map port aa
—ed. 6, *Edin* 1766. aa
—ed. 7, *Dub* 1766. D [6] 140 front. aa

—rptd. *Edin* 1787, D [6] 150 front.; *Edin* 1792, D 156 front.; n.p. 1794, D 24 a
—other eds.: variant titles—"Authentic narrative . . .," "Life and adventures . . .," "Life and astonishing adventures . . .," "Life and curious adventures . . .," "Surprising history . . ." *Aberdeen* [1800?]; *Aberdeen* 1801; *Stirling* 1803; *Edin* 1805; *L* 1806; *L* n.d.; *Liv* 1807 [2issues, one dated 1808 on cover] a
—Am. ed. *N Y* 1807. D [2] 5–38 front. a
—later eds., both Eng. & Am.
Among British readers the most popular of all Indian captivities; describes the 1755 Oswego expedition.

[WILLIAMSON, PETER]?   **501**
Occasional reflections on the importance of the war in America . . . In a letter to a member of parliament. *L* 1758. O [4] 139 aa

WILLIAMSON, PETER   **502**
Some considerations on the present state of affairs . . . *York* 1758. O [4] 56 b Hn NYP

WILLIAMSON (PETER).   **503**
The travels of: . . . among . . . savage Indians . . . *Edin* 1768. D [8] 184 3pls b N NYP PaH
Not to be confused with his captivity account; it is entirely different.

WILLIAMSON, R. S.   **504**
Report of a reconnaissance . . . in California. [With geological report by William P. Blake.] House Ex. Doc. 129. [*Wash* 1855]. O 61 + 80 a
For series of which this is a part, *see Pacific railroad explorations.*

WILLIAMSON, WILLIAM D.   **505**
The history of . . . Maine . . . *Hallowell* 1832. O 2v: [12] 9–660; 714 2 pls aa
—anr. ed., from sheets of original ed., with adds., same impr. 1839. O 2v: [12] 9–696; 729. 2pls aa 330 cops ptd.

WILLIS, WILLIAM   **506**
The history of Portland [Me.] . . . *Port Me* 1831–[1833]. O 2v: 243; 355. 3maps 2pls a
—ed. 2, enl., same impr. 1865. O [16] 9–928. map pls Part of ed. burned in 1866.

[WILLISTON, H. C.]   **507**
California characters, and mining scenes and sketches. Pt. I [all]. *S F* [*ca* 1854]. O 24 b
—rptd. with pt.II added, [*ca* 1855]. b

WILLOCK (JOHN).   **508**
Voyages and adventures of: . . . with remarks on different countries in Europe, Africa and America . . . *Penrith* [1789]. O [16] 328 aa
—Am. ed. *Phil* 1798. D [2] 9–283 [8] front. a
This English mariner voyaged to Virginia and New York several times before 1780; deserting to

an American ship he made coast-wise voyages for several years; then crossed the ocean and was captured and held prisoner by the Algerines.

WILLRICH, GEORG   **509**
Erinnerungen aus Texas . . . *Leip* 1854. 16° 3v: 173 + adv-p; 176; 174 + 2adv-p aa

[WILLS, THOMAS?]   **510**
A correct statement of the late . . . affair of honor, between General Hamilton and Col. Burr. *N Y* 1804. O 78 a
Attributed also to Burr's second in this duel, William P. Van Ness.

WILLSON, BECKLES   **511**
The great company . . . *Tor* 1899. O [22] 17–541 13pls a
—Eng. ed., with new pref. & slight adds., *L* 1900. O 2v: [32] 339; [12] 369. 20maps & pls facs

WILLSON (DON ESTEVAN JULIAN)   **512**
and EXTER (DON RICHARD).
Documents relating to grants of lands, made to: in Texas. *N Y* 1831. O 48 aa

[WILMER, JAMES J.]   **513**
The American Nepos . . . lives of . . . men, who have contributed to the discovery, the settlement, . . . of America. *Balt* 1805. D [16] 384 port a
—ed. 2, *Balt* 1811. D 408

[WILMER, JAMES J.]   **514**
Narrative respecting the conduct of the British, from their first landing on Spesutia island, till their progress to Havre de Grace . . . *Balt* 1813. O 38 [misnumb 21] a

WILSON, AMOS   **515**
The sweets of solitude . . . Annexed is a sketch of the life of said Wilson . . . *B* 1821. D 36 [incl. port] aa
—rptd., same impr. & collat., 1822. a
—anr. ed. "The Pennsylvania hermit . . . narrative of the extraordinary life of Amos Wilson . . .," *N Y* 1838. O 24 [incl. port]
—rptd. *Phil* 1839. same collat.
—other *Phil* eds.: 1839, O 24; 1839, 16° 48; 1840, O 24

WILSON, MRS AUGUSTUS   **516**
Memorial sketch of the first national convention of cattlemen . . . *St L* [1884]. O 95 map 3pls b
—rptd. in "Parson's memorial . . . magazine". *St L* 1885. O [14] 409 [incl. advs] port aa

WILSON, C[HARLES] H.   **517**
The wanderer in America . . . *Northallerton Eng* 1820. D 112 aa
—ed. 2, *Thirsk Eng* 1822. D 108 a
—ed. 3, with app., same impr. 1822. D 120
—ed. 4, same impr. & collat. 1823.

—ed. 5, same impr. & collat. 1824. [dated 1823 on cover] rptd 1826
—ed. 6, same impr. & collat. 1828.
Acrid commentary. Claims that Birkbeck discovered his folly in purchasing Illinois land and issued his books with the hope of unloading his losses on gullible lunatics.

WILSON, EDWARD   518
The golden land; a narrative of early travels in California . . . B 1852. O 56[incl. 14adv-p] port aa

WILSON, EDWARD   519
An unwritten history . . . of early Arizona. [*Phoenix* 1915]. D 78 a

WILSON, ELIJAH N.   520
Among the Shoshones. *S L C* [1910]. D 222 8pls most of ed. suppressed aa
—rptd. same impr. & date. D 247 8pls a
Blunt, unrestrained narrative of a trapper, Indian fighter, etc., of the Rocky Mountains, from Wyoming and Montana to Idaho and Utah. The 247 page reprint omits account of how he lost his Mormon fiancée [given on pp. 194 to 200 of original edition].

WILSON, F. MARION   521
History of Hickory county, Missouri. [*Hermitage, Mo.* 1907] O 189 a

WILSON, FRANK I.   522
The battle of Great Bethel . . . *Raleigh* 1864. 16° 28 [4] aa

WILSON, H. T.   523
Historical sketch of Santa Fe. *Chi* [1880] O 74 [12] front. aa
—rptd. *Chi* [1884] O 68 + 32adv-p a

WILSON, HENRY   524
History of the rise and fall of the slave power in America. *B* 1872–7. O 3v: [28] 670; [22] 720; [22] 774 a
—vol. 1 rptd. several times

[WILSON, JAMES]   525
Considerations on the Bank of America. *Phil* 1785. D 35 aa

[WILSON, JAMES]   526
Considerations on the nature and extent of the . . . authority of the British parliament. *Phil* 1774. O [4] 35 aa
Ascribed also to John Witherspoon.

WILSON, JAMES G., ed.   527
The memorial history of the city of New York . . . *N Y* 1892–3. Q 4v: [24] 605; [22] 634 [5]; [22] 664; [24] 650 [82]. 23pls aa

WILSON, JAMES H.   528
The life . . . of . . . General Andrew J. Alexander . . . *N Y* 1887. sm Q 135 port a
Services in the Rebellion and in Indian wars from 1866 to 1880.

WILSON (MRS. JANE ADELINE).   529
Thrilling narrative of the sufferings of . . .: during her captivity among the Camanche Indians. *Rochester* [ca 1853]. D 23 b NYP [of 2copies known]
Cf., Narrative of Mrs. Clarissa Plummer.

[WILSON, JOHN] 1804–75   530
The life of John Eliot, the apostle of the Indians . . . *Edin* 1828. 18° 300 a
—Am. eds.: *Phil* 1841; *N Y* 1841.

[WILSON, JOHN A.]   531
History of Los Angeles county. *Oakland* 1880. Q [6] 11–192 map pls b
—rptd. 1959.

WILSON, L[EWIS] A.   532
History and directory for southeast Missouri and southern Illinois . . . *Cape Girardeau Mo* 1875–6. O 350 map aa

WILSON, OBED G.   533
My adventures in the Sierras. *Franklin O* 1902. D [2] 215 port a

WILSON, RICHARD L.
Short ravelings from a long yarn . . . *Chi* 1847. *See* Taylor, Benjamin F.

WILSON (ROBERT) . . . pedestrian.   534
The travels of: . . . *L* 1807. D [28] 244 4pls b LC NYP
Served with British army in Florida in the revolution; includes his adventures in the Gulf states.

[WILSON, SAMUEL]   535
An account of the province of Carolina . . . *L* 1682. D 27 map [not in all cops]
—iss. 1, p10, 11, 14, 15, 25, 26, 27 misnumb c H JCB LC
—iss. 2, first 4 of mispaginats corrected b NYP
—ed. 2, identical with above, but no paginat errors b NYH Hn
Glowing account of South Carolina as an emigrant's paradise.

WILSON (THOMAS). [Quaker]   536
A brief journal of the life, travels . . . in the work of the ministry of: *Dub* 1728. 16° [48] 98 + 2adv-p a
—anr. ed. *L* 1730. D [48] 96
—rptd. *L* 1784. D [48] 98 + 2adv-p
Visited America in 1690 and in 1713; but, like most Quaker narratives, very dull.

WILSON, THOMAS, of Manchester 537
Information from the United States, with directions to emigrants . . . *Manch* 1817. D 43 a

WILSON, THOMAS, of Pa. 538
The biography of . . . American military and naval heroes . . . *N Y* 1817. D 2v: [10] 13–324; [4] 320. 6ports a
—rptd. same impr. & collat. 1819
—ed. 2, same impr. 1821. D 2v: 360; 336. 6ports
—rptd. same impr. 1822. D 2v: 370; 336. 6ports
—anr. ed. *N Y* 1823. D [4] 320 port

WILSON, THOMAS, of Pa.
Picture of Philadelphia, for 1824. *See* Mease, James.

WILSON, THOMAS W. 539
An authentic narrative of the piratical descents upon Cuba . . . by hordes from the United States, headed by Narciso Lopez. *Havana* 1851. O 44 aa

WILSON, VEAZIE 540
Glimpses of the Yukon gold fields and Dawson route. *Vancouver* [1895]. D 96 pls a
—anr. ed. "Glimpses of Alaska, Klondike and the gold fields," *Chi* 1897. D same collat.

WILSON, V[EAZIE] 541
Guide to the Yukon gold fields . . . *Seattle* 1895. D 74, 16 incl. adv pp, 24 24maps & pls aa
—rev. ed., same impr. 1897. a

WILSON, WILLIAM B. 542
History of the Pennsylvania railroad company . . . *Phil* 1899. O 2v: [10 incl. port] 418; [8] 323. 126pls Suppressed aa

WILSON COUNTY, KANSAS. 543
Handbook of: *Chi* 1886. O 40 a

WILSON'S . . . ORDERLY BOOK 544
Wilson's [Commissary] orderly book. Expedition . . . against Ticonderoga and Crown Point, 1759. *Alb* 1857. Q [12] 220 fold.map 110 copies ptd.[10 on L.P.] aa

WILSTACH, FRANK J. 545
Wild Bill Hickok, the prince of pistoleers. *N Y* 1926. O [20] 304 8pls a

WILSTACH, PAUL 546
Potomac landings. *N Y* 1921. O [14] 376 fold. map 26pls aa
—rptd. *Indp* [1932]; *N Y* [1937]. a

WILTSEE, ERNEST A. 547
The pioneer miner and the pack mule express. *S F* 1931. Q 112 maps pls a

[WIMER, JAMES] 548
Events in Indian history . . . *Lancaster Pa* 1841. O 633 8pls aa
—rptd., same collat., *Phil* 1842; *Lancaster* 1843. a

WIMMEL, HEINRICH 549
Californien, sein minen-bergbau . . . *Cassel* 1867. D [6] 200 front. pl a

WINCHELL, ALEXANDER 549a
The Grand Traverse region [Michigan]. *Ann Arbor* 1866. O 97 fold.map a

WINCHELL, N[EWTON] H., ed. 550
The aborigines of Minnesota . . . *St P* 1911. F [16 incl. final blank lf] 761 61maps and pls a

WINCHELL, N[EWTON] H., NEILL, 551
EDEARD D., et al
History of the upper Mississippi valley. *Minneap* 1881. Q [6] 717 + 3adv-p aa
Histories of Minnesota and eleven of its counties.

WINCHESTER, B[ENJAMIN] 552
The origin of the Spaulding story, concerning the manuscript found . . . showing it to be a mere fabrication, so far as its connection with the Book of Mormon is concerned. *Phil* 1840. D 24 aa
—Eng. ed. "Plain facts, shewing the origin of the Spalding story," *Bedford Eng* 1841. a

WINCHESTER, ELHANAN 553
An oration on the discovery of America . . . *L* 1792. O 32 aa
—ed. 2, with app. on Washington, D. C., *L* [1792]. O 78 | 2adv-p plan tab a

WINCHESTER, ELHANAN 554
The reigning abominations, especially the slave trade . . . *L* 1788. O 32 a

[WINCHESTER, JAMES] 555
Historical details, having relation to the campaign of the northwestern army under Generals Harrison and Winchester. *Lex* 1818. O 88 c N NYP [of 10 cops loc]
Attempt by the author to answer McAfee's allegations against his conduct at the river Raisin, etc.

WINCHESTER, CAPT. J[AMES] D. 556
. . . experience in a voyage . . . to San Francisco, and to the Alaskan gold fields. *Salem Mass* 1900. O 251 27pls a

[WINDER, R. H.] 557
Remarks on a pamphlet, entitled "An enquiry respecting the capture of Washington [D. C.] by the British . . ." *Balt* 1816. O [4, incl. blank lf] 72 map a

[WINDER, WILLIAM H.]   558
Secrets of the American bastile . . . *Phil* 1863.
O [8] 47 a
—ed. 2, same impr. & date. O [8] 64
—ed. 3, same impr. & date. O [8] 72

WINDLE, MARY J.   559
Life in Washington [D. C.] . . . *Phil* 1859. D 384 a
By a Pennsylvanian with Southern sympathies,
written when the air was surcharged with imminent
disunion.

[WINES, ENOCH C.]   560
A trip to Boston, in a series of letters . . . *B* 1838.
D 224 a

WINFIELD, CHARLES H.   561
History of the county of Hudson, New Jersey
. . . *N Y* 1874. O [8] 568 12pls a

WING, GEORGE C.   562
Early years on the Western Reserve . . . *Clev*
1916. O 142 fold.chart a 150copies ptd.

WING, JACK   563
The great Union stock yards of Chicago . . .
Chi 1865. O 32 + 10adv-p front. aa
—rev. ed. *Chi* 1866. O 32 + 10adv-p front. a

WINGET, DAN H.   564
Anecdotes of "Buffalo Bill" . . . *Clinton, Ia.*
1912. D 224 aa
—rptd. *Chi* 1927. D 230 a

WINGFIELD, EDWARD M.   565
A discourse of Virginia. *B* 1860. O 45 100 copies
ptd.
First printing of a 1613 manuscript.

WINGFIELD, MARSHALL   566
A history of Caroline county, Virginia, 1727–
1924. *Rich* 1924. O [16] 528[incl. front.] a

WINKFIELD ([MRS.] UNCA ELIZA),   567
The female American; or, the adventures of: *L*
1767. D 2v: [4] 193 + 2adv-p; [2] 171 + 9adv-p aa
—Am. eds.: *Newburyport* [1800?], D 213 port:
Vergennes Vt 1814, 18° 270 a
Fiction.

WINKLER, MRS. ANGELINA V.   568
[WALTON]
The Confederate capital and Hood's Texas
brigade . . . *Austin* 1894. O [16] 312 10pls a

WINNEBAGO INDIANS (THE).   569
Letter from the Secretary of War, transmitting
information in relation to . . . the treaty of 1837
with: [H. Doc. 229]. *Wash* 1839. O 112 a
—rptd., to discredit Cameron, *Harrisburg* 1839.
O 38

Plot of Simon Cameron and fellow rascals to
defraud these Indians of half a million dollars,
frustrated by a young army officer, E. A. Hitchcock.

WINONA.   570
City of: and southern Minnesota . . . their
growth and prospects . . . *Winona* 1858. O 36 a

WINSHIP, GEORGE P., ed.   571
The Coronado expedition, 1540-42 . . . *Wash*
1896. Q In 14th Annual Report, pt. 1, Bureau of
Am. Ethnol., of which it occupies p329–637, with
pls & maps numb. 38 to 84. a
—rptd., text. only, *N Y* 1904. 16° [34] 251 map
front.
—anr. ed. *S F* Grabhorn 1933. Q 550copies
ptd. aa
—anr. ed., ed. by Hammond & Rey, with adds.,
Albuquerque 1940. O [12] 413 front a
For original edition of the basic narrative, *see*
Castaneda de Nagera.

WINSHIP, GEORGE P., ed.   572
Sailors narratives of voyages along the New
England coast, 1524–1624. *B* 1905. O [8] 292 fold.
map 5pls a

WINSLOW, D. A.   574
History of St. Joseph, Michigan . . . *Chi* 1869.
D 98 aa
First history of the St. Joseph Valley, based
largely on relations of its pioneers.

WINSOR, JUSTIN   575
A history of . . . Duxbury, Massachusetts . . . *B*
1849. O 360 front. a

WINSOR, JUSTIN, ed.   576
The memorial history of Boston . . . *B* 1880–81.
Q 4v: [32] 596; [58] 577; [12] 691; [10] 713. maps
pls aa
—rptd., same impr. & collat.: 1882; 1883; 1890.

WINSOR, JUSTIN   577
The Mississippi basin . . . struggle in America
between England and France, 1697–1763. *B* 1895.
O [10] 484 + adv-l. at front a
—rptd. 1898.

WINSOR, JUSTIN, ed.   578
Narrative and critical history of America [to
1850]. *B* 1889. Q 8v some sets on L.P. aa
If competently revised and brought more nearly
to date, would be the most useful single work on
the Western hemisphere, its history, cartography
and bibliography.

WINSOR, JUSTIN   579
The westward movement . . . 1763–1798. *B*
1897. O [8] 595 a
—rptd. *B* 1899

WINSOR, M., and SCARBROUGH,   **580**
JAMES A.
History of Jewell county [Kansas]: its early set-
tlements . . . *Jewell City* 1878. O 37 + 11adv-p aa

WINTER EVENING'S TALE (A).
See Brackett, Geo. A.

WINTER (A) IN THE WEST.
By a New Yorker. *See* Hoffman, Chas. F.

WINTERBOTHAM, W[ILLIAM]   **581**
An historical . . . view of the . . . United States
. . . *L* 1795. O 4v: [10] 591; [4] 493; [4] 525; [4]
416, 54 [20]. 11maps & plans 22pls 7tabs[on 4 lvs].
List of pls calls for Niagara Falls in error for St.
Anthony's Falls aa
—ed. 2, *L* 1799. O 4v: [18] 591; [4] 493; [4] 525;
[4] 416, 96 [10]. 11maps & plans 22pls[1 col] 7tabs
[on 4 lvs] a
—anr. ed., same collat., *L* 1819.
—Am. ed. "A geographical [etc.] view of the present situation of the United States . . .," *N Y* 1795–
[1796]. O 33weekly nos. or 4v: [2] 590; [2] 493; [4]
519; [4] 328; [8] 329–516 [8] a
—anr.—and best—ed., with adds., "An historical
[etc.] view of the United States," *N Y* 1796. O 4v:
[8] 590; [4] 493; [4] 519; [4] 516 [16]. 2plans 24pls
[1 col] + atlas F [2] 20pls[in some copies an add.
unlisted plan of Washington] b

WINTERFIELD (CAPTAIN).   **582**
The voyages, distresses and wonderful adventures of: . . . his transactions in America, during
the late war . . . *L* 1788. D [2] 74 front. aa
—rptd.: *L* 1798, D 46 + adv-p front.; *L* 1799, D
48 front.; *L* 1800, same collat.; *L* 1802, D [2] 5–38;
Manch [*ca* 1800], O 48 a
—anr. ed. "The exile of Ireland; or, the life . . . of
Captain Winterfield . . .," *L* [*ca* 1800]. D 36 a
A farrago of incredible miracles.

WINTHROP, JOHN   **583**
A journal of . . . occurences in the settlement of
Massachusetts . . . 1630—1644. *Hart* 1790. O [6]
364 [4] aa
—complete ed., with adds. to 1649, "The history
of New England . . .," ed. Savage, *B* 1825–1826.
O 2v: [12] 424; 429. port facs a
—best ed., with adds. & index, *B* 1853. O 2v: [20]
514; 504 facs port a
Minute, faithful and graphic. The original edition was edited by Noah Webster.

WINTHROP, THEODORE   **584**
The canoe and the saddle . . . among the northwestern rivers . . . *B* 1863. D 375 + 18adv-p [2 at
front, 16 at rear] a
—rptd. many times.
—best ed., with adds., ed. by J. H. Williams,
Tacoma 1913. O [26] 332 16col.pls a

[WIRT, WILLIAM]   **585**
The letters of a British spy . . . *Rich* 1803. O 43
aa
—ed. 2, same impr. & date. O 88 a
—rptd. "The British spy . . .," *Newburyport* 1804.
16° 105
—ed. 3, same impr. 1805. 16° 128
—ed. 4, *Balt* 1811. 18° 186 + 2adv-p
—ed. 5, *Balt* 1813. 24° 186 + eng.t.& 4 adv-p
front.
—6 other eds. before 1840

WIRT, WILLIAM   **586**
Sketches of the life . . . of Patrick Henry. *Phil*
1817. O [16] 427 [13] port a
—ed. 2, same impr. 1818. O [16] 427 [12]
—ed. 3, same impr., date & collat.
—ed. 4, "Life of Patrick Henry," *N Y* 1831. O 444
[2] 19 eng.t. port
—6 other eds. before 1840

WIRT (WILLIAM).   **587**
The two principal arguments of: on the trial of
Aaron Burr . . . *Rich* 1808. 24° [4] 221

WISCONSIN.   **588**
Description of the Wisconsin territory. *Liv* [1843].
16° 20 aa
—ed. 2, enl. *Liv* 1844. D 48 a
—Welsh tr. *Bangor* 1845. D 46 [2]

Hand book of Wisconsin. [*Milw*? 1855?]   **589**
D 72 [8] aa
—ed. 2, enl. Milw. 1855. D 177 + 26adv-p a
—anr. ed., same impr. 1856. D 117 + 10adv-p
Intended to accompany the same publisher's -
Chapman's - separately published Wisconsin map.

**The home of the badgers, or a sketch of the early
history of Wisconsin** . . . By Oculus. *See* Grinnell,
Josiah B.

Observations on the Wisconsin territory. *See*
Smith, Wm. Rudolph.

WISDOM (THE)
Wisdom (The) and policy of the French . . . *See*
McCulloch, Henry.

WISE, BARTON H.   **590**
The life of Henry A. Wise of Virginia. *N Y* 1899.
O [14] 434 port a

WISE, GEORGE   **591**
Campaigns . . . of the Army of Northern Virginia. *N Y* 1916. O 432 2ports a

[WISE, GEORGE]   **592**
History of the Seventeenth Virginia Infantry,
C. S. A. *Balt* 1870. D 312 a

WISE, LIEUT. [HENRY A.]   **593**
Los Gringos; or, an inside view of Mexico and California . . . *N Y* 1849. D [16] 453 a
—rptd., same impr. & collat. 1850; 1857.
—Eng. ed. *L* 1849. D [16] 406
—anr. issue, same impr. & date. D [16] 453
—Ger. tr. *Leip* 1851. 16° 3v: [6] 218; [4] 268; [4] 224

[WISE, REV. JOHN]   **594**
The churches quarrel espoused . . . *N Y* 1713. O 152 b PaH
—ed. 2, au. named, *B* 1715. O [2] 116 aa
—for later eds. *see* next entry.

WISE, REV. JOHN   **595**
A vindication of the government of New-England churches . . . *B* 1717. O 105 12 aa
—rptd. *B* 1722. D 3pts in 1: 80; 96; 68 + adv-p a
—anr. ed., same impr. 1772. O 4pts in 1: 272 + 12p subscribers' list a
The most authoritative defense of Congregational polity, recognized as such even in law courts. For earlier editions, *see* preceding entry.

WISLIZENUS, FREDERICK A.   **596**
Ein Ausflüg nach den Felsen-Gebirgen im Jahre 1839. *St L* 1840. D 122 [4] map dd B Y
—Eng. tr. "A journey to the Rocky mountains." *St L* 1912. O [2] 162 port map 500 copies aa

WISLIZENUS, FREDERICK A.   **597**
Memoir of a tour to northern Mexico . . . with Col. Doniphan's expedition . . . *Wash* 1848. O 141 3maps a
—Ger. tr. *Braunschweig* 1850. O [8] 211 3maps a

WISTAR (ISAAC J.)   **598**
Autobiography of: *Phil* 1914. Q 2v: [10] 341; [6] 191. map 2pls b N NYP Y 250 copies ptd.
—rptd. *Phil* 1937. O [8] 528 fold.map 6pls a
—anr. ed. *N Y* Harper n.d. O 530 fold.map 6pls
Largely devoted to the opening and development of the far West from 1849 to 1860, in which Wistar played a conspicuous part before achieving fame and fortune in Pennsylvania.

WITBECK, H. P., and ROWLEY, J. P.   **599**
Wisconsin and the city of Racine . . . *Racine* 1856. O 16 + 24adv-p map aa

WITCHER, WALTER C.   **600**
The reign of terror in Oklahoma . . . the Klan's barbarous practices . . . *Ft Worth* [1923]. O 144 [incl. wraps] a Suppressed

WITHERS, ALEXANDER S. [ed.]   **601**
Chronicles of border warfare . . . *Clarksburg Va* 1831. D 320 + adv-l. Some copies have, inserted, a 4-p list of contents, which was ptd later. aa
—rptd., ed. by Thwaites and Draper: *Cin* 1895, O [22] 447 port; *Cin* 1903. a

Compiled largely by William Powers and William Hacker, but cited always as by Withers.

WITHERSPOON, JOHN   **602**
The dominion of Providence over the passions of men. A sermon . . . *Phil* 1776. O [4] 78 [1] aa
—Eng. ed. *Glas* 1777. O 54 a
—3 other Eng. eds. by 1778

WITLENBORGER, J.   **603**
Der Rathgeber und Wegweiser für Auswanderer nach den Vereinigten Staaten . . . und Texas . . . Ed. 2, enl. *Heilbronn* 1848. D [4] 144 map aa
No copy of the first edition located.

WITTE, AUGUST   **604**
Kurze Schilderung der Vereinigten Staaten . . . *Hannover* 1833. D [6] 118 a

WIXSON, FRANKLIN   **605**
The Black hills gold mines . . . *Yankton* 1875. O 100 2maps pl c WisH Y

[WODENOTH? OR WOODENOTH?,   **606**
ARTHUR]
A short collection of the most remarkable passages . . . of the Virginia Company. *L* 1651. SmQ [4] 20 c Hn JCB N
Defends company management.

WOELMONT, ARNOLD, Baron de   **607**
Ma vie nomade aux montagnes Rocheuses. *P* 1878. 16° [6] 366 map pl a

WOELMONT, ARNOLD, Baron de   **608**
Souvenirs du Far-West. *P* 1883. 16° [6] 269 a

WOGAN (EMILE, Baron de).   **609**
Voyages et aventures du: *P* [1863]. D [4] 326 [2] a
—ed. 2, "Six mois dans le Far-West . . .," *P* 1875. D same paginat, but port. added
—Eng. ed. "Adventures in the Rocky mountains," *L* 1867.

WOLCOTT, ANSON   **610**
Eighteen months in Louisiana, or criticisms on slavery. *Lockport N Y* 1843. D 41 aa

[WOLCOTT, OLIVER]   **611**
British influence on the affairs of the United States . . . *B* 1804. O 23 a

WOLDT, A., ed.   **612**
Captain Jacobsen's Reise an der Nordwestküste Amerikas, 1881–3 . . . *Leip* 1884. O [8] 431 3maps a
—Norw tr. *Christiania* 1887. O [38] 329

WOLFE, J. M. [comp.]   **613**
Guide, gazetteer . . . of cities . . . villages and government forts along the Union Pacific . . . railroads and the towns in the Black hills . . . *Omaha* 1878. O 326 map tab b

WOLFE, J. M. [comp.]   **614**
Guide, gazetteer . . . of Nebraska railroads . . .
Omaha 1872. D 210 fold.map 6pls + unnumb
adv-pp throughout aa

WOLFE, J. M. [comp.]   **615**
Lincoln city directory, for 1873–4. Containing
historical sketches [etc.]. *Lincoln* 1873. O 146 [incl.
advs] + col inserts & end leaves pl a
—rev. ed. *Lincoln* 1873. O [2] 146 [incl. advs] +
inserts & end leaves 2pls

WOLFE, J. M. [comp.]
Nebraska City directory . . . *see* Nebraska City.

WOLFE, J. M. [comp.]   **616**
Omaha directory for 1874–5, containing histori-
cal sketches of the city [etc.]. *Omaha* 1874. O [16]
340 [3] incl. advs + pls & unnumb adv-p aa
—for 1876–7, *Omaha* 1876. O 288 [incl. advs] +
adv-pls aa

WOLFE, J. M. [comp.]   **617**
Omaha in 1873; containing historical sketches
[etc.]. *Omaha* 1874. O 32, 33a–40a, 33–98 [incl.
advs] aa

WOLFE, SAMUEL M.   **618**
Helper's Impending crisis dissected. *Phil* 1860.
16° [4] 223 a

[WOLL, ADRIAN]   **619**
Expedicion hecha en Tejas . . . *Monterrey* 1842.
O 60 2 tabs c B G TxU Y
Capture of San Antonio, in 1842, etc.

W[OLLEY], C[HARLES]   **620**
A two years journal in New York . . . *L* for John
Wyat 1701. D [8] 104[incl. advs] dd JCB N
—anr. issue, same sheets with new t-p, *L* for D.
Boys [etc.] 1701. dd Hn NYP
—rptd.: ed. O'Callaghan, *N Y* 1860; ed. Bourne,
Clev 1902. 250 cops ptd
Most interesting description of New York in the
late 17th century.

WOOD, AARON   **621**
Sketches of things and people of Indiana. *Indp*
1883. O 48 port a

WOOD, E. T.   **622**
Mobile directory . . . for 1844. *Mobile* 1844. D
120 [57] b AA AlaU

WOOD, EDWIN O.   **623**
Historic Mackinac. *N Y* 1918. O 2v: [20] 697
35pls; [18] 774 + 4adv-p 28pls aa

WOOD, ELLEN L.   **624**
George Yount . . . *S F* [Grabhorn] 1941. Q [10]
126 3pls fldg chart 200 cops ptd aa

Trapped for furs in the southwest, along with
Ewing Young and the Patties, in the 1820's; later
one of the pioneer American settlers in California.

WOOD, GEORGE W.   **625**
Report of [his] visit to the Choctaw and Chero-
kee missions. *B* 1855. D 24 aa

WOOD, H. CLAY]   **626**
The status of Young Joseph and his band of
Nez-Perce Indians . . . *Port Ore* 1876. D [4] 49 aa

WOOD, ISAIAH   **627**
The Massachusetts compendium . . . with a par-
ticular description of the district of Maine . . .
Hallowell 1814. 16° 72 a
—ed. 2, enl., *Port* 1816. 16° 99

WOOD, J. C.   **628**
Report . . . on . . . the United States overland
mail route between San Antonio . . . and San
Diego . . . [*Wash* 1858]? O 43 capt.t.only b BP Hn.

WOOD, JOHN, of N. Y.   **629**
A correct statement of the . . . sources from
which the History of the administration of John
Adams was compiled, and the motives for its sup-
pression by Col. Burr. *N Y* 1802. O 49 a
—ed. 2, cor., *N Y* 1802. O 58
Reply, by the author of the suppressed book, to
James Cheetham's *Narrative* . . .

WOOD, JOHN, of N.Y.   **630**
A full exposition of the Clintonian faction.
Newark 1802. O 56 a

WOOD, JOHN, of N.Y.   **631**
A full statement of the trial and acquittal of
Aaron Burr . . . at Frankfort . . . *Alexandria* 1807.
O 36 aa

WOOD, JOHN of N.Y.   **632**
The history of the administration of John Adams
. . . *N Y* Barlas & Ward 1802. O [2] 506 a Most
copies bought up and destroyed by Burr. Apparently he didn't get all; but copies found usually
have pub's. impr. cut out. Some cops carry
Napthall Judah's imprint.
—anr. issue, with new t-p, *N Y* no pub's. impr.
1802. same collat.
—rptd. *Phil* 1846. [2issues, each with port]

WOOD, JOHN, of Ohio   **633**
Journal . . . from Cincinnati to the gold diggings
in California . . . 1850. *Chillicothe O* 1852. O 76 d
AA G NYH S Y
—rptd. *Columbus* 1871. D 112p b N Y

[WOOD, JOHN P.]   **634**
A sketch of the life . . . of John Law . . . *Edin*
1791. F [2] 48 a

—enl. ed. "Memoirs of the life of John Law . . .," *Edin* 1824. D [4] 234 port

Based on a manuscript account owned by Law's nephew.

WOOD, R. E., ed.   **635**

Life and confessions of James Gilbert Jenkins, the murderer of eighteen men . . . *Napa City Cal.* 1864. O 56 front. pl aa

WOOD, REV. S[AMUEL]   **636**

Letters from the United States. [*L* Smallfield 1837]. O 11 a

—rptd. [*L* 1838]. O 27

WOOD, SAMUEL N.   **637**

The boomer. The true story of Oklahoma . . . *Topeka* 1885. D 90 map port aa

WOOD, S[AMUEL S.] pub.   **638**

The cries of New York. *N Y* 1808. 32° 47 [incl. wraps] aa

—other eds.: same impr. & collat. 1809; 1814, same impr. & collat. [2 issues one with 26, one with 31 cries] aa

—anr. ed., 31 cries, same collat. *Balt* 1818 aa

—rptd. *N Y* 1830 a

WOOD, SILAS   **639**

A sketch of the first settlement of the several towns on Long Island. *Bklyn* 1824. O 66 250copies ptd. aa

—rev. ed. *Bklyn* 1826. O 112 100copies ptd a

—new. ed. *Bklyn* 1828. O 184 100copies ptd a

—rptd., with adds., *Bklyn* 1865. O [22] 206 3 pls 250 copies [50 on L.P.] a

The first history of Long Island.

WOOD, SILAS   **640**

A sketch of . . . the town of Huntington [L. I.]. *Wash* 1824. O 30 Of the few copies ptd most were burned aa

—rptd. *N Y* 1898. O [12] 63 port a

[WOOD, SILAS]   **641**

Thoughts on the state of the American Indians . . . *N Y* 1794. D 36 b Hn

WOOD, LIEUT. W. N.   **642**

Reminiscences of big I. *Charlottesville Va* 1909. D 107 a

Reminiscences by a member of the Nineteenth Virginia Infantry.

WOOD (WILLIAM).   **643**

Autobiography of: *N Y* 1895. O 2v: [6] 464; [4] 528. 3pls a Small ed.

Includes travels in Louisiana, Mississippi and Arkansas.

WOOD, WILLIAM [C. H.], ed.   **644**

Select British documents of the Canadian war of 1812. *Tor* Champlain Soc. 1920–23–26–28. O 3v in 4: [16] 678 [10] 11pls 8maps; [10] 518; [8] 540 [11]; [8] 541–1062 [11] aa

WOOD, W[ILLIAM] D.   **645**

Reminiscences of reconstruction in Texas . . . n.p. 1902. O 58 a

WOOD, WILLIAM M.   **646**

Wandering sketches . . . in South America, Polynesia, California . . . *Phil* 1849. D [10] 13–386 a

WOODMAN, DAVID   **647**

Guide to Texas emigrants. *B* 1835. D [6] 13–192 map pl aa

WOODRUFF, GEORGE H.   **648**

Forty years ago! . . . early history of Joliet and Will county [Ill.]. *Joliet* 1874. O [4] 108 aa

—rptd. with adds "Fifty years ago . . .," same impr. 1883. O 62

WOODRUFF, WILFORD   **649**

Leaves from my journal. *S L C* 1881. D 96 a

—ed. 2, same impr. & collat., 1882.

Mormon affairs in Ohio, Illinois and Utah, from 1833.

WOODRUFF, WILLIAM E.   **650**

With the light guns in '61–'65 . . . *L. Rock* 1903. O 115 map front aa

WOODS, DANIEL B.   **651**

Sixteen months at the gold diggings. *N Y* 1851. D 199[incl. prelim. blank 1f] + 8adv-p in some copies aa

—rptd. 1852, same collat. a

—Eng. ed. *L* [ca 1851]. a

WOODS, EDGAR   **652**

Albemarle county in Virginia . . . [*Charlottesville* 1901]. O [4] 412 a

—rptd.: 1932; [1956]

WOODS, HARRIET F.   **653**

Historical sketches of Brookline, Massachusetts. *B* 1874. D 431 a 100copies ptd.

WOODS, JOHN   **654**

Two years' residence in the . . . Illinois country . . . *L* 1822. O [4] 310 plan 2maps aa

—other less desirable, but possibly earlier, issues have either only 1 or 2maps. aa

Favorable appraisal of his adopted country.

WOODS, NEANDER M.   **655**

The Woods-McAfee memorial . . . *Louisv* 1905. Q 503 maps & illus aa

Contains the journals of James and Robert McAfee through Kentucky, in 1773.

WOODSON, CARTER G.   656
The education of the Negro prior to 1861 . . .
N Y 1915. D [6] 454a

WOODWARD, AUGUSTUS B.   657
Considerations on the executive government of
the United States . . . *Flatbush* 1809. O 87 [incl.
blank lf] a

WOODWARD, A[UGUSTUS] B.   658
The presidency of the United States. *Wash* 1825.
O 88 a
—anr. ed., same collat., *N Y* 1825.
—ed. 2, same collat., *Frederick-Town* 1826.

WOODWARD, CORODON R.   659
Recollections . . . of seventy years. n.p. [1906].
O 916 aa
Served as steamboat pilot and captain out of St.
Louis from 1848 to 1862, later became a financial
leader in Cairo, Illinois.

WOODWARD, JOHN   660
Arguments and observations on the empresario
contracts in Texas. *N Y* 1837. O 35 aa

WOODWARD (JOHN).   661
The empresario rights in Texas of: . . . *N Y*
1841. O 24 aa
This land grant was made originally by Mexico
to Beale in 1832.

WOODWARD, K., pub.   662
The Augusta directory . . . for 1841. *Augusta Ga*
1841. D 82 + 24adv-p[numb. 1–12 & 25–36] aa

WOODWARD, SAMUEL   663
The help of the Lord . . . A sermon, preached at
Lexington, Apr. 19, 1779; in commemoration of
. . . the nineteenth of April, 1775 . . . *B* 1779. O
29 aa

WOODWARD, SAMUEL   664
A sermon . . . on occasion of the reduction of
Montreal . . . by the troops . . . under the com-
mand of General Amherst. *B* [1760]. O 30 aa

WOODWARD, THOMAS S.   665
. . . reminiscences of the Creek . . . Indians . . .
Montg 1859. O 168 b AlaA N
—rptd. *Tuscaloosa* 1939. O 168 a
By the best informed man of his time on this
tribe.

WOODWARD, W[ILLIAM] ELLIOT, ed.   666
Records of Salem witchcraft . . . *Roxbury* 1864.
Q 2v: [6, 5–10] 9–279; [4] 287 a 250 copies ptd[15
on L.P.]

WOODWORTH, SAMUEL   667
The life and confession of James Hudson . . .

executed . . . for the murder of Logan, an Indian
chief . . . *Indpls* 1825. O 24 b IndH [only cop loc]

WOOLMAN, JOHN   667a
Considerations on keeping Negroes . . . Part
second. *Phil* 1762. D 52 aa

WOOLMAN, JOHN   668
Some considerations on the keeping of Negroes
. . . *B* 1754. D [6] 24 [2] aa

WOOLMAN (JOHN).   669
The works of: *Phil* 1774. O 2v in 1: [16] 436 aa
—ed. 2, abr *Phil* 1775. O [16] 432 a
—ed. 3, abr *L* 1775. O [16] 319 a
—anr. ed. complete. *Dub* 1776. O [16] 434 +
2adv-p a
—many later Eng. & Am. eds.
Includes his famous *Journal*, of which innumerable separate editions, both American and English,
have since appeared. An autobiographical masterpiece, rivalled in 18th century America only by
that of Franklin.

WOOLWORTH, JAMES M.   670
Nebraska in 1857. *Omaha* [*N Y* ptd] 1857. D
[2] 105 + 23adv-p map b N NYP Y

WOOLWORTH, JAMES M.   671
Omaha City . . . Its history [etc.]. *Omaha* 1857.
16° 64 b OS[only copy known]

[WOOLWORTH, S. B.] pub.   672
Guide to Denver, Utah, [etc.]. *Omaha* 1862. D
28 [8] [the only copy known has a fragmentary
map] d S

WOOTEN, DUDLEY G., ed.   673
A comprehensive history of Texas . . . *Dallas*
1898. roy O 2v: [24] 890; [8] 5–851. 23pls b
Includes complete text of Yoakum's *History*,
with additions.

[WORCESTER, SAMUEL M., et al]   674
Essays on slavery . . . *Amherst* 1826. O 83 a

WORD
Word (A) of consolation to the scattered saints.
See Briggs, Jason W.

WORK (JOHN).   675
The journal of: a chief-trader of the Hudson's
Bay Co., during his expedition from Vancouver to
the Flatheads and Blackfeet . . . *Clev* 1923. O 209
[incl. front and 5pls] a

WORKMAN, JAMES   676
Essays and letters on various political subjects.
N Y 1809. D 165 aa
Styles itself "second American edition," as por-
tions had appeared previously.

[WORKMAN, JAMES]   677
A faithful picture of the political situation
of New Orleans... [*N O*] 1807. O [4] 38 b
AA Hn
—rptd. *B* 1808. O 48 aa
Relates to Wilkinson's conduct in the Burr
affair. Attributed also to Edward Livingston.

WORKMAN, JAMES   678
A letter to the respectable citizens... of the
county of Orleans. *N O* 1807. O [16] 30 b NYP

WORKMAN (THE HONB. JAMES) and
KERR (COL. LEWIS).
The trials of: *See* Castera, F.

WORRELL, JOHN   679
A diamond in the rough... *Indp* 1906. D 282
port a
Sam Houston, Texas war, etc.

WORSHAM, JOHN H.   680
One of Jackson's foot cavalry... *N Y* 1912. O
353 8 pls a

WORSHAM, WILLIAM J.   681
The old Nineteenth Tennessee regiment...
Knoxv 1902. O [4] 235 a

[WORTH, GORHAM A.]   682
Random recollections of Albany... 1800–1808.
Alb 1849. O 57 a
—ed. 2, enl., under pseud. of Ignatius Jones, *Alb*
1850. O 90 78
—ed. 3, further enl., au. named, *Alb* 1866. O [8
incl. front.] 17–144 450copies ptd. [50 on L. P.]

[WORTH, GORHAM A.]   683
Random recollections of Cincinnati... 1817–
1821. *Alb* 1851. O 88 a
Some copies have, bound in, the second edition
of this author's *Random recollections of Albany*.

WORTHINGTON, ERASTUS   684
The history of... Dedham, Massachusetts. *B*
1827. O 146 a

[WORTHINGTON, COL. THOMAS]   685
Shiloh, or the Tennessee campaign of 1862...
Wash 1869–72. O 164 map facs a
—rptd. "Shiloh, the only correct... history of U.
S. Grant...," *Wash* 1872. O 179 map facs
—anr. ed. "A correct history of... Shiloh," *Wash*
1880. O 164 [15]
A startling philippic, accusing Halleck, Grant
and Sherman with carrying out a plot to protract
the war into 1864 or 1865, thus insuring the 1864
election to the Republican party. An earlier effort
in 1869 to issue the work in parts was abandoned
after bringing out the initial one [in twelve pages],
which is incorporated herein.

WORTLEY, EMMELINE STUART   686
"&c". [i.e. et cetera].
L 1853. D [12] 450 errata lf front a
A continuation of the next entry.

WORTLEY, EMMELINE STUART   687
Travels in the United States... *L* 1851. D 3v:
[16] 307; [2, 5–12] 351; [8] 316 a
—Am. ed. *N Y* 1851. D 463
—anr. ed., in Eng., *P* 1851. O [4] 236

[WORTLEY, VICTORIA S.]   688
A young traveller's journal of a tour in North
and South America... *L* 1852. 16° [12] 260 16pls aa
—ed. 2 *L* 1855. same collat a
Unusual diary, kept by the thirteen-year old
daughter of Lady Emmeline Wortley, describing
her trip to Pittsburgh and down river to Natchez,
New Orleans, etc.

WRANGEL, FERDINAND VON
Reise... längs der Nordküste von Sibirien...
See Engelhardt, G.

WRANGEL, FERDINAND VON   689
Statistische und ethnographische Nachrichten
über die Russischen Besitzungen an der Nordwestküste von Amerika... *St Ptbg* 1839. O [40]
332 map tab aa

WRAXALL, SIR F. C. LASCELLES [ed.]
The backwoodsman, or life on the Indian frontier. *See* Strubberg, F. A.

WREDE, FRIEDRICH W. VON   690
Lebensbilder aus den Vereinigten Staaten...
und Texas... *Cassell* 1844. O 2pts in 1: [6] 160;
[6] 161–324 aa

[WRIFFORD, ALISON or ANSON]   691
Traits of character... manifested by the inhab-
itants of the northeastern states. *Port Me* 1837
O 68 a

WRIGHT, DAVID   692
Memoir of Alvan Stone... *Northampton* 1837.
16° [4] 9–256 a
Stone was an Illinois pioneer.

WRIGHT, E[DGAR] W. ed.   693
Lewis and Dryden's marine history of the Pacific northwest... *Port Ore* 1895. F [24] 494 [incl.
pls] aa
—rptd. *N Y* 1959. 2v a

WRIGHT (EDMUND).   694
Narrative of: his adventures with... the
Knights of the Golden Circle. *N Y* 1864. O [6]
15–150 15pls a
—anr. issue carries *Cin* impr.
—rptd. 1865.

WRIGHT, FANNY
See under D'Arusmont.

WRIGHT'S . . . CAMPAIGN   695
Wright's (Colonel George) late campaign against the Indians in Oregon and Washington . . . Topographical memoir . . . of: [Sen. Ex. Doc. 32]. *Wash* 1859. O 82 2maps aa

WRIGHT, JAMES A.   696
History of . . . Moravia [N. Y.]. *Auburn* 1874. O 289 errata lf a

WRIGHT, J[OHN]   697
The American negotiator . . . currencies of the British colonies . . . *L* 1761. O [6] 464 aa
—3 other eds. pub. by 1767. a

[WRIGHT, JOHN]?   698
A compleat history of the late war . . . in Europe, Asia, Africa and America . . . *Dub* 1763. O [16] 572 5maps 11pls aa
—rptd. *L* 1763–5. O 2v: [16] 112, 121–248; [2] 249–559. 3maps 10pls aa
—anr. ed. same impr. & collat. 1765. aa
—ed. 4, *Dub* 1766. O [16] 559 6maps 10pls aa
—anr. ed., called ed. 6, *Dub* 1774. O [20] 627 5maps 12pls aa
Ascribed also to John Exshaw, publisher of the Dublin edition. Possibly the work of Edmund Burke using the name of Wright as a pseudonym.

WRIGHT, JOHN A.   699
A paper on the character . . . of the country on the southern border. *Phil* 1876. O [2] 114 a

WRIGHT, JOHN S.   700
Chicago: past, present, future. *Chi* 1868. O 404 fold.map a
—ed. 2, with adds., same impr. 1870. O [2 46] 432 + ¹/₂ sheet["To fellow citizens"] tipped in at front, 2maps 5pls

WRIGHT, JOHN S.   701
Letters from the west . . . *Salem N Y* 1819. O [10] 72 b ChiH [only copy known]

WRIGHT, MARCUS J., comp.   702
List of field officers, regiments . . . in the Confederate States army. [*Wash* 1891?]. O 131 91 25copies ptd. aa

WRIGHT, MARCUS J.   703
Reminiscences of the early settlement . . . of Mc Nairy county, Tenn. *Wash* 1882. O 96 16ports a

WRIGHT, MARCUS J.   704
Some account of the life and services of William Blount . . . *Wash* [1884]. O 142 port a

WRIGHT, ROBERT   705
A memoir of General James Oglethorpe . . . founder of Georgia . . . *L* 1867. D 414 map a

WRIGHT, ROBERT M.   706
Dodge City, the cowboy capital . . . [*Wichita* 1913]. D 344 col.front. 40pls aa
—rptd. n.d.[*ca* 1930]. same collat., but col. front. replaced by port a

[WRIGHT, THOMAS]   707
The famous voyage of Sir Francis Drake . . . *L* 1742. O [4] 54 map b JCB N NYP
Attributed also to Francis Pretty; Wagner thinks it the work of Richard Hakluyt, in whose collection of *Voyages* [1589] it first appeared.

WRIGHT, CAPT. T[HOMAS] J.   708
History of the Eighth regiment Kentucky Volunteer infantry . . . *St Joseph Mo* 1880. D 286 [2] + errata slip at p. 128 a

[WRIGHT, WILLIAM, and JOHN W.] of Eng.   709
Recollections of western Texas. By two of the U. S. Mounted Rifles. *L* 1857. O 88 erratum slip b G Pn

[WRIGHT, WILLIAM] of Nevada   710
History of the big bonanza . . . By Dan De Quille [pseud.] *Hart* 1876. O 569 2pls at front [others incl. in paginat.] aa
—rptd., same impr. & collat., 1877. a
—anr. ed. *N Y* 1947. O
Most interesting chronicle of "flush times" in Nevada following the "silver strike." In the first edition plate no. 44 (residence of J. P. Jones) was omitted.

[WRIGHT, WILLIAM] of Nevada   711
A history of the Comstock silver lode . . . *Virginia Nev* [1889]. D 158 a

WRITINGS (THE) OF LACO . . .
See Higginson, Stephen.

WÜRTTEMBURG, prince of
Reise in Nordamerika . . . *See* Paul Wilhelm, Friedrich.

WULSTEN, CARL   712
The silver region of Sierra Mojada . . . Colorado. *Denver* 1876. O 100 [2] + adv-p 2maps aa

WYANDOTTE COUNTY, OHIO.   713
Historical sketch of: . . . *Sandusky* 1877. O 170 [10] a

WYATT (HENRY).   714
Life and confessions of: . . . made shortly before his execution. *Auburn N Y* 1846. O 56 aa

Career of a consistent villain throughout the West and in Texas.

WYATT, WILLIAM N.   715
Wyatt's travel diary, 1836 . . . *Chi* 1930. O 78 [2] port 2maps a
Travels in Arkansas.

WYETH, JOHN A.   716
Life of General Nathan Bedford Forrest. *N Y* 1899. O [22] 656 55pls & maps aa
—ed. 2, *N Y* 1900. same collat a
—ed. 3 *N Y* [1908] O [22] 668 maps pls a

WYETH, JOHN B.   717
Oregon; or a short history of a long journey . . . [Ed. and partially written by Dr. Benjamin Waterhouse.] *C* 1833. D [4] 87 errata slip c AA N NYP Y
First printed account of the first emigrant party to cross the plains.

WYETH (CAPTAIN NATHANIEL J.)   718
. . . correspondence and journals of: 1831–6. *Eugene Ore* 1899. O [20] 262 3maps a
Wyeth, with Sublette, led expeditions to Oregon, in 1832 and in 1834, and established Fort Hall.

WYLD, JAMES, pub.   719
Geographical . . . notes, to accompany . . . map of the gold regions of California. *L* 1849. O [2] 32 + adv. lf map a

WYLD, JAMES   720
A guide to the gold country of California . . . *L* [1849?]. O 62 map a
Compiled from American official documents.

WYLIE, ANDREW   721
Discourse before the Indiana Historical Society . . . *Indp* 1831. O 26 a

WYLLY, CHARLES S.   722
Annals . . . of Glynn county, Georgia. *Brunswick* 1897. D 27 [3] a
—rptd. with adds., same impr. [1917] D 76 a

WYLLY, CHARLES S.   723
The seed that was sown in the colony of Georgia. *N Y* 1910. D 163 a

—abr. ed., "Memories," [*Brunswick Ga*] 1916. O 41

WYMAN (SETH.).   724
The life and adventures of: . . . *Manchester N H* 1843. D 310 a
A worthy successor to two earlier New England practicioners of roguery, Stephen Burroughs and Henry Tufts.

WYNN, WILLIAM O.   725
Biographical sketch of an old Confederate soldier, also three years as a cowboy on the frontier of Texas. *Greenville, Tex.* 1916. D 159 a

WYNNE, [JOHN H.]   726
The history of the British empire in America . . . in three volumes. [only two pub.] *L* 1769–70. O 2v: [8] 520; [8] 546. 4maps & plans 3pls aa
—issue 2, with new title to v.I "A general history . . .," [dated 1770 and stating "in two volumes"]. O 2v: [14] 520; [8] 546. 4maps & plans 3pls a [some copies contain only the large fold.map] aa
—ed. 2, *L* 1776. O 2v same collat. a
The first volume is devoted to the French and Indian War.

WYOMING   727
Brands owned by members of the Wyoming stock growers association. *Chi* 1882. D 58 [2] b
—ed. 2, *Chi* 1883. D 82 [2] a
—ed. 3, *Cheyenne* [1884] D [4] 128 [unpaged] a
—ed. 4, Cheyenne 1885. D [4] 118 [unpaged]

Diary of the Wyoming bear hunt. [*Bklyn*   728
ca 1900]. O 59 pl a Small ed.

Letters from old friends and members of   729
the Wyoming Stock Grower's Association. *Cheyenne* 1923. O 55 a

The Territory of Wyoming its history . . . 1874. *See* Jeffrey, J. K.

WYSE, FRANCIS   730
America, its realities and resources . . . Texas and Oregon questions, etc. *L* 1846. O 3v: [4] 494; 440; 389 [78] aa
—Ger tr. *Leip* 1846. O 3v in 1: 243; 240; 168 a

X

XÁNTUS, JÁNOS   1
Levelei Éjszakemirikábol [tr. "Letters from North America"]. *Pesten* [i.e. *Budapest*] 1858. O 176 [incl. final adv-p] 12pls aa
Unauthorized edition of letters by a Hungarian

exile and scientist who accompanied a railroad survey through the Southwest and California. The incompetent editor, Prépost, produced rather chaotic information, much of it borrowed from Marcy's Red River report.

XÁNTUS, JÁNOS   **2**
Utazás Kalifornia déli részeiben [tr. "Travels in southern California"]. *Pesten* 1860. O [10] 192 + 3adv-p. map 8pls aa

Authorized edition of this scientist's letters on California; they embody, without acknowledgment, much from the reports of Abert and Emory.

Y

Y . . ., A.
The theatre of the present war . . . *See* Young, Arthur.

YANCEY, WILLIAM L.   **1**
An address on . . . Calhoun. *Montg* 1851. O 72 a

YATES, JOHN V. N., and MOULTON, JOSEPH W.   **2**
History of the state of New York, including its aboriginal and colonial annals. Vol. I, pts. 1 & 2 [all]. *N Y* 1824–6. O 2v: [4] 325 [11]; [8] 333–418. 7maps a
See Moulton, Joseph W., for two entries supplementing this work.

YATES, ROBERT, comp.   **3**
Secret proceedings and debates of the convention assembled at Philadelphia in 1787, for . . . forming the constitution. *Alb* 1821. O 308 a
—rptd. many times.

YAZOO CLAIMS.   **4**
Sundry papers, in relation to: . . . *Wash* 1809. O 195 aa 300 cops ptd.

YEADON, RICHARD   **5**
The amenability of northern incendiaries, as well to southern as to northern laws . . . *Charleston S C* 1835. O 48 a

YELLOWSTONE   **6**
An illustrated history of the Yellowstone valley embracing the counties of Park, Sweet Grass . . . Montana. *Spokane* [1907]. O [22] 669 32pls a

Journey through the Yellowstone . . . park   **7**
etc. [*Wash*] 1883. Q 43 43photo pls b
Only a few copies printed for members of the elaborate expedition of 1883 headed by President Arthur.

Yellowstone valley (The) and the town of   **8**
Glendive. *St P* 1882. O 108 fold.map plan aa

Yellowstone valley (The) in the Territory of   **9**
Montana . . . *St P* 1882. O 80 fold.map a

YLARREGUI, JOSÉ SALAZAR
Datos de los trabajos astronómicos y topográficos . . . *see* Salazar Ylarregui, José.

YOAKUM, HENDERSON K.   **10**
History of Texas . . . *N Y* 1855. O 2v: 482; 576. 4maps 5pls facs b
—anr. issue, identical, but dated 1856. aa
—rptd. *Austin* 1935. O 2v a

YOLO COUNTY, CALIF.   **11**
The western shore gazetteer and commercial directory for: *Woodland, Cal* 1870. O 602 aa

[YONGE, FRANCIS]   **11a**
A narrative of the proceedings of the people of South-Carolina . . . and of the true causes . . . that induced them . . . to put themselves under the . . . government of the Crown. *L* 1726. Q 40 b AA Hn LC
—rptd. [*Wash* 1837]. O 40 a

YORKTOWN.   **12**
Orderly book of the siege of: 1781. *Phil* 1865. Q [4] 66 a 60copies ptd[10 on plate paper] aa

YOSEMITE BOOK (THE) . . .
See Whitney, Josiah D.

YOUNG, ALEXANDER   **13**
Chronicles of the first planters of . . . Massachusetts Bay, 1623–6 . . . *B* 1846. O [8] 572 map port a

YOUNG, ALEXANDER   **14**
Chronicles of the pilgrim fathers of . . . Plymouth, 1602–5. *B* 1841. O [16] 504 port 2maps a
—ed. 2, same impr. & collat. 1844.

YOUNG, ANDREW W.   **15**
History of . . . Warsaw, New York . . . *Buf* 1869. O 400 40ports 6views a

[YOUNG, ARTHUR]?   **16**
American husbandry . . . By an American. *L* 1775. O 2v: [4] 472; [4] 319 [16] a
—Sp. tr. "Cultura Americana . . .," *Lis* 1799. Q 2v

[YOUNG, ARTHUR]   **17**
Observations on the present state of the waste lands . . . on the occasion of the establishment of a new colony on the Ohio . . . *L* 1773. O 83 b JCB N NYP VaU Y
Refers to colonies in the western territory projected by Thomas Walpole and associates. Intended to discourage emigration to America.

[YOUNG, ARTHUR]   **18**
Political essays concerning the present state of the British empire . . . *L* 1772. Q [8] 552 aa
Half of the book relates to the American colonies; their revolt and victory is foreseen. Ascribed also to Dr. John Campbell.

[YOUNG, ARTHUR]   **19**
The theatre of the present war in North America . . . *L* 1758. O [12] 56 aa

YOUNG, BENNETT H.   **20**
The battle of the Thames . . . *Louisv* Filson club 1903. Q [16] 274 4pls & plans a

YOUNG, BENNETT H.   **21**
Confederate wizards of the saddle. *B* 1914. O [22] 633 33maps & pls a
—rptd. same collat, *Kenesaw Ga* 1958
Practically a history of cavalry operations in the last war to employ extensively that romantic arm.

YOUNG, BENNETT H.   **22**
The prehistoric men of Kentucky . . . *Louisv* Filson club 1910. Q [16] 343[incl. pls] front. a

YOUNG, CHARLES E., and GIBBS, OLIVER, [pubs.]   **23**
First annual review of Pierce county, Wisconsin. *Prescott Wis* 1856. D 46 aa

YOUNG, E. H.   **24**
History of Round Prairie and Plymouth [Ill].. *Chi* 1876. O 302 aa

YOUNG, FRANK C.   **25**
Across the plains in '65 . . . *Denver* 1905. D [16] 224 map 200copies ptd. aa
Day-by-day journal of a trip from Atchison to Julesburg and Denver. Properly a companion volume to the entry following.

YOUNG, FRANK C.   **26**
Echoes from Arcadia. The story of Central City . . . *Denver* 1903. D [14] 220 200copies ptd. aa
Minute record of fifteen golden years, reviving a unique social life and a ghost-town's departed glory.

YOUNG, HARRY   **27**
Hard knocks: a life story of the vanishing west. *Port Ore* 1915. D 242 25pls aa
—rptd. *Chi* n.d. same paginat., but only 18pls a

YOUNG, J. P.   **28**
The Seventh Tennessee Cavalry. A history . . . *Nashv* 1890. O 227 4pls a

YOUNG (JOHN R.). Utah pioneer.   **29**
Memoirs of: . . . *S L C* 1920. D [6] 9–341 4ports a
By Brigham's nephew who accompanied the 1847 migration.

[YOUNG, ROBERT]   **30**
Abraham Lincoln: a study. *Liv* 1865. D 32 cov. t. only aa

YOUNG, SAMUEL   **31**
The history of my life . . . *Pitt* 1890. D 147 port a
Record of events in western Pennsylvania, from 1833.

YOUNG, VAN BUREN   **32**
An outline history of Bath county [Ky.]. *Lex* 1876. O [2] 54 aa

[YOUNG, W. A.]   **33**
The history of North and South America . . . *L* 1776. 16° 2v: [10] 276; [6] 280 2pls aa
—rptd, au named. *L*, Lane, 1776. 16° 2v: [8] 276; [8] 280 2pls a
First issued in 16 parts. Vol I devoted to North America.

YOUNG TRAVELLER'S JOURNAL [A] . . .
See Wortley, Victoria S.

YOUNGBLOOD (CHARLES L.)   **34**
Adventures of: during ten years on the plains. *Boonville Ind* 1882. D 199 port b Y
—rptd., on execrable wood-pulp paper, "A mighty hunter . . .," *Chi* 1890. D 362[incl. front.] + 4adv-p 47pls a

YOUNGER (COLE).   **35**
The story of: *Chi* 1903. D 124 + adv-p 10pls a

YOUNGER BROTHERS (THE).
The true life of: *see* Appler, A. C.

[YRUJO Y TACON, CARLOS M.]?   **36**
Letters of Verus . . . to the native American. *Phil* 1797. O [6] 75 aa
—Fr. tr. [*Phil* 1797?]. O [6] 68 a
Defense of Marquis Yrugo, Spanish Minister to the United States against charges made by Timothy Pickering. Ascribed also to Yrugo's secretary, Philip Fatio, and to John Armstrong.

YUBA COUNTY, CALIFORNIA.
History of: . . . *See* Chamberlain, Wm. H.

YUKON MINERS.   **37**
Appeal of: to the Dominion of Canada . . . *Ottawa* [1898]. 16° 128 a
The appeal, bearing over 2500 signatures, gives information on many Alaskan mining regions.

YULE, P[ATRICK]   **38**
Remarks on the disputed north-western boundary of New Brunswick, bordering on the United States . . . *L* 1838. O 28 map aa
—ed. 2, same impr., date & collat. a

YUMA COUNTY, ARIZONA.
Resources of: . . . *See* King, Cameron H.

Z

ZAGOSKIN, LIEUT. LAURENTII A.   1
Peshekhodnaia opisj Tschasti russikh vladienli v Amerikie. *St Ptbg* 1847–8. O 2 pts in 1: 20, [2] 182; [2] 120 44 [2], map a
Pedestrian trips in Alaska, etc.

ZAHM, J. A.   2
The great southwest: its attractions, resources and people. *Notre Dame* 1883. O 39 fold.map a

ZAVALA, LORENZO DE   3
Viage à los Estados-Unidos . . . *P* 1834. O [12] 374 aa
—rptd., with adds., *Merida Yucatan* 1846. O 57 382[5] By the first vice-president of the Texas republic.

ZEISBERGER (DAVID).   4
A brief narrative of the life of: . . . *L* 1821. O 38 a
—rptd. *Dub* 1822. 16° 58

ZEISBERGER (DAVID).   5
Diary of: *Cin* 1885. O 2v: [32] 464; 535 aa

ZELL, T. ELWOOD & CO., pubs.
A guide to . . . Chicago . . . *Chi* 1868. *See* under Chicago

ZENGER (JOHN P.)   6
A brief narrative of the . . . tryal of: [capt.t.] *N Y* 1736. F 40 [misnumbered 42] b NYP WisH
—rptd. [capt. t.] *B* 1738. Q 48 b AA NYP
—other Am. eds.: *Lancaster* 1756, F 39 a; *N Y* 1770, O [2] 54; *N Y* 1790, O 48; *B* 1799, [capt. t.] O 48 aa
—Eng. eds.: *L* 1738, Q [2] 32; *Dub* 1738. aa
—eds. 2, 3 & 4, same impr., date & collat.; *L* 1750, D 60; *L* 1752, O [4] 74 [2]; *L* 1765, O 59 [1]; *L* 1784, O [4] 64 a
One of the famous decisions in legal history, establishing the epochal doctrine of the freedom of the press; probably written by James Alexander, one of Zenger's attorneys.

ZENNERN, GOTTFRIED   7
Neu-Europa oder die Alte in der Neuen Welt . . . *Leip* 1720. O [26 incl. fold. t.] 205 [6] map aa

ZESTERMANN, C[HRISTIAN] A. A.   8
. . . Memoir on the European colonization of America, in ante-historic times . . . [*L* 1851]. O 32 a
Separate from American Ethnological Society *Proceedings*.

ZEVALLOS, FRANCISCO   9
Carta . . . sobre la apostólica vida y virtudes del P. Fernando Konsag . . . missionero de la Califor-

nia. *Mex* 1764. Q [6] 32 c Hn Y [of 3 cops in U.S.]
Konsag's 1746 exploration to the Colorado confirmed Ugarte's earlier doubt of California's insularity. For note on Ugarte *see* Villavicencio's *Vida*.

ZHIZNEOPISANIE
Zhizneopisanie Aleksandra Andreecicha Baranova glavnago pravitelia rossiskikh kolonii v Amerikie. *See* Kheliebnikov, Kiril T.

ZIEGENFUSS, C. O.   10
Western Montana . . . *Butte* 1886. O 176 map aa

ZIEGLER, ALEXANDER   11
Der Geleitsmann: Katechismus für Auswanderer nach den Vereinigten Staaten . . . *Leip* 1856. D [12] 235[incl.front.] map a

ZIEGLER, ALEXANDER   12
Skizzen einer 'Reise durch Nordamerika . . . *Dresden* 1848. D 2v in 1: [10] 310; [6] 289 aa
—anr. ed. "Der deutsche Auswanderer nach den Vereinigten Staaten," *Leip* 1849. D [4 3–6] 366 [2[a
—Dutch tr. abr., "Reis door de Vereenigde Staten," *Amst* 1849. D [10] 296 front. eng.t. 2maps a

ZIMMERMANN, E[BERHARD] A. W.   13
Frankreich und die Freistaaten von Nordamerika . . . *Berlin & Braunschweig* 1795–[9]. 16° 2v: [12] 446; [96] 612 [2] pl c Y
—anr. issue, *Berlin* 1795–1800. 16° 2v b NYP
—Fr. tr. of v.I, "Essai de comparison entre la France et les États-Unis . . .," *Leip* 1797. D 2v: [6, 3–8] 272; [2] 273–494 a
—Swed. tr. *Stockh* 1817. D [4] 426 [2] map 2pls tab a

ZIMMERMANN, HEINRICH   14
Reise um die welt, mit Capitain Cook. *Mannheim* 1781. O 110 c [said to have been suppressed] N NYP
—Fr. tr. with biog. of Cook added, *Berne* 1782. O [16] 200 b
—anr. ed. *Mannheim* 1783. O b Y
—Dutch tr. *Leyd* 1784. aa
—Eng. tr. *Wellington N Z* 1926. O 49 map 2pls a
—Eng. tr. *Toronto* [1930]. O 250copies ptd. aa
—Rus. tr. "Posliednee puteshestvie okolo svieta Kap. Kuka . . .," *St Ptbg* 1786. O 265 b
—ed. 2, *St Ptbg* 1788. O 411
With possible exception of John Rickman's *Journal*, earliest account of Cook's last voyage.

ZIMMERMANN, DR. W. F. A. [pseud.]
See Vollmer, Carl G. W.

ZIMMERMANN, DR. W. F. A. [pseud.]
Californien und das Goldfieber . . . *See* Vollmer,
Carl G. W.

ZINCKE, F. BARHAM   **15**
Last winter in the United States . . . *L* 1868. D
[16] 314 + 6adv-p a

**[ZINZENDORF, NICOLAUS LUDWIG,
Graf von]**
Pennsylvanische   Nachrichten . . .   [*Büdingen*
1742?]. O 191 aa

ZIRCKEL, OTTO   **16**
Skizzen aus den und über die Vereinigten Staa-
ten . . . *Berlin* 1850. O [10] 182 a

ZIRCKEL, OTTO   **17**
Tagebuch geschrieben Während der nordameri-
kanisch-mexikanischer Campagne, 1847–8. *Halle*
1849. O 179 aa
Services, as Captain of Ohio Volunteers, by a
former Prussian officer.

ZITTLE, CAPT. JOHN H.   **18**
Correct history of the John Brown invasion . . .
Hagerstown 1905. O 259 a
Eye-witness account by a Virginia militiaman.

ZOG, ANTON   **19**
Achtzehn Jahre in Peoria . . . *Peoria* 1869. O
213 a

ZORN, JOHN H. [comp.]   **20**
Annual city directory of Lincoln, Nebraska, for
1876–7 . . . and a historical sketch of the city.
[*Lincoln* 1876]. O 161 + advs aa

[ZUBLY, JOHN J.]   **21**
Great Britain's right to tax her colonies; placed
in the clearest light. *L* 1774. O [4] 55 aa
—Am. ed. [*Phil*? 1775]. O [2] 55 aa
American ed has ¹/₂ t. only; it was undoubtedly
the English sheets, with title leaf excised.

[ZUBLY, JOHN J.]   **22**
An humble enquiry into the nature of the dependency of the American colonies upon the Parliament of Great Britain . . . [*Charleston*?] 1769. Q
[2] 26 aa

ZUBLY, JOHN J.   **23**
The law of liberty. A sermon on American affairs
. . . *Phil* Miller 1775. O [20] 42 aa
—issue 2, same collat., but impr. lengthened to
include booksellers in New York, Charleston &
Savannah. a
—Eng. ed. *L* 1775. O [2] 5–73 a

ZUBLY, JOHN J.   **24**
The stamp-act repealed . . . Second edition. *Sav*
1766. D 30 a
—rptd.: *Charleston S C* 1776, O 24; *Phil* 1766.
Of the first edition of this sermon no copy is
known; it was delivered at Savannah in 1766, and
undoubtedly printed there, possibly in a newspaper.

ZUÑIGA, IGNACIO   **25**
Rapida ojeada al estado de Sonora . . . *Méjico*
1835. O 66 c B NYP Y
—Fr. tr. 1842. aa
Account of his attempt to establish a colony in
present Arizona [on the Colorado and Gila] with
a view of uniting New Mexico and California.

ZURLA, PLACIDO   **26**
Dizzertazione intorno ai viaggi e scoperte set-
tentrionali di . . . Fratelli Zeni. *Venice* 1808. O [16]
144 map a

ZURLA, PLACIDO   **27**
Lettera ai viaggi e scoperte . . . di Nicolò e
Antonio Zeno . . . [*Venice* 1813]. O 31 a

ZUVERLÄSSIGE NACHRICHTEN   **28**
Zuverlässige Nachrichten über die Vorbedingun-
gen unter welchen Auswanderungen nach den Vereinigten Staaten . . . *St Gall* 1818. 16° 30 aa